Z DAY

Saturday, 1st July 1916
The First Day of the Battle of the Somme

The Attack of the VIII Corps
at Beaumont Hamel and
Serre

For my Father
Ewen MacDonald MacCormick, 1921-2010

Z DAY

Saturday, 1st July 1916

The First Day of the Battle of the Somme

The Attack of the VIII Corps At Beaumont Hamel and Serre

Alan MacDonald

Iona Books

British Library Cataloguing In Publication Data
A Record of this Publication is available
from the British Library

ISBN 978-0-9558119-2-0

Published March 2014 by Iona Books
and printed by Lightning Source, Milton Keynes

Typeset in 10pt Garamond

Also by Alan MacDonald
*Pro Patria Mori: The 56th (1st London) Division
at Gommecourt, 1st July 1916*
*A Lack of Offensive Spirit? The 46th (North Midland) Division
at Gommecourt, 1st July 1916*

Pro Patria Mori
Website: www.gommecourt.co.uk

Front cover photograph: The Danger Tree in Newfoundland Memorial Park, Beaumont Hamel. The petrified remains of a tree which stood in No Man's Land on 1st July 1916 and which marks the possible 'High water mark' of the advance of the 1st Battalion, The Royal Newfoundland Regiment, at about 9.30 a.m. on that day. The battalion suffered 90% casualties in an isolated attack in the face of the massed machine guns and artillery of the German 26. Reserve Division. It was described by one witness as 'The most devoted thing I saw in the war'. We will remember them.

CONTENTS

USE OF FOOTNOTES & ENDNOTES

Both footnotes and endnotes are used in this book.

Footnotes are marked with Roman numerals (i.e. [ii]) and normally refer to people or events within the text. Footnotes are to be found at the bottom of the relevant page.

Endnotes are marked with ordinary numbers (i.e. [2]) and normally refer to sources or information not directly related to events within the text. Endnotes are to be found at the end of each chapter.

PHOTOGRAPHS

MAPS

FIGURES

TABLES

CHARTS

"No plan survives first contact with the enemy."

Field Marshal Helmuth Karl
Bernhard Graf von Moltke
Großer Generalstab
(1800-1891)

1. Introduction

This is the third of a planned six books in which I hope to provide a detailed account of the planning and conduct of the opening day of the Battle of the Somme on 1st July 1916. The first two books, *'Pro Patria Mori'* and *'A Lack of Offensive Spirit?'* describe the diversionary attacks of the 56th (1st London) and 46th (North Midland) Divisions of the VII Corps, Third Army, on the village of Gommecourt. The three remaining volumes will cover the planning of the offensive by the French and British High Commands; the attacks of the X and III Corps on Thiepval, Ovillers le Boisselle and La Boisselle; and the attacks of the XV and XIII Corps on Fricourt, Mametz and Montauban. This last book will also include a detailed account of the operations of the French 6th Army on either bank of the River Somme.

The most notable book about the opening of the Somme battle is Martin Middlebrook's seminal work *'The First Day on the Somme'* which, as it approaches the 50th anniversary of its publication, still stands as a landmark in the historiography of the Great War. There are numerous other accounts of the first day in other volumes which cover the entire Somme campaign. Some describe the action from the point of view of the young officers and ordinary soldiers who delivered the attack and others attempt to provide some analysis of the action and the reasons for the outcome. We are also fortunate that, courtesy of Jack Sheldon and Ralph Whitehead, detailed descriptions of the campaign are now available which see the fighting from the German perspective. Sadly, little currently exists on the French involvement in the Somme campaign although William Philpott's excellent *'Blood on the Somme'* does look at the entire battle from both the French and British points of view. Detailed accounts of the hugely successful French attacks at the beginning of the Battle of the Somme do not yet exist in either English or French.

I hope that my books will differ from existing accounts of the Somme in that that they will focus very much on the *local* planning of each Corps' attack, on the quality of staff work, on the use and effectiveness of the heavy and field artillery and trench mortar batteries, on the use and misuse of intelligence by senior officers and of the response of the enemy, areas about which little has been written to date. In this book about the VIII Corps, descriptions of the fighting will also attempt to analyse how and why so many false reports from British observers caused so many disastrous decisions to be made on the use of reserves and of the artillery. At the same time I will endeavour to come to some conclusions about the truth of the various reports of British troops making deep but ultimately unsuccessful penetrations of the German positions. Lastly, using contemporary and post-war documents, these books will try to explain what precisely went wrong (or right, but not in this book) on 1st July both in the words of the generals and units officers present on the day and through interpretation of the various official records. Inevitably, responsibility for failure (and success where achieved) will be allocated according to the weight of evidence available.

Although the 1st July 1916 stands alone as by far the worst day in the history of the British Army, the performance of the VIII Corps opposite the small villages of Beaumont Hamel and Serre was definitely the most disastrous and arguably generated the most controversy of any of the attacks launched by the Fourth Army on that terrible day. Two facts are not open to debate: that VIII Corps lost more men than any other Fourth Army Corps involved in the opening day of the Somme; and VIII Corps was the only Fourth Army Corps that failed to gain permanently any enemy territory whatsoever[i].

In addition, there were more, and more persistent, reports of British troops having penetrated the German defences which then resulted in additional troops being erroneously and expensively committed to the fighting than on any other Corps front. The 31st Division was said to have had men in Serre and Pendant Copse. Observers reported the 4th Division in Munich Trench and also Pendant Copse. The reports on the 29th Division's front suggesting incursions into Station Road and as far as Beaucourt resulted in the most catastrophic and tragic event of the day anywhere on the Somme front: the isolated advance and annihilation of the brave officers and men of the 1st Newfoundland Regt. One of the purposes of this book will be to look at each of these reported advances in order to determine whether all, or any of them, actually took place.

In coming to any conclusions, appropriate weight has been placed on German reports and accounts of the fighting. These come mainly from *'Somme Nord'*, a German account of the opening stages of the Somme battle between Gommecourt and Curlu on the north bank of the Somme, and on regimental and other histories. Readers may think that too much weight has been placed on these accounts. These accounts do accept that British troops entered the German trenches in various locations on 1st July but then dispute the depth and duration of such break-ins. Where British accounts state that sections of German trenches were occupied for several hours or even longer these German documents uniformly often agree with these statements. There is no attempt to cover up or minimise such incursions. For example, the desperate twelve hour defence of captured German trenches by the 56th Division at Gommecourt, the fighting at the Heidenkopf which continued into 2nd July and the great initial success of the 36th Division at the Schwaben Redoubt at Thiepval are all recorded in detail and do not materially differ from British accounts. In this latter example, *'Somme Nord'* makes no bones about the degree of disorganisation and luck involved in the German counter-attacks which drove the exhausted Ulstermen back to their jump-off trenches. Further south, where Allied success was nearly complete, the state of the German defences and the collapse of the defending troops are frankly described. Given that German troops were far closer to the action within their own positions than the British it seems to me reasonable to assume that they knew where and how far British troops had penetrated. Furthermore, as no British troops ever returned alive from places like Serre, Pendant Copse, Munich Trench or Beaucourt to give first-hand accounts of any fighting in these locations one must even more firmly come to the conclusion that the chances of small parties of British troops reaching these places were so slim as to be non-existent.

---

[i] One these two points, the 34th Division of III Corps had the highest divisional casualty total and III Corps only managed to hold onto a very small part of the Leipzig redoubt.

Undoubtedly some readers will dispute these conclusions and others reached about who should shoulder the majority of the responsibility of the failure of VIII Corps. All I can say is that they are based on a detailed analysis of British war diaries and other official reports from GHQ down to machine gun companies and field ambulances. These documents and the views of officers expressed both in the summer of 1916 and post-war, allied to the findings of the German reports confirm me in believing in the accuracy of these conclusions.

Any errors of fact in the book are mine alone, as are any incorrect interpretations or opinions based on factual errors. I freely admit that I am not a 'trained' historian. I have no degree or doctorate with which to embellish the title page of these books. I have, however, spent the last fifteen years researching the very limited subject matter of the fighting on the 1st July 1916 and feel I know as much as some and more than most of what happened on that day. My opinions are, as with any writer, my own and are likely to be disputed. I look forward to it. I should also say that, on occasion, my opinions are expressed in a less than academic manner but, as author, editor and publisher I don't feel obliged to write a history book in any particular way. If, in my opinion, an order or action is clearly absurd and the person responsible an idiot I am inclined to say so. One has to have some small reward after spending so much time on the research for and the writing of these laughably long books.

I make no apology for the quality of some of the photgraphs of officers and men included within nor for the amount of biographical information included in the footnotes. I would like readers to think of those shown and mentioned as men with lives and families and not just a number on a casualty report or a name on a CWGC memorial. I would like to have been able to provide more images and details about the 'rank and file' soldiers mentioned but, unfortunately, less information about the 'other ranks' is easily accessible and constraints of time and space meant that, if the book was ever to be finished, I had to draw the research line somewhere.

Finally, two of my relatives fought on the Somme. One died at Gommecourt on 1st July, the other, my grandfather, nearly died at Leuze Wood in September after winning the Military Cross a few days earlier. These books are intended as a written memorial to them and to the men of all armies who fought, suffered and died on both banks of the River Somme during the summer and autumn of 1916.

Alan MacDonald,
West Wickham,
January, 2014.

ACKNOWLEDGEMENTS

I WOULD LIKE TO THANK the following people for their help and support during the writing of this book.

Pride of place must go to Martin Middlebrook, whose book, *'The First Day on the Somme'*, I read soon after my initial visit to Thiepval and Newfoundland Memorial Park in about 1988. His book inspired my long term fascination with the opening day of the Battle of the Somme and it remains a classic of military history.

I must also acknowledge the far more recent but hugely significant contributions of Jack Sheldon and Ralph Whitehead whose research into and writing on the German Army on the Somme has proved invaluable in improving our understanding of the fighting during this dreadful campaign.

I must thank the staff at the Brotherton Library, Leeds University for helping with access to, and permission to quote from, documents held by the Liddle Collection. Similar gratitude must be expressed to the staff at the National Archives, Kew, the staff at the Newspaper Archive of the British Museum, Colindale and the Imperial War Museum Library and Photographic Library for their assistance in meeting many requests made over many years.

Everyone should thank the Bibliothèque Nationale de France for making freely available on-line the narrative volumes and annexes of the French Official History: *'Les Armées Françaises dans la Grande Guerre'*.

More specifically I must acknowledge the assistance of the following (whether they know about it or not!):

The excellent *Newfoundland Regiment and the Great War* website and database at: *http://www.therooms.ca/regiment/part1_entering_the_great_war.asp;*

Great War Forum member Andy Pay for information concerning the 1st Rifle Brigade on 1st July 1916;

Dick Flory for supplying biographical details of several officers from the various VIII Corps' units;

Andrew Jackson's superb web site notionally about the *Accrington Pals* but which covers so much more territory to do with other Pals battalions and the men who fought with them: *http://www.pals.org.uk/pals_e.htm#intro;* and

Jonathan Viser's excellent and comprehensive web site *'The Prussian Machine'* at *http://home.comcast.net/~jcviser/*

Also, thanks to Avril Williams and her many guests, all met at *Ocean Villas*, her excellent and hospitable guest house at Auchonvillers, over the past few summers.

WHERE POSSIBLE I have attempted to gain permission for the use of the quotations found in this book, however, if I have unknowingly infringed copyright in the writing of this book I would hope that my apologies are accepted.

Photographs, unless otherwise credited, are the author's.

FINALLY, NO-ONE CAN RESEARCH AND WRITE a book without the support and encouragement of their families. Over many years my wife, Helen, has helped and, when necessary, nagged me into completing these books when my own enthusiasm and energy have flagged. Living with a nerd is never easy at the best of times but her patience and tolerance of my obsessions and foibles is postively saintly. She now knows numerous empty fields in Picardy almost as well as I do but, as part of a not wholly unselfish arrangement, she also knows and has enjoyed some excellent hotels and their restaurants in northern France which, but for these books, we might never have visited. Every cloud…

A.M.
February. 2014

2. FOURTH ARMY

ON 6TH MARCH 1916 Lt. Gen. Sir Henry Seymour Rawlinson, KCB, convened a meeting at his new headquarters, the imposing Chateau de Querrieu located some five miles east of the cathedral city of Amiens. The men he had invited were the commanders of the three British Army Corps which now formed the new Fourth Army of the British Expeditionary Force of which Rawlinson was the recently appointed GOC or General Officer Commanding. Fourth Army had started existence, made up of just its GOC and his staff, on 5th February 1916 at Tilques near St Omer. On 1st March the Army came into being officially, taking over the right of the extended Third Army's line from Foncquevillers down to the north bank of the River Somme. Rawlinson then set up his HQ at the chateau at Querrieu. The Third Army, meanwhile, progressively extended its left around Arras and Vimy. It took over stretches of line still occupied by the French 10th Army thereby allowing these troops to bolster the French Army to the south of the Somme as it struggled to deal with the continuous and heavy casualties it was suffering at Verdun.

Plate I Sir Henry Rawlinson's HQ at Querrieu

The three Corps which now formed the Fourth Army were the:
XIII Corps – 7th, 30th and 18th Divisions;
X Corps – 32nd, 36th, 48th and 49th Divisions; and
VIII Corps – 31st Division.

The three Corps commanders called to the chateau at Querrieu were Lt. Gen. Walter Norris Congreve VC, CB, MVO, GOC of XIII Corps, Lt. Gen. Thomas Lethbridge Napier Morland, KCB, DSO, of X Corps and Lt. Gen. Aylmer Gould Hunter-Weston, CB, DSO, commanding VIII Corps. Also present were Rawlinson's Chief of Staff, Maj. Gen. Archibald Amar Montgomery and Sir Douglas Haig's artillery adviser, Maj. Gen. James Frederick Noel Birch. The purpose of the conference was to allow Rawlinson to set out his thinking on the great French-led Allied offensive due to take place in the summer. Rawlinson had been entrusted by the CinC, Sir Douglas Haig, with the planning of the British supporting element of the offensive and he had devised a conservative plan of phased attacks with limited objectives designed to force the enemy into hurried and expensive counter-attacks. It was a technique known as 'Bite and Hold' which, at its heart, had the rationale of attrition, i.e. killing more of the enemy than they were able to kill of your own troops. In its ultimate expression the war's winner would be the last man standing. Rawlinson, however, believed it was possible to force the German Army into a series of such disadvantageous counter attacks that their strength would be so eroded as to make possible, at some as yet undetermined date, an offensive which might actually be able to break through the enemy's lines and bring about a speedy resolution of the conflict.

His offensive theories were, at least in part, in tune with the current tactics of Gen. Ferdinand Foch, the senior French commander in Northern France and Flanders. Foch commanded GAN, the Groupe des Armées du Nord, which essentially comprised the French 6th and 10th Armies, and he had been instructed by the French CinC, Joffre, to plan and deliver a major offensive south of the River Somme with the British co-operating with a supporting attack between the Somme and a point near to the tiny village of Serre. Although Foch fundamentally disagreed with the Somme as a productive location for this joint offensive, favouring, instead, the area to the north of Arras, he set to planning the proposed 35+ division attack with a freedom from tactical interference from his Commander in Chief not to be enjoyed by his British opposite number.

Foch had absorbed the lessons of the severe and mainly unproductive fighting in the summer and autumn of 1915 in Artois in which the French 10th Army had been heavily involved. He had come to the view (not accepted by Joffre) that, within the existing limitations of offensive technology, a breakthrough of the German lines was not yet possible. This was a sea change in attitude by Foch who, pre-war, had been a devout advocate of the power of 'the offensive', but the change was the result of a detailed study of the various French offensives in Artois and Champagne in 1915. His conclusions were supported by another highly experienced French General whose name would come to national prominence during the defence of Verdun: Gen Philippe Pétain[i].

As a result of their deliberations Foch and Pétain had come to the following conclusions:

- A breakthrough of the German defences was currently impossible;
- An offensive needed to be conducted in staged advances with limited objectives between which the artillery should be brought forward in order to deliver a new, and precise, bombardment of the new position to be taken;

[ii] Pétain had been rapidly promoted from command of a brigade on the outbreak of war to command of the XXXIII Corps during the Foch-directed 2nd Battle of Artois in May and June 1915. He was then promoted to command the 2nd Army which fought in the 2nd Battle of Champagne between 25th September and 6th November 1915. He went on to direct the defence of Verdun, being promoted to command of GAC, Groupe des Armées du Centre, in May 1916.

- The width of the offensive should be determined by the availability of heavy guns with a prescribed frontage of trench per heavy howitzer;
- The depth of the offensive should be determined by the ability of ground observers to accurately observe the results of the artillery preparation which, in the main, limited the first stage of an offensive to taking the German 1st position;
- Effective counter-battery fire was crucial with sufficient guns of sufficient weight and a considerable supply of ammunition allocated to the task (Gen. Fayolle, the commander of the French 6th Army which would deliver the French attack on 1st July, went even further instructing all battery commanders within range to respond to information that a German battery was firing); and that
- The maximum width of No Man's Land which the infantry had to cross should be no more 200 metres.

As a result, Foch, with the commander of 6th Army, Gen Emile Fayolle, planned a series of limited depth, phased assaults on the successive German positions south of the Somme. These were designed to drive the enemy's troops eastwards and up against the barrier of the River Somme to their rear which, on this part of the front, ran parallel to the lines of trenches which formed the opposing front lines. All of the principles set out above were to be applied to the attack with Foch making it very clear that his intention was to conserve his infantry and, as far as possible, leave the bulk of the task of destroying the enemy and his fortifications to a great concentration of French trench, field and heavy artillery.

It would seem as though Rawlinson was broadly in agreement with Foch's ideas. At the conference he informed the three Corps commanders that, after the addition of a fourth Corps[i], the Fourth Army would seek to capture the 1st German position between Mametz and Serre in an offensive to take place at some time in June or July. Depending on events at Verdun, however, Rawlinson advised the generals that some kind of attack might be required in April or early May in order to relieve pressure on the French Army. Otherwise, they were to devote their time to planning and organising what was to be the Allies' main offensive on the Western Front in 1916.

The plan devised by Rawlinson and his staff, and forwarded to Haig at GHQ on 3rd April, was reasonably in tune with Foch's ideas or, at least, those concerning staged attacks and limited depth. In other essentials, though, it was still far behind French tactical developments on the Western Front. In view of the resources he had been allocated, Rawlinson concluded that the maximum width of the front to be attacked could be no more than 20,000 yards. In determining this distance Rawlinson diverged from Foch's principle of basing the width of an attack on the number of available heavy howitzers. Rawlinson, instead, made his decision on the basis of the quantity of available infantry,

---

[i] The fourth Corps arrived in late March. It was the III Corps, commanded by Lt. Gen. Sir William Pulteney Pulteney, and its 8th Division was put into the line between the left of the XIII Corps and the right of the X Corps around Ovillers la Boisselle. Its other divisions, the 19th and 34th, did not arrive in the Somme sector until the beginning of May.

making 8 or 9 men per yard of front (for both the initial and follow up attacks) his yardstick. Had Rawlinson based the width of the Fourth Army's attack on Foch's ideas then the front attacked would have been no more than 10,000 yards wide. Rawlinson knew, however, that such a narrow front would not be acceptable to Haig. From the very start, therefore, the British artillery was never going to be able to produce the concentration of fire demanded and delivered by Foch. Other decisions would dilute the British concentration still further.

Another key ingredient of Foch's planning which escaped both Rawlinson and Haig was that Foch insisted that a close study be made of every section of trench to be attacked. The number of artillery rounds required to destroy each part was to be calculated and then the number of suitable guns within range identified and, if need be, adjusted. For Foch, the devil was very much in the detail. The British should have been very well aware of this detailed artillery planning. On 17th June, Capt. Edward Spears, the British liaison officer with the French 6th Army, wrote to both GHQ and Fourth Army explaining this approach, an approach which inevitably led to artillery being concentrated where needed most rather than scattered evenly along the entire front. If read, Spear's letter was either ignored or dismissed[i]. It was probably already too late to change the way the bombardment and attack were to be delivered and, anyway, Haig and Rawlinson were convinced that their plan of attack would be successful.

THE FRONTAGE RAWLINSON HAD SELECTED ran from the left of the Maricourt salient near the Somme to just short of the tiny village of Serre north of the River Ancre. Rawlinson divided the initial attack into two phases with each dictated by the need to be able to see clearly the results of the artillery's work on the German trenches to be attacked. On the Somme front, the German defences consisted of a 1st position comprising fire, support and reserve trenches, an intermediate position (the Zwischen Stellung) sometimes of two lines of trenches and studded wiith defensive redoubts, and a 2nd Position, also of two trench lines and usually 3-4,000 yards behind the front line trench. A third defensive position further to the rear was in the early stages of preparation. Given the strength of the German 2nd position and the difficulties of observing it from within the British lines, Rawlinson concluded that the first attack should be limited to the German 1st position between Mametz and Serre. On average this would require an advance of some 2,000 yards and the capture of a number of German front line fortified villages: Beaumont Hamel, Thiepval, Ovillers la Boisselle, La Boisselle and Fricourt. The second phase, once the necessary artillery had been moved forward, involved a second advance of 1,000 yards from south of Pozieres to Grandcourt on the south bank of the Ancre. The villages of Contalmaison and Pozieres and the strongpoint of Mouquet Farm were included

---

[i] Spears was not universally popular. A fluent French speaker born in France he was something of an outsider and was especially unpopular with the cavalry officer deputed to act as liaison with Foch at GAN. In June, Col. Eric Dillon demanded that all reports submitted by Spears be copied to him at GAN and that GHQ should take no action on these reports until they had been 'verified' by Dillon. An increasingly bitter dispute between the two officers persisted up to and beyond the Armistice.

in this attack's objectives. North of the Ancre the VIII Corps would hold fast awaiting developments on their right.

This was a conservative even cautious proposal but it was, in Rawlinson's own words, one designed to:

"Kill as many Germans as possible with the least loss to ourselves."

He believed that the Germans would be forced, both tactically and by defensive doctrine, to launch extemporised counter attacks against these newly gained positions which, through supporting artillery and machine gun fire, Forth Army wouild be able to destroy in detail.

It was also a plan with which his Corps commanders, without exception, were in agreement. Congreve, Morland and Hunter-Weston all supported an attack with limited objectives. Nor, most tellingly, did Maj. Gen. Birch, artillery adviser to the Commander in Chief, demur from this conclusion.

Hunter-Weston was the most outspoken in his support of restricting the initial advance, stressing he was:

"... strongly opposed to a wild rush... for an objective 4,000 yards away."[1]

He went on the remind Rawlinson that:

"... to lose the substance by grasping at the shadow is a mistake that has been made too often in this war."

Given Hunter-Weston's track record at Gallipoli and the events about to unfold there is a certain irony in these comments. It is, however, remarkable that, in spite of the coincidence of views expressed at Querrieu, their Commander in Chief should then override them all in pursuit of the 'shadow' mentioned by VIII Corps' commanding General.

Nevertheless, and without using the word, Rawlinson had introduced the concept of 'attrition' as the purpose of the forthcoming battle. This was not the first time Rawlinson had considered the necessity of playing a long game of wearing out the enemy both militarily and economically. On 24th December 1914 he had addressed a lengthy letter to Edward Stanley, the 17th Earl of Derby and driving force behind the recruitment of the Pals battalions. In the letter he stated quite clearly that no major change could be expected on the Western Front until the British and French Armies were at full strength, which needed the completion of the training of Kitchener's New Armies, and until the artillery had a sufficient supply of shells. In the long term, however, he did not doubt that the Allies would be victorious. The victory might have to be gained over a considerable period of time and at great cost:

"There is no manner of doubt that we are going to succeed in crushing the German Empire. It may be a war of exhaustion, it may take one, two or three years to complete, but we shall be daily gaining strength and wealth whilst Germany will be daily losing theirs."[2]

Rawlinson's 'war of exhaustion' is attrition by another name and it is the explanation which Haig would belatedly adopt as the true purpose for the Battle of the Somme and he would trumpet its success in his final despatch concerning the battle in November. That this was not Haig's real view, pre-1st July 1916 at least, can be assumed from Rawlinson's diary note of 30th March 1916, i.e. before Haig had even seen his initial plan of attack:

> "I shall have a tussle with (Haig) over the limited objective for I hear he is inclined to favour the unlimited with the chance of breaking the German line."[3]

As he was to discover within the week, Rawlinson knew his ever optimistic CinC only too well.

Rawlinson's comment was based on his previous experience of working under Haig. In February 1915 Rawly, then commanding IV Corps, part of Haig's First Army, was asked to prepare plans for an attack at Neuve Chapelle. We shall leave to one side his rather odd behaviour of inviting suggestions from his two Divisional commanders as to how an attack might be organised without any input from himself and then not chasing up the one who failed to reply (Capper) and rejecting and then recycling the unworkable plan of the one who did (Davies). Rather we should concentrate on the way the attack developed in scope and ambition once Sir Douglas got his mitts on it. Intervening in the process was the unseemly competition between Haig, First Army, and Smith-Dorrien, Second Army, as to who should have the opportunity of leading the first major British offensive of the war: Haig at Neuve Chapelle or Smith-Dorrien at Messines. Haig 'won' by adding Aubers Ridge to the objectives and then, in cooperation with the French about Arras, planning a drive towards La Bassee and, who knows, even Lille.

Under huge pressure to provide a workable plan for the attack on Neuve Chapelle and Aubers Ridge, Rawlinson managed to produce an unworkable one, i.e. a minor re-working of an inordinately complex, double flanking manoeuvre first dreamed up by Maj. Gen. Davies of 8th Division. Sensibly, Haig rejected it out of hand and, under threat of dismissal, Rawlinson and his staff rapidly improvised a plan which would be the one eventually employed. But it was only a plan for the capture of the village of Neuve Chapelle. The more ambitious objective of Aubers Ridge was notably absent from his considerations. Although this had been the original objective of the attack set by Haig, now the Army Commander had bigger fish to fry and suddenly Rawlinson's limited, staged plan simply wouldn't do. Rawlinson intended to stop, re-group and move the artillery after the taking of Neuve Chapelle and before moving on to Aubers Ridge but this was completely unacceptable to Haig who, at a conference on 5th March 1915 in Béthune, demanded as rapid an advance as possible. The reasons for Haig's urgency would be echoed just over twelve months later when he demanded more ambition, greater speed and greater scope from Rawlinson in his plan for the Somme. In Haig's eyes Neuve Chapelle was no longer a 'minor operation' but one with potentially far reaching consequences:

> "The advance to be made is not a minor operation. It must be understood that we are embarking on a serious offensive movement with the object of breaking the German line and consequently our advance is to be pushed vigorously. Very likely an operation of considerable magnitude may result. The idea is not to capture a trench here or a trench there, but to carry the operation right through; in a sense surprise the Germans, carry them right off their legs, push forward to Aubers… ridge with as little delay as

possible, and exploit the success thus gained by pushing forward mounted troops forthwith."[4]

One could almost substitute the names of locations on the Somme and one would have the same formula – rupture, breakthrough, cavalry! No wonder Rawlinson thought Haig 'inclined to favour the unlimited with the chance of breaking the German line' in March 1916; it appears to have been his Commander in Chief's permanent mind-set.

So, when Haig called Rawlinson and his Chief Staff Officer, Maj. Gen. Montgomery, to a meeting at GHQ on 5th April 1916, Rawlinson must have had a very good idea what to expect. Douglas Haig had not come to the same conclusions as Foch in his analysis of the British experience of the 1915 fighting. As commander of the First Army, Haig had been directly involved in every British offensive action in the year: Neuve Chapelle, Aubers Ridge, Festubert, Givenchy and, finally, Loos. Not one of these offensives had been successful but Haig had 'detected' the seeds of potential success in two of these actions: Neuve Chapelle; and the opening of the biggest British offensive to date: the Battle of Loos. On both occasions British troops had broken into the German lines and, in the case of Loos, Haig believed it would have been possible to break through the entire German position had it not been for the mishandling of the reserves by the then CinC Sir John French. Consequently, still believing in the possibility of a breakthrough, Haig wanted a more ambitious Somme plan, one which held out the hope of a rupture of the German lines through which might pour the cavalry. As a result, at the meeting and, subsequently, in writing, Haig set out his objections to Rawlinson's conservative proposal and demanded one which was both wider and deeper in its initial penetration. In short, one more likely to result in a significant breach in the German lines, destabilising their entire position on the Somme and, thereby, possibly creating the conditions for a return to a more fluid and open style of warfare.

The only problem was that there would be no more troops and, far more significantly, no more guns to help Rawlinson produce this breach. Haig had 'previous' as far as this issue of 'more from less' is concerned – the disastrous attack on Aubers Ridge on 8th May 1915, again overseen by the Haig/Rawlinson combination. The concentration of artillery at Neuve Chapelle had been considerable given the limitations of the time. So considerable, in fact, that no attack up to an including the opening day of the Somme managed such a relative concentration and intensity of firepower. One gun every six yards was brought together for Neuve Chapelle and, more significantly, a sufficient number of howitzers of 6 in. and larger, one every thirty yards, with which to give the German front line a heavy pounding. For a while, this formula became a yardstick by which the scope of forthcoming battles would be measured. But then discipline weakened in the face of Haig's ever ambitious demands for the results of any attack on First Army's front. He was always seeking the breakthrough with the cavalry pouring through. One could not achieve this on very narrow fronts and so, in spite of the limitations on the numbers of guns, howitzers and ammunition, fronts of attack widened, and widened again. According to the Neuve Chapelle 'formula' there were sufficient medium/heavy howitzers to bombard the German front line at Aubers Ridge across a width of

600 yards. By the time Haig had chivvied Rawlinson into a more expansionist programme that front had more than doubled. Now it was 1,500 yards but with no additional howitzers to deal with the greatly expanded yardage. To make matters worse, the defences here consisted of three lines of trenches along with a number of strongpoints and all of these positions had to be taken under fire. On a simple basis, the expanded front had increased the ratio of howitzers to yardage from the thirty yards per howitzer at Neuve Chapelle to fifty yards per howitzer at Aubers Ridge. Add in the need to bombard three lines of trenches rather than one and the various strongpoints which were now part of the bombardment programme and it has been estimated that the Aubers Ridge bombardment was only 20% as powerful as the one fired at Neuve Chapelle[5]. Leaving to one side some fairly madcap tactical instructions to the 'Poor Bloody Infantry' which simply served to increase the casualty lists still further, the results of the bombardment were feeble and the attack collapsed in a welter of blood: 11,000 casualties in one day for no gain. From experience 'More from less' did not seem like a good idea but the concept remained tucked away in Sir Douglas Haig's brain to be brought out again as the Somme offensive was planned.

WHAT WERE HAIG'S GEOGRAPHIC EXTENSIONS of the front to be attacked as set out at the meeting on 5th April? The first change was to the width of the attack. Haig wanted to widen the front at either end so as to include in the first attack the fortified villages of Serre and Beaucourt sur Ancre on the northern flank and Mametz and Montauban on the southern flank, as well as the three main objectives of Rawlinson's second phase attack: Contalmaison, Pozieres and Mouquet Farm. Other than the significant lateral expansion of the front these objectives alone increased the depth of the overall attack as they required the taking of the Zwischen Stellung, or Switch Trench, within the first phase. But Haig's grandiose ideas did not stop there. From Pozieres north to Serre, he wanted Fourth Army to take the German 2nd Position too. North of the Ancre, on the VIII Corps' front, this would leave the front line overlooking the villages of Miraumont and Grandcourt, to the north and south of the Ancre respectively, thus threatening the German positions on both banks of the meandering and swampy little river. Instead of a limited advance of about 1,000 yards, the VIII Corps would now have to get its leading troops forward nearly 4,000 yards, and this on a front significantly wider than Rawlinson had first proposed. Haig's main interest was in how the possession of the high ground around Montauban and above Miraumont would assist Fourth Army in its next advance. The issue of how the troops would go about taking these areas was another matter. That was a problem Rawlinson and his Corps commanders had to solve.

It was clear that the existing numbers of men and guns would have to be stretched thin to deal with Haig's massive extension of the original width and depth of front Rawlinson had initially envisaged. And 'stretching' was the word used by Maj. Gen. James Frederick Noel Birch, Haig's own Artillery Adviser, when he fulfilled his advisory role and informed his CinC that the British artillery would be over-extended if his proposed extensions to the limits of the attack were insisted upon. Birch's advice was ignored and the 'Learning curve', the phrase so beloved of modern historians as a means of explaining the 'steady' improvement of the BEF and its Generals between 1914 and 1918, flat-lined again.

Thus were sown the first seeds of disaster on the northern wing of the Fourth Army and, most especially, on the front of the VIII Corps. Rawlinson, owing perhaps his career[i] and certainly his position to Sir Douglas Haig, had no alternative but to agree to his CinC's demands. The consequences would be dramatic and tragic and would lead to the carnage of the 4½ month Somme campaign. The Somme may have been 'the bloody grave of the German Army' but it was also the grave of many of the enthusiastic volunteers of Kitchener's New Armies. Neither Army would be the same.

In recent years much has been made of the eventual damaging impact on the German Army of the Battle of the Somme and this is used to justify Haig's determination to continue to battle until the middle of November. The success of the French attack with its carefully limited objectives begs the question as to what might have been the effect on the German Army, its strategic and tactical position and the morale of its troops, had such a success attended both Allied armies at the opening of the battle. The French, through careful planning and a great concentration of artillery, took the German 1st Position and the Zwischen Stellung on successive days and was up against the left bank of the Somme within a week. What if, after a two or three stage advance, Rawlinson's men had stood on the top of the Pozieres plateau on 4th July with the first two and possibly the third line of German trenches in their hands from the Ancre to Contalmaison? But such speculation is pointless. The die was cast and the hand that cast it was that of the Commander in Chief of the British Armies in France and Flanders. Sir Henry Rawlinson was but the monkey. The organ grinder was miles away at GHQ.

A week after the meeting Kiggell put into writing the main issues concerning the overall direction of the attack. At that point, i.e. 13th April, the offensive was still to be a French-dominated offensive with the largest part of the Allied force involved south of the Somme. The axis of attack for the French on either bank was eastwards. The intention was to outflank Peronne from the north while, to the south, the German troops were either crushed up against the barrier of the river or forced back with the French 6th and 10th Armies in hot pursuit. In consequence, therefore, after the initial advance to the Pozieres plateau and the taking of Fricourt, Mametz and Montauban, the British too would turn east and north east, taking the Ginchy-Bazentin le Grand ridge and then directly east towards Combles. In this manner, the British would protect the left flank of the French units advancing to the north of Peronne towards Mont St Quentin. Rawlinson was told that his purpose was:

> "… to cooperate with and assist the French Army on your right in effecting the passage of the River Somme."[6]

---

[i] He had been caught out accusing one of his subordinates for the failings of Neuve Chapelle when the faults were, in fact, his own. Some, including Sir William Robertson, wanted him sent home in consequence but Haig intervened and Rawlinson prospered. He was, however, Haig's 'poodle' from now on.

Keeping in close touch and working in co-operation with Foch and his Armies was essential, however, Rawlinson was also given some leeway, as according to Haig and transmitted by Kiggell, it was also the case that:

> "… the object will continue to be to prevent the enemy from re-establishing his line of defence and to exploit to the full all opportunities opened up for defeating his forces within reach, always, however, with due regard to the need to assist the French Army to effect the passage of the River Somme."[7]

So said Kiggell's first note (dated 12th April). Another was appended, dated the following day. It addressed more specifically the details of Fourth Army's offensive and one section highlights Haig's gung-ho attitude towards the opening stages of the assault. It should be reproduced in full:

> "One of the most important problems raised by you is the question of the objectives to be attained in the first instance, a point discussed in paragraphs 21-24 of your paper.
> It is, of course, inadvisable to push on isolated and disorganised bodies of troops beyond the reach of possible support, in face of an enemy who is still capable of delivering organised counter-attacks on a scale which these troops, unsupported, could not be expected to be capable of beating off.
> On the other hand, the importance of using every endeavour to surprise the enemy at the outset and to take full advantage of the confusion and disorganisation in his forces resulting from our first assault can scarcely be over-rated.
> Experience shows that tactical advantage may be secured with comparative ease during the first few hours of an attack which, if not secured then, are very costly and difficult to capture later. The further a first success can be pushed the greater will be the enemy's demoralisation and confusion, the better prospects there will be of capturing his guns, and the easier will be our subsequent advance. It is therefore usually wiser to act boldly in order to secure, at the outset, points of tactical value which it may be possible to reach, rather than to determine beforehand to stop short of what may prove to be possible in order to avoid risks.
> The risks to be incurred can be foreseen and to a great extent guarded against by careful previous arrangement providing artillery support, for throwing in reinforcements as required to fill gaps in the line and to cover flanks that become exposed, for ensuring an adequate supply of munitions, food, and water, and, generally, for providing the means of holding what may be gained.
> The first advance therefore should be pushed as far as the furthest objectives of tactical value which we can reasonably hope by forethought and. tactical skill to be able to retain after capturing."[8]

From this analysis sprang Haig's desire for Rawlinson to give:

> "… further consideration … to the possibility of pushing our first advance further than is contemplated in your plan…"[9]

As far as the VIII Corps was concerned, this meant taking the Serre to Miraumont spur. This was a huge enlargement of its initial planned assault area. This note also pressed Rawlinson on the time scale to be adopted. Haig's views on this fly in the face of Foch's, Petain's and, it is reasonable to assume, Rawlinson's analysis of the previous fighting:

> "As regards the time that must elapse between different phases of the operation there is no room for doubt that the more rapidly you can pass from one phase to the next the more far-reaching is success likely to be, and the less the losses likely to be suffered - always provided that such artillery preparation and reorganisation as may be really necessary are carried out; but remembering that the more the enemy can be pressed while he is shaken the less need there will be for a long artillery preparation."[10]

For Haig this also strongly suggested the early employment of cavalry and Rawly was invited to consider his CinC's remarks on the subject made at a previous Army Commanders' Conference held at Aire on 16th March. The prospect of a mass of cavalry, pennants fluttering on lances, streaming through a shattered German front loomed large in Haig's thinking:

> "Opportunities to use Cavalry, supported by guns, machine guns, &c., and infantry, should be sought for, both during the early stages of the attack and subsequently.
> So far as possible probable opportunities should be foreseen and all possible preparations made beforehand to enable them to be taken advantage of."[11]

So, according to Haig, this could be war on the Western Front – but not as Foch, Petain, Fayolle and Rawlinson knew it.

Rawlinson's response to the meeting and the two notes from GHQ was despatched on 19th April. Given the subject matter of this particular book we shall concentrate on those parts affecting VIII Corps which, in fact, are very few as Rawlinson appears to have immediately given in on VIII Corps' objectives which are now referred to as a line from Serre to Grandcourt with a possible push further forward to Miraumont[i].

Rawlinson, however, wanted to establish that, although the front to be attacked had both widened and deepened as a result of Haig's intervention, this did not mean that any more troops or guns were to be made available:

> "The troops that will be available for the Fourth Army offensive remain, I understand, as laid down in your letter No. O.A.D. 644 of the 25th March, that is to say, 17 divisions with approximately 200 heavy howitzers."

He then established his 'get out' clause should the whole affair go pear-shaped:

> "Before suggesting the limits of the first phase of the attack, I gave all the factors which affected the selection most careful consideration, after

[i] A full account of the planning of the Anglo-French Somme offensive will be found in the author's forthcoming book *Z Day, Planning the Somme.*

personally studying the ground and weighing the pros and cons from every point of view.
These factors were explained in paragraphs 24 to 30 of my letter of the 3rd of April.
I came to the conclusion that two courses were open to me. The first, and most alluring one, was to attempt to capture the whole of the enemy's lines of defence as far south as the Albert – Bapaume road in one attack. The second, less ambitious but in my opinion more certain, to divide the attack into two phases, the first of which would give us possession of the enemy's front system and all the important tactical points between the front system and the second line. The second phase to follow as soon as possible after the first, so as to give the enemy as little time as possible to construct new defences and bring up guns and reserves.
The first alternative, I considered, was a gamble which involved considerable risks."

For Rawlinson, the 'risks' were quite clear:

- The sheer distance between the various elements of the German defences;
- The strength of Pozieres and Contalmaison;
- The strength of the German second position consisting of two lines of well-wired trenches;
- The difficulties of cutting the wire in front of these trenches which lay some 3-4,000 yards away from the British front line;
- The likelihood that German reserves would reach this position before the advancing British troops;
- The difficulty of arranging accurate artillery support at such a range especially given the inexperience of many of the gunners; and
- The inexperience of the bulk of the troops to be employed and the possibility of inexperienced junior officers losing control during such a long advance.

Rawlinson stated quite clearly that, in his view, an advance of this type involved 'considerable risks'. He was, however, in no position to resist his superior's demands. He had, though, made clear his serious and sensible objections to the plan his CinC was forcing on him. Haig, however, was not to be denied. The result was that VIII Corps was asked to bombard and then capture up to eight lines of trenches in three different positions spread over a depth of 4,000 yards, a depth of penetration no British troops had come close to achieving at any point during the war to date.

There was another issue, however, which materially affected VIII Corps and that was what to do about the Gommecourt salient just to the north of Serre. Rawlinson had all along firmly stating that he did not have the troops and guns to mount an effective attack on this heavily fortified salient. The problem was eventually passed to Allenby's Third Army to the north but earlier, when invited to suggest a diversionary attack on their front which might assist Fourth Army, Gen. Allenby, GOC Third Army, in consultation with his Chief of Staff, Brig. Gen. Louis Jean Bols, CB, DSO, had first suggested Vimy Ridge. Their reasoning was tactically sound. The ridge was such an important tactical location that the

Germans would be sure to divert troops and guns to help defend it if it became apparent that a serious attempt was about to be made to take this prominent geographical feature. Given its distance from the main Somme front, i.e. 35 kilometres from Serre, even if OHL realised quickly that the Vimy Ridge attack was a feint it would take time to disengage infantry and artillery and ship it south. This, thought Allenby and Bols, was the main purpose of a 'diversion' – to stop troops interfering in the real offensive.

GHQ, however, thought the Vimy attack too ambitious and asked for an alternative. Third Army's second choice was a less high profile part of the German line, the shallow salient at Monchy-au-Bois and the trenches between there and Ransart to the north. These lay some 5,000 metres and more north of Gommecourt and 9 kilometres north of Serre. Although significantly closer to the left wing of the main attack, one of the main virtues of an attack here was that most of the field guns available to the Germans, i.e. the 77 mm FK 96 nA with a maximum range of 8,400 metres, would be unable to interfere with the main offensive or, at least, not until the attack at Monchy-au-Bois/Ransart had been defeated or been shown to be a diversion. By this time, as the main work of the VIII Corps would be over by the early afternoon of the first day of attack, the diversion would have done its job. In other words, Monchy-au-Bois too was a tactically sound recommendation from Allenby and Bols if the prime requirement of the diversion was to take German guns and infantry far enough away from the grand offensive that they could not interfere with its initial phases.

GHQ clearly agreed with Third Army's analysis and, on 13th April, put them to work planning an assault on this otherwise insignificant French village. At the same time, the 48th Division was ordered to prepare the ground south of Gommecourt for a single brigade assault on the village, thus giving the Germans early warning of a potential threat against the salient. But Haig still brooded on Gommecourt and, as he contemplated the most optimistic outcome of the offensive, he began to see how taking the ridges behind Gommecourt would greatly assist in his emerging plan to drive north from the town of Bapaume, thereby taking in the rear all of the German troops trapped south of Arras[i]. It was a tantalising prospect. Too tantalising for Haig and soon Third Army was ordered to switch objectives from Monchy-au-Bois to Gommecourt. As will be seen this was a disastrous decision, not only for the two Territorial Force divisions chosen to make the attack, but also for the two divisions on the extreme left of Fourth Army's offensive – the 31st and 4th Divisions of VIII Corps.

The scene was set for one of the bloodiest defeats in the long history of the British Army. It now needs to be seen how the decisions at GHQ and Fourth

---

[i] This overall change in emphasis, away from the easterly drive supporting the French and towards the north east (and away from the French), was a result of the slow but steady weakening of the French commitment to the Somme offensive caused by their losses at Verdun. On 21st April, Joffre informed Haig that the number of French divisions in the attack was being reduced from 39 to 30. On 20th May it was reduced from 30 to 26, on 31st May from 26 to 20 (with Rawlinson being warned he may have to attack on his own) and on 6th June from 20 to 12. Six were actually involved on the first day. On 14th June the main axis of the British attack was officially switched from eastwards towards Peronne to north east towards Bapaume.

Army were compounded by decisions on the ground by VIII Corps in order to ensure that the result was as grave a setback as could be imagined.

---

[1] Fourth Army Conference 30th March 1916, Fourth Army Papers V1, Imperial War Museum, quoted in Robin Prior and Trevor Wilson, *The Somme*, Yale University Press, 2005, pages 39-40.

[2] Jeffery, Keith, *Field Marshal Sir Henry Wilson: A Political Soldier.* Oxford University Press, page 139. 2006.

[3] Rawlinson Diary, 30th March 1916

[4] *'Notes on Conference on 5th March 1915'*, WO 95/708, quoted in *'Command on the Western Front'*, Robin Prior and Trevor Wilson, Blackwell, 1992, page 31.

[5] Op. cit. Prior and Wilson, page 85.

[6] NA, GHQ, OAD 710, 12th April 1916.

[7] Ibid.

[8] NA, GHQ, OAD710/1, 13th April 1916.

[9] Ibid.

[10] Ibid.

[11] Ibid.

3. VIII Corps

THE THREE BRITISH CORPS MOST AFFECTED BY THE CHANGES demanded by Haig were, from south to north, III Corps, X Corps and VIII Corps. X and III Corps had considerable depth added to their attack plans in the sectors between La Boisselle and Thiepval. VIII Corps, however, had additional width and depth to cope with and on a front on which, over the previous 21 months, the Germans had made enormous defensive efforts, turning places like Beaumont Hamel and Serre into small, modern fortresses. VIII Corps' task, therefore, had become immeasurably more difficult to achieve. It would require excellent leadership, superb planning by the staff and a fair degree of creativity and cunning if the Corps was to succeed in takings Haig's objectives. Sadly, all of these factors would be in short supply in the run up to 1st July 1916.

The VIII Corps was originally formed in Gallipoli in May 1915 as the British Army Corps. In June, it was renamed the VIII Corps. Commanded by Lt. Gen. Sir Aylmer Hunter-Weston, the Corps contained during its time on the peninsula various Divisions which included Hunter-Weston's previous command, the Regular 29th Division (later transferred to the IX Corps), 42nd (East Lancashire) Division, 52nd (Lowland) Division, the Royal Naval Division and sundry other units. The Corps was to remain at Gallipoli until the evacuation in early January 1916. Various elements, including the Corps commander and his staff and the 29th Division returned to France in March 1916 where they were reunited as part of a new version of VIII Corps which now consisted of the 29th Division, the 'Regular' 4th Division, the Territorial 48th (South Midland) Division and the New Army 31st Division.

The commander of the VIII Corps, Lt. Gen. Sir Aylmer Gould Hunter-Weston[i], was an intriguing fellow. His hard-earned reputation as an archetypal 'butcher/blunderer' has proved difficult to shift over the decades. One or two historians have attempted some sort of rehabilitation, e.g. Robin Prior in

[i] John Bourne's biographical sketch of the colourful Hunter-Weston from the University of Birmingham's Centre For First World War Studies:
Sir Aylmer Hunter-Weston ('Hunter-Bunter')
Lieutenant-General Sir Aylmer Gould Hunter-Weston (1864-1940) was one of the best known officers in the British Army. He was undoubtedly a 'card' and more stories were told about him and his eccentricities than any other general. He also had a flair for self-publicity unusual among his contemporaries. He was elected Unionist [Conservative] MP for North Ayrshire in October 1916. He held this seat and then that of Buteshire and North Ayrshire until 1935. His visits to subordinate formations and to the trenches often seemed more like an MP's visits to his constituency than military inspections. Hunter-Weston is best remembered for his long tenure of the command of VIII Corps, both on Gallipoli and on the Western Front. Hunter-Weston had a bad case of sunstroke on Gallipoli. Charles Carrington thought he was 'not quite sane' and dismissed VIII Corps as 'deplorable'. On 1st July 1916, the first day of the battle of the Somme, VIII Corps suffered the highest casualties of any corps and achieved nothing. It spent much of the remainder of the war in quiet sectors and back areas. Sir Aylmer Hunter-Weston died in a mysterious fall from a turret of his ancestral home, at Hunterston, Ayrshire, on 18th March 1940.

'Gallipoli: The End of the Myth' and most recently, Gordon Corrigan in *'Mud, Blood and Poppycock'* and there is a mood amongst some others to, at least, further investigate his performance as commander. Currently, Corrigan's opinion is the most favourable. He describes his performance at Gallipoli as 'competent'[1] and states the belief that he has since been unfairly vilified for an extraordinarily strange decision prior to the attack on Beaumont Hamel involving. the timing of the blowing of the Hawthorn Ridge mine. This, Maj. Corrigan suggests, has rather coloured most historians' views of the VIII Corps commander. Were it the case that this was the only complaint against Hunter-Weston and his staff at this time then one might have more sympathy for Corrigan's view but it was not. Perhaps we should let the actions of the no-less controversial Commander in Chief, Sir Douglas Haig, speak on Hunter-Weston's behalf. Haig never used him and his staff again in a major action on the Western Front[i]. He was, perhaps, too senior to sack and when, extraordinarily, he fought and won a Parliamentary by-election in the autumn of 1916 he was, perhaps, too well positioned to dismiss. The by-election, in the Northern Ayrshire constituency, fell on 11th October 1916 and Hunter-Weston garnered 85% of the vote[ii]. He would remain an MP until 1935.

Haig, of course, knew Hunter-Weston both professionally and, certainly, socially. Both were lowland Scots, although from opposite sides of the country, and, within the tight social circles within which they moved, reasonable acquaintance, at the very least, was certain. They had also served together in South Africa where Haig had been Sir John French's Chief Staff Officer and Hunter-Weston, for a period, head of his administrative staff.

There are those who suggest that the war-time link was very close and that, for Haig, having such a man in Parliament at a time when he was facing increasing pressure from such as Lloyd George, was a certain asset. What is odd, if this is the case, is the almost total absence of references to Hunter-Weston after 1st July 1916 in Haig's own diaries and the accounts of close colleagues. John Charteris, Haig's loyal Intelligence chief, makes but one reference to Hunter-Weston in each of his two post-war books on Haig. His biography mentions the South African connection. In *'At GHQ'* there is a passing reference to Hunter-Weston having done well in the Dardanelles and an anonymous one which, given

---

[i] Hunter-Weston rarely features in any memoires or histories thereafter, however, in January 1918, when his Corps was on the defensive in the Ypres sector, his Army commander, Sir Henry Rawlinson, was to voice displeasure at their failure to follow adequately instructions to improve the defences in anticipation of a major German offensive. Rawlinson's diary entry for the 2nd January 1918 contains the following: 'I was not at all pleased with the progress made and told H[unter] W[eston] so'.

[ii] His opponent, the Rev. H Chalmers who stood as a 'Peace by Negotiation' candidate, was supported by the Union of Democratic Control, a pressure group formed by Charles Trevelyan, MP, who had resigned from the Liberal Government in protest at the declaration of war, and Ramsey MacDonald, previously the Chairman of the Labour Party. It opposed censorship and conscription and was funded mainly by wealthy Quakers and, by 1917, had some 10,000 members and the support of affiliated organisations representing 650,000 people. It survived into the 1960s as a pressure group linked to the Labour Party.

The result of the by-election was: Hunter-Weston 7,149 votes, Chalmers 1,300 votes.

Haig's expressed reservations about the preparations of the VIII Corps in his own diaries, can only be about Hunter-Weston. Otherwise, Charteris makes no further mention of Hunter-Weston, nor does he refer to the outcome of this 'anonymous' general's attack.

Other Haig biographers, Terraine, Dewar, Duff Cooper, for example, make only passing or no references at all to the VIII Corps commander, which hardly suggests he loomed large in the thinking of the CinC either as general or politician. Although commanding one of the Army Corps resident in the 'Salient' prior to the Third Battle of Ypres his command was eased to one side and took no part in the fighting. He seems mainly to have spent his time meeting and entertaining foreign and other dignitaries whilst making infrequent speeches in the Commons, his maiden speech, made sixteen months after his election, being a somewhat bombastic contribution during a debate on Clause 2 of the Military Service Bill on 24th January 1918. It 'played to the gallery' within the B.E.F. as much as to those at home and the Conservative *'Daily Sketch'* acclaimed it as 'The Greatest War Speech of the War'. As the *'Sketch'* went on to become the *'Daily Mail'* in later years then the less said about that endorsement the better.

Plate 2 Lt. Gen. Sir Aylmer Hunter-Weston, DSO, CB, KCB, GOC VIII Corps

Hunter-Weston, or 'Hunter-Bunter' as he was nicknamed at Staff College in the 1890s, was, perhaps, an excellent example of an officer promoted too far, too fast, a man who epitomised the Peter Principle in action, that 'employees (or, in this case, Generals) tend to rise to their level of incompetence'. The GOC of the 11th Brigade at the outbreak of war, having taken command on 1st February 1914, he was given command of the regular 29th Division in time for the landings at Cape Helles on the Gallipoli peninsula on 25th April 1915. In spite of the dreadful casualties and repeated setbacks suffered by the Division, Hunter-Weston was promoted to command the British Army Corps and given the rank of temporary Lieutenant General on 24th May 1915. Having supervised two lamentable attacks at Krithia as Divisional commander, the hallmarks of which were bad planning, absurd tactics and a long casualty list, he took the chance as Corps commander to add to these characteristics by deciding to reinforce failure in the Third Battle of Krithia. It is, perhaps, no surprise that he became known as the 'Butcher of Helles' and that he was described by Aubrey Herbert[i] as 'more hated than most of the generals'. Such a reputation was then undoubtedly enhanced by the equally awful Battle of Gully Ravine where the 156th Brigade of the untried 52nd (Lowland) Division was hung out to dry and Hunter-Bunter, a keen fox hunter, congratulated himself on taking the opportunity to 'blood the pups'. The Brigade lost some, 1,400 men, of whom 800 were dead, and, after the battle, their commander, Maj. Gen. Egerton, is reputed to have introduced each battalion to the Expedition's visiting commander, Sir Ian Hamilton, as 'the remnants of the…battalion' until testily ordered to desist by his CinC.

Sir Aylmer Gould Hunter-Weston was born on the 23rd September 1864. His father, Lt. Col. Gould Weston, assumed the name Hunter-Weston seventeen years after marrying Jane Hunter, the daughter and heiress of Robert Hunter, 25th Laird of Hunterston in Ayrshire. Lt. Col. Weston had served in India during the Mutiny, being involved in the defence of the Lucknow Residency and in the later siege and recapture of Lucknow in 1858, and his son was always destined for a military career. The young Hunter-Weston was educated at Wellington College before attending the Royal Military Academy at Woolwich. He was commissioned into the Royal Engineers in 1884 and went to India where he served on the North West Frontier with some distinction, being rewarded with the Brevet of Major in 1895. His commander on the Waziristan Delimitation Escort, Brig. Gen. A H Turner, mentioned him in his despatch published in the *London Gazette* of 14th June 1895:

> "Captain A. G Hunter-Weston, Commanding No. 2 Company, Bengal Sappers and Miners, is an Officer of great energy, who, by his ability and readiness to undertake work, has been of great service to me."[2]

Further action was seen in Egypt and the Sudan in the later 1890s before he was sent to South Africa in 1899 where he climbed to be Gen. French's Chief Staff Officer before successfully commanding a cavalry column of his own. He was involved in numerous actions, being awarded the DSO in April 1901. He ended the campaign with a Brevet Lt. Colonelcy. He then served a long period as a Staff Officer, first under French with Eastern Command (1904-08) and then as Chief General Staff Officer for Scottish Command until 1911. He then spent three years as the Assistant Director of Military Training at the War Office until given command of 11th Brigade.

It was a more than decent pedigree. He went to France with his Brigade, part of the 4th Division, and was again mentioned in despatches. This time it was in

---

[i] Capt. Aubrey Nigel Henry Molyneux Herbert, JP, DL, FRGS, Irish Guards, diplomat, linguist, orientalist and Conservative and Unionist MP, was, at this time, a liaison officer on the staff of General Birdwood's ANZAC Corps. Born in 1880, he was the son of the 4th Earl of Carnarvon and was educated at Eton and Balliol College, Oxford. A diplomat who had served in Tokyo and Constantinople, he was elected Conservative MP for South Somerset in the December 1910 General Election. He served in France, Gallipoli, Mesopotamia and Salonika. He was elected MP for Yeovil in the 1918 General Election. He died in 1923.

Field Marshal Sir John French's despatch of 27th November 1914 in which his Brigade's counter attack in support of some exposed cavalry was described as:

> "… entirely successful, the Germans being driven back with great loss and the abandoned trenches reoccupied. Two hundred prisoners were taken and about forty of our prisoners released."[3]

His later use of his battalions was described by French as 'skilful'. So far, so good.

At Gallipoli things did not go quite so swimmingly and it was here that he gained the dubious nickname of 'The Butcher of Helles'. He is also reputedly to have commented to the GOC of a Division recently decimated in one of the attacks he had planned, "Casualties? What do I care for casualties?"

This comment was addressed to Maj. Gen. Archibald Paris, GOC of the Royal Naval Division. In an article in the Western Front Association's magazine *'Stand To!'*, Elizabeth Balmer attempts to put this comment into some form of context:

> "He is remembered mainly for his remark, 'Casualties? What do I care for casualties?' quoted by Compton Mackenzie, but Mackenzie's rider to this remark is not remembered. He continues that it was because the General never hesitated to talk in this 'ruthless strain' that he achieved the reputation of butcher on Gallipoli. He goes on to say 'Actually no man I have ever met brimmed over more richly with human sympathy. He was a logician of war…and believed that…provided the objective was gained, casualties were of no importance.' While this attitude may offend modern sensibilities, it was the unquestioned and unsentimental approach at the time."[4]

Compton Mackenzie seems not to have considered that it was the hideous casualties in futile attacks that earned Hunter-Weston his reputation rather than words the average junior officer and 'rank and filer' were never likely to hear. And, while Elizabeth Balmer may believe such an approach was unquestioned, an enormous and unsubstantiated claim which flies in the face of the conduct of numerous British Generals of WW1, the quote and the context explain why Hunter-Weston's reputation amongst the officers and men at the sharp end was so low. Lastly, had any of Hunter-Weston's attacks attained their objectives then these words from a 'logician of war' might have had some merit. But none did.

One General in particular to have a different perspective was Maj. Gen. Granville Egerton[i] who commanded the 52nd (Lowland) Division and whose three Brigades were frittered away in failed Hunter-Weston commanded attacks in June and July 1915. His particular complaint was about the fighting on the 12th and 13th July which witnessed the destruction of his 155th and 157th Brigades:

---

[i] Maj. Gen. Granville George Algernon Egerton, Seaforth Highlanders, was born in 1859 and, after Charterhouse and the RMC, Sandhurst, joined the 72nd Highlanders in 1879. He served in Afghanistan, Egypt and the Sudan. The Commandant of the Hythe School of Musketry between 1907 and 1909 he took command of the 52nd Division in 1914. He was appointed Inspector of Infantry in 1916. He died in 1951.

"It seems to me that the fighting of this battle was premature and at the actual moment worse than unnecessary – I submit that it was cruel and wasteful. The troops on the Peninsula were tired and worn out; there were only two Infantry Brigades, the 155th and the 157th, that had not been seriously engaged. It was well known to the higher command that large reinforcements were arriving from England (i.e. IX Corps) and a grand attack was to be made at Suvla. Was it not therefore obvious that the exhausted garrison at Helles should be given a fortnight's respite and that the fresh attacks from that position should synchronise with those at Suvla and Anzac? I contend that the Battle of July 12th-13th was due to a complete want of a true appreciation of the situation. If the conception of the battle was wrong the tactics of the action were far worse. The division of the attack of two Brigades on a narrow front into two phases, no less than 9 hours apart, was positively wicked."[5]

The 155th Brigade lost 48 officers and 1,268 men during 12th July 1915 and the 157th Brigade 39 officers and 938 men advancing later in the day over the same corpse-littered ground. There was no logic to Hunter-Weston's tactics whatsoever.

Equally, the impact of Hunter-Weston's tactics on his old Division, the 29th, was devastating. Maj. Jack Churchill[i], Winston's brother and a member of Hamilton's and later Birdwood's staff, was to report:

"The 29th Div. is down to small numbers now … These continual frontal attacks are terrible, and I fear the Generals will be called butchers by the troops. H[unter] W[eston] already has that name with the 29th."[6]

In his favour, it must be stressed that Hunter-Weston had opposed the idea of the landings on Gallipoli, regarding them as a 'big gamble', however, his alternative strategy for dealing with the Turks lacked substance and genuine realism. Credit for appreciating the essential flaws in the campaign's strategy should, though, be his. It is a sad irony that he was equally opposed to the greatly extended scope of Haig's concept for the beginning of the attack on the Somme but, as at Gallipoli, once given an objective he threw himself with enormous enthusiasm but no great skill or imagination into planning and organising the required attack.

Given his overall performance in Gallipoli, his next appearance in a despatch is nothing short of remarkable. It comes in the report of the CinC, Sir Ian Hamilton, published in the *London Gazette* on 2nd July 1915. It hints at something of the character of Hunter-Weston who, had it been written at the time, might well have found his favourite song to be Monty Python's *'Always look on the bright side of life'*. Hamilton's opinion of his subordinate was:

"Major-General A. G. Hunter-Weston, C.B., D.S.O., was tried very highly, not only during the landings, but more especially in the day and night attacks and counter attacks which ensued. Untiring, resourceful and ever

[i] Maj. John 'Jack' Strange Spencer Churchill, DSO, TD, 1/1st Queen's Own Oxfordshire Hussars, was aged 35 at this time. Born in 1880, he was the younger brother of Winston Spencer Churchill. He served in South Africa, MiD. His DSO was gazetted on 31st May 1918. He died in 1947.

more cheerful as the outlook (on occasion) grew darker, he possesses, in my opinion, very special qualifications as a Commander of troops in the field."[7]

Within a few days, Hunter-Weston had been invalided home suffering from, and one may 'perm' any one (or more) from five: sunstroke, exhaustion, enteric fever, dysentery and/or a breakdown (sunstroke is the generally, though not universally, accepted condition). Whether H-W's medical collapse had any long lasting effects one cannot say. Perhaps his contemporaries could not tell. Certainly, one more madman in the House of Commons would hardly have stood out from the crowd.

He was described, however, by Cuthbert Headlam[i], then GSO2 in VIII Corps and later a Conservative MP, as, variously, 'not all there' and a 'madman', while, according to Headlam, a fellow officer described H-W as 'on heat' and raving mad. Charles Carrington[ii], a staff officer in the 48th (South Midland) Division who was in the front line trenches on 1st July between the VII and VIII Corps' attacks, regarded Hunter-Weston as 'not quite sane' and the performance of the VIII Corps' staff as 'deplorable'.

After the fiasco of the 1st July 1916, when his Corps had the dubious honour of suffering the heaviest casualties of the five involved in the main attack and of being the only one to make no gains whatsoever, Hunter-Weston's military career dawdled along until he retired from the Army in 1919. After his withdrawal from active politics in 1935 he retreated to his estate at Hunterston where, on the 18th March, 1940, he fell to his death from a turret in slightly odd circumstances.

The potential picture of Hunter-Weston is not an encouraging one: promoted beyond his level of competence, callous, pompous, vainglorious, perhaps slightly deranged and something of a show-off. He liked nothing more than to descend on his battalions on horseback at the gallop, then to direct a few platitudes in their general direction before belting off to irritate the next unit on his roster. Once elected to the House of Commons he chose to introduce himself by his full military title to which was appended 'MP'. He was renowned for his pomposity and even Field Marshal Haig poked gentle fun at this aspect of his character after the war. The story is told in a memoire by Ruth du Pree (née Haig), the daughter of Douglas Haig's older brother John. With a visit from Hunter-Weston imminent an officer discovered a corporal comatose through drink. Showing

[i] Capt., later Lt. Col., Rt. Hon. Sir Cuthbert Morley Headlam, 1st Baronet, DSO, OBE, TD, DL, Bedfordshire Yeomanry, was born in 1876. He was educated at King's School, Canterbury and at Magdalen College, Oxford. He was a Clerk in the House of Lords 1897-1924 and became a barrister, Inner Temple in 1906. He was three times elected a Conservative MP, once as an Independent Conservative, between 1924 and 1940 (Barnard Castle 1924-29 and 1931-5, North Newcastle 1940-51, before retiring in 1951. He was, until 1942, the editor of the *Army Quarterly*. He died in 1964.

[ii] Brig. Gen Charles Ronald Brownlow Carrington, DSO, OBE, Royal Artillery, was born in 1880. Educated at Eton, he joined the Kent Artillery (Eastern Division), Royal Artillery, Militia, in 1899, later transferring to the Royal Horse Artillery. He was appointed Brigade Major in April 1916. DSO, 1916, six times MiD, Bt. Lt. Col. He was the commander Royal Artillery, 48th (South Midland) Division, TF, between 1931 and 1933. OBE, 1942. He died in 1948.

great initiative he managed to cover the drunkard with a military greatcoat. Haig's account continued:

> "Great quietness reigned and in marched the General. He stopped dead, saluted, and exclaimed, 'Salute the glorious dead'."

The late Richard Holmes, in his *'Tommy: The British Soldier on the Western Front'*, tells an anecdote which also speaks volumes about the man:

> "In the bitter winter of 1917-18 'Hunter-Bunter' decided to wish troops departing on leave trains a merry Christmas. An aide-de-camp would open the carriage door and the general would intone: 'I am Lieutenant General Sir Aylmer Hunter-Weston, MP, your Corps commander, and I wish you a Happy Christmas'. From the smoky fug of one carriage a disembodied voice declared: 'And I'm the Prince of Wales, and wish you'd shut the bloody door'."[8]

It must have been with mixed feelings that the surviving officers and men of the 'Incomparable' 29th Division learnt they would be under the command of 'The Butcher of Helles' once more when they landed back in France in the early spring of 1916.

AFTER HAIG MADE CLEAR TO RAWLINSON HIS REQUIREMENTS for the offensive, the VIII Corps started to assess the German defences, what was needed to overcome them and the resources available for the task. Meanwhile, the troops assembled.

The 29th Division had been evacuated from Gallipoli on the nights of the 7th and 8th January 1916 and they then spent the best part of two months in the somewhat safer surroundings of Egypt. Orders were received to move to the Western Front on the 25th February and in early March they took ship for Marseilles. The component parts of the Division concentrated in the area around Pont Remy between 15th and 29th March before moving into position on the Somme. Another Egypt-based unit, the 31st Division, which had been in that country since the end of December 1915, was shipped off to France a few days earlier. Unlike the Regular 29th Division, the 31st, a New Army unit raised in Yorkshire, Lancashire and Co. Durham in the autumn of 1914, had not seen any serious action. Furthermore, it had not had an opportunity to work with its own Divisional artillery as, when they embarked for Egypt in December, they had been accompanied by the artillery of the 32nd Division. The various elements of the original division were reunited in France in the spring of 1916 to become the first division to join the reformed VIII Corps. In early April the 29th Division arrived from Marseille via their concentration area around Pont Remy to join the 31st Division and bolster the Corps' strength. Next, the Regular 4th Division, in France since the Battle of Le Cateau, and the Territorial 48th (South Midland) Division were transferred to the Corps from VII Corps. The 48th Division had spent the previous nine months thinly spread along both the southern and western faces of the Gommecourt salient. With the arrival of the two divisions tasked with taking Gommecourt – the 56th (1st London) and the 46th (North Midland) Divisions – the 48th Division occupied the short stretch of trench from just north of Serre to the east of Hebuterne.

THE 31ST DIVISION WAS THE ONLY NEW ARMY DIVISION within VIII Corps and the attack on the village of Serre would be its first involvement in a major attack. For such an inexperienced Division the task given to it was a formidable one. Its role was to cover the extreme left flank of the main attack on the Somme and, if the attack developed according to Haig's expectations, it was to be the hinge on which the whole offensive swung in a great arc to the north-east towards Arras and Douai.

The 31st Division was formed as part of Kitchener's Fifth New Army and, originally, was designated the 38th Division. In April 1915 the then Fourth New Army was broken up and the Fifth became the Fourth New Army. As a result, its Divisions, originally numbered 37th to 42nd, were re-designated the 30th to 35th. The 38th Division became the 31st Division as a result.

Plate 3 Maj. Gen. Robert Wanless-O'Gowan, GOC 31st Division

The commander of the 31st Division was the experienced Irish officer Maj. Gen. Robert Wanless-O'Gowan. Wanless-O'Gowan was born Robert Wanless Smith in Bray and Rathmichael, Dublin in 1864, the son of a wealthy cattle breeder Edward John Smith and his wife Dorcas Maria Kelley. The name Wanless came from his maternal grandfather, Robert Wanless Kelley of Islanmore, Limerick. The surname Smith, however, was the Anglicization of the Irish surname MacGowan/O'Gowan (from the Gaelic Mac an Ghaghain or Mac Gabhann). Gowan is the Gaelic for 'smith' and, during the long period of English domination in Ireland, Smith became a more socially and politically acceptable surname. Quite what event triggered Wanless-Gowan's decision is not clear but, in 1895, he changed his name by deed-poll from Smith to the hyphenated Wanless-O'Gowan in something of a return to his original Gaelic roots.

By this time, he was already a soldier. After a private education, he entered the 8th KRRC before transferring to The Cameronians (Scottish Rifles) in 1886. He was steadily promoted and saw extensive action in South Africa, fighting in some of the more lamentably conducted actions such as Colenso and Spion Kop, where he was severely wounded, and at the siege of Ladysmith. By now a Brevet

Major he transferred to the East Lancashire Regt. in 1906 and was promoted Lt. Colonel of the 1st Battalion in September 1909. He served as OC of the 1st East Lancashires until 1913 when he was promoted full Colonel but put on half pay. In January 1914 he was appointed AQMG of Eastern Command and, on the outbreak of war, AAG, Lines of Communication. In October he was appointed AA and QMG of the 6th Division and he was MiD by Sir John French that November. In early 1915 he was given his first outright wartime command when he took over the 13th Brigade, 5th Division, which then saw some heavy fighting in the Spring. The Brigade took Hill 60 near Ypres on 17th April 1915 and fought at the 2nd Battle of Ypres before again seeing action in a failed attempt to re-capture Hill 60 lost in a heavy gas attack on 15th May. In August, Wanless-O'Gowan was given command of the 31st Division still training in England, which Division he commanded until after the Battle of Arras.

His Division was made up of three infantry Brigades, the 92nd, 93rd and 94th, four Brigades of Field Artillery, 165th, 169th, 170th and 171st, five trench mortar batteries, S/31, X/31, V/31, Y/31 and Z/31, three Leeds-based Royal Engineer Field Companies, 210th, 211th and 223rd, the 93rd, 94th and 95th Field Ambulances with the 12th King's Own Yorkshire Light Infantry (Leeds' Miners) as the Pioneer Battalion.

The 92nd Brigade was made up of four battalions raised in and around Hull and the East Riding. Its GOC in 1916 was the 41 year old Brig. Gen. Oliver de Lancey Williams[i], DSO, the younger brother of Brig. Gen. Weir de Lancey Williams of the 86th Brigade, 29th Division. The son of Lt. Gen. Sir W G Williams, KCB, he joined the 2nd Royal Welsh Fusiliers from Sandhurst in 1894 after being educated at Oxford Military College[ii]. He served in South Africa and briefly was seconded to the Chinese Regiment of Infantry in 1901. He gained one of the first Pilot's Licences, No. 356, in 1912. He was awarded the DSO in the *London Gazette* of the 23rd March 1915 having been an acting Lt. Col. since early in the war and having been CO of the 2nd Royal Welsh Fusiliers (19th Brigade, 6th Division) since the end of October 1914 to May 1915.

The battalions of the brigade were the:

10th East Yorkshire Regt. (Hull Commercials)
11th East Yorkshire Regt. (Hull Tradesmen)
12th East Yorkshire Regt. (Hull Sportsmen)
13th East Yorkshire Regt. (T'Others)

---

[i] Post-war, Brig, Gen, Williams was the unfortunate victim of a strange woman, Una Hanley (née Bowen), who married him bigamously in 1921 under the false name of Margaret Patricia Crawford, the supposed widow of a naval surgeon killed at the Battle of Jutland, She then proceeded to trade on his name and reputation to falsely claim medical qualifications through which she took jobs in a Dublin Hospital and as a temporary GP. She was prosecuted for bigamy and for impersonating a doctor as well as for several frauds and thefts. The marriage was dissolved and he subsequently married Mildred Ramsey-Hill in 1924.

[ii] Oxford Military College was a private boarding school and military academy founded in Cowley in 1876. In spite of an eminent school council which listed, amongst others, Lord Wolseley (Field Marshal 1894, Commander in Chief 1895), the school went bankrupt in 1896.

These battalions, raised between August and October 1914, were originally designated the 1st to 4th Hull Battalions before being retitled the 10th to 13th (Service) Battalions, East Yorkshire Regt. Between them, they formed the 113th (Hull) Brigade, 38th Division, Fifth New Army, until the renumbering triggered in the Spring of 1915.

The 93rd Brigade's GOC in 1916 was the 44 year old Brig. Gen. John Darnley Ingles. He was educated at Cheltenham College and the United Services College[i] at Westward Ho! in Devon where both Rudyard Kipling and the WW1 cartoonist Bruce Bairnsfather went to school. Ingles joined the Devonshire Regt. in 1894 and served in the South African War. He started the war as a Captain, being promoted Major in October and given command of a battalion in October 1915. He took command of the 93rd Brigade in June 1916 on the death of Brig. Gen. Henry B Kirk who died of pneumonia on 12th May 1916.

The 93rd Brigade comprised three Battalions raised from Bradford and Leeds and a Pals battalion formed in Durham:

15th West Yorkshire Regt. (Leeds Pals)
16th West Yorkshire Regt. (1st Bradford Pals)
18th West Yorkshire Regt. (2nd Bradford Pals)
18th Durham Light Infantry (Durham Pals)

The Leeds Pals, formed in early September 1914, was a non-manual workers' battalion made up of office workers, teachers, sportsmen, both professional and amateur, and was a well-educated, middle class unit. Many of its officers were drawn from the Leeds University and Leeds Grammar School OTCs, whilst others were well-educated sons of prominent businessmen.

The two Bradford Pals battalions were recruited over a far longer period of time with the 1st Battalion being full to capacity within six days of the opening of recruitment on 20th September 1914. The 2nd Battalion, however, did not start to recruit until 8th February 1915 and, now that the first flush of enthusiasm for teaching the Hun a lesson had waned (and the casualty lists had grown), it was not until 29th April that the fourth company reached the required numbers. The battalion would have to work extra hard to catch up on the seven months training lead enjoyed by the other battalions in the Division.

The officers of the 1st Battalion were a mixture of 'Dugouts', retired officers with either regular of Volunteer experience, some of whom had served in Egypt and South Africa, and younger men who had either come through one of various OTCs or were the sons of leading businessmen within the community. The rank and file, however, came from all walks of life: clerks, warehousemen, bricklayers, insurance agents, wool combers, mechanics, tramway conductors and others[9].

The 18th Durham Light Infantry, called the Durham Pals, were, in fact, drawn from across the county with recruiting starting on 24th September 1914. Contingents came from Durham City, South Shields, Sunderland, Hartlepool and Darlington and the battalion was, like the Leeds pals, another well educated, middle class battalion of clerks, tradesmen, students, teachers and the like. For a time, the battalion was part of the Tyne and Tees Defences and, as such, suffered its first losses when five men were killed and eleven wounded when three

[i] The USC at Westward Ho! failed financially in 1903 and relocated to St George's, Harpenden, in the spring of 1904.

German Battle cruisers, the *Derfflinger, Blücher* and *Von der Tann*, bombarded Hartlepool on 16th December 1914. This battalion, therefore, became the first Service battalion to come under enemy fire during the war. The battalion was originally part of the 122nd Brigade, 41st Division, Fifth New Army, and it was not until the end of May 1915 that it joined up with the rest of the 93rd Brigade.

The 94th Brigade was made up of three Service battalions of the York and Lancaster Regt. and one from the East Lancashire Regt. Its GOC in 1916 was the 46 year old Brig. Gen. George Tupper Campbell Carter-Campbell, DSO, though Brig. Gen. Hubert Conway Rees, DSO, would be in command on 1st July 1916 when Carter-Campbell fell ill. Rees was considerably younger than his fellow Brigadiers, being just 34 years old in 1916. The son of a churchman and educated at Charterhouse, he joined the 3rd East Surrey Regt. of the Militia before being commissioned into the 2nd Welch Regt. in 1903. He started the war as a company commander fighting at Mons, winning the DSO at Langemarck in October 1914 and taking part in the Battle of Neuve Chapelle. He took temporary command of the Brigade on 15th June.

The 94th Brigade's battalions were:

11th East Lancashire Regt (Accrington Pals)
12th York and Lancaster Regt. (Sheffield City Battalion)
13th York and Lancaster Regt. (1st Barnsley Pals)
14th York and Lancaster Regt. (2nd Barnsley Pals)

The Accrington Pals were actually raised from four main towns – Accrington, Blackburn, Burnley and Chorley – and several nearby villages as it was clear that Accrington itself, with a population of 45,000, would struggle to recruit the 1,000 or so men required to form a Service battalion in Kitchener's New Army. The battalion, originally designated the 7th (Service) Battalion of the East Lancashire Regt., was, like the 1st Bradford Pals, a mixture of men drawn from across the community. With unemployment at very high levels locally, the attraction of regular meals, pay, exercise and excitement appealed to many and the ranks were soon filled. The four companies were as follows:

A Company – Accrington
B Company – the surrounding villages of Clayton-le-Moors, Oswaldtwistle. Rishton and Great Harwood
C Company – Chorley and Blackburn (mainly Chorley)
D Company – Burnley

On 10th December, when the Fifth New Army was officially formed, the 7th (Accrington) Service Battalion became the 11th (Accrington) Service Battalion of the East Lancashire Regiment, part of the 112th Brigade, 37th Division. In February 1915, whilst training in Wales, the battalion was put under the command of Lt. Col. Arthur Wilmot Rickman who, except for periods recovering from wounds and temporary secondments, would retain command for the rest of the war. One of his first actions was to change the company titles from A, B, C and D to W, X, Y and Z and they kept these titles throughout the war.

The Sheffield City Battalion was predominantly a middle class unit, as its original title of 'The Sheffield University and City Special Battalion, York and Lancaster Regt.' suggests. There were, however, a number of miners and railwaymen recruited from the Penistone area outside the city. Sheffield, however, was a city crammed with essential war factories producing weapons and munitions and it was in the best interests of the war effort that the majority of the manual and skilled workers in these factories remained where they were. The resulting companies had the following characteristics[10]:

A Company – University students, teachers, bankers, businessmen;

B Company – Tradesmen, railwaymen and contingents from Penistone and Chesterfield;

C Company – Teachers, students, Town Hall clerks; and

D Company – Teachers, students, clerks, employees of the Sheffield *Daily Telegraph*.

The battalion was originally part of the 115th Brigade of the 38th Division, along with the 10th Lincolnshire Regt. (Grimsby Chums) and the two Barnsley Pals battalions.

There were two main 'occupations' in Barnsley in September 1914: mining and being unemployed. Young men flocked to enlist in the local Pals battalion from the pit head, the street corner and the public bar. With a surplus of men generated by the first wave of recruitment the formation of a 2nd Battalion was put in hand. Enthusiasm for this unit waned, however, and various schemes were attempted, including cash incentives for the enlisted men who could recruit the largest number of new additions, but it was not until April that the battalion's full complement was approached.

With the replacement of the Grimsby battalion by the Accrington lads and the renumbering of the Brigade from 115th to 94th and the Division from 38th to 31st the formation of the infantry of this New Army Division was complete. They now had to await their baptism of fire.

The Divisional Pioneers were another locally raised unit. The 12th King's Own Yorkshire Light Infantry was known as the Leeds' Miners. Raised under the auspices of the West Yorkshire Coalowners' Association in mid-September 1914, they were known as the 'T'Owd Twelfth'. Many of the men came from the coal mines owned by J & J Charlesworth around Leeds, Wakefield and Rotherham.

Initial training took place near to the cities and towns from which they had been raised until the entire Division moved to South Camp near Ripon in North Yorkshire. Their final training, including live firing with newly supplied rifles, took place at Fovant on Salisbury Plain in September and October 1915. Initially ordered to go to France in November, these orders were countermanded in early December and, instead, the Division, minus its field artillery, was shipped off to Egypt where it formed part of the Suez Canal defences for the rest of the winter. In early March the Division was brought back across the Mediterranean to Marseille and, from there, it wended a weary way along the ramshackle French railway system, ending up in the trenches initially to the south of Serre. So leisurely was this railway journey north that the history of the Durham Pals recalls how two men who fell out of one of the '40-homes ou 8-chevaux' trucks on a tight bend south of the town of Orange still reached the station only a few minutes after the arrival of the train.

THE 29TH DIVISION WAS COMMANDED by Maj. Gen. Sir Henry de Beauvoir de Lisle, CB, DSO. Its divisional troops consisted of four artillery brigades, one made up of three 18 pdr batteries from the Royal Horse Artillery (15th Brigade,

RHA), and the other three Royal Field Artillery Brigades each comprising three 18 pdr and one 4.5 in. howitzer batteries (17th, 132nd and 147th Brigades, RFA). Its trench mortar batteries were: X/29, Y/29 and Z/29[i]. The three Royal Engineers companies were all Territorial units: 1/1st West Riding (455th), 1/3rd Kent (497th) and 1/2nd London (510th) Field Companies. Medical support was provided by the 87th (1st West Lancashire), 88th (1st East Anglian) and 89th (1st Highland) Field Ambulances. Lastly, the divisional pioneers were the 1/2nd Monmouthshire Regt. This unit was a late addition to the division having originally been attached as an infantry battalion to the 12th Brigade, 4th Division. A Territorial Force battalion based at Pontypool, the Monmouths had arrived in France on 7th November 1914 where it joined the 12th Brigade. At the end of May 1915, having suffered heavy casualties, it was merged with the 1/1st and 1/3rd Monmouthshire Regt. to form a temporary composite battalion. Two months later it was reconstituted and re-joined the 12th Brigade. At the end of January 1916 the battalion was removed and, as part of the process of changing to a pioneer battalion, it became a Lines of Communication unit. It was allocated to the 29th Division on 1st May 1916, becoming the last of the three 1st line battalions of the Monmouthshire Regt. to become a pioneer battalion[ii].

Plate 4 Maj. Gen. Sir Henry de Beauvoir de Lisle, GOC 29th Division

The GOC, De Beauvoir de Lisle, was aged 52 and came from a military family. His father had served as an Army surgeon for 18 years, seeing service in the Crimean War with the 4th (King's Own) Foot and, after Henry's private education on Jersey was completed, he entered the Royal Military College at Sandhurst. He came out an infantryman and was gazetted into the 2nd Durham Light Infantry in 1883. Within two years he had been awarded a DSO and

---

[i] Y/23 Battery from the 23rd Division was attached during the pre-attack bombardment.

[ii] The 1/1st Monmouthshire Regt. became the pioneer battalion of the 46th (North Midland) Division and the 1/3rd Monmouthshire Regt. the pioneer battalion of the 49th (West Riding) Division in September 1915

recommended for a VC as a result of his involvement in the rescue of the garrison of Ambigole Wells Fort in August 1885. He was then sent to India where his passion for, and excellence at, polo emerged. Described by one commentator as 'the inventor of modern polo', de Lisle took his infantry polo team to an unprecedented Championship of India in 1898, much to the chagrin of the various cavalry regiments more used to winning such a prestigious competition.

After attending the Staff College at Camberley, de Lisle commanded the 6th Mounted Infantry in the South African War and, having been badly wounded at Venterskroon in 1900, his talents as a potential cavalryman were recognised by none other than Field Marshal Lord Roberts and, in 1902, a transfer was arranged to the 5th Dragoon Guards. He was to stay with the cavalry until 1915, rising to command the 2nd Cavalry Brigade in 1911, which unit he took to France on the outbreak of war. His performance during the retreat from Mons saw an auspicious promotion to Major General and command of the 1st Cavalry Division. On 4th June 1915 he replaced Hunter-Weston as commander of the 29th Division at Gallipoli on Hunter-Weston's promotion to the command of VIII Corps. He would remain in command of the Division, with temporary commands at both Corps and Army level, until the end of the war.

Created in January 1915, the 29th Division was the last of the 'regular' divisions to be formed and, initially, was made up of eleven regular battalions brought back from the far flung posts of Empire[i] along with the 1/5th Royal Scots (Queen's Edinburgh Rifles), an Edinburgh Territorial unit[ii]. On its return to France the division was made up as below:

86th Brigade	
2nd Royal Fusiliers	1st Lancashire Fusiliers
1st Royal Dublin Fusiliers	16th Middlesex Regt. (Public Schools B'n.)
87th Brigade	
1st Border Regt.	1st King's Own Scottish Borderers
1st Royal Inniskilling Fusiliers	2nd South Wales Borderers
88th Brigade	
1st Essex Regt.	2nd Hampshire Regt.
4th Worcestershire Regt.	1st Newfoundland Regt.

The eleven original regular battalions of the division had been hurriedly returned from various locations scattered across the Empire, although the majority had been serving somewhere in or near India on the outbreak of war. The battalions returned from the following locations:

86th Brigade:

2nd Royal Fusiliers – Calcutta (now Kolkata), returned December 1914

1st Lancashire Fusiliers – Karachi, January 1915

[i] The 1st Royal Munster Fusiliers was replaced by the 16th Middlesex Regt. in April 1916. Pre-war the Munsters had been garrisoned in Rangoon, Burma.

[ii] For reasons not clear, the 1/5th Royal Scots was never to receive any drafts to replace losses suffered at Gallipoli and when, eventually, reduced to Company strength it was replaced by the 1st Newfoundland Regt. in September 1915. The 1/5th Royal Scots was amalgamated with the 1/6th Royal Scots becoming the 5/6th Royal Scots which joined the 14th Brigade, 32nd Division, on 29th July 1916.

1st Royal Dublin Fusiliers – Madras (now Chennai), December 1914

Replacing the 1st Royal Munster Fusiliers, the 16th (Service Battalion) Middlesex Regt. (Public Schools) was a New Army battalion raised in London in September 1914. After training in England the battalion joined the 100th Brigade, 33rd Division, with which it went to France in November 1915. It left the division in February 1916 and joined the 86th Brigade on 25th April 1916.

87th Brigade:

1st Border Regt. – Maymyo (now Pyin Oo Lwin), Burma, January 1915

1st King's Own Scottish Borderers – Lucknow, December 1914

1st Royal Inniskilling Fusiliers – Trimulgherrey (now Tirumalagiri, a suburb of Secunderabad), India, January 1915

2nd South Wales Borderers – Tientsin (Tianjin), China

88th Brigade:

1st Essex Regt. – Mauritius, December 1914

2nd Hampshire Regt. – Mhow, India, December 1914

4th Worcestershire Regt. – Meiktila, Burma (now Myanmar), February 1915

The 1st Newfoundland Regt. was raised by the Government of Newfoundland on the outbreak of war and the initial contingent was sent to England for training before the complete battalion was sent out to Egypt before replacing the 5th Royal Scots at the end of September 1915.

The three Brigadiers who commanded the Brigades of the 29th Division were:

86th Brigade – Brig. Gen. Weir de Lancey Williams who was the elder brother of Oliver de Lancey Williams, GOC of the 92nd Brigade, 31st Division. Educated at the United Services College, Westward Ho! and Sandhurst he joined the Hampshire Regt. in 1891. Between 1897 and 1900 he fought in, and was severely wounded in each of, the Tirah Campaign in India, the Benin Hinterland and Siama Expedition in West Africa and the South African War. He was awarded the DSO in 1899. From 1903 he was seconded to the Indian Army rising to be a Divisional Staff Officer. On his return to England he was appointed GSO2 of the Welsh Division, Western Command, and, on the outbreak of war, GSO1, 1/1st Welsh Division. He was a GSO1 on Sir Ian Hamilton's Staff in Gallipoli where he distinguished himself on V Beach during the initial landings. He briefly commanded the 88th Brigade before taking command of the 86th Brigade late in 1915.

87th Brigade – was commanded by Brig. Gen Cuthbert Henry Tindall Lucas. Lucas was 37 years old and had been educated at Marlborough and Sandhurst from where he joined the 2nd Royal Berkshire Regt. He spent two years involved in the South African War before being seconded to the Egyptian Army and the Sudan Civil Service. In 1913 he attended the Staff College at Camberley. Briefly the CO of the 1st Royal Berkshire Regt., he fulfilled a variety of staff positions before becoming the GOC, 87th Brigade in 1915.

88th Brigade – was commanded by 46 year old Brig. Gen. Douglas Edward Cayley. Educated at Clifton College and Sandhurst he was commissioned into the 2nd Worcestershire Regt. based in Limerick but was soon transferred to the 1st Battalion and sent to India. He remained there until going to South Africa with the battalion on the outbreak of war. In 1905 he returned to the 2nd Battalion being posted to Ceylon. In 1914, he was sent to Burma to take command of the

4th Worcestershire Regt. which then returned to England to join the 29th Division. He was promoted to command the 88th Brigade in 1915.

Plate 5 Brig. Gen. Douglas Edward Cayley, GOC, 88th Brigade

The 29th Division first saw action on the morning of the 25th April 1915 when two of its Brigades, the 86th and the 87th, landed on the beaches at Cape Helles, Gallipoli. It was here, on W Beach, that the 1st Lancashire Fusiliers won their 'six Victoria Crosses before breakfast' and on V Beach that the 1st Royal Munster Fusiliers were slaughtered in their attempt to land. And it was here that the then Divisional commander, Sir Aylmer Hunter-Weston, put down the first marker for his serial incompetence that was to identify him and his unfortunate commands throughout the war. The Division would stay on the peninsula until the end of the disastrous campaign, being evacuated in January 1916 to join up with their erstwhile Corps commander opposite Beaumont Hamel in April 1916.

But it was not the same Division. The experienced and trained Regular Army veterans who had made up more than 90% of the infantry before the Gallipoli shambles were long since killed, wounded or dead from disease. According to the Divisional History[11] the average rifle strength of the Division had been 7,300. Only 21% of those that landed in April 1915 came through unscathed[i]. Another 19% started and ended the campaign though wounded or sick at some point in the nine month occupation[ii]. Total casualties had been 34,011. This was the equivalent of the entire Division being replaced every two months. A staggering 1,100 officers had been lost during the campaign. The 29th may have earned its 'Incomparable' name tag in hard fighting along the rugged Turkish peninsula but the vast majority of the officers and men who now faced the German defenders of Beaumont Hamel had neither the experience nor the training of their forebears. Many were as near novices as the men of the New Army Divisions about to be bloodied in 'The Big Push'.

---

[i] 14 officers, 1,523 other ranks according to *'The Story of the 29th Division'*.

[ii] 18 officers, 1,405 other ranks.

Taking the 1st Border Regt as an example of how different the battalion was from its former days as regular unit, the war diary shows that a quarter of the other ranks present on 1st July 1916 were men sent out from the base depot since the middle of April 1916 and one third of the officers had come from the same source since the second week in May. Eleven officers alone had joined the battalion from the base depot between the 9th May and 29th June. Five of them would become casualties on 1st July. Overall, the battalion had lost over 550 officers and men killed since the beginning of the war – half a battalion's worth of fatalities. Of these, 95% had died at, or as a result of wounds or illness suffered at, Gallipoli. For the 2nd Hampshire Regt. these figures were even worse. By the beginning of May 1916 the battalion had suffered 835 fatalities. Just eight of these had not been caused by action or illness incurred at Gallipoli. The regular battalions that had started the war effectively disappeared on that infamous peninsula.

THE 4TH DIVISION HAD BEEN COMMANDED by a succession of Generals who had gone on to bigger and better things. On the outbreak of war it was commanded by Maj. Gen. Sir Thomas D'Oyly Snow until an accident after the division's first engagement, the Battle of Le Cateau, in which his horse rolled over him, saw him sent back to England to recover from his injuries. His health improved sufficiently for him to return to the Western Front but he was never fully fit and required regular trips back to London for treatment. By 1916 he had been elevated to the command of the VII Corps which was to conduct the disastrous 'diversionary' attack on Gommecourt a short distance to the north of the VIII Corps' left flank near Serre. Snow had briefly been replaced by Sir Henry Rawlinson who, after a few weeks in command, was promoted to command IV Corps. In his place came Maj. Gen. Henry Wilson who took over the division having commanded its 12th Brigade since the beginning of the war. He took the 4th Division through the heavy and costly fighting on the Aisne, at Messines and during the 1st and 2nd Battles of Ypres.

In September 1915, Wilson was promoted to Lieutenant General and given command of the XII Corps with which he went to Salonika. His place was taken by Maj. Gen. Hon. Sir William Lambton, the 52 year old son of George Lambton, the 2nd Earl of Durham, and Lady Beatrix Frances Hamilton, daughter of James Hamilton, 1st Duke of Abercorn.

Lambton was the eighth of thirteen children born to the severely overworked Lady Beatrix, a lady who seems to have been permanently pregnant between the autumn of 1854 and 18th January 1871 when their last child was born. Sadly, she died three days later aged just 35. Born on the 4th December 1863, Lambton attended Eton and the Royal Military College, Sandhurst, and was commissioned into the Coldstream Guards in 1884. After four years he was appointed battalion Adjutant and, in 1892, he was promoted Captain. In 1897 he was seconded to the Egyptian Army and fought at the Battles at Atbara and Omdurman during the Sudan campaign. He then fought in South Africa, where he was wounded, and was rewarded with the DSO for his services during that war. After four years as the Military Secretary to Lord Milner (Administrator and then Governor of the Transvaal and Orange River Colony), Lambton was promoted to Lieutenant Colonel in 1906 and given command of the 1st Coldstream Guards in 1910. In the same year, his connections in high places were underlined when he was appointed a Groom of the Bedchamber in Waiting to His Majesty. He spent the two years before the war as the Assistant Adjutant and Quartermaster General of the London District before becoming the Military Secretary to Sir John French when he was appointed the CinC in France. Command of the 4th Division was his first senior appointment and the Somme his first battle in command.

Plate 6 Maj. Gen. Hon. Sir William Lambton, GOC 4th Division

In the early summer of 1916, the infantry of the 4th Division was made up as follows:

10th Brigade:

1st Royal Warwickshire Regt.	1st Royal Irish Fusiliers
2nd Royal Dublin Fusiliers	2nd Seaforth Highlanders

11th Brigade:

1st Rifle Brigade	1st Hampshire Regt.
1st East Lancashire Regt.	1st Somerset Light Infantry

12th Brigade:

2nd Lancashire Fusiliers	1st King's Own Royal Lancaster Regt.
2nd Essex Regt	2nd Duke of Wellington's (West Riding Regt.

Eleven of the twelve battalions had been part of the pre-war 4th Division which had been based in Kent and Essex. The exception was the 2nd Duke of Wellington's Regt. which was part of the 13th Brigade, 5th Division in August 1914, based in Dublin. This battalion went to France with the 5th Division in mid-August 1914 and remained with this division until transferred to the 12th Brigade on 14th January 1916, replacing the 1/2nd Monmouthshire Regt. which was then converted into a pioneer battalion, joining the 29th Division at the beginning of May. The 4th Division had initially been retained in England for home defence before being rushed out to France where its infantry arrived just in time to play an important role at the Battle of Le Cateau on 26th August 1914.

The Division went on to be involved in hard fighting on the Marne, Aisne and at Messines.

On 22nd April 1915, the Germans launched the first poison gas attack on the Western Front, releasing 168 tons of chlorine gas from 5,730 gas cylinders against the French 45th and 78th Divisions[i]. Thus started the 2nd Battle of Ypres in which the 4th Division, as part of Sir Horace Smith-Dorrien's Second Army, would play a major role in the Battles of St Julien (24th April to 5th May) and Frezenberg (8th to 13th May). The fighting here was intense and vicious and the 4th Division suffered enormous casualties. The 2nd Royal Dublin Fusiliers, who fought in the salient from 25th April through to the end of Frezenberg, lost over 470 officers and men killed and died of wounds during this period, with half of that number dying on the 25th and 26th April alone. With losses of another 165 men killed between their arrival in France and the beginning of the fighting at St Julien it is clear that the experienced Regular Army battalion that had been based in Gravesend at the beginning of the war had long since ceased to exist. Although these casualty numbers are extreme they are not out of line with the losses suffered by other battalions of the Division. The 1st Rifle Brigade, for example, lost 550 officers and men killed and died of wounds between the beginning of the war and their joining the VIII Corps in April 1916 and the 2nd Seaforth Highlanders 500. If one adds to these figures those wounded and unable to return to the ranks then, again, these battalions on 1st July 1916 would have born very little resemblance in terms of knowledge and experience from the ones that embarked for Boulogne and the Western Front in the third week of August 1914.

The divisional troops of the 4th Division were its three Field Artillery Brigades – the 14th (two 18 pdr and one 4.5 in. howitzer batteries), 29th and 32nd Brigades (these two made up of three 18 pdr and one 4.5 in. howitzer batteries). As they were one Artillery Brigade 'light' each 18 pdr battery contained six rather than the normal four guns. Thus the number of 18 pdrs was brought up to the 48-gun compliment expected for each Division.

The trench mortar batteries were V/4 and W/4, both to be armed with the 240 mm heavy trench mortar, and S, T, X, Y and Z/4 Batteries equipped with the 2 in. 'Toffee Apple' trench mortar. Its Royal Engineer companies consisted of one Regular Army Field Company, the 9th, and two Territorial companies: the 1/1st Renfrew (406th) and 1/1st Durham (526th) Field Companies. Medical services were provided by the 10th, 11th and 12th Field Ambulances. The divisional pioneers were to be the 21st (Service) Battalion, West Yorkshire Regt. also known as the Wool Textile Pioneers. This New Army unit had been formed in late September 1915 in Halifax and did not arrive in France until 16th June. It was then thrown in at the deepest end of the British Army's Western Front experience to date.

THE 48TH (SOUTH MIDLAND) DIVISION, TF, was embodied for service in August 1914 and went to France in late March 1915. Its three brigades were made up of South Midland and Home Counties Territorial battalions and, having

[i] Some 6,000 French and colonial troops died in this attack or as a result of chlorine gas poisoning. The resulting hole in the Allied lines was plugged by Canadian troops who managed to hold the German advance until further troops were brought up.

seen very limited action, the men who trained pre-war with the division would have been very much the same men who were part of the division at the end of June 1916. The Division was made up of the following infantry units:

143rd Brigade:
1/5th, 1/6th, 1/7th and 1/8th Royal Warwickshire Regt.
144th Brigade:
1/4th and 1/6th Gloucestershire Regt.
1/7th and 1/8th Worcestershire Regt.
145th Brigade:
1/5th Gloucestershire Regt.
1/4th Oxfordshire & Buckinghamshire Light Infantry
1st Buckinghamshire Battalion (Ox & Bucks Light Infantry)
1/4th Royal Berkshire Regt.

The 1/5th, 1/6th and 1/8th Battalions of the Royal Warwickshire Regt. were Birmingham raised Territorial battalions. The 1/5th and 1/6th Battalions were both based at the Thorp Street Drill Hall in central Birmingham and the 1/8th Battalion's HQ trained at the Aston Manor Drill Hall, to the north of the city. The 1/8th Battalion was a more working class battalion than its central Birmingham partners and pre-war, when it was a unit made up of eight companies, there were companies sponsored by various large local businesses such as Dunlop Rubber and Ansell's Brewery, and public utilities like the Birmingham Corporation Gas Department, but it also included a company recruited from amongst the trainee teachers at St Peter's College at Saltley. The 1/7th Battalion came from the Coventry area.

The two battalions of the Gloucestershire Regt. in the 144th Brigade were both recruited in Bristol with the 1/4th (City of Bristol) Battalion being based in Clifton and the 1/6th Battalion at St Michael's Hill. The two battalions of the Worcestershires were recruited from around Kidderminster, the 1/7th Battalion, and Worcester, 1/8th Battalion.

The recruiting areas for the battalions of the 145th Brigade were:
1/5th Gloucestershire Regt. – Gloucester
1/4th Oxfordshire and Buckinghamshire Light Infantry – Oxford
1st Buckinghamshire Battalion – Aylesbury
1/4th Royal Berkshire Regt. – Reading

The Divisional commander was the 53 year old Maj. Gen. Robert Fanshawe. The youngest son of the Rev. H L Fanshawe, he was educated at Marlborough before joining the 2nd Oxfordshire Light Infantry in 1883. He spent a large part of the next sixteen years in India with his regiment before entering the Staff College, Camberley, at the beginning of 1899. On the outbreak of the South African War he joined the Inspector-General's staff and fought at the relief of Kimberley and the Battle of Paardeberg. For a time he was the adjutant of the 6th Mounted Infantry (then commanded by de Beauvoir de Lisle) before he was given command of his own mounted column. At the end of the war he was awarded the DSO and, in 1903, he was appointed Deputy Assistant Adjutant General of the 4th Division. Between 1907 and 1911 he commanded the 2nd Oxfordshires before being appointed GSO1 of the 1st Division in which position he served until 1914. On the 20th September 1914 he was given command of the

6th Brigade, 3rd Division, which he led through the heavy fighting of the 1st Battle of Ypres and, in 1915, he commanded the brigade at the Battle of Festubert. He was given command of the 48th Division in June 1915 when the commander of the Division fell ill.

Only a few of the units from the 48th Division were due to be actively involved in the VIII Corps attack. The 1/6th and 1/8th Royal Warwickshires would be attached to the 4th Division for their attack on Redan Ridge. The four artillery brigades would either assist the other divisions in wirecutting and trench bombardment or would attempt (and fail) to persuade the German Infanterie Regiment Nr. 66 opposite their front line positions at the northern end of the VIII Corps' front that something might happen on this front when the offensive started. These four artillery brigades were:

240th South Midland Brigade – made up of three 18 pdr and one 4.5 in. Howitzer batteries from Gloucester;

241st South Midland Brigade – as above with its batteries from Worcester;

242nd South Midland Brigade – again the same, this time from Warwick; and

243rd South Midland Brigade – of three 18 pdr batteries.

The trench mortar batteries, V, X, Y and Z/48 were also involved in the diversionary bombardment or in battering the northern end of the 31st Division's front while its Field Ambulances, the 1/1st, 1/2nd and 1/3rd South Midland Field Ambulances, would all assist the other divisions with the flood of casualties unleashed by the failure of the VIII Corps' attack.

---

1 Corrigan, G, *'Mud, Blood and Poppycock'*, page 199.

2 *London Gazette*, 14th June 1895, page 3382.

3 *London Gazette*, 27th November 1914, page 10128.

4 Balmer, E, *'General Hunter-Weston's 'Appreciation' of the Dardanelles Expedition'*, *Stand To!*, No. 79, April 2007.

5 Egerton, G G A, Typescript account, IWM.

6 Churchill Maj. J. *'Gallipoli Diary'*,

7 *London Gazette*, 2nd July 1915, page 29217.

8 Holmes, R, *'Tommy: The British Soldier on the Western Front'*, Harper, 2004, page 234-5.

9 A full list of these men and their occupations can be found in Appendix 5 of *'The Bradford Pals'* by Ralph N Hudson, published by Bradford Libraries Archives and Information Service, 2000.

10 Gibson R and Oldfield P, *'The Sheffield City Battalion'*, Pen & Sword, 1988, page 27.

11 Gillon Capt. S, *'The Story of the 29th Division: A Record of Gallant Deeds'*, Thomas Nelson & Sons, 1925, page 71.

4. THE PLAN OF ATTACK

ON THE 6TH MARCH, AT THE FIRST FOURTH ARMY CONFERENCE at Rawlinson's Querrieu HQ, Aylmer Hunter-Weston had vigorously argued against the idea of a 'wild rush … for an objective 4,000 yards away'. And yet, as spring moved into early summer, this was precisely the task he had been set. As had been his wont at Gallipoli, once instructed he proceeded without argument. He was a soldier and he did as he was ordered. Religiously. So, when he met with his commander in chief on Wednesday, 10th May, he took careful note of his superior's words of wisdom and then applied them to the job in hand. Again, religiously.

Haig's message had been unambiguous and so Hunter-Weston took his words as holy writ and applied them without deviation to the VIII Corps' plan of attack. According to the CinC's own diary his words to Hunter Bunter were:

> "I impressed upon him that there must be no halting attacks at each trench in succession for rear lines to pass through! The objective must be as far as our guns can prepare the Enemy's position for attack – and when the attack starts it must be pushed through to the final objective with as little delay as possible. His experiences at Gallipoli were under very different conditions: then he landed from ships, a slow proceeding: now his troops can be forward in succession of lines in great depth, and all can start at the same moment!"[1]

It would seem a shame that Haig did not listen to his own words about 'objectives (being) as far as our guns can prepare' because, as Foch, Fayolle and, apparently Rawlinson and his Corps commanders had learned from experience, such objectives were extremely limited and fell far short of those imposed by Haig on Fourth Army. Clearly, also, Haig had paid scant attention to the fighting at Gallipoli where, when he was Corps commander, all of Hunter-Weston's fighting had been land-based. He may have commanded the 29th Division at the Cape Helles' landings but, thereafter, with the troops ashore, the Turks were fought from one trench line to another. A small-scale oriental version of the Western Front but fought in terrain and in conditions far more troublesome than anywhere on the British front in France and Belgium. No matter, the oracle had spoken and Hunter-Weston obeyed. Haig had set the distant objectives, now he had set the style of the attack and Hunter-Weston was only too happy to oblige.

With their objectives, and tactics dictated by higher and distant authority, VIII Corps staff, under Hunter-Weston's direction, decided to leave nothing to chance. Every eventuality or, at least, every eventuality which fitted in with their fervently held belief that the great offensive would be a resounding success, was covered in the reams of paper printed and distributed down to every Division, Brigade and Battalion. By the time they had finished, the VIII Corps' scheme of attack ran to over 70 pages under 28 headings. If there was a detail to be considered it was addressed: timings, formations, speed, direction, consolidation, use of weapons, treatment of prisoners, dealing with the dead, roads, communications, transport, ammunition, water supply, etc., etc., etc.

Everything, except the response of the enemy and the means by which they might defend themselves and how this might be countered. Everything except the means by which the men would get across the 'fire swept zone' of No Man's Land in sufficient numbers to quell the enemy's resistance. Everything except what happened if things didn't go to plan, the problem otherwise known as Sod's Law. Because there was no Plan B, perhaps because by admitting the need for a Plan B was to admit of the possibility of failure – and failure was not only not an option, it was not even a consideration. As a result, Hunter-Weston would confide to his wife in a letter written on the night of the 30th June that:

> "I have, with my excellent staff, done all possible to ensure success… I have nothing more to do now till well after the attack has taken place."[2]

This smacks of a hands-off approach but nothing could be further from the truth. Everything, with the exception of the the wire targets of the Divisional artillery which remained under Divisional control, was in the hands of VIII Corps. They had, however, set the timetables to which the infantry and artillery had to adhere once the attack began, although it would be up to infantry, whose pace they could not control, to keep up with the artillery which they could control. The targets for the bombardment were a Corps responsibility. The use of the heavy guns and howitzers, which trenches to bombard, when and how often, counter battery work, control over the barrages on Z Day were all Corps functions. Any requests for artillery action which did not appear in the VIII Corps scheme were made to the Corps staff and it was up to them to make a decision as to whether to respond. Whilst the scheme covered every apparently conceivable possibility it was also inherently inflexible and unresponsive to what would actually happen on the ground.

In addition, Fourth Army had issued to every officer above the rank of captain, its now infamous *'Tactical Notes'*. Running to another 31 pages, its most famous section is the one which suggests, with rather typical Rawlinsonian vagueness, the formation to be adopted by the infantry in the attack. This formation, indeed the only formation, contained within *'Tactical Notes'* is the 'wave', i.e. the men would advance in long lines, each man three paces away from the one next to him and with about 100 yards between each wave. The number of lines, or waves, of troops in the advance would depend on the distance to be covered and the number of objectives to be taken. The greater the distance and the larger the number of objectives then the larger the number of waves as each one would pass through its predecessor and on to the next target. This formation is not specified in so many words but rather hinted at, with a wink here and a nudge there. For example:

> "The assaulting force must push forward at a steady pace in successive lines, each line adding fresh impetus to the preceding line."[3]

Or:

> "There can be no definite rules as to the best formation for attack… Probably the two best formations for a battalion if conditions permit are…"[4]

And:

"As a general guide, the leading lines should not be more than 100 yards apart."[5]

The problem this presented to those who religiously adopted these vague recommendations, i.e. to VIII Corps and most of the other Corps south towards Fricourt, was that a large number of waves would be above ground and marching slowly and for some considerable time towards and, hopefully, across the German trenches, irrespective of the state of the German defences and whether their machine guns had survived. Indeed, *'Tactical Notes'* demanded this:

"16. Each line of assaulting troops must leave its trenches simultaneously and make the assault as one man. This is of the highest importance."[6]

If the enemy's Maxims survived in any number then these waves would present the most extraordinary and tempting targets. VIII Corps, whether through laziness, a lack of imagination or out of a genuine belief that this formation was the best one, adopted the repeated 'wave' approach along its entire front. The only variations would be the starting points for the leading elements which, for some, would be the front line trench and, for others, would involve the risky expedient of forming up in No Man's Land several minutes in advance of zero hour.

Interestingly, on 3rd June, GQG issued to the French Army a tactical note from Joffre that showed, again, that the French were ahead of the British tactically by some margin. This document, *'Note pour les armées'*, stated unequivocally that:

"Assault waves composed of men shoulder to shoulder are to be absolutely forbidden."[7]

French tactics now dictated that the initial attack be delivered by the smallest number of men possible, with the mass of the troops available to reinforce, exploit or assist these troops as was required. Further tactical instructions issued to battalions on 20th June insisted that an attack by the infantry was the follow-up to a successful preparation by the artillery. They were to occupy the ground made ready by the overwhelming firepower of concentrated artillery. The infantry was to be employed with 'strict economy' and was to be 'conserved at all costs'[8]. This was, as yet, a philosophy unknown to the British Army and, sadly, totally contrary to the manner in which Aylmer Hunter Weston had conducted his battles whilst on the Gallipoli peninsula.

BUT WHAT OF THE PLAN OF ATTACK DEVISED BY HUNTER WESTON and his staff? It simple, painfully simple. And rigid in its timing. Restrictingly so. It was devoid of subtlety, creativity, flexibility – of intelligence.

It would involve 8½ of Hunter-Weston's twelve brigades while, on the extreme right, half a brigade of Ulstermen from the 36th Division, III Corps, would endeavour to capture the north bank of the Ancre before re-joining their parent unit south of the river. From south to north the 29th Division would attack with two brigades up and one coming behind to take the German 2nd Position; the 4th Division went with one brigade plus half of the 143rd Brigade, 48th Division, leading with two brigades to leap frog them and take the final objective; the 31st Division would attack on a two brigade, but only three battalion front, with one brigade held back in reserve (and not to be committed); and the 48th Division would hold the line between Serre and Hebuterne with 1½ brigades while the third would be ready to move south to follow up the advance nearer to the Ancre.

After a five day bombardment, which involved the field and long guns cutting the wire in front of six, seven or even eight lines of enemy trenches, the demolition of the various small villages – Serre, Beaumont Hamel and Beaucourt sur Ancre – and reduction of the trenches and redoubts by the heavy artillery, it was felt that the Germans would have suffered so many casualties and be so worn down by the constant explosions and destruction that they would be incapable of any organised defence. On this basis, it was concluded that the infantry would attack arrayed in a series of long, slow moving lines which would wash over the German positions like an incoming spring tide. The lead battalions would overrun the three trenches of the German 1st Position and occupy the fourth line some 200 to 150 yards beyond. The next lines of troops would then push through the men now consolidating this new position and advance to take the Zwischen Stellung. There would be a brief pause before the final lines of the follow-up brigades, who had already marched 2,500 yards and more to reach this position, went forward to take the German 2nd Position which they would consolidate, reversing the trenches and building strong points. They would come under the protective fire of field batteries brought forward as the advance went on and which would occupy new positions in and around the old German front line trenches. In front of the advancing infantry, the artillery would provide a barrage which would either move forward in bounds or creep across the ground between objectives. This would happen to a precise timetable at the end of which they would establish a long range curtain of fire in front of the newly gained trenches.

It was concluded that, in order for the flow of infantry to be uninterrupted, the infantry should advance over the open, even from the rear most trenches. This inevitably meant that at some point, and for quite a long period of time, almost every man involved in the advance would be out in the open and striding forward at the prescribed 50 yards a minute. Although, even if only momentarily, some officers might have been concerned at the unmissable target such an enormous and slow moving body of men would present to the enemy's artillery and machine guns, such worries were dismissed by the enthusiasm with which the Corps commander pronounced that any German soldiers in the front lines would either be dead or incapacitated by that time. There was no need to worry about such eventualities as unmissable, slow moving targets. So no-one did.

This overwhelming confidence which radiated from Hunter-Weston like heat from the sun permeated nearly every level of the Corps and turned otherwise sensible men's brains to mush. Capt. William Carden-Roe, the Adjutant of the 1st Royal Irish Fusiliers, 10th Brigade, 4th Division, attended a senior officers' conference of the 10th Brigade at which the plans were presented. Carden-Roe's battalion was to be in the last waves of 4th Division's advance with their objective the German 2nd Position some 4,000 yards distant:

> "The Brigadier explained the whole scheme simply, but with a great air of confidence, and his enthusiasm rapidly infected us all. An advance of two

> miles was such as had never been contemplated before, and though it was hardly possible that the whole plan would go like clockwork, we were one and all determined to win through."[9]

Green troops, inexperienced gunners already spread too thin and now an advance of such depth as 'had never been contemplated before' – hardly a reliable recipe for success.

On the 23rd June, as the weather turned oppressively thundery and a heavy storm threatened, the Divisional and Brigade commanders of the VIII Corps met at Gen. Hunter-Weston's HQ at Marieux. The conference was the second of two, the first being held two days earlier, which discussed the plans for the forthcoming offensive. In particular, it was felt essential that the GOCs of the Brigades that were to operate alongside one another should meet, thoroughly understand each other's plans as well as those of the artillery supporting them. The GOCs concerned were those of the lead Brigades of the 29th and 4th Divisions, the 11th and 86th, the neighbouring Brigades of the 31st and 4th Divisions, the 93rd and 12th, and the two Brigades with the furthest to advance, the 88th and 10th. The Brigadiers were also advised to ensure that the officers commanding all flank battalions, companies and platoons should be in contact in order to be aware of the attack formation and plan of their corresponding unit from the neighbouring Division.

The conference then went on to discuss a number of key general points for the offensive. These included:

The use of reserves;
Instructions on the advance and the consolidation of captured positions;
Disposal of the dead;
The use of trench bridges;
Road construction in the captured areas;
Forward movement of the artillery;
Raids;
The use of gas by both sides; and, lastly,
Cheering and doubling.

Hunter-Weston, reflecting his CinC's concerns on the subject, was insistent that all Divisional commanders should hold some troops in reserve and that these should be held under each commander's control as long as possible. These reserves were not to be 'frittered away as soon as help is called for'. Apart from the tactical flexibility this provided the GOCs, it also would prevent the forward areas in both the British and German lines from becoming congested, a result which would provide excellent shooting for the enemy's artillery and machine guns. It was thus recommended that reserves should not be brought up too close to the front line. The notes of the conference make interesting reading on the 'proper use of reserves' especially in the light of what was about to happen on two of the three Division's fronts where, it might be argued, almost every single instruction on the use of reserves was to be ignored:

> "The proper use of reserves requires the highest form of moral courage as well as deep military knowledge. It requires courage to say no to appeals for help, and it requires a highly developed military instinct to realise that the troops calling for help can generally be best helped by using the

> reserve in some other place. As a rough and ready rule it is usually not necessary to accede to the request for reinforcements as troops can always hold out longer than they think and, as suggested above, reinforcements can be often most profitably employed at the places where our troops are meeting with success."[10]

In the light of his own failings using reserves at the Third Battle of Krithia such comments suggest Hunter-Weston had learnt a valuable lesson. But it was only a valuable lesson if the units involved actually adhered to the basic concept and if the overall scheme had sufficient flexibility built into it to allow for some local or overall initiative. But, with the plans as set down strictly specifying the timetable for the advance of every unit in every Brigade in every Division in the Corps, this flexibility was lacking and, therefore, Hunter-Weston's dictums on the 'proper use of reserves' became irrelevant. Support and reserve battalions would move off according to the clock not according the situation in front of them because that is what VIII Corps' scheme required. It was not a popular scheme, therefore, with several of the officers lower down the food chain.

The central reserves of the VIII Corps were specified and a comment made that these were the only available reserves north of the River Ancre as all others were held as Fourth Army reserves for exploitation of the anticipated successes further south. The reserves available to VIII Corps were: two infantry Brigades, two Royal Engineer Field Companies, one Pioneer Battalion, one motor machine gun battery and six Hotchkiss guns of the Lancashire Hussars. It was made clear that this reserve was to be used to exploit or consolidate success and, unless any failure was catastrophic, it was not be used to support attacking units that felt themselves hard-pressed. And, in any case, the two infantry Brigades were not immediately available as they would be on the move south in order to be in position behind the attacking divisions at some point during the day.

Divisional reserves, in terms of distinct units allocated to that role, did not properly exist as, with the exception of the 92nd Brigade of the 31st Division, all units were in some way involved in the advance. For example, every battalion of all three Brigades of the 4th and 29th Divisions had a role to play in taking one of the three lines of German defences which were their objective. Apparently, as far as these Divisions were concerned, God helped those who helped themselves. Any reserve available for use after the initial advance had to be put together from troops previously involved in the attack. One might call it military 'recycling'. The instruction is somewhat convoluted:

> "Divisions must understand that they will have to depend on themselves and on the indirect assistance of the formations on the flank. They must be determined not to engage their reserves without good cause, and must make careful arrangements for the immediate collection of an efficient reserve distinct from the troops told off to consolidate and hold the present reserve line of German front system of trenches, as soon as the troops detailed for the second objective have crossed over this reserve line."[11]

Basically, a reserve had to be made up from any spare men from the battalions used in the initial attack who were not being employed to consolidate the newly won trenches and were not either dead or wounded. Such instructions presume low casualties amongst the attacking troops. Such instructions even seem to suggest the advance as an occupation rather than territory gained by hard fighting. These instructions, however, do beg the question: what was to be done about the 'proper use of reserves' if there were none? If every unit had a role to play in the attack, then how could Divisional or Brigade commanders reinforce anything, let alone reinforce success?

Hunter-Weston also made it clear that every unit had to press on to its objective irrespective of the progress, or failure, of the units on its flanks. Such tactics had already proved disastrous in several of the Gallipoli battles over which he'd had control. Against a resolute, intelligent and flexible defence this is a policy which, potentially, dooms the most successful unit to ultimate failure. It is, however, a policy which might be appropriate to an inexperienced body of troops not familiar with the concepts of mutual support and at a time when, once 'over the top', the attacking troops were often out of reach of further orders from any senior officer. Had the VIII Corps' objectives been more limited, then it is a policy which might have worked. Otherwise it risked exposing the leading, perhaps more aggressive, perhaps just luckier, troops to counter-attack potentially out of the range of the Divisional artillery and, even worse, out of sight of the British trenches. This is, effectively, what happened to the leading units of the 36th Division at the Schwaben Redoubt on 1st July. They continued to advance even though the attacks on either flank had failed and, as a result, were left horribly exposed to counter attack and ended up back in their own trenches having suffered terrible casualties.

Broadly, this policy of pushing on come what may only worked if the enemy's defences had broken down and/or the enemy artillery was unable to assist in the defence of the position. To achieve the latter required an investment in guns, ammunition and observational resources on counter battery fire which the B.E.F. was, as yet, either unwilling or unable to make. Killing or neutralising the forward elements of the enemy infantry should have been the artillery's highest priority but instead their fire was spread over a huge area. To make matters worse, preventing their own attacking infantry from being destroyed or cut off by a German artillery barrage seems not have been a priority.

There appears to have been an acceptance at the conference that casualties might be heavy though whether these were thought likely to be mainly British or German is not made clear. The instructions for the disposal of the dead, however, give some flavour of the dismal outcome of any large scale battle in an 'industrial' war:

> "Cremation is by far the most sanitary means of disposal of dead bodies but is not practicable for great numbers.
> If the dead are buried in large pits the bodies should be laid about 1 foot apart, the intervening space being filled with earth. There should also be 1 foot of earth between layers. The earth acts as an absorbent and prevents liquid matter percolating through the ground and contaminating sources of water supply."[12]

Forward communications once the German line had been broken was a high priority in the planning of the offensive. Any advance over a multi-line trench system presents problems for the attacking Army. First, the attacking infantry needed to surge relentlessly forward in wave after unbroken wave if the plan was to function to time. Using communication trenches (as found by several Divisions and battalions on 1st July[i]) was not a recipe for a smooth onward flow of men. The solution was to bridge the various lines of trenches forward to the British front line and then the laying of similar bridges across the captured German trenches. Following on behind the infantry, certain field artillery batteries were to be rushed forward in order to be able to support the troops in the furthest German trench captured, i.e. the 2nd Position. Wagons hauling ammunition would need to reach them and thus these bridges had to be both wide and robust. Their forward movement and installation in the German lines were jobs that would have taxed the Royal Engineers tasked with this role had any been required during the attack. The RE would also be involved in the rapid construction of metalled roads so that motor lorries carrying supplies could reach the forward areas. They were also expected to link and repair the British and German trench tramway systems across No Man's Land. No wonder the men of these RE units were described as 'very precious' in the conference notes.

Raids were always high on the agenda of the B.E.F. Not for them any 'live and let live' policy. Unfortunately for VIII Corps, the German XIV Reserve Armeekorps under Generalleutnant Hermann Christlieb Matthäus von Stein had developed a reputation for dominating No Man's Land with an aggressive and constantly changing regime of patrols. Having taken on the French until the middle of 1915 they then found the British troops deployed north of the Somme far more aggressive but also far less experienced in the niceties of trench warfare. In February 1916, a document entitled *'Patrolling Experiences'* was issued under von Stein's signature. It itemised the manner in which German patrols had continued to control No Man's Land through a programme of raids which was regularly adapted as the British attempted to respond. Every change made by the British in an effort to improve their night-time success rate was quickly met by a subtle or, sometimes, major alteration in tactics which kept the German patrols 'ahead of the game'. Von Stein's document was not only sent down the chain of command, it also went up to 2. Armee HQ and beyond. At last one Armeekorps, VI Armeekorps, simply retitled it and distributed it amongst all of its units.

During the early days of the 29th Division's time north of the Ancre the 2nd South Wales Borderers were twice the victims of the greater raiding efficiency and expertise of the Reserve Infanterie Regiment Nr. 119 (RIR 119). The first event occurred on the night of the 6th/7th April near the Mary Redan where an excellently planned raid by officers and men of the II Bataillon, RIR 119, resulted in the SWB losing 112 officers and men, 34 of whom were killed and 19 taken prisoner, at a cost to the enemy of just three men dead and one wounded. An attempted retaliation on the night of the 29th/30th April was so clumsily and obviously planned that the raid's commander, Capt. Edmund Byrne, and five of his men were killed by German patrols lying in wait for them[ii].

---

[i] For example, 46th Division at Gommecourt and the 1st Essex Regt. at Beaumont Hamel.

[ii] Capt. Edmund James Widdrington Byrne, 3rd att. 2nd South Wales Borderers, was aged 35. He was the second son and fourth of nine children born to the late Hon. Sir Edmund Widdrington Byrne, a barrister and High Court judge, and Dame Henrietta Johnstone Byrne (née Gulland) of 35 Lansdowne Road, Notting Hill, London. A solicitor, admitted

This relative British failure to defend enemy raids and to mount effective ones of their own would be repeated over and over again along not only the VIII Corps' front but throughout much of Fourth Army's sector. From time to time there were signs that the British were learning the necessary lessons but the area north of the Ancre tended to remain a problem for all concerned. Success was achieved, however, on the night of the 3rd/4th June when two raids, one by the 1st Lancashire Fusiliers north of Hawthorn Ridge and another by the 14th York and Lancaster Regt. opposite Matthew Copse, entered the German trenches and explored the dugouts but such successes were and would be few and far between in the run up to the offensive. Occasionally, too, the normal German thoroughness deserted them and they experienced the grief and frustration of a failed raid. Such an event occurred on the night of the 10th/11th June in front of Hamel down by the River Ancre when the co-ordination between the infantry and artillery was poor and 'friendly fire' caused casualties amongst the raiders and the abandonment of the action.

Otherwise, however, it was the Germans who topped the raiding 'league table' north of Ancre even if, progressively, this was in defensive rather than offensive mode. As a result, the raids mounted on VIII Corps' front during the last week of June 1916 would be a series of poorly executed failures which served only to confirm the strength and resilience of the German troops in the front line trenches. One might have thought these results alone should have informed higher authority that their planned 'annihilation' bombardment was not performing the prescribed function. It did not.

AT THE TIME OF THIS CONFERENCE, THE BOMBARDMENT was expected to last for five days. Y/Z night was, therefore, the last before the planned assault on Z Day and the discussions on raids were framed accordingly. All Divisions were instructed to mount raids on the last two nights but one of the bombardment, i.e. W/X and X/Y nights. To assist, two 1 hour intervals in the artillery preparation had been pre-arranged, between 10:30 p.m. and 11:30 p.m. on W/X night and between midnight and 1 a.m. on X/Y nights. The conference notes betray the excessive confidence in the outcome of the attack which was all pervading in the VIII Corps:

> "If on W/X night we find that there are few or none of the enemy in the front trench, the raiding parties on X/Y night must push on to the second trench.
> As the artillery lifts off the front trench for an hour the raiding parties should be able to explore a very considerable extent of the enemy's trenches."[13]

---

in 1903 and practising at 7, Lothbury, London, EC, he enlisted as a Private in the Inns of Court OTC before being commissioned into the 3rd South Wales Borderers on 23rd September 1914. Promoted Captain May 1915. Served in Gallipoli. His body was never found and his name is inscribed on the Thiepval Memorial, Pier & Face 4 A.

The five men were 19882 Pte John Harris, 13822 Pte David John Jones, 24661 L/Cpl. David James, 3/25574 Pte Percy Powell and 19634 Pte John Sidebottom. They are buried together in what appears to have been a communal grave in Auchonvillers Military Cemetery, graves II. C. 22-24.

Date/Unit	Results	Casualties
Night of 26th/27th June		
1st Newfoundland Regt., 88th Brigade	Failed. Uncut wire	Nil
1st R Warwickshire Regt., 10th Brigade	Cancelled	
11th E Yorkshire Regt., 92nd Brigade	Failed.	4 officers wounded, 1 shell shock 3 OR killed, 5 wounded, 1 missing
1/5th R. Warwickshire Regt., 143rd Brigade	Failed.	1 officer wounded 14 OR wounded
Night of 27th/28th June		
2nd Royal Fusiliers, 86th Brigade	Failed, wire uncut	1 OR wounded, 2 missing
16th Middlesex Regt., 86th Brigade	Failed.	2 OR slightly wounded
1st Lancashire Fus., 86th Brigade	Failed. Wire insufficiently cut.	1 officer missing 1 OR killed, 5 wounded, 1 missing
1st Border Regt., 87th Brigade	Failed. Uncut wire.	Nil
1st Newfoundland Regt., 88th Brigade	Failed. Wire cut but trench heavily manned.	3 officers wounded 2 OR killed, 10 wounded, 7 missing
12th E Yorkshire Regt., 92nd Brigade	Failed.	
1/5th R Warwickshire Regt., 143rd Brigade	Failed.	1 officer wounded 20 ORs wounded
Night of 28th/29th June		
1st Royal Dublin Fusiliers, 88th Brigade	Failed. Uncut wire.	2 officers wounded 4 OR killed, 14 wounded, 6 missing
1st Somerset LI., 11th Brigade	Failed. Uncut wire.	1 Officer wounded 1 OR missing, 2 wounded
12th E Yorkshire Regt., 92nd Brigade	Failed. Wire repaired by Germans or uncut.	2 officers killed, 1 wounded 4 ORs killed, 15 wounded
1/7th Worcestershire Regt., 144th Brigade	Failed.	
Night of 29th/30th June		
1st South Wales Borderers, 86th Brigade	Partial success. 1 German killed.	Nil
1st Essex Regt., 88th Brigade	Partial success. 1 German killed.	1 OR slightly wounded
1st Rifle Brigade, 11th Brigade	Failed. Uncut wire.	
18th W Yorkshire Regt., 93rd Brigade	Failed.	1 officer wounded, 2 missing 1 OR killed, 18 wounded, 9 missing
1/5th R Warwickshire Regt., 143rd Brigade	Failed.	2 ORs wounded
1/4th Ox & Bucks LI., 145th Brigade	Failed.	

Table 1 Details of VIII Corps' Raids, 26th to 29th June 1916

By the night of 30th June, with two extra nights available for raids, the VIII Corps would be able to 'boast' of just one entry into the German lines – by the 1st Essex Regt. of the 29th Division on the night of Thursday, 29th June. Two Germans were known to have been killed at a cost to VIII Corps of one officer missing and 13 wounded, and eleven ORs killed, 27 missing and 80 wounded. Hardly a cost-efficient way of conducting warfare.

Gas was planned for use at various times during the day and night in the run up to the assault. At this time, the British were still reliant on gas released from cumbersome canisters lugged up to the front and set up by the Royal Engineers of the Special Brigade. The officer in charge of the gas canisters was the final arbiter when it came to decisions about its use. It was employed on several occasions. It always drew a heavy artillery response from the Germans and it caused several deaths and dozens of gassings amongst the RE and the nearby infantry. It is not thought that it caused many casualties amongst the enemy.

The last comment in the notes covered the issue of 'cheering and doubling'. Cheering was not to be allowed as, apart from a large mine on Hawthorn Ridge ten minutes before zero hour and a seven day bombardment, 'it only warns the enemy that we are coming'. Doubling, i.e. running or trotting in the advance, was also frowned upon and was not to be allowed. The reason given explains the slow methodical advance used by all but those who had the sense to ignore this instruction:

> "With the heavy weight men will be carrying it is very exhausting except for the very shortest distances such as 20 yards."[14]

KNOWLEDGE OF THE STRENGTH of the German positions north (and, indeed, south) of the Ancre was widespread amongst all senior ranks. The German use of deep dugouts in the front line areas was also well known throughout the Army and Rawlinson had factored this into his planning from the very beginning. Writing on 19th April, in response to Haig's initial criticisms of his plan for the Somme, Rawly, while discussing the issue of the length of the proposed preliminary bombardment, talked about:

> "… the existence of numerous dug-outs and cellars in the enemy lines."

What is never made explicit is how best to deal with these dugouts and the German troops and machine guns concealed by and protected within them. Haig's thinking seemed to be gas shell. The underlining in the Rawlinson quote is in the original document in the National Archives and is in Haig's typical blue pencil. Haig's appended hand-written note goes on to say:

> "[re: dugouts and cellars] We must have gas shells for these."

Haig may have believed that the British Army would have access to supplies of gas shells by the time of the attack but, at least in terms of lethal gas shell, this was not the case though there was a small supply of SK, tear gas, shell for certain guns[i]. The French did have, and employed extensively, two forms of lethal gas shell. Those fired by the field and heavy artillery were mainly aimed at German

[i] SK = South Kensington and was the codename for Ethyl Idoacetate, a formula for tear gas developed at Imperial College, South Kensington.

artillery positions. Those fired by trench mortars were used on the front line. The main issue about the gasses used was that they dissipated quickly and it really required a mass of quick firing weapon such as the French 75 mm field gun if a sufficiently dense cloud of the poisonous gas was to envelop the target in a sustained and, therefore, effective manner. The very quick firing British 3 in. Stokes mortar might have provided an option for smothering the front line German lines with gas shells which could have been dropped into the bottom of their trenches (and, therefore, allowed the heavier than air gas to enter the openings of the deep dugouts). It could certainly fire at a fast enough rate, however, no such shells existed or were planned and experiments later in the war proved fruitless. It would seem, therefore, that neither Haig nor Rawlinson had any clear idea as to how to deal with the German dugouts and their occupants, indeed, Rawlinson just seemed to hope that the enemy would be so demoralised by his planned 60 hour bombardment that they would be unable to resist the infantry attack.

Ironically, back in May 1915, when Haig's predecessor, Sir John French, had still be in control, his then artillery adviser, Brig. Gen. J du Cane, requested a supply of delayed action fuzes for high explosive shells precisely because of the German tactic of housing his machine gun teams in protected dugouts. Delayed action fuzes, similar to the type that penetrated the armour and then blew up the shells stores of several British battlecruisers at Jutland, might well have helped collapse the German dugouts on the Somme. The concussion from shells so fused exploding several feet or even yards underground would radiate out from the centre causing severe shock to any nearby underground shelters. Close enough and it might even collapse the dugout or, at least, its entrances. If the walls of the dugout were ruptured then the powerful blast wave or the lethal fumes from the explosives would quickly kill the occupants. There was no special call, however, for delayed action fuzes for this purpose.

If there was any doubt about the existence of this network of deep dugouts on VIII Corps' front then this view should have been firmly corrected by the results of two successful entries into the German trenches near Beaumont Hamel and opposite Serre early in June 1916.

On the night of the 3rd/4th June 1916, after a one hour bombardment, several groups of heavily armed men slipped through gaps in the British wire and headed across the pockmarked grassland of No Man's Land towards the German front line trenches along the whole of the VIII Corps' front. Nearly everywhere the raiding parties were repelled. All except two.

One, comprising two officers and 48 other ranks, led by Lt. S M W Sheppard of the 1st Lancashire Fusiliers, moved towards the German lines just to the north of the Hawthorn Redoubt. Their intention was to break into the German trenches to see what they could find. This night they were lucky. The German defenders of the 8. Kompanie, RIR 119, were otherwise engaged and the party took the opportunity to investigate thoroughly the stretch of trench entered. Deep dugouts under the parapet were entered and ransacked and the trenches searched for 50 yards to north and south. After ten minutes, carrying papers and notice boards, the party withdrew as per the timetable. They were hurried on their way by German machine guns which belatedly opened up. One man was wounded in the withdrawal.

Sheppard's findings were reported up the chain of command through Division, to VIII Corps HQ and, no doubt, beyond. His report was detailed:

> "The trench was found to be from 9 to 10 feet deep, 3 feet wide at the bottom and 10-12 feet wide at the top with gradually sloping sides. The firestep was made of wood about four feet above the bottom of the trench… the trench was for the most part revetted with brushwood and was in excellent repair and scrupulously clean. The traverses were very large and the parados very high. Dugouts were about 20 feet deep and connected. Communication trenches had the same profile as the firing line but without fire step. The wire was 40 to 50 yards wide, very strong and breast high."[15]

They key sentence comes towards the end: 'Dugouts were about 20 feet deep and connected'.

On the same night, a raiding party of the 14th York and Lancasters from the 31st Division also entered the German lines, this time opposite Matthew Copse. A party organised and led by Capt. Alphonse Wood consisting of three officers and 72 men with four Lewis guns, was to mount the raid. An artillery bombardment had been laid down to cover their advance and, after using a Bangalore torpedo and cutting through the remaining wire, some of the men, led by the rhyming couple of 2nd Lts. George Herbert Thomas Best and Harold Quest, got into the German trenches where they bombed two dugouts and killed at least two German soldiers but lost one of their own in the fight[i]. The party had become somewhat disorganised, however, and Capt. Wood decided to withdraw after only a brief period. Overall, the party lost three dead and four wounded, two of the wounded being Capt. Wood and 2nd Lt. Quest[ii]. Overall, the raid was something of a shambles, with three casualties, two men killed and Lt. Quest wounded, being caused by 'friendly fire' before reaching the German trenches. The incursion itself had lasted three mad minutes but, it was thought, two German dugouts had been identified and bombed.

The important issue, again, was the existence of the front line dugouts. Both of these raids featured in the VIII Corps Summary of Operations for the week 2nd to 9th June. The accounts do not express any surprise at the existence of these

---

[i] 14/149 Pte. George Galloway, 14th York and Lancaster Regt. (2nd Barnsley Pals), was aged 30. He was the son of the late George and Mary Galloway. His body was never found and his name is inscribed on the Thiepval Memorial, Pier & Face 14 A & 14 B.

[ii] Capt. Harold Quest, MC, A Company, 14th York and Lancaster Regt. (2nd Barnsley Pals), died on 3rd November 1916. Aged 22, he was the son of Arthur Charles Quest, Deputy Chief Constable of the West Riding, and Jane Hannah Quest, of Wakefield. He is buried in Hebuterne Communal Cemetery, grave I. D. 2. He was awarded the MC for his conduct during the raid. The citation in the *London Gazette* of 25th July 1916 reads: "For conspicuous gallantry during a raid on the enemy's trenches. Though wounded at the outset he stuck to his post and led his party personally accounting for one of the enemy. On the withdrawal he remained with two other officers till all the party had left the trench, and later assisted in bringing in the wounded."

dugouts, they are described in matter of fact terms, although Lt. Sheppard's detailed description is remarked upon.

These reports on the condition of the German defences at Beaumont Hamel and Serre should have set alarm bells ringing at all levels of the B.E.F., especially as a similar, and more detailed, report emerged from the 8th Division of III Corps at Ovillers La Boisselle only two days later (and certainly found its way to Fourth Army HQ). When combined with other earlier reports from such places as Gommecourt just to the north, the strength and security of the protection afforded to the German troops defending the Somme by their deep dugouts should have come as no surprise to officers at every level.

The 8th Division's report from Ovillers sector had been even more detailed and included both a vertical and a floor plan of a dugout found in the trenches there. Furthermore, their report reinforced the point that these deep dugouts were connected both laterally and to the rear.

But the findings of these raids were nothing new. On the night of the 25th November 1915, a raiding party from C Company of the 1/6th Gloucestershire Regt., of the 48th (South Midland) Division, had entered the German trenches at the south east corner of Gommecourt Park. Their findings were similarly ominous:

> "Shelters are very deep with some spiral staircases. All appeared to be connected with underground passages to each other and back to the second line."[16]

And again, at Ovillers on 17th January 1916, a German prisoner described dugouts six metres deep capable of housing securely a dozen men.

This information was all confirmed by a German soldier captured on the same night as the Lancashire Fusiliers conducted their inspection. Reservist Robert Kirchstetter of the 3. Kompanie, IR 110, was captured in front of Becourt on the III Corps' front after he became lost in No Man's Land whilst part of badly conducted raid. Interrogated by the Corps' Intelligence Officer, Capt. William Wyndham Torre Torr[i], MC, (under whose name the report on the Ovillers trench raid had been submitted), Kirchstetter explained in his interview that the whole of his battalion front was accessible underground through deep inter-connecting dugouts.[17]

In short, the existence of the network of deep, essentially shell-proof interconnected dugouts which were to shelter enemy troops was common knowledge at all levels of the B.E.F. After all, the man at the top of Fourth Army, Rawlinson, acknowledged their existence in his response to Haig's challenge about the length of the preliminary bombardment. Indeed, Rawlinson had previously noted the use of dugouts, though not so deep and robust, in use during the fighting at Givenchy in the summer of 1915.

[i] A pre-war regular, Capt. William Wyndham Torre Torr, MC, West Yorkshire Regt., was awarded the DSO (1917), MC (1916) and Croix de Guerre (1st June 1917) for his war-time service. ADC to Maj. Gen. R N R Reade, CB, 1914. GSO3, May 1915. GSO2 in August 1916. He continued in staff appointments until 1933. Military attaché Washington DC, 1934. GSO1, 1939. CMG, 1942, whilst military attaché in Madrid (by then a Brigadier). He died in 1963 aged 73.

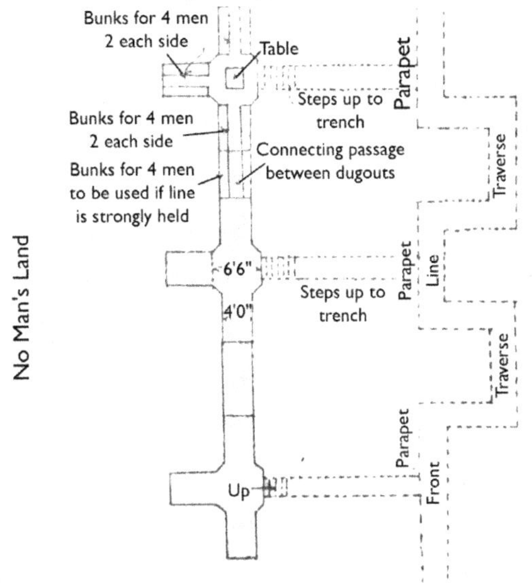

Figure I Floor plan of German dugouts explored on 5th June 1916

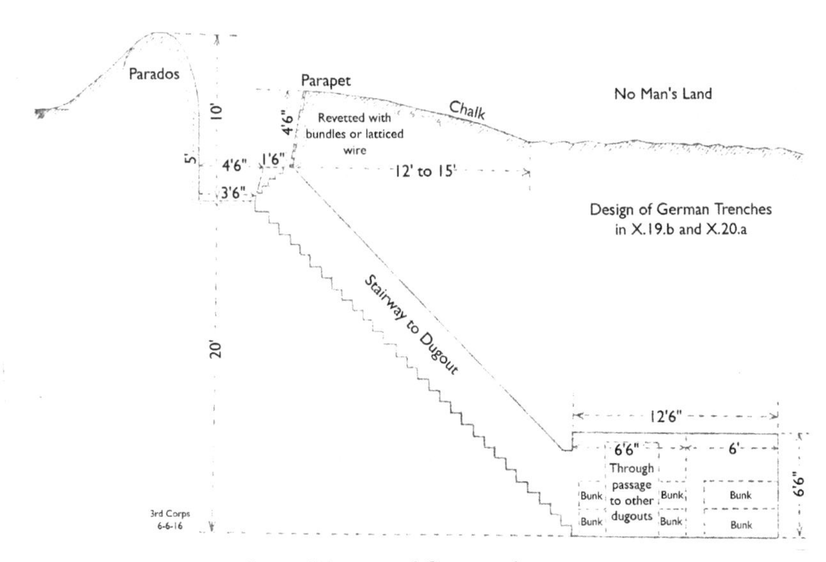

Figure 2 Layout of German dugouts

Taken from III Corps, Fourth Army Intelligence Report dated 8th June 1916 of a trench raid conducted on 5th June 1916, (Source: NA, WO157/171)

It is because these dugouts were known about thatm further down the chain of command, every Brigade allocated follow-up troops to the job of clearing any remaining enemy soldiers from the front line trenches and dugouts whilst the rest of the waves advanced to their final objectives.

And yet, the immediate implications for the attacking troops of the presence of secure accommodation for the German infantry in their 1st Position seems to have been lost on all. If the opposition front line troops and their machine guns survived the bombardment intact then the battle would come down to a 'race for the parapet' of the German front line trench. But, as previously mentioned, the British infantry was not about to 'race' anywhere. The speed of their advance was a prescribed 50 yards a minute and, according to VIII Corps' own orders, there was not to be any 'doubling' as (and it bears repeating):

> "With the heavy weight men will be carrying it is very exhausting except for the very shortest distances such as 20 yards."[18]

From their repeated mentions after the battle as an explanation for the unexpected survival of the German garrisons, it would appear that many senior officers either ignored these dugouts or did not appreciate the reasons for their existence and/or the strength of their construction. Certainly, the subsequent failure to employ the heaviest howitzers available on the German front line trenches must have contributed greatly to the survival of the German troops huddled in their depths. But, of course, because of the substantial increase in the area of ground to be prepared by the gunners as a result of Haig's intervention, these guns had multiple targets with which to deal and the decision was made that the German front line could be left mainly to the mercies of the field artillery and lighter howitzers and the trench mortars. Unfortunately for many men of the VIII Corps, where evidence of the resilience of the men lurking in these dugouts would be proved almost every night until the attack went in, the consequences of ignoring these essential facts would be fatal.

GIVEN THE PHYSICAL STRENGTH AND THE GREAT DEPTH of the German defences north of the River Ancre what plan was developed at VIII Corps' HQ to overcome their adversary? In brief it was one of great detail, it was precise, it shunned initiative and it involved some extraordinary manoeuvres by certain battalions in full view of the enemy. It was not, however, a scheme of any great subtlety. Reduced to its simplest, however, the British artillery would fire a lot of shells at the German trenches and wire and then the British infantry would walk forward and occupy what was left.

And 'occupy' was about the only word one could use to describe the process envisaged. For example, the troops from the 4th Division with the task of taking the most distant objective, the German 2nd Position, were given 3½ hours (i.e. 210 minutes) to complete the task. Given that the regulation pace of their advance was 50 yards a minute and that their assembly trenches were 1,600 yards behind the British front line and that the distance from there to the German 2nd Position was another 3,400 yards, they would be walking for 100 minutes in order to advance the required 5,000 yards to their objective. Some of the remaining 110 minutes was given up to reorganisation as they passed through the troops currently consolidating the first two objectives and more time was allowed for the artillery to engage its next targets in front of the advancing troops. One might also imagine that the pace might drop as the men crossed the cratered landscape of previously German held territory and also as they bunched to cross the trench bridges laid by the Royal Engineers and then shook out into waves on the other side. It is not difficult to imagine another 30 minutes being occupied in this way which means that all but 80 minutes of their morning's work, assuming no delays caused by obstinate Germans, would be taken up by the walk from their starting trench to the German 2nd position. In other words, there was not a lot of time allowed for actually fighting any of the enemy they might find. Just that 80 minutes, in fact. Give or take.

Such a tight timescale suggests two things:

1. Serious resistance was not expected; or (and whisper it quietly)
2. If serious resistance was encountered then a potentially serious dislocation between the timing of the artillery programme and the advance of the infantry would rapidly develop.

But more on that issue later.

One key decision was made early on and this applied to more or less the entire British front on the Somme. The decision, made after discussions at the highest level, was that there would be no reduction in the width of No Man's Land. No new, advanced, jump-off trenches would be dug. The men would advance from wherever their front lines happened to be in May or June.

The reason? The maintenance of a wholly spurious secrecy. Lt. Col. Cuthbert Graham Fuller, GSO1 29th Division, wrote after the war that:

> "… about a month before the attack the whole question had been discussed by the CinC, CGS, Fourth Army, VIII Corps and 29th Divisional commanders in conference and they had come to the conclusion that it was undesirable to dig trenches closer to the Germans as it would make them realise we intended to attack."[19]

Not one of the great and the good listed above seemed to think that the introduction of numerous new British batteries, the laying of new light and trench railways and the metalling of roads, a significant increase in aerial activity (including a co-ordinated attack on all German observation balloons) and then a five day bombardment by guns of all calibres might suggest to the German commanders that something was brewing in the neighbourhood. If it weren't for the tragedy that ensued one might laugh at such absurdity.

A few miles further south, however, the French were not so precious. Work on reducing No Man's Land to a maximum of 200 metres had been on-going for weeks. Foch and Fayolle insisted on it. But not so on Fourth Army's front. It is interesting to note that one division did make a major effort to reduce the distance it had to cross to get into the German lines. This was the 56th (1st London) Division of Third Army attacking just to the south of Gommecourt. In three nights towards the end of May the division dug an entire new forward trench system by the simple expedient of having a Brigade's worth of men out overnight in No Man's Land digging. This audacious enterprise reduced the gap between the two front lines by half, from 500 to 250 yards, and, on 1st July, the advance elements of the division would all penetrate the first three German lines and some would remain there for some twelve hours, a result few British divisions came close to achieving except on the southern end of the battlefield[i].

The consequences of this decision not to narrow No Man's Land would be severe for the infantry (and would apply on other parts of the front where No Man's Land was especially wide, e.g. opposite Ovillers la Boisselle where the 8th Division attacked). When allied to the approved formation for the advance, i.e. extended waves, 100 yards apart for as far back as was required to get sufficient troops forward to occupy the furthest objective, this meant one thing: the attacking infantry would spend many minutes trying to get to the German front line trench all the while exposed to enemy artillery, machine gun and rifle fire.

On VIII Corps' front No Man's Land narrowed the further north one went. Next to the Ancre, in front of Hamel, where two battalions of the neighbouring 36th (Ulster) Division were to attack, No Man's Land was between 550 and 650 yards wide although somewhat narrower on either flank, i.e. 400 yards by the railway line on the north bank of the Ancre and 220 yards opposite the projection of the Mary Redan.

On the 29th Division's front, No Man's Land was c. 450 yards wide south of the Y Ravine narrowing to 330 yards at its western tip. The distance into the re-entrant south of the Hawthorn Ridge redoubt was 450 yards and to what would become the near edge of the mine crater some 275 yards. With the front line taking a sharp curve westwards on either side of the Beaumont to Auchonvillers road No Man's Land briefly widened to over 550 yards, narrowing again in front of the Sunken Lane, from which the 1st Lancashire Fusiliers were to advance, to not much more than 220 yards.

The southern flank of the 4th Division's front was 450 yards wide narrowing sharply to just 100 yards where the Redan faced the German Ridge Redoubt across the old mine crater field. It expanded to 330 yards to the north before again narrowing sharply to just 100 yards opposite the tip of the Heidenkopf.

For the 31st Division, No Man's Land was less daunting, ranging from 150 yards opposite the end of Ten Tree Alley to 220 yards near to John Copse, the extreme northern end of the front to be attacked. To the north, however, No Man's Land steadily widened to a maximum of nearly 800 yards at the point where the sunken road from Hebuterne to Puisieux cut across the front line trenches. One of the issues of complaint from the 31st Division, especially the troops on the left wing, was that no effort was made to close this huge gap as part of a programme to persuade the Germans that this sector might also be attacked.

If No Man's Land varied significantly, so did the complexity of the German trench systems and the distances between the 1st Position, the Zwischen Stellung (Munich Trench) and the 2nd Position. Again, the further north one went the smaller the distances were between the three lines of trenches that made up the

---

[i] Technically the other unit at Gommecourt, the 46th (North Midland) Division, dug an advanced trench. It was a fiasco. Ordered to be dug against the Divisional commander's wishes, it was started the day before the bombardment was due to begin and the alert German artillery and machine guns caught the men out in No Man's Land during the night. The results were numerous casualties and a trench system not fit for purpose. It was so bad one battalion commander refused to use it.

German 1st Position – the front, support and reserve lines – and then between the 1st Position and the Zwischen Stellung and between that trench and the 2nd Position.

The German fire trench, support and reserve lines were, on average, about 100 yards apart with a considerable depth of wire in front of all three trench lines.

Current German tactical thinking had resulted in two things:

1. The placing of the advanced trenches predominantly on forward slopes, although this not the case in front of Beaumont Hamel because of the nature of the localised terrain. While this gave the defenders long and wide fields of fire it also meant that most, if not all, of the front three trenches could be observed from the ground from the British lines. Again, though, this was not the case at Beaumont Hamel;
2. The placing of the main defensive garrison, usually two battalions, in the 1st Position, normally with one company per sector in the front line and another company in the reserve line. The third battalion was usually found in the Zwischen Stellung. The 2nd Position was normally garrisoned by men from reserve regiments based in villages further to the rear.

This combination of factors should have given the British artillery a distinct advantage as two thirds of the German forward defence occupied just three lines of trenches. Had the heavier artillery been able to concentrate almost solely on these trenches then it is possible that far greater damage could have been done to both defences and defenders. On the XIII Corps' front and on the French front there was such a concentration and, towards the end of the bombardment, the Germans had, in some places, been forced to abandon their fire trench and, in a few locations, even their support trench. With up to seven lines of trenches to bombard (1st Position three, Tübinger Stellung/Nagel Graben one, Zwischen Stellung two, 2nd Position one/two) the VIII Corps' heavy guns had no option but to spread their allocation of shells far more thinly, with the result that much of the apparent damage to the German 1st Position was cosmetic and casualties amongst the defending troops remarkably light.

In places, for example to the west of Serre, there was an additional line of wired trench between the 1st Position and the Zwischen Stellung, complete with dugouts, in which the reserve company of the front line German battalions were often located. This line extended from north-west of Serre into the north of Beaumont Hamel being known to the Germans as Tübinger Stellung on the 52. Division's front at Serre and Nagel Graben on the front of the RIR 121 of the 26. Reserve Division on Redan Ridge. To the British they were known as Serre and Beaumont Trenches. On the 31st and 4th Division's front this would be the 1st objective of the assault. For the 29th Division it was the trench on the ridge to the east of, and overlooking, Station Road. Around Serre, Tübinger Stellung was 200 yards or more behind the reserve line and a similar distance in front of the Zwischen Stellung. As it ran further south Nagel Graben closed up with and, eventually, became the reserve line of the 1st Position. At Beaumont Hamel and down to the Ancre, this line again ran 200-250 yards behind the reserve line using the high ground to the east of the village and on the ridge above Station Road.

The 2nd objective was to be the far side of Serre village and the long, twin trench system running south across the plateau of Redan Ridge and thence down along the length of the Beaucourt to Beaumont Road. This system was the Zwischen Stellung, the switch line, the intermediate trench or, to the British, Munich Trench (for most of its length). In many places this system was difficult or impossible to observe from the ground and assistance from the observers in the BE2cs of the RFC would be essential if the wire was to be cut and the trenches accurately bombarded. Sod's Law, the 'what can go wrong, will go wrong' affecting most human affairs, would intervene heavily here with the late June weather failing to cooperate for a large proportion of the preliminary bombardment. This trench line got progressively further away from the 1st objective as one went south. At the south-west corner of Serre the gap was a mere 200 yards but, in the middle of Redan Ridge and on the road from Beaumont Hamel down to Beaucourt this gap expanded to 750 yards. This meant that the distance from the British front line to their 2nd Objective, the Zwischen Stellung, varied from about 900 yards at Serre to nearly 1,800 yards behind Beaumont Hamel.

On average, the distance between the British front line and the German 2nd Position was:

29th Division – 4,400 yards
4th Division – 3,400 yards
31st Division – 2,700 yards

Those were not, however, the distances which the attacking infantry had to travel in the open in order to reach this objective. The attacking battalions were staggered back across a series of assembly trenches with the troops nearest to the German front having the shortest distance to travel to reach their objective and the troops at the rear having by far the longest distance to travel as each successive wave leap-frogged the one in front. In the case of the 4th Division, for example, this gave the battalions charged with taking the German 2nd position an additional 1,200 to 1,650 yards of terrain behind the British front line to cross before embarking on the 3,400 yard hike towards their distant objective. The consequences were that these supporting battalions, walking at the prescribed 50 yards a minute, would take between 20 and 30 minutes just to reach the British front line, all the while exposed to anything the Germans might be able to throw at them. This period of time alone explains the incredibly heavy casualties suffered by supporting battalions, some of which failed to get any men into No Man's Land let alone the German trenches.

Unfortunately for the British troops, it was also the case that the Germans had an excellent view across the British rear areas almost everywhere along VIII Corps' frontage. Certainly the men of the 31st and 4th Divisions would be horribly exposed as soon as they left their trenches. This problem extended to the rear area of the 1st Lancashire Fusiliers and the 16th Middlesex Regt. on the extreme left of the 29th Division's front but, from there southwards, the division's problem was a different one. Here, wherever possible, the Germans had placed their front line trench on a reverse slope or, at least, below the level of the British front line trench. As a result, in order to be able to approach the British front line, let alone get into the German trenches, the attacking infantry would have to cross the sky-line, thereby presenting excellent targets to the machine guns in the tiers of German trenches stretched out across the opposite ridge[i]. To make matters worse, those machine guns further back, and slightly higher up, had a view over the British support and reserve lines from which the supporting battalions were due to advance and, therefore, were able to take the slow moving lines of infantry under fire several hundred yards behind the British front line.

This issue is nicely illustrated by a post-war sketch by Maj. Geoffrey Raikes of the 2nd South Wales Borderers of the area around the Y Ravine attacked by his battalion (see Figure 3 below). The arrowed lines from left to right indicate the lines of fire of German machine guns located in the three trenches indicated. Guns in the German front and support trenches would fire at troops as they appeared over the sky-line and those on Beaucourt Ridge were able to fire at troops emerging from all three British trenches.

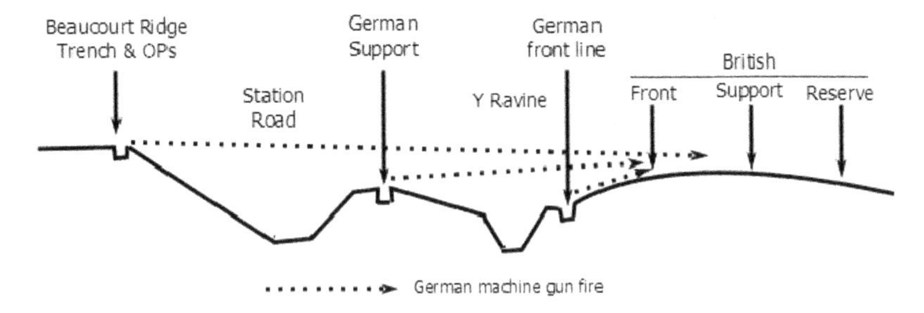

Figure 3 Maj. G T Raikes' (2nd SWB) sketch of the Y Ravine position

The attacking and supporting infantry of every division was, therefore, exposed for long periods of time to the fire of any machine guns which avoided destruction during the bombardment. If the counter battery fire failed to do its work then the German artillery would also have a wonderful slowmoving target at which to fire. The question would be: could the British artillery do the job of destroying or neutralising the German defences during the five day bombardment? The answer seemed to be 'no', if the results of VIII Corps' raids were anything to go by.

WHEREAS THE RELENTLESS FAILURE OF THE VIII CORPS' raids did not seem to disturb Hunter-Weston and his Staff there were concerns at a higher level. Hunter Bunter had been to GHQ on the 29th June and shared lunch with Haig. The CinC described VIII Corps' commander as 'satisfied and confident' but a report later in the day from Noel Birch, Haig's artillery adviser, clearly painted a more worrying picture for his superior. In his diary entry Haig was scathing in his assessment of the senior commanders and staff of the Corps:

> "The conclusion I come to is that the majority (of VIII Corps) are amateurs and some thought that they knew more than they did of this kind of warfare because they had been at Gallipoli. Adversity, shortage of

[i] This local topography caused other problems as flat firing guns, like the 18 and 60 pdrs, struggled to get their rounds up and over the British front lines and then down onto their German targets. Instead, they fired into the British front line trenches. 'Friendly fire' from some heavy howitzers firing short would also be troublesome before and during 1st July.

ammunition and fighting under difficulties against a superior enemy has taught us much!"[20]

Whatever the truth of Haig's opening statement his condescension and his ignorance of, or ability to ignore, the facts pertaining to the fighting at Gallipoli do him little credit. Neither does the fact that nothing appears to have been done to remedy the VIII Corps' shortcomings which would soon result in the highest casualties anywhere on the British front on 1st July 1916.

Interestingly, on the subject of VIII Corps, there are variations in the contents of the two versions of Haig's diaries. The quote given above is taken from the original handwritten (Ms) diary. There are additions to the later typed version (Ts diary) which, at least to this writer, are suggestive either of being wise after the event or of a degree of back covering given the calamitous defeat about to be inflicted on the entire left wing of Haig's offensive. The first amendment comes at the end of a sentence in which he professes to have 'full confidence in their (VIII Corps) abilities to reap success in the coming fighting'. In the typed manuscript the sentence has these words appended:

"… but I still was anxious regarding the leading of the small units (platoons and companies) because their raids had failed."[21]

It can be argued, however, that the battalion officers of all of the Divisions in the Corps were, in the main, sadly lacking in fighting experience. Their military knowledge was based on the every day drudgery of trench warfare and the long days of tactical and physical training behind the lines. Two of the Divisions, the New Army 31st Division and the Territorial Force 48th Division, had, as yet, seen no serious action. One might expect to have been able to look to the officers in the two Regular Divisions for the necessary battlefield experience but, as a result of these Divisions' previous heavy losses, the number of officers still with these infantry battalions who had seen hard fighting were few and far between. One need only look at the details of the officers who went 'over the top' on 1st July to see that the majority of them were war-time commissions or came from Reserve, Territorial or Service battalions, transferred to the first line battalions to make up for previous casualties.

In the 29th Division. for example, the figures are revealing. Ten infantry battalions were committed to the attack on 1st July and the figures below give an indication of how seriously inexperienced these officers from a supposedly Regular Division were:

1st KOSB	Four from the 1st Battalion
	Four from the 3rd (Reserve) Battalion
	One from the 7th (Service) Battalion
	Six from the 9th (Reserve) Battalion (New Army)
	Five from New Army battalions of other regiments

Of the four officers from the 1st KOSB, three were war-time commissions aged 19 to 22 and the fourth was a pre-war professional, Maj. George Hilton.

1st Border Regt.	Six from the 1st Battalion
	Three from the 3rd (Reserve) Battalion
	One from the 8th (Service) Battalion
	Six from the 10th (Reserve) battalion (New Army)
	Three from New Army battalions of other regiments

One from a TF battalion

Of the six officers from the 1st Border Regt. four were pre-war professionals, including the CO, Lt. Col. Ellis, and two were war-time commissions.

1st Royal Inniskilling Fusiliers	Four from the 1st Battalion
	Three from the 3rd (Reserve) Battalion
	One from the 4th (Extra Reserve) Battalion
	Three from the 6th (Service) Battalion
	One from a 1st Line battalion of another regiment
	One from an Extra Reserve battalion of another regiment
	Six from Service battalions of other regiments

Of the four officers from the 1st Battalion, two were pre-war regulars (including Lt. Col. Pierce) and two were war-time commissions.

2nd Royal Fusiliers	Eight from the 2nd Battalion
	One from the 4th Battalion
	Three from the 5th & 6th (Reserve) Battalions
	One from the 8th (Service) Battalion
	Five from the 16th (Reserve) Battalion (New Army)
	One from the 18th (Service) Battalion
	One from the 28th (Reserve) Battalion (New Army)
	One from a Service Battalion of another regiment

Of the eight officers from the 2nd Battalion, one was a pre-war regular, the others were all wartime commissions of which five were from the ranks and three were promoted in April 1916.

From the above it is clear to see how dependent every battalion would be on newly commissioned, young and inexperienced officers to lead their newly recruited, young and inexperienced troops. It is, perhaps, even more extraordinary that their CinC would demand such a deep advance through some of the most heavily fortified and well-defended terrain on the Western Front of such 'green' officers and men. With his first experience employing New Army Divisions at Loos[i] having been such a costly fiasco it is strange that Haig should not have learnt an important lesson that these troops needed to 'walk before they could run'. An advance of 4,000 yards across seven trench lines hardly represented an easy introduction to offensive warfare in France and Flanders. Indeed, in the context of 'walking and running' this advance represented more of a sprint than a stroll.

Haig then went onto a more explicit criticism of Hunter Weston and his Staff based on Birch's report and 'and as a result of my own observation' which reads:

> "Hunter Weston and the majority of his officers… are amateurs in hard fighting".[22]

[i] The completely inexperienced 21st and 24th Divisions of the New Army were ordered by Haig to attack unsupported between Hulluch and Hill 70 on the second day of the Battle of Loos on 26th September. Dreadfully exposed they were slaughtered, losing over 8,200 men in a few hours. It was said that some German troops were so sickened by the mayhem that they stopped firing on the retreating men.

Haig then reinforced his lack of faith in VIII Corps by his diary entry of 30th June assessing Fourth Army's overall prospects. The adverse comment appears only in the later, typed, version of the diary:

> "The only doubt I have is regarding the VIII Corps (Hunter-Weston) which had no experience of fighting in France and has not carried out one successful raid."[23]

Although surely correct in his concerns about Hunter-Weston and his Staff, Haig's thinking here seems confused. On the one hand he is critical of the Corps commander and his senior officers because of their lack of experience in French conditions whilst, on the other, junior officers are the cause of his concern. One might think that, if platoon and company commanders were lacking, that this points a finger at battalion, Brigade and Divisional commanders too. If then, as hinted at, the entire Corps was failing why were not major changes in the command structure made, either at the time or later? Instead, of course, Hunter-Weston survived as VIII Corps' commander. Unaccountably, he remained in command of VIII Corps until it was disbanded in June 1918, although it was not entrusted with any major offensive operations after 1st July 1916. This latter fact, perhaps, more correctly sums up Haig's attitude towards a General too well-connected to sack but too incompetent to employ.

The truth is, however, that the German commanders from Army down to Brigade level had a great advantage over their British equivalents in terms of both overall experience and staff training. The average age of VIII Corps' GOC and his four divisional commanders was 52 (also Rawlinson's age) whereas the average age of the German Army commander, von Below, and the Corps and divisional commanders on the other side of No Man's Land was 62. The average age of British Brigade commanders was 44 whilst that of the German Brigade generals was 58. Although one might imagine that energy and stamina were on the side of the British generals, one of the inevitable consequences of this age difference was the level of experience of commanding Brigade or large sized units. On average, German commanders had at least four years' experience commanding formations of this size and complexity, with most of them having gone to war in 1914 in charge of a unit at least the size which they commanded on the Somme in June 1916. On the British side, however, experience of leading such large units was a rarity. The most experience 'large unit' commander was de Lisle of 29th Division who had commanded Brigade and Division-sized formations for five years. Hunter-Weston and Fanshawe of the 48th Division had two years' experience each. Other than these three officers, British divisional and brigade GOCs had at most a year or, in four cases, less than six months experience of higher command.

Furthermore, whereas every German General had attended both the Prussian Kriegsakademie and been a member of the Großer Generalstab (Great General Staff) in Berlin and then gone on to serve in staff positions at Divisional, Corps and Army level, the same could not be said of the British General Officers of the VIII Corps. Six[i] had attended the Staff College at Camberley and only five of the eight senior officers actively involved in the attack (i.e. excluding the 48th

[i] Hunter-Weston, Lambton, de Lisle, Fanshawe, Lucas, Weir de Lancey Williams.

Division) had any direct experience of Staff work. Whilst Haig as CinC actively sought out younger, more energetic, thrusting and aggressive General Officers, the downside of their relative youth and inexperience was an absence of the planning, organisational and logistical skills and experience of the trained staff officer. These weaknesses would be harshly exposed during both the planning and delivery of the VIII Corps' attack.

As to Haig's criticism of junior officers one wonders how fair this is especially as the failure of raids was not isolated to just the VIII Corps' front? The issues preventing the successful prosecution of the numerous raids mounted by VIII Corps were surely far more to do with poor staff work, the inadequately cut wire and the failure of the Corps artillery to destroy or neutralise the enemy troops defending the front line than any failures of skill or valour on the part of the officers and men involved. These problems do not reflect on the abilities of the infantry officers who did their best to fulfil their objectives but more on the performance of the Divisional and Corps artillery and the ability of the various staffs to assess the results of their work and alter their priorities where necessary. Of course, the work of the artillery was circumscribed by the necessity of preparing an area far deeper than anywhere south of Pozieres and this requirement was placed on them by Sir Douglas Haig's decision to override Rawlinson's initial plan of attack.

Staff work, intelligence gathering and analysis had undoubtedly been poor on VIII Corps front. In spite of the evidence gathered from the failure of most of the raids, details of which are shown in Table 1 on page 46, there had been no significant adaptations to the conduct of the bombardment or the plans for the attack. It was clear that the German front line was heavily held and that machine guns were present and active and yet no changes were made to the timings set in stone by Corps for the explosion of the great mine under Hawthorn Ridge or the lifts of the heavy guns from the front line trenches. Criminally, the infantry were still supposed to walk slowly across No Man's Land towards their objectives.

Furthermore, there was very little information about the nature and location of the German artillery ranged against them. German artillery tactics had been subtle. Many batteries did not fire much during the seven day bombardment and, usually, only when gas or smoke was released. As a result, aerial and ground observers had been unable to pinpoint the location of many of the well camouflaged German batteries. In addition, numerous alternate battery positions had been created to which guns were often relocated during the last week of June. Generally, counter-battery fire was not yet a high enough priority within the BEF as Noel Birch would later admit. Whereas Foch and Fayolle regarded the destruction or, at least, the neutralisation of the enemy's guns as an essential prerequisite of any successful attack, for the British it was a rather burdensome add-on to the main bombardment. To make matters worse for the VIII Corps, the Gommecourt diversion had only served to sharply increase the number of guns opposing it and the weight of artillery fire that was to fall on the 31st and 4th Divisions on Z Day would come as a complete shock to both the infantry and their commanders.

It was the failure of the VIII Corps' counter battery work that most concerned Rawlinson. On 28th June he recorded in his diary that the Corps:

"… have not been doing their counter battery work well."[24]

Sadly, that was not all that had gone wrong and others, apparently, sensed this fact. Brig. Gen. Charteris makes an extraordinary claim in his book *'At GHQ'* in which he describes a visit to an unnamed Corps HQ the day before the attack. Given Haig's own fears about their VIII Corps' preparations, it is difficult to see how his observations can have been about any unit other than VIII Corps. And if there were any residual doubts then the final comment by the anonymous Corps' commander feeling 'like Napoleon at Austerlitz' should be enough to identify Hunter-Weston's pompous bluster beyond all doubt:

> "I went to one Corps where the preparations had not been so thorough, to advise whether that part of the attack should be held back. I had been given power to countermand the attack of the Corps if I considered it advisable, a most unpleasant responsibility, for it had little chance of complete success and there was a certainty of many casualties. But even partial success might mean much to other parts of the line. The Corps commander was more than satisfied. He was convinced of a great success. The Divisional commanders are almost equally confident. Eventually I decided to let the attack go on, and came back feeling very miserable. The Corps commander said he felt 'like Napoleon before the battle of Austerlitz'."[25]

Or Waterloo, as it would turn out.

---

1 Gary Sheffield and John Bourne, eds., *Douglas Haig: War Diaries and Letters 1914-1918*, Weidenfeld and Nicholson, 2005, page 187.
2 Hunter-Weston Papers, BL, no. 48365.
3 Fourth Army, *Tactical Notes*, para. 12
4 Ibid., para. 17.
5 Ibid., para. 20.
6 *OH*, 1916, Appendices, Appendix 18, *'Tactical Notes'*, page 134.
7 *AFGG*, Tome IV, Annexes Vol. 2, annex 868.
8 *AFGG*, Tome IV, Annexes Vol. 2, annex 1369, *'Note a communiquer jusqu'aux bataillons'*.
9 Carden-Roe papers, IWM.
10 NA WO 95/820, *Notes of two conferences held at Corps headquarters 21st and 23rd June 1916.*
11 Ibid.
12 Ibid.
13 Ibid.
14 Ibid.
15 NA WO/95/820, *VIII Corps summary of operations, 2nd June to 9th June, 1916*
16 NA WO95/2745.
17 Whitehead, R J *'The Other Side of the Wire'*, Volume 1, page 433.
18 NA WO 95/820, *Notes of two conferences held at Corps headquarters 21st and 23rd June 1916.*
19 NA CAB45/133, *Comments on draft of Official History, Authors D-F.*
20 Sheffield & Bourne, op. cit., page, 194.
21 Ibid.
22 Ibid.
23 Ibid., page 195.
24 Rawlinson Diary, 28th June 1916.
25 Charteris, J, *'At GHQ'*, page 150.

5. The Defenders

THE GERMAN ARMY CAME TO BEAUMONT HAMEL on the morning of the 5th October 1914 when it was captured by troops from Reserve Infanterie Regiment Nr. 99 (RIR 99) of the 26. Reserve Infanterie Division. The men had been recruited from the area around Mönchengladbach in the Rhineland, although the Division to which they belonged originated from the Southern German Kingdom of Württemberg (Königreich Württemberg). Sandwiched between Bavaria (Bayern) to the east and Baden to the west, this region provided the bulk of the men of the Division and they would occupy and fortify the area around Beaumont Hamel and Redan Ridge north of the River Ancre as well as Thiepval away to the south over the next 20 months.

The long term garrison of the village, the Württembergische Reserve Infanterie Regiment Nr. 119 (RIR 119), was recruited from Stuttgart, Württemberg's largest city, and its surrounding areas. This regiment took over the Beaumont Hamel and Beaucourt sectors on 7th May 1915 with RIR 99 moving south of the river to the area around the Schwaben redoubt and Thiepval. Happily for RIR 119, its predecessors from the Rhineland had within its ranks numerous miners and, as commander of its 14. Kompanie, one Hauptmann Franz Leiling.

In the seven months of their occupation, the RIR 99, under the guidance of Hptm. Leiling, had embarked upon an extraordinary series of building and mining works which, with the continued efforts of the Württembergers over the following year, resulted in the construction of one of the strongest fortifications anywhere on the Somme front. So significant were the efforts of Leiling that some of the results of his efforts were given his name. What was known to the British, because of its distinctive shape, as the Y Ravine was known on the other side of the wire as the Leilingschlucht. At the far end of the Leilingschlucht was the Schluchtstollen, a large dugout mined out of the chalk which lay under No Man's Land and contained, by June 1916, a Moritz listening station capable of tapping into indiscreet telephone conversations in the British lines. Then there was the Leilingstollen, a large dugout mined into the reverse slope of the valley that runs south from Beaumont Hamel towards Beaucourt Station and the River Ancre (Station Road). Linked to the rear by a light railway, this dugout was one of the largest of many quarried into the sides of the valley and was used as accommodation by the garrison. Leiling was busy along the whole front of the sector and, indeed, was heavily involved in the construction of the complex of dugouts at St Pierre Divion on the south side of the Ancre which, after its capture in November 1916, was thought capable of housing up to 1,000 men in secure, underground accommodation.

Leiling's regiment, the RIR 99, was the only major element of the 26. Reserve Infanterie Division not to come from Württemberg. The Division consisted of two infantry brigades each of two three-battalion regiments, an artillery brigade made up of two field artillery regiments to which were attached a whole series of mortar, pioneer, medical, mining, labour and cyclist companies, a field recruit depot (in which new recruits were tutored in the ways of the Western Front usually from a relatively safe distance), a cavalry detachment, seven machine gun companies and attached units, plus additional artillery attached from 6. Army, XIV Reserve Corps and neighbouring and reserve divisions.

Plate 7 Generalleutnant Franz Freiherr von Soden-Frauenhofen, 26. Reserve Infanterie Division

The Divisional commander was the 60 year old General der Infanterie Franz Freiherr von Soden[i]. Von Soden was born in Stuttgart and volunteered in 1873, joining the Grenadier-Regiment Königin Olga (1. Württembergische). He was obviously identified as a candidate for the Staff, attending the Prussian Kriegsakademie in 1880 and becoming part of the Großer Generalstab in Berlin in 1886. A variety of Corps and Divisional Staff roles ensued through until 1898 when he was given command of a battalion of Infanterie-Regiment von Wittich (3. Kurhessisches) Nr. 83. By 1900 he was the Chief of Staff of the X Armeekorps and, three years later, the commander of Infanterie-Regiment, Kaiser Friedrich König von Preußen, (7. Württembergisches) Nr. 125. In 1906 he was give command first of the 51. Infanterie Brigade (1. Königlich Württembergische) and then, in 1910, of the 26. Infanterie Division. On the outbreak of war he took command of the 26. Reserve Infanterie Division and he proved to be a vigorous and thoughtful commanding officer. He learned much during the heavy French attacks in front of Redan Ridge in the summer of 1915 and applied those lessons to the defence of Beaumont Hamel in the summer of 1916. Energetic and flexible, he would later take command of three different Army Corps.

His troops in the sector north of the River Ancre consisted of the two regiments of the 51. Reserve Infanterie Brigade commanded by Generalleutnant Theodor von Wundt[ii]. Von Wundt was two years younger than his Divisional

[i] Freiherr = Baron

[ii] The second brigade, 52. Reserve Infanterie Brigade (RIR 99 and RIR 180) defended the Schwaben, Thiepval, Liepzig Redoubt and Ovillers La Boiselle sectors.

commander and had been born in Ludwigsburg, a small city with a population of about 25,000 some 8 miles north of Stuttgart[i]. He was the son of a previous War Minister for Württemberg and was another career officer having commanded the 59. Infanterie Brigade before the war. He was also a prolific writer about his favourite pastime, mountain climbing, having published seven books on the subject before the outbreak of war. He was married to an English woman, Maud Walters, who accompanied him on his many holidays in the Alps, Dolomites and Tatra Mountains, one of which trips was their honeymoon. One of their children, Max, was killed in the first weeks of the war. Von Wundt was given command of the 51. Reserve Infanterie Brigade on the outbreak of war, commanding them through until the autumn of 1916. Clearly a man of many parts, he commissioned artist Albert Heim to produce a series of 80 colourful cartoons of life at the front, some of which poked gentle fun at senior officers. Von Wundt even appears in one of the pictures[ii].

Plate 8 Generalleutnant Theodor von Wundt, 51. Reserve Infanterie Brigade

His two infantry regiments were the Württembergisches Reserve-Infanterie-Regiment Nr. 119 and Württembergisches Reserve-Infanterie-Regiment Nr. 121 which had been recruited around Stuttgart and Ludwigsburg respectively. Attached to the two regiments were three Machine Gun companies (two with the RIR 119) whilst the RIR 121 also could draw on the guns of Maschinengewehr-Scharfschützen-Abteilung[iii] Nr. 198 and the six Maxim machine guns of Fortress Maschinengewehr-Kompanie Fassbender. Nine captured Russian and twelve captured Belgian machine guns were in their armoury. The two infantry regiments consisted of three battalions, each of four companies. Each battalion

[i] For a time, von Wundt's headquarters was at the Thiepval chateau and a nearby field work, the Wundtwerk, was named after him.

[ii] The collection was sold for £13,750 at Bonham's, the London auctioneers, in April 2012 by von Wundt's now American-based family.

[iii] Machine Gun Sharpshooter Detachment.

comprised some 900 men which meant that there about 2,500 infantry[i] opposing the 29th Division with its three Brigades of around 3,700 infantry each plus a Pioneer battalion of about 1,000, i.e. 12,100 officers and men. Of course, on both sides of No Man's Land, not all of the troops were fighting men and not all would be involved, however, it is not unfair to put the ratio of British attackers to German defenders as something close to 5 to 1.

Artillery support for the Beaumont Hamel and Redan Ridge defences came from batteries drawn from the two field artillery regiments of the 26. Reserve Feldartillerie-Brigade: Württembergisches Reserve-Feldartillerie-Regiment Nr. 26 (RFAR 26) and Nr. 27 (RFAR 27). These were made up of four gun batteries of either 77 mm field guns, the equivalents of the British 18 pdr. and the French 75 mm, or 10.5 cm field howitzers[ii], the equivalent of the British 4.5 in. field howitzer. They were supported by a number of batteries drawn from the Feldartillerie (Field Artillery) and Fußartillerie (Foot Artillery) regiments and battalions specially attached to the Division.

A Feldartillerie-Brigade was organised thus:

- Two Feldartillerie-Regiments; each comprising
- Two Feldartillerie-Abteilung, I and II, (Field Artillery Groups); each made up of
- Three Feldartillerie Batteries, numbered 1 to 3 and 4 to 6, each of four field guns or howitzers;

In the case of RFAR 26, the six batteries were all armed with the 77 mm Feldkanone 96[iii]. In RFAR 27, one Abteilung was armed with the 77 mm field gun and the other with the 10.5 cm leichte Feldhaubitze 98/09[iv] (Light Field Howitzer). This gave a total of 36 field guns and 12 field howitzers per Brigade and those of the 26. Reserve Division were distributed north and south of the River Ancre.

All of these units, along with the 52. Infanterie Division defending Serre and the southern front of the Gommecourt salient, had been involved in very heavy fighting in early June 1915 in the sector east of Hebuterne and west of a small salient that was now called the Heidenkopf. The French launched a series of attacks south of Hebuterne gaining some ground either side of Toutvent Farm to the west of Serre but failed in their objective of taking the village. Fighting went on for the best part of a week but eventually, after suffering 11,000 casualties, the French stabilised their position based on the trench systems from which the 4th and 31st Divisions of the VIII Corps would attack on the 1st July 1916. The one

---

[i] A portion of the RIR 119 faced the two battalions of the Ulster Division attacking between the Mary Redan and the River Ancre.

[ii] Most first line German artillery batteries started the war with six guns but the Reserve formations which were introduced from October 1914 only had four guns per battery. By the beginning of 1915 all batteries became four gun batteries, partly to improve ammunition supply, because of the rate that quick firing guns went through shells, but also because it created 300 new batteries. *[Thanks to Jack Sheldon for this information].*

[iii] The 77 mm Feldkanone 96 had a maximum range of 9,200 yards (8,400 m) and could fire up to 10 rounds per minute. It fired either a 15lb (6.8 Kg) shrapnel, HE or gas shell.

[iv] The 10.5 cm leichte Feldhaubitze 98/09 had a maximum range of 6,890 yards (6,300 m). It fired either a 35 lb. (15.7 Kg) HE or 28 lb. (12.8 Kg) shrapnel shell.

reminder that the Germans had occupied more French territory in the farmland south of Hebuterne was the existence in the front line of the Heidenkopf (known to the British as the Quadrilateral), in front of Redan Ridge and just to the east of the Serre to Mailly Maillet road[i]. Previously, at this point, the German front line had run north west and around Toutvent Farm but now the Heidenkopf was just a rather difficult to defend projection into a low lying area of No Man's Land overlooked by the British trenches. Rather like the human appendix it was rather useless but difficult to get rid of.

The German defences consisted of three trench systems, the:

- First position, consisting of three lines of trenches, front, support and reserve, roughly 100 yards apart, which, around Hawthorn Ridge and the Y Ravine, used reverse slopes to conceal them from direct observation from the British trenches. The areas in front of the first two trench lines and parts of the reserve trench were heavily wired and even this wire, in certain places, was not visible from the British front line making wirecutting a difficult business. In addition, there were two strongpoints built into the front line trench both of which projected out into No Man's Land which made it possible for the defenders to enfilade any troops attacking to left or right. These two were the redoubts on Redan Ridge, the Ridge Redoubt, and, to the south and in front of Beaumont Hamel on Hawthorn Ridge, what the British called the Hawthorn Redoubt;
- Intermediate position (known to the Germans as the Zwischen Stellung and the central part of which became known to the British as Munich Trench) which consisted of two heavily wired trenches which ran from Star Wood north of Serre, around that village and then across the plateau of Redan Ridge, turning south east when it hit the Beaucourt to Beaumont Hamel road. From there it followed the road to Beaucourt sur Ancre and the river. Serre village was encircled by these trenches and, further south, a series of three redoubts had been constructed: one behind the Heidenkopf on Redan Ridge called the Feste Soden (after the commander of the 26. Reserve Infanterie Division, General der Infanterie von Soden), another called the Grallsburg (Battle HQ of the RIR 121), which lay behind Beaumont Hamel where the Zwischen Stellung met the Beaucourt Road, and the third known as the Feste Alt Württemberg (Battle HQ of the RIR 119) which lay above Beaucourt and was known to the British as the Beaucourt Redoubt; and lastly the
- Second Position (known to the Germans as the 2. Stellung) which ran around the western edge of Puisieux and then due south to reach the Ancre to the west of Baillescourt Farm and opposite the western end of Grandcourt on the southern bank of the river. A large proportion of this position was not visible from the British trenches. There were two redoubts along this line, the Alte Garde Stellung (Battle HQ of the 51. Reserve Infanterie Brigade) which was 1,000 metres due east of Serre, and

[i] The site of the Heidenkopf lies in the field some 50 metres to the north of the northern wall of Serre Road No. 2 Cemetery with its front edge running nearly parallel to, and about 20 metres behind, the front of the cemetery.

one around a ruined windmill, the Moulin Ruiné, which lay midway between the Alte Garde Stellung and the northern bank of the River Ancre.

To increase the strength of the defences there was the previously mentioned trench line which ran between the reserve line of the 1st position and the Zwischen Stellung. In front of Serre it was called Tübinger Stellung (British: Serre Trench) and along Redan Ridge it was known as Nagel Graben (British: Beaumont Trench). From Beaumont Hamel southwards this trench line was intermittent and ran along the western side of Station Road. To the rear, the headquarters of the artillery commander, von Maur, was in the village of Grévillers and von Soden's divisional HQ was at Biefvillers.

The objective of the VIII Corps was to take the German 2nd Position to the east of Serre down to the River Ancre, i.e. six or seven separate lines of trenches including seven redoubts, in the space of the morning of Z Day which, before the weather intervened, was due to be Thursday, 29th June 1916.

At this time, German defensive tactics required the front line trenches to be heavily manned and the explicit instructions to local commanders were that any ground lost was to be regained by immediate counter attacks. This front line garrison was housed in the many deep dugouts, tunnels and caves that either already existed or had been constructed over the 21 months during which the Beaumont Hamel area had been occupied.

Fortunately for the defenders, the area around Beaumont Hamel had been quarried and mined for chalk over many centuries and, to the north of the village, was an area known as the 'Mine' to the west of which was the defensive position called the Bergwerk. The 'Mine' was a large cave[i] lying to the east of the road which ran over Redan Ridge towards Serre. During the many wars over previous centuries that had swept this land, the villagers would retreat into these caves as enemy forces approached. Now it, and another smaller cave to the west of the road to Serre, were perfect locations for the accommodation of the men of the Reserve Infanterie Regiment Nr. 121 who defended the Bergwerk and the southern end of Redan Ridge.

The RIR 121's front had been split into six sectors, H1 to H6, and it was sector H6, which straddled what was known as the New Beaumont Road, which was to be the northern limit of the 29th Division's front opposite. The road ran along a shallow valley from the centre of Beaumont Hamel to the northern end of the British occupied village of Auchonvillers, or 'Ocean Villas' as it was known to the men of the 29th Division. Startinng on the northern side, sector H6 ran a short distance south of the road and up the slope to what the British called Hawthorn Ridge, so called because of the hawthorn bushes that flowered there. On the top of this slope was the fortified strongpoint known to the Germans as the Weißdornfeste, or whitethorn fortress, whitethorn being the same as the British hawthorn. To the British, this area was known as Hawthorn Ridge and the fate of the Weißdornfeste and its garrison would provide one of the most controversial incidents of the entire day's fighting on 1st July.

[i] British trench maps from November 1916 suggest it occupied an area some 200 yards square.

The Weißdornfeste was in Sector B1 of RIR 119's position, and six other sectors, B2 to B7 occupied by the regiment ran south and then east around the Y Ravine before turning down to the River Ancre over undulating slopes of open farmland.

The village of Beaumont Hamel is set into a depression between Redan and Hawthorn Ridges to the north and west and higher ground to the east which rises gently before sloping away south east towards Beaucourt sur Ancre. At the village's heart lies a junction of six roads:

- The previously mentioned New Beaumont Road which runs west towards Auchonvillers between the slopes of Redan and Hawthorn Ridges;
- Station Road, which runs south east towards Beaucourt railway station on the banks of the River Ancre, along a valley in which many dugouts and tunnels had been excavated. This area was known as the Kolonie. The entrance to the Y Ravine ran west off Station Road just to the south of the village cemetery;
- Beaucourt Road, which runs north west from Beaucourt sur Ancre, the first half running just east of the Zwischen Stellung and the rest, which entered Beaumont Hamel, being just to the north of an important German communication trench – Landsturm Graben (Beaucourt Alley);
- Wagon Road, which runs north east, up onto the plateau across Redan Ridge and on to Serre;
- A road, Frontier Lane, which ran due north between the German front line trenches, up and over Redan Ridge and behind the front line fortification, the Heidenkopf, to join the Mailly Maillet to Serre road opposite what is now Serre Road Cemetery No. 1; and
- What was known to the British as Watling Street, a track which ran off the Serre to Mailly Maillet Road well behind the British front lines, then drove south east across No Man's Land and into the north west of the village.

The key feature of the terrain behind the German lines everywhere was that the land was tiered like the rows of seats in a stadium with each area of high ground to the east higher than the one before. Apart from the advantages of observation this gave the Germans it also, and crucially, allowed them to place machine guns at each level and these weapons, with their interlocking fields of fire, were capable of sweeping the entire British front line from all three trenches of the 1st Position and also from most of the Zwischen Stellung. In addition, south of the Ancre, there were several machine gun emplacements located around the tiny riverside hamlet of St Pierre Divion capable of firing north, across the river, and into the flank of any attacking troops. Their range would allow them to fire as far north as the Y Ravine if required.

Along the entire front of the 26. Reserve Division, both north and south of the Ancre, it was able to deploy 90 machine guns, most of which were German MG08s, but some of which were captured Russian and Belgian guns. In addition, attached to the Division was the 1. Kompanie of Musketen Bataillon Nr. 1. Equipped with 30 mobile Danish Madsen Light Machine Guns[i], the equivalent of

---

[i] The Madsen was developed by Julius A. Rasmussen and Theodor Schoubue and adopted by the Danish Army in 1902. Lightweight, 20 lbs. (9.1 Kg), it used a magazine containing

the British Lewis Gun, these provided much needed mobile firepower and were usually kept out of the front line trench, instead being deployed as circumstances dictated. Two gun teams from this company would feature in the confused fighting around the Hawthorn Ridge crater on the day of the attack.

The heavy machine gun was the Maschinengewehr 08, or MG08, which was a variant on the original Maxim Machine Gun and had been adopted by the German Army in 1908. Water-cooled, it fired 7.92 mm bullets from 250 round belts at a notional rate of 400 rounds per minute. It had a maximum range of 3,800 yards (3,500 metres) but just over 2,000 yards was deemed its effective range. Over the previous 21 months, the German machine gun teams had been given plenty of time to identify the best possible positions to produce interlocking fields of fire covering the whole of the divisional front. South of Beaumont Hamel, for example, there were nearly 30 gun positions of which only six were in the German front trench. The rest were deployed in the support and reserve lines, on the ridge above Station Road and in the Zwischen Stellung. Half of all the guns were in these two latter positions. There was not one square yard of No Man's Land onto which a machine gun could not be trained. The front to be attacked by the 87th Brigade, for example, was overlooked by thirteen machine gun positions of which eight were either on the Station Road ridge or along the Beaucourt Road, i.e. out of the immediate reach of any attacking infantry. In addition, at least two positions at St Pierre Divion covered the British front with enfilade fire from the Ancre up to the southern side of the Y Ravine, a distance well within an MG08's effective range.

To prevent these machine guns from slaughtering the advancing troops in No Man's Land, the German front line dugouts would need to be destroyed and the trenches above Station Road and along the Beaucourt Road would have to be kept under continuous artillery and machine gun fire as the British attack progressed. Disastrously, however, as the plan for the attack was firmly fixed on a timetable rather than reflecting actual progress on the ground, none of these criteria were achieved.

In addition to the ideal terrain for the deployment of multiple machine guns, the Germans had also made use of the lie of the land to conceal their artillery from ground level observers. The artillery of the 26. Reserve Infanterie Division was commanded by a highly experienced officer, the 53-year-old Generalmajor Karl Theodor Alexander Heinrich von Maur from Ulm, who had been rushed back from the Eastern Front on 5th June 1916 to take control of a unit that had lost most of its heavy howitzers to the Verdun campaign. Von Maur had joined Feldartillerie-Regiment Prinzregent Luitpold von Bayer (2. Württembergisches) Nr. 29 in 1881 and, after a lengthy career learning his trade, was appointed commander of his original regiment in March 1913. He took the regiment to war on the Western Front in 1914 being involved in heavy fighting around Lille and Ypres. At the end of December 1914 he was sent to the Eastern Front to take command of the 79. Reserve-Feldartillerie-Brigade of the 79. Reserve Infanterie Division with which he fought at the Masurian Lakes, Kovno and Vilnius. Von

25, 30 or 40 rounds. In appearance it was similar to the later Czech-derived Bren Gun used extensively by the British in WW2 and beyond and was first widely used by the Russian Army in the Russo-Japanese War.

Maur was promoted Generalmajor on 27th January 1916 and returned to the Western Front at the beginning of June to take command of the 26. Reserve Artillerie Brigade[i]. For the fighting at the end of June, von Maur would delegate tactical control of the field guns and howitzers to his two regimental commanders, Oberstleutnant Erlenbusch of 26. RFAR based at Miraumont, and Maj. Reiniger, 27 RFAR based at Pys, however, from his HQ at Grévillers he retained direct control over some heavier guns, two captured Russian heavy howitzers, and two obsolete 10 cm Ringkanone.

Plate 9 Generalmajor Heinrich von Maur, 26. Reserve Artillerie Brigade

The division's artillery had been reinforced by several batteries supplied by the Army or Corps and, in early June, they had been divided into two groups. Group Pys was deployed south of the Ancre and supported the defenders of Thiepval and Ovillers la Boisselle. Group Miraumont, commanded by Oberst Erlenbusch of RFAR 26, undertook the defence of Redan Ridge and Beaumont Hamel. Group Miraumont was itself sub-divided into two sub-groups: Gruppe Adolf and Gruppe Beauregard. The battery positions of Gruppe Adolf were along the north bank of the Ancre between Beaucourt and Baillescourt Farm and on the western (reverse) slope of the Artillerie Mulde, a shallow dry valley which ran north from Beaucourt sur Ancre towards Puisieux between the Zwischen Stellung and the 2nd Position. Gruppe Beauregard was dug in to the east of the 2nd Position along the Puisieux to Baillescourt Farm Road (see Map 1).

Covering the 29th Division's front were:

[i] Von Maur commanded his Brigade throughout the Battle of the Somme and, on 12th March 1917 was given command of the 27. Infanterie Division (2. Königlich Württembergische) which he commanded throughout the heavy fighting in 1917 and 1918 on the Western Front. He was awarded Pour le Mérite on 20th May 1917. He died on 10th April 1947.

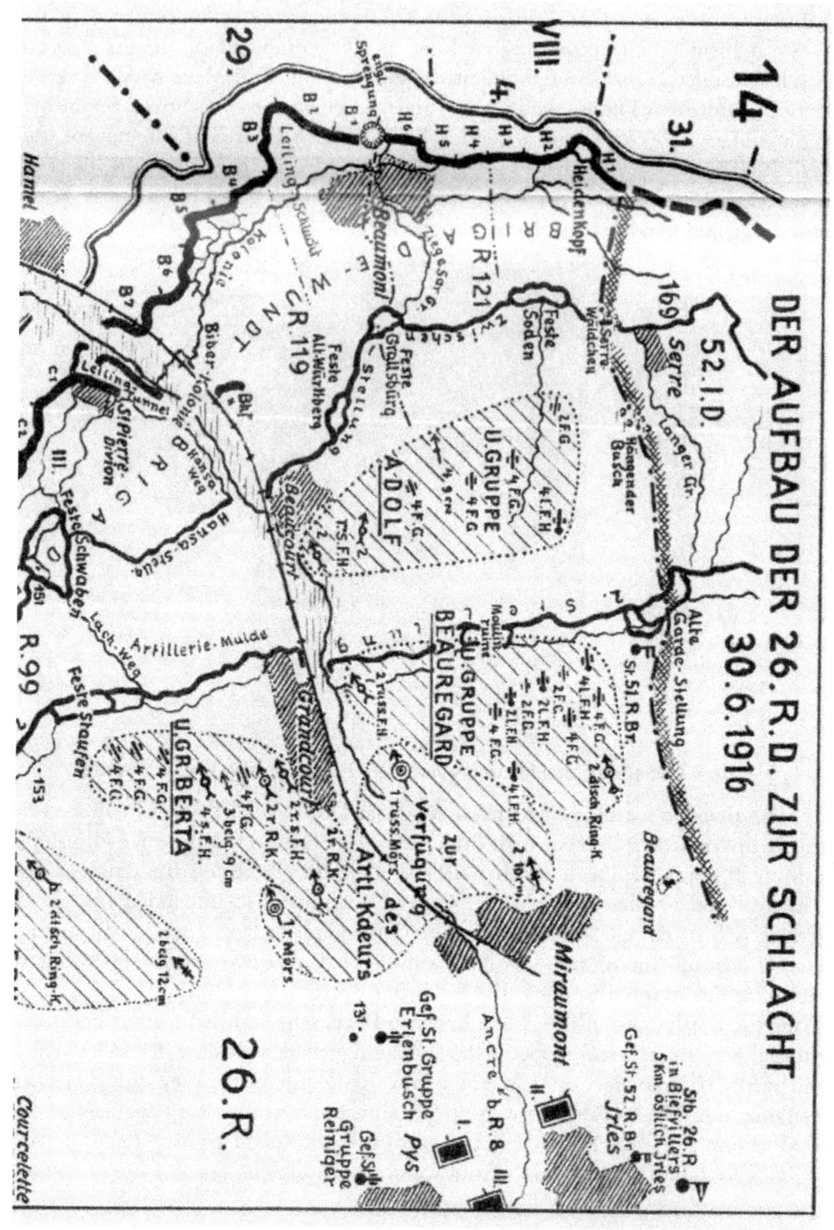

Map 1 Distribution of artillery of the 26. Reserve Division
[Source: Klaus, M. *Das Württembergische Reserve-Feldartillerie-Regiment Nr. 26*, 1929]

Key: F.G. = 77 mm Field Gun l.F.H. = 10.5 cm Light Field Howitzer
S.F.H. = 15 cm Heavy Field Howitzer Ring K. = Ring Kanone
Russ.F.H./Mörs. = Captured Russian Field Howitzer/Heavy Howitzer

- 3. Batterie (four 77 mm field guns), RFAR 26, Gruppe Adolf, in position 721 which covered sector H5 and the right of sector H6, the area of the 1st Lancashire Fusiliers and the Sunken Road opposite the Bergwerk;
- A battery of four obsolete 9 cm guns, Gruppe Adolf, in position 720 which covered the left of sector H6, the ground over which the 16th Middlesex were to advance to the north of the Hawthorn Redoubt;
- 6. Batterie (four 10.5 cm field howitzers), RFAR 27, Gruppe Beauregard, in position 708, which covered the area opposite the Hawthorn Redoubt and the re-entrant to the south to be attacked by the 2nd Royal Fusiliers;
- 4. Batterie (four 10.5 cm field howitzers), Kgl. Bayerisches Feldartillerie-Regiment Nr. 20, 10. Königlich Bayerische Division (10th Bavarian Division and 10. KB Division hereafter), Gruppe Beauregard, in battery positions 710 and 712, which covered the area to the west of the Y Ravine to be attacked by the 2nd South Wales Borderers;
- 3. Batterie (four 77 mm field guns), RFAR 27, Gruppe Beauregard, in positions 709 and 711, which covered the area south of the Y Ravine where the left and right of the South Wales Borderers and 1st Royal Inniskilling Fusiliers met;
- 6. Batterie (four 10.5 cm field howitzers), Kgl. Bayerisches Feldartillerie-Regiment Nr. 20, 10. KB Division, Gruppe Beauregard, in battery position 714, which covered the area either side of the Mary Redan.
- Half of Fußartillerie-Batterie Nr. 683 (two 15 cm Ringkanone) in position 733, Gruppe Beauregard, which covered the trenches to the rear of the Mary Redan.

From there to the river, the guns of the 1. Batterie, Badisches Feldartillerie-Regiment Nr. 104 of the 52. Division, position 756, 3. Batterie, FAR 104, in position 757 (both four 77 mm field guns), and half of the 2. Batterie (two captured Russian 15 cm field howitzers) of Fußartillerie-Bataillon Nr. 51 in position 114, all Gruppe Adolf, would cover sectors B5 to B7, the area to be attacked by two battalions of the 108th Brigade, 36th (Ulster) Division.

On average, each battery was allocated a frontage of between 300 and 400 metres to cover (see Map 3) but a total of eight field guns, twelve field howitzers and six obsolete long guns hardly compared to the weight of artillery that 29th Division and VIII Corps Heavy Artillery brought to the table. The key difference was this: whereas the British artillery had to bombard the trenches as well as destroy the wire in front of the three German positions, whilst also trying to deal with the German guns, the German artillery had just one objective – to destroy the British infantry in and just in front of the British trench system. They could, and mostly would, ignore the British artillery but if, in conjunction with their machine guns, they could stop the British infantry advancing and cut off any that got across No Man's Land with an impenetrable barrier of HE, shrapnel and MG bullets then their battle would be won.

To win this battle the German gunners had trained and worked hard. Their gun positions, personnel dugouts and ammunition bunkers were robust and well concealed. Spare battery positions had been prepared in case it proved necessary or useful for a battery to move and dummy positions were also constructed in an effort to confuse British observers and divert counter battery guns. Communications, by telephone, rocket and runner, had been tested and re-tested. Targets had been identified, plotted and registered. Tactics had been decided and battery and gun commanders briefed. Initiative and flexibility, as with the infantry, were encouraged, even expected. Although each battery had been allocated an area on which to fire they were also expected to change targets to areas of apparent British strength or German weakness in an instant. There was no need to refer requests up and down the Army or Corps chain of command. If the Division or a Gruppe commander concluded that concentrated fire needed to be poured on a particular sector then the guns were expected to comply and quickly. Their speed of response to special requests from the front line infantry would be shown on the day of the attack with batteries responding in minutes to requests for a special barrage or with details of a specific target. How envious must have been the British infantry of such co-operation as they watched the barrages of their heavy and field guns march away into the distance as they grimly battled their way into No Man's Land on 1st July.

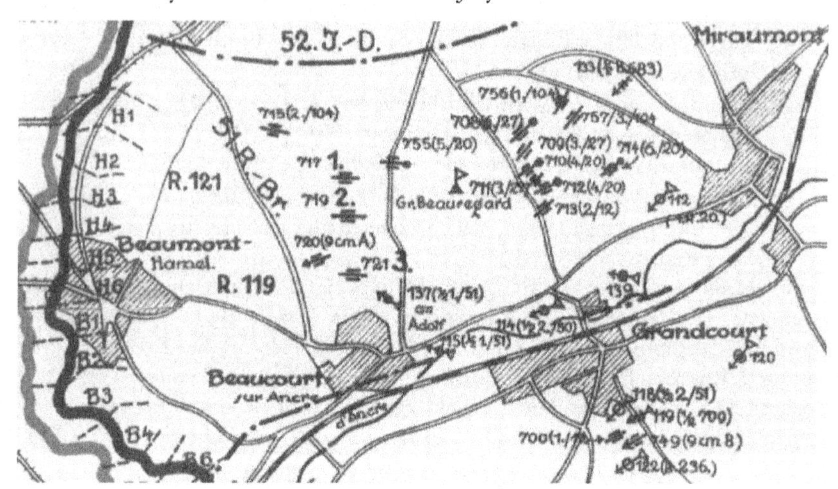

Map 2 26. Reserve Division battery positions by number

The artillery supporting the RIR 121 on Redan Ridge also fired from the valleys running north from the Ancre. Their locations and targets were as follows:

- Half of the 2. Batterie, Badisches FAR 104 (two 77 mm field guns), Gruppe Adolf, firing from Position 715 at Sector H1;
- Half of the 1. Batterie, (two captured Russian 15 cm field howitzers) of Fußartillerie-Bataillon Nr. 51, Gruppe Adolf, in position 137 firing to the rear of the British lines opposite the Heidenkopf;
- 5. Batterie, RFAR 20, (four field howitzers), Gruppe Adolf, firing on sector H2 from position 755;
- 1. Batterie, RFAR 26 (four 77 mm field guns), Gruppe Adolf, firing on sector H3 from position 717;
- Half of the 7. Batterie, 2. Garde Fußartillerie Artillerie Regt. (one captured 15.2 cm Russian Mörser), in position 139 fired to the rear of sector H3.

This gun was under the control of the artillery commander of RFAR 26, Gen. von Maur;

- 2. Batterie, RFAR 26 (four 77 mm field guns), Gruppe Adolf, firing on sector H4 from position 719;
- Half of the 1. Batterie, (two captured Russian 15 cm field howitzers) of Fußartillerie-Bataillon Nr. 51, Gruppe Adolf, in position 115 firing to the rear of the British lines north of the Bergwerk.

A total of ten 77 mm guns, four 10.5 cm field howitzers, four Russian 15 cm howitzers and one 15.2 cm Russian Mörser. Nineteen guns in all. Each of the batteries firing on the British front line trenches again had a front of between 300 and 400 yards to cover.

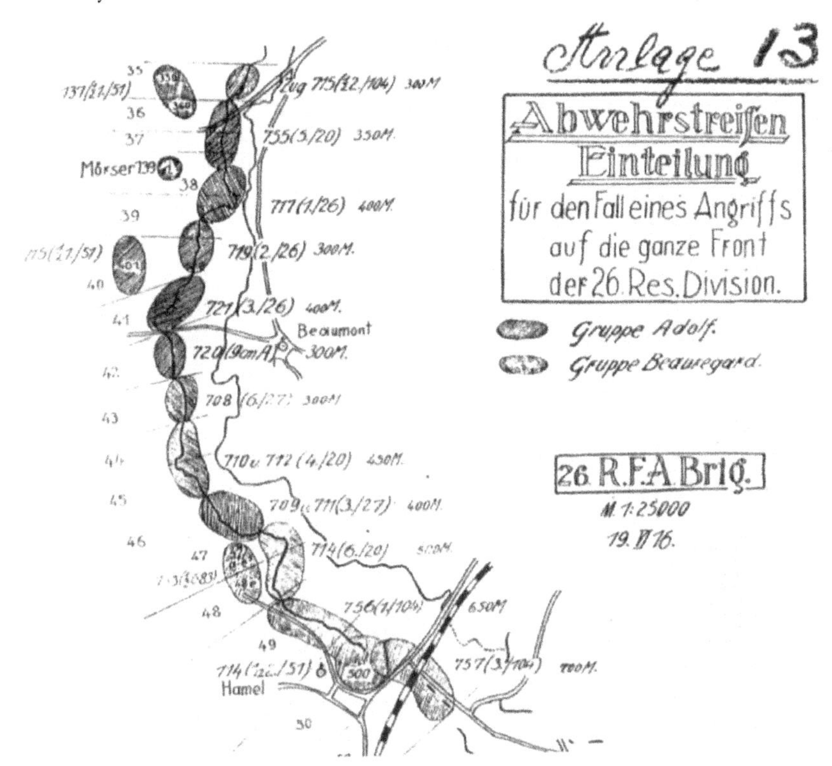

Map 3 Target areas for artillery of 26. Reserve Division. Ancre North

The northern most sector of the RIR 121's area, H1, ended just south of where Frontier Lane joined the Serre to Mailly Maillet road. The border between the 26. Reserve Division and the 52. Division[i] was the long communication trench known to the British as Ten Tree Alley which, more than 2,000 yards to the rear, ran to the south of a small copse called on the maps Pendant Copse (and by the Germans Serre Waldchen). To the British infantry expected to take the

[i] The 52. Infanterie Division was formed on 6th March 1915 with IR 66 coming from the 7. Division and IR 169 and 1700 from the 29. Division.

place it was rather less flatteringly known as 'Pending Corpses'. From here to the German front line opposite the northern limit of John Copse was the zone of 8. Badisches Infanterie Regiment Nr. 169 (IR 169) of the 104. Infanterie Brigade of the 52. Infanterie Division. The regimental front was divided into four sectors: S1 in the north down to S4 in the south. This front line, as far south as the southern edge of the Heidenkopf, was the line that had been established after the very hard fighting with the French 2nd Army in the summer of 1915. Until then, the German front line had run 1,000 yards further to the west in a large semi-circular salient south and east of Hebuterne that had taken in all four of the Gospel copses as well as Toutvent, or (on later British maps) Touvent Farm.

Since then, the Germans had developed a defensive system of three lines of trenches in front of Serre as well as two defensive trenches which encircled the village. From these trenches, running north and south, was the Zwischen Stellung position, heavily fortified and wired. Further to the east, the 2nd Position ran south from Puisieux towards the north bank of the Ancre. As with all of the German defences on the Somme, the garrison was able to retreat into the security of a large number of deep and interconnected dugouts and it was here that the men were securely if uncomfortably sheltered throughout the British bombardment.

Immediately to the north of Serre the front line was occupied by the 3. Magdeburgisches Infanterie-Regiment Nr. 66 (IR 66) also of the 52. Infanterie Division. As the British planned no attack to the north of Serre, the IR 66 was in the happy position of having no-one to occupy it except for the demonstrations and smoke screens mounted on the inactive front of the 48th (South Midland) Division. The third battalion of the 104. Infanterie Brigade, the 9. Badisches Infanterie-Regiment Nr. 170 (IR 170), was opposite the centre and right of the 56th (1st London) Division's front north of Hebuterne and would face the attack launched by this Division as part of the diversionary attack on Gommecourt. It was this diversion, mounted so close to the northern flank of the main British attack at Serre, that was to have untold consequences for the men of the 31st Division.

The commander of the 52. Infantry Division was Gen. Lt. Karl Julius Wilhelm Leo von Borries. Born in 1854 Von Borries served in the Franco-Prussian War in 1870 as a one year volunteer in the 1. Proviant-Kolonne[i] of the XIII Armeekorps. In 1872 he became a cadet in Füsilier-Regiment Prinz Heinrich von Preußen (Brandenburgisches) Nr. 35 in which he served for four years before attending the Prussian Military Academy, the Kriegsakademie. He then served in various Jäger battalions becoming a company commander before being promoted Major and the commander of the II Bataillon, 1. Badische Leib-Grenadier-Regiment Nr. 109 in 1896. Between 1897 and 1909 von Borries commanded Kurhessische Jäger-Bataillon Nr. 11 and then 3. Posenschen Infanterie-Regiment Nr. 58 before being promoted to Generalmajor and given command of the 84. Infanterie Brigade. A further promotion to Generalleutnant followed in 1911 and, shortly after the outbreak of war, he was given command

[i] Provision column.

of the 33. Reserve Infanterie Brigade. On the 3rd March 1915 he took over the 52. Infanterie Division which he commanded until October 1918.

There was only one Brigade in the 52. Infanterie Division, the 104. Infanterie Brigade of three regiments, IR 66, IR 169 and IR 170. The brigade commander was the 55 year old Generalmajor Arnold Lequis. Lequis had joined the 1. Rheinisches Pionier-Bataillon Nr. 8 in 1880 and had risen to the rank of major by 1900 during which time he had spent a spell on the Großer Generalstab in Berlin. With a brief gap to act as an instructor at the Kriegsakademie in 1902, Lequis spent most of the next ten years abroad or in various German colonies. Initially he commanded the Ostasiatischen Pionier-Bataillon in the German Expeditionary Force to China during the Boxer Rebellion. In 1904 he joined the General Staff of the German Forces in South West Africa. Here he participated in the attempted genocide of the indigenous Herero and Nama populations with those not murdered by German troops being forced into the Kalahari Desert to starve or die of thirst. The extreme treatment of the survivors, including slave labour and medical experiments, the establishment of concentration camps and the description of the campaign by Alfred von Schlieffen as a 'racial struggle' were all a terrible warning of the willingness of German officialdom to perpetrate any outrage in pursuit of their national objectives and were a blueprint for what was to come with the Final Solution in Hitler's Reich.

Plate 10 Generalmajor Arnold Lequis, 104. Infanterie Brigade

After South West Africa, Lequis was sent to the Cameroons (Kamerun), a German colony in which they had been actively trading since the 1860s. With the local peoples being exploited as cheap labour rather than being slaughtered or driven out, the issue here was the maximisation of profit for German companies under German military protection. As the prospect of war loomed, Lequis returned to Germany to take command of the Pioniers of the 1. Armeekorps in 1913 and then to become Oberquartiermeister of the 2. Armee in 1914. Promoted Generalmajor he was given command of the 104. Infanterie Brigade in 1916 and, later, the 12. Infanterie Division. Whatever the details of his track record, Lequis had built up years of experience and training as a Staff Officer which would have stood him in good stead when organising the defence of Serre.

ALTHOUGH THERE WOULD NO ATTACK against the trenches held by IR 66, there was only a small gap between the left of the main British assault by Fourth Army and the right of the diversionary attack against the Gommecourt salient mounted by two divisions of the VII Corps of Third Army.

Haig ordered Lt. Gen. Thomas Snow, commanding VII Corps, in whose sector Gommecourt fell, to make his preparations as obvious as possible[i]. Haig wanted troops drawn in to defend Gommecourt, preferably from somewhere on the main Somme front or, at the very least, ones that might otherwise be sent to the main front when it became obvious an Allied offensive was about to be unleashed. The Germans read Haig's intentions only too well, alerted, perhaps, by the initial preparations made in April for a single brigade attack on the village to be launched by the 48th Division in that month. Gommecourt was already comprehensively fortified, now it would be reinforced. An experienced and trusted unit, the 2. Garde Reserve Division, then resting out of the line after a stint at Vimy, was sent in to strengthen the position at the end of the first week in May, just a few days after the 56th and 46th Divisions took over the British front lines opposite. The attacking divisions may have only just arrived but the intent of the British was clear and the deliberate preparations being made opposite the Gommecourt salient persuaded von Below that this was the place requiring reinforcement.[1]

The 2. Garde Reserve Division took over the western face of the Gommecourt salient and the area around the Park and to the south of the village. By so doing, it halved the length of line previously held by the 52. Division which now concentrated its troops, machine guns and artillery to the north and south of Serre. Other adjustments further south allowed the 26. Reserve Division to move the IR 180 from north of the Ancre to the sector in front of Ovillers La Boisselle where they would face (and comprehensively defeat) the 8th Division on 1st July.

It is, of course, possible that these dispositions might have gone unchanged even had the obvious preparations for the British diversion been made further to the north around Monchy-au-Bois. This too was an area believed by OHL to be threatened by Allied plans, however, and one might imagine that resources would have been moved to reinforce the endangered sector. Given the overall paucity of both infantry and artillery at 2 Armee's disposal it would seem reasonable to assume that there would have been some shift northwards of men and guns from the recently reinforced area around Gommecourt and towards Monchy. As it was, with Snow, at Haig's request, ensuring that the preparations around Gommecourt were obvious, all that happened here was a still greater reinforcement of the artillery available both to defend this village and interfere with any attack on Serre.

In other words, Haig, by deliberately attracting troops and artillery to Gommecourt, had significantly reinforced Serre and, as a knock-on effect, Redan Ridge and even Ovillers La Boisselle. It was a disastrous decision – well, for the men of the VIII, III and X Corps anyway.

---

[i] "They'll know we're comng alright," was Snow's response.

Crucially, neither VII Corps nor VIII Corps were fully aware of the units facing them throughout the planning and preparation for the attack. On a map dated 27th June 1916 and entitled *'Order of Battle of Enemy's Forces Opposite VIII Corps'*, three regiments of only two German Divisions were shown to be facing the VIII Corps: IR 66 (52. Division) opposite the 48th (South Midland) Division and RIR 121 and RIR 119 (26. Reserve Division) to the south opposite the three assaulting Divisions, with the RIR 119 facing the 29th Division and RIR 121 opposite both the 31st and 4th Divisions. Further north, the IR 169 is shown as defending Gommecourt to the north and south of the village while the IR 170 is in the front line to the north away towards Monchy au Bois. On the right of the map there was a question mark next to the 2. Garde Reserve Division. This Division had, in fact, been inserted into the German line opposite Hebuterne and Foncquevillers in May. With them they had brought not only their own artillery, Reserve-Feldartillerie-Regiment Nr. 20, but also additional field batteries on loan from the 10. Kgl. Bayerisches Division[i] as well as half a dozen howitzer batteries specially attached from the Second Army to help with the defence of Gommecourt. Although some of these batteries were placed to the north of the town of Bucquoy they were still only 6,000 metres from Serre, i.e. both 77 mm field guns and 10.5 cm field howitzers would be able to fire at the northern end of the VIII Corps' position if required.

On its own this was a serious enhancement to the artillery north of the Ancre but they were not the only new guns in the vicinity. The 52. Division, whose line is shown on this British map running from Monchy au Bois to Serre (whereas it actually ran less than half that distance, i.e. from east of Hebuterne to Serre), had not only been reinforced by Field and Foot Artillery batteries from the 10. Kgl. Bayerisches Division[ii] but also by six Howitzer batteries from 2. Armee. Many of these batteries were placed around Puisieux, a mere 3,000 metres from the 31st Division's front line trenches. This enhancement provided the 52. Division with a powerful artillery presence which, on 1st July, would help produce what the British Official History described as the heaviest German artillery barrage anywhere on the Somme front.

The artillery at 52. Division's disposal was:

52. Feldartillerie Brigade comprising the Badisches Feldartillerie-Regiments Nr. 103 and 104[iii] and the Fußartillerie-Bataillon Nr. 52 (minus the II Abteilung[iv]);

2. and 3. Batterie, Fußartillerie-Regiment Nr. 7;

Two guns from 7. Batterie of Garde Fußartillerie Regiment Nr. 2[v]

Three guns from Fußartillerie-Batterie Nr. 472;

Four guns from Fußartillerie-Batterie Nr. 471[vi];

Fußartillerie-Batterie Nr.10;

---

[i] I/Kgl. Bayerisches Feldartillerie-Regiment Nr. 19.

[ii] II/Kgl. Bayerisches Feldartillerie-Regiment Nr. 19 and 2/Kgl. Bayerisches Fußartillerie-Regiment Nr. 10

[iii] The I Abteilung, less two guns from 2. Batterie, had been temporarily attached to 26. Reserve Division.

[iv] Attached to the 2. Garde Reserve Division.

[v] Other guns attached to 26. Reserve Division.

[vi] Other guns attached to 26. Reserve Division.

1. & 2. Batterie, II Bayerisches Landsturm Fußartillerie-Bataillon, from II Armeekorps;

2. Batterie, Ersatz Fußartillerie-Regiment Nr. 18

Three captured Belgian 5.7 cm guns

These batteries were divided into three groups: north, centre and south. Each had the responsibility of supporting one of the regimental sectors in the front line, with the South Group looking after the frontage of the IR 169 at Serre. The Centre Group, because IR 66 was not directly attacked, was able to respond to appeals for assistance from both IR 169 at Serre and IR 170 at Gommecourt. The fighting at Gommecourt would be by far the most prolonged.

To complete the picture, 26. Reserve Division's two regiments of field artillery[i] had also been enhanced by field guns and minenwerfers from 10. Kgl. Bayerisches Division as well as field batteries from the 12. Reserve Infanterie Division, three batteries of howitzers from XIV Reserve Armeekorps and eight howitzer batteries from 2. Armee. To worsen the picture still further, with the frontage of the 52. Division having been more than halved, the resulting concentration of machine guns on its front had been more than doubled. Much of this was unknown to the British. There was a general feeling, given the relatively lightweight response of the German guns to the British bombardment, that the German artillery was rather weak whereas it was actually stronger north of the Ancre than anywhere else on the Anglo-French Somme front. Their existence would add to the shock created by the unexpectedly strong resistance encountered by the British infantry after they went over the top.

Confirmation of the presence of the 2. Garde Reserve Division was only obtained late on the 29th June when a prisoner from Reserve Infanterie Regiment Nr. 55 was captured at Gommecourt during the night of the 29th/30th. On 30th June, Charteris issued a summary of information from GHQ which correctly identified the component parts of the Division but which placed three rather than two of its regiments in the front line[ii]. The report then went on to describe the change of the positioning of the 52. Division after the dramatic reduction in the length of line it now held. The report, however, erroneously placed the IR 169 in reserve at Achiet le Petit rather than in the trenches in front of Serre. The presence of this regiment in the front line made a significant difference to the concentration of troops and, most particularly, machine guns which the 31st Division would have to face. The report also suggested that the RIR 121 of the 26. Reserve Division might be in reserve instead of holding the front line from Beaumont Hamel to the northern side of Redan Ridge as was actually the case. As a result of this analysis, British commanders on the VIII Corps front may well have gone into action believing they were up against just 1½ German regiments (six battalions) instead of the three (twelve battalions) which actually manned the front to be attack with a fourth, IR 66, being unoccupied on its front and able, therefore, to interfere with the flanks of the attacks on Serre and Gommecourt.

In addition to these changes, the infantry of 10. Kgl. Bayerisches Infanterie Division had been brought up from south of the Somme in mid-June to lie

---

[i] Württembergisches Reserve-Feldartillerie-Regiment Nr. 26 and Nr. 27.

[ii] RIR 91 and RIR 55 were in the front line and RIR 15 and RIR 77 in reserve. Charteris's report has RIR 77 in the front line.

behind the XIV Reserve Armeekorps in areas south and east of Bapaume. But, on 1st July, its main contributions would come from the guns of Kgl. Bayerisches Feldartillerie-Regiments (KBFAR) Nr. 19 and Nr. 20. These two regiments' batteries were deployed from Gommecourt in the north down to Pozieres in the south in support of the 2. Garde Reserve, 52. Infanterie, 26. and 28. Reserve Infanterie Divisions. The batteries of these regiments were introduced rather late into their defensive positions on the night of the 19th June so it is, perhaps, not surprising that these units were not on the British list of artillery units they might face. The batteries were distributed thus:

1. Batterie, KBFAR Nr. 19 and 2. Battery, KBFAR Nr. 20 were attached to the northern group of RFAR Nr. 20, 2. Garde Reserve Division to the north of Bucquoy;

3. Batterie, KBFAR Nr. 19 attached to the southern group of RFAR Nr. 20;

4. Batterie, KBFAR Nr. 19 attached to the northern group of the 52. Division;

5. Batterie, KBFAR Nr. 19 attached to the middle group of the 52. Division;

6. Batterie, KBFAR Nr. 19 attached to the southern group of the 52. Division.

These last three batteries fell under the overall command of the 52. Feldartillerie Brigade and were distributed south of Bucquoy and around Puisieux. The commander of KBFAR Nr. 19 was the highly experienced Oberst von Belli who had gained great experience from the very heavy fighting around Arras in 1915. His first instruction was to greatly increase the supplies of ammunition available to each gun and these were delivered prior to the beginning of the bombardment after which communications and transport became increasingly difficult. These batteries would play an important role in the forthcoming defence of Serre.

The 2. Battery, KBFAR Nr. 19, meanwhile, was attached to the artillery defending Ovillers La Boisselle while the remaining batteries of KBFAR Nr. 20 were placed to support the 26. Reserve Division at Beaumont Hamel (4., 5. and 6. Batteries), Thiepval (1. Batterie) and Ovillers (3. Batterie). Between the two regiments, they brought much needed reinforcements of 36 extra field guns and howitzers to the northern defences of the German Somme front.

The infantry of the two divisions was deployed with two battalions defending the 1st position and the third battalion in reserve, normally in the Zwischen Stellung. Each company was given a sector to defend and each sector was given a letter, for each regimental front, and a number. On the regimental fronts to be attacked these were (low numbers north to high numbers south):

IR 169 – S1 to 4

RIR 121 – H1 to 6

RIR 119 – B1 to 7

Although battalions and companies would be rotated in and out of the front line positions, the deployment of battalions and companies at the end of June was:

IR 169

I Bataillon

S1 front line – 4. Kompanie

S1 reserve line – 1. Kompanie
S2 front line – 3. Kompanie
S2 reserve line – 2. Kompanie
II Bataillon
S3 front line – 6. Kompanie
S3 reserve line – 8. Kompanie
S4 front line – 7. Kompanie
S4 reserve line – 5. Kompanie
III Bataillon
Tübinger Stellung – 10., 9. and 11. Kompanie (north to south)
Zwischen Stellung – 12. Kompanie
RIR 121
I Bataillon
H1 front line – 3. Kompanie
H2 front line – 2. Kompanie
H3 front line – 1. Kompanie
H1-3 reserve line – 4. Kompanie
II Bataillon
H4 front line – 7. Kompanie
H5 front line – 6. Kompanie
H6 front line – 5. Kompanie
H4-6 reserve line – 8. Kompanie
III Bataillon
Zwischen Stellung
RIR 119
III Bataillon
B1 front line – 9. Kompanie
B2 front line – 10. Kompanie
B3 front line – 11. Kompanie
B1-3 reserve line – 12. Kompanie
I Bataillon
B4 front line – 2. Kompanie
B5 & 6 front line – unknown
B7 front line- 3. Kompanie
B4-7 reserve line - unknown
II Bataillon
B1 reserve line – 7. Kompanie
B2-7 reserve line – 5., 6. and 8. Kompanie

THE COMMANDERS OF THE 2. ARMEE, XIV Reserve Armeekorps, 26. Reserve and 52. Divisions had learnt a lot from the French attacks in June 1915. Although the ground gained by the French at great cost had been restricted to an area from just to the north of the Serre-Mailly Road (opposite Serre Road No. 2 Cemetery) for a distance of around two miles, including Toutvent Farm, the attack had highlighted certain shortcomings in the defensive system then employed. Although a number of deep dugouts had already been constructed prior to the attack the construction limited the entrances to just one per dugout. This restricted the speed with which men could exit the dugouts in order to man the trenches and, allied to a lack of adequate alarm systems to alert the men to an attack, had resulted in several parts of the original front line being overrun by the French infantry with the German defenders still trapped underground. Von Below issued instructions, therefore, that every dugout must have at least two exits, that these exits should be wider than previously and that an array of systems should be put in place to allow lookouts to alert the garrison of enemy activity. Additional dugouts were to be constructed in the new front line and, generally, the engineers were advised that excessive depth was not a necessity. Three metres of head cover was deemed sufficient to protect the garrison from a direct hit by a 6 in. shell and new dugouts were to be built to that standard. As it turned out, these new dugouts and others already in existence, were then connected to one another by tunnels through which men might exit should the entrances to their dugout become blocked.

Von Below also made it clear that the occupants of the dugouts needed to be regularly drilled in the process of exiting their dugouts and manning their defensive positions. A dugout 'commander' was to be appointed and it was he, under threat of court martial, who was responsible for drilling the men and ensuring they were in place in the required time in order to repel attacks. The timings for these drills were, no doubt, based on the French method of attack which involved speed of movement and mutual support. As a result, when faced with the ponderous and deliberate methods employed by the British on 1st July, it is little surprise that the German defenders of Serre and Beaumont Hamel easily won the all-important 'race to the parapet'. Generalmajor Friemel, 2. Armee's commander of the Pioniers (Engineers), conducted a tour of inspection of the front lines of the 26. Reserve Division in mid-May and his report gave detailed instructions about the construction or extension of trenches, improvements to signage and the construction of OPs and a myriad of other tiny but significant details[2].

As with their skills at raiding, improving their depth and the detail of their defences was a constant process, one given added impetus once the build-up on the other side of No Man's Land became apparent. Von Soden records the deepening of dugouts still further, a special squad tasked with constructing reinforced concrete observation posts, a great extension of the fields of barbed wire laid out in front of most of the trenches from the Zwischen Stellung forward. Telephone communications to the front were improved and the number of Moritz listening posts used to intercept Allied telephone and Morse traffic increased. Ammunition stocks and ammunition bunkers were improved especially near the front line.

The French attack in June 1915 had given the 2. Armee a year in which to transform and improve their defences based on a detailed analysis of the fighting. In the areas of the 26. Reserve and 52. Divisions every moment of this time was employed in an effort to turn the area from Thiepval to Serre into a veritable fortress based on the principles of strength and depth of defences, mutual support and speed of action. As was to be proved in November 1916, this area was not impregnable but it was a defensive system that would need power and precision creatively employed if it was to be breached. These attributes would be in short supply on the British front in the early summer of 1916.

Throughout this period, General der Infanterie Fritz von Below, the commander of the 2. Armee, had been keeping an increasingly anxious eye on Anglo-French activity astride the River Somme. Von Below was an astute fellow and, as early as March, he had proposed a pre-emptive strike against the Fourth Army and the French positions south of the Somme in order to forestall any planned offensive. At this time, Foch's plans for the French offensive south of the river involving the 6th and 10th Armies were still extensive as the impact of casualties at Verdun had yet to make a significant impact on the resources Joffre had made available. Von Below's plan was ambitious and would have required the commitment of much of the reserve force currently being husbanded by von Falkenhayn. The plan involved a preliminary drive against Fourth Army followed up by a secondary assault on the French. The total width of the offensive was to run from the Ancre to Foucaucourt on the southern edge of the Flaucourt plateau on the southern bank of the Somme opposite Peronne and von Below intended it to be delivered in a series of phases. Unfortunately for von Below, von Falkenhayn and his staff at OHL though that, if there was to be an Allied attack, it would come further north. Rather more pertinently, however, they wished to retain their reserve to use against an enfeebled French Army once the effects of the murderous fighting at Verdun had devastated their reserves. At the end of May, having watched the massive preparations on the other side of No Man's Land and being even more convinced that the British planned a major attack on the Somme, von Below forwarded his proposal to OHL for a second time. Their simple solution to his inconvenient suggestion was to ignore it. When nothing was forthcoming from OHL, the commander of 2. Armee made a plea that he at least be allowed to attack from the Ancre down to Ovillers. Clearly, he felt anything to slow down the progress being made for the British assault was better than nothing. Events elsewhere, however, had overtaken him. The initially hugely successful Russian offensive commanded by Gen. Brusilov on the Eastern Front, an achievement which surprised Russia's allies almost as much as its enemies, required reserves of men and ammunition to be shipped east with all haste. With these reserves shipped east and Verdun consuming as many German soldiers as it did French, Von Below would now have to stand on the defensive and make the best of it. After a study of the ground and opposition, it was concluded that reinforcing the area between Serre and the Somme made the most sense. To the later great benefit of the French, the 10. Kgl. Bayerisches Infanterie Division was moved from the south to the north of the Somme and its component parts spread behind the entire front of the XIV Reserve Armeekorps.

Other than elements of the 10. Kgl. Bayerisches Infanterie Division which, north of the Ancre mainly came in the shape of additional artillery support, a number of other units were added to the roster of the two divisions then occupying the sector. The machine gun strength of the 26. Reserve Division was augmented by the guns of Maschinengewehr-Kompanie Fassbender along with half a dozen captured Belgian machine guns. A few batteries, some of obsolete 15 cm guns, were added to the strength of the 26. Reserve Feldartillerie-Brigade. Then, with the insertion of the 2. Garde Reserve Division at Gommecourt, came the biggest accretion of strength north of the Ancre. It triggered a wholesale reorganisation of the deployment of both the 52. and 26. Reserve Divisions. The

52. Division kept all three of its regiments in line but on a greatly reduced frontage. For 26. Reserve Division the changes were far more substantial. The 10. Württembergisches Infanterie Regiment Nr. 180 was moved out of the line north of the Ancre and switched to the Ovillers la Boisselle sector (where they destroyed the 8th Division on 1st July). RIR 121 came into the line but only to take over part of the IR 180's former position while RIR 119 around Beaumont Hamel shortened its front by handing over three of its sectors to RIR 121. The shortened fronts for all of these regiments meant that it was now possible to retain a complete battalion in reserve and, in the front line battalions, one company was held back in reserve to assist where necessary. All of these improvements to the defence were the unlooked for consequences of the very obvious preparations to attack Gommecourt being made, at Haig's request, by VII Corps. Given OHL's conviction that the British were likely to attack further north it is possible that the 2. Garde Reserve Division might have been given Gommecourt to defend anyway but VII Corps' obvious activity only served to confirm OHL's beliefs and the powerful reinforcement of the salient was assured. The consequences of these moves were far reaching and impacted on the attacks of all three Corps being asked to make the deepest penetrations of the German lines on the opening day. Every German sector on the VIII, X and III Corps' fronts had been reinforced as a result of the arrival of the 2. Garde Reserve Division. It is difficult to believe that this is what Haig had intended.

---

[1] See Duffy, Christopher, *Through German Eyes: The British and the Somme 1916*, Weidenfeld and Nicholson, 2006, page 122.
[2] See Sheldon, Jack, *The German Army on the Somme*, Pen & Sword Books, 2005, pages 111-3.

6. THE BOMBARDMENT

OTHER THAN DETERMINING THE OVERALL FRAMEWORK and then the detail of the attack plan, VIII Corps' other main responsibility was the use of the heavy artillery. In all previous British battles on the Western Front there had been an acute shortage of both guns and ammunition. Under the energetic guidance of Lloyd George the ammunition supply issue was being addressed and, at least in terms of quantity, the number of shells made available to the Fourth Army was unprecedented. As in any industrial enterprise where an enormous increase in output is demanded within a very short period, there was an issue about the quality of the ammunition now being stored by the guns and in dumps further to the rear. Shells produced in the USA were viewed with considerable suspicion by both the gunners and any infantry who were positioned under the line of fire. There were also significant variations in the size and weight of shells. Those for the modern 26 cwt. 6 in. howitzers were said, in some cases, to vary by as much as four inches in length which made precise accuracy round by round almost impossible. There was also a problem with fuzes. These, too, were being rushed into service with one, the Percussion Nose Fuze for high explosive shells, being taken from design to production within ten days in 1914. Unsurprisingly it had a poor performance record. Some fuzes failed to detonate, others fell out in flight, some simply didn't fit the shells for which they were designed. The 9.2 in. howitzer shell, the most common super heavy howitzer in the B.E.F., was extremely prone to 'blinds', i.e. shells that failed to detonate on impact. There are some suggestions that as many as a quarter of these shells failed to explode.

Then there was the weather to contend with and its effect on ground and aerial observation. The Northern French climate of 1916 seemed intent on working against the plans of the B.E.F. throughout the last days of June. The VIII Corps war diary recorded each day's climatic conditions. It rained every day bar one.

23rd June – Heavy thunderstorm in the afternoon.
24th June – Heavy rain in early morning, fine later.
25th June – Heavy rain in the evening.
26th June – Heavy rain in the evening.
27th June – Rain at intervals all day.
28th June – Heavy rain in morning. Cleared about 6 p.m.
29th June – Fine day.
30th June – Some rain in early morning. Cleared up later. Strong wind west to South West all day.

According to the more detailed weather reports of the neighbouring Third Army, nearly an inch of rain fell during the seven days of the bombardment. This could be added to the nearly three inches that had fallen in the first three weeks of June and which included over ½ inch that fell in the thunderstorm on the afternoon of the 23rd June. These figures were well above the seasonal average and had left all of the trenches, at best, muddy and, at worst, filled with several inches of slime and cold water. Living and working in them was a deeply unpleasant and very tiring experience and all the battalions manning and working in the trenches became exhausted as a result. When their workload also included training over the replica trench systems laid out miles behind the front line, supplying working parties to assist the Royal Engineers in their numerous tasks and route marches and other physical fitness then it was no surprise that the men, especially the older ones, started to feel the strain.

Plate 11 Brig. Gen. Thomas Angus Tancred, CMG, CRA, VIII Corps

BRIG. GEN. THOMAS ANGUS TANCRED, CMG, was the Commander, Royal Artillery, for VIII Corps. A Scotsman, Tancred was aged 49 and had been educated at Harrow before joining the Royal Artillery in 1886. In 1893 he was seconded to the Bechuanaland Border Police with which he served in Matabeleland over the next two years. In 1899 he was sent to India and, in 1900, China. Throughout this time, therefore, he failed to serve in any of the Empire's hotspots – the Sudan, South Africa or the North West Frontier – where so many of the current generation of generals had learnt their trade. By 1904 he was a major in the Royal Garrison Artillery and from then onwards his career somewhat drifted along and, during this period, he commanded various siege and heavy batteries both in the UK and India. Promotion to Lt. Colonel in May 1914 came with command of the 1st Heavy Brigade based at Fareham. When the batteries of this group were split up he was given command of the 3rd Heavy Brigade[i] attached to the 7th Division during the early part of the war and was mentioned in Sir John French's despatch of 14th January 1915. His award of the CMG was also listed in the same edition of the *London Gazette* as published French's MiD list (16th February 1915). On 18th August 1915 he was promoted temporary Brigadier General and he took command of No. 5 Group Heavy Artillery reserve. His batteries were used to support I Corps during the Battle of Loos. His was given command of the newly reformed VIII Corps heavy artillery in March 1916. After the opening of the Somme battle he was transferred to III

[i] 111th and 112th Batteries, each equipped with 4 x 4.7-inch QF guns.

Corps where he was CRA through the battles around the Ancre, at Cambrai and during the German offensive in the Spring of 1918. Later that year he was appointed CRA, Mesopotamian Expeditionary Force. He ended the war as a temporary Major General, with a CB and DSO to his name.

To confuse the chain of command, GHQ decided in March 1916 that every Corps should have a Commander, Heavy Artillery (CHA), as well as a Commander, Royal Artillery (CRA). Both positions were to be filled by men of equal rank, i.e. Brigadier Generals. Each Corps was allocated two Heavy Artillery Groups (HAGs) and the CHA was put in command of them. In the memorandum announcing the new appointment, the CHA was described as 'Brig. Gen., R.A., of the Corps'. Such was the confusion caused by this memo that at least two Army commanders, those of Second and Fourth Armies, issued notes making clear it clear that the CRA's status had not altered and that the CHA was a subordinate officer. Further confusion was caused by GHQ when, in May, an attempted clarification of the two roles only served to muddy the waters still further such that the CHA appears to have had a certain degree of independence from the CRA when the Somme offensive began. It should be noted that the Operational Orders issued to the VIII Corps heavy artillery and the account of the activities of these guns up to and including 1st July 1916 came from the office of the CHA, in this case Brig. Gen. David Finlay Hosken Logan, CMG.

Brig. Gen. Logan[i] was Tancred's senior by five years and had joined the Royal Artillery in 1883, having been educated privately before attending the Royal Military Academy at Woolwich. Originally, he was an officer in the 1st Glamorganshire Volunteer Corps, R.A, being promoted Captain and Adjutant in 1890. Having served in the South African War with the Cape Garrison Artillery he was promoted Lt. Col. in the Royal Garrison Artillery in 1911. His appointment as CHA was published on 7th April 1916. It would appear from the official diaries that it was Logan who had the hands-on direction of the VIII Corps' heavy artillery during the bombardment and on 1st July even though Tancred was his superior by dint of seniority.

Tancred and Logan commanded 103 heavy howitzers and guns:

3 x 15 in. RMA howitzers
2 x 12 in. howitzers
12 x 9.2 in. howitzers
16 x 8 in. howitzers
12 x 6 in. 26 cwt. howitzers
12 x 6 in. 30 cwt. howitzers
32 x 60 pdr. guns
6 x 6 in. Mk VIII guns
8 x 4.7 in. guns

Also temporarily attached to the Corps artillery were four 4.5 in. howitzers from D/242 Battery and three French batteries, the 4e, 5e and 6e, of the 2e

[i] Brig. Gen. Logan died on 17th June 1923. His only son, 2nd Lt. David Herbert Hosken Logan, 2nd Border Regt., was killed on 1st July 1916, aged 19. He is buried in the Citadel New Military Cemetery, Fricourt, grave II. D. 12.

Groupe, 37e Régiment d'Artillerie de Campagne, each comprising four 75 mm field guns.

The key figure here is the number of howitzers of 6 in. or heavier as these were the weapons capable of doing real damage to the German fortifications. VIII Corps' front was approximately 4,500 yards wide[i] and there were 57 howitzers of 6 in. or larger. This meant that there would be one medium or heavy howitzer for every 79 yards of front. How does this concentration of firepower compare to previous bombardments on the Western Front as well as the French bombardment prior to the offensive ? At Neuve Chapelle fifteen months earlier Haig and Rawlinson had managed to achieve a concentration of one medium or heavy howitzer for every 30 yards of front. This yardage per howitzer doubled and doubled again at the subsequent Battles of Aubers Ridge and then Loos. More recently, the Germans had achieved at Verdun a concentration surprisingly similar to that of Neuve Chapelle, i.e. one medium or heavy howitzer per 31 yards. The French for their bombardment on either bank of the Somme had accumulated sufficient medium and heavy howitzers to give one for every 36 yards of front. In other words, at Neuve Chapelle, Verdun and for the French on the Somme, the concentration of medium and heavy howitzers had been between 2 and 2.5 times greater than was available to the VIII Corps.

Looking at it another way, Table 2 below shows, in the *'VIII Corps'* column, the actual number of medium and heavy howitzers deployed by VIII Corps between 24th June and 1st July. The column marked *'Germans Verdun'* shows how many howitzers would have been available to VIII Corps had it been possible to achieve the same concentration of howitzers as did the Germans for the preliminary bombardment at Verdun. The column marked *'French Somme'* shows how many howitzers VIII Corps would have needed to achieve the same concentration of howitzers as were used by the French 6th Army in the bombardment prior to their completely successful attacks on 1st July.

	VIII Corps	Germans Verdun	French Somme
6 in. (15 cm) Howitzer	24	79	53
8 & 9.2 in. (20+ cm) How	28	40	51
12 & 15 in. (30+ cm) How	5	7	8
Total	57	126	112

Table 2 Howitzers available to VIII Corps & if same as Germans at Verdun & French 6th Army

The issues which these raw numbers fail to take into account, however, are the quantity and quality of trenches which were to be bombarded in each case. With the exception of VIII Corps, all of the other bombardments concentrated on the front line position which, in every case, was less robustly fortified with, in particular, nothing like the quantity and quality of underground protection provided to the German defenders north of the Ancre. This latter consideration alone would have diluted the intensity of howitzer fire on VIII Corps' front when compared to Verdun and the French on the Somme. When one adds into the

[i] This excludes the German front line from Mary Redan to the River Ancre which was the responsibility of the heavy artillery of X Corps.

equation the two additional sets of trenches which the VIII Corps artillery needed to prepare (the Zwischen Stellung and the 2nd Position) one rapidly sees how lightweight would be the bombardment on VIII Corps' front compared to the others cited. It is reasonable to say that the German initial bombardment at Verdun and that of the French on the Somme were approximately six times more powerful than that achieved by VIII Corps on the enemy's key front line position.

One should remember that, on both the British and French fronts on 1st July, the greatest success was achieved in the areas where the shallowest penetration was required. The VIII Corps may have had more guns per yard of front than several other more successful Corps but, in terms of square yardage to prepare, they were not so favourably placed because of the demands heaped upon them by their Commander in Chief in his attempt to enhance the prospects for a genuine breakthrough. As previously mentioned the VIII Corps possessed 57 howitzers of 6 in. calibre and above with one medium/heavy howitzer for c.80 yards of front. The figures for the rest of Fourth Army are given in below:

Corps	No of Yards of front	No of Howitzers	Yards per Howitzer
VIII	4532	57	80
X	4560	48	95
III	3920	52	75
XV	4524	38	119(1)
XIII	3760	58	65
Total	25023	253	99

Table 3 Medium and Heavy Howitzers per yard per Corps, 1st July 1916

(1) This is the number of yards for the entire front of XV Corps. Part of this front immediately south of Fricourt was not attacked on 1st July

From this table it would appear that VIII Corps was reasonably generously supplied with medium and heavy howitzers and this might have been true had their objectives been restricted to those initially proposed by Rawlinson. The fact is, however, that with a maximum depth of 4,000 yards along their front and with seven lines of trenches to be prepared this concentration of fire was substantially enfeebled. On a simple calculation, each howitzer had an area 562 yards square[i] to deal with or, to look at it another way, they had to fire on 553 yards of fire trench[ii] spread across all three German positions (i.e. excluding communication trenches). As these guns were not able to take these trenches in enfilade, which would have significantly improved their prospects of landing a shell in or close to a German trench, the accuracy of their shells when fired face on to a trench would have been low. Aerial photographs support this contention. Although the front line trenches are cosmetically battered by light metal from the field guns and howitzers, large craters caused by heavy howitzers are few and far between.

[i] 4500 yds x 4000 yds = 18,000,000 sq yds. That divided by 57 (no. of howitzers) = 315,789 sq yds per howitzer. √ 315,789 = 562 yds, therefore area to be bombarded is 562 yds by 562 yds square.

[ii] 4500 yds ÷ 57 = 79, the number of yards of front per howitzer. Times seven for the number of trench lines to be bombarded = 553 yards of trench per howitzer.

Large craters in or close to German trenches are a relative rarity. Had these guns only had to fire at the 1st German position then the length of trench to be prepared would have been reduced to 237 yards per gun[i]. The square yardage of the area to be bombarded, i.e. an area 126 yards square[ii], also reduces dramatically as these trenches are close together which of itself brings about another benefit, a shell missing one trench has a far better chance of damaging another even if by accident. There can be little doubt that, with the number of howitzers available, the inexperience of many of the gun crews fresh from the UK and with the inexperienced infantry at hand, Rawlinson's initial concept for the attack was correct. As a result, the heaviest burden of blame for the disasters that befell Fourth Army on 1st July should be laid squarely at the feet of Sir Douglas Haig. Others compounded his original and catastrophic error by devising absurd and rigid tactics but the fundamental error was his as must be the majority of the blame for the outcome.

THE ROYAL GARRISON ARTILLERY BATTERIES OF VIII CORPS were notionally organised into four groups:

1st Heavy Artillery Group, Maj. Robert Norman Lockhart

4th Heavy Artillery Group, Lt. Col. Charles Fosbett Phipps

16th Heavy Artillery Group, Lt. Col. Hugh Robert Palmer

17th Heavy Artillery Group, Lt. Col. Thomas Richard Phillips

In practice, batteries and guns were used in various combinations as required by the artillery programme.

The batteries employed by VIII Corps were a mixture of fairly experienced ones that had been in France for some time and others fresh from training in the UK. Present on and before 2nd May were the 19th Heavy Battery, 25th Heavy Battery, 139th Heavy Battery, 14th Siege Battery, No. 5 Gun, Royal Marine Artillery and a section of 60th Siege Battery. These came under the control of the OC, 16th HAG, on 2nd May. In addition, No. 3 Gun, Royal Marine Artillery joined 4th HAG and 16th Siege Battery and 77th Siege Battery became part of 17th HAG. The timetable for the arrival of the other batteries to be employed on the VIII Corps' front was as follows:

4th May – 46th Siege Battery joined 1st HAG. 111th Heavy Battery came into action. 48th Heavy Battery joined 18th HAG.

5th May – One section, 71st Siege Battery came into action.

7th May – 79th Siege Battery arrived.

11th May – Second section, 71st Siege Battery came into action.

17th May – 25th Heavy Battery came into action.

20th May – Right section, 79th Siege Battery, came into action. Left section 112th Heavy Battery came into action.

26th May – Right section, 112th Heavy Battery, came into action.

3rd June – 71st Siege Battery pulled out of action and sent to Ypres.

---

[i] 4500 yds ÷ 57 = 79, the number of yards of front per howitzer. Times three for the number of trench lines to be bombarded = 237 yards of trench per howitzer.

[ii] 4500 yds x 200 yds = 900,000 sq yds. That divided by 57 (no. of howitzers) = 15,789 sq yds per howitzer. √ 15,789 = 562 yds, therefore area to be bombarded is 126 yds by 126 yds square.

6th June – 65th Siege Battery, No. 1 Gun, Royal Marine Artillery arrived and joined 1st HAG. 29th Siege Battery arrived and joined 17th HAG.

7th June – 23rd Siege Battery, one gun into position.

8th June – 23rd Siege Battery, remaining guns into position.

9th June – One section, 14th Siege Battery into position. One section 36th Siege Battery arrived and joined 16th HAG. One section of 54th and 55th Siege Batteries and 1/1st Welsh and 1/1st Highland Heavy Batteries arrived and joined 1st HAG.

10th June – One section, 14th Siege Battery, into position. One section, 36th Siege Battery into position. 16th Heavy Battery arrived and joined 4th HAG. 81st Siege Battery joined 16th HAG.

11th June – 16th Heavy Battery into position.

12th June – One section, 49th Siege Battery, arrived. One gun, 29th Siege Battery, in position.

13th June – No 1 gun, RMA, ready for action. 139th Heavy Battery into position. One section, 54th Siege Battery, ready for action.

14th June – A section of 1/1st Highland and of 1/1st Welsh Heavy Batteries, into position.

15th June – Second sections of 1/1st Highland, 1/1st Welsh Heavy Batteries and 35th, 49th, 54th, 55th, 56th and 81st Siege Batteries arrived. 113th Heavy Battery into position.

16th June – Second sections of 1/1st Highland and of 1/1st Welsh Heavy Batteries, into position.

17th June – 71st Siege Battery returned from Ypres and took up old position.

18th June – One section, 55th Siege Battery, into position.

19th June – Second section, 55th Siege Battery, into position.

23rd June – All guns in position and ready for action.

With many of the batteries still arriving in their positions in early to mid-June and with gun positions taking several days and sometimes weeks to prepare, several of the bigger howitzers were still completing their preparatory work on the day the bombardment began. For example, the detachment manning No. 3 Gun, Royal Marine Artillery, one of the huge and unwieldy 15 in. howitzers, took from the 1st to the 23rd June preparing their position during which time they constructed Observation Posts, dugouts and a magazine in which they stockpiled 172 of their 1,400 lb. shells. With the weather being damp and cold for a lot of the time this was hard and unpleasant work.

The two 12 in. howitzers[i] of the 65th Siege Battery were still in position west of Arras on 3rd June. The unit's war diary gives an excellent idea as to the huge workload involved in transporting and preparing these guns for their role in the attack, with much of the work being done under cover of darkness in order to avoid observation by enemy aircraft or balloon observers:

---

[i] The right section of 65th Siege Battery went out to France & Flanders on 19th January 1916 armed with one 12 in. Howitzer, Road Mounted. The Left Section went out on the 5th February 1916 armed the same. These guns were 12 in. variants on the original, and successful, 9.2 in. howitzers designed by Vickers in 1913, the first of which had gone to France in November 1914. These howitzers, which were transported in six pieces, weighed in at nearly 37 tons and fired a 750 lb. projectile out to a maximum range of 11,340 yards.

3rd June. 8.05 p.m. Working till 4 a.m. morning of 4th dismounting 12 in. howitzer. Gun, carriage and cradle on to road and ready to move off.
4th June. 8 p.m. to 12 midnight. Working all night dismounting gun platform. 3 loads cleared and all six loads moved at Dainville by daylight, 5th June.
5th June. 8.30 p.m. Gun stores were loaded in lorries and left billets Arras for Dainville thence with gun. Caterpillar tractor to Frevent en route Beauquesne in accordance with orders received from GHQ to join Fourth Army… All loads parked on Frevent to Doullens road as they arrived night 5th/6th. Billets in Le Chateau.
6th June. 7 a.m. All vehicles arrived and parked. Resting in billets during day.
8 p.m. Battery and ASC (MT) section attached left for Beauquesne via Doullens-Huteux road. Lorries arrived Beauquesne 11 p.m., parked on road Rue du Doullens.
7th June. OC (Maj. G F S Tuke) proceeded to VIII Corps HA Office to report for orders and then proceeded to No. 1 HAG and arranged reference to taking up gun positions allotted near Mailly Maillet. Working parties to start on 8th.
8th June. 9 a.m. OC, 4 officers and 123 ORs (includes 6 ASC) proceeded to Mailly Maillet, billeted there and started work digging gun pits 2 p.m. Worked in reliefs throughout night of 8th/9th. Very wet. 88 rounds of ammunition arrived from railhead 1 a.m., 9th, offloaded at position.
9th June. 3 a.m. Stopped work at gun position. Both pits completed except for accurate levelling. Very wet weather.
10 a.m. Work re-commenced at gun positions P.6.d.95.60 and Q.1.c.00.80. All day preparing positions. 25 rounds.
10th June. 9 a.m. Levelled both gun pits and getting ready for platform load night 10th/11th. June.
8.30 p.m. Mounting platforms Nos. 1 and 2 guns until 2 a.m. morning of 11th June. Lorries arrived at position at 10 p.m. Got in front of transom and beam of No. 1 gun and near transom of No. 2 gun. Ground in latter position very difficult to handle loads owing to restricted space and greasy surface of ground.
11th June. 7.45 p.m. Work re-commenced mounting platforms, etc., at position. By 3 a.m. 12th finished platform of No. 1 gun and also No. 2 gun except for holding down beam. Ground very wet and greasy. 25 rounds received and dumped.
12th June. 10 p.m. to 4 a.m., 13th. Carriage and cradle for No. 1 gun and carriage for No. 2 gun brought in and mounted by daylight 13th. Very heavy downpour of rain all night, loads skidded considerably on greasy chalk surface. 25 rounds received and dumped.
13th June. 5 p.m. Work resumed at gun position.
9.30 p.m. to 3 a.m., 14th. No. 1 gun and No. 2 gun and cradle brought in and all mounted by daybreak 14th. Very heavy rain as on night 13th/14th. 25 rounds received and dumped.

June 14th. 5 p.m. Work resumed at battery position constructing cartridge recesses and dugouts.
8 p.m. Guns prepared for action and laid on night lines Serre. OC visited OP Aintree.
9.30 p.m. 25 rounds received from railhead.
June 15th. 9 a.m. to 8 p.m. Worked on gun position. OC visited alternative OP Epsom.
16th June. Work on battery position throughout the day. GOC RA VIII Corps visited position 6 p.m.
17th June. 2 a.m. 33 rounds of ammunition dumped at battery.
1 p.m. Established communication by telephone with wireless station through 46th Siege Battery. Work at position carried out throughout day and night. 75 rounds dumped at battery night of 17th/18th.
18th June. Work on battery position throughout day.
167 rounds of ammunition dumped to battery position 11 p.m.
19th June. Work on battery position throughout the day.
4 p.m. Battery visited by Gen. Budworth and GOC RA VIII Corps HA. Met by OC. Very pleased with work done.
5 p.m. Vacated billets 65A and 39 in village of Mailly Maillet and moved the entire battery to dugouts at gun position.
20th June. Working on dugouts, etc., throughout the day.
21st June. Working on dugouts, etc., throughout the day.
7 p.m. Aintree OP manned for Group night of 21st/22nd to 8 a.m. 22nd.
22nd June. 9 a.m. Work on battery throughout day.
9 p.m. Telephonic communication with buried cable established from battery position with Aintree OP, 1st HAG, wireless station 46th Siege Battery, Dressing Station, AA battery in rear of position.
23rd June. 9 a.m. Work on battery throughout day.
10.30 a.m. Commenced permanent manning of OP Aintree day and night.
4 p.m. Violent thunder storm with deluge of rain. Roads flooded in low lying ground also several dugouts. Heavy rain at intervals night of 23rd/24th.
24th June.
6 a.m. First day of bombardment. Field guns and lighter natures of HA employed wire cutting.
5.30 p.m. Registered on Pendant Copse L.31.a.70.60, 6500 yards. 2nd charge in 2nd round per gun. Line correct. Results satisfactory.[1]

It was three weeks from the date of dismantling their guns near Arras to the time 65th Siege Battery fired their first shell at the German positions opposite VIII Corps. Apart from the enormous workload involved in this operation what it also clearly spelled out was the necessarily slow pace of siege warfare in France and Flanders. Had the war moved, as Haig hoped, from static trench warfare to open, mobile fighting then guns like these and the 9.2 in. and 15 in. howitzers and the railway mounted guns and howitzers would soon become an irrelevance as they would never have been able to keep up with an advance of any speed. These were siege weapons which could perform a useful function only if an advance was relatively slow and incremental, i.e. the pace that Rawlinson had envisaged when first asked to prepare a plan of action for the Somme offensive. A genuine breakthrough would make them redundant. They were still in use at the end of the war.

The various guns and howitzers were to be used for specific purposes:

The 15 in. RMA howitzers with their heavy shell, but limited range of 10,000 yards, were going to be used to batter the villages of Serre, Beaumont Hamel and Beaucourt sur Ancre as well as the Beaucourt Redoubt. The 15 in. BL (Breech Loading) howitzer was a private development by the Coventry Ordnance Works of the previous and successful 9.2 in. variant. A director of the company, the retired Admiral Bacon, contacted the Admiralty about this development expecting them to pass the information on to the Army, however, Winston Churchill, the First Lord of the Admiralty and ever one to spot an opportunity for the Navy to get in on any act in the war, decided to 'crew' the first gun with Royal Marines and send them off to the Western Front with their sou'westers at the ready. Eventually a dozen of these guns were roaming northern France until the Navy, with more than enough to do protecting shipping and trying to defeat the High Seas Fleet, withdrew the gun crews leaving it to the Army to decide what to do with them. The Army Ordnance Board was less than delighted to be lumbered with guns which they regarded as a waste of money and material, but gun crews were duly formed and, with decreasing frequency, they were employed to fire slowly, between frequent breakdowns, at the German trenches. But, whatever their shortcomings, they were the heaviest weapons currently available to the B.E.F. and thus their employment on the Somme front. In spite of their weight of shell, 1,400 lbs. filled with 200 lbs. of Amatol, they were not fired at the front line trenches and were not, therefore, given the chance of collapsing the front line dugouts built to resist a mere 6 in, howitzer shell.

The 12 in. howitzers were also spin-offs from the original 9.2 in. howitzer and were a development by Vickers of a 12 in. railway mounted howitzer. It was decided to build some versions transportable by road and these two guns were amongst the first off the production lines. As with the 15 in. howitzers, they were based on the pattern of the 9.2 in. howitzer which had been the first British heavy howitzer in the field in 1913, but these 36 ton beasts had another 1,000 yards of range over Churchill's pet 15 in. white elephant. As with all of these howitzers, one of its obvious features was a huge metal box which was attached to the front of the gun. When filled with several tons of earth it prevented the gun from rearing up and toppling over when fired at low elevations. Erecting, filling and emptying these boxes was yet another reason why these guns only made any sense in siege warfare conditions. The two guns of the 65th Siege Battery would join in with the destruction of Serre with occasional shoots at a little wood called Pendant Copse, a location which would assume unlooked for prominence on the day of the attack and was given the nickname 'Pending Corpses' by the more cynical elements of the infantry.

The other howitzers, the 9.2 in., the 8 in., and the two versions of the 6 in. howitzers, were given the tasks of trench and strongpoint bombardment. Whilst some of their targets included front line trenches, the area each battery of four guns was given was large, stretching usually from the front line to the Zwischen Stellung (Munich Trench) in terms of depth with a frontage of about 400 yards.

For example, for the 9.2 in. howitzers of the 46th Siege Battery this meant, in practice, firing at five lines of trenches from just north of the Heidenkopf back to Munich Trench (inclusive) and south to a line approximately that of Lager Alley. This was 2,000 yards of fire trench, excluding the communication trenches, of which there were four each more than 800 yards long. Interestingly, these howitzers did not join in with the bombardment until W Day, 26th June, two days after the 18 pdrs. and 4.5 in. howitzers had started to cut the wire and bombard the frontal areas. According to the original bombardment plan, the medium and heavy howitzers were to complete their work within three days, i.e. 26th, 27th and 28th June, with Z Day being 29th June.[2]

Destroying the German defences was not to be 46th Siege Battery's only task, however, as on occasion it might be called upon to fire at a German battery. The guns, on a good day, would fire about 100 rounds each, of which about a quarter might be fired at various German batteries. That left c. 300 rounds containing a total of 10,000 lbs. of high explosive to be fired at the German trenches which covered an area of approximately 320,000 square yards or density of about 1 lb. of Amatol to every 32 square yards. If one assumed, a very big assumption, that all of the guns' shells were delivered on, or sufficiently near to, a trench to cause damage[i], then they might expect to deposit one load of 34 lbs. of Amatol for every 17 yards of German fire, support and communication trench. Accuracy, of course, was considerably less than 100%, indeed firing was predicated on the notion of the '50% zone', i.e. an area, long and relatively thin, in which it was expected just half of all shells fired by a single gun would land. It was for this reason that all guns tried, whenever possible, to fire along the length of a trench rather than at its face as it was far more likely for a gun to land a shell in or very close to a length of trench than it was in its width. Added to this general inaccuracy is the previously mentioned estimate of a 25% rate of 'blinds' amongst the 9.2 in. shells. This alone decreased the density of HE per square yard from 1 lb. to 32 sq. yards to 1lb to every 42 sq. yards and the quantity of HE per yard of trench to 34 lbs. to every 23 yards. In practice, nothing like this density was achieved. In addition, as Sir John Keegan observed in his book '*The Face of Battle*':

> "… the greater part of that small explosive load was dissipated in the air, flinging upwards, to be sure, a visually impressive mass of surface material and an aurally terrifying shower of steel splinters but transmitting a proportionately quite trifling concussion downwards towards the hiding places of the German trench garrisons."[3]

The other weapons available to the Corps artillery were the various long guns, pieces that could fire a lighter weight of shell considerably further than the various howitzers. These guns consisted of six 6 in. BL Mk VIII guns, thirty two

---

[i] A study of various aerial photographs taken on the 56th Division's front in front of Gommecourt on the evening of 30th June suggests, for example, that less than 33% of the 9.2 in. howitzer shells that exploded landed in or near to a German trench. Aerial photographs taken in front of Serre and at the Heidenkopf on the morning of the attack suggest a similar pattern (but also reveal a concentration of shell holes just in front of the British trenches opposite Serre as a result of the highly effective German barrage fired on 1st July).

60 pounder BL Mk I Field guns and eight 4.7 in. QF Field Guns. The 6 in. and 4.7 in. guns both shared the same parentage. They were the brainchild of Capt. Percy Scott, RN, who, realising the shortage of suitable artillery in the South Africa War, dismounted several 4.7 in. coastal and naval guns and mounted them on improvised carriages[i]. After the war trials were conducted using dismounted 6 in. Mk VII coastal guns and several batteries of these were sent to France early in 1915. The range and weight of shell fired for these guns were as follows:

4.7 in. QF Field Gun: range 10,000 yards, shell 46 lb. 9 oz.;

60 pounder BL Mk I Field Gun: range 12,300 yards, shell 60 lb.; and

6 in. BL Mk VII Field Gun: range 13,700 yards, shell 100 lb.

These guns were allocated the following tasks:

Six batteries of 60 pounders – counter battery (C/B) work;

Two batteries of 60 pounders and the two 4.7 in. batteries – to shell German OPs, working parties and any troops, supply movements; and

The 6 in. MK VII guns were to fire on the rear villages, Bucquoy, Puisieux, Ablainzeville, Achiet le Grand and Achiet le Petit, plus Irles and Miraumont at night, and road and rail communications, dumps and certain woods thought to conceal troops or supplies.

On occasions, some of the heavier howitzers were used to bombard German artillery positions but, generally speaking, the British had not woken up to the need to allocate both heavy weapons and large numbers of shells to the destruction or suppression of German guns. This was not the case on the French front, however, where Gen. Fayolle, commander of the 6th Army, repeatedly emphasised to his junior commanders the essential nature of counter battery fire even to the exclusion of other artillery priorities. To be a German gunner on the French front during the bombardment and on 1st July was not an experience any would have wished to repeat. German gunners opposite the VIII Corps, however, had a relatively easy time of it by comparison.

On the British front, however, the use of the 60 pounders as the main C/B weapon was a considerable error. Because of the far greater stresses placed on a shell in a long gun compared to one from a howitzer, the ratio of explosive to overall shell weight was far smaller. A 60 lb. HE shell contained just 6 lbs. of Amatol or 4 lbs. of Lyddite, a ratio of 1:10 or 1:15 explosive to weight of shell whereas the 100 lb. projectile from the 30 cwt. 6 in. howitzer contained 14 lb. 4 oz. of Lyddite, a ratio of 1:7. The other issue was that the 60 pounder had a maximum elevation of 21.5° as opposed to the 45° and more of the modern 6 in.

---

[i] Capt., later Admiral, Sir Percy Moreton Scott, 1st Baronet, GCB, KCVO, entered the navy in 1866, aged 13. He was present at the bombardment of the Egyptian forts at Alexandria in 1882, noting the appalling shooting. In 1896 he was given command of *HMS Scylla*, an Apollo Class light protected cruiser armed with 6 in. and 4.7 in. guns. During the 1897 gunnery trials his ship scored an 80% success rate, an unprecedented level of accuracy. His reward was to be accused of cheating, removed from his command and placed on half pay. Only the intervention of Jackie Fisher saved his career. Reinstated he later took command of the 1st Cruiser Squadron where he twice came into conflict with the commander of the Channel Fleet, Lord Charles Beresford. On the second occasion, Beresford attempted to have Scott court-martialled but the Admiralty refused. During WW1 he established the London Air Defence Area to defend London against German Gotha and Zeppelin attacks. He died in 1924.

and 9.2 in. howitzers. This meant that the 60 pounder shell had a relatively flat trajectory which required great accuracy if it was to do much damage to a well dug in German battery. The plunging and penetrating shell of a heavy howitzer had the potential to wreak havoc on these positions but, in the main, these weapons were used to bombard strongpoints and villages.

In addition to their counter battery function, the 60 pdrs. and 4.7 in. guns were also used to cut the more distant wire in front of the Zwischen Stellung and the German 2nd Position. They were required to perform this function because:

a. The plan of attack required the wire to be cleared so as to facilitate the infantry's advance all the way to the 2nd Position; and
b. The 18 pdrs. could not reach this wire or, even if they could, the range would be too extreme to allow for effective wire cutting which required an accuracy of height and range and a trajectory at the burst point simply not achievable at these distances.

This operation occupied these batteries for several hours every day thereby still further diluting the counter battery effort.

THE 19TH, 20TH AND 21ST JUNE WERE USED by those heavy batteries ready for action to register their various targets. Out of necessity, this process continued into the opening days of the bombardment proper, with the afternoon of the 23rd June having been a write off because of the heavy thunderstorm which flooded the trenches and played havoc with the observers in their delicate, tethered balloon. Four balloons, those of III, VII, VIII and X Corps, all broke away from their moorings with that of the VIII Corps eventually landing at Sailly au Bois.

On the 24th June various 15 in., 9.2 in., 8 in. and 6 in. howitzers continued the registration process while the 60 pdrs. fired off 1,050 shells and the 4.7 in. guns 218 rounds mainly at the distant wire although one battery, the 112th Heavy Battery, fired at three active German batteries and stopped one from firing on another 60 pounder battery, the 16th Heavy Battery. Unfortunately, there was no point in the howitzers joining in on the counter battery work as 'observation (was) impossible' and none of the shells fired at hostile batteries by the 46th and 54th Siege Batteries could be seen. An effort to register the newly arrived 8 in. howitzers on their prospective targets had to be abandoned until the following day. Two of the 15 in. howitzers were briefly in action. No. 3 Gun, RMA, fired two 'blinds'[i] and No. 5 Gun started as it meant to carry on. One shell was fired, immediately putting the gun out of action until 5 a.m. on the 26th June.

The next day the 8 in. howitzers again attempted to complete their registration but the weather was overcast and 'observation difficult'. Four howitzer batteries from the 1st HAG spent the day registering points on their bombardment schedules. Two 9.2 in., one 8 in. and one 6 in. battery[ii] spread their shells over the wide area they were required to prepare for the forthcoming attack. These ranged from the front line trenches north of the Heidenkopf, to trenches in front of Serre and the area around Pendant Copse deep in the German lines.[4]

---

[i] Shells that failed to explode.
[ii] 46th and 55th (Australian) Siege Batteries, 9.2 in. howitzers, 54th (Australian) Siege Battery, 8 in. howitzer and the 71st (Transvaal) Siege Battery, 6 in. 26 cwt. howitzers.

The two 4.7 in. batteries spent most of their day attempting wire cutting in front of the German 2nd line trench, firing between them 385 of their HE shells.

A total of 44 German artillery targets were engaged throughout the day but without any reports of obvious success. Some of the guns were, however, already beginning to show signs of the unusually heavy use the bombardment demanded. One 60 pounder and a 6 in. howitzer were exhibited symptoms of excessive wear and another 60 pounder and No. 5 Gun, RMA, were out of action.

An overall increase in British artillery activity had already been noted on the other side of No Man's Land and, in response, various adjustments were made to the dispositions of the defending infantry. RIR 121 made two moves: its III Bataillon marched up to the Zwischen Stellung while the I Bataillon moved forward to the Nagel Graben behind and to the north of the Heidenkopf. Not long after this change, the commander of the I Bataillon, Hauptmann Hans Freiherr von Ziegesar, was seriously wounded. He would die in the Reserve Feld Lazaret I near Bapaume the following day. Von Ziegesar was regarded as a considerable loss to the regiment. He had gone to war commanding 11. Kompanie and had shown himself a capable officer.

Overnight, RIR 119 also responded to the increased threat from VIII Corps by moving some companies from its II Bataillon up from Miraumont towards Beaumont Hamel. Villages like Miraumont were already becoming unhealthy places to be and, today, the church was hit and partially destroyed. It was enough to convince the few remaining villagers that it was time to move on and, in the same way as the British cleared villages like Mailly Maillet as the battle approached, so Miraumont was emptied of its last French residents.

Things did not materially improve on the 26th June, the day all of the heavies were supposed to join in with the field artillery in the bombardment of the enemy's positions. The CHA's war diary records:

> "Sharp, short showers during the day. Rather misty at times, greatly interfered with registration."[5]

In general, the German gunners were quiet, as per their tactical instructions from on high, but there was one thing which almost certainly brought them into action and this was a release of either gas or smoke (until it arrived at the trench it was not possible to discern whether it was noxious or simply an attempt to conceal, thus the German guns were instructed to open up whenever either was released). This happened on the 26th and five new German positions were noted opening fire to the north and south of Bucquoy. Already it had been mentioned in the CRA's report there appeared to be an 'unusual number' of hostile batteries opposing the VIII Corps. It was a fact that should have been noted and acted upon. It was not. Nor was the observation that German artillery action had increased most particularly on the 31st Division's front. Nor was the method used by the front line units to call up artillery support. As it was assumed that gas and/or smoke presaged an infantry attack, whenever a thick cloud of gas or smoke appeared the signal sent up from the German front lines was two red rockets which indicated a British infantry attack. Over the coming days, this signal was used repeatedly during both day and night. It appears that no-one of importance recognised this signal and put 'cause', red rockets, together with 'effect', i.e. the sudden opening of a German barrage. This failure was to be of huge importance as, in an act of singular stupidity, the British adopted the firing of red rockets during the advance as a signal that an objective had been taken. Thus, the rash of red rockets fired on 1st July did not indicate, as some optimists believed, the gaining of some important point but rather the imminent arrival of numerous German shells.

Finally, to complete a less than perfect day, the batteries reported another three guns, two howitzers and a 60 pounder, out of action.

27th June was much the same and, again, the weather interfered with any attempts to employ the heavy howitzers on active German batteries:

> "Heavy rain showers throughout the day… Heavy batteries engaged numerous hostile batteries but light was too bad for effective work with heavy howitzers on hostile batteries."[6]

Again, it was left to the 60 pounders to be the main counter battery weapon but these guns, as on previous days, were also cutting the wire in front of the Zwischen Stellung and the German 2nd position. To cut this wire these guns and the 4.7 in. batteries fired shrapnel shells using the 87C fuze. This fuze was causing increasing problems and the batteries had started to report numerous mis-fires. Three more guns were temporarily out of action and one 6 in howitzer from the 122nd Siege Battery, was permanently put out of action when a shell burst prematurely in the barrel rupturing the tube.

Today some of the heavy howitzers devoted all of their energies to battering the trenches of the Zwischen Stellung and the German 2nd Position[i]. The 71st Siege Battery expended 563 shells, the 46th Siege Battery 307 shells, the 55th Siege Battery 370 shells and the 54th Siege Battery 307 shells on the most distant parts of the battlefield on the 31st Division's front. But, as Haig had demanded these trenches be taken, there was no alternative but to bombard these locations and 1,547 shells were wasted on positions the British would not reach until the spring of 1917 when the Germans withdrew to the Hindenburg line. Alternatively, of course, these guns might have been better employed on either the front line trenches or on counter battery work. Instead, only 206 shells were fired by these guns on this latter and crucial task.

Some temporary success was gained by the 240 mm trench mortars on the 29th Division's front. The bombs launched by these weapons caused an almighty mess and were often mistaken for the explosion of a heavy howitzer shell. Today they managed to block the entrances to the Leiling Stollen, a large dugout on a reverse slope overlooking Station Road just to the south of the Y Ravine. Blocked dugout entrances were about as bad as it got for the defenders north of the Ancre and, during the day and night, men had to expose themselves to the dangers of shell fire as they hurriedly cleared away the earth and rubble in order to ensure quick and easy access to and from these deep shelters.

[i] The 1st HAG's war diary talks of the 3rd and 4th line trenches but then goes on the explain that the: "Trench referred in future as 3rd line trench is that from NE of Star Wood through L.36.a and c to Beaucourt Redoubt. Trench referred to in future as 4th line trench is that from Puisieux through L.32.a and c to R.8.b." These are the Zwischen Stellung and 2nd German position. [Source: NA, WO/95/208].

It would appear that the 28th June was the best day for weather during the bombardment (the 30th was a clear day but very windy thus affecting the accuracy of the firing), though it still rained from time to time. Though better, the weather was still less than perfect and the batteries trying to neutralise the German artillery had to spend most of the day firing 'off map' as effective liaison with the RFC proved impossible. In this manner, 48 targets were fired on but, without proper observation, it was impossible to say whether the shelling of these positions was effective, although the 55th and 46th Siege Batteries both claimed direct hits on three German positions around Puisieux.

Again, many of the heavy and medium howitzer batteries were employed on the destruction of the Zwischen Stellung and 2nd Position with the 46th, 54th, 55th and 71st Siege Batteries wasting 1,356 shells which would have been far better employed on the German front line trenches. They would be at it again on the 29th when, in a much reduced programme because of the postponement of Z Day, 938 shells were frittered away on these distant lines while only 73 were used to suppress the German artillery.

Numerous guns were out now temporarily or permanently out of action. A 6 in. MK VII was condemned by the IoM for scoring and wear and both 6 in. Mk VII guns of the right section, 29th Siege Battery, were out of action. Two 6 in. howitzers were out of action and three 4.7 in. guns from the 1/1st Welsh Heavy Battery needed repair. No. 1 Gun, RMA, had broken its traversing arc and slewed 45° to the south. Lastly, two 60 pounders from the 16th Heavy Battery were out of action, significantly reducing this battery's contribution to the day's shooting.

On the 29th the CHA war diary recorded:

"Conditions were against accurate air observation."[7]

On the 30th June it was claimed that 'Counter battery work was energetically continued'[8], however, throughout the entire seven day bombardment hits on only nine German battery positions were recorded anywhere on the Corps' front. 'Energetically', as far as the 1st HAG was concerned, meant the expenditure of 89 of the lightweight 4.7 in. shells and 181 shells from the heavy and medium howitzers. Given that these howitzers otherwise spent the fourth day running bombarding the 2nd and 3rd German Positions (881 shells from four batteries) and the final contribution of the Corps artillery along large stretches of the front of the VIII Corps might be said to have been of little or no use to the infantry waiting to attack the following day. To add to this, much of the shooting by all batteries had been done 'off map' with little or no aerial or ground observation as the war diary of the 1st HAG makes clear:

> "This completes deliberate bombardment of seven days before final infantry assault. A large amount of shooting had to be done off the map for several reasons. Enemy batteries in most cases invisible. Targets for 6 in. Mk VII too far back to be seen with any degree of accuracy except by balloon. Observation by balloon and in several cases from the OPs rendered impossible during several days owing to the bad weather."[9]

GENERALLY, THE RESPONSE OF THE GERMAN ARTILLERY was described as 'feeble' or 'slight'. Only when gas and/or smoke were released and when British raids were mounted did the German guns fire with any intensity. It was a deliberate part of the German defensive plan that not all guns should fire during the preliminary British bombardment and, as a result, they were often forced to refuse requests from the front line infantry for artillery support. The benefits of this would be seen on the day of the attack when the German artillery response at both Gommecourt and, in particular, Serre was of a weight and intensity which caught both the British infantry and its commanders completely by surprise.

What should have been of concern to both the British artillery and infantry was the significant fall-off in intensity of the British bombardment once it had been decided to postpone the attack from the 29th June to the 1st July.

The super-heavy howitzers, 9.2 in. and upwards, fired 1,636 rounds on 27th June, 1,755 on the 28th June, the day of the postponement, 975 on the 29th June and just 889 on the 30th June. This was necessary not only to conserve ammunition for the day of the attack but also to allow for a reserve supply for any subsequent fighting (although, had there been a genuine breakthrough, these guns would have been rapidly left behind). The result was that, on the day before the attack, the super heavies fired 50% fewer shells than on the peak day of the 28th June which had been the original day immediately prior to the attack.

With the medium howitzers, the 8 in. and 6 in., the position was not quite so dramatic:

27th June – 4,640
28th June – 5,646
29th June – 3,982
30th June – 4,764

This still represents a 15% drop in intensity over the two extension days of the bombardment compared to the previous two days. Similar reductions in the numbers of shells fired occurred with the batteries of long guns.

Table 4 below shows the daily expenditure for each type of gun from the 27th June onwards.

	15 in How	12 in How	9.2 in How	8 in How	6 in How	6 in Gun	60 pdr	4.7 in
27th June	84	117	1435	1518	3122	515	?	?
28th June	118	193	1444	1825	3821	544	3967	742
29th June	98	49	828	1348	2634	522	3323	?
30th June	66	34	789	1329	3435	376	3516	291
1st July	70	?	1518	2562	4374	575	6105	1722
Total	436	393	6014	8582	17386	2532	16911	

Table 4 Ammunition expenditure by VIII Corps Heavy Artillery, 27th June to 1st July[10]

What might have been the consequences of this reduction in the intensity of the British barrage over the last two days of the bombardment? Given the targets the heaviest howitzers were firing on probably not a great deal. The 15 in. and 12 in. howitzers spent their time flattening three villages: Serre, Beaumont Hamel and Beaucourt-sur-Ancre and, on occasions, pummelling the Beaucourt redoubt. The German defenders of these villages were not concentrated in the houses and cellars but predominantly in the dugouts in front of them or to their rear. A proportion of the other howitzers were firing on the Zwischen Stellung and the German 2nd positions which were areas where the reserve companies of the defending regiments and other reserves were located but, with the possible exception of the 9.2 in. howitzers, their shells were not heavy enough to collapse the deep dugouts which sheltered them. A reduction in shelling in these areas might well have allowed for the bringing up of supplies: food, water, ammunition but the supply parties would still have experienced enormous difficulties in getting their loads to the front.

What about the front lines? Were they affected by the scaling down of the bombardment? The answer is: yes. Not only did the Corps artillery reduce the number of shells fired, so did the Divisional artillery, most particularly in the last 17 hours before the final bombardment began at 5 a.m. on 1st July. Detailed figures exist for several of the bombardment groups of the Divisional artillery. In the main they show the same trend in the intensity of the bombardment designed to prevent the wire and trenches being repaired and supplies from being brought up to the front line.

	Grand totals				
	18 Pdr		4.5 in. Howitzer		
	A	AX	B	BX	Total
Noon U – Noon V	3710	35	0	404	4149
Noon V – Noon W	3506	696	0	645	4847
Noon W – Noon X	3181	901	0	880	4962
Noon X – Noon Y	3950	1608	0	580	6138
Noon Y – Noon Y1	3374	580	0	640	4594
Noon Y1 – Noon Y2	1597	2396	0	976	4969
Noon Y2 – 0500 Z	560	166	52	257	1035
Totals	19878	6382	52	4382	30694

Table 5 Total shells fired by Right Group, 29th Division, 24th to 30th June 1916.[11]

On the 29th Division's front figures are given in the war diary of the 17th Brigade, RFA, for the nine batteries which formed the Right Group and which was commanded by Lt. Col. W P Monkhouse, CMG, MVO, the CO of the 17th Brigade[i]. The totals for the seven day bombardment are shown in Table 5 above (A = 18 pdr. shrapnel, AX = 18 pdr. HE, B = 4.5 in. Field Howitzer shrapnel and BX = 4.5 in. HE). These batteries were responsible for cutting the wire and other bombardment responsibilities from the northern arm of the Y Ravine to the Mary Redan. The figures show that for the 24 hours between midday on Thursday, 29th June (Y1 Day), to midday on Friday, 30th June (Y2 Day), the batteries involved fired an average of 207 rounds per hour, most of which would have been fired in daylight hours. At their peak, from midday on X day to midday on Y Day, these batteries fired an average of 255 rounds per hour. But, during the 17 hours before the final bombardment started on Saturday morning, these nine batteries fired together an average of just 61 rounds per hour, less than a quarter of the number fired at the bombardment's peak time which, barring the postponement, would have been just before the attack was due to start.

[i] The Right Group consisted of the 26th, 92nd, 13th and 460th (D/17) Batteries from the 17th Brigade, RFA, the 370th and 371st Batteries from the 132nd Brigade, the 10th Battery from the 147th Brigade and B/243 and A/241 Batteries from the 48th Division's artillery.

The change in the daily volumes fired is, perhaps, better shown in a bar chart as in Chart 1 below which shows the combined totals for shrapnel, combined total for High Explosive and the grand total for all shells fired by this group during the seven day bombardment. Two things are made clear in this graph: the dramatic reduction in activity on the last day of the bombardment and the sharp reduction in wire cutting activity as indicated by the more than 50% reduction in shrapnel used on Y2 Day compared to the first four days of the bombardment.

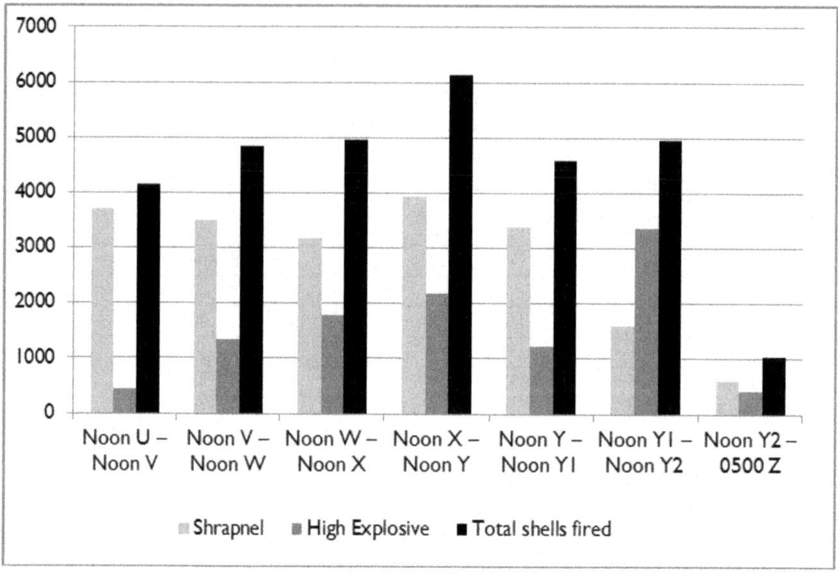

Chart 1 Shrapnel and HE shells fired by Right Group, 29th Division, 24th to 30th June.

Interestingly, the detailed figures for the 147th Brigade, three batteries of which supported the 86th Brigade on the left wing of the 29th Division, do not show the same trend. These batteries, 97th, 368th and D/147 (two 18 pdr. and one 4.5 in. howitzer), maintained a consistently increasing volume of fire over the seven days, there being a dip on the 29th June which rebounded on the 30th back to the levels of Y Day. Oddly, it was from 6 a.m. onwards on Z Day, that there was a significant fall-off in intensity with both 368th Battery (down 64%) and D/147 (down 80%).

On the 4th Division's front a similar pattern to that of the Right Group, 29th Division, held good. The four batteries of the 29th Brigade, RFA, the 125th, 126th, 127th (18 pdr.) and 128th (4.5 in. howitzer) Batteries bombarded the left wing of the 4th Division's front from positions near the Sucrerie[i]. Chart 2 below shows the significant reduction in the intensity of the Brigade's bombardment over the final two days of the bombardment, with Y1 Day totals showing a 44% reduction over Y Day and Y2 Day a 32% reduction over that same day. This Brigade's area, however, was one where the wire proved fairly well cut thus the reduction in

[i] They were joined for the last day of the bombardment by B/241 and C/241 from the 48th Division but they were only registering targets with a view to a greater level of activity on Z Day.

shrapnel fired over the last two days may not have proved too costly. On the other hand, given that these guns were the only ones to maintain any level of activity over the German forward lines both day and night the decrease in intensity might well have given the defenders an opportunity to make some repairs and bring forward supplies.

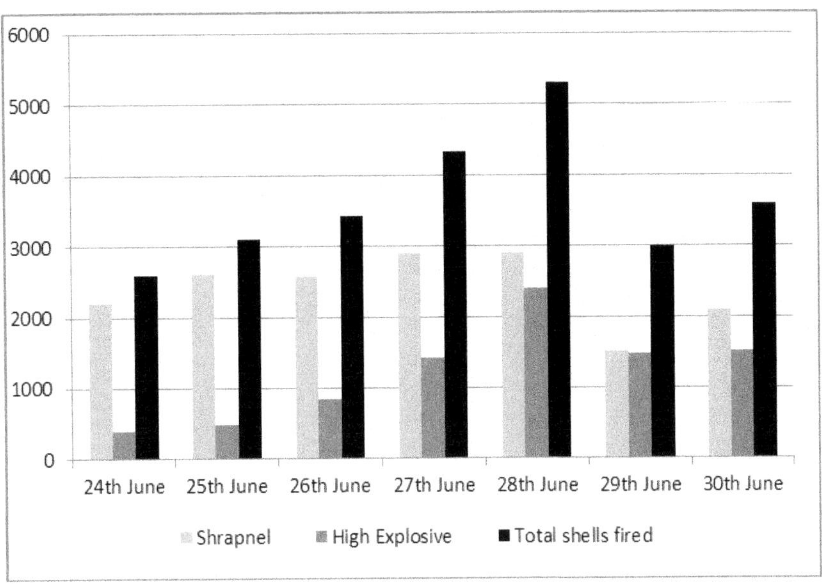

Chart 2 Shrapnel and HE shells fired by 29th Brigade, RFA, 4th Division, 24th to 30th June.[12]

On the 31st Division's front detailed figures only survive for the four 18 pdr. batteries under the control of the 165th Brigade, RFA. These were A/165, B/165, C/165 and A/171 Batteries and they had the task of cutting the wire in front of the first four lines of German trenches on the 94th Brigade's front. Although Chart 3 below clearly shows a reduction in firing on the 29th June, down 40% compared to the 28th June, there was a corresponding bounce back the following day during which the four batteries fired 3,900 shrapnel shells compared to 4,096 on the 28th June (and 2,243 on the 29th). What is interesting about these figures is that nothing but shrapnel was fired on the last three days of the bombardment and this is because the Brigade was still trying (and failing in many places) to cut the German wire right up until the time of the attack. Although the war diary does not specify where the wire was being cut on 30th June it is clear that, on the day before, their efforts were entirely devoted to the German front line wire:

> "A/165 – engaged on front line wire. Left of wire badly damaged for 10 yards. Right of this wire is badly damaged.
> B/165 - engaged on front line wire. Large pile of cut wire and knife rests on right of zone at K.29.b.60.81.
> C/165 – engaged on front line wire. With exception of three small patches, front line wire appears to be completely cut from K.29.b.23.23 to K.29.b.15.10.

A/171 – engaged on front line wire. Another lane 5 yards wide cut through wire at K.29.b.33.40."[13]

The fact that the second largest number of shrapnel shells fired during the bombardment was expended the day before the attack strongly suggests that the wire which was to hold up the 12th York and Lancasters and the 11th East Lancashires was inadequately cut and, in spite of claims to the contrary made by officers of the Field Artillery, was known to be inadequately cut.

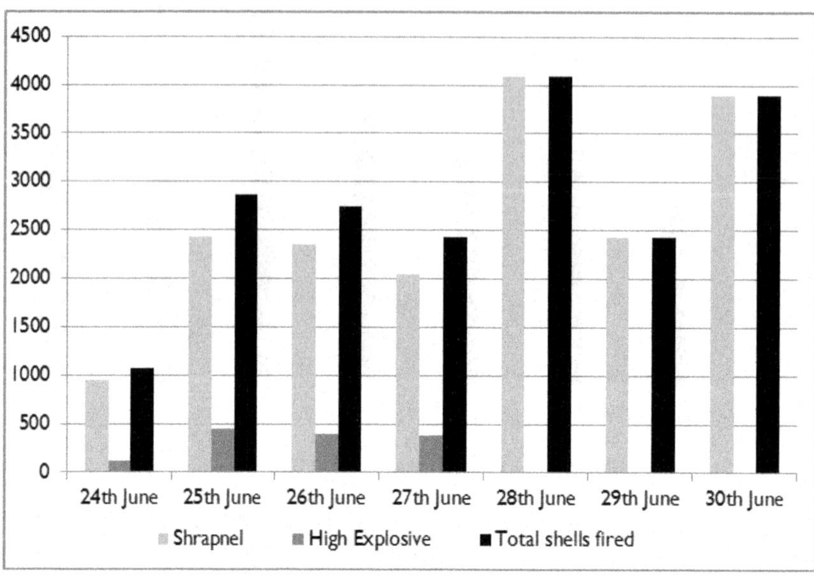

Chart 3 Shrapnel and HE shells fired by 165th Brigade, RFA, 31st Division, 24th to 30th June.

The bombardment of the German trenches carried on throughout the night of the 30th June/1st July and steadily intensified as the first signs of dawn streaked the eastern sky. As everywhere north of the River Somme, the last 65 minutes of the bombardment, i.e. from 6.25 a.m. onwards, was to be intense with that intensity growing as the time neared zero. For the last ten minutes all guns of the Corps and Divisional artillery, as well as the Stokes trench mortars of the Brigade Trench Mortar Batteries, were to fire as fast as possible. The only proviso was that the heavy artillery firing on the German front line was to lift ten minutes before zero, shifting their fire to the reserve line of trenches. Then, at 7.25 a.m., i.e. five minutes before zero, the heavy howitzers firing on the German support line were also to lift and join the others firing on the reserve line. This left only the 18 pdr field guns firing HE to bombard the two German front line trenches for the final five minutes of the bombardment. At this time, the men from several of the attacking infantry battalions would be forming up in No Man's Land, with one, the 1st Royal Inniskilling Fusiliers, performing a right wheel in full view of these front line enemy trenches in order to be properly aligned with their objective.

There does, however, appear to have been some confusion about the lifts of the heavy batteries in the last ten minutes. The war diary of the 1st Heavy Artillery Group notes that at 7.06 a.m. they received an order that appeared to contradict the original plan in which the howitzers firing on the front line moved to the reseve line at 7.20 a.m. while those firing on the support line should not shift onto the German reserve line until 7.25 a.m. The diary states:

> "7.06 a.m. Message received warning that all howitzers are to lift to 3rd line at 7.20 a.m."[14]

'All howitzers', not just those firing on the front German trench. According to this instruction, therefore, the medium and heavy howitzer batteries of the 1st HAG which had been firing on either the front *or* support lines were to lift onto the reserve line at 7.20 a.m., thus leaving these two trench lines solely to the tender mercies of the 18 pdrs and Stokes mortars. Indeed, some batteries, for example the 46th Siege Battery of four 9.2 in. howitzers, had moved off the front line at 7.10 a.m. having fired 110 rounds at this target between 6.05 a.m. and 7.10 a.m. Prior to that the battery had fired nearly forty rounds at either the German reserve line or the fourth line of trenches between the 1st Position and the Zwischen Stellung. At 7.10 a.m., however, the guns switched targets yet again, firing 92 rounds on the German reserve line.

Since 6.25 a.m. the 4th HAG had two 6 in. howitzer batteries, the 112th Siege Battery and 23rd Siege Battery, firing on the front line trench. At 7.20 a.m. they were planning to increase their rate of fire to the maximum possible when an order was passed to the battery commanders by the Brigade Major. It read:

> "7.20 a.m. Brigade Major ordered all howitzer batteries firing on front line to lift at 7.20 a.m. whether at 250 yards from our trenches or not."[15]

This order suggests a great deal of confusion over the instruction to take the howitzers off the front line trench and, allied to the 7.06 a.m. order to the 1st HAG, even suggests that someone was making decisions on the hoof about the bombardment. First of all, the 7.06 a.m. order meant that those batteries firing on the German support trench were to move five minute earlier than planned. The order to the 4th HAG hints at something altogether more serious. It suggests that the 7.20 a.m. lifts off the front line trench by the howitzers were originally only to take place in those areas where No Man's Land was 250 yards wide or less. This was presumably done in order to avoid these guns firing on their own troops, some of which were to form up in No Man's Land. Such a plan might well have been sensible on 31st Division's front where No Man's Land was only between 200 and 300 yards wide as well as around the Heidenkopf and the Ridge Redoubt on 4th Division's front. But, if this is true, then it also meant that in the sectors where No Man's Land was considerably wider this lift off the front line trench was not originally planned to take place ten minutes before zero. This would have applied, for example, to the southern end of 4th Division's front and most of the 29th Division's front. As a result, the German front line would have been kept under fire by the heavy guns for an additional five minutes. An instruction for variably timed lifts based on the width of No Man's Land, if issued, makes considerable sense. The 4th HAG Brigade Major's order at 7.20 a.m., however, appears to override any such flexible instructions and instead meant that all howitzers firing on the German front line at 7.20 a.m. were to move to the reserve line however wide No Man's Land might be. In other words, this order applied to the entire VIII Corps' front from Serre to Mary Redan.

It was a recipe for disaster.

Thereafter, the artillery was to perform five further lifts onto targets progressively further to the east. The lifts for the field artillery were:

Off the first objective (Serre and Beaumont Trenches) at between 15 to 20 minutes after zero (depending on the distance between the British front line and the first objective);

Off the second objective (the Zwischen Stellung/Munich Trench) at between 40 and 45 minutes after zero (though after 80 minutes in the area around Beaucourt);

Off two intermediate positions at 95 minutes and 2 hours 40 minutes after zero; and

Off the third objective (the German 2nd Position) at 3 hours and 30 minutes after zero.

The heavy artillery was to lift five minutes before the field artillery in each case and, unlike the field guns, was to lift straight onto the next objective, e.g. off Serre and Beaumont Trenches at between 10 and 15 minutes after zero and straight onto Munich Trench. The field guns (18 pdrs), however, were to attempt something akin to the 'creeping barrage' that would become the norm in future assaults. When, according to the timetable, the infantry should have been ready to launch the second advance, e.g. from Serre Trench to Munich Trench, the field guns were to start firing 100 yards in front of the infantry, lengthening their range by 50 yards a minute in which time each gun was to fire three rounds. 50 yards a minute was, of course, the prescribed speed of the infantry advance. While the 18 pdrs provided this moving curtain of fire, their colleagues manning the 4.5 in. howitzers were to take under fire any identified machine gun positions and OPs.

The timings of each artillery lift and of the increases in range of the 18 pdrs were precise and it would be up to the infantry to keep pace with the artillery. It is interesting to note that, in the instructions issued by Corps setting out the artillery plan for the attack, VIII Corps only considered the possibility of the infantry moving too fast rather than too slowly:

> "The times (for lifts) once settled cannot be altered. The infantry therefore must make their pace conform to the rate of the artillery lifts. If the infantry find themselves checked by our own barrage, they must halt and wait until the barrage moves forward."[16]

The onus for the success of the attack was placed squarely on the infantry and their ability to understand and conform to 'the creeping method of the artillery'. There was nothing in the plan for what the artillery should do if the infantry were held up.

At 3 hours and 30 minutes after zero, i.e. 11 a.m., the infantry should have occupied the German 2nd Position and the new northern flank above Serre. At this time the longer range guns and the field gun batteries which had been moved forward into new positions on the German side of No Man's Land[i] were to provide a covering barrage to the east and north of these positions in order to prevent or break-up any attempted German counter-attacks.

It all looked remarkably straight forward – as long as the German troops in the front line trenches did the decent thing and either died or surrendered. Life, however, was not to be that simple and even the weather continued to intervene in a particularly unhelpful way.

BEFORE MOVING ONTO THE DETAILED ACCOUNTS of each Division's attack, it is important that the reader bears in mind the weather conditions and how they, and subsequent events, affected the ability of the British observers and commanders to discern what precisely was going on in front of them. Saturday, 1st July 1916, is commonly described as a glorious, hot summer's day with clear blue skies. And so it became. But not before the early morning mist, which was notorious in the Somme area, had burned off. Douglas Haig records in his diary that the day started misty; expressing the hope that it might conceal the concentrations of troops in their assembly trenches[17]. What he did not record was the problem it caused the RFC observers and the Corps and Divisional artilleries as they endeavoured to deluge the German positions with shells during the final 2½ hours of the bombardment immediately prior to the attack.

The war diary of the 1st Heavy Artillery Group recorded the problems of observation for each of its batteries:

No 1 Gun, RMA, taking on Beaucourt and the redoubt and Grandcourt – 'No observation owing to bad weather and smoke'[ii].

65th Siege Battery (12 in. howitzers) firing at Serre, Pendant Copse and Puisieux – 'Very little observation possible. Impossible to give any good results'.

55th Siege Battery (9.2 in. howitzers) firing on Serre and positions further east – 'Practically no observation possible owing to smoke. Results therefore unknown'.

54th Siege Battery (8 in. howitzers) firing on front line trenches on 48th Division's front, Serre and positions further east – 'Observation practically impossible owing to mist and smoke'.

71st Siege Battery (6 in. howitzers) firing on an area to the rear of the Heidenkopf, on the German 2nd Position and used on counter battery work – 'No observation possible… mostly from map'.

46th Siege Battery (9.2 in. howitzers) firing on the area to the rear of Heidenkopf, Munich Trench and the German 2nd Position – 'Visual but few bursts seen owing to mist, dust, smoke, etc.'

29th Siege Battery (6 in. Mk VII guns) firing on Puisieux and Achiet le Petit – 'All map shooting. Observation impossible'.

---

[i] Each Division was instructed to have two 18 pdr batteries ready to move forward over bridges provided by the Royal Engineers in order to be within range of the eastern side of the German 2nd Position by the time the infantry arrived there.

[ii] To add to their problems the diary goes on to record: "Platform slewed and tilted so much that it is not advisable to fire again."

1/1st Welsh and 1/1st Highland Heavy Batteries (4.7 in. guns) firing on counter battery work, Puisieux, Beaucourt and the 2nd Position – ' Practically all map shooting'.[18]

Other batteries in other groups reported the same problems. Neither No. 3 nor No. 5 Gun, RMA, could see the results of their firing with No 5 Gun's diary reporting at 6.25 a.m. that 'Observation was almost impossible owing to smoke clouds'. Later in the day the same problem persisted with 19 rounds fired at the Beaucourt Redoubt at about 8.45 a.m. proving impossible to see 'owing to smoke clouds'. It was not until midday, after most of the fighting had died down, that they reported 'moderately good' conditions for observation. [19]

There are not as many comments about the visibility in the Field Artillery war diaries but there are some, all from the 31st Division which, given the repeated observations of deep penetrations in this area, poses some interesting questions about what the observers could genuinely see. The 169th Brigade, RFA, talks of 'a very misty early morning' and, at 6.30 a.m. that the 'enemy's line and our front lines were completely hidden in a dense cloud of smoke'.[20] The 165th Brigade, RFA, recorded that, at 6.25 a.m., the start time for the final intense bombardment, 'observation (was) impossible owing to mist'. Then, at 7.13 a.m., 17 minutes before the attack was due to start, it states 'mist cleared a little but still impossible to observe fire'. At 7.39 a.m., with the attack already underway, the 'smoke rendered observation very difficult'. [21]

Apart from the issue of the effectiveness of the artillery during the bombardment and the attack, these comments should be borne in mind when assessing the likely accuracy of many of the observer reports that came in during the morning of 1st July, some of which led to disastrous decisions about the deployment of battalions supporting the initial advance.

On the other side of No Man's Land, except for where the front line wire had been properly cut, the majority of the damage was cosmetic. No dugouts had been collapsed. Some entrances had been blocked but, in the main, they had been quickly cleared. Some trenches had been flattened or significantly eroded but they still existed and gave shelter to the defenders. Supplies of food, water and ammunition to the front line troops had been severely interrupted and many of the roads and villages to the rear were dangerous places to pass along and through during daylight hours. Overall, however, casualties amongst the defending regiments had been very light. RIR 119 at Beaumont Hamel had lost twenty dead and 83 wounded and RIR 121 on Redan Ridge twenty four dead, 122 wounded and one man missing[i]. Losses amongst the artillery batteries had been similarly slight. The seven day bombardment had looked and sounded impressive, most especially to the officers and men watching from the relative safety of the British lines, but its impact was minimal. All of the evidence gathered from raids and patrols would confirm that the German soldiers in the front line trenches had been little disturbed by the shelling. Nervous, tired, hungry and thirsty they may have been, but they remained a formidable fighting force and one which was increasingly anxious to take out their frustrations and anger on the British 'Tommy' once he showed himself in No Man's Land.

[i] Figures for IR 169 and IR 66 losses during the bombardment are not available.

[1] NA, WO95/221, *War Diary 65th Siege Battery.*
[2] NA, WO95/217, *War Diary 46th Siege Battery.*
[3] Keegan, Sir J, *The Face of Battle*, 1976, page 239.
[4] NA, WO95/208, *War Diary 1st HAG.*
[5] NA, WO95/285, *War Diary, CHA, VIII Corps.*
[6] Ibid.
[7] Ibid.
[8] Ibid.
[9] NA, WO95/208.
[10] NA, WO95/285.
[11] NA, WO 95/2291/3, *War Diary, 17th Brigade, RFA.*
[12] NA, WO 95/1466/5, *War Diary, 29th Brigade, RFA.*
[13] NA, WO 95/2349/3, *War Diary, 165th Brigade, RFA.*
[14] NA, WO95/208.
[15] NA. WO95/298, *War Diary 4th HAG.*
[16] *VIII Artillery Instructions* quoted in *BOH*, 1916, Vol.1, page 428.
[17] Sheffield & Bourne, op. cit., page 195.
[18] NA, WO95/208.
[19] NA, WO95/483, *War Diary No. 5 Gun., RMA.*
[20] NA, WO 95/2349/4, *War Diary, 169th Brigade, RFA.*
[21] NA, WO 95/2349/3.

7. THE 29TH DIVISION AT BEAUMONT HAMEL

PLANS FOR THE ATTACK ON BEAUMONT HAMEL were sent out by the Staff of the 29th Division on 14th June. As Table 6 below shows the plan was complex and yet this intricate operation was to be done and dusted by 12.10 p.m., just four hours and forty minutes after the whistles were to blow at zero hour. On a less well-defended front a penetration to a depth of 4,000 yards in this time would have been a tall order but to take such a heavily fortified position incorporating seven sets of trenches was asking the impossible.

The topology of the ground was also heavily in the favour of defenders. The ravines and depressions in which Beaumont Hamel lay provided numerous opportunities for both ancient and modern mined shelters for the defending troops and the tiered nature of the ground, which rose onto two increasingly high ridges to the east gave the defenders the ability to fire over the heads of their colleagues in the front trenches. To stand a chance of success the men of the 29th Division needed the occupants of five lines of trenches to have been killed or neutralised by the artillery. The gunners, meanwhile, had another line of trenches much further to the east to batter – the German 2nd Position and the Division's final objective.

The task of taking these five lines of trenches would fall to the battalions of the 86th and 87th Brigades with, on the extreme right, the assistance of two battalions of the 108th Brigade of the 36th (Ulster) Division. The success, or otherwise, of these battalions' parent Division would have a material effect on the prospects of the 29th Division as, should the Ulstermen fail, then the right wing of the 29th Division would be horribly exposed to machine gun fire from the southern bank of the Ancre. Of course, were the opposite to happen, then it would be the fate of the Irish troops to be raked by enfilade machine gun fire from their left. Success for both was the only guarantee of success overall.

To the immediate north of the these two Ulster battalions and the large expanse of open No Man's Land they had to cross, two battalions of the 87th Brigade were to lead the assault. Because of an absurd decision taken by the highest authority not to close or otherwise re-align their trenches both of these units would have a tricky start to their busy day. The battalion on the right of the 29th Division's line was the 1st Royal Inniskilling Fusiliers who would start from a northerly facing stretch of trench to the west of the fortification called the Mary Redan. Their problem was that the German trenches they were to take were to the east. The solution was a difficult manoeuvre at the best of times – a right wheel. This right wheel, however, was to take place in full view of the enemy several minutes before zero but at a time when all of the supporting heavy artillery had moved off the first two lines of German trench. It should have been enough to make even the most optimistic senior officer nervous. But not, apparently in the 29th Division and VIII Corps.

On their left, the other lead battalion was the 2nd South Wales Borderers and they had problems of their own. Their task was to take a position called the Y Ravine before moving onto Station Road and their other tasks. The Y Ravine was a small, steep faced valley which projected out from the German position towards the British trenches. It had been riddled with dugouts by assiduous German engineers and these bolt holes were pretty much artillery proof. Some of the SWB would attack the nose of the ravine and others would have to cross its southern face before turning left to attack their enemy. As with the Inniskillings and the Ulster battalions the Borderers would be in full view of any German machine guns in any of the five sets of trenches they were to attack.

Neither of the lead battalions of the 86th Brigade on the left of the Division's front had easy tasks. Part of Z Company of the 2nd Royal Fusiliers was to grab the near and far edges of the crater to be created by the explosion of the huge mine under the Hawthorn Redoubt. German troops had always seemed to get the upper hand in crater fighting on the Western Front and this could not be allowed to happen on Z Day. If neither the crater or the Y Ravine fell then the rest of the Royal Fusiliers would be in trouble as they advanced into a re-entrant between the two locations. To make matters worse, the German front line here was on a reverse slope and, come the day of the attack, no-one could be sure if the wire here was cut. The fate of the German garrison was also an unknown quantity so everyone just hoped for the best.

On their left, to the north of the Beaumont to Auchnovillers Road, two things would happen. First, at 7.20 a.m., Geoffrey Malins, an Official War Office Kinematographer, would film the monstrous eruption of the great mine and would record one of the iconic images of the Great War. Ten minutes later two companies of the 1st Lancashire Fusiliers would emerge from the undergrowth lining a small sunken lane out in front of the main British trench system and attempt to drive through the German front line to the northern end of Beaumont Hamel. Later in the day, Malins would film the hurried retreat of the remains of two battalions from around the crater and the roll call of the sorry remains of the Fusiliers whose repeated gallant efforts were to founder on the German wire.

But all of this was to come. The planners foresaw none of this debacle. Envisioning only success they imagine these first four battalions sweeping all before them until they reached the line of Waggon Road at the northern end of Beaumont and Station Road, which ran away to the south east, and the ruined station at its southern end. This line was to be reached after just twenty minutes. Forty minutes later, the next four battalions of the two Brigades would move out to maintain their sedate advance eastwards towards the 2nd Objective, the Beaucourt Ridge on which sat the Beaucourt Redoubt, known to the Germans as the Feste Alt Württemberg. By zero + one hour and twenty minutes this line too would have fallen, to be followed fifteen minutes later by Beaucourt village. Just before this they would leave the Ulstermen behind guarding the river bank and the nearby mill.

Finally, at 10 a.m., the men of the 88th Brigade were to take over from their no doubt tired but happy colleagues and they would advance to the Puisieux Road and on towards their 3rd and final objective, the German 2nd Position. At this point, to be quite honest, the timings started to get a trifle silly. At zero + three hours and 27 minutes precisely they would assault the first element of the 3rd objective. This would take three minutes. Then they would take the second line of trenches. By 12 noon it would be all over. The guns would cease fire ten minutes later. Lunch would be served shortly afterwards.

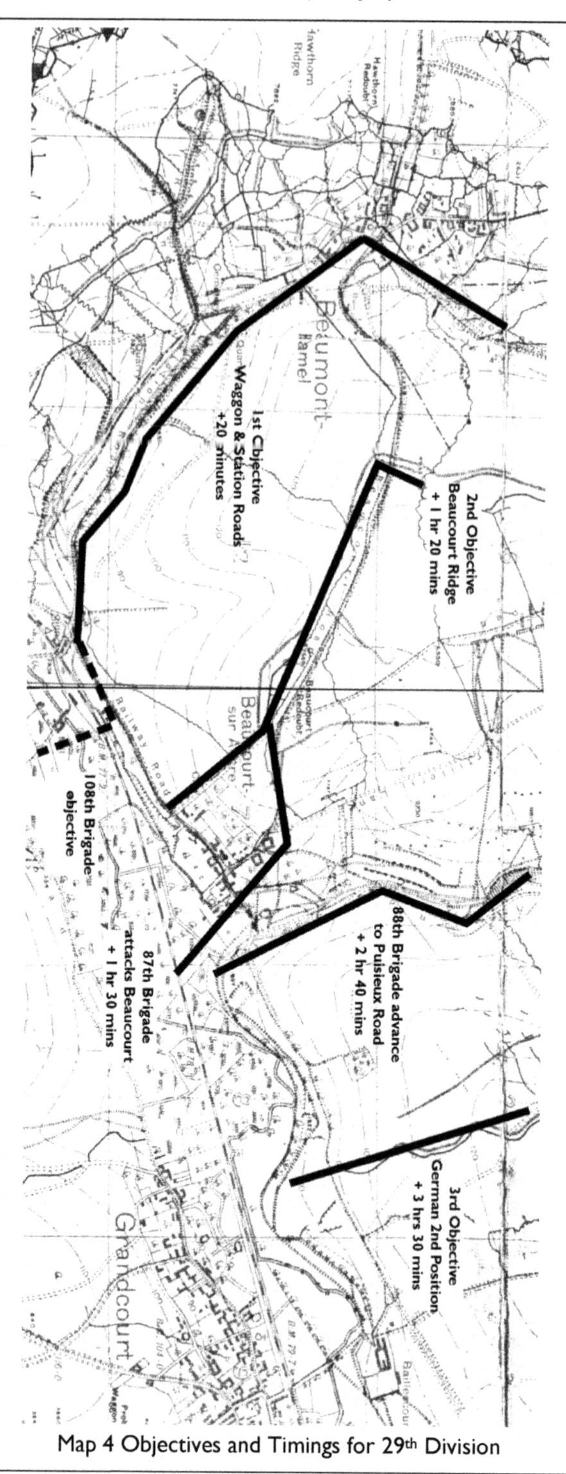

Map 4 Objectives and Timings for 29th Division

Time	Moves of infantry	Trench mortars/ Divl artillery	Heavy artillery
-0.10		Stokes mortars open hurricane bombardment	
-0.5			Lift to new trench in Q.11.d & Q.12.c
Zero	87th & 86th Bde assault 1st objective & advance at rate not exceeding 50 yards a minute	All trench mortars cease fire. Field Artillery - Lift to enemy support trench or minimum of 100 yards beyond front line	
+0.2		Stokes mortars cease fire Field Artillery - Lift another 100 yds	
+0.4		Lift another 100 yards & continue lifting at rate of 100 yards every 2 minutes until they reach line 400 yards east of Station & Wagon Roads where they remain till 1.5 Howitzers remain on new trench in Q.12.c	
+0.15			Lift to 2nd objective
+0.20	87th & 86th Bdes reach Station & Wagon Roads	Howitzers lift off new trench	
+1.0	87th & 86th Bdes advance from Station & Wagon Roads against 2nd objective at rate not exceeding 50 yards a minute		
+1.5		Lift 100 yards and continue lifting at rate of 100 yards every 2 minutes until they reach Beaucourt Ridge where they will remain till +1.20	Lift to Beaucourt village
+1.20	87th & 86th Bdes assault second objective	Lift to line of wire R.7.a.5.2 to R.1.c.25.50 (where they will remain until 1.35) & also to Beaucourt village	
+1.25			Lift to 3rd objective
+1.30	87th & 86th Bdes send out patrols to cut line of wire R.7.a.3.2 to R.1.c.25.50. 87th Bde assault Beaucourt village	Lift off Beaucourt village	
+1.35	87th & 86th Bdes cut wire	Lift off line of wire to east of Artillery Lane and maintain barrage until +2.30	

+2.30	88th Bde advance through wire to Puisieux Road at rate not exceeding 50 yards a minute	Lift to the Puisieux Road	
+2.40	88th Bde reach Puisieux Road	Lift to a line 300 yards east of the Puisieux Road and remain there till +3.10	
+3.10	88th Bde advance from Puisieux Road towards third objective	Lift 100 yards and continue lifting at rate of 100 yards every 2 minutes until they reach front trench of third objective where they remain till +3.27	
+3.22			Lift on to Baillescourt and ground SW of it
+3.27	88th Bde assault front trench of 3rd objective	Lift to support trench of third objective	
+3.30	88th Bde assault support line of 3rd objective	Lift to sunken road	
+4.25			Cease fire
+4.30	88th Bde push forward small parties to establish themselves as an outpost line in sunken road and at Baillescourt	Lift 400 yards east of sunken road	
+4.40		Cease fire	

Table 6 Infantry and Artillery Programme, 29th Division[1]

ON THE SAME DAY AS THE DIVISIONAL INSTRUCTIONS were distributed to every unit, so the four Brigades of Royal Field Artillery attached to the 29th Division received the details of the programme and targets from the commander of the Divisional Royal Artillery, Brig. Gen. Malcolm Peake. The 51 year old Peake was a Midlander from Melton Mowbray. He entered the Royal Military Academy, Woolwich, from Charterhouse and was commissioned into the Royal Artillery in 1884. Ten years, between 1895 and 1905, were spent commanding guns in the Egyptian Army during which time he took part in the Battles of Atbara and Khartoum. He spent the first twenty months of the war at home as Assistant Adjutant General at the War Office. Command of the 29th Division's artillery was, therefore, his first active command and, when he took over on 22nd April 1916, he had but nine weeks in which to get to grips with the men and weapons at his disposal before the bombardment was to begin[i].

The Divisional artillery comprised four brigades: the 15th Brigade, Royal Horse Artillery (three batteries of 18 pdr. QF guns), and 17th, 132nd and 147th

[i] Brig. Gen. Malcolm Peake, CMG, Royal Artillery, was killed on 27th August 1917 at Hill 70 near Loos. He had been promoted BGRA I Corps on 19th December 1916. Aged 52, he was the 3rd son of Frederick and Charlotte Peake of Burrough, Melton Mowbray, Leicestershire. Married Louisa, eldest daughter of Patrick H Osborne, NSW, in 1900. He is buried in Noeux-les-Mines Communal Cemetery, grave I. U. 2.

Brigades, Royal Field Artillery (three batteries of 18 pdr. QF guns and one of 4.5 in. QF howitzers). In addition, there were four batteries of trench mortars: X/29, Y/29 and Z/29 plus Y/23 attached from the 23rd Division. Whilst these batteries prepared positions for their guns, organised Observation Posts and communications, brought up and stockpiled ammunition, fitted out dugouts for men and stores alike, some were training hard for the anticipated advance. Y Battery of the 15th Brigade, RHA, for example, spent 16th June in driving drill and the training of its horse teams for the expected move forward and the crossing of both British and German trenches over wooden bridges specially constructed for them by the Royal Engineers.

The Royal Engineers, meanwhile, were busy both above and below ground. On the 18th June, the 1st West Riding Field Company, RE, completed the tram line which ran from Auchonvillers, just behind the front line, to Mailly Maillet. In less than a fortnight it would be heavily used by the men of the Divisional Field Ambulances to remove the wounded and dead from the battlefield. Not its anticipated purpose. Their colleagues in the 1/3rd Kent Field Company, RE, and the 1/2nd London Field Company, RE, meanwhile, were busy building roads, OPs, digging trenches, constructing dugouts, aid posts and dressing stations. They were helped by working parties from the infantry. No-one was to be spared from either work or training during the last two weeks of June.

The work underground, however, by the men of the 252nd Tunnelling Company, was, perhaps, the most arduous, the most unpleasant and just as dangerous as anything on the surface. The men of the Company had been digging tunnels and now Russian Saps along the whole length of the VIII Corps front. The work on one tunnel, designated H3, would culminate in the filming of one of the abiding images of the entire Battle of the Somme: the explosion of the huge mine under the Hawthorn Ridge redoubt.

The tunnellers had been clawing their way through the chalk and flint underlying the battlefield for months and the unit was proud of its achievements. In the War Diary for the 30th April 1916 it recorded:

> "This company has every record for the Army beaten by the driving in the Hawthorn mine. In this mine we made 35 feet in 24 hours, 200 feet in one week of 7 days, 322 feet in fourteen days, and 565 feet in 26 days. This in one tunnel with one face only and the length to destroy the enemy trench will be 1055 feet."[2]

It would be H3 that was to be filled with 40,600 lbs. of Ammonal explosive[i] and which would send the German garrison of part of the Hawthorn Redoubt sky high at 7.21 a.m. on the 1st July 1916. But this was not the only underground work in progress on the 29th Division's front. Two tunnels, shallower than the 75 foot deep H3 at 33 and 32 feet respectively, were being pushed out from 1st Avenue, opposite the Y Ravine, and Mary Redan, the southern limit of the 29th Division's front. The purpose of these two tunnels was to provide emplacements relatively close to the German front line from which the new quick firing Stokes mortars could bombard the enemy trenches during the last frantic 10 minute

[i] Ammonal is an explosive made up of Ammonium Nitrate, Trinitrotoluene (TNT) and Aluminium powder.

hurricane bombardment. Work on these tunnels averaged some 15 feet of excavation a day and on the 9th May the Company registered another record for underground digging on the Western Front, managing 277 feet in 24 hours across the 13 tunnels being dug. A few days later, however, problems began to emerge at the big mine under Hawthorn Ridge. Describing the work as 'extraordinarily difficult', the 252nd Tunnelling Company War Diary entry for 20th May went on to say:

> "The length is now 900 feet and work is being carried on silently by wetting the face and working the chalk out with bayonets. This face is now almost entirely flint and progress is very slow."[3]

Five days later, 29th Division added to their workload with a request for another tunnel, this time from Sap 7 towards the sunken lane which ran north from the New Beaumont Road on the British side of No Man's Land. This tunnel was started on 1st June and was dug down to a depth of 26 feet. Its purpose was to connect the British front line with the natural trench of this sunken road. Here would be photographed another iconic image of the first day on the Somme: the men of the 1st Lancashire Fusiliers nervously waiting to jump off at 7.30 a.m. on the morning of the 1st July 1916.

Although the Germans interfered with some of the tunnels on other parts of the VIII Corps' front, nothing untoward occurred for the tunnellers digging for the 29th Division. Their objective was to have all work completed by 20th June. And so, on they went.

The reason for the 20th June deadline was that, in the original timetable, this was the day on which the 'annihilation bombardment', as the 86th Brigade War Diary starkly describes it, was supposed to have started[4]. As has been explained earlier, this date had been postponed until the 24th June with Z Day on the 29th June. This delay gave everyone much needed extra time to prepare for the attack and, in the case of a significant part of the British artillery, time to register their targets and, in many cases, simply get used to firing their guns in anger.

This period was especially useful for the 4e and 5e Batteries of French 75 mm field guns from the 2e Groupe, 37e Regiment d'Artillerie de Campagne, which had been put at the disposal of VIII Corps on 19th June[i]. These two batteries occupied positions just to the east of Englebelmer, with the Group's HQ at Mailly Maillet. Apart from a very high rate of fire[ii], the 75 mm had two other advantages over the British 18 pdr. The first was that they had available an instantaneous graze fuse for their HE shells. Although somewhat unstable in flight and potentially dangerous to handle, this fuse made the 75 mm gun a very effective wire cutter. The reason for this was that the shell exploded as soon as the fuse touched anything. In other words, it would blow up the wire on contact rather than bury itself in the ground and create a crater full of wire. It would be some months before the British had supplies of a similar fuse and the benefits to the French of this fuse would be seen on their front to the south where the German wire presented little obstacle on the day of the attack.

---

[i] The third battery, the 6e Battery, was attached to the 48th (South Midland) Division and was located at Sailly au Bois.

[ii] A rate of 15 to 18 rounds per minute could be sustained for short periods.

Their other bonus was that they could fire two types of gas shell – the No. 4 shell contained *'Vincennite'*, a mixture of Cyanide and Arsenic, and the No. 5 shell contained Phosgene. For the British to use gas meant bulky and potentially lethal gas canisters being installed in the front line trench where men of the Special Brigade, RE., would wield large spanners with which to release the valves and the gas. Leaks, whether accidental or caused by the enemy, were frequent and barely a gas release went by without both Engineers and infantry suffering casualties from the gas. The 75s, however, could pepper a location with their lethal gas shells and, with their high rate of fire, the batteries were capable of creating a gas cloud over the target which, though quick to disperse, was potentially fatal to any German not wearing his mask. Targeting enemy artillery with gas shell was, therefore, a common tactic on the French front. Bearing these two points in mind, the allocation of targets in the area around Beaucourt sur Ancre and the lines of communication to the rear, seems to have been somewhat of a waste of these guns' special talents.

On 22nd June the gunners of the 17th Brigade, RFA, smothered the German trenches and wire with a flurry of 18 pdr and 4.5 in. howitzer shells. The 17th Brigade formed part of the Right Group of the 29th Divisional Artillery which was commanded by 17th Brigade's CO, Lt. Col. William Percival Monkhouse, CMG, MVO. Today, both the Brigade and the Group moved their HQs forward from the village of Englebelmer to dugouts in the Mesnil valley. The Right Group consisted mainly of 18 pdr batteries with the addition of one field howitzer battery:

17th Brigade: 26th, 92nd, 13th and 460th (D/17, Howitzer) Batteries

132nd Brigade: 370th, 371st Batteries

147th Brigade: 10th Battery

Attached from the 48th Division's artillery were B/243 and A/241 Batteries.

The total number of guns available to the Right Group was, therefore, 32 x 18 pdrs and 4 x 4.5 in. Howitzers.

The Left Group was commanded by Lt. Col. Douglas Evans Forman, CMG, of the 147th Brigade and was made up as follows:

147th Brigade: 97th, 368th, D/147 (Howitzer) Batteries

15th Brigade RHA: B, L and Y Batteries

132nd Brigade: 369th and D/132 (Howitzer) Batteries

Total number of guns available: 24 x 18 pdrs and 8 x 4.5 in. Howitzers.

The key job of the 18 pdrs of the Divisional artillery was the cutting of the German wire in front of the German support line, bombarding the German front line and, along two stretches of trench, cutting the front line wire. The 4.5 in. howitzers were mainly used to cut the wire in front of the Zwischen Stellung along the Beaucourt Road in conjunction with the 4.7 in. and 60 pdr guns of the Corps artillery, as well as set up permanent barrages on five key communication trenches running up from the village and Station Road to the front. The entire length of the Y Ravine was one of these targets.

The weapons tasked with cutting the majority of the front line wire were the 2 in. trench mortars, the famous 'toffee apples', which tests had shown to be excellent at cutting wire. There were three areas where this task was either shared or taken over by the 18 pdrs and these were the re-entrant between the

Hawthorn Redoubt and the Y Ravine where L Battery, 15th Brigade, RHA, assisted; the trenches immediately north of the Bergwerk (369th Battery); and on the trenches on the south side of the Y Ravine down to a point north east of Mary Redan where the 26th and 368th Batteries cut the wire.

From north to south, the front line bombardment targets of the 18 pdr batteries were:

369th – front line wire north of the Bergwerk and the Bergwerk

B/15 – trenches north of the Bergwerk

Y/15 – wire in front of support line behind the Bergwerk

L/15 – front line between the Hawthorn Redoubt and the New Beaumont Road and the front line in the re-entrant to the south of the redoubt

368th – the Hawthorn Redoubt

97th – the front line trenches in the re-entrant

10th – the front line trenches to the north of the end of the Y Ravine

13th – the front line trenches at the head of the Y Ravine

92nd – the front line trenches on the southern side of the Y Ravine

26th – the wire on the southern side of the Y Ravine and the front line trenches around the point where the German trenches turned south

368th – the front line wire to the north east of the Mary Redan

370th – the front line trenches to the north east of the Mary Redan

371st – the front line trenches opposite the Mary Redan

In addition, the 2 in. mortars of the Divisional Medium Trench Mortar Batteries were to take on certain sections of wire which the 18 pdrs, with their flatter trajectory, might find difficult to bombard. These turned out to be key areas for the attack: the Bergwerk, Hawthorn Ridge, the approaches to the Y Ravine and the area opposite Mary Redan. The central area opposite the Hawthorn Redoubt and the Y Ravine would prove to be a difficult target for the 18 pdrs as some guns, trying to fire over the ridge on which lay the British trenches, failed to clear it, causing alarm and possible casualties amongst the troops in the front lines. 'Friendly fire' by heavier guns was to prove a particular problem on the day of the attack. The 4.5 in. howitzers were to target certain key trench junctions and suspected machine gun and observation posts. During the night, the guns fired on 'night lines' to prevent German reliefs, working parties, ration parties, etc., moving to and from the front lines.

All of this was due to start at 5 a.m. on the morning of 24th June but, in the meantime, frantic activities continued in and behind the front lines. On the morning of the 23rd June all remaining civilians in the village of Mailly Maillet were ordered to leave and transport was provided to help move the families to a place of safety. They were sent on their way by a deluge of rain which started to fall at 3.30 p.m. The thunderstorm caused havoc in the trenches, flooding many and leaving most inches deep in a thick glutinous mud which made work and movement a slow and filthy process. Its impact on the timetable for the attack was not yet apparent.

In addition to the artillery preparation the 29th Division had other activities up their sleeve for the coming days. Along the whole length of the line from Gommecourt to Montauban there would be releases of gas and smoke, sometimes lacking any co-ordination with the activities of the neighbouring units and, at night, there would be a vigorous programme of patrols and raids. It was intended that these should serve a number of purposes:

1. To check the progress of wire cutting;
2. To explore the damage done to the German front line system;
3. To ascertain the alertness and strength of the defenders; and
4. To collect intelligence about the units opposite and, whenever possible, bring back a prisoner or two for interrogation.

These raids should indicate clearly the impact of the bombardment on the defenders of Beaumont Hamel and, one would imagine, the results, good or bad, would then be factored into the plan for the assault.

THE 24TH JUNE DAWNED DAMP. More heavy rain delayed the start of the field guns' activities but, as the day progressed and a persistent mist cleared, the sharp crack of the field guns followed seconds later by the puffs of smoke over the leading edges of the German wire showed that the wire cutting programme had begun in earnest. The 18 pdrs and trench mortars started to cut lanes in front of the 1st German line while the 4.5 in howitzers and 60 pdrs of the Corps artillery embarked upon a similar activity on the Zwischen Stellung. Progress with the wirecutting was deemed satisfactory, with obvious damage being caused in at least eight locations along the enemy front.

The 18 pdrs were allocated 160 shells per gun per day (i.e. 640 per battery) but because of the late start and the difficult observation not all of the available shells were used in the first 24 hours. The 17th Brigade, for example, fired, between 6 a.m. on the 24th and 6 a.m. on the 25th June[5]:

26th Battery 352 A (A = shrapnel)
13th Battery 444 A
92nd Battery 422 A
460th/D/17 404 BX (BX = 4.5 in. high explosive)

These batteries were firing at the western and southern edge of the area around the Y Ravine but not all of these shells were used to cut wire as there was a need to keep back a proportion for the night time firing with which to keep the gaps clear and German heads down. Every night a Battery Section was designated to keep firing with an allocation of 172 rounds per section per night. To help with this, the Division's Machine Gun Companies fired their guns at intervals both into gaps cut in the wire and along German communication trenches. Movement of any sort within the German lines was, therefore, a risky business. On the British side, though, life was not entirely trouble free. Given the huge number of shells manufactured in advance of the offensive it was inevitable that some would be faulty and there were 'prematures' in both the 18 pdr and 4.5 in. Howitzer ammunition which caused some casualties, most notably on this day, amongst the men of the 132nd Brigade.

Ammunition was replenished using the light railway which ran from the railhead at Acheux to the station at Auchonvillers and then on behind the British lines to Mesnil. Here there was a concentration of battery positions and, every night, wagons from the batteries and from the Divisional Ammunition Column shifted the shells from the railway trucks to the guns. All, except the 368th Battery, were serviced in this way but this unfortunate unit had to bring their ammunition up in wagons from the rear as the light railway was not able to supply them.

The German artillery response was muted, being most intense either side of lunchtime. General der Infanterie von Soden had ordered his artillery to be careful with its ammunition in view of the expected attack but, in order to help protect his limited array of mainly field guns and howitzers, they withheld fire unless it appeared essential, for example when gas and/or smoke were released by the British. By this means, they concealed themselves from the prying eyes of British observers in both aircraft and balloons. As a result, across most of the battlefield north of the Ancre, the inadequate quantity of British artillery devoted to counter battery work found targets to be either limited or, in the cases of guns like the 4.7 in. allocated to C/B work, simply out of range.

But not all German batteries escaped unscathed. In a shallow valley running north from Beaucourt between the Serre and Puisieux roads was an area called the Artillerie Mulde (Mulde = hollow) in which six German batteries were dug in, three from the I Abteilung, Württembergisches Reserve-Feldartillerie-Regiment Nr. 26. These positions were heavily targeted but, protected as they were by well-constructed and reinforced emplacements and with the gun crews and ammunition sheltered in nearby dugouts, the numerous 4.7 in. shells which fell around them did sparse damage, though some positions in the Artillerie Mulde and further back on the north bank of the Ancre were hit and severely damaged.

German observation of the British lines was mainly by means of tethered balloons of which six could be seen hanging in the sky from Bapaume north to the Bois de Logeast to the east of Bucquoy. Plans were afoot to deal with these Hun 'eyes in the sky'. But, otherwise, German air activity was minimal, allowing one British flyer to sweep low over the German front line without a care. As the war diary of the 29th Division's CRA noted:

> "One of our aeroplanes flew low over the enemy's trenches, very low but no enemy machine gun fired at it. It is thought that their machine guns are either in deep dugouts or have been removed as aeroplanes have never previously been permitted to fly so low without being fired on."[6]

Again, this report acknowledges the presence of the enemy's deep dugouts without commenting on the danger that machine guns kept securely away from the British artillery would present to the attacking infantry.

There had been a plan to release gas on the 29th Division's front at 10 p.m. but a shift in the wind put this on hold. The 4th Division on their left had no such problems and, at 10.11 p.m. the men of the Special Brigade, Royal Engineers, wielded their large spanners and released the valves on the White Star[i] canisters. The German response was immediate with a heavy artillery barrage falling on the 4th Division's front. The decision by the 29th Division not to release gas seems to have been vindicated by the fact that some of their neighbour's gas blew back into the British trenches to the north causing several casualties amongst both the infantry occupying the front lines and the Royal Engineers responsible for the release[ii].

---

[i] White Star was a poison gas mixture of 50% phosgene and 50% chlorine.

[ii] See chapter *'The 4th Division at Redan Ridge'*, for details of this mishap.

On a more cheerful note, a concert party was held at the Brigade HQ of the 88th Brigade. The GOC, 29th Division, Maj. Gen. de Lisle, was in attendance and minds were, at least for a time, taken off the forthcoming operation.

During the night the long guns of the Corps artillery and the field guns and howitzers started their planned barrage fire designed to cut off the German front line troops from food, equipment and their reserves. In addition, efforts were made to sweep the areas where the wire had been cut in front of the German front and support lines and in front of the Zwischen Stellung on the Beaucourt Road. The impact was immediate and the roads either side of the Ancre leading to Beaucourt and Grandcourt became impassable for any German wheeled transport and the light railways also found it impossible to function. Carrying parties were employed to bring supplies up hazardous routes along interminable communication trenches and, further to the rear, the centre of villages and other transport junctions became targets with Miraumont, Irles and Pys being especially badly hit. Within two days in Miraumont, the church belfry, an old Divisional HQ, the memorial to the dead of the 26. Reserve Division and a cinema were all destroyed by the British guns. Other than disruption to traffic, however, little material or human damage was inflicted on German troops defending the sector.

THE WEATHER ON THE 25TH JUNE WAS A MIRROR IMAGE of the day before. This time the heavy rain came in the evening, creating more mud in the trenches and softening the ground generally. Gas was released in the morning on the front of the 87th Brigade on the right of the Divisional front. The release was supervised by 2nd Lt. Wilfred Stanley Pheasey of the Royal Engineers and, after a short delay caused by a shift in the wind, the gas was released at 10.30 a.m., generating the standard German artillery response whenever gas or smoke were released. Mailly Maillet was briefly shelled and some casualties caused. The enemy seemed ready for the gas as, two minutes before the taps were turned on, a horn started to sound in the German lines only stopping when the gas had passed. It is impossible to say what, if any, casualties were caused but, again, gas leaked in the British lines and the operator in one bay was disabled before he had been able to turn on four of the eight cylinders under his charge.

The artillery programme continued as before with lanes being cut in the German 1st and 2nd trench line wire and in the wire in front of Beaucourt Ridge. The daily allocation for the 18 pdrs was now increased to 200 rounds per gun as the bombardment intensified. Today most of the Corps Heavy Artillery joined in, the exceptions being the two 12 in. Howitzers of the 65th Siege Battery and the three 15 in. Howitzers of the Royal Marine Artillery. They would start to pound their targets in Serre, Beaucourt and Beaumont Hamel on Monday, 26th June.

The job of cutting the more distant wire, which was out of the range of the 18 pdrs, was given to the 1/1st Highland and 1/1st Welsh Heavy Batteries (each four 4.7 in. guns) and the 139th Heavy Battery made up of four 60 pdr guns. To be honest, there was precious little else to be done with these obsolete 4.7 in. guns except interdicting roads and communications. How useful these guns were at these tasks is impossible to say accurately but it is thought that the wire in front of the German 2nd Position was damaged. Two other 60 pdr batteries, the 19th and 25th, were used to bombard some of the German positions but were also used for counter battery work and the barraging of roads and rear villages. The long guns had started firing on the 24th June but the weather had worked against them. The aeroplanes of the R.F.C. were unable to observe because of the wet and stormy weather and the wirecutting in front of the Beaucourt Road by such batteries as the 1/1st Welsh and 1/1st Highland (4.7 in. guns) could only be observed from the ground.

The howitzers' main objectives were the destruction of the German field fortifications in the German 1st Position and the Zwischen Stellung. The majority of the heavy howitzers had not fired on the 24th June except for two batteries, the 46th and 54th Siege Batteries, both of which tried their hands at some counter battery work. None of their 34 shells were observed and the shoot was halted. Around the 8 in. howitzers of the 54th Siege Battery the ground was so wet that the gun platforms sank into the mud, requiring several hours of back breaking work before they could shoot again.

Others continued to register their targets with the odd shot here and there. For No. 5 Howitzer of the Royal Marine Artillery one shot was enough. Capt. Hugh Boffey's men had laboriously loaded and fired one of their 1,400 lb. shells only for the equipment to fail. It didn't fire again until 5 a.m. on the 26th June.[7]

On the 25th June more of the medium howitzers joined in although they were still, mainly, registering targets rather than getting down to the serious business of destroying the enemy positions. The long guns continued cutting the distant wire, this time with some aerial observation which suggested good work was being done. The observers in the BE2cs of the R.F.C. were still struggling to identify the results of the firing because of the low cloud and poor observation but their colleagues in the 4th Brigade, R.F.C., had a more productive day, joining in a concerted attack on all 23 German balloons in the air along the B.E.F.'s front in the middle of the afternoon and bringing down three of them in the VIII Corps' area. Six enemy balloons had been noted on the previous day. They were:

In the direction of Warlencourt
In the direction of Bapaume
Over the Bois de Logeast
At Point G.34
South west of Le Sars
Over Grévillers

At 2 p.m. on 26th June the first German balloon fell burning to the ground to the south of the Bois de Logeast. A few minutes later the dracken hanging in the sky to the south west of Le Sars exploded and plummeted to the earth. A third fell at 7.15 p.m. near the village of Courcelles la Comte. As the aircraft attacked the balloons, the long range 6 in. Mk VII guns fired on the men manning the winches as they desperately tried to lower the balloons and their two observers to the ground.

The 26. Reserve Division's tethered balloon was attached to a winch in a grove of trees near the village of Grévillers, a village a couple of miles due west of Bapaume. Attacked by British aircraft firing incendiary rockets, the balloon was caught in the air and burst into flames. Its two occupants, Vizewachtmeister Thomas Auchter[i] and Leutnant der Reserve Eugen Welte[i], both died, Auchter

[i] Vizewachtmeister Thomas Auchter, 6th Battery, Reserve Feldartillerie Regiment Nr. 26, came from Zwiefalten.

during the attack and Welte on the way to the Reserve-Feld-Lazaret Nr. 2 in Vélu near Bapaume.

For the British infantry it was either working parties or training. Two battalions, the 1st Royal Dublin Fusiliers and the 16th Middlesex Regt. of the 86th Brigade due to attack Hawthorn Ridge on Z Day, were at the Divisional training ground at Louvencourt. Other parties were endeavouring to keep the front line and assembly trenches in reasonable order after the heavy rain of the past two days. They were fortunate that the enemy did not add to their travails by bombarding the lines in any meaningful way. The 88th Brigade was also busy training and rehearsing. The 4th Worcesters used the Louvencourt facility, this time working on keeping in touch with aeroplane contact patrols which would be essential as their anticipated advance moved out of front line observation. The 1st Essex Regt, meanwhile, rehearsed their attack which was to follow on from the initial advance by the other two Brigades of the Division. Apart from some casualties caused in a bombing accident, a Lt. Bartlett and four men were wounded, everything seemed to run smoothly. Gen. de Lisle was at the training ground and here he watched the Newfoundland Regt. practice for a raid due to take place the following night.

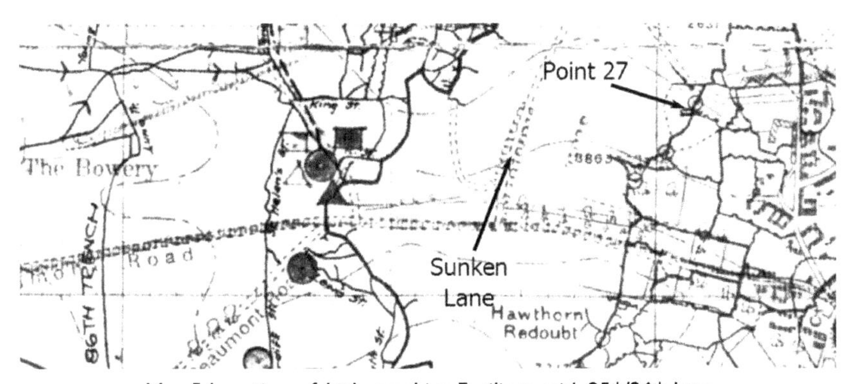

Map 5 Location of 1st Lancashire Fusiliers raid, 25th/26th June

Patrols and raids were very much the night time activity of choice. Demanded by Haig, heartily disliked by most front line troops, their regularity was a yardstick by which younger, 'thrusting' generals were judged. On the night of the 25th, five patrols from C Company of the 1st Lancashire Fusiliers slipped out of their trenches and cut five lanes through the German wire. 2nd Lt. Caseby's patrol opposite the end of Watling Street examined the wire about Point 27. His report showed the German wire defences to be dauntingly thick:

> "... the wire is about 40 yards deep reaching up to the enemy's parapet. At front edge of the wire (are) large iron knife rests which are unmoved, behind the knife rests the wire is much blown about and there are large holes in it 5 or 6 yards in diameter. There is no clear passage infantry

[i] Leutnant der Reserve Eugen Welte, 3rd Battery, Reserve Feldartillerie Regiment Nr. 26, is buried in the Kriegsgräberstätte in Villers au-Flos, Block 3, Grave 414. He came from Bavensdorf near Ravensburg and was commander of the Balloon detachment.

> could work through with little difficulty. The enemy have made no attempt to renew the wire in this sector."[8]

Clearly the gunners of the RFA had much work still to do.

MONDAY, 26TH JUNE WAS WARMER BUT STILL WET, with heavy rain, again in the evening. Gas was again discharged but precisely when would depend on which war diary one might favour. VIII Corps suggests 10.30 a.m. on the 86th Brigade front and 10.35 a.m. on the 87th Brigade front. The 29th Division diary talks of 10.45 a.m. and 11.20 a.m., while 132nd Brigade, RFA, mentions 'about 10 o'clock' and the 147th Brigade, RFA, states 10.15 a.m. while the 86th Brigade records the times as 10.30 a.m. and 1.30 p.m. Mid to late morning will have to suffice. 2nd Lt. Henry Charles Stephens, RE, on the 86th Brigade's front described a 5 mph south westerly wind which took the gas into the southern section of Beaumont Hamel and down Station Road. Although German retaliation was relatively light, one shell did blow a pipe back over the parapet and into the trench where four men were gassed, one seriously. This incident prompted some criticism from Stephens over the box respirator which he described as:

> "…clumsy with mouthpiece too short and difficult to hold in mouth both on that account and because there is no ridge on it."[9]

Not encouraging given the regularity with which gas was to be released in the coming days.

The 87th Brigade tried its hand at a smoke screen using smoke candles placed on the parapet of the front line trench. These belched noxious clouds of green, brown or yellow smoke but only if one was able to light them and here the weather made life difficult. Many of the candles were wet and only after stripping off the cases and setting fire direct to the powder within was anything possible. Several German snipers were sufficiently annoyed by the stinking cloud of fumes that enveloped their trenches that popping one's head over the British parapet to chart the cloud's progress was unwise in the extreme. Capt. Edward Vere Slater of the Royal Engineers, the man in charge of this little escapade, was prudent enough not to try this but he still had to watch as his hard won smoke cloud rolled off to the south and the valley of the Ancre, barely reaching the German front trenches.

With all of the heavy guns as well as the trench mortars, both 2 in. and 240 mm, involved in the bombardment the intensity had moved up several notches. The 2 in. trench mortars were especially feared by the German front line troops and the defences of the 9. Kompanie of the RIR 119 in the Hawthorn Redoubt were particularly badly hit by mortar bombs mainly fired to clear away the wire. Of course, the front line dugouts were excavated under No Man's Land so that the entrances faced away from the British guns, and so these bombs, some causing craters nearly 15 feet deep, had the capacity to badly shake the dugouts and their occupants.

The two lumbering 15 in. howitzers of the Royal Marine Artillery allocated to the 29th Division's front today started the process of the destruction of Beaumont Hamel and Beaucourt sur Ancre. These unassuming and ancient villages were to be flattened by the 1400 lb. shells of Nos. 1 and 5 Howitzers, RMA. No. 1 Howitzer had the most fun firing 40 rounds during the day at Beaumont,

Beaucourt and the Beaucourt Redoubt. No. 5 Howitzer's day was less satisfactory. Having targeted and demolished two houses at the north end of the village near to the church with six rounds the gun then failed to run out to its normal position and was unusable from 7 a.m. on the 26th to 8 a.m. on the 27th June. To make up for this, the 240 mm heavy trench mortars dug in at Tenderloin, lobbed a few of their 180 lb. bombs over the Bergwerk and into the village which was, 'much knocked about', according to the 29th Division diary.[10]

According to the report of the 46th Siege Battery, a German 15 cm battery, possibly the 1. Batterie, Fußartillerie-Bataillon Nr. 51, which occupied two battery positions east and north east of Beaucourt, was more than 'knocked about' by its 290 lb. Amatol filled 9.2 in shells:

"Gun seen to be blown to bits. Position completely destroyed."[11]

The 8 in. howitzers of the 56th Siege Battery dug in around Courcelles, fired 365 rounds during the day, ranging from Puisieux away to the north east at 4 a.m., to the rear of Beaumont Hamel and the Bergwerk and positions behind the Redan Ridge redoubt on the 4th Division's front. The other howitzer batteries firing on the German lines on the 29th Division's front were the:

- 81st Siege Battery, four 6 in. howitzers 30 cwt. pattern, firing on the north end of Beaumont Hamel, eastwards to the junctions with Munich Trench;
- 77th and 79th Siege Batteries, four 8 in. and 9.2 in. howitzers respectively, bombarding the Beaucourt Redoubt with the 79th also dealing with the three lines of trench of the Bergwerk and the 77th the three lines of trenches north east of the Mary Redan;
- 14th Siege Battery, four 6 in. howitzers 30 cwt. pattern, which, with assistance from the 56th and 81st Siege Batteries and the 19th and 25th Heavy Batteries, bombarded Wagon Road as far south as Beaumont Hamel church; and
- 23rd Siege Battery, four 6 in. howitzers 26 cwt. pattern, which, with assistance from 77th, 79th, 81st Siege Batteries and the 1/1st Highland and 1/1st Welsh Heavy Batteries fired on Station Road from Beaumont Hamel Church southwards as well as dealing with all of the trenches around the Y Ravine.

In other words, twelve howitzers were to deal with the three trenches of the German 1st Position, with each four gun battery having to cover an area 500 yards wide and 250 yards deep. Each battery's zone of 125,000 square yards contained at least 2,500 yards of fire and communication trenches. In addition, the howitzers had to fire on their other designated targets and in the special bombardments which occurred on a daily basis and lasted 1 hour and 20 minutes.

In addition, it was the view of the VIII Corps' Staff that the main line of resistance in the German lines would be the support trench which generally ran some 100 to 150 yards behind the front line trench. This trench, according to a document entitled *'Particulars Concerning Corps Heavy Artillery'*[12], was to be 'severely bombarded'. If one assumes, therefore, that the efforts of the heavy howitzers fell disproportionately on and around the support trench then it inevitably meant that the front line trenches were less heavily punished. The vast majority of the shells that fell on the German front trench came from the 18 pdr and 4.5 in.

howitzers of the field artillery which, though capable of firing very large quantities of shells, did not fire shells of the necessary weight to cause undue trouble to the men waiting in the dugouts. Some two thirds of all of the shells fired during the seven day bombardment were fired by the 18 pdrs, the vast majority of which was shrapnel fired either to cut wire or to prevent it from being repaired. The small proportion of 18 pdr HE shell, a large element of which was fired in the final 65 minute intense bombardment, made use of a shell containing just 13 oz. (368 gms) of the explosive Amatol. The HE shell of a 6 in. howitzer contained nearly ten times as much Amatol while that of a 9.2 in. howitzer sixty times more but these shells were falling predominantly on the support line and other areas much further to the rear.

The other weapon which might damage the first line trenches, and which certainly concerned the German front line infantry, was the 2 in. medium trench mortar. A 'toffee apple' bomb contained some 12.5 lbs. (5.6 Kgs) of Amatol or Ammonal. The ratio of explosive weight to shell weight was approximately 1 to 4 as the stresses on the bomb itself when fired were nowhere near as great as one fired along the rifled tube of a field gun (ratio of explosive to weight of shell for an 18 pdr HE shells was approximately 1 to 20). Though these bombs gouged out large craters and made life distinctly uncomfortable for the men within, they were still not capable of collapsing a deep German dugout. Furthermore, these weapons were mainly being used the cut the front line wire and, because of their locations in or close to the front line (their maximum range was 570 yards), they were favourite targets of the German artillery and minenwerfers and very difficult to conceal, as the heavy casualties amongst trench mortar crews would testify.

As a result, not only was the German front line trench not battered by sufficient shells heavy enough to do real damage to the dugouts, those that did fall tended to fall on the support line rather than the front line where, raids had clearly shown, a large proportion of the German garrison was concentrated.

Today, though, the weather, showers and mist, made observation both from the ground and the air tricky but the field guns stuck to their task and continued to wear a way through the German wire. It was not, however, entirely one way traffic. A 4.2 in. German shell burst to the rear of Y Battery of the 15th Brigade, Royal Horse Artillery, and killed 2nd Lt. Walter Drake[i].

The 2 in. medium mortars were now assisting with the wire cutting in those hard to reach sections of the German defences. Y/29 medium battery was attached to the 147th Brigade, RFA, which was bombarding the wire on Hawthorn Ridge. They did not enjoy an auspicious opening to the campaign. No. 1 mortar blew in its gun pit with its first faulty round. No. 2 gun fired just 30 rounds which, for a gun capable of one round a minute when pushed, was not an earth shattering output. Misfires were a regular complaint. At the same time Y/23 Battery, on loan from the 23rd Division, managed to fire 200 rounds in its first day's action, an altogether more satisfactory result.

---

[i] 2nd Lt. Walter Drake, Y Battery, 15th Brigade, Royal Horse Artillery, was aged 30. He was the son of Thomas Drake of Norwich; husband of Sophia Kate Drake of 21, Bantoft Terrace, Felixstowe Rd., Ipswich. He is remembered in Mailly Wood Cemetery, Mailly Maillet, Spec. Mem. North of Row Q., Plot 1.

More raids were planned for tonight. The 1st Lancashire Fusiliers were again out and about the German wire. Two officer patrols disappeared into No Man's Land at about 10.30 p.m. On the left a patrol of three officers and 40 men set to work hacking five lanes through the wire in readiness for the attack. Another two lanes were started and rendered passable. On the Lancashire's right three more officers with a party of other ranks examined the wire. In general, it appeared as though the 18 pdrs and 2 in. mortars were doing a decent job. The wire was being cut but the lanes needed widening and clearing in order to give easier access. The problem lay along the front edge of the barbed wire barrier. Here, a row of heavy iron knife rests were fastened to each other by very thick wire and fixed to the ground by strong iron screw staples. It was clear that only a direct hit by a shell (and not the shrapnel being fired at it) would disturb their forbidding presence.

To their right, three officer patrols of the 2nd Royal Fusiliers scouted the wire near Point 89, towards the northern end of the Y Ravine, but did not attempt to gain access. Here, they reported, the wire was little damaged. To their right, three officer patrols of the 2nd South Wales Borderers took advantage of the hour 'quiet period' when the artillery and machine guns did not fire, to examine the wire at the nose of the Y Ravine salient and the area further south. They found three passable gaps within 250 yards of one another on the southern shoulder of the salient. In general terms, the wire to the south of the Y Ravine seemed easier to cut than that to the north and along the Hawthorn Ridge.

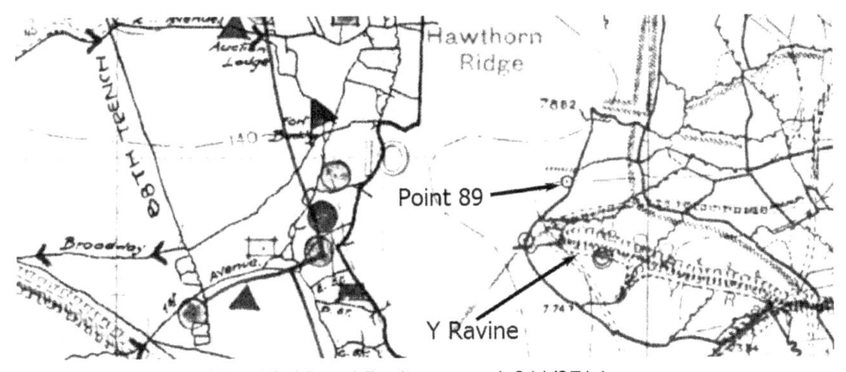

Map 6 2nd Royal Fusiliers patrol, 26th/27th June.

The big event of the night was to be a raid by the Newfoundland Regt., the preparations for which had been witnessed by Maj. Gen. de Lisle at Louvencourt. The raid was led by Capt. Bertram Butler. Butler was from Topsail, Newfoundland, and had been a banker before the war. He would finish the war with the DSO, an MC and Bar and having been Mentioned in Despatches. But tonight he would be frustrated. His party left their trenches at 11.30 p.m. as per programme. The covering fire from the artillery started at midnight and went on until 12.15 a.m. at which time a Bangalore torpedo was successfully blown in the German wire but failed to clear the necessary path. A second five minute barrage was ordered and the party withdrew to their forming up position before advancing again. A second Bangalore torpedo was placed in the partial gap blown but this one refused to detonate. They then resorted to wire cutters but these too failed. Sentries were on the alert in the German trenches, however, and Lt. der Reserve Breitmeyer, 9. Kompanie, RIR 119, and his men engaged Butler's party with rifle fire. Sensibly, discretion overcame valour and Butler withdrew his men to the relative safety of the British trenches.

A short time after they returned, at 2 a.m., the gas from 18 cylinders not used the day before was released.

Brig. Gen. Cayley, GOC 88th Brigade, appended a handwritten note to Butler's report to Division. It read:

"To raid same place again tonight."[13]

Not, perhaps, the news the Newfoundlanders were hoping to hear.

Butler's report reached VIII Corps HQ on the 27th along with the details of four other failed raids on the Corps' front but, rather than be disappointed with the outcome, the Corps commander considered:

> "...they attained most useful results, as it has been established the enemy's front line trenches are strongly occupied."[14]

Quite why this should have been regarded as good news is something of a mystery.

Plate 12 Capt. Bertram Butler, 1st Newfoundland Regt.

TO MAKE EVERYONE FEEL A BIT BETTER No. 1 Howitzer, RMA, and the Division's heavy trench mortars flattened Beaumont Hamel on the 27th June. 107 240 mm mortar shells and 25 15 in. howitzer shells rained down on the sad remains of the village. Another 25 15 in. shells were contributed by No. 5 RMA now back in action. Its targets were around, and to the south, of the church and nine direct hits on houses were observed, though the dust and smoke enveloping the remains of the village made observation of the other sixteen shells impossible. The medium howitzer batteries, the 6 in., 8 in. and 9.2 in. had now moved off the German support lines and Zwischen Stellung and were bombarding trenches away to the east with, they reported, very satisfactory results. That the majority of the German garrison were sheltering in their deep dugouts and in the medieval tunnels burrowed into the surrounding slopes might have tempered the enthusiastic reports of the destruction as none of these guns were bombarding the front line areas where lurked the main German garrison.

Otherwise, the day was not an especially auspicious one for the field gunners. It rained heavily – again – and observation was consequently poor. But 'prematures' seemed the order of the day and these caused casualties. One officer and four men of the 17th Brigade, RFA, were wounded by the early explosions of shells[i]. The OC, 371st Battery, Capt. C G Hetherington, was also rushed to hospital when an 18 pdr shell blew up prematurely. In total, the Divisional artillery lost six men killed and 34 wounded. And to complete the picture, the remaining gun of Y/29 medium trench mortar battery was put out of action when a mortar shell burst at the muzzle. On the up side, however, Y/23 happily fired another 200 'toffee apples' into the German wire and D/147 Battery proved the effectiveness of its respirators when twice showered with gas shells by the enemy.

Enemy artillery activity was a bit more vigorous than on previous days. The day before a direct hit had destroyed the northern OP of the 29th Division, killing a telephonist based there. Today the enemy artillery concentrated on the trenches, causing some damage in the front and support lines and adding to the repair work the heavy rain had already caused.

Somewhat further back numerous raiding parties were busy being briefed and equipping themselves because tonight the world and its wife would be out in No Man's Land. Raids were planned by the Lancashire Fusiliers, the Royal Fusiliers, the Middlesex Regt., the Border Regt. and the Newfoundland Regt. Very soon they would all be blundering around in the dark hoping that the German sentries would not hear them. Unfortunately, the lookouts from the 2., 10. and 11. Kompanien, RIR 119, were on the alert.

The Lancashire Fusiliers sent out fifteen NCOs and men under 2nd Lt. Eric William Sheppard and 2nd Lt. Clement Rudd from Sap 7 towards Point 27. The intention was to enter the German lines and seize a prisoner for interrogation. They were allowed one hour for the task and, given the ease with which C Company's patrols had wandered up and down the German wire the night before, they somewhat rushed the approach to the enemy positions. But, instead of easy access through the wire, they found it insufficiently cut to admit a large party and, as the officers and three men struggled through the gap, flares were sent skywards from the German lines. The result was predictable. Thoroughly alerted, the Germans in their front line subjected the raiders to heavy rifle and machine gun fire with a few grenades thrown in for good measure. After sheltering in some shell holes, from which they lobbed the odd Mills bomb hopefully in the direction of the enemy, the Fusiliers withdrew to be greeted by a German artillery barrage on the British front line. 2nd Lt. Rudd was wounded, two men killed and five others wounded.

---

[i] The casualties were: Maj. Robert Carlisle Williams, 92nd Battery, with a severe chest wound, and 80989 Act/Bdr Sidney Goodwright, 53812 Gnr. Frederick S Fitch, 32953 Gnr. Henry Hurst and 42383 Gnr. Arthur Robinson, all 460th (Howitzer) Battery.

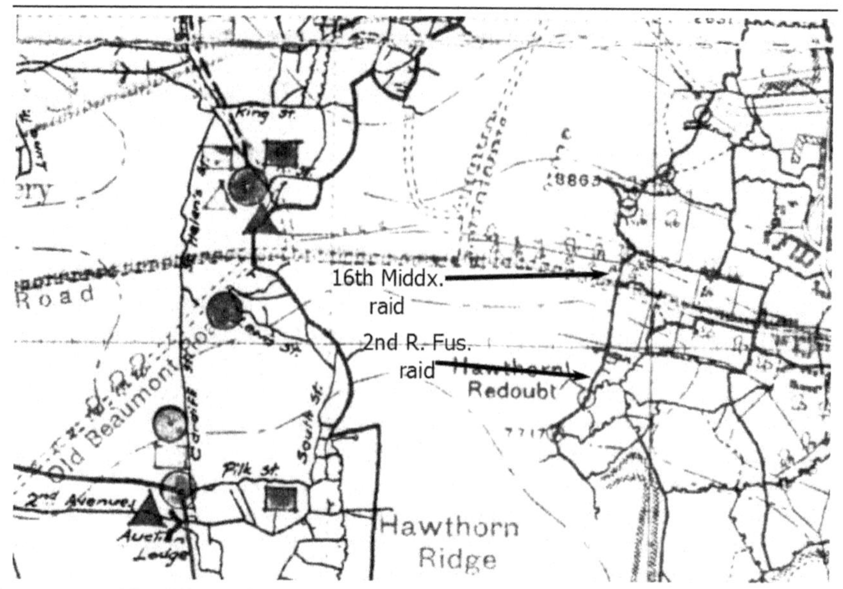

Map 7 Sites of Royal Fusiliers and Middlesex raids, 27th/28th June.

The Royal Fusiliers were not much luckier. Their objective was the German line just to the north of the Hawthorn Redoubt. Fifteen other ranks under 2nd Lt. Hurle and Sgt. Turner from W Company, 2nd Royal Fusiliers, followed a Lancashire Fusilier guide out from Bridge End towards a gap cut by C Company of the Lancashires the night before. The guide took them to the correct place but there, behind the wire previously cut, was another row through which the party could not find a way. Hurle took his men back through the first gap before he and Turner crept through the wire to the parapet of the German trench. They were challenged and fire was opened on them. In the hurried withdrawal one man was wounded and touch was lost with Sgt. Turner and another man. Both men survived.

One thing nobody noticed at the time was a man slipping away from the patrol and into the German lines. Pte. Josef Lipmann was a 23 year old Russian Jew who had lived in England for two years before the outbreak of the war. Now, seriously disillusioned after nine months of purgatory on the Gallipoli peninsula, he had had enough. He had decided to desert and saw his opportunity when volunteers for the patrol were called for and, when he approached the enemy trench, his few words of German prevented him from being shot out of hand by the German defenders. With him went more than a little information about the plan for the attack along Hawthorn Ridge. Of course, he was not to know that Z Day was about to be postponed but he knew enough to tell his German interrogators that there was to be five days of bombardment before an early morning attack (the precise time of zero hour was not yet public). Details of which regiments were to attack, how his particular battalion was to be employed and even the colour codes for rockets and flares were all passed on. In all, it was a disastrous breach of security undoubtedly made worse by information less willingly gathered from badly wounded survivors of the various patrols who were taken prisoner by the men of RIR 119. After the battle there were suspicions of other damaging leaks, perhaps telephone or buzzer calls intercepted by the German listening post at the head of the Leiling Schlucht.

Meanwhile, the twelve men of the 16th Middlesex Regt., under Lt. Charles Cleghorn, at least had the satisfaction of getting in, or close to, the German trenches. Taken across No Man's Land by another Lancashire Fusilier guide at 11.10 p.m., they left from south of the Horseshoe and moved along the New Beaumont Road to attempt an entry at the Bergwerk. They found a partial gap in the wire and only Cleghorn and two men managed to get into the German trench. Whilst they waited for the rest of the patrol to arrive they were subjected to a barrage of rifle grenades and bombs from a traverse to the north occupied by men of the RIR 121. A machine gun opened up and, in apparent response to two red rockets, a shrapnel barrage was opened over the Sunken Lane. Cleghorn[i] ordered a withdrawal but not before he chucked two Mills bombs in the direction of the machine gun which was firing from a position some 30 yards behind the front line. Two men were slightly wounded in the raid and it took the last two men nearly three hours to get back to the British lines.

In all, the 86th Brigade's raids had been failures. Casualties were mercifully light but the findings of the officers leading the patrols were ominous. Sheppard of the Lancashire Fusiliers concluded:

> "The wire is not sufficiently cut to allow of the passage of a large number of men, at any rate at night, and it appears the line is strongly held at night."[15]

Hurle of the Royal Fusiliers reported:

> "… that the sentries are doubled and that there are sentry groups about every three bays. Machine guns were very active and the officer reports that he saw at least five firing."[16]

And Cleghorn wrote:

> "The wire was not very well cut and a large body of men would have great difficulty in getting through."[17]

The raiders of the 1st Border Regt., of the 87th Brigade fared little better. Fifty men from D Company under Lt. David Bremner left Acheux during the afternoon. Their objective was opposite the Mary Redan and the party left Knightsbridge at 10.45 p.m. in two groups. Bremner and the main group worked their way up the mud-filled communication trenches at the top of Shaftesbury Avenue where they expected to meet a smaller party carrying two Bangalore torpedoes led by a guide from the Royal Inniskilling Fusiliers. This party eventually arrived 15 minutes late, at five minutes past midnight, having gone overground because the trenches were too muddy and congested to accommodate the lengths of pipe. But all to no avail. The fuse holes were choked

[i] Temp. Lt. Charles Reid Cleghorn, 16th Middlesex Regt., was awarded the MC for his actions on 27th June 1916. The citation in the *London Gazette* of 22nd September 1916 reads: "For conspicuous gallantry. He raided the enemy's front trench with a small party to see if it was strongly held, forcing his way through the wire with great difficulty. He showed the greatest determination under heavy rifle, grenade and bomb fire".

with mud and the torpedoes useless. Undaunted, Bremner and his men struck out through the British wire towards the expected gap in the German wire. Finding it still standing they steadily cut through it that is until the final eight feet where they came up against a thick mass of iron knife rests. When several machine guns opened fire as a result of the Newfoundland raid off to their left, and the German illuminated No Man's Land with a number of flares, Bremner and his men prudently retired to their own lines, where they arrived at 1.20 a.m. Casualties, like the results of the raid, were nil.

The last, and most intense, raid of the night was the repeat of the Newfoundland Regt.'s foray of the night before against the southern flank of the Y Ravine. The bare facts are these: the raiding party formed up under cover of an artillery barrage at 11.30 p.m., moving forward at midnight when the barrage lifted onto the German support line. The Bangalore torpedoes were not needed as the wire was well cut but the German trench was thronged with men. After a brisk fire fight, in which it was thought casualties were inflicted on the enemy as evidenced from the 'groans coming from the German trenches', the party withdrew. All three officers were wounded, two men killed and ten wounded. A further seven were missing. Capt. Butler's report, however, paints a more detailed and graphic picture:

> "Party left our trenches at 2325 and formed up in front of hedge in Q.16.b
> 2335 Moved in three lines in file towards enemy trenches halting at a point about 150 yards from enemy wire, four scouts going ahead to a point about 50 yards further. Waiting there until midnight.
> 0003 Left forming up place and proceeded to a point about 60 yards from wire and waited. In the meantime Bangalore torpedo men carried torpedoes forward and NCO reconnoitred wire. Bombers went up with this party.

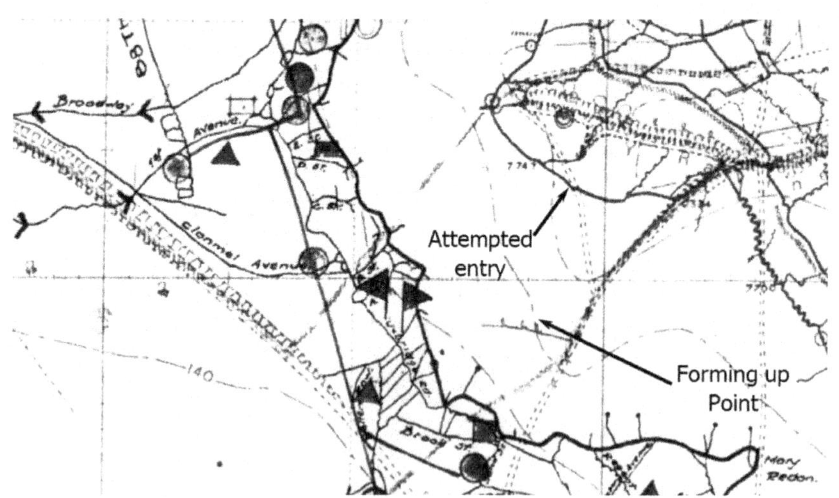

Map 8 Newfoundland Regt. failed raids, 26th/27th & 27th/28th June.

0020 As torpedo had not been heard to explode OC Party moved up to the torpedo men who were along a large gap practically straight through enemy wire (which was about 15 yards in width at this point).
The wire was reconnoitred and the gap was found to be complete, hardly a strand being in the way. The gap would be about 5 yards wide but all the wire in the vicinity was badly cut up and in daylight ought not to present any difficulty to infantry getting through with ease.
At 0030 a man was sent back to main party with the order to advance, the bombers remaining in the wire and the scouts laying tape also advancing.
At 0057 Head of party arrived at entrance of gap (progress had been slow owing to the numerous flares which were being sent up all along enemy front. Most of these flares were sent up from his support trench). The party was fired on from the front trench, a burst of rifle fire and bombs coming from directly in front of gap.
We immediately extended to single rank and faced enemy trench, every man throwing bombs which were very effective, many landing direct into enemy trench. This continued for about 5 minutes, two of the officers being hit by bombs that fell in front of enemy wire. Some of our men (about four) were on enemy parapet and one German was bayoneted and another shot by them.
Owing to the number of bombs thrown by us the supply was getting rather low and, as the German trenches were heavily manned, it was deemed inadvisable to go further. Our casualties were increasing rapidly so it was decided to retire with the wounded back to the hedge, the gap in wire being held by our bombers and riflemen.
The fight lasted about 25 minutes, the covering party being withdrawn at 0115.
The enemy used bombs and rifle fire mostly but machine guns were busy on either flank. Most of their fire was wild but their bombs were very effective. Trench mortars also placed a few bombs in their own wire, whilst their artillery put several lachrymatory shells in No Man's Land about 100 yards from their wire. Three of our men were gassed but recovered soon afterwards. These shells were sent over about 0105.
The wounded were got back to the trees in hedge at Q.16.b and several cases of exemplary conduct were observed, some men going back to enemy wire 3 or 4 times for wounded comrades. Covering party returned to trees about 0125 reporting that the only men that were still out had been examined and found dead. As they were in the enemy wire it was thought inadvisable to send out for them.
The party returned to our trenches and were found to be 21 short.
This deficit was made up as follows: killed 2, missing 8, wounded 11. Later information gives: killed 3, missing believed killed 3, missing 1, wounded 13[i].

---

[i] The CWGC records four men of the 1st Newfoundland Regt. as having died on Wednesday, 28th June 1916. Their bodies were not found and they are remembered on the Beaumont Hamel (Newfoundland) Memorial:

Plate 13 547 Pte. John Thomas Lukins, 1st Newfoundland Regt.

At least three of our men penetrated into enemy trench. Two were apparently bayoneted and fell in the trench. The third returned to our wire just before daylight. His story is as follows:
He was a wire cutter and consequently well to the front with three or four more men. As soon as fire was opened from enemy trench he rushed forward to enemy parapet. He stabbed two men with his bayonet, one had a round cap on with a badge like two buttons in front. The other wore a helmet with a spike.
He lay on the parapet for a while apparently undetected and as enemy fire directly in front of him had subsided he entered the trench. This bay was unoccupied and was blocked with sandbags at either end, apparently very recent work.
In this bay there was a dugout entrance which might have led to other bays. His last bomb was thrown in here. He was unable to find any identification as there was nothing in this place and the bays on either side were occupied.
He cannot say how long he was in the trench but when he left it he had to cut a way through with his wire cutters. His appearance on return looked as if he had been through a lot of barbed wire. On arriving outside the wire he lay in some tall nettles and fired all his ammunition, 120 rounds at enemy parapet where flashes were seen. By the light of flares he got some good shots in and thinks he accounted for some of the enemy. While he was in German trench he afterwards heard many groans and he says the bombs from our men must have done considerable damage. He retired to a shell hole about 100 yards from enemy wire and lay there with two others until machine gun fire had subsided."[18]

195 Pte Edward Louis Cole, aged 20. He was the son of Edward James and Fanny Jane Cole, of 46, Gilbert St., St. John's.
547 Pte John Thomas Lukins, A Company, was aged 26. He was the son of Frederick and Johanna Lukins and husband of May Campbell, of 12, Bell St., St. John's. They had three daughters. Lukins worked as a clerk. His body was recovered by the Germans who notified the Red Cross that he had been shot through the heart. His remains were subsequently lost. His half-brother Pte George Wilson Lukins was killed on 1st July 1916.
1588 Pte Edward West, aged 20. He was the son of Mrs Rose Shelley, of Apsey Cove, Fogo. A fisherman, he lived at Ladle Cove, Fogo.
944 Pte Arthur Wight, D Company, was aged 26. He was the son of Samuel and Annie Wight, of Shoal Brook. Bonne Bay. He was a carpenter.

The man whose exploits Butler recounts in his report was 1164 Pte. George Phillips of Whitbourne, Trinity Bay. At the recommendation of both Col. Hadow, CO of the Newfoundlanders, and Brig. Gen. Cayley, GOC 88th Brigade, he was subsequently awarded the Military Medal and the Russian Order of St George, 3rd Class, for his actions[i]. He would receive neither award before he was killed on the Somme in October.

Capt. Butler[ii] was also decorated with the first of the two Military Crosses he was to win.

One man not to win an award was 408 Pte. Frederick Michael O'Neill. One cannot understand why. His action is described thus in Richard Cramm's *'The First Five Hundred'*:

> "Private F M O'Neill, seeing an enemy bomb thrown in the midst of his party and realizing the danger to the entire party picked up the bomb and threw it back. It exploded on leaving his hands and severely wounded him, but his quick and brave act undoubtedly saved several of his company." [19]

Evacuated to England on 1st July, O'Neill returned to Newfoundland at the end of September. He was discharged from the Army as medically unfit on 31st January 1917 with two fingers in his left hand paralysed by bomb fragments that

---

[i] 1164 Pte George Phillips, MM, 1st Newfoundland Regt., was aged 27. He was the son of William and Sarah Phillips, of Whitbourne, Newfoundland. He was a lumberman. He survived 1st July with a gun shot wound to his right hand and left ear. He rejoined the battalion on 8th September and was killed at Gueudcourt on 12th October 1916. His body was never found and he is remembered on the Beaumont Hamel (Newfoundland) Memorial. The citation for the Military Medal, listed in the *London Gazette* of 19th December 1916, reads: "For gallantry in the raid on the night of 28th/29th (sic) June 1916. Displayed conspicuous gallantry in the raid 27th/28th June south of Beaumont Hamel. He entered the enemy trench and accounted for several of the enemy single handed. After getting out of the trench he went back again to try and obtain some identification. Remained out all night and had to cut his way back through enemy's wire. This man also took part in the attack south of Beaumont Hamel on July 1st and showed great gallantry. He was wounded on this date".

His two awards were formally presented on 4th June 1917 by Lt. Col. Sir W E Davidson, KCMG, then commanding the Newfoundland Regt. Although undoubtedly brave, Phillips was also something of a trouble maker and was brought up on charges in front of his officers no less than eleven times between May 1915 and March 1916. Drink appears to have been the problem and he was four times accused of being drunk, on which occasions he twice resisted arrest, once struck an NCO and once abused an NCO.

[ii] Capt. Butler's MC was listed in the *London Gazette*, September 22nd, 1916. Action date, June 26th/27th, 1916, Beaumont-Hamel. Raid. "For conspicuous gallantry during operations. He commanded a raiding party on two successive nights with great determination in face of heavy opposition. A few days later he took part in an attack on the enemy's lines and did fine work". He was also mentioned in the 88th Brigade Lists: "On the night of June 26th/27th, 1916, south of Beaumont-Hamel, he was in command of a raiding party which failed to achieve its objective. On the following night the raid was repeated. This officer led the raid with courage and ability. A severe fight took place and the party only returned after all three officers, including Capt. Butler, had been wounded".

could not be removed and no use of his right thumb. Rather belatedly (and inadequately) he was Mentioned in Despatches on 1st June 1917[i].

966 Pte. John Joseph Cahill from St John's was another hero that night. He brought in one of the wounded and, later, on his own initiative he went back out into No Man's Land in an effort to bring in another casualty. He was never seen again. The sad conclusion to the story is that Cahill was severely wounded and taken prisoner whilst on his mission of mercy. He died a week later, on 5th July, and is buried behind the German lines at Achiet le Grand[ii]. He, too, was belatedly Mentioned in Despatches though rather earlier than O'Neill with Cahill's appearing on 8th January 1917.

23-year old seaman 809 Pte. John Cox from Harbour Breton was awarded the Military Medal for his conduct during the raid. The citation reads:

> "For gallantry in the raid on the night of 28th/29th June 1916. During a raid in connection with the operations of July 1st south of Beaumont Hamel when, owing to severe fire the raiding party had to retire after very heavy losses, he showed conspicuous gallantry and contempt of danger in covering the retirement, remaining out all night to perform his task".[20]

Pte. Cox survived the war to live in the USA in spite of being severely wounded in mid-October 1916 at Gueudcourt in the fighting in which George Phillips, MM, died.

At the same time as the raids were taking place the 2nd South Wales Borderers had three officer patrols out in No Man's Land on the southern flank of the Y Ravine salient. The three patrols left Sap 3 close to the Mary Redan at intervals between 11.35 p.m. and midnight. The left patrol managed to clear or enlarge three existing gaps created by the artillery before the rumpus caused by the Newfoundlanders made wandering around No Man's Land somewhat unsafe. The centre patrol found the wire generally well cut but hacked away another 21 foot gap for good measure before German machine guns and red rockets presaging an artillery barrage made it prudent to withdraw. The right patrol was

---

[i] 408 Pte. Frederick Michael O'Neill was aged 20. He was the brother of John O'Neill of 49, Angel Place, St John's. He was a labourer. The MiD, listed in the *London Gazette* on 1st June 1917, reads: "Displayed the greatest gallantry and coolness during a raid on the night of 28th June 1916. A bomb was thrown by the enemy which he at once picked up and threw back at the enemy. The bomb burst on leaving his hand and he was severely wounded. But for his promptitude the bomb would undoubtedly have caused other casualties in the raiding party. The case had only just been brought to notice owing to the man being invalided out of the Service from his wounds and others who witnessed the action having become casualties during the raid."

[ii] 966 Pte John Joseph Cahill died of wounds on 5th July 1916. Aged 36, he was the son of the late Joseph and the late Mary Cahill, of St. John's, Newfoundland. He lived at 208, Water Street West, St John's, with his stepbrother Edward Croke. He was a fireman. He is buried in Achiet le Grand Communal Cemetery Extensions, grave IV. X. 8. He was mentioned in 88th Brigade Despatches for his action. Oddly, according to his personal file, he died of his wounds, gunshot wounds to the lung and neck, in hospital in Minden, Germany. Pte Cahill's MiD reads: "Took part in a raid on the night 27th/28th June south of Beaumont Hamel displayed conspicuous gallantry in bringing in a wounded man, and after the raid went out on his own initiative to bring in another wounded man and was never seen again."

the latest to leave and arrived at the German wire at 12.20 a.m. Here they found two gaps about ten yards apart. The gaps, however, were only six feet wide and the patrol was about to start work widening the breach when enemy machine gun and rifle fire and a barrage on the British front line prompted their immediate withdrawal.

Typically, VIII Corps' diary the following morning, 28th June, managed to find a silver lining in the cloud of 100% failed raids in their sector, stating that:

> "...some useful information (was) obtained as to occupation of trenches by enemy and progress of wire cutting."[21]

Brig. Gen. Lucas of 87th Brigade expressed a rather more serious concern in his personal diary. It was one that would trouble a battalion commander in 86th Brigade, Lt. Col. Nelson of the Dublin Fusiliers, within 24 hours:

> "28th June
> Last night's wire cutting and raiding parties were not a great success anywhere. The Germans seem to have expected it as all the parties were fired upon, and so came back."[22]

With the Germans having a listening post in the Y Ravine, the possibility that the arrangements for the raids had been overheard as a result of the indiscreet use of a front line telephone or buzzer is very real. One wonders just how much other information had been given away as a result of indisciplined use of communications equipment close to the British front line?

THE CORPS NEEDED SOME CHEERING UP because the weather was still bad on Wednesday, 28th June, with heavy rain and poor light hindering the work of the gunners once again. Cutting wire was still the main task of the 18 pdrs and 2 in. trench mortars and today, like previous days, was a tale of two trench mortar batteries. Y/29 at last managed to get one gun into action. Then the rifle mechanism jammed after a few rounds. Next, as they tried to repair that, the pit was blown in by a German shell. Meanwhile, those smug 'so and sos' from Y/23 fired another 200 rounds before happily going home for their tea.

Again, the medium howitzers were away bombarding distant trenches to the east. The two 15 in. RMA howitzers continued their blitz on Beaumont Hamel and Beaucourt villages with 48 rounds on Beaumont and 31 on Beaucourt and the redoubt. More houses were destroyed and more debris seen to shoot skyward. The wear on the guns was, however, beginning to tell. One 6 in. gun had been condemned and was out of action, a 6 in. howitzer was also out of action because of a broken sight bracket, while three of the eight 4.7 in. guns needed to be repaired during the day. There was also a big problem with No. 1 Howitzer RMA. Its traversing arc had broken and required replacing. As a result, the gun had slewed 45° to the south making firing at its two village targets an interesting exercise for the gun team.

The big news of the day, however, came from on high. Z Day was postponed 48 hours. Apparently, the weather had done its work and the cancellation was just as well according to the 86th Brigade diary which described the trenches as a 'muddy stream'. But then again, the progress with wire cutting was clearly highly variable and more time to do the job was certainly useful. On the 29th Division's front only the Newfoundlanders had experienced little trouble from barbed wire when approaching the German lines but all of the other raiding parties had found it was insufficiently cut to allow to them get through with any ease or, indeed, at all. How this can be squared with VIII Corps' wire report on the morning of the 29th June is difficult to fathom. Certainly, on the southern side of the Y Ravine the comments are supported by the Newfoundlanders' findings, i.e. the wire was 'absolutely cleared away or well cut'[23]. But the reports from patrols sent out to examine the wire between Point 89 and the Hawthorn redoubt were worrying: 'Two parties report wire very much damaged, other two report not much damaged'. Given that the three raids to the north of the redoubt all showed the wire either incompletely cut or passable by only a few men at a time and one gets an impression that a considerable amount of work was still required by the artillery if the northern half of the divisional front was to be acceptably clear of German wire. Perhaps the interference from the weather provided the powers that be with a good excuse for delaying the attack 48 hours as wire reports like those from the Beaumont Hamel sector weren't that uncommon on other parts of the front. Who knows what disaster might have befallen the attacking troops had the attack gone ahead as scheduled?

And on the 29th Division's front there was another issue. The 'annihilation bombardment' had clearly not annihilated anything much. The German front lines, however battered they appeared to be, were still full of men with plenty of fight and armed with plenty of machine guns. Those dugouts discovered in previous weeks and months seemed to be doing their job of sheltering the garrison most effectively. The Germans might be tired, hungry, thirsty and even frightened but they were still there, still alert, still fighting – still very dangerous.

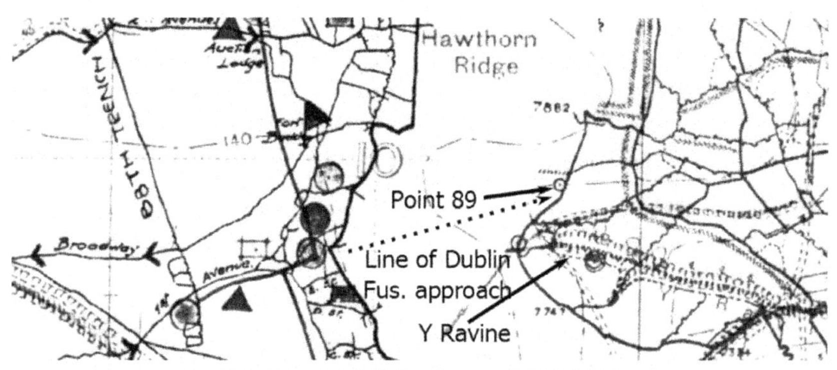

Map 9 1st Royal Dublin Fusiliers raid, 28th 29th June.

The men of the 1st Royal Dublin Fusiliers were to find out precisely how dangerous on another disastrous night of raids for VIII Corps. This raiding party was large: three officers, Lt. Robert George Arthur Gun-Cuninghame[i], Lt. Angus

[i] Lt. Robert George Arthur Gun-Cuninghame, 1st Royal Dublin Fusiliers, was aged 20. He was the fourth child and first son of Maj. Cornwallis Robert Ducarel Gun-Cuninghame DL, JP, High Sheriff of County Wicklow, of Mount Kennedy, Co. Wicklow and his first wife, Isabella Wingfield. He was commissioned into the 3rd Royal Dublin Fusiliers on 10th October 1914 and was promoted Lt. on 26th August 1915. He married Emily Frances Grace O'Callaghan in 1927, two daughters, one son. He died in 1970.

John Willans Pearson[i] and 2nd Lt. Joseph Devoy, DCM[ii], and 80 other ranks. Their task was to enter the German lines, seize a prisoner if possible or at least identify the unit opposite and cut any wire obstructing progress. The objective was the German line at Point 89. To achieve this, the party was divided into two portions: one to enter the enemy trench and the other to cut wire and act as a covering party. 2nd Lt. Devoy was sent out first from the junction of 1st Avenue and the front line trench to lay guide tape in No Man's Land across to the German wire under cover of the barrage but, at about 1.20 a.m., he was slightly wounded in the hand and this caused some delays with the result that the two groups did not leave the British trenches until 1.30 a.m. Gun-Cuninghame led the trench party while the battalion intelligence officer, Lt. Pearson, took over from 2nd Lt. Devoy in charge of the covering party.

Gun-Cuninghame's party crossed No Man's Land unmolested and found the wire at Point 89 well cut. Worryingly, however, the wire either side was, in places, still 15 yards deep. As they approached the edge of the German wire an enemy patrol was seen to be crawling back into their trenches and, perhaps because the defenders were on the lookout for their own men, the Dubliners were spotted. Heavy rifle and machine gun fire was brought to bear and German trench mortars started to bombard No Man's Land and their own wire. With both officers now wounded and several of the leading men killed, the withdrawal, constantly illuminated by German flares, was slow and costly with more men wounded. Some of the party did not return to the British lines until after daybreak such was the difficulty of moving out in No Man's Land. Initially, reported casualties were: two officers wounded, 3 other ranks killed, 7 wounded and 14 missing. Of the missing, six men came in during the early hours of the morning having sheltered in shell holes in No Man's Land and another two were confirmed as dead[iii].

The CO of the Dublins, Lt. Col. Herbert Nelson[iv], DSO (Border Regt.), wrote after the war that he believed the raid was expected:

---

[i] 2nd Lt. Angus John Willans Pearson, 14th Royal Fusiliers att. 1st Royal Dublin Fusiliers, was killed on 1st July 1916. Aged 21, he was the elder son of Ernest William and Jessie Borland Pearson of 66, Brook Green, Hammersmith, London. Born at Minnedosa, Manitoba, he was educated at Colet Court and St Paul's School where he played for the cricket 1st XI for four years and for the rugby 1st XV. A leg break bowler he played for The Rest v Lord's Schools at Lord's and for the Public Schools against the MCC. He was also selected for the Young Amateurs of Middlesex. He had gained a Classics scholarship at Pembroke College, Oxford, in May 1914. He enlisted in the Public Schools' Battalion in September 1914 and was commissioned into the Royal Fusiliers in October 1914. He went to Gallipoli in July 1915 with a draft for the Royal Dublin Fusiliers. He is buried in Auchonvillers Military Cemetery, grave II. A. 7.

[ii] 2nd Lt. Joseph Devoy. 1st Royal Dublin Fusiliers, was commissioned on 5th March 1916. As 10335 Sgt. Joseph Devoy he had been awarded the DCM for his conduct on 21st August 1915 at Suvla Bay, Gallipoli.

[iii] Eight men of the 1st Royal Dublin Fusiliers are recorded as having died on the 28th June 1916.

[iv] Lt. Col. Herbert Nelson, 1st Border Regt., att. 1st Royal Dublin Fusiliers, was commissioned into the 1st Border Regt. in 1895. He was promoted Captain in 1903. He served in South Africa (Queen's Medal with one clasp). Promoted Major, April 1915, and

> "It was rather short notice as my battalion was in reserve... They did splendidly but were smashed to pieces by minenwerfers... It would seem that the raid was expected and there was no element of surprise in it from the moment they went over the top."[24]

One wonders whether, again, the Moritz listening station at the head of the Y Ravine had anything to do with the apparent German anticipation of the Dubliners' raid?

Brig. Gen. Lucas, 87th Brigade. commented in his personal diary on the failure of the Dublins' raid. His complaint was not directed at the battalion and its officers but at VIII Corps for demanding raids at far too short notice which could then not be properly planned and organised:

> "The Dublins carried out a raid and struck the only place where the wire was not cut and so they did not get it in. The Corps are making us carry out these raids at a moment's notice, & therefore without adequate preparation they are not a success."

Apart from the dead and wounded, these raids might have had another effect. A crucial loss to the Germans of vital intelligence. Nelson touched upon this potentially worrying aspect of losing men wounded so close to the German lines:

> "In the dawn several of my men were seen to be pulled into the German lines. Those men were Irishmen as loyal as any in the Army but they were in possession of all details regarding the assault to be made on 1st July and it is my firm conviction that they were prevailed upon by the Germans to give unwittingly very valuable information about that assault which led to its repulse[i]."[25]

Writing after the raid on 29th June, Lt. Col. Nelson's conclusions about the state of the German defences and the troops should have been concerning:

> "... though the German front line may be badly smashed in places, fire from a line or lines in rear very effectively sweeps the ground in front of their front line and... the troops holding this line or lines were able to fire despite our artillery bombardment."[26]

Brig. Gen. Williams, GOC 86th Brigade, added to the air of concern with his note attached to Nelson's report of the attack:

> "By day the enemy line appears to be empty, doubtless it is well held by machine guns but these do not fire. Artillery FOOs in the front line stand head and shoulders over the parapet for hours at a time and are not fired at. By night the line is undoubtedly strongly held."[27]

VIII Corps' response to this intelligence seems complacent in the extreme:

Temp. Lt. Col. June 1915. Fought at Gallipoli. DSO February 1916 and Bar, February 1918. Temp. Brig. Gen.

[i] It is believed the same happened in the case of Pte Victor Wheat of the 1/5th North Staffordshire Regt., who was wounded and taken prisoner in No Man's Land on the night of the 24th June at Gommecourt. A German document later reported the details of the planned attack by the VII Corps on the village. The date of the attack is wrong but the fact that it was to be a pincer movement which avoided attacking Gommecourt Park was explicit.

> "Raids on the enemy's trenches were made by all four Divisions. Owing to the alertness of the enemy and the strength in which his front line trenches were held none of the raiders succeeded in entering his trenches. The fact that his front line trenches are held in force is, however, fully established."[28]

In spite of the evidence in their own report on the raid, i.e. the raiding party 'found the enemy's wire difficult to get through', in spite of the fact that the 87th Brigade had parties out from both front line battalions trying to clear the enemy wire, and in spite of the fact that VIII Corps' reported two out four officer patrols found the wire between Point 89 and the Hawthorn redoubt 'not much damaged', the 29th Division's general report as to the condition of the German wire was optimistic:

> "The enemy's wire is reported destroyed almost entirely along his front trench and badly damaged in front of his support and reserve trenches."[29]

Certainly, as noted before, wire cutting appears to have been more effective on the western and southern sides of the Y Ravine salient. Two officer patrols of the 2nd South Wales Borderers had gone out at 11.30 p.m., before the Dubliners' raid, and inspected the wire in both areas. The right patrol started to cut some wire when interrupted by machine gun fire from the German second trench whilst the left patrol, at the nose of the salient, found the wire well cut and passable almost everywhere. They returned at 12.45 a.m., fifteen minutes before 2nd Lt. Devoy started laying out the tape for the Dublin's raid, and so missed the excitement of the Irish regiment's sally.

THE BETTER WEATHER AND THE EXPECTED DRYING OUT of the trenches and roads on 29th June seem to have improved the mood amongst 29th Division Staff in spite of significant evidence that affairs were not running smoothly. For the men in the front line, however, things were not quite so rosy. The South Wales Borderers reported the front line trenches still very wet and increasingly knocked about by the German guns, especially around C Street where lurked some of the Divisional trench mortar batteries and around the workings for the Russian sap at Sap 6. The 18 pdrs and the trench mortars, however, continued to cut the wire which, given the fact that it was supposed to be 'destroyed', speaks more to the reality of the situation than does the 29th Division's wire report.

Problems were increasing amongst the Divisional trench mortar batteries. It was difficult to conceal their location and, as a result, they were a favoured target for retaliation. As a result, Y/29 was still unable to fire with both gun pits blown in and Z/29 had three men killed when an explosion in a gun pit, possibly caused by a faulty charge, destroyed the gun and blew the men to pieces[i]. As a result,

[i] It has been possible to identify two of these men:
5212 Bombardier Frederick J Howe, Z/29 Trench Mortar Battery, Royal Field Artillery, was aged 23. He was the son of Mrs M J Howe of Williams Buildings, East Quay, Bridgwater, Somerset. His body was never found and his name is inscribed on the Thiepval Memorial, Pier and Face 1 A & 8 A.
97573 Cpl Haydn Isaiah Price Thomas, Z/29 Trench Mortar Battery, Royal Field Artillery, was aged 22. He was the son of Mr and Mrs D W Thomas of Pleasant View, Trealaw

368th Battery of the 147th Brigade, RFA, had to take over wirecutting from a trench mortar battery. Y/23 battery, however, was still working effectively and efficiently, another 130 bombs today, and the SWB were able to observe the wire south of the nose of the Y Ravine salient increasingly well cut. The field guns, though, were beginning to feel the strain of a continuous programme of firing for which there was no precedent. 132nd Brigade reported on the 29th that springs on the 18 pdrs were beginning to break – a sure sign that wear and tear was eroding both the productivity and accuracy of the guns.

The heavy howitzers and the 240 mm trench mortars had, meanwhile, completed the destruction of every house in Beaumont Hamel, a fact mentioned in both Divisional and Brigade war diaries. Had this meant that the garrison had also been destroyed then this might have been some cause for celebration but, as they clearly had not, the diary entries and the destruction itself served no useful purpose. Briefly, one of these big guns was turned on an area of front line trench in which the German garrison was concentrated. No. 1 Howitzer, RMA, is recorded in the 1st Heavy Artillery Group's (HAG) diary as having sent eight shells into the central part of the Y Ravine. To what effect was unknown as observation was difficult. In addition, on other shoots that day, nearly one in five of the 15 in shells was a 'blind', i.e. a dud, and so this brief excursion towards the enemy front line might not have achieved a great deal which would have been of assistance to the infantry. No. 5 Howitzer, RMA, meanwhile was happily blowing up the few remaining walls of Beaumont Hamel north of the church. During the bombardment a German trench mortar position was revealed and engaged with nine heavyweight rounds. Little remained when the smoke cleared. Otherwise, with the medium howitzers again off to the east bombarding Beaucourt and Puisieux Trenches, the heavy howitzers contributed nothing to the destruction of the German front line trenches where the dugouts were known to be packed with men.

On the night of Thursday, 29th June, two battalions sent out parties with the intention of doing more than just checking the wire. The 2nd South Wales Borderers went first with two officer patrols slipping into No Man's Land as the guns fell silent for sixty minutes late in the evening. The plan was for one party under Lt. John Bowler Karran to try to snatch an enemy soldier from the German front trench while away to the left the one other examined the wire at the nose of the Y Ravine salient. Karran's party left Sap 3 at 10.20 p.m. With him went one sergeant and five other ranks and, as it was still not yet completely dark, they paused for thirty minutes in a sunken lane which ran diagonally across No Man's Land towards the centre of the ravine. When the light had completely faded, the small group advanced cautiously to the German wire where Karran ordered three men to remain on look out while he led the others to the German front line. Undetected, Karran peered over the parapet to find himself immediately above the entrance to a German dugout. With no firestep to jump onto Karran was forced to stay where he was. A few moments later an unsuspecting German appeared from his left and walked directly underneath him and towards a turning in the trench. Karran shot the unfortunate man with this

(Rhondda), Glam. His body was never found and his name is inscribed on the Thiepval Memorial, Pier and Face 1 A & 8 A.

service revolver and he fell with a grunt into the bottom of the trench. Shortly afterwards, as Lt. Karran tried to find a way into the trench, he was alerted by the sound of men climbing the stairs of the dugout beneath him and he prudently withdrew, taking his party with him. Later Karran reported on the condition of the trenches. It should be recalled this description was written on the morning (i.e. the 30th June) of the day after the attack was originally planned to have taken place:

> "The trench was about 7 ft. broad at the top and from 8 to 10 ft. deep. The fire step appeared to be made of wood along the top and also along the side. The parapet was much knocked about by our shells but the bay did not appear to be much damaged. The dugout I saw was in the right hand corner of the bay looking at it from my direction and was under the parapet. The entrance appeared to be larger than those of our deep dugouts. The trench appeared to be quite dry. I went in through a good gap in the wire about 4 yds. wide. The rest of the wire at this point appeared fairly strong."[30]

There is much in Karran's report which should have concerned the Divisional and Corps Staff: uncut wire, defensible trenches and secure and occupied deep dugouts. There was little the artillery would be able to do about this in the time remaining to them. And the unknown German soldier shot by Karran would be avenged. 23 year old John Bowler Karran from the Isle of Man would be one of eleven SWB officers to die on the morning of 1st July[i].

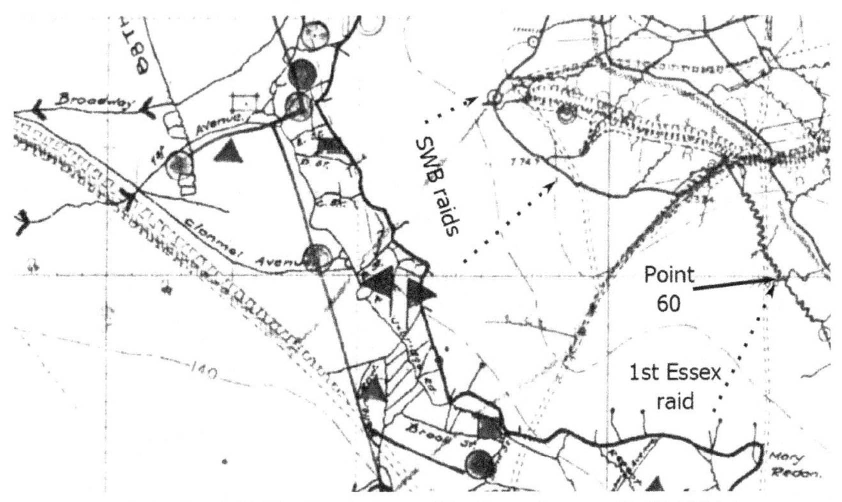

Map 10 2nd South Wales Borderers and 1st Essex Regt. raids, 29th/30th June.

At 12.25 a.m. another raiding party, this one from the 1st Essex Regt., left the British trenches from near the Mary Redan with their objective being Point 60.

---

[i] 2nd Lt. John Bowler Karran, 9th att. 2nd South Wales Borderers, was aged 23. He was the son of George Christian Karran, a shipowner of Sea Mount, Scarlett, Castletown, Isle of Man, and Matilda May Woolf of Otago, New Zealand. He was commissioned on 13th November 1914. He is buried in Y Ravine Cemetery, Beaumont-Hamel, B. 10.

Lt. Henry Branfill Russell[i] and two NCOs had already been out in No Man's Land laying tape from a sap near Charing Cross to within twenty yards of the German trenches and now the party proceeded in single file following the tape. The thirty men led by Lt. Russell, 2nd Lt. Warner and 2nd Lt. Morison[ii] were somewhat delayed in their progress across No Man's Land and they did not arrive at the German trench until 12.50 a.m., 20 minutes after the covering bombardment had ceased. In spite of this, this raid became the first and only one from 29th Division to achieve an effective entry into the German trenches. With the wire here well cut, the party divided into three groups and, on a signal, they rushed the front line. One party moved left, another right and a third held the top of a communication trench with a few men acting as a covering party. They found a relatively shallow trench, 5 ft. deep, which was easy to access. The right group came up against a trench barricade three bays along the trench and withdrew when hand grenades were lobbed over it. The left group ran into a German soldier who, after appearing to surrender, tried to escape and was shot with his helmet evidence of their success. The raid was quickly over. At 1.05 a.m., with German flares illuminating the scene and machine guns firing from three directions the order was given to withdraw. A few bombs were lobbed down a nearby dugout before they came under fire from troops coming down two communication trenches and, with only one man slightly wounded, they successfully withdrew, bringing with them another trophy – a trench noticeboard.

These two raids would be the only successful ones carried out during the seven days of the bombardment on not only the 29th Division's front but the entire front of the VIII Corps. These results, however, did not seem to concern Hunter-Weston and his Staff as no alterations were made to the plan for the bombardment or the attack.

AFTER SOME EARLY RAIN WAS BLOWN AWAY on a fresh south westerly wind, Friday, 30th June, was a significant improvement on the previous days' weather. In places, though, the trenches were still very wet but, otherwise, there was little to undermine the confidence in success which pervaded the whole front north of the River Ancre. 29th Division reported the enemy wire on its front as 'no longer a serious obstacle' and, as final preparations were made at the front, the assault troops readied themselves in their village billets, wrote letters home and other ones only to be opened if they were killed. Last minute wills were hastily written and kit separated out with packs and greatcoats being discarded for the attack.

---

[i] Lt. Henry Branfill Russell, 1st Essex Regt., died on 11th July 1916. Aged 21, he was the second son of Champion Branfill Russell, JP, and the Hon. Isabel Ellen Russell née Bruce (daughter of the 1st Baron Aberdare of Duffryn), of Stubbers, North Ockendon, Essex. He was commissioned on 20th October 1914. He was buried in Gezaincourt Communal Cemetery Extension, grave I. B. 11.

[ii] 2nd Lt., later Capt., Alfred James Morison, 3rd att. 1st Essex Regt., died on 20th November 1917. Aged 33, he was the son of James Robertson Morison, a company secretary, and Catherine McLerret of The White House, Cannon Road, Southgate, London. He was educated at Clifton Bank and St Andrew's and worked on the London Stock Exchange. He enlisted as a Private in the Royal Fusiliers in August 1914 and was commissioned into the 3rd Essex Regt. in April 1915. Served at Gallipoli. Killed at Cambrai, he is buried in Flesquieres Hill British Cemetery, grave III. D. 34.

The night before, all available estaminets did a serious trade as men pooled their money for a final 'night out' before the advance on Berlin began. Overhead the BE2cs kept watch as the gunners continued to toil, pouring yet more shells of all calibres into the German positions.

For No. 1 Howitzer, RMA, issues with its platform were now more than just a nuisance. The gun had slewed so far to the south west that ten rounds had to be fired at Ovillers La Boisselle in order force it back onto its normal line. It then sent eleven rounds into the mess that was the Beaucourt redoubt for good measure. No. 5 Howitzer at last fired some rounds specifically at the entrances to the caves behind the Bergwerk but it was only ten rounds and it was a case of too little, too late. Otherwise, it was the field guns and howitzers and the 2 in. trench mortars which did their level best to disturb the equilibrium of the front line German troops and only the 'toffee apples' caused them any great concern.

The infantry, meanwhile, were distributed thus:

86th Brigade – elements of the 2nd Royal Fusiliers and 1st Lancashire Fusiliers in the front line, remainder in Mailly Wood. The 1st Royal Dublin Fusiliers and the 16th Middlesex Regt., at Acheux.

87th Brigade – three companies each of the 1st Royal Inniskilling Fusiliers and 2nd South Wales Borderers in the front line, remainder in Englebelmer. The 1st King's Own Scottish Borderers and the 1st Border Regt. in huts at Acheux.

88th Brigade – in billets at Louvencourt.

Casualties until now had been light which was a function of the British front line being thinly held, the resilience of the reasonable dugouts in which the front line infantry were sheltered and the moderately heavy German artillery retaliation.

During the evening of the 30th, the assaulting battalions began to move to the front via pre-determined routes. As they went they picked up tools and other equipment from dumps along the way. These were to be used to consolidate the captured German positions. Even the leading waves of the infantry would be heavily laden:

> "The leading troops all carried 170 rounds of SAA, two days rations in haversack on the back, two bombs and two sandbags. The leading companies in addition carried 50 shovels and 10 picks whilst wire cutters were distributed amongst the leading sections. Each platoon also of the leading battalions carried two trench bridges."[31]

The following waves would carry extra sandbags and additional tools and rolls of wire, mauls, stakes and 100 heavy entrenching tools per battalion had been dumped in the front line trench to be carried forward by the supporting troops. Officers had been instructed to dress and arm themselves as ordinary soldiers in the hope that they would not be targeted by German snipers. A good idea in theory but one that failed to work in practice. Any soldier worth his salt would target an obvious leader and, whatever they were dressed in, officers were meant to lead and so became targets. As a result, for example, nearly 80% of all officers who went over the top from the 86th Brigade became casualties.

The troops around Acheux left for the front in the middle of the evening. Ahead of them, final preparations were being made by the Royal Engineers for the Hawthorn Ridge mine, for the opening of the tunnels and positioning of the Stokes mortars and, on the 1st Lancashire Fusiliers front, for the opening of a tunnel from Sap 7 to the Sunken Road in No Man's Land which was to be occupied by the leading troops of the battalion. Pioneers from No. 2 Platoon, A Company, 1/2nd Monmouthshire Regt. were to dig a seven yard trench from Sap 7 to the end of the Sunken Road. This they finished by 2.30 a.m.

The 86th Brigade had all of their men in place before midnight. They were distributed as follows from right to left:

2nd Royal Fusiliers – Three companies in the front line from F Street to Bridge End. One company in deep dug outs in Support line;

1st Lancashire Fusiliers – Two companies with four Stokes guns and two guns of MG Company in the sunken road; one company in front line from Bridge End to New Beaumont Road; one company in Lanwick Street;

1st Royal Dublin Fusiliers – Two companies in Essex Street, two companies in 88 Trench;

16th Middlesex Regt. – Two companies in Cripps Street, two companies in Cardiff Street.

The men were described as 'cheerful and full of confidence' although this confidence was not necessarily shared everywhere if a comment in the 86th Brigade war diary for 30th June is any indicator. It summed up their experience during the bombardment:

> "…three small raiding parties entered the enemy trenches but were always driven off without being able to secure prisoners. A stronger raiding party of 40 R Dublin Fus., also failed to enter the enemy lines. All reconnaissance proved the line to be well held and little shaken by the bombardment."[32]

Although the trenches were very crowded, a hot meal was served to the men between 4 and 5.30 a.m. Otherwise, all they could do was find a space and wait. Sleep was pretty much impossible given the still constant roar of the guns.

To assist the infantry in the work of consolidation, two platoons of the 1/2nd Monmouths were attached to each attacking Brigade and a company to the 88th Brigade which, all being well, had the furthest to travel.

Amongst the men of the field artillery batteries there was the greatest confidence that they had done the job of cutting the wire well. Some batteries, for example 371st and D/132 (targeting the 2nd line), claimed to have completely swept the wire away. Others, such as those of the 147th Brigade and the 369th and 370th Batteries of the 132nd Brigade, claimed to have cut lanes from the front edge of the wire to the trench parapet. 29th Division recorded the German wire as 'almost completely destroyed along the whole front'. There seemed little to stop the advance.

And then there was the great mine. The painstaking digging and the hauling of tin after tin of Ammonal to the cavity which lay just under the forward lip of the Hawthorn Redoubt had been completed on 23rd June. The mine was 1,015 feet long, 80 feet deep in places and was filled with 40,600 lbs. (18.125 tons) of the deadly explosive. Now it sat and waited to be sprung under the unfortunate occupants of the dugouts in the trenches 50 feet above.

Discussions about the best time to explode the mine had been lengthy and, to this day, the final decision causes controversy. It had been decided to fire the mine at 7.20 a.m., ten minutes before the infantry were due to go over the top.

This time was a compromise. Originally, Hunter-Weston had wanted to blow the mine at 3.30 a.m. It would have been followed up by a swift infantry assault which would take the near lip. Then things would go quiet, or so the thinking went, and the all-out attack at 7.30 a.m. would come as a surprise to defenders convinced the blowing of the mine was a small scale local action. It is a fairly implausible scenario given that the Germans had been subjected to a seven day bombardment and, anyway, given the information provided by Josef Lipmann and possibly by wounded PoWs, they would have been on the alert for anything suggestive of the launch of the offensive. In addition, British infantry had a rather lousy track record when it came to crater fighting and this was pointed out by the Inspector of Mines. In his view, the likely outcome was that the Germans would occupy the entire crater giving them almost as strong a position as had previously existed and significant notice of an imminent attack. As all of the other mines on the Somme front were due to be fired at just before 7.30 a.m. it was suggested that H3 should go at the same time but someone, either at VIII Corps or in 29th Division, apparently expressed concerns about the possible damage done by debris falling on the advancing men of the 2nd Royal Fusiliers. As experience showed that all heavy rocks and stones came back to earth within 20 seconds of a mine explosion this view, if expressed, should have been given short shrift. Instead, and against all experience and logic, it was agreed to fire the mine at 7.20 a.m. At this point, the attacking elements of the 2nd Royal Fusiliers would rush the crater lip, followed, ten minutes later, by the attack of the rest of the Division. Rather more significantly, it was also concluded that, in order to protect the onrushing Royal Fusiliers from possible 'friendly fire', the heavy artillery should lift off the German front line at the same time as the mine went up. And not just on Hawthorn Ridge – along the whole Corps front!

It is impossible to find an officer writing after the war, from Gen. de Lisle down to the lowliest subaltern, who does not blame in some way the blowing of the Hawthorn Redoubt mine at 7.20 a.m. for the utter defeat of the 29th Division on 1st July. The timing had, apparently, been known for some days and was a constant topic of conversation amongst those involved in the attack. It was only the widespread, though inexplicable, belief that the bombardment had crushed German resistance that persuaded participants all would be well. Otherwise, the decision appears to have been absurd, bordering on the insane.

Or was it?

Lt. Col. Clement Graham Fuller, RE, was GSO1, 29th Division. He was the senior Staff Officer of the Division. One feels he was in a position to know about such affairs as this and, indeed, he contributed some illuminating comments about the initial draft of the British Official History in January 1930. He expressed views about a number of aspects of the attack but his most significant, and previously completely ignored comment, is about the timing of the firing of the H3, Hawthorn Redoubt, mine. The compilers of the Official History chose to ignore Fuller's remarks in spite of the fact that his explanation makes definite sense. Hunter-Weston has tended to shoulder the blame for the decision. Some have even suggested 29th Division requested the 7.20 a.m. explosion. The answer, as given by Fuller, is rather more mundane:

"The explosion of the mine ten minutes before the assault was only agreed to at the express request of the OC Tunnelling Company who was in charge of the tunnels and mine. He stated he must have ten minutes grace in which to ensure that the mine exploded so as, if necessary, to remedy defects. The Inspector of Mines when he made his report was probably unaware of the action of the OC Tunnelling Company."[33]

Now, it must be said that someone, somewhere had to accept this request. Some senior officer had to have endorsed Major Reginald Graham Trower's demand. So, perhaps, one should not blame the OC, 252nd Tunnelling Company. Whoever weighed in the balance the effect of the mine failing to go off against the ten minutes' notice given to the Germans by its explosion clearly had a difficult decision. The Germans had fortified a strong point on the northern end of the Hawthorn Ridge for excellent tactical reasons. Machine guns placed there had the potential to take in enfilade the attacks on Y Ravine, the Bergwerk and even the right flank of the 4th Division on Redan Ridge. But, if German resistance really was at or beyond breaking point then an early blowing of the mine might be worth the risk. Alternatively, if the German defences truly were that fragile then what difference would be the failure of the mine make? Such are the decisions of generalship. Whoever it was, and as de Lisle steadfastly denies involvement one must look to his superior at VIII Corps, they wrecked whatever slim chances the 29th Division had of taking any of its objectives. And whoever gave the order (or misinterpreted the order) that the heavy guns were to be moved off the German front line trenches five minutes before the infantry attack along the entire VIII Corps front (followed by half the field artillery) rather than just the area around the redoubt has, perhaps, an even greater responsibility to bear. No claim for responsibility for this decision has ever been made.

At 12.10 a.m. Divisional HQ received message G719 from VIII Corps in which Gen. Rawlinson wished all ranks good luck for the coming offensive. This message was certainly intercepted away to the south by one of the German listening posts and, no doubt, was passed up and down the front as a matter of urgency.

During the early hours the infantry filtered into their assembly positions and now waited for the off. The strength of the Division immediately prior to the attack is shown in Table 7 below: In total, just over 8,000 officers and men would be committed to the fighting during the day. The strength of the battalions actually used in the attack varied considerably, with the 2nd Royal Fusiliers (22 officers and 906 OR) being the strongest battalion and the 2nd South Wales Borderers the weakest (22 officers and 623 OR). Overall, the Royal Fusiliers deployed 30% more men in the attack than the Borderers.

On the Division's left, at midnight, the Lancashire Fusiliers had moved to occupy the Sunken Road via the new tunnel without incident. B Company, on the right, and D Company, on the left, were supported by a special bombing company of 100 men drawn from all four battalions of the 86th Brigade, two platoons each of 25 men flanked the other companies. Behind them in Lanwick Street, just behind the front line, was A Company and Battalion HQ. C Company was in Tenderloin Trench near to the White City along with two sections of the 1/2nd Monmouths, the main battalion HQ and the Regimental Aid Post. Waiting to advance from Sap 7 were two Vickers Machine Gun teams, a battery of four Stokes mortars and a carrying party. As they waited, a working party from the Monmouths toiled furiously to complete a covered communication trench from the road back to the front line. This was finished by 3 a.m.

Bde	Regiment	Available		10% Held to reinforce		In actual assault	
		Off	OR	Off	OR	Off	OR
86th	2nd R Fus.	33	1006	11	100	22	906
	1st Lanc Fus.	36	983	14	98	22	885
	1st Dublin F	27	918	5	92	22	826
	16th Middx	35	773	13	77	22	696
	Total	131	3680	43	367	88	3313
87th	2nd SWB	33	692	11	69	22	623
	1st KOSB	34	927	12	93	22	834
	1st Innisk F	36	874	14	87	22	787
	1st Border	32	976	10	98	22	878
	Total	135	3469	47	347	88	3122
88th	4th Worcs	34	852	12	85	Not in actual assault, held in reserve	
	2nd Hants	34	949	12	95		
	1st Essex	36	910	14	91	22	819
	1st Newfdld	45	842	23	84	22	758
	Total	149	3553	61	355	44	1577
1/2nd Monmouths		31	649	0	0	6	170
Total Officers and Other Ranks in attack						226	8182

Table 7 29th Division: Battalion total strength & numbers used in the attack[34]

To their right, a party of the 2nd Royal Fusiliers waited for their sprint to the Hawthorn Redoubt crater. X, Y and Z Companies occupied the front line with W Company in the support line. They suffered a few casualties overnight, one officer, 2nd Lt. Keith Barrett, would miss the attack as a result[i]. Z Company had been tasked with taking the lip of the crater and one can but imagine the nervousness amongst the young officers and men who were to make their isolated rush across No Man's Land several minutes before any other men left the trenches.

[i] 2nd Lt., later Capt., Keith Joy Barrett, 2nd Royal Fusiliers, died of wounds on 16th April 1917 at No. 20 General Hospital, Dannes Camiers. Aged 25, he was the son of Dr James William and Marian Barrett (née Rennick), of Palmyra, Lansell Rd., Toorak, Melbourne, Australia. An agricultural student at Ormond College, University of Melbourne, he enlisted in the 2nd Australian Field Ambulance, leaving for Europe from Melbourne on 19th October 1914 on *HMAT Wiltshire*. He was commissioned into the Royal Fusiliers in April 1915. Mentioned in Despatches, his diary was published in 1921 under the title *'The Diary of an Australian Soldier'*. His father, Sir James William Barrett, KBE, CB (1862-1945) was a controversial figure who served in the Australian and British medical services in Egypt writing several books about his experiences after the war. Capt. Barrett is buried in Etaples Military Cemetery, grave XVII. C. 5.

Behind them the men of the 16th Middlesex Regt. and the 1st Royal Dublin Fusiliers waited for their opportunity to advance. The Middlesex were to advance to the left of the crater, i.e. between the right of the Lancashire Fusiliers and the left of the Royal Fusiliers while the Dublin Fusiliers would advance to the right of the crater into the re-entrant between the Hawthorn redoubt and the Y Ravine salient, following the supporting companies of the 2nd Royal Fusiliers. The Middlesex men occupied two lines of assembly trenches in the slope above the junction of the Old and New Beaumont Roads: Cripp's Cut and Cardiff Street. From left to right in Cripp's Cut were D Company, Battalion HQ and C Company. Each Company was to be accompanied by one Stokes gun. 100 yards to their rear A Company (right) and B Company (left) occupied Cardiff Street. Two sections of the 1/2nd Monmouths were to the right of A Company.

To their right, the Dublins had moved into position via Broadway communication trench and by 1 a.m. two companies were established in Essex Street with W Company on the left and X Company on the right. 250 yards behind them Y Company (right) and Z Company (left) were in 88 Trench.

This completed the dispositions of the 86th Brigade. Their role was to take the front line trenches, Beaumont Hamel village, the majority of the ruins being on their front, and then move to the Beaucourt Ridge.

On their right, the battalions of the 87th Brigade had moved up to the front line and support trenches opposite and to the south of the Y Ravine salient. The troops here would be attacking in a variety of directions. The 2nd South Wales Borderers would attack into the 'jaws' of the Y Ravine. A Company, on the left of the battalion, was to assault the nose of the Y Ravine salient behind which lay the northern and more pronounced depression of the ravine. Their line of attack was due east. On their left would be the 2nd Royal Fusiliers supported by the Dublin Fusiliers. On the right of A Company came C Company, the centre company. They were to attack the southern side of the salient where the two front lines diverged. No Man's Land here was some 500 yards across and remained so until the projection of Mary Redan sharply closed the gap. D Company was on the right and they were to attack due east towards a point in the German lines where they turned 90° to the south. Their line of attack, as a result, ran parallel to the German front line on the southern side of the Y Ravine salient and was over 600 yards from trench to trench. This was an uncomfortable prospect for the men involved should C Company's attack not go well. B Company was the support company whose job it was to mop up in the German first and second trenches. Each company was to attack on a front of 140 yards. The three attacking companies were instructed to move into No Man's Land before zero hour so as to be within 100 yards of the German trenches when the whistles blew. In other words, they were to be out in No Man's Land at about the same time as the Hawthorn Ridge mine was to go up and the heavy and then field artillery moved off the German front trenches. They would be in the open without any artillery protection for nearly ten minutes.

On the right of the 87th Brigade front the 1st Royal Inniskilling Fusiliers had to exit their northerly facing trenches to the left of the Mary Redan but then attack east-north-east after conducting a right wheel in the middle of No Man's Land. They too were to be aligned and ready 100 yards from the German trenches by 7.30 a.m. and this right wheel manoeuvre and advance was to take place in full view of the three tiers of German trenches. Once through the first three lines of German trenches, the Inniskillings were to push on across Station Road to take a new German trench running just to the east.

Behind the SWB came the 1st Border Regt. while the 1st King's Own Scottish Borderers followed the Inniskillings. These two battalions were to assault the second German position on the Beaucourt Ridge as well as Beaucourt chateau and village before the 88th Brigade took over responsibility for the last element of the plan – the taking of the German 2nd Position beyond the Puisieux Road. The KOSB would have to replicate thc wheeling manoeuvre of the Inniskillings out in No Man's Land. It was to be hoped that no German machine guns were trained on them as they performed this rather tricky parade ground movement.

The attack of the 29th Division was an ambitious and complex arrangement as Table 6 (page 116) shows. It was made even trickier by the irregularities of the terrain. Furthermore, the Germans had selected a position where three lines of defence were arranged in tiers, allowing the British front and support trenches and No Man's Land to be fired on from the German front line, mainly on a reverse slope and therefore invisible to British observers, the German support trench, running in front of Station Road, and, finally, the Zwischen Stellung on the Beaucourt Ridge. Each trench line stood higher than the one in front allowing the machine gun teams excellent fields of fire across the entire position of the 87th Brigade. Unless these positions were effectively neutralised by the field and heavy artillery, the advance of the infantry would be, at the very best, a highly costly exercise and, at the worst, a disaster.

The Inniskillings and the South Wales Borderers had taken up their assembly positions in Regent's Street (the new front line), and the old firing line by 11 p.m. Behind them the 1st KOSB and 1st Border Regt., which had left Acheux Wood at 9.15 and 9.30 p.m. respectively, marched up via Rotten Row, Withington and Tipperary Avenues and occupied the line of trenches: Buckingham Palace Road, St James' Street, Brooke Street and Fethard Street soon after 12 midnight. No casualties were suffered while moving up to the assembly trenches. The men settled down to wait for the big event to 'kick off'.

At 5 a.m. the Corps artillery and 4.5 in. howitzers of the Divisional artillery started to ratchet up the intensity of the bombardment on the lines opposite. Every minute ten of the field howitzers deposited one of their 35 lb. Amatol filled shells on selected locations in the German trenches. Three medium howitzer batteries, 23rd, 77th and 79th, were firing on or close to the German front line. The 8 in. howitzers of the 77th Siege Battery were firing on the objectives of the 1st Royal Inniskilling Fusiliers, the trenches opposite Mary Redan and on the near side of Station Road. The 6 in. howitzers were engaging the objectives of the 2nd South Wales Borderers around the Y Ravine and the 9.2 in. howitzers of the 79th Siege Battery pummelled the area the 1st Lancashire Fusiliers were to attack, the Bergwerk. Otherwise it was only the field batteries and medium trench mortars that were keeping the German sentries' heads down.

These continuous explosions and the heavier rumbles of the bigger howitzers must have been reassuring sights and sounds to the men watching from the British side of No Man's Land. At 5.15 a.m., however, came an ominous increase in the intensity of the German reply. Several batteries were shelled as were the approach roads to the front. Fortunately, the front line trenches, now crammed with men, were not yet a target.

29th Division reported the morning rather misty and a light breeze from the south west failed to shift the covering of low lying grey that obscured the German positions from the view of the R.F.C. observers circling above. For Haig, the mist was a bonus which 'concealed the concentrations of our troops'. For the artillery it was a pain in the neck. They couldn't see their targets and observers were unable to advise on the necessary corrections in length and line. With the failure of the seven day bombardment to neutralise the German infantry and artillery this was just the icing on the cake for VIII Corps.

At 6.10 a.m. the field howitzers ceased firing for 20 minutes. It was time to register on their targets for the intense bombardment due to start at 6.25 a.m. and for the Forward Observation Officers (FOOs) to try and spot the results of their previous firing. But, with VIII Corps describing the mist at this time as 'thick … which made observation very difficult' this was easier said than done.[35]

At 6.25 a.m. the heavy and field artillery of all batteries opened a rapid and intense fire on the German trenches. The 4.5 in. howitzers of 2½ batteries[i] fired at rate of one round per gun per minute, doubling this rate at 7 a.m. At the same time eleven 18 pdr batteries of the 29th Division and the 48th Division[ii] opened fire with HE on the German front line at one round per minute. Two more fired from advance positions on the trench in front of Beaucourt while the last one, dug in close to the front line, reserved its fire for Zero hour.

All the while the Corps artillery was firing – but many batteries were firing blind. Nos. 1 and 5 Howitzers, RMA, were battering the Beaucourt Redoubt with 36 of their 1400 lb. shells but with what result it was nearly impossible to say. The 1st Heavy Artillery Group's war diary reports No. 1 Howitzer as having 'No observation owing to bad weather and smoke'. No. 5 Howitzer reported:

> "Observation was almost impossible owing to smoke clouds. Out of four rounds actually observed[iii] two were reported as direct hits."[36]

The 4.7 in. guns of the 1/1st Highland and 1/1st Welsh Heavy Batteries spent the day firing 'off map' as observation was so poor.

All this was unknown to the infantry waiting in the front line trenches. For them, the sound and fury of the bombardment provided much needed, if groundless, optimism about the prospects for the attack. According to the war diary of the 147th Brigade, RFA, sound and fury was all it amounted to:

> "The infantry assault was timed to take place at 7.30 a.m. It was preceded by 65 minutes intense bombardment of the front line trenches by 18 pounders. All natures of artillery participated and some of the heavy batteries commenced as early as 5 a.m. But it was obvious that no weight of heavy metal was on the enemy front line."[37]

---

[i] D/132, D/147 and half of D/17 (460th) Batteries. The other section of D/17 was employed on counter battery work.

[ii] A/241 and B/243 Batteries.

[iii] They fired 19 rounds at this target.

The gunners of the Field Artillery and Divisional Trench Mortar Batteries had fired a prodigious quantity of rounds as Table 8 below shows. On average, the Division's 18 pdr guns would fire 1,903 rounds per gun and the 4.5 in. howitzers gunners had managed 1,449 rounds per gun by the evening of 1st July. In the seven days of the bombardment each 18 pdr averaged 180 rounds per gun per day and the howitzers 150 per gun per day. It was little wonder that the guns were breaking down on a regular basis as both the equipment, and the men for that matter, had never before experienced such a prolonged and intense programme of firing. And yet, for all their extraordinary efforts, the weight of shell delivered was inadequate and the infantry would suffer cruelly as a result.

	Hours	18 pdrs		4.5 in. Hows	Trench mortars	
		Shrapnel A	HE AX	HE BX	2 in. Medium	240 mm Hvy
U	1200 23rd – 1200 24th	1164	0	316	0	0
	1200 24th – 2000 24th	3667	84	185	0	0
V	2000 24th – 1200 25th	5824	39	1006	0	0
	1200 25th – 2000 25th	3390	7	612	0	0
W	2000 25th – 1200 26th	3656	1483	1166	0	0
	1200 26th – 2000 26th	3099	132	1111	0	0
X	2000 26th – 1200 27th	3576	1621	1081	1090	76
	1200 27th – 2000 27th	4641	396	725	0	0
Y	2000 27th – 1200 28th	3638	2608	1049	1005	107
	1200 28th – 2000 28th	3177	405	975	0	0
Y1	2000 28th – 1200 29th	2705	717	917	1115	55
	1200 29th – 2000 29th	2313	1907	780	735	0
Y2	2000 29th – 1200 30th	959	615	359	0	0
	1200 30th – 2000 30th	2096	2437	1513	1022	112
Preliminary bombardment		43905	12451	11795	4967	350
2000 30th – 1200 1st July		13537	5080	3538	0	0
1200 1st – 2000 1st		6655	2109	1994	0	0
		20192	7189	5532	0	0
Grand totals		64097	19640	17327	4967	350

Table 8 29th Divisional Field Artillery & Trench Mortar ammunition expenditure 24th June to 1st July[38]

The first signs that things might be about to get tricky occurred at 7 a.m. The companies of the 1st Lancashire Fusiliers and the mixed bombing party had been sheltering patiently and unnoticed in the Sunken Road throughout the early morning. This was about to end as suddenly twenty 77 mm shells burst in and around the lane causing 20 casualties. It was later thought that an observer had spotted the entrance to the tunnel and had put two and two together. Two hundred yards away, the defenders of the Bergwerk would have been alerted and put in a state of instant readiness for the race to the parapet.

The tunnel entrance was visible because the Royal Engineers had slightly misjudged its direction:

> "Unfortunately this exit came out a few yards too far north, at a point where it was exposed to enemy fire in part and so that we had to use it on hands and knees. Its purpose was to serve as a sort of concealed communication trench for the sunken lane."[39]

Two hundred yards to the south, the men of the 9. Kompanie, RIR 119, waited in their dugouts under the front parapet of the Hawthorn Redoubt (Weißdomfeste to the Germans) none expecting their imminent oblivion. The 9. Kompanie was part of the III Battalion commanded by Major Schäfer and they were unaware of the fatal danger immediately beneath their feet.

At 7.20 a.m. the earth erupted with unprecedented violence[i]. A huge cone of earth and smoke surged into the air, taking with it three sections of No. 1 Platoon, 9. Kompanie, commanded by Leutnant Renz. The adjacent dugouts of nearly 1½ platoons were either crushed or had their entrances blocked. Parts of No. 2 Platoon, Leutnant Böhm, were buried in their dugouts (although Böhm was to survive) and many of the entrances were blocked by great chunks of falling chalk. All of the entrances of No. 3 Platoon, Lt. Breitmeyer, were filled with rubble, trapping the officer and his men and the company commander, Oberleutnant der Reserve Anton Mühlbayer, underground for hours as the air slowly ran out. Those men not killed immediately by either the explosion or the collapse of their dugout were now either asphyxiated by the poisonous gasses released by the explosion, or died starved of oxygen. Those trapped inside an air pocket began the frantic task of digging themselves out through the tons of chalk that now obstructed the entrances. Some would succeed. Others not.

As a great cloud of smoke hovered over the ridge, drifting slowly over the German lines, tons of chalk rocks and other debris started to rain down over a crater some 50 yards in diameter. A lip nearly six yards high had been thrown up and the rubble covered an area some 120 yards across.

NOW THE RACE FOR THE CRATER'S EDGE BEGAN.

And the British heavy artillery firing on the German front trench lifted onto the reserve trench everywhere on the VIII Corps front. On the 29th Division's front the 79th Siege Battery started to fire on the eastern edge of Beaumont Hamel, the 23rd Siege Battery moved onto the northern half and the 77th Siege Battery the southern half of Station Road. For the next ten minutes, as the attacking troops started to emerge into No Man's Land ready for the assault, no shell of any weight fell on the German front line and, for the last five minutes of the bombardment, no heavy shells fell on the German support trench either. Only the 18 pdrs and the Stokes trench mortars were left to fire at the German front trenches. Even firing three rounds per gun per minute the fifty two 18 pdrs firing had 2,000 yards of front to cover and their lightweight shells were hardly going to keep the German infantry and their machine guns below ground.

---

[i] To be exceeded eight minutes later when the 60,000 lbs. of the Lochnagar mine exploded at La Boisselle.

Plate 14 Lt. Samuel MacDonnell Campbell, 13th Lancashire Fusiliers att. 86th Trench Mortar Battery

Many high ranking officers had placed their hopes on the storm of shells fired from the 3 in. Stokes mortars. At 7.20 a.m. four guns of the 87th Trench Mortar Battery revealed themselves at the end of the Mary Tunnel and started to fire at a furious rate into the nearby German trenches[i]. The eight guns of the 88th TMB were in emplacements at the end of a tunnel driven 111 yards out from the end of Sap 6 and they joined in with the frantic delivery of hundreds of the 10¾ lb. bombs onto the already battered trench lines opposite. The gunners of the 86th TMB were also involved at the northern end of the Division's front with four firing on the German trenches and four more going with the Royal Fusiliers as they attacked the Hawthorn Ridge crater. 88th TMB managed to fire 1,200 rounds in the ten minutes allowed, an average of 15 rounds per gun per minute, although they could not see where the shells were landing as a result of the configuration of the ground on its front. They lost one man, a sergeant, in the process. The four guns of the 87th TMB ceased firing at 7.32 a.m., possibly as an indication of the longer distance its battalions had to travel to reach the German wire, but came out unscathed. This was not the case for the 86th TMB but then they would have four guns out in the thick of the fighting around the crater. Casualties amongst these gun teams would be heavy: one officer killed and another wounded with two other ranks killed, five missing and another nine wounded[ii]. Previous demonstrations of these new weapons had raised expectations and now

---

[i] Two guns from 87th TMB were attached to each of the 1st Border Regt. and 1st KOSB.

[ii] The officer casualties were:

2nd Lt. Samuel MacDonnell Campbell, 13th Lancashire Fusiliers att. 86th Trench Mortar Battery, who was the second son of Mr. Robert M. Campbell of Dungiven, Larne. Before the war he was a cashier in the Larne Branch of the Northern Banking Company. Served in Egypt. He had been transferred on 30th May 1916. He is buried in Beaumont-Hamel British Cemetery, grave B. 52.

2nd Lt. Archibald Pollock, 3rd att. 1st Lancashire Fusiliers, was wounded.

was their chance to impress, but they did not, nor could they, make up for the absence of the truly heavy guns now firing at targets more than 200 yards behind the German front line.

The consequences of the inadequate bombardment of the frontal zones and the early lift of the heavier guns were well summed up by the writer of the war diary of the 147th Brigade, RFA:

> "…except in isolated cases, the enemy front line was scarcely entered. The enemy front line trench had not been sufficiently damaged to prevent movement in and out of the dugouts and even before our 18 pdrs lifted off the enemy front line many of the enemy machine guns were up on the parapet."[40]

What the attacking troops and the commanding Generals did not know was that, in spite of the tens of thousands of shells fired at the German trenches occupied by the RIR 119 and RIR 121, they had suffered hardly any casualties. The RIR 119 reported 20 men killed and 83 wounded as a result of the seven day bombardment. To the north the RIR 121 had lost 24 dead, 122 wounded and one missing. Just 250 casualties after seven days of the severest bombardment the British Army had delivered in its history. As a result, the attacking British battalions were about to suffer two or three times that number of casualties *each* in barely a few minutes.

The effect of the Corps counter-battery fire was no more successful. The 26. RFAR had lost just nine men killed since the beginning of the bombardment and three of those had been attached to one of the two Leichte Munitions-Kolonne (Light Ammunition Column). The gunners at the batteries had lost just five men from three of the batteries in seven days. On the southern wing of the Somme front, however, the French 6th Army and the French-assisted XIII Corps had been making mincemeat out of the German gunners and their guns such was the concentration of heavy and light HE, shrapnel and gas shell poured on any German battery with the temerity to open fire.

ON HAWTHORN RIDGE, THE TWO PLATOONS OF Z COMPANY, 2nd Royal Fusiliers, led by Lt. Leonard Charles Russell were already out in No Man's Land as the lumps of chalk and clay crashed to earth. Russell had been an accountant before the war[i] and nothing in his previous experience could have prepared him for the next few hours. Now he watched as his men spread out on either side of him and then set off for all they were worth towards the still smoking crater. Already the insistent chatter of Maxim machine guns could be heard and bullets whistled and whined around the men. Men walked and ran and fell, scythed down by cross fire now trained on them. There was no-one else for the German machine guns to fire at until the South Wales Borderers and Inniskillings moved out into No Man's Land away to the right and so the Royal Fusiliers hurried and fell and died. Running with them were two Lewis gun teams, a section of bombers, four Vickers machine gun teams commanded by the Brigade Machine

[i] He lived at 44, Hillcourt Road, East Dulwich.

Gun Officer, Lt. Kenneth Fergus McAlpin[i], 14th Royal Fusiliers, and men lugging four Stokes mortars and their ammunition. These weapons would only be of any use if all the elements of the team made it to the appointed spot. A Stokes without its base plate, or tripod or bombs was useless, as was a Vickers without its tripod, water coolant and belts of .303 bullets.

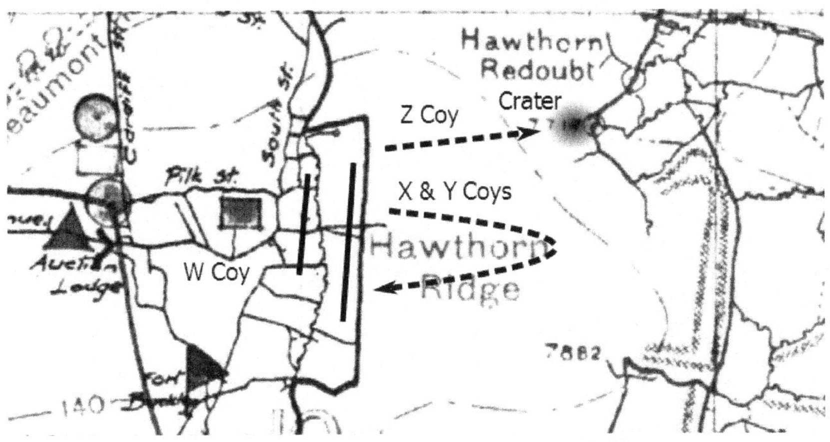

Map 11 The attack of 2nd Royal Fusiliers, 0730.

Z Company split into two parties as they charged towards the crater lip, one party to the left and another, under Russell, to the right. The vicious cross fire through which they ran accounted for two officers, many of the infantry and the majority of the Stokes mortar teams. The four machine guns and some of the mortars with about 20 rounds per gun reached the crater. Two Vickers each were sent to the left and to the right and the mortars were set up centrally under the lip of the crater.

Within five minutes of their arrival these machine guns were in action sweeping the German front lines to the north and south and the two northern guns cleared the 15 to 20 enemy infantry they saw in the German trench running away down the slope towards the New Beaumont Road. Lt. McAlpin had good observation over the German trenches running north towards the Bergwerk. He later reported that these trenches were badly knocked about and that he could see parties of the enemy moving about from the waist upwards. They presented excellent targets to his two gun teams. The guns to the south of the crater, however, had little at which to fire as the front German trenches in the re-entrant were concealed by the slope. The Stokes mortars started firing at about 7.35 a.m. but with so few rounds available were soon quiet.

Although barely two sections of the 9. Kompanie, RIR 119, had escaped the carnage of the mine detonation relatively unscathed these men rushed to the

[i] Lt., Temp. Capt., Kenneth Fergus McAlpin, 14th Royal Fusiliers att. 86th Machine Gun Company, had been appointed Brigade Machine Gun Officer on 25th November 1915. He transferred to the Machine Gun Corps in August 1916. Served at Gallipoli, in France and Palestine. He remained in the Regular Reserve of Officers until 1935 when he resigned his commission with the rank of Major. Twice MiD. Before the war he was a medical student at Guy's Hospital.

crater edge determined to defend their position. Within 15 minutes of the explosion two German machine guns had been set up on the far side of the crater. In addition, in neighbouring trenches, between four and six Maxims had been brought up from dugouts and they were now sweeping the British front line, focusing on the gaps in the British wire through which the attacking infantry was filtering and where the congestion was already considerable.

The 147th Brigade, RFA, noted the problems with the British wire:

> "Our own wire had been insufficiently cut and our dead were soon in bunches in the gaps therein."[41]

This view was later supported by Maj. Richard Osbaldeston Spencer Smith[i], 2iC of the 2nd Hampshire Regt., who wrote after the war:

> "There is no doubt that our wire was a serious obstacle to the assault, the paths that had been cut were much too small causing men to bunch. It should have been bodily removed in certain clearly marked places and in sufficient width. As the attack took place in the early morning this could have been done under nightfall. Men just got entangled in loose tangles and strands of wire."[42]

The supporting companies of the Royal Fusiliers were being mown down in heaps and soon it became clear that very few reinforcements would ever reach Russell's and McAlpin's men at the crater. In addition, the German artillery belonging to Artillery Group Miraumont[ii], Oberst Erlenbusch, R.F.A.R. 26, had now opened on the British front line with shrapnel and the communication trenches with Howitzer HE and this, plus the trenches becoming clogged with wounded, slowed the forward progress of W Company of the Royal Fusiliers and of the supporting battalions.

The commanders of two of the supporting Companies of the Royal Fusiliers were the only officers of the battalion not to be wounded or killed. Captains Dearden and Baldwin somehow managed to get through the day unscathed or nearly, in the case of James Ferrand Dearden. He was saved from death by his Brodie helmet which deflected a bullet, even though the impact knocked him out for a while. Nothing daunted, when he came round, Dearden continued to lead his men and was one of the last to come in from No Man's Land when the withdrawal took place[iii]. Other young officers did their utmost. 2nd Lt. Stanley

---

[i] Maj. Richard Osbaldeston Spencer Smith, 2nd Hampshire Regt., was born in 1885. Educated at St John's College, Oxford University, he was commissioned into the Hampshire Regt. in 1909. He married Murielle Alethe Victoria Wingfield-Stratford (dec. 1931) in 1912. He was promoted Captain in 1914. He joined the staff of Sandhurst in 1917. He remarried in 1932 Christian Louis Passy. He was the Lt. Col. of Princess Beatrice's Isle of Wight Rifles, 8th Battalion, The Hampshire Regiment, from 1932 to 1936. He died in 1962.

[ii] Artillery Sub-Group Adolf, Maj. Bornemann (I/RFAR 26) and Artillery Sub-Group Beauregard, Major Kollen (I/FAR 104).

[iii] Capt. James Ferrand Dearden, DSO, MC & 2 Bars, 2nd Royal Fusiliers, died on 6th October 1919. Aged 23, he was the son of Peregrine Robert and Annie Abbott Dearden (née Grigg), of the Hotel Curtis, Cheltenham. Born in Canterbury, New Zealand, he entered the RMC, Sandhurst, in 1913. He passed out in September 1914 but was initially deemed medically unfit (irregular heartbeat). He was then passed fit and commissioned

Pakeman[i] had seen officers and men cut down like corn before the German machine guns and he did his best to collect the survivors and urge them forwards before himself collapsing severely wounded. He would survive. 2nd Lt. Ferdinand Reiss[ii] saw his company commander killed and assumed command. Wounded, he stayed out throughout the night helping his men get back to their trenches. Both would be awarded the Military Cross.

Lt. Albert Walter Whitlock was with W Company and he watched as X and Y Companies tried to get across No Man's Land:

> "…the major portion of the first wave of the three companies of the 2nd RF were placed out of action almost immediately with no one getting into the enemy's trenches.
> My own company which followed shortly afterwards as second wave was also put out of action after which no more troops could leave our trenches mainly owing to the constant machine gun barrage on our parapet from the Redoubt."[43]

Whitlock encouraged his men forward into No Man's Land but was wounded as soon as he stepped over the parapet[iii].

But the German guns were not the only ones causing trouble in the British trenches:

> "The enemy retaliated heavily on our front system of trenches and on our main communication trenches, completely blocking many of them. Our

---

into the 2nd Royal Fusiliers. MiD and MC 1916. MiD, DSO and MC 1917 and wounded at Cambrai. MiD twice and MC 1918. Diagnosed with Pulmonary Tuberculosis in August 1918 he was sent to the Home Sanatorium in Bournemouth. He was declared medically unfit in July 1919 and returned to his home where he died eleven weeks later. He is buried in St Peter's Churchyard, Leckhampton, to the south of the church. His brother, Midshipman Percy Dearden served on *HMS Queen Elizabeth* in the Dardanelles and was on *HMS Queen Mary* when it blew up and sank on the first day of the Battle of Jutland. He was one of the few survivors and was picked up by a German destroyer and made a PoW for 18 months. He was later interned in Holland.

Lt. (temp Capt.) Dearden was awarded an MC for his actions on 1st July 1916. The citation in the *London Gazette* of 22nd September 1916 reads: "For conspicuous gallantry in action. He led his company with great dash against the enemy trenches. He was knocked over and rendered unconscious by a bullet on his steel helmet. When he recovered, he continued to command, and was one of the last to withdraw".

[i] 2nd Lt. Stanley Edward Pakeman, 2nd Royal Fusiliers, was awarded an MC for his conduct on 1st July 1916. The citation in the *London Gazette* of 22nd September 1916 reads: "For conspicuous gallantry in action. After his command had suffered severe casualties he went up and down the line collecting men to lead on, till he was severely wounded himself".

[ii] 2nd Lt. Ferdinand Edward Reiss, 28th Royal Fusiliers att. 2nd Royal Fusiliers, was awarded an MC for his conduct on 1st July 1916. The citation in the *London Gazette* of 22nd September 1916 reads: "For conspicuous gallantry in action. After his Captain had been killed, he led his company, and continued to urge on the men till he was badly wounded himself. He remained out till night, refusing to leave his men".

[iii] 2nd Lt. Albert Walter Whitlock, 2nd Royal Fusiliers, was awarded the MC for his conduct on 1st July 1916. His citation in the *London Gazette* of 26th September 1916 reads: "For conspicuous gallantry in action. He led the reserve company of his battalion against the enemy's first line, directing and cheering them on till he fell wounded".

heavy artillery, even 9.2 howitzers, put many shorts into our own trenches adding greatly to the horrors that our own infantry had to undergo."[44]

The effect of the German machine guns, artillery barrage and the 'friendly fire' was to delay the departure of the supporting battalions from the British trenches until close to 8 a.m. and to drive those in No Man's Land to earth.

A German account later described the effect of the heavy German fire on the morale of the attacking infantry:

"According to later statements from prisoners the attacking British troops had been assured that the advance would be a 'walk over'; all the defenders in the front German lines would have been killed by their artillery and the only serious resistance was to be expected in the German 3rd line. The success of the 10. and 11. Kompanien in defending their position convinced them otherwise."[45]

As a result, back at the crater, Russell and his men were on their own. The German line in the re-entrant to the south was rapidly filling with men from the 10. and 11. Kompanien, RIR 119. They had brought with them from their dugouts the half a dozen machine guns already mentioned.

At the crater, however, both defenders and attackers believed their positions to be in jeopardy. The bombing parties and the two Lewis gun teams that had advanced with Lt. Russell had pushed towards the south of the crater where rubble blocking the exits of their dugout had trapped the men of No. 3 Platoon of 9. Kompanie, RIR 119. One small hole existed in one of the four exits and now a German was trying to enlarge it when some of the attackers appeared. They killed this chalk-dust covered soldier who fell back down the stairs into the bottom of the dugout. Behind him Lt. der Reserve Meier and the Company commander, Oberleutnant der Reserve Anton Mühlbayer, along with several men stood on the stairs waiting to escape. One of them clutched a flare gun which normally he would have used to call up artillery support but now this man, Vizefeldwebel Davidsohn, turned it to another purpose. He fired the flare into the face of the British soldier who had just killed his colleague. The British retaliated with bombs, driving Mühlbayer and his men into the bottom of the dugout from where they heard shouted demands for their surrender. After yelling their refusal they retreated to the far end of the dugout to await the help of their comrades.

Back above ground, Russell pushed round the edge of the crater and led a group of about 15 men into a German trench only to come face to face with one of the German machine guns, almost certainly Machine Gun No. 2 of the 2. Maschinengewehr Kompanie, RIR 119, commanded by Utffz. Aicheler. Aicheler's gun and team had been on the surface when the mine exploded and had been knocked into the bottom the trench by the power of the detonation. Perhaps here the gun was jammed by dirt, anyway, when Russell and his men charged them the gun jammed twice after only twenty rounds and they had no option but to retreat into the next traverse where the gun was rapidly got back into action. For Russell and his men there was no alternative but to charge the gun again but, cleared of the jam and firing at full tilt, most of his men were killed or wounded in the act. Russell, left with just a corporal and two other men, was forced to retire down then trench where his small band tried to keep the enemy at bay with grenades. Meanwhile, above their heads, a fire fight was developing nearby between the Lewis guns by the crater and Aicheler's gun team.

For the Germans at the crater matters were critical. All of the available troops were in the front line and the dugouts and tunnels under Beaumont Hamel were empty of reserves. If the Royal Fusiliers and the Middlesex had been able to push onwards then the entire position of the RIR 119 would have been threatened. The German soldier on the Somme at this time, however, was not short of initiative. Indeed, the German accounts of the Somme fighting count this as one of the crucial differences between the brave but inexperienced and over-rehearsed British troops and their own men amongst whom independent and speedy action was positively encouraged. In the next line of trenches behind the crater were two platoons of infantry. These men of the 7. and 12. Kompanien under Lt. der Landwehr Heinz Rupp[i] and Lt. d. Res. Gerster rushed across the open to the crater, Gerster bringing with him two Madsen light machine guns of the 1. Kompanie of the 1. Musketen Bataillon. Leaping into shell holes they took the few British infantry still advancing under fire, preventing them joining up with Russell and his men at the crater's edge.

Russell and his beleaguered men urgently needed reinforcements and the young officer decided to risk a glance back across No Man's Land to see if anyone was on their way. He spotted a small group of men lying in a depression out in No Man's Land but before he could do anything a German sniper hit him on the helmet, bowling him over. Russell's luck was in, however, and the result was a messy but slight flesh wound over the left eye. Feeling it essential that a status report and a request for reinforcement was urgently sent back to his CO, the lieutenant tried throwing a message sheet to the men out in the German wire. It landed short and so he made a dash for it. The distance was no more than six yards and he nearly made it. As he tried to flatten himself into the grass a machine raked the area catching him in the head and face and, rather more seriously, in the left shoulder.

He now discovered that most of the men were either dead or wounded. One of them was another officer, a Lt. Arthur Hedges, who Russell had passed earlier applying a field dressing to a leg wound. Russell suggested to Hedges that he might try to take some of the wounded back and pass a message on at the same time. After a while, Hedges and half a dozen men made a dash for it. The officer and three men reached a shell crater in which they were later found and made prisoners of war. Russell[ii] would share the same fate later having survived several nearby shell explosions as well as German bullets and bombs liberally distributed over No Man's Land to finish off any possibility of a renewed attack.

A DEGREE OF CHAOS WAS RAPIDLY DEVELOPING IN THE BRITISH TRENCHES. Wounded men by the dozen were flooding back through the wire and were trying, by all means possible, to get to medical assistance in the rear. As they went, they discarded equipment and some even their clothing. Trying to get forward in the opposite direction were the remnants of the three companies of

---

[i] Killed 29th September 1916.

[ii] Lt. Leonard Charles Russell, 2nd Royal Fusiliers, was taken prisoner but escaped 17 months later. See *Appendix 1* – Prisoners of War.

the 2nd Royal Fusiliers who had failed to get forward in support of their colleagues in Z Company. In addition, members of the 86th Machine Gun Company were attempting to get forward as were carrying and consolidating parties made up of Nos. 5 and 6 Sections of No. 14 Platoon, 1/2nd Monmouths. Not sure whether to advance or stay where they were, they were eventually withdrawn into a deep dugout but not before losing one man killed, two wounded and three missing.

Behind them came the men of the 1st Royal Dublin Fusiliers and the 16th Middlesex Regt. W Company of the Dublin Fusiliers with Y Company in support tried to move up F Street and Broadway while X Company with Z in support went up Bloomfield and 2nd Avenue. Their task was to be ready to move out against the German second line system of trenches on Beaucourt Ridge, south east of Beaumont Hamel but this could only be achieved once the Royal Fusiliers had taken the redoubt and the front line system and this they seemed unable to do. So, instead of advancing, the Dubliners added to the congestion in the trenches. As did their carrying parties from the Monmouths: Nos. 7 and 8 Sections of No. 14 Platoon. They too eventually withdrew to a deep dugout in the support lines having spent some time helping with the wounded and in carrying bombs and ammunition forward from the reserve dump.

Lt. Col. Herbert Nelson, DSO, CO of the 1st Dublins, confirmed just how bad the logjam was in the front line trenches when writing after the war:

> "At zero hour the battalion started filing down the various communication trenches towards the front line and very soon found progress almost impossible owing to stretcher bearer parties trying to struggle back along the same way.
> Eventually most of the battalion did manage to reach the front trench to find that parties of the Royal Fusiliers were still in it.
> Utter chaos prevailed. Looking over the parapet one could see the wire entanglements uncut and the various passages through it choked with the bodies of the dead and dying."[46]

W and X Companies of the Dublins were the first to try to enter No Man's Land but by now it was gone 8 a.m. As they clambered out of the front line trenches the two leading companies and then Y Company following on behind encountered a problem which was to be a recurring theme along the 29th Division's front and speaks ill of the Staff work of that formation:

> "Our own barbed wire was cut only at intervals of about 40 yards and by this time the Germans had machine guns trained on these gaps, the result being that our casualties were very heavy and only a few of our men ever got through our own wire and still fewer of these succeeded in advancing more than 50 to 60 yards before being shot down. W Company and Y Company both behaved exceptionally well under fire."[47]

Those few men of the Dublins who got through their own wire failed to reach the enemy's wire entanglements. 2nd Lt. Douglas Warner went forward with his men until fatally wounded. His corporal offered to carry him back to safety but Warner told the NCO to leave him behind and carry on advancing. His body was not found until the battlefield was cleared in the Spring of 1917[i].

Taking a heavy toll of the support companies of the Royal Fusiliers and of those few men of the Dublins who got through their own wire was Machine Gun No. 3 of the 2. Maschinengewehr Kompanie. Commanded by an Uttfz. Boehme this gun was located in the second German trench just to the north of the Y Ravine. It had a perfect view over the ground between the British front line and the lip of the crater and, even nearer, the re-entrant which lay between the crater and the northern end of the Y Ravine. If no targets presented themselves in this sector, then the gun easily swing round to the south and take on the British troops struggling across the wide expanse of No Man's Land between the Y Ravine and the Mary Redan. Some men, possibly from 2nd Lt. Wilson's party mentioned above, optimistically tried to throw Mills bombs in the the gun team's direction, possibly in an interval when the gun briefly jammed, but to no avail. One nearby explosion knocked the gun and its team into the bottom of the trench but they were soon back in action and, like Machine Gun No. 1, began to run out of targets.

Capt. F A Wilson of the Dublin Fusiliers complained after the war about the inability of the infantry to move at any speed across No Man's Land such was the load they were forced to carry. More heavily laden than the Royal Fusiliers, his men provided a slow moving target as they walked stolidly into a hail of machine gun cross-fire. They stood little chance.

> "Loaded up as the infantry were it was quite impossible for any man to move at any pace faster than a walk, whereas had the troops been able to move quickly across No Man's Land the enemy machine gunners would have had much harder shooting.
>
> It was the enemy machine guns that stopped us, far more than their artillery. One of our officers who was wounded that day and whom I met afterwards in London told me he was hit in the thigh by no less than thirteen machine gun bullets.
>
> Application was made by one of our officers for the battalion to be allowed to travel as light as possible but permission was refused and the men went over loaded up more like beasts of burden than anything else."[48]

Lt. Col. Nelson and his staff were to move to a position in the Y Ravine once the enemy front line had been taken by the Royal Fusiliers. Unlike his men, who even now were struggling to get through the narrow gaps in the British wire, Nelson had been instructed to cross No Man's Land using the 1st Avenue tunnel dug by the Royal Engineers opposite the northern end of Y Ravine. When he arrived at the opened out end of the sap all he found was the dead body one of

[i] 2nd Lt. Douglas Redston Warner, 4th att. 1st Royal Dublin Fusiliers, was aged 28. He was educated at Woodcote House, Windlesham, and Bradfield. He trained as an engineer at Messrs Marshall's at Gainsborough and then went to Vancouver. He returned on the outbreak of war and enlisted in the 1st Sportsman's Battalion and was commissioned into the RDF in April 1915. He spent five months at Gallipoli. He is buried in Hawthorn Ridge Cemetery No. 1, Auchonvillers, grave B. 7.

the men from the Stokes mortar teams which had used the saps during the final 10 minute hurricane bombardment of the German front lines. Nelson peered over the edge and found himself close to the German wire. No one was moving in No Man's Land to his right, the 87th Brigade front, or left, where the Royal Fusiliers were supposed to be. He sensibly concluded that the attack had failed and returned to his HQ.

Affairs had not improved in the front line trenches:

> "The confusion in the front trench was terrible and control was out of the question. Stretcher cases and the slightly wounded of both battalions made communication by trench almost impossible and very few reports reached me as to the progress of my left leading company.
> I did learn later however that a small party of my battalion on the left had been found in the front trench by the Brigadier who ordered the two officers with him to take them forward. It was certain death but they went and were all killed."[49]

It has not proved possible to identify either of these officers.

EXTRAORDINARY AND CONTRADICTORY REPORTS of success and failure were now flying between Brigade, Division and Corps.

At 7.52 a.m. the 29th Division diary erroneously stated that:

> "86th Brigade report that the Dublin Fusiliers have gone through the Royal Fusiliers and that Germans are running down Beaumont Alley."[50]

Such a report makes no appearance in the 86th Brigade war diary. Indeed, the 86th Brigade diary paints a completely different and wholly depressing picture of failure:

> "It was not until 7.55 a.m. that the two 2nd line battalions were able to leave the parapet. By this time the enemy had marked down our passages through our wire and the fire on them was very heavy. The two leading companies of the Dublins followed shortly by a third did their best to gain ground but they also failed to reach the enemy's wire and were shot down all along the front."[51]

The 7.55 a.m. report from the 86th Brigade diary went on to describe the fate of the left hand battalion, the 16th Middlesex, some of whom were seen to reach the German lines just north of the crater:

> "The 16th Middlesex moved forward on the left very steadily and reached the crater though not without considerable loss."[52]

The 16th Middlesex Regt. was to advance on a rather narrow front. C and D Companies led the way, on the right and left respectively, each on a front of 100 yards. Behind and to the right of C was A Company with B Company following D. The advance was in columns of platoons. This extended mass of men must have made a perfect target for machine guns and artillery alike.

To the left of the crater at least some of the 16th Middlesex Regt. managed to reach the German lines along the slope running down to the New Beaumont Road and the northern rim of the enormous white hole in Hawthorn Rdige. The crater, however, was much larger than expected, as the battalion CO, Lt. Col. John Hamilton-Hall[i] explained after the war:

> "Of the 200 yards of frontage assigned to me quite one third in the middle was occupied by this obstacle. The broken earth round about the crater also, no doubt with its hope of affording some cover from the machine gun swept surface, had a certain amount of magnetism for troops whose line of direction passed near its flanks. Possibly it was not realised how vast the crater would be. Personally I expected to see one of not more than half of its extent."[53]

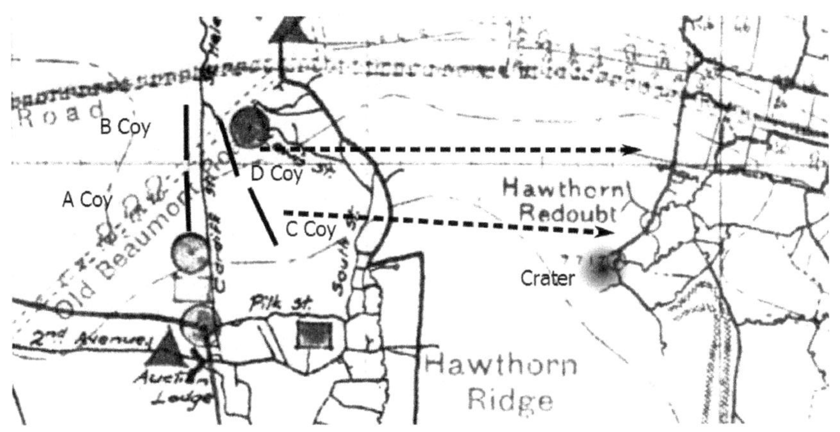

Map 12 The attack of the 16th Middlesex Regt., 0730.

Although their role was to drive into the northern section of Beaumont Hamel alongside the Lancashire Fusiliers, the battalion was almost inevitably drawn into the fighting on the northern edge of the still smoking mine crater. As they approached the German position they were taken under fire by Machine Gun No. 1 of 2. Maschinengewehr Kompanie commanded by Uttfz. Braungart. Before the first 250 round belt had been finished the gun's bullets had taken down most of the first wave and two of the battalion's officers. Belt after belt was reloaded as Braungart's gun team swept the hillside above the Beaumont to Auchonvillers Road clean of the officers and men of the 16th Middlesex Regt. It was like shooting fish in a barrel.

[i] Maj. (Temp. Lt.Col.) later Brig. Gen. John Hamilton-Hall, CMG, DSO & Bar, was born at Harrou, North West Frontier Province, on 23rd February 1871. He was the son of the late Major John Greive Hall, RE, and Agnes Robertson of Edinburgh. He was educated at the United Services College, Fettes College, Edinburgh and the RMC, Sandhurst. He was commissioned into the Middlesex Regt in 1891 being promoted Captain in 1890. He served in the South African War (medal, 4 clasps) and was a Staff Capt., DAQMG and DAAG in South Africa from 1902 to 1907 being promoted Major in 1908. Assistant Inspector of Recruiting, Eastern Command, 1913-1914, he took command of the 16th Middlesex on 19th September 1914. He was promoted Lt. Col. in 1916 and Brig. Gen. between 1918 and 1919. MiD four times. He was promoted Colonel in 1921 and was in charge of the Record Office, Lichfield, 1921-1925. He died, single, on 12th April 1953.

In spite of being dressed like their men, the officers of the Middlesex advancing over the exposed hillside were rapidly identified and targeted. Capt. Eric Hall went down wounded in the knee about 80 yards from the German front line trench. Unable to move he became a prisoner of war later in the day[i].

Plate 15 2nd Lt. Eric Rupert Heaton, 14th att. 16th Middlesex Regt

Plate 16 Capt. George Henry Heslop, 16th Middlesex Regt

Another casualty was 2nd Lt. Eric Rupert Heaton[ii] who was attached to the 16th Middlesex from the 14th Battalion. He wrote a final and moving letter to his parents on the evening of Wednesday, 28th June, when it was still expected that the attack would be on Thursday, 29th June:

> "I'm writing this on the eve of my first action. Tomorrow we go to the attack in the greatest battle the British Army has ever fought. I cannot quite express my feelings on this night, and I cannot tell you if it's God's will that I shall come through, but if I fall in battle, then I have no regrets, save for my loved ones I leave behind. It is a great cause, and I came out willingly to serve my King and country. My greatest concern is that I may have the courage and determination necessary to lead my platoon well. No one had such parents as you have been to me, giving me such splendid opportunities and always thinking of my welfare at great self-sacrifice to yourself. My life has been full of faults, but I've tried at all times to live as

---

[i] Capt. Eric Walter Hall, 16th Middlesex Regt., was educated at Malvern College and Trinity College, Oxford. He was a director of Peter Jones Ltd., and was a member of Chelsea Borough Council after the war.

[ii] 2nd Lt. Eric Rupert Heaton, 14th att. 16th Middlesex Regt., was aged 20. He was the youngest son of the late Rev. Daniel Heaton and of Mrs Heaton of Cressbrook, 46, Pembroke Crescent, Hove, Sussex. Educated at the Royal Grammar School, Guildford, he was a medical student at Birkbeck College, London and played cricket for Woking CC. He was a member of London University OTC. He is buried in Hawthorn Ridge Cemetery No. 1, Auchonvillers, grave A. 89.

a man and thus follow the example of my father. This life abroad has taught me many things, chiefly the fine character of the British race to put up with hardships with wonderful cheerfulness. How I have learned to love my men. My great aim has been to win their respect, which I trust I have accomplished and hope that, when the time comes, I shall not fail them. If I fall, do not let things be black for you. Be cheerful, and you will be living then always to my memory."[54]

Heaton led his men towards the chalk strewn perimeter of the crater but was shot in the leg. He was last seen alive lying in the long grass that covered No Man's Land. His remains were found and buried in 1917.

Talented sportsman Capt. George Henry Heslop[i] also fell. Leaving the trenches at 7.55 a.m. he led D Company along the left of the battalion's advance, exposed to machine gun and rifle fire from the ridge and the Bergwerk on the other side of the New Beaumont Road. Heslop was only 21 years old but had been rapidly promoted: 2nd Lieutenant in September 1914, Lieutenant in January 1915 and Captain in May 1915. A promotion to Major had only been turned down on the basis of his age. He was a musketry instructor, had done courses on bombing and machine guns and was now a company commander. He was struck down somewhere between the British front line and the edge of the crater. One of his men wrote later that he advanced:

"… not minding the shells and bullets, but just leading us on as if nothing was happening."

The CO, Hamilton-Hall, wrote to his parents that 'no one's death would be more deeply felt'.

Coming on behind with B Company was 24 year old 2nd Lt. Frederic Baron Tanqueray, a solicitor from Woburn in Bedfordshire. The last recorded sight of him was as he shouted a cheery 'Good luck' to a wounded fellow officer. His body was recovered after the fall of Beaumont Hamel in November[ii].

---

[i] Capt. George Henry Heslop, 16th Middlesex Regt., was aged 21. Born in Sandback, Cheshire, he was the only son of George Heslop, MA, headmaster of Sevenoaks School, and Gertrude Heslop of 41, The Park, Mitcham, Surrey. He was educated at Lancing College, where he was in the OTC, and was due to attend Trinity College, Cambridge, in September 1914. He was in the Lancing cricket 1st XI, being captain in 1913-14, and the school football XI, captaining from 1912-14. A prolific batsman, he scored one double century and four centuries in the summer of 1914, topping the batting averages. He was also the leading wicket taker and Wisden describd him as 'the most promising young all-rounder who had yet to appear in a first class match'. He enlisted as Pte 433 in the Public Schools' Battalion in September 1914 and was commissioned on 29th September 1914. Previously wounded in January 1916 near the Hohenzollern Redoubt, his body was found in 1917 and he is buried in Hawthorn Ridge Cemetery No. 1, Auchonvillers, grave B. 40. On October 28th 1916 the following appeared in the Sussex Daily News: "In memory of Captain G H Heslop, Middlesex Regiment, who fell in action last July, and who was very prominent in athletics at Lancing College, an anonymous gift has been provided, by means of which a cricket bat will be presented annually for the best individual performance in the Brighton College match". The first recipient was Maurice Cyril Philpot Tuckett in 1916 who was commissioned into the RFC in June 1917.

[ii] 2nd Lt. Frederic Baron Tanqueray, B Company, 16th Middlesex Regt., was aged 24. He was the son of Frederic Thomas, solicitor, and Catherine Tanqueray of Woburn, Beds. He

Plate 17 2nd Lt. Eustace Roland Whitby, 16th Middlesex Regt

Plate 18 2nd Lt. Frederic Baron Tanqueray, 16th Middlesex Regt.

Lt. Henry Heath[i] was older than average at 39 years of age. Nonetheless, he bravely took his men towards the German lines and, even when mortally wounded, continued to encourage and direct their actions.

2nd Lt. Dudley Starnes[ii], attached from the 14th Middlesex, seeing his fellow officers fall, took control of the faltering troops and guided them forward until he too was struck down, another to become a prisoner of war.

2nd Lt. Eustace Whitby, attached from the 24th Middlesex, was amongst the last officers to be hit. Collecting the leaderless men from other platoons he took them onward until he fell unconscious to the ground. He would survive this day

---

was educated at The Knoll, Woburn Sands, and Tonbridge, leaving in 1906 to be articled to his father. He was a member of the Cadet Corps at Tonbridge. Having passed the final Law Examination in January 1914, he practised with his father in Woburn, Beds. Enlisted Sept. 1914, as 117 Private, 16th Middlesex Regt. Promoted sergeant, he was commissioned in 1915. Went to France November 1915. His body was recovered in 1917 and he is buried in Beaumont Hamel British Cemetery, grave B. 62.

[i] Lt. Henry James Heath, MC, 16th Middlesexas aged 39. He was the son of George and Eliza Barbara Heath. Born at Alton, Hants, he was educated at Farnham Grammar School and he was a member of the United Empire Club, 117 Piccadilly. He is buried in Hawthorn Ridge Cemetery No. 1, Auchonvillers, grave A. 84. He was awarded a posthumous MC for his conduct on 1st July 1916. The citation in the *London Gazette* of 22nd September 1916 reads: "For conspicuous gallantry in action. He commanded his platoon with great coolness and courage, and, when severely wounded, continued to urge on his men and to issue instructions".

[ii] 2nd Lt. Dudley Sampson Blyth Starnes, 14th Middlesex Regt., att. 16th Middlesex Regt., was awarded an MC for his conduct on 1st July 1916. The citation in the *London Gazette* of 22nd September 1916 reads: "For conspicuous gallantry in action. He led a platoon in an attack with great coolness and bravery, and reorganised men of other platoons whose leaders had fallen. He was finally himself severely wounded".

but not the war[i]. Heath, Starnes and Whitby were all awarded the Military Cross, Heath posthumously.

Attached to B Company of the Middlesex as carrying parties were Nos. 3 and 4 Sections of No. 13 Platoon, D Company, 1/2nd Monmouthshire Regt. The Pioneers were carrying rolls of wire and Bangalore torpedoes and they followed B Company towards the German trenches, lying down in No Man's Land about three-quarters of the way across when it became clear that the advance had stalled. They could see that some of the Middlesex men had got into the German trenches on the northern edge of the crater but, with nothing else happening, they eventually withdrew to the British lines. They lost one man killed and another 12 wounded.

The crater acted as a magnet for any British troops still in the area. They were drawn inexorably to the apparent shelter of the lip as, elsewhere, the machine gun swept expanse of No Man's Land remained a killing field for the men of the Royal Fusiliers, Middlesex and, just to their north, the 1st Lancashire Fusiliers. For now, fighting was still heavy around the crater and the area just to the south.

One of the men of the Middlesex drawn to the crater was Capt. Frederick Sydney Cockram and, if any man deserved the highest accolade of the Victoria Cross, it was the Adjutant of the 16th Middlesex. Three times Capt. Cockram led a dwindling band of men forward in a desperate effort to hold the crater. Three times he was wounded. Three times he struggled to his feet and went forward once more. On the fourth occasion he was struck again, 'riddled with bullets' the 86th Brigade diary says, and he fell for the last time. The last words he spoke were passed to his CO, Lt. Col. Hamilton-Hall. The CO recorded them in a letter to Cockram's mother in which he expressed his desperate sadness at his Adjutant's assumed death:

> "Tell the Commanding Officer," he was reported as saying, "I have endeavoured to get the men forward as far as I was able to".

His heroic efforts were not unnoticed by his enemy. German troops had been pinned down by the resolute fire of a Lewis gunner just to the south of the crater rim who was causing serious casualties. Vizefeldwebel Mögle of the 7. Kompanie tried to bomb the British out but it was not until Utffz. Hess and Rapp, 12. Kompanie, shot the Lewis gunner that progress could be made. Lt. der Landwehr Blessing[ii] led a bombing party of the 10. Kompanie against the other positions

---

[i] 2nd Lt. Eustace Roland Whitby, 24th Middlesex Regt., att. 16th Middlesex Regt., was awarded the MC for his conduct on 1st July 1916. The citation in the *London Gazette* of 26th September 1916 reads: "For conspicuous gallantry in action. When all the other officers of his company became casualties in the advance, he took command and, though wounded, endeavoured to gain more ground till he finally became unconscious".
He was killed while attached to the 1st Royal Munster Fusiliers, on 20th November 1917. Aged 28, he was the son of Robert and Florence Whitby, of Edinburgh House, Clevedon, Somerset. He was educated at Mill Hill and was a chartered accountant. Previously a sergeant in the 24th Middlesex Regt., he was commissioned in January 1916. His body was never found and his name is inscribed on the Arras Memorial, Bay 9.

[ii] Lt. der Landwehr Blessing was killed on the 22nd October 1917.

still obstinately holding out at the crater and Vizefeldwebel Eugen Mögle[i] rallied elements of the 7. and 12. Kompanien to renew the attack. At last the British gave way and 'a brave wounded English officer (Cockram) was taken prisoner'[55].

Plate 19 Capt. Frederick Sydney Cockram, 16th Middlesex Regt.

Plate 20 2nd Lt. Archibald Ronald Grant-Suttie, B Battery, 15th Brigade, RHA

Presumably from reports sent in, VIII Corps assumed that Capt. Cockram had been killed whereas, though seriously wounded, he was taken prisoner and eventually ended up in a Swiss Hospital. Capt. Frederick Sydney Cockram, 16th Middlesex Regt., was recommended for a VC by his CO, Lt. Col. Hamilton-Hall, but, instead, he was awarded the DSO in the New Year's Honours List of 1917. In spite of the severity of his wounds he returned to London after the war, married, had two daughters and lived to 82 in spite of losing part of a lung and living the rest of his life with shrapnel in his body[ii].

---

[i] Vizefeldwebel Mögle, RIR 119, was mortally wounded in the fighting at Stuff Redoubt on 29th September 1916. He died the following day and is buried in Sapignies German Cemetery, Block 2, grave 150. [Source: Jack Sheldon, *The Germans at Beaumont Hamel*, Pen & Sword, page 81].

[ii] Capt. Cockram's mother received letters of condolence from both the Battalion's CO and Chaplain so convinced were they by reports that he was dead. Hamilton-Hall's letter to Cockram's mother reads:

Dear Madam,

It is with deepest regret that I have to tell you of the sad news of the death of your son. Although he has to be reported officially as 'missing believed killed', owing to the fact that we have been unable to recover his body, I am sorry not to be able to hold out any hopes of his having only been wounded. During the action on the 1st July, your son, who as you know was my Adjutant, got separated from me and when our men found themselves up against an impassable obstacle he went forward and endeavoured to break through at their head; he was wounded three times and on each occasion rose up and pushed forward. The fourth occasion on which he was hit he was unable to rise, and, with almost the last words he was heard to utter said, "Tell the Commanding Officer I have endeavoured to get the men forward as far as I was able to".

In spite of Cockram's fall, the men at the crater still clung on. With them, having gone forward with the 16th Middlesex, was a party from the 15th Brigade, Royal Horse Artillery. 2nd Lt. Archibald Ronald Grant Suttie, the Forward Observation Officer, and a party of telephonists from B Battery had advanced with Lt. Col. Hamilton-Hall with the intention of connecting the crater to the artillery and Battalion HQ by a telephone cable unrolled as they went. From there it was intended that they would direct the fire of the guns onto the second German trench line ready for the next phase of the advance. Instead they were witnesses to the carnage at the crater. Grant Suttie reported that the Germans, armed with machine guns and small minenwerfers, were:

> "…simply killing our man as they pleased, jeering at them and telling them to come on."[56]

The men of his party then became casualties. 71947 Bdr. Albert J Port, B Battery, was wounded and Bdr. Herbert Brockett[i] and Dvr. Sidney Indge[ii], also B Battery, were reported missing from the party. Bdr. Port and his officer retired, Grant Suttie[iii] helping the wounded Hamilton-Hall back to the British lines.

Meanwhile, another Lewis gun had been brought into position just 15 yards from the German positions. In an act of bravery nearly the equal of Cockram's, Marskman Hermann, part of the team of Gun No. 2 of the 2. Maschinengewehr Kompanie, rushed their position, killed the Lewis gun team, then jumped forward and retrieved the gun from No Man's Land.

Although out of the 25 officers of the battalion who went into action 24 were either killed or wounded, there is no one's loss which will be more deeply felt amongst us all than that of your son; he was not only respected, but almost worshipped by all - officers, N.C.O.s and men. As for myself, his death is an irreparable loss. As an Adjutant and officer I know no equal; as a companion and friend I especially valued him; he was always so cheery and sympathetic. He died a most glorious death leading men on to attempt the almost impossible; if ever there was a hero, he was one. I only wish to Heaven that he had been left even if all my other officers had been taken, and I am certain that this is the feeling right through the battalion.
(signed) J. Hamilton Hall
In a letter dated 12th December 1916 Cockram wrote to her from a hospital in Hannover where he was seriously ill but recovering and out of danger. He received his DSO at Buckingham Palace in February 1919. In April 1919 Brig. Gen. Hamilton-Hall, GOC 39th Division, wrote to him explaining how hard he had tried to get him awarded a VC.

[i] 53518 Acting Bombardier Herbert James Brockett, B Battery, 15th Brigade, Royal Horse Artillery, was aged 26. He was the son of Charles and Mary Brockett. He is buried in Hawthorn Ridge Cemetery No. 1, Auchonvillers, grave B. 34.

[ii] 52590 Driver Sidney John Indge, B Battery, 15th Brigade, Royal Horse Artillery, was aged 26. He was the son of Harry George and Elizabeth Mary Indge, of 45, Ramridge Rd., Roundgreen, Luton, Beds. His body was never found and his name is inscribed on the Thiepval Memorial, Pier & Face 1 A and 8 A.

[iii] 2nd Lt. Archibald Ronald Grant-Suttie, L Battery, 15th Brigade, Royal Horse Artillery, died on 23rd July 1917. Aged 20, he was the son of Robert and the Hon. Mrs Edith Mary Grant-Suttie (nee Dawnay), of Balgone, North Berwick. Educated at Rottingdean, Malvern College and the RMC, Sandhurst, he was commissioned into the Royal Horst Artillery in July 1915. Served in Gallipoli. Transferred to L Battery and was killed near Ypres. He is buried in Dozinghem Military Cemetery, grave I. G. 20.

The fighting was swinging in favour of the Germans now. The remnants of Lt. Breitmeyer's No. 3 Platoon along with the commander of the 9. Kompanie, Oberleutnant d. R. Mühlbayer, had been dug out of their ruined bunker and joined the men in the front line just in time to help sweep the remaining British troops off the ridge. They formed up behind Uttfz. Aicheler and Machine Gun No. 2 which, with the Lewis Gun teams disposed of, was now able to sweep the ground to their front across which the rest of the Royal Fusiliers and some of the Dublin Fusiliers were still trying, and failing, to advance. Oberleutnant d. R. Mühlbayer, however, would not survive to enjoy his regiment's victory. At some point during the day he was shot in the head and killed.

To the north of the crater Braungart's Machine Gun No. 1 had run out of immediate targets and now, lengthening their range and firing into the flank of the 4th Division away to the north, the gun took on targets well behind the British front line firing at ranges of up to 1,000 yards. Even with this significant extension of its field of fire, however, by now targets were hard to come by and, by the end of the day, the gun had only fired about eleven belts of ammunition or about 2,600 rounds. On other parts of the Somme front on 1st July, German Maxims were known to have fired eight times as many rounds but the attack of the 86th Brigade was over so quickly there was little else to do other than pick off any British soldier in No Man's Land foolish enough to move.

Together, the combined rifle and machine gun fire of the 7., 9., 10. and 12. Kompanien of the RIR 119 scattered any British troops still moving and the men at the crater lip were taken in enfilade by a machine gun of RIR 121 to the north. The final straw was the fire of a heavy trench mortar which started to drop big bombs amongst them. Exhausted, the withdrawal became a rout as the remnants of the Fusiliers and Middlesex abandoned positions, weapons and wounded and fled towards the safety of nearby shell holes. Lt. Col. Hamilton-Hall[i] did his best to rally them but the men were spent and their spirit broken.

Lt. McAlpin and his machine gunners were amongst the last to leave the crater. They gave what covering fire they could as the infantry retired but, with ammunition running out, McAlpin and his men at last withdrew. Sixteen had been either killed or wounded and, as a result of not having enough men to bring all the guns back, he was compelled to destroy one of the guns with a rifle grenade to prevent it from falling into the enemy's hands. At the front of the crater the Stokes mortars were abandoned in No Man's Land, though they would be recovered that night by a party of the Dublin Fusiliers under Capt. Oulton.

Back in the British trenches, the rest of the 86th Machine Gun Company was stuck, unable to get forward because of congestion in the trenches and the heavy German machine gun fire that swept their parapet and wire. As the chaos spread, concerns started to grow that the Germans might follow the retreating infantry across No Man's Land so the surviving Vickers guns were set up in the British

[i] Maj. (Temp Lt. Col) John Hamilton-Hall, 16th Middlesex Regt., was awarded the DSO for his conduct on 1st July 1916. His citation in the *London Gazette* to the 26th September 1916 reads: "For conspicuous gallantry in action. He led his battalion to consolidate a mine crater in the enemy's front line. In spite of very heavy casualties, he conducted the operation with the greatest determination, and succeeded in holding his position all day".

front line under Lts. O P Byrne and Duffy and the Adjutant, Lt. J F B Wilkinson, ready to repel any counter attack.

ALL THE WHILE, THE DIVISIONAL ARTILLERY was firing away at a line 400 yards east of Station and Wagon Roads, the roads which the infantry should have arrived at just short of 7.50 a.m. According to the plan, at 8.30 a.m. the two attacking Brigades were due to resume the advance with the field guns sweeping the ground in front of them in 100 yard lifts and, even though the infantry were either stuck in their own trenches, pinned down in No Man's land or dead, the field gunners duly started their next series of lifts, arriving on the Beaucourt Road at 8.45 a.m., a position which the heavier guns had been pounding since 7.45 a.m. The battery commanders were following orders as laid down in the Corps artillery plan from which there was to be no deviation unless so instructed by higher authority. Higher authority duly and belatedly intervened at 8.45 a.m. in the form of the 29th Division's commander of Royal Artillery, Brig. Gen. Peake. He ordered the 18 pdrs back to their previous line but even this was of no use to the struggling infantry. This barrage fell 1,200 yards in front of their furthest advance and on this target the 18 pdr batteries fired uselessly until 11 a.m.

Amongst those gunners who could see what was going on the frustration was immense. 2nd Lt. Charles Ball of B Battery, 15th Brigade, RHA, was in a perfect position to witness the shambles unfolding in front of him. His battery was dug in on a forward slope between Auchonvillers and the White City and, from there, they were firing to the north of Beaumont Hamel over open sights at a range of 1,700 yards. B Battery was required by the plan to fire at Munich Trench on the 4th Division's front but, from their position, they could clearly see the action around the crater. Writing after the war, 2nd Lt. Ball stated:

> "Unfortunately although we were able to see all that was happening at the crater we had to comply with the barrage table and continue shelling Munich Trench when we could have dealt directly with the Boche on the far lip of the crater who could be clearly seen from the guns.
> Standing in B's position we saw the enormous cone of earth go up from the Hawthorn Redoubt and within 5 minutes it seemed that every Boche machine gun along the line was shooting full belt, the bullets simply whistling like hail over our position. We could see our fellows caught forming up and knew from that moment they hadn't a chance. The rest was just useless sacrifice."[57]

By 10.30 a.m. the sacrifice at the crater was over. All that remained were the bodies of the dead and wounded from both sides, piled in tangled heaps in places. Such was the nature of the vicious close quarter fighting that several British soldiers had been cut in half by short range machine gun fire. It was a charnel house, the chalk spoil stained crimson by the blood of scores of men.

Only for the defenders was there some cheerful news. Between midday and 1 p.m. Lt. der Reserve Renz and the survivors of No. 1 Platoon of the 9. Kompanie, RIR 119, trapped by the explosion of the mine, managed to dig themselves out through a hole on the edge of the crater. Their dugout had survived the explosion but every entrance had been blocked and their air was close to giving out when they broke through to the bright sunshine of a beautiful summer's day.

On the British side there was no silver lining. Apart from Capt. Cockram and his bravery and luck, there is little more to say about the actions of the 16th Middlesex Regt. With 24 officers as casualties there was no-one left to write a report. Thus the war diary is painfully brief:

> "Battalion in action 7.30 a.m. from support trenches. Casualties: officers killed 3; wounded 10; missing believed killed 6; missing 5; other ranks killed 19; wounded 306; missing believed killed 37; missing 138."[58]

Plate 21 2nd Lt. James Kenneth Orr, 14th att. 16th Middlesex Regt.

Plate 22 Capt. Arthur Channing Purnell, 16th Middlesex Regt.

Plate 23 Capt. Talbot Hamilton Watts, 16th Middlesex Regt.

The casualties of the battalion were recorded as:
Officers
Killed:
2nd Lt. H E Asser[i], att. 1st Middlesex
Lt. H W Barker[ii]
Lt. H D Goodwin[iii]
Lt. H J Heath
2nd Lt. E R Heaton
2nd Lt. H C Hertslet[iv], att. 6th Middlesex
Capt. G H Heslop
2nd Lt. J K Orr[v], att. 14th Middlesex
Capt. A C Purnell[vi], Brigade Bombing Officer
2nd Lt. F B Tanqueray
Capt. T H Watts[i]

---

[i] 2nd Lt. Harold Edward Asser, 1st att. 16th Middlesex Regt., was the son of Edith Marian Asser of 65, Windsor Rd., Ealing, London, and the late Arthur Edward Asser. He was an Assistant Scoutmaster with the St. Mellitus (3rd Hanwell) Troop. He enlisted as 2856 Pte in the 9th London Regt. (Queen Victoria's Rifles) and was commissioned from Cpl. on 24th September 1915. His body was never found and his name is inscribed on the Thiepval Memorial, Pier & Face 12D & 13B.

[ii] Lt. Harold William Barker, 16th Middlesex Regt., was never found and his name is inscribed on the Thiepval Memorial, Pier & Face 12D & 13B. He was commissioned on 19th March 1915. Believed to be remembered on the Washingborough and Heighington War Memorial, Lincolnshire.

[iii] Lt. Harold Desborough Goodwin, 16th Middlesex Regt., was aged 25. He was the youngest son of Albert Frederick Goodwin, R.W.S., and Alice Goodwin (née Desborough). He was born in Ilfracombe, Devon, and educated at Mr Beale's Preparatory School at Ellerslie. He graduated from Trinity College, Cambridge, in 1909. He is buried in Hawthorn Ridge Cemetery No. 1, Auchonvillers, grave A. 88.

[iv] 2nd Lt. Harold Cecil Hertslet, 6th att. 16th Middlesex Regt., was 27. He was the son of Gerald and Ethel Hertslet (née Barry); husband of Helen Dorothy Hertslet (née Beardsley) of Nosoton Heights, Conn., U.S.A., married February 1912. He emigrated to New York in 1906 becoming a US citizen. He was commissioned into the 6th Middlesex Regt. on 21st April 1915. He is buried in Auchonvillers Military Cemetery, grave II. E. 21.

[v] 2nd Lt. James Kenneth Orr, 14th att. 16th Middlesex Regt., was aged 21. He was the eldest son of Dr and Mrs W R Orr of Clydesdale, East Finchley, Middx. He was educated at Highgate School and King's College, London, where he was studying engineering. He was a member of the OTC. He was commissioned on 10th March 1915 and went to France in February 1916. His body was never found and his name is inscribed on the Thiepval Memorial, Pier & Face 12D & 13B. His brother, 2nd Lt. John Compton Orr, 2nd att. 5th Royal Berkshire Regt., died on 28th April 1917. He is buried in the Faubourg d'Amiens Cemetery, Arras.

[vi] Capt. Arthur Channing Purnell, 16th Middlesex Regt., was aged 34. He was the son of the late John Alfred Purnell and Emily Blandford Purnell of St Clair, Ryde, Isle of Wight. An excellent oarsman, he won the double sculls championship on the Thames between 1911 and 1913. He also won the skiff marathon in 1912 and 1913. He was commissioned on 28th January 1915 and was promoted captain on 10th February 1916. His body was never found and his name is inscribed on the Thiepval Memorial, Pier & Face 12D & 13B. He is remembered on the All Saints Church War Memorial Chapel, Ryde, IoW.

Died of wounds:
2nd Lt. C J Addington[ii], 2nd July 1916
2nd Lt. C J J K Deakin[iii], 2nd July 1916
2nd Lt. R F Michelmore[iv], att. 5th Middlesex, 7th July 1916, in German hands
Wounded and prisoner of war:
Capt. Frederick Sydney Cockram
Capt. Eric Walter Hall
2nd Lt. Dudley Sampson Blyth Starnes, att. 14th Middlesex Regt.
Wounded:
2nd Lt. Frank Edgar Bennet, att. 15th Middlesex Regt
2nd Lt. Edward Arthur Cuffe Adams
Maj. Francis Rowley Hill
2nd Lt. George Henry Fitzjames Lushington, att. 24th Middlesex Regt
2nd Lt. John Shearstone
2nd Lt. Duncan Beresford Tuck[v]
2nd Lt. Eustace Roland Whitby, att. 24th Middlesex Regt

The casualties amongst other ranks are given as 614 in various places, however, the actual total is 500 of which 19 were known to have been killed, 306 were wounded, 37 were missing believed to be killed and 138 were missing. Officer casualties are given variously as 22 or 24, the latter being correct. The original figures were: killed 3, wounded 10, missing believed killed 6 and missing 5. These figures were subsequently revised to: killed 11, missing believed killed 3, died of wounds 3 and wounded 7. At least four officers became prisoners of war:

[i] Capt. Talbot Hamilton Watts, 16th Middlesex Regt., was aged 27. He was the youngest son of the late Dr. Fred Watts of London. He was a member of Messers Killick, Nixon & Co., Bombay, and was at home on leave when he enlisted in the Public Schools Battalion. He was commissioned in September 1914 and promoted Captain in January 1916. He went to France in November 1915. His body was never found and his name is inscribed on the Thiepval Memorial, Pier & Face 12D & 13B.

[ii] 2nd Lt. Cyril John Flintan Addington, 16th Middlesex Regt., was aged 22. He was the son of Paul Flintan Addington and Mary Louisa Addington of 49, Merton Hall Rd., Wimbledon, Surrey. He was commissioned on 11th September 1915. He is buried in Auchonvillers Military Cemetery, grave II. E. 11.

[iii] 2nd Lt. Charles Joseph John King Deakin, 16th Middlesex Regt., was aged 25. He was the son of the late Charles Frank and Ellen Louise Deakin of Burton-on-Trent. Educated at Aldenham School, where he was the wicketkeeper in the cricket 1st XI, he was a managing clerk with Messrs. Onions & Davies, solicitors, of Market Drayton. He played cricket for Market Drayton CC. Joined Sept. 1914, as Private in Public School Batt., promoted Sergeant Jan. 1915. Gazetted 2nd Lt. 16th Middlesex Regt. May 1915. He is buried in Doullens Communal Cemetery Extension No. 1, grave II. A. 5.

[iv] 2nd Lt. Robert Frank Michelmore, 5th att. 16th Middlesex Regt., was aged 24. He was the only son of Robert Frank, a farmer, and Harriet Elizabeth Michelmore of Rickham Farm, East Portlemouth, Salcombe, Devon. He was educated at Allhallows School near Honiton. From 1909 he was a trooper in the Devon Yeomanry. He was commissioned in February 1915. He was a machine gun instructor. He is buried in Lebucquiere Communal Cemetery Extension, grave II. C. 24.

[v] Capt. Duncan Beresford Tuck, 16th Middlesex Regt., died on 30th March 1918. Aged 21, he was the son of Mr. and Mrs. W. R. Tuck, of 'Ripple', Fairfield Rd., Woodford Green, Essex. He is buried in St Sever Cemetery, Rouen, grave Officers, B. 8. 10.

Capt. F S Cockram, Capt. E W Hall, 2nd Lt. D S B Starnes and 2nd Lt. R F Michelmore, who died of his wounds in German hands on 7th July 1916. The strength of the 16th Middlesex going into action was 22 officers and 689 other ranks. Their total casualties of 524 represent 74% of those who went into action[i].

WHILST THIS DISASTER WAS UNFOLDING AT THE CRATER, the flow of information between the various headquarters seems not to have improved. As 29th Division was receiving some absurdly optimistic reports about progress on the 87th Brigade's front, reports which would directly lead to perhaps the greatest tragedy of a day of tragedies, their view of progress on the 86th Brigade's front seemed far more realistic. It was clear to Division and 86th Brigade that the attack on the crater had, at the very best, stalled and that the attack of the 1st Lancashire Fusiliers on the Bergwerk, of which more later, was going the same way.

At 8.20 a.m. the 29th Division reported the Royal Fusiliers and Dublin Fusiliers 'held up'. Something of an understatement, but at least a reasonable recognition that things were not going well at the crater. This report throws into sharp relief the contradictory and totally inaccurate report in VIII Corps' war diary eight minutes later from Corps Observation Post No. 2 that:

> "…our troops believed through Beaumont Hamel which Germans are now shelling."[59]

At 8.29 a.m. 29th Division were reporting a heavy German barrage on their front line while, one minute later, VIII Corps were repeating their belief that all was going well with reports of Very lights being seen in Beaumont Hamel meaning:

> "…that our troops had reached their objective."[60]

In the same report, however, VIII Corps recorded that 86th Brigade had reported their attack held up. It was as if they either could not or did not want to believe the news coming from the commanders on the ground.

86th Brigade, however, had accepted that affairs were running ill and, with the news coming through of the excessive casualties amongst officers in the attacking battalions, Brig. Gen. Williams despatched the Brigade's Staff Captain, Capt. Robert Gee of the Royal Fusiliers, to reorganise and move the attack onwards. On arriving at the front line, Gee was almost immediately wounded but refused to leave his position. He managed to send in two reports to Brigade HQ from just out in No Man's Land before the nearby landing of a, thankfully, dud 5.9 in shell lifted Gee clear into the British front trench[ii].

---

[i] 172 men of, or attached to, the 16th Middlesex are recorded as having died on 1st and 2nd July 1916. In other words, the vast majority, something approaching 90%, of the missing had been killed in action. The full strength of the battalion on 1st July 1916 was 35 officers and 773 other ranks of which 13 officers and 79 other ranks were kept back to form a cadre in case of heavy casualties.

[ii] Capt. Robert Gee, VC, MC, 2nd Royal Fusiliers, was aged 41 and was the son of Robert and Amy Gee of Leicester. Apprenticed to the Ornamental Metal & Iron Works at Aylestone, Leicestershire, at aged 16 he joined the 2nd Royal Fusiliers the following year. He was commissioned in 1915 and served at Gallipoli. He was three times MiD. He won his VC for his actions on 30th November 1917 at Masnières. The citation in the *London Gazette* reads: "For most conspicuous bravery and initiative and determination when an

Plate 24 Capt. Robert Gee, VC, MC, 2nd Royal Fusiliers

Capt. Gee was awarded an MC for his actions, the citation in the *London Gazette* of 22nd September 1916 reads:

> "For conspicuous gallantry in action. He encouraged his men during the attack by fearlessly exposing himself and cheering them on. When wounded he refused to retire, and urged his men on till, after being blown into the air by a shell, he was carried in half unconscious."

Brigade also sent forward the Brigade Major, Capt. Ian Cameron Grant, 1st Cameron Highlanders, to try to get the remains of the Dublin Fusiliers forward. The 150 relatively organised men of this unit were all that Brig. Gen. Williams had in hand after the destruction of the 16th Middlesex and 2nd Royal Fusiliers. His fourth battalion, the 1st Lancashire Fusiliers, were otherwise engaged as we shall see. The rest of the Dublins were either casualties, caught in the trenches or trapped out in No Man's Land. Grant went across the open with two orderlies

---

attack by a strong enemy force pierced our line and captured Brigade Headquarters and ammunition dump. Captain Gee finding himself a prisoner, killed one of the enemy with his spiked stick, and succeeded in escaping. He then organized a party of the Brigade Staff, with which he attacked the enemy fiercely, closely followed and supported by two companies of Infantry. By his own personal bravery and prompt action he, aided by his orderlies, cleared the locality. Captain Gee established a defensive flank on the outskirts of the village, then finding that an enemy machine gun was still in action, with a revolver in each hand, and followed by one man, he rushed and captured the gun, killing eight of the crew. At this time he was wounded, but refused to have the wound dressed until he was satisfied the defence was organised."

After the war Gee went into politics, fighting the 1918 General Election at Consett as a National Democratic Party candidate (he lost) and then, as a Conservative and Unionist, a by-election in Woolwich East in March 1921 where he defeated Labour's Ramsay MacDonald, the campaign focusing entirely on MacDonald's pacifism and opposition to the war. Gee lost the seat to Labour in the 1922 General Election but was elected to represent Bosworth in the General Election of 1924. He resigned his seat in 1927 and emigrated to Western Australia where he died on 2nd August, 1960.

from the advanced Brigade HQ in the support line and was trying to get this small group of Dublins to advance when he was struck by machine gun bullets fired from the right[i]. To replace these two Staff Officers, Capt. Fulton was ordered forward from Divisional HQ to the 86th Brigade's advanced battle headquarters at 9.42 a.m. Later, Major Henry Harrison Cripps, 2iC of the 2nd Royal Fusiliers and in command of the 10% cadre, who had stepped into Capt. Grant's role as Brigade Major at 1 p.m., was also seriously wounded at about 3 p.m. Clearly, it was not a good day to be a staff officer with 86th Brigade

Plate 25 Lt. Alan Foster Paterson, 14th att. 2nd Royal Fusiliers

Plate 26 2nd Lt. Charles Francis Roope, 16th Royal Fusiliers att. 2nd Royal Fusiliers

Cripps' battalion, the 2nd Royal Fusiliers, had suffered severe casualties around the crater and in the attempt by the following companies to advance into the re-entrant to the south of the Hawthorn Redoubt. Their casualties were reported as: Officers killed 3, wounded 11, missing 5, missing believed killed 2, shell shock 2 and Other Ranks: killed 51, wounded 216, missing 247. A total of 23 officers and

---

[i] Capt. (later Major Gen) Ian Cameron Grant, CB, CBE, DSO, 1st Cameron Highlanders, was aged 25 and was the oldest son of James Cameron Grant of Albert Lodge, Albert Place. He was educated at St Neots, Cheltenham College and the RMC Sandhurst. He was commissioned into the Cameron Highlanders in 1910. He was promoted Lt. Col. in 1931 and Major Gen in 1941, commanding the 1st Cameron Highlanders between 1931 and 1935, the 160th (South Wales) Infantry Brigade TA from 1935 to 1938 and the Cairo Infantry Brigade 1938-39. He was ADC to the King in 1944. Wounded twice, he was MiD three times. He died on 26th August 1955.
He was severely wounded on 1st July and was out of the front line war. For three months in 1917 he acted as Assistant Private Secretary (unpaid) to Rt. Hon. John Hodge, PC, MP, Minister of Labour. He then became the DAAG at the War Office. He was awarded a DSO for his actions on 1st July. His DSO was gazetted on 22nd September 1916. The citation reads: "For conspicuous gallantry in action. When the attack was wavering he went forward into the front line and cheered on the troops till he was badly wounded. As Brigade Major he has set a fine example to all the officers in the Brigade".

514 other ranks[i]. 22 officers and 906 men had gone into action which means a casualty rate of 55%[ii]. The casualties, of course, were highly concentrated in Z Company which had attacked the crater.

The officer casualties were:

Killed:

2nd Lt. C Blackwell[iii]
Lt. A F Paterson[iv]
2nd Lt. C F Roope[v]

Missing:

2nd Lt. W F Bennett, att. 18th Royal Fusiliers
Lt. F M Drinkill[vi]
Lt. A M Haycraft[vii]
2nd Lt.A Hedges[viii], PoW
Lt. L C Russell, att. 4th Royal Fusiliers, PoW

Missing reported killed:

Lt. & Adjutant J W Nicholls[ix]

---

[i] These numbers were revised in the Official History to:
Officers: killed 6, wounded 15, missing 2, total 23; Other ranks: killed 158, wounded 334, missing 46, total 538. This increases the percentage casualty rate to 60%.

[ii] The difference between the number of officers in action, 22, and the number wounded, is explained by Maj. Cripps who was originally in charge of the 10% cadre and was not counted as one of the original 22. To add to the confusion, however, Capt. Goodliffe who temporarily took over command of the Battalion after Lt. Col. Johnson and Maj. Cripps were rendered *hors de combat*, states that two of the Company commanders, Capts. Dearden and Baldwin, were unwounded which gives a total of 25 officers having been involved on the day. Capt. Francis William Swifte took command later in the day and Goodliffe became 2iC pending officer replacements.

[iii] 2nd Lt. Cyril Blackwell, 16th att. 2nd Royal Fusiliers, was aged 33. He was the son of Marion Whelan Blackwell of Fairfield House, North Avenue, Salisbury, Rhodesia, and the late John Blackwell (B & N W Railways, Bengal, India). His body was never found and his name is inscribed on the Thiepval Memorial, Pier & Face 8C 9A & 16A.

[iv] Lt. Alan Foster Paterson, 14th Middlesex Regt. att. 2nd Royal Fusiliers, was never found and his name is inscribed on the Thiepval Memorial, Pier & Face 12D & 13B.

[v] 2nd Lt. Charles Francis Roope, 16th Royal Fusiliers att. 2nd Royal Fusiliers, was aged 32. He was the only son of Charles H and Millicent M Roope of Briar Knoll, Lake, Sandown, IoW. He was educated at St Augustine's, Ramsgate, and was commissioned in December 1915. He is buried in Hawthorn Ridge Cemetery No. 2, Auchonvillers, grave B. 57.

[vi] Lt. Frederick Maurice Drinkill, 5th att. 2nd Royal Fusiliers, was aged 24. He was the son of Richard and Ellen Rosanna Drinkill of 43, Walton St., Chelsea, London. He was educated at Keble House School and King's College. A member of London University OTC he was commissioned in November 1914. He fought at Gallipoli. He was a member of the Guild of St Gregory, the altar servers at Westminster Cathedral. He is buried in Auchonvillers Military Cemetery, grave II. F. 1.

[vii] Lt. Alan Montague Haycraft, 6th att. 2nd Royal Fusiliers, was aged 34. He was the son of Charles Frederich Haycraft. He enlisted as 2324 Private in the Honourable Artillery Company and went to France in April 1916. He is buried in Hawthorn Ridge Cemetery No. 2, Auchonvillers, grave B. 44.

[viii] Commissioned from Bombardier in the Royal Horse Artillery (TF) on 7th November 1915.

[ix] Lt. & Adjutant John Watson Nicholls, 5th att. 2nd Royal Fusiliers, was aged 25. He was the only son of John Frederick and Annie Elizabeth Nicholls of 31, Coleraine Rd., Blackheath, London. He was educated at Felsted and Rouen and was foreign correspondent at the *Comptoir National d'Escompte de Paris* in Paris. Gazetted, Feb., 1915.

2nd Lt. L T Westaway[i]
Wounded:
2nd Lt. Keith Joy Barrett
2nd Lt. Edward Jonathan Bowie, att. 16th Royal Fusiliers
2nd Lt. John Stephens Cox, att. 16th Royal Fusiliers
Maj. Henry Harrison Cripps
2nd Lt. Bernard Durnford[ii]
2nd Lt. Charles William Field, att. 8th Royal Welsh Fusiliers
2nd Lt. Stanley Edward Pakeman
2nd Lt. Ferdinand Edward Reiss, att. 28th Royal Fusiliers
2nd Lt. Leslie Edward Smith[iii]
2nd Lt. Arthur Henry Tytherleigh, att. 16th Royal Fusiliers
Lt. Albert Walter Whitlock[iv]
Shell shock:
Lt. Col. Allen Victor Johnson 2nd Lt. W Hyett

THE RIGHT SUPPORTING BATTALION, THE 1ST ROYAL DUBLIN FUSILIERS, had barely seen a German but had still suffered badly. They had gone into action with 22 officers and 826 men. Four officers were killed, one died of wounds and another was missing believed killed. Six more were wounded. Amongst the men 29 were known to be dead, 123 were wounded and 54 were missing of which half were later shown to have been killed. A casualty rate of 25% does not seem a lot when compared to, say, the 16th Middlesex Regt., but, for a unit that barely got any men through the British wire it still represents a heavy casualty list[v].

Officers killed were:
Capt. E R L Maunsell[vi] 2nd Lt. A J W Pearson

Also served at Gallipoli. His body was never found and his name is inscribed on the Thiepval Memorial, Pier & Face 8C, 9A & 16A.

[i] 2nd Lt. Leslie Thomas Westaway, 2nd Royal Fusiliers, was aged 22. He was the son of John and Sarah Westaway of 120, Melrose Avenue, Cricklewood, London. Attended Goldsmith's College. He enlisted in the Honourable Artillery Company and was commissioned into the Royal Fusiliers on 23rd April 1916. He is buried in Hawthorn Ridge Cemetery No. 2, Auchonvillers, grave B. 98.

[ii] Commissioned out of the 15th Hussars on 30th April 1916.

[iii] Commissioned out of a London Mounted Brigade Field Ambulance (TF) on 7th November 1915.

[iv] Commissioned out of a Service Battalion of the Royal Fusiliers on 23rd April 1916.

[v] One of the Other Ranks 'missing' was 12923 Pte Albert Rickman. For whatever reason, and there were good and bad reasons aplenty, he left his post. He was eventually arrested on the lines of communication to the rear on 20th July. Six and a half weeks later he was brought to trial, faced the court without representation and was found guilty of desertion. Pte Rickman was shot at dawn on 15th September 1916. Aged 27, he was the son of Charles and Anne Rickman, of 4, Carrington Terrace, Milford-on-Sea, Hants. He had served at Gallipoli from April 1915 to January 1916. He is buried in Vlamertinghe Military Cemetery, grave IV. D. 7.

[vi] Capt. Edwin Richard Lloyd Maunsell, 1st Royal Dublin Fusiliers, was aged 25. He was the second son of Maj. John Drought Maunsell and Euphemia Sullivan Maunsell (née Bush) of Ballywilliam, Ferndown, Wimborne and Taunton, Somerset. He was educated at the Royal Naval School, Eltham, Sir Anthony Browne's School, Brentwood, and the RMC,

2nd Lt. C F Greenlees[i] 2nd Lt. A M B Rose-Cleland[ii]
Died of wounds:
2nd Lt. T W R Neill[iii], died of wounds 3rd July 1916
Missing:
2nd Lt. D R Warner
Wounded:
Lt. Richard Elphick, att. 1st Royal Welch Fusiliers
2nd Lt. Ronald Gibson Stewart Durward[iv], att. 14th Royal Scots
2nd Lt. W J Robertson, att. 9th Royal Scots Fusiliers
2nd Lt. John Edmond Bush Maunsell, att. 3rd Royal Dublin Fusiliers
2nd Lt. Hugh Vernon Spankie, att. 4th Royal Dublin Fusiliers
2nd Lt. Macartan Hubert Tighe, att. 1st Royal Welch Fusiliers

WE LEFT THE 1ST LANCASHIRE FUSILIERS, the left hand battalion of the 86th Brigade's attack, just after their position had been discovered by the Germans at 7 a.m. and taken under the fire of several 77 cm field guns. Their heads were being kept well down now as they contemplated their task of swarming over the Bergwerk just to the north of the New Beaumont Road and taking the northern part of Beaumont Hamel, the remains of which were located to the rear of this German strongpoint. To their right, the ground sloped sharply up to Hawthorn Ridge and to their left it rose more gently towards Redan Ridge on which stood

Sandhurst. He was commissioned into the Royal Dublin Fusiliers from RMC, Sandhurst, in March 1911. Seconded to the 1st Nigeria Regt., 1913. OC commanding Kaduna, Northern Nigeria, and Captain, 1915. Invalided home with sun-stroke. Involved in suppressing Sinn Fein Easter Rising in Cork. Went to France May 1916. He is buried in Auchonvillers Military Cemetery, grave I. A. 11. Also wounded was his brother, 2nd Lt. John Edmond Bush Maunsell who was commissioned into the 3rd Royal Dublin Fusiliers on 29th January 1916 after he had first enlisted in the Australian Imperial Force. He was born in Calcutta in 1887. A farmer in Western Australia he enlisted in Perth, WA, in January 1915 and joined the 5th Reinforcement, 11th Battalion as 1978 Pte. He went to Gallipoli where he was wounded on 6th August 1915. He was evacuated via Egypt to the 2nd Southern General Hospital, Southmead, Bristol. He joined the 1st RDF on 20th June 1916 after training at the Dublin University School of Instruction.

[i] 2nd Lt. Charles Fouracres Greenlees, 9th Queen's att. 1st Royal Dublin Fusiliers, was aged 21. He was the son of Archibald and Jessie Mary Greenlees of 198, Park Lane, Tottenham, London. Educated at St John's School, Leatherhead, he was due to go to University College, Oxford, in September, 1914. He is buried in Auchonvillers Military Cemetery, grave I. A. 4.

[ii] 2nd Lt. Alfred Middleton Blackwood Rose-Cleland, 4th att. 1st Royal Dublin Fusiliers, was aged 21. He was the son of Henry S and Elizabeth A Rose-Cleland of Redford House, Moy, Co. Tyrone, Ireland. Educated at Dungannon School and St Columba's College, Dublin, he had been working in Essex for the building company of McLaughlin and Harvey when war broke out. Returning home, he enlisted in the 9th Royal Inniskilling Fusiliers. He is buried in Auchonvillers Military Cemetery, grave II. B. 3.

[iii] 2nd Lt. Thomas William Robertson Neill, 9th Royal Scots Fusiliers att. 1st Royal Dublin Fusiliers, was aged 21. He was the son of the late John and Mary Neill of 60, Ardrossan Road, Saltcoats. He is buried in Louvencourt Military Cemetery, Plot 1. Row B. Grave 25.

[iv] Lt. Ronald Gibson Stewart Durward, 1st Royal Scots, died on 11th August 1918. Aged 24, he was the son of James Stewart Durward and Mary Wilson Jardine Durward, of 127, Mayfield Rd., Edinburgh. He is buried in Bouchoir New British Cemetery, grave V. C. 18.

the Ridge Redoubt, this German fortification providing an excellent position from which to sweep the area over which the Lancashire Fusiliers were to advance. 2nd Lt. Eric Sheppard gave an excellent description of the ground after the war:

> "The road from Auchonvillers to Beaumont Hamel ran up a shallow trough from which the ground rose on the south to Hawthorn Ridge (on the crest of which the big mine was blown) and on the north to another more distant crest on which was situated the redoubt. Halfway across No Man's Land (here about 400 yards wide) a sunken lane ran due north from this road, gradually flattening out to ground level on the northern ridge. Halfway again between this and the German line lay a small bank … giving some shelter from enemy fire. Apart from these features No Man's Land was open and bare of cover."[61]

At 7.20 a.m. three Stokes mortars[i] joined in with the final frantic hurricane bombardment of the German front trenches and, on the slope to their right, the enormous cone of chalk and clay erupted from under the Hawthorn Redoubt, the signal to all that the big push was on. Tucked away as they were under the steep bank of the sunken road that faced the German lines, the men of D and B Companies felt rather than saw the mine explode. The ground around them shook and shuddered. D Company were doing their best to conceal themselves from the enemy's fire as the northern end of the sunken lane became increasingly shallow and any movement threatened exposure to the already flying Maxim bullets. B Company had a different problem with which to contend. At the southern end of the road the bank was steep and overgrown and finding places through which to exit was an issue. Whichever gap they went though, though, their exit was sure to be slow.

At 7.30 a.m. along the whole British front, the whistles blew and the men advanced. Two waves of Fusiliers moved out of the sunken road and headed towards the bank midway between the two sets of trenches. Beyond was the fringe of the remaining German wire and set back from that the battered line of trenches and shell holes which, even now, were filling fast with German troops from the 5. Kompanie, RIR 121.

One the left, D Company was led by 2nd Lts. Craig, Gorfunkle[ii] and Spencer. On the right, B Company had 2nd Lts. Prescott[iii], Edwards and Kershaw[iv] at its head. As they advanced in extended order a platoon of B Company under Lt.

---

[i] One had been damaged and was unable to fire.

[ii] Lt. Isaac Gorfunkle, 13th att. 1st Lancashire Fusiliers, died on 12th August 1918. Aged 25, he was the son of Samuel Gorfunkle and Hilda Gorfunkle (née Levensohn). His parents moved to Lancashire from Poland and Isaac was born in West Derby, Liverpool. They layer moved to Belfast. He is buried in Outtersteene Communal Cemetery Extension, Bailleul.

[iii] 2nd Lt. Robert Stewart Prescott, 10th East Lancashire Regt., att. 1st Lancashire Fusiliers, was commissioned on 10th April 1915. He is buried in Beaumont Hamel British Cemetery, grave A. 78.

[iv] 2nd Lt. Ellis Kershaw, 13th att. 1st Lancashire Fusiliers, was aged 22. He lived at 23, Alexandra Road, Moss Side, Manchester. His body was never found and his name is inscribed on the Thiepval Memorial, Pier & Face 3C & 3D.

Francis Whittam and two platoons of bombers left their trenches just to the south of the New Beaumont Road and moved across the base of the shallow valley in line with the two supporting companies of the 2nd Royal Fusiliers. Meanwhile, A Company, under Capt. Edward Matthey, advanced from Lanwick Trench in support of the main attack. Behind them, C Company emerged from Tenderloin Trench along with two sections of the 1/2nd Monmouths.

After a few seconds grace, a storm of machine gun cross fire swept No Man's Land. The first two waves reached the edge of the German wire or took shelter under the low bank in the middle of No Man's Land.

> "A party of about fifty men with two officers got as far as the (bank) where they stayed till night gave them a chance to re-join the unit in safety. From where they were they could not see the enemy front and would have been quite unable to defend themselves against a counter attack. It is worth mentioning none reached the enemy wire as far as I know."[62]

Plate 27 Capt. George Paterson Nunneley, 4th Bedfordshire Regt., att. 1st Lancashire Fusiliers

Plate 28 Lt. Col. Meredith Magniac, DSO, 1st Lancashire Fusiliers

Behind them, the third and fourth waves of D and B Companies were caught a few yards from the edge of the sunken road and cut down almost to a man. Only some wounded, including Capts. Nunneley[i] and Wells, the two Company

---

[i] Capt. George Paterson Nunneley, 4th Bedfordshire Regt., att. 1st Lancashire Fusiliers, was awarded the MC for his conduct on 1st July 1916. His citation in the *London Gazette* of 26th September 1916 reads: "For conspicuous gallantry in action. Though wounded early in the attack, he remained in command of his company, and handled it with great skill under very trying circumstances". Maj. Nunneley was killed in action on 27th March 1918. Aged 36, he was the son of Rev. F B Nunneley, M.A., M.D. He is buried in Ovillers Military Cemetery, grave: I. C. 30. His brother, Lt. Charles Francis Nunneley, 3rd Northumberland Fusiliers att. King's Own Yorkshire Light Infantry, was killed between 25th and 27th October 1914.

commanders, managed to crawl back to the dubious shelter of the road. To their right, 2nd Lt. Whittam[i] and his men were nearly annihilated before they drew level with the southern end of the sunken road. To their rear, A Company, exposed on ground above the sunken road, were shattered by a storm of bullets and all three subalterns were hit before reaching the lane. Capt. Matthey and a few men dashed forward and gained the minimal shelter of the northern end of the lane which was now rapidly filling with dead and wounded Fusiliers. C Company was equally exposed and equally badly mauled. Caught by machine gun fire on the parapet, Capt. Edmund McNaghten Dawson[ii], OC C Company, and CSM Nelson, were both knocked out as they encouraged the men forward. Only about 60 men under 2nd Lt. Caseby reached the sunken road while another platoon under 2nd Lt. Jones found themselves blocked in a communication trench by the wounded already streaming to the rear.

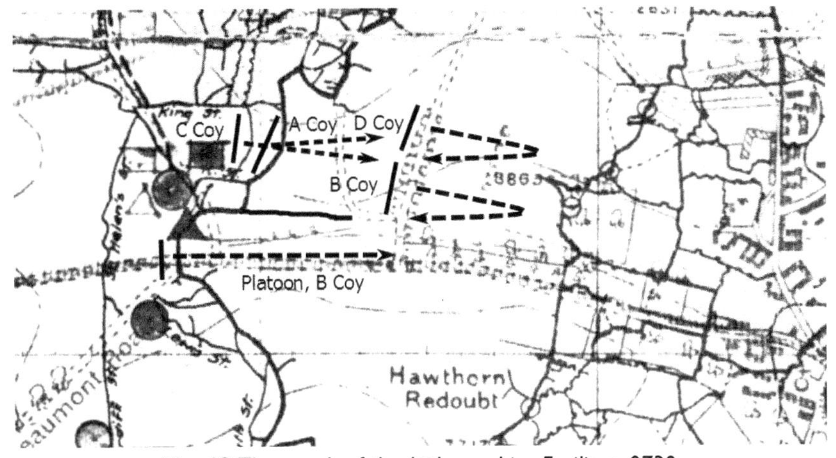

Map 13 The attack of the 1st Lancashire Fusiliers, 0730.

For the men of A and C Companies, accessing the sunken road was a tricky business. It ran some 15 feet below, down a steep bank and many of the men who arrived at the edge were carrying coils of wire and tools for consolidation. They had no option but to join the dead and wounded falling into the lane by rolling down the slope, adding bumps and bruises to any other injuries already incurred.

With so few men available to him to renew the attack Lt. Col. Magniac[iii], the CO of the 1st Lancashire Fusiliers, ordered the Battalion Intelligence Officer, 2nd

---

[i] 2nd Lt. Francis Joseph Whittam, 3rd att. 1st Lancashire Fusiliers, was aged 38 and was the second son of Major and Mrs James Whittam, of Prestwich Park, Manchester. He was educated at Ampleforth and Ushaw and he had returned from Canada to offer his services. Married with one son, he served at Gallipoli. His body was never found and his name is inscribed on the Thiepval Memorial, Pier & Face 3C & 3D.

[ii] Capt. Dawson, or 'Pongo' as he was known to his fellow officers, can be seen in Malins' film footage of the 1st Lancashire Fusiliers moving up a trench prior to the advance of C Company.

[iii] Lt. Col. Meredith Magniac, DSO, 1st Lancashire Fusiliers, was killed on 25th April 1917. Aged 36, he was the third son of the late Maj. Gen. Francis Lane Magniac (5th Madras

Lt. Sheppard, to bring forward any men he could find. During the search Sheppard was hit in the head and, bloodied but unbowed, he returned to the lane and took his place amongst the men waiting there.

With 100 wounded men sheltering in the road, the chaotic arrival of the survivors of the advance of A and C Companies resulted in all units becoming mixed up. An immediate advance was out of the question and the surviving officers set to reorganising the men, separating the wounded and preparing the rest for an advance that already looked foredoomed. With them were Nos. 1 and 2 Sections, No. 13 Platoon, 1/2nd Monmouthshire Regt. They had followed Caseby and his party from C Company and had managed to get into the sunken road though its southern entrance. They were laden with stakes and wire, ready to consolidate the positions captured but now they were turned back into infantry. Ordered to dump all of their material they prepared themselves to join in with the next attempted advance.

As the men were organised, a process that took over half an hour, Sgt. Caulfield, a Lewis gunner, spotted a Maxim placed behind some debris in the ruins of Beaumont Hamel. This he pointed out to Lt. Col. Magniac. Two Lewis guns were placed to provide converging fire in an effort to put it out of action but German artillery observers spotted the guns and 77 cm fire was immediately brought down on them. One of the Lewis guns was hit but the German machine gun ceased firing from that position.

At 8.15 a.m. the able-bodied officers and men in the sunken road were ready to make another desperate charge. Magniac ordered the three Stokes guns to provide some covering fire under which 2nd Lt. Caseby and some 75 other ranks dashed from the northern end of the lane towards the German wire. The forlorn hope was that they might make it to the higher ground above the northern end of the village but, on leaving the shelter of the lane, all but Caseby[i] and about ten men were cut down by machine gun fire within ten yards. Some of these men

---

Light Cavalry) and of Mrs Edith Magniac (née Parkinson), of Coombe Cot, Abbotsham, Devon, husband of Winifred Ethel Magniac (née Dacres), the sister of Capt. Hugh Winfield Sayres also killed 1st July 1916, of The Austen, Rye, Sussex. Educated at Clifton College, where he played for the cricket 1st XI, and RMC, Sandhurst. He played cricket for the South African Army team against the touring MCC at Pretoria in 1906. Commissioned into the Lancashire Fusiliers in 1899. Promoted Captain, 1904. Attended the Staff College at Quetta, 1914, qualified 1916. Brigade Major, Ireland, then GSO3 and GSO2, IX Corps, 1915. Served at Gallipoli. DSO, June 1916, three times MiD. He is buried in Beaurains Road Cemetery, grave B. 4. His younger brother, Lt. Col. Erskine Magniac, 27th Punjab Regt., died on 28th April 1917. He is remembered on the Basra Memorial, Panel 54.

[i] 2nd Lt. William Robert Brown Caseby, Royal Scots att. 1st Lancashire Fusiliers, was awarded the MC for his conduct on 1st July 1916. His citation, in the *London Gazette* of 22nd September 1916, reads: "For conspicuous gallantry in action. He led his platoon-with great dash, and, when all other company officers had fallen, reorganised the men and led forward a second attack".

2nd Lt. Caseby was to die by the side of his CO, Lt. Col. Magniac, during the Battle of Arras. 2nd Lt. William Robert Brown Caseby, MC, Royal Scots att. 1st Lancashire Fusiliers, was killed on 25th April 1917. Aged 21, he was the son of David and Margaret Caseby, of 30, Argyle St., St. Andrews, Fife. Also served at Gallipoli. His body was never found and his name is inscribed on the Arras Memorial, Bay 1 & 2.

were Pioneers and, having reached the lee of the low bank in No Man's Land some 50 yards from the German trench, they dug in and waited[i]. Amongst those to fall was Capt. Matthey who had collected his few men together and helped lead the charge towards the German lines. 'They followed him over splendidly,' wrote a fellow officer, 'It was a magnificent thing to do, but he never came back.'[ii]

Sometime later, some reinforcements, in the shape of two extra machine guns from the 86th Machine Gun Company, arrived from the Brigade front near Rooney's Sap (opposite the re-entrant south of the crater). Informed by a runner that two of the officers, Lt. J O Laker and Lt. Charles William Creasey[iii], in charge of teams on the Lancashire Fusiliers front had been wounded, the Company CO accompanied by Lt. J B Stevenson and two Vickers guns moved to support the Brigade's left battalion. By the time they arrived they found three guns back in the old front line and the new ones were mounted alongside so as to cover the whole of the Lancashire Fusiliers' front. Lt. Col. Magniac was informed by runner of this reorganisation.

At 8.30 a.m., with the withering away of Caseby's attack and with no news coming back from the men thought to be out in No Man's Land, Lt. Col. Magniac returned to the old front line in order to assess the situation on both his and the neighbouring battalions' fronts. There he met Maj. Henry Kelso Utterson who was in command of the 10% reserve which he had brought up to the front line system. In addition to Utterson's small body of men another thirty or so were found in the trenches, men who had been unable to get forward with the rest owing to the congestion in the communication trenches caused by the flood of wounded escaping to the rear.

Together Magniac and Utterson studied the German lines. Little movement could be seen opposite and Beaumont Hamel seemed clear of troops or, at least, clear of British troops. Only around the crater was there any movement and here a German officer and about 25 men could be seen. One of the newly positioned machine guns was brought to bear on them but the German artillery observers again showed their excellence by calling up accurate fire within three minutes. The Vickers ceased firing when the parapet was blown in.

Back at the lane there were about 100 fit men and another 100 wounded. It was impossible to say how many men were still alive out in No Man's Land. At about 9.45 a.m. men from the Middlesex and Royal Fusiliers were seen to start retreating from the crater. The threat of being left out in the lane panicked many

---

[i] No. 13 Platoon, 1/2nd Monmouthshires, lost one officer wounded, Lt. Thomas Edward Roper Williams, two other ranks killed, 8 other ranks wounded and two other ranks missing during this time.

[ii] Capt. Edward Granville Matthey, 1st Lancashire Fusiliers, was aged 23. He was the son of Cara T Granville Matthey of 76, Lexham Gardens, Kensington, London, and the late Capt. Granville E Matthey (Royal Inniskilling Fusiliers). He was educated at Cheltenham College and the RMC Sandhurst. He was commissioned in February 1913 and went to France attached to the East Lancashire Regt. in October 1914. He was wounded at Neuve Chapelle and he returned to the battalion in May 1916. He is buried in Redan Ridge Cemetery No. 2, Beaumont-Hamel, grave C. 44.

[iii] Lt.Charles William Creasey, Loyal North Lancashire Regt., att. 86th Machine Gun Company, was commissioned from CQMS on 28th April 1915.

of the wounded and a mad scramble for the tunnel ensued. Such was the demoralisation that, as the 1st Lancashire Fusiliers diary records:

> "Everyone thought for the moment the Germans were counter-attacking, nothing seemed more possible from our point of view."[63]

> 2nd Lt. Eric Sheppard remembered this incident clearly:

> "... at the sight of these (Royal Fusiliers) coming back there was an incipient panic among the wounded and unwounded but badly shaken men in the lane. A number of them tried to escape through the tunnel and swarmed round the entrance but the CO drew his revolver and threatened to use it and the officers and NCOs managed to restore order and quieten the men and organise the lane for defence."[64]

It is a sad indicator of the utter chaos within the British trenches north of the River Ancre that this fear of a German counterattack across No Man's Land was widespread. It is mentioned in accounts from Gommecourt through Serre to Beaumont Hamel and is an indicator of the total shock and panic felt by all units at the complete collapse of the VIII Corps' attack.

In the lane, some sort of order was restored and an effort was made to turn it into a defensible position. Fifty fit men were lined up along the bank facing the Germans while 25 men under Sgt. Green started to construct a barricade at the southern end and another 35 attempted the same at the northern exit.

Further south, on the 87th Brigade's front, fighting was on-going as more battalions were thrown into the furnace of No Man's Land. On the 86th Brigade's front, however, things were somewhat quieter. The attack on the crater was at an end. Those that could move of the Middlesex, Royal Fusiliers and Dublin Fusiliers were back in their trenches. Those that couldn't were either sheltering in No Man's Land or dead. Nevertheless, Lt. Col. Magniac had decided to reinforce his men in the sunken road and, at noon, he informed the OC of the 86th Machine Gun Company that he planned to get all available men into the lane at 12.30 p.m. It was arranged that the machine guns on his front would start laying down bursts of fire on the German front line trenches from 12.15 pm. onwards. By now, and far too late, some of the Divisional artillery had been brought back to the German forward positions in anticipation of yet another suicidal attack by the last two remaining battalions of the 88th Brigade.

At 12.30 p.m. Maj. Utterson collected the men left over from the original advance and, leaving the 10% cadre in the trenches, advanced as ordered by Magniac to the sunken road. From there, Utterson was to lead his men and those in the lane forward in a third attack on the Bergwerk. Frankly, it was an insane idea as anyone who ventured into No Man's Land immediately attracted the attentions of the numerous German machine gun teams just looking for some British soldiers to slaughter. It was, however, thought that, with another attack planned down towards the Y Ravine (by the Worcesters and Hampshires), the pointless loss of a few dozen more Lancashire Fusiliers might, in some misguided way, help the men of the 88th Brigade achieve what the two other Brigades had failed to manage. The total futility of the exercise was reinforced first when Utterson and only four men arrived at the sunken road and second when no-one moved from the 88th Brigade away on their right.

Plate 29 2nd Lt. Frank Westall Anderton, 3rd att. 1st Lancashire Fusiliers

There was nothing left to do but improve the defences of the lane, evacuate the seriously wounded and let the walking wounded retire to medical aid near the White City by crawling through the tunnel, which was itself not a wholly healthy thing to attempt given the entrance was partially visible from the German lines.

Thankfully, the same air of reality had dawned at 86th Brigade HQ. At 12.30 p.m. Brig. Gen. Williams accepted the inevitable:

> "I realised that further attack could only mean needless loss of life. I had heard that the Brigade on my right had failed and I had seen the Brigade on my left could not advance. I instructed Lanc Fus. to hold the Sunken Road and with the remainder of the troops took up the defence of our own line."[65]

Work continued until 2.10 p.m. when Magniac was blessed with a visit from Capt. Fulton, attached by Division to the 86th Brigade staff as replacement for the wounded Gee and Grant. Fulton informed the unhappy CO that it was now his duty to hold the sunken road at all costs. Again, this betrays the widespread, if preposterous, concern that the Germans might take advantage of the heavy losses and general confusion to charge across No Man's Land at any moment. And so the small group of men under Utterson remained in the lane, creating some sort of fortification and losing the odd man here and there to German shells lobbed into the lane for the sake of amusement.

Out in No Man's Land the trapped and wounded kept their heads down and tried not to move. Detection meant the attentions of one of the many snipers whose fun it was now to pick off the defenceless men who were roasting gently in the strong mid-afternoon sun.

At 6 p.m. all but one officer and 25 men were withdrawn from the sunken road. The fight was over for the Lancashire Fusiliers. Casualties were reported as 7 officers killed, 14 wounded and 500 ORs. The officer casualties were:

Killed:
2nd Lt. A F D Anderson[i], att. 4th Lancashire Fusiliers
2nd Lt. F W Anderton[ii], att. 3rd Lancashire Fusiliers
2nd Lt. H N Grant[iii]
2nd Lt. E Kershaw
Capt. E G Matthey
2nd Lt. R S Prescott
Lt. F J Whittam
Wounded:
2nd Lt. George Arthur Bateson
Lt. George Edward Beaumont
Capt. Edmund Mcnaghten Dawson
2nd Lt. Edwards, att. 3rd Lancashire Fusiliers
Lt. William Edward England, att. 16th King's (Liverpool) Regt.
2nd Lt. Thomas George Mahony, att. Queen's Royal West Surrey Regt.
Capt. George Paterson Nunneley, att. 4th Bedfordshire Regt.
Capt. William Pottle, att. 4th Bedfordshire Regt.
2nd Lt. Peter Quentin Reiss[iv]
2nd Lt. George Riley Spencer, att. 3rd Lancashire Fusiliers
2nd Lt. Eric William Sheppard[v], att. 1st Royal West Kent Regt.
Capt. Cecil Francis Wells[vi], att. 3rd Lancashire Fusiliers
2nd Lt. Heneage Gervase Noel Yates
The casualty numbers as recorded in the 29th Division diary were:
Officers: missing 7, wounded 13, total 20
Other ranks: killed 13, wounded 204, missing 247, total 464.

---

[i] 2nd Lt. Arthur Furneaux Dalgairns Anderson, 4th att. 1st Lancashire Fusiliers, was aged 22. He was the son of Mr A W H and Florence E Anderson of 12, Park Avenue, Barrow-in-Furness. He is buried in Beaumont Hamel British Cemetery, grave A. 6.

[ii] 2nd Lt. Frank Westall Anderton, 3rd att. 1st Lancashire Fusiliers, was aged 21. He was the son of James Anderton a cotton manufacturer of Brookfield Mill, Preston, Lancs., and Alice Anderton of Glenroyd, 50, North Drive, St. Annes-on-Sea. He was educated at Mill Hill where he was in the OTC. He worked for Wood Milne Ltd at the Ajax Rubber Works, Leyland. He enlisted as a Private in the 1/4th Loyal North Lancashire Regt., and was commissioned into the Lancashire Fusiliers in March 1915. He is buried in Redan Ridge Cemetery No. 2, Beaumont-Hamel, grave C. 33.

[iii] 2nd Lt. Henry Norman Grant, A Company, 1st Lancashire Fusiliers, was aged 23. He was the son of Henry Richard and Jane Victoria Grant of 6, Castle St., Hay, Breconshire. He is buried in Redan Ridge Cemetery No. 2, Beaumont-Hamel, grave C. 31.

[iv] 2nd Lt. Peter Quentin Reiss joined the R.F.C. in 1917. He was a friend and suitor of the aviator Amy Johnson in the 1930s.

[v] 2nd Lt. Eric William Sheppard, 1st Royal West Kent Regt. att. 1st Lancashire Fusiliers, was awarded an MC for his conduct on 1st July. The citation in the *London Gazette* of 26th September 1916 reads: "For conspicuous gallantry in action. He went forward under heavy fire and brought back a clear report of the situation. Though wounded, he insisted on remaining at duty".

[vi] Capt. Cecil Francis Wells, 3rd Lancashire Fusiliers att. 1st Lancashire Fusiliers, was awarded the MC for his conduct on 1st July 1916. The citation in the *London Gazette* of 26th September 1916 reads: "For conspicuous gallantry and devotion to duty in action. Though wounded early in the action he remained at his post for six hours until compelled by weakness to go back. He set a fine example to his men".

They had gone into action with 22 officers and 885 men, giving a casualty rate of 53%[i].

Progressively, the exchanges of artillery dwindled. 86th Brigade put the remnants of its four battalions in the line, from right to left the Dublin Fusiliers, Royal Fusiliers, 16th Middlesex and 1st Lancashire Fusiliers. Now the effort was in evacuating the wounded, clearing the debris and discarded equipment from the trenches and removing the dead.

During the night the Sunken Road was cleared of all wounded except five. About 12 midnight 2nd Lts. Spencer (wounded), Gorfunkle, Craig and Caseby got back with about 20 men. They had spent the day in a small hollow just short of the German wire.

Battalion	Available		Held to reinforce		In actual assault(1)		Casualties	
	Off	OR	Off	OR	Off	OR	Off	OR
2nd R Fus.	33	1006	11	100	22	906	21	507
1st Lancs Fus.	36	983	14	98	22	885	20	464
1st Dublin F	27	918	5	92	22	826	11	206
16th Middx	35	773	13	77	22	696	22	614
Total	131	3680	43	367	88	3313	74	1791
					Percentage casualties		84%	54%

Table 9 86th Brigade Strength and Casualties[66]

(1) This includes Brigade & Battalion carrying parties, stretcher bearers, battle police, etc.

Battalion	Killed		Wounded		Missing		Total
	Off	OR	Off	OR	Off	OR	
2nd R Fus.	3	51	11	196	7	260	528
1st Lancs Fus.	0	13	13	204	7	247	484
1st Dublin F	4	29	6	123	1	54	217
16th Middx	0	0	8	0	14	0	636(1)
86th MGC	0	4	3	24	0	9	40
86th TMB	1	2	1	9	0	4	17
86th Bde Staff	0	0	2	0	0	0	2
	8	99	44	556	29	574	

Table 10 Details of casualties, 86th Brigade[67]

(1) Detailed figures for Other Ranks not then reported

LET US NOW CONSIDER THE EVENTS UNFOLDING on the 87th Brigade's front to the south.

Without the mine crater to concern them, the objectives of the Brigade were to take three lines of German trenches in 20 minutes at which time they were to arrive at Station Road, the valley that runs from the south of Beaumont Hamel down to the railway station by the Ancre. There would be a 40 minute pause while reorganisation took place and the two supporting battalions came up at which point, i.e. 8.30 a.m., the Brigade would advance at a speed not exceeding

[i] Again, the Official History's numbers are slightly different: Officers 8 killed and 10 wounded, Other Ranks 156 killed, 298 wounded and 11 missing.

50 yards a minute until, at Zero + 1 hour 20 minutes, they would assault the second objective, the Zwischen Stellung along the Beaucourt Road. Five minutes later, the 1st KOSB on the right of the 87th Brigade would assault Beaucourt chateau and village while, on the rest of the front, the Brigade cut any remaining wire not cleared during the bombardment. Whilst this happened, the 88th Brigade was to come forward ready to go through the 86th and 87th Brigades. At 10 a.m., i.e. Zero + 2 hours 30 minutes, the 88th Brigade would continue to advance, again at a speed not exceeding 50 yards a minute, until they reached the Puisieux Road ten minutes later. There they would wait while the field and heavy artillery gave one last pummelling to the third objective before, at 10.57 a.m., they were to attack and take the first line of the third objective, swiftly followed three minutes later, by the support line. Simple.

Meanwhile, on their right, two battalions of the 108th Brigade of the 36th (Ulster) Division were to advance from the trenches south of the Mary Redan which ran down the slope towards the railway line which runs along the north bank of the Ancre. At this point another fortification, the William Redan, projected out into No Man's Land towards a depression half way across No Man's Land known as the 'Ravine'. The task of these two battalions, the 12th Royal Irish Rifles and the 9th Royal Irish Fusiliers, was to cross the first three lines of German trenches down as far as the marshland on the banks of the river and then push north east on an ever decreasing front until they took and passed the railway station which gave Station Road its name. It would probably be the brave, brief and costly entry by a few of their men into the German front line trench which caused the chaos and heavy losses that was to cripple the 29th Division over the next two hours.

According to the programme, however, everything on this part of the front would be done and dusted no later than 11.25 a.m., at which point the Corps artillery would cease firing, the field guns continuing to provide a protective barrage 400 yards to the east. The 18 pdrs would stop firing at 12.10 p.m. Everyone could then sit down for their well-earned lunch. It would probably include some captured Bratwurst, sloshed down with some liberated champagne, all the while modelling some dead German officer's ornate pickelhaube (except, of course, that looting was a court martial 'shooting' offence). Anyway, the thing would be that the Fourth Army's left wing would be sitting on the objective demanded of Sir Henry Rawlinson by the CinC, Sir Douglas Haig, back in the spring. At the same time, some cavalry would, undoubtedly, be trotting up the road towards Bapaume with grinning Indian lancers indulging in some pig-sticking practice at the expense of the backsides of various terrified Huns. Next stop Berlin.

Perhaps there were some men hunkered down in the assembly trenches who truly believed this would be the outcome. Others might have contemplated the series of failures to enter the German trenches by numerous raids and wondered how was it these supposedly dead Germans fought so well.

The KOSB had everyone in their correct place by 2 a.m. D Company was in Brook Street, B Company and the Trench Mortar Section in Piccadilly, A Company and the Machine Gun Section were in St James' Street and C Company and a platoon of 1/2nd Monmouth Regt. waited in Buckingham Palace Road.

They had suffered a few casualties as these arrangements were made with 2nd Lt. James Gow[i], C Company, being killed while getting his platoon into position and 2 men, also of C Company, wounded. The new advance Battalion HQ, meanwhile, was established in a dug out at the junction of Piccadilly and Bond Street. They, like every battalion in the Brigade, would employ the same attack formation. They were to advance in lines of platoons in column of sections. Wire cutters and bridge carriers were in the first line, Lewis gunners and bombers for clearing the trenches in the 2nd and 3rd lines with the consolidating parties in the 4th line. Two machine guns went forward with each battalion reserve and the two Stokes mortars with the reserve of the two rear battalions. There is something about this formation that smacks of the idea that this was an occupation rather than an attack. The wire cutters and bridge carriers were there to assist with a trouble-free advance. They were not going to be thrown at the enemy if they inconveniently neglected to die or surrender.

At 5 a.m. the leading waves of South Wales Borderers filtered into the front line trenches. The ground ahead dropped gently away towards the German trenches in front of the two branches of the ravine. Mist filled the valleys and hollows only disturbed by the flash and roar of British shells as they plunged blindly into the German lines. At 6 a.m. tea was passed around, still tasting of the previous contents of the petrol cans from which it was poured.

As everywhere along the line the artillery bombardment built in intensity towards the final 10 minutes madness in which the Stokes mortars would join from their positions at the end of the tunnels at 1st Avenue and Mary Redan. But how effective was this continuous shelling? Not very, according to the 87th Brigade diary:

> "The actual bombardment by the artillery immediately previous to the assault does not appear to have knocked the enemy trenches about or filled in the deep dugouts."[68]

Chilling words for the infantry now crammed into the front lines.

At 7.20 a.m. all hell broke loose. The COs of the South Wales Borderers and Border Regt., Maj. Raikes and Lt. Col. Ellis, watched from the steps of a front line dugout as the mine erupted, flinging chalk and the unfortunate occupants of several German dugouts to kingdom come. Then the batteries of Stokes mortars started firing at a furious rate from the two tunnels which had been opened up just 30 yards from the German trenches at either end of the Brigade front. And, at the same moment, the British heavy artillery moved off the German front line and, within minutes, the killing began.

In the British trenches officers ushered their men over the parapet and towards the gaps cut in the British wire just after the mine exploded. On the left of the South Wales Borderers, where distances across No Man's Land were shorter, A Company moved off at 7.27 a.m. On the right where, especially for D Company, distances were considerably greater, they left the trenches at 7.24 a.m.

---

[i] 2nd Lt. James Lightfoot Gow, 9th att. 1st Kings Own Scottish Borderers, was aged 26. He was the son of the late Mr David Gow and Mrs Gow of Glencairn Cottage, Dunfermline. He was commissioned on 10th April 1915. He is buried in Knightsbridge Cemetery, Mesnil-Martinsart, grave C. 42.

It is thought that three German machine guns lay in wait for the South Wales battalion.

Lt. Col. Ellis of the 1st Border Regt., watched their advance with alarm:

> "Within a very few moments of the first waves of the SWB coming out into the open it was abundantly clear to observers from the front line that the bombardment had completely failed to subdue the German MGs.
> The moment the barrage lifted from the German front line … German machine gunners could be seen quite distinctly at the head of Y Ravine getting their guns into action. The guns very soon began to take heavy toll of the SWB and it was pretty obvious that while troops on our flanks met with an easier ride the attack on our immediate front was foredoomed to failure.
> So convinced was I of this that just previous to the time for my own battalion to advance I tapped in on the Brigade line and told Brigade what was happening on my own front.
> Gen. Lucas spoke to me and said that things were going well with the R(oyal). Innisk(illing). Fus(iliers). and the R(oyal). F(usiliers). and that my attack was to go as arranged."[69]

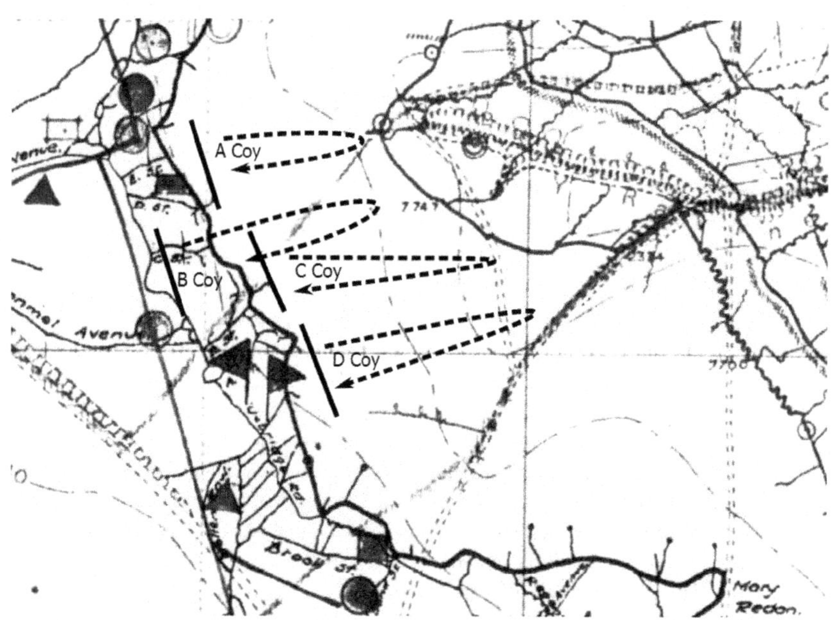

Map 14 Attack of the 2nd South Wales Borderers, 0730,

Maj. Geoffrey Taunton Raikes[i], ex-Egyptian Army and the CO of the SWB, described what happened after the war:

---

[i] Maj., later Maj. Gen., Sir Geoffrey Taunton Raikes, DSO & 2 Bars, South Wales Borderers, was born in 1884, the fourth son of Robert Taunton Raikes of Treberfydd, Bwlch, Breconshire, and 171, Victoria Street, London, SW, and Rosa Margaret, fourth daughter of Henry William Cripps, QC. He married Dorothy Annabel Wilson in 1923.

"It was of course broad daylight. Warned partly by the mine at the Hawthorn Redoubt and partly by direct observation, the German Machine Gun and rifle fire opened on the leading companies while they were advancing before zero."[70]

The 29th Division war diary description of this moment is almost shockingly understated:

"The appearance of our troops on the parapet was the signal for a very heavy machine gun fire from the enemy and many casualties ensued."[71]

The entry in the diary of the 2nd South Wales Borderers is rather more explicit but still does not convey the full scale of the carnage that occurred within a few yards of the British lines:

"As the leading companies reached the outer edge of our wire machine gun fire was opened on them which rapidly increased in intensity. Enemy also opened percussion shrapnel on the advancing lines. By about 0730 the leading companies had lost nearly all their officers and 70% of the men."[72]

In spite of this slaughter the men advanced grimly into a torrent of machine gun bullets and shrapnel. What was left of A Company on the left reached a point 20 yards short of the German trenches opposite the nose of the salient. There they were finally stopped by close range machine gun fire and hand grenades. Lt. Charles Frank Dutton[i] ordered his men to take to shell holes from where they lobbed Mills bombs at the enemy. Dutton is himself reported to have shot three of the enemy. C Company crossed over a hollow by a sunken road and were within 60 yards of the German wire when stopped by heavy machine gun fire from their right. D Company, with the furthest to travel, struggled forward for 300 yards before being forced to ground with another 300 yards to go. It had been practically wiped out by machine guns that could be seen mounted on the German front line parapet.

B Company started from the support trenches and, so as not to be blocked in the communication trenches, advanced over the open towards the front line trench. Men were dropping before they even reached their own wire. There they

---

They had three daughters. He was educated at Radley College and the RMC, Sandhurst. He joined the Army in 1903, served with the Egyptian Army between 1913-15. He was MiD, awarded the DSO, 1916, and two bars (first 1918) and the Croix de Guerre, 1919. Chief Instructor, Military History and Tactics, RMA, 1928-30; CO 1st South Wales Borderers 1932-34; GOC 9th Infantry Brigade 1935-37; Major General 1937; Retired 1938; commander Territorial Army Division 1939-40; Lord Lieutenant Brecknock 1948-59. He died in 1975. His five brothers served in the war, one with the RFA, three with the Machine Gun Corps and one as a submariner. Four of the six were awarded DSOs and another the MC and all survived the war except the eldest, 2nd Lt. Frederick Munro Raikes, South Wales Borderers att. Machine Gun Corps, who died on 22nd February 1917 in Mesopotamia and is buried in the Amara War Cemetery.

[i] 2nd Lt. Charles Frank Dutton, 2nd South Wales Borderers, was awarded an MC for his actions on 1st July 1916. The citation in the *London Gazette* of 22nd September 1916 reads: "For conspicuous gallantry in action. In spite of heavy losses he led his men on till he was hung up by the enemy wire. He then got the remains of his company into shell holes and bombed the enemy. He personally shot three of the enemy".

bunched as they tried to move into No Man's Land. Still they went on. The Company commander, Capt. Alexander Arbuthnott Hughes[i], was last seen alive about 50 yards from the German trenches stubbornly leading half a dozen men onwards. Within a few yards they were all seen to fall. The battalion CO, Maj. Raikes, advanced with B Company but COs had been told not to advance into No Man's Land and he could only watch the destruction of his command. He spent the night supervising the removal of his wounded[ii].

Plate 30 Maj. Geoffrey Taunton Raikes, 2nd South Wales Borderers

Plate 31 2nd Lt. Thomas Frederick Breene, 87th Machine Gun Company

Coming up with B Company were Nos. 1 and 2 machine guns of No. 1 Section, 87th Machine Gun Company. They too marched stolidly into the maelstrom, their OC, 2nd Lt. Thomas Frederick Breene[iii], shot through the heart, disappeared forever from the sight of man.

---

[i] Capt. Alexander Arbuthnott Hughes, 4th att. 2nd South Wales Borderers, was aged 29. He was the elder son of Col. Arbuthnott James Hughes, RFA, and Caroline Mabel Hughes of Presteign, Warwick Park, Tunbridge Wells. Born at Woolwich, he was educated at Clifton and entered the RMC, Sandhurst, in 1906. He was commissioned into the 24th Regt. (SWB) in 1907 in Karachi, being appointed Adjutant. In 1911 he was posted to the 3rd King's African Rifles in British East Africa in 1912. In 1913 he was transferred to the 3rd King's African Rifles' Camel Corps in Jubaland and was promoted to command it three months later, fighting in the Jubaland uprising of 1913-14. He was promoted captain in 1914. He was injured in an accident with a camel in November 1915 and invalided home. He joined the battalion in April 1916 and went to France on 14th June to command a Company. He is buried in Y Ravine Cemetery, Beaumont-Hamel, grave C. 9.

[ii] Maj. Geoffrey Taunton Raikes, 2nd South Wales Borderers, was awarded the DSO for his conduct on 1st July 1916. His citation, in the *London Gazette* of 22nd September 1916, reads: "For conspicuous gallantry in action. He led forward his reserve under very great difficulty with the greatest coolness and courage. After dark he personally supervised the withdrawal of his wounded".

[iii] 2nd Lt. Thomas Frederick Breene, 1st Royal Warwickshire Regt. att. 87th Machine Gun Company, was aged 28. He was the son of Thomas John and Mary Breene of 99, Fitzroy

According to Raikes, by 7.35 a.m. their attack was over:

"...all that was left of the battalion was scattered individuals lying out some 10 to 100 yards from the German trench."[73]

The 2nd South Wales Borderers had not gone into the attack in great strength. 21 officers had led 578 other ranks into No Man's Land. Five minutes after the attack proper commenced, two thirds of them were casualties. It was such a crippling disaster for the battalion that, as early as 9.30 a.m., the 10% reserve was called up from Englebelmer to help man and clear the trenches. The casualties given in the war diary were:

	Killed	Wounded	Missing	Missing/killed	Total
Officers	2	4	5	4	15
Other ranks	21	160	203	0	384
Total	23	164	208	4	399

Table 11 2nd South Wales Borderers' Casualties[74]

This represents a casualty rate of 66%[i]. The battalion war diary notes that:

"None reached the enemy trench and it was impossible to bring the bodies in, practically all those reported missing were probably killed."[75]

142 men of, or attached to, the 2nd South Wales Borderers who are likely to be casualties from 1st July are recorded as having died between 1st and 15th July. There may be others who died of wounds at a later date. One man died of wounds in German hands. It should be noted that four officers noted as wounded but 'at duty' by the SWB war diary are not included in 'Officers wounded' element given in Table 11 above. It is not possible to ascertain how many 'Other ranks' fell into this category.

The officer casualties were:

Killed:

2nd Lt. D F Don[ii], att. 14th Sherwood Foresters

2nd Lt. F Rice[i], att. 8th SWB

Avenue, Belfast. He started work at the Head Office of the Northern Bank in 1906. He worked for numerous branches of the bank before returning to Head Officer in 1914. A member of the Queens' University OTC in 1915. He was commissioned into the 1st Royal Warwickshire Regt. in May, 1915. His body was never found and his name is inscribed on the Thiepval Memorial, Pier & Face 9A 9B & 10B.

[i] The Official History revised these figures down to: Officers: killed 9, wounded 6, missing 2, total 17; Other ranks: killed 141, wounded 212, missing 2, total 355. It should also be noted that the actual number of officers killed was 10 with another attached to the 87th MGC and not 9 as in the Official History.

[ii] 2nd Lt. David Fairweather Don, 14th Sherwood Foresters att. 2nd South Wales Borderers, was aged 22. He was the youngest son of Surgeon General William Gerard Don, RAMC ret., and Jean Ann Don née Fairweather, of 52, Canfield Gardens, West Hampstead. He was educated at University College School and worked for the National Bank of India. He enlisted in the HAC in January 1915 and was commissioned into the Sherwood Foresters in July 1915. He went to Egypt in October 1915 and was attached to the 2nd South Wales Borderers. His body was never found and his name is inscribed on the Thiepval Memorial, Pier & Face 10C 10D & 11A.

Plate 32 2nd Lt. George Henry Bowyer, 2nd South Wales Borderers

Missing:
2nd Lt. G H Bowyer[ii]
Capt. R J McLaren[iii], att. 14th Cheshire Regt.
2nd Lt. J E Murray[iv], att. 9th SWB
2nd Lt. J Robinson[v], att. 3rd SWB
2nd Lt. T W M Wells[vi]

---

[i] 2nd Lt. Frederick Rice, 8th att. 2nd South Wales Borderers, is buried in Y Ravine Cemetery, Beaumont-Hamel, Sp. Mem. A. 3.

[ii] 2nd Lt. George Henry Bowyer, 2nd South Wales Borderers att. 87th Machine Gun Company, was aged 25. He was the son of W S Bowyer of 'Heathcote', 36, Christchurch Rd., Streatham Hill, London. Educated at Dulwich College he played for the Old Alleynian Football Club rugby 1st XV between 1911 and 1914. He joined the Hon. Artillery Company in 1909. Mobilized, Aug., 1914, proceeded to Egypt, April, 1915. Joined School of Instruction at Zietoun and was commissioned into the 2nd SWB in November, 1915. His body was never found and his name is inscribed on the Thiepval Memorial, Pier & Face 4 A.

[iii] Capt. Robert John McLaren, 14th Cheshire Regt att. 2nd South Wales Borderers, is buried in Hawthorn Ridge Cemetery No. 1, Auchonvillers, grave A. 48.

[iv] 2nd Lt. John Claude Murray, 9th att. 2nd South Wales Borderers, was aged 31. He was the son of William and Elizabeth Murray of Treberth Farm, Saundersfoot, Pembrokeshire. He was educated at Greenhill Grammar School, Tenby. His body was never found and his name is inscribed on the Thiepval Memorial, Pier & Face 4A. (The Commonwealth War Graves Commission records his death as being on the 9th July 1916 however the 2nd SWB's War Diary includes him amongst the missing of 1st July 1916. There is no mention of any casualties on 9th July 1916 when the battalion was many miles from the front line).

[v] 2nd Lt. John Robinson, 3rd att. 2nd South Wales Borderers, was aged 29. He was the son of Richard Syer Robinson and Alice Louise Robinson of 8, Vicarage Terrace, Kendal, Westmorland. Born at Barry, Glam. He joined the battalion on 8th June 1916. He is buried in Hawthorn Ridge Cemetery No. 2, Auchonvillers, grave B. 74.

[vi] 2nd Lt. Thomas William Maurice Wells, MM, 2nd South Wales Borderers, came from Colchester. Originally 8796 Sergeant in the Essex Regt., he was commissioned into the

Missing believed killed:
Capt. F S Blake[i], att. 15th King's Liverpool Regt.
Capt. A A Hughes, att. 3rd SWB
Lt. H P Evans[ii]
2nd Lt. J B Karran, att. 9th SWB
Wounded:
Capt. & Adjutant Desmond Henry Sykes Somerville MC
Lt. Charles Christopher Fowkes[iii]
2nd Lt. William Miles Mason, att. 9th SWB
2nd Lt. William Henry Kelly
Wounded at duty
2nd Lt. Eric Glanville Jones, att. 9th SWB
2nd Lt. Charles Richard Wardle, att. 9th SWB
2nd Lt. William Maurice Evans, att. 3rd SWB
2nd Lt. Albert Edward Morgan

IT SEEMS ABOUT NOW THAT OBSERVERS from 87th Brigade started having trouble believing what they were seeing. They had been assured by the Corps commander, no less, that the Germans were all either dead or so demoralised that resistance would be feeble and yet here, in front of their appalled eyes, was the clearest possible evidence that 'higher authority' had got things seriously wrong. It was a difficult concept to swallow for men trained to believe in their senior officers' infallibility. Their problem now was that, spread across the long grass between the front lines, was the torn and bloodied human wreckage of a once proud battalion. And yet, from the very place which, according to timetable they should now be, came rockets. Rockets of the same colour that would indicate the troops had arrived at their first objective. With the greatest reluctance, however, the Brigade war diary came to the only sensible conclusion:

> "These lights may have been enemy as no troops on our left got as far as the German front line."[76]

'May'? To quote a popular American cartoon character with a large belly, a fondness for beer and low intelligence, 'Doh!' Yes, all that remained of the 2nd South Wales Borderers, alive and dead, were out in No Man's Land, ergo, the rockets being sent up behind the German lines were German rockets sending

South Wales Borderers in April 1916. His body was never found and his name is inscribed on the Thiepval Memorial, Pier & Face 4A.

[i] Capt. Francis Seymour Blake, 15th King's Liverpool Regt att. 2nd South Wales Borderers, was aged 38. He was the husband of Florence Blake of 31, Newstead Rd., Lee, London. He worked in the Comptroller of the Council's office of the London County Council. His body was never found and his name is inscribed on the Thiepval Memorial, Pier & Face 1D, 8B & 8C.

[ii] Lt. Humphrey Pennefather Evans, 2nd South Wales Borderers, was commissioned on 19th April 1915. His body was never found and his name is inscribed on the Thiepval Memorial, Pier & Face 4A.

[iii] Lt. Charles Christopher Fowkes, DSO, MC, 2nd South Wales Borderers, went on to become a Major General, serving in East Africa (GOC, 12th African Division) and Burma (GOC, 11th East African Division) in the Second World War. He retired in 1946 and died in 1966. His unlikely nickname was 'Fluffy'.

signals to German units. The artillery fire coming from their side of the wire might have been some hint as to what the signals had meant.

Behind the SWB, previously tucked safely away in the support line, was the 1st Border Regt. Like B Company of the SWB, it had been arranged that the Border Regt. would advance over the open so as to avoid any potential congestion in the communication trenches. Unlike B Company they had nearly twice as far to go before arriving at the British wire. To get across the British lateral trenches the men had to bunch together to cross the bridges laid there and then, when they reached the wire, they had to bunch again to get through the inadequately numbered and sized gaps prepared for the advance. The bridges and the gaps in the wire were now perfect targets for the machine guns in all three tiers of the German defence system. The men of the Border Regt. fell in heaps at each bottleneck. It is a wonder that any of them made it out into No Man's Land but there, impossible as it is for us to believe nowadays, those that were left formed up, inclined to the right and set off towards the enemy's trenches 'at a slow walk'. Such stubborn bravery is beyond comprehension. Within a few yards the advance was reduced to a few small groups of men and, within a few yards more, those that still lived took to shell holes or any form of cover they could find. All, that is, except for a small group, led by 39 year old 2nd Lt. Arthur William Fraser[i], which reached the uncut German wire to the south of the nose of the Y Ravine. Uncut Boche wire was not about to prevent the indomitable 39 year old Fraser from getting at the Germans. Although twice wounded by grenade fragments and once by a bullet, he ordered his few remaining men to cut a way through the wire before collapsing unconscious. But there was no way through and his men were all shot down. Someone in authority noted his actions, however, and Fraser was awarded a posthumous DSO.

It was, perhaps, Fraser's forlorn and hopeless advance which led to another of those erroneous and tragically misleading reports to reach VIII Corps:

> "Reports state that the first line of the Border Regiment crossed the enemy's front trenches, but little confirmation of this is forthcoming."[77]

Lt. John Boustead Sinclair[ii] was hit three times as he led his men through the wire but carried on advancing at the head of his men until a superior ordered him

---

[i] 2nd Lt. (temp Capt.) Arthur William Fraser, DSO, 8th att. 1st Border Regt., was aged 39. He was the son of Capt. James Kemp Fraser (14th King's Hussars); husband of Mary Ann Fraser. He is buried in Hawthorn Ridge Cemetery No.2, Auchonvillers, grave A. 33. He was awarded the DSO for his conduct on 1st July 1916. The citation in the *London Gazette* of 22nd September 1916 reads: "For conspicuous gallantry in action. After suffering heavy casualties he led his company up to the enemy wire at a place where it was uncut. Though severely wounded, twice by bombs and once by rifle fire, he continued to direct the wire-cutting till he lost consciousness".

[ii] Lt. John Boustead Sinclair, 10th Border Regt., att. 1st Border Regt., was awarded the MC for his conduct on 1st July 1916. The citation in the *London Gazette* of 26th September 1916 reads: "For conspicuous gallantry in action. He continued to lead his men forward after he had been wounded three times. He was then ordered back to have his wounds dressed, but immediately afterwards resumed his duties in the trenches till again ordered back". Previously a member of the OTC he was commissioned on 28th September 1914. After recovering from his wounds he was transferred to the Training Reserve in March 1917

back to get his wounds dressed. This he did before hurrying back to the front lines to resume command of what was left of his men. It was only when directed to seek medical help for a second time that he was persuaded to leave the field.

Amongst the last to negotiate the death trap that was the British front line was No. 15 Platoon of the 1/2nd Monmouthshire Regt. attached to the Borders for the attack. These men were not going anywhere very fast, laden, as they were, with eight full water bottles in a sandbag and also signalling equipment. Their departure point was Fethard Street just to the south of 1st Avenue. This was the support line and to get to No Man's Land it was necessary to get through two rows of wire, one between Fethard Street and the front line and another outside the front line trench. The men filed over the parapet through the Fethard Street wire then got into extended order. To cross the front line they again got into file until clear of the wire, all the while visible to the German machine gunners. They were now in No Man's Land and horribly exposed. As the advance had clearly stalled the men lay down amongst the dead and wounded and waited. And waited. After about 2 hours they were ordered back into the front line. The platoon spent the rest of the day giving what help they could to the wounded[i].

These were not the only men of the Divisional pioneers trying to perform their allotted tasks. Part of the plans for the advance was the digging of two communication trenches across a relatively short space of No Man's Land from the ends of the two tunnels dug by the Royal Engineers on either flank of the 87th Brigade front. Nos. 5 and 6 Platoons, B Company, 1/2nd Monmouthshire Regt., were given the job of digging the trench from the end of the 1st Avenue tunnel. They started out for the tunnel at 7.50 a.m. via Yellow Street, Tipperary and 1st Avenue but, try as the might, the men were unable to get to their posts. The trenches and tunnel were so full of wounded, signallers and orderlies that they were unable to move beyond the support line where they stayed all day, suffering under the German barrage.

The collapse of the attack and the destruction of his battalion were observed at the very closest quarters by the CO of the 1st Border Regt., Lt. Col. Archibald Jenner Ellis[ii]:

---

before returning to the Border Regt. He relinquished his commission on the grounds of ill health caused by wounds in May 1919.

[i] Their casualties were, happily, remarkably light: Capt. Alfred Courtenay Sales wounded, 3 other ranks missing and 7 other ranks wounded.

[ii] Lt. Col. Archibald Jenner Ellis, DSO, OBE, 1st Border Regt., was born on 18th May 1881. He was commissioned into the 3rd Border Regt. in 1901 serving in South Africa (1901) and Southern Nigeria (1905). Promoted Captain in 1912, and Adjutant in 1913, he went to war in that position. Served in Gallipoli. DSO, 1916, and Bar, 1918. Attended Staff College in 1922 and went to the North West Frontier with the 1st Border Regt. In April 1923, while at Kohat, his wife, Ellen Mary Ellis, was murdered and his 17 year old daughter Mollie abducted by Afridi tribesmen led by an Ajab Khan. On his daughter's release he returned to England and took command of the 2nd Border Regt. Promoted Colonel he was given command of the Tientsin Brigade in China but ill-health forced his resignation. Appointed Commandant, South Nigerian Regt., until ill-health again forced his resignation. Retired from the Army in 1935 to live in Sussex. Appointed to a Staff position on the outbreak of WW2 he then commanded the 22nd Battalion, Sussex Home Guard and was awarded the OBE. Re-married in 1930 to Marguerite Johnston. He died in 1953.

> "By this time the German barrage had come down one our front, support and reserve trenches and my battalion suffered severely from it before even they reached our own wire. By the time my leading platoons were filing through the lanes cut in our wire our own barrage was half way up the hill towards the Beaucourt Redoubt and was therefore giving us no help at all.
> By this time all the lanes through our wire (which were too few and too narrow) were thoroughly 'taped' and before my supporting company got to them were in most cases completely blocked with dead and wounded.
> The whole of my battalion eventually got clear of our front line trench and I went forward with my HQ not through one of the lanes but through a place where the wire was not very deep or thick and where it had been blown away to a great extent by the German barrage.
> When I got about 20 yards clear of the wire I was shot in the thigh and fell into a deep shell hole in which there was already a dead man and two wounded men of the SWBs."[78]

Lt. Col. Ellis lay in the shell hole observing the action through a small periscope he had thought to take with him. About 9 a.m. he was spotted and brought in by one of his HQ runners, No. 8408 Pte. John Newcombe[i] who crawled out into No Man's Land and dragged his commanding officer back into the relative safety of the front line trenches. Whilst waiting to be rescued Ellis[ii] watched events on the 87th Brigade's front:

> "On my own front all movement had practically ceased though I saw occasional small parties still making headway from shell hole to shell hole. On my right conditions seemed much the same. A few KOSBs still moving forward... By this time our barrage had reached the Beaucourt Redoubt and as far as I could observe never came back from there. About 8.30 a.m. the German MG fire died down appreciably, the reason being I imagine that there was nothing left to shoot at as all movement within my range of vision had entirely ceased."[79]

The second in command, Major James Ross Conrad Meiklejohn had been put in charge of the 10% reserve and these men were hurried forward as the scale of casualties became clear. The sight that greeted the Major was a terrible one:

> "I myself was with the 10 p.c.s (10%) and arrived in the line about 7.30[iii] a.m. to find everything in a very bad way. The front trenches were choked with dead and wounded of the successive waves which had gone over to

---

[i] 8408 Pte John Newcombe MM, 1st Border Regt, died on 24th April 1917. He was the son of Mr J F Newcombe of 85, Woodborough Rd., Nottingham. He is buried in Duisans British Cemetery, Etrun, grave IV. A. 25. His Military Medal was gazetted on 21st September 1916.

[ii] Maj. (temp. Lt. Col.) Archibald Jenner Ellis, 1st Border Regt., was awarded the DSO for his conduct on 1st July 1916. The citation in the Londonj Gazette of 22nd September 1916 reads: "For conspicuous gallantry in action. He led his reserve under very heavy machine gun fire till he was severely wounded. After this he continued to direct operations and to re-organise men in No Man's Land".

[iii] This time is incorrect and is given as 9.15 a.m. by the 1st Border Regt. war diary.

be mown down in turn. The communication trenches were the same. Lt. Col. A J Ellis, my CO, was very severely wounded through both thighs and I found him only after a long search deposited behind one of the traverses in the front line… Another officer had 18 bullet wounds from machine guns and survived… the whole of the casualties occurred in our own wire or in No Man's Land. Our whole battalion HQ for instance, with the exception of the Intelligence Officer, fell in our own wire. This included runners, servants, etc., complete."[80]

By 8 a.m. the 1st Border Regiment's war diary simply recorded that:

"The advance was brought entirely to a standstill."[81]

Meiklejohn reported his battalion's status to Brig. Gen. Lucas, GOC 87th Brigade, and the sensible advice given was to remain in the front line system and attempt nothing. Indeed, so severe were the casualties there was very little that could be done except mount some machine guns against the possibility of a German counter attack and start to clear the dead and wounded. With the German artillery relentlessly dropping 4.2 and 5.9 in. howitzer shells in the front line trenches and along the communication trenches the numbers of dead and wounded were continuously added to.

Amazingly, given that the 1st Border Regt., was a support battalion whose main task was to attack the second objective, they were to suffer the highest actual (though not proportional) casualties of any of the eight battalions in the 86th or 87th Brigades. Casualties at the time were recorded as being over 600 from the 22 officers and 878 other ranks involved in the attack – a 66% casualty rate. An unhappy record, although one all too soon to be exceeded[i].

The officer casualties were:

Killed

Capt. T H Beves[ii]

---

[i] The Official History's figures are Officers: killed 10, wounded 6, total 16; Other ranks: killed 173, wounded 362, missing 22, prisoners of war 2, total 559. A percentage casualty rate of 63%. It should be noted that the actual casualties amongst officers were: killed/DoW 11, wounded 9. It should also be noted that the wounded figure from the war diary is a precise 411, 49 more than the Official History total. Whilst some men would have died of wounds, and some 14 can be identified as having done so over the following fortnight, this still leaves over 30 additional wounded relative to the Official History's figures. These may have been lightly wounded men 'at duty' but wounded they still were. Furthermore, 199 officers and men of the 1st Border Regt are recorded as having died on 1st July 1916 by the CWGC, 16 more than the total given by the Official History. Some of these may have been 'missing' but the discrepancies lead this writer to believe that the 1st Border Regt.'s actual casualty total for 1st July is likely to be nearer the 600 figure originally given. The 29th Division War Diary gives a figure of 608 casualties of which 18 were officers. This discrepancy amongst the officers can be accounted for by the two officers who died of wounds over a week after the attack.

[ii] Capt. Trevor Howard Beves, MC, 1st Border Regt., was aged 25. He was the son of Lt. Col. Edward Leslie and Clare Beves of Brighton. He was educated at Wellington College and Woolwich. Commissioned into the Border Regt., in 1910 he was promoted Captain in May 1915. He was thrice wounded, once at Ypres, October 1914, and twice at Neuve Chapelle in March 1915 when he was awarded the MC. He is buried in Auchonvillers Military Cemetery, grave II. C. 2.

Capt. F R Jessup[i]
Wounded believed killed
2nd Lt. J Y Baxendine[ii], att. 5th Royal Scots
2nd Lt. A W Fraser, DSO, att. 8th Border Regt.
2nd Lt. L Jackson[iii], att. 10th Border Regt.
2nd Lt. W K Sanderson[iv], att. Royal West Kent Regt.

Plate 33 Capt. Francis Reginald Jessup, 1st Border Regt.

Plate 34 2nd Lt. John Young Baxendine, 5th Royal Scots att. 1st Border Regt.

Wounded and missing
2nd Lt. H L Cholmeley[i], att. 3rd Border Regt.

---

[i] Capt. Francis Reginald Jessup, 1st Border Regt., was aged 29. He was the son of the late George James and Emma Mary Jessup of 34, Queen Anne's Gardens, Enfield. He joined the battalion in January 1915 and was promoted Temp. Capt. in April 1916. His body was never found and his name is inscribed on the Thiepval Memorial, Pier & Face 6A & 7C.

[ii] 2nd Lt. John Young Baxendine, 5th Royal Scots att. 1st Border Regt., was aged 22. He was the eldest son of Andrew and Alice Baxendine of 10, McLaren Rd., Edinburgh. He was educated at George Watson's College and was a member of the Edinburgh University OTC. He worked for his father's bookselling business. Commissioned in April 1915 he fought at Gallipoli where he contracted dysentery. He is buried in Hawthorn Ridge Cemetery No.2, Auchonvillers, grave B. 42. His younger brother, Pte Andrew Richard Baxendine, 3rd Royal Scots att. 1st Garrison Battalion, Seaforth Highlanders, died from pneumonia on 18th December 1918 on the way back from Salonika.

[iii] 2nd Lt. Lancelot Jackson, 10th att. 1st Border Regt., was never found and his name is inscribed on the Thiepval Memorial, Pier & Face 6A & 7C.

[iv] 2nd Lt. Walter Kerr Sanderson, 1st Border Regt., was aged 35. He was the only surviving son of Mrs E A Sanderson of Fairfield, Penrith, Cumberland, and the late Dr. Sanderson. He was educated at Sedbergh School. He worked for 11 years in the Vote Office of the House of Commons. He enlisted in the Public Schools Battalion and was commissioned into the Royal West Kent Regt. before transferring to the Border Regt. His body was never found and his name is inscribed on the Thiepval Memorial, Pier & Face 6A and 7C.

2nd Lt. W P Rettie[ii], att. 10th Border Regt.
Died of wounds
2nd Lt. D Bremner[iii], att. 10th Border Regt., 9th July 1916
2nd Lt. F H Talbot, att. 13th Royal Warwicks[iv], 15th July 1916
2nd Lt. F T Wilkins, att. 15th Northumberland Fus.[v], 3rd July 1916

Plate 35 Lt. Harry Lewin Cholmeley, 1st Border Regt.

Plate 36 2nd Lt. Douglas Cecil Rees Stuart, 1st Border Regt.

[i] Lt. Harry Lewin Cholmeley, 3rd att. 1st Border Regt., was aged 23. He was the son of Lewin Charles and Elizabeth Maud Cholmeley of 19, Hamilton Terrace, St. John's Wood, London. Educated at Eton College, he graduated from Magdalen College, Oxford, in 1912. He had intended to take Holy Orders. He was previously wounded with the 2nd Bn. March, 1915. His brother Hugh Valentine lies in Ypres Reservoir Cemetery. His body was never found and his name is inscribed on the Thiepval Memorial, Pier & Face 6A & 7C.

[ii] 2nd Lt. William Philip Rettie, 10th att. 1st Border Regt., was aged 24. He was the son of Mr and Mrs William Rettie of Balcairn, Dundee. Educated at Fettes College and St Andrew's University. His body was never found and his name is inscribed on the Thiepval Memorial, Pier & Face 6A & 7C.

[iii] 2nd Lt. David Bremner, 10th att. 1st Border Regt., died on 9th July 1916 of wounds received on 1st July 1916. Aged 27, he was the oldest son of Alex. Hamilton Bremner and Grace Clark Bremner (née Raphael) of 5, Cobden Crescent, Edinburgh. He was born in Strathblane and educated at Merchiston Castle School. He returned from British Columbia on the outbreak of war and was commissioned in November 1914. He is buried in Doullens Communal Cemetery Extension No.1, grave II. A. 8. His younger brother, Lt. James Bremner, 1/8th Royal Scots, was killed on 24th June 1917. He is buried in Lijssenthoek Military Cemetery.

[iv] 2nd Lt. Francis Henry Talbot, 13th Royal Warwickshire Regt. att. 1st Border Regt., was the son of Frank Talbot. He is buried in Harpsden (St. Margaret) Churchyard Extension, Adjacent to the central pathway.

[v] 2nd Lt. Frank Trevor Wilkins, 15th Northumberland Fusiliers att. 1st Border Regt., was aged 26. He was the son of Samuel Griffen Wilkins and Eliza Maria Wilkins of 58, Gladstone Rd., Sparkbrook, Birmingham. M.Sc., Bowen Scholar, G.I.M.E. He is buried in Gezaincourt Communal Cemetery Extension, grave I. A. 12.

Wounded
2nd Lt. Alfred William Howard Barnes, att. 10th Border Regt.
2nd Lt. Donald Cargill, att. 3rd Border Regt .
Lt. Col. Archibald Jenner Ellis
Capt. & Adjutant John Geoffrey Heyder[i]
Lt. Bernard Lawrence Austin Kennett, att. 10th Border Regt.
2nd Lt. George William Nathaniel Rowsell
Lt. Harold Fehrsen Sampson[ii]
Lt. John Boustead Sinclair, att. 10th Border Regt.
2nd Lt. Douglas Cecil Rees Stuart[iii], att. 3rd Border Regt.

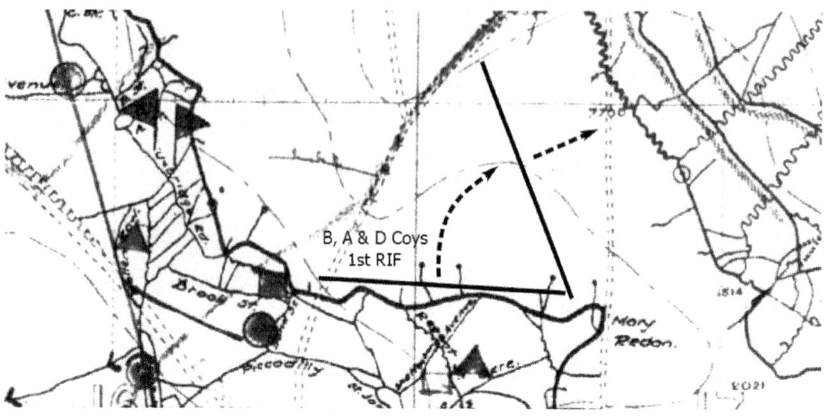

Map 15 The right wheel of the 1st Royal Inniskilling Fusiliers, 0730.

ON THE RIGHT OF THE 87TH BRIGADE FRONT the 1st Royal Inniskilling Fusiliers advanced with three companies, B, A and D, leading while C Company was held

---

[i] Capt. John Geoffrey Heyder, 1st Border Regt., was awarded the MC for his conduct on 1st July 1916. His citation in the *London Gazette* of 26th September 1916 reads: "For conspicuous gallantry in action. He advanced with the reserves, and, though wounded in two places, continued to give his C.O. every assistance. He set a fine example of bravery and devotion to duty".

[ii] Lt. Harold Fehrsen Sampson, 1st Border Regt., was born in 1890 in Grahamstown, South Africa. He was the youngest son of Mr Justice Victor Sampson. A Rhodes scholar he studied law at Trinity College, Oxford. After the war he was called to the Bar in London and South Africa. He became a Professor of Law at Rhodes University. He published three volumes of poetry between 1915 and 1937. He died in 1937.

[iii] 2nd Lt. Douglas Cecil Rees Stuart, 3rd att. 1st Border Regt., was born in 1885. He was the son of Mantague Pelham Stuart and Mary Rees of Steynton, Surbiton. Educated at Cheltenham College, where he won his boating colours, he rowed for Kingston Rowing Club. He went to Trinity Hall, Cambridge, where he won the Colquhoun Sculls. Trinity Hall were head of the river, 1907 and 1909. Stroked the Cambridge VIII to successive victories in the Varsity Boat Race between 1906 and 1908. Stroke of the VIII which won a bronze medal at the 1908 Olympic Games. President Cambridge University Boat Club in 1909 but lost to Oxford. 3rd Class degree in the Law Tripos and became a solicitor. He was commissioned into the 1st Border Regt. on 27th May 1915. September 1917, Captain of the Courts Martial. Assistant Chief Clerk in the Solicitor's Department at the Inland Revenue, 1920. Died in 1969.

in reserve in the front line. They had three trenches of the first German position to take then, crossing Station Road, another trench newly dug. 22 officers and 787 other ranks were given this task and, as the mine went up away to their left, they clambered out of the trenches and made ready for their advance. To achieve this, the battalion had to conduct a right wheel to change their alignment from facing north to facing east. This they did in the middle of No Man's Land. The battalion was immediately taken under a heavy cross fire by several machine guns. Whole ranks were swept away as they manoeuvred and then advanced with, as the battalion war diary records:

"…none being able to gain further ground than the enemy's wire."[82]

Note the word 'none'.

Officers from the 1st Essex Regt. were watching the advance from the reserve trenches and the impression of the attack, written in the war diary, was:

"7.30 a.m. 86th and 87th Brigade left our 1st line trenches to assault their objective. Heavy artillery and machine gun fire and difficulty of getting through our own wire caused these Brigades very heavy losses. Very few men survived long enough to enable them to reach half way across No Man's Land."

Note closely that last sentence.

Unfortunately for several hundred men from Newfoundland, someone apparently saw the Inniskillings march up to the German wire and 'place' their trench bridges over the German front line trench. Admittedly, according to this unknown observer, they were 'very small in number' but this element of the report was to make little difference to decisions about to be made.

Brig. Gen. Lucas, GOC 87th Brigade, recorded this 'event' in his own diary, writing:

"One party of RIF were seen to place their bridge over the German 1st line, look down into the trench and then pass on."

'Were seen'. Not seen by Lucas, therefore, or by anyone he could name or whose rank and position he could note. It has not proved possible to identify any specific officer who actually saw this happen but, once the report was in the system, it was repeated and repeated up the chain of command as if it were an undeniable fact and it was on the basis of this report and others that hundreds of men's lives were to be squandered over the next three hours. Totally inaccurate reports compounded into fictions that would have tragic outcomes. By the time the 'report' of trench bridges being placed on the German lines had reached 29th Division HQ it had been inflated with dire consequences:

"As regards the 87th Brigade some of the 1st R Inniskilling Fus. on the right were seen to march up to the enemy's first line, as if on parade, place their trench bridges across the trench and advance over the crest to the support line."[83]

It then goes on to relate the reality of the situation, but this part of the report seems to have been ignored by de Lisle and his staff. The result would be the greatest tragedy anywhere on the Somme front on this terrible day. This is what the 29th Division's account goes on to say:

"The bulk of the battalion was however held up on the line of the German wire."

It confirms what the Inniskilling Fusiliers themselves reported, but substitutes the phrase 'the bulk… was held up' for the battalion's own wording that '…none (were) able to gain further ground than the enemy's wire'. This discrepancy, affected by over-optimism or stupidity or inexperience, seems to have been either an 87th Brigade or 29th Division Staff issue. Brig. Gen. Lucas in his diary recorded that:

"… it was reported that parties of the 87th had been seen fighting down by Beaumont Hamel cemetery and the station buildings[i]."

But he then concludes that:

"It was subsequently discovered that hardly a single man had reached the German frontline and that the best part of six battns were lying out casualties in no man's land."

Why 'subsequently' when it appears that some at 87th Brigade HQ knew the true picture? Capt. Grant, the 86th Brigade's Brigade Major, soon to be wounded trying to reorganise that Brigade's disaster, recalled distinctly after the war the information coming from 87th Brigade HQ:

"I cannot understand how the success of the 87th Brigade elements that got on was so exaggerated at Divisional HQ. Immediately before I went forward I spoke on the phone to the B(rigade)M(ajor), 87th Bde, Capt. J C Brand[ii], DSO, MC, Coldstream Guards, and my recollection is that he definitely stated 'their attack had broken down everywhere and our right supporting battalion didn't appear to have left their trenches'."[84]

Meanwhile, so fierce was the fire in No Man's Land that C Company of the Inniskillings was unable to leave the trenches.

Watching the advance from higher ground to the south west was 2nd Lt. George Hamilton Moberly, Royal Lancaster Regt., the adjutant of the 87th Machine Gun Company. After the war he recorded several essential points which, in his view, led to the collapse of the attack. They were:

"The comparatively long time taken between the getting out of the trenches and actually starting the advance;

The extreme slowness of the advance in the initial stages. It was carried out at a slow walking pace;

The German wire seemed to be very little damaged;

---

[i] This report apparently came from 36th Division and suggested that the 9th Royal Irish Fusiliers at Station Buildings (Beaucourt Station) had joined hands with the 1st Royal Inniskilling Fusiliers at Station Road though how the 36th Division could possibly know this is not clear.

[ii] Capt., Later Lt. Col., John Charles Brand, DSO, MC, 1st Coldstream Guards, was born in 1885. He was the son of Maj. Hon. Charles Brand and Alice Emma Sturgis Van de Weyer. He married Lady Rosabelle Millicent St. Clair-Erskine, the daughter of the 5th Earl of Rosslyn, in May 1916. Brigade Major, November 1915. MiD, MC 1916, DSO 1918. He died in 1929.

After a time there were parties of Germans standing up on the parapet firing on the attackers in No Man's Land at close range (as soon as this was observed one of our machine guns was trained on these German parties and caused them to get back into their trenches).
Very few attackers on the sector which I could see appeared even to reach the German wire and I saw none beyond the wire."[85]

Given the complex right wheel procedure which the Inniskillings (and later the 1st KOSB) had to adopt in order to be face on to their objective it is, perhaps, not surprising that the advance was slow in starting. Had, as every senior officer at VIII Corps and many further down the food chain firmly believed, the Germans been mainly killed or neutralised then this would have been of little concern but, to attempt this manoeuvre and then have to walk between 250 and 500 yards to reach an enemy's line fully manned and with multiple machine guns firing from various directions and from succeeding lines of trenches, invited the disaster which befell them.

Typically, casualties amongst the Inniskilling's officers had been horrendous. 19 out of 22 were hit and, as a result, direction and control was non-existent for much of the day. In addition, the battalion reported 540 casualties amongst the other ranks[i]. Just short of 70% of the battalion became casualties and, with C Company never leaving the front line trench, the percentage losses in the other three companies must have been closer to 90%. Amongst the dead was the commanding officer, Lt. Col. Robert Campbell Pierce[ii]. He had been shot down by machine gun fire soon after leaving the front line trench. Alongside him, the artillery's FOO, 2nd Lt. D T Davis, 26th Battery, 17th Brigade RFA, was wounded at the same moment. Another eight of his fellow officers had also died.

The officer casualties were:

Killed:

Lt. F M S Bowen[iii], att. 9th Queen's Own Royal West Kent Regt.

Capt. B St G French[iv], att. 15th Liverpool Regt.

---

[i] The Official History has revised these figures to officers: killed 9, wounded 11, total 20; Other ranks killed 236, wounded 308, missing 3, prisoner of war 1, total 548.

[ii] Lt. Col. Robert Campbell Pierce, 1st Royal Inniskilling Fusiliers, was the son of the late Rev. W. Edward Pierce, B. A., Vicar of St. Michael and All Angels, Jamaica, afterwards of British Guiana. He married Marion MacGregor Greer in 1897. They had one daughter, Patricia. He was commissioned into the 2nd Royal Inniskilling Fusiliers from the RMC, Sandhurst, on 9th November 1889 and was promoted Captain in 1897. Adjutant, 3rd Battalion in 1904. Promoted Major in 1906. He served in Burma 1891-2 and on the NW Frontier 1897-8. Served in the Tirah Expeditionary Force. In 1914 he commanded the 3rd Battalion (Royal Tyrone Militia) at Omagh. Promoted Lt. Col. 10th September 1915. He is buried in the Ancre British Cemetery, Beaumont-Hamel, grave VI. D. 18.

[iii] Lt. Francis Moull Storer Bowen, 9th Queen's Own Royal West Kent Regt. att. 1st Royal Inniskilling Fusiliers, was aged 32. He was the son of Henry Storer Bowen and Beatrice Bowen, of Littlebourne, Canterbury. He is buried in Ancre British Cemetery, Beaumont-Hamel, grave VII. D. 44.

[iv] Capt. Bertram St George French, 15th The King's (Liverpool Regiment) att. 1st Royal Inniskilling Fusiliers, was aged 25. He was the son of the Rev. Arthur Thomas William French and Magdalene Gibb of 4066, Tupper St., Westmount, P.Q., Canada. Graduate in Arts, McGill University, Montreal. Undergraduate Trinity College, Oxford. Born at

Plate 37 Lt. Sidney Todd Martin, 6th att. 1st Royal Inniskilling Fusiliers

Lt. G A L Harbord[i], att. 3rd Royal Inniskilling Fusiliers
Lt. Col. R C Pierce
2nd Lt. W Porter[ii], att. 6th Royal Inniskilling Fusiliers
Lt. A D L Wilson[iii], att. 9th Queen's Own Royal West Kent Regt.
Missing:
Lt. S T Martin[iv], att. 6th Royal Inniskilling Fusiliers
2nd Lt. C A Stonor[v], att. 3rd Royal Inniskilling Fusiliers

Montreal. He had served at Gallipoli and Salonika. He is buried in Ancre British Cemetery, Beaumont-Hamel, grave I. A. 13.

[i] Lt. George Alfred Lionel Harbord, 3rd att. 1st Royal Inniskilling Fusiliers, was aged 20. He was the son of the Rev Richard Charles M Harbord, B.D. and Margaret Grace Harbord of Murragh Rectory, Enniskean, Co. Cork. Also served at Gallipoli. His body was never found and his name is inscribed on the Thiepval Memorial, Pier & Face 4D & 5B.

[ii] 2nd Lt. William Porter, 6th att. 1st Royal Inniskilling Fusiliers, was aged 31. He was the son of William and Mary Porter of 'Beechview', Balmoral Avenue, Belfast. He is buried in Ancre British Cemetery, Beaumont-Hamel, grave V. E. 11.

[iii] Lt. Arthur Desmond Lloyd Wilson, 9th Queen's Own Royal West Kent Regt. att. 1st Royal Inniskilling Fusiliers, is buried in Y Ravine Cemetery, Beaumont-Hamel, grave D. 42.

[iv] Lt. Sidney Todd Martin, 6th att. 1st Royal Inniskilling Fusiliers, was aged 26. He was the son of the Very Rev Dr William Todd Marton, MA, DD, DLit, Professor of Ethics and Apologetics at the Presbyterian (Assembly's) College in Belfast, and Catherine Mary Martin. He was educated at Campbell College where he played for the rugby 1st XV and cricket 1st XI. He graduated in Classics from Sidney Sussex College, Cambridge. He was studying for the Bar when he was commissioned into the 6th Royal Inniskilling Fusiliers in September 1914. Previously wounded at Gallipoli, his body was never found and his name is inscribed on the Thiepval Memorial, Pier & Face 4D & 5B.

[v] 2nd Lt. Cuthbert Mary Anthony Stonor, 3rd att. 1st Royal Inniskilling Fusiliers, was aged 28. He was the youngest son and 10th of eleven children of Charles Joseph Stonor, JP, and Maude Mary Welman of Llanvair, Ascot, Berkshire. He had connections with the Bukit Rajah Estate at Klang, Malaya. He was commissioned out of the OTC in July 1915. 2nd Lt.

Wounded:
Lt. Robert Murray Clarkson, att. 4th Highland Light Infantry
Capt. John Ralph Congreve Dent, MC
Lt. William Tillie Dickson, att. 6th Royal Inniskilling Fusiliers
2nd Lt. Arthur Fortescue
2nd Lt. Samuel John Jenkins
2nd Lt. Bertram John Keene, att. 13th West Yorkshire Regt.
2nd Lt. Philip Mauleverer Lindesay, att. 3rd Royal Inniskilling Fusiliers
2nd Lt. Alexander Lucas, att. 12th Scottish Rifles
Lt. William Francis Copson Peake, att. 1st Queen's Own Royal West Kent Regt.
2nd Lt. Lawrence David Watts, att. 12th Royal Warwickshire Regt.
2nd Lt. Ernest Arthur Worskett, att. 4th Royal Inniskilling Fusiliers
Other ranks
Killed 50, Missing 225, wounded 265.

IN ADDITION, NOS. 1 AND 2 GUNS OF NO. 3 SECTION of the 87th Machine Gun Company had tried to get forward. The 19 year old officer in command, Lt. Edward Costello[i], was last seen along with several of his men moving close up to the German wire. There Costello was shot in the head and killed instantly.

The 1st King's Own Scottish Borderers were scheduled to leave the British front line at the time when the last waves of C Company of the Inniskillings reached the German wire. Here, the German barrage falling on the Border Regt. also crashed into the Scottish Borderers and, as they waited for the Inniskillings to clear the German wire, they reported:

"0740 1st RIF held up by machine gun fire."[86]

Capt. George Ernest Malcolm was the OC, D Company, and his command advanced at 7.50 a.m. His report shows the absurd complexity of the manoeuvre the 1st KOSB were required to do in the middle of No Man's Land whilst under heavy machine gun fire. The battalion left their trenches facing north. Their objective was to the east. Like the Inniskillings, they were, therefore, required to perform a right wheel in full view of the enemy before continuing their advance:

> "On the morning of Z Day at 0.20 (zero 0.00) D Company received the whistle signal to advance.
> On leaving the trenches they came under very heavy machine gun fire. The company moved forward in line of platoons in column of sections in single file, No. 13 Platoon on the left and No. 16 Platoon on the right. At 60 yards from our own trenches I gave the signal to lie down as I intended to make the right wheel on to our objective at that point and C Company

Stonor was originally found and buried along with twelve other men on the night of 25th August 1916 by a burial party led by Lt. William Edward Brandt of the 2nd Sherwood Foresters. He is now buried in Y Ravine Cemetery, Beaumont-Hamel, grave D. 99.

[i] Lt. Edward William Costello, 3rd Royal Inniskilling Fusiliers att. 87th Machine Gun Company, was aged 19. He was the eldest son of Mr and Mrs Thomas D Costello of 55, Pembroke Rd., Ballsbridge, Dublin. He was educated at St Vincent's College, Castleknock. Commissioned on 12th December 1914, he fought at Gallipoli. His body was never found and his name is inscribed on the Thiepval Memorial, Pier & Face 4D & 5B.

> and the Border Regt were not yet in position. Owing to casualties I had 3 men of No. 13 (2 wounded) and 1 of No. 14 Platoon left; I could see no one of the other platoons.
>
> At 0.35 (i.e. 8.05 a.m.) I sent a message to the Adjutant, 1st KOSB, by Private Douglas stating estimated casualties."[87]

As the 1st KOSB went into action with 22 officers and 834 other ranks it would seem as though Malcolm's company command had been reduced by 95% within just 15 minutes. Malcolm and his small group of men lay in the long grass in No Man's Land for the next hour wondering just what to do next.

Plate 38 2nd Lt, Howard Frank Byrne Cooper, 1st King's Own Scottish Borderers

Many of the Borderers were caught behind or just in front of the British lines. Capt. Jonathan Ainslie, OC A Company, recalled their advance and the death of his 'best subaltern', 2nd Lt. Howard Cooper[i]:

> "When the battalion attacked on 1st July we did not do so directly from the front trench but had to get out into the open from a trench in the rear and advance over the front trench into No Man's Land. I was speaking to (2nd Lt. Cooper) just before he left the rear trench – he went over at the head of my company. He was very cheerful and keen to start. Between the rear and front trenches we were under pretty heavy artillery and machine gun fire. I saw him several times during this time but did not see him reach our front line. He was hit only a few yards over this front trench and must have been killed immediately. I cannot say for certain what hit

---

[i] 2nd Lt. Howard Frank Byrne Cooper, A Company, 1st Kings Own Scottish Borderers, was aged 19. He was the elder son of Capt. Frank Alexander Cooper, Government Educational Service, India, and Mabel Ellen Cooper (née Byrne) of Aligarh, United Provinces, India. Born at Musoorie, India, he was educated at Bedford School and the RMC, Sandhurst and he was commissioned on 16th March 1915. Served in Egypt. He is buried in Ancre British Cemetery, Beaumont-Hamel, grave VIII. D. 44.

> him but nearly all our casualties were from machine gun fire and the place where we crossed was swept by it. His death was a blow to everybody, both officers and men, for he was very much liked. He was far and away the best of the six subalterns I had at the time. That is why I detailed him to lead the company, as I had been forbidden to do so myself."[88]

In spite of what was happening on the ground, more cheerful news arrived at VIII Corps HQ from 29th Division at 7.41 a.m. The two leading battalions of the 87th Brigade had, apparently, successfully crossed the enemy's front line and even now the reserve battalions were advancing in support. One can, perhaps, imagine the smiles of satisfaction amongst the officers staring at the maps in order to follow the progress of the attack.

29th Division then provided another extraordinary report from Observation Posts manned by its officers:

> "7.48 a.m. Southern OP reports that the 87th Brigade are in the German front line trench."[89]

Given the reports from the battalions involved it is difficult to understand what these observers thought they were seeing. But, on the basis of these reports, battalions from the 88th Brigade were made to ready to exploit the 'success' of the 87th Brigade.

At 7.52 a.m. came two contradictory reports. The important one, given what would happen later, is recorded in the 29th Division diary:

> "7.52 a.m. GSO2 with 87th Brigade reports 3 Very lights have been sent up from Beaumont Hamel and from the Royal Inniskilling Fusiliers on the right of the 87th Brigade indicating that they have attained their objective, the 86th Brigade report that the Dublin Fusiliers have gone through the Royal Fusiliers and that Germans are running down Beaumont Alley."[90]

A rather feeble note was then appended at a later time:

> "… from later information this does not appear to have been the case but the situation became rather involved at this period."[91]

The other report, given little or no emphasis, came from the 1st KOSB whose men were about to add to the burgeoning casualty lists by 'going over the top':

> "0752 1st RIF attack not progressing. Battalion moved out under heavy machine gun fire."[92]

The further to the rear these reports reached, the more optimistic was their interpretation. VIII Corps' war diary entry for 7.59 a.m. came to the conclusion from 29th Division's report that:

> "7:59 a.m. 29th Division report Inniskilling Fusiliers got to 0.20 line. Three red flares sent up in Beaumont Hamel. Second-line battalions all gone through… Germans are running up Beaumont Alley."[93]

Clearly, no-one seems to have thought that, just maybe, the Germans employed red flares, and white ones and various other colours, as a means to sending signals when, for example, phone lines were cut. No, red flares had to mean success achieved in spite of the evidence of hundreds of dead and wounded men lying in No Man's Land and the British trenches. In fact, red rockets *were* the signal used by the Germans to call up artillery support (as the men in the British trenches were currently experiencing) and, had anyone remembered it, red rockets had been used during the course of several abortive British raids prior to Z Day for precisely this purpose. One might ask, therefore, why red flares were chosen to indicate the achieving of an objective when it should have been realised that confusion was more than possible as the Germans employed the same colour but for a wholly different purpose? Another failing of Staff work?

To add to this heady mixture of inaccurate Divisional observations, the Corps and Royal Artillery observers decided they too should make a contribution to the apparently imminent success of the entire enterprise. At 8.03 a.m. Corps observation post No. 1 reported:

> "… another wave of 29th Division gone out and filed along German trenches to their left."[94]

This may refer to the advance of the 1st KOSB (no other troops were moving at this point) but they got nowhere near the German trenches.

Three minutes later the Royal Artillery got in on the act:

> "8.06 a.m. RA reports a rumour that a stubborn bombing fight is going on in Y Ravine
> 8.10 a.m. RA report that our infantry have reached Station Road without difficulty and that our men can be seen bombing dugouts."[95]

Quite what is meant by a 'rumour' of a bombing fight is difficult to understand. A man who told a mate who passed it on to his friend? As far as is known, no British troops entered the Y Ravine. Well, not until November 1916, at least. The report on the activity on Station Road is even more difficult to fathom. Who were these phantom troops bombing German dugouts? The men of the 1st Royal Inniskilling Fusiliers, apparently. The battalion of which, one might recall:

> "…none (were) able to gain further ground than the enemy's wire."[96]

Again, it fell to the men on the spot to record the appalling truth of the situation. At the same time as the RA observers were gleefully reporting success, the KOSB, one of the battalions supposedly backing up this success wrote:

> "0810 Our attack not progressing owing to intense enemy machine gun fire. Attack on left observed to be equally unsuccessful."[97]

At 8.15 a.m. an entry appears in the 29th Division's war diary which fully exposes the wild assumptions and utter breakdown in information processing that was taking place at its HQ. It reads:

> "8.15 a.m. GSO3 reports Very lights have been sent up from both of the leading battalions of the 87th Brigade.
> NOTE: From the above report it appears that portions of the enemy's third line have been captured between Y Ravine and the River Ancre and possibly some of our troops actually reached the Station Road but from this time onwards no more was heard of any such success except from unreliable statements of wounded men who say our men got into the 2nd and 3rd German lines of trenches. The Inniskilling Fusiliers completely disappeared and no news has been heard of them."[98]

The conclusions drawn from all of this were that the problems being experienced by the Border Regt., i.e. suffering 600 casualties within a few yards of their own wire, and the 1st KOSB, who were about to give up their advance as they were running out of men, were being caused by some German machine guns in the front line somehow by-passed by the SWB and Inniskillings in their enthusiastic assault on Station Road. Indeed, the 29th Division war diary at 8.25 a.m. pretty much states this:

> "8.25 a.m. GSO2 reports some Germans with machine guns are still holding their front line and have checked the Border Regt and KOSB."[99]

The VIII Corps war diary entry for 8.30 a.m. actually sets out this scenario in rather more detail and concludes with a statement as to the action the GOC, 29th Division, intended to take to resolve this little problem:

> "At this juncture General de Lisle decided to make a further effort to capture the front line and thus support parties of the 87th Brigade who he believed were fighting in the enemy's trenches."[100]

To achieve this objective two battalions of the 88th Brigade were called forward: the 1st Essex Regt. and the 1st Newfoundland Regt. Their orders were timed at 8.37 a.m. The passing minutes were a countdown to tragedy.

IT NOW SEEMS APPROPRIATE TO ATTEMPT TO DESCRIBE what had happened on the southern flank of the 29th Division's front because, there, events had unfolded which might explain the reports of a British entry into the German front line system near to the Mary Redan. From the reports made by the battalions of the 87th Brigade it is clear that, as far as they were concerned, none of their men had gained entry into the German front line. To their right, however, the story was slightly different.

Between the Mary Redan and the north bank of the Ancre, two battalions of the Ulster Division had, with the exception of a small narrow area immediately south of the Mary Redan, nearly six hundred yards of open hillside over which to attack. They were to do so in full view of four lines of German trenches as well as the machine guns dug in and firing north-west from St Pierre Divion on the south bank of the Ancre. At the northern end of their area a road ran southwards across No Man's Land from the eastern end of the Y Ravine, cutting the tip of the Mary Redan before entering the British lines north of Hamel. In the 108th Brigade's sector the road ran between banks, providing yet another 'sunken road' on the Somme battlefield. On the southern end of No Man's Land, a 'Ravine' ran south-east down to the road and railway line. Its sides became increasingly steep as it neared the valley of the Ancre and it was a significant feature in the landscape[i]. It lay about mid-way between the opposing sets of trenches.

The objectives of the two Ulster battalions were limited but complex. Their task was to capture the railway station at the southern end of Station Road, then called Beaucourt Station (now le Gare de Beaumont Hamel), and two houses 250 yards further east which lay just under halfway between the village of Beaucourt

[i] It now contains Ancre British Cemetery which is the result of concentrations from seven other cemeteries into Ancre River No. 1 British Cemetery which was started in the Spring of 1917 after the German withdrawal to the Hindenburg Line.

sur Ancre and the station. Before doing any of this, they needed to clear a German position which ran out into the marshy ground on the north side of the Ancre as well as Railway Sap which, as the name suggests, projected out into No Man's Land parallel to, and to the north of, the railway line. It also led to the position in the marsh. These two tasks were given to two platoons of B Company, 12th Royal Irish Rifles, commanded by Lt. Col. George Bull[i]. Bull was a professional, imported from the 1st Royal Irish Fusiliers, but his men were amateurs – Protestants who were mainly previous members of the Central Antrim Volunteers of the Ulster Volunteer Force raised before the war to contest the prospect of a united Ireland.

No. 8 Platoon was given the task of clearing 'the marsh' as the defensive position in the flood plain of the Ancre was called. It was to start from Lancashire Post, a position on the south side of the railway line facing towards a small area of dry ground above the river called The Mound, fifty yards behind the German position. On their left, and to the north of the railway line, was No. 6 Platoon. Their task was to take Railway Sap which ran into No Man's Land parallel and to the north of the railway before cutting under the railway and road and entering the marsh.

The rest of B Company, Nos. 5 and 7 Platoons, formed up in the hedge rows which formed the north-east boundary of the village of Hamel. In front of them, assembled in the trenches of the William Redan were the 9th Royal Irish Fusiliers. Here the front line of the Redan, as it ran north-west, turned away from the German lines thus widening No Man's Land by 150 yards. As a result, the Irish Fusiliers had to attack across some 550 yards of open grassland, in the process negotiating the 'Ravine' which ran across their entire line of advance. This battalion was commanded by Lt. Col. Stewart Blacker[ii], Royal Artillery, who had

---

[i] Lt. Col. George Bull, DSO, 12th Royal Irish Rifles, then Brigadier General commanding 8th Brigade, 3rd Division, died on 11th December 1916 of wounds received on 6th December. Aged 39, he was the third and last surviving son of Mr R George Bull, late Resident Magistrate, of Downshire House, Newry, Co. Down and Mary Bull, and the husband of Norah Bull (née Warburton). Served in South Africa with the 5th Royal Irish Rifles (Militia) into which he was commissioned in 1901. Queen's Medal & 4 clasps, King's Medal & 2 clasps. He was commissioned into the Royal Garrison Regt. in 1903 joining the Leinster Regt. in 1905 when the Royal Garrison Regt., was disbanded. He transferred into the Royal Irish Fusiliers in 1907, being promoted Captain in 1912. He was Adjutant, 5th East Lancashire Regt., in 1909 rejoining the Royal Irish Fusiliers in April 1914. Went to France with 1st Royal Irish Fusiliers. He took command of the 12th RIR in November 1915. Three times MiD he was awarded the DSO in June 1916. He is buried in Varennes Military Cemetery, grave I. C. 31. His two brothers both pre-deceased him, Lt. Arthur Harcourt Bull, Inniskilling Mounted Infantry, was killed in South Africa in 1902 and Edward J Bull, an engineer working for the Indian Government, died accidentally in 1915.

[ii] Lt. Col. Stewart Ward William Blacker, DSO, JP, DL, Royal Artillery cmdg 9th Royal Irish Fusiliers, was aged 51. He was the son of the Reverend Robert Shapland Carew Blacker and Theodosia Charlotte Sophia Meara. He married Eva Mary Lucy St. John FitzRoy, daughter of Lt. Col. Edward Albert Fitzroy, in 1903 and they lived at Carrickblacker, Portadown, Co. Armagh, and Woodbrook House, Enniscorthy, County Wexford. He was educated at the Royal Military Academy, Woolwich, and commissioned into the RA in 1885. Adjutant, Bermuda Militia Artillery, 1895. He was severely wounded on the North West Frontier in 1897 and MiD. Served in South Africa (Queen's Medal

overall command of the two detached battalions of the 36th Division. His unit was raised from the counties of Armagh, Monaghan and Cavan and, like the whole of the 36th Division, the men were mainly pre-war UVF members.

Lt. Col. Blacker and his battalion had been in position just to the north of the Ancre since February 1916 and the Colonel, an ex-Artillery officer, knew the ground well and was able to appreciate both the strength of the enemy's position as well as the weakness of the artillery preparation. He was of the view that X Corps' heavy guns and the 36th Division's artillery had concentrated disproportionately on the sector south of the river where the bulk of the Division was to attack. With VIII Corps' heavies concentrated on the 29th Division's front this meant that his area to be attacked was something of a forgotten afterthought. As a result, his post-war view was that the German wire and trenches, occupied by three companies of I/RIR 119 (the fourth company was in reserve), were:

> "'very little impaired... and it was evident to me that the artillery bombardment was insufficient." [101]

Blacker advised Maj. Gen. Nugent, the GOC, 36th Division, of this some days before the attack but to no effect. Then, on the morning of the 30th June, Nugent came to his battalion HQ to wish him and his officers 'good luck'. Blacker used the opportunity to repeat his criticism of the artillery work on his front, again with no result. As his General left the dugout Blacker could not resist a sardonic attempt at black humour. 'Morituri te Salutant', he remarked. 'Those about to die salute you' were the parting words of the gladiators of ancient Rome before they set to slaughtering one another for the amusement of the baying crowd.

Blacker regarded the task given him and his battalion as 'hopeless'. His men, however, did their level best to prove him wrong.

To the left of Blacker's men were, in order, C, D and A Companies of the 12th Royal Irish Rifles. C Company was in the front line trenches between Louvercy and Winchester Streets, a frontage of barely 200 yards, while D and A Companies covered a front 800 yards wide with a No Man's Land that narrowed from nearly 600 yards on the right to barely 300 yards on the left by the south-eastern face of the Mary Redan.

The overall plan was this:

- No. 8 Platoon, 12th Royal Irish Rifles, under 2nd Lt. M Neill, supported by a Lewis gun team, was to reconnoitre the marsh as far as Beaucourt Station, always keeping between the river and the railway line;
- No. 6 Platoon, 12th Royal Irish Rifles, under Lt. Lemon, also supported by a Lewis gun team, was to enter Railway Sap and then clear its entire length to the north-east before pushing up the railway line to the station. They were to keep in touch on the right with 2nd Lt. Neill's party and on the left with the 9th Royal Irish Fusiliers;

with clasp). Retired from the Army, 1905. Raised and commanded the 9th Royal Irish Fusiliers, Lt. Col. 15th September 1914. Commanded 20th Reserve Battalion, Royal Irish Rifles, April 1917. MiD three times and Legion d'Honneur. He died on 6th September 1935. His first son, Lt. Col. William Desmond Blacker, DSO, RA, cmdg 179th Field Regt., RA., was killed in action in Normandy on 11th July 1944. He is buried in St. Manvieu War Cemetery, Cheux, Calvados.

- The 9th Royal Irish Fusiliers were to go forward in four waves supported by Nos. 5 and 7 Platoons of the 12th Royal Irish Rifles. They were to take the three lines of German trenches immediately to their front then move to Beaucourt Station where they would occupy the trenches to the east of the village, two houses beyond that and the mill on the far side of the Ancre. The Lewis guns were to advance with the 1st wave, two Stokes mortars with the 2nd wave and five Vickers machine guns with the 3rd wave;
- C Company, 12th Royal Irish Rifles, was to attack with two Lewis and two Vickers machine guns on a platoon frontage in four waves. They were to take and clear the three lines of trenches on their front in a north easterly direction;
- D and A Companies, 12th Royal Irish Rifles, were to attack in eight waves of alternating platoons, accompanied by their Lewis Guns. Their job was to take the shallow German salient south east of the Mary Redan, occupying the front and support trenches before A Company cleared the trenches northwards and made contact with the 87th Brigade on their left and D Company cleared the trenches eastwards and made contact with C Company;
- When all objectives had been taken, the 12th Royal Irish Rifles were to reform in No Man's Land preparatory to moving south of the Ancre to assist the main body of the Division, leaving the 9th Royal Irish Fusiliers to occupy and fortify their newly won positions.

The only advantage the battalions of the 108th Brigade had over the attacking troops of the 29th Division was that their artillery lifts conformed to those of the main body of the X Corps south of the river, i.e. there would be no lifting of the Heavy artillery off the front line trenches ten minutes before zero. They would lift at zero and, in spite of the distance the Ulstermen had to travel to attack their enemy, this seems to have made some difference.

Opposed to them were the four companies of the I Battalion, RIR 119, which occupied sectors B5, B6 and B7, that is, from opposite the Mary Redan to the Ancre. Three companies were in the front and support line and the fourth was held in reserve. Supporting them directly were two machine guns from the regiment's 2. Maschinengewehr Kompanie (Machine Gun Company) whilst other guns at St Pierre Divion were ready to take the attackers under enfilade fire. In total, the RIR 119 had deployed about 600 to 650 men in the front two trenches of these three sectors. As confirmation of Blacker's prediction of the failure of the British artillery bombardment here, the casualties amongst these units had been very low from 24th to 30th June. Over the seven days of the bombardment the four companies of the I Battalion, RIR 119, had lost 16 men killed or died of wounds and the 2. Maschinengewehr Kompanie lost two men dead. Another 45 of all units were wounded but some of these were so slight that they were able to participate in the battle to come.

Further back in the Feste Alt-Württemberg was the 2. Rekrut Kompanie of the Württembergisches Feldrekrutendepot. These men were still under training but, if required, could be brought into action, as several such companies were along the German front on 1st July.

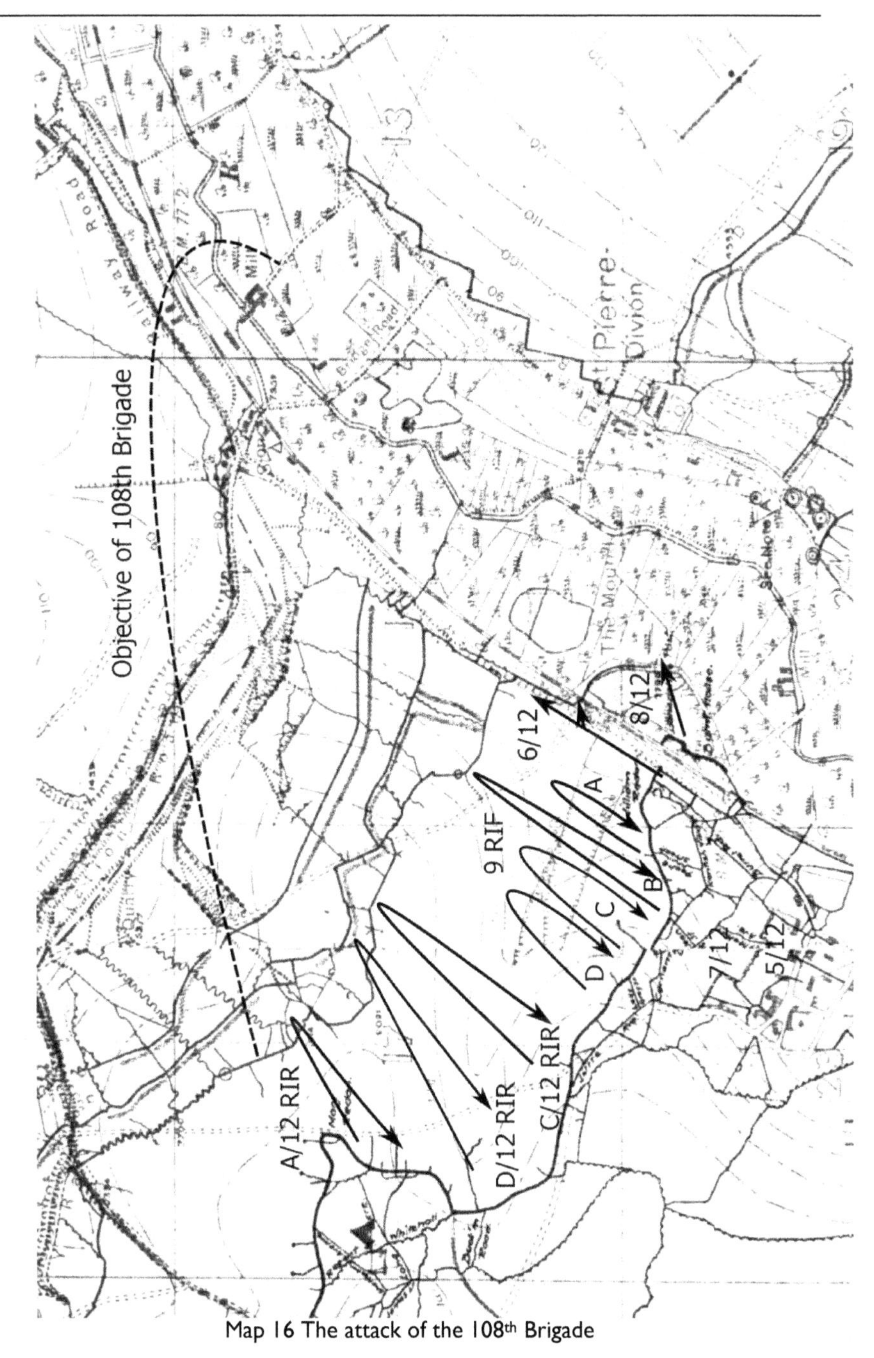

Map 16 The attack of the 108th Brigade

A/12 RIR = Companies of the 12th Royal Irish Rifles, 6/12 = Platoons of the 12th Royal Irish Rifles. D, C, B, A = Companies of the 9th Royal Irish Fusiliers.

As elsewhere, the German 1st Position consisted of three lines of trenches all heavily wired. The unusual element of the position was in the valley of the slow moving Ancre with its marshy flood plain. The slopes of the hills rising away to the north from the railway and river had been the subject of much mining and here were located several secure caves in which the infantry could shelter. A trench, Railway Sap to the British and Tal Stellung to the Germans, ran parallel to the river before branching out into the marsh where the fortification ran above ground to avoid flooding. It was this final stretch of trench that No. 8 Platoon of the 12th Royal Irish Rifles was to attack while No. 6 Platoon dealt with the 'dry' section of the sap.

The 9th Royal Irish Fusiliers had been relieved by the Rifles on the evening of the 28th June and had been sent for a brief rest in Mesnil prior to the attack. Even there they were not out of the action and seven men were wounded during a brief German strafe on the following day. They marched up to the front lines in the early hours of the 1st July. No special assembly trenches had been dug for the operation and so the Fusiliers went straight into three lines of trenches east of Hamel. The battalion was deployed as follows:

> "... on a four platoon front on the following order: Right Company, A, Capt. C Ensor, Right centre company, B, Maj. T J Atkinson, Left centre company, C, Capt. C M Johnston, Left Company, D, Capt. J G Brew[i], each company being on a platoon front, making four waves; each wave advancing 60 yards distance. The two leading waves assembled in the front line trench. The 3rd wave consisting of supporting platoons in communication trenches. The 4th wave consisting of consolidating platoons in 2nd line trench."[102]

By 3 a.m. they were in position and, during the 4½ hour wait they now had to endure, lost some 50 men to German artillery fire. As they waited, officers studied the German wire and trenches. The wire appeared well enough cut with clear lanes through to the German parapet. The trenches, however, were a different matter with the battalion reporting that they appeared 'not to have suffered materially from the previous bombardment'. A comment supported by the remarkably low casualties incurred by the RIR 119.

The width of No Man's Land here varied from 400 yards on the right to nearly 600 yards on the left. The ravine was described as being:

> "...some 70 yards in width about half way between the opposing trenches, the banks of which were 15 ft. to 20 ft. high in places and steep."[103]

Everywhere the ground fell from left to right down to the valley floor.

Because of the width of No Man's Land the Fusiliers started to leave their trenches twenty minutes before Zero. Their departure timetable was:

1st wave across the parapet at 7.10 a.m.
2nd wave across the parapet at 7.15 a.m.
3rd wave across the parapet at 7.20 a.m.

---

[i] Maj. John George Brew, 9th Royal Irish Fusiliers, died on 6th April 1918. He was the husband of Annie Moffat Brew of 'Rathlin', Portadown, Ireland. He is buried in Roye New British Cemetery, grave IV. D. 9.

4th wave across the parapet at 7.30 a.m.

Even though they were moving when the artillery barrage was still playing on the front line positions they immediately came under machine gun fire, especially from the left flank. As a result, the 1st wave got through their own wire relatively unscathed but started to lose heavily as they advanced towards the rim of the ravine. The 2nd wave was caught getting through the British wire, again by flanking machine gun fire, and suffered badly. As for the 1st wave, the highest casualties were on the left and here, C and D Companies lost practically all of their officers before they reached the ravine. Using the ravine as cover the two leading waves were reorganised into one line before resuming their advance.

Behind them, the 3rd and 4th waves caught a perfect storm of flanking and frontal machine gun fire and a hail of shrapnel and HE as the German artillery got in on the act. Both waves are described as having been 'practically annihilated' before they reached the ravine.

Emerging from the shelter of the ravine the remnants of the battalion continued to advance until again swept by heavy machine gun fire 150 yards from the German trenches. The explanation for the pause in the German machine gun fire may be explained by the account of the gun team of No. 7 gun of the 2. Maschinengewehr-Kompanie commanded by Uttfz. Kaesar. The gun had opened fire from the support line on the Fusiliers as they approached the ravine when, having fired 250 rounds, a British shell exploded in front of the gun, burying the MG08 and slightly wounding the gun layer, one Gefreiter Leuze. The gun was quickly dug out and Leuze resumed his work as the Fusiliers emerged from the cover of the ravine. He fired another 2,250 rounds before the attack collapsed. To the north of No. 7 gun was No. 9 gun. It too was subject to artillery fire and Schütze Gustav Bäzner from Petersmühle, Nagold, was fatally wounded in the head by a shell splinter. The gun, though subject to further shell fire and a short interruption caused by a faulty cartridge, fired over 2,500 rounds during the morning, helping to cut down the attackers on either side of the ravine.

In addition, maps show the existence of a machine gun post just above the road next to the Ancre and in front of the German first line trench in sector B7 which was able to take the whole advance in enfilade. The position was later inspected by a 108th Brigade Staff Officer, Maj. 'Jake' Duke[i], Royal Warwicks, who found that a tunnel had been dug into the slope next to the road, at the end of which a vertical shaft with steps led to the concealed position. The existence and devastating fire of a machine gun out in front of the German trenches was remarked upon in the report on the attack of the 12th Royal Irish Rifles.

Small groups of men reached the lanes cut in the wire and charged the trenches. The battalion report suggests that some Germans appeared to surrender

---

[i] Maj., later Brig. Gen., Jesse Pevensey Duke, DSO. MC, 2nd Royal Warwickshire Regt., was born in 1890. He was the son of Maj. & Hon. Lt. Col. Oliver Thomas Duke, 5th Rifle Brigade (Militia), and Blanche Wheeler of 84, Bouverie Road, Folkestone. He was five times MiD. Staff Capt., 1916. MC, 1915. DSO, 1916. 1920, GSO2. 1929-33, Chief Instructor, RMC, Sandhurst. 1936-8 GSO1, War Office. 1938-9 AAG, Eastern Command. 1939-40 GOC, 158th Brigade. 1940-1 AAG, Home Forces. 1941-2 AAG Army HQ, India. 1942-3 Dir. of Organisation, Army HQ, India. He married Marion Clarke in 1925. He died in 1980.

until they realised how few in number the Fusiliers were. It was also thought that elements of Maj. Thomas Atkinson's[i] B Company somehow fought their way across three lines of trenches, with a few reaching Beaucourt Station. There is no evidence to support this claim which, one must assume, stands as one of the many reports where optimism exceeded realism on or near VIII Corps' front. In particular, there is no mention of any such incursion within the various German histories, both regimental and divisional, which cover the fighting north of the Ancre. German histories are prepared to describe events where the performance of the German troops involved is less than ideal. For example, their descriptions of the counter-attacks against the 36th Division south of the Ancre reveal an unexpected lack of co-ordination amongst the units trying to regain the Schwaben redoubt. They accept there were elements of good luck rather the renowned Teutonic thoroughness involved in their success. In addition, the regimental history of the RIR 119 admits that, a few hundred yards further north, the 12th Royal Irish Rifles did enter the first line trench in a few places but were swiftly ejected. All too often when British accounts describe deep penetrations by small but gallant groups of men from which there were no survivors and, therefore, no witnesses, for example at Serre village, Pendant Copse and now Beaucourt Station on the VIII Corps' front, these find no place in German accounts. As a result, this writer, at least, suspects they never happened and emerged only from either wishful thinking or persistent bad observation and interpretation of the results.

Plate 39 Maj. Thomas Joyce Atkinson, 9th Royal Irish Fusiliers

[i] Maj. Thomas Joyce Atkinson, M.A., LL.B., T.C.D., 9th Royal Irish Fusiliers, was aged 38. He was the only son of Wolsey Richard and Alice Atkinson of Eden Villa, Bachelor's Walk in Edenderry. He graduated from Trinity College, Dublin in 1898 and was a partner in the firm of Messrs Carleton, Atkinson and Sloan, Solicitors, Portadown. He had been 2iC of the Portadown Battalion of the UVF commanded by the then Major Stewart Blacker. He is buried in Ancre British Cemetery, Beaumont-Hamel, grave VIII. A. 5.

Back in No Man's Land the German machine gun and artillery fire was so severe that only one runner made it back to battalion HQ. His report came from Capt. Johnston[i] of C Company. What was left of his unit was lying out in No Man's Land 30 yards short of the ravine. His message was simple:

"Cannot advance without support."[104]

The available support was No. 7 Platoon, B Company, 12th Royal Irish Rifles. It was sent forward and wiped out. Survivors now huddled together under the cover of the ravine until the Germans started to bombard the area with their heavy erdmörsers. The terrifying effect of their 25 lb. charges was sufficient to persuade those able to move to risk returning to their own lines whatever the risks from the scything machine guns.

And with that, the attack of the 9th Royal Irish Fusiliers was over. Casualties were appalling. The report in the war diary estimates that 15 officers and about 600[ii] other ranks were in the attack from a total of 41 officers and 860 other ranks on the strength of the battalion on 30th June. According to the war diary, all 15 officers were casualties as were 518 other ranks – a staggering 85% casualty rate[iii].

One of the officers to die was Lt. Arthur Carson Hollywood[iv] of A Company. The various accounts of his demise highlight the problems of eye-witness

---

[i] Capt. Charles Moore Johnston, 9th Royal Irish Fusiliers, was aged 30. He was the son of Charles Johnston D.L. and Marian Johnston of Portadown. He married Muriel Florence Edmeston Mellon of Carrickblacker Avenue, Portadown. Their son, Charles Collier Johnston, was an Honorary Treasurer of the Conservative Party (1984-7) and became Baron Johnston of Rockport in 1987. His father was educated at Lurgan College before going to Campbell College. He then attended the Royal School of Mines. Joined the UVF before the war. He is buried in Mesnil Communal Cemetery Extension, grave III. B. 17.

[ii] A figure of 615 OR is given in other sources.

[iii] According to the war diary, the total ration strength of the battalion at noon on 2nd July was 281, including officers and all detachments. It is not unreasonable to assume that several unwounded or very lightly wounded men might have returned in the following days. Certainly, searches of No Man's Land went on to the night of the 5th July. This still leaves a significant number unaccounted for, anything up to 87 based on a battalion strength on 30th June of 901 officers and men.

[iv] Lt. Arthur Carson Hollywood, 9th Royal Irish Fusiliers, was aged 24. He was the son of Elizabeth Hollywood and the late James Hollywood of 'Bayswater', Princetown Road, Bangor and later of Red Gorton, Helen's Bay, Co. Down. James was a property broker and insurance agent. He was educated at Friend's School, Lisburn, from September 1903 to July 1906 and the Royal Belfast Academical Institution. He joined the Royal University of Ireland in September 1909, and served as the company commander of F Company of the Willowfield Battalion of the UVF in 1913 and 1914. He worked in his father's business on the Albertbridge Road, Belfast, as a rent agent, and lived in Helen's Bay, Co. Down. He joined the 108th Field Ambulance on 12th September 1914, as a Staff Sergeant. He was commissioned into the Royal Inniskilling Fusiliers on 19th April 1915, and joined the 9th Royal Irish Fusiliers in January 1916, being posted to A Company. He was subsequently appointed Lieutenant on 29th February 1916. A Sgt. Slater reported that his body had been buried in Hamel village graveyard but it was lost and his name is inscribed on the Thiepval Memorial, Pier & Face 15A. His younger brother James, serving with the 12th Royal Irish Rifles, was also killed on 1st July 1916. The telegram announcing his death arrived one day apart from that announcing the death of his brother.

accounts from men caught up in the extreme stress and confusion of the battlefield. A Sgt. Whitsell apparently saw:

> "The first wave of men left the British trenches followed by the second wave to which Lt. Hollywood belonged. I followed them with the 3rd wave of men. I saw Lt. Hollywood jump into the German trench. I was then wounded and saw no more. Before this attack, Lt. Hollywood showed me the rips in his steel helmet where he had been hit, but seemed to be all right then."

Two Privates, Stewart and Coppleton, then testified to seeing Arthur Hollywood killed around 1 p.m. just after leaving the German first line trench. Bull's account shows the men of his battalion having been outside the German trenches for upwards of four hours by this time. Another witness, Pte. Cobain, has Lt. Hollywood 'hit by a machine gun bullet during the advance'. Lastly, a Pte. Nelson, who was wounded during the attack, claims to have spent the night lying next to the dead officer before returning to the British lines. The complete truth will never be known.

Plate 40 Lt. Arthur Carson Hollywood, 9th Royal Irish Fusiliers

Two weeks later, as his battalion rested and re-built far from the front line, Lt. Col. Blacker wrote to Col. Fitzgerald, CO of the 10th Royal Irish Fusiliers. He was clearly devastated by the loss of so many men who were his friends as much his soldiers.

> "Ensor, Atkinson, Johnston C, and Brew were in command respectively and 11 other platoon officers, that was all that were allowed in the actual assault, and about 600 men. Of these Johnston was killed. Atkinson, Townsend, Hollywood, Montgomery, Seggie, Stewart are missing, believed killed. Brew, Gibson, Jackson, Shillington, Andrews, Smith, Barcroft, Capt. Ensor are wounded and 516 other ranks are casualties …
> The gallant and splendid leading of the officers and the steady advance of the men even after their officers were down, was magnificent, and makes

me proud indeed to have been associated with such heroes. For four nights after, parties went out and searched for the wounded and brought in several (Ensor and three others on the 4th night), and then we were moved back 12 miles and the Border Regiment continued the search and rescued many of which we owe them deep gratitude. Cather was killed bringing in wounded in daylight, and Menaul[i] slightly wounded. Alas, many of our best have gone and we only marched back 281 strong, including transport. The Battalion in the hour of trial was splendid as I knew it would be, but I am heartbroken. The gallant friends and comrades we shall see no more. So few have come back unwounded it is hard to get any information as to individuals. Of the 48 Lewis Gunners, only 7 are left.

In A Company, Sgts More, Whitsitt, Hegan, Kirkwood, McCourt are wounded and Sgt. Wilson[ii] is missing believed killed. In B Company, Sgt. Porter[iii] is killed and Sgts Caulfield, Keith, Barr, Courtney, Johnston wounded. In C Company, Sgts Hobbs[iv] and Bryans[v] are killed and Sgts Brown[vi], Love[vii] missing. In D Company, Sgts Mullen[viii], Gordon[ix], Thornberry[x] killed, Sgts Hare, Balmer, Sewell, Hughes[xi] wounded and Sgt.

---

[i] Lt. William John Menaul was the Battalion Intelligence Officer and had observed the 1st July attack from a position called Shooters Hill. He was awarded an MC for his conduct on 1st July. The citation in the *London Gazette* of 14th November 1916 reads: "With five scouts he observed the operations from an exposed position only 400 yards from the enemy's lines. He was under heavy shell and machine gun fire throughout the day, but sent in 21 clear messages to his CO. He has also done fine work on patrol".

[ii] 14815 Sgt. Edward Wilson, 9th Royal Irish Fusiliers, was never found and his name is inscribed on the Thiepval Memorial, Pier & Face 15 A.

[iii] It has not proved possible to identify this man.

[iv] 14302 Sgt. Robert Hobbs, 9th Royal Irish Fusiliers, was never found and his name is inscribed on the Thiepval Memorial, Pier & Face 15 A. His two brothers, 14259 Pte Andrew Hobbs and 14305 Pte Andrew Hobbs were also both killed on 1st July 1916. Neither body was found and they join their brother on the Thiepval Memorial. Andrew Hobbs was married to Elizabeth Hobbs of 140, Union St., Lurgan, Co. Armagh. A fourth brother, 14273 Pte Herbert G Hobbs, survived having been wounded. They all came from Lurgan, Co Armagh, and the three brothers' names are side by side on this town's War Memorial.

[v] 13987 Sgt. John Bryans, 9th Royal Irish Fusiliers, was never found and his name is inscribed on the Thiepval Memorial, Pier & Face 15 A.

[vi] 14033 Sgt. John Brown, 9th Royal Irish Fusiliers, is buried in Ancre British Cemetery, grave VIII. A. 71.

[vii] It has not proved possible to identify this man.

[viii] 16090 Sgt. William Mullen, 9th Royal Irish Fusiliers, is buried in Ancre British Cemetery, grave II. F. 9.

[ix] 14221 Sgt. William Gordon, 9th Royal Irish Fusiliers, was aged 27. He was the son of Thomas Scott Jackson, of 36, Stranmillis Gardens, Belfast, and the late Minnie Louisa Jackson. He is buried in Hamel Military Cemetery, grave I. B. 7.

[x] 11947 Sgt. Joseph Thornbury, 9th Royal Irish Fusiliers, is buried in Ancre British Cemetery, grave VIII. A. 26.

[xi] 14321 Sgt. William Hughes, 9th Royal Irish Fusiliers, died of his wounds on 11th July 1916 and is buried in Boulogne Eastern Cemetery, grave VIII. D. 104.

Bunting[i] missing. McClurg, the Primate's chauffeur wounded. We want Lewis gunners badly, the Signallers escaped well, we still have over 30 available. Your draft of 53 came last night and I saw them today, very well turned out and a good lot.
What can you do further? I fear little – nearly all our bombing teams are gone. We are right back now, not more than 30 miles from Boulogne and are hoping to get drafts and trying to refit and sort things out. Fortunately the four Company Sgt. Majors and four Company Quarter Master Sgts were not allowed over the parapet so the Company Staff is intact. Cather's loss is a severe one, he was quite wonderful as an Adjutant, but his was a glorious death and his name has gone in for a posthumous Victoria Cross. He brought in one wounded man from about 150 yards from German wire in daylight! and was killed going out to a wounded man who feebly waved to him on his calling out to see if there were any more near.
There has [sic] been a lot of extravagant words written and published in the Press, which is a great pity. The Division behaved magnificently and the point does not want labouring. Please be careful that this epistle does not get into the Press. I am still dazed at the blow and the prospect in front of us all, but we must not be downcast; and must remember the glorious example of the gallant band who so nobly upheld the honour of the Battalion, and who have died so gloriously, leaving their example to live after them, and to inspire those who are left."[105]

THE FATE OF THE 12TH ROYAL IRISH RIFLES WAS NOT DISSIMILAR. A week after the attack Lt. Col. Bull wrote a full report, having taken the time to interview survivors and observers of the battle. It appears below verbatim:

"Right (No. 8) Platoon
During the last ten minutes or so of the intense bombardment No. 8 Platoon under Sgt. Hoare left the Crow's Nest and lay outside their own wire. At zero and under cover of the barrage of smoke put up by the Trench Mortar Officer they commenced the advance. This platoon was divided into three parts, one under Sgt. Hamilton who went to the left, one under Sgt. Benison who went to the right and one under Sgt. Hoare who remained in the centre. This platoon was very heavily shelled going out and while out were under very heavy machine gun fire from both right and left and Sgt. Hoare's party soon all became casualties. The left party under Sgt. Hamilton also suffered very heavily but he managed to get into the German sap with three or four men but owing to the heavy machine gun fire were unable to remain and had to leave the sap. On the right Sgt. Benison[ii] was killed and this party with its Lewis gun came under very heavy machine gun from the right and were unable to get forward at all. The casualties were heavy and Sgt. Hoare sent back a man to Lt. Col.

---

[i] 13997 Lce. Sgt. Thomas Bunting, 9th Royal Irish Fusiliers, was never found and his name is inscribed on the Thiepval Memorial, Pier & Face 15 A.

[ii] 17256 Sgt. James Benison, 12th Royal Irish Rifles, was aged 22. He was the son of Jonathan and Liza Benison of 8, School Row, Monkstown, Co. Antrim. His body was never found and his name is inscribed on the Thiepval Memorial, Pier & Face 15A & 15B.

Blacker for orders as he could not advance. He received orders to retire; he did so with what was left of the platoon.

Plate 41 Lt. Archie Dunlop Lemon, 12th Royal Irish Rifles

No. 6 Platoon
This platoon was under Lt. Lemon and was made responsible for the Railway Sap. The platoon left our trenches before zero at the same time and on the right of the 9th R. Irish Fus. But, before reaching the ravine, the whole platoon with the exception of Lt. Lemon and twelve men were all casualties. On reaching the ravine Lt. Lemon looked for some supports but as none were available he advanced with his twelve men to enter the Sap. When he reached the sap he had only nine men left but he entered the sap at the railway bank. L/Sgt. Millar and three men moved to the right and the remainder of the men advanced up the main sap. The thick wires running into the first large tunnel[i] were cut by Rfn. Gamble who was the first bayonet man. There was a machine gun firing across the sap from the small tunnel. Lt. Lemon, however, climbed above the small tunnel with some bombs in order to catch any Germans who might come out and sent the men on. Lt. Lemon[ii] was then shot by two German officers who fired their rifles at him from the top of a dugout which apparently led into the tunnel. The two German officers were immediately afterwards killed by a bomb which exploded right at their feet[iii]. The

---

[i] The tunnels mentioned here are two tunnels dug through the railway embankment through which Railway sap entered into the marsh to the north of the Ancre.

[ii] Lt. Archibald 'Archie' Dunlop Lemon, B Company, 12th Royal Irish Rifles, was aged 41. He was the son of the late A D Lemon, J.P., and Mrs Lemon of Edgcumbe House, Strandtown, Belfast. His body was never found and his name is inscribed on the Thiepval Memorial, Pier & Face 15A & 15B.

[iii] Two German officers from No. 3 Kompanie were killed on 1st July, they were Lt. der Reserve Otto Frech from the village of Reichenberg near Backnang north of Stuttgart who

remaining men got cut off between the 1st and 2nd German line and only two of them escaped.

Nos. 7 and 5 Platoons

No. 7 Platoon advanced behind the 9th R. Irish Fus. but as the Fus. were held up this platoon only got just beyond our own wire. No. 5 was the carrying platoon and did not leave our own wire. Capt. C S Murray[i] was in command of these two platoons but was wounded at the very start.
The two machine guns which caught No. 6 Platoon so badly were right outside the German trench and the shelling was also very severe in the ravine. The Lewis gun team which was with No. 6 Platoon became casualties before reaching the ravine and the gun was put out of action by shrapnel. Cpl. Burgess and Rfn. McNeilly were the two men who escaped from the sap. Rfn. McNeilly lost Cpl. Burgess on the way back and reported himself to two NCOs of the 9th R. Irish Fus.
C Company's attack
Before zero C Company, who were on the left of the 9th R. Irish Fus., left our wire and immediately came under very heavy machine gun fire. At zero the company advanced led by No. 10 Platoon and followed by No. 11. No. 10 were held up by the wire which had only two small gaps cut in it at this point. No. 10 Platoon at once split in two, each going for a gap. Some of this party succeeded in getting into the German line but, as there was a machine gun opposite each gap, the casualties were very heavy. No. 11 Platoon immediately reinforced No. 10 and at once rushed the gaps and a few more men succeeded in getting through. The casualties were very severe but Capt. Griffiths[ii] collected Nos. 9 and 12 Platoons and gave orders to charge. He was killed immediately he had given the order. At the same time an order came to retire. The remaining men retired with the exception of Sgt. Cunningham, Cpl. Herbison and L/Cpl. Jackson who remained and fired at the Germans who were standing on their parapet firing and throwing bombs at our men. They killed or wounded at least ten Germans. Rfn. Craig with a Lewis gun kept up a good fire by himself all the rest of the team having been killed or wounded. L/Cpl. Harvey

---

is buried in Fricourt German Cemetery, Block 2, grave 80, and Lt. der Res. Karl Sütterlin from Vienna who was originally buried near Miraumont but now has no known grave.

[i] Capt. Charles Stephenson Murray, 12th Royal Irish Rifles, died of his wounds on 2nd July 1916. Aged 44, he was the son of Col. Murray of Portrush, Co. Antrim. He served with the British South Africa Company 1889-92. He was was taken prisoner during the Jameson Raid, 1896. He is buried in Warloy-Baillon Communal Cemetery Extension, grave I. A. 13.

[ii] Capt. John Griffiths, 12th Royal Irish Rifles, was aged 34. He was the son of John and Jane Griffiths of Chester. He graduated with a BSc from the University of Wales and taught Mathematics and Science at Larne Grammar School from 1908 where he taught Lt. William McCluggage of A Company also killed on 1st July 1916. He was hugely popular in Larne and in 1923 the Griffiths Memorial Cup for Athletics was donated by a lady from Larne in his memory. A pre-war Territorial, he was posthumously Mentioned in Despatches for his 'gallant and distinguished service in the field'. He is buried in Ancre British Cemetery, Beaumont-Hamel, grave I. D. 38.

then rallied all the men he could find and rushed the gaps again but had to retire for the third time. The company had then to retire to the Sunken Road. Sgt. Cunningham and Cpl. Herbison again did good work by helping wounded men to get under cover in the Sunken Road. The Road was being shelled very heavily all the time.

D Company's attack

D Company attack was led by 2nd Lt. Sir E H Macnaghten[i], Bart, and No. 16 Platoon. Sir Harry was on the right of his platoon and Sgt. McFall on the left. At zero this platoon rushed the German front line and entered it. Sgt. McFall found some dugouts on the left and detailed two bombers to attend to each. The German second line was very strongly held and the machine gun fire from the salient on the left (Q.17.b) was very heavy. The Germans stood up on the parapet of their second line and threw bombs into the front line while they kept a steady fire up against the other advancing platoons (13, 14 and 15). These suffered very heavily as they approached the German wire and line. No. 14 Platoon lost half its men before No. 16 had gained the German front line. An order to retire was shouted out and Sir Harry got out of the trench to order the men not to retire but to come on and, just as he got out, he was shot in the legs by a machine gun only a few yards away and fell back into the trench[ii]. Rfn Kane, who was quite close to Sir Harry, bayoneted the German who was firing the machine gun. D Company then fell back behind the ridge and was at once reassembled with the remains of A Company by 2nd Lt. Dickson who ordered a second charge at the German trenches. He was very severely wounded almost as soon as he had given the order but carried on for a time till he fell and then Sgt. McFall at once rallied the companies and they advanced a second time. The machine gun fire from the salient was very severe and their casualties were very heavy and they had to eventually fall back on our own trenches.

A Company's attack

A Company, who were on the extreme left of the battalion front, were in touch with the 29th Division. They left their new trench before zero and assembled along the Sunken Road. At zero they began to advance and at once came under very heavy artillery and machine gun fire. No. 4 Platoon led the attack and was badly cut up but what men remained entered the

---

[i] 2nd Lt. Sir Edward Harry Macnaghten, Bart, 1st Black Watch att. 12th Royal Irish Rifles, was aged 20. He was the son of the late Hon. Sir Edward Charles Macnaghten, 5th Bart., K.C., D.L., of Dundarave, Co. Antrim, and of Edith Minnie Powell, the Hon. Lady Macnaghten of Sandhurst Lodge, Berks. He was the 6th Baronet and was educated at Eton. His body was never found and his name is inscribed on the Thiepval Memorial, Pier & Face 10A. His younger brother, the 19 year old 2nd Lt. Sir Arthur Douglas Macnaghten, 8th Rifle Brigade, the 7th Baronet, was killed in action on 15th September 1916 and is buried in Caterpillar Valley Cemetery, Longueval.

[ii] According to a Private Galloway, on home leave to Ballycastle a month after the 20-year-old was reported missing, Sir Harry was badly wounded on the parapet of an enemy trench. Three Germans then climbed out to take the officer a prisoner, fighting off and killing a soldier who attempted to thwart them. Sir Harry was last seen being carried towards the rear by his captors.

German front line. They were closely followed by No. 3 who at once reinforced them. The wire was well cut here but there were two machine guns on each side of the gap and three or four in the salient as well as a German bombing party. Lt. McCluggage[i] at once collected his men and tried to rush on to the German second line but was killed in the attempt.

Plate 42 Lt. Thomas Greenwood Haughton, 12th Royal Irish Rifles

The Germans in the front line, it was noticed, all wore caps while those in the second line wore helmets. The German second line was full of men and there was a considerable number at the back of the large mound on the left. All these men fired at Nos. 1 and 2 Platoons while they were advancing and threw bombs at Nos. 3 and 4 while in the German front line. The men of Nos. 3 and 4 Platoons bombed three dugouts and shot a good many Germans. All these four platoons suffered very heavily from an exceedingly intense machine gun fire. An order to retire was passed along and, as there were no supports on the spot, A Company did so. Lt. Thomas Haughton[ii], No. 4 Platoon, had been wounded in the leg soon

---

[i] Lt. William McCluggage, A Company, 12th Royal Irish Rifles, was aged 23. He was the son of Thomas and Annie McCluggage of Ballyboley, Larne, Co. Antrim. He was educated at Larne Grammar School (where he was taught by Capt. John Griffiths who also died on 1st July 1916) where he played rugby for the 1st XV. He graduated from Queen's College with a B.Sc. (Civil Engineering) in 1914. He played rugby both for Queen's and Larne Town Rugby Club. Joined the UVF before the war. He is buried in Serre Road Cemetery No. 2, grave VII. J. 3.

[ii] Lt. Thomas Greenwood Haughton, 12th Royal Irish Rifles, was aged 25. He was the youngest son of Thomas Wilfred and Catherine Isabel Haughton of Hillmount, Cullybackey, Co. Antrim. Educated at Edgbaston Prep School, Birmingham and St Edward's School, Oxford, where he was in the OTC, he worked for the family firm of Messrs. Frazer and Haughton, Cullybackey. He was the OC, E Company, 1st Battalion, North Antrim Volunteers, UVF. He is buried in Hamel Military Cemetery, Beaumont-Hamel, grave I. A. 15.

after leaving our front line but led his platoon on. He was wounded a second time during the retirement and killed[i].
The company then retired to the Sunken Road when 2nd Lt. Dickson, who was the only officer left, assembled the men there and ordered another advance. He was immediately wounded. The men advanced again but were met with a terrific fire from all machine guns in the salient (Q.17.b) and had to ultimately retire to the new trench. Rfn McMullan, being the only man left of his team of Lewis gunners, entered the German line with the gun and two magazines and fired from his shoulder at the Germans in the second line. He retired with the company and brought the gun with him.
All companies had now been badly cut up and had very few men left. We were ordered to attack again at 10.12 a.m. with what men we could collect. Maj. C G Cole-Hamilton[ii], DSO, took command of the front line, collected all the men he could find, about 100, assembled them in the new trench and prepared to launch the attack. Sgt. McFall and Sgt. A Smith of D Company and L/Cpl. W Harvey of C Company were conspicuous for their coolness and skill under a very heavy fire and in helping Maj. C G Cole-Hamilton, DSO, to form up the men and carry out the attack. The attack was made under very heavy shrapnel fire from the time of assembly and was finally stopped by machine gun fire. When in advance of the Sunken Road the same three NCOs did magnificent work in steadying the men, while L/Cpl. Harvey brought a wounded man in on his back. About 11 a.m. another attack was ordered for 12.30 p.m. in conjunction with the 29th Division. Every available man was collected and assembled in the new trench. The total number this time was 46. The men went forward before 12.30 p.m. and were lying under cover by 12.30 p.m. Maj. C G Cole-Hamilton, DSO, finding that the 29th Division did not launch an attack at 12.30 p.m. and not having a sufficient number of men to carry out an attack, sent a message to the commanding officer to this effect. The commanding officer ordered the men to be brought back and the front line to be reorganised and held. Sgt. McFall, Sgt. A Smith and L/Cpl. W Harvey again did splendid work in getting the men back and reorganised under very adverse conditions.
By 2 p.m. all the men were back and sentries were posted all along the line. This state of affairs continued until the few men who were left in the line were relieved by the York and Lancs at 6.30 p.m."[106]

---

[i] An eyewitness, 12/207 Pte William Gray, claims that Lt. Haughton was shot in the head and killed instantly at about 8 a.m. as he topped the bank of the sunken road.

[ii] Maj., later Lt. Col., Claud George Cole-Hamilton, DSO, 12th Royal Irish Rifles, was born in 1869. He was the son of Captain William Claud Cole-Hamilton, Royal Marines, and Caroline Elizabeth Josephine Stuart. Educated at Bedford and Ripon, he served with the 5th Royal Irish Rifles in South Africa, MiD. Transferred to 6th Battalion and the 4th Special Reseve Battalion in 1907. DSO, 1902 (and Bar, 1919). Joined 12th Battalion in February 1915. Commanded 15th Battalion in September 1917. MiD four times, thrice wounded and gassed. PoW 21st March to 14th December 1918. CMG, 1917. Chief Constable of Breconshire. He married Lucy Charlewood Thorold in 1893. He died in 1957.

The key points in Lt. Col. Bull's excellent post-battle report concern the performance of A and D Companies. These two companies attacked from the line immediately south of the Mary Redan, i.e. on the right of the 1st Royal Inniskilling Fusiliers. It is the Inniskillings, one should recall, whose apparent entry into the German lines would trigger the disastrous attacks of the Newfoundland and 1st Essex. It was the Inniskillings whose own report stated unequivocally that of its attacking troops:

"…none (were) able to gain further ground than the enemy's wire."

A few hundred yards to the south, however, elements of all platoons of A Company and men from No. 16 Platoon of D Company, 12th Royal Irish Rifles, entered the German lines and this is confirmed in the history of the RIR 119. Sector B5 was the area immediately south of the Mary Redan and it was in this sector that the German account concedes that the Ulstermen entered, however briefly, their front trench. Here they were vigorously counter-attacked from the flanks and from the support line and ejected, the German capturing two Lewis guns in the process.

The persistence with which junior officers of the 12th Royal Irish Rifles attempted to re-launch their attack meant that fighting would have seemed continuous in this sector for some time after the attackers had been forced back into No Man's Land. One can only surmise that observers, confused by the smoke, their adrenalin-fuelled hearts pumping, perhaps inexperienced and naïve, confused what they saw in Sector B5 with the failed attack of the Inniskilling Fusiliers. The brief and hugely costly entrance into the German front line of the 12th Royal Irish Rifles might, tragically, have resulted in the squandering of many more lives when reports of success became inflated and hopes of snatching victory from the jaws of defeat were raised.

The casualties of the two gallant Ulster battalions were heartbreakingly high.

For the 9th Royal Irish Fusiliers they were:

Officers

Killed in Action

Capt. C M Johnston

Missing: Believed killed

Major T J Atkinson	Lt. A C Hollywood
2nd Lt. R T Montgomery[i]	2nd Lt. A Seggie[ii]

Missing

2nd Lt. W J Stewart[i]

---

[i] 2nd Lt. Robert Taylor Montgomery, 9th Royal Irish Fusiliers, was the son of Thomas and Sarah Montgomery. His body was never found and his name is inscribed on the Thiepval Memorial, Pier & Face 15A.

[ii] 2nd Lt. Alexander Seggie, B Company, 9th Royal Irish Fusiliers, was aged 24. Born in Dubllin, he was the son of William Fergusson Seggie and Janet Seggie of 28, Prince's St., Prospect Rd., Tunbridge Wells. B.A. (Lond.). Graduated from University College, Reading. Enlisted in the Public Schools' Battalion in 1914, he was commissioned into the 3rd Royal Irish Fusiliers in May 1915. He joined the battalion on 20th January 1916. He is buried in Ancre British Cemetery, Beaumont-Hamel, grave VIII. A. 86.

Wounded
2nd Lt. Arthur Alexander Andrews
2nd Lt. Gilbert Evelyn Barcroft
Capt. John George Brew
Capt. Charles Howard Ensor
Lt. John Edgar Gibson
Lt. Henry Kelleth Jackson
Lt. Thomas Graham Shillington[ii]
Lt. Edgar Montague Smith
Lt. Richard Stapleton Barry Townsend[iii]
Shell Shock
2nd Lt. George Daly Craig

Plate 43 2nd Lt. Alexander Seggie, 9th Royal Irish Fusiliers

Other Ranks	
Killed	56
Wounded	303
Missing	159
Total	518[i]

[i] 2nd Lt. William Johnston Stewart, 10th att. 9th Royal Irish Fusiliers, was a student at Glasgow University. He was commissioned in January 1916. His body was never found and his name is inscribed on the Thiepval Memorial, Pier & Face 15A.

[ii] Capt. Thomas Graham Shillington, 9th Royal Irish Fusiliers, died on 18th August 1917. Aged 19, he was the son of Major and Mrs D Graham Shillington of 'Ardeevin', Portadown, Co. Armagh. He is buried in Brandhoek New Military Cemetery No.3, grave II. E. 31.

[iii] Lt. Richard Stapleton Barry Townsend, 9th Royal Irish Fusiliers, was aged 32. He was the youngest son of Norman Lionel Townsend (Resident Magistrate) and Annabella Harriett Townsend (née Barry), daughter of Maj. Gen. Philip Barry, RE, of 14, Cathedral Close, Armagh. He is buried in Ancre British Cemetery, Beaumont-Hamel, grave VIII. A. 18. He is also remembered in St. Patrick's Cathedral, Armagh.

In addition, Lt. and Adjutant Geoffrey Cather[ii], was killed on the morning of 2nd July 1916 whilst out searching No Man's Land for wounded. He was one of two men from the 108th Brigade to be awarded a VC, although, unlike the other recipient, his was posthumous. The citation in the *'The London Gazette'*, dated 8th September 1916, reads:

> "For most conspicuous bravery. From 7 p.m. till midnight he searched 'No Man's Land ', and brought in three wounded men. Next morning at 8 a.m. he continued his search, brought in another wounded man, and gave water to others, arranging for their rescue later. Finally, at 10.30 a.m., he took out water to another man, and was proceeding further on when he was himself killed. All this was carried out in full view of the enemy, and under direct machine gun fire and intermittent artillery fire. He set a splendid example of courage and self-sacrifice".

Losses for the 12th Royal Irish Rifles were:
Officer casualties
Killed:

Lt. L B Campbell[iii]	Capt. J Griffiths
Lt. T G Haughton	2nd Lt. J Hollywood[iv]

[i] 222 officers and men of the 9th Royal Irish Fusiliers are recorded as having died on 1st July 1916. Lt. Cather was killed on the 2nd July and a further 19 are recorded as having died over the next three weeks. Given the locations of their burials it is reasonable to assume that the majority, possibly all, died of wounds incurred on or about 1st July 1916. Only one man is recorded as having died as a Prisoner of War which information further suggests that no men from this battalion penetrated deep into German lines. There were two British cemeteries created in the winter and spring of 1916/17 in areas near to Beaucourt Station in which any burials found from 1st July might be expected: Ancre River British Cemetery No. 2 (400 yards east of No. 1) and Beaucourt Station Cemetery. The CWGC records them as only having contained casualties from September 1916 to March 1917.

[ii] Lt. & Adjutant Geoffrey St George Shillington Cather, VC, 9th Royal Irish Fusiliers, was aged 25. He was the son of the late Mr R G Cather and of Mrs M M Cather of Limpsfield, Surrey. Educated at Rugby School, he joined the Public Schools' Battalion, Royal Fusiliers, being commissioned in May 1915. His body was never found and his name is inscribed on the Thiepval Memorial, Pier & Face 15A. He was related to Lt. T G Shillington who also died on 1st July 1916. Cather was a nephew of Shillington's father.

[iii] Lt. Lawford Burne Campbell, C Company, 12th Royal Irish Rifles, was aged 20. He was the son of Robert Garrett Campbell and Alicia Anna Campbell (née Ferguson) of Coolgreany, Fortwilliam Park, Belfast. His body was never found and his name is inscribed on the Thiepval Memorial, Pier & Face 15A & 15B. He is also remembered in St. Anne's Cathedral, Donegall Street, Belfast and in Carnmoney (Holy Evangelists) Churchyard.

iv 2nd Lt. James Hollywood, 18th att. 12th Royal Irish Rifles, was aged 23. He was the son of Elizabeth Hollywood and the late James Hollywood of 'Bayswater', Pricetown Road, Bangor and later of Red Gorton, Helen's Bay, Co. Down. He was educated at Friend's School, Lisburn, from September 1904 to July 1906 and the Royal Belfast Academical Institution. He spent one year in the Young Citizen Volunteers, and six months in the Ulster Volunteer Force. He worked for Ross Brothers Linen Merchants in Linenhall Street, joining the 18th Royal Irish Rifles on 14th September 1914 as a Corporal, being appointed Company Quartermaster Sergeant on 14th October 1914 and subsequently being gazetted 2nd Lt. with the 12th Battalion on 5th May 1915. His body was found later in

Lt. A D Lemon
Lt. W McCluggage
2nd Lt. Sir E H Macnaghten
Died of wounds:
Capt. C S Murray, 2nd July 1916
Capt. J E Jenks[i], 4th July 1916
Wounded:
2nd Lt. Thomas Reid Cambridge
Maj. Claud George Cole-Hamilton
2nd Lt. Alexander Dickson
2nd Lt. Cecil Robert Kellock
Capt. Sydney James Lyle
2nd Lt. Joseph Roger Moore
Other ranks:
Killed 56
Wounded 236
Missing 94
Total 386

154 men of the 12th Royal Irish Rifles are recorded as having died between 1st July and 25th July 1916, of which 140 died on the day of the attack and the others at times and in locations which suggests deaths from wounds received on that day. Two men died as Prisoners of War.

Plate 44 2nd Lt. James Hollywood, 12th Royal Irish Rifles

The disappearance of 2nd Lt. Sir Edward Harry Macnaghten, 6th Baronet, was the cause of the award of one of four Victoria Crosses given to men of the 36th

---

the year by men of the 2nd Hampshire Regiment but was subsequently lost and his name is inscribed on the Thiepval Memorial, Pier & Face 15A & 15B.

[i] Capt. John Edward Jenks, 12th Royal Irish Rifles, was aged 36. He was the son of the late John Jenks, V.S., and Annie Jenks of Larne Harbour, Co. Antrim; husband of Gladys Jenks, of Moyle, Larne Harbour, Co. Antrim. He was commissioned on 1st December 1914. He is buried in Puchevillers British Cemetery, grave I. A. 28.

Division on this day. 31-year old 12/18645 Pte. Robert Quigg was part of No. 16 Platoon, D Company, 12th Royal Irish Rifles, and he went forward behind Macnaghten to the attack, participating in all three of the failed assaults launched by the battalion that morning. Quigg was a notoriously fearless man who had been sent to the cookhouse in an effort to keep him out of the front line, such was his determination to take on the entire German Army single-handed. In the early hours of 2nd July, he heard a story that his young officer was somewhere out on the battlefield seriously wounded. Quigg had worked on the Macnaghten estate at Dundarave near Bushmills on the north Antrim coast and his platoon officer was the heir to the estate. Now, Quigg went out to look for the young gentleman under heavy artillery and machine gun fire. Seven times. On each occasion, he brought in a wounded man, dragging the last from just outside the German wire across No Man's Land on a waterproof sheet.

Plate 45 2nd Lt. Sir Edward Harry Macnaghten, 12th Royal Irish Rifles

Plate 46 12/18645 Pte. Robert Quigg, VC, 12th Royal Irish Rifles

Robert Quigg received his VC from King George V at York Cottage at Sandringham[i]. On his return to Bushmills, Edith, Harry Macnaghten's mother, presented him with a gold watch for his bravery in trying to find her son. He was also later presented with the Russian Medal of St George (Fourth Class), Russia's highest award for junior officers and other ranks. Robert Quigg, VC, died on 14th May 1955.

NORTH OF THE 108TH BRIGADE THE COLLAPSE OF THEIR ATTACK was being replicated on the 87th Brigade's front.

---

[i] The citation in the *London Gazette* of 9th September 1916 reads: "For most conspicuous bravery. He advanced to the assault with his platoon three times. Early next morning, hearing a rumour that his platoon officer was lying wounded, he went out seven times to look for him, under heavy shell and machine-gun fire, each time bringing back a wounded man. The last man he dragged on a waterproof sheet from within yards of the enemy's wire. He was seven hours engaged in this most gallant work, and was finally so exhausted that he had to give it up".

By 8.31 a.m. the 1st KOSB were close to giving up. Any attempt to move was being 'constantly checked' and men were returning to their jumping off point as there were no further reinforcements. Also giving up were the two platoons of the 1/2nd Monmouthshires whose job it was to stand out in No Man's Land and dig a communication trench from the end of the Mary Tunnel to the German front line. Nos. 7 and 8 Platoons of B Company had been given this now impossible task. After two attempts to get up the tunnel, the near end of which was full of wounded sheltering from the German artillery, their project was postponed until later in the day. Then they did manage to get out to 'do a little sapping', digging ten yards of soon abandoned trench at the cost of several men killed and wounded in the process. In this activity they were joined by colleagues from No. 16 Platoon. These men had been scheduled to follow A Company, 1st KOSB, across to the German lines and had advanced over the open from the British support lines towards Mary Redan. By the time they reached the front line A Company had disappeared as had, for all intents and purposes, all of the King's Own Scottish Borderers. So, having suffered 16 casualties in the process, they went to the Mary Tunnel where they helped as they could under the direction of Capt. G B Cox, 1st KOSB.

Unbelievably, at 8.35 a.m., that is within four minutes of the 1st KOSB recording the imminent collapse of their advance, VIII Corps observer post No. 2 reported the Division to be 'crossing the second objective' with the artillery barrage advancing in 100 yard lifts in front of it.

In order to get a balanced view of proceedings, tt might well be appropriate, at this point, to describe this attack from the other side of No Man's Land. The account in *Somme Nord* is brief:

> "Thick waves of the 1st Inniskilling Fusiliers and the 1st [sic] South Wales Borderers (87th Brigade, 29th Division) emerged from their trenches and climbed the slope. Waves of the 1st King's Own Scottish Borderers and the 1st Border Regt. followed. The men of the I/RIR 119, Hptm. v. Breuning, immediately occupied the ruined trenches and opened fire. Red rockets were the signal for the artillery barrage. Rifle and M.G. fire swept the hostile waves and stopped them. In a few places where the British entered the front line they were attacked in the flank and in the front by courageous troops and thrown out. Two Lewis guns were captured[i]."[107]

And that, as far as the attack of the 87th Brigade is concerned, is it. Of course it is possible that this German account underplays the successes of the British south of Beaumont Hamel but, given their frankness about their failures and problems elsewhere during the attack, there is no particular reason to believe this is anything other than a fair account. It has the added bonus of fundamentally agreeing with the British battalion reports. Its mention of the red rockets explains, in a way that should have been considered by Division and Corps, what was happening on the 29th Division's front. It is believable and, therefore, probably true whereas stories of stubborn bombing fights in Y Ravine and easy advances to Station Road had no basis in truth unless one allowed optimism to

[i] This comment actually refers to the attack of the 12th Royal Irish Rifles immediately to the south.

overcome realism and unless one explained the disappearance of the attacking troops as meaning they were in the German lines rather than dead and wounded in front of them.

Within British GOCs and staff officers' minds, however, fantasy still ruled fact when it came to making crucial decisions. Gen. de Lisle, on this basis:

> "... decided to make another effort to capture the front line and thus support the parties of the 87th Brigade who were, I believed, fighting in the enemy's trenches. At 8.37 a.m., consequently, I ordered the 88th Brigade to attack the enemy's front between points 03 and 89 but to keep two battalions in hand as Divisional reserve and not to utilise them without my express instructions.
> 88th Brigade
> Orders were consequently issued to the 1st Essex and 1st Newfoundland Regts to support the right attack, the objective of the former being from point 03 to the north of point 60, and of the 1st Newfoundland from this latter to point 89."[108]

Whilst the 1st KOSB, now back in their trenches, were reporting the heavy shelling of Mary Redan, VIII Corps were reporting:

> "8:40 a.m. forward observation officer reports 29th Division crossing Munich trench."[109]

At 8.45 a.m. de Lisle ordered the 87th Brigade to 'push on'. Who was to push on where is moot, especially as one of the units which was presumably supposed to be 'pushing on', the 1st KOSB, was simultaneously recording in its diary that its attack had ceased. All they could do now was to collect as many fit and wounded men together as possible and Capt. Ainslie set to this task, reorganising the men to the left of the Mary Redan. The battalion, which had barely got into No Man's Land had suffered heavily. It reported losses of 20 officers and 548[i] other ranks of the 22 officers and 834 other ranks who had gone into action, a 66% casualty rate.

The officer casualties were:
Killed
2nd Lt. P T Bent[ii]
2nd Lt. H F B Cooper
2nd Lt. W Dickie[iii], att. 9th KOSB

---

[i] The Official History revises these figures to: Officers: killed 11, wounded 8, total 19; Other ranks killed 145, wounded 388, total 533. Overall total 552.

[ii] 2nd Lt. Percy Temple Bent, 12th att. 1st Kings Own Scottish Borderers, was aged 21. He was the son of Capt. Percy Salisbury Bent, M.C. Served as a private in the South Wales Borderers, 1914-1915, in China. Took part in the fall of Tsing Tau. Gazetted in 1915. His body was never found and his name is inscribed on the Thiepval Memorial, Pier & Face 4A & 4D.

[iii] 2nd Lt. William Dickie, 6th Border Regt. att. 9th Kings Own Scottish Borderers att. 1st Kings Own Scottish Borderers, was aged 24. He was the elder son of Mr William Dickie, the editor of the *Dumfries Standard*. He was educated at Dumfries Academy and Edinburgh University, graduating with an MA in 1913. He was a bible scholar at Oriel College, Oxford, 1913-14, and a member of the OTC. He was commissioned into the KOSB in

Plate 47 2nd Lt. Ian Archibald Sawers Scott, 1st King's Own Scottish Borderers

Plate 48 2nd Lt. Robert Stewart, 1st King's Own Scottish Borderers

2nd Lt. J H Glennie[i]
2nd Lt. J L Gow, att. 9th KOSB
2nd Lt. J A S Graham-Clarke[ii], att. 9th KOSB
2nd Lt. F Paterson[iii], att. 9th KOSB
2nd Lt. R Reid[iv], att. 9th KOSB
2nd Lt. I A S Scott[v], att. 3rd KOSB

October 1914 and served at Gallipoli. His body was never found and his name is inscribed on the Thiepval Memorial, Pier & Face 6A & 7C.

[i] 2nd Lt. John Herbert Glennie, 1st Kings Own Scottish Borderers, was aged 22. He was the son of Jane Glennie of 22, Wellington St., Portobello, Midlothian, and the late David Graham Glennie. He is buried in Knightsbridge Cemetery, Mesnil-Martinsart, grave B. 10.

[ii] 2nd Lt. John Altham Stobart Graham-Clarke, 9th Border Regt., att. 1st Kings Own Scottish Borderers, was aged 19. He was the only son of Capt. L A Graham-Clarke, DSO, RA, and Mrs A Graham Clarke of Frocester Lodge, Stonehouse, Glos. He was educated at Wye College. He enlisted in a Service battalion and was commissioned into the 9th Border Regt. He served, and was wounded, in Gallipoli and transferred to the KOSB in Egypt. He is buried in Ancre British Cemetery, Beaumont-Hamel, grave II. A. 26.

[iii] 2nd Lt. Frank Paterson, 9th att. 1st Kings Own Scottish Borderers, was never found and his name is inscribed on the Thiepval Memorial, Pier & Face 4A & 4D.

[iv] 2nd Lt. Robert Reid, 9th att. 1st Kings Own Scottish Borderers, was aged 26. He was the son of John and Elizabeth Reid of 5, Ferguslie Buildings, 77, Maxwellton Rd., Paisley. Educated at Paisley Grammar School he graduated from Glasgow University with a Divinity degree. He played football for the Paisley Grammar School Former Pupils' football team. He is buried in Knightsbridge Cemetery, Mesnil-Martinsart, grave F. 53. His younger brother, 4585 Pte John G Reid, 1/6th Argyll & Sutherland Highlanders, was killed in action on 8th June 1915.

[v] 2nd Lt. Ian Archibald Sawers Scott, 3rd att. 1st Kings Own Scottish Borderers, was aged 19. He was the youngest son of the late Dr William Sawers Scott, M.D. of Withington, Manchester and of Margaret S Scott of 28, Romilly Rd., Barry, Glam. He was educated at

Capt. A J M Shaw[i], att. 14th KRRC
2nd Lt. R Stewart[ii], att. 9th KOSB
Wounded
2nd Lt. David Burns Dempster[iii], att. 3rd KOSB
2nd Lt. Hugh Francis Dixon, att. 3rd KOSB
Maj. George Hilton
2nd Lt. Richard Barton Howey, att. 7th KOSB
Lt. Arthur Kennedy, att. 12th Scottish Rifles
Capt. George Ernest Malcolm, att. 11th Royal Highlanders
2nd Lt. Donald McLaren, att. 9th KOSB
2nd Lt. Claude Anthony Moreton
Temp Capt. Eric Robertson, att. 3rd KOSB
Other ranks:
Killed 83, wounded 406, missing 59

MEANWHILE, FURTHER BACK IN THE BRITISH TRENCH SYSTEM, the two battalions earmarked for the clearance of the enemy front line began their preparations.

The 1st Essex diary records:

> "8.40 a.m. Orders received cancelling our previous objective and ordering the Essex and Newfoundlands to advance and clear the German 1st line trenches. Worcs and Hants remaining in reserve.
> Newfoundlands were ordered to advance to the attack from their positions in St John's Road. Essex, owing to ground between St John's Road and our front line being under heavy fire, were ordered to advance via communication trenches and take up a position in our front line from which to commence the assault. Essex and Newfoundland Regts to advance to the assault independently as soon as they were ready."[110]

Manchester Grammar School, Fettes College and Edinburgh University. He was commissioned in June 1915. He is buried in Knightsbridge Cemetery, Mesnil-Martinsart, grave G. 9. His brother, 2nd Lt. Norman Sawers Scott, 2nd KOSB, died on 23rd April 1915. They and their father are remembered on a memorial window in St Chad's Church, Ladybarn, Lancashire.

[i] Capt. Alexander James Mackintosh Shaw, 14th KRRC att. 1st Kings Own Scottish Borderers, is buried in Ancre British Cemetery, Beaumont-Hamel, grave I. A. 18. His date of death is incorrectly given as 9th July 1916 by CWGC. The battalion suffered no casualties on that date and he is listed amongst those died on 1st July 1916.

[ii] 2nd Lt. Robert Stewart, 9th att. 1st Kings Own Scottish Borderers, was aged 25. He was the son of James and Mary Stewart of Hawthorn Cottage, Station Rd., Kelty, Fife. Educated at Dunfermline High School and Edinburgh University he was awarded his MA in 1912. A schoolmaster, he was in the College Company of the 8th Royal Scots. He enlisted as a Private in September 1915 before being commissioned into the KOSB. His body was never found and his name is inscribed on the Thiepval Memorial, Pier & Face 4A & 4D.

[iii] Capt. David Burns Dempster, MC, 3rd Kings Own Scottish Borderers att. 2nd Border Regt. died on 26th October 1917. Aged 22, he was the son of Robert and Cecilia Dempster of 'Carresden', George St., Dumfries. He was a student at Glasgow University. His body was never found and his name is inscribed on the Tyne Cot Memorial, Panel 66 to 68.

At the same time, the Divisional artillery barrage was ordered to return from the useless bombardment of areas far to the east to the equally useless bombardment of an area 400 yards to the east of Station and Wagon Roads. The theory was that this barrage would give the phantom troops fighting in Station Road some protection to the east while the two new battalions cleared up the minor irritants lurking in the German front line.

To achieve this, the two battalions organised themselves independently for their attacks. These two battalions had been waiting in the area of St John's Road and it was from these areas that they were to advance. The 1st Essex were in the Southern end of St. John's Road, from east of Fort Jackson to the junction of St. John's Road and Uxbridge Road. The 1st Newfoundland Regt. was drawn up from the junction of St. John's Road and Uxbridge Road, along St. John's Road to the junction of Clonmel Avenue with the extension of Pompadour (from 1st Avenue). The other two battalions of the 88th Brigade were in reserve, the 2nd Hampshires being in the trenches around Fort Jackson, i.e. to the rear of the Essex, and the 4th Worcester Regt. were located in the extension of Pompadour and the trenches to the rear back to Thurles Dump (excluding 1st Avenue) with X Company in the Redoubt Line between Tipperary Avenue and Fort Anley, Z Company in Pompadour, Y Company in Clonmel, and W Company round Haymarket. Battalion HQ was in The Trocadero. C Company of the 1/2nd Monmouthshires, attached to the Brigade for the purposes of consolidating the positions away beyond the Puisieux Road to the east, was in the trenches between Withington and Gabion Avenues.

On the southern side of the Y Ravine salient, the 1st Essex issued orders to its companies at 8.45 a.m. to move up to the trenches to the west of Mary Redan. Once there, Y Company was to take up position with its right on a point 100 yards north of Mary Redan, X Company was to prolong to the left with W and Z Companies being in the support trenches.

At the same time the 1st Newfoundlands were seeking clarification of the orders they had received. They understood their task which was to:

> "… to move forward in conjunction with 1st Essex Regt and occupy enemy's first line trench, our objective being Point 89 to just north of Point 60 and work forward to Station Road clearing the enemy trenches, and move as soon as possible."[111]

There were two points, however, on which Lt. Col. Hadow of the Newfoundlanders was not entirely clear:

> "Asked Brigade if enemy's first trench had been taken and received reply to the effect that the situation was not cleared up. Asked Brigade if we were to move off to attack independently of Essex Regt. and received reply in affirmative."[112]

As to the first point not being cleared up, it is certain that 29th Division knew that there were, at least, German machine guns established at Point 89. They reported as such at 9 a.m. The significance of Point 89 was that it was the very tip of the Y Ravine salient and these guns, lying to the north of the Newfoundland Regiment's line of attack, would be able to take them in enfilade as they moved forward. In addition, VIII Corps reported, just before the Newfoundland Regt.

started to advance, that German machine guns were known to be at points 60 and 03, i.e. the positions between which the 1st Essex were due to attack with Point 60 being the extreme right of the section of trenches which the Newfoundland Regt was to attack on the Essex's left. No attempt was made, however, to destroy or neutralises these guns. Indeed, the only recorded support provided to the two battalions was a machine gun barrage provided by some of the 88th Machine Gun Company's guns dug in in front of Fort Jackson. Because of the clever placing of the German front line trench they were unable to bring their guns to bear on the Maxims that were about to slaughter the Newfoundlanders.

At VIII Corps HQ the conviction that the two lead battalions of the 87th Brigade had gone clean through the German front line system was still strong:

> "Two battalions of 87th Brigade went right through to Station Road. Machine guns brought out by enemy are now firing into backs of these."[113]

Plate 49 Lt. Col. Arthur Lovell Hadow, cmdg 1st Newfoundland Regt.

It was now 9.15 a.m. At this time VIII Corps ordered the 48th Division away to the north to move to Mailly Maillet. This division formed the Corps reserve and was to finish its move south not long after the various battalions along the line had reached their final objectives. Striding, driving and trotting down roads to the west of the fighting were two infantry brigades, the 144th and 145th, the 13th Motor Machine Gun Battery and a gun detachment of the Lancashire Hussars. The only unit missing was the 143rd Brigade which was either fighting grimly on Redan Ridge or holding the inactive part of the front line between VIII and VII Corps.

At the same time, back in St John's Road, the men of the Newfoundland Regt. were ready to advance. Lt. Col. Hadow had been ordered to attack as soon as his battalion was ready. There was to be no attempt to co-ordinate the attacks, indeed, the fact that the two battalions were ordered to approach the front lines by different means, i.e. the Newfoundlanders over the open, the Essex along communication trenches, meant that 29th Division knew this would be impossible. The 1st Essex was, even now, struggling at a snail's pace up the clogged and damaged communication trenches towards their jump off position to the west of Mary Redan. Hadow, therefore, had no alternative but to inform 88th Brigade he was going forward alone. Incredibly, Division was providing the Germans with the perfect opportunity to destroy the 88th Brigade in detail, one unit at a time.

The Newfoundlanders' first wave was made up of A and B Companies, with A Company on the left. They were followed by C and D Companies, with C on the left. The formation was lines of platoons in file or single file at 40 paces interval and 26 paces between sections with a gap of 100 yards between the leading and supporting companies. Of the four companies, C Company was the most heavily laden. Designated as the consolidation company, the men were weighed down with all sorts of additional equipment and material. Given the apparent urgency of the situation, the Newfoundlanders followed the lead of the South Wales Borderers and 1st Border Regt., whose dead and wounded even now littered the ground between the British support and front lines, and advanced above ground. It was clear that, had they used the communication trenches, then much valuable time would have been lost in getting men forward. The Newfoundlanders would go straight into action above ground. On their own.

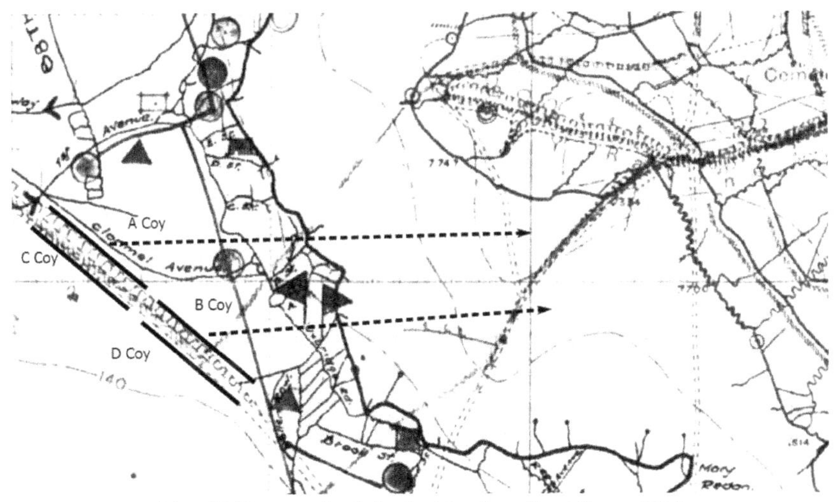

Map 17 The attack of the 1st Newfoundland Regt., 0915

At orders from their officers the men of the Newfoundland Regt. clambered out of their trenches along side St John's Road and Clonmel Avenue, formed up and started to walk steadily forward. In front of them, bands of British wire had been pulled to one side to allow men access to the bridges across the various lines of trenches they must cross before reaching the British front line wire. Overall, the left hand companies had some 650 yards to travel to the German front line, B and D Companies on the right had nearly 900 yards to go. At the prescribed speed of advance of 50 yards a minute this translated into a walk above ground of between 13 and 18 minutes before they reached the German trenches. The ground over which they travelled started just behind the top of a shallow ridge running south from Auchonvillers which then fell away slowly towards the German front line. As soon as they crested the ridge they were visible from every line of German trenches opposite. They might as well have had bulls eye targets pinned to their chests.

The advancing men could now see that the gaps and bridges in front of Fethard Street were already littered with the dead and wounded of the SWB and Border Regt. It was obvious that the German machine guns had had plenty of practice lining up these deadly routes towards No Man's Land. But on they went.

Heavy machine gun fire opened up, especially from around Point 60, where both Division and Corps already knew the Germans to have positioned some Maxims. Men started to fall immediately but, still, on they went, watched in horrified amazement by the survivors of the other battalions huddled in the battered trenches.

Plate 50 Capt. Eric Stanley Ayre, 1st Newfoundland Regt.

When they reached the inadequately cut front line wire the enemy machine guns concentrated their fire. The defenders, the 2. and 11. Kompanien, RIR 119, added rifle fire to that of their machine guns. The machine guns of the 11. Kompanie were located in the support line along Station Road and, from there, they fired over the top of the front German trenches. The Newfoundlanders were cut down in heaps as they struggled to get through the too narrow and too few gaps in their own wire. Amongst those seen to fall was Capt. Eric Ayre, caught by machine gun fire according to evidence provided two weeks later by 874 Pte Edmund Shea from his bed in St Thomas's Hospital[i]. At some time

[i] Capt. Eric Stanley Ayre, 1st Newfoundland Regt., was aged 27. He was the elder son of Robert Chesley Ayre and Lydia Gertrude Ayre of Brookdale, St. John's, Newfoundland. He was the husband of Janet Ayre of St. John's, Newfoundland, but who was living at Rodney House, 39, Bedford Square, London, WC., at the time of his death. He was

during the day, Capt. Ayre's younger brother, Capt. Bernard Ayre of the 8th Norfolks, was to die at the southern end of the Fourth Army front near Carnoy.

Plate 51 2nd Lt. Wilfred Douglas Ayre, 1st Newfoundland Regt.

Capt. Ayre's cousin, 2nd Lt. Wilfred Ayre, was in command of No. 14 Platoon, D Company. He advanced further than most, falling some one hundred yards into No Man's Land. His sergeant, 1513 Sgt. William Phelan, saw him go down without a word, killed instantly[i]. His body was retrieved during the day to be buried in what was then grave No. 5 in the fast-growing cemetery at Knightsbridge. The Rev. H S Reid presided.

Lt. Frederick Mellor was the Battalion Signalling Officer and one of the battalion who failed to reach the British front line. A witness, 1152 Pte Eric Burt[ii], told a second-hand tale from his bed in No. 8 Stationary Hospital in Boulogne. Burt had himself been badly wounded in the right wrist very early in the advance and had been able to crawl back into the trenches. From there, he walked to the ADS at Mailly Maillet. While he waited to be evacuated another man came in, a wounded signaller from the battalion. This man told Burt that 31 of the 36 signallers were either dead or wounded. The officer in charge, Lt. Mellor, had been killed outright by a machine gun bullet almost as soon as the attack started[iii].

---

educated at the Methodist College, St John's, Newfoundland, and The Leys School, Cambridge, where he played football for the 1st XI. He was commissioned in September 1914 and helped train the first Newfoundland contingent. He was promoted Captain in January 1915. Originally buried to the south of Beaumont Hamel he was re-buried in 1920 in Ancre British Cemetery, Beaumont-Hamel, grave II. E. 12. His brother, 24 year old Capt. Bernard Pitts Ayre, 8th Norfolk Regt. also fell on 1st July and is buried in Carnoy Military Cemetery, grave D. 10.

[i] 2nd Lt. Wilfred Douglas Ayre, 1st Newfoundland Regt., was aged 21. He was the son of Charles P and Diana Ayre of Waterford Bridge Road, St. John's, Newfoundland. He was educated at the Methodist College, St John's, Newfoundland and The Leys School, Cambridge. After working for the family business in Newfoundland he came to England to take his Chartered Accountant examinations. He enlisted as a Private in September 1914, was promoted Sgt and CQMS and was commissioned in October 1915. He is buried in Knightsbridge Cemetery, Mesnil-Martinsart, grave B. 10.

[ii] 1152 Pte Eric Burt, 1st Newfoundland Regt., died on 19th October 1917. Aged 20, he was the son of John and Jemima Burt, of Battery Rd., St. John's. His body was never found and his name is inscribed on the Beaumont-Hamel (Newfoundland) Memorial.

[iii] Lt. Frederick Courtney Mellor, No. 7 Platoon, B Company, 1st Newfoundland Regt., was aged 28. He was the son of Rev. Thomas C and Mary L Mellor of St Luke's Rectory,

2nd Lt. William Warren was also of the view that Mellor had been killed early on. Warren was wounded in the left leg out in No Man's Land and, unable to move, lay out amongst the dead and wounded from 9.20 a.m. on Saturday to 11.30 p.m. on Sunday and, as a result, was recorded as 'missing'. Also in the 3rd London General Hospital, Warren recalled his belief that, in addition to Mellor, 2nd Lts. Robert Reid[i] and George Taylor[ii] were both almost certainly dead. Sadly, in both cases he was correct. He was also correct in his statement that neither officer had been brought in from No Man's Land for neither was seen again. Further confirmation of Reid's demise was provided in September by 278 Pte John Mackay of B Company, a patient in an infirmary on the Walmsley Road in Bury, Lancashire. Meanwhile, 2nd Lt. Taylor's death was seen by one of his brothers. There had been three Taylor brothers in the 1st Newfoundland Regt. on the morning of 1st July 1916. Less than a year later, all three were dead, their bodies never to be found.

Another officer whose death was witnessed was the recently commissioned 2nd Lt. Clifford Jupp. Enlisting as a Private in September 1914 he had risen to be a CQMS before he received his commission just over three weeks before he died. 492 Pte Archibald Coombe provided the necessary confirmation of the young officer's death from his bed in the 3rd London General Hospital in Wandsworth. Already wounded and sprawled in the long, lank grass, Coombe then saw 2nd Lt. Jupp hit in the chest and collapse. He did not move again[iii].

It is almost certain that the majority of the Newfoundlanders' casualties occurred on the British side of their own wire but still the survivors marched steadfastly forwards towards and past the Danger Tree which stood forlorn and

---

Annapolis Royal, Nova Scotia, Canada. Native of Eastern Passage, Dartmouth, Nova Scotia. He was a cable operator. He enlisted in September 1914 and was commissioned in April 1915. He is buried in Knightsbridge Cemetery, Mesnil-Martinsart, grave B. 9.

[i] 2nd Lt. Robert Bruce Reid, 1st Newfoundland Regt., was aged 21. He was the son of Sir William Duff Reid, President of the Reid Newfoundland Railway & Steamship Company, and Lady Reid of 'Bartra', Circular Rd., St. John's, Newfoundland. Born in Montreal, he was educated at Harrow School and Trinity College, Cambridge. He enlisted as 593 Private in the 1st Newfoundland Regt. in August 1914 and was commissioned in August 1915. He fought at Gallipoli from August 1915 as Machine Gun Officer. His body was never found and his name is inscribed on the Beaumont-Hamel (Newfoundland) Memorial.

[ii] 2nd Lt. George Hayward Taylor, 1st Newfoundland Regt., was aged 24. He was the son of Eugene F and Mary Taylor of 5, Maxse St., St. John's, Newfoundland. He enlisted in September 1914, was promoted Sgt., Colour Sgt., CQMS, and CSM, before being commissioned in September 1915. Fought at Gallipoli. His younger brothers 1973 Pte Richard H Taylor and 2525 Pte Eugene Fred Taylor, 1st Newfoundland Regt., both died on 14th April 1917. None of the brothers' bodies were found and their names are inscribed on the Beaumont-Hamel (Newfoundland) Memorial. It would appear that 2nd Lt. Taylor's body may have been found in August 1917 by the 3rd Army Mobile Graves Registration Unit because, at this time, the Officer Commanding confirmed him as having been killed. Details of the grave were subsequently lost.

[iii] 2nd Lt. Clifford Henry Oliver Jupp, 1st Newfoundland Regt., was aged 25. He was the son of William and Marion Jupp of Pulborough Sussex, England. A dry goods clerk living in St John's, he enlisted as 157 Pte in September 1914, was promoted L/Cpl., Cpl., Sgt., and CQMS, and was commissioned on 5th June 1916. His body was never found and his name is inscribed on the Beaumont-Hamel (Newfoundland) Memorial.

leafless in the middle of No Man's Land. Some even reached the edge of the German wire where they managed to throw a few bombs before being shot down. Credited with having advanced the furthest was 39 year old 274 Sgt. Thomas Carroll[i] from Harbor Grace. He died close to the German lines.

Plate 52 274 Sgt. Thomas Carroll, 1st Newfoundland Regt.

A Lt. Menzies of D/17 Battery, 17th Brigade, RFA, was attached to the 1st Newfoundland Regt as their Forward Observation Officer. He advanced with Lt. Col. Hadow[ii]. After the war, 2nd Lt, later Major, C J P Ball, DSO, MC, of B Battery, RHA, who had talked to Menzies after the attack, recalled:

> "In his words the MG fire was too awful, men were dropping like flies but not faltering. We had lost so many between the support and the front line that as we reached the front line Col. Hadow dropped into it and I was thankful to join him. The rest of the men swept on falling as they went till the last remnants reached the wire and disappeared into the German trench."[114]

Without doubt, the advance of the 1st Newfoundland Regt. ranks beyond even the Charge of the Light Brigade as the most gallant but pointless sacrifice in the annals of the British Army. It was witnessed by Lt. Col. Harry Marriott-Smith, DSO, the CO of the 132nd Brigade, RFA. Writing after the war he stated:

> "The isolated attack of the Newfoundland Regt was the most devoted thing I saw in the war. I witnessed it from our support trench and saw no

---

[i] 274 Sgt. Thomas Carroll, 1st Newfoundland Regt., was aged 39. He was the son of Thomas and Ellen Carroll, of Harbor Grace, Newfoundland. He was married to Elizabeth Carroll and with their three children they lived at Bell Island, St John's East. His body was found the following year and he was buried in Hawthorn Ridge Cemetery No. 2, Auchonvillers, grave A. 40, in August 1917.

[ii] Lt. Col. Arthur Lovell Hadow, CMG, Norfolk Regt. cmdg 1st Newfoundland Regt., was aged 39. He was the son of Rev. John Lovell Gwatkin Hadow, vicar of Sutton Valence, and Fanny Burness. He was educated at Repton and Oriel College, Oxford. He married Adela Maude Bayly, daughter of Lt. Col. Edward Richard Bayly in April 1916. Two children. Commissioned into Norfolk Regt. 1898. Served in South Africa. Served in Waziristan 1901. Served in Tibet, 1904, MiD. Seconded to Egyptian Army and Sudan Civil Service, 1906-15. Served at Gallipoli, MiD. Staff Captain, 88th Brigade, Brigade Major, 34th Brigade. Took command 1st Newfoundland Regt., 6th December 1915. CMG, January 1916. Cmdg Southern Labour Centre, Labour Corps, April 1918. Twice MiD. He died in 1968. His son, 122121 Flying Officer John Maude Hadow, 137 Squadron, RAF Volunteer Reserve, died on 16th April 1943. He is buried in Margate Cemetery.

> man falter. One incident sticks in my memory. Two Newfoundlanders carrying a trench ladder well up with their leading men. One falls, another picks up the end and is shot almost at once. The survivor staggers forward with the ladder another 100 yards and falls too."[115]

Maj. Spencer Smith, 2iC of the Newfoundlanders' Brigade colleagues the 2nd Hampshires, was damning in his criticism of higher authority for leaving the Newfoundland Regt. and, later, the 1st Essex Regt., hanging out to dry in full view of the enemy, an action for which no-one at Division or Corps had any excuse:

> "I consider the attack of the Newfoundland and Essex battalions a grave error of judgement being preordained to failure and having no chance of success. On the scanty information available it should have not have taken place. It should have been evident to anyone in our front line system that the enemy's fire was in no way subdued. It should not have been made until the existing situation had been cleared up and superiority over the enemy's fire had been obtained.
> 'The climax of the infantry attack is the assault which is alone made possible by superiority of fire' (*Field Service Regulations*, *Part 1*, quote from memory).
> It was an extremely gallant effort but all to no purpose. The Newfoundland Regt. was practically wiped out and I don't think any reached the German lines.
> Was our artillery cooperating with the attack? If an attack which had taken months to prepare under cover of a bombardment of a week failed I can see no reasons to suppose the attack of the Newfoundland and Essex battalions improvised on the spur of the moment and without adequate support should succeed."[116]

Precisely.

Out in No Man's Land, a small group of Newfoundlanders who had drifted far to the right, stumbled over the remains of D Company, 1st King's Own Scottish Borderers, still lying out in No Man's Land. Capt. Malcolm appears to have collected a few more men around him and, on the appearance of this hapless band of officer-less infantry, he ordered his men to rise and they advanced together towards the German wire. Capt. Malcolm's objective was laudable if grossly optimistic given what had gone before:

> "I hoped to get a footing in the enemy trenches and so hinder the machine gun fire. I was wounded 60 yards from the enemy trenches. The advance ceased 20 yards further on."[117]

Thus ended the last vestige of the attack by the 1st Newfoundland Regt. They went into action 22 officers and 758 men strong. At Roll Call the following morning, with the exception of the 10% reserve, runners and stretcher bearers, just 68 men answered their names. Nearly half of the 780 officers and men who had gone into action were dead.

The report of their casualties makes grim reading:

Officers:

Killed 12, missing 3, died of wounds 2, wounded 9, total 26 (four officers from the reserve also became casualties as they attempted to assist in the attack).

Other ranks:

Killed 66, wounded 362, died of wounds 21, missing (believed killed) 209, total 658.

The battalion had suffered a casualty rate of 88% although, if you take the Official History's figures as accurate, this number stands at 91%. 46% of the men involved were killed or died of wounds. That the battalion and the people of Newfoundland recovered from such a savage blow speaks volumes about the character of the men and their families from this rugged Atlantic province.

Plate 53 2nd Lt. Gerald Walter Ayre, 1st Newfoundland Regt.

The details of the officer casualties are:

Killed (inc. one missing, believed killed)

Capt. E S Ayre	2nd Lt. G W Ayre[i]
2nd Lt. W D Ayre	2nd Lt. J R Ferguson[ii]

[i] 2nd Lt. Gerald Walter Ayre, 1st Newfoundland Regt., was aged 25. He was the son of Frederick William and Mary Julia Ayre of Circular Road, St. John's. He was educated at the Methodist College, St John's, Newfoundland and Rossall College. He enlisted in January 1915, being promoted Corporal and Sergeant, and was commissioned in July 1915. Unfortunately, a wounded soldier removed 2nd Lt. Ayre's ID disc and his revolver which were later discovered at No. 29 CCS. As a result, his body was never identified and his name is inscribed on the Beaumont-Hamel (Newfoundland) Memorial.

[ii] 2nd Lt. John Roy Ferguson, 1st Newfoundland Regt., was aged 27. He was the son of Daniel and Isabella Ferguson of 39, Leslie Street, St. John's; husband of Jeannette Herbert Ferguson of 67, Springdale Street, St John's, and later Grand Falls, with whom he had a son. He enlisted on 4th January 1915, was promoted Sergeant and CSM was commissioned in June 1916. His body was never found and his name is inscribed on the Beaumont-Hamel (Newfoundland) Memorial. His younger brother, 95 Sgt. Stewart Small Ferguson, 1st Newfoundland Regt., aged 26, was also killed on 1st July. His body was never found and his name too is inscribed on the Beaumont-Hamel (Newfoundland) Memorial. Unfortunately, owing to his wife moving house twice since he had enlisted, 2nd Lt. Ferguson's widow first heard of his death from a friend and from a list in the newspapers.

Lt. H C Herder[i]	2nd Lt. C H O Jupp
Lt. F C Mellor	2nd Lt. R B Reid
2nd Lt. R W Ross[ii]	2nd Lt. W T Ryall[iii]
Lt. R A Shortall[iv]	2nd Lt. G H Taylor

Missing:
Lt. R G Paterson[v], wounded
2nd Lt. William Valence Warren, wounded
Died of wounds
2nd Lt. H J R Rowsell[vi], died of wounds, 8th July 1916
Capt. & QM M F Summers, died of wounds, 16th July 1916
2nd Lt. C Rendell[vii], died of wounds, 22nd July 1916

---

[i] Lt. Hubert Clifford Herder, 1st Newfoundland Regt., was aged 25. He was the son of William James and Elizabeth Herder of 40, Rennie Mille Road, St. John's, Newfoundland. He enlisted in September 1914, was promoted L/Cpl and Cpl. and was commissioned in in April 1915. He is buried in Y Ravine Cemetery, Beaumont-Hamel, grave C. 69. His brother, Lt. Arthur Herder, died of wounds on 3rd December 1917 and is buried in Tincourt New British Cemetery, and another was wounded, both serving with the Newfoundland Regt. Unfortunately, there was a mix up over the location of Hubert and Arthur's graves with the family being informed that they were both buried at Tincourt. This was not resolved until 1920.

[ii] 2nd Lt. Robert Wallace Ross, 1st Newfoundland Regt., was aged 22. He was the son of Hector and Elizabeth Ross of 14, Victoria Street, St John's, and later Toronto, Ontario, Canada. He enlisted as 1182 Pte in March 1915 and was commissioned in November 1915. He is buried in Hawthorn Ridge Cemetery No.2, Auchonvillers, grave A. 51.

[iii] 2nd Lt. William Thomas Ryall, 1st Newfoundland Regt., was aged 28. He was the son of Robert and Elizabeth Ann Ryall of 40, Hayward Avenue, St. John's. He was a jeweller He enlisted as 53 Pte in September 1914, being promoted L/Cpl., Cpl., Sgt, and CQMS, and commissioned in November 1915. His body was never found and his name is inscribed on the Beaumont-Hamel (Newfoundland) Memorial.

[iv] Lt. Richard Aloysius Shortall, 1st Newfoundland Regt., was aged 25, He was the son of Richard and Catherine Shortall of Waterford Bridge Road, St. John's, Newfoundland. He enlisted as 595 Pte in September 1914, was promoted L/Cpl., and commissioned in April 1915. Previously wounded at Gallipoli, he is buried in Y Ravine Cemetery, Beaumont-Hamel, grave C. 44.

[v] Lt. Reginald Grant Paterson, MC & Bar, suffered a wound to his right thumb and was evacuated via Rouen to the 3rd London General Hospital. He received his MCs for his conduct in 1917 and 1918. He was also wounded in 1915 at Gallipoli and in 1918.

[vi] 2nd Lt. H John R 'Jack' Rowsell, 1st Newfoundland Regt., was aged 21. He was the son of John and Lydia G Rowsell of Bonavista, Newfoundland. He was studying for the Anglican Ministry at St. Augustine College, Canterbury. Although originally deemed unfit because of defective eyesight he enlisted as 619 Pte in March 1915 at Edinburgh Castle, was promoted L/Cpl. and commissioned in July 1915. Wounded in the thighs and abdomen he was sent to the 2nd Stationary Hospital at Abbeville. He died on 8th July and is buried in Abbeville Communal Cemetery, grave IV. C. 17. His older brother, Capt. Reginald S Rowsell, was wounded on 1st July and later killed during the Battle of Arras on 14th April 1917.

[vii] 2nd Lt. Clifford Rendell, 1st Newfoundland Regt., died of wounds on 22nd July 1916. Aged 21, he was the son of Dr Herbert and Lizzie Rendell, of Duckworth Street, St. John's, Newfoundland. He enlisted as 621 Pte in December 1914, being promoted Cpl. and Sgt., and was commissioned in July 1915. He was originally described as 'missing' but

Plate 54 Capt. James A Ledingham, 1st Newfoundland Regt.

Plate 55 Capt. Joseph Nunns, 1st Newfoundland Regt

Plate 56 Capt. Reginald S Rowsell, 1st Newfoundland Regt.

Plate 57 Capt. and QM Michael Francis Summers, 1st Newfoundland Regt.

Wounded:

2nd Lt. Christopher Bertram Dicks

2nd Lt. Harold Kenneth Goodyear, GSW right elbow, permanently unfit

2nd Lt. Henry George Hicks, GSW left shoulder, returned to duty, MC & Bar

Capt. James Allan Ledingham

2nd Lt. Henry Morton Maddick, shell wounds left shoulder and head, permanently unfit, returned to Newfoundland

Capt. Joseph Nunns. GSW left calf, awarded MC, permanently unfit

Lt. Stanley Robertson, GSW back, broken ribs, did not return to the front

Capt. Reginald S Rowsell[i], GSW left hip and buttock, awarded the MC, killed in action 14th April 1917

---

was found with a severe gun shot wound to the right thigh and was sent to the Duchess of Westminster's Hospital at Le Touquet where his condition was described as critical. His right leg was amputated and it was hoped he might recover. His father and sister Mary were at his bed-side but he contracted septicaemia as a result of gas gangrene and died on 22nd July. He is buried in Etaples Military Cemetery, grave I. A. 38.

[i] Capt. Reginald Rowsell was awarded the MC in the New Year's Honours List of 1917. In the 88th Brigade Lists the citation reads: "Served continuously with the Regiment since it landed at Gallipoli until he was wounded whilst leading his company on 1st July in the attack near Beaumont Hamel. He has shown great devotion to duty."

Capt. Reginald S Rowsell, MC, 1st Newfoundland Regt., died on 14th April 1917. Aged 27, he was the son of John and Lydia Rowsell, of Bonavista. His body was never found and his name is inscribed on the Beaumont Hamel (Newfoundland) Memorial. His younger brother, 2nd Lt. Jack Rowsell, was killed on 1st July 1916.

2nd Lt. John Robin Stick, GSW left leg, broken fibula, returned to action, shell shock in November 1917, awarded MC

One young officer who approached the day of battle with the same calm organisation as he employed on his role in the battalion was Capt. Michael Summers, the Quarter Master, who would die of his wounds on the 16th July. His last letter to his parents was dated 18th June. He took comfort from his religion, telling his mother and father that 'If it is God's Will that I should not come through, His Holy Will be done'. Beyond that, he left everything to his parents except for a series of small personal bequests the details of which are, in their small way, unutterably moving. He left a fountain pen to 870 Pte James Lang 'who has been my batman-orderly and who has served me faithfully'. 930 L/Cpl. Gordon Bastow, who had worked with Summers in the stores, was to receive a cigarette case. His bed and washstand went to 31 RQMS Hector McNeill and a penknife to 664 Cpl. Edward Nicholls who had also worked in the regimental stores. 24 Pte Ernest McLeod received his pocket book. There were three final items to dispose of: his signet ring, watch and identity disc. The signet ring was left to his grieving father. The last two items went, respectively, to a 'Vincent' and a 'Harold'. Family members, perhaps, to be received by them 'as a small souvenir of me… just a small remembrance…".[i]

Plate 58 20 Private Stewart Dewling, MM, 1st Newfoundland Regt.

That some had survived was due in no small part to the actions of 20 Pte. Stewart Dewling[ii], a 22 year old plumber from 25, Flemming Street, St John's, and 856 Pte. Thomas White McGrath[iii]. Under heavy machine gun and shell fire

---

[i] Capt. Michael Francis Summers, 1st Newfoundland Regt., was aged 26. He was the son of Michael and Catherine Summers, of 330, Water St., St. John's, Newfoundland. He was appointed Quarter Master in September 1914 and promoted Captain in November 1915. He died at 49th Casualty Clearing Station and is buried in Gezaincourt Communal Cemetery Extension, grave II. A. 18.

[ii] The citation for the Military Medal listed in the *London Gazette*, 21st September 1916, reads: Pte S Dewling. "For bravery in the field. On July 1st under machine gun fire south of Beaumont Hamel brought in two wounded men and worked continuously under heavy shell fire. On July 2nd brought in six wounded men under shell fire and machine gun fire in daylight. On July 3rd went out and looked for wounded men in daylight".

Pte Dewling survived the war although wounded once and was a Company Sergeant Major at the end of the war.

[iii] The citation for the Military Medal listed in the *London Gazette* of 21st December 1916, awarded the Pte McGrath reads: "For conspicuous bravery on July 1st in attending to the wounded under very heavy fire. On July 1st near Beaumont Hamel showed conspicuous

they went about the battlefield bringing in the wounded. Dewling brought in wounded men on three successive days and in broad daylight. Both men were awarded the Military Medal.

It took nearly a month before the people back home in Newfoundland became aware of the true scale of the disaster which had overtaken their boys in France. On 6th July, a local newspaper, *The Telegram*, reported eight men as having died in the attack. That number soon grew to 48 casualties. On 8th July, *The Telegram* reported a statement from the Prime Minister of Newfoundland, Edward Morris. This announced a figure of 230 men killed, wounded and missing. By 22nd July, the figure stood at 524 of which 44 were dead. The full extent of the tragedy became clear when *The Evening Telegram* published Lt. Col. Hadow's report on the attack. It contained the news that 110 of their men were dead, 115 were missing and 495 had been wounded. The soldiers, alive or dead, were eulogised, their advance became the stuff of legend, their contribution to the 'greater good' of the offensive endorsed by none other than Sir Douglas Haig. But not a word was raised against the officers who had sent them to their deaths. Everyone had done their duty 'to the best of their abilities' but the abilities of those of senior rank were never questioned[118].

AN INEVITABLY SHATTERED LT. COL. HADOW[i] appeared at the 88th Brigade's Battle HQ 100 yards behind the firing line at 9.45 a.m. to report the utter failure of the attack and the destruction of his battalion.

Whilst his men were being massacred reports recorded in the VIII Corps' war diary were positively chirpy:

> "9:33 a.m. 29th Division report situation improving. We have cleared point 89 and Newfoundland and Essex Regiments are going straight on to clear the whole front system."[119]

By this time, the majority of the 1st Newfoundlands were dead or wounded and the 1st Essex had not yet managed to leave the front line trenches such was the congestion in the communication trenches leading to the trenches to the left of the Mary Redan.

---

devotion to duty as a Red Cross attendant under heavy shell and machine gun fire during daylight bringing in wounded men after the attack had failed. His conduct was most gallant". 856 Pte Thomas White McGrath, MM, was killed in action on 11th October 1916. Aged 20, he was the son of T J and Annie M McGrath, of 46, Water St. East, St. John's. His body was never found and his name is inscribed on the Beaumont Hamel (Newfoundland) Memorial.

[i] Lt. Col. Hadow continued to command the battalion until 27th November when, worn out, he was replaced by Maj. James Forbes-Robertson, 1st Border Regt., who had been made 2iC of the battalion in the middle of June. Hadow returned in May 1917 a few weeks after the 1st Newfoundland Regt. suffered another days of heavy losses at Monchy le Preux in April 1917. Forbes-Robertson had instituted a fearsome routine of fitness and other training after 1st July in order to give the survivors something else to think about. Unpopular at the time it had the required effect. Forbes-Robertson went on to command the 16th Middlesex Regt. and the 1st Border Regt. and was awarded the VC (gazetted 22nd May 1918), a DSO and Bar and the MC. Unusually, he was riding a horse during the action which won him the VC. He died in 1955.

The news of the disaster reached 29th Division at 10.05 a.m. and, at last, some sense of reality dawned, if only temporarily. De Lisle ordered that no more troops should be sent forward. But only for the time being. Unfortunately, this information does not appear to have reached the 1st Essex Regt. A few minutes later, the 36th Division asked for assistance in the failing attack of that part of the 108th Brigade which was attacking from the Mary Redan to the Ancre. There was nothing, in the circumstances, that 29th Division could do to help as there were no troops available.

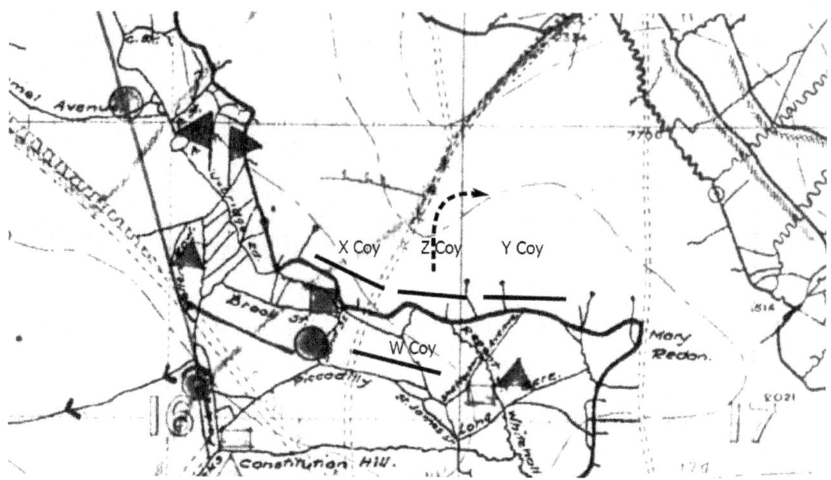

Map 18 The attack of the 1st Essex Regt., 1050.

It was not until 10.50 a.m., according to the 1st Essex war diary, i.e. 95 minutes after the Newfoundlanders had launched their attack and 45 minutes after the GOC had ordered the attacks to cease, that the battalion's lead companies were in position. Quite what the point was of their attack is a mystery. Again, they were the only battalion advancing and a target for every rifle, machine gun and artillery piece that could be brought to bear. Nevertheless, they went 'over the top'.

> "Y Company reported that they were in front line in touch with W Company. Z Company had taken up a position between X and Y Companies owing to the congestion of the trenches. Due to being checked with wounded and badly damaged by shell fire it had taken Companies two hours to get into position. Orders issued to companies to attack. Companies came under heavy artillery and machine gun barrage immediately they appeared over the parapet causing heavy losses. Report received from OC X Company that our wire on his front was uncut, that further advance was impossible and that he had suffered heavy casualties. Z Company in centre was able to make better progress. One platoon under 2nd Lt. Chawner getting about half way across No Man's Land. W Company attempted to support but were unable to make progress."[120]

So reads the war diary entry. Twenty minutes later their RFA FOO, a 2nd Lt. Montague Skitt, advised them that, at last, the field batteries were going to bombard the German 1st line between 11.10 a.m. and 12.30 p.m. The reason for this re-bombardment of the German front lines was that yet another attack was being organised. The immediate problem, though, was that the remnants of the battalion were scattered over No Man's Land and were busily trying to advance into an area the British guns were about the bombard. Hurried instructions were sent out by runner to the various companies cancelling their attack and ordering them to return and reorganise in St John's Road.

The runners were unable to find two platoons of Z Company. Z Company was commanded by Capt. George Archibald Mackay Paxton. After the long and tortuous trek up the shambles of the communications trenches he had been unable to get his men into the front line trench:

> "In my case" he wrote later, "the front line trench was blocked and the company went over from the second line about 10:50 a.m. We deployed in artillery formation (13 and 15 Platoons in front and 14 and 16 in support), but at the same time I was told our guns were shelling the German front line and ordered to hold up my attack. This was impossible as I had launched the Company upon its offensive. However I collected as many men as I could and withdrew them to our forming up position. The fire was hellish and many men were unable to get back from No Man's Land until 24 hours after the attack died down. I was never able to get in touch with Lt. A P Chawner's[i] Platoon or Lt. Cheshire's[ii]."[121]

2nd Lt. Cheshire was but one of nine officer casualties in the brief time the battalion was out in No Man's Land. In addition, 19 other ranks had been killed, a further 40 were missing and 148 were wounded, a total of 216 officers and men. The officer casualties were:

Killed:
2nd Lt. R B Horwood[iii], att. 3rd Essex Regt.
2nd Lt. W R Cheshire
Died of wounds:
Capt. T A C Brabazon[i], 3rd August 1916

---

[i] 2nd Lt. Alain Percy March Chawner, 3rd Essex Regt. att. 1st Essex Regt., survived this attack but not the war. He was killed on 21st October 1916. Aged 22, he was the son of Major Hampden Chawner and Jeanne Chawner (née Lederry), of Shotters, Alton, Hants. Born in Shajahanpur, West Bengal, India, he was educated at Haileybury School and enlisted in the East Surrey Regt., in August 1914. MiD. He is buried in Bernafay Wood British Cemetery, Montauban, grave F. 30. His younger brother, Capt. Meredith Andre Chawner, 2nd Essex Regt., was killed on 21st May 1917.

[ii] 2nd Lt. William Robert Cheshire, 3rd Essex Regt. att. 1st Essex Regt., was aged 27. He was the son of William and Emma Jane Cheshire of 1, Meyrick Crescent, Colchester. He had worked in Ceylon since 1911 ending as an assistant at the Colombo Stores Company of Ceylon. He served in F Company, No. 1 Section of the Ceylon Planters' Rifle Corps Overseas Contingent and went to Egypt in November 1914, transferring to the OTC in April 1915. He was commissioned into the 3rd Essex Regt. He is buried in Knightsbridge Cemetery, Mesnil-Martinsart, grave G. 18.

[iii] 2nd Lt. Ronald Bentall Horwood, 3rd att. 1st Essex Regt., was aged 22. He was the son of Henry Samuel and Caroline Sarah Horwood of Leighton House, Victoria Rd., Colchester. Previously wounded at Gallipoli. He is buried in Ancre British Cemetery, Beaumont-Hamel, grave V. C. 3.

Wounded:
Lt. Frederick Francis Cooke
Capt. Archie Douglas Henderson, att. 10th Norfolk Regt.
2nd Lt. Ernest Thomas H Hill, att. 12th Essex Regt.
2nd Lt. Harry Alfred Jackson
2nd Lt. Alfred James Morison, att. 3rd Essex Regt.
2nd Lt. Bernard Oldershaw Warner[ii], att. 3rd Essex Regt.

Plate 59 2nd Lt. Alfred James Morison, 1st Essex Regt.

ONE CAN BUT GUESS AT THE LEVEL OF PANIC AND CONFUSION that now existed at de Lisle's HQ. News was coming in that the Divisions to both left and right were advancing. The 4th Division was, according to some reports, sweeping over Redan Ridge and the 36th Division was actually disappearing from view after taking the Schwaben Redoubt with some apparent ease. And yet the 'Incomparable 29th' was hung up with the majority of its troops dead or wounded. What should they do next?

---

[i] Capt. Terence Anthony Chaworth Brabazon, 1st Essex Regt., died of septic pneumonia on 3rd August 1916. Aged 20, he was the only son of Lt. Col. William B. Brabazon, Essex Regt. and the Naval Ordnance Dept., and Mrs Mabel Brabazon. Born at Rochester, Kent, he was educated at the King's School, Rochester, 1907-1913. He played for the cricket 1st XI for two seasons, scoring 109 runs against Forest School. He was also in the football 1st XI and a good runner. A silver cup was presented to the school by his parents in his memory which is still presented to the winner of the annual Preparatory School one mile race. A King's Scout he entered RMC, Sandhurst, in July 1913, passed out 13th, and was commissioned into the Essex Regt., on 12th August 1914. He served with the 2nd Essex Regt. from November 1914 to May 1915 when he was wounded at 2nd Ypres. He re-joined the 1st Essex Regt. in August 1915 and served in Gallipoli. He died at the Countess of Pembroke's private military hospital Wilton House, Salisbury, and is buried in Wilton Cemetery, Wiltshire, grave D. 193.

[ii] Lt. Bernard Oldershaw Warner, 3rd att. 1st Essex Regt., died on 19th May 1917. He is buried in Orange Trench Cemetery, Monchy le Preux.

Perhaps thankfully from their point of view, higher authority intervened. Hunter-Weston and his Staff assessed the situation and, with ten of the 29th Division's twelve battalions already 'hors de combat', they concluded there was only one thing to do. It was a ploy taken straight from Hunter-Weston's Gallipoli playbook: he would do precisely what he had warned lesser officers not to do, he would reinforce failure. He would throw in the last remaining Divisional reserve in the shape of the two remaining battalions, the 2nd Hampshires and the 4th Worcesters. They were to commit suicide in No Man's Land along with any other troops that could be gathered together. Amongst them were to be the remains of the 1st Essex. The objective would be the Y Ravine and their advance would be synchronised with a new attack by the 4th Division on a line between points 84 and 94. The Divisional artillery at 11 a.m., and the Corps artillery at noon, was to be brought back, at last, onto the German front line, with the attack to go in at 12.25 p.m.

Throwing away one's last two battalions in such a fashion seems a somewhat reckless decision but it is clear from the VIII Corps assessment of the situation at 10.20 a.m. that they really did not have a clue about the true position on the ground:

> "29th Division reported several parties got through. Inniskillings got through and part of South Wales Borderers. Germans came out of dugouts in front line, re-took trench and cut these troops off. Germans now got machine guns along whole front line except crater. We have crater. In front of Beaumont Hamel Germans got front-line back."[122]

But, by the battalions' own assessments, neither the Inniskillings nor the South Wales Borderers had got anyone into the German lines. No troops, therefore, were cut off. The Germans had never lost control of their front line except briefly around the crater and, even here, they had now regained control and the British troops had withdrawn. Otherwise, VIII Corps were perfectly 'correct' in their appraisal of the position on the 29th Division's front.

Indeed, the position at the crater had been so poor that 86th Brigade had asked 88th Brigade at 10.20 a.m. whether they could throw in a battalion to assist. 88th Brigade's response was polite but negative:

> "Under the circumstances this request could not be complied with."[123]

More troops were, however, arriving at the front. The 87th Brigade had called up the 10% reserves of its battalions and these started to arrive at 10.30 a.m. The 2iC of the 1st KOSB, Maj. George Hilton, took his men into the front line and was wounded some time later. The 1st Border Regt. placed its 10% in the reserve line whilst, at the same time, recording in their war diary the telling sentence:

> "1030. Advance definitely given up in this sector."[124]

At this moment, De Lisle and Hunter-Weston were conferring by telephone as to the best course of action. Their decision was that the field artillery was to bombard the German front line from Point 03 to Point 89, i.e. the same area of German trench on which the Newfoundlanders had just been squandered. They would start at 11 a.m. The heavy guns would join in between noon and 12.25 p.m. at which moment, in a bizarre echo of what had happened at 7.20 a.m., the heavy guns would move off, and a single battalion would attack five minutes later. Although there were very few officers still standing, those that were able to move were to go out and warn the men lying out in No Man's Land of the imminent bombardment. Quite what the point of this exercise was is unclear. One assumes that those lying out in No Man's Land were doing so for a reason: they were dead, wounded or pinned down. Being shouted at by an officer that they were about to be blown up by their own artillery was not likely to improve their day a great deal.

The battalion selected for this great enterprise was the 4th Worcester Regt. At 10.50 a.m. they were ordered to assemble in the trenches opposite Point 89. Unfortunately, the Germans inconsiderately chose this moment to severely bombard the British front line trenches with HE and shrapnel. To add to the fun some of the heavier guns supposedly bombarding the German front lines still couldn't get their range right and dropped several shells into the crowded British front line. Amongst the casualties caused by these shells falling short was Lt. Col. Allen Victor Johnson[i] of the 2nd Royal Fusiliers. At about 11 a.m., he was buried in the front line by the explosion of a British 6 in howitzer shell. He was dug out by Capt. Guy Vernon Goodliffe who recalled after the war:

> "I helped to dig him out and found the fuse lying against his cheek. I later sent it back to Gunner HQ who told me that it was fired by the South African 6 inch battery[ii].
> Lt. Col. Johnson insisted in remaining on but, owing to shock, was really quite incapable of commanding and was evacuated the same night."[125]

Goodliffe had been given the task of taking command of the German front line once captured. He could do nothing at the moment other than enquire of the wounded pouring back into the front lines how things appeared to be going beyond No Man's Land. In spite of his injuries, one man was keen that the Major should know what he'd seen:

> "One poor fellow, whose jaw was shattered, could only mumble, but he insisted on telling his story. A guess was made at his meaning, 'We are doing no good on the right.' When this was repeated to him, he nodded and smiled, and went off to the dressing-station. Such was the spirit of the men in one of the worst experiences of the war."[126]

The communication trenches were already filled with dead and wounded and they were littered with discarded equipment. The progress of the Worcesters was, therefore, gratifyingly slow. They did not arrive at the front line until the time at

---

[i] Lt. Col. Allen Victor Johnson, DSO, 2nd Royal Fusiliers, was aged 45. He was the fourth son of Gen. Sir Charles Cooper Johsnon, GCB, of the Bengal Staff Corps, and Jemima Anne Frances Martin. He married Angela Mary Hibbert, daughter of Hubert Hibbert and the widow of Brig. Gen. Paul Aloysius Kenna, VC, DSO, in 1919. He was educated at Wellington College and the RMC, Sandhurst. He served in Tibet in 1904. He was promoted Captain in 1898 and Major in 1906. He took command of the 3rd Royal Fusiliers in March 1915 and was promoted Lt. Col. in March 1916. He was wounded three times between 1914-18, was MiD and was awarded the DSO, gazetted December 1917. He died in 1939.

[ii] 71st (Transvaal) Siege Battery commanded by Maj. P N G Fitzpatrick and firing four 6 inch 26 cwt. howitzers. It was part of the 1st Heavy Artillery Group.

which they were due to go over the top and so a 15 minute extension to the bombardment was arranged while the infantry got themselves ready. During their journey to the front line the battalion had already suffered significant casualties: 5 officers[i] and 96 other ranks. They had not yet seen a German. To add to the chaos and impending sense of doom, the telephone lines were now cut by the German shelling and the only form of communication with Brigade and Division was by 'runners' who, at this time, certainly could not 'run' anywhere in the British trenches such was the congestion.

In the meantime, orders had been sent out to other battalions that they, too, should participate in this attack. Thus, twenty minutes after their attack had been aborted, the 1st Essex was told to be ready to go again at 12.30 p.m.

Reports from artillery observers of fighting behind the German lines continued to come in and, at 11.48 a.m., Brig. Gen. Peake, CRA 29th Division, passed on a report that a bombing fight was going on at the eastern end of the Y Ravine by the cemetery on Station Road south of the village. Mind you, at noon, Peake was reporting that his observers had seen Pendant Copse captured away to the north between the 31st and 4th Divisions and that fighting was taking place on the Puisieux Road, all flights of the purest fancy.

Nevertheless, by 12.17 p.m. 29th Division was reporting to VIII Corps that arrangements had been made for the 12.30 p.m. attack, followed three minutes later by its postponement to 12.45 p.m.

12.45 p.m. came and went. The guns dutifully lifted off their targets and started to move back in 100 yards lifts in the expectation of the infantry attack and yet, around Fethard Street and the front line, nothing happened. The 4th Worcesters, caught under the German barrage and still trying to get its men in place, had not moved. Behind them, the 2nd Hampshire Regt. was horribly held up by the carnage in the trenches and would not arrive in position until 2.30 p.m., two hours after the attack should have taken place. For their pains the battalion lost 2nd Lt. William C Riggs of X Company slightly wounded as well as 3 other ranks killed and 11 wounded. Meanwhile, Division was informed of this second delay and the artillery was ordered back onto the German front lines pending a decision about what should happen next. The minutes ticked by until, at 1.10 p.m., 88th Brigade ordered the Worcesters to suspend their advance. The news was passed upwards to Division and Corps and, while it was digested, the field guns kept up a desultory fire on the German front lines.

As activity decreased, the opportunity was taken to try to clear the dead and wounded so badly choking the trenches. The 1st West Riding Field Company, RE, was split up and sent along the sector to help the battalion and Field Ambulance stretcher bearers. They now used the canvass stretchers which had been improvised to carry forward stores to bring out the casualties. As some space was cleared they found numerous dugouts full of wounded men who had crawled into them to get away from the heavy German bombardment.

---

[i] All five officers were wounded. They were: Capt. Robert Charles Wynter, Lt. Lionel Thomas Hillies Leland, att. 5th Worcestershire Regt., 2nd Lt. Albert Edward Allsopp, 2nd Lt. Joseph Sydney Wesson, att. 6th Worcestershire Regt. and 2nd Lt. J Scott, att. 10th Leicestershire Regt. All five officers would survive the war.

At VIII Corps HQ the reality of the scale of the defeat of the 29th Division was beginning to dawn. At 1.40 p.m. a report came through from the Division which, at last, encapsulated the true magnitude of the casualties suffered by the attacking battalions:

> "1:40 p.m. 29th Division report: from left to right, 86th Brigade practically no one left and can muster only 150 men in front line trenches, exclusive of 10% reserve; 87th Brigade have all been used up, also two battalions of 88th Brigade, of which leading Battalion, the Worcesters, are now filling up the first line trenches opposite to point 89 ready to attack as soon as they are fully assembled. Owing to communication trenches been blocked and number of wounded in front line there has been great delay in getting forward. Do not intend to attack until everything is ready."[127]

Hunter-Weston immediately called de Lisle and the discussion was brief. The attack was at an end. The Worcesters were to stand down and, along with the remaining men of the 88th Brigade, take over the right of the Divisional front. The 86th were to stay where they were and the 87th move back into reserve. The threat to the men of the 4th Worcesters and the 2nd Hampshires was not over, however, as Hunter-Weston told de Lisle they should be made ready to re-launch the offensive the next day, this time with the help of elements of the 48th (South Midland) Division. For the rest of the day the men were to clear the trenches and put them into a defensible state. The attack was over. Ironically, fifteen minutes later 88th Brigade reported that the Worcesters were, at long last, in position to attack.

At 2.20 p.m. the 18 pdrs ceased firing while the 4.5 in howitzers kept up a slow rate of fire on various points in and around the Y Ravine. They were, however, to be ready to open a barrage on the enemy front line at very short notice. The reason for this was not that Hunter-Weston might change his mind and launch the Worcesters in some suicidal assault but because the fears of a German counter-attack across No Man's Land still loomed large:

> "At 2.30 p.m. orders were received (by the 4th Worcesters) to hold the line at all cost as the Germans would in all probability deliver an attack. Everyone worked hard in repairing the broken trenches under most trying conditions."[128]

Every attack, both north and south of the River Ancre, was going pear-shaped by now. The 31st Division at Serre had long since collapsed (although the same issues of unreliable observations being taken as gospel dogged both them and the 4th Division), the 4th Division had been driven back into a small foothold in the Heidenkopf, the few remaining men of the 108th Brigade of the 36th Division, fighting on the north bank of the Ancre, were back in their trenches and the main body of the 36th Division south of the Ancre was coming under increasing pressure from counter-attacks it could hold up but not hold off. In fact, with one very small exception (at the Leipzig Redoubt) the entire offensive north of the Albert to Bapaume Road had come unstuck in a costly and embarrassing fashion.

On the 29th Division's left, the attack by the 10th Brigade supposedly synchronised with that of the 4th Worcesters had been cancelled when it became clear that there would no advance at the Y Ravine. Furthermore, the 4th Division's position was crumbling rapidly and the optimistic forecasts about easy progress had now been replaced by news of heavy German counter-attacks and desperate defence by isolated parties of men of the few trenches won. As for the 29th Division, it was all about defence along the length of the VIII Corps' front.

The focus for the 29th Division was to prepare a position and dispose of troops in such a manner that they might defend against a German counter-attack. The 88th Brigade, now the strongest in the Division by some margin, issued the following orders with this in mind:

> "About 2.30 p.m. a message was received from the 29th Division that the 86th and 88th Brigades were to reorganise a line of defence ready for counter attack; two Battalions of the 88th Brigade to be disposed ready for an attack if ordered later. Orders were immediately sent out, and the following dispositions taken up. Worcestershire Regt. remain in their present position in the firing line opposite point (89). Essex Regt. to hold remainder of the firing line on the right of the Worcestershire and support trenches in rear. Hampshire Regt. to hold Fethard Street. Newfoundland Regt. to hold support trenches from St. James Street to the right. 10% reinforcements to re-join their Battalions. The Worcestershire and Hampshire Regt. to be prepared to attack in depth if ordered, each Battalion in two lines, Worcestershire Regt. leading, Hampshire Regt. in support. The 88th Machine Gun Company to take up position to cover the front against possible counter attack."[129]

The 88th Machine Gun Company deployed ten of its guns in the front line and six in the redoubt line covering the bulk of the Division's area. The purpose of their deployment was clear:

> "Everything was prepared with a view to a probable counter attack that night. Each gun was supplied with 6500 SAA rounds and a tin of reserve water while spare numbers were accommodated in deep dugouts while all precautions were taken against gas."[130]

These comments and these dispositions (and similar ones as far north as Gommecourt) show how rapidly affairs had spun out of British control north of the Ancre. Instead of a rapid advance and occupation of the German trenches up to their 2nd Position, the British Divisional and Corps commands were now genuinely fearful that a strong German counter thrust might deprive them of their own front line trenches and perhaps more. It is an appalling reflection on the scale of the defeat of the VIII Corps that such fears were openly expressed in war diaries at a variety of levels. It is not sufficient to argue that putting the front line into a defensive stance was prudent generalship. The German attack they were preparing against would have been an unprecedented event. Never before, since trench warfare had begun on the Western Front, had troops on either side risked their own positions by attempting to follow a defeated enemy back across No Man's Land in an attempt to capture additional territory. Clearly, the total defeat of the VIII Corps had shattered morale at the very highest level.

Above the battlefield, the BE2cs of the R.F.C. were still trying to make sense of the scene below them. A message dropped at 4.07 p.m. for VIII Corps' attention showed the facts of the situation which the front line troops had known for several hours:

> "2:30 p.m. Line River Ancre to Hawthorn redoubt occupied by German sentry groups.
> 2:33 p.m. German front-line West of Beaumont Hamel very weakly occupied, apparently by Germans. Crater at Hawthorn redoubt occupied on West edge by British troops. Crater a very large one."[131]

Of course, the troops at the crater were long since gone. Perhaps the observer, buffeted by passing shells, shot at by small arms and AA guns and with the ground still obscured by smoke and dust, took the bodies of the dead and wounded for those of still active British soldiers.

Indeed, according to Lt. Col. Hamilton-Hall of the 16th Middlesex, things were so quiet around the crater that German stretcher bearers were seen moving about No Man's Land clearing the wounded of both sides. He later wryly commented that:

> "… he no doubt was helping himself to the machine guns, Lewis guns, rifles, etc. lying about close to his front line (these in any case he would have had no difficulty in collecting at night)."[132]

This was, indeed, the case but there was a humanitarian aim as well. An English-speaking member of the RIR 119 had noticed several wounded British soldiers struggling in No Man's Land and had called on them to surrender. Eventually a group came in carrying a wounded lieutenant. After this, members of the 9. Kompanie, whose colleagues had been so recently blown sky-high by the great mine, went out from their trenches and brought in five wounded officers and 31 wounded Other ranks. Seeing this, Hamilton-Hall sent a message to Brigade asking for permission to send his bearers out to collect the wounded near to the British front line. Instead he was instructed to fire on the German stretcher bearers. The dire consequences of such a decision were soon felt by the wounded and even the men in the supposed relative safety of their own trenches:

> "These instructions were not acted on with any enthusiasm by our rifle men in the front line. Shortly after, our heavy artillery opened fire, presumably meant for the enemy's front line, but most of their shells fell into our front lines, some even into our support lines. This was stopped in about 20 minutes through Brigade HQ. Thereafter, whilst daylight lasted, the enemy was reported as firing on any wounded man in No Man's Land who showed the slightest movement."[133]

The stupidity of it all is hard to credit and was the result of another decision of genius from Corps who had control of the heavy guns but precious little else.

At 4 p.m. the 4th Worcesters received the grand news that they were to attack Point 89 at 3.15 a.m. on 2nd July. Preparations were made but, at 11.45 p.m., the attack was cancelled. The gung-ho bravado of the comment in the battalion war diary is, perhaps, understandable if somewhat forced:

> "This order I am sure was disappointing, we were looking forward to capturing the German front line. The battalion remained in the trenches hoping the Germans would attack but no luck came our way."[134]

As anything but defensive activity on the 29th Division's front died away, the news coming in from elsewhere became increasingly grim. At 4.47 p.m. a message arrived from the neighbouring 36th Division. The Schwaben Redoubt, taken with such apparent ease in the morning, had now succumbed to heavy German counter-attacks. Everywhere, it seemed, the British were being forced back into their starting positions.

At 6 p.m. the 1st Lancashire Fusiliers withdrew every man bar 2 officer and 25 other ranks from the Sunken Road. Later, the 1st West Riding Field Company, RE, would fortify the road, cover over the trench, barricade the ends and construct a firestep and thus provide the one permanent 'gain' on the VIII Corps' front. But, before they could do this, the dead and wounded had to be removed and the Engineers grimly joined in this unhappy task.

The 1/2nd Monmouths were also withdrawn to reorganise in Mailly Wood, leaving a few small parties to help clear the communication trenches: 1st, 2nd and 3rd Avenues, Broadway, Withington and Gabion. Their casualties had been relatively light, in the context of the entire Division: four officers wounded[i], eleven other ranks killed, 74 wounded and nine missing.

Apart from being alert to any movements in the enemy trenches, the task of all able-bodied men was now the evacuation of the wounded, the removal of the dead, the clearing and repairing of the trenches and wire and the salvaging of any equipment, especially the more valuable material such as Stokes mortars and Lewis guns. Four Stokes mortars had been abandoned on the near side the crater in the morning and, at 7 p.m., the Royal Dublin Fusiliers were instructed to send a party to recover them. Capt. W P Oulton and 20 men managed to retrieve all four during the night without suffering any casualties under cover of the barrage timed for 10.30 to 11.30 p.m.

BY THE MIDDLE OF THE EVENING REPORTS BEGAN TO COME IN to Division showing the true extent of the casualties suffered during the attack. Brig. Gen. Lucas reported his command, 87th Brigade, could summon barely 600 men from its four battalions. Their approximate strengths were given as:

2nd South Wales Borderers – 11 officers, 102 OR

1st King's Own Scottish Borderers – 15 officers, 150 OR

1st Royal Inniskilling Fusiliers – 8 officers, 100 OR

1st Border Regt – 11 officers, 255 OR

Total: 45 officers and 607 other ranks.

These figures *included* the 10% reserve.

At 9.40 p.m., Brig. Gen. Cayley, 88th Brigade reported his approximate strength:

4th Worcestershire Regt. – 750

---

[i] Capt. Alfred Courtney Sales, D Company, Lt. Thomas Edward Roper Williams, D Company, 2nd Lt. Edgar Victor Hunt, A Company, and 2nd Lt. Walter Searl Bartlett, B Company. Casualties within the companies were:

A Company: killed 3, wounded 10, total 14

B Company: killed 3, wounded 21, total 24

C Company: nil

D Company: killed 5, wounded 43, missing 9, total 57

2nd Hampshire Regt – 750
1st Essex Regt – 280
1st Newfoundland Regt – 80
Total: 1,860

These paltry numbers were undoubtedly high on the agenda of a crisis meeting held at VIII Corps and attended by Hunter-Weston and two Divisional commanders: de Lisle and Fanshawe of the 48th Division. Plans were discussed for further action and, although the diary writer of the 4th Worcesters might think otherwise, much to everyone's relief the attack planned for early on Sunday morning was cancelled.

At Corps level the sheer scale of the catastrophe began to sink in as the evening wore on. Rumours abounded and reached every level. The Deputy Director of Medical Services noted at about 10 p.m. that total casualties were now estimated at some 12,000. One third of these losses were thought to be concentrated in six battalions which, it was whispered, had been taken prisoner in their entirety once they had crossed the German front line. The rumour mongers suggested that enemy troops had emerged from their deep dugouts after these battalions had crossed the front line and, cut off, these units had then surrendered en masse. That, noted the DDMS with an edge of disbelief, 'is the explanation at present'. Clearly, VIII Corps staff still could not deal with the notion that the majority of the casualties had occurred either out in No Man's Land or behind the British front line. So divorced were they from any sense of reality that mass surrenderings seemed a better explanation of the losses than an even greater mass of dead and wounded most of whom were lying in plain view of any sensible observer.

The initial casualty returns for the infantry involved in the attack are contained in the 29th Division's War Diary and are displayed in Table 12 below. What immediately springs to notice is the truly dreadful casualty rate amongst junior officers. Overall, eight out of ten officers between the ranks of Lt. Col. and 2nd. Lt. were casualties. Three battalions lost more than 90% of their officers; one, the 16th Middlesex, lost every officer involved; and another, the 1st Newfoundland Regt., achieved the apparently impossible, losing 118% of the officers committed to the battle. The explanation for this clearly anomalous statistic is that four officers from the 10% reserve rushed to the assistance of the main body of their battalion and became casualties in the process. Two battalions lost either side of 90% casualties amongst the Other Ranks – the 16th Middlesex and the 1st Newfoundland Regt. These two battalions between them were responsible for over 25% of the casualties suffered by the entire 29th Division.

Another noteworthy statistic is the uniformity of the casualties within the 87th Brigade, all of which lost two thirds or more of their strength. Whilst the losses of the South Wales Borderers and Inniskilling Fusiliers can be explained by the fact that they led the attack, the losses of the Border Regt. and KOSB are truly staggering as many of these casualties occurred behind the British front line and none of their men reached the German wire.

What makes these figures even worse is that the numbers of officers and men given as taking part in the actual assault include such bodies of men as stretcher bearers, battalion and Brigade carrying parties, Battle Police, etc., i.e. men who would not expect to leave the trenches until the fighting soldiers had reached their immediate objectives. The casualties amongst the assaulting infantry must, therefore, have been close to 100% in several battalions.

Bde	Battalion	In actual assault		Casualties		% Casualties	
		Off	OR	Off	OR	Off	OR
86th	2nd R Fus.	22	906	21	507	95%	56%
	1st Lanc Fus.	22	885	20	464	91%	52%
	1st Dublin F	22	826	11	206	50%	25%
	16th Middx	22	696	22	614	100%	88%
	Total	88	3313	74	1791	84%	54%
87th	2nd SWB	22	623	15	431	68%	69%
	1st KOSB	22	834	20	550	91%	66%
	1st Innisk F	22	787	19	551	86%	70%
	1st Border	22	878	18	590	82%	67%
	Total	88	3122	72	2122	82%	68%
88th	4th Worcs	Not in actual assault, held in reserve		5	48		
	2nd Hants			0	25		
	1st Essex	22	819	9	207	41%	25%
	1st Newfdld	22	758	26	710	118%	94%
	Total	44	1577	40	990	91%	58%
1/2nd Monmouths		6	170	4	96	67%	56%
					Total casualties	190	4999
					Percentage casualties	84%	61%

Table 12 29th Division: Initial Casualty Returns[135]

LOOKED AT FROM THE OTHER SIDE OF NO MAN'S LAND the battle had been a great victory for the Württembergers of the RIR 119. They claimed 5 British officers and 100 other ranks had been taken prisoner. In all, they had inflicted huge casualties on their enemy. The Official History gives casualty figures of 223 officers and 5,017 other ranks for all units of the 29th Division. In addition, there were the 1,200 casualties of the two Ulster battalions to add to the balance sheet. Against these dreadful numbers should be balanced just eight officers and 93 other ranks killed and three officers and 188 other ranks wounded from the RIR 119.

The officers killed were: Oblt. der Reserve Anton Mühlbayer[i] (9. Kompanie), Lts. der Reserve Karl Sieber[ii] (8. Kompanie), Karl Sütterlin (3. Kompanie), Otto Frech (3. Kompanie), Erwin Rothacker[iii] (1. Maschinengewehr Kompanie), Hermann Moll[iv] (11. Kompanie), Richard Barthelmäs[i] (10. Kompanie) and Lt. der

[i] Oblt. der Reserve Anton Mühlbayer, Württembergische Reserve Infanterie Regiment Nr. 119, was born on 6th November 1881 and came from Hall. He is buried in Fricourt German Cemetery, Block 3, grave 306.

[ii] Lt. der Reserve Karl Sieber came from Stuttgart.

[iii] Lt. der Reserve Erwin Rothacker came from Eschach.

[iv] Lt. der Reserve Hermann Moll came from Stuttgart.

der Landwehr Otto Schrempf[ii] (5. Kompanie). Lt. de Landwehr Heinrich Voegele[iii] (7. Kompanie) died of wounds the following day.

Whilst the 1st Lancashire Fusiliers came up against men of the neighbouring RIR 121, the RIR 119 also fought off the attack of two battalions of the 108th Brigade, 36th Division, between the Mary Redan and the north bank of the River Ancre. Taken all together, the ratio of British to German casualties from Beaumont Hamel to the Ancre appears to have been in the region of 20:1. The 'incomparable 29th' had suffered as crushing a defeat as almost any Division in the history of the British Army. The 1st July 1916 provided no redeeming features except in the exemplary behaviour of the young officers and men who had gone 'over the top' throughout the day at the order of their superior officers.

Company	Killed	Died of Wounds	Severely Wounded	Slightly Wounded	Total
I Bataillon					
1. Kompanie	3	3	7	28	41
2. Kompanie	4	1	14	25	44
3. Kompanie	12	0	8	29	49
4. Kompanie	9	5	8	18	40
Total	28	9	37	100	174
II Bataillon					
5. Kompanie	4	1	3	24	32
6. Kompanie	1	1	5	19	26
7. Kompanie	8	1	4	10	23
8. Kompanie	1	0	1	8	10
Total	14	3	13	61	91
III Bataillon					
9. Kompanie	39	0	5	32	76
10. Kompanie	12	0	6	18	36
11. Kompanie	8	1	2	28	39
12. Kompanie	2	0	3	22	27
Total	61	1	16	100	178
1. MGK	4	0	8	8	20
2. MGK	3	1	3	10	17
2. Rekrut K.	1	0	0	0	1
Total	111	14	77	279	481

Table 13 Casualties by Company, RIR 119[136]

WITH THE FIGHTING AT LAST AT AN END A GREAT EFFORT was made during the night to evacuate the wounded and to make a start at burying the dead. Capt. G V Goodliffe of the 2nd Royal Fusiliers saw men coming in from No Man's Land throughout the latter part of the day. Many crawled in, some seriously wounded. Others suffered from severe shell shock, their minds unable to cope with the sounds and sights they had witnessed that day:

[i] Lt. der Reserve Richard Barthelmäs came from Mergentheim.
[ii] Lt. der Landwehr Otto Schrempf came from Ludwigshafen.
[iii] Lt. de Landwehr Heinrich Voegele came from Ulm.

> "Two ... were quite mad (one had taken off all his clothing) and fired at their own trenches whenever anyone showed himself."[137]

Brig. Gen. Lucas of the 87th Brigade wrote later that:

> "During the night about 300 unwounded men of the brigade were collected, most of whom had crawled back from No Man's Land, including about 6 officers of about 80 who had gone over the parapet. A large number of the wounded were got in including a number of officers. Raikes (SWB) came in about 10.30 p.m., he had previously been reported killed. Welch (KOSBs) had fortunately not taken his hd qrs forward so was all right, all other COs and adjutants were killed or wounded."

Maj. Spencer Smith of the 2nd Hampshires remembers a mass of dead and wounded being collected near Hyde Park Corner and, to give the burial teams the shortest distance to move the cadavers and body parts, the 1st KOSB had an officer and 20 men dig a mass grave at the Collecting Post near Knightsbridge during the night[i].

The dead could suffer no more, for the wounded their journey to safety and treatment began at the front line.

The system for medical evacuation was as follows:

At the front the battalion stretcher bearers assisted by men from the Bearer sub-divisions of the Field Ambulances brought men into the Regimental Aid Post (RAP), walking cases made their own way to medical collecting posts in the reserve lines or the Advanced Dressing Stations (ADS).

For the 86th Brigade, Collecting Posts (CP) had been set up at: the Red Barn and White House in Auchonvillers and in the Tenderloin and were manned by the 87th Field Ambulance. Behind the 87th Brigade the collecting posts were manned by the 88th (1st East Anglian) Field Ambulance. They were located at Knightsbridge Barracks and the Mesnil Station dugouts.

There were two Advanced Dressing Stations: one at Mailly Maillet (86th Brigade) and another at the church at Vitermont[ii] (87th Brigade), run by 87th and 88th Field Ambulances respectively and used for emergency treatment, dressing and assessing of wounds, recording and labelling of the wounded, provision of hot drinks and food (if appropriate), administering morphine, etc. These ADS also performed the function of Divisional Collecting Stations (DCS) for the lightly wounded. Attached to the 88th Brigade were two bearer sub-divisions and one tent sub-division of the 1/1st South Midland Field Ambulance attached from the 48th (South Midland) Division. This Field Ambulance was commanded by Lt. Col. C H Howkins and he had some of his units at Vitermont and others at Mailly Maillet. This field ambulance also manned the Divisional Rest Station (DRS) based at Arqueves.

The two Main Dressing Stations (MDS) were at Acheux, manned by the 89th Field Ambulance, which served the right of the Division, and at Louvencourt which was manned by the 87th Field Ambulance and served the Division's left units. Here was conducted emergency surgery, the dressing of wounds and any

---

[i] 83 officers and men of the 29th Division and 108th Brigade, 36th Division, are buried in this cemetery, i.e. Knightsbridge Cemetery, Mesnil-Martinsart.

[ii] Vitermont church is at the eastern end of the village of Englebelmer.

other necessities before the casualty was shipped off to a Casualty Clearing Station (CCS) further to the rear.

The Corps Collecting Station at Acheux was used by the walking wounded and was manned by the 89th Field Ambulance. Also based there, and to be used as circumstances required, was 16 Sanitary Section.

Onward evacuation was by means of the ambulances of No. 20 Motor Ambulance Company (MAC) which were to take wounded to Nos. 4 and 35 Casualty Clearing Stations at Beauval and Doullens respectively. Abdominal cases, always a specialist issue, were to be sent to 93rd Field Ambulance at Authie while more lightly injured men were to be sent to No. 29 CCS. The narrow gauge railway to Gezaincourt was also made available and was used to move cases to Acheux.

The 87th (1st West Lancashire) Field Ambulance was commanded by Lt. Col. Creighton Hutchison Lindsay and they would deal with the majority of the 86th Brigade's casualties over the coming days. Lindsay had arranged for a significant quantity of transport to be brought up to Mailly Maillet in the early morning in the expectation of a busy day. Four GS wagons adapted for transport of sitting up cases, three two-horsed ambulance wagons and ten motor ambulance wagons arrived at Mailly Maillet at 7 a.m. In addition, Capt. Walsh and 35 OR of his bearer sub division of the 89th (1st Highland) Field Ambulance were kept in readiness in the village. As Mailly was likely to be shelled during operations, the motor ambulances were parked up in three different locations to the south of the village. The horsed transport, however, was kept close to the ADS ready to start the evacuation process.

Lindsay arranged for his men to be fed and then for a supply of hot food and drink to be ready for the incoming wounded before he went forward to the collecting stations in Auchonvillers.

Lindsay had disposed of his units as follows:

One officer and one bearer sub division at Tenderloin;

Three squads at Thurles Dump[i] under an NCO;

Four squads at 2nd Avenue near the Regimental Aid Post of the 2nd Royal Fusiliers;

Two squads were at the chateau with stretchers and wheeled carriers under an NCO;

One bearer sub-division at Auchonvillers under an NCO;

Two officers, four nursing orderlies and various other staff at the Red Barn.

All posts had been cleared and been stocked up with large supplies of dressings and anti-tetanus serum.

The 88th (1st East Anglian) Field Ambulance was commanded by Lt. Col. Alfred Edward Weld and they had set up two collecting posts, one at Knightsbridge Barracks and the other at Mesnil Station to deal with the 87th Brigade's wounded.

One MO, Lt. Raffan and the bearer subdivision of C Section were based in the hospital dugouts at Knightsbridge Barracks. This post had been well supplied

[i] A position on St John's Road about 700 yards south east of Auchonvillers.

with extra surgical material, extra rations and medical comforts and water in petrol tins. One end was fitted as an improvised theatre for doing dressings.

The routes for evacuating wounded were for walking cases via Gabion Avenue or across the open to the Vitermont ADS, and for sitting and lying cases by trolleys on the trench tramway and light railway to Mesnil. The trench trolleys held four stretcher cases or six sitting and those of the light railway three stretcher or eight sitting cases.

The Mesnil station collecting post was set up in dugouts in a bank by the railway station and was staffed by Sgt. Maj. Towers and seven men of B Tent sub division.

From Vitermont and Mesnil motor ambulances, horse ambulances and converted GS wagons would carry the casualties to the Corps collecting station at Acheux.

The Advanced Dressing Station was established at the church at Vitermont and the cellars of an adjacent house by the tent sub division of C Section under Capts. Cogan and Langdon and Lt. Gordon. This was also well supplied with extra medical comforts, rations and surgical material. The church and cellars having stretchers on trestles set out in them and a theatre in the house.

Reserve bearers in the form of the bearer sub divisions of A Section under Lt. Johnson, and of B Section under Capt. Caesar were moved into the catacomb dugouts at Mesnil with instructions to move up to Knightsbridge Barracks on the morning of 1st July.

Lastly, back at Acheux, the tent sub divisions of A and B Sections were parked with packed wagons ready to move. Also at Acheux were eight motor ambulances (six from the 88th FA and two from the 1/1st South Midland FA), six horse drawn ambulances from the two Field Ambulances and five improvised GS wagons for sitting cases.

Communications from the RAPs to Knightsbridge and from there to Vitermont and Mesnil was by runner. From there, messages would be carried by motor bike and the ambulances.

Walking cases from the 86th Brigade started to arrive at the Red Barn at 8.15 a.m. and Lindsay quickly realised that casualties were going to be heavy on this front. The 89th FA bearer sub-division at Mailly Maillet was immediately called up along with all of the horsed wagons parked up by the ADS and four of the motor ambulances. The transport arrived at 9 a.m. by which time a large number of men had accumulated and those that could sit up and had been processed were loaded onto the wagons and sent off to Mailly. Before they went all the necessary paperwork was done including the medical label, the AF (Army Form) W 3118 or Field Medical Card (also known as the Patients 'Ticket') which was completed and attached to every patient[i]. Food and drink was provided to all casualties for whom it was appropriate.

[i] Clerks had to make out Field Medical Cards (A.F. W.3118) whenever a casualty was first admitted to a field medical unit. These were clinical cards, containing the personal particulars of the casualty, diagnosis and date of admission. They were pinned on to the patients during their evacuation from the front. Whenever each of these patients entered a field ambulance, C.C.S. or hospital, an entry was made on the card stating the unit to which admitted, latest diagnosis, and treatment given, or other observations.

The more seriously wounded started to arrive at 8.40 a.m. They were assessed, processed, food and drink given if suitable and then shipped off to the MDS at Louvencourt in one of the motor ambulances. From then, until 4 p.m. on Sunday, 2nd July, the procedure carried on without a break.

When the attack started A and B bearer sub-divisions of the 88th FA moved forward to Knightsbridge to join C sub-division. A and C sub-divisions had been ear-marked to advance with the infantry but, instead, spent the day bringing the wounded back to the collecting post at Knightsbridge from where B sub-division carried stretcher cases down the hill to Mesnil. The system of evacuation appeared to work successfully with practically all of the walking wounded going across country to Vitermont church and the stretcher cases and those unable to walk being taken to Mesnil and then evacuated on the trolleys.

To assist at the Vitermont ADS, another MO, Capt. Ellis, was sent to assist Capt. Cogan while Lt. Col. Weld went to Mesnil for the rest of the day.

Lt. Col. Howkins of the 1/1st South Midland FA visited the redoubt line at 9.30 a.m. and found walking cases moving along a communication trench called Gabion Avenue towards the Vitermont ADS. He examined several of these men and he independently decided to set up a small 'rest station' at this position using a Lt. Davies-Jones and orderlies of his unit stationed nearby. Here, his men re-fixed bandages and replaced dressings. If the man was bleeding heavily procedures were conducted to stop the haemorrhage. Every man who passed was examined and, when necessary treated. Dressings and other supplies were brought up from the Vitermont ADS.

At 12.45 p.m. Howkins received a message from Brig. Gen. Cayley, GOC 88th Brigade, requesting help evacuating the large numbers of wounded now in the trenches. Bearers were sent forward to the front line trenches and another party was sent to assist the Medical Officer at the CP at Knightsbridge Barracks which was becoming congested with wounded. Howkins went up the trenches to see the conditions at first hand and it became clear that a major effort was needed to clear the trenches and a bearer sub-division commanded by Capt. W Bowater was sent forward. Their work was slow and difficult with the communication trenches being narrow and badly congested by men and discarded equipment. As the men being moved were the more seriously injured, great care had to be taken as sudden movements could easily compound problems with the wounds already suffered.

The walking cases directed to Mailly were there fed and their wounds re-dressed if required. Then, under the command of an NCO, they were sent onwards in batches of 15-20 to the Corps Collecting Station at Acheux. Casualties who could not walk were sent on in horsed transport but, by about 2.30 p.m., they were unable to deal with the flood of wounded needing such help.

By 6.30 p.m. the detachments from the 1/1st South Midland FA had cleared many of the wounded and Brig. Gen. Cayley ordered them to rest until 10 p.m. when it was hoped that No Man's Land might be cleared under the protection of an artillery barrage. The bearer-sub divisions returned to the area around the temporary rest station at the junction of Gabion Avenue and the redoubt line where they had tea and a much needed rest.

Fortunately, the OC of the Motor Lorry Transport based at Acheux was able to loan Lindsay six lorries and these were put to the task of moving all but the seriously wounded from Mailly to Acheux until 3 p.m. on the 2nd. By this means, Lindsay was able to keep the roads and the villages of Mailly and Beaussart clear all of which were shelled during the night.

Capt. Walsh of the 89th FA assisted two officers from the 87th FA, Capts. McCausland and Andrews, at Auchonvillers while his bearers assisted in the clearance of the aid posts in 2nd Avenue. At Mailly, Lindsay had requested additional help from the DADMS and another two officers of the 89th FA, Capts. Blandy and Morris, had been sent up to assist Capt. Seddon in his work there. By 8 p.m. all sitting up and walking cases had been despatched to Acheux from Mailly by either horse drawn wagon or motor lorry.

Work at the RAPs seemed to be progressing smoothly as Lindsay found when he toured those of the Newfoundland Regt., the 16th Middlesex, the 2nd Royal Fusiliers and the 1st Lancashire Fusiliers in the late morning. He found an average of only four cases waiting in each RAP and the wounded were being moved out of the RAPs faster than they arrived. Only at his CP at Tenderloin were more men accumulating but it was nothing which caused great concern.

At 9.15 p.m. the bearers from the 1/1st South Midland FA returned to Knightsbridge Barracks. One sub-division under Capt. Bowater set to clear the RAP of the South Wales Borderers in B Street which Howkins had noticed was still clogged with cases. Howkins himself, along with the Liaison Officer, Capt. H P Thomason, took the other bearer sub-division to the 88th Brigade Advanced HQ in order to ascertain how best they might be employed. As they moved along the communication trenches German machine guns were playing on the British lines and overhead shrapnel burst regularly, forcing the men to duck and take shelter. Unluckily, one shell burst over the trench where Howkins and Thomason were standing, wounding both officers and two bearers. Before being evacuated, Howkins put his bearer sub-division to work under the control of Capt. Sanders, the MO of the 1st Essex, while messages were despatched to Capt. Bowater and Maj. McCall, the 2iC 1/1st South Midland FA, who was officer commanding the HQ and hospital at Arqueves. McCall came forward to Englebelmer to take control of the work of the bearers, his place at Arqueves being taken by Maj. H F W Boedicker who had recently returned from commanding the tent sub-division at Mailly Maillet. For Lt. Col. Howkins it was the end of the Big Push for now and his report on proceedings was forwarded on 5th July from his bed at the 1st Southern General Hospital at Edgbaston, in Birmingham.

Before midnight on 1st July reports started to come in from the OCs of the 88th FA's bearer sub-divisions. Lt. Johnson commanded A Section and he was working between the front lines and Knightsbridge:

> "No Man's Land has not yet been attempted as regards clearing wounded. I am still at Knightsbridge with Capt. Caesar and Lt. Raffan. The KOSB RAP is still in our firing line."[138]

On the basis of this Weld ordered Johnson to use his bearers to clear the RAPs and trenches, bringing the wounded into Knightsbridge. At midnight he add a further report:

> "I am still at Knightsbridge with my party. The runners from the MOs of the KOSB and Border Regts have returned. The KOSB evacuate through us here but the Borders found it more convenient to evacuate through 87th FA. I have had no casualties among my men. The Essex Regt sent down for stretcher bearers and I sent a party of 8 bearers from my squad. Mary Redan and Constitution Hill are being dealt with.
> The motor ambulance cars and horsed wagons began at 7.30 to run to Vitermont and Mesnil were started with two motors and 2 horsed wagons every 15 minutes. It was found that the horsed wagons took five hours to do the round trip and the motors 2 hours excluding the time of waiting at the Corps collecting station. In all 155 trips were made up to midnight."[139]

Capt. Caesar, B Section, gave a detailed report on conditions and the evacuation route down to Mesnil:

> "The cases are very easily dealt with as far as removal to the dump at the junction of the trench tram and light railways (i.e. Mesnil). Thence the removal has been slow. There are only four trolleys to work with. I have now plenty of bearers but no trench stretchers but the wounded are coming in well. The ambulance wagons could not be used between Mesnil and Knightsbridge owing to the bad state of the road. It has been suggested that about 800 to 900 cases have been dealt with during the day possibly about 250 by rail. We are dealing with all our wounded as arranged but the Regimental MOs have not left the trenches and thus are evacuating through us in the usual way and also through the 87th FA. It is very difficult to clear the trenches but this is being done as rapidly as possible. Mary Redan and Constitution Hill are being dealt with. The railway to Auchonvillers is being used by 87th FA. A large supply of blankets is needed."[140]

Weld asked Lindsay whether they could get access to more trolleys but such was the pressure at Auchonvillers Lindsay was unable to comply. As a result, another attempt was made to get a horsed ambulance up the track to Knightsbridge but this, too, failed.

The report from Lt. Raffan, OC C Section, clearly indicated the terrible pressures under which the medical units were operating:

> "I have to report that last night the casualties were somewhat heavier than usual. The wounded have arrived in such numbers that we have been extremely busy. Owing to the very large numbers I have found it impossible to make an accurate account. The stretcher bearers have as far as possible kept in touch with the regimental MOs. The arrival of Lt. Johnson and then of Capt. Caesar and their parties made the work very much lighter. Up to twelve midnight the wounded are still coming in.
> At Mesnil I found that the wounded were coming in faster than the cars could evacuate them and I sent an urgent message for more convoy … Two convoys of 12 and 15 GS wagons were obtained and sent to Mesnil and this with the diverting of the cars from Vitermont which had reported clear enabled us to cope with the numbers."[141]

At the ADS at Vitermont church Capt. Cogan had been busy since the early morning:

> "The first cars arrived between 6 and 8 a.m. and from then until 4 p.m. cases in a continual stream. A certain number of cases did not require redressing. All cases received an injection of anti-tetanus, all who required it were fed and given hot drinks. At about 4.30 the motor ambulances failed to arrive and the ADS began to get congested. I commandeered two empty motor lorries which relieved the congestion. Only the severe cases were sent on the motor ambulance cars, the slight cases either walked or were sent in horsed ambulances. Wheeled stretchers and dressings were supplied to Knightsbridge and stretchers and ground sheets to Mesnil, also dressings to an aid party of 1/1st South Midland FA. As Vitermont was shelled the previous night tents were erected in an adjacent orchard for patients if necessary. These however were not required. Enquiry as to the failure of the motor ambulances showed that this was due to their being held up in the Acheux collecting station."[142]

Because of the congestion at Vitermont, Weld and sent Capt. Ellis to assist and his brief report showed the pressure under which they were working:

> "On joining Capt. Cogan at midday I helped to dress, inoculate with anti-tetanus and to evacuate about 600 cases."[143]

On the evening of 1st July, Weld ordered an NCO and ten men of A Tent sub-division to go Vitermont to prepare cellars for the reception of the wounded.

The wounded continued to flood in throughout the night and by 9 p.m. on the 1st July, the A&D books recorded 22 officers and 1,635 other ranks as having gone through Knightsbridge.

The overnight efforts to collect as many wounded as possible from No Man's Land and the forward trenches dramatically increased the pressure on all concerned as these tended to be the most seriously injured. Lindsay and Weld's bearers had been working continuously now for over 15 hours and the numbers of seriously wounded had increased. These cases needed careful transportation down the long communication trenches and the bearers were close to exhaustion. As a result, stretcher cases were now beginning to clog the RAPs which, being well within the range of German guns, was an unhealthy position for all concerned.

At 1.15 a.m. on the morning of the 2nd, Lindsay took a calculated risk and sent some of his GS wagons down the Old Beaumont Road towards the front lines. They collected their loads and returned without attracting the attentions of the German artillery and machine guns and so he sent down two horse drawn ambulances which started to shuttle the wounded from the front lines to waiting motor ambulances in Auchonvillers. Still the Germans did not interfere. As a result, at 2 a.m. Lindsay instructed the officer in charge of the collecting post at Tenderloin to bring as many cases as possible over ground to a point where they could be loaded on to his wagons.

The sun rose on the morning of the 2nd July and the horses trotted up and down the Old Beaumont Road in full view of the enemy trenches. No shots were fired. By 8 a.m. the horses were exhausted and had to be taken off this duty.

Lindsay took another chance and started to send his two motor ambulances down the road. The guns opposite remained silent. There was still a backlog of wounded at the Newfoundlanders' RAP at Thurles Dump. With nothing ventured, nothing gained, Lindsay set his motor ambulances to the task of evacuating the casualties from there too. By this means, Lindsay was able to evacuate the wounded lying out at four RAPs direct to his dressing station without interference from the enemy. Between 1.15 a.m. and 3.30 p.m. Lindsay estimates he was able to evacuate 682 stretcher or sitting cases by these means. Had the Germans chosen to stop this essential work they could easily have done so. It is to their credit that they refrained from firing on the ambulance transports at any time during this process.

Lindsay's policy had other benefits. At 11 a.m. stretcher bearers from the battalions and from the 87th FA ventured into No Man's Land. They were able to bring in the wounded unmolested by the German troops manning the trenches a few hundred yards away. And not only were the Germans allowing the wounded to be cleared from areas just in front of the British lines. Lindsay saw two men brought in who had clearly been dressed by German medical orderlies.

All was running smoothly and hopes were raised that all or, at least, the vast majority of the wounded out in No Man's Land would be brought in before night fall. Until, that is, higher authority intervened. This was a war, after all, and the job of soldiers is to kill one another. At 3.20 p.m. Lindsay was informed that the artillery was going to bombard the German front line trenches at 3.31 p.m. Reluctantly, Lindsay had to withdraw his bearers from No Man's Land and discontinue sending his motor ambulances out towards the RAPs and Tenderloin while 'business as usual' resumed. He had, however, managed to clear the RAPs and, by the time normal evacuation routes had resumed, only 30 cases were left at Tenderloin.

At the Main Dressing Station, Major Taylor of the 87th FA had kept things running smoothly and, with the cooperation of No. 20 Motor Ambulance Convoy, they kept the number of men awaiting evacuation at any one time to no more than 100. Other units also lent a helping hand. The 1/1st South Midland Field Ambulance placed four motor ambulances at Lindsay's disposal for the evacuations to Acheux. Capt. L H Guest and 18 OR of 16 Sanitary Section had helped out at the MDS throughout the 1st July and then went down to the front lines in the later morning of the 2nd where they stayed until 9 a.m. on the 3rd July helping tend to and evacuate the wounded. At 2 p.m. on the 2nd an officer and 21 other ranks from the 1/1st South Midland FA arrived at Auchonvillers where they remained until 6 p.m. on the 3rd. The scale of the casualties made this 'all hands to the pump' approach essential.

The work was such that it was not until 4.30 p.m. on the 2nd that the flow of casualties started to ebb and by 8.50 p.m. the station at Auchonvillers was clear of wounded for the first time in 36 hours. 1,700 men had been dealt with in that time. Capts. McCausland and Andrews and their men had been in action continuously for 40 hours with no rest and hardly any food. Lindsay was fulsome in his praise:

> "Capt. S MacCausland and Andrews displayed a fine spirit of zeal and energy in continuing to work at high pressure all the time under the most

dangerous and difficult conditions imaginable. Their example spread to the other ranks who exhibited an equal devotion to duty."[144]

At 5 p.m. on the 2nd July, Capt. Caesar reported from Knightsbridge that the evacuation of the wounded in their sector was complete. The railway had been used to move 40 cases an hour. This slackening in the rate of admissions was confirmed by Lt. Raffan who stated that the collecting post dugout had been empty except for some serious stretcher cases most of the afternoon. Prior to that, though, the pressure of work had been such that no detailed count was made of the wounded coming through between sunset on the 1st and noon on the 2nd July. During the afternoon, only two officers and 34 men were admitted and this trench carried on throughout the 3rd July when two officers and 138 other ranks came in, some of these suffering from injuries caused while clearing the trenches of debris, equipment, dead and wounded.

At the Corps Collecting Station at Acheux the 89th (1st Highland) Field Ambulance had also been busy. Small numbers of wounded had started to arrive in the early hours, of 1st July mainly wounds caused by the intermittent German artillery fire. The first ambulance train, carrying 91 cases, was despatched at 10 a.m. Soon after, the trickle became a flood as men started to arrive on foot, in horsed and motor ambulances and in wagons.

Lt. Col. Bell, the CO of the 89th FA, had arranged for a large supply of straw to be made available at the collecting post and another ten tons had arrived the previous evening to spread across a nearby field. Their stock of 7,000 blankets was soon in use by the men not requiring urgent surgical treatment and, after being fed, these men tried to sleep out in the open. Thankfully it was a warm and dry night. In the evening, a mixed party of bearers from the 1/1st South Midland FA and C Section, 89th FA., under Capt. J B Foubister, was sent to Knightsbridge via Vitermont. This left the Corps Collecting station short-handed and help was enlisted from the Divisional Reserve Company, Machine Gunners and the Divisional Band who were employed as stretcher bearers and to perform other necessary functions. With the despatch of Capts. Blandy and Morris to Mailly, the pressure on the 89th FA grew further.

It was clear from the later arrivals that the pressure had been telling on the units at the front. During the morning, all arrivals had arrived properly labelled and having had an anti-tetanus shot but, as the day drew on, more and more casualties arrived without a label and not having been injected. This piled more work onto the staff at Collecting Post who now had to properly record and label each new patient and then arrange the necessary injections. This process carried on throughout the night without a rest for the hard-pressed medical staff and they were grateful for the help of four Army chaplains who assisted in the feeding of the mass of men they were now accommodating.

Lt. Col. Bell's men were exhausted by the morning of the 2nd July and it was some relief to all when 25 men were obtained from other units. Access to the collecting post had been slow during the night as the road had become congested such was the number of horse drawn and motorised transport trying to deliver casualties. The men were dealt with as fast as possible and, nearly every hour, an ambulance train set off with a load of patients destined for Casualty Clearing Stations or the Base and General Hospitals in large towns or along the Channel coast. The evacuation by ambulance train was organised by Capt. Thomson who oversaw the shipping of 124 lying cases and 997 sitting cases by 8.30 p.m. on the night of the 1st July.

At midnight the numbers crammed into the collecting post and the neighbouring field were large: 135 lying cases, 1,555 sitting cases and, Lt. Col. Bell estimated, 2,000 more men sleeping in the field who had not yet been processed. By 11.10 p.m. the number of men Capt. Thomson had managed to get away by train had sharply increased to 246 lying and 1,739 sitting cases. A further 290 sitting cases had been sent on by requisitioned motor buses. In all, therefore, they had received and sent on 2,275 casualties in some 16 hours. Gratifyingly, given the numbers involved, there was only one death and that in the early hours of 2nd July[i].

Even though the numbers of men being dealt with were way beyond expectations, the sanitary, cooking and feeding arrangements survived the strain with the men being provided with anything from tea, cocoa, Bovril, Macconachie stew, porridge and milk pudding. There was also a constantly available supply of hot and cold milk. Hot drinks for those able to take them would become even more important during 2nd July as, at about 8 a.m., it started to rain and, with it, the temperature dropped.

Throughout the morning of the 2nd the numbers at the Collecting Post remained high. At 8.30 a.m. 98 lying cases and 1,901 sitting cases were awaiting evacuation. The number already evacuated as of 8 a.m. stood at:

By train: lying 442, sitting 3,102, total 3,544

By bus: sitting 490

Total: lying 442, sitting 3,592. Total 4,014

As the morning wore on, Lt. Col. Bell ordered up as a precaution more supplies of food, dressings and anti-tetanus serum although, by noon, the numbers waiting to be evacuated had declined to lying 70 and sitting 683.

By 7.30 p.m. the numbers evacuated had risen to well over 6,000.

By train: lying 756, sitting 5,061, total 5,817

By bus: sitting 490

Total: lying 756, sitting 5,551. Total 6,307

Bell had now managed to obtain 15 motor lorries through the good offices of the ADMS and these were sent off at 11 p.m. filled with walking and sitting cases to Gezaincourt.

Out in No Man's Land rescue parties were venturing further and further afield in a desperate effort to recover wounded men. One private from the 4th Worcesters eventually found an injured man close up to the front of the German wire. He was spotted from the enemy's trenches:

> "…a German officer (who must have been in the Staff by his dress) shouted to him 'you must not stop there with him, if you want to come in come along or else go back to your own trenches', the lad replied 'I'll go back to my own trenches, Sir'. Two stretcher bearers were sent out and brought in the wounded man. At this time the Germans were acting

[i] Three men are buried in Acheux Military Cemetery who died on 2nd July 1916. Two more died on the 3rd July.

> straight allowing our fellows to bring in the wounded from No Man's Land."[145]

A certain chivalry still existed on this blasted and blackened battlefield.

By the morning of the 3rd July the pressure had slackened significantly. Only small numbers of stretcher cases came in during the night and the MOs, working all night, were able to complete the dressing of all wounds. The convoy of lorries late the previous night had cleared the post of all sitting and walking cases and, by Monday morning, there were only 70 stretcher cases awaiting removal. As things quietened down time was taken to bury the five men who had died over the previous 24 hours.

By 11.30 a.m. a few more sitting cases had arrived and the total awaiting evacuation was lying 20 and sitting 73. The total evacuations now stood at 7,109.

By train: lying 1,064, sitting 5,318, total 6,382

By bus and motor lorry: sitting 727

Total: lying 1,064, sitting 6,045. Total 7,109

In addition to those evacuated under the auspices of the hard working Capt. Thomson another 1,469 walking cases from Clairfaye had been put on trains thereby increasing the total number of cases evacuated from Acheux by train to 7,851.

Meanwhile, in addition to overseeing the medical aspects of the post, Lt. Col. Bell had also been required to entertain the DDG, the DDMS VIII Corps, the DMS Fourth Army, Maj. Barclay Black RAMC, and an American newspaper correspondent, one Mr Palmer.

During the three days in which his men treated and evacuated the wounded Lt. Col. Lindsay was able to make a judgement about the wounds he had seen. For some, perhaps, hoping for a decent long term 'Blighty' wound, his impressions would not be regarded as especially good news:

> "My impression during the first three days of the battle enable me to say that quite 45% of the wounded should with proper care and attention be able to return to the fighting line in from 3 to 5 weeks. It was also observed that although our troops advanced under a perfect shower of shrapnel shell fire the proportion of head wounds were the lowest I have ever seen."[146]

He attributed this to the newly introduced Brodie helmets, however, Lt. Col. Lindsay's optimism about the wounded returning quickly to the ranks appears to have been sadly misplaced. A study of 116 wounded men of the 1st Newfoundland Regt. showed that 53% of them returned to the Western Front at some point during the next two years. The other 47% were either declared medically unfit or were given positions out of the front line at home or in the UK. Of those that returned to active service with the regiment just 3, or 3%, returned within the 3 to 5 week period. Another 13% (15) returned by the end of 1916 meaning just 16% returned within six months. Another 32% (37) returned in 1917 and a further 6% (7) by July 1918. How representative of the wounded this sample is one cannot be sure but it suggests that, when calculating permanent losses in action, one should always include a significant proportion of the wounded and not just those known to be dead.

By noon on the 3rd July, although wounded still crawled in or were found in No Man's Land for several days, the bulk of Lindsay's work was done. The 87th Field Ambulance had admitted, assessed, treated and evacuated 2,111 men.

Cases kept appearing at the collecting post over the next few days. They tended to be serious ones involving men who had been lying out in No Man's Land for three or four days. Maj. R O Spencer Smith, the 2iC of the 2nd Hampshires, recalled the continuing work to bring in casualties:

> "My battalion, 2nd Hampshires, continued to hold the front line for 10 days during which hundreds of dead and wounded were collected each night. The battalion had, I think, about 70 casualties during this 10 days which was a heavy toll considering they never left the trenches except for patrols and rescue parties.
>
> One wounded man crawled into our lines eight days after the attack having lain out in No Man's Land the whole time taking water and rations off his dead comrades. The ground was so pitted with shell holes and dry so that respectable cover could easily be found. This man had lost all sense of direction and time and thought he had only been out one night."[147]

Broadly speaking, however, the medical crisis on the VIII Corps' front was over by 3rd July, though the stench of the unburied dead would linger for weeks.

---

[1] Ibid.
[2] NA, WO95/406, *War Diary, 252nd Tunnelling Company, RE.*
[3] Ibid.
[4] NA, WO95/2298, *War Diary 86th Brigade.*
[5] NA, WO95/2291/3.
[6] NA, WO95/2287, *War Diary 29th Division CRA.*
[7] NA, WO95/483.
[8] NA, WO95/2280, *War Diary 29th Division.*
[9] Ibid.
[10] Ibid.
[11] NA, WO95/217.
[12] NA, WO95/2287.
[13] NA, WO95/2280.
[14] NA, WO95/820, *War Diary VIII Corps.*
[15] Ibid.
[16] Ibid.
[17] Ibid.
[18] NA, WO95/2280.
[19] Cramm, R, *The First Five Hundred,* C.F. Williams & Son, Inc., Albany, New York, p. 42.
[20] 88th Brigade Lists.
[21] NA, WO95/2280.
[22] NA, WO95/2303, *War Diary 87th Brigade.*
[23] NA, WO95/820.
[24] NA, WO95/2301, *War Diary, 1st Royal Dublin Fusiliers.*
[25] Ibid.
[26] Ibid.
[27] NA, WO95/2280.
[28] NA, WO95/820.

[29] NA, WO95/2280.
[30] Ibid.
[31] Ibid.
[32] NA, WO95/2298.
[33] NA, CAB45/133, *Comment on the Official History (OH) by Lt. Col. C G Fuller.*
[34] NA, WO95/2280.
[35] NA, WO95/820.
[36] NA, WO95/483.
[37] NA, WO 95/2292/2, *War Diary 147th Brigade, RFA.*
[38] NA, WO95/2280.
[39] NA, CAB45/137, *Comment on the OH by Lt. E W Sheppard.*
[40] NA, WO 95/2292/2.
[41] Ibid.
[42] NA, CAB45/137 *Comment on the OH by Lt. Col. R O Spencer Smith.*
[43] NA, CAB45/138, *Comment on the OH by Lt. A W Whitlock.*
[44] NA, WO 95/2292/2.
[45] *Somme Nord.*
[46] NA, CAB45/136, *Comment on the OH by Brig. Gen. H Nelson.*
[47] NA, WO95/2301.
[48] NA, CAB45/138, *Comment on the OH by Capt. F A Wilson.*
[49] Op. cit. *Nelson.*
[50] NA, WO95/2280.
[51] NA, WO95/2298.
[52] Ibid.
[53] NA, CAB45/134, *Comment on the OH by Brig. Gen. J Hamilton Hall.*
[54] Quoted by Reed, P. *Walking the Somme*, Pen & Sword Books, page 46.
[55] *Somme Nord.*
[56] NA, CAB45/132, *Comment on the OH by 2nd Lt. Ball, B Battery, RHA.*
[57] Ibid.
[58] NA, WO95/2302, *War Diary, 16th Middlesex Regt.*
[59] NA, WO95/820.
[60] Ibid.
[61] Op. cit. *Sheppard.*
[62] Ibid.
[63] NA, WO95/2300, *1st Lancashire Fusiliers.*
[64] Op. cit. *Sheppard.*
[65] NA, WO95/2298.
[66] NA, WO95/2280.
[67] Ibid.
[68] NA, WO95/2303
[69] NA, CAB45/133, *Comment on the OH by Lt. Col. A J Ellis.*
[70] NA, CAB45/137, *Comment on the OH by Maj. G T Raikes.*
[71] NA, WO95/2280.
[72] NA, WO95/2304, *War Diary, 2nd South Wales Borderers.*
[73] Op. cit. *Raikes.*
[74] NA, WO95/2304.
[75] Ibid.
[76] NA, WO95/2303.
[77] NA, WO95/820.
[78] Op. cit. *Ellis.*
[79] Ibid.
[80] NA, CAB45/136, *Comment on the OH by Maj. J R Meiklejohn.*

[81] NA, WO95/2305, *War Diary 1st Border Regt.*
[82] NA, WO95/2305, *War Diary 1st Inniskilling Fusiliers.*
[83] NA, WO95/2280.
[84] NA, CAB45/134, *Comment on the OH by Capt. I C Grant.*
[85] NA, CAB45/136, *Comment on the OH by Capt. G H Moberly.*
[86] NA, WO95/2304, *War Diary 1st Royal Inniskllіng Fusiliers.*
[87] NA, WO95/2308, *War Diary, 1st Newfoundland Regt.* Malcolm's report is to the Adjutant, 1st KOSB. A copy is in the Newfoundland diary because of its reference to their advance.
[88] *De Ruvigny's Roll of Honour,* Volume 3, page 62.
[89] NA, WO95/2280.
[90] Ibid.
[91] Ibid.
[92] NA, WO95/2304, *War Diary, 1st King's Own Scottish Borderers.*
[93] NA, WO95/820.
[94] Ibid.
[95] NA, WO95/2280.
[96] NA, WO95/2305
[97] NA, WO95/2304.
[98] NA, WO95/2280.
[99] Ibid.
[100] NA, WO95/820.
[101] NA, CAB45/132, *Comment on the OH by Lt. Col. S W W Blacker.*
[102] NA, WO95/2505, *War Diary 9th Royal Irish Fusiliers.*
[103] Ibid.
[104] Ibid.
[105] Ibid.
[106] NA, WO95/2506, *War Diary, 12th Royal Irish Rifles.*
[107] *Somme Nord.*
[108] NA, WO95/2280.
[109] NA, WO95/820.
[110] NA, WO95/2309, *War Diary 1st Essex Regt.*
[111] NA, WO95/2308.
[112] Ibid.
[113] NA, WO95/820.
[114] Op. cit. *Ball.*
[115] NA, CAB45/136, *Lt. Col. H Marriott Smith.*
[116] Op. cit. *Spencer Smith.*
[117] NA, WO95/2308.
[118] Harding, R J A, *'Glorious Tragedy: Newfoundland's Cultural Memory of the Battle of Beaumont Hamel 1916-1949'.* MA Thesis, Dalhousie University, Halifax, Nova Scotia, 2004.
[119] NA, WO95/820.
[120] NA, WO95/2309.
[121] NA, CAB45/136, *Comment on the OH by Maj. G A Mackay Paxton.*
[122] NA, WO95/820.
[123] NA, WO95/2306, *War Diary 88th Brigade.*
[124] NA, WO95/2305.
[125] NA, CAB45/134, *Comment on the OH by Capt. G V Goodliffe.*
[126] *The Royal Fusiliers in the Great War.*
[127] NA, WO95/820.
[128] NA, WO95/4312, *War Diary 4th Worcestershire Regt.*
[129] NA, WO95/2306.
[130] NA, WO95/2309/7.

[131] NA, WO95/820.
[132] Op. Cit. *Hamilton Hall.*
[133] Ibid.
[134] NA, WO95/4312.
[135] NA, WO95/820.
[136] Whitehead, R, *The Other Side of the Wire, Vol. 2*, Helion, 2013. Compiled from casualty CD.
[137] Op. cit. *Goodliffe.*
[138] NA, WO95/2296/2, *War Diary, 88th Field Ambulance.*
[139] Ibid.
[140] Ibid.
[141] Ibid.
[142] Ibid.
[143] Ibid.
[144] NA, WO95/2269/1, *War Diaray 87th Field Ambulance.*
[145] NA, WO95/4312.
[146] NA, WO95/2269/1.
[147] Op. cit. *Spencer Smith.*

8. THE 4TH DIVISION AT REDAN RIDGE

REDAN RIDGE WAS THE NAME GIVEN TO THE PLATEAU that separates Serre to the north from Beaumont Hamel to the south and was the key to the defence of both positions. The ridge was mainly in German hands and had been since the fighting of the autumn of 1914. The main body of the plateau is a large flat, featureless expanse of farmland. Now it is littered with small and difficult to access CWGC cemeteries, some from the fighting of July 1916, others from the second effort to take Beaumont Hamel, Redan Ridge and Serre in the snow and freezing cold of November 1916[i]. Then, Beaumont Hamel and Beaucourt station fell. Not so Redan Ridge and Serre. Serre would be attacked again by the 31st Division with the same costly results. On 12th November, Redan Ridge was the objective of the 2nd Division. After fierce fighting in appalling conditions into which elements of the 37th Division and the whole of the 32nd Division were involved, the first German position, including the Heidenkopf, was prised from German hands. Attacks on Munich Trench failed, however, and, on 18th November the offensive, and the Somme battle, technically came to an end. That the fighting locally did not stop was due to the heroic defence of a small section of Frankfurt Trench, deep behind the German front line. Here a small party of the 16th Highland Light Infantry, 11th Border Regt. and 2nd KOYLI, completely cut off from their colleagues, held out for eight days in the freezing weather against repeated German attacks before overwhelming force, a lack of water and food and 90% casualties amongst the officers and men forced their surrender on 25th November.

The ground across which these men fought, that is the heart of the Redan Ridge plateau, is more or less completely flat. It drops very slowly away to the east and, on its southern flank, is cut by several dry valleys which run away into the Ancre valleys, valleys which proved to be a valuable hiding place for most of the artillery of the German 26. Reserve Division. Towards the western end of the plateau its shoulders drop away to north and south whilst a narrowing strip of land continues westwards, across the German front line and No Man's Land, through the British front line and on towards the Euston to Auchonvillers Road. It is across this area, the 'throat' of the ridge, that the two front lines came closest and it is here that the Germans placed the formidable Ridge Redoubt. On the other side of No Man's Land, the British inherited the redan which gave the ridge its name, originally constructed by the French opposite this German stronghold. Extensive mining and counter-mining had taken place between the redoubt and the redan, with both sides busily trying to get under the other's front line trenches. The result, along the narrow strip of No Man's Land that separated the combatants, was an area scarred by numerous small and large craters which was, as a result, difficult for infantry to cross en masse.

Just off the northern shoulder of the ridge was the Heidenkopf, or Quadrilateral as it was known to the British. This small salient was a vestige of

[i] There was an attack made astride the Ancre on 3rd September involving the 39th Division on the northern bank and the 49th Division on the southern bank. Both attacks failed.

the old German front line which had run northwest towards Hebuterne before the French attacks of June 1915 had driven in the German line to its current position. Now, this area of trenches which projected out into No Man's Land, was a difficult to defend, low lying system overlooked by the British trenches and, as a result, hugely vulnerable to attack. This point had been accepted by the Germans who had constructed a surprise for any attacking troops by digging four mines out into No Man's Land which were designed to blow the advancing enemy sky high. As it turns out, through a combination of circumstances, these mines would prove less effective than hoped and, as a tactic, were later thought hardly worth the effort of the German miners and Pioniers.

There was one aspect of the Heidenkopf which did not become truly apparent until the day of the attack and which worked to the advantage of the attackers. At its north west corner, where No Man's Land was very narrow, an area of partially 'dead ground' existed, that is terrain which could not be swept by the machine guns positioned in the Ridge Redoubt. Though vulnerable to fire from the north, i.e. around Serre, this combination of proximity to the British front line and relative protection from the heavy fire from the south would allow reserves and supplies to reach the British troops in and around the Heidenkopf, thus sustaining them in their captured trenches for many hours.

South of the Ridge Redoubt and to its front, however, the view over the British trenches was complete. Machine guns in the redoubt could not only take in enfilade any troops attacking to the south of the crater field, they could also see and, therefore, fire deep into the territory behind the British front line making any support troops advancing over the open horribly vulnerable to the concentrated fire of these guns. The southern end of the 4th Division's position was also exposed to fire from the higher ground north of Beaumont Hamel, technically on the front of the German RIR 119. German machine gun teams, however, were trained to make independent decisions about targets and regimental, divisional and Corps boundaries meant nothing if there were attacking troops to be destroyed.

On the northern side of the ridge, the troops of the 4th Division would be open to enfilade fire if the attack of the 31st Division were to fail. As the instructions from Hunter Weston were for successful units to advance come what may, this meant that, were the 4th Division to succeed and others on either flank fail, they might well find themselves in a highly exposed position from which it might prove difficult to withdraw. It was known that there were enemy machine guns setback just in front of Serre which, if deprived of targets on their immediate front, could, and would, cause havoc amongst the left supporting battalions of the 4th Division as they swept forward to take the Zwischen Stellung and the German 2nd Position. What no-one could predict, however, was the speed at which the attacks of both the 31st and 29th Divisions would fail and, with Corps instructing troops to advance to a set timetable rather than to the tactical requirements of the actual attack, these failures would lead to supporting battalions of the 4th Division becoming the main targets of enemy machine guns from Beaumont Hamel to Serre from very early in the day.

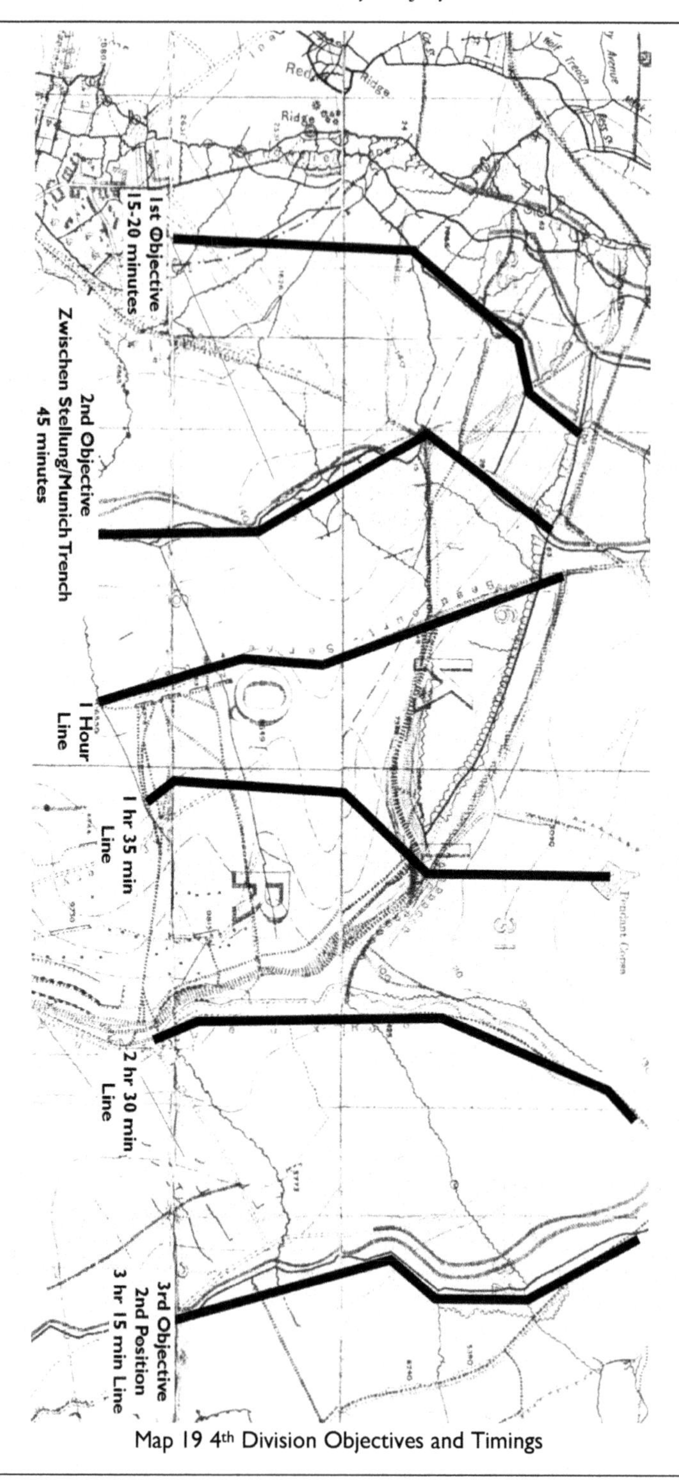

Map 19 4th Division Objectives and Timings

The details and timetable for the 4th Division's attack were set out in Operation Order No. 38, dated 18th June. It was an ambitious programme and much would depend on the success of the neighbouring Divisions.

The basic concept was that the initial attack would be delivered by the four battalions of the 11th Brigade reinforced by two battalions borrowed from the 143rd Brigade of the 48th Division. These units were split into two attacking groups each of three battalions and the first would take the first objective – Serre and Beaumont Trenches – in a time of between 15 and 20 minutes depending on the distance to be travelled (i.e. there was a greater distance to travel on the left, northern, wing of the Division). The second group would then move through these battalions to take the second objective which was the Zwischen Stellung or Munich Trench, as it was known to the British. This line was to be taken in 45 minues, i.e. at 8.15 a.m.

The first objectives was the to be the target of, from right to left, the 1st East Lancashire Regt., the 1st Rifle Brigade and the 1/8th Royal Warwickshire Regt. from the 143rd Brigade[i]. The men of the Rifle Brigade would have the tricky job of taking on the Ridge Redoubt while the Warwicks dealt with the Heidenkopf and the trenches up to the Divisional boundary of Ten Tree Alley. Once successfully established they were to send bombing parties to left and right in order to join hands with the Divisions on either flank. Six strong points were also to be established with material brought up by later carrying parties. Behind them, men of the Pioneers and the Royal Engineers would set to joining up the British and captured German trenches, to laying trench bridges to allow the movement forward of certain 18 pdr artillery batteries and to start the process of creating roadways forward for supplies and ammunition.

At this point, the artillery barrage should have moved forward to bombard the 2nd objective, the Zwischen Stellung while, from the British trenches, the second wave of the attack moved up and through the first to capture this line of German trenches. The battalions involved in this advance were, again from right to left, the 1st Hampshire Regt., the 1st Somerset Light Infantry and the 1/6th Royal Warwickshire Regt. Once again, after occupying the trenches they were to send bombers to left and right and start on building another six strongpoints at intervals along the captured trenches. The guns would now have moved forward to barrage the line of the Beaucourt to Serre road on the far side of which on the right flank of the attack were several German battery positions. At one hour thirty minutes after zero, i.e. 9 a.m., a special party was to be sent forward to capture any surviving guns while the British artillery moved onto its next firing line. At the same time, special parties were to be sent forward to cut gaps in the wire running north-south between the Beaucourt-Serre Road and the Puisieux Road further east.

Meanwhile, behind the 11th Brigade, the men of the 10th and 12th Brigades would be moving forward in order to be ready to advance on the German 2nd Position at 9.30 a.m., the 4th Divisions 3rd and final objective. The dividing line between these two Brigades ran due east from a point just to the north of the Ridge Redoubt and thence along a track which ran east from the Zwischen

[i] Operation Order No. 38 actually has the 1/6th Warwicks leading the attack but this was an error.

Stellung, across the Beaucourt-Serre Road until it reach the far end of Ten Tree Alley. At 8.45 a.m. the leading elements of these battalions were to push out strong patrols beyond the line reached by 11th Brigade. At 9.30 a.m. the two lead battalions of each Brigade were to start the advance beyond the Zwischen Stellung while, behind them, the remaining four battalions set out for the British front line. As with all of these advances within the British position, these men were to advance above ground rather than along the communication trenches. The four lead battalions were, on the right, 2nd Royal Dublin Fusiliers and the 2nd Seaforth Highlanders (10th Brigade) and, on the left, the 1st King's Own Royal Lancaster Regt., and the 2nd Essex Regt. At Zero + 2 hours and 40 minutes these troops were to arrive at the line of the Puisieux Road, extending north to Pendant Copse.

The heavy artillery and any guns of the field artillery able to reach it were now pounding the 3rd objective, the German 2nd Position. This was to be assaulted at 10.45 a.m. and, once taken, contact was to be eastablished with the neighbouring Divisions, work was to start on another six strongpoints and strong patrols were to move to the Puisieux to Baillescourt Road where advanced OPs were to be established. As the battalions of the 10th and 12th Brigades would be advancing into areas which could not be observed from the British trenches they were all equipped with a supply of red rockets. Should they encounter difficulties and need help then the SOS signal was the firing of five of these devices. These rockets should, therefore, not only call down an artillery barrage to the east of the troops' position but would also give an idea as to how far the men of the Division had advanced. As has already been seen on the 29th Division's front, the use of red rockets would cause more problems than they solved.

The maximum distance to be travelled by the men of the Division was 4,000 yards and they were given three hours and fifteen minutes to achieve all of their objectives.

AS EVERYWHERE ON THE FOURTH ARMY FRONT, the prospects for success depended almost entirely on the success of the artillery preparation. In certain places there were aspects of the defences and of the terrain, for example the Heidenkopf, which allowed for a certain degree of success come what may but, if the German trenches were not flattened and the dugout entrances at least blocked or, better still, the dugouts collapsed then, in the main, there was very little prospect of success. As everywhere on the VIII Corps front, however, very little use was made of the medium and heavy howitzers on the German front line. Whilst cutting the forward wire was an 18 pdr field gun and 2 in. trench mortar task so, it seems, was it their role to bombard the German front line trench. The inadequate weight of metal deposited on these trenches would cost the infantry dear. And, of course, the same insane decision to shift the heavy weapons involved in the last 65 minute intense bombardment prior to the attack from the front line trench ten minutes before zero and from the support trench five minutes before zero applied on 4th Division's front as much as it did around the Hawthorn Redoubt away to the south.

The 4th Division's field artillery consisted of only eight batteries of 18 pdr field guns unlike the twelve batteries for each of the other two Divisions. To compensate for this reduced number, each of the batteries was equipped with six

18 pdr guns rather than the normal four. All three divisions, therefore, were able to deploy forty eight 18 pdrs. The field howitzer batteries of the 4th Division contained the regulation four 4.5 in. howitzers.

The field artillery was organised into three groups: Left, Centre and Right. Each group was allocated a sector of the German front due east of their positions. In addition, two 18 pdr batteries from the 48th (South Midland) Division were dug in just 500 yards behind the British front line. Their task was to bombard and barrage the Zwischen Stellung prior to the attack as the range was too great for the other 18 pdr batteries. As it turned out, neither of these two batteries came into action. Another 18 pdr battery of the 14th Brigade, RFA, was dug in 1,200 yards behind the front line and this was to be employed in cutting some of the more distant wire, i.e. that in front of the German 2nd position, which, again, was out of the effective range of the other 18 pdr batteries. This battery started to fire on V Day, the second day of the bombardment. The roles of the 18 pdr batteries of the Left and Centre groups, supplemented by one from the Right group, were wire cutting by day and barrages to block communications at night. The Right group (minus the one battery) fired at night and was specially detailed to keep open the lanes cut during the day and to disrupt communications by periodic concentrations on selected points in the rear areas of the German position. Each evening, the OCs of the Left and Centre groups advised the OC, Right group, of the lanes cut so that he might direct his fire accordingly. The 4.5 in. howitzers were used to bombard selected points – OPs, suspected machine gun positions, trench junctions, etc., – and to assist in the various barrages put down during the day and night.

The 2 in. toffee apple trench mortars of the Divisional Trench Mortar batteries were to cut the wire in front of the first trench and to bombard the forward positions. The heavy 240 mm trench mortars, the 'flying pigs', were all to bombard the northern end of Beaumont Hamel and the trenches immediately to the north of the village. Two batteries of the 32nd Brigade, RFA, the 134th and 135th, which were firing at the greatest range from the German trenches, would come out of action at 10 p.m. on the night before the assault and be ready to advance as quickly as possible to new forward positions from where they could be brought into action against the German 2nd Position before the infantry assault. Then, by stages, the rest of the 32nd Brigade, followed by the 29th Brigade, RFA, would be taken out of action as the attack progressed, ready to be brought forward and put in a position to defend the newly won German 2nd Position.

On the day of the attack an artillery officer was to be attached to each Infantry Brigade HQ and he, along with an NCO and some signallers, were to go forward with each infantry battalion. In addition, Forward Observation Officers, or FOOs, were to set up OPs in the German Zwischen Stellung as soon as it was occupied. With them would go parties of visual signallers.

A large stockpile of ammunition of all sorts was dumped at Bertrancourt in early June. It consisted of:

45,000 18 pdr shrapnel
15,000 18 pdr HE
12,600 4.5 in. How HE
500 (SK) Lachrymatory shells

1,200 4.7 in. HE
1,600 6 in. How 30 cwt.
800 6 in. How 26 cwt.
200 240 mm bombs (French)
1,000,000 SAA
10,000 2 in. bombs of 50 lbs. each
16,000 Stokes bombs
5,000 No. 3 and No. 10 rifle grenades
40,000 Mills grenades
Red, green and white rockets, red flares, roman candles

This ammunition was not all to be used for the initial assault and some, indeed an increasing amount, was kept back for further activities as higher command anticipated a further advance east and north east. Each field gun and howitzer was to have an immediate supply of 1,000 rounds placed in shell proof dumps at the battery position. In addition, 4,000 2 in. bombs, 16,000 Stokes bombs and 100 240 mm bombs had to be transported from the dump at Bertrancourt to the area bounded by the Quarry – Euston – Tenderloin – White City near to the Sucrerie to Auchonvillers Road. These were to be shifted between the 11th and 20th June. All such work had to be done after 10 p.m. and before 2.30 a.m. so as to avoid too much interference from the German artillery.

During the bombardment itself, ammunition was constantly supplied by the 4th Divisional Ammunition Column to the battery positions and, given the number of trips required and the distance travelled to and from the guns, the casualties suffered by the men of the 4th DAC were surprisingly light. Three men were wounded on the 27th and 28th June but on that day an incident occurred which highlighted the dangerous work the men of the Ammunition Columns undertook and the bravery it often required. A horsed wagon from No. 2 Section came under artillery fire as it attempted to take a wagon load of shells to a battery position. A shell fell close by, killing one of the men, 41673 Dvr. Walter Hammond[i], and wounding another, Dvr. Kirby. In addition, two of the six horses were killed and another two wounded. A third man, 22021 Dvr. Richard Hindle[ii], got the casualties, human and equine, away, re-harnessed the two remaining horses and, under continuous shell fire, coolly proceeded to deliver the ammunition.

Prior to this, the men of the Divisional Field Artillery had to labour hard throughout early and mid-June to prepare their gun pits, ammunition and personnel dugouts and communications. All too often, materials were hard to come by, especially suitable wood. Unlike the Germans, who as an occupying

[i] 41673 Dvr. Walter Hammond, No. 2 Section, 4th Divisional Ammunition Column, was aged 29. He was the son of Edward Hammond; husband of Amy Hammond, of 11, Maythorne Cottages, Hither Green, Lewisham, London. Born at Cambridge, Haverhill. He is buried in Sucrerie Military Cemetery, Colincamps, grave I. I. 75.

[ii] Dvr. Hindle was awarded the DCM. The citation in the *London Gazette* of the 18th August 1916 reads: 22021 Dvr. Richard Hindle RFA. For conspicuous gallantry. When driving ammunition along a heavily-shelled road one man and two horses were killed. Driver Hindle coolly removed the man and horses, readjusted his harness and proceeded to the guns, where he delivered his ammunition.

power commandeered whatever supplies and manpower they needed, the B.E.F. had to negotiate with local farmers and landowners for materials. Some were more forthcoming than others.

One of the key components of their work was the installation of a robust, hopefully shell-proof, communications system. A good and comprehensive system was designed but, according to the CRA of 4th Division, Brig. Gen. Cyril Prescott-Decie, there was simply not enough cable to complete the network. The system that was completed, however, did survive throughout the attack even if some of the messages passed along it were of doubtful quality. The lac of sufficient cable was not the only problem, however, as the trenches dug to conceal and protect the cable were supposed to contain all of the various telephone lines required by Corps, Division and Brigade and by the heavy and field artillery. Lt. Col. Norman Eccles Tilney, CO, 29th Brigade, RFA, may have been feeling somewhat jaundiced by the loss of ten men from his 127th Battery when a 15 cm shell hit their position, but his comment in the War Diary of the 23rd June suggests some chaos in the Corps' staff arrangements for these communications:

> "While the Brigade were digging gun pits and OPs, etc., cable trenches for the communications of the whole division were being dug under Corps' arrangements. The principle being to minimise digging as far as possible and allowing the Corps, Divisions and other units to have cables in the same trench. This scheme did not work, for as soon as the Corps cables were laid in a trench that trench was filled in whether the other units who, under the scheme, were entitled to use that trench, had their cables in or not! These remarks apply equally to smaller formations, e.g. Divisions, infantry Brigades."[1]

The Divisional trench mortars too needed 'comms' and these had to be run up very close to the front line give these weapons short range. The Divisional trench mortars comprised five batteries of 2 in. medium mortars firing the famous 'toffee apple' bombs and two batteries of 240 mm heavy mortar. Known as the 'flying pig', this mortar had been designed by the French company Dumezil-Batignolles in 1915 and, being built under licence in the UK, they were only now coming into service with the B.E.F. They arrived, or sometimes failed to arrive, in the run up to or during the course of the bombardment. Each 2 in. mortar had a total ammunition supply of 500 bombs of which 150 were dumped with each gun, 75 each at the Quarry and the Roman Road forward dumps and the remaining 200 at Bertrancourt. For the 240 mm trench mortars the ammunition allowance for each gun was 100 rounds. Each round weighed 69 Kgs (nearly 11 stone) and it took its seven man team some six minutes to load and fire each one of these beasts.

In addition, each Brigade had Trench Mortar Batteries equipped with eight Stokes light trench mortars. The Stokes batteries had a supply of 480 bombs of which a minimum of 300, and preferably 400, were to be with each gun and the balance split between the two forward dumps. The bulk of the Stokes bombs were to be fired during the final ten minute intensive bombardment, though some guns were to go forward with the attacking troops where they performed with varying but all too often very brief results.

In total, therefore, and assuming all of the 240 mm (or 9.45 in. as the British designated it) mortars arrived in time the 4th Division would be able to dispose of:

8 x 240 mm trench mortars with 800 rounds (100/gun);

20 x 2 in. trench mortars with 10,000 rounds (500/gun); and

33 x Stokes light trench mortars with 16,000 rounds (480/gun).

On paper, at least, it was a formidable concentration of firepower.

Life for a member of a trench mortar gun team was one of the least pleasant on the Western Front. Because of their short range they were always placed in or near to the front line trench where they were often quickly identified by the enemy opposite. As a result, they were the regular targets of German trench mortars and artillery making their location extremely dangerous and their presence amongst the local infantry extremely unpopular. Finding themselves more or less alone in the front lines when firing was in progress was a constant complaint from the gun teams as, understandably, the neighbouring troops moved as far away as possible in order to avoid the inevitable and heavy enemy response[i].

AS EVERYWHERE ALONG THE FOURTH ARMY FRONT, the bombardment started on the morning of the 24th June with the 18 pdr batteries and 2 in. trench mortars concentrating on wire cutting. The areas given to the field batteries were quite large. The 14th Brigade, RFA, had two batteries cutting wire and one 4.5 in howitzer battery bombarding selected points. The 18 pdr batteries tasks were:

68th Battery – the wire in front of the German 1st, 2nd, 3rd and 4th trenches from the area immediately to the north of Beaumont Hamel to the centre of the Ridge Redoubt. This is a frontage of 600 yards;

88th Battery – the wire in front of Munich Trench from Point 53, just north of the Beaucourt Road, to Point 15, where it starts to run parallel and just to the west of Wagon Road, a frontage of 1,000 yards;

The 86th Battery of field howitzers was to bombard strongpoints and trench junctions in the entire area covered by the two 18 pdr batteries, an area approximately 1,000 yards deep by 650 yards wide.

The 29th Brigade was to perform the same functions starting from the northern boundary of the 14th Brigade's area up to Ten Tree Alley.

For wire cutting purposes the idea was to attempt to sweep away all wire in front of the German 1st trench and then to cut a 5 yard wide lane every 20 yards in all other wire up to an including Munich Trench. In addition, the 128th Howitzer Battery was to perform the same function as the 86th Battery within its area of responsibility. The 29th Brigade's war diary noted on the 24th June that:

> "None of the wire to be cut by the Brigade, except the portions of front line wire allotted, could be seen from any part of the trenches so an aeroplane was allotted to the Brigade nominally for 2 hours daily. Owing to weather this plane could not observe today."[2]

---

[i] Unfortunately, no records remain of the activities of the 4th Divisional Trench Mortar Batteries, however, there are detailed accounts for the 31st Division which give a very good indication of the trials and tribulations of the men of the trench mortar batteries. These are included in the chapter describing the 31st Division's attack on Serre.

The batteries, delayed by the weather, opened fire at 9 a.m. firing first on the more distant of their targets but they were hampered by the frequent showers and resulting poor visibility.

The 32nd Brigade, RFA, from which the 68th and 86th Batteries had been detached and attached to the 14th Brigade, were to use their remaining guns to cut wire to the rear of the Ridge Redoubt and to fire at night on those areas where the wire had been cut during the day by the other two Brigades.

All three Brigades were to participate in a ten minute shrapnel barrage on the German front line at 10 p.m. which was due to coincide with a release of 'Dresden', that night's code word for gas.

Behind the lines the voluntary evacuation of French civilians still living in Mailly Maillet had started the day before. Now, as the guns started firing, this task was completed.

The day was sultry with thunder never far away. The East Lancashires spent the middle of the day training on the practice ground at Louvencourt, returning to their camp at 1.30 p.m. The war diary records that:

"... the men are still very tired and have to be worked very lightly."[3]

Concerns were also expressed about the shortage of officers available for the assault. Two officers, Capt. H T MacMullen and Lt. Scott, had been sent off to Paris to give evidence in the case against a battalion officer, 2nd Lt. Harold Vincent, who was to be tried for absence without leave in April 1916 amongst other offences. Two other officers, Capt. Richards and Lt. Cyril Watson were away at the Third Army School and an application for their urgent return was sent in. Watson would return and be killed on 1st July.

The gas discharge, when it came, was something of a fiasco. Gas canisters containing White Star[i] had been brought up the men of the Special Brigade, RE, commanded by Lt. Jones. They were placed in the front line trench then occupied by the 1st Royal Warwickshire Regt in sectors 4 to 7 in K34, the area between the Heidenkopf and the Ridge Redoubt. The wind was variable as the time for the release drew near but it was deemed sufficient both in speed and direction for a safe release of the gas. Just after 10 p.m., the taps were turned and the gas leaked slowly from the nozzles on the parapet. On the slight westerly breeze it drifted towards and over the German lines, the chlorine bleaching the grass white as it went. As per the German artillery plan, any discharge of gas (or smoke, as it was not possible to tell the difference) was the signal for an artillery barrage on the British front line trenches. Some longer range German guns searched the rear areas and the villages where the British infantry was billeted. In response to red rockets and white flares, salvoes of 5.9s, 4.2s and 77 mm 'whizz bangs' started to fall on the Warwicks and Royal Engineers causing heavy casualties. The minenwerfers then joined in the fun. At about 10.30 p.m. a cylinder in the British front trench was hit by a shell fragment and started to leak. To make matters worse, at 10.45 p.m. the breeze veered to the ESE and some of the gas started to move back towards the British lines. Lt. Jones immediately turned off the remaining cylinders but some of his men were badly gassed and he was wounded.

---

[i] A mixture of 50% chlorine and 50% phosgene.

Fortunately, the men of the Warwicks had donned their gas helmets soon after the start of the discharge but, otherwise, the night was something of a disaster. Two officers were killed, 2nd Lts. Charles Lukey[i] and James Gamble[ii], two more wounded, 2nd Lts. Arthur Clifford Giles and Leslie Beresford Pugh, while 10 other ranks were killed, 51 wounded and 31 sent to hospital suffering the effects of gas. Although the German artillery kept up their barrage until 12.15 a.m., with gas lingering at the bottom of the trench, it was another two hours before the front line trench could be re-occupied by the Warwicks. There was then a lot of work to do as the damage to the trenches was considerable. This was unfortunate as the Warwicks had been occupying the Divisional front since 18th June where they had been working extremely hard to ready the front lines for the attack. This had not been helped when, on 22nd June, the Germans dumped fifteen heavy trench mortar shells into C Company's sector[iii]. After this, and with the heavy work load made worse by the poor weather, the war diary confided that the older men of the battalion were 'very tired after nine days shelling and gas'.

The casualties caused by the gas discharge did not just fall on the RE and Warwicks. The 2nd Seaforth Highlanders were billeted in Mailly Maillet and, as the German bombardment tailed off at about 1.30 a.m., two 5.9 in shells fell near the battalion's bivouacs. The firing was too close for comfort and the men were formed up to march out into the countryside. A third 5.9 then fell amongst the Battalion Scouts and men of C Company. The effect was devastating. 14 men were killed instantly and another 34 were wounded, six of whom died of their wounds. Only three of the Battalion Scouts survived and 2nd Lt. Harrison, OC Scouts, had to rapidly select and train a group of men to perform this function. Two sergeants, 9377 Sgt. Hugh Hendry[iv] of the Scouts and 8163 Sgt. John Wood[v] of C Company, were amongst the dead buried on the eastern edge of Mailly Wood the same night. The following day, the 4th Division's War Diary would blithely describe the night's events as a 'successful action by ourselves'.

---

[i] 2nd Lt. Charles Ximines Lukey, 1st Royal Warwickshire Regt., was aged 36. He was the son of Edward and Ellen Mary Lukey of Dover. He fought in the South African War as a Private in the 33rd (Royal East Kent) Squadron, 1st Battalion, Imperial Yeomanry. He was a Squadron Quartermaster Sergeant with the 4th (Royal Irish) Dragoon Guards and was commissioned into the Royal Warwickshire Regt. on 16th February 1916. He was buried in Auchonvillers Military Cemetery, grave II. B. 4.

[ii] 2nd Lt. James Frederick Gamble, 1st Royal Warwickshire Regt. was aged 25. He was the son of Joseph Frederick and the late Sarah Mary Gamble, née Punch, died 1893, of 86 Park Crescent, North Shields, Northumberland; nephew and adopted son of Charles William and Mary Elizabeth Simmons, of York. Born at Middlesbrough, he was the assistant surveyor at York Corporation. He attended the RMC Sandhurst, passing out top of 148 candidates, before being commissioned into the Royal Warwickshire Regt. in June 1915. He was buried in Auchonvillers Military Cemetery, grave II. B. 5.

[iii] Fortunately, casualties were light. One man, 1373 Pte J Botterill, died of wounds and he is buried in Gezaincourt Communal Cemetery Extension, grave I. E. 1.

[iv] 9377 Sgt. Hugh Kelso Hendry, 2nd Seaforth Highlanders, was aged 31. He was the son of James and Margaret Hendry, of 11, Morrison St., Govan, Glasgow; husband of the late Sarah Procter Hendry. He is buried in Mailly Wood Cemetery, Mailly Maillet, grave I. A. 1.

[v] 8163 Sgt. John Wood, 2nd Seaforth Highlanders, is buried in Mailly Wood Cemetery, Mailly Maillet, grave I. A. 3.

One of the less dramatic events of the day was the opening of the Divisional trench tramway, known rather precisely by the 1/1st Renfrew Field Company, RE, as the Decauville railway. This system came into the Divisional sector from Mailly Maillet with the line dividing a few hundred yards west of the Sucrerie to Auchonvillers road, with one branch heading south east and the other north east towards the Mailly to Serre Road. The southern branch divided again immediately to the east of the Sucrerie-Auchonvillers Road with a track running towards the rear of the White City. The northern branch re-joined the track running parallel to and just south of the Mailly-Serre Road immediately to the east of Elles Square where one branch continued into the rear of the northern end of the Division's front and another, turning back on itself, returned to the Sucrerie running alongside a trench called Roman Road. It would become a target for German gunners but also a significant means of getting supplies and ammunition in to the sector and, from 1st July onwards, casualties out.

THE 25TH JUNE WAS A SLIGHTLY BETTER DAY weather-wise than the previous one and the artillery were able to fire with a degree of observation from the BE2cs of the R.F.C. The system employed was for the batteries to fire in turn on pre-arranged areas of wire so that the observer could send down corrections to their length. The 29th Brigade, RFA, was allocated two hours, from noon to 2 p.m., to work with an aircraft with each battery taking it in turns to fire on a pre-determined section of wire. It was a system that seemed to work quite well but, of course, the more the 18 pdrs fired and heated up, the less accurate would be their unadjusted fire so, once the aircraft moved on, they were very much on their own again. And, on only the second day, wear to the barrels and hydraulics and other issues was beginning to take teir toll. The 86th Battery of the 14th Brigade suffered a premature and the 126th Battery of the 29th Brigade already had one gun with a worn piston rod.

The batteries of the 29th Brigade had been given an allocation of 900 rounds per day per 18 pdr battery, i.e. 225 rounds per gun, and 240 rounds per day per howitzer battery, i.e. 60 rounds per gun. The number of shells actually fired was:

125th Battery (18 pdr) – 1020 shrapnel;
126th Battery (18 pdr) – 780 shrapnel, 76 HE;
127th Battery (18 pdr) – 821 shrapnel, 55 HE; and
128th Battery (How.) – 348 HE

For all concerned, firing this number of shells for this long was a novel experience and no-one was quite sure how the guns and their gun teams would react to the pressure.

With the heavy guns still yet to enter the fray, German casualties were light, however, one shell exploded near to Hauptmann Hans Freiherr von Ziegesar, the OC of the I Bataillon, RIR 121, as he observed the effects of the bombardment. Severely wounded, he was rushed back along the medical evacuation route to Reserve-Feld-Lazaret Nr. 1 at Bapaume. His wounds were too severe and he died the following day. His place in charge of the I Bataillon was taken by Hptm. Winter.

To the rear, the infantry not occupying the trenches was involved in training either in particular skills or, like the 1st Royal Irish Fusiliers, over the training ground prepared at Louvencourt. Every division had attempted to identify some ground which shared similarities with that over which they were to attack and then, using tapes, the various German trenches had been indicated. Then, whilst Brigade, Division and Corps officers observed, the men marched across the field carrying pennants to indicate their current position. Today, before the Fusiliers got started, there was a short delay as six German aircraft droned overhead, a rare occurrence on the Western Front at this time given the Allies' overwhelming air superiority. But then the marching and counter-marching got under way until the observing officers were all sharply brought to attention as a party of men galloped up. The Corps commander, Sir Aylmer Hunter-Weston, had come calling. 'Hunter Bunter' was a flamboyant little man who had an eye for the dramatic entrance (and exit) and usually exuded confident good cheer. Now he congratulated the CO of the Fusiliers, Lt. Col. William Findlater, on the fine body of men that was his command and directed him to pass on his best wishes to the men for the forthcoming attack. He expressed the greatest pleasure that the battalion should be under his command as he recalled well them being on his left during the fighting around Messines when he was GOC, 11th Brigade in 1914. With that he remounted and galloped off followed by his Staff, keen to bring some sunshine into another unit's life.

Gas was again discharged during the night but this time without the heavy casualties suffered the night before. The gas was released at 2.30 a.m. in the early morning of the 26th June and, initially, it hung around the British front line. After 30 minutes the white cloud drifted slowly across No Mans' Land carried by a light 3 mph breeze. Then, like the previous night, having blown over the German trenches, it then blew back but the British gas helmets seemed to work. Although the German severely bombarded the trenches, especially the support line, the casualties were moderate. The 1st Warwicks lost two officers, Capt. Richard Horace Baily and 2nd Lt. Henry Thomas Elliott, and 18 other ranks wounded. The men of the Special Brigade were not so lucky, with two being killed and another seven sent to hospital all as a result of inhaling their own gas. In the villages, the lesson had been learnt from the night before and several of the battalions had de-camped into the local fields.

Other than firing their ten minute barrage to coincide with the release of the gas and regular firing by the 32nd Brigade, RFA, to keep to gaps in the wire open, the most excitement of the night for the artillery came when the White Star gas was blown so far west, on a now easterly breeze, that that men of the 29th Brigade, RFA, had to hurriedly put on their gas masks. Thankfully, the cloud had pretty much dispersed and the concentrations of chlorine and phosgene were so weak it was safe to remove their masks after just ten minutes.

WIRECUTTING CONTINUED THROUGHOUT THE 26TH JUNE. It was an OK day interspersed with heavy showers and the 125th and 127th Batteries of the 29th Brigade started on the front line wire. From time to time there were special bombardments in which both the Corps and Divisional artillery joined. Sometimes these were of a particular area. Alternatively, they rehearsed the lifts that the guns would make when the infantry assault went in. Worryingly, more of the guns were beginning to show signs of wear and tear with buffer springs and piston rods of the recuperation system showing the most obvious signs of strain.

Today was the first day of the heavy artillery's bombardment. Firing, though not exclusively, on the 4th Division's front were:

14th Siege Battery of the 16th HAG of four 6 in. 30 cwt. Howitzers;
36th Siege Battery of the 16th HAG of four 8 in. Howitzers;
46th Siege Battery of the 1st HAG of four 9.2 in. Howitzers;
56th Siege Battery of the 17th HAG of four 8 in. Howitzers;
81st Siege Battery of the 16th HAG of four 6 in. 30 cwt. Howitzers;
112th Heavy Battery of the 4th HAG of four 60 pdr guns;
139th Heavy Battery of the 16th HAG of four 60 pdr guns; and
Firing on the long distance wire of the German 2nd Position were:
1/1st Highland Heavy Battery of the 1st HAG of four 4.7 in. guns
1/1st Welsh Heavy Battery of the 1st HAG of four 4.7 in. guns;
25th Heavy Battery of the 16th HAG of four 60 pdr guns; and
139th Heavy Battery of the 16th HAG of four 60 pdr guns.

None of these batteries would fire solely on the 4th Division's front and, rather more importantly, very few of their shells would land on the German front line, especially on either the Ridge Redoubt and Heidenkopf where No Man's Land was so narrow long range fire from the heavy howitzers would almost be as dangerous to the British troops in their trenches as to the enemy. Otherwise, these guns would range across all three Divisions' fronts often taking on distant targets which they quite often fired at 'off map' because the weather conditions were such that aerial observation was impossible. Guns like the 60 pdrs and 4.7 in. guns spent a lot of their time and ammunition endeavouring to cut the wire in front of the 2nd Position or in firing relatively lightweight, flat trajectory shells at German gun emplacements only likely to be put out of action by a decent number of high trajectory and much heavier howitzer shells. The heavy howitzer batteries did have some of the front line trenches to bombard but they had huge areas containing as many as six lines of trenches to attack. The 9.2 in. howitzers of the 46th Siege Battery, for example, fired nearly 100 rounds each per day with some 50% being aimed at junctions in Serre Trench and the Zwischen Stellung and another 25% being fired at enemy batteries. It left little with which to demolish the numerous German dugouts in the 1st Position.

At the Louvencourt practice ground the Royal Irish Fusiliers were at it again and so was Gen. Hunter-Weston. At 2.10 p.m. he galloped up to Lt. Col. Findlater to whom he imparted the good news that his Corps commander wished to address the battalion. The men were hurriedly formed up in a square and the General gave a ringing oration:

> "I am glad to have the opportunity of addressing the Royal Irish Fusiliers. A finer body of men I have never seen. We all belonged to the 4th Division at Le Cateau, etc., and during the coming fight we hope we shall live up to and, if possible, improve on the traditions of the Division on that occasion. You know your work and you know the part you are to play in the battle. In the Corps we have 600 pieces of ordnance from the 15 inch howitzer down to the Stokes gun. Now, in the early days we did so well with almost no artillery support, what will we do now? I give to each officer, NCO and man of the Royal Irish Fusiliers my very best wishes and hope you have the best of luck in the battle."[4]

The speech obviously raised morale as, just before midnight, the battalion marched off to encamp near Bertrancourt. The weather was bad again and it poured with rain en route but the men were described as in 'excellent spirits'.

Lt. Col. Green of the East Lancashires was not so contented. His concern about the shortage of officers was apparently met when five young subalterns arrived from the 10th East Lancashires at the battalion's bivouacs at Mailly Maillet. They would be followed, in another two days, by two more. None of these officers would take part in the attack but they would form part of the nucleus of the battalion afterwards. Which was all very well, but Green's worry was that these young men 'had little or no training' and would not replace the experienced officers now scattered across training schools or in Paris for the court martial.

The 12th Brigade, meanwhile, was at Louvencourt practising its long, slow walk from the rear most British trenches to the German 2nd Position. It appears to have been done in 'real time', as it were, as the programme took 3½ hours to complete, starting at 6 a.m. The exercise was somewhat cryptically described as 'The advance from Line B' in the King's Own's war diary. Whatever its use, it was a pleasant morning for a long stroll.

A raid was planned for this night with men from the 1st Royal Warwicks attempting to get into the German trenches to the south of the Heidenkopf. Six 18 pdr batteries opened up on the German front lines at 11.30 p.m. while two 4.5 in. howitzers barraged communications by bombarding key trench junctions in the support and reserve trenches. The raiding party, comprising Lt. James Lister Shute and 2nd Lt. Raymond Watts Gorton and 20 men, was ready to leave their trenches at the appointed time of 11.40 p.m. but, as a result of an action by the 31st Division which, one would think, should have been prevented by VIII Corps Staff, the whole raid was put off. The postponement came because, at the same time as their barrage opened, the 31st Division lit smoke candles and, with an efficiency which was becoming all too obvious, the German barrage crashed down on No Man's Land and the front trenches within a few minutes of the candles being lit.

The 1st Rifle Brigade did manage to get some men out into No Man's Land to inspect the German front line wire which they reported as generally well cut. A patrol from the 6th Warwicks was also due to enter No Man's Land to investigate the state of the German wire but, in another example of less than wonderful Staff work, they were unable to get close as the British guns were still firing in the area to be checked.

IN THE EARLY HOURS OF THE 27TH JUNE smoke was again discharged twice, each time drawing the anticipated response from the German guns. At 3.45 a.m. it was the turn of the 4th Division to try out the foul smelling smoke candles. Three red rockets later and their front line trench was being pounded. Then, at 5.10 a.m., they had another go with the same predictable and accurate response. With dawn breaking there was something to see from the German trenches and machine gun and rifle fire also opened on the British parapet. The 4th Division war diary remarked that the 'enemy trenches appear strongly held', a comment which it might well have been prudent to act on in the remaining days of the bombardment.

The 18 pdrs continued to cut the wire with each of the field batteries firing about 1,000 rounds of shrapnel during the day plus a few hundred HE as part of the special bombardments. The batteries had the help of a BE2c overhead during the early evening which sent down good reports of the wirecutting on some of the more distant targets.

Back at Bertrancourt, the Irish Fusiliers were busy with working parties during the day with 100 men under 2nd Lt. Wilson being sent up the Sucrerie to haul trench mortar ammunition up the gun emplacements in the front lines. At 10 p.m. all four companies sent working parties forward under Capts. Barefoot and Wilson to the Sunken Road between the Sucrerie and Auchonvillers. It was from this line that the battalion was to advance on Z Day and the task of these troops was to cut the necessary gaps in the lines of British wire between the various trench lines between the Sunken Road and Tenderloin. It was a job that could only be done at night and it was not until 5 a.m. that they returned to their tents at Bertrancourt. They had been pleased to find the assembly trenches dry and undamaged by the German guns (even though the 4th Division diary talked about the trenches having 'a considerable amount of water in them and general very muddy'). The men left at Bertrancourt had time off to enjoy themselves, perhaps buoyed by the confident words of Hunter-Weston the day before. The war diary describes an extemporised cricket match with a pair of old socks as the ball and part of ration box as the bat:

> "The men's behaviour on this evening was most gratifying, tails right up and all in good fettle. A strong feeling of comradeship was keenly felt by all. The PRI (Maj. P Penn) sent into Doullens and obtained 4,000 eggs to supplement rations on Y Day and 100 French loaves."[5]

The 11th Brigade's battalions had wire patrols out during the night. Men from the 1st Hampshires and the 1st East Lancashires were despatched to inspect the wire between Beaumont Hamel and the Ridge Redoubt. As they crossed the sunken road rockets and flares were sent up from the German lines followed by an immediate shrapnel barrage accompanied by machine gun and rifle fire. It was not the 11th Brigade patrols which had been spotted but those of a raiding party from the 86th Brigade on their right. In spite of this unplanned disruption, the patrols hung about in No Man's Land until 1.20 a.m. but, as there was no way of getting close to the German wire, the attempted inspection was abandoned. A patrol of the 1st Somerset Light Infantry had somewhat better luck. Entering No Man's Land from the end of Beet Street the patrol, commanded by 2nd Lt. George Winstanley[i], worked their way from the northern end of the Ridge Redoubt towards the southern flank of the Heidenkopf but hostile artillery fire prevented them from getting too close. The wire they were able to inspect, however, was regarded as well cut and no real obstacle. Further north still, the 6th Warwicks had another frustrating night as they were again prevented from getting out into No Man's Land by the heavy German shelling.

---

[i] 2nd Lt. George Clement Winstanley, 1st Somerset Light Infantry, was killed early on the 2nd July 1916. A CQMS with the Army Service Corps, he was commissioned on 1st March 1916. His body was never found and his name is inscribed on the Thiepval Memorial, Pier & Face 2A, and remembered on the Slough St Mary War Memorial.

One activity that was possible, however, was the cutting of the British front line wire. Here, in order to attempt to conceal such an obvious preparation for an attack, the lanes through the wire were cut on a diagonal. Though possibly not obvious from the ground any aerial observer should have been able to spot the results of the night time's work and, as a result, realised the implications of such a move. The fact that the weather was about to intervene to give the Germans two extra days to detect this was more than unfortunate.

THE 28TH JUNE WAS ANOTHER WET DAY with repeated heavy showers. The ground, according to the 4th Division war diary, was becoming impassable and, as a result, the date for Z Day was put back 48 hours. The field artillery, guided by the belief that the front German wire was cut, was concentrating on areas in front of the 3rd trench and the Zwischen Stellung.

Maj. Gen. Lambton, who had spent much of the previous day touring the battalions of the 12th Brigade and talking to the troops, now focussed on the 10th Brigade. Elsewhere it was work as usual. The 1st Royal Irish Fusiliers, having consumed the 4,000 eggs obtained from Doullens in anticipation of the 29th June being Z Day, went on a route march to burn them off. Six young subalterns joined the 1st Rifle Brigade and all would count themselves fortunate they arrived too late to take part in the attack. Three of the six, though, would be dead before the end of October[i].

During the night another raid was attempted, this time by the Somerset Light Infantry. The patrol, under 2nd Lt. Armstrong and 2nd Lt. Ralph Dunn, left the trenches at the head of Borden Street, opposite the south west face of the Heidenkopf, at 1.10 a.m. There was no pre-arranged bombardment by the field artillery and so the men crept across No Man's Land hoping not to be noticed or caught by a sudden German strafe. No Man's Land here was about 300 yards wide and it took the party 20 minutes to get through the German wire. The report talks of 'great difficulty' being experienced in getting through the wire which, of itself, was bad news as previous reports had suggested it had been swept away. As they approached within 5 yards of the 'apparently little damaged' German parapet the Germans opened fire. Armstrong and three men were immediately hit. Dunn[ii] ordered the patrol to withdraw and he brought the wounded Armstrong in with him. Two NCOs, L/Cpl. Briggs of H Company and L/Cpl. Vranch of C Company, were wounded and one man was missing. A search party sent out at 2.45 a.m. brought in an unwounded man sheltering in a shell hole but of 6657 Pte. Albert Thomas Swift, C Company, there was no sign[iii].

[i] 2nd Lts. James Oswald Haldane and Reginald Stuart Handford (both KiA 9th August), and 2nd Lt. John Stewart Blackie (KiA 18th October).

[ii] 2nd Lt. Ralph Ellis Dunn, 1st Somerset Light Infantry, was killed on 1st July 1916. Aged 20, he was the son of Mrs H Ellis Dunn of Myre Cottage, Clatworthy, Wiveliscombe, Somerset and the late Rev H Ellis Dunn. Joined as Trooper in 2nd King Edward's Horse, Jan., 1915, went to France in March, 1915. Obtained his Lieutenancy 1916. His body was never found and his name is inscribed on the Thiepval Memorial, Pier & Face 2A.

[iii] 6657 Pte Albert Thomas Swift, 1st Somerset Light Infantry, from Peasedown St John, Somerset, was never found and his name is inscribed on the Thiepval Memorial, Pier & Face 2A.

Officer patrols from the other battalions went out overnight to check the state of the German wire. According to the 4th Division diary the reports were, in the main, encouraging. From the northern tip of the Heidenkopf to Ten Tree Alley the wire was reported to be blown away and passable anywhere. From the southern corner of the Heidenkopf to the mid-point of the Ridge Redoubt all the wire was badly damaged and well cut, although 2nd Lt. Winstanley of the Somersets, out again inspecting the wire, observed he was unable to get near to the Heidenkopf during his patrol. From the Ridge Redoubt south to the border with the 29th Division at the northern end of the Sunken Road, where 2nd Lt. Myles Sayers and 18575 Sgt. Miles Redmayne of the 1st East Lancashires were out on patrol, the trip wire out in front was cut but behind that was a heavy row of concertina and barbed wire which was only damaged in places.

Other nocturnal activities took place that reflected the reasons why Z Day had been postponed. 2nd Lt. William Treasure[i], the Stokes mortar officer of the Somersets, spent several hours with a fatigue party armed with 39 buckets bailing out the front trenches such was the volume of water that was accumulating in them.

ON THE 29TH JUNE, AS BEFORE, THE 18 PDRS CARRIED ON cutting wire where it was known to present an obstacle, however, with the 48 hour extension of the bombardment, the intensity of the shelling was sharply reduced. The 29th Brigade, for example, cut its consumption of shrapnel and HE by nearly half.

	28th June	29th June	Difference	% Change
Shrapnel	2,899	1,518	-1,381	-48%
HE	2,406	1,474	-932	-39%
Total	5,305	2,992	-2,313	-44%

Table 14 Change in ammunition use by 29th Brigade, RFA, 28th to 29th June[6]

At the same time, the 4th Division noted an increase in enemy artillery activity with the raid triggering a widespread response spread across the front and support lines. Machine guns were also quick to open up from various locations along the front and an array of coloured rockets were sent up which resulted in a barrage concentrated between the two final red flares. Furthermore, to the right, on the 29th Division's front, a raid was bloodily repulsed. All of this indicated an enemy thoroughly on the alert and able to bring down both artillery and machine gun barrages in short order and on specific locations as required. With just two days to go before the assault this should surely have set alarm bells ringing at nearly every HQ from Brigade to GHQ. If it did there was no evidence of any planned response.

Heavy showers had characterised the night of the 28th and 29th June and, although the day was fine and mainly dry, more showers moved in during the night of the 29th. The infantry spent the day continuing their training with

---

[i] 2nd Lt. William Herbert Treasure, 1st Somerset Light Infantry, was killed on 1st July. Aged 19, he was the only son of Herbert George and Grace Georgina Treasure of 2, Hyde Lodge, Bristol. Educated at Merchant Taylor's School at Sutton Courtenay, he entered RMC, Sandhurst, in December 1914 and was commissioned on 13th July 1915. His body was never found and his name is inscribed on the Thiepval Memorial, Pier & Face 2A.

lectures and route marches. In the evening, before the rain came, the senior officers of the 1st Royal Irish Fusiliers played a keenly contested game of rounders against the senior sergeants. Lt. Col. Findlater was, no doubt, satisfied with the 5-1 win.

Around the front line trenches, other officers and men were preparing for rather more serious activities. The 1st Rifle Brigade was to attempt a raid on the German trenches while others were again to go out to check the wire. The Rifle Brigade's plan was to send out two parties, each of an officer, two NCOs and nine Riflemen at 11.30 p.m. The first, Party A, assembling in Beet Street and under the command of 2nd Lt. Robert Patterson[i], was to creep and then crawl diagonally south east across No Man's Land in order to arrive just outside the German trenches at Point 20 in the centre of the Ridge Redoubt at 12.20 a.m. Party B, commanded by 2nd Lt. Fred Kirkland, would leave the sap at the end of Cat Street and move straight across No Man's Land to reach Point 24 at the same time. Their approach was to be covered by a trench mortar barrage of the German front lines which was to cease at 12.30 a.m. Their instructions were then to rush the trench 'as quickly and quietly as possible' and snatch up any German soldier they found. Should the trenches be empty then each party was to work 50 yards towards one another looking for any wounded left over from the mortar barrage. As soon as they were successful they were to leave the German trenches independently and return, though they would probably find it necessary to hang around in No Man's Land while the enemy artillery vented its fury with a bombardment of the British front line.

Plate 60 2nd Lt. Frederick William Kirkland, 1st Rifle Brigade

At 11.30 p.m. the two parties assembled, each man equipped with a rifle with fixed bayonet, or 'sword' as the Rifle Brigade would have it, and two bombs and

[i] 2nd Lt. Robert Arthur Patterson, 6th Rifle Brigade, died on 12th April 1917. He was commissioned into the 6th Rifle Brigade on 16th December 1914. He is buried in Point du Jour Military Cemetery, Athies.

set off under cover of the dark, damp and overcast night. Ahead of them the trench mortars were busily bombarding the German trenches. Or so they thought. Later 2nd Lt. Kirkland would complain that, at least in front of Party B, the bombs fell 60 yards short of the German front line, causing no damage but delaying their approach. Eventually each party reached the German wire safely but then made the disconcerting discovery that the German wire was not sufficiently cut to allow access. They set to work cutting through the obstacles but the wire was so thick it proved almost impossible and even special heavy duty wire cutters supplied to the patrols were useless. Almost inevitably, given the fate of previous raids, they were seen by the German sentries. Within minutes Party A came under artillery fire while Party B was showered with bombs and then chased away by rifle and shell fire. Harassed by artillery fire the two parties withdrew hurriedly but were then forced to stay out in No Man's Land as the predicted German bombardment crashed down on the British front line trenches until 2.30 p.m. Altogether, a most unsatisfactory evening's work. Only the fact that just three men from Party B were wounded during the raid saved it from being a disaster. But that was mainly because of the conduct of Kirkland and an unknown sergeant. One of the wounded men was hit just outside the German wire and Kirkland and the NCO stayed out with the casualty until they were able to drag him back to safety. One of his fellow officers wrote later to the family that he had been recommended for a VC for his conduct, though no award was forthcoming. Having saved one life, Kirkland's own could now be measured in hours.

Three wire patrols were also out that night. Their reports were moderately discouraging. 2nd Lt. Winstanley of the Somersets was out on the south side of the Heidenkopf. As a result of his previous night's excursion in this area, the officer had visited the artillery OP in Taupin Trench and asked for more artillery fire on this sector. The results were, he found, not especially effective. He also checked the position along the main front line from the southern corner of the Heidenkopf along the re-entrant towards the Ridge Redoubt. Here the wire was far better cut and the knife rests that had presented a genuine obstacle had been blown onto the German parapet. Winstanley did observe, however, that the enemy's front and support lines were held and the sentries on the alert. Three times he was fired on but luck was on his side. At least for now.

Further north, on the far side of the Heidenkopf, the situation appeared better. A patrol from the 1/8th Warwicks found the wire well cut.

On the right flank, 2nd Lt. Sayers and a patrol were out again to see if there had been any improvement in the wire cutting between the Ridge Redoubt and the northern end of Beaumont Hamel. The patrol was rather larger than last night's. This time, Sayers and Sgt. Redmayne were accompanied by 2nd Lt. Eric Mallett, 10460 L/Cpl. Joseph W Wallace[i] and another subaltern, the son of a world-renowned Englishman. 2nd Lt. Arthur Alleyne Kingsley Conan Doyle, 1st Hampshire Regt., was the second child and first son of Arthur Conan Doyle, author of the famous Sherlock Holmes books, and of his first wife Louisa

[i] Wallace would win the DCM and the MM before the end of the war and was the RSM of the 1st Hampshires in the 1930s.

Hawkins[i]. Now he was out in No Man's Land to find out for himself the state of the German wire which his battalion must negotiate on Z Day.

Plate 61 Lt. Arthur Alleyne Kingsley Conan Doyle, 1st Hampshire Regt. (with his brothers Denis and Adrian)

The joint report of Sayers and Conan Doyle was a detailed one:

"Patrol left front line trench 100 yards south of junction of 4th Avenue at Q.4.d.4.6 passed north to Q.4.b.6.0 thence crossing Watling Street to 0 in 2601. Here a shell crater (9.2 in). 3 NCOs and men left here to watch while both officers proceeded to German wire about 50 yards north of Lone Tree.

German tripwire completely destroyed leaving stakes; behind this a single line of concertina wire with barbed wire interwired; this had been damaged in places by artillery fire but in no place had been entirely cut through still presenting an obstacle to infantry advance. Stakes supporting this wire (up to 3 in. diameter) had been cut about by shell fire but in most cases still held good. Ground along the immediate front of this wire is not cut about by field artillery fire but presents occasional large craters. Stakes in rear of this were completely stripped of wire.

Very lights were fired from German second line also from sap at Q.5.a.2.4½.

Sector examined:

Pt. 2608 – north to sap at Q.5.a.2.4½.

Time of leaving German wire 2 a.m.

---

[i] 2nd Lt. Arthur Alleyne Kingsley Conan Doyle, 1st Hampshire Regt., was born in 1892 and was the son of Arthur Ignatius Conan Doyle and his first wife the late Louisa Hawkins. He enlisted as 1145 Driver in the Royal Army Medical Corps before being commissioned into the Hampshire Regt. He died from Spanish influenza on 28th October 1918 whilst convalescing from wounds received on 1st July 1916. He is buried in St Luke's Churchyard, Grayshott, Hants, grave 23D.191.

Raids were made north and south of our position which caused delay owing to Very lights being fired in great numbers.
Our artillery was exceedingly helpful in firing on German 2nd and 3rd lines over our heads.
We returned along Watling Street to our own front line."[7]

In spite of the evidence contained in Sayers' and Conan Doyle's report, as well as that of Winstanley, 4th Division summed up the evening's work as 'all reported wire well cut', which was not remotely close to the officers' views of the state of the German wire on the southern flank and centre of the Division.

30TH JUNE WAS A COOL, BRIGHTER IF WINDIER DAY which helped with the slow process of drying out the trenches but must also have made the task of the gunners more difficult. The 18 pdr batteries were continuing in their efforts to cut the remaining wire and, as a result, over a third more shrapnel was expended than on the previous day. 29th Brigade, RFA, records their ammunition use as:

	29th June	30th June	Difference	% Change
Shrapnel	1,518	2,091	+573	+38%
HE	1,474	1,507	+33	+0.2%
Total	2,992	3,598	+606	+20%

Table 15 Change in ammunition use, 29th Brigade, RFA, 29th to 30th June[8]

Overall, these figures still represented a decrease in weight of shell of almost a third compared to the last full day of the bombardment (28th June). This was not, necessarily, because of a decrease in targets. Haig had already impressed upon Rawlinson the need to keep back ammunition for the fighting to come and, as a result, some of the planned intense bombardments had been either scaled down or abandoned altogether. This policy also applied to those batteries trying to cut the German wire and, already, VIII Corps had refused a request from 4th Division for 2,462 shrapnel shells to bring the stocks at the guns up to normal strength. 900 shells were all they were prepared, or able, to release.

For the infantry, Friday, 30th June, was a much needed day of rest, at least, that was, until they started the march up to the front line trenches. Many of the men had written their letters home two days before in the expectation that the attack was to be on the 29th but now, as a few men made last minute efforts to write down their thoughts for their loved ones, and some penned wills, many men attended open air church services for the various denominations. One of the officers writing home was 2nd Lt. Frederick Bertram Key of D Company, 1/8th Royal Warwickshires. His battalion would lead the division's attack on the left wing and Key would be at the forefront of the action. A keen cricketer who had played for Lichfield Grammar School 1st XI and Lichfield Cricket Club pre-war, he couched his final letter in terms clearly close to his heart. If the letter was sent, he wrote, then that meant he had been 'bowled out middle peg'. He promised, however, that he would have 'batted well'. The body of the cricket-loving Sunday School teacher would never be found.[i]

---

[i] 2nd Lt. Frederick Bertram Key, 1/8th Royal Warwickshire Regt., was aged 27. He was the only son of Frederick and Edith Key of 30, Queen St., Lichfield, Staffs. Educated at Lichfield Grammar School, he played for the school 1st XI and Lichfield CC. He taught in

Plate 62 2nd Lt. Frederick Bertram Key, 1/8th Royal Warwickshire Regt.

The mood amongst the men was generally of great optimism about the forthcoming operation. Almost every officer with a red tab had assured them that the seven day bombardment and the final intensive pummelling of the German lines would leave the soldiers opposite either dead or incapable of serious resistance. All the evidence to the contrary collected over the previous week was conveniently ignored. The failure of the raids, the uncut wire at the centre and southern end of the sector, the robust nature of the German defenders and their trench defences and the obvious and rapid forms of communication with their artillery were all swept to one side such was the certainty of success.

It was left to the incurably optimistic Hunter-Weston to add the final dollop of froth to this sickly confection of over-confidence and unreality. During the afternoon he arrived at the encampment of the 2nd Lancashire Fusiliers where Lt. Col. Freeth[i], the CO, was chatting to Capt. John Collis-Browne, one of his

---

the Sunday School at Christ Church, Lichfield, where there is a memorial plaque. He was commissioned from Lance Sergeant on 30th April 1916. His body was never found and his name is inscribed on the Thiepval Memorial, Pier & Face 9A, 9B & 10B.

[i] Lt. Col. (later Maj. Gen.) George Henry Basil Freeth, CB, CMG, DSO, Lancashire Fusiliers, was born in 1872. He was the son of Colonel William Freeth, MVO, Chief Constable, Isle of Man, and Helen Macpherson, daughter of General Macpherson, of Inverness. He was educated at Merchant Taylors' School, London; King William's College, Isle of Man, and the RMC, Sandhurst. He joined the Lancashire Fusiliers in 1892 and was promoted Lieutenant 1894. He served in India and on the Nile Expedition of 1898. Present at the Battle of Khartoum, Medal and the Egyptian Medal with clasp. Promoted Captain 1899. He served during occupation of Crete. Served in South Africa, MiD, Queen's Medal & 3 clasps, and King's Medal and 2 clasps. DSO 1901. Adjutant, Militia 1902-5. Staff College, 1909. DAAG, Northern Command, 1911-4. DAAG and AAG, GHQ, to 1915. GOC, 167th Brigade. MiD four times. CMG, 1916, CB, 1919. Promoted Maj. Gen. 1921. Southern Command, 1923. DAG and Director Personal Service, Army HQ, India, 1927. Retired 1931. Col, Lancashire Fusiliers 1926-46. Married to Ruth Elaine Scott, 1903, two daughters. He died in 1949.

company commanders. 'Hunter Bunter' was in the highest of high spirits and was intent on communicating his mood of unsupportable enthusiasm to all and sundry:

> "Splendid, Freeth (he remarked), the enemy's front line trenches are full of Germans. They will all be blown to pieces by the morning."[9]

Collis-Browne, writing after the war, explained how their General's certainty was passed onto the men and how it put them all in 'good heart':

> "In fact, we thought this must be the start of the end of the war!!!"[10]

For rather too many men on Saturday, 1st July, 1916, this this would prove to be sadly true.

According to the regimental history of the 1st East Lancashire Regt., another wire patrol led by 2nd Lt. Sayers was sent out on the night before the attack. There is no record of this in the battalion war diary but the regimental history is quite explicit about the problems experienced by the patrol and the catastrophic effects of these issues:

> "The same patrol (i.e. 2nd Lts. Sayers, Mallett and Conan Doyle, Sgt. Redmayne and L/Cpl. Wallace) went out on the following night. On this occasion the patrol definitely reported that the enemy wire was insufficiently cut on that portion of the line it had been able to examine. Unfortunately it has been impossible to arrange for a temporary cessation of the bombardment long enough to allow of a reconnaissance of the whole of the wire. Consequently it was not discovered that the enemy wire opposite the right and centre companies was practically intact. If a longer cessation of the bombardment had been possible a thorough reconnaissance could have been made and the information thus gained would have considerably altered the plan of the attack."[11]

Both the failure to discover this uncut wire and the failure of the co-ordination of the patrol and the bombardment speaks very badly of the staff work of all involved from Brigade upwards. Quite how it is possible for the failure of the wirecutting along two thirds of a battalion's front to go undiscovered until the infantry were on top of it on the morning of the assault is difficult if not impossible to fathom. The consequences for the men of the East Lancashires and Hampshires would be profound.

Getting ready for the attack the 11th Brigade and its two attached battalions from the 48th (South Midland) Division were held in three main areas:

In billets in Mailly Maillet – Brigade HQ, the 1st Somerset LI, the 1st Hampshires and the 1/6th Royal Warwickshires; and

In bivouacs in Wood P.17 – 2 companies each of the 1st Rifle Brigade, 1st East Lancashires and the 1/8th Royal Warwickshires as well as three sections of the 11th Machine Gun Company and the 11th Trench Mortar Battery;

Already in the front lines were the remaining companies of 1st East Lancashires, holding trenches from Q.4.d.3.8 to Maxim Trench inclusive, the 1st Rifle Brigade, holding trenches from Maxim Trench exclusive to Serre Road inclusive, and the 1/8th Royal Warwickshires, holding trenches from Serre Road exclusive to K.35.a.3.7. One section of the 11th Machine Gun Company was held on the line Elles Square-5th Avenue.

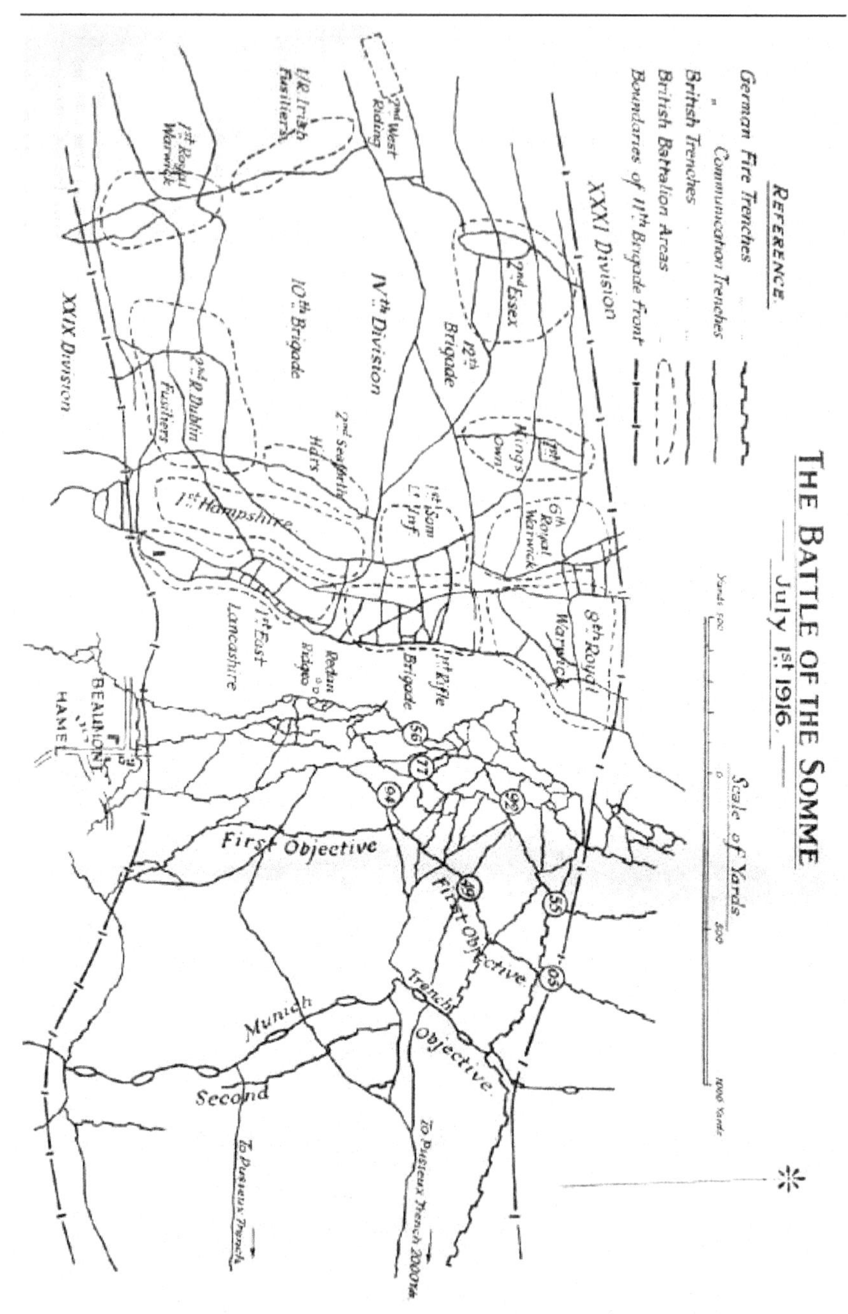

Figure 4 Assembly areas and initial objectives of 4th Division

[Source: *History of the East Lancashire Regt. in the Great War*, Nicholson & McMullen, 1936]

The movement towards the front lines began during the afternoon of Friday, 30th June. Advance parties, which included three sections of machine guns, all of the Stokes mortars of the Trench Mortar Battery due to go forward with the attacking troops and the Brigade carriers, left their billets and bivouacs in order to be in place by 8 p.m. These units, approaching the battle zone in daylight, moved via the long communication trenches that snaked eastwards to the north and south of the Serre to Mailly Maillet Road.

The main bodies of the 11th Brigade infantry moved out once night had fallen and marched via pre-arranged marked tracks over the open until they entered the front line system. The right column, the East Lancashires, Somersets and Hampshires in that order started forward at 10 p.m. while the left column, marching to the north of the Sucrerie, moved off in the order: 1/8th Warwicks, 1st Rifle Brigade and finally 1/6th Warwicks. Interference from German artillery was, thankfully, minimal during the night with some shelling near the left column at the Sucrerie and on the Auchonvillers to Mailly Maillet Road near which the right column marched. All of these units moved to their assembly trenches over the open, the exceptions being the two Warwickshire battalions who approached the lines north of the Serre to Mailly Road via Cheeroh Avenue entering it at its junction with Taupin Trench. The four battalions going over the open made better time and were in position by 2 a.m. on the morning of 1st July. The two Warwickshire battalions, however, were delayed until 3.30 a.m. by congestion caused by too many troops being in the trench at the same time and by the 8th Warwicks finding the front assembly trench too badly damaged by shell fire to use. The retirement of the leading wave to the support trench caused yet further delays.

Behind these battalions came the 10th Brigade on the right and the 12th Brigade on the left. The 10th Brigade, advancing from its billets in Bertrancourt and Beaussart, passed their starting point at 10.15 p.m. marching over the open in a single column north of Mailly Maillet and Auchonvillers before arriving at the sunken road from the Sucrerie to Auchonvillers just south of 4th Avenue. Two battalions, the 1st Royal Irish Fusiliers and 1st Royal Warwickshires were left in the road, the Warwickshires between 3rd and 5th Avenues and the Fusiliers to their left, while the two other battalions made their way via communication trenches to their assembly trenches, the 2nd Seaforth Highlanders forming up behind the left of the East Lancashires and Hampshires and the 2nd Dublin Fusiliers astride 3rd, 4th and 5th Avenues to the west of the White City and Tenderloin. They were all in position by 1.45 p.m. having lost just one officer and one man slightly wounded by the weak German artillery fire. Once in place, they met up with their machine gunners and the Trench Mortar Battery which, like those of the 11th Brigade, had moved into position by 8 p.m. the previous evening. Also waiting for them were the ladders, trench bridges and other RE stores which had been deposited previously in their assembly trenches.

North of the Serre to Mailly Road the 12th Brigade was in place by 3 a.m. The 1st King's Own Royal Lancaster Regt's approach had been via the Sucrerie and then along the north side of 6th Avenue before crossing the Serre-Mailly Road to their concentration area around the Lyceum in Green Trench and Bow Street between Newgate Street and Borden Avenue. They had left Bertrancourt just as the Germans had started to shell the village but, in spite of their approach being over the open throughout, they suffered injuries to only six men during the march. The 2nd Essex followed on and occupied Elles Square and the surrounding trenches while the 2nd Duke of Wellington's (West Riding) Regt. waited around the Sucrerie. Further west, and to the south of the Mailly Road, the 2nd Lancashire Fusiliers occupied two lines of trenches ready for their advance towards the German 2nd Position.

Elements of the most recent addition to the Division were also in the trenches waiting for the 'off'. The 21st West Yorkshire Regt. – the Wool Textile Pioneers from Halifax and environs – had arrived in France just two weeks previously[i] and, on 21st June, had met their new divisional commander when Maj. Gen. Lambton inspected them at Vauchelles. Three companies of these completely green troops were to be involved in some way in the attack. B Company was to go forward with the attacking troops. C Company was to man the front line trenches. A Company had the most interesting task. They were to go out into No Man's Land and convert some of the Russian saps into communication trenches. Standing around under fire in No Man's Land armed with a pick or shovel – not everyone's idea of a fun day out.

Last minute preparations were now conducted. Breakfast was distributed amongst the men and RE parties set out to lay bridges across the rear British trenches to allow a constant flow of men forward during the attack, uninterrupted by the need to use the communication trenches or find a way across the numerous trenches strewn across their paths.

The artillery, meanwhile, continued to bombard the German positions. German retaliation was sporadic and was mainly aimed at the British lines east of the reserve trenches of Vallade, Tournai and Tenderloin. From 5 a.m. to 6.05 a.m. the 18 pdrs of the field artillery fired at a rate of 1 round per gun per 1½ minutes on the wire in their sectors. The 4.5 in. howitzer batteries bombarded trenches in the second and third lines of the German 1st Position. At 6.25 a.m. all of the field batteries, 18 pdrs and 4.5 in. howitzers, fired on the German front trench at a rate of one round per gun per minute. The resulting explosions in and around the German trenches may have looked impressive to the waiting infantry but the weight of shell falling could only ever do cosmetic damage to the German positions. The defenders, waiting in their dugouts, were safe, their only concerns being to keep the entrances clear so as to enable them to sprint to their positions once the barrage lifted. Deeper into the German lines the heavy howitzers and long guns pounded all sorts of targets many in areas which the infantry would never reach. It is easy to see why the officers and men of the attacking battalions believed what they had been told: all of the defenders would be dead or disabled by the time the whistles blew for the 'off'. No-one had ever seen or heard anything quite like it: the noise, the smoke, the explosions. It was only too easy to believe that no-one could survive. The shock, to morale and self-confidence, when the truth was revealed would be like a blow to the solar plexus.

At 7.20 a.m. the 18 pdrs increased their rate of fire to 3 rounds per gun per minute and the 4.5 in. howitzers doubled their output. At the same time, the

[i] The battalion left for France aboard two ships, the *'Courtfield'* and *'Marguerite'*, on 16th June.

three heavy howitzer batteries firing on the German front line, i.e. 46th Siege Battery, 71st Siege Battery and the 56th Siege Battery, lifted onto the reserve line. Simultaneously, 500 yards to the south of the 1st East Lancashires on the right of the Division's front, the Hawthorn Ridge mine exploded. Adding their fire to the intense bombardment, the Brigade light trench mortar crews fired as quickly as they could. The Stokes mortars of the 12th Trench Mortar Battery with its two sections in Vallade and Wolf Trenches, fired 700 rounds in the ten minutes intense bombardment before allowing their guns to cool ready to move forward after the infantry. The three sections of the 11th Trench Mortar Batteries were in Maxim Trench which ran along the base of the British redan opposite the Ridge Redoubt. This was their target and the men worked their guns furiously in an effort to subdue the riflemen and machine gunners known to inhabit the redoubt's dugouts[i].

But at 7.25 a.m., and some observers say earlier, the intense fire on the front trench slackened as the rest of the heavy guns and the 4.5 in. howitzers shifted targets from the support to the reserve trench and beyond and the 2 in. trench mortars and 240 mm heavy mortars ceased firing altogether. Now it was just the 18 pdrs firing HE who were trying to keep the defenders' heads down. And they failed. The premature explosion of the mine, the lifting of the heavier guns and, no doubt, advance warnings from higher authority, meant that the troops of Reserve Infanterie Regiment Nr. 121 were all too ready for the race to the parapet. Indeed some, amongst them several machine gun teams, were already out and in position and, as the heavier shells moved away, they started to sweep the British parapet, with other guns in supporting positions providing a deadly crossfire through which the British infantry must now advance.

At 7.30 a.m. the batteries of the RGA allocated to the 4th Division's front lifted from the German reserve trench onto the British 1st objective, Nagel Graben, which ran between 200 and 400 yards east of the German front line. The batteries were, from north to south, the 46th Siege Battery (9.2 in. howitzers), 71st (6 in. 30 cwt. howitzers), 56th Siege Battery (8 in. howitzers), 79th Siege Battery (9.2 in. howitzers) and half of the 81st Siege Battery (6 in. 30 cwt. howitzers). They were to bombard this trench as well as the northern end of Beaumont Hamel and the southern end of Waggon Road for ten minutes. At zero+10 these guns all lifted onto Munich Trench (Zwischen Stellung) except for those of the 79th and 81st Siege Batteries which had other fish to fry and their place was taken by the 14th Siege Battery (6 in. 30 cwt. howitzers). The two lines of trenches making up the Zwischen Stellung were to be shelled for 30 minutes. At zero+40, by which time the leading waves of the support battalions should have been approaching this area, the guns shifted again, some straight onto the German 2nd Position, e.g. 46th Siege Battery, while others moved onto intermediate targets before taking on this remote line of trenches. The 14th and 71st Siege Batteries had the task of firing on an area along the Serre to Beaucourt Road which concealed a number of German battery positions. They devoted 30 minutes to this past-time before moving eastwards to the 2nd Position. There they were

[i] 11/1, 11/2 and 11/3 Trench Mortar sections were to advance with the 11th Brigade. 12/1 and 12/2 sections returned to 12th Brigade, getting ready to follow its advance and 10/1, 10/2 and 10/3 sections, in reserve in Tenderloin Street, were to advance with 10th Brigade.

joined by the 56th, 23rd and one section of 81st Siege Batteries and all of these guns would continue to pound this line until 3 hours and 25 minutes had elapsed since the whistles had blown for zero hour. By now the final elements of the infantry should be waiting to move forward to occupy the final objective. Unfortunately, most of the infantry wouldn't reach the 10 minute line let alone the Zwischen Stellung or the 2nd Position and a significant proportion wouldn't even reach the British front line.

On the far right, the men of the 1st East Lancashires had, no doubt, witnessed the eruption of the Hawthorn mine with awe and a degree of expectation. In front of them lay more than 400 yards of No Man's Land. To their right, the two companies of the 1st Lancashire Fusiliers were about to deploy from the Sunken Lane 100 or so yards in advance of their position. At 7.26 a.m. the leading platoons started to leave the front line trench. The battalion was to attack on a three company front, each company having two platoons in each wave. On the extreme right was C Company under Capt. Heinrich William Max Thomas from Crouch End in North London. They occupied the front line in sectors 11, 12 and 13. On their left were the two platoons of A Company led by Capt. Arthur Hugh Penny, a pre-war Sandhurst cadet. They held the line to the junctions of 16 and 17 sectors. B Company held the rest of the battalion front to their border with the 1st Rifle Brigade at the junction of sectors 19 and 20. B Company was commanded by Capt. Meyrick Gouldsburg Browne, a pre-war subaltern from 12th Battalion, London Regt. (The Rangers). The second wave was aligned in Minden Trench, Green Trench and Ludgate Street. Behind them, in Chatham Trench, came D Company, Capt. Frederick Edmund Hatfield, and the Battalion HQ.

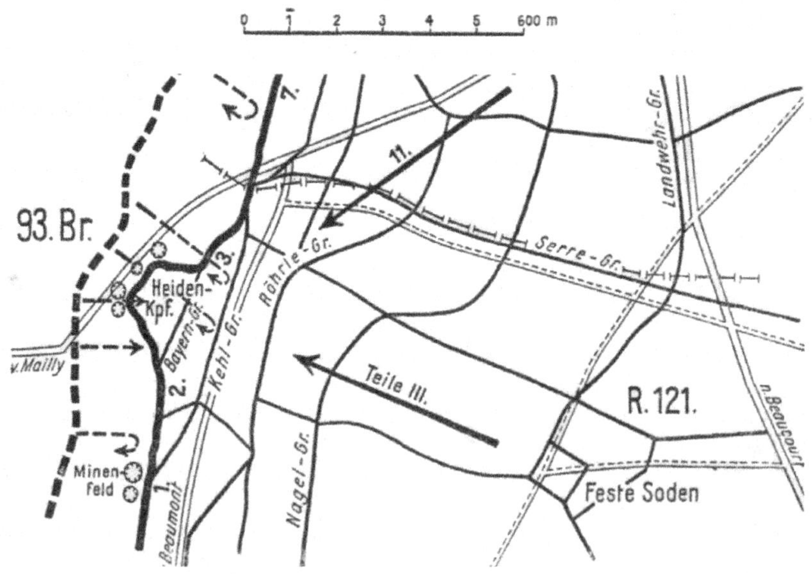

Figure 5 German map of the attack of the 4th Division

(N.B. The 93rd Brigade is incorrectly shown as attacking the Heidenkopf)
[Source: *Somme Nord*]

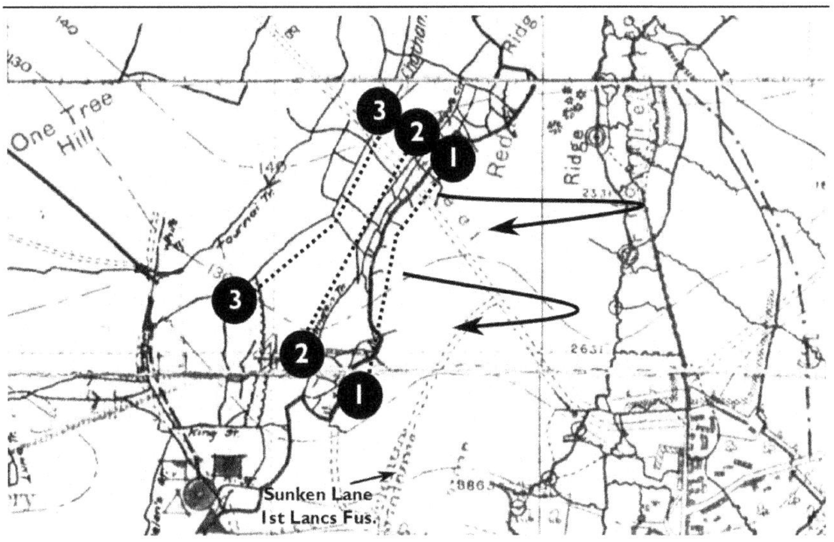

Map 20 Attack of the 1st East Lancashire Regt., 0730

Key:
1 to 1 = Two platoons each of C, A and B Companies (from right to left)
2 to 2 = Two platoons each of C, A and B Companies (from right to left)
3 to 3 = D Company and Battalion HQ

At zero, as the 18 pdrs lifted off the German front line trench, the men out in No Man's Land started to advance and the second wave which had, in the meantime, moved into the British front line left the cover of the trenches. They were immediately met by heavy machine gun fire from both flanks as they walked slowly forward and, at the same time, the German artillery increased the intensity of their fire on the British front lines. As the waves pushed on, C Company on the right withered away in the face of flanking fire from Beaumont Hamel while the other companies were raked by machine guns located on the southern face of the Ridge redoubt. The machine gun fire from the area around Beaumont Hamel was not from guns of the RIR 121 but from Maschinengewehr Kompanien Nr. 2 of RIR 119. The German defensive ethos was all about flexibility and mutual support. If a neighbouring regiment could assist its fellows then it did so without needing to ask permission from higher authority. If a target presented itself, like the long lines of the 1st East Lancashires slowly trudging towards the trenches south of the Ridge redoubt, then any machine guns in the area without an immediate target would open fire. In this case, it was Machine Gun No. 1, commanded by Unteroffizier Braungart, and, most especially, a captured Belgian machine gun B1 commanded by Gefreiter Bürk. The former gun had responsibility for the German numbered sectors 40 and 41 within the British trench lines. Sector 41 was the area of the Sunken Lane from which the 1st Lancashire Fusiliers were attacking. Sector 40 was the right flank of the 1st East Lancashire Fusiliers and, with the attack from the Sunken Lane collapsing within minutes and after helping to destroy the attack of the 16th Middlesex just to the north of the mine crater, Braungart re-targeted his gun onto the British troops to the north. Bürk's gun had responsibility for almost the entire front of the East Lancashires, designated sectors 38 to 40 according to German trench maps. These guns, plus others firing from the Ridge Redoubt, took a heavy toll of the East Lancashires, all but stopping their advance in its tracks.

At 7.32 a.m. D Company and the Battalion HQ moved out from Chatham Trench, moving across the open towards the front line, but, with so much further to travel to reach the German wire, they suffered the same fate as the preceding waves and the survivors were soon taking shelter from the vicious machine gun fire in any cover they could find. The remnants of Battalion HQ pushed on to a large shell hole just outside the German wire. Here they found a signaller, 9358 L/Cpl. James McDonald, who had carried forward a telephone and cable in the expectation of setting up communications with Brigade from the German front trench. His telephone wire was already cut but, pinned down, McDonald[i] and the men from HQ remained in the shell throughout the day.

Seven young officers were killed in No Man's Land: Capt. Heinrich Thomas[ii] of C Company, Capt. Cyril Watson[iii], Lts. Thomas Fisher[iv] and Richard Newcombe and 2nd Lt. Charles Watson[v], Charles Sadler[vi] and Harold Tompkins[i].

---

[i] 9358 L/Cpl James McDonald, 1st East Lancashire Regt., was awarded the DCM and the Russian Medal of St George, 3rd Class, (gazetted 13th February 1917) for his conduct on 1st July 1916.

[ii] Capt. Heinrich William Max Thomas, 1st East Lancashire Regt., was aged 24. Born in France, he was the son of M. and Helena Thomas of 31, Wolseley Rd., Crouch End, London. He was commissioned into the East Lancashires from the 28th (London Regt.), Artists' Rifles, on 11th June 1915. He is buried in Munich Trench British Cemetery, Beaumont-Hamel, grave A. 12.

[iii] Capt. Cyril Pennefather Watson, 3rd att. 1st East Lancashire Regt., was killed on 1st July 1916. Aged 32, he was the eldest son of Brig. Gen. A G Watson (late East Lancashire Regt.) and Mrs Watson of Sheringham, Norfolk. He worked for Simmer & Jack Mines in the Transvaal and enlisted in King Edward's Horse on the outbreak of war. He was commissioned on 9th January 1915 and seconded as Brigade Machine Gun Officer on 27th August 1915, being promoted Temporary Captain. He was wounded in September 1915, re-joining the battalion in December. An instructor at the Third Army School. His body was never found and his name is inscribed on the Thiepval Memorial, Pier & Face 6C.

[iv] Lt. Thomas Edward Coney Fisher, 1st East Lancashire Regt., was aged 19. He was the son of Major Edward and Edith Mabel Fisher of Braywick, Budleigh Salterton, Devon (formerly of La Guilaumerie, St Saviour, Jersey). Born in Chislehurst, Kent, he was educated at Victoria College, Jersey, Felsted and Sandhurst. He was commissioned on 15th June 1915. He was originally buried in Waggon Hill Cemetery, Beaumont Hamel, but his body was subsequently lost and his name is inscribed on the Thiepval Memorial, Pier & Face 6C.

[v] 2nd Lt. Charles Edward Stephens Watson, 1st East Lancashire Regt., was aged 20. He was the son of William Stephens Watson and Alice Maude Watson (née Attwell) of Cape Town. Educated at the High School, Rondebosch, Cape Province; Kent College, Canterbury, England; and R.M.C. Sandhurst. Served with the Royal Naval Reserve at Simonstown, 1914. Gazetted July, 1915. His body was never found and his name is inscribed on the Thiepval Memorial, Pier & Face 6C.

[vi] 2nd Lt. Charles Edward Sadler, 10th att. 1st East Lancashire Regt., was aged 21. He was the son of William E and Sarah Sadler of Heath Rd., Holmewood, Chesterfield. A student at Borough Road College, London University. He was commissioned on 2nd September

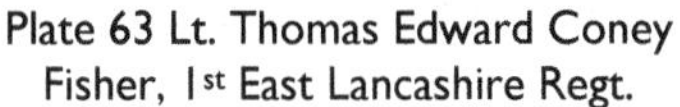

Plate 63 Lt. Thomas Edward Coney Fisher, 1st East Lancashire Regt.

Plate 64 2nd Lt. Charles Edward Stephens Watson, 1st East Lancashire Regt.

Lt. Newcombe[ii] was the Machine Gun Officer and he advanced from Chatham Trench along with the rest of Battalion HQ and D Company. With him was 2nd Lt. William J Page, the Battalion Intelligence Officer. Page had been commissioned from the rank of L/Cpl. from the Royal Irish Regt. on 30th January 1916 and would eventually become a Major in the Royal Sussex Regt. Now he was hurrying nervously across No Man's Land in the face of vicious machine gun fire while alongside him 'Newky', as Lt. Newcombe was known to his fellow officers, nonchalantly strolled along whilst lighting a cigarette extracted from his case. But Newky's advance was cut brutally short by a German bullet and Page was left to scurry forward to the edge of the uncut German wire alone. On the way he crossed Watling Street, the shallow track that ran diagonally across No Man's Land from the north-west into the top of Beaumont Hamel. Here he found a few men sheltering from the scything Maxim fire and he encouraged them to move forwards. As he neared the front edge of the German wire he ran into 2nd Lt. Albert Duncan Layton with whom he had a quick word before continuing to advance. Layton, promoted into the battalion as an NCO in the Honourable Artillery Company in September 1915, would be one of the handful of subalterns not to be wounded in the East Lancashire Regt[iii].

1915. His body was never found and his name is inscribed on the Thiepval Memorial, Pier & Face 6C.

[i] 2nd Lt. Harold Arthur Tompkins, 10th att. 1st East Lancashire Regt., was commissioned on 27th November 1915. His body was never found and his name is inscribed on the Thiepval Memorial, Pier & Face 6C.

[ii] Lt. Richard Newcombe, 1st East Lancashire Regt., was aged 23. He was the son of Charles Henry and Emily Newcombe of 28, Herne Hill, London. He enlisted in the Artists' Rifles before being commissioned into the 1st East Lancashire Regt. His body was never found and his name is inscribed on the Thiepval Memorial, Pier & Face 6C.

[iii] 2nd Lt. Albert Duncan Layton, 1st East Lancashire Regt., was awarded the MC for his conduct in action in May 1917. *London Gazette*, 18th July 1917.

Plate 65 Capt. Cyril Pennefather Watson, 3rd att. 1st East Lancashire Regt.

Plate 66 Lt. Richard Newcombe, 1st East Lancashire Regt.

Plate 67 18575 Sgt. Miles Benjamin Redmayne, DCM, 1st East Lancashire Regt.

The CO, Lt. Col. Green, was one of those who had gone forward into No Man's Land. As he left the front trench, the man in front, 18575 Sgt. Miles Benjamin Redmayne[i] of A Company, was shot in the head and killed. Redmayne had been awarded the DCM for his conduct in taking a German prisoner on 23rd

---

[i] 18575 Sgt. Miles Benjamin Redmayne, DCM, 1st East Lancashire Regt., came from Nelson, Lancashire. He worked at the Catlow Quarries, Nelson and lived at Southfield Cottages, Nelson. He was married. His body was never found and his name is inscribed on the Thiepval Memorial, Pier & Face 6C. He is remembered in Southfield Methodist Church, Southfield, Nelson, Lancashire.

September 1915. It had been Redmayne, along with Lts. Sayers and Mallett and L/Cpl. Wallace of the East Lancashires and 2nd Lt. Conan Doyle of the Hampshires, who had discovered the uncut German wire on the two previous nights. Uncut wire which, too late, was found to extend across most of the fronts of C and A Companies on the right and centre of the attack.

By about 7.40 a.m. 2nd Lt. Page was lurking outside this wire and, a few yards away, a group of German bombers were taunting the men trapped in No Man's Land, calling them to come on into range of the stick grenades they brandished. Page took a few pot shots at them but their bravado was rather more brutally ended by a British shell which, presumably falling short, ploughed into them. Prudence then dominated Page's thinking and he settled into a shell hole aware that any movement was likely to bring down machine gun fire as well as a German grenade or two. He was soon joined by 2nd Lt. William Daly who, correctly believing the attack to have been a complete failure and that any attempt to advance was hopeless, advised Page that it was now time to dig even further in and wait for nightfall before withdrawing. This they did.

Plate 68 2nd Lt. Eric Sidney Mallett, 1st East Lancashire Regt.

A few men, some suggest as many as 40, of the centre and left companies, A and B Companies, managed to penetrate the first German trench but there they were quickly overwhelmed by bombing counter-attacks from the II/RIR 121. It was here that Capt. Penny[i] of A Company was killed and Capt. Browne[ii] of B

---

[i] Capt. Arthur Hugh Penny, 1st East LancashireRegt., went to RMC, Sandhurst, was commissioned on 5th February 1913. He was promoted Captain on 6th August 1915. His body was never found and his name is inscribed on the Thiepval Memorial, Pier & Face 6C.

[ii] Capt. Meyrick Gouldsburg Browne, 3rd att. 1st East Lancashire Regt., had been commissioned into the 3rd East Lancashire Battalion out of the Special Reserve of Officers on 15th August 1914. He had previously been a 2nd Lt. in the 12th London Regt. (The Rangers), resigning his commission on 22nd March 1911. He was promoted Captain on 3rd January 1916. He was taken prisoner during the attack.

Company was made a Prisoner of War. In addition, 2nd Lts. Mallett[i] and Jones[ii] were killed.

Browne was fortunate to survive. He had been hit in the thigh in No Man's Land and his servant, 18517 Pte. Arthur Laverack, had helped dress the wound before Browne ordered him forward to find out how the attack was progressing. The twice wounded Capt. Penny appeared briefly before going off in search of the rest of A Company never to be seen again. As Browne attempted to move forward Laverack rushed back with the news that the men in the German trenches were being counter-attacked and that the few survivors were withdrawing. Within a few moments they were met by a dozen or so men retiring through the German wire. When they reached Browne they turned and opened fire on several Germans clearly visible above the parapet. Browne now set out in search of other men to rally and lead forward but, finding no-one alive, he was again wounded and forced to take shelter in a shell hole up close to the edge of the German wire where he remained all day until found by a German patrol and taken into their forward trenches. His faithful servant, Pte. Laverack, was never seen again[iii].

The 1st East Lancashire's attack was over and the remaining men, trapped in No Man's Land, waited hopefully for the long day to pass, the light to fade and a chance to escape.

Behind the East Lancashires, the men of the 1st Hampshire Regt. had started to advance over the open from the support and reserve lines at 7.40 a.m. The battalion was spread over three lines of assembly trenches behind Chatham and Minden Trenches. Colchester Trench was home to, from right to left, one platoon of C Company, two platoons of B Company and two of A Company. To their rear, the three remaining platoons of C Company were in Albuera Trench, the rest of B Company was in Winchester Trench between 4th Avenue and Tournai Trench and A Company's remaining two platoons were in Tournai

---

[i] 2nd Lt. Eric Sydney Mallett, 1st East Lancashire Regt., was aged 22. He was educated at Dulwich College and the Ecole de Commerce, Neuchatel. He joined the North British and Mercantile Insurance Company in 1911, working in their London Head Office. He enlisted as 1904 Private in the 28th London Regt., Artists' Rifles, going to France in December 1914. He was commissioned into the 1st East Lancashire Regt. in June 1915. His body was never found and his name is inscribed on the Thiepval Memorial, Pier & Face 6C.

[ii] 2nd Lt. Kenneth Champion Jones, 1st East Lancashire Regt., was aged 26. He was the fifth and youngest son of Frederick and Rose Jones of Lanherne, Beckenham, Kent. Educated at Oundle he was articled to a firm of chartered accountants. He joined the Artists' Rifles in September 1914 as a Private and went to France in December 1914. He was commissioned in July 1915. His body was never found and his name is inscribed on the Thiepval Memorial, Pier & Face 6C.

[iii] 18517 Pte Arthur Laverack, 1st East Lancashire Regt., was aged 29. He was the son of Thomas and Harriett Laverack, of Station Rd., Rawcliffe; husband of Edith Laverack (née Earl), of Rose Hill, Rawcliffe Bridge, Goole, Yorks. He worked at the Thorne Brewery. His body was never found and his name is inscribed on the Thiepval Memorial, Pier & Face 6C. A younger brother, 18480 Pte Clayton Laverack, 8th King's Own Yorkshire Light Infantry, aged 23, was also killed on 1st July near Ovillers la Boisselle and is remembered on the Thiepval Memorial, Pier & Face 11C.

Trench between Fox Street and 6th Avenue. D Company occupied Oscar Alley from just north of 4th Avenue to its junction with 6th Avenue. Battalion HQ, battalion carriers and a gun of the Brigade Trench Mortar Battery occupied Hampshire Trench and a short section at the southern end of Oscar Alley. The advanced battalion HQ was in a dugout on the southern side of 4th Avenue between Albuera and Hampshire Trenches.

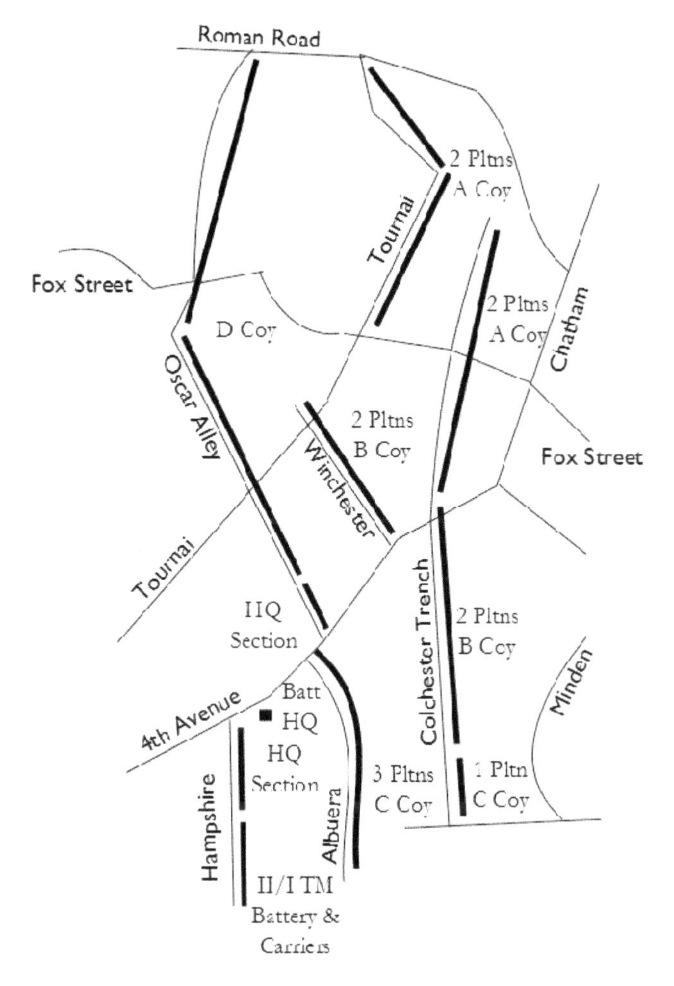

Figure 6 Assembly areas of 1st Hampshire Regt.

Artillery had caused the Hampshires some concerns before the attack started but the most serious damage was done to a section of the battalion buried by a British shell falling short! It took nearly an hour to dig the casualties out. When the order came to advance, therefore, it was almost a case of out of the frying pan into the fire but nothing could have prepared the men for the storm of machine gun fire which swept the British front lines as well as No Man's Land. They had observed the advance of the East Lancashires and witnessed its collapse but now they trudged forward, leaning into the hail of bullets as if into a gusting downpour. Many fell well short of their own wire but the few that survived battled onwards into No Man's Land passing the dead and wounded of the East Lancashires until forced to find shelter alongside their north country colleagues.

The Hampshires' 45 year old CO, Lt. Col. the Hon. Lawrence Charles Walter Palk, DSO, went into the attack armed with his stick. Palk was a popular CO. He had taken command of the battalion when his predecessor, Col. Hicks, had been wounded during the 2nd Battle of Ypres on 8th May 1915. Well educated and fluent in both German and French he had a reputation for reading sections of Gibbon's *'Decline and Fall of the Roman Empire'* to his junior officers.

One of his officers later remembered meeting Palk for the first time. His CO's views about how an officer should conduct himself were firmly enounced:

> "'The first time I met him he said, 'There are three things I will never have said to me: "it always 'as been done, Sir"; "never 'as been done, Sir" and "I thought". It is your business to know and to act"'.[12]

Such forthright views extended beyond the battalion and, as a result, he was heartily disliked by staff officers at most levels.

Palk was a veteran of the South African War and had served in the Hampshire Regt. for 22 years. Being armed only with a stick, however, was a perfect invitation to a German sniper or machine gunner and he was shot down early on and died in the Advanced Dressing Station a short time later[i]. As with the East Lancashire men, a few bombers were thought to have penetrated the German front trench where they were swiftly killed or ejected. The rest of the survivors found shelter in the already crowded shell holes where the remnants of the East Lancashire battalion now lay.

Lt. Errol Shearn[ii] was shot and wounded early in the attack but having found *only* 'a very neat hole under my left ribs from which a little blood was coming' he decided to 'get on with the war', moving forward with a fellow officer and friend 2nd Lt. Donald Day who, away to his left, was walking stolidly forward with his

---

[i] Lt. Col. the Hon. Lawrence Charles Walter Palk, DSO, 1st Hampshire Regt., was aged 45. He was the younger son of the late Lawrence Hesketh Palk, 2nd Baron Haldon and Baroness Haldon (née the Hon. Constance Mary Barrington and the daughter of the 7th Viscount Barrington of Ardglass). Educated at Wellington College, he joined the 8th Hussars in 1890. He was promoted from Sergeant to 2nd Lt. in the Hampshire Regt. on 4th July 1894, being promoted Lt. in 1897 and Brevet Major 11th November 1901. He served in India and in the South African War. Queen's Medal & 5 clasps. In 1906/07, now a Captain, he was twice temporarily put on half pay because of ill health. He was promoted Major on 20th December 1914. He was awarded the DSO for meritorious service during the retreat from Mons on 24th March 1915 and promoted Temp. Lt. Col. on 8th June 1915. MiD, he was also awarded the Legion d'Honneur. He is buried in the Sucrerie Military Cemetery, Colincamps, grave I. H. 14.

[ii] Lt. Errol David Shearn had been commissioned out of the 20th Royal Fusiliers on 15th May 1915. A solicitor, he moved to Malaya after the war joining Pooley & Co. in Kuala Lumpur, which company he took over in 1925. The company, Shearn Delamore & Co., still practices in Kuala Lumpur and Penang. Shearn became a Flying Officer in the RAF during WW2, was captured by the Japanese in 1942 and spent over three years in various Prisoner of War camps which he survived. His account of his war-time activities are held by the Imperial War Museum.

head down 'as though it were raining'. Shearn carried on, even saluting his company commander, Capt. Cyril Dalton Fawkes, an act which did not go down well with his superior who did not want it made obvious to German snipers he was an officer. Shearn now came to Watling Street, the sunken track which ran diagonally across No Man's Land. Here he found his friend 2nd Lt. Day being attended to by three men. Day had been wounded in the knee and was sheltering on the far side of the track under cover of a shallow bank. Shearn collected two of the three men and continued his increasingly forlorn advance. Within fifteen yards he was hit again, being spun around and knocked to the ground. Day's location in the sunken lane now seemed rather attractive and Shearn dragged himself back, finding Day still there and sensibly keeping his head down. Another man lurking there helped him dress his wounds pouring iodine into all available injuries, which now also included holes in his left bicep. When he enquired of the man whether that was the lot he was told:

"The lot? You've got a 'ole in your back you could put 'alf your 'and in!"

Shearn would survive (as would Donald Day), spending months in Bathurst House in Belgravia and recuperating in Folkestone. He would not return to the front, though, and spent his time on Army and RAF legal matters for which he was rather more formally trained.

Capt. Fawkes[i] was also badly wounded and lay out in No Man's Land encouraging his men to stick at it. For his pains and fortitude he became one of three men to win an MC amongst the ranks of the 1st Hampshires on 1st July 1916. The others were 2nd Lt. Guy Douglas Clifford Money[ii] and 5395 CSM John Palmer[iii].

Within half an hour the attack on the right flank of the 11th Brigade had completely collapsed, caught up on uncut wire and shredded by the German machine guns. Lt. Col. Green of the 1st East Lancashires, who was to be wounded out in No Man's Land some two hours later, related later that he had counted eight Maxims firing on his battalion's front. These guns would have been set up to provide interlocking fields of fire through which it was nearly impossible to advance without being hit. As a result, over 1,000 casualties from the 1st East Lancashires and 1st Hampshires now lay scattered across No Man's Land or between first lines of British trenches.

---

[i] Lt. (temp. Capt.) Cyril Dalton Fawkes, 1st Hampshire Regt., was awarded an MC for his conduct on 1st July 1916. The citation in the *London Gazette* of 22nd September 1916 reads: "For conspicuous gallantry in action. Though badly wounded early in the attack and unable to get on, he continued to encourage and cheer his men". Capt. Fawkes survived the war.

[ii] 2nd Lt. Guy Douglas Clifford Money, 1st Hampshire Regt., was awarded an MC for his conduct on 1st July 1916. The citation in the *London Gazette* of 22nd September 1916 reads: "For conspicuous gallantry in action. He kept his men together and led them into action under heavy machine-gun, shell and rifle fire. He showed the greatest coolness, and did fine work throughout the day".

[iii] 5395 CSM John Palmer, 1st Hampshire Regt., was awarded an MC for his conduct on 1st July 1916. The citation in the *London Gazette* of 22nd September 1916 reads: "For conspicuous gallantry in action. When all his company officers had become casualties he took command, led on the men, and set a splendid example".

Immediately to the left of the 1st East Lancashires no attack was to take place because of the state of the ground after the extensive mining warfare in the area. Consequently, the centre of the Ridge Redoubt would not be directly attacked leaving its occupants to interfere with any advances to both north and south. North of the crater field, it was the role of the 1st Rifle Brigade to attack the northern end of the Ridge Redoubt and the shallow re-entrant which lay between this Redoubt and the Heidenkopf. Driving on between these two fortifications, they were to establish themselves in the third line of trenches of the German 1st Position broadly along a line running from Points 62, via 94 to Point 49.

The battalion approached the front line trenches in two columns. On the right, and approaching the front lines via Vallade Corner, came I and A Companies and the Battalion HQ. To the left, and coming up Borden Avenue, were B and C Companies and the Battalion bombers. Final dispositions were: I Company on the right, A Company centre and B Company on the left. C Company was the support company. Each company had two platoons in the front line, one in support and one in the third line. I Company[i] occupied sectors 3 and 4 in the front line, with the third platoon in slits trenches off Cat and Beet Streets and the fourth platoon in Chatham Trench. A Company occupied sectors 5 and 6 in the front line, with its third platoon at the head of Dog Street and the fourth in a new trench to the rear. B Company took over sectors 7 and 8 with some men in slit trenches off Borden Avenue and Egg Street, the third platoon was in a new trench to the rear and the fourth in Burrow Trench. C Company, in support of I Company, was at the north end of Chatham Street and in the areas around Freddy and Buster Streets. Battalion HQ and scouts were in Freddy Street and the Battalion bombers in Buster Street.

The men settled down to wait for the off, being fed a breakfast of cocoa, bacon and potted meat sandwiches before facing the enemy and rum was issued two hours before zero. Some would need extra stamina for the attack. Every man would carry two of the 1 lb. 11 oz. (765 gm.) Mills bombs across to the enemy's lines and, in total, the battalion would take a total of 2,120 Mills bombs into the attack of which a third would be carried by the battalion scouts and bombers. But, some in the lead companies had a far heavier weight to handle. Twenty men had been given a large 'bomb bucket' to carry. Each bucket contained twelve Mills bombs at a total weight of 20 lbs (9.2 Kg). Ten of the officers and NCOs would take a small bucket with six bombs into the attack. Each company would have some 400 bombs between them assuming, of course, that all of these slower moving targets made it across No Man's Land. It might have seemed a lot at the time. It was not.

Two tunnels had been dug across No Man's Land to within a few feet of the front edge of the German wire. These two tunnels started at the heads of Beet

---

[i] The existence of I Company, as opposed to D Company, in the 1st Rifle Brigade is thought to derive from an incident in the 2nd Kaffir War of 1852-3 when the regiment consisted of ten companies, A to J. I Company was attached to the GOC, Lt. Gen Cathcart, as his 'camp bodyguard' in an operation against the Basuto north of the Orange River at Berea Hill where it so distinguished itself in the ensuing fighting that I Company became a traditional part of the 1st Battalion from then onwards. When the battalion was reorganised to four companies, I Company was retained as part of this tradition.

and Cat Streets and were opposite the northern end of the Ridge Redoubt. A Lewis gun team was concealed at the head of each tunnel and, at 7.25 a.m. the time when the heavy guns and howitzers moved off the German support trench, the ends of the tunnels were broken open and the guns were mounted in the wire. The first shock was that the wire here was uncut. At 7.28 a.m. the gun teams started to see activity in the German front trenches. Fire was opened on the parapet but was not sufficient to supress the growing volume of machine gun fire that was now sweeping both the infantry advancing behind them or was being directed at their positions.

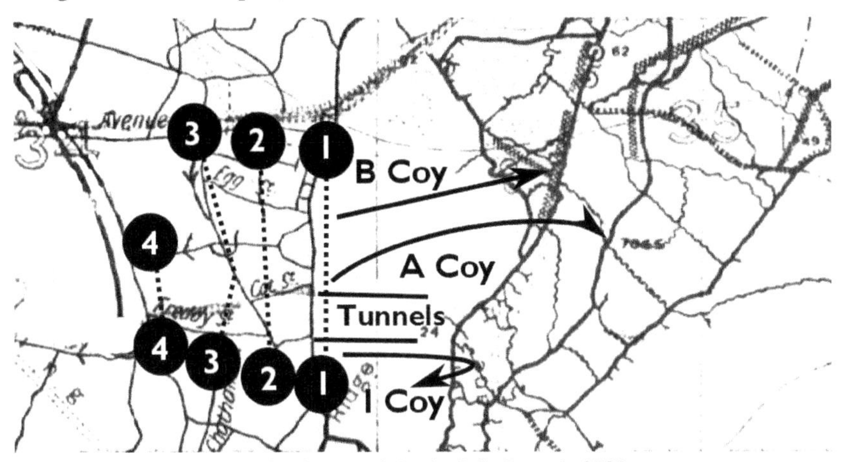

Map 21 Attack of the 1st Rifle Brigade 0730

Key:
I to I = 2 Platoons each of I, A and B Companies (from right to left)
2 to 2 = 1 Platoon each of I, A and B Companies (from right to left)
3 to 3 = 1 Platoon each of I, A and B Companies (from right to left)
4 to 4 = C Company

The diminutive Lt. George Glover late recalled how the men had advanced:

> "They got up out of the trenches (rather envying the officers the privilege of going first), lay down, and at the given signal all stood up and moved off. Not a charge, no running, no shouting, just a steady walk keeping perfect alignment."[13]

The men of the Rifle Brigade had managed to get most of the way across No Man's Land before two machine guns on the parapet of the northern flank of the Ridge Redoubt and others to the rear and left started to sweep their lines. The majority of I Company on the right, also exposed to two more machine guns on the face of the redoubt and those firing in enfilade from about the northern end of Beaumont Hamel, was cut down. Here the ground was badly broken up, partly by the craters left over from the efforts at mine warfare aimed at either side's fortified position on the ridge, the Redan and the Ridge Redoubt, and partly by the work of the British 2 in. trench mortars during the bombardment. No Man's Land was little more than 100 yards wide and the mortars had not only cut the German wire but also badly damaged the German trenches including the entrances to some of the deep dugouts. As a result, the defenders took somewhat longer to get into position than on other less damaged parts of the German line, and a party estimated at one officer and ten bombers somehow found their way through the craters and into the German front line. Initial resistance from some men from the 4/Württemberg Pionier Bataillon, Nr. 13 failed to prevent the incursion which, fortuitously, had occurred at the junction of two companies of two different battalions of the RIR 121: the 7. Kompanie to the south and the 1. Kompanie to the north. Independent initiative, however, was the hallmark of the German officer and NCO and, seeing the break-in from the German support trench, Hptm. der Reserve Gonsor, the OC of the 1. Kompanie, collected some men together and counter-attacked over the open. Covered by a machine gun he had brought up and which now prevented any British reinforcements from reaching their now beleaguered colleagues in the German front line, Gonsor and his men proved irresistible. With both flanks in the air and under savage counter-attack also from the 7. Kompanie on their right, the position of this small group rapidly became untenable and they were forced back out into the shelter of shell holes in No Man's Land. Within minutes the attack of I Company was over and all four of its officers were killed or fatally wounded.

The company commander, Capt. Hugh Russell-Smith[i], a Fellow of St John's College, Cambridge, and a lecturer in History and Political Science, was gravely wounded and would die five days later at a base hospital in Rouen. Seeing his commander down, the gallant 2nd Lt. Frederick Kirkland[ii] briefly took command before a bullet to the head ended his life. The other officers from I Company, 2nd Lt. James Morum[iii] and 2nd Lt. Cyril Volkers[iv], were both cut down, neither to

---

[i] Capt. Hugh Francis Russell-Smith, 6th att. 1st Rifle Brigade, died on 5th July 1916. Aged 28, he was the son of Henry and Ellen Russell-Smith of Heathside, Potters Bar. Graduate of St. John's College, Cambridge (Classical Tripos 1909, History Tripos 1910). Awarded Thirlwall Prize, 1911, for dissertation on *'The Theory of Religious Liberty in the reigns of Charles II and James II'*. Elected Allen Scholar. Elected Fellow of St John's College, Cambridge, 1912, and lecturer in History and Political Science. Commissioned into the Cambridge University Contingent OTC on 21st February 1915 and into the 6th Rifle Brigade on 22nd May 1915. He is buried in St. Sever Cemetery, Rouen, grave Officers, A. 3. 10.

[ii] 2nd Lt. Frederick William Kirkland, 6th att. 1st Rifle Brigade, was aged 20. He was the son of Charles Frederick Kirkland, an engineer and spindlemaker, and Edith Bottomley of Islay Cottage, 7, Braeside Avenue, Rutherglen. He was educated at North Eastern County School, Barnard Castle, where he was head monitor and a member of the Cadet Corps. He received a scholarship to Emmanuel College, Cambridge. He was commissioned into the 6th Rifle Brigade on 28th November 1914 and went to France in June 1915. Invalided home sick he returned to join the 1st Rife Brigade on 24th February 1916. His body was never found and his name is inscribed on the Thiepval Memorial, Pier & Face 16B & 16C.

[iii] 2nd Lt. James Pearse Morum, 6th att. 1st Rifle Brigade, was aged 20. He was the eldest son of William E and Florence S Morum of Chislehurst, Kent. He was born in Queenstown, Cape Colony, South Africa. He was educated at Merton Court School, Sidcup, and Wellington College and was an undergraduate at Pembroke College, Cambridge. He joined the Army in Cambridge and was commissioned on 16th December 1914. He is buried in Sucrerie Military Cemetery, Colincamps, grave I. H. 1.

[iv] 2nd Lt. Frederick Cyril Stowell Volkers, 1st Rifle Brigade, was aged 20. He was the son of Robert Charles Francis Volkers, C.I.E., of 5, Lovelace Rd., Dulwich, London, and of Ellen Volkers (deceased). He was educated at Dulwich College where he was in the rugby 1st

survive the day. With this, the entire attack of the 4th Division from the northern edge of the Ridge Redoubt down to Beaumont Hamel was over. According to German accounts the entire operation took less than an hour.

Behind them, the two Lewis gun teams in the tunnels on the edge of the German wire had come under heavy machine gun fire and by 7.35 a.m. both guns were out of action and had been withdrawn into the shelter of the tunnels. 2nd Lt. George Albert Robson had been given the task of commanding and taking forward the Lewis guns and he now sent back for a new gun to replace the damaged ones. Some German troops in the front line, noting that the guns had ceased fire, rushed the exits to the tunnels and bombed the men there. Robson withdrew his men and built a block in the total darkness of the tunnel where, for the next two hours, he and his dwindling band of men defied the enemy bombers. For his leadership and conduct, 2nd Lt. Robson[i] was awarded the MC.

Meanwhile, above ground, ferocious fighting continued. To the left of I Company, the two lead platoons of A Company had advanced accompanied by 2nd Lt. Neil Fagan, the battalion bombing officer. As men started to fall in dozens around him the 20 year old officer stopped to help one of the wounded and was himself hit three times. Fagan fell in No Man's Land and was to lie there for 48 hours before being found and brought in by one of the search parties sent out repeatedly to recover the numerous wounded men unable to move. He clung to life for nearly three weeks before dying in hospital in Chichester on 20th July[ii].

The remnants of A Company, endeavouring to get away from the vicious machine gun fire pouring from the Ridge Redoubt, veered away to the left towards where B Company was taking advantage of a slight change in the ground which helped conceal them from these guns. Again, all A Company officers had become casualties: Capt. Rowland Fraser[iii] and Lt. Malcolm White were killed and

XV. He enlisted in the 5th London Regt. (London Rifle Brigade) ten days after leaving school and went to France in November 1914. He was invalided home in April 1915 and returned to the front in August. He entered the Cadet School, St Omer, in November and was commissioned into the 1st Rifle Brigade on 13th December 1915. His body was never found and his name is inscribed on the Thiepval Memorial, Pier & Face 16B & 16C.

[i] 2nd Lt. George Albert Robson, 1st Rifle Brigade, who joined the battalion on 26th October 1915, was awarded an MC for his conduct on 1st July 1916. The citation in the *London Gazette* of 22nd September 1916 reads: "For conspicuous gallantry in action. Just before the assault he mounted his two machine-guns, and fired them till they were both put out of action by shell-fire. While bringing up a new gun the enemy bombed his party, but he built a block and held up their bombing attacks for two hours in a tunnel in total darkness, though most of his party had become casualties".

[ii] 2nd Lt. Neil Fagan, 6th att. 1st Rifle Brigade, was aged 20. He was the younger son of Sir Patrick James Fagan, C.S.I., I.C.S., the Financial Commissioner of the Punjab, and Emily Fagan of The Boundary, Simla. Born at Montgomery, Punjab, India, he was educated at Woolton Court, Canterbury, Rugby School, 1909-1911, and entered Pembroke College, Cambridge, in October 1914 where he joined the OTC. He was commissioned into the 6th Rifle Brigade in November 1914 and went to France in July 1915. He is buried in Chichester Cemetery, grave 126. 13.

[iii] Capt. Rowland Fraser, 6th att. 1st Rifle Brigade, was aged 26. He was the son of J M Fraser Esq., an Auctioneer and Live Stock Agent, and Alice Fraser of Invermay, Forgandenny. He was married to Mary Dorothy Fraser of Invermay, Forgandenny, Perthshire. Educated at Merchiston Castle, Edinburgh, (Cadet Corps 1903-8), Pembroke

Lt. George Glover wounded, though Glover and a few men reached the German trenches.

Plate 69 Capt. Hugh Francis Russell-Smith, 1st Rifle Brigade

Plate 70 2nd Lt. Frederick Cyril Stowell Volkers, 1st Rifle Brigade

Plate 71 2nd Lt. Neil Fagan, 1st Rifle Brigade

Plate 72 Capt. Rowland Fraser, 1st Rifle Brigade

College, Cambridge (graduated 1908) and Edinburgh University, where he studied Law. He was in the Merchiston cricket 1st XI for four years and the rugby 1st XV and played for the Grange CC and Perthshire. He was the captain of the Cambridge Rugby XV, 1910-11, and was a Scottish rugby International winning four caps against France, Wales, Ireland and England in 1911. Promoted 2nd Lt. from the OTC into the 6th Rifle Brigade on 15th August 1914, he went to France on 5th January 1915. His body was never found and his name is inscribed on the Thiepval Memorial, Pier & Face 16B & 16C.

Plate 73 Lt. George Wright Glover, 1st Rifle Brigade

Glover[i] was a small man, just 5 ft. 2 in. tall, and had previously been rejected for service for being too short. He was not to be denied and this South African-born lecturer in German at Princeton University resigned his comfortable post in New Jersey and returned to the UK in June 1915. He was commissioned into the Rifle Brigade on 2nd November 1915. Now he led his men forward into the German lines. His platoon was one of the support platoons and he recalled later, in a letter written from hospital in France and sent to Maj. Geoffrey Barclay, how things had seemed to run smoothly in the first few minutes, although he was almost immediately wounded in the left arm.:

> "…. Things seemed going quite well till we, or rather our first wave, reached the German front line; they slowed and we bunched rather and the most fearsome hail of rifle and machine gun fire with continuous shelling opened on us. Most of us seemed to be knocked out."

[i] Lt. George Wright Glover, DSO, 6th att. 1st Rifle Brigade, died on 1st September 1918. Aged 33, he was the son of Thomas and Marannah Glover of Pretoria, South Africa. He was educated at Leigh Grammar School and Manchester University where he was a member of the OTC. MA, 1st Class, Modern Languages, 1913. He joined the staff at the University of Marburg, Germany, before becoming a German lecturer at Princeton University. He resigned from Princeton in June 1915 and returned to England to enlist. He was rejected for service several times because of his height but joined the battalion on 21st April 1916. The George Wright Glover Memorial Scholarship was established at Princeton in his memory after he died of wounds at the Drocourt-Queant Switch Line on 31st August, 1918. He is buried in Aubigny Communal Cemetery Extension, grave IV. G. 40. Glover was awarded the DSO for his actions on 1st July. The citation reads: "For conspicuous gallantry in action. Though twice wounded in the advance, he continued to lead his men forward under heavy machine gun and artillery fire into the enemy's third line, where he organised the defences. Although his left arm was useless, he threw bombs as long as there was any supply. He set a splendid example all day".

An account of his day and news of the award of the DSO were carried in the *New York Times* on 12th October 1916:

> "Most of our casualties were in the first few minutes, myself amongst them. But such is the effect of imagination that, since I couldn't see any hole in my tunic nor at first any blood, and since I got the two bullets absolutely simultaneously, I imagined that a shell had gone off somewhere and that two piece had given me rather hard knocks, one of which had certainly bruised my shoulder. So after feeling sick for a second or two, I picked myself up and decided that I was still very much alive, and that I would be foolish to stop for that, so I proceeded. And, anyway, an officer doesn't altogether need his arms, provided he keeps his head."[14]

Still having his right arm with which to throw bombs, 2nd Lt. Glover[i] and Sgt. Smith and Cpl. Halls[ii] started to lob them at a group of Germans who appeared in a nearby trench. The bombs sent them off to the right in a hurry and Glover and a few others, now accompanied by some men from the Somersets who had somehow made it across No Man's Land, advanced until they reached the second German trench. Here Glover met up with 9703 CSM Tom Selway[iii] and Sgt. Hunt and, together with Sgt. Smith[iv], they started to consolidate their position and explore the trenches to the north in the hope of making contact with B Company and the two battalions of Royal Warwickshires who should, by now, have been on their left.

B Company, on the 1st Rifle Brigade's left, was to attack just to the south of the Heidenkopf and here some men of the 1st wave entered the German trenches from where they started to bomb southwards towards the expected position of A Company. Instead they met strong German bombing parties and, with any further progress impossible, set to building a trench block while they waited for the anticipated support from C Company and the 1st Somerset Light Infantry, the support battalion. The OC of B Company was a youthful looking 21 year old Old Harrovian, Capt. William Henry Beever. A graduate of the Royal Military College, Sandhurst, he had joined the 3rd Rifle Brigade before transferring to the 1st

[i] Glover was lucky with his wounds. He described one as 'a mere scratch, but half an inch would have meant my spine'. The other, he wrote, 'might easily have shattered the humerus at the joint but the bullet took a bit out and passed straight on, not even turning'. Such, he said, was 'the advantage of being shot at close range'.

[ii] 5093 Cpl James John Halls, DCM, 1st Rifle Brigade, was killed on 1st July 1916. Aged 20, he was the son of James J. and Elizabeth Halls, of 13, Museum St., Saffron Walden, Essex. He is buried in Sucrerie Military Cemetery, Colincamps, grave I. E. 16. He had won his DCM for his conduct on 13th May 1915 at Mousetrap Farm near Ypres when he and a Cpl H E Shunnuck were cut off for nine hours but held their post.

[iii] 9703 CSM Thomas Upton Selway, MC, DCM, 1st Rifle Brigade, survived the war and was awarded the DCM on 31st December 1918. His MC was gazetted on 20th October 1916. The citation reads: "For conspicuous gallantry in action. When all his officers had become casualties, he took command, and led his company forward to the enemy third line, where he assisted an officer in organising the defences. When finally relieved by another regiment he would not leave the trench till all the men of his regiment had got back. He has done fine service throughout the campaign".

[iv] 4080 Actg. Sgt. Charles E Smith, 1st Rifle Brigade, was awarded the MM for his conduct on 1st July 1916. It was gazetted on 1st September 1916.

Battalion at the end of 1915. He had managed to get at least some of his men into the enemy lines but was wounded and, during the fighting, he slipped from view forever[i].

Plate 74 Capt. William Henry Beever, 1st Rifle Brigade

It was here that the second line of German trenches ran very close to their front line and just west of Frontier Lane, the track that ran from Beaumont Hamel north to Serre. Almost certainly it is in this area that the few men from A Company under 2nd Lt. Glover and some survivors from the Company's 2nd and 3rd waves joined up with the men from B Company. A short while later, they were reinforced by the remnants of C Company and the leading elements of the Somersets. A few men from the leading waves of the 8th Royal Warwickshires also filtered through the network of trenches at the base of the Heidenkopf to swell the numbers still further.

The Somersets had surged forward from their positions in and around Vallade Trench as soon as the Rifle Brigade left their trenches. A, on the right, and B Companies led with two platoons in each of two waves, with C and H Companies in support deployed in the same scheme. To get to the British front line the Somersets had some 300 yards to advance over the open in full view of the German machine guns sweeping No Man's Land and the front trenches. Men started to fall immediately and, amongst those lost even before No Man's Land

[i] Capt. William Henry Beever, B Company, 1st Rifle Brigade, was aged 21. He was the elder son of Major Henry Holt Beever, RFA and Katherine Leonide Brocklebank of Littleton House, Blandford, Dorset. He was educated at Harrow School and the RMC, Sandhurst, where he won the Riding Prize in 1913. He was commissioned into the 3rd Rifle Brigade in August 1914, going to France in October 1914. He transferred to the 1st Rifle Brigade in autumn 1915, was promoted Captain and given command of B Company. His body was never found and his name is inscribed on the Thiepval Memorial, Pier & Face 16B & 16C. His younger brother, Lt. Jonathan Holt Beever, G Battery, 17th Brigade, Royal Horse Artillery, died on 25th March 1918. He is remembered on the Pozieres Memorial.

was reached, were Lt. Col. John Audley Thicknesse[i] and the Adjutant, Capt. Charles Ford[ii].

Plate 75 Lt. Col. John Audley Thicknesse, 1st Somerset Light Infantry

As with the Rifle Brigade, the sheer weight of fire from their right pushed the line of the advance north east instead of eastwards as the men did anything to avoid the withering fire of the two machine guns in the northern face of the Ridge Redoubt and those further south. Writing after the war, the Brigade Major of the 11th Brigade, Maj. William 'Bunt' Somerville of the King's Own[iii], blamed the failure of the left wing of the 4th Division's attack almost entirely on these two guns. These guns and the early lift of the artillery off the German front line:

---

[i] Lt. Col. John Audley Thicknesse, 1st Somerset Light Infantry, was aged 46. He was the fifth and youngest son of the Right Rev. Dr Francis Henry Thicknesse, D.D., late Bishop of Leicester and Anne Thicknesse; and husband of Phyllis Margaret Thicknesse (née Woodcock) of South Luffenham Hall and Minster Precincts, Peterborough. The grandson of Ralph Thicknesse, MP for Wigan. Born at Middleton Cheney, Northants, he was educated at Charterhouse. He was commissioned into the 3rd Leicestershire Regt., in October 1888, being promoted Lt. in 1890 and transferring to the Somerset LI in 1891. He served on the North-West Frontier of India and in the South African War. Promoted Captain in 1901 he became the Adjutant of the 3rd SLI in May 1904 before being promoted Major in 1911. He started the war as a Brigade Major and was given command of the 1st Somerset LI in August 1915. He is buried in Sucrerie Military Cemetery, Colincamps, grave I. H. 15.

[ii] Capt. & Adjt. Charles Clement Ford, 1st Somerset Light Infantry, was aged 21. He was the son of the late Commander C R Ford, Royal Indian Marine. He was educated at the United Services College. Commissioned in February 1914, he was promoted Lieutenant on 18th May 1915 and Captain on 21st February 1916. He was wounded in May 1915. He is buried in Sucrerie Military Cemetery, Colincamps, grave I. I. 67.

[iii] Maj., later Lt. Col., William Arthur Tennison Bellingham Somerville, DSO & Bar, King's Own Royal Lancaster Regt., won his first DSO in 1915 and his second in 1917. He was mentioned in despatches five times.

"About this time, two enemy machine guns opened from the Ridge Redoubt. These guns, to my mind, were the main cause of the failure of the 4th Division attack in the Northern sector.
The Redoubt was never taken and was held strongly throughout the morning and the guns… facing north swept the whole area over No Man's Land and the front line systems. The havoc they caused was immense, the rear waves of the Rifle Brigade and 8th R Warwicks Regt., the supporting battalions… and again the lines of battalions of the 10th and 12th Brigades were all taken in enfilade at close range."[15]

9090 Sgt. Arthur Henry Cook was amongst the leading waves being thinned by enemy gunfire with every step across No Man's Land. 2nd Lt. H M Tilley, his platoon commander, was wounded close to the German lines[i] and with his platoon sergeant dead, Cook assumed command of what little was left. The planned attack in well-ordered waves had now broken down into small mad dashes from one form of cover to another, from shell hole to shell hole and into the German front line trench. Cook admitted later he had lost control of his men as they moved into the German trench system. The ground was covered with the dead and wounded of the Rifle Brigade and the enfilade fire from the Ridge Redoubt was brutal. After a brief pause Cook led his little band to the second German trench to join the likes of 2nd Lt. Glover and the men from B Company of the Rifle Brigade.

Everywhere the ground was churned up by the fire of the British 18 pdrs, field howitzers and trench mortars but it was immediately apparent that the German dugouts were intact. Because of this, and because the supporting waves of the advancing battalions were either dead or wounded or dreadfully thinned by the heavy casualties, the process of clearing the captured trenches and dugouts was hardly thorough and groups of German soldiers were able to appear in unexpected places ready to attack from the rear or flank when least expected.

On the far left of the 4th Division's front the job of taking the German 1st position had been given to the 1/8th Royal Warwickshires of the 143rd Brigade, 48th (South Midland) Division, supported by the 1/6th Battalion. These two battalions were Territorial units drawn from in and around Birmingham. Their jumping off trenches were aligned towards the east and south east and faced either side of the nose of the Heidenkopf salient which projected out from the German trenches on a shallow slope which ran down towards the Serre to Mailly Maillet Road.

The Heidenkopf, or Quadrilateral as it was known to the British, was a relic of the old German front line the rest of which had been lost during French attacks the previous summer. Previously, the German lines had here crossed the Serre-Mailly Road before turning north towards Toutvent Farm but, as a result of the French advance, all that was left was the small salient overlooked from the British lines. The German accepted that the Heidenkopf was fundamentally indefensible. In consequence, there was to be no serious attempt at defending the area and, instead, a trap was planned for any advancing infantry. Whilst mining opposite the Ridge Redoubt had been extensive, nothing had previously taken

---

[i] 2nd Lt. Tilley was made a Prisoner of War.

place around the Heidenkopf. As a result, the men from 4/Württemberg Pionier Bataillon, Nr. 13 under Leutnant der Reserve Eitel, were left undisturbed as they excavated four chambers under No Man's Land around the face of the salient. In each of them charges were laid with the intention that, as the British advanced, they would be destroyed by the simultaneous blowing of the four mines just as they reached the edge of the German wire. The effectiveness of this ploy would be disputed later. Suffice to say that the Germans believed it to have been successful whilst it is mentioned only in passing in British accounts[i]. What is not in dispute is that members of the demolition team died in some of the explosions, thought to have been premature, and that these mines may have taken with them a machine gun helping to defend the German position. Such a result does not really support the German claim that the mines exploded 'according to plan'[16], however, the account does state that men from the 1/RIR 121, defending the Ridge Redoubt, noticed the surge forward of British troops falter at the time the mines were blown. Later, after the attack had finished, a large number of British dead were found in the area of the resulting craters but whether they were killed by the mines or died for other reasons is not clear.

Writing after the war, however, Capt. D R Adams, C Company, 1/8th Royal Warwickshire Regt., talked of a 'mine under the Heidenkopf Redoubt (being) exploded while the forward elements of the 1/8th Warwicks were actually crossing the German front line trench', which suggests the explosions may well have been effective. He also noticed a dead German machine gun detachment which, he believed, had been put out of action by the Stokes mortar barrage. What appears to have happened is that two of the mines were detonated early on, whether prematurely or not no-one can say, and that these may have killed or wounded some of the 1/8th Royal Warwicks. It is thought that the other two mines may have been detonated later, either deliberately or accidentally, and that these caught some men of the 2nd Lancashire Fusiliers. No authoritative report was possible as the officer in charge of the Pioniers, Lt. d Res. Eitel[ii], was later found dead in Bayern Graben, the trench that ran along the base of the Heidenkopf.

Before all of this took place, the men of the 1/8th Royal Warwicks had readied themselves for the assault by lying out on the British parapet at 7.28 a.m. The war diary notes that German machine guns had already been firing for three minutes, i.e. from the time the heavier guns and field howitzers had left the German support line. At 7.30 a.m. the whistles blew and the men advanced. On the far left, D Company immediately found themselves exposed to heavy machine gun fire from their left. Here the ground rises gently towards the village of Serre, the objective of the 31st Division. Unfortunately, the right company of the 15th West Yorkshires, which was supposed to be advancing on the 1/8th Warwicks' left, was almost completely destroyed by the heavy and accurate German artillery barrage which crashed down on their forming up trenches just

[i] Although they were remarked upon by Lt. Col. Simonds, CO, 170th Brigade, RFA, of the 31st Division, whose OP looked out over the Heidenkopf as well as Serre.

[ii] According to *Somme Nord*, though his name does not appear in the Verlustlisten of the 4/Württemberg Pionier Bataillon, Nr. 13.

before zero[i]. As a result of the almost immediate collapse of their attack, the German machine gunners in and around the village took the opportunity to switch their targets to the men advancing from the 4th Division's lines. Thankfully, the initial bursts of fire were too high and the 1/8th Warwicks pressed on towards the German front line but the range was soon adjusted and D Company and to a lesser extent, C Company to their right, started to suffer heavy casualties. L/Cpl. Williamson saw the lines of men start to dissolve as they advanced under the increasingly accurate fire from Serre. The Battalion Signalling Officer, Lt. H M Jones, was one of the early wounded as was CSM Haines. Everywhere men were collapsing to the ground and the attack was reduced to small groups of men advancing in short rushes. Behind them, while still inside the British lines, the CO, Lt. Col. Edgar Innes[ii] and the Adjutant, Lt. Arthur Procter[iii], were both killed.

Another officer to be wounded early on was the battalion Medical Officer, Lt. Fred Newton Walsh. Alongside him the majority of the stretcher bearers were also caught by the German machine gun and artillery fire. One, unknown, stretcher bearer did survive and manned the Regimental Aid Post more or less single-handed. He collected wounded and gave what treatment he could. In the grand scheme of things it was a small matter but, without this man, there would have been no organised collection and treatment of casualties until the replacement MO, Lt. Fairley from the 1/3rd South Midland Field Ambulance, arrived well into the afternoon. It was observed, however, that many fatalities resulted from German shells falling amongst the seriously wounded and immobile men out in No Man's Land who could not be moved due the lack of stretcher bearers. Meanwhile, those wounded able to shift themselves tended to by-pass the overcrowded RAP and, instead, trailed down the long, crowded and muddy communication trenches to arrive untreated at the ADS at Euston in ever increasing numbers. The resulting strain on the doctors and medical orderlies at this facility rapidly became overwhelming.

---

[i] Capt. D R Adams of the 1/8th Royal Warwicks visited the trenches of this company: "I would state that later in the day I went through the forming up trenches of the right Company of the 15th W. Yorks and they were so blocked with dead and dying that progress through the trench was impossible."

[ii] Lt. Col. Edgar Arthur Innes, CMG, 1/8th Royal Warwickshire Regt., was aged 43. He was the son of the late Mr Innes of Harborne Hill House, Birmingham. He lived at Metchley Abbey, Metchley Lane, Harborne and was a partner in Innes, Smith & Co., Wine Merchants of Burlington Passage, 124a New Street, Birmingham. A pre-war Territorial, he was commissioned into the 1st Birmingham Volunteer Battalion, Royal Warwickshire Regt., on 18th April 1900 and promoted Major into the 8th Royal Warwickshire Regt., on 1st April 1908. He was promoted Lt. Col. on 17th May 1913. He was awarded the CMG in the New Year's Honours List of 14th January 1916. His body was never found and his name is inscribed on the Thiepval Memorial, Pier & Face 9A, 9B & 10B.

[iii] Lt. & Adjutant Arthur Procter, MC, 1/8th Royal Warwickshire Regt., was aged 28. He was the son of Mr and Mrs W Procter of 91, Trafalgar Rd., Moseley, Birmingham. He was awarded the MC for his conduct during a trench raid. It was gazetted on 16th May 1916. His body was never found and his name is inscribed on the Thiepval Memorial, Pier & Face 9A, 9B & 10B.

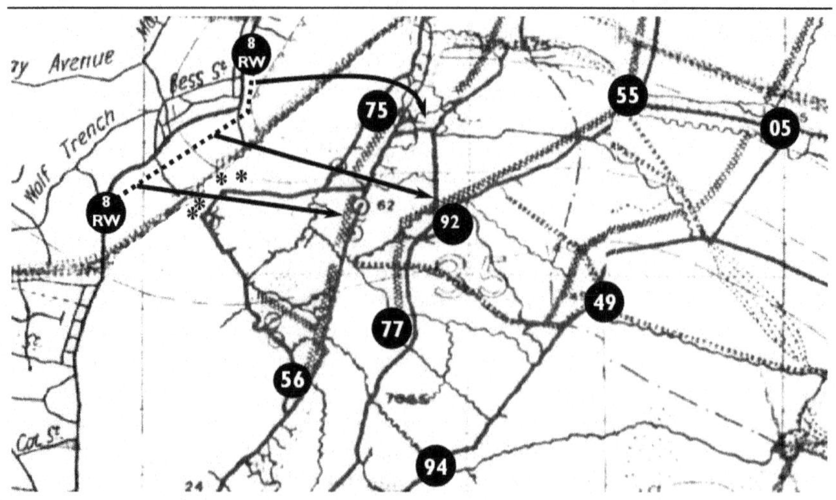

Map 22 Attack of the 1/8th Royal Warwickshire Regt., 0730

Q = Site of German mine craters detonated during advance

On a slightly more positive note, however, the initially swift advance of the Warwicks had caught the men of the 2 and 3/RIR 121 unawares and many men were either still trying to get out of their dugouts or were trapped as a result of damage caused by the bombardment and, possibly, the German's own mine explosions. As a result, on the battalion's right the Warwicks swept over the front German line with little resistance from the isolated parties of the left section of the 3. Kompanie, RIR 121, and then moved to attack the rest of this company from the flank and rear. Several of the 3. Kompanie were caught underground trapped in their bunkers by the rapid advance. Amongst them was the company commander, Oberleutnant Max Lutz. Already slightly wounded Lutz decided that caution was the best option and he and his men waited below ground until, hopefully, their comrades could come to the aid.

Currently, therefore, the main resistance to the British advance seemed to be coming from the machine guns from Serre and from three machine guns thought to be in the German third trench. German demands for artillery support were now urgently made. A Leutnant der Reserve Beck of the 3. Kompanie was established in a concrete reinforced OP between the first and second line of trenches that ran along the base of the Heidenkopf. He had previously spent time liaising with the artillery by spotting targets and then the fall of their shot when these targets were engaged. Now, with his telephone wire to the rear cut by a British artillery shell, he sent up red flares, the German signal for urgent artillery intervention (and the British signal that a position had been taken). Covering the front line trenches of the 1st Rifle Brigade and 1/8th Royal Warwicks (sectors 35 to 37 according to German maps) were just six guns, two 77 mm field guns of the 2. Batterie. FAR 104 and four 10.5 cm field howitzers of 5. Batterie, RFAR 20. In addition, two captured Russian 15 cm field howitzers from 1. Batterie of Fußartillerie-Bataillon Nr. 51 covered the area to the rear over which the supporting battalions of the 11th and 12th Brigades were now advancing. It was hardly a powerful force of artillery but the exposed masses of British infantry presented such excellent targets that every shell seemed to find a billet amongst their ranks.

In addition, the two heavy, one medium and one light minenwerfers of the Württembergisches Minenwerfer-Kompanie Nr. 226 joined in on the entire front line of RIR 121 along with the regiment's own extemporised heavy Erdmörsers and Albrecht mörsers and the lightweight Priestermörsers. The first two, made from a wooden, wire bound cylinder, fired large 25 cm projectiles with a huge killing radius. The Erdmörser, or 'earth mortar', was literally dug into the ground and fired on a fixed line and trajectory but, with a projectile weighing over 50 lbs. (23.5 Kgs), its effect could be devastating over a radius of more than ten metres. The Priestermörsers was a small, mobile mortar firing a 2 Kg round akin to a grenade and was, apparently, invented by a Hungarian priest names Vecer (thus the name). Originally in service with the Austro-Hungarian Army it was adopted into the German Army as the Granatwerfer 16 and manufactured under licence. These shorter range pieces too fired on No Man's Land and the British front line helping to cut off the lead elements of the British attack from their reserves and supplies.

With the German machine guns now finding the range, casualties swiftly mounted and the surviving troops resorted to isolated rushes in small parties towards the German support line some 200 yards distant. Capt. Douglas Raymond Adams of C Company was one of those who made it into the German second trench in an area where the ground rose towards the ridge behind the far left corner of the Heidenkopf. Here he was wounded at about 7.50 a.m., becoming one of the six officer casualties from the company. He remembers seeing the remnants of D Company still struggling forward on his left. With him was the commander of C Company, Capt. Stratford Ludlow, the son of Col. W R Ludlow who had been in command of the 8th Royal Warwickshire Regt. when it was formed in 1908. Ludlow had been wounded in the crossing of No Man's Land and he was last seen with a group of his men in the German 2nd trench[i].

Another thing that Capt. Adams clearly recalled after the war was that any 'further advance was impossible' on the part of the 1/8th Warwicks though it is thought that some men may have reached Serre Trench. Later suggestions that elements of his battalion reached Munich Trench can, therefore, be discounted for this reason and one other – Serre Trench, a couple of hundred yards west of Munich Trench, was their final objective. It was the task of the 1/6th Warwicks to take Munich Trench.

The troops now sheltering in the second (support) trench were still under fire from the machine guns in the third (reserve) trench around Point 92 and this caused a delay as various intrepid groups rushed forward to dislodge the enemy.

[i] Capt. Stratford Walter Ludlow, C Company, 1/8th Royal Warwickshire Regt., was aged 22. He was the youngest of the six children of Brig. Gen. Walter Robert Ludlow, C.B., and Helen Florence Ludlow (née Hart) of Lovelace Hill, Solihull. Brig. Gen. Ludlow had been the Lt. Col. and Hon. Col. of the 8th Royal Warwickshire Regt. from 1908 to 1913. Capt. Ludlow was educated at the King's Cathedral School, Worcester, where he was in the OTC. He was commissioned in November 1911 and promoted Captain in December 1914. He is buried in Serre Road Cemetery No. 2, grave XXXIX. E. 12.

With this section of the third trench taken some time after 8 a.m.[i], the men, commanded by Capt. Cecil Watson Martin of A Company and 2nd Lt. John Turner[ii] of B Company, started to consolidate the position and clean their rifles. They had been advancing for some 40 minutes and had yet to reach their objective at which they should have arrived, according to the timetable, at 7.50 a.m. They now awaited the anticipated arrival of the 1/6th Warwicks who were due to follow up and move through them at any moment. The pathetically small numbers that eventually arrived gave ample testimony to the ferocity of the German machine gun and artillery fire sweeping the ground to their rear. These men joined in the process of preparing the trench for counter-attack. There was no question now of any further advance[iii].

Plate 76 Capt. Stratford Walter Ludlow, 1/8th Royal Warwickshire Regt.

The 1/6th Royal Warwickshires had started out at 7.40 a.m. by which time the German machine guns to their left and front had found the range. Two of these on the left were thought to be in specially constructed emplacements on the site of two old haystacks a short distance south west Serre. Lt. Col. Simonds of the 31st Division's 170th Brigade, RFA, had tried to get the Corps Heavy Artillery to bombard the spot which was identifiable from burn marks on the ground where the haystacks had once stood. He was told to use his 4.5 in. howitzers although he knew they were inadequate to the task. Now these machine guns swept the left wing of the 4th Division as it tried to advance.

---

[i] The war diary of the 1/8th Royal Warwicks claims these men reached the fourth German trench, however the diary of the 1/6th Royal Warwicks equally firmly states that they caught up with the 1/8th Royal Warwicks in the German third (reserve) trench. In other words they were well short of their objective.

[ii] Lt. John Turner, 1/8th Royal Warwickshire Regt., was awarded the MC for his conduct on 1st July 1916. It was listed in the *London Gazette* of 1st January 1917.

[iii] Although it was later claimed that some men had reach the trench between Points 49 and 05.

There was another incident with a German machine gun which may also have significantly reduced the manpower of the 1/6th Warwicks. Lt. der Reserve Wilhelm Bühler of the Reserve Machine Gun Company of RIR 121 had been wounded and his gun put out of action earlier in the attack but in his dugout was a spare Maxim which he now brought to the surface and, placing it on the parapet, the gun team fired at near point blank range into the advancing troops causing heavy casualties and stopping the forward movement of the battalion at least temporarily[17].

Plate 77 Lt. Col. William Hodgson Franklin, 1/6th Royal Warwickshire Regt.

It is estimated that at least 80 men, about 20% of the battalion's total casualties, fell before the battalion reached the British front line trench. The CO, Lt. Col. William Franklin[i], advanced with his battalion's 4th wave. He started out

---

[i] Lt. Col. William Hodgson Franklin, CMG, CBE, DSO, Royal Newfoundland Regt., att. 1/6th Royal Warwickshire Regt., was born in 1871, the son of W Franklin, a Liverpool merchant. He was educated at Liverpool Institute. He settled in Newfoundland in 1891 setting up an import/export business. He was, before the war, a senior officer in the Church Lads' Brigade in Newfoundland. He was heavily involved in the recruitment of the 1st Newfoundland Regt. and in its training. He was given a commission as Captain in September 1914. He came to England in October 1914 and was attached to the 1st Suffolk Regt. He then transferred to the 1/6th Royal Warwickshire Regt. and was promoted Major in March 1915 and given command of the 1/6th Royal Warwickshire Regt. in April 1916 and the rank of Lt. Col. He was awarded the DSO for his conduct on 1st July and the citation in the *London Gazette* of 20th October 1916 reads: "For conspicuous gallantry in action. He led his men in the attack with great dash and directed a bombing party after being severely wounded". Badly affected by his wounds (he was still having operations at the Special Military Surgical Hospital, Ducane Road, Shepherd's Bush, in 1919) he acted as an instructor in Devon, co-authored a handbook on Tactical Exercises and was a member of the Imperial Organisation Committee. Twice MiD, he retired in November 1919. CBE, June 1919. He was appointed HM Trade Commissioner in East Africa after the war, 1919-33. CMG, 1933. Married to Mrs Sarah Franklin (née Knowling) of St John's Newfoundland. One son, four daughters. He died in Nairobi in 1941.

with some seven men behind him but all of these had disappeared by the time he entered the German trenches. He had just arrived in the German front line when Lt. Col. Donald Wood, CO of the 1st Rifle Brigade, started to run across the open towards him. Franklin could see the remains of the Rifle Brigade held up to his right and Wood had just started to yell at him, "Franklin, we must ch…" when he fell, shot by a German soldier who had been missed in the advance[i]. Franklin shot and killed the German but was then hit in the back and knocked out, possibly by a nearby shell explosion. He had suffered, amongst other wounds, a compound fracture of the right femur, an injury only too often fatal, but he survived the day and the war although he was still requiring operations in the spring of 1919.[ii]

With the Warwicks being enfiladed from the left and the Rifle Brigade and Somersets under bombing attack from the right there was now nowhere for the men to go accept to man their line, build sandbag trench blocks and hope for reinforcements and supplies. The first counter-attacks came from the 4. Kompanie of RIR 121 which had been placed in close support in the support and reserve trenches of the 1st Position. Instructions from the very highest level, from von Falkenhayn at OHL no less, stated unequivocally that no ground was to be given up voluntarily and any position lost was to be re-taken by immediate counter-attack. These instructions would later be held responsible for the very heavy casualties suffered by German units on the Somme as the battle developed. Nevertheless, an order is an order and, seeing British troops occupying trenches in and to the east of the Heidenkopf, the 4. Kompanie first endeavoured to limit the break-in and then moved forward in an attempt to evict the intruders.

The weapon of choice for the troops ordered to undertake the attack was the stick grenade. The Model 24 Stielhandgranate was designed in 1915 and was a grenade designed to kill and injure by means of its blast. Weighing in at 595 gms (20% lighter than the British Mills bomb) and with the stick giving additional leverage to the thrower, it had a greater range than the Mills grenade with estimates suggesting a 30 to 40 metre range with reasonable accuracy against a 15 metre range for the British bomb. Specialist bombing teams armed with nothing other than a canvass bag of bombs but many wearing, and to British eyes for the first time, the now highly recognisable 'coal scuttle' helmet, were supported by rifle-bearing infantrymen. These teams now filtered down the communication

---

[i] Lt. Col. Donald Wood, 1st Rifle Brigade, was aged 38. He was the youngest son of Mr A H Wood of Duddleswell, Uckfield. A career soldier, he joined the Army from the Militia in 1899 and fought in the South African War including the Siege of Ladysmith. He was promoted Captain in May 1904. He was the Adjutant of the 10th (Service) Battalion, Rifle Brigade, in September 1914 and Brigade Major on 7th October 1914. He was promoted Major on 15th March 1915 and Temp. Lt. Col. on 5th December 1915. He joined the battalion on 28th November 1915. His body was never found and his name is inscribed on the Thiepval Memorial, Pier & Face 16B & 16C.

[ii] Franklin was later struck down by a severe kidney infection and, with one leg now shorter than the other, was deemed unable to work in terrain and weather such as applied in Newfoundland. He would spend the rest of his life in the warmer climes of East Africa. He was invited to participate in the Victory Parade on 19th July 1919 but was forced to decline on medical grounds. His health was never good and the effects of his wounds and subsequent operations contributed to his death in 1941.

trenches or rushed from shell hole to shell hole in order to attack the disorganised British-held trenches. Further to the rear in the Zwischen Stellung Oberst Josenhans, CO of the RIR 121, was organising other bombing parties from amongst the men of the regimental reserve, the III Battalion of the RIR 121.

Glover described the situation in his letter to Maj. Barclay:

> "We were enfiladed from the left but some Warwicks came up and apart from shelling we were fairly comfortable. Trevor turned up and Greetham of the Somersets and we decided to carry on, stretch out our right as far as we could with the bombers, about half a dozen, on our right flank.
> We were attacked by the German bombers and resisted them falling back slightly then they seemed to work round to our right rear. However, we kept up a lookout on that side and a Lewis gun on the parapet of a communication trench running back dominated the open. A Capt. Martin of the 8th Warwicks kept the men as well as he could at strengthening our left but it was hard work, the men seemed dazed and careless. With rifle fire we drove off an attack on the left front and we managed by scraping shallow trenches to get in some of the men from the shell holes beyond. Others came in over the top – or didn't."[18]

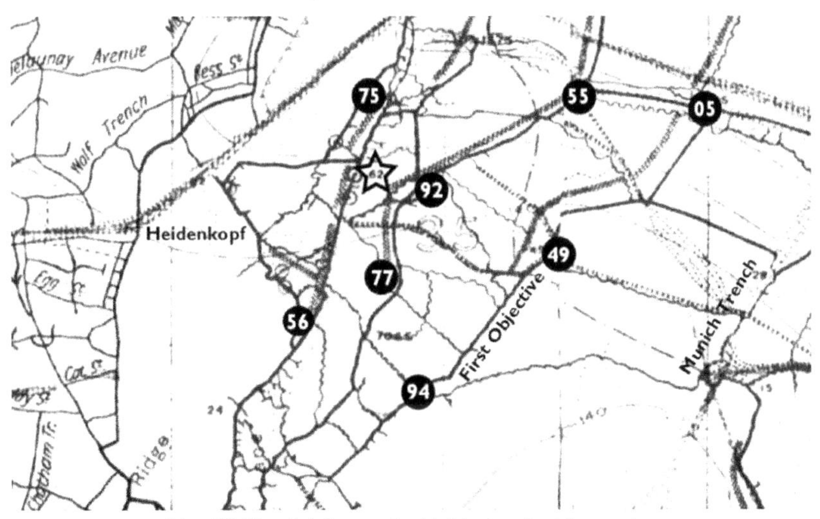

Map 23 The fighting at the Heidenkopf mid-morning

Key: The 4th Division's perimeter ran through points 56-77-92-75
The Division's 1st Objective ran through points 05-49-94 and south towards Beaumont Hamel
Part of Munich Trench (the Zwischen Stellung) appears bottom right
This represents Point 62 and the OP of Lt. d Reserve Beck (see page 334)

These troops occupied a line running approximately from Point 56 in the front line through Point 77 to Point 92 and from there back to the German front line north of the Heidenkopf (Point 75), though it appears there was a gap between the men in the front line and those in the third line of trenches as no contact was made between them until much later in the day. Officers in the forward position were few in number. 2nd Lt. Glover, though wounded, was still actively leading the defence as were Capt. Martin[i] and 2nd Lt. Turner of the 1/8th Warwicks. Another officer was also present, identified only as 'Trevor' by Glover. He was, presumably, either the Rifle Brigade's Adjutant, Capt. George Trevor Cartland[ii], or 2nd Lt. Evan Edward Trevor-Jones[iii] who was killed later bringing in a wounded man. Whatever this officer's identity, he survived most of the day only to be killed by a shell late in the afternoon a couple of yards from the British front line while returning to the British lines.

The Somersets were represented by Capt. Allan James Harington and Lt. Guy Cochrane Veale Greetham[iv]. Harington took command over the remains of the Somersets until he was wounded early in the afternoon[v]. Somewhere nearby, within earshot of Capt. Martin, was the CO of the 1/6th Warwicks, Lt. Col. Franklin, but he was wounded twice more and then knocked unconscious and played no part in the defence of the position. He was carried into a German dugout for safe-keeping. The only unwounded officer of the 1/6th Warwicks was now 2nd Lt. J G Cooper[vi]. Otherwise, the line was manned by NCOs and ordinary soldiers, Privates and Riflemen of the various battalions squeezed into this small section of German trench.

---

[i] Capt. Charles Watson Martin, 1/8th Royal Warwickshire Regt., was awarded the DSO for his conduct on 1st July 1916. The citation in the *London Gazette* of 20th October 1916 reads: "For conspicuous gallantry in action. He led his company in the attack with great dash, repelled bombing attacks, and displayed great courage in endeavouring to consolidate the position".

[ii] Capt. & Adjutant George Trevor Cartland, 1st Rifle Brigade, was aged 23. He was the only son of George and Lilian Cartland of Bevere Cottage, near Worcester. Educated at Winchester College he entered the RMC, Sandhurst. He passed out 1st with honours, receiving the King's sword and gold medal in August, 1912. He joined the Rifle Brigade in October, 1912 and went to France in August, 1914. He served on Gen. Hunter-Weston's staff for five months and was then ADC to Gen. Wilson. He re-joined the battalion in June 1915, being appointed Adjutant in September. He is buried in Serre Road Cemetery No. 2, grave III. E. 14.

[iii] 2nd Lt. Evan Edward Trevor-Jones, 6th att. 1st Rifle Brigade, was aged 20. He was the elder son of Lt. Col. Evan James Trevor Cory, O.B.E., T.D., RAMC, of 38, Hyde Park Gate, South Kensington, London. He was educated at Downside School, where he played cricket for the 1st XI, and Clare College, Cambridge. A member of the OTC, he enlisted in 1914. He lived at 36, Alexandra Road, Sheerness, Kent. He was commissioned on 16th December 1914 and went to France in June 1915. His body was never found and his name is inscribed on the Thiepval Memorial, Pier & Face 16B and 16C. His younger brother, Capt. & Adjt. John Eric Trevor-Jones, MC, 6th att. 1st Rifle Brigade, (also Clare College. Cambridge) was killed on 22nd April 1918.

[iv] Lt. Guy Cochrane Veale Greetham, 1st Somerset Light Infantry, was awarded the MC for his conduct on 1st July 1916. It was listed in the *London Gazette* of 1st January 1917.

[v] Lt. (Temp. Capt.) Allan James Harington, 1st Somerset Light Infantry, was awarded a Bar to the MC for his conduct on 1st July (MC previously gazetted 14th January 1916). The citation in the *London Gazette* of 9th September 1916 reads: "For conspicuous gallantry in action. Soon after entering the enemy trenches, he found himself in command of the battalion and did fine work organising bombing parties, consolidating the ground won and repelling counter attacks. He was finally wounded and forced to retire".

[vi] Eleven officers of the 1/6th Royal Warwickshire Regt. were killed and eleven were wounded.

One German who was counting his lucky stars was Lt. der Reserve Beck, the artillery observer for the RIR 121. Having sent up his red flares to call down artillery fire on the advancing British troops he had remained in his one-man OP between the German front and support lines immediately behind the Heidenkopf. This was an area overrun by the advancing British troops who, spotting his hidey-hole, shouted a challenge followed immediately by two grenades. Fortunately for Beck, these exploded short of his refuge but were deemed sufficient to deal with anyone within. A second party, seeing the damage to the OP's entrance, decided it wasn't worth bothering with and passed on towards the second German trench. A while later, Beck discovered his escape route obstructed by a British-built sandbag block and a machine gun team all, happily for him, looking the other way. He also noted what he thought was a wireless set which would have been an unusual item to employ at this stage of the war. Two sets had been supplied to 12th Brigade, however, with the intention that one would be taken forward during the advance and used to communicate with the other established at Brigade HQ pending the establishment of a telephone cable. The wireless set was set up at Point 62 in the German lines but was then damaged by machine gun fire before it could be used. It was later abandoned. For Beck, though, this group of enemy soldiers meant it would be nightfall before he could make good his escape.[19]

Back in the British trenches the battalions of the two remaining Brigades of the 4th Division were moving forward towards the front line. In and about the front line trenches were the three companies of the pioneer battalion, the 21st West Yorkshires. The men from Halifax, who had been happily training in England just two weeks earlier, must have wondered what they had let themselves in for, especially A Company. Commanded by Capt. George Seymour Noon[i] and accompanied by his 2iC Capt. Edmund Boulnois[ii] this company had the task of opening out the Russian saps across No Man's Land in order to transform them into communication trenches. This was a task that required unarmed men to stand in No Man's Land whilst wielding a pick or a shovel, orders that were only remotely reasonable had the German defences completely collapsed with the assault of the leading battalions. But, with machine guns sweeping the corpse strewn areas between the two opposing front lines, asking

[i] Noon and Boulnois as well as the CO, Sir Edward Henry St Lawrence Clarke, 4th Bt, had been transfers from the 6th and 12th (Reserve) Battalions, Worcestershire Regt. to the 21st West Yorkshire Regt. in 1915. Capt. Noon was commissioned on 26th November 1914 and relinquished his commission on 15th May 1918 as a result of wounds suffered during the war. Lt. Col. E H St L Clarke, DSO, CMG, commanded the battalion throughout the war, retiring on 26th March 1919.

[ii] Capt. Edmund Boulnois, 21st West Yorkshire Regt. (Wool Textile Pioneers), was killed on 23rd October 1916. Aged 31, he was the son of Arthur and Annie Louisa Boulnois of The Homestead, Aylesbury, Canterbury, New Zealand. His grandfather was the late Edmund Boulnois, from 1889 to 1906 the Conservative MP for Marylebone East and the first mayor of the Metropolitan Borough of St Marylebone. Born and educated in New Zealand, he attended Selwyn College, Cambridge, and volunteered on the outbreak of war whilst visiting his widowed grandmother. He was commissioned into the Worcestershire Regt. before transferring to the 21st West Yorkshire Regt. His body was never found and his name is inscribed on the Thiepval Memorial, Pier & Face 2A, 2C & 2D.

anyone to do this job was clearly highly unreasonable and Noon and Boulnois sensibly kept their men as far out of harm's way as they could manage. B and C Companies, too, kept their heads down but remained in the front trenches throughout the day. The War Diary states that nine officers and 296 Other Ranks were engaged in the action. One officer was wounded, two other ranks killed and nine other ranks wounded. Helping to clear the trenches of the dead and wounded would become their chief role over the coming few days.

THE TASKS OF THE BATTALIONS OF THE 10TH AND 12TH BRIGADES were to advance through the 11th Brigade to take the intermediate (Zwischen Stellung) and 2nd (II Stellung) German positions, the latter 3,600 yards distant, as well as the German gun lines in the shallow valleys running south off the Redan Ridge plateau. The 10th Brigade's battalions were in assembly areas to the rear of the East Lancashires and Hampshires on the southern flank, opposite and to the south of the Ridge Redoubt. The 2nd Royal Dublin Fusiliers were on the right in assembly trenches around Tenderloin and the 2nd Seaforth Highlanders on the left in Mountjoy Trench and an assembly trench 100 yards behind. The remaining two battalions, the 1st Royal Warwickshire Regt., between 3rd and 5th Avenues and in Rostrum Trench, and the 1st Royal Irish Fusiliers, north of Kilometre Lane, lay in the relative shelter of the sunken road between the Sucrerie and Auchonvillers. On the left of the Division the 12th Brigade, arrayed behind the two Warwickshire Territorial battalions, was advancing. In the lead was the 1st King's Own Royal Lancaster Regt., starting from the Lyceum, with the 2nd Essex Regt. at Elles Square, the 2nd Duke of Wellington's (West Riding) Regt., at the Sucrerie and the 2nd Lancashire Fusiliers further west along the Serre to Mailly Maillet Road beyond the Sucrerie.

On the 10th Brigade's front all the battalions advanced with three companies leading, each on a frontage of 125 yards and the fourth company, laden with consolidating material, 200 yards behind the last man of the preceding waves. The leading waves of the supporting battalions, i.e. the 1st Warwicks and the Irish Fusiliers, were to move off 200 yards behind the last man of the support companies of the Seaforths and Dublins. The machine guns of the 10th Machine Gun Company, with the exception of four held in reserve at Tenderloin, were to advance with the two leading battalions, six guns supporting each battalion of which two were with the leading waves and four came up with the final wave.

The 2nd Royal Dublin Fusiliers on the extreme right started to move out of their assembly trenches at 9 a.m. A, B and C Companies led, with D Company in support in Young Trench. Although some of the battalion advanced through an area of dead ground, immediately they crested a small rise in the ground they were subject to heavy enfilade machine gun fire from the northern end of Beaumont Hamel. Their problem was that the failure of the left battalion of the 29th Division, the 1st Lancashire Fusiliers, to clear their front meant that the machine guns supporting the II/RIR 119 in the front and support trenches and on the ridge behind the village could now turn their attention to the right wing of the 4th Division. Their fire was devastating and men from all companies started to fall. Lt. William Thomas Colyer was leading his platoon on the left corner of his company which was advancing in a diamond formation. In front of him Lt. James Berthune Moffat was at the head of the company and to his right, Lt.

Robert MacIlroy Stobart, attached from the 3rd Wiltshire Regt., led the right-hand element. The fourth platoon, coming up behind, was commanded by a sergeant. As they crested the low ridge so the panorama of the battlefield was laid before them, the ruins of Beaumont Hamel on their right and the smoke covered expanse of Redan Ridge to their front. They immediately came under machine gun fire. Colyer's platoon started taking casualties and, with German shells now adding to the chaos, he and those left of his men took shelter in a nearby trench. It was a shell bursting close by that did for Colyer or at least scrambled his brain:

> "... my whole nervous system seemed to be jangled up and I ran like a hare down the trench. I don't know where I thought I was going. I was much too agitated. I went tumbling along until I saw what I took to be a dugout opening which I made for at once. There were a couple of men and an officer sitting just inside the opening. They looked at me as if I had taken leave of my senses – which, for the time being, really, I suppose I had."

Shell shock. For some men enough to see their war ended. For Colyer a temporary respite from the madness around him[i]. He would survive[ii].

Plate 78 Lt. Col. Harold Martin Cliff, 2nd Royal Dublin Fusiliers

News of the total failure of the East Lancashires and Hampshires attack had, meanwhile, reached 10th Brigade's HQ and orders were immediately sent out to all four battalions to hold fast while the true position was ascertained. The order sent to the Dublin Fusiliers arrived at 9.05 a.m. and was followed by another ordering the CO, the recently appointed and not very physically fit Lt. Col.

---

[i] Lt. William Thomas Colyer, 2nd Royal Dublin Fusiliers, enlisted as 1691 Private with the 1/28th London Regt. (Artists Rifles) serving in France from August 1914 to January 1915 before being commissioned into the Dublin Fusiliers. He fought at the 2nd Battle of Ypres, was wounded on 1st July and later served as a Rations Officer with the 16th (Irish) Division and an instructor with IX Corps School.

[ii] As would both James Moffatt and Robert Stobart.

Harold Martin Cliff[i], not to allow his battalion 'to go beyond English front line trenches till further orders'. With his men struggling forward under heavy fire Lt. Col. Cliff immediately despatched two runners to every company while he went after A Company himself, fortunately coming up with a sergeant in rear of the company who then doubled forward with the urgent verbal order. For the 54-year old Cliff such exertions must have been extremely taxing. He had been severely wounded in Gallipoli in early August 1915 and had only assumed command of the battalion on 21st May. His tenure would be brief. Ill-health would force him to relinquish command on 13th July and he would die from a heart condition in a London hospital on 1st February 1917. Nevertheless, his gallant pursuit of A Company undoubtedly saved lives – just.

The messages were nearly late in arriving. Each of the three leading companies had reached the British front line and was now under heavy fire from the German front line trench as well as the machine guns around Beaumont Hamel. But here, undoubtedly to their relief, they were stopped. All, that is, except for a few platoons who were already out in No Man's Land. Their fate is tersely described in the battalion War Diary:

"These, without exception, became casualties including 5 officers."[20]

For a battalion that barely left the trenches, the 2nd Royal Dublin Fusiliers had suffered badly. Fourteen officers, including all four company commanders, had been hit. Two of the company commanders would lie out wounded for most of the day. Only one would survive.

One of them, Major Lionel Walsh, was hit by three machine gun bullets fired from one of the machine guns taking the Dublins in enfilade from around Beaumont Hamel. The bullets broke his femur, a horribly dangerous injury. With the ground around him swept by fire the stretcher bearers were unable to get to him for twelve hours during which time he lost a large amount of blood. When

---

[i] Lt. Col. Harold Martin Cliff, Royal Irish Rifles cdg. 2nd Royal Dublin Fusiliers, was appointed to take command of the battalion on 21st May, replacing Maj. Lionel Walsh who had been in temporary command since February. Born in 1862, he was the younger son of William Cliff, JP, shipping merchant, and Marion Frater of Claremont, West Derby, Liverpool. He married Marion Watt, eldest daughter of William McCulloch of Melbourne, in 1889 and lived at 8 Allardstown, Co. Louth and later Fane Valley, Dundalk. He was the Master of the Dundalk Hunt. He was educated at Clifton College and passed out of the RMC, Sandhurst in 1883 joining the Royal Irish Rifles being promoted Captain in 1888. In 1889 he was put on half-pay due to ill health but re-joined in February 1890. He was the Adjutant of the 6th Royal Irish Rifles (Louth Militia) from 1897-1902. He fought in South Africa, att. to 2nd Royal Irish Rifles. He retired in December 1902. He re-joined the Royal Irish Rifles on the outbreak of war and in March 1915 was promoted Major and transferred from the 7th (Service) Battalion, Royal Irish Rifles to command 6th (Service) Battalion, Royal Inniskilling Fusiliers, 31st Brigade, 10th (Irish) Division. He was severely wounded in Gallipoli at Chocolate Hill on 7th August, 1915. After recovering he was given command of the 2nd Royal Dublin Fusiliers on 21st May 1916 but relinquished command on 13th July 1916 due to ill-health. In October 1916 he was appointed to command a School of Instruction. He died from a heart condition in the Swedish Military Hospital, 16, Paddington Street, London, on 1st February 1917. He is buried in Kensal Green (All Soul's) Cemetery, grave 118. 6. 45445. He is remembered on the Castlebellingham War Memorial, Co. Louth.

found he was rushed to the ADS and then on to No. 4 Casualty Clearing Station at Beauval at which he arrived on the morning on 2nd July. His wounds were dressed, his leg set and, remarkably, he was able to dictate at letter to his sister, Mrs Beatrice Scott-Smith of Banks Hall, Cawthorne, near Barnsley. On Tuesday, 3rd July, Maj. Walsh took a dangerous turn for the worse. As happened to so many of the wounded, the bullets that struck him had taken dirt, detritus and bacteria into his wounds. One of these bacteria would have been *Clostridium perfringens*, a bacterium found in rotting vegetation, the human intestine and soil. Ingested it is a common cause of food poisoning. Given access to tissue and blood and the resulting infection can be catastrophic. Lionel Walsh developed such an infection. The result was gas gangrene, invariably fatal in those days, and he lost consciousness as the bacterium's alpha toxin wreaked havoc in his weakened body. He died, aged 41, at 6 a.m. on 4th July[i].

Between serving in South Africa with the Imperial Yeomanry and sailing from New York on 8th August 1914 to enlist in the Army, Lionel Walsh had been a noted comic actor on the American stage playing in theatres from San Francisco to Chicago and New York. He frequented the noted Players' Club at 16 Gramercy Park, New York, founded by Edwin Booth, the brother of the infamous John Wilkes Booth, the assassin of Abraham Lincoln. It was a social club for actors, artists, writers and other creative thinkers of which Samuel Clemens, better known as Mark Twain, and the inventor Nikola Tesla were members. He was also well known at Lamb's Club at 128 West 44th Street, another New York haunt of thespians and the like. He was about to appear on Broadway with Elsie Janis, a hugely popular singer, songwriter, actress and, later, Hollywood screen writer and composer who would be known as the 'Sweetheart of the American Expeditionary Force' towards the end of the war.

On his death, the husband of his sister, Beatrice, wrote to the Players' Club describing his death, burial and commemoration. The letter later appeared in the *New York Times* on 10th September 1916 in an article entitled *'Exit Lionel Walsh'*. It is most moving and an extract appears below:

> "It was a singular coincidence that the Casualty Clearing Hospital to which he was taken was in the lines of his old regiment, the Yorkshire Dragoons, which one of my brothers commands. They all heard he was there. The CO and all those who knew him attended the funeral. They

---

[i] Maj. Lionel Percy Walsh, Hampshire Regt. att. 2nd Royal Dublin Fusiliers, was aged 41. He was the third son of the Rev. Lionel E Walsh, late Lt., RN, Chaplain to HM Forces. He was the brother of Mrs Beatrice Scott-Smith of Banks Hall, Barnsley. He was educated at Pocklington and graduated from Wadham College, Oxford, in 1894. He fought in the South African War, serving with the 19th Battalion, Imperial Yeomanry (King's Medal & 4 clasps). On leaving the Army in 1903 he took up as a comic actor, sailed from Liverpool on the *SS Celtic* to the USA where he performed in numerous musical comedies. In New York on the outbreak of war he sailed to London and enlisted in the Inns of Court Volunteers. He was then commissioned into the Yorkshire Dragoons (Queen's Own) Yeomanry on 15th September 1914 before transferring to the 3rd Royal Dublin Fusiliers on 4th May 1915. He was promoted Captain on 13th May 1915 and Major on 4th January 1916. He acted as CO from February to June 1916, returning to take command of his company just before the attack. He is buried in Beauval Communal Cemetery, grave A. 12.

sent a carrying party and escort and the Trumpet Major and trumpeters to sound 'Last Post'. He was buried in the French cemetery at Beauval… His grave is marked by a wooden cross, with his name on a metal plate and is properly looked after by a resident in the village. It is a pathetic, yet comforting, circumstance that he should have died and have been buried in the lines of his old regiment, and carried to his last rest by the troopers of his old squadron, who loved him so well… His brigade went into rest billets on July 20, and his Colonel writes that a service was held over his grave on the twenty-first of July by Mr Waldegrave, the Chaplain. It was attended by the General commanding and the majority of the officers of the different regiments. Every officer of his battalion except those on duty was present and many of the NCOs and men of his company. He says, 'I wish to impress on you that this was entirely a voluntary service, and that the General and officers consider it a privilege to be able to join and show their respect to one who had earned the respect of his brother officers and men of his company. I realised his value both as a man and a soldier. I wish we had more like him. He died a soldier's death and that cheerfully, as he was cheerful to the last. His loss is keenly felt, not only in the regiment, but in the brigade'.

So Lionel Walsh played his last part well. Surely no comedian ever made a finer exit."[21]

One of the other company commanders, Capt. William Francis Jeffries, was hit within ten minutes of leaving the assembly trenches and lay out in the open for the next eight hours unable to see anything that was going on. He would survive to play a major role in intelligence operations in post-war Ireland and, promoted Brigadier General, would become the commandant of the Intelligence Corps between 1940 and 1942[i].

Behind the Dublins the 1st Royal Warwicks were more fortunate. Their orders to stop advancing reached them in time to hold them up between Tenderloin and the front line where, with wounded streaming down the communication trenches from the front trenches, they could see at first hand the effects of rifle and machine gun fire on their Divisional colleagues. The same good news applied to the 1st Royal Irish Fusiliers. They were due to move off from the Sucrerie end of the Sunken Road at 9.30 p.m. and were forming up ready for their advance on

---

[i] Capt., later Brig. Gen., William Francis Jeffries, CBE, DSO, 2nd Royal Dublin Fusiliers, was born in 1891 and was the only son of William Carey Jeffries, MD, of Coolcarron, Co. Cork, and Maud Grace Kennedy of Ballinamultina, Co. Waterford. He was educated at Downside and Trinity College, Cambridge. He was commissioned out of the Royal Monmouth Royal Engineers into the 3rd Royal Dublin Fusiliers on 15th August 1914 and was wounded at the 2nd Battle of Ypres, 1915. He was awarded the DSO in 1918. He was on the Intelligence Staff in Dublin and Horse Guards between 1920-21, running the London Spy School. An administrative officer in Nigeria until 1927 he joined the General Staff in 1938 and was the Commandant, Intelligence Corps, 1940-42, Deputy Head of Psychological Warfare, Middle East and Central Mediterranean Forces, 1943-45. CBE 1945. He married Leila Downing, daughter of Francis Downing of Ballyvelly, Tralee, Co. Kerry in 1920. He died in 1969.

the normal three company front. Lt. Col. William Findlater[i] and his Adjutant Capt. William Carden Roe[ii], MC, were watching the attack unfold before them. The signal to be sent up when a unit reached its objective was three white lights and, at about the time that the first line battalions should have been entering Munich Trench, a series of white flares were seen over the battlefield. 'This is too good to be true', Findlater told his Adjutant before instructing him to call Brigade with the news they were moving off. Carden Roe hurried to the dugout where he heard a voice calling from below: 'Adjutant wanted on the phone by the Brigade Major – hurry upstairs and find him'. Carden Roe recalled the conversation well after the battle:

> "The Brigade Major was talking in hurried, jerky sentences. 'Hullo, is that you, Carden Roe? Look here, have your people started yet? Well, then, hurry up and stop them, you are not to move until further orders. The whole show is hung up. We will let you know more when we have something definite'. 'But', I stammered, 'what about the white lights?' 'Those ruddy white lights mean "Held up by machine gun fire", and the damned things are going up everywhere'. The whole rotten truth suddenly dawned on me."[22]

An orderly was sent hurrying away with the new orders that the Irish Fusiliers were to stop at the line Mountjoy Trench-Tenderloin. There, under persistent artillery fire, they waited further orders.

On the left of the Brigade, the 2nd Seaforths were not so lucky. At 8.45 a.m., with no news from either the 11th or 10th Brigade HQs, the advanced patrols under 20 year old Lt. William Harrison left the assembly trenches and moved towards the German lines. They were immediately swept by heavy machine gun fire, again, predominantly from the north of Beaumont Hamel. Lt. Harrison[iii] was severely wounded. He would die at a Casualty Clearing Station in Doullens five days later.

Lt. Col. John Hopkinson, the CO of the Seaforths, was now in something of a quandary. He was undoubtedly aware of the earlier failure of the two battalions

---

[i] Lt. Col. William Alexander Victor Findlater, DSO, 1st Royal Irish Fusiliers, was born in 1880. He was the son of Sir William Huffington Findlater and Marion Park, daughter of Lt. Col. Archibald Park, son of the explorer Mungo Park. He was educated at Harrow and Trinity College, Dublin. He was commissioned into the 3rd Devonshire Regt., of the Militia in 1899. He transferred to the 2nd Royal Irish Fusiliers in 1900 and served in South Africa (Queen's Medal & 5 clasps). He was promoted Captain and Adjutant, 4th Royal Irish Fusiliers (Cavan Militia). Promoted Lt. Col. May 1916. Retired 1926. He married Leila Blackwell, daughter of Thomas Blackwell of Merrion Square in 1904. They had two sons and three daughters. He died in 1957. His brother, Capt. Percival St George Findlater, Army Service Corps, 21st Divisional Train, died on 28th March 1918.

[ii] Carden Roe was originally called William H Liesching and changed his name in March 1916 presumably because of the name's Germanic overtones. He was awarded the MC in December 1914.

[iii] 2nd Lt. William Harrison, 3rd Gordon Highlanders att. 2nd Seaforth Highlanders, died on 5th July 1916. Aged 20, he was the son of Dr John Harrison MD and Elizabeth Campbell Harrison, of St Machutes, Lesmahagow, Lanarkshire. He was a student at Glasgow University and was commissioned on 17th March 1915. He is buried in Doullens Communal Cemetery Extension No.1, grave II. A. 7.

of the 11th Brigade to his right and, perhaps, could see that the Dublin Fusiliers seemed to be taking up positions in the front line rather than advancing but, in the absence of alternative orders, he had to throw his men into the battle. With his telephone connection to Brigade HQ out of order, he sent two runners off in the hope they might return with fresh instructions. With neither having returned by 9 a.m., the appointed time for their advance, he had no options and the whole battalion left the trenches and marched out into No Man's Land. B Company was on the right, A Company in the centre and C Company on the left. D Company followed on in support. Away to their left, the 1st King's Own and the 2nd Essex were also moving forward north of the Serre to Mailly Road. They all came under heavy machine gun fire.

Plate 79 Lt. William Harrison, 2nd Seaforth Highlanders

Plate 80 2nd Lt. Miles Harry Blackwood, 2nd Seaforth Highlanders

Like the Rifle Brigade and Somersets before them, the majority of the Seaforths inclined to the left in an effort to avoid the murderous machine gun fire from Beaumont Hamel and the Ridge Redoubt. Although a machine gun firing from the front of the redoubt was eventually silenced by the battalion Lewis guns, it had the effect of forcing D Company to leave their trenches to the south of the crater field opposite the redoubt where they made little headway in No Man's Land. The rest of the battalion, however, followed the more northerly path. As they went, 19 year old 2nd Lt. Miles 'Daddy' Blackwood[i] laughed and chatted with his men. A fellow officer wrote of him:

[i] 2nd Lt. Miles Harry Blackwood, 2nd Seaforth Highlanders, was aged 19. He was the only son of Major Harry Officer Blackwood and Isla Jessie Blackwood of Kincurdie, Rosemarkie, Ross-shire and Arthur's, St. James's, London. Born at Fawley, he was educated at Stone House, Broadstairs, and Harrow School. He represented Harrow as a bantamweight in the Public Schools Boxing Competition at Aldershot, 1913. Joined 5th Bn. Royal Fusiliers in 1914. Passed through RMC, Sandhurst, and posted to 2nd Bn. Seaforth Highlanders, July, 1915. He joined the battalion in France on 7th June 1916. He is buried in Sucrerie Military Cemetery, Colincamps, grave I. H. 21.

"Miles or 'Daddy' Blackwood, as he was always known in the Regiment, was a most charming person and his loss will be felt deeply by all who knew him; he had a greater number of friends than most people and was especially loved by his men. Miles was killed today leading his Platoon to the assault like a soldier and a gentleman. I was not with him at the time but met some of this Platoon afterwards. They all loved him dearly and, before they went over the top, he was giving them cigarettes and was remarked by all to be especially cheery."

Five minutes after the main body of the Seaforths left their trenches a message ordering them to hold fast was sent by 10th Brigade HQ. None of the runners sent by Brigade arrived in time to stop the advance. The battalion was committed to the fray and those that survived the crossing of No Man's Land were even now disappearing into the German trenches around Point 56. The battalion to their rear, the 1st Royal Irish Fusiliers who were now moving across the open preparatory to their advance, were contacted, as mentioned above, and they were ordered to halt in the recently vacated Mountjoy Trench.

NORTH OF THE SERRE – MAILLY ROAD THE 12TH BRIGADE was also on the move and here, again, confusion reigned. Although the battalions were strung out in a line from the Lyceum westwards the idea of their attack was that they should advance with two battalions each side by side, with the 1st King's Own on the left and the 2nd Essex on the right followed by the 2nd Duke's on the left and the 2nd Lancashire Fusiliers on the right and slightly to the rear. The role of the Fusiliers and Duke's was mainly to consolidate the newly won German 2nd Position (Fusiliers) and the area around Pendant Copse (Duke's) and, as a result, two each of their four companies were laden with RE materials. In addition, 125 men were detailed to act as carriers for rations, bombs and ammunition, etc.

In order to arrive to timetable, the battalions furthest from the front moved off between 8 and 9 a.m. It would seem that, as they came under artillery fire, the two supporting battalions could not resist the natural tendency to move as quickly as possible through the fire zone and, as a result, they arrived near the front lines too early. The 2nd Lancashire Fusiliers recorded that they crossed Vallade Trench at about 9 a.m. and immediately came under heavy artillery, machine gun and rifle fire which intensified as they crossed the front line into No Man's Land. The speed of the advance which, until they came under fire, had been the regulation stroll of 50 yards a minute now became 'naturally faster'[23] under the bombardment but, in these few short minutes, and before crossing the front line, two of their officers were killed, Capt. Hugh Sayres[i] and the Battalion

---

[i] Capt. Hugh Wingfield Sayres, 1st att. 2nd Lancashire Fusiliers, was aged 27. He was the only son of William Borrett Sayres and Ellen Harriet Sayres (née Wingfield) of 38, Kensington Mansions, London SW. He was educated at Allen House, Guildford, Army House, Bradfield College, and Loudwater, Westgate. He entered Sandhurst in 1908, received his commission in November, 1909, and served with the Lancashire Fusiliers in India till the outbreak of war. He was severely wounded after the landing at the Dardanelles on 25th April at Lancashire Landing. He is buried in Sucrerie Military Cemetery, Colincamps, grave I. I. 7.

Signalling Officer, 2nd Lt. Charlie Roberton[i], and two more wounded, Capt. John Collis-Browne[ii], with a knee wound that ended his war, and Lt. Geoffrey Grenside Bowen[iii]. Collis-Browne advanced alongside the senior NCO, CSM Holden:

> "I wish more could have seen him beside myself. He was an elderly man but he marched along as if it were on a ceremonial parade in barracks. I never saw him duck and as you can guess the enemy were being pretty prodigal with bullets. Before we reached our support trenches I was hit below the knee so I sent Pte. Murphy, my runner, and excellent servant (I never had a better) with a message to my second in command (Lt. R S MacIver) that I had been wounded and to tell him to take command. I heard after that Murphy[iv] was never heard of again and that MacIver[v] was killed."[24]

Further forward, the 2nd Essex had left their assembly trenches at 8.36 a.m. with A and D Companies leading. They immediately came under heavy fire from both flanks and the front but pushed on until the survivors entered the German lines. Casualties amongst officers and men were heavy and amongst the dead was 37 year old 2nd Lt. Herbert Robert White. White had been in the Army for 21 years, first as a ranker, then becoming the Regimental Quartermaster Sergeant of the 2nd Essex. A South African veteran he had been commissioned in May 1915

---

[i] 2nd Lt. Charlie Drinnan Roberton, 4th att. 2nd Lancashire Fusiliers, was aged 23. He was the son of Mrs J R Roberton of 31, Elgin Terrace, Dowanhill, Glasgow, and the late Mr C G Roberton, O.B.E., of Barrow in Furness. He is buried in Euston Road Cemetery, Colincamps, grave V. E. 10.

[ii] Capt., later Major, John Collis-Browne, 4th att. 2nd Lancashire Fusiliers, was the son of Maj. William Alfred and Mrs Mary Anne Collis-Browne of Monteagle, Godalming, Surrey. He was educated at Radley College. He was commissioned into the 6th Lancashire Fusiliers (Militia) in 1904 and transferred to the 4th Lancashire Fusiliers in 1908. He married Kathleen Lucas in 1916. His brother, Lt. Alfred Ulick Collis-Browne, 1st King's Own Yorkshire Light Infantry, died on 13th April 1915. He is remembered on the Ypres (Menin Gate) Memorial. Maj. John 'Jack' Collis-Browne died in 1969.

[iii] Capt. Geoffrey Grenside Bowen, MC, B Company, 2nd Lancashire Fusiliers, died on 2nd September 1918. Aged 23, he was the son of Mr J. C. G. and Mrs W. M. Bowen, of Durmast Cottage, Burley, Brockenhurst, Hants. He is buried in Windmill British Cemetery, Monchy-le-Preux. His MC was gazetted on 18th July 1917.

[iv] 9989 Pte William Murphy, 2nd Lancashire Fusiliers, was aged 32. He was the son of Mrs Ann Otine, of 35, Boond St., Greengate, Salford, Manchester. His body was never found and his name is inscribed on the Thiepval Memorial, Pier & Face 3 C & 3 D.

[v] Lt. Reginald Squarey MacIver, 4th att. 2nd Lancashire Fusiliers, was aged 24. He was the eleventh of twelve children of ship owner and MP for Liverpool, Kirkdale (1898-1907), the late David MacIver and Edith Eleanor MacIver (née Squarey) of Wanlass How, Ambleside, Westmorland. He was educated at Mostyn House, Parkgate, and Shrewsbury School and gained a science scholarship to Christ Church, Oxford in 1911. He rowed in the college boat in 1913 and 1914 and was a member of the Leander Club. He was commissioned in August 1914 in the 4th Lancashire Fusiliers. He transferred to the 2nd Lancashire Fusiliers on 15th February 1915 and went to France in May 1915. He is buried in Sucrerie Military Cemetery, Colincamps, grave I. H. 5. His brother, Capt. Andrew Tucker Squarey MacIver, Cheshire Field Company, RE, died on 24th April 1915. He is buried in La Clytte Military Cemetery.

as a reward for, and in recognition of, services in the field. One of his men followed him out into No Man's Land. Three quarters of the way across White turned 'as if to shout an order' but was shot and killed outright[i]. He'd been a popular officer, a man from the ranks but 'a gentleman right through'. One of his men wrote later:

> "How I wish Mr White had come through; he was well liked by his platoon, a gentleman and a soldier. Always had a kind word for the men, and one whom any solider would follow."[25]

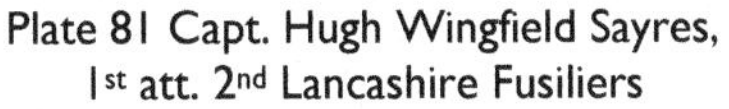

Plate 81 Capt. Hugh Wingfield Sayres, 1st att. 2nd Lancashire Fusiliers

Plate 82 2nd Lt. Herbert Robert White, 2nd Essex Regt.

With the survivors went a number of Lewis gun teams designed to provide mobile firepower until the arrival of the heavy Vickers machine guns. The leading team on the right, following D Company, lost four men crossing their own front line, amongst them being the men carrying the majority of the magazines. The remains of the team eventually joined some men of D Company in the German front line behind a barricade they had constructed where they used their one remaining magazine against enemy bombing parties. A search was made and some discarded Lewis gun drums were found and the first was fired but, after about 25 rounds, the gun jammed possibly from grit in the drum. This was a common complaint and was commented on by a number of the gun teams. Another gun team coming on behind came into action between the first and

[i] 2nd Lt. Herbert Robert White, 3rd att. 2nd Essex Regt., was aged 37. He was the son of William Henry and Sara White (nee Brookes) of East Ham. He married Marguerite Blanche Emmeline White (nee Twiss) of St. Margaret's, Kiltegan, Co. Wicklow, in 1910. Three daughters. Enlisted in 1st Essex Regt. in 1895. Served in the South African War (Queen's Medal and King's Medal, seven clasps). Transferred to 2nd Essex Regt., served in Malta and at home. Promoted RQMS he went to France in August, 1914. He was commissioned on 9th May 1915. His body was never found and his name is inscribed on the Thiepval Memorial, Pier & Face 10D.

second German trenches, taking on a machine gun to their right which, it was thought, was put out of action. They too had suffered casualties amongst the ammunition carriers and, having reached the second German trench, they used what drums the remaining man had brought over against German bombing parties. The third gun on the right was disabled in No Man's Land by a nearby shell burst which filled the gun with dirt. Having arrived in the German front trench they set up behind a barricade blocking a communication trench. After stripping and cleaning the gun, the team got it working and fired off 100 rounds at various bombing parties. Again their complaint was against the magazine panniers which easily filled with dirt and, if a man flung himself to the ground for any reason, the malleable metal allowed the drums to be dented. The last gun team arrived in the second German trench with only one man to fire the gun. There were adequate supplies of drums and spare parts, however, and the gun was kept in action until the evening when they ran out of ammunition while covering the withdrawal. The remaining men managed to get the gun back to the British trenches.

Behind A Company two guns made it into the Heidenkopf where one was found to be damaged by a bullet. While the gun was stripped and repaired the second gun fired off six drums before it too jammed. The cartridge guide spring was broken and, with no spare parts available, the gun became useless. Another gun arrived in the second German trench with just one man to man the gun and eight magazines carried by others. Brought into action against the numerous bombing parties, other members of the team found two more abandoned Lewis guns but these had to be destroyed when the Essex withdrew towards the German front line later in the day. The original gun, however, covered the left flank against bombing parties after this withdrawal and later, when they were driven back into the first German trench, took on German snipers who had crawled out onto the parapet to fire on the men in the trenches. Again, the gun had to be regularly cleaned after firing from dirty drums. The Lewis guns had, whatever their shortcomings, provided valuable help in supporting the infantry in the trenches who, otherwise, spent the day depending on an ever dwindling supply of British and then German grenades.

On the left of the Essex the 1st King's Own pushed out a screen of four scout patrols at 8.41 a.m. Two hundred yards behind them came two fighting patrols each supported by a Lewis gun and in the centre was the Scout Officer accompanied by two runners, two signallers and an observer. The officer who had drawn this particular short straw was 24 year old 2nd Lt. Charles Christopher MacWalter[i] from Kent. He and his men trudged into the maelstrom and isappeared. MacWalter's body was never found.

---

[i] 2nd Lt. Charles Christopher MacWalter, 1st King's Own Royal Lancaster Regt., was aged 24. He was the son of Lt. Robert MacWalter of the 13th (Princess of Wales) Hussars and was born in Canterbury. He was educated at Dover County School for Boys, leaving in 1907. He enlisted in The Buffs (East Kent Regt.) and was promoted sergeant. He was commissioned into the King's Own Royal Lancaster Regt., on 7th November 1915. His body was never found and his name is inscribed on the Thiepval Memorial, Pier & Face 5D & 12B.

Plate 83 2nd Lt. Charles Christopher MacWalter, 1st King's Own Royal Lancaster Regt.

Five minutes later the whole of the battalion left their assembly trenches on a 400 yard, four company front, in columns of platoons. They were not to know that ten minutes earlier 4th Division had issued instructions that 12th Brigade was not to move until the situation became clear. Again, instructions that did not arrive in time.

The companies were deployed A to D, with A Company on the right. Behind them came Battalion HQ, comprising the CO, Maj. John Bromilow[i], the Adjutant, the Lewis Gun Officer, 2nd Lt. Ivo Robinson, the Signal Officer, 2nd Lt. Joseph Rowley, DCM,[ii] five signallers, 16 runners and 16 men carrying Lewis gun ammunition who had all been specifically trained in filling the guns' drums. The battalion started to lose men well before entering No Man's Land. The two left hand companies of the battalion, C and D, were especially badly hit, mauled, no doubt, by the machine gun fire from about Serre and Pendant Copse and the very heavy artillery barrage being deposited on the 31st Division's front and which here extended down towards the Heidenkopf. The right hand companies made better progress across No Man's Land and pushed forward towards the second German trench. The war diary remarked later on the difference between the left and right companies. The left hand companies lost most men killed and wounded

[i] Major John Nisket Bromilow, 1st King's Own Royal Lancaster Regt., was the son of Mrs H J Bromilow of Rann Lea, Ramhill, Lancs. A pre-war Territorial, he was promoted Lt. in November 1908 and Captain in December 1914. He served with the 1st King's Own Royal Lancaster Regt in India at Lucknow, commanding the Maxim Gun Section. He was appointed to a Staff position, Brigade Major, before taking command. His body was found in August 1917. He is buried in Serre Road Cemetery No. 1, grave I. B. 51.

[ii] 2nd Lt. Joseph Rowley, DCM, 1st King's Own Royal Lancaster Regt., was aged 29. He was the only son of Mrs Davies (formerly Rowley), of 24 Havelock Street, Bowerham, Lancaster. He was educated at Scotforth C of E and Bowerham schools. His father, the late Mr Brian Rowley, was an engineering contractor. Fourteen years in the ranks he was a Company Sergeant Major before he was commissioned on 16th December 1915. He was awarded the DCM on 9th September 1914. His body was never found and his name is inscribed on the Thiepval Memorial, Pier & Face 5D & 12B.

in No Man's Land. The right companies recorded a large number of men as 'missing'. These had been killed or captured inside the German lines[i].

Those men of the left companies who got across ended up mainly in the front German trench. An unnamed officer of the left centre company recalls seeing no-one advancing on his left but on the right he saw men of the King's Own and Seaforths disappear into the German second trench, there to meet up with the rag-tag army of Warwicks, Somersets and men of the Rifle Brigade who had been fighting there for nearly 90 minutes. This officer also reported that the German second line to his front and left was strongly held by German troops who had machine guns out in the open in advance of the trench which were able to sweep the entire area of the 12th Brigade's advance.

Plate 84 Brig. Gen. Charles Bertie Prowse, GOC 11th Brigade

At 8.45 a.m. Brig. Gen. Bertie Prowse, DSO, GOC 11th Brigade, telephoned Brig. Gen. James Crosbie, GOC 12th Brigade. His news was something of a curate's egg – only good in places. He reported that some of his men had got through to the third German trench. Though encouraging, this was still 700 yards short of Munich Trench, the second objective. Prowse then told Crosbie that, in response, the Germans had dropped a barrage on their own third trench to the rear of the Heidenkopf and that this barrage was now creeping forward towards the German front line. When pressed by Crosbie as to whether his men had reached Munich Trench Prowse was equivocal. He had received no precise

[i] It has been suggested (*The Other Side of the Wire*, Vol. 2, Ralph Whitehead, page 86) that the King's Own suffered some casualties from the detonation of two of the mines laid out in No Man's Land in front of the Heidenkopf and that these were blown by men of the 4/13 Pioniers lurking in a dugout near the front. This idea may come from a post-war account of a 2nd Lt. H S Vincent, Lancashire Fusiliers, attached to 12th Brigade staff. The King's Own, however, advanced to the north of the Heidenkopf and were not in the correct area. Another officer of the 2nd Lancashire Fusiliers does, however, mention his battalion being affected by two large explosions in front of the Heidenkopf as they advanced.

messages to this effect but signals which might have come from his men had been seen in the vicinity. Crosbie advised Prowse that his leading patrols were now starting to advance. Prowse replied that he was pleased to hear this and rang off.

At 8.50 a.m. Prowse called the other Brigadier, Brig. Gen. Charles Wilding of 10th Brigade. He advised Wilding that the 12th Brigade were on the move, something Wilding had himself seen from his own position. Prowse then left his advanced Brigade HQ at the Lyceum with the intention of going over No Man's Land in order to assess the position at first hand[i]. He had also ordered No. 2 Section, 1/1st Durham Field Company, RE, commanded by Lt. James Aitken, to advance from Vallade Trench to the German lines, with one half going to the north of the Heidenkopf and the other to the south. Prowse then set off through the trenches towards the two tunnels in No Man's Land. With him went Maj. Arthur Michael Terry, OC, 1/1st Durham Field Company as well as a 2nd Lt. Herford and the General's servant, 8867 Pte. W R Bailey. The Brigadier, brandishing only his swagger stick, entered No Man's Land at the junction of the front line and Cat Street, opposite Point 56. Almost immediately he was struck in the back by a machine gun bullet probably fired from the Ridge Redoubt. It was thought that the bullet had entered his stomach, and such wounds had a very poor prognosis. Maj. Terry rushed off to inform the Brigade Major, Maj. Somerville, who assumed command of the Brigade as all of the battalion COs were, by now themselves casualties. 2nd Lt. Herford urgently sought out an MO or some stretcher bearers while Bailey desperately tended to his officer:

> "I, myself, did all in my power for my beloved master holding my hand over his wound for quite half an hour or so to keep the blood in... We then started on our journey back, after we had procured a stretcher, which took a considerable time. It was a terrible journey moving up these small trenches... He was conscious and happy until we reached Divisional Headquarters, when he grew weaker. We got to the hospital as soon as possible. He practically died in my arms, breathing his last at the hospital."[26]

Bertie Prowse arrived at the 12th Field Ambulance ADS near the Sucrerie at 11 a.m. He was immediately examined and was diagnosed as having suffered a shrapnel wound in the 'left loin'. Given the severity of the wound, and the poor survival rate associated with stomach wounds, he was sent off in an ambulance to the abdominal specialists at Authie for an immediate operation. He died soon after arrival. He is buried in Louvencourt Military Cemetery[ii].

---

[i] Writing after the war, Maj. William Somerville, Brigade Major of the 11th Brigade, states that Prowse went forward to organise an attack against the two German machine guns on the northern face of the Ridge Redoubt which, the major contended, were almost single-handedly holding up the advance of the left wing of the 4th Division. It may have been a bullet from one of these guns which caused his fatal wound.

[ii] Brig. Gen. Charles Bertie Prowse, DSO, 1st Somerset Light Infantry cmdg. 11th Brigade, was aged 47. He was the third son of Captain George James William Prowse, J.P. and Emmeline Lucy Prowse of St Edith's, Bromham, Wilts. Born at West Monkton, Taunton, Somerset. Husband of Violet Stanley Prowse of Bromham, Fleet, Hants. Educated at Cornish's School, Clevedon, and Marlborough College, he joined the 2nd Somerset Light

At 9.05 a.m. Crosbie called 11th Brigade to find that Prowse had gone forward. In his absence, the staff at 11th Brigade informed Crosbie that they thought Munich Trench had been taken. They were wrong.

Divisional HQ was now growing increasingly concerned about the position in the German trenches. Three out of the four battalions of the 10th Brigade had been held back on their orders and now similar orders were issued to 12th Brigade. Until further notice, there should be no further committing of troops to the battle. In spite of this decision, the King's Own and the 2nd Essex had already gone over but runners were despatched from 12th Brigade HQ in an effort to intercept the Duke's and Lancashire Fusiliers. These two battalions were not due to leave the British trenches until just before 10 a.m. but, with men hurrying on in order to avoid the worst of the German barrage, the runners arrived too late to stop the Fusiliers and only in time to hold back one company of the Duke's. The rest of these battalions had hastened across No Man's Land suffering heavy casualties all the way. Except for a few reports and what are described as 'confused incoherent messages' from the wounded, Brig. Gen. Crosbie had, for all intents and purposes, lost contact with, and control of, 90% of his Brigade by 10 a.m.

To the south of the Heidenkopf, Lt. Col. Hopkinson and his Seaforths had joined the men in the third German trench between Points 62 and 94. There is a common belief that some of these men 'may have' reached Munich Trench some 750 yards further forward but, if this was true then, as the Seaforth's War Diary states: "there was no possible communication and none returned"[27]. As German accounts make no mention of such a deep penetration it is, perhaps, sensible to assume that, like several other claims, this was more fantasy that reality. There were no messages and no-one returned simply because no British troops were there. Indeed, many of the reports about the presence of British troops at far distant points within the German defences such as Munich Trench and Pendant Copse are hedged about with such indefinite words and phrases as 'thinks' or 'may have' and 'believed to have'. In the absence of precise information, and with the German accounts making no mention of any such events, it seems sensible to place such claims in the trays marked 'wishful thinking' or 'inaccurate reporting'. There was certainly going to be plenty of the latter as the day drew on.

BY NOW IT WAS CLEAR THAT THE ATTACKS OF THE TWO DIVISIONS on either flank had collapsed in total disarray. At 9.07 a.m. 4th Division received a message from 29th Division to the effect that a planned renewal of their attack timed to go in at 9.20 a.m. had been postponed – for 4½ hours! And, the message admitted,

Infantry from the Militia on 12th December 1892. He served in the South African War (1899-1902), and was Adjutant between November 1900 and November 1904. He was Adjutant of the 1st Volunteer Battalion, Somerset Light Infantry, and then the 4th Somerset Light Infantry between 1904 and 1908. He spent the opening months of the war as a Major in the 1st Somerset Light Infantry before being given command of the 1st Leinster Regt. in January 1915. He fought at Le Cateau, the Aisne and Ypres. In April 1915 he was promoted to command the 11th Brigade. Five times MiD, he was awarded the DSO on 3rd June 1916. He is buried in Louvencourt Military Cemetery, Plot 1. Row E. Grave 9. His brother, Capt. Cecil Irby Prowse, RN, *HMS Queen Mary*, had been killed on 31st May 1916 at the Battle of Jutland.

"The attack may possibly not be made then".[28] Confusion was also rife within 4th Division. At exactly the same time, i.e. 9.12 a.m., as a Maj. MacGrath was reporting from a Divisional OP that the 11th Brigade had not reached their objective, the Divisional Artillery HQ Staff was advising the 31st Divisional Artillery that 11th Brigade was in their objective and not to fire on the southern section of their trench.

Three minutes later the 2nd Lancashire Fusiliers, still unaware of the fact that they should have stood fast in the British trenches, started to cross the front line into No Man's Land. With every step the casualties amongst officers and men grew. By now, with the 31st Division's attack a bloody shambles, the men defending the Serre sector's southern flank in S4, 7. Kompanie, IR 169, assisted by a platoon from the 1. Kompanie, Kgl. Bayerisches Pionier Regiment Nr. 1 commanded by Lt. Stumpf, independently switched targets to the left flank of the 4th Division plodding forward from well behind the British front line all the way into No Man's Land. If the advance of the first line battalions had been slow, theirs was even slower, laden as many were, with material with which to consolidate the trenches they expected to occupy. The funereal speed of the advance was noted by the Bavarians and the Fusiliers' casualties mounted as rifle and machine gun fire poured into their left flank.

The message, which should also have stopped the Lancashire Fusiliers, arrived with the Duke's at 9.25 a.m. Orders were rushed to the companies but only No. 4 Company received them in time to halt inside the British wire. The other three, already out in No Man's Land, concluded that, with a heavy German barrage falling on the British front trenches to their rear, advance was preferable to withdrawal and so on they pushed into the German lines, some of them joining the miscellaneous bunch of men crowding into the second German trench.

This heavy German barrage now fell from opposite the Ridge Redoubt northwards along the rest of the 4th Division's and the whole of the 31st Division's front. A group of 10th Brigade carriers, waiting to move forward with supplies, were stopped in their tracks by the hail of 77 mm and 10.5 cm shrapnel and high explosive being poured on the British front from the batteries of Gruppe Adolf and Gruppe Beauregard lurking in the shallow valleys away to the east.

Maj. MacGrath in his exposed OP was still trying to make sense of what he could see and, at 9.30 a.m., he repeated his opinion that British troops were *not* in Munich Trench whatever his HQ Staff might think. Confirmation came two minutes later with a report from 14th Brigade, RFA, which stated that Munich Trench was "certainly not taken".[29] It was now that the 'confused incoherent messages' from wounded men which so concerned Brig. Gen. Crosbie began to further muddy the murky waters of intelligence. As men returned wounded, exhausted, terrified, they passed other units and it was only natural that officers and men from these units would ask for news of the advance. What was 'unnatural' and certainly unprofessional was then to take these men's comments and pass them up the chain of command as somehow reliable statements from credible eyewitnesses. Unfortunately, at 9.42 a.m. this started to happen. Maj. Robinson of the 128th Battery, 29th Brigade, RFA, accosted a wounded man from one of the Warwickshire Territorial battalions. It is impossible to know whether the man thought what he said was true, whether he was badly confused or whether he said what he thought an officer might want to hear but his comment that "…our infantry are pushing on from German 4th line and there is not much resistance"[30], began to be reflected in certain other reports that continued to come in, in spite of all of the evidence to the contrary, well into the late afternoon.

The reports from the battalions painted an altogether different and more realistic picture. By 9.45 a.m. the 2nd Lancashire Fusiliers, who, of course, should have been somewhat more safely established on the British side of No Man's Land, were held up in the third German trench with both flanks in the air. They started to dig in while elements of the battalion still in the British lines tried to organise a system to keep them supplied with ammunition and grenades.

The 2nd Essex was in a similar position. Some elements had reached a position which they took to be 50 yards short of the 2nd German Position, i.e. Munich Trench. Here, though, there were four lines of German trenches to cross before reaching the 300 yards which separated Serre Trench from Munich Trench and, from German accounts, it seems more likely that Serre Trench was as far as they penetrated (Point 81). Although reported by both the Essex War Diary and others it is extremely unlikely that any troops of this or any other unit reached Pendant Copse as claimed. Coming under heavy machine gun fire from about Serre and also from their right (Munich Trench) the men of the Essex tried to consolidate a line of craters which they manfully held for several hours.

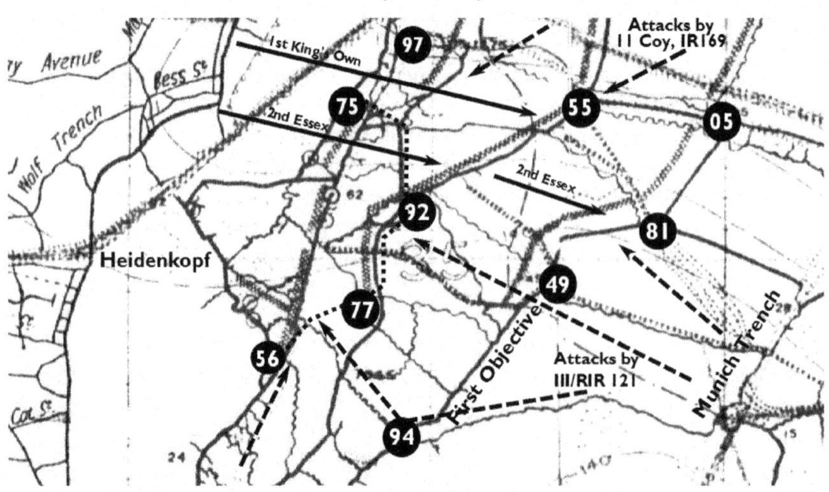

Map 24 The advance of the 1st King's Own and 2nd Essex

Key: Point 81, furthest advance by 1st Essex and location of Lt. Martineau
Point 97, remains of left companies of 1st King's Own
The 11. Kompanie of IR 169 launch attacks agsinst the left of 4th Division
The III Bataillon, RIR 121, advance from Feste Soden and Munich Trench
1. Kompanie, RIR 121, attacks Heidenkopf from the south

During the advance, casualties amongst the officers of the Essex had been most severe and, by the end of the day, all bar one was either dead or wounded.

15951 Pte. J Adkins saw what may have been the final moments of his platoon officer, 2nd Lt. Gilbert Waterhouse from C Company. Adkins reported what he had witnessed from his bed in the St John's Hospital in Etaples ten days after the attack:

> "I last saw Lt. Waterhouse on the 1st July about 9.30 am two hours after the start. He was a very brave man and he stood out more conspicuously than anyone. He seemed so fearless… On the 1st July between Serre Wood and Beaumont, about 9.30 in the morning, I had got over one German trench and was advancing to a second when I was hit in the back. I was carrying bombs and I was going on again when I caught sight of Lt. Waterhouse about 30 yards from me. He had a revolver in his hand and he stood out, a solitary figure. I saw him drop to his knees and begin to crawl and I did the same and so did his platoon. I thought at the time he had seen an MG and was avoiding the fire but he may have been hit."

Waterhouse's[i] body was recovered in July 1917 and buried in the cemetery that occupies the area of No Man's Land just to the south of the site of the Heidenkopf Redoubt – Serre Road No. 2 Cemetery.

Plate 85 2nd Lt. Gilbert Waterhouse, 2nd Essex Regt.

In the main, 4th Division HQ accepted the reality of the situation that, basically, all of the men in the German lines were squeezed into one of the three trenches that ran along the base of the Heidenkopf and that Munich Trench had not been occupied and, instead, was the route being used by German bombing parties moving to the counter attack. Rather oddly, though, the War Diary does

[i] 2nd Lt. Gilbert Waterhouse, C Company, 2nd Essex Regt., was aged 33. He was born in Chatham, the son of a shipbroker, and was educated at Bancroft's School and the University of London. He qualified as an architect. He enlisted as a Private in the 18th Royal Fusiliers and was commissioned into the 3rd Essex Regt., in May 1915. He is buried in Serre Road Cemetery No. 2, grave I. K. 23. Waterhouse was a poet and a volume of 24 poems entitled *'Rail-Head and other poems'* was published posthumously in 1916.

record a report from 10th Brigade at 10.07 a.m. that the Royal Dublin Fusiliers, even now waiting in the British trenches for further instructions, had somehow taken the two front German trenches opposite them. In reality, they were waiting for an attempted renewal of the attack by the 29th Division on their right at some time after midday. It would not take place.

Back in the German trenches, more and more British troops were filtering into position at the base of the Heidenkopf as 2nd Lt. Glover later described:

> "Gradually our bit of trench filled in with a great many of the 12th Brigade and some of the 10th. I afterwards learnt that some of the 10th had stayed in the (German) front line but didn't know till about 5 p.m. otherwise we should have tried to make connection. We were a fearful squash in the trench, everybody in the way of everybody else and it was extremely difficult to move or dig. I did try, but not very successfully, to spread the 11th out to the right and Capt. Martin also tried to get the 10th and 12th to the left but they were held back and we couldn't get along the single trench."[31]

Further north and somewhat isolated, those men of the left companies of the 1st King's Own who had reached the German lines had drifted to their left and were at Point 97 near the end of Ten Tree Alley. On their left the 93rd Brigade of the 31st Division should have been driving eastwards towards Pendant Copse but, with few exceptions, the battalions of this Brigade had been dreadfully cut up and the survivors were either in No Man's Land or back in their jump-off trenches. So chaotic were the scenes here that the men of the 93rd and 12th Brigades in these trenches become intermingled. Opposite them, though, the small group of the King's Own had come under attack by bombers from the 11. Kompanie of IR 169 pressing down from the direction of Serre. A request for help from the 93rd Brigade sent at 10.25 a.m. was rejected as there were no troops available to assist and the King's Own were forced to retire.

The intervention from 11/IR 169 had come on their initiative not at the request of the RIR 121. The men attacking the King's Own came from the platoon of Leutnant der Reserve Gattner who went to the aid of 1. Kompanie, RIR 121. No. 3 Platoon, commanded by Leutnant Johannes Hoppe, occupied the front line around the western end of Ten Tree Alley and helped stop any British reinforcements get across No Man's Land and into the German lines. A third platoon, No.1 Platoon under 20 year old Leutnant Friedrich Hoppe, moved towards the position of the hard-pressed 3. Kompanie, RIR 121 where they vigorously bombed towards the base of the Heidenkopf. They advanced down the trenches protected by a shower of bombs and, on their way, liberated a number of men trapped in dugouts. One of these was Oberleutnant Max Lutz, the wounded commander of the 3. Kompanie, whose face apparently betrayed the strain he had been under waiting for help. Hoppe left some men with Lutz before leading the forty remaining men under his command against a series of four British trench blocks hurriedly built during the morning. Each one was taken, a flurry of bombs preceding a frantic rush down the trench before their last bomb was thrown at the overthrow of the fourth trench block. Now, Hoppe's men, like the British opposite, were completely out of grenades.

The only troops now in the German lines were the mixed bag of men from nine battalions from three Brigades in and around the Heidenkopf. Further south, however, the men of the 11th Brigade trapped in No Man's Land were still taking casualties. At about 10.30 a.m., Lt. Col. James Green, DSO, of the East Lancashires, who had been lying in a shallow depression out in front of the German wire with his Adjutant, Capt. Sidney Heath, found it not deep enough when he was hit in the shoulder by a bullet. Green stayed where he was as retiring across a machine gun-swept No Man's Land was not a sensible option. Behind him, the battalion medical officer, Capt. John Richard Menzies Whigham[i], MC, RAMC, had been tending to the wounded lying out in No Man's Land. He had already been slightly wounded but now, at the same time as his CO, he was shot in the shoulder and forced to seek medical attention. He left behind his medical orderly, 6583 Pte. Edward J Brightmore[ii], who carried on the work of helping the numerous casualties and was later awarded the Military Medal for his bravery. Unless the Germans in the Ridge Redoubt and further south could be dislodged, all the East Lancashire men could do was wait in their shell holes and scrapes and hope to survive until night fall.

BY MID-MORNING, 10TH BRIGADE STAFF COULD SEE the enemy front line gradually filling with German troops, some appearing to emerge from dugouts in the forward trenches. Machine guns were sweeping No Man's Land as well as the British front lines. The only way forward was to come at these troops from the flank and rear. At 10.35 a.m. a message was sent by runner from Brigade HQ to Lt. Col. Hopkinson of the Seaforths in the Heidenkopf requiring him to attempt just that. He was ordered to bomb down the trenches from Point 77 towards the rear of the redoubt. Then the men of the East Lancashires, Hampshires and Dublin Fusiliers currently pinned down could push through and the advance renewed. It appeared a plausible scenario from the position of the Staff at Brigade HQ. But the very machine guns that were scything down anyone in No Man's Land effectively cut all communications between HQ and the men on the other side. The order to Hopkinson was never delivered.

In spite of this, optimistic reports were still coming in. At 10.42 a.m. the HQ of the 4th Division's Artillery received a report from the 29th Brigade, RFA, that the Somerset Light Infantry had reached their final objective. This artillery unit, the reader may recall, was the source of the news that, 60 minutes earlier, the Warwickshires were at the German 4th line and that there was little German resistance. This information was equally incorrect. The facts of the matter around the Heidenkopf were rather different, as 2nd Lt. Glover recalled:

> "Suddenly our right seemed to be rushed by German bombers and the men next to our Battalion Bombing squad rushed back, the bombing

---

[i] Born in 1891, Whigham was awarded his MC in the New Year's Honours List in the *London Gazette*, 11th January 1916. He later became a Fellow of the Royal College of Surgeons and wrote *'An Introduction to First Aid'*, published in 1942.

[ii] 6583 Pte Edward James Brightmore, MM, 1st East Lancashire Regt., was awarded the MM in the *London Gazette* of 21st September 1916. Brightmore lived in Burnley and his three brothers also served. One of them, 8268 Pte Sydney Brightmore, 6th East Lancashire Regt., was killed in Mesopotamia in April 1917.

> squad was apparently cut off. This was about 11 a.m. to 12 noon and we were short of bombs and the Lewis guns were more or less out of action."[32]

At this time 4th Division reported the surge in German bombing counter attacks which forced the British troops to retire and, by noon, the 3rd trench had been abandoned and the line now occupied was between Point 77 and Point 92. The withdrawal had been sudden and precipitate in places with some men bolting for the German front line and beyond. 9090 Sergeant Arthur Henry Cook, 1st Somerset Light Infantry, was near to Lt. Col. Hopkinson when the withdrawal took place and, for a few moments, it looked as if the whole position might collapse in an instant:

> "Col. Hopkinson of the Seaforths was doing excellent work, he seemed to be the only officer here, and was seen walking around the Quadrilateral giving encouragement to all. He saved a dangerous situation; someone gave an order to retire, there was an immediate panic, and some four to five hundred retired, in spite of great efforts to stem the rush by the Colonel and us sergeants present. The Colonel then ordered a bugler of the Seaforths to sound the 'charge'; this had the immediate effect and saved the situation."[33]

It was at this moment that the only Victoria Cross awarded to a man of the 4th Division on 1st July 1916 was won. 68 Pte. Walter Potter Ritchie was 24 years old and a drummer in the 2nd Seaforths' Pipe Band. He had been carrying messages since he arrived in the German lines but now, as the men wavered under this concerted bombing attack, he stood on the parapet of the trench, in full view of everyone, and repeatedly blew the 'charge' on a bugle[i].

With the position stabilised 2nd Lt. Glover and the other officers still standing attempted to consolidate their new position:

> "All the bombs we had and could spare from the left were passed up and, with the help of a corporal, I managed to get together about four throwers who absolutely kept the trench for us for hours. They were a magnificent lot and splendid fellows, they deserve any praise or reward. There was another even finer, the runner of the Colonel of the 8th Warwicks, I believe. (But I have all their names only unfortunately I left it with the

---

[i] Not a drum as shown in several inaccurate portrayals of the event, the most notable being one from *'Deeds that Thrill the Empire'*. 68 Pte Walter Potter Ritchie, 2nd Seaforth Highlanders, was awarded the Victoria Cross for his conduct on 1st July 1916. The citation, in the *London Gazette* of 8th September 1916, reads: "For most conspicuous bravery and resource, when on his own initiative he stood on the parapet of an enemy trench, and, under heavy machine gun fire and bomb attacks, repeatedly sounded the 'Charge', thereby rallying many men of various units who, having lost their leaders, were wavering and beginning to retire. This action showed the highest type of courage and personal initiative. Throughout the day Drummer Ritchie carried messages over fire-swept ground, showing the greatest devotion to duty".

Ritchie was born in Glasgow in 1892 and died in Edinburgh in 1965. He enlisted in the 8th Scottish Rifles, transferring to the 2nd Seaforth Highlanders in 1908. He received his VC from the King at Buckingham Palace on 25th November 1916. He was also awarded the Croix de Guerre.

> things to be returned to my kit but I will let you have the names when I get my kit and want you, if you can, to do what you can for any who are left). This runner made the trip between that trench and our own at least 20 times, bringing bombs and LG ammunition. He did more than any single individual to keep things going."[34]

Back at 12th Brigade HQ Brig. Gen. Crosbie was increasingly concerned by the total absence of any reliable information about the whereabouts of his Brigade. Runners had been sent to both of the forward battalions, the King's Own and the Essex, but the men had not returned. At 10.47 a.m. came the first detailed news. Capt. Kenneth James Milln, OC of the Duke's No. 1 Company, had been wounded whilst in the Heidenkopf and was on his way back for medical treatment. No. 1 Company had been the right hand company of the Duke's and Milln was able to report to Crosbie that, in spite of heavy casualties, his company, along with elements from the three other battalions of the Brigade, were established in the second German trench on the line 58-92-85. Men of the Lancashire Fusiliers were on their right and those of the King's Own and Essex in the third trench.

What Milln did not know was that the commanders of two companies from the Dukes were already dead. Capt. Cecil Lyon Hart[i], No. 3 Company, had been killed by a shell fragment and the body of Capt. Noel Waugh Hadwen, No. 2 Company, was never found[ii].

Hadwen had written home on the day before the attack with the confidence widespread amongst the VIII Corps:

> "You will have seen in the paper about activity here. We go over to see the Boches at dawn tomorrow. I believe that if our Division, the 4th, is successful, it will mean a good deal. I don't think the attack can fail, but at present my head hasn't room for any idea except my own little Company patch. I know they will do well, and this is all that seems to matter after five days' bombardment. The troops are full of life. I've never seen them in such good form. The weather is improving which means a lot for us."[35]

---

[i] Capt. Cecil Lyon Hart, No .3 Company, 3rd att. 2nd Duke of Wellington's (West Riding) Regt., was aged 27. He was the only son of Moss Alexander and Marguerite Hart of 12, Alexandra Mansions, West End Lane, Hampstead. Born in Kimberley, South Africa, he was educated at University College School, Hampstead, and was a graduate of University College, London where he was in the OTC. Active in the Jewish Lads' Brigade, he had just passed his bar examinations at the Inner Temple when he enlisted and was commissioned into the 3rd Duke of Wellington's on 15th August 1914. He joined the 2nd Duke's in France on 29th December 1914 and was promoted Captain on 10th June 1915. He is buried in Sucrerie Military Cemetery, Colincamps, grave I. H. 10.

[ii] Capt. Noel Waugh Hadwen, No. 2 Company, 2nd Duke of Wellington's (West Riding) Regt., was aged 30. He was the second son of Frederick W Hadwen, an Architect, and Anna M Hadwen of The Dene, Kebroyd Triangle, Yorks. Educated at Lockers Park and Harrow School, he was an architect in partnership with Mr E Guy Dawber of Buckingham Street, Adelphi, London. He joined the battalion in September 1914 and went to France in April 1915. He was badly, nearly fatally, gassed at Hill 60 in May 1915, returning to the front in October 1915. His body was never found and his name is inscribed on the Thiepval Memorial, Pier & Face 6A & 6B.

Hadwen was a popular and energetic officer who had been keen to get to grips with the enemy and bring an end to the war. He had nearly died in a gas attack on Hill 60 where he had been so badly poisoned that he was being carried away to be buried when something brought him round. He recovered to return to France in October 1915 where he remained, viewing trench warfare with increasing frustration. 2nd Lt. Cyril Grimley was Noel Hadwen's best friend in the battalion and they had been together on the night before the attack but had lost track of one another during the day. Grimley was wounded and hurried off to the Advanced Dressing Station when he found himself lying next to a man from Hadwen's company. When Grimley asked how his company had got on the man replied that he wouldn't care what happened to him as long as he knew Mr Hadwen was safe. The man then told him that he had been near to his company commander when they had both been hit. He had survived but Noel Hadwen's life had finally been brought to an end by a shell.[i]

Plate 86 Capt. Cecil Lyon Hart, 2nd Duke of Wellington's Regt.

Plate 87 Capt. Noel Waugh Hadwen, 2nd Duke of Wellington's Regt.

Some minutes later a more up to date message came in, one of the few sent by one of the visual messaging systems. It came from Lt. Col. George Freeth of the Lancashire Fusiliers and was later confirmed by a written message delivered by a runner who had crossed No Man's Land from the tip of the Heidenkopf.

---

[i] 2nd Lt., later Brig. Gen., Cyril Walter Gaitskell Grimley, 2nd Duke of Wellington;s Regt. was born in India in 1896. He was the son of Edith Grimley (widow), of 29, Landsdown Crest, Cheltenham. He was commissioned into the Duke of Wellington's Regt. in December 1914. He transferred to the Machine Gun Corps on 6th November 1916 and was then seconded to the Tank Corps in August 1917. Won the MC at Cambrai. He was appointed Adjutant of the Central School, Tank Corps, in 1919 and then served in the West African Frontier Force up to 1927 when he rejoined the regiment. He returned to West Africa in 1934, acting as OC, 6th Battalion, The Nigeria Regt. He served as GOC, 4th West African Brigade, West Africa, 1941-2, and GOC, 145th Brigade, 1942-3. He retired in 1947 and died in 1963.

The message read 'that the advance was slow but practical and that casualties had been severe and that reinforcements were required'.

Somehow these two messages were translated by Crosbie into a report to 4th Division at 11.10 a.m. that the 11th Brigade had achieved its objective and that the King's Own and Essex, supported by the Lancashire Fusiliers were advancing steadily. This, in spite of his report also stating that 'I have no information from King's Own or Essex since operation began'. Fifteen minutes later 4th Division was reporting the East Lancashires and the Hampshires were established in the 2nd German trench south of Ridge Redoubt. The source for this erroneous news was not provided.

With all efforts to reach the King's Own and Essex failing but with garbled reports from the wounded streaming up Roman Road past the Brigade HQ suggesting that, somehow, the two battalions had reached Munich Trench, Crosbie became increasingly desperate for news. Was the attack teetering on the brink of victory or, more likely, defeat?

At 11.50 a.m. this news came. A Lt. Martineau, the 12th Brigade Signalling Officer[i], sent a visual signal from a position thought to be 100 yards south west of Point 81. Point 81, if this was correct, was in Serre Trench and about as close to Munich Trench as anyone was likely to have got during the fighting (though still 200 yards short of it). His message was brief: "Essex held up here, Boches bombing towards them".

This message confirmed the fact that the 12th Brigade had not reached Munich Trench but, rather more to the point, it indicated that strong German counter attacks from III/RIR 121 and Lt. Friedrich Hoppe's platoon from 11. Kompanie IR 169 were converging on the 4th Division's lodgement within the German lines. Behind Hoppe and his dwindling band, now reduced to twenty tiring men, came Vizefeldwebel Haid and a few others from 11/IR 169 and they joined in the continuous bombing battles that took place along the slowly reducing British perimeter.

The attacks on the scattered elements of the 2nd Essex were made in strength and vigorously pushed home. Coming in from the front, i.e. Munich Trench (III/RIR 121), and from the flank, i.e. from Ten Tree Alley (11. Kompanie IR 169), they rapidly pushed the Essex back to the 77-92 line where the men met up with two of their officers, Capt. Andrew de la Mare[ii] of B Company and 2nd Lt. Leslie Ward[iii], the battalion Bombing Officer, who were trying to reorganise the

---

[i] Thought to be Lt. Wilfrid Martineau, Royal Warwickshire Regt.

[ii] 2nd Lt. (temp Capt.) Andrew Guy de la Mare, 2nd Essex Regt., was awarded the MC for his conduct on 1st July 1916. The citation in the *London Gazette* of 22nd September 1916 reads: "For conspicuous gallantry in action. At a critical moment in the attack, assisted by an officer and a company serjeant-major, he organised a party of about forty men of different units and manned and held a crater. They kept the enemy in check with some of the enemy's own bombs which they found. They were subjected throughout to heavy artillery and bombing attacks".

[iii] 5550 Pte. Leslie Jack Ward, Honourable Artillery Company, was commissioned into the 2nd Essex and attained the rank of Captain in August 1916. Alone of the three Essex officers mentioned he did not receive an award in recognition of his conduct on 1st July. He relinquished his commission on 4th June 1917 as a result of ill-health caused by wounds.

troops now packed into the trenches. De la Mare had already ransacked captured German dugouts in an effort to find supplies of bombs with which to resist the German attacks and these he used to great effect. With their CO, Lt. Col. Sir George Stirling[i] twice wounded early on, command of the battalion had been assumed by Lt. Lawrence Cadic, the Adjutant. Along with de la Mare and Ward, Cadic, although three times wounded, did much by example to stabilise the position and bring some sense of order to the crowded trenches. Cadic and de la Mare would both win the Military Cross[ii].

2nd Lt. Ward had advanced with forty bombers, each carrying 15 bombs in two sandbags carried round the neck. They were organised in four sections of ten NCOs and men and had gone over with the fourth wave of the 2nd Essex. They were split into two parties of 20 on each flank. Casualties were heavy as they went over and one section on the right, arrived in the German support line at about 10 a.m. with only Ward and one man left. Here they found de la Mare in a short stretch of trench crowded with men, the Germans having retreated at speed down two communication trenches. With most of the supply of bombs lying out in No Man's Land with the other carriers it was clear that there were not sufficient supplies to act aggressively and a trench barricade was hurriedly built and, a few yards behind, another, this one supported by a Lewis gun. Because of the press of men in the trench it was not possible to leave much of a gap between the two barricades but, until about 5 p.m. in the afternoon, this position was held. With attacks coming in from both ends of the trench it became clear that their position was untenable and they were forced to withdraw into the German front line trench. By this time, owing to a shortage of trained bombers, the men competent to use the bombs were exhausted. They had also used up both their

---

[i] Lt. Col. Sir George Murray Home Stirling, DSO, 2nd Essex Regt., was the 9th Baronet of Glorat. Born in 1869, he was the son of Sir Charles Elphinstone Fleming Stirling, 8th Baronet, of Glorat (Nova Scotia Baronetcy, 1666), formerly Highland Borderers Militia, JP and DL for Stirlingshire, and of Anne Georgina, eldest daughter of James Murray. He was educated at Eton College, and the RMC, Sandhurst; and was commissioned into the 2nd Essex Regiment on 9th November 1889. He served in the Chitral and Tirah Campaigns and in South Africa where he was awarded the DSO for his part in saving the guns in an action at Sanna's Post. He commanded the 7th Somali Camel Corps (1903-4) and was later DAAG, Mhow Division, India. Initially Provost Marshal with IX Corps he was given command of the 2nd Essex in November 1915. The Lord Lieutenant of Stirling 1936-49, he died in 1949.

[ii] Lt. & Adjt. Lawrence William Ludovic Cadic, 2nd Essex Regt., was awarded the MC for his conduct on 1st July 1916. The citation in the *London Gazette* of 22nd September 1916 reads: "For conspicuous gallantry in action. When his C.O. was wounded, he continued to reorganise the men in the second line of the enemy's trench under heavy shell and machine gun fire. His fine example did much to steady the men under trying circumstances".

Capt. Lawrence William Ludovic Cadic, MC, 2nd Essex Regt., died of wounds on 10th October 1917. Aged 20, he was the second son of Lt. Col. Louis Stephen Cadic (Royal Engineers), of Manor House, Chalk, Gravesend, Kent. Educated at King's School, Rochester, he joined the 2nd Essex Regt in March 1915. He is buried in Cement House Cemetery, Langemarck, grave VI. D. 21. His older brother, Capt. Bernard Francis Cadic, Royal Garrison Artillery, died of wounds on 20th August 1916 and is buried in Gravesend Cemetery.

own supplies and the bags of stick grenades found in the German dugouts. 2nd Lt. Ward remembered the Germans as very aggressive and several were shot in the open while passing up bags of bombs or while directing their throwers. He also described them as both stronger and more accurate than the British bombers. Back at 12th Brigade HQ Crosbie, meanwhile, had organised carrying parties to get more grenades over to the Heidenkopf as soon as possible.

Meanwhile, the artillery persisted in claiming that men of the Essex were in Munich Trench. Messages from the 32nd and 29th Brigades, RFA, either side of 11.50 a.m., had the Essex in or very near to Munich Trench with one suggesting they were at Point 63, the junction of Munich Trench with Ten Tree Alley. At the same time, Lt. Martineau was signalling from a position 400 yards short of Point 63 that the 'Essex held up here, Boches bombing towards them'. But, acting on their interpretation of the situation, the two Artillery Brigades independently ordered D/32 Battery of 4.5 in howitzers and 127th Battery of 18 pdrs to place a barrage 200 yards to the east of Munich Trench. The 2nd Essex position was, however, some 400 yards to the west of the trench. All the while, the guns of 14th Brigade, RFA, were happily barraging the southern end of Munich Trench, an area no-one had ever claimed British troops to be anywhere near. It was all a nonsense.

From just after noon, orders emanating from 4th Division had, as a result of all this inaccurate and contradictory information, ventured into fantasy land. According to their assessment of the situation the position was this:

- The 2nd Essex were in Munich Trench with both flanks in the air and were threatened by bombing attacks which were being held off by an artillery barrage 200 yards to the east;
- The Lancashire Fusiliers were in the Heidenkopf – somewhere;
- The 11th Brigade was holding a line 81-49-77; and
- The 1st East Lancashires held the 2nd German trench between Points 62 and 59.

The reality of the situation was that what was left of the Essex was back in the 77-92 line. The remnants of the Lancashire Fusiliers actually were in the Heidenkopf – somewhere. Fragments of the 11th Brigade (and the Seaforths) were arrayed over various trenches from the second line (77-92) back to the front line of the Heidenkopf. And the remains of the East Lancashires were littered across No Man's Land and the British front line.

But, on the basis of their interpretation, and with news that the 29th Division hoped to re-launch their sorry excuse for an assault at 12.30 p.m., the Dublin Fusiliers were ordered to push through the East Lancashires to the third German trench while the Seaforths bombed south along this trench to Point 86. Thoughtfully, the orders did suggest that the Dubliners should:

> "Take care of (their) left flank as there are still some Germans in position opposite the Redan".[36]

The absurdity of this analysis of the situation and the orders given was more than amply highlighted when Lt. Col. Cliff of the Dublin Fusiliers was unable to collect more than 60 men for this venture. With the battalion having already lost 14 officers and over 300 men during their advance from their assembly trenches to the British front line and with the rest of the battalion scattered in trenches and shell holes over an area several hundred yards deep behind the British front, there just were not the troops available to launch on this fool's errand across No Man's Land.

12.30 p.m. came and went and neither the Dublin Fusiliers nor the 29th Division attacked. Around the Heidenkopf fighting continued with all battalions and Brigades reporting heavy casualties amongst the units involved. On the left, the 12th Brigade reported at 12.45 p.m. that the 93rd Brigade, their immediate neighbours to the north, were retiring from their own front line and it appeared they were being heavily counter-attacked from the direction of Serre. Brig. Gen. Crosbie repeated his view that it was unlikely that the Essex were in Munich Trench. He also advised Division that, including carrying parties, he only had 500 men at his disposal and, taking account of the retrograde movement of the 93rd Brigade, he was trying to collect and keep as many man as he could lay his hands on. In response to Crosbie's concerns about the 93rd Brigade, 31st Division sent to 4th Division one of the more extraordinary messages of the day. Arriving at 12.55 p.m. it stated:

> "First four waves of 31st in possession of Serre and Pendant Copse line. 93rd Brigade being counter attacked by small detachments only. Probably fallen back because of bad state of our trenches – very little fear of Germans getting round 4th Division left."[37]

These extraordinary claims seem to have been taken with several truckloads of salt at 4th Division HQ who recorded at 1 p.m. that the 'attack of the 31st Division had failed' but, clearly, Crosbie had been told the same nonsense, as he forwarded, at the same time, a message stating that the 94th Brigade had somehow taken the Serre-Pendant Copse line.

There was no such ludicrous optimism from the 29th Division as another attempt to renew the attack came and went. The Dublin Fusiliers, instead of being flung across No Man's Land to support a non-existent incursion by the East Lancashires and Hampshires, were withdrawn to their original assembly trenches whilst their officers tried to collect as many men as they could find. Their place was taken by the 1st Royal Warwickshires who sent a strong patrol under Lt. Reginald Waters from A Company to try to enter the German lines at Point 27. Had this been successful, Lt. Col. George Forster of the Warwicks had intended pushing over A Company in small groups with the intention of bombing northwards towards the Ridge Redoubt. But it was not to be. The patrol got to about the point where the Sunken Road, i.e. the one occupied by the 1st Lancashire Fusiliers, joined Watling Street when they were halted by intense machine gun fire from Beaumont Hamel and had to return, arriving back in the British lines at 2.15 p.m. Typically, an order cancelling this patrol was received by Col. Forster after the men had gone. The unfortunate Lt. Waters survived this escapade but not the Battle of the Somme[i]. Thereafter, any attempt to exit the

---

[i] Capt. Reginald Rigden Waters, 4th att. 1st Royal Warwickshire Regt., died on 24th October 1916. Aged 22, he was the son of the late Hubert David and Lucy Fownes Waters of Oakhurst, Coundon, Coventry. He was educated at Rugby School and Corpus Christi College, Oxford, where he was in the OTC. He was commissioned into the 4th (Extra

British trenches on the southern flank of the 4th Division was met by heavy machine gun fire. It was 2.30 p.m. when reality dawned and the Warwicks were ordered to hold the front line with a single company while the rest were withdrawn out of the way in trenches further to the rear.

Plate 88 Capt. Reginald Rigden Waters, 1st Royal Warwickshire Regt.

As part of this abortive movement, first by the Dublins and then by the Warwicks, it was hoped that the men of the Seaforths in the German trenches would be able to bomb down to the rear of the Ridge Redoubt. All attempts to get messages to this effect across to Lt. Col. Hopkinson failed and, instead, the Seaforths and other troops within the German lines came under increasing pressure from aggressive German bombing parties. Heavy bombing attacks on both flanks had already forced the abandonment of the German 3rd trench. Pressure was also growing on the other battalions. At 1.14 p.m. the 10th Brigade War Diary records a message sent via 11th Brigade from the 2nd Essex. It was disconcertingly straightforward: "For goodness sake send reinforcements".

The artillery, at last, also seem to have realised they were firing too far to the east to be of any help to the infantry where they actually held up. Currently, the guns were still firing at where the infantry were *supposed to be* according to the timetable. At around 1.30 p.m. instructions were sent to the Artillery Brigades to start firing to the west rather than the east of Munich Trench and to fire a barrage only 200 yards east of the 55-92-77 line, i.e. the 2nd German trench. At the same time, 32nd Brigade, RFA, passed on a somewhat desperate message taken from a visual signal received from the Heidenkopf. It called for grenades – urgently. A carrying party laden with 500 Mills bombs in boxes set off but every man became a casualty in No Man's Land.

Reserve) Battalion of the Royal Warwickshire Regt. in December 1914. Went to France in May 1915 and joined the 1st Battalion. Wounded on 15th July, he was fatally wounded on 23rd October near Le Transloy. His body was never found and his name is inscribed on the Thiepval Memorial, Pier & Face 9 A, 9 B & 10 B.

Messages were now flying in as the full extent of the danger facing the troops in the German trenches became apparent. No longer were any men thought to be 700 yards further forward in Munich Trench. Now, with the messages like the one picked up at 1.05 p.m. by D/32 Battery and passed to 10th Brigade at 1.35 p.m. which read: "For God's sake reinforcements", reality rapidly dawned. Maj. Gen. Lambton summed the situation up in the 4th Division war diary:

> "As it was now evident that the objective of the VIII Corps could not be obtained without fresh artillery preparations, at 1.40 p.m. I ordered the GOCs 10th and 12th Brigades to organise the defence of our own line, allotting the right sector to the 10th Brigade and the left to the 12th Brigade, the dividing line being an east and west line through Point 56. The GOC 12th Brigade was entrusted with the defence of the German trenches held by us with orders to consolidate and hold them. The scattered units of the 11th Brigade were to be collected within our own lines and to be reformed as a Divisional Reserve."[38]

Lambton's comments do rather beg the question: what did he expect to achieve with a brief ad hoc bombardment that the seven day's planned bombardment could not? Whatever his expectations, the job in hand now was to reorganise the troops in his own lines and reinforce and supply those hemmed in around the Heidenkopf. At 1.15 p.m. an order was sent to the CO of the 1st Royal Irish Fusiliers, Lt. Col. William Findlater, which required him to send a company of the battalion over to support Lt. Col. Hopkinson in the Heidenkopf. By 1.40 p.m., however, news was coming back that men from the Rifle Brigade and the Somersets were filtering back to the British trenches and that those of the Warwicks, Seaforths and the 12th Brigade were under increasing pressure. In addition, a party of Germans had entered the tunnel at Beet Street but had been ejected. The only Brigade with any organised troops left was 10th Brigade and, as a result, Brig. Gen. Wilding ordered a company of the Royal Irish Fusiliers over to the Heidenkopf with a supply of bombs to accompany them. At the same time, the 10% reserve of the 11th Brigade was called forward to swell, even if only slightly, the much depleted ranks of its hard hit battalions.

At 2 p.m. C Company of the Royal Irish Fusiliers, commanded by Capt. Edward Rowland Wilson, assembled north of the Redan (i.e. opposite Ridge Redoubt) with the intention of following the Seaforths into the German trenches around Point 56 but any attempt at leaving their trenches was met by intense machine gun fire from front and flanks. Capt. Wilson was badly wounded in the attempted crossing and the movement was abandoned. It would be another two hours before Lt. Col. Findlater was to hear of the failure.

From the German lines a steady stream of wounded crawled their painful way across No Man's Land. By 1.30 p.m. both officers of the Somersets, Capt. Harington and Lt. Greetham, had been wounded and sent back. Command of the dwindling band of men from the battalion now passed to 7578 CSM Percy Chappell. He also collected to himself men of any other unit in the surrounding trenches and organised a vigorous bombing defence of his little section of

German trench. He was not to be dislodged until relieved around midnight[i]. He had been joined in the Heidenkopf by 4812 RSM Edgar Paul and some of the Brigade carriers who Paul had brought over. His party, initially of 50 men, had tried to get across before but came under heavy machine gun fire so Paul had brought them back to the British trenches and led them round to the northern end of the Heidenkopf where the terrain gave some respite from the fire from the Ridge Redoubt. Having deposited his load of consolidating material he returned to the British lines with an invaluable update of the situation opposite[ii]. Two other men from the Somersets played a crucial role in the defence of the Heidenkopf. 9224 Sgt Sidney Imber[iii] and 8685 Pte. William Hodges[iv] did excellent work in signalling from German trenches for supplies of grenades, the positioning of barrages, etc.

The field artillery, meanwhile, had been told to barrage Beaumont Trench (Nagel Graben), the third German trench which ran from behind the north end of the Ridge Redoubt down and into the northern end of Beaumont Hamel. Given that the only British troops within the German lines were to the north of this trench, this seems a strange area to bombard but it was, perhaps, a hangover from the belief that men of the East Lancashires and Hampshires were occupying the second German trench in front of Beaumont Trench. At 2.15 p.m. 12th Brigade asked for a barrage on the eastern side of the line Point 92-77, i.e. in the area in front of Serre Trench which was the extension of Beaumont Trench north of Lager Alley. This was a far more sensible place for the field guns and howitzers to barrage as it was the area directly in front of the trenches which were still being held, albeit tenuously, by the motley group of officers and men collected there. In addition, the 12th Brigade sent in an urgent request for supplies

---

[i] 7578 CSM Percy Edgar Eyres Chappell, 1st Somerset Light Infantry, from Bath was 30 years old and a pre-war regular of twelve years' standing. He was awarded the DCM for his conduct on 1st July 1916. The citation in the *London Gazette* of 22nd September 1916 reads: "For conspicuous gallantry in action. When all his officers had become casualties, he collected all available men, including many of other regiments. He then organised bombing parties, and arranged the defences generally. He held on to the ground won till relieved at midnight". He was later commissioned, was briefly Adjutant in the Welsh Regt., was awarded the MBE in 1923 and promoted Major.

[ii] 4812 RSM Edgar Paul, MC & Bar, 1st Somerset Light Infantry, was awarded the DCM for his conduct on 1st July 1916. The citation in the *London Gazette* of 22nd September 1916 reads: "For conspicuous gallantry in action. He took charge of a party of fifty men, who were carrying R.E. stores to the captured enemy line. When hung up by heavy machine-gun fire he skilfully got his party through by a circuitous route. He then returned with most valuable information as to the state of affairs. Throughout the rest of the day he did fine work". Capt. & Adjutant Edgar Paul, MC, DCM, 1st Somerset Light Infantry, died on 10th September 1918 of wounds suffered on 2nd September 1918. He is buried in Aubigny Communal Cemetery Extension, grave IV. B. 15. His MC was gazetted on 25th August 1915. He was posthumously awarded a bar to his MC in the *London Gazette* of 31st January 1919 for his actions during which he was fatally wounded.

[iii] 9224 Sgt. Sidney Imber, 1st Somerset Light Infantry, was awarded the MM for his conduct on 1st July 1916. It was gazetted on 1st September 1916.

[iv] 8685 Pte William J Hodges, 1st Somerset Light Infantry, was awarded the MM for his conduct on 1st July 1916. It was gazetted on 1st September 1916.

of machine gun belts as there were only two Brigade machine guns still in operation and their ammunition supplies needed replenishing.

The Machine Gun Companies of all three Brigades had been actively involved in the fighting for many hours. In the 11th Brigade sections of the MGC had been attached to four of the attacking battalions:

No. 1 Section attached to the 1/8th Warwicks
No. 2 Section attached to the 1st Hampshires
No. 3 Section attached to the 1st Somersets
No. 4 Section attached to the 1st Rifle Brigade

These guns went forward with these battalions and it is not possible to give an account of their actions. Suffice to say the 11th Machine Gun Company suffered 55% losses of which four were officers. In addition, 7 other ranks were killed, 9 were missing and 63 wounded. The officer casualties were:

Plate 89 Capt. Francis George Ross Mockler, MC, 2nd Royal Irish Regt., att. 11th Machine Gun Company

Killed:
Capt. F G R Mockler[i], Commanding
2nd Lt. P C Knight[ii], No. 1 Section

---

[i] Capt. Francis George Ross Mockler, MC, 2nd Royal Irish Regt., att. 11th Machine Gun Company, was aged 26. He was the youngest son of Maj. Gen Edward Mockler (Indian Army) and Mrs Mockler of Rochford, Grange, Guernsey. He was educated at Elizabeth College, Guernsey and RMC, Sandhurst. His body was never found and his name is inscribed on the Thiepval Memorial, Pier & Face 3 A.

[ii] 2nd Lt. Philip Clifford Knight, 1st Somerset Light Infantry att. 11th Machine Gun Company, was aged 23. He was the younger son of Alexander and Josephine Knight of Long Lynch, Child Okeford, Blandford, Dorset. He was educated at Uppingham and went to Trinity College, Cambridge, in 1911, graduating with Classical honours in 1914. He enlisted in the HAC on the outbreak of war and was commissioned on 14th February 1915. He was wounded in April 1915. His body was never found and his name is inscribed on the Thiepval Memorial, Pier & Face 2 A.

Died of wounds:
2nd Lt. T St John[i], No. 2 Section
Wounded:
2nd Lt. H R Wood, No. 4 Section

The sixteen guns of the 12th Machine Gun Company were spread over various units with a variety of functions, much to the displeasure of the OC, Capt. George Basil Sleigh of the King's Own. Sleigh was already unhappy because he and his men, and the majority of 12th Brigade, had been billeted in Bertrancourt, a village well within the range of the German guns. Every night, or so it seemed to him after the war, the village was shelled and every night he and everyone else dutifully tramped off into the nearby fields in an effort to get some sleep. Clearly this memory, and some others, had festered with the good Captain as his post-war remarks reveal:

> "I could never understand why, in the warm fine summer weather, we should tamely sit like sardines in a place that asked for a shelling and so everyone's sleep and freshness was undermined."[39]

But it was Brig. Gen. Crosbie's plans for Sleigh's precious machine guns that really grated:

> "I was given orders to send six machine guns forward to advance with the attacking battalions of our Brigade (1st Kings and 2nd Essex) and four guns on a special mission of the Brigadier's beyond the Heidenkopf Redoubt, and to advance myself about 15 or 20 minutes later with my remaining six guns (as a reserve) in the direction of the Heidenkopf Redoubt and to use my discretion as to how to act. I did not like the plan of scattering these sixteen guns so widely. It seemed to me to be treating machine guns like Lewis Guns! Especially as the ground could hardly have been better suited to overhead supporting barrage fire. But I was too blunt spoken and too keen on using a machine gun company as a unit to be popular with my Brigadier and so my opinion had little weight (this of course is not meant in any insubordinate sense, it's a question of understanding facts)."[40]

Notwithstanding his reservations, the Captain and his men went over on time, Sleigh and his six guns following on the rest. Just as Sleigh was about to leave the British trenches an Artillery officer in a nearby OP informed him that Serre had been taken, news that proceeded to rather interfere with the discretion he had been granted by Crosbie in his pre-battle instructions. Nonetheless, Sleigh and his men doubled into No Man's Land, each man carrying a heavy load of tripod or barrel, ammunition belts or water cans, and they headed towards the Heidenkopf. Sleigh later recalled his men going 'just like a line of football forwards'. One of his men, to whom Sleigh had given a hefty dose of Field Punishment No. 1 just a few days before, grinned at him and shouted over the hubbub, 'Just like the beach at Brighton, sir'. Their spirit delighted him. Advancing in extended order,

[i] 2nd Lt. Thomas St John, DCM, 1st East Lancashire Regt att. 11th Machine Gun Company, was aged 24. He was the son of John and Catherine St. John of Longsight, Manchester. He was seconded to the 11th MGC on 23rd December 1915. He is buried in Auchonvillers Military Cemetery, grave II. E. 37.

they reached the Heidenkopf but there began to suffer casualties from bullets being fired from their left, i.e. from the direction of Serre. Sleigh was perplexed:

> "That information (i.e. the capture of Serre) tied my hands all along... then I found that some of my men and one officer were being hit by bullets from our left flank, i.e. from the direction of Serre and I was puzzled, thinking that Serre was captured. So I halted my guns in a bit of a trench and signalled back by semaphore myself to the direction of 12th Brigade HQ (which I could see) to say where I was and ask for information about the left flank. I was told after the battle by Maj. Thompson (2nd Essex), the 12th Brigade Bombing Officer then, that he had personally taken my message to Brigade HQ. But I received no information or orders in reply, only the signal 'message received'. I should certainly have opened fire on Serre but for the fear that our troops were in it and that this shooting from the left flank was only from some isolated party of Germans left unnoticed in the advance. I stared and stared at Serre and the ground between it and me with my field glasses but could not find a trace of men at all and so could deduce nothing on which to act."[41]

Sleigh was himself then hit in the left shoulder by a bullet from the left and, as it was near to his heart, he was sent back with his condition marked 'serious' (though it proved not to be). His wound having been dressed at the ADS he continued his trip to the rear. On his way he found the mortally wounded Bertie Prowse lying in the back of an ambulance. The Brigadier had but one thought on his mind. 'Are we advancing?' he repeatedly asked and, in an attempt to reassure the dying General, all who were asked, including Sleigh, 'swore it was so, though we did not know'.[42]

Another officer of the 12th MGC had better fortune. Lt. Kenneth Robert Gordon Browne, 2nd Essex Regt., got his machine gun section into the Heidenkopf and his four Vickers guns were hastily dug in. Here they helped hold back the German attacks until, one by one, the guns were put of action and his men were killed or disabled. Browne, though, stayed in position until ordered to withdraw at 2 a.m. on 2nd July. His post-war comments about the day are self-deprecating in the extreme:

> "We were pretty well isolated all day and came back to our own lines at nightfall; but, at the time, I was too young and scared to understand what was going on anywhere but in my immediate neighbourhood."[43]

Lt. Browne was awarded the Military Cross for his conduct[i].

The machine guns of the 10th Brigade also experienced differing fortunes. Two guns went forward with the Seaforths towards Point 56. The guns arrived in spite of the officer in charge and both NCOs being wounded before the British

[i] The citation for Lt. Kenneth Edward Gordon Browne, MC, 2nd Essex Regt., att. 12th Machine Gun Company, in the *London Gazette* of 22nd September 1916 reads: "For conspicuous gallantry in action. He led his machine-gun section in the attack with great skill and total disregard of personal danger, entering the enemy's lines with the leading troops. He continued to do fine work throughout that day and the ensuing night, and finally cleared out several enemy dug-outs and sent back many prisoners".

front line was passed. Nevertheless, both guns came into action, at least for a time. One gun was eventually destroyed and the other returned during the night carried by the two remaining men of the team. On their right, the two guns due to go forward with the Dublin Fusiliers got no further than the British front line where they were employed giving barrage fire in the direction of the Ridge Redoubt and areas to the south.

Of the remaining twelve guns, four were to go forward behind the Seaforths, four behind the Dublins while the remaining four stayed in reserve in Tenderloin. One of the guns following the Dublins got across No Man's Land but was destroyed by shell fire. The other three teams set up their guns in the front line and joined their colleagues in providing barrage fire on the German lines.

Plate 90 Capt. George Newdegate Alison, 2nd Seaforth Highlanders att. 10th Machine Gun Company

All four guns following the Seaforths managed to get into the German trenches but not without cost. Capt. George Newdegate Alison, attached from the Seaforths, was with the guns out in No Man's Land where a section had laid down in extended order under heavy fire. Little appeared to phase Alison. On the outbreak of war Capt. Alison was in Hong Kong acting as ADC to the Governor, Sir Francis Henry May. The trip back to his battalion necessitated an arduous journey across Russia via St Petersburg and Archangel. Since then, he had been twice wounded but now he could be seen strolling nonchalantly around No Man's Land encouraging his men. According to a letter to his parents from Brig. Gen. Wilding, GOC, 10th Brigade, he approached Lt. Charles Buckworth, the officer commanding the section lying out in the grass:

> "Alison strolled over to them with one hand in his pocket – an attitude he was used to – and told them to move on. Buckworth commanded that section. 'Bucky, I think you had better get on', is what he said. He then re-joined his orderly, a man by the name of Gould. The next thing was Alison was shot, a rifle bullet through, I think, the heart, for he merely said to Gould, 'I am hit; go and tell Mr Low to take command', but before

Gould left him he was dead. Gould says he is quite sure his Captain could not have suffered, as he was perfectly quiet and cool, and died almost at once. Your son was one of the most remarkably plucky men I ever met. I was very fond of him and often asked his opinion and advice concerning the employment of his guns. I only wish I had him with me still. We recovered his body at night and buried him alongside about a hundred Seaforth Highlanders[i]. I am sure he would prefer to be near them."[44]

Two guns were later destroyed in the German lines and two brought back after dark. Lt. Charles Buckworth had command of two of these guns and these he brought up to a point just south of Point 92. Buckworth so positioned his guns that he was able to bring enfilade fire to bear on the German front line trenches to the north around Point 87 and his two Vickers guns were thought to have caused substantial casualties amongst the defenders before one of them was destroyed. When last seen Lt. Buckworth had been severely wounded. He failed to survive[ii].

Four officers of the 10th Machine Gun Company became casualties, of whom three died, all from the Seaforth Highlanders. Two of them were the sons of Knights of the Realm:

Lt. C R Buckworth
Capt. G N Alison
Lt. J M Low[iii]

AT 2.45 PM., 4TH DIVISION RECEIVED CONFIRMATION from the 29th Division that no further attacks would take place on their front during the day. With the 31st Division long since either back in their trenches or dead, wounded and trapped in No Man's Land this news confirmed the fact that the dwindling bunch of men around the Heidenkopf were very much on their own. A route had been found which allowed carriers to bring up some supplies to Lt. Col. Hopkinson

[i] Capt. George Newdegate Alison, 2nd Seaforth Highlanders att. 10th Brigade Machine Gun Company, was aged 26. He was the second son of the late Sir Archibald Alison, 3rd Bart., Colonial Secretary for Bermuda, and of Lady Georgina Alison (née Bond-Cabbell) of 'Possil House', Budleigh Salterton, Devon. Born in Bermuda, he was educated at Malvern College and RMC, Sandhurst. He played cricket for the Incogniti and the battalion. He was commissioned in December 1909 and was ADC to Sir Henry May, the Governor of Hong Kong from November 1913 to October 1914. He was seconded to the 10th MGC on 22nd December 1915. MiD in Sir John French's final despatch, 1st January 1916. Wounded twice in 1914 and 1915, he is buried in Sucrerie Military Cemetery, Colincamps, grave I. H. 36. His two brothers served in the Royal Navy.

[ii] Lt. Charles Raymond Buckworth, 2nd Seaforth Highlanders, was aged 19. He was the son of Mr and Mrs Buckworth of Ardgay, Ross-shire. He attended the RMC, Sandhurst, and was commissioned into the Seaforth Highlanders on 16th December 1914. He was seconded to the 10th MGC on 22nd December 1915. He is buried in Serre Road Cemetery No. 2, grave I. K. 22.

[iii] Lt. James Morrison Low, 2nd Seaforth Highlanders att. 10th Brigade Machine Gun Company, was aged 24. He was the elder son of the late Sir James Low Low, 1st Bart., and Katherine Mary Duff Munro, Lady Low, of Kilmaron Castle, Cupar, Fife. He was educated at Glenalmond College before going to Merton College, Oxford, in 1910. He was seconded to the 10th MGC on 22nd December 1915. His body was never found and his name is inscribed on the Thiepval Memorial, Pier & Face 15C.

and his men. The area of No Man's Land to the left of the redoubt was partially concealed from the machine guns in the Ridge Redoubt and, though exposed to fire from the north, still allowed some men to get across with much needed supplies of bombs and some machine gun belts.

Between 2 and 3 p.m. a message arrived with 2nd Lt. Glover from Lt. Col. Hopkinson in the German front line around Point 56. It was again brought by the intrepid but sadly unknown runner from the 8th Warwicks. Hopkinson promised to send Glover a supply of bombs but that he had to hold on until they arrived. The bomb throwers in his little bit of trench were now exhausted and it took some persuasion to get half a dozen men to carry on with the task while others were cajoled into being bomb carriers. Some of the wounded were willing to help but were not fit enough to be useful. Behind their trench there was a run of about 35 yards of straight trench and, as a fall-back position, Glover and the other officers, organised a barricade to be built at the far end and placed a Lewis gun on top of a traverse which covered the trench. Until it was needed they kept up the fight around their existing stretch of German line, wondering, no doubt, what was to come.

Progressively, the field guns had been reducing their range in order to keep a barrage just in front of the areas thought to be occupied by British troops. Unfortunately, these still included areas to the south of the Ridge Redoubt which were assiduously bombarded by the 14th Brigade, RFA. Hopkinson, however, wanted a barrage on his flanks as well as on his front but with men from the 12th Brigade still thought to be in the German front line to the north of the Heidenkopf as well as 11th Brigade men to the south of the Ridge Redoubt this proved to be a problem.

But for the men still fighting in the German lines affairs were about to take a turn for the worse. At 4 p.m., with the sun beating down on the bloody battlefield from a clear blue sky, Lt. Col. Findlater learnt that C Company, 1st Royal Irish Fusiliers, had been unable to cross No Man's Land in support of the Seaforths and so he ordered D Company, plus a carrying party loaded with 500 Mills grenades, to reinforce Hopkinson's men. This time, the Fusiliers moved further north, away from the Ridge Redoubt and towards the northern end of the Heidenkopf where previous experience had shown it was possible to get men and supplies across No Man's Land. Two platoons went over and the other two remained in the front line trench ready to move when required. The process was slow and great care had to be taken but it could be done. D Company's journey would take nearly an hour but, during their careful advance, the balance of power in the German trenches again shifted dramatically in the enemy's favour.

At about 4.30 p.m. Glover's first barricade was rushed by German bombers and his men retired behind the second one built some time before. For a while the German bombers contented themselves by lobbing stick grenades into the now empty stretch of trench between the two blocks. Fortunately, as it was to turn out, the men who had been crowded into the trench behind the new barricade had themselves retired crawling, so it appeared, into the fire trench further to the rear where the main bulk of Hopkinson's Seaforths now were concentrated. Glover had lookouts watching to each side and one observing the long straight stretch of trench back to their former position. Nothing untoward was happening. The odd German bomb exploded harmlessly in the empty trench. Glover was called away by an officer, possibly wounded, who was in a German dugout and they chatted for no more than three minutes.

> "As I came up the end came with a rush. How they managed it I don't know, possibly they had worked into a trench near our front line, but the Germans suddenly threw some bombs, some of which fell on the traverse by the L(ewis)G(un) and drove our men out of the trench. An attempt to make a stand at the next traverse was unsuccessful. In the new trench – the front line – the base of the Quadrilateral – there seemed to be no definite plan, except that they were manning it facing left. Some of the men there and some of ours out of the advanced trench, I mean not necessarily R(ifle)B(rigade)s, got out and back to our trenches. Some lay on the parapet facing the Germans who put some heavy shells into the middle of them, more went back."[45]

The bombing attacks came from the south and east and, from the British lines, it was clear that the men were in trouble. At 4.52 p.m. a surge of men retiring from the front line of the Heidenkopf was observed by the 29th Brigade, RFA, who sensibly put a barrage from 126th Battery on the trench across the base of the Quadrilateral.

In the Heidenkopf Glover was again trying to organise some sort of defence with a view to a more orderly retirement if required. It seemed that there were about 50 men in the front German trenches and Glover, along with Sgt. Charters, got them manning the ground outside the parapet, i.e. the side of the trench facing the British lines, ready to retreat if the time came. As this happened, a Staff Captain turned up with orders for Hopkinson and, as he and Glover went to find him, Glover realised for the first time just how many men were occupying the front line above Point 56. Hopkinson had accumulated some 200 troops from nearly all of the battalions involved in the attack. Here, Glover found Capt. Martin of the 1/8th Warwicks, his Rifle Brigade colleague, the unidentified 'Trevor', another called Billington[i], CSM Selway, Sgt. Hunt, a Rfn. Carty and one or two others he recognised from earlier in the day. There were also several officers from the 2nd Lancashire Fusiliers who had been in the Heidenkopf since mid-morning: Capt. William Du Pré Mansel[ii] and 2nd Lts. Herbert Ravenscroft, William Foster Hall, James William Watkins and Charles Leslie Rougier. Ravenscroft and Rougier[iii] were wounded. With them were 685 CSM James W

---

[i] Possibly 2nd Lt. Francis Billington.

[ii] Capt. William Du Pré Mansel, 2nd Lancashire Fusiliers, was killed on 12th October 1916. Aged 47, he was the son of the Rev. Owen Luttrell Mansel and Louisa Catherine Montagu. He was commissioned into the 4th King's Own Regt., before transferring to the 2nd Lancashire Fusiliers. He had previously been the Assistant Commissioner for Basutoland. His body was never found and his name is inscribed on the Thiepval Memorial, Pier & Face 3C and 3D. His younger brother, Lt. Cdr Charles Pleydell Mansel, RN, died 26th March 1915 and is remembered on the Portsmouth Naval Memorial.

[iii] 2nd Lt., later Lt. Col., Charles Leslie Rougier, MC, 2nd Lancashire Fusiliers, died on 22nd May 1940, aged 44. He was the son of Charles and Jean Rougier (née Crookston); husband of Marjorie Alice Rougier (née Tanner). He was killed commanding the 2nd Lancashire

Laverick[i] and 893 Sgt. George W Albon. These two had found an abandoned Stokes mortar and, though neither had seen one before let alone been trained to fire one, they worked the gun until all available ammunition was expended.

Hopkinson now ordered all of the wounded away and Glover and 'Trevor' both worked their way to a point where they could exit the Heidenkopf with a reasonable chance of getting back across No Man's Land. They had nearly made it when 'Trevor', lagging some way behind Glover was killed by a German shell within a few yards of the relative safety of the British trenches. Another to die on the return journey was 2nd Lt. Brian Farrow[ii], 2nd Lancashire Fusiliers, who had spent the day fighting in the German trenches.

Plate 91 2nd Lt. Francis Ramsay MacKenzie, 2nd Seaforth Highlanders

Orders were sent out at 5.15 p.m. from 10th Brigade HQ instructing Hopkinson to bring his men back as soon as possible and to hand over defence of the Heidenkopf to the Company of the 1st Royal Irish Fusiliers recently sent over. Hopkinson replied he would rather wait until night fell when he would try to get away as many of his wounded as possible. Hopkinson requested that his party be met by stretcher bearers in the front line. While they waited for darkness

---

Fusiliers which formed part of the rear guard of the BEF at Dunkirk. He is buried in Waarmaarde Churchyard, grave 4. His MC was gazetted in August 1918.

[i] 685 CSM James William Laverick, 2nd Lancashire Fusiliers, was awarded the DCM for his conduct on 1st July 1916. The citation in the *London Gazette* of 22nd September 1916 reads: "For conspicuous gallantry in action, he greatly assisted his officer in organising men of different units. He then found and brought into action a trench gun, which he fired as long as ammunition lasted. He behaved with the greatest coolness, and set a fine example".

[ii] 2nd Lt. Brian Farrow, 4th att. 2nd Lancashire Fusiliers, was aged 24. He was the son of Capt. Jacob Frederick Farrow, MC, (R.A.M.C.), and Clara S Farrow of 248, Upper Chorlton Rd., Manchester. Born at Cleckheaton, Yorks. Enlisted in the Public Schools Battalion, Royal Fusiliers, Sept., 1914. He was commissioned on 20th May 1915. He is buried in Serre Road Cemetery No. 1, grave I. C. 6. His father won the MC in 1916 and served as the MO with the 17th Manchester Regt.

to fall, some of the more seriously wounded were evacuated and some men from other units made good their escape. A search was made for one officer from C Company of the Seaforths, 2nd Lt. Frank Ramsay MacKenzie from Glasgow, who had been wounded in the initial advance. He had last been seen sheltering in a shell hole with his head bandaged but now he could not be found. The uncertainty as to his fate lasted for months until he was eventually declared dead in 1917. His body was never found[i].

To assist in the withdrawal, the Divisional field artillery was now mounting a barrage very close to the British held trenches. So close, in fact, that at 5.25 p.m. 12th Brigade asked for the range to be lengthened by 200 yards.

Although the area now occupied was just the front line trench and that across the base of the Heidenkopf, the supply of bombs was such that it proved possible to resist any further attacks. The pressure on the perimeter had also been eased by the fact that Lt. Hoppe's platoon from IR/169 had long since run out of stick grenades. His platoon, however, had claimed nearly forty prisoners of war as well as three abandoned machine guns. A certain degree of mutual exhaustion had set in and Lt. Col. Hopkinson took advantage. He organised double blocks on the trenches on either flank and, with a large supply of bombs which arrived around 5.30 p.m., bomb dumps were formed by each of the barricades. The war diary of the Seaforth Highlanders records:

> "… after this the enemy made no serious attack and was easily driven back when he attempted to bomb us."[46]

It was at about this time that one of the more curious reports of the entire day was forwarded to 4th Division HQ. It came from the Forward Observation Officer of the 170th Brigade, RFA, of the 31st Division and read:

> "170th Brigade FOO reports from bits of information that are coming into battalion headquarters[ii] that a junction has been affected in Serre between our troops and the 4th Division."[47]

Thankfully, this message, reported without comment in the 4th Division's documents, was then ignored by those in charge of the Division's field artillery who were now concentrating solely on placing barrages on the eastern side of the Heidenkopf and anywhere else 12th Brigade requested. VIII Corps, however, were rather more easily led astray and it was, perhaps, on the basis of this report that an order came through from VIII Corps Artillery for the guns to fire on Ten

---

[i] 2nd Lt. Francis Ramsay MacKenzie, 2nd Seaforth Highlanders, was aged 32. He was the son of the late Thomas Dingwall Mackenzie and Jessie Jeffrey Mackenzie (née Ramsay); husband of Elizabeth Mary Stark Mackenzie of 13, Princes Gardens, Glasgow; father of Frances Elma Mackenzie. He was educated at Hillhead High School. He was a pre-war member of the 1st Lanarkshire (Glasgow 1st Western) Rifle Volunteers and the 5th Scottish Rifles. A drapery warehouseman at Messrs J & W Campbell, Ingram Street, Glasgow, he joined the Glasgow University OTC in August 1915 and was commissioned into the 10th Seaforth Highlanders in November 1915. He went to France in March 1916 and was attached to the 2nd Seaforth Highlanders. His body was never found and his name is inscribed on the Thiepval Memorial, Pier & Face 15C.

[ii] The Forward Observation Officers or FOOs were attached to infantry battalions and went forward with them in an attack.

Tree Alley in order 'to prevent Germans reaching Serre'. The long standing, and hugely damaging, conviction that as many as two battalions of the 94th Brigade had occupied Serre clearly still lingered at VIII Corps HQ in spite of all the evidence lying about in No Man's Land and in the forward trenches of the 31st Division that the majority of the two attacking Brigades were either dead or wounded.

On the 4th Division's front, though, another concern was growing. In spite of the fact that it had never happened before, each Division of the VIII Corps, when it became clear that their attacks had catastrophically failed, began to believe that the Germans might leave their own trenches and mount a counter attack across No Man's Land. Lt. Col. Lloyd of the 14th Brigade, RFA, first raised the possibility at 5.50 p.m. when he noted German troops concentrating around Point 35, south of the Ridge Redoubt. He was ordered to use his own initiative as to whether to engage these men but his report was forwarded by the CRA to 4th Division for their consideration.

Whether this was a serious move on the part of the Germans is extremely unlikely but this movement may have been a response to the attempted withdrawal of some of the men of the East Lancashires and the Hampshires trapped since the early hours of the attack just outside the German wire in this sector. One of those who tried to escape was the Adjutant of the 1st East Lancashires, Capt. Heath, who had been lying out with his CO, Lt. Col. Green, close to the German wire for some ten hours. He was severely wounded at 6 p.m. as he tried to crawl back to the British lines. It would be another 2½ hours before he and Lt. Col. Green could get back and have their wounds dressed.

To the north of the Heidenkopf other men were finding a way back to their lines. It was a traumatic journey. 2nd Lt. John Turner of the 1/8th Royal Warwicks, who had done much to assist Capt. Martin in establishing a defensive perimeter earlier in the day, described 'that awful journey' passing the dead and the dying, some lying still others still painfully crawling to where they knew not. L/Cpl. Williamson of the same battalion saw 'hundreds of dead soldiers everywhere' as he approached the British trenches, the dead of six battalions who had crossed this dreadful ground.

At 6.20 p.m. the Staff Captain of the 10th Brigade, the officer who had met up with 2nd Lt. Glover in the Heidenkopf, returned to HQ with a relatively reassuring report. Hopkinson was in command of approximately 100 men from all three Brigades. They were holding out well and now had plenty of grenades. Hopkinson was of the view that there were no other 4th Division troops nearby. It was his plan to withdraw his men and anything, or anyone, he could bring with him, after dark.

As evening set in both sides seemed to relax somewhat. Bombing attacks on the Heidenkopf were desultory affairs as if everyone was exhausted and waiting for night to fall. The Divisional artillery was barraging the furthest edges of the Quadrilateral of trenches and now, at last, the German front line further south. Inside the British lines defences were reorganised and men redeployed. The 1st Warwicks took over the front line from the boundary with the 29th Division at the northern end of the Sunken Road to Maxim Trench, which lay just behind the Redan. The Irish Fusiliers occupied the front to the north as far as the dividing line between the 10th and 12th Brigades. The Dublin Fusiliers were in Young Street behind Tenderloin and the remains of the Seaforths were in the Sucrerie to Auchonvillers Sunken Road.

At about 7 p.m. Hopkinson's exhausted garrison was reinforced by two platoons of the Irish Fusiliers who brought with them a good supply of bombs. They were directed to the right hand trench blocks which they took over. By that time the evacuation of the remaining men of the 11th Brigade, i.e. those of the Rifle Brigade and Somersets, was complete. There were still rumours that, somehow, men of the Rifle Brigade were in the German lines north and south of the Ridge Redoubt but this was more of the wishful thinking that so beset the thoughts of officers from VIII Corps during this day.

The full impact of the fighting on the battalions involved was beginning to become apparent. The Brigade Major of the 11th Brigade reported that the Rifle Brigade, the remains of which were now congregating in Elles Square, comprised a total of 120 men excluding carrying parties. Fifty stragglers from the Hampshires and East Lancashires had been rounded up in Tenderloin, otherwise nothing had been heard of the East Lancashires since they had gone over the top at 7.30 a.m. Eighty or so men of the Somersets and the two Warwickshire Territorial battalions were in the support trenches. 250 men from the more than 3,000 who had advanced with such high hopes twelve hours before. In spite of the carnage, the reports of British troops trapped in Serre still dominated VIII Corps thinking.

The companies of the 1st Royal Irish Fusiliers were spread across the lines between the Redan and the Serre to Mailly Road. Two platoons of D Company had already gone over to the Heidenkopf where they held the right flank defences. Another two platoons waited to advance in the trenches on the other side of No Man's Land. Capt. George Barefoot, OC D Company, was instructed that he had to hold onto the Heidenkopf at all costs. The Germans had abandoned the Heidenkopf early in the day as they believed it to be nearly impossible to defend. In the medium to long term the same applied to the British. It would not be possible to integrate it into the British trench system, it was overlooked and horribly vulnerable. So what reason could there be for the 'at all costs' instruction? The explanation was rooted in VIII Corps' unshakeable belief that Serre was occupied by British troops. The Heidenkopf needed to be held 'at all costs' so that what was left of the 12th Brigade could attack to the north and link up with these fictitious troops in the village.

The first 'at all costs' message had arrived at 9 p.m. and was directed to Lt. Col. Hopkinson. Perversely, the runner who brought this message, untimed but with the number H18, also brought a second message, also untimed, J22. H18 ordered him to hold at all costs. J22 ordered him to return to the British lines. With the arrival of the first two platoons of the Irish Fusiliers, Hopkinson determined that logic suggested message J22 was the later of the two orders. But, as the order also said two more platoons of the Fusiliers were to arrive, he decided to await their arrival before moving off. They would wait for another four hours.

Any sense of confusion was relieved by the arrival of the Irish Fusiliers' Adjutant, Capt. William Carden-Roe. He confirmed that Hopkinson was to withdraw his men and that it was Capt. Barefoot's responsibility to hold 'at all costs'. While Hopkinson, who had, by now, been wounded in the face and shoulder, set to organising the evacuation of his men, Capt. Barefoot assumed command and waited for the anticipated arrival of the rest of D Company later in the evening.

AS THE LIGHT BEGAN TO FADE ACROSS THE BATTLEFIELD, those able to move started to crawl carefully back towards the British lines. Lt. Col. Green and his Adjutant, Capt. Heath, struggled back into the front trench at about 8.20 pm. News of their wounding reached 4th Division HQ 85 minutes later. Heath, in attempting to crawl back to the British lines had lost all sense of direction. He was found by the last two officers of the East Lancashires to leave No Man's Land alive, 2nd Lts. Page and Daly, who had been lying out under the German wire since 7.30 a.m. Page and Daly had sent back from around them those men that could move and they had then slowly crept back towards what they believed were the British lines. As they retired a familiar voice called out. It was that of their Adjutant, Capt. Sidney Heath. He had been severely wounded in the arm and leg and they found him on the Rifle Brigade's front opposite the Ridge Redoubt. Page went off to find help and a volunteer Private from the Royal Irish Fusiliers went with him to retrieve the wounded officer. Daly, enervated by the day's activities, collapsed on his return to the British lines.

Before this, the news of the death of Brig. Gen. Prowse was confirmed by the 1/2nd South Midland Field Ambulance and his burial at Vauchelles was authorised. Meanwhile, the field guns continued to fire to the east of the Heidenkopf and were later joined by the Corps heavy artillery at 9.54 p.m.

The two platoons of D Company, 1st Royal Irish Fusiliers, eventually set off to occupy the Heidenkopf after 10 a.m. With the gathering gloom came also a German barrage on No Man's Land and it was 1 a.m. before they arrived to relieve Hopkinson's men. The relief took an hour to complete during which time the Germans were gratifyingly inactive. All the wounded who could be found were evacuated as well as any equipment, etc., not needed by Barefoot's command. Hopkinson's exhausted men quietly withdrew across No Man's Land and then marched across to the Sunken Road between Auchonvillers and the Sucrerie where they joined the 10% reserve who had arrived from Bertrancourt at 10 p.m. With Hopkinson[i] all day had been his Adjutant, Capt. John Laurie[ii], Capt.

[i] Lt. Col. John Oliver Hopkinson, 2nd Seaforth Highlanders, was awarded a DSO for his actions on 1st July. The citation in the *London Gazette* of 22nd September 1916 reads: "For conspicuous gallantry in action. He led his battalion against the enemy trenches, captured them, and held his ground for 13 hours under heavy fire, repulsing constant attacks. He continued to command after being wounded".

[ii] Capt., later Maj. Gen., John Emilius Laurie, 2nd Seaforth Highlanders, was awarded a DSO for his actions on 1st July. The citation in the *London Gazette* of 22nd September 1916 reads: "For conspicuous gallantry in action. At a critical time he rallied men of various units who were without leaders, did fine work consolidating the position and helped to repel a bomb attack". Born in 1892, was the son of Sir Wilfrid Emilius Laurie, 5th Bt. and Marian Isabel Stirling of Maxwelton. He was educated at Eton and Sandhurst. He went on to become Maj. Gen. Sir John Emilius Laurie, Bt., CBE, DSO & Bar, Colonel of the Seaforth Highlanders, commanding the 157th Brigade, 52nd (Lowland) Division, in the

William Gordon[i], OC B Company, and 7095 CSM William George Fenoulhet[ii] and 8859 CSM William Aitken[iii] of B and D Companies respectively and 3/7171 Sgt. K MacLeod[iv] of A Company, who had been left very early in the day as the senior NCO in his company when all the officers and senior NCOs had been killed. McLeod was later was awarded the DCM.

It was during the early part of this laborious process that 10th Brigade learnt that, at last, VIII Corps appeared to have accepted that there were no British troops in Serre. Well, not live ones anyway. There would be no need for the 12th Brigade to attack and, equally, no need to hold onto the Heidenkopf either. Two runners were given messages to this effect at 11.35 p.m. and, receiving no response, runners were again sent at 12.35 a.m. on the 2nd July. None of these messages arrived and it was not until 8.45 a.m. that a message got through. Barefoot coolly evacuated his men in broad daylight at 11.35 a.m. on the 2nd, bringing all of his wounded, three German prisoners and a quantity of equipment which included: two Lewis guns belonging to D Company and one belonging to another unit, one machine gun and two Stokes mortars abandoned in No Man's Land just in front of the British front line. In the process his men suffered just one casualty. Barefoot received the Military Cross in recognition of his excellent work[v]. Another officer to perform work of note was 2nd Lt. Ralph Le Mare. The

B.E.F. in 1940 and commanding the Division between 1940 and 1942. He commanded the Combined Operations Training Centre in Inverary 1943–45. He died in 1983.

[i] Capt. William Longman Gordon, 2nd Seaforth Highlanders, was awarded the MC for his conduct on 1st July 1916. The citation, in the *London Gazette* of 22nd September 1916 reads: "For conspicuous gallantry in action. He led his company with great dash and took an active part in repelling bombing attacks throughout the day".

[ii] 7095 CSM William George Fenoulhet, 2nd Seaforth Highlanders, was awarded the MC for his conduct on 1st July 1916. The citation, in the *London Gazette* of 22nd September 1916 reads: "For conspicuous gallantry in action. He did fine work at a critical time, rallying men of a number of units who were held up by machine-gun fire combined with bombing attacks. His splendid example gave great confidence to the men".

[iii] 8859 CSM William Aitken, 2nd Seaforth Highlanders, was awarded the MC for his conduct on 1st July 1916. The citation, in the *London Gazette* of 22nd September 1916 reads: "For conspicuous gallantry in action. When all his officers had become casualties he took command of the company, organised bombing parties, and did fine work reorganising the defences".

[iv] 3/7171 Sgt. K MacLeod, 2nd Seaforth Highlanders, was awarded the DCM for his conduct on 1st July 1916. The citation in the *London Gazette* of 22nd September 1916 reads: "For conspicuous gallantry in action. When his platoon officer was killed early in the advance he led the platoon with great dash under very heavy fire. He got as far as anyone in the battalion, and, though he had only five men left, he set to work to consolidate the captured trench. He then led a bombing attack with great vigour as long as his bombs lasted".

[v] Lt. (temp Capt.) George William Norman Barefoot, 1st Royal Irish Fusiliers, was awarded the MC for his actions on 1st July 1916. The citation in the *London Gazette* of 22nd September 1916 reads: "For conspicuous gallantry in action. He held on to the position gained until ordered to withdraw eighteen hours later, having successfully repulsed three enemy attacks. When he withdrew he brought back a trench gun, a machine-gun, three prisoners and all his wounded".

23 year old, who had been commissioned out of the Artists' Rifles in March 1915, spent his time in the Heidenkopf doing little else than throw bombs at the enemy. The regimental history credits him with having thrown 'some hundreds' which, if even half true, was a remarkable performance.

As Barefoot and his men withdrew the Germans advanced slowly through the wreckage of the Heidenkopf, freeing their own men who had either been temporary Prisoners of War or who had been hiding in the deep dugouts.

With that, and except for the recovery and treatment of the wounded and the burial of the dead, the 4th Division's attack on Redan Ridge was at an end. They had suffered crippling casualties, occupied a small and insignificant section of German trench for 28 hours and otherwise achieved nothing.

THE CASUALTIES WERE APPALLING, most especially within the 11th Brigade and its two attached battalions. Each one of the six battalions had more than 475 casualties with the highest number being from a battalion which lost the vast majority of its men behind the British lines or in No Man's Land – the 1st Hampshires.

According to the 4th Division's war diary the numbers were:

	Officers					
10th Brigade	Killed	Wounded	Missing	Wounded & Missing	Missing believed killed	Total
1st R Warwicks	0	2	0	0	0	2
2nd Seaforths	12	10	0	2	0	24
1st R Irish Fus.	0	5	0	0	0	5
2nd Dublin Fus.	2	12	0	0	0	14
10th MGC	1	1	1	0	1	4
10th TMB	0	0	0	0	0	0
Officer total	15	30	1	2	1	49
	Other Ranks					
1st R Warwicks	15	57	0	0	3	75
2nd Seaforths	56	218	100	0	0	374
1st R Irish Fus.	14	111	11	0	0	136
2nd Dublin Fus.	52	222	40	0	0	314
10th MGC	2	15	7	0	0	24
10th TMB	0	2	0	0	0	2
Other Ranks total	139	625	158	0	3	925
10th Brigade totals	154	655	159	2	4	974

Capt., later Lt. Col., George William Norman Barefoot, CB, CMG, MC, 1st Royal Irish Fusiliers, was the only son of Col. George H Barefoot, CB, CMG, RAMC. He was educated aat Epsom College and the RMC, Sandhurst, joining the Fusiliers in September, 1913. He was appointed Staff Captain in February, 1918. He married Dorothy Elizabeth Winter, second daughter of Col. G F Winter, Military Secretary in Ottawa, in 1917. He was an Instructor at the Small Arms School of the Indian Army between 1930-33. He retired from the Army in 1936.

11th Brigade	Officers					
1st Somerset LI	4	9	5	1	7	26
1st East Lancs	3	6	1	4	3	17
1st Hants	10	16	0	0	0	26
1st Rifle Bde	7	7	1	2	3	20
1/6th R Warwicks	5	11	3	3	0	22
1/8th R Warwicks	6	16	0	3	0	25
11th MGC	1	2	0	0	1	4
11th TMB	1	4	0	0	0	5
Officers total	37	71	10	13	14	145
	Other Ranks					
1st Somerset LI	47	171	232	0	0	450
1st East Lancs	65	251	169	0	0	485
1st Hants	113	249	197	0	0	559
1st Rifle Bde	52	239	165	0	0	454
1/6th R Warwicks	43	173	234	0	0	450
1/8th R Warwicks	52	238	275	0	0	563
11th MGC	3	54	6	0	0	65
11th TMB	5	17	12	0	0	34
Other Ranks total	380	1392	1290	0	0	3060
11th Brigade totals	417	1463	1300	13	14	3207
12th Brigade	Officers					
1st King's Own	6	13	3	0	0	22
2nd Lancs Fus.	5	12	1	1	0	19
2nd Essex	5	13	1	3	0	22
2nd West Riding	3	17	0	0	0	20
12th MGC	1	3	0	0	0	4
12th TMB	0	2	0	0	0	2
Officers total	20	60	5	4	0	89
	Other Ranks					
1st King's Own	37	209	177	0	0	423
2nd Lancs Fus.	21	241	101	0	0	363
2nd Essex	43	167	205	0	0	415
2nd West Riding	21	292	61	0	0	374
12th MGC	9	47	6	0	0	61
12th TMB	3	21	26	0	0	50
Other Ranks total	134	977	576	0	0	1687
12th Brigade total	154	1037	581	4	0	1776
	Other Ranks					
1/1st Durham Fd Coy RE	1	12	8	0	0	21
4th Signal Coy	1	9	4	0	0	14
Other Ranks totals	2	21	12	0	0	35
4th Division totals	610	2592	1903	30	28	5163

Table 16 4th Division Casualties[48]

11th Brigade
From right to left the losses in the first wave were:
1st East Lancashire Regt.
Strength, 22 officers and approximately 700 other ranks.
Casualties:
Officers
Killed:
2nd Lt. K C Jones
Lt. R Newcombe
Capt. A H Penny
2nd Lt. R S Prescott[i]
2nd Lt. C E Sadler
Capt. H W M Thomas
2nd Lt. C E S Watson
Capt. C P Watson
Missing:
Capt. M G Browne (afterwards reported prisoner of war)
Lt. T E C Fisher
2nd Lt. E S Mallett (afterwards reported killed in action)
Died of wounds:
2nd Lt. H A Tompkins
Wounded:
Lt. Col. James Edward Green
T/Capt. Frederick Edmund Hatfield
Capt. Sidney John Heath
2nd Lt. C E Henderson
2nd Lt. Charles Morgan Jenkins
2nd Lt. Myles Sayers
Capt. John Richard Menzies Whigham, RAMC
The immediate estimate of casualties amongst the other ranks was:
Killed 65
Wounded 251
Missing 169
Total 485

192 men of the 1st East Lancashire Regt., are recorded as having been killed or died as a result of wounds received on 1st July 1916 (20 men and 2nd Lt. St John attached to the 11th MGC dying from wounds from the 2nd July onwards). Three of these casualties died in German hands. Their casualties amounted to 70% of those who went over the top and the overwhelming majority of these men were killed or wounded in No Man's Land.

1st Rifle Brigade
Casualties:
Officers
Killed
Capt. & Adjutant G T Cartland
Lt. (Temp Capt.) R Fraser
Lt. (Temp Capt.) A W Henderson[ii]
2nd Lt. J P Morum

[i] 2nd Lt. Robert Stewart Prescott, 10th att. 1st East Lancashire Regt., was commissioned on 10th April 1915. He is buried in Beaumont-Hamel British Cemetery, grave A. 78.

[ii] Capt. Andrew William Henderson, 1st Rifle Brigade, was aged 22. He was the elder son of the late William Henderson of 4, Windsor Terrace, Glasgow. Educated at Kelvinside

Plate 92 2nd Lt. Evan Edward Trevor-Jones, 6th att. 1st Rifle Brigade

Plate 93 Capt. Andrew William Henderson, 1st Rifle Brigade

2nd Lt. E E Trevor-Jones
Lt. Col. D Wood
Died of wounds
2nd Lt. N Fagan, Bombing Officer, 20th July 1916
2nd Lt. (Temp Capt.) H F Russell-Smith[i], 5th July 1916
Missing believed killed
2nd Lt. C A Clark[ii]
2nd Lt. A G Clarke[iii]
Temp Lt. G C L Dewhurst[i]
Lt. M G White

Academy, Winchester and Balliol College, Oxford, (entered 1913), he was commissioned into the 1st Rifle Brigade on 26th August 1914. His body was never found and his name is inscribed on the Thiepval Memorial, Pier & Face 16B and 16C. His younger brother, Capt. & Adjt. Thomas Harvey Henderson, MC, 6th att. 10th Rifle Brigade, died on 30th November 1917 and is remembered on the Cambrai Memorial.

[i] Capt. Hugh Francis Russell-Smith, 6th att. 1st Rifle Brigade, was aged 28. He was the son of Henry and Ellen Russell-Smith of London. Graduate and Fellow of St. John's College, Cambridge (Fellow 1912), he was a lecturer in History. He was commissioned in the Cambridge University Contingent OTC on 21st February 1915 and the 6th Rifle Brigade on 22nd May 1915. He is buried in St. Sever Cemetery, Rouen, grave Officers, A. 3. 10.

[ii] 2nd Lt. Charles Augustus Clark, 5th att. 1st Rifle Brigade, was aged 30. He was the son of Arthur Clark of Matlock Bath, Derbyshire, and the late Mary Francis Clark. He was commissioned on 7th May 1915. His body was never found and his name is inscribed on the Thiepval Memorial, Pier & Face 16B & 16C.

[iii] 2nd Lt. Arundell Geoffrey Clarke, 5th att. 1st Rifle Brigade, was aged 33. He was the younger son of the late Rev. Arthur Edward Clarke, headmaster of Oxford Preparatory School. Born at Oxford, he was educated at Oxford Preparatory School and Winchester College. He graduated from New College, Oxford, in 1902. He lived at Tolvadden, East Cowes, Isle of Wight and was an assistant master at the Royal Naval College, Osborne, IoW. He helped organise Boys' Clubs in Bethnal Green. He joined the Royal Fusiliers on December 1914 and was commissioned on 9th May 1915 into the Rifle Brigade. He was seconded to the Intelligence Corps on 9th December 1915 and later re-joined his battalion. He is buried in A.I.F. Burial Ground, Flers, grave XIII. A. 13.

Wounded and missing
Lt. (Temp Capt.) W H Beever
Missing
2nd Lt. F W Kirkland 2nd Lt. F C S Volkers
Wounded
2nd Lt. M F Buller
2nd Lt. Lewis Edmund Cording
2nd Lt. George Wright Glover
2nd Lt. Hugh le Geyt Kensington
2nd Lt. R A Pattisson
The estimate of casualties amongst other ranks was:
Killed 52
Wounded 239
Missing 165
Total 454

Plate 94 Capt. Murray Hulme Paterson, RAMC

The only officers to get through the day unscathed were 2nd Lt. Alfred Geoffrey Lole of B Company who survived the war and Lt. Thomas Alfred Greville Rouse-Boughton-Knight[ii] of C Company and the Canadian MO, Capt. Murray Hulme Paterson, RAMC, who did not. Capt. Paterson was awarded an MC for his conduct on 1st July 1916 during which he repeatedly brought wounded men in from No Man's Land under heavy fire. One man he was carrying was killed as he brought him in and another was wounded for a second time[iii].

---

[i] Capt. George Charnley Littleton Dewhurst, 6th att. 1st Rifle Brigade, was aged 24. He was the only son of Mrs Annie Maude Jones (formerly Dewhurst, née Davidson) of Aberuchill Castle, Comrie, Perthshire, and the late George Littleton Dewhurst, JP, DL, of Beechwood, Cheshire. He was educated at Eton College and graduated from Trinity College, Cambridge in 1910. He was commissioned on 15th August 1914. He joined the battalion on 16th October 1915. He is buried in Serre Road Cemetery No. 2, grave I. G. 38.

[ii] Lt. Thomas Andrew Greville Rouse-Boughton-Knight, 1st Rifle Brigade, died on 18th October 1916. Aged 19, he was the only son and third child of Andrew Greville Rouse-Boughton-Knight JP and Isabel Harriet Heber-Percy of Wormesley Grange, Downton, Herefordshire. He was buried in the Peronne Road Cemetery, Maricourt.

[iii] Capt. Murray Hulme Paterson, MC, Canadian Army Medical Corps, died on 15th September 1917. Aged 26, he was the son of D. S. and Mattie Paterson, of 108, Stanley Avenue, Chatham, Ontario. He was educated at Chatham Public School and the Toronto

180 men of the 1st Rifle Brigade are recorded as having been killed or died as a result of wounds received on 1st July 1916 (2 officers and 15 men dying from wounds from the 2nd July onwards). One man died in German hands. Precise details about the number of men taking into battle by the 1st Rifle Brigade do not exist but their rifle strength was very similar to that of the 1st East Lancashires and, therefore, it is a reasonable assumption that their casualty rate was approximately 62%. Before the end of the day, with the CO and Adjutant dead, two company commanders dead, one missing and the other fatally wounded, command of the battalion devolved to a subaltern, 2nd Lt. Edward Temple Leigh Gurdon, one of the 10% reserve. He recalled after the war that, though the front line was inhabited by men of four or five battalions there were only two 2nd Lts. from two different battalions, one of them himself, left to take command such had been the carnage amongst the officers of all units. Gurdon was awarded the MC for his role in reorganising the remaining men of his and other battalions[i].

One of the officers to die and whose body was never found was Lt. Malcolm Graham White of A Company[ii]. White was a hugely talented musician having

Medical School and was on the staff of St Michael's and the Sick Children's Hospital, Toronto. He joined the RAMC in May 1915 and went to France in July, joining the 1st Rifle Brigade. He transferred to the CAMC in the summer of 1917. He was killed accidentally when he was hit by a train near Orpington, Kent. He is buried in Brookwood Military Cemetery.
The citation in the London Gazette of 22nd September 1916 reads: "For conspicuous gallantry and devotion to duty during operations. He went out twice by daylight into No Man's Land and brought in wounded men. When his battalion was relieved he remained in his Aid Post till it was cleared of wounded. He did fine work"

[i] 2nd Lt., later Maj. Gen., Edward Temple Leigh Gurdon, CB, CBE, MC, 1st Rifle Brigade, was born in 1896 and was the only son of the late Right Rev. Francis Gurdon, DD, Bishop of Hull and Florence Hoskyns. He was educated at Summerfields, Oxford, Rugby School and the RMC, Sandhurst. He was commissioned into the Rifle Brigade in May 1915. King's African Rifles, 1917-20. AdC to Gov. of Uganda, 1919-20. Transferred to the Black Watch, 1922. AdC District Commander, India, 1927. He passed out of the Quetta Staff College in 1931. GSO3, War Office, 1932-4. Brig. Maj., Northern Command, 1934-5. GSO2, Palestine & Transjordan, 1936. Instructor Quetta,1937-40. CO, 1st Black Watch, 1940, AA+QMG, 51st Division. GOC, 25th Brigade, 1941. BGGS, IV Corps, 1941. BGGS, Eastern Army, India, 1942. Director of Military Training, Army Headquarters India, 1943-5. MGGS, Home Forces, 1945. Divisional command, BAOR, 1945-6. District Officer Commanding, Salisbury Plain District, 1947-8. Retired 1948. He married Elizabeth Madeleine Wilson in 1923, two sons, two daughters. He died in 1959.
The citation in the London Gazette of 22nd September 1916 reads: "For conspicuous gallantry in action. When all his senior officers became casualties he took command of the battalion, and showed great ability, coolness and courage throughout the day".

[ii] Lt. Malcolm Graham White, 6th att. 1st Rifle Brigade, was aged 29. He was the son of the late John Arnold White of Mere Cottage, Birkenhead. He was educated at Birkenhead School where he played in the football and cricket 1st XIs. He was also a talented musician. Went to King's College, Cambridge, in 1905 becoming the Master of the King's Choir School. He was an assistant master at Marlborough College and Shrewsbury School where he was Captain of the O.T.C. He was commissioned in May 1915, and joined the battalion on 8th February 1916. His body was never found and his name is inscribed on the Thiepval Memorial, Pier & Face 16B & 16C. He was a great friend and colleague of Capt. Evelyn Herbert Lightfoot Southwell, 13th Rifle Brigade, (KiA 15th September 1916, Thiepval

been the master of the King's College Choir School at Cambridge. He went on to become a master at Shrewsbury School and was active in the OTC. His great friend and fellow Shrewsbury master was Capt. Evelyn Southwell of the 13th Rifle Brigade, and their letters to one another and family and friends were published in 1919. White's last letter home is dated 29th June 1916. It speaks to the special qualities of the men, officers and other ranks who formed this great volunteer army.

> "I dare say this will not reach you, but I have asked a friend to send it for me when censorship does not apply any longer. We are taking part in a big attack, and I go up to the trenches this afternoon and shall not be able to write again between now and the beginning of it. All hope that this attack will bring us a little nearer the end of the War. There is little doubt that it will be a difficult business, but we hope for success after the bombardment that is going on. Our business is to take the front system of German trenches in the area we are in.
> And now, I just want to say to you all, that, if I don't come through it, you must all be quite cheerful about it. I am quite happy about it, though of course I can't deny that I am very keen to come home again. I look at all this from a very personal point of view, almost a selfish point of view. It seems to me that, if I die in this action, it gives me a great simple chance of making up for a lot of selfishness in the past. And when I want to reconcile myself to the idea of not coming back again, I just think of all those selfish mistakes I've made, and I am almost glad of the opportunity to put them right. That's my view of it. It is not priggish – I hope it doesn't sound like that.
> It is also a great comfort to think of you all going on, living the same happy lives that we have led together, and of the new generation coming into it all.
> I can't write more. My dearest love to you all.
> I am very fit."

A fellow officer later wrote about White:

> "I have never known such a real Christian. That was a fine letter of his which was shown me. Fancy Malcolm talking about being selfish. I doubt if he knew what selfishness meant. If he did, it was only the more fully to understand unselfishness. It was that and his utter sincerity and genuineness which made him what he was. His ideal was always so high, and he was never falling short of it. His ideas were just wonderful, and in the six years that I have known him I have learnt more of what real religion means than anyhow else."

Both men forever lost, the names of Lt. Malcolm Graham White and his dear friend and colleague Capt. Evelyn Herbert Lightfoot Southwell can now be found on the Memorial to the Missing of the Somme at Thiepval.

Memorial) who was also a master at Shrewsbury and an account of their time at the school and their letters from the front are contained in *'Two Men: A Memoir'* by H E E Howson published by OUP in 1919.

Plate 95 Lt. Malcolm Graham White, 6th att. 1st Rifle Brigade

Plate 96 Maj. Alfred Armstrong Caddick, 1/8th Royal Warwickshire Regt.

143rd Brigade (attached 11th Brigade)
1/8th Royal Warwickshire Regt.
Officer casualties:
Killed:

Lt. R Adams, MC, C Company[i]
Lt. J G Fussell, A Company[iii]
Lt. Col. E A Innes, CMG, commanding
Capt. S W Ludlow, C Company
2nd Lt. E R Shuttleworth, B Company[i]
Maj. A A Caddick, D Company[ii]
Lt. C Hoskins, B Company[iv]
2nd Lt. F B Key, D Company
Lt. & Adjutant A Procter, MC

---

[i] Lt. Ralph Adams, MC & Bar, 1/8th Royal Warwickshire Regt., was aged 23. He was the son of John and Minnie Adams of 301, Gillatt Rd., Birmingham. He was awarded his first MC in the New Year's Honours List of 14th January 1916 and his second for gallantry during a trench raid which was gazetted on 22nd September 1916. He is buried in Serre Road Cemetery No. 2, grave I. A. 33.

[ii] Maj. Alfred Armstrong Caddick, OC D Company, 1/8th Royal Warwickshire Regt., was aged 44. He was the son of Alfred and Anne Jessie Caddick of The Firs, Ockford Rd., Godalming, Surrey. His father was a solicitor and, for some time, Deputy Town Clerk and Deputy Clerk of the Peace at West Bromwich. Member of Caddick & Walker, solicitors, of West Bromwich and Birmingham. Once MiD. His body was never found and his name is inscribed on the Thiepval Memorial, Pier & Face 9A, 9B & 10B.

[iii] Lt. James Gerald Fussell, 1/8th Royal Warwickshire Regt., was aged 23. He was the son of Ada Fussell of The Hincks, Lilleshall, Wellington, Salop, and the late H S C Fussell. He was commissioned on 24th September 1914. His body was never found and his name is inscribed on the Thiepval Memorial, Pier & Face 9A, 9B & 10B.

[iv] Lt. Cyril Hoskins, 1/8th Royal Warwickshire Regt., was aged 25. He was the son of Mrs J E Hoskins of The Limes, Yardley, Birmingham, and the late J E Hoskins, J.P. Mobilized in Aug., 1914. Twice previously wounded. His body was never found and his name is inscribed on the Thiepval Memorial, Pier & Face 9A, 9B & 10B.

Lt. F W Wareham, D Company[ii]
Wounded and missing:
2nd Lt. F B Freeman, C Company[iii]
Wounded and Prisoner of War
2nd Lt. F A Brettell[iv], C Company
Wounded:
Lt. Douglas Raymond Adams, C Company
2nd Lt. Sidney Henry Anstey, B Company
Lt. Leslie Whorwood Auster, A Company
Capt. Stephen Howard Neale Coxon, D Company
2nd Lt. Reginald Harry Fish, A Company
2nd Lt. Leonard Griffiths, B Company
2nd Lt. Frederick H Heath, C Company
Lt. H M Jones, Signalling Officer
Capt. Cecil Watson Martin, A Company
Lt. Fred Newton Walsh, RAMC
2nd Lt. Sydney Whitelock Pepper[v], B Company

---

[i] 2nd Lt. Ernest Ronald Shuttleworth, 1/8th Royal Warwickshire Regt., was aged 22. He was the son of Thomas Ernest and Mary Edith Shuttleworth (née Travis) of 5, Park Avenue, Riverdale Rd., Sheffield. Educated at the Quenford House School, Jersey, he was a Chartered Accountants' Articled Clerk. He enlisted as an Ordinary Seaman in the Public Schools' Battalion, Royal Naval Division and was commissioned on 10th April 1915. His body was never found and his name is inscribed on the Thiepval Memorial, Pier & Face 9A, 9B & 10B.

[ii] Lt. Frederick William Wareham, 1/8th Royal Warwickshire Regt., was aged 25. He was the son of Frederick and Harriett Wareham of 'Lydgate', Carlton Rd., Malvern Link, Malvern, Worcs. He was educated at Malvern Link CE School and Worcester Royal Grammar School. He was a troop leader in the Malvern Link 1st Scout Troop. He trained as a teacher at Saltley Training College and was employed by the Education Department of the London County Council as a teacher at St Matthew's Boys School, Westminster. He enlisted in the 1/12th London Regt. (The Rangers) going to France in December 1914. Wounded, he was commissioned in June 1915 and promoted Lieutenant in November 1915. His body was never found and his name is inscribed on the Thiepval Memorial, Pier & Face 9A, 9B & 10B.

[iii] 2nd Lt. Francis Basil Freeman, 1/8th Royal Warwickshire Regt., was aged 26. He was the younger son of Albert Francis and Ellen Louise Freeman of 77, King's Rd., Bengeworth, Evesham, Worcs. Born at Hednesford, Staffs. Educated at Berkeley School, Evesham Grammar School and Saltley College. He worked in the Education Department of the London County Council. He joined the 2nd Volunteer Battalion, Worcestershire Regt., in 1907, joining the 8th Worcestershire Regt., on the formation of the Territorial Force in 1908. He transferred to the 8th Warwickshire Regt in 1910, being commissioned from Sergeant on 2nd April 1916. He was reported as having been shot in the stomach between the German 2nd and 3rd lines. He is buried in Cerisy-Gailly French National Cemetery, grave II. G. 16.

[iv] 2nd Lt. Frank Austin Brettell, 1/8th Royal Warwickshire Regt., was commissioned into the 1/8th Warwicks on 3rd April 1915 from the Fort Garry Horse, Canadian Expeditionary Force, with which he had been a Trooper. He was wounded on 1st July and had been placed in a German dugout where he was found and taken prisoner.

[v] 2nd Lt., later Capt., Sydney Whitelock Pepper, 1/8th Royal Warwickshire Regt., was killed on 27th August 1917. Aged 25, he was the son of Edwin and Emma E Pepper, of 4,

2nd Lt. John Teague, D Company
Maj. James Newman Townsend, DSO, 2iC
2nd Lt. John Turner, B Company
The casualties amongst the other ranks were:
Killed 57
Wounded 255
Missing 251
Total 563

Every officer who went into the attack was either killed or wounded. Four company officers were kept out of the fighting but not all would survive the war. 2nd Lt. Reginald Robin John Laing survived apparently unscathed, 2nd Lt. R A Block resigned his commission as a result of his wounds, 2nd Lt. Robert Charles Denison[i] was killed on the Somme in August 1916 and 2nd Lt. Joseph Arthur Richards[ii] died seven days before the war ended.

235 men of the 1/8th Royal Warwickshire Regt. are recorded as having been killed on 1st July 1916 and it is reasonable to assume another ten other ranks died as a result of wounds received on 1st July 1916. One of these men died in German hands. Excluding officers, the battalion's strength on 30th June was 1,035. 128 of these men were assigned to various carrying parties and, of the remaining 907, another 90 or so were assigned to the 10% reserve. Excluding the MO and stretcher bearers, etc., it is believed not more than 800 officers and men went into action, quite possible fewer, and the minimum casualty rate suffered by the battalion was 73%.

At roll call at 11 a.m. on the 2nd July L/Cpl. Williamson was horrified when only 45 men answered to their names, the rest being dead, wounded or scattered across No Man's Land and the British trenches. 2nd Lt. John Turner summed up the disaster that had befallen the battalion when he wrote home:

'The 8th that you knew is a memory only'.

THE CASUALTIES AMONGST THE SUPPORTING BATTALIONS WERE, from right to left:
11th Brigade
1st Hampshire Regt.
Officers
Killed:
Lt. H I Adams[iii] 2nd Lt. H T Alexander[i]

Radnor Rd., Handsworth, Birmingham. His body was never found and his name is inscribed on the Tyne Cot Memorial, Panel 23 to 28 and 163A.

[i] 2nd Lt., later Capt., Robert Charles Denison, 1/8th Royal Warwickshire Regt., died on 27th August 1916. Aged 26, he was the son f Robert Henry and Emily Denison, of Avino, Fowey, Cornwall. He is buried in Mill Road Cemetery, Thiepval.

[ii] 2nd Lt., later Capt., Joseph Arthur Richards, 18th Royal Warwickshire Regt., died on 4th November 1918. Aged 26, he was the son of James and Anne Richards of 45, Cartland Rd., Stirchley, Birmingham. Native of Shustoke. Birmingham. He is buried in Landrecies British Cemetery.

[iii] Lt. Hugh Irving Adams, 1st Hampshire Regt., was born in India in 1882 and lived at 8, Sydenham Villas Road, Upper High Street, Cheltenham. He passed out of the RMC, Sandhurst, in May 1901 He joined the 5th Light Infantry in the Indian Army in 1902,

2nd Lt. N H Bell[ii]	Capt. A T Bonham-Carter[iii]
2nd Lt. G H J Bramble[iv]	2nd Lt. E S Cane[v]
Lt. C J H Goodford[vi]	Lt. W G Nixon[vii], att. 11th TMB
Lt. Col. Hon. L C W Palk	2nd Lt. F P Thompson[i]

resigning in 1909. He was appointed Lt. in the Hampshire Regt. on 17th September 1915. He was buried in Sucrerie Military Cemetery, Colincamps, grave I. H. 12.

[i] 2nd Lt. Henry Talbot Alexander, 1st Hampshire Regt., was aged 28. He was the son of Alfred Alexander of 90, Fernhead Rd., Maida Hill, London, and the late Susanne Alexander (née Talbot). He joined the Civil Service in 1904 as a boy clerk and, in 1907, he was promoted to Registry Assistant in the Secretary's Office of the Post Office in London. He was commissioned on 10th June 1915. His body was buried in Redan Ridge Cemetery No.2, Beaumont-Hamel, grave C. 8. His younger brother, S/8446 L/Sgt. Alfred Reginald Alexander, 9th Rifle Brigade, died on 11th September 1915 and his name is on the Ypres (Menin Gate) Memorial.

[ii] 2nd Lt. Norman Henderson Bell, 3rd att. 1st Hampshire Regt., came from Southampton and is remembered on the Peartree Green United Reformed Church Memorial. He went to the RMC, Sandhurst, and was commissioned on 10th August 1915. His body was never found and his name is inscribed on the Thiepval Memorial, Pier & Face 7C & 7B.

[iii] Capt. Arthur Thomas Bonham-Carter, 3rd att. 1st Hampshire Regt., was aged 47. He was the youngest son of John 'Jack' Bonham Carter and Mary Baring. Born in Adhurst St Mary, Petersfield, Hampshire. Educated at Winchester, he went to Trinity College, Cambridge, in 1887 and attended the Inner Temple. Served with the Volunteer Company, Hampshire Regt., in South Africa 1899-1901 and became a magistrate in the Transvaal in 1902. Appointed the town magistrate in Mombasa in 1905 he served as a judge in the High Court, East Africa until 1915. He joined the 1st Volunteer Battalion, The Hampshire Regt., on 15th July 1896 (resigned as Captain, December 1902) he was promoted Captain in the 3rd Hampshire Regt., on 29th July 1915. He is buried in Serre Road Cemetery No. 2, grave XVI. D. 13.

[iv] 2nd Lt. Gerald Henry Joseph Bramble, 3rd att. 1st Hampshire Regt., was aged 21. He was the son of John and Rose Bramble of 'Avon', Christchurch, Hants. Enlisted in the Grenadier Guards, Sept., 1914, he was commissioned into the 3rd Hampshire Regt. on 25th March 1915. His body was never found and his name is inscribed on the Thiepval Memorial, Pier & Face 7C & 7B. His brother 100825 Bdr. John Gamble, 109th Heavy Battery, RGA, was killed on 3rd July 1916 and is buried in Vlamertinghe Military Cemetery. There is a memorial in the Church of St Michaels and All Angels, Sopley, Hampshire.

[v] 2nd Lt. Reginald Shapland Cane, 1st Hampshire Regt., was aged 34. He was the son of John James and Annie Cane of 18, Byron Rd., Ealing, London. He had been commissioned into the Hampshire Regt. from Z2888 Private in the Rifle Brigade on 27th June 1916. His body was never found and his name is inscribed on the Thiepval Memorial, Pier & Face 7C & 7B.

[vi] Lt. Charles James Henry Goodford, MC, 1st Hampshire Regt., was aged 20. He was the only son of Henry Frank and Katharine Goodford of 69, Frances Rd., Windsor and the grandson of the late Revd. C O Goodford, Provost of Eton College. He was educated at Eton College and was due to attend King's College, Cambridge. He was commissioned out of Sandhurst on 22nd December 1914 and went to the front in January 1915. He is remembered on a memorial in All Saints' Church, Windsor. He is buried in Sucrerie Military Cemetery, Colincamps, grave I. H. 13.

[vii] Lt. William Gerald Nixon, 3rd att. 1st Hampshire Regt. att. 11th Trench Mortar Battery, was commissioned on 3rd February 1915. His body was never found and his name is inscribed on the Thiepval Memorial, Pier & Face 7 C & 7 B.

2nd Lt. L A Westmore[ii]
Died of wounds:
2nd Lt. E W M Price[iii]
Wounded:
2nd Lt. Arthur Alleyne Kingsley Conan Doyle
2nd Lt. Donald Day
Capt. Cyril Dalton Fawkes
2nd Lt. J P Hall
2nd Lt. Henry George Harding
2nd Lt. William Athelstan Hiddingh
Capt. Hubert Nutcombe Hume
2nd Lt. John Victor Reed Jacob
Capt. Kenneth Alfred Johnston
2nd Lt. Horace Claude Charles Newnham
Lt. Shearer
2nd Lt. John James Sims
2nd Lt. Robert Sweetenham
2nd Lt. Walter George Welhams
Capt. John William Fortescue Wyld[iv]
The casualties amongst the other ranks were:
Killed 113
Wounded 249
Missing 197
Total 559

243 men of the 1st Hampshire Regt. are recorded as having been killed or died as a result of wounds received on 1st July 1916 (19 men dying from wounds from the 2nd July onwards). Two men died in German hands. Precise details about the number of men taken into battle by the 1st Hampshire Regt. do not exist but their rifle strength was very similar to that of the 1st East Lancashires and, therefore, it is a reasonable assumption that their casualty rate was approximately 80%, a remarkable figure given that many casualties were suffered behind the British front trench and no further forward than the German wire.

[i] 2nd Lt. Fendall Powney Thompson, 3rd att. 1st Hampshire Regt., was aged 19. He was the only son of Lt. Col. Cyril Powney Thompson (Indian Army) and Mary Alice Helen Thompson (née Clifford). He was born at Fort Munro, Punjab. He was commissioned on 26th May 1915. He is buried in Sucrerie Military Cemetery, Colincamps, grave I. H. 7.
[ii] 2nd Lt. Lawrence Arthur Westmore, 1st Hampshire Regt., was aged 22. He was the son of Arthur Sydney and Gertrude Mary Westmore of 9, Wimborne Rd., Bournemouth. Exhibitioner of Wadham College, Oxford (entered 1913). He was commissioned into the 1st Hampshire Regt. in December 1915. He is buried in Sucrerie Military Cemetery, Colincamps, grave I. I. 72.
[iii] 2nd Lt. Eric William Manning Price, 1st Hampshire Regt., was aged 19. He was the only child of Alfred Manning Price and Hannah Headley Price of 144, Hill Lane, Southampton. He was educated at Highfield School, Liphook and Sherborne School. He went to the RMC, Sandhurst, and was commissioned on 14th July 1915. He went to France in May 1916. He is buried in Bertrancourt Military Cemetery, Plot 1. Row G. Grave 15.
[iv] Capt. Wyld lost his leg as a result of his wounds.

1st Somerset Light Infantry
Officers
Killed:

Capt. & Adjt. C C Ford	Lt. Col. J A Thicknesse
Missing believed killed	
2nd Lt. R E Dunn	2nd Lt. G P C Fair[i]
2nd Lt. J A Hellard[ii]	2nd Lt. J A Johnston[iii]
Capt. R J R Leacroft, MC[iv]	2nd Lt. A V C Lèche[v]
Lt. E C MacBryan[vi]	Capt. G H Neville, MC[i]

---

[i] 2nd Lt. George Patrick Conroy Fair, 1st Somerset Light Infantry, was aged 20. He was the younger son of Catherine Fair of Woodside, Walton-by-Clevedon, Somerset, and the late Thomas Conroy Fair. He was educated at Eastington, Clevedon, Lambrook Bracknell and Uppingham Schools where, at the latter, he was the heavyweight boxing champion in 1914. He attended the RMC, Sandhurst, passing out 3rd. He went to France in June 1915. He is buried in Sucrerie Military Cemetery, Colincamps, grave I. H. 8. His brother, 2nd Lt. James Conroy Fair, 1st Coldstream Guards, was killed on 27th September 1915 and is commemorated on the Loos Memorial.

[ii] 2nd Lt. John Alexander Hellard, 3rd att. 1st Somerset Light Infantry, was aged 34. He was the second son of Edwin and Alice Jane Hellard of 'The Knoll', Stogumber, Somerset. He was educated at King's School, Canterbury, where he played for the cricket 1st XI and rugby 1st XV. He was a member of the OTC. He twice played cricket for Somerset. He practised as a solicitor in Colombo and served with the Town Guard Artillery, Colombo, 1914 to 1915. Gazetted 2nd Lt. in the 3rd (Reserve) Batt. Somerset Light Infantry June 1915 and attached 1st Batt. May 1916. He is buried in Serre Road Cemetery No. 2, grave II. A. 1.

[iii] 2nd Lt. James Annandale Johnston, 3rd att. 1st Somerset Light Infantry, was the son of the late Lt. James Johnston, R.N. and Mrs A R Johnston; husband of Mrs Gladys H Johnston, of 89, Westcourt Rd., Worthing. He was educated at Christ's Hospital. He is remembered on the Broadwater (Worthing) Parish Church War Memorial. His body was never found and his name is inscribed on the Thiepval Memorial, Pier & Face 2A.

[iv] Capt. Ronald John Ranulph Leacroft, MC, 1st Somerset Light Infantry, was aged 22. He was the younger son of Edward Ranulph and Alice Leacroft of Rowberrow Manor, Winscombe, Somerset. Born at Weston near Stafford, he was educated at Blundell's School, Tiverton. He was gazetted to the Somerset LI in 1913. He was wounded at Mons and promoted Captain in February 1915. His MC was gazetted on 3rd June 1916. He is buried in Redan Ridge Cemetery No.1, Beaumont-Hamel, grave C. 40. His original wooden battlefield cross is at the Church of St Michael, Rowberrow, Somerset.

[v] 2nd Lt. Arthur Victor Carleton Lèche, 3rd att. 1st Somerset Light Infantry, was aged 20. He was the third child and second son of Arthur Victor Carlyon Lèche, of Elmcroft, Axbridge and Sarah Charletta Ludlow of Philadelphia, USA. His father was the GP in Axbridge. Educated at Sexey's School, Bruton where he was in the OTC. He was commissioned into the 3rd Somerset LI on 15th August 1914 and went to France in May 1915. He is buried in Serre Road Cemetery No. 2, grave I. A. 31. There is a memorial in the Church of St John the Baptist, Axbridge.

[vi] Lt. Edward Crozier MacBryan, 1st Somerset Light Infantry, was aged 22. He was the second son of Dr Henry Crawford MacBryan of Kingsdown House, Box, Wilts. Educated Mr Trask's School (St Christopher's), Bath, at Oundle School, where he captained the cricket 1st XI and played for the 1st XV, and Jesus College, Cambridge. He also played cricket for Wiltshire. He was commissioned on 14th August 1914. Previously wounded in 1916, his body was never found and his name is inscribed on the Thiepval Memorial, Pier & Face 2A. His brother, John Crawford William (Jack) MacBryan, Somerset Light Infantry, was made a Prisoner of War at Le Cateau in 1914. Jack MacBryan won an

Plate 97 2nd Lt. Arthur Victor Carleton Lèche, 1st Somerset Light Infantry (Copyright Axbridge Town Trust)

Plate 98 2nd Lt. Thomas Marriott Dodington, 1st Somerset Light Infantry

2nd Lt. W H Treasure, 11th TMB	
Wounded and missing	
2nd Lt. F A Pearse[ii]	2nd Lt. H M Tilley, PoW
Missing	
Lt. V A Braithwaite, MC[iii]	2nd Lt. T M Dodington[iv]

Olympic Gold Medal in 1920 (hockey), played one cricket test match for England (1924 v South Africa) and was a Wisden Cricketer of the Year in 1925. His other brother, Lt. R A MacBryan, King's Own Scottish Borderers was wounded.

[i] Capt. George Henry Neville, MC, 1st Somerset Light Infantry, was aged 35. He was the son of Mr and Mrs T Neville of Dunchurch, Rugby; husband of Alice Ethel Pearl (formerly Neville) of 107, Chiswell, Portland, Dorset. He was awarded his MC in the New Year's Honours List, 14th January 1916 and promoted Captain on 21st February 1916. Before being commissioned he was a Company Sergeant Major. He is buried in Serre Road Cemetery No. 2, grave XIV. G. 12.

[ii] 2nd Lt. Frank Arthur Pearse, 1st Somerset Light Infantry, was aged 24. He was the son of Henry Charles and Clara Pearse of 14, Eaton Place, Brighton. A Private in the Honourable Artillery Company he was commissioned on 27th July 1915. His body was never found and his name is inscribed on the Thiepval Memorial, Pier & Face 2A.

[iii] Lt. Valentine Ashworth Braithwaite, MC, 1st Somerset Light Infantry, was aged 20. He was the only son of Gen. Sir Walter Pipon Braithwaite, K.C.B., A.D.C. and Jessie, Lady Braithwaite (née Ashworth) of 35, Sloane Gardens, Westminster, London. He was commissioned on 14th August 1914. He won his MC at Mons in 1914. His body was never found and his name is inscribed on the Thiepval Memorial, Pier & Face 2A. There is a special memorial to Lt. Braithwaite outside Serre Road Cemetery No. 2.

[iv] 2nd Lt. Thomas Marriott Dodington, 1st Somerset Light Infantry, was aged 20. He was the eldest son of Lt. Col. Roger Marriott Dodington, JP, Deputy Lieutenant of Somerset, and Mary Emiline Bertha Dodington (née Couper) of Horsington House, Templecombe. Lt. Col. Dodington commanded the West Somerset Yeomanry. He attended the RMC, Sandhurst, and was commissioned on 16th December 1914. He went to France on 3rd

2nd Lt. H E Whitgreave[i] 2nd Lt. G C Winstanley
Died of wounds:
2nd Lt. H L Colville[ii], DoW 6th July 1916

Plate 99 Lt. Charles John Odinel Daubeny, 3rd att. 1st Somerset Light Infantry

Wounded
2nd Lt. Alfred H Collins, Brigade carriers
Lt. Charles John Odinel Daubeny[iii]
Lt. Guy Cochrane Veale Greetham

February 1915 and was wounded on 13th May 1915. He returned to France on 22nd May 1916. His body was never found and his name is inscribed on the Thiepval Memorial, Pier & Face 2A.

[i] 2nd Lt. Henry Egerton Whitgreave, 1st Somerset Light Infantry, was aged 34. He was the eldest son of Robert Whitgreave and Marian Clare Whitgreave (née Smith) of Bushbury Lodge, Walton-by-Clevedon, Somerset, and of Moseley Court, Staffordshire. Born at Stafford, he was educated at Radford House School, Coventry, and Beaumont College, Old Windsor. He was seventh in line from the Thomas Whitgreave who sheltered Charles II after the Battle of Worcester, 1651. A Lance Sergeant in the 6th (Service) Battalion, Somerset Light Infantry, he was commissioned on 13th August 1915. He is buried in Redan Ridge Cemetery No.1, Beaumont-Hamel, grave A. 51.

[ii] 2nd Lt. Harold Linklater Colville, 9th att. 1st Somerset Light Infantry, was aged 22. He was the son of George and Mary Colville. He graduated from St Chad's College, Durham University where he was a member of the OTC. He was commissioned on 22nd June 1915. He is buried in St. Sever Cemetery, Rouen, grave Officers, A. 3. 5.

[iii] Capt. Charles John Odinel Daubeny, 3rd att. 1st Somerset Light Infaantry, died of wounds on 16th June 1917. Aged 21, he was the son of Capt. Charles William and Mrs Edith Daubeny of The Brow, Combe Down, Bath. Educated at St Christopher's School, Bath, and Tonbridge, where he was in the OTC, he was commissioned into the Special Reserve of the Somerset Light Infantry in October 1914. He went to France in May, 1915, and was promoted Lt. in April 1916. He was wounded in the thigh on 1st July, returned in December and was wounded again on 12th April 1917. He was fatally wounded at Monchy le Preux on 15th June 1917 and is buried in Aubigny Communal Cemetery Extension.

Capt. Allan James Harington, MC
Capt. William Wynn Llewellyn
Lt. Reginald Willis Shannon
2nd Lt. Richard Clive Strachey
2nd Lt. Alexander Richard Waugh
The casualties amongst the other ranks were initially estimated as:
Killed 47
Wounded 171
Missing 232
Total 450

181 men of the 1st Somerset Light Infantry are recorded as having been killed or died as a result of wounds received on 1st July 1916 (One officer and 8 men dying from wounds from the 2nd July onwards). One man appears to have died in German hands. Precise details about the number of men taking into battle by the 1st Somerset Light Infantry do not exist but their rifle strength was very similar to that of the 1st East Lancashires and, therefore, it is a reasonable assumption that their casualty rate was approximately 62%.

As a footnote to these casualties, the battalion returned to the front line trenches opposite the Heidenkopf on 10th July. Two night-time patrols had gone out on successive nights to see what, if anything, the Germans were doing to repair their trenches. It may be possible that, during these patrols, wounded from the 1st July were found still alive out in No Man's Land as, on the night of the 12th, the battalion Medical Officer, Capt. John Henry Dyke Acland, went out beyond the British wire to look for wounded. Aged 36, Acland was an experienced and dedicated doctor who had trained at St Thomas's Hospital and then worked in London and in Bulawayo (then Southern Rhodesia now Zimbabwe). On the outbreak of war he returned to England and was commissioned into the RAMC in October 1914 being attached as MO to the 1st Somerset Light Infantry. At some point on the night of the 12th July Capt. Acland was shot by a sniper and killed. One of the two unwounded officer survivors of the 1st July, he was buried in the same cemetery as his late commanding officer, Lt. Col. Thicknesse, and they lie together under the trees in the Sucrerie Cemetery near Colincamps[i].

---

[i] Capt. John Henry Dyke Acland, Royal Army Medical Corps att. 1st Somerset Light Infantry was aged 36. He was the second son of the late Rev. Henry Dyke Acland, vicar of Luccombe, Somersetshire, and Mrs. Adelaide Clementina Hart Acland (née Davis), of Devon. One of six children, his older brother became a Rear Admiral in the Royal Navy and his younger brother the Bishop of Bombay. He married Elizabeth Margaret Corner on 4th November 1914 and they lived at 7, Gloucester Place, Marylebone, London. He was educated at Blundell's School and St Thomas's Hospital, where he took the diplomas of M.R.C.S. and L.R.C.P. London in 1905. He was house-surgeon to the East London Hospital for Children, Shadwell, and house-physician to the West London Hospital; afterwards he went to South Africa, and after serving as medical officer of the Beira railways, began to practise at Bulawayo, the chief town of Southern Rhodesia, where he was medical officer of the Bulawayo Government Schools. He took a temporary commission as Lieutenant in the R.A.M.C. on October 7th 1914, was promoted to captain in 1915. He is buried in the Sucrerie Military Cemetery, Colincamps, grave I. H. 16.

Maj. Vivian Henry Bruce Majendie, previously the 2inC of the battalion and now its new CO, wrote to his parents:

> "He went out into the front of our line to try and find a wounded man who was reported to be there. By the greatest misfortune, he was hit by a bullet and died almost at once. He is a very great loss to us; besides being a skilful doctor he was a most cheery companion and we all miss him dreadfully, he did most gallant work in the attack on July 1st. I immediately recommended him for the Military Cross and if he had been spared I have not the least doubt that he would have been awarded it. He died while trying to perform an act of mercy."[49]

143rd Brigade (attached to 11th Brigade)
1/6th Royal Warwickshire Regt.
Casualties
Officers
Killed:

2nd Lt. J Balkwill[i]	Capt. J E B Dixon[ii]
2nd Lt. H L Field[iii]	2nd Lt. R V Rose[iv]

---

[i] 2nd Lt. John Balkwill, 1/6th Royal Warwickshire Regt., was aged 33. He was the son of Francis and Mary Vince Balkwill of Forest Hill, London. Educated privately by J. O. Boyes at 45 Houston Road, Forest Hill and went to St. Dunstan's in Sept. 1893 (Entrance Scholarship, Governor's Scholarship, School Prize, prizes for French and Science; Head Prefect 1898-99, Leaving Prize, Rugby 1st XV, Lacrosse 1st XII, Cricket 1st XI; Captain of Athletics; left in 1899). Played Rugby for Catford Bridge A XV, 1899-1901; Committee of the Old Dunstonian Club, 1902-03 and 1908. Joined Northern Assurance Col. Ltd in 1899, transferring to Birmingham as a surveyor in July 1908. After moving to Birmingham he cricket for the Knowle Club. Volunteered for the 6th Royal Warwickshire Regt., in September 1914 and was commissioned on 19th September 1915. He is buried in Pargny British Cemetery, grave III. E. 36. His younger brother. 2nd Lt. Charles Vince Balkwill, 1/5th London Regt. (London Rifle Brigade), was also killed on 1st July 1916 in the attack on Gommecourt. [*Sources:* Dick Flory, *The War Record of the Northern Assurance Co. Ltd 1914-1918* and *St. Dunstan's College Roll of Honour 1914-19* by David W. Collett].

[ii] Capt. James Evelyn Bevan Dixon, 1/6th Royal Warwickshire Regt., was aged 22. He was the younger son of Mr and Mrs Arthur Stansfield Dixon of Deddington, Oxon., and the grandson of the late George Dixon, MP for Birmingham, Edgbaston. Born at Edgbaston, Birmingham. Educated at Oundle School, he went to Trinity College, Cambridge, in 1913. He was commissioned on 19th October 1914 and went to France in March 1915. He is buried in Serre Road Cemetery No. 2, grave I. K. 7.

[iii] 2nd Lt. Henry Lionel Field, 1/6th Royal Warwickshire Regt., was aged 22. He was the second son of Henry Cromwell Field and Ruth Field of Courtlands, Edgbaston, Birmingham, and the grandson of Rt. Hon. Jesse Collings, MP for Birmingham, Bordesley. A descendant of Oliver Cromwell. He was educated at Marlborough and the Birmingham School of Art. He was commissioned on 19th September 1914. A poet he wrote *'Poems and Drawings'* by H L Field. He is buried in Serre Road Cemetery No. 2, grave II. C. 10.

[iv] 2nd Lt. Reginald Vincent Rose, B Company, 1/6th Royal Warwickshire Regt., was aged 19. He was the son of Louise Rose of 58, Gillott Rd., Edgbaston, Birmingham, and the late Ethelbert Rose. As 2665 Cpl he was commissioned into the battalion on 7th May 1916. His body was never found and his name is inscribed on the Thiepval Memorial, Pier & Face 9A, 9B & 10B.

Plate 100 2nd Lt. John Balkwill, 1/6th Royal Warwickshire Regt.

Plate 101 Capt. James Evelyn Bevan Dixon, 1/6th Royal Warwickshire Regt.

Plate 102 2nd Lt. Henry Lionel Field, 1/6th Royal Warwickshire Regt.

Plate 103 Capt. Arthur Brian Rabone, 1/6th Royal Warwickshire Regt.

Lt. G R C Martin[i]

Capt. A B Rabone[ii]

[i] Lt. George Russell Courtney Martin, 1/6th Royal Warwickshire Regt., was aged 25. He was the son of George Martin and lived at Hartop Court, Four Oaks, Sutton Coldfield. He was commissioned on 19th October 1914. He is buried in Miraumont Communal Cemetery, grave C. 5.

[ii] Capt. Arthur Brian Rabone, 1/6th Royal Warwickshire Regt., was aged 28. He was the only son of Arthur J and Maud Mary Rabone of Elmwood, Handsworth, Birmingham; husband of Jessie D Rabone (née Best). He was educated at Lickey Hill School and Uppingham and was a director of Messrs J Rabone & Son Ltd of Whitmore Street,

2nd Lt. S J Winkley[i]
Missing believed killed:
Capt. C T M Davies[ii] 2nd Lt. R Price[iii]
2nd Lt. W P Wheeler[iv], 2nd July 1916
Wounded and missing:
2nd Lt. A E Clarke[v], died of wounds 9th July 1916, in German hands
Wounded:
Lt. William Hendley Bruce Baxter
Lt. K Brown
Maj. Francis Henry Deakin
2nd Lt. Alec Neville Downing
Lt. Col. William Hodgson Franklin, att. Newfoundland Regt.
2nd Lt. Keith Thomas Colrick Herne
Capt. Eric Wynne Jones
Lt. Frank Leslie Morgan
Capt. James Neilson Greenlees Stafford[vi]
Capt. Arthur Brooke Turner
Lt. Arthur D Wilcox

Birmingham. Pre-war he was commissioned into the 6th Royal Warwickshire Regt., on 26th May 1908. He was promoted Captain on 10th June 1915. His body was never found and his name is inscribed on the Thiepval Memorial, Pier & Face 9A, 9B & 10B.

[i] 2nd Lt. Sydney Joseph Winkley, 1/6th Royal Warwickshire Regt., was a sergeant and was commissioned on 3rd October 1915. His body was never found and his name is inscribed on the Thiepval Memorial, Pier & Face 9A, 9B & 10B.

[ii] Capt. Cyril Thomas Morris Davies, 1/6th Royal Warwickshire Regt., was aged 31. He was the son of Morris and Mary Laura Davies, of Llanllwchaiarn. He had enlisted as a Private into the Royal Warwickshire Regiment at the outbreak of war being promoted Corporal. He was commissioned on 19th September 1915. He was promoted Temp. Capt. on 11th March 1916. His body was never found and his name is inscribed on the Thiepval Memorial, Pier & Face 9A, 9B & 10B.

[iii] 2nd Lt. Reginald Price, 1/6th Royal Warwickshire Regt., was aged 37. He was the son of the late Rev. Thomas Price and of Anne Price late of Claverdon Vicarage, Warwickshire. He was educated at Warwick School and the Birmingham School of Art. He was the art master at Rossall School. He was commissioned from Cpl. on 19th September 1915. His body was never found and his name is inscribed on the Thiepval Memorial, Pier & Face 9A, 9B & 10B.

[iv] 2nd Lt. William Pierce Wheeler, 1/6th Royal Warwickshire Regt., was aged 20. He was the son of Edward and Edith Wheeler of 'Westbourne', Beech Hill Rd., Wylde Green, Birmingham. Commissioned from Cpl. on 7th May 1916. His body was never found and his name is inscribed on the Thiepval Memorial, Pier & Face 9A, 9B & 10B.

[v] 2nd Lt. Albert Edward Clarke, B Company, 1/6th Royal Warwickshire Regt., was aged 23. He was the only son of Clara Clarke of the Bungalow, Lincoln Rd., Saxilby, Lincs., and the late James Clarke. He was commissioned on 26th November 1915. He is buried in Cologne Southern Cemetery, grave VII. E. 22.

[vi] Capt. James Neilson Greenlees Stafford, 1/6th Royal Warwickshire Regt., was killed in action at Epéhy on 16th April 1917. Aged 28, he was the second son of Thomas Stafford of Bristol Road, Birmingham. Returned to front three months after being wounded on 1st July 1916. He is buried in Saulcourt Churchyard Extension, Guyencourt-Saulcourt, grave B. 2.

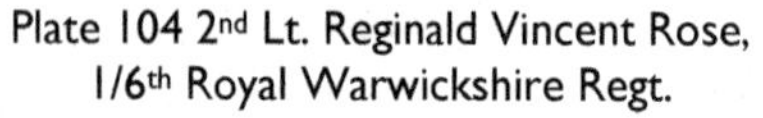

Plate 104 2nd Lt. Reginald Vincent Rose, 1/6th Royal Warwickshire Regt.

Plate 105 Capt. James Neilson Greenlees Stafford, 1/6th Royal Warwickshire Regt.

The casualties amongst the other ranks were initially estimated as:
Killed: 43
Wounded: 173
Missing: 234
Total 450

163 men of the 1/6th Royal Warwickshire Regt. are recorded as having been killed or died as a result of wounds received on 1st July 1916 (7 men dying from wounds from the 2nd July onwards). Three men appear to have died in German hands. Precise details about the number of men taking into battle by the 1/6th Royal Warwickshire Regt. do not exist but their rifle strength was considerably less than the majority of other battalions and, therefore, it is a reasonable assumption that their casualty rate was approximately 73%.

10th Brigade
2nd Seaforth Highlanders
Casualties
Officers:
Killed:

Capt. C E Baird, C Company[i]
2nd Lt. M H Blackwood, B Company
2nd Lt. F G Broom, A Company[ii]
2nd Lt. D Buchanan, B Company[i]

---

[i] Capt. Charles Edward Baird, 2nd Seaforth Highlanders, was aged 21. He was the eldest son of Brig. Gen. Edward W D Baird and Millicent Bessie Baird of Kelloe, Edrom, Berwickshire, and Forse, Caithness and the grandson of the late Maj. Gen Sir Stanley Clarke. He was educated at Eton College and Sandhurst. He was commissioned in October 1913. Twice wounded, he is buried in Serre Road Cemetery No. 2, grave I. K. 21.

[ii] 2nd Lt. Frederick Gordon Broom, 2nd Seaforth Highlanders, was from Greenock. He is buried in Sucrerie Military Cemetery, Colincamps, grave I. H. 20.

2nd Lt. F A Conner, A Company[ii] 2nd Lt. S A Crum, D Company[iii]
2nd Lt. J N Gourlay, C Company[iv] 2nd Lt. J Harvey, D Company[v]
2nd Lt. T E Lancaster, D Company[vi]
2nd Lt. W Shaw, C Company[vii]
2nd Lt. H F L Sillars, B Company[viii] 2nd Lt. J Williamson, A Company[ix]
Died of wounds
2nd Lt. W Harrison, Scout officer, died 5th July 1916

---

[i] 2nd Lt. David Buchanan, 2nd Seaforth Highlanders, was aged 23. He was the younger son of William and Margaret Bryson Buchanan of Alt-an-Aros, Northland Road, Londonderry. He was educated at Foyle College and enlisted as Private in the 6th Black Watch serving at Festubert before being commissioned into the Seaforths in August 1915. He is buried in Sucrerie Military Cemetery, Colincamps, grave I. H. 35.
[ii] 2nd Lt. Frederic Attenborrow Conner, 2nd Seaforth Highlanders, was aged 21. He was the son of James Conner (Sheriff Clerk Depute Aberdeen) of 58, Gladstone Place, Aberdeen. He was educated at Aberdeen Grammar School and Aberdeen University where he matriculated in agriculture in 1913. He played rugby for Aberdeen Grammar FPs and Aberdeenshire Cricket Club. He enlisted in the Grammar School Company of the 4th Gordon Highlanders, being promoted sergeant before being commissioned into the Seaforth Highlanders in August 1915. His body was never found and his name is inscribed on the Thiepval Memorial, Pier & Face 15C.
[iii] 2nd Lt. Stewart Alexander Crum, 2nd Seaforth Highlanders, was aged 19. He was the son of the late J L Crum. He was educated at Aldeburgh Lodge, Wellington College and Sandhurst and was commissioned in September 1915. He joined the battalion on 7th June 1916. He is buried in Serre Road Cemetery No. 2, grave I. C. 32.
[iv] 2nd Lt. John Norman Gourlay, 2nd Seaforth Highlanders, was aged 21. He was the son of Dr Frederick Gourlay and Mary Gourlay 0née Connor) of Rathmore, Seafield Street, Elgin. A student he enlisted in October 1914. He joined the battalion on 14th June 1916. He is buried in Pargny British Cemetery, grave III. A. 41.
[v] 2nd Lt. James Harvey, 2nd Seaforth Highlanders, was aged 24. He was the son of Jessie Harvey of 47, Palatine Rd., Douglas, Isle of Man, and the late James Harvey, of Greenock. He was commissioned from Company Sergeant Major on 18th November 1915. His body was never found and his name is inscribed on the Thiepval Memorial, Pier & Face 15C.
[vi] 2nd Lt. Thomas Erwin Lancaster, 2nd Seaforth Highlanders, was aged 18. He was the second son of Henry Percy and Elizabeth Lancaster of 17, St. James Mansions, West Hampstead, London. He was educated at York House Preparatory School and Highgate School where he played for the cricket and football 1st XIs. He entered Sandhurst on the outbreak of war where he qualified for the Army Lightweight Boxing Championship. He joined the battalion on 14th June 1916. His body was never found and his name is inscribed on the Thiepval Memorial, Pier & Face 15C.
[vii] 2nd Lt. William Shaw, 2nd Seaforth Highlanders, was aged 38. He was the son of William Shaw of Dunfermline and Christina Shaw (née Wilson); and the husband of Ellen O'Regan. He was born in Elgin and enlisted at Fort George. His body was never found and his name is inscribed on the Thiepval Memorial, Pier & Face 15C.
[viii] 2nd Lt. Harry Frederick Lionel Sillars, 4th Argyll & Sutherland Highlanders att. 2nd Seaforth Highlanders, was aged 21. He was the son of H J Sillars, J.P. and Mrs Sillars of Garden Cottage, Grove Rd., Richmond, Surrey, formerly of Saltcoats, Ayrshire. He was educated at Ardrossan Academy. His body was never found and his name is inscribed on the Thiepval Memorial, Pier & Face 15A & 16C.
[ix] 2nd Lt. John Williamson, 2nd Seaforth Highlanders, was aged 19. He was the son of the Rev James Alexander and Martha Winder Williamson (née Thomson) of The Manse, Alva, Clackmannanshire. He is buried in Sucrerie Military Cemetery, Colincamps, grave I. H. 22.

Capt. F L Cleland[i], RAMC, died 4th July 1916
Wounded and missing:
2nd Lt. F R MacKenzie, C Company   Capt. N I MacWatt, A Company[ii]

Plate 106 2nd Lt. Frederic Attenborrow Conner, 2nd Seaforth Highlanders

Wounded:
2nd Lt. Alex Bonthrone, C Company
Capt. Hamilton Barrett Goulding, RAMC
Lt. Andrew St Clair Jameson, Lewis Gun officer
2nd Lt. John Arthur McKinnell, C Company
Lt. R E Paterson, B Company
2nd Lt. Frederick Alfred Phillips, B Company
Capt. Alexander Welsh Somerville, D Company
Wounded at duty:
Lt. Col. J O Hopkinson, commanding
Other ranks
Killed 59
Wounded 255
Missing believed killed 1
Missing 53
Wounded at duty 5
Total 373

---

[i] Capt. Frank Lee Cleland, Royal Army Medical Corps, died of wounds on 4th July 1916. Aged 28, he was the elder son of Mary and the late Francis Lee Cleland, of Breda House, Newtownbreda, Co. Down. He was educated at the Methodist College and Queen's University, Belfast. He graduated MB, BCh and BAO in January 1915 and joined the RAMC on 1st February 1915. He is buried in St Sever Cmetery, Rouen, Officers, A. 3. 11.

[ii] Lt. Norman Ian MacWatt, 2nd Seaforth Highlanders, was aged 24. He was the son of Norman MacWatt of Alloa. His body was never found and his name is inscribed on the Thiepval Memorial, Pier & Face 15C.

140 men of the 2nd Seaforth Highlanders are recorded as having been killed or died as a result of wounds received on 1st July 1916 (13 men dying from wounds from the 2nd July onwards). Precise details about the number of men taken into battle by the 2nd Seaforth Highlanders do not exist but it is a reasonable assumption that 22 officers and about 640 other ranks went into action[i] and that their casualty rate was, therefore, approximately 60%. The bodies of Capt. Alison, 2nd Lts. Williamson, Brown, Buchanan, Blackwood and 25 other ranks were collected over the coming days and were buried side by side in the large British cemetery 200 yards NW of the Sucrerie[ii].

2nd Royal Dublin Fusiliers
Casualties
Officers:
Killed:

2nd Lt. R H Ingoldby[iii]
2nd Lt. J W R Morgan[iv]

Died of wounds:

2nd Lt. W H A Damiano[v], 2nd July 1916
Maj. L P Walsh, 4th July 1916

Wounded:

Lt. Hugh S Anderson
Capt. Thomas Brady
2nd Lt. John Cyril Joseph Chadwick[vi]
Lt. William Thomas Colyer
2nd Lt. Arthur Joseph Franklin
Capt. William Francis Jeffries
2nd Lt. Thomas William Hobart Mason
2nd Lt. George Francis Mulholland

---

[i] Trench strength is given as 35 officers and 848 other ranks. 13 officers and 10% of the men were put into reserve and 125 men were used as carriers.

[ii] Now Sucrerie Military Cemetery, Colincamps.

[iii] 2nd Lt. Roger Hugh Ingoldby, 2nd Royal Dublin Fusiliers, was aged 30. He was the fourth of eight children of Mr Frederick John and Mrs Madeline A Ingoldby (née Kerr) of Westgate House, Louth, Lincs. He graduated from Emanuel College, Cambridge, in 1905. In Canada when war broke out, he joined the 19th Alberta Dragoons as a private, going to France in Feb., 1915. He was gazetted to a Commission a few months later. He is buried in A.I.F. Burial Ground, Flers, grave VI. H. 26.

[iv] 2nd Lt. John Walter Rees Morgan, 4th att. 2nd Royal Dublin Fusiliers, was aged 25. He was the younger son of the late Rees Powell Morgan of Brynhyfryd, Neath, and the late Mrs Mary Evelyn Morgan (née Matthews). He was educated at Bilton Grange, Rugby, and Rugby School. Articled to L R Morgan, solicitors, of Neath. Joined Oct. 8th, 1914, as 281 Private, 1st Sportsman's Batt. Royal Fusiliers. Gazetted 2nd Lt. 4th Batt. Royal Dublin Fusiliers April 1915 and went to France July 1915. He is buried in Sucrerie Military Cemetery, Colincamps, grave I. D. 61.

[v] 2nd Lt. Walter Henry Alexander Damiano, 2nd Royal Dublin Fusiliers, was aged 19. He was the son of Nicholas and Enid Damiano of 2, Church Lane, Calcutta, India. He is buried in Beauval Communal Cemetery, grave A. 9.

[vi] 2nd Lt. John Cyril Joseph Chadwick, 5th att. 2nd Royal Dublin Fusiliers, was articled to Louis Chadwick, solicitors, of 60 Carey Street, Lincoln's Inn, W.C. Joined Sept. 2nd 1914, as Private, 18th Service Bn. (1st Public Schools), Royal Fusiliers. Gazetted 2nd Lt. 5th (Special Reserve) Royal Dublin Fusiliers 23rd May 1915, promoted Lt. July 1917.

2nd Lt. Arthur William Sainsbury
Capt. James Owen William Shine

2nd Lt. Mulholland had been commissioned from the rank of sergeant only nine days earlier. He did not return to the battalion, being sent to train soldiers in Nigeria after he recovered from his wounds.

The casualties amongst the other ranks were initially estimated as:
Killed: 52
Wounded: 222
Missing: 40
Total: 314

74 men of the 2nd Royal Dublin Fusiliers are recorded as having been killed or died as a result of wounds received on 1st July 1916 (one officer and 12 men dying from wounds from the 2nd July onwards). The fighting strength of the 2nd Royal Dublin Fusiliers as of 30th June was given as 31 officers and 870 other ranks. 22 officers and approximately 780 other ranks would have gone into action giving a casualty rate of approximately 41%, this for a battalion which did not advance any further than the British front line.

1st Royal Irish Fusiliers
Casualties
Officers
Wounded
2nd Lt. W Johnson
2nd Lt. Cecil Tucker Parker
Capt. Edward Roland Wilson
Other ranks
Killed: 10
Wounded: 90
Missing 7
Total 107

16 men of the 1st Royal Irish Fusiliers are recorded as having been killed or died as a result of wounds received on 1st July 1916 (4 men dying from wounds on the 2nd July). Given that the 1st Royal Irish Fusiliers had two companies heavily involved in the fighting, with one occupying the Heidenkopf for nearly 18 hours, its casualty rate of approximately 15% is remarkably low.

1st Royal Warwickshire Regt.
Casualties
Officers
Wounded
Lt. Reginald R Waters, 4th att. 1st Royal Warwicks
Other ranks
Killed: 9
Wounded: 27
Missing: 1
Total: 37

13 men of the 1st Royal Warwickshire Regt. are recorded as having died on the 1st and 2nd July 1916. The 1st Royal Warwickshire Regt. was the weakest

battalion in the Division on this date and only the 1/6th Royal Warwickshires had fewer men available on the day. It would seem probable that the battalion went into action with approximately 22 officers and 600 other ranks. The reason for this relative weakness was the loss they had sustained whilst occupying the front line during the bulk of the bombardment. On 23rd June the battalion had numbered 42 officers and 1,031 other ranks. By the evening of the 30th June, these numbers had been reduced to 33 officers and 843 other ranks, a net loss of 9 officers and 188 other ranks. All bar one of the officer losses were suffered in action[i] while amongst the other ranks 13 were killed, 83 wounded and the rest went to hospital, the bulk of whom, i.e. about 90, had been affected by gas during the various gas releases. The discrepancy in the totals was made up by men returning to the battalion from hospital, of whom there were 26 during this period, and seven reinforcements.

12th Brigade
1st King's Own Royal Lancaster Regt.
Casualties
Officers
Killed

2nd Lt. P Clegg[ii]
2nd Lt. G R Hablutzel[iii]
2nd Lt. C C MacWalter, Scout Officer
2nd Lt. H P Melly[iv]
2nd Lt. R Minor[v]
2nd Lt. J Rowley, Signalling Officer

---

[i] The exception was 2nd Lt. Ethelbert Godwin Stockwall Wagner who joined the R.F.C. Originally 28015 Cpl Wagner, Royal Engineers, he was commissioned into the Royal Warwickshire Regt., before transferring to the R.F.C. where he joined No. 32 Squadron. He was the son of Christian and Anne Francis Wagner (née Marples). Born in Taiping in the Malay States, he was educated at Lord Williams School, Thame, and Birmingham University and lived at 110, Bristol Road, Edgbaston, Birmingham. He was flying DH2 7851 on 7th January 1917 when he was shot down by Lt. Erwin Bohme of Jasta 2. He was Bohme's 9th victory. He died aged 23, and is buried in Achiet le Grand Communal Cemetery Extension, grave II. M. 25.

[ii] 2nd Lt. Percy Clegg, 1st King's Own Royal Lancaster Regt., was aged 21. He was the son of Robert and Margaret A Clegg of Higher Lomax, Heywood, Lancs. He was commissioned on 4th December 1915. He is buried in Sucrerie Military Cemetery, Colincamps, grave I. H. 3.

[iii] 2nd Lt. George Rudolph Hablutzel, 1st King's Own Royal Lancaster Regt., was aged 39. He was the husband of L A Hablutzel of Hatfield Rd., Northallerton, Yorks. He served in the South African War, receiving the Queen's South Africa Medal with two bars and a Long Service Good Conduct Medal. A Company Sergeant Major, he was commissioned on 30th May 1916. His body was never found and his name is inscribed on the Thiepval Memorial, Pier & Face 5D & 12B.

[iv] 2nd Lt. Hugh Peter Egerton Mesnard Melly, 4th att. 1st King's Own Royal Lancaster Regt., was aged 19. He was the elder son of Hon Col. Hugh Mesnard Melly, V.D. and Eleanor Lawrence Melly (née Own) of The Quinta, Greenheys Rd., Liverpool. He was educated at Malvern College, 1911-1914. Passed into Royal Military College, Sandhurst, but did not enter. He was commissioned on 5th March 1915. He is buried in Sucrerie Military Cemetery, Colincamps, grave I. H. 11.

[v] 2nd Lt. Roland Minor, 3rd att. 1st King's Own Royal Lancaster Regt., was aged 21. He was the son of Philip Scott Minor LL.B. and Susan Helen Minor of Avonmore, Alderley Edge, Manchester. Articled to H W Minor, solicitors, of Manchester. Joined Sept. 1914, as

Capt. J F H Young[i]

Missing

Maj. J N Bromilow

2nd Lt. A H W Hudson[ii]

Capt. A Weatherhead[iii]

Plate 107 Capt. Andrew Weatherhead, 3rd att. 1st King's Own Royal Lancaster Regt

Wounded

Capt. Frank Montague Barnes RAMC

2nd Lt. L A Hall (shell shock)

2nd Lt. C H Hallett

2nd Lt. Frederick Arnuff Markham

2nd Lt. Lionel Leasowe Mortlock

2nd Lt. Albert Percy Myers (shell shock)

Capt. Archibald Hugh Read, att. 3rd Royal Sussex Regt.

Private, Public Schools Batt. Gazetted 2nd Lt. King's Own Royal Lancaster Regt. May 26th, 1915. He is buried in Euston Road Cemetery, Colincamps, grave I. B. 43.

[i] Capt. John Ferrers Harrington Young, 1st King's Own Royal Lancaster Regt., was aged 19. He was the son of Mrs Patrick Stewart (formerly Young) of 8, Vicarage Gate, Kensington, London, and the late Capt. J E H Young (R.A.). Educated at Wellington College, he was commissioned out of the RMC, Sandhurst, on 11th November 1914 and was promoted Captain on 28th January 1916. He is buried in Sucrerie Military Cemetery, Colincamps, grave I. G. 41.

[ii] 2nd Lt. Arthur Henry William Hudson, 1st King's Own Royal Lancaster Regt., was aged 19. He was the son of Arthur John Hudson of 341, Fairfax Drive, Westcliff, Southend, and the late Hannah Hudson. His body was never found and his name is inscribed on the Thiepval Memorial, Pier & Face 5D & 12B.

[iii] Capt. Andrew Weatherhead, 3rd att. 1st King's Own Royal Lancaster Regt., was the fourth son of the late Canon Robert Johnston Weatherhead, vicar of Seacombe, Cheshire, and Anna Bagot Weatherhead. His body was never found and his name is inscribed on the Thiepval Memorial, Pier & Face 5D & 12B. His brother, Capt. & Adjt. G E Weatherhead, 2nd King's Own Royal Lancaster Regt., died on 9th May 1915 and is buried in Ypres Town Cemetery Extension.

2nd Lt. Ivo Pearl Robinson, Lewis Gun officer
2nd Lt. Harry Sedgwick Sever
Capt. Stanley Stanmore Skeats, att. 21st (Empress of India's) Lancers
2nd Lt. Wilfred Richard Thompson
2nd Lt. Charles Stanley Whitworth
2nd Lt. Christopher Other Wright
The casualties amongst the other ranks were initially estimated as:
Killed: 37
Wounded: 209
Missing: 177
Total: 423

132 men of the 1st King's Own Royal Lancaster Regt. are recorded as having been killed or died as a result of wounds received on 1st July 1916 (10 men dying from wounds from the 2nd July onwards). Precise details about the number of men taking into battle by the 1st King's Own Royal Lancaster Regt. do not exist but it is a reasonable assumption that their casualty rate was approximately 63%.

2nd Essex Regt.
Casualties
Killed:
2nd Lt. G A Allen[i]
Lt. T Fraser[ii]
2nd Lt. S C Goodchild[iii]
2nd Lt. A Holmes[iv]
Lt. A M Middleditch[v]
2nd Lt. L G Smith[i]

[i] 2nd Lt. Geoffrey Austin Allen, 2nd Essex Regt., was born in Halstead, Essex, in 1887 and enlisted in the Artists' Rifles before being commissioned into the 2nd Essex Regt. He graduated from St John's College, Cambridge, in 1905. His body was never found and his name is inscribed on the Thiepval Memorial, Pier & Face 10D.
[ii] Lt. Thomas Fraser, 2nd Essex Regt., was never found and his name is inscribed on the Thiepval Memorial, Pier & Face 10D. He is remembered in the parish church of All Saints, Witham, now the [Catholic] Church of the Holy Family and All Saints.
[iii] 2nd Lt. Stanley Cecil Goodchild, 2nd Essex Regt., lived at 3, Cambridge Gardens, Notting Hill. He enlisted as a Private in the Essex Regt., and was commissioned on 15th August 1915. His body was never found and his name is inscribed on the Thiepval Memorial, Pier & Face 10D.
[iv] 2nd Lt. Aubrey Holmes, 2nd Essex Regt., was aged 36. He was the son of the late Benjamin and Alice Holmes of 80, Oakwood Court, London and Llandrindod Wells. Educated at Harrow School and Balliol College, Oxford, (graduated 1898) he was called to the Bar at Lincoln's Inn in 1902. He enlisted as 5859 Private in Queen Victoria's Rifles (London Regt.) in August 1914 going to France in November before being commissioned into the Essex Regt. He is buried in Redan Ridge Cemetery No.1, Beaumont-Hamel, grave A.50. His brother, Lt. Cyril Holmes, Welsh Regt., died at Mudros on 21st December, 1915.
[v] Lt. Archibald Milne Middleditch, 12th att. 2nd Essex Regt., was aged 19. He was the son of Benjamin Bernard Middleditch, solicitor, and Mary Charlotte Milne of 28, Bolton St., Piccadilly, London. Born at Bardwell, Bury St. Edmunds. Educated at Merchant Taylors' and St. Paul's Schools. Worked for Messrs. Morton & Co., Export Merchants. Enlisted in the Artists' Rifles, 10th August 1914. Commissioned into 12th Essex Regt., 3rd December, 1914. Attached to 2nd Essex Regt., October 1915. Three times wounded, his body was found in May 1917. He is buried in Serre Road Cemetery No. 1, grave I. H. 35. His

Capt. B Smith-Masters[ii] 2nd Lt. G Waterhouse
2nd Lt. H R White

Plate 108 2nd Lt. Aubrey Holmes, 2nd Essex Regt.

Wounded:
Lt. Col. Sir George Murray Home Stirling and twelve other officers including:
Lt. Finlison
The casualties amongst the other ranks were initially estimated as:
Killed: 43
Wounded: 167
Missing: 205
Total: 415

---

brother, 2nd Lt. Arnold Warden Middleditch, Oxford and Bucks Light Infantry, died of wounds on the 19th June 1916 and is buried in New Southgate Cemetery, grave H. 1575.

[i] 2nd Lt. Leonard George Smith, B Company, 2nd Essex Regt., was aged 20. He was the eldest son of Alexander and Alice B Smith of 'Verulam', London Rd., Pitsea, Essex. He was educated at Cowper Street School, the City of London School and the Technical School, Southend on Sea. He enlisted in the 13th Middlesex Regt in September 1914 and was commissioned into February 1915. His body was never found and his name is inscribed on the Thiepval Memorial, Pier & Face 10D.

[ii] Capt. Bruce Swinton Smith-Masters, MC, 2nd Essex Regt., was aged 24. He was the third son of the Rev. John Ernest and Eliza Margaret Smith-Masters of Warren Lodge, near Newbury. His father was the vicar of Stewkley. Native of Kidmore End, Oxon. He was educated at Eversley School, Haileybury College, where he was captain of the cricket 2nd XI and rugby 2nd XV, and the RMC, Sandhurst where he played cricket for the college and his regiment. He was commissioned into the Essex Regt., on 14th February 1912 and promoted Temp. Captain on 2nd June 1915. He fought at Le Cateau, on the Marne and the Aisne and at Meteren. Twice wounded, he returned to the front in March 1915 and fought at the 2nd Battle of Ypres. He was awarded the MC in the Birthday Honours of 1916. He is buried in the Sucrerie Military Cemetery, Colincamps, grave I. H. 9. His brother, Lt. George Arthur Smith-Masters, 6th Bedfordshire Regt., died on 18th August 1915 and is buried in Dranoutre Military Cemetery.

161 men of the 2nd Essex Regt. are recorded as having been killed or died as a result of wounds received on 1st July 1916 (10 men dying from wounds from the 2nd July onwards). Precise details about the number of men taking into battle by the 2nd Essex Regt. do not exist but it is a reasonable assumption that their casualty rate was approximately 60%.

2nd Duke of Wellington's (West Riding) Regt.
Casualties
Officers
Killed:
2nd Lt. C H Bowes[i]
Capt. N W Hadwen, OC No. 2 Company
Capt. C L Hart, OC No. 3 Company
Died of wounds:
2nd Lt. J S Millican[ii], 3rd July 1916 2nd Lt. H R Thelwell[iii], 8th July 1916
Wounded:
Lt. Lewis Cochrane Adye
2nd Lt. Donald McKenzie Browne[iv]
2nd Lt. Cyril Walter Gaitskell Grimley
Lt. Arthur Francis Hemming
2nd Lt. George Douglas Johnston
2nd Lt. Stewart Brabayor Kington
Lt. Sydney Riley Lord
Capt. Kenneth James Milln, att. Somerset LI
2nd Lt. Edward Stephen Plumb
Lt. Paul James Sainsbury
2nd Lt. Charles Rupert Sanderson
Shell shock:
2nd Lt. Joseph Aspinall Linton Brooke
The casualties amongst the other ranks were initially estimated as:
Killed: 18

[i] 2nd Lt. Cyril Hulme Bowes, 2nd Duke of Wellington's (West Riding) Regt., was aged 24. He was the only son of George Henry Poynter Bowes and Lilian Bowes (née Briggs). He had been commissioned on 18th April 1916 having previously been a sergeant in a Service battalion. He is buried in Serre Road Cemetery No. 2, grave II. B. 15.

[ii] 2nd Lt. John Stanley Millican, 2nd Duke of Wellington's (West Riding) Regt., was aged 23. He was the son of Thomas and Katherine Millican of 'Holcombe', Ellesmere Park, Eccles, Manchester. He is buried in Beauval Communal Cemetery, grave A. 10.

[iii] 2nd Lt. Harry Rowland Thelwell, 2nd Duke of Wellington's (West Riding) Regt., died of wounds on 8th July 1916. Aged 23, he was the only son of the late George Thelwell and Mrs Thelwell of Commercial Street, Leeds. He was educated at St Cuthbert's College, Worksop. A pre-war territorial in the 1/9th Queen Victoria's Rifles (London Reg.), he went to France in October 1914 fighting at Hill 60 where he was wounded. He was commissioned into the Duke of Wellington's Regt. on 27th March 1915. He is buried in Etaples Military Cemetery, grave I. A. 34.

[iv] 2nd Lt. Donald McKenzie Brown, 2nd Duke of Wellington's (West Riding) Regt., enlisted as 2246 in the 9th Royal Scots and was commissioned into the Dukes on 23rd November 1915.

Wounded: 251

Missing: 40

Total: 309

67 men of the 2nd Duke of Wellington's (West Riding) Regt. are recorded as having been killed or died as a result of wounds received on 1st July 1916 (two officers and 12 men dying from wounds from the 2nd July onwards). Precise details about the number of men taking into battle by the 2nd Duke of Wellington's (West Riding) Regt. do not exist but it is a reasonable assumption that their casualty rate was approximately 45%.

2nd Lancashire Fusiliers

Strength 24 officers and 611 other ranks

Casualties

Officers

Killed:

2nd Lt. B Farrow — Capt. M P Gamon, Intelligence Officer[i]

2nd Lt. H C Kenion[ii] — 2nd Lt. R S MacIver

2nd Lt. C D Roberton, Signalling Officer — Capt. H W Sayres

Missing:

2nd Lt. Alfred Valentine Davies, prisoner of war

Wounded:

2nd Lt. J Anderson

Lt. Geoffrey Grenside Bowen[iii]

Capt. John Collis-Browne

2nd Lt. Cornelius Gregory

Lt. Alan David W MacDonald, Lewis Gun officer

2nd Lt. Harold Ravenscroft

2nd Lt. Charles Leslie Rougier

Capt. George Macdonald Scott[i], RAMC

---

[i] Capt. Maurice Partridge Gamon, 3rd att. 2nd Lancashire Fusiliers, was the founder and Scoutmaster of the Wellington Troop based in Lambeth and Assistant Commissioner for Scouts, South London. He was educated at King's School, Canterbury, and in Germany. He was a member of the South London Harriers. He originally joined the Honourable Artillery Company with which he had served pre-war before being commissioned into the Lancashire Fusiliers. He was married with one son. He was badly gassed at the 2nd Battle of Ypres. He was married to Ethel Elizabeth Gamon and they lived at Cossington, Leicestershire. Their son, also Maurice Partridge Gamon, was born on 2nd March 1916. A lieutenant on the cruiser *HMS Ajax*, he was killed on 12th October 1940 at the Battle of Cape Passero. He also fought at the Battle of the River Plate. His father is buried in Serre Road Cemetery No. 2, grave I. E. 35.

[ii] 2nd Lt. Hugh Cyril 'Nipper' Kenion, 2nd Lancashire Fusiliers, was aged 32. The fifth son of J H Kenion of Liverpool, he was educated at Charterhouse. He was a clerk at Messrs Harwood, Banner & Sons, chartered accountants and lived at The Rosslands, Rock Ferry, Cheshire. He was previously a Sergeant in A Squadron, King Edward's Horse. He was commissioned into the Lancashire Fusiliers on 4th April 1916. He is buried in Serre Road Cemetery No. 1, grave VIII. A. 6.

[iii] Capt. Geoffrey Grenside Bowen, MC, 2nd Lancashire Fusiliers, died on 2nd September 1918. He is buried in Windmill British Cemetery, Monchy le Preux.

2nd Lt. M T Williams
Other Ranks
Killed 24
Wounded 273
Died from wounds 7
Missing 48
Total: 352

84 men of the 2nd Lancashire Fusiliers are recorded as having been killed or died as a result of wounds received on 1st July 1916 (one officer and 12 men dying from wounds from the 2nd July onwards). The casualty rate of the 2nd Lancashire Fusiliers was 58%. Seven officers came through the fighting unscathed: the Adjutant, Lt. G C Martin, Capt. W D P Mansell, Capt. L B L Seckham, 2nd Lt. C P Ranger, 2nd Lt. J W Watkins, 2nd Lt. J Riley and 2nd Lt. W F Hall. All went on to survive the war.

Plate 109 2nd Lt. Geoffrey Grenside Bowen, 2nd Lancashire Fusiliers

THE PICTURE ON THE OTHER SIDE OF NO MAN'S LAND was sharply different. The regimental history of the RIR 121 paints a graphic picture of the devastation caused by the heavy fighting in and around the Heidenkopf. Its details of casualties, moreover, underline just how one-sided the contest had been and how feeble had been the effect of the seven day bombardment on the Germans safe in their dugouts:.

---

[i] Capt. George Macdonald Scott, RAMC, was awarded the MC for his conduct on 1st July 1916. The citation in the *London Gazette* of 22nd September 1916 reads:
"For conspicuous gallantry and devotion to duty in tending the wounded in No Man's Land under heavy artillery and machine gun fire. Finally he carried in a wounded officer on his back but collapsed from his efforts. When he recovered he insisted on returning at once to duty and continued dressing the wounded between the lines till he was knocked over by a hsell and incapacitated."

"Already during the fighting on the 1st of July a number of prisoners had been taken and when on the 2nd of July the dugouts of the recaptured position were searched, still another quantity of Englishmen were found inside one or more. There were also still men in the shell holes close in front of the position, so that the overall number of prisoners amounted to 200. Also a number of our men, who were already in English captivity, were released. However, what does it look like in the Heidenkopf? Body next to body, and at individual positions whole piles of Germans and Englishmen under each other, not to mention the mass of weapons and material lying around. A horrible picture of destruction. Approximately 150 German dead lay in the comparatively small area of the Heidenkopf and approximately triple that number of Englishmen. Altogether the regimental losses were:

24th to 30th June: 24 dead, 122 wounded, 1 missing;

1st to 10th July: 179 dead, 291 wounded, 70 missing, most of them on the 1st of July.

Among these were the following officers:

Killed: 1st July – Leutnant der Reserve Hans Lutz[i] (2. Kompanie), Lt. der Landwehr Kurt Seidel[ii] (3. Kompanie), Lt. de Res. Max Freiherr von Gaisberg-Schöckingen[iii] (3. Kompanie), Lt. de Res. Emil Bauer (3. Kompanie), Lt. de Res. Erich Rapp[iv] (4. Kompanie), Offizierstellvertreter Michael Stadelmaier[v] (4. Kompanie), Lt. de Res. Siegfried Schlößer[vi] (5. Kompanie).

Wounded: Leutnant der Reserve Karl Dobler[vii] (1. Kompanie), Oberleutnant der Reserve Karl Weiger (2. Kompanie), Oberleutnant Max Lutz (slightly wounded, 3. Kompanie), Lt. d R Theodor Förster[viii] (slightly wounded, 6. Kompanie), Lt. d R Erwin Schwaderer (severely wounded, 7. Kompanie), Offizierstellvertreters Jäger and Heinrich Häusler[ix] (slightly wounded, 11. Kompanie), Lt. d R Friedrich Scheu (slightly wounded, 12. Kompanie), Hauptmann der Landwehr Hans Bösenberg[x] (slightly wounded, 12. Kompanie), Lt. der Reserve Bühler (Reserve Maschinengewehr Kompanien RIR 121).

---

[i] Leutnant der Reserve Hans Lutz came from Bissingen.

[ii] Leutnant der Landwehr Kurt Seidel, RIR 121, is buried in the Kriegsgräberstätte in Fricourt, Block 1 Grave 54. He came from Möckmühl near the town of Neckarsulm.

[iii] Leutnant der Reserve Max Freiherr von Gaisberg-Schöckingen came from Leonberg near Stuttgart and was one of four members of the family to become casualties.

[iv] Leutnant der Reserve Erich Rapp, RIR 121, is buried in the Kriegsgräberstätte in Fricourt, Block 4 Grave 101. He came from Ulm.

[v] Offizierstellvertreter Michael Stadelmaier, RIR 121, came from Gmünd and is buried in the Kriegsgräberstätte in Fricourt, Block 1 Grave 139.

[vi] Leutnant Siegfried Schlößer came from Jena.

[vii] Lt. d R Karl Dobler came from Pflugfelden, Ludwigsburg.

[viii] Lt. d R Theodor Förster came from Vaihringen.

[ix] Offizierstellvertreter Heinrich Häusler came from Unterjettingen near Herrenberg.

[x] Hauptmann der Landwehr Hans Bösenberg from Hamburg was attached to the 12. Kompanie from Reserve Feldartillerie Regiment Nr. 26.

1,200 dead Englishmen were counted in and in front of the position of the I Battalion, 576 in front of the sector of the II Battalion. 28 machine guns, 4 mine throwers (i.e. Stokes mortars), and a great deal of material: arms, ammunition, entrenching tools, signal and telephone apparatus were captured. The Englishmen had been splendidly equipped. The prisoners made an excellent impression, large strong, well maintained people. Each man had his shaving things with him and one was occupied with shaving during his capture in the dugout, so important was the thing to him."

With data taken from the Verlustlisten for the RIR 121 it is possible to see how savage the fighting was that involved the I Bataillon, RIR 121 in particular. 53% of all casualties came from this battalion and 32% alone from the units defending the Heidenkopf, the 2. and 3. Kompanien. In addition, all bar one of the 27 Prisoners of War lost by the regiment came from these two units[i]. What is notable is that 38% of all casualties were either killed or died of wounds, a significantly high proportion and suggestive of extremely hard and vicious fighting. Deaths from wounds extended over several weeks with the last listed man to succumb to wounds attributable to the fighting on the 1st July being Musketier August Öhler, 11. Kompanie, who died on 30th July.

Kompanie	Killed	Died of wounds	Severely wounded	Slightly wounded	PoW	Total
I Bataillon						
1. Kompanie	26	4	1	47	0	78
2. Kompanie	41	2	12	54	9	118
3. Kompanie	53	4	9	44	18	128
4. Kompanie	34	3	2	46	0	85
Total	154	13	24	191	27	409
II Bataillon						
5. Kompanie	12	6	9	23	0	50
6. Kompanie	9	1	1	24	0	35
7. Kompanie	13	6	5	21	0	45
8. Kompanie	4	1	2	6	0	13
Total	38	14	17	74	0	143
III Bataillon						
9. Kompanie	5	3	3	12	0	23
10. Kompanie	9	1	1	9	0	20
11. Kompanie	13	3	11	11	0	38
12. Kompanie	7	0	2	20	0	29
Total	34	7	17	52	0	110
Res MGK.	8	1	8	10	0	27
Minenwerfer K. 226	14	0	7	12	0	33
Reserve Sanitäts K. 26	3	0	0	5	0	8
4. Pionier Coy /13 Pionier Bn	10	0	10	19	1	40
Total	261	35	83	363	28	770

Table 17 Casualties by Company, RIR 121

[i] The other PoW, Pionier Anton Deutinger, 4. Pionier Kompanie, 13. Pionier Bataillon, was, presumably one of the group ordered to blow the mines in the Heidenkopf.

The next ten days were spent collecting the bodies of the dead of both Armies. German soldiers were buried in a mass grave behind the Feste Soden which lay due east of the Heidenkopf in the Zwischen Stellung. According to the regimental history of RIR 121 a large birch wood cross stood over this grave of some 150 bodies. The remains of some of the British troops collected were buried in a special grave nearby. Others were buried where they fell within the German lines. The heat and moisture of the erratic July weather contributed to the decomposition of the corpses littering the area and the smell of corruption poisoned the air until all the dead that could be reached safely were below ground. Those hundreds of bodies out in No Man's Land, however, could not be collected for burial and the stench of decay would hang over the battlefield until the flesh had rotted and only skeletons remained.

ACROSS THE ENTIRE FRONT OF THE 4TH DIVISION the priority was now the finding, treating and evacuation of the wounded. The dead would be dealt with when and where possible, otherwise they must lie out in No Man's Land, a gloomy, festering reminder of the day's failures.

Everywhere there were stories of the bravery of ordinary man from every battalion who went out to tend to and bring in the wounded.

The wounded were scattered on both sides of the British front line but, wherever they were, men risked death and injury to go out to them. The response to a man helping the wounded after the fighting had stopped drew a varied response from the Germans. Sometimes they were left to attend to their missions of mercy, at other times they immediately drew fire. It didn't just depend on the temper of the men in Field Grey. All too often, quiet periods in which medical orderlies and MOs were able to tend to the wounded, were followed by British strafes of the German trenches. An irritable response was, therefore, not surprising. But, whatever the mood of the men opposite, climbing out of a trench, exposed to sniper or shell, was an act of the greatest courage – and many ordinary soldiers did just that. Those few that we know of deserve their names and acts recorded:

7909 Acting Lance Sgt. Frederick Bone[i], 1st Hampshire Regt. He was in charge of the battalion stretcher bearers and organised the clearing of the front line trench under four hours of heavy shelling. He also went out and brought wounded men in from the open. He was awarded the Distinguished Conduct Medal.

17442 Pte. Harry Pidgeley[ii], 1st Hampshire Regt. He collected wounded men under very heavy fire and set an excellent example to all around him. He was awarded the Distinguished Conduct Medal.

---

[i] 7909 Actg. L/Sgt. Frederick William Bone was awarded a DCM for his conduct on and after 1st July 1916. The citation in the *London Gazette* of 22nd September 1916 reads: "For conspicuous bravery and devotion to duty when in charge of stretcher-bearers. For nearly four hours he continued at his duties under very heavy shell fire. On numerous occasions he went out to rescue wounded. He successfully organised parties to clear the front-line trenches of wounded".

[ii] 17442 Pte Harry Pidgeley, 1st Hampshire Regt., was awarded the DCM for his conduct on and after 1st July 1916. The citation in the *London Gazette* of 22nd September 1916 reads:

14262 Pte. Sidney J Mildenhall[i], 1st Hampshire Regt., who was constantly out in No Man's Land bandaging and helping wounded men. He was awarded the Military Medal.

Ptes Barton, Morgan and Parkinson, all of the 1st Hampshire Regt., who displayed great devotion to duty when out in No Man's Land at night collecting the wounded. They were all awarded the Military Medal.

6583 Pte. Edward J Brightmore[ii], 1st East Lancashire Regt., who treated men in No Man's Land as the fighting went on around him. He was awarded the Military Medal.

8198 Pte. Albert Greenwood[iii] and 82231 Pte. Frank Coker[iv], both of the 12th Field Ambulance, killed carrying the wounded and Ptes Woodcock, Gingell, Poulton, Engleberg, Pull, Harvey, Richardson, Franklin and Hampson, also 12th Field Ambulance, wounded whilst doing their duty.

20192 Pte. Frederick Fensome[v], MM, C Section Bearer Sub Division, 10th Field Ambulance, who was dangerously wounded while on duty in the trenches and died later of wounds to the head.

78338 Pte. William Bowden, 11th Field Ambulance, wounded while doing his duty.

Capt. George Allman Bridge, 11th Field Ambulance, who was temporarily attached to the 2nd Essex Regt. after their MO was wounded and went repeatedly out into No Man's Land to bring in the wounded amongst whom was Lt. Col. Franklin of the 1/6th Warwickshires.

THE MAIN MEDICAL SERVICES WERE PROVIDED by the Division's three Field Ambulances: the 10th, 11th and 12th FA. Their efforts were supplement by those of the 48th Division, in particular the 1/3rd South Midland Field Ambulance.

"For conspicuous bravery and devotion to duty in collecting wounded men under very heavy fire. His inspiring conduct and devotion to duty were invaluable".

[i] The award of the MM to 14262 Pte Sidney J Mildenhall, 1st Hampshire Regt., was posthumously gazetted on 8th December 1916. 14262 Pte Sidney James Mildenhall, MM, was killed on 18th October 1916. Aged 19, he was the son of Mr J T and Mrs E J Mildenhall of Brimpton Common Farm, Reading, Berks. His body was never found and his name is inscribed on the Thiepval Memorial, Pier & Face 7 C & 7 B.

[ii] 6583 Pte Edward James Brightmore, MM, 1st East Lancashire Regt., was awarded the MM in the *London Gazette* of 21st September 1916. Brightmore lived in Burnley and his three brothers also served. One 8268 Pte Sydney Brightmore, 6th East Lancashire Regt., was killed in Mesopotamia in April 1917.

[iii] 8198 Pte Albert Greenwood, 12th Field Ambulance RAMC, was aged 19. He was the son of Joseph and Sarah A Greenwood of Burnley, Lancs. He is buried in Bertrancourt Military Cemetery, Plot 1. Row G. Grave 19.

[iv] 82231 Pte Frank Coker, 12th Field Ambulance, RAMC, was aged 25. He was the son of William Vince Coker and Mary Coker of Droitwich, Worcestershire. He is buried in Bertrancourt Military Cemetery, Plot 1. Row H. Grave 9.

[v] 20192 Pte Frederick Fensome, MM, 10th Field Ambulance, RAMC, was aged 23. He was the son of George and Sarah Fensome of Bedford; husband of Gladys Mary Fensome of 36, Park Road West, Bedford. He is buried in Bertrancourt Military Cemetery, Plot 1. Row G. Grave 20. Pte Fensome's award of the Military Medal appeared in the *London Gazette*, 3rd June 1916.

The 'front line' medical services were provided by the 12th Field Ambulance which had the responsibility of constructing the forward medical facilities and then of manning them on the day of the attack. The Field Ambulance had established a network of dugouts through which casualties could be filtered. There were Collecting Posts in dugouts at the Sucrerie, Bordon and Cheeroh Trenches and Stirling Street and Tenderloin; dugouts in the Sucrerie to Auchonvillers Road and Tenderloin Street; with the Advanced Dressing Stations at the Red House and in Mailly Maillet; and the Main Dressing Station at Bertancourt. Further to the rear the Divisional Collecting Station for lightly wounded was at Beaussart and was manned by the 10th Field Ambulance and from there, such men would go to the rest centre or onto a Casualty Clearing Station if further treatment was required. The bearer and tent sub-divisions of the 11th Field Ambulance were to be used as required and, as it turned out, the bearers spent most of the day of the attack and afterwards in the front line areas supporting directly their colleagues of the 12th Field Ambulance. The rest of the 11th FA manned the Divisional Rest Station at Vauchelles. Their last unit, 3a Sanitary Section, helped out at Bertrancourt or were to be used as required.

Work was still going on preparing these various positions until just before the bombardment started with the CO of 12th Field Ambulance, Lt. Col. F G Fitzgerald, spending hours of each day liaising with everyone from the Royal Engineers who were to put bursting layers[i] over the dugouts to the Trench Railway Officer who agreed to let him have eight trollies with which to evacuate the wounded from near the front line. Four of these trollies were planned for Tenderloin and the others for Vallade Trench. He also arranged with the OC, 3a Sanitary Section to have some of this unit's men available to help unload the ambulances at the ADS.

When the bombardment started, these facilities were soon in use with the first large batch of patients on 25th June containing 22 men accidentally gassed in the front line the night before. Those that needed to be evacuated from the MDS at Mailly were carried by the motor transport of No. 20 Motor Ambulance Convoy. The following night's patients were predominantly men again accidentally gassed, this time 28 out of a total of 32. Lt. Col. Fitzgerald spent the day moving his men into position, visiting both the Main and Advanced Dressing Stations and greeting two new MOs temporarily attached to the Field Ambulance.

The problem with accidental gassing occurred again on the 27th June (this really did seem to cause the 4th Division more trouble than it did the Germans) and, again, the day was spent tweaking dispositions of bearers and medical orderlies as well as ensuring that the trench trollies were in place.

The casualty evacuation process Fitzgerald had in place was as follows. A and C Bearer Sub-divisions were to be placed in Tenderloin the night before the attack. After the attack started C Bearers were to collect the wounded from between the front line and Tenderloin. A Bearer Sub-division was to go forward and their task was to bring in casualties from the between the British front line and the, by now, captured 1st objective. All of these casualties were to be returned to the British front line where C Sub-division would take over. The evacuation

[i] A system of earth, timber and other materials designed to absorb and reduce the impact of an HE shell.

routes were down Fox Street and Tournai Trench on the right of the Divisional front and down 5th Avenue on the left. Fitzgerald had divided his remaining men as below:

B Bearer Sub-division evacuating men from the front line to the Collecting Post in Stirling Street;

One squad in the Cheeroh Collecting Post;

An NCO, one squad RAMC and one squad from the Divisional Reserve Company in the Stirling Street Collecting Post;

An NCO and one squad RAMC and one squad Divisional Reserve Company in the CP at the Sucrerie;

An NCO and one squad RAMC and one squad Divisional Reserve Company in the CP at Tenderloin;

One squad Sanitary Section and one squad Divisional Reserve Company at the Collecting Post in the Sunken Lane (Sucrerie to Auchonvillers Road);

Five squads Divisional Reserve Company in a dugout at Point 160

The MDS at Mailly and the ADS at the Red House were both to be run by C Tent Sub-division (with B Bearer Sub-division from the 11th Field Ambulance in attendance from 30th June onwards);

The Field Ambulance's wheeled stretchers as well as five on loan from the 10th and 11th Field Ambulances were split between the Sucrerie and Sunken Lane CPs.

The 28th June saw another large group of accidentally gassed men, some 50 according to the 12th FA's war diary, but mild ones this time, and the men were sent off to 11th Field Ambulance for a couple of days to recover. Fitzgerald, however, had another concern. Several batteries of 18 pdrs were firing from positions to the west of the Sucrerie to Auchonvillers road and the very low trajectory of their shells as they crossed the lane was a worry to the Colonel. One of his staff, Capt. Gray, was sent off to chat with the battery commanders in an effort to find out just how safe road traffic was in this area.

Over the next two days other roads loomed large in Fitzgerald's thinking. The evacuation route from Mailly Maillet to Courcelles was along a well-used road which the constant traffic and the heavy rain had made nearly impassable to a loaded ambulance. He contacted the CRE and got permission to use some road metalling materials to repair it. A team from the Field Ambulance was then sent off to do the work. As a backup to this move, he also asked Corps for permission to send ambulances carrying badly injured men along the better quality Mailly to Beaussart Road.

His bearer sub-divisions started to move into their battle positions at 3 p.m. on 30th June in the order C, B and A. They were commanded by Capt. Albert Edward Quine, Capt. James Rafter[i] and Capt. Esler respectively. From this point,

[i] Capt., later Maj., James Rafter, MC, Royal Army Medical Corps, died on 5th October 1919. Aged 32, he was the son of Dr. John Rafter, L.R.C.P.S.I., and Mary Mortelle of 338, Stanley Rd., Bootle. His father was the first Roman Catholic Mayor of Bootle. He was a graduate of Liverpool University and worked at the Liverpool David Lewis Northern Hospital. A doctor on the cruise ship *Mauretania*, he died from heart failure related to Trench Fever in St.Vincent's Hospital, New York City, and is buried in Liverpool (Ford) Roman Catholic Cemetery, grave F.739. He was awarded his MC in October, 1917.

Fitzgerald's previously detailed entries in the war diary are reduced to brief edited highlights:

> "1st July
> Have been evacuating since 7.30 a.m. Ran cars up to Sucrerie all the time and wheeled stretchers up sunken road. Ran the cars in relays one at a time to Sucrerie. Got all cars of 10th and 11th Field Ambulances. Went up to Bordon and brought Capt. Lipp, 11th Field Ambulance, and bearer sub-division at 1 a.m. Got 100 men of West Yorkshires (Pioneers) to help carry wounded. Sent 20 squads to work on left sector and five to work on right."[50]

This brief account hints at the growing pressure on the medical services as the 4th Division's casualties started to flood in. Such were the numbers of wounded that A and C Bearer Sub-divisions from the 11th Field Ambulance were sent up to the MDS and ADS respectively. With casualties amongst the regimental MOs leaving vacancies in the front line two officers were despatched as replacements. Capt. Raymond William Ryan was sent to the 1st King's Own and Capt. George Allman Bridge to the 2nd Essex. Bridge was to have an eventful day.

Capt., later Col., George Allman Bridge was a 26 year old Irishman from Roscrea in Co. Tipperary. To get to the battalion, Bridge moved up to the front via the Sucrerie and along a communication trench towards the fighting. By the time he arrived the front line trenches were clogged with wounded who had crawled in from No Man's Land and the areas behind the British front line. Bridge set to treating and clearing the wounded using whichever stretcher bearers happened to be nearby. It soon became clear that medical help was needed across in the German lines and Bridge made his way into the Heidenkopf, probably by means of the area of defiladed ground by its western tip. He decided to check the various dugouts to see whether any wounded needed his assistance by the simple expedient of shouting down the stairs. At one, he received a reply. The account of his actions was later written by his daughter and lodged with the Liddle Collection at Leeds University:

> "He walked along a trench which had been made by the Germans and called into a deep dugout below 'is there anyone there?' and a rather depressed voice from the colonel of one of the Warwickshire regiments (NB Lt. Col. Franklin, 1/6th R Warwicks) called out and he said 'My medical officer is here but no bearer has come here'. Father went on as the MO was there but later, passing the same place, the voice still feebly said that the bearers hadn't come to which (Bridge) replied that no one would come unless the MO went out and called them. The colonel was a very big, tall man and the steps from the dugout were very steep. They got him on to a stretcher and pulled him up and the bearers tried to get him up with little success until a gallant little man got under the stretcher and took some of the weight and then they were able to get him out. The MO was overcome. They had never seen anything like it before. I believe my father said that the colonel had a thigh wound.
> That evening and things were a bit clearer, (Bridge) found the HQ of the Essex Regt. and reported to the Adjutant and then went out to collect more wounded and get them back. He did this two or three times.

Eventually the Adjutant told him he should lie down. Later the Adjutant, Maj. Maitland, asked him what he had gone out for and he told him that he had gone out again after lying down and had been brought back by two of his bearers."[51]

Capt., later Col., Bridge was awarded the MC in 1918 and went on to serve in WW2. He died in 1983.

The war diary of Lt. Col. D M O'Callaghan, Assistant Director Medical Services (ADMS), 4th Division, reveals a more detailed picture of a break down in the system as it became completely overloaded by the dreadful numbers of wounded men being brought in:

"The evacuation of casualties was extremely difficult in the first place over No Man's Land and then in our crowded and partly demolished communication trenches. Another difficulty was that regimental stretcher bearers dumped wounded in places other than the collecting points that had been arranged, with the result that the casualties there swelled in numbers till someone discovered them and phoned or wired into ADMS when orders were phoned out for stretcher bearers to proceed to the places indicated and clear the casualties. A lot of casualties and also some of our own personnel were kept lying in No Man's Land during the afternoon unable to move on account of hostile machine gun fire. The casualties became so numerous that we had to ask the Division to help us and they gave us 100 Pioneers to whom we issued stretchers and these men brought a certain number in to the main collecting posts and thence on to the ADS. Also we had 40 men from the Divisional Reserve Company and 20 men from 3a Sanitary Section. Our shortage of MOs embarrassed us very much. Before the action started we had to detach 2 MOs from F(ield) Ambulances for duty at CCS so we started 2 short. In a very short time we had to replace 4 casualties amongst regimental MOs[i]. The Divisional Collecting Station worked very well and evacuated a great number by making them walk to Acheux to the Corps Collecting Station and sending sitting cases in horse ambulances and GS wagons. At one time there was a block in Main Dressing of 12th FA owing to the shortage of MOs as the cases were arriving faster than they could be dressed. The two main collecting posts and the ADS were under fire all day and it was not advisable to allow cases to collect in any number in any of these places which explains the large number of cases that arrived at the MDS that had to be dressed and get their anti-tetanus serum. We then got extra help for the MDS and this matter righted itself and then blocked again as the cases were being attended to faster that the Convoy could evacuate. 20 ambulances were pouring in patients and only 4 were available for evacuating stretcher cases to Acheux. The DDMS was notified and promised 4 extra ambulance cars from the Convoy. He also gave us a motor bus to use for sitting cases.

[i] The MOs of the Seaforths, 2nd Essex, 1st East Lancashires and 1/8th Royal Warwicks were all wounded during the day. That of the 1/8th Warwicks was replaced by Lt. Fairley from the 1/3rd South Midland Field Ambulance.

> Just before midnight orders came from the DDMS that the Corps Collecting Station was full and that no more cases were to be sent there. The OCs FA concerned were notified and extra ambulances again asked for from DDMS as the round the cars will have to go to the CCS will take much longer than that to Acheux and consequently delay the evacuation."[52]

The first walking wounded arrived at the Divisional Collecting Station at Beaussart at 9 a.m. Late in the morning 10th Field Ambulance sent off a Capt. Darlington to replace the wounded MO of the Seaforths but otherwise the feeding and treatment of the growing crowd at the DCS was going smoothly. At 1.15 p.m. the atmosphere changed when the 2-300 men resting before carrying on to the Corps Collecting Station at Acheux were suddenly shelled by a German long range battery. Thankfully no further injuries were caused from this strafe nor from another later in the afternoon. In the 12 hours from the first arrival to 9.15 p.m. seven officers and 1,130 other ranks were treated, fed and evacuated through the DCS.

During the early hours of 2nd July it became apparent that large numbers of wounded men were lying unattended in various trenches and Lt. Col. O'Callaghan had to phone both the ADS at the Red House and the Collecting Post in Tenderloin to ask them to send all available stretcher bearers out the Freddy Street, Chatham Street and Minden Street which were all clogged with casualties. He then got the AA+QMG to release an officer and forty men of the Pioneers to act as bearers between Tenderloin and the ADS via the sunken road because every stretcher bearer of the 12th Field Ambulance was out collecting men from the trenches and No Man's Land.

The problem with regimental stretcher bearers dumping the wounded in the first bit of trench they came to was still an issue and at 2.55 a.m. on Sunday, the ADMS was forced to call 10th Brigade's HQ with an instruction that casualties should be taken to the recognised Collecting Posts and not left lying around willy-nilly.

At 5.10 a.m. O'Callaghan was on the blower to Corps, this time asking for more motor vehicles to help clear the clogged up MDS and ADS of 12th Field Ambulance. Ten minutes later the MO of the 1st Rifle Brigade called him. He needed more stretcher bearer squads as his own could not deal with the numbers.

With the withdrawal of the Royal Irish Fusiliers from the Heidenkopf by late morning the exchanges of fire died away. The work of the men of the RAMC, however, continued at the same level of intensity as O'Callaghan's diary entry confirms:

> "This was a very quiet day as far as hostilities on the Divisional front were concerned but an extraordinary hard day for stretcher bearers. The communication trenches were damaged and clogged with dead and this combined with the lengths of the carries rendered the work slow and very tiring. No Man's Land was being cleared by permission of the enemy and then they started shooting so that had to be stopped till dark when squads went out all along our line and brought in all they could find.
>
> Our bearers tried to clear casualties along the open instead of along communication trenches but shrapnel stopped this. In the evening our

dugout post west of Hyde Park Corner was blown in and the bearers there became casualties. About 5 p.m. the position as far as medical arrangements were concerned was good and only a very few casualties were beyond the ADS and at midnight all cases were in and dressed and awaiting the Convoy to evacuate them.

From 6 a.m. 1st to 6 p.m. 2nd roughly 2000 cases were dressed and evacuated."[53]

Sunday at the Divisional Collecting Station was fairly busy. Throughout the day seven officers and 727 other ranks, one of them a German PoW, were processed and sent onwards which, together with another officer and 102 other ranks admitted overnight, meant some 2,000 cases had been dealt with over the two days. The details of eight of the officers' wounds (they were a mixture of 29th and 4th Division casualties) were recorded in the war diary and give an indication of the nature of the injuries regarded as light enough to be handled by the DCS:

Lt. George Edward Beaumont, 1st Lancashire Fusiliers, gun shot wound face

Capt. George Paterson Nunneley 4th Bedfordshire Regt., att. 1st Lancashires Fusiliers, GSW right arm.

Capt. Cecil Francis Wells, 1st Lancashire Fusiliers, GSW face

2nd Lt. Joseph Aspinall Linton Brooke, 2nd West Riding Regt., shell shock

Lt. H Finlison, 2nd Essex Regt., GSW right arm

2nd Lt. Wilfrid Darley Wynne, 2nd Royal Irish Regt., att. 11th Trench Mortar Battery, GSW right shoulder (slight)

2nd Lt. Charles Leslie Rougier, 2nd Lancashire Fusiliers, GSW right arm

2nd Lt. Henry George Harding, 1st Hampshire Regt., GSW left hand

With its main work done, the DCS was closed early on Monday, 3rd July.

The 3rd July was a quieter day for all concerned. About 100 wounded men were found and evacuated, some having been brought in from No Man's Land. There were others who would remain out there for several days more before either being found or dying the loneliest of deaths. During the day the exhausted bearers of the 12th Field Ambulance were relieved by bearers from the 10th and 11th FAs. The 12th Field Ambulance had dealt with some 2,000 casualties of whom 160 were officers. These cases were predominantly stretcher cases as the walking wounded had been directed the Divisional Collecting Station.

Five more wounded men were brought in from No Man's Land on the night of the 4th/5th July. Some of the men were able to tell their rescuers about others, still alive and as yet undiscovered. Lt. Col. Fitzgerald decided to ask Lambton for permission to send out volunteer officers and men under a Red Cross flag during the daylight hours of the 5th July. The plan was agreed to and, at 4 p.m. the flag was warily raised above the British parapet. An eyewitness account continues:

"When, after a few minutes, no shots were fired, two medical officers (one of them Lieutenant-Colonel Fitzgerald, R.A.M.C.) scrambled on to the parapet on either side of the flag. Still the enemy held their fire, and so, after a short pause, the two officers advanced across No Man's Land with the bearer of the flag moving between them. By this time a mass of curious heads appeared above the parapet of the German trench, and a German officer, wearing the Red Cross brassard and carrying a white handkerchief tied on to a walking-stick, hastily sprang out of their lines

> and advanced across No Man's Land to meet the British party. He was closely followed by several others, all presumably of the medical corps. It was an impressive sight. He waited until our party had come as far as he considered fit, then raised his hand signalling to them to halt. The parties of both sides stiffened to a ceremonious salute, following which he commenced to point out all the British wounded lying close to his lines. A signal from our two medical officers brought forward several stretcher-parties, who at once set about their task. At the same time German parties carried wounded who had been lying close to the parapet of the German trench as far as the middle of No Man's Land, whence they were carried off by the British bearers."

It is not recounted how many men were saved by this simple act of humanity on the part of the RIR 121.

WOUNDED BRITISH PRISONERS OF WAR as well as the casualties of the RIR 121 were initially taken to regimental aid post in the Feste Soden. Here the medical team was led by Oberstabsarzt Dr. Schwarz. During the early part of the day the only men to arrive were the walking wounded who were patched up, given a meal of sausage, bread and coffee and moved on their way to the larger medical facility at Miraumont. The seriously wounded cases started to arrive in the afternoon and more flowed in during the night when the stretcher bearers were able to move more freely around the battered frontal trenches. With the arrival of those sufficiently injured to require more detailed medical intervention the medical dugout quickly ran out of space. A number of men with fatal head injuries were helped out of this world with morphine or chloroform. Those with survivable wounds were retained in the dugout until night fell and they could be sent to rear under cover of darkness. The problem for the stretcher bearers was that it was a long way to the nearest road along which motor and horse ambulances could travel. This was the Miraumont to Beaucourt road and so these badly wounded men, for whom the slightest disturbance was agony, had to be carried along battered communication trenches to the head of the Artillerie Mulde. They were then carried down the shallow valley, past the numerous artillery positions dug in on the reverse slope, until they reached the road. It was a journey of some 3,000 yards. It was not risk free as the death of one and the wounding of two other stretcher bearers testified. Just over 200 wounded were evacuated from the Feste Soden in this manner, a third of them British PoWs. The last wounded British soldier was brought in from No Man's Land on 6th July.

The medical facility at Miraumont was clearly under strain as some of the British PoWs recall being left lying for five or six hours before their wounds were dressed. For those unable to walk they were then conveyed by horse drawn cart to the next port of call which was likely to be the more organised Feld Lazarets at Bapaume or Vélu. Such was the strain at Vélu that British PoWs were kept outdoors in the grounds of a large chateau on poor quality straw while the only two tents were reserved for German wounded. Some men had to put up with these conditions for three days and nights. To make matters worse, it rained heavily on the 3rd July and these men were kept soaked and some without proper clothing until they were moved further to the rear.

The next stop for those needing further treatment was a hospital, almost certainly at Caudry, where a significant number of British casualties were buried. Transport there was by grossly overcrowded ambulance train with the journey lasting many hours. The hospital at Caudry was located in a large converted lace factory and, at this time, there were some 200 British wounded including a dozen officers waiting for treatment. The operating theatres were rudimentary and, with some of the more minor operations being carried out without anaesthetic, the noises coming from behind the screens must have been extremely disturbing to those awaiting their turn. The place appears to have been severely understaffed with Lt. Russell of the Royal Fusiliers who had fought so hard at the mine crater, seeing only two doctors and six nurses to attend to the 400 wounded in their care. The food was also very poor in Russell's opinion. Lt. Frank Brettell of the 1/8th Royal Warwickshire Regt. was kept at Caudry for some eight days during which time he was aware of some thirty men having limbs amputated while three or four British soldiers succumbed to their wounds every day. Brettell was fortunate as, being an officer, he was then shipped off to the Camp Lazaret in the Gütersloh Offiziers-Lager which was regarded as, perhaps, the best Prisoner of War Camp within Germany.

The other main hospitals for men from this part of the front were based at St Quentin, a train journey of some seven hours, and Cambrai. The hospital at St Quentin was based in an old cotton mill and had a capacity of over 1,000. Although the men were regularly and reasonably well fed and the nurses seemed friendly, treatment here could be painfully slow as the large number of German casualties being brought in were, understandably, given priority. This lead to considerable suffering and even the deaths of some men whose relatively minor wounds were allowed to become infected. Pte Gill of the Seaforths recalled a man with a slight knee injury who lost his leg and then his life as a result of being left untreated for days.

At these hospitals the men were allowed to send a postcard home which could not say where they were but did at least carry the message home that the man was alive and as well as could be expected. As all of these PoWs would have been reported as missing and some, undoubtedly, missing believed killed, these simple postcards would have come as an immense relief to the fretful relatives waiting daily for news of their loved ones.

The rest of Russell's, Brettell's, Gill's and several other PoWs' stories can be found in the Appendix: *Prisoners of War.*

ONE SHOULD, PERHAPS, LEAVE THE FINAL WORD about this terrible day on Redan Ridge to the diminutive yet indomitable 2nd Lt. George Glover of the 1st Rifle Brigade who had fought so hard and so long in the Heidenkopf. His words give an insight into the minds of the young men of both sides who had risked and so prodigally sacrificed their lives in a cause one doubts many truly understood.

> "I had the day of my life; and am not exactly hankering for another immediately, though I wouldn't have missed it for anything. The noise was fearful. I found difficulty in making myself heard at a couple of yards part of the time. Well, I got through all right, though I don't know how –

three men were killed beside me and two more bullets came along and made the acquaintance of my tunic, one going through my shirt as well. Once the tension was relaxed I slept like everything. The strange part about it was that I did not feel any physical fear at all, though as the day wore on I developed a loathing at the thought of a head wound (the result of seeing skulls shattered, British and German) and my first sensation on being wounded was of intense surprise that I was wounded. For the men once cannot have anything but the greatest admiration. They were perfectly calm.

Perhaps the most merciful thing about it is that everything is on such a scale that you can't realize it, both the danger and the pain and suffering all around you. One attains a curious stoical courage; as you can't possibly know what will come next, or where, you might just as well go on. But it is absolutely incredible how one can go through such a sweep of bullets and rain of shells and still come out alive. And the strange silent way men put up with such tortures, almost with the dumb fright of wounded animals, is the most touching part of it. You realize how merciful a thing a clean, quick death is, even if it should blot out a fresh young life."[54]

Of the wounded, Glover was equally eloquent:

"The quiet, resigned way they bore fearful wounds was quite wonderful, no groaning or complaining, even if they had to be moved – the most exquisite torture – to allow work to be carried on. Even the mortally wounded looked the fact in the face without a sign. But it was touching to see men whose pals were badly hurt; just for a few moments and then the work had to be done. Of course, one hears these things often, but to see them is the greatest revelation. That has been one of my privileges. There are men of all shades and types of character among them, but the more I have seen, the more I have admired them."[55]

The results of the fighting were felt well beyond the survivors of the attack itself. A month later the officers and men of the 7th (Service) Battalion of the Somerset Light Infantry took over the front line between the Ridge Redoubt and the Heidenkopf. Capt. Henry Arthur Foley and his company were given the task of clearing and repairing the trenches. There was nothing good one could say about this task. Even adding names to bodies in order to given grieving relatives a grave to visit a war's end proved beyond them:

"Our work now was to clear this ghastly shambles and make it once more into the semblance of a trench. In many places earth, tumbled sand bags and bodies were so hopelessly intermingled that any thought of a decent burial were impossible, and we could but hack a way through the deadly nauseating debris. The atmosphere of the place, after the days that had elapsed since the attack, was unutterably vile. It did not do to let oneself think too much in a place like that. These torn fragments of flesh and bone had once been splendid men. And now 'missing' would, after many months, be their epitaph."[56]

[1] NA, WO 95/1466/5, *War Diary 29th Brigade, RFA.*
[2] Ibid.
[3] NA, WO95/1498/1, *War Diary 1st East Lancashire Regt.*
[4] NA, WO95/1482, *War Diary 1st Royal Irish Fusiliers.*
[5] Ibid.
[6] WO 95/1466/5.
[7] NA, WO95/1490, *War Diary 11th Brigade.*
[8] WO 95/1466/5.
[9] *Capt. J Collis-Browne Papers*, IWM.
[10] Ibid.
[11] NA, WO95/1498/1.
[12] *The Hampshire Regt.*
[13] *Princeton Alumni Weekly*, Vol. XVII, pages 41-2.
[14] Op. cit. *Princeton Alumni Weekly.*
[15] NA, CAB 45/132-8, *Comment on the OH by Brigade Major, 11th Brigade.*
[16] *Somme Nord.*
[17] Whitehead, J, *The Other Side of the Wire*, Volume 2, page 81. Helion & Co., 2012.
[18] Op. cit. *Princeton Alumni Weekly.*
[19] Sheldon, J, *The Germans at Beaumont Hamel*, page 87, Pen & Sword Books, 2006.
[20] NA, WO95/1481, *War Diary, 2nd Royal Dublin Fusiliers.*
[21] *New York Times*, 10th September 1916.
[22] *Brig. Gen. W Carden Roe's Papers*, IWM
[23] War Diary, 2nd Lancashire Fusiliers.
[24] Op. cit. *Collis-Browne.*
[25] *De Ruvigny's Roll of Honour*, Volume 3.
[26] From a letter to Mrs Prowse.
[27] NA, WO95/1483, *War Diary, 2nd Seaforth Highlanders.*
[28] NA, WO95/2280.
[29] NA, WO 95/1466/4, *War Diary, 14th Brigade, RFA.*
[30] NA, WO 95/1466/5.
[31] Op. cit. *Princeton Alumni Weekly.*
[32] Ibid.
[33] Ibid.
[34] Ibid.
[35] *Harrow Memorials of the Great War*, Volume III.
[36] NA, WO95/1481.
[37] NA, WO95/1445, *War Diary 4th Division.*
[38] Ibid.
[39] NA, CAB45/137, *Comment on the OH by Capt. G Basil Sleigh.*
[40] Ibid.
[41] Ibid.
[42] Ibid.
[43] NA, CAB45/132, *Comment on the OH by Lt. K R G Browne.*
[44] *De Ruvigny's Roll of Honour*, Volume 2.
[45] Op. cit. *Princeton Alumni Weekly.*
[46] NA, WO95/1483.
[47] NA, WO95/1445.
[48] Ibid.
[49] Source: http://www.blundells.org/archive/in-memoriam/acland_jhd.html
[50] NA, WO 95/1474, *War Diary 12th Field Ambulance.*
[51] *Papers of Lt. Col. F A Bridge*, Liddle Collection, Leeds University.
[52] NA, WO96/1462, *War Diary Assistant Director Medical Services, 4th Division.*

[53] Ibid.
[54] Op. cit. *Princeton Alumni Weekly*.
[55] Ibid.
[56] Moorhouse B, *Forged by Fire: The Battle Tactics and Soldiers of a WWI Battalion, the 7th Somerset Light Infantry*, Spellmount Publishers Ltd., 2002.

9. THE 31ST DIVISION AT SERRE

THE 31ST DIVISION ARRIVED IN THE VIII CORPS' SECTOR at the end of March and were soon taking turns in the front line initially around the Auchonvillers area. It was not until mid-May that the Division took over the front line opposite Serre. Here they found trenches of a very inferior quality overlooked from the German positions in front of the village and flanked to the south by the troublesome Heidenkopf from which a constant stream of trench mortar bombs seemed to emanate. Here they continued their education in the dangers of the trenches, Western Front-style.

The task given to the 31st Division was, for a completely inexperienced unit, particularly complex. It not only involved the taking of anything up to seven lines of German trenches spread over a distance of nearly 4,000 yards, it also involved the entire division performing a half left-wheel about a third of the way to their final objectives. Commenting on the complexity of the 31st Division's scheme in response to the draft of the volume of the Official History describing the attack of the 1st July, Lt. Francis MacAlpine, the signals officer of the 11th East Lancashire Regt., the Accrington Pals, wrote:

> "The attack on 1st July gave the troops employed almost parade ground changes of direction to be carried out during the attack and this would not have been considered for a moment later in the war. The depth of penetration was also very considerable."

This comment highlights the huge problems which the Division had to overcome. Initially, all battalions advanced in line eastwards until they reached the western edge of Serre and the Zwischen Stellung running towards Redan Ridge from the south-east corner of the village. At this point, whilst some of the 93rd Brigade drove due east towards Pendant Copse and the German 2nd Position, the rest of the battalions had to turn half-left in order to advance on the long German communication trench which would form the new northern front of the Division and the Fourth Army. Such manoeuvres in the middle of a battlefield were difficult enough for units with experienced officers and NCOs but the 31st Division had few such men. Even if they were able to take the five lines of trenches to the west of Serre, those battalions tasked with performing the left wheel would need to be under firm control if the change of direction was to be performed successfully. The capacity for chaos was considerable as such a complex scheme would require the Division to be in good order and with sufficient battalion officers and senior NCOs available to direct the troops appropriately. Heavy casualties amongst these ranks in particular and stiff resistance from the enemy had the potential to reduce the Division's advance to a shambles, however, without such an advance, the left wing of the 4th Division would be horribly exposed to German counter attacks and enfilade fire. It was asking an awful lot of a novice Division to perform the twin tasks of successfully completing a complicated battlefield manoeuvre in good order, and at speed, as well as act as the left flank guard of the entire Fourth Army's attack.

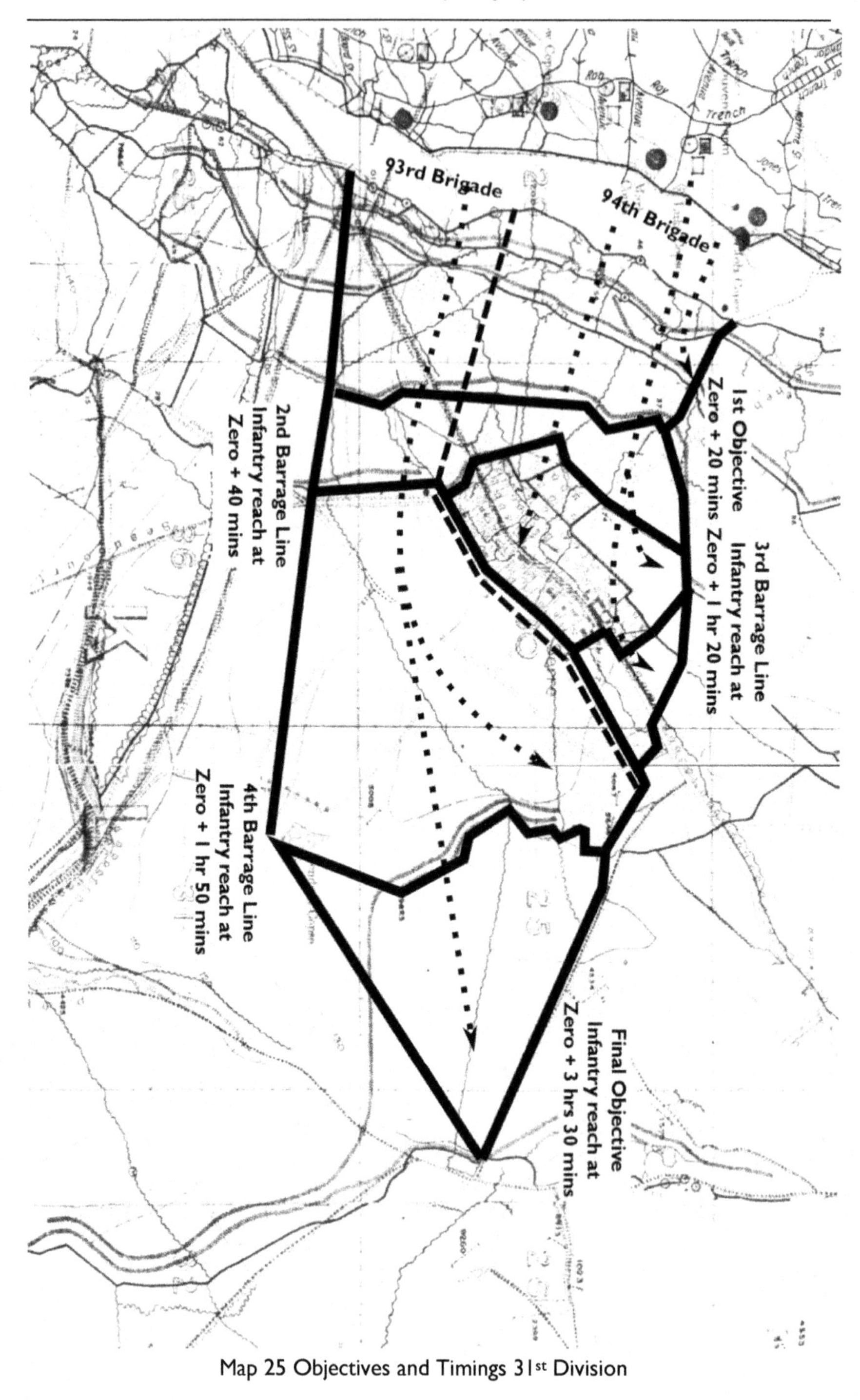

Map 25 Objectives and Timings 31st Division

The timings for the advance of the 31st Division were, to start with, the same as for the 4th and 29th Divisions. The three lead battalions, which were (from north to south) the 12th York and Lancaster Regt. (Sheffield City), 11th East Lancashire Regt. (Accrington Pals) and the 15th West Yorkshire Regt. (Leeds Pals), were to take the first three lines of the German 1st Position and the fourth intermediate line just to the west of Serre in twenty minutes. Ahead of them, the artillery was to 'creep forwards' at a rate of 100 yards every 2 minutes. The infantry had to conform to this speed if they were not to lose contact with their protective barrage. For ten minutes the attacking troops were to reorganise whilst the artillery fired 'occasional bursts' on positions to the east for ten minutes.

At zero + 30 minutes the artillery placed its fire on the northern end of Munich Trench (south from where it met the corner of Serre village) and the trench line running around the western and northwestern fringe of the village (the 2nd Barrage Line in Map 25, page 432). This line was to be shelled for ten minutes at which time, i.e. zero + 40 minutes, the infantry should have arrived to occupy the trench. The village itself was to be the next objective and, to assist the advance of the infantry through the ruins of the tiny hamlet, the field guns would place a barrage across the width of the village and then march up the road towards Puisieux initially at the regulation 100 yards every two minutes. After 200 yards this advance slowed to 100 yards every four minutes. This meant the entire village should have been barraged and occupied in twenty minutes, i.e. by 8.30 a.m.. Not much additional time was to be given for the clearing of any pockets of resistance. These would have to be dealt with troops following on.

There was now another pause for reorganisation and for the rear battalions to advance through the leading ones for the final stages of the advance. At the same time, the artillery placed a ten minute bombardment on certain special points further east. At zero + one hour thirty minutes (9 a.m.) the infantry were to start their advance on their next objective which was to be Pendant Copse and Pendant Trench running north from it. Again, the artillery was to place a barrage 200 yards in front of the troops which was to move forward as a curtain of fire at the required speed of 100 yards for every 2 minutes. After twenty minutes the infantry was to arrive and occupy Pendant Copse and Trench and at this time, zero + one hour fifty minutes (9.20 a.m.), the troops were to reorganise, start consolidating and, on the northern flank, carry on the work of turning the German communication trench which was to be the new northern facing flank of Fourth Army into a fire trench. This work was to be started by the 14th York and Lancaster Regt. which had been given the task of joining the two opposing front lines with a new communication trench across No Man's Land and converting the first stretch of German communication trench from the front line to the first objective into a fire trench.

All being well, the time would be approaching for the final phase of the operation, the advance to the German 2nd Position south of Puisieux. For eighty minutes the artillery fired at targets to the east of Pendant Copse and Trench until, at zero + 3 hours ten minutes (10.40 a.m.), the infantry would start to move forward, preceded as ever by the creeping artillery barrage. Twenty minutes later, at 11 a.m., the infantry's advance would be complete and the artillery were to place a barrage 300 yards north and east of the final objective. At noon, this barrage was to be extended by another 300 yards and would then cease fire 10 minutes later. 'Job done' as they say on those annoying DIY television shows.

As with all of the attacks, success at Serre depended almost wholly on the artillery successfully destroying the garrisons of the German 1st Position and the intermediate line west of Serre. The distraction and, hopefully, destruction of the otherwise unoccupied elements of the troops and machine guns of the IR 66 off the northern flank of the Division's attack would also be key. A smoke screen might help but heavy artillery fire was the key (and was not forthcoming). As everywhere else north of La Boisselle the artillery also had the problem of the preparation of three groups of German trenches and, on 31st Division's front, the village of Serre itself. It would be the task of all of the super-heavy howitzers to flatten the houses and farm buildings and an inordinate amount of time and weight of shell was expended on an area which lay behind the trench lines where sheltered the main elements of the German garrison.

SERRE, THE VILLAGE THEY WERE TO ATTACK, was an uninspiring straggle of houses and farm buildings running north-east/south-west alongside the road from Puisieux to Colincamps. It lies on a slight rise in the ground which, to the west, slopes almost imperceptibly down towards a line of trees which run north to south and which were, in 1916, a string of separate small copses. Then, collectively, they were known as the Gospel Copses and were named Matthew, Mark, Luke and John from south to north. The last three ran immediately behind the British front line trenches (and now form the belt of trees which includes the Accrington Memorial Park). Matthew Copse, at the southern end, no longer exists but was set back from the others being just behind the British support line and opposite the southern end of the village a few hundred yards to the east.

Immediately behind the British front line trenches was a shallow depression along which ran a light railway which helped supply the front line troops. Thus its name – Railway Hollow. This area was, however, prone to flooding and the front line trenches themselves were not robust examples of the trench diggers' 'art'. This line had been established after some very hard fighting by the French 2nd Army in the summer of 1915. Until then, the German front line had run 1,000 yards further to the west in a large semi-circular salient south east of Hebuterne which had taken in all four of the Gospel Copses as well as Toutvent, or Touvent, Farm. In a week's heavy fighting starting on 7th June 1915 the French had forced the Germans back beyond the copses to the line now occupied, but at a cost of over 11,000 casualties. One residue of this assault was the Heidenkopf or Quadrilateral, the small salient projecting from the German lines south west of Serre which was the remains of the old German front line which had run north-west prior to the French attack.

The existence of the Gommecourt salient to the north and what do to neutralise it had occupied Rawlinson's thoughts considerably during the planning stages of the offensive. He had long since concluded that he had neither the men nor the guns to deal with a front extending beyond Serre and it had been left to Haig and Allenby, commander of the neighbouring Third Army, to decide what best to do about this position. Discussions about Gommecourt and the concept of some sort of diversionary attack had been on-going since March. Post war, Allenby's GSO1, Brig. Gen. Louis Bols, CB, DSO, had maintained that Third

Army's preferred locations for a diversion had been first Vimy Ridge and, when it was clear that the troops and artillery required for such an enterprise were not available, the small salient to the north of Gommecourt at Monchy-au-Bois. Bols' argument was that, to succeed as a diversion, the location of any attack had to have some tactical significance to the Germans, which Vimy Ridge undeniably did, and it also needed to be sufficiently far enough away from the main attack that German troops drawn in to defend against the diversion could neither directly interfere with nor quickly reinforce the area being assaulted by Fourth Army. With Vimy a non-starter, Monchy-au-Bois just about fulfilled these requirements and, as a result, Third Army set to planning an attack on this village with GHQ's approval. That still left the troops and guns defending Gommecourt as a problem to be resolved by Haig, Rawlinson and Allenby. This issue, however, was not as pressing as it might first have appeared.

At the end of April, the 52. Division had the task of defending not only the village of Serre but Gommecourt and the trenches further north towards Monchy-au-Bois. As a result, this Division, ironically like the 48th (South Midland) Division then opposite, was stretched very thin by the great length of line it was required to defend. Gommecourt, however, was a strongly fortified position and was also of significance for propaganda purposes as, within Gommecourt Park, lay the most westerly point occupied by the German Army on the Western Front. The oak tree at this point was known as the 'Kaiser's Oak'. Gommecourt, and the area to the north which included Monchy-au-Bois, was also one which the German High Command, OHL, thought likely to be attacked by the British in the event of a major Allied offensive. They were, as a result, very sensitive to any prospect of Gommecourt being attacked and were ready to reinforce the area in a manner which nowhere else on Fourth Army's proposed Somme front might expect.

Haig's belated decision, therefore, to switch the diversion from the Monchy-au-Bois sector to Gommecourt was of great significance, not only for the troops involved but also to their neighbours to the south in the 31st Division. The decision to launch an all-out attack, and one which was required to be obvious in its preparation, is one of Haig's more bizarre decisions. The intention was that it should draw men and guns to the Gommecourt sector which might otherwise have been employed elsewhere on the Somme front. As it was, it drew in a highly experienced unit, the 2. Garde Reserve Division, which had been resting near Cambrai after a stint at Vimy. This was not a unit that might have otherwise been sent further south as it was always in OHL's mind for the reinforcement of the anticipated attack from Gommecourt northwards. Thus, when the preparations for the two Division assault on Gommecourt became apparent, the Division was hurried south to take over the trenches opposite Foncquevillers to the west and Hebuterne to the south of Gommecourt. With them came a greatly enhanced body of artillery with contributions made by 6. Army, XIV Reserve Corps and by other Divisions including the 52. and the 10. Bayerische Division. In addition, with the insertion of the 2. Garde Reserve Division at Gommecourt (a fact not picked up by British Intelligence until the attack itself), not only was the Gommecourt sector heavily reinforced but, as a result of a dramatic 50%+ reduction in the length of the 52. Division's sector, so were the defences around

Serre. The consequence of this was that the combined strengths of the 2. Garde Reserve and 52. Division's artillery provided the heaviest German bombardment on the Somme front on the morning of 1st July 1916, the more so as to the north of Gommecourt, the 111. Division was idle and their Divisional artillery was able to participate in the destruction of the 46th (North Midland) Division, the left wing of the Gommecourt diversion.

By choosing to attack Gommecourt, and by deciding to make the preparations obvious (at his direct request), Haig had ensured that the defences of Serre were greatly enhanced. The 31st Division, in its first ever attack, would be greeted by more artillery and more machine guns than would ever have been the case had the diversion taken place at Vimy or Monchy-au-Bois. By attacking Gommecourt, Haig more or less ensured the failure at Serre and the knock-on effects of this would be felt keenly by the 4th Division at Redan Ridge and further south.

The effect of the insertion of the 2. Garde Reserve Division to the north and south of Gommecourt was to significantly reduce the frontage of the 52. Division such that a new regiment now defended Serre – the 8. Badisches Infanterie Regiment Nr. 169. Previously it had been further to the north in the area now occupied by the regiments of the 2. Garde Reserve Division. On the IR 169's right was the 3. Magdeburgisches Infanterie-Regiment Nr. 66 which occupied the sector opposite the 48th (South Midland) Division. Both of these regiments would be involved in the defence of Serre and both adopted similar formations. Each regimental frontage was split into four sectors, M1-4 on the IR 66's front and S1-4 on the IR 169's front. Their battalions and companies were organised as follows:

IR 66 (opposite 48th Division)
Right sector
III Bataillon
M1 – 11. Kompanie, front and support trenches
M1b – 10. Kompanie, front and support trenches
M2 – 12. Kompanie, front and support trenches
9. Kompanie, reserve trench and Gardegraben
Left sector
I and II Bataillon
M3a – 6. Kompanie, front and support trenches
M3b – 7. Kompanie, front and support trenches
M4 – 5. Kompanie, front and support trenches
8. Kompanie, southern half of reserve trench
3. Kompanie, northern half of reserve trench
2. Kompanie, Zwischen Stellung
1. and 4. Kompanien, in reserve with two machine guns.
IR 169 (opposite 31st Division and extreme left of 4th Division)
Right sector
I Bataillon
S1 – 4. Kompanie, front trench, 1. Kompanie, reserve trench
S2 – 3. Kompanie, front trench, 2. Kompanie, reserve trench
1. Maschinengewehr Kompanie, six guns

Left sector
II Bataillon
S3 – 6. Kompanie, front trench, 8. Kompanie, reserve trench
S4 – 7. Kompanie, front trench. 5. Kompanie, reserve trench
2. Maschinengewehr Kompanie, four guns
III Bataillon
10., 9., 11. and 12 Kompanien, Tübinger Stellung from north to south.

The key units in these two regiments would be the I and II Bataillons, IR 169, defending the first lines trenches in front of Serre and II Bataillon, IR 66, immediately to the north which, apart from British artillery fire, would be free to interfere with the attack of the 31st Division. The III Bataillon would be able to do the same to the right wing of the 56th Division in front of Gommecourt as the decision to leave the front of the 48th Division inactive would leave its neighbours on either flank woefully exposed.

GIVEN THE OPEN NATURE OF NO MAN'S LAND it was decided very early on that, to assist in the advance of the infantry and to provide positions from which machine guns and Stokes mortars might easily barrage the German trenches, tunnels would be excavated from the front line trenches, finishing just short of the German front line trench. Such tunnels, known as Russian saps, were dug on all three Division's fronts and then, for reasons not entirely clear, used only for purposes of housing either Stokes mortars or Lewis guns.

On the 31st Division five tunnels were embarked upon by the 252nd Tunnelling Company at the end of April. They were located as follows (from north to south):

K23 John
K29 Mark
Excema
Grey
Bleneau

A sixth Russian sap would also be dug from the end of Nairne Street immediately to the north of John Copse and this, extended into the German lines, was to form the new northern boundary of the 31st Division, the VIII Corps and the Fourth Army[i].

To assist the Tunnellers, some 1,900 men drawn from the infantry battalions of the VIII Corps were attached. The tunnels, some 30 feet below the surface, progressed rapidly with the miners managing progress of some 15 feet a day. From early on it was thought that these tunnels were to be used as more than just firing positions with the 252nd Tunnelling Company's war diary of 2nd May describing them as 'underground communication tunnels'. By 16th May, these tunnels were all more than 200 feet out under No Man's Land and were progressing well. By the end of the month most of the tunnels were over 400 feet long and were sufficiently close to the German line that silent work had been commenced. This would slow progress but it also helped to ensure that the mines

[i] These saps would also be known as Saps A to F but from south to north, i.e. Bleneau was Sap A and the new Russian Sap on the northern flank was Sap F.

and their occupants would not fall victim to any counter-mining operations mounted by the enemy.

Above ground, huge amounts of work were required by the Royal Engineer Field Companies attached to the 31st Division. The workload of the 210th Field Company alone provides ample testimony to the enormous demands placed on the RE and on the infantry attached to them as working parties. Between the 1st and 29th June, the 210th Field Company performed the following tasks:

- Constructed four ration, ammunition and water dumps;
- Constructed 17 artillery bridges, placed ten in position and carried remainder to suitable dumps for replacement of destroyed bridges;
- Formed RE dump in Observation Wood;
- Constructed eight bomb stores in second trench;
- Constructed six artillery OPs;
- Constructed two Brigade OPs;
- Constructed 35 feet of Russian sap, total length 70 feet. Note: a large proportion of the time occupied on this work was taken up in clearing out the sap after a bombardment;
- Commenced four deep dugouts, reached an average of 20 feet;
- Supplied RE supervision clearing and opening out eight assembly trenches and four communication trenches;
- Construction of four small emplacements. Supplied RE supervision for erection of same in front line;
- Constructed bombardment slit trenches (24) in front line area;
- Two plumbers repairing and supervising water supply for front area;
- Constructed extra entrance to BHQ dugout in Dunmow;
- Construction of Signals dugout in Le Cateau, gallery completed. Further work stopped as working parties could not be spared;
- Supervised cutting and removal of barbed wire in front of Rob Roy, Monk and Campion;
- General supervision and RE assistance in ordinary trench maintenance in area allotted to 210th Field Company;
- Traversed, deepened and revetted Pylon Avenue and Palestine (Yellow line);
- Wells at Bus les Artois: Erection of two engines and pumps, three tanks and four stand pipes. Sinking of wells continued. Depth of each well 130 feet;
- Wells at Warnimont: Improvements and repairs, wire fencing, etc.;
- Couin-Bus water supply. Construction of reservoir at Bus les Artois (near wooden water tank), 20 feet x 18 feet x 6 feet. Laying 4 in. pipeline from this reservoir to 4th Division watering area. Erection of troughs, fittings and connections throughout the 4th Division water supply; and
- Completion of:
  Section room and officers' quarters Divisional School, Bus les Artois;
  Dugout for motor lorry, Courcelles;
  Felling trees, cutting same into suitable lengths, making pickets, etc.[1]

Unfortunately for the Royal Engineers, a lot of the work required was in the making good of the less than robust trenches which the 31st Division had inherited from their previous occupants. Subject to intermittent German bombardments and prey to the vagaries of this particularly unsettled French summer, this work was unrelenting. Overall, the three Royal Engineer companies of the Division dug and repaired 38 miles of trench, excavated and reinforced 86 dugouts in the forward areas and constructed or improved 34 observation posts.

Whilst these preparations were made by the Engineers, the officers and men of the Divisional Field Artillery were also hard at it constructing gun positions, dugouts for both personnel and ammunition, laying communications cable and installing telephone systems, and constructing Observation Posts from which they would judge the effectiveness of their firing. They had been in the area for some time, not having gone to Egypt with the rest of the Division, but had gained something of a reputation for wild shooting, with the diary of the 1/8th Worcestershire Regt. (48th (South Midland) Division) recording that some of their casualties had been caused by the shells of the 31st Division's field guns falling short. It was suggested that the quality of the US-manufactured shells also may have had something to do with it. Overall, however, there were some concerns about the experience and expertise of the Division's gunners.

It was not only the gun teams manning the 18 pdrs and 4.5 in howitzers who were digging for all they were worth. Much further forward and, therefore, much more vulnerable to enemy action, were the men of the Divisional Trench mortar batteries. Six batteries were, or rather should have been, available to the Division for the purposes of wire cutting and barraging the German front line. Three batteries, X/31 (Lt. Percy Charles Binns), Y/31 (Capt. Charles Gordon Kirk, replaced by 2nd Lt. Walter Dann) and Z/31 (Lt. Reginald Murray Alexander) had previously been formed and a fourth, S/31, was hurriedly put together from officers and men from the Divisional Artillery who had been sent on a one week trench mortar course. 2nd Lt. Charles Axten was given command of this unit. In addition, Z/23 Battery (Lt. George) was attached from the 23rd Division for the duration of the bombardment and its two mortars bombarded the positions of the IR 66 opposite the right flank of the 48th Division. These batteries were all armed with the 2 in. Trench Mortar, the 'toffee apple', which consisted of an explosive filled sphere screwed onto the end of a stick, the stick being fired from the mortar's tube. It was anticipated that a sixth battery, V/31 Heavy Trench Mortar Battery, would also take part in the attack. This French-designed 240 mm mortar fired bombs which might have proved a useful addition to the weaponry aimed at the enemy front line and its dugouts but, unfortunately, although Capt. Frederick Joseph Haney, RFA, and his men arrived on 4th June and although two gun pits and two ammunition dumps were dug in expectation of the arrival of the guns, they failed to materialise being diverted to the 29th Division where they wasted most of their ammunition demolishing buildings in Beaumont Hamel. To make up for the absence of V/31, assistance was given on the northern flank of the division by V/48 battery of the 48th Division. It would join in with the attack on the trenches to the north west of Serre on the 26th June and fire some twenty rounds a day throughout the bombardment. X/48, Y/48 and Z/48 medium trench mortar batteries fired on the wire opposite the 48th Division's front and came under some heavy German artillery retaliation. Only three guns remained in action by 1st July but casualties amongst the gun team personnel were remarkably light.

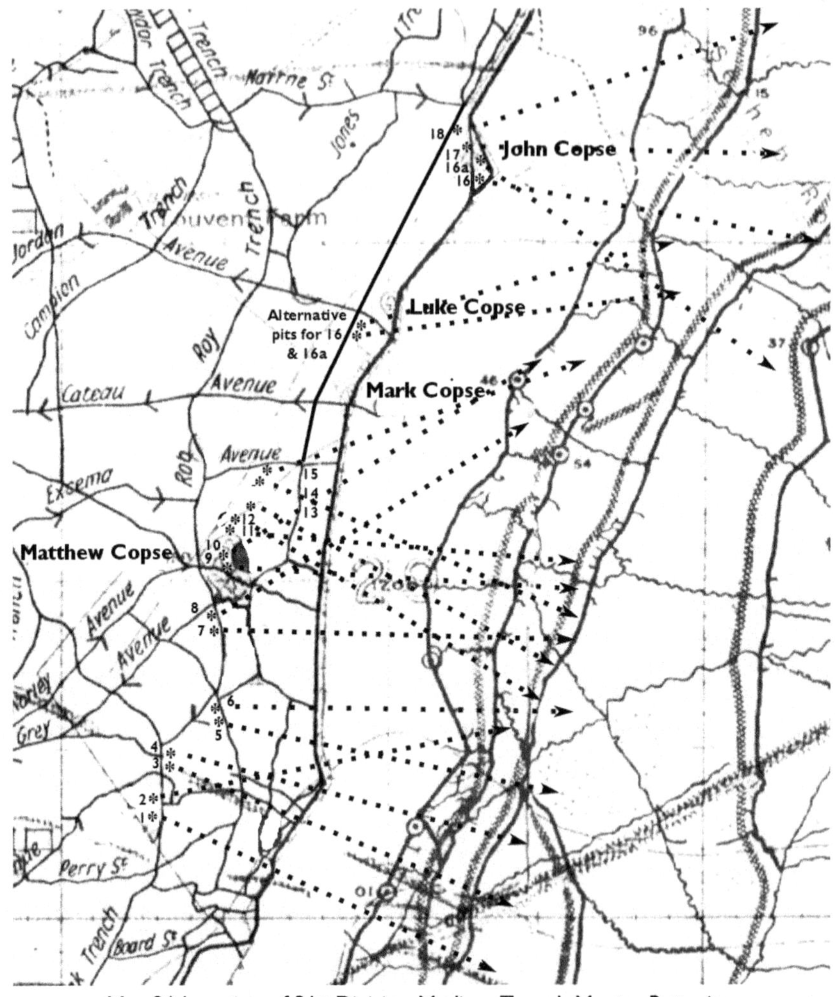

Map 26 Location of 31st Division Medium Trench Mortar Batteries

---➔ Centre line for direction and range of trench mortar's fire

Q Position of mortar

Y/31 Battery = Guns Nos. 1-4 Z/31 Battery = Guns Nos. 5-8
X/31 Battery = Guns Nos. 9-12 S/31 Battery = Guns Nos. 13-15
Z/23 Battery = Guns Nos. 17-18 (These guns fired on the 48th Division's front)

On 8th June, 2nd Lt. Henry Brian Bates, RFA, was made the Divisional Trench Mortar Officer (TMO) and he oversaw the work needed to prepare 18 gun positions and ammunition dumps which were to house some of the 6,000 rounds available for firing. In addition to the men of the batteries, 53 men from the Divisional Pioneers, later increased to 100, helped with the work. Getting the cumbersome ammunition to the trench positions was heavy and exhausting work. Each 2 in. mortar bomb weighed 42 lbs (19 Kg) and, with the fuze and stick, this increased the weight to 51 lbs (23 Kg). These bombs were brought up to Colincamps by motor lorry, then by horsed GS wagon to Euston Dump and from there were transported by hand to the various battery positions. The task was enormous:

> "The weather was wet and the trenches muddy and very heavy to walk through and it was almost impossible to get the men carrying bombs to do more than one journey by night… The Pioneers had to work day and night shifts during the last 10 days and the ammunition required actually 9000 men to carry it from first to last, including replenishment of gun pits during the bombardment."[2]

1,000 each of the rounds were stored in three dumps at Sackville Street, Observation Wood and Matthew Copse and the rest were stored in deep dugouts by the guns. The battery positions were located along the entire length of the Division front. S/31 and Z/23 Batteries were in or behind John Copse at the northern end of the front[i]. X/31 Battery was behind the British support line to the north of Matthew Copse with secondary positions in the copse itself and immediately to the north of it. Z/31 Battery's guns were aligned in groups south of Matthew Copse and Y/31's positions were just to the rear of Monk Street further south still. Once these guns opened fire then they, and the neighbouring infantry, would be in for a torrid time. No-one, probably on either side of No Man's Land, looked forward to being a close neighbour to a trench mortar. They immediately attracted heavy retaliatory fire and, quite often, it was the infantry nearby who suffered the consequences when a trench mortar battery came into action.

In addition to the Divisional Trench Mortar Batteries, the Brigade Trench Mortar Batteries, armed with the new Stokes quick firing mortars, were also beavering away getting ready for their much more brief participation in the pre-attack bombardment. Their guns were to be used as part of the hurricane bombardment due to be delivered during the last ten minute onslaught immediately prior to the attack when every artillery piece and mortar would fire as fast as they were able. For them, much of June was spent training the men so that they could step into action should one or more of the gun teams be put out of action. They were also trained and used as ammunition carriers, getting the 10 lb. 11 oz. (4.84 Kg) rounds from the dumps up to the near ends of the saps from the far ends of which some guns would fire on the morning of Z Day. 94th Trench Mortar Battery was to use D and E Saps as positions for its Stokes mortars and, by 29th June, the carriers had moved 3,600 rounds into place in readiness to be brought up to the guns just before the attack.

In mid-June it became apparent that the Germans were aware of some of the preparations being made for the attack. Although silent working on the tunnels

---

[i] S/31 later moved to positions to the rear of Luke Copse as a result of damage caused to their original positions.

had been the norm for over two weeks an attack on the end of John Tunnel on the night of the 17th June showed that they were no longer a well-kept secret. Although patrols were sent out in an effort to intercept any curious Germans, an enemy party, despatched specifically to destroy the mortar emplacements at the end of the tunnel, managed to evade them and placed explosive charges in both of the gun positions running at right angles to left and right of the head of the tunnel. These positions were known as N1 and S1. Both gun emplacements were blown in and 132630 Spr. W Pearson[i] of the 252nd Tunnelling Company and three men from the 13th York and Lancaster Regt. (1st Barnsley Pals) were killed[ii].

Three days later another unfortunate event occurred which, allied to the increasingly uncertain weather, contributed significantly to the deteriorating state of the trenches. The Royal Engineers had laid a water main towards the front line which ran near to the Mailly to Serre Road. Just beyond the Auchonvillers to Hebuterne road junction, the terrain slopes down towards the junction of the 31st and 4th Division fronts. The severing of the main by a German shell on the 20th June not only cut off the water supply to the front line troops in the vicinity until the 22nd June, it also flooded parts of the communication and front line trenches which were already more than just damp. The heavy thunderstorm a day later added to the misery of the men in the trenches and made movement increasingly difficult and tiring.

The 12th King's Own Yorkshire Light Infantry, the Divisional Pioneers, was hard at work trying to maintain the condition of the trenches. They were known as the Leeds' Miners, with many of the men coming from the pits around Leeds and neighbouring Wakefield and Rotherham. Their tasks during the attack had already been allocated. Two companies, A and D, were to accompany the 94th and 93rd Brigades respectively during the advance and the other two companies were to follow up and clear the German communication trenches from the front line to the 2nd Position once captured. They were also to dig trenches from the far ends of saps A, B, C, D and E across the remaining stretch of No Man's Land in order to connect them to the ends of the German communication trenches. Thus, if required, men and supplies would be able to move from the British rear lines all the way to the new front line under some sort of cover.

A lot of this cover would be provided by the tunnels across No Man's Land and, after the attack on the 17th, the 252nd Tunnelling Company tried to ensure there was no repeat of the damage done to the trench mortar emplacements at the head of John Tunnel. From the 22nd June onwards, the tunnels were guarded by the officers and 160 men of the company who would also be present when the tunnel faces were to be opened just before zero hour on Z Day.

Further to the rear, the Divisional artillery batteries were completing their work and testing newly installed communications systems. The trench mortar batteries were registering their targets in the German wire and putting the finishing touches to their battery positions before they took up permanent residence.

---

[i] 132630 Spr. W Pearson, 252nd Tunnelling Company, RE., was killed on 17th June 1916. He is buried in the Sucrerie Military Cemetery, grave I. G. 1.

[ii] A number of men of this battalion died on this day and it has not proved possible to identify those killed in John Tunnel.

The following day, the 23rd June, the Brigade Machine Gun Companies and Trench Mortar Batteries took up positions in the front line. The 92nd Trench Mortar Battery, commanded by Capt. Wilfred Horsley, tried their hands at some test firing of their Stokes guns and 72 rounds were sent over towards the German lines from the front line emplacements.

To the rear, the attacking troops were still practising their advance over the training ground at Gezaincourt observed, as ever, by officers from Brigade and Division. Today the 2nd Bradford Pals and the machine gun teams from the 93rd Machine Gun Company selected to advance with the attacking troops rehearsed their movements. For 23 NCOs and men of the 93rd MGC the operation would have been a new experience. They had all been transferred to the company from 2nd King Edward's Horse to replace 51 men deemed unsuitable as machine gunners. Those men had all joined from Bantam battalions and clearly a certain height was a minimum requirement for the Machine Gun Corps.

ON THE NEXT MORNING, THE 24TH JUNE AT 6 A.M., the field artillery started their bombardment. This was an hour later than planned but the weather had been poor and observation difficult. As conditions improved, the 18 pdrs began the tricky task of cutting the German wire in front of the 2nd, 3rd, 4th and 5th trenches. For the time being, it was left to the 2 in. trench mortars to cut the front line wire.

The batteries of the 31st Division had been divided into four groups:

Right Group (OC 170th Brigade, RFA): A/170, B/170, C/170 and C/171;

Left Group (OC 165th Brigade, RFA): A/165, B/165, C/165 and A/171;

Reserve Group (OC 169th Brigade, RFA): A/169, B/169, C/169 and B/171; and

Howitzer Group (OC 171st Brigade, RFA): D/165, D/169, D/170 and D/171.

The 18 pdr batteries were each given a lane to cut through the wire in front of each trench line and initial observation suggested the work went well even though the numbers of shells fired was not great. The four 18 pdr batteries under the overall command of the 165th Brigade fired an average of 250 shrapnel shells during the day at the wire in front of the 2nd, 3rd and 4th trenches. Given such a small number of shells fired the reports of the effect seem unusually positive:

"A/165 – 2nd, 3rd and 4th line lanes 'Y' satisfactorily cut.

B/165 – 2nd, 3rd and 4th line lanes 'Z' 2nd line fairly well cut, 3rd line needs few more rounds, 4th line not visible.

C/165 – 2nd, 3rd and 4th line lanes 'W' 2nd line appears satisfactory, 3rd and 4th not yet finished.

A/171 – 2nd and 3rd lines cut, 4th damaged but not yet finished."[3]

The reports from the four batteries of the 170th Brigade group were equally positive. Three of the batteries were cutting wire for the 93rd Brigade and the fourth for the 94th Brigade and the impression of their observers was unreservedly optimistic:

"A/170 – 3rd and 4th line lanes cut 10 yards broad. 2nd line partially.

B/170 – 3rd line lane cut, 4th line considerable damaged.

C/170 – 3rd line lane passable, 15 yards broad. 4th line considerably damaged.

C/171 – 5th line lane 15 yards on either side of Serre Road."[4]

For one day's firing these were exceptional results. If, that is, one accepts that the reports were accurate.

Further to the rear, some of the heavier weapons were continuing the process of registration but they were kept well away from the area where wire was to be cut so as not to confuse the Divisional artillery observers trying to judge the line, length and height of the shrapnel shells' explosions.

German retaliation was not slow in materialising. At 6.20 a.m. some medium and heavy howitzer shells started to fall close to the front line trenches but then moved back towards the Sucrerie and the nearby light railway which was cut and some nearby equipment badly damaged. The enemy artillery continued to fire in short bursts every two or three hours but damage was slight.

On the night of the 24th, in spite of the 252nd Tunnelling Company's precautions, the Germans again successfully attacked the far end of John Tunnel. Although damage was slight the noxious gas from the explosion caused casualties. Sgt. West[i] and Spr. Langlands[ii] were killed by the gas and 2nd Lt. Davidson and eight men were only rescued with the greatest difficulty. On the same day, a German shell blew in the mouth of Mark Tunnel but the damage was repairable and the men of the 252nd set to the task.

Within the German lines, casualties amongst the men of the IR 169 were slight: six dead, one missing and 14 wounded[5]. As yet, though, the heaviest guns in the British arsenal had not fired in anger.

AS THE FIELD ARTILLERY TRIED TO CARRY ON WITH ITS WIRE CUTTING the strength of the German retaliation grew. The 92nd Brigade occupied the front line trenches and, from 4.40 a.m. on the 25th June onwards, they reported increasing damage being done to the already less than robust trenches. In addition to the high explosive that was blasting the front line and communication trenches, gas shells were fired into Mark Copse. From time to time the German guns ranged further back and both Colincamps and the Sucrerie became unhealthy places in which to linger during the afternoon.

Meanwhile, the early morning weather had made life difficult for the gun crews of the 18 pdrs with rain and mist preventing observation for several hours and making the early morning 'useless for wirecutting' according to the 170th Brigade War Diary. Such climatic conditions were of no concern to the German

---

[i] 139428 Sgt. George West, MM, 252nd Tunnelling Company, Royal Engineers, was aged 40. The name West was an alias and his true name was Park. He was the brother of Mrs Margaret Marshall of 27, Kingscavil, Linlithgow. Native of Kilbirnie, Ayrshire. He was previously 4145 Private in the Royal Highlanders (Black Watch). He is buried in Bertrancourt Military Cemetery, Plot 1, Row D, Grave 13.

[ii] 139430 Spr. Alexander Langlands, 252nd Tunnelling Company, Royal Engineers, was aged 36. He was the son of the late Alexander Langlands of Burntisland, Fife; husband of Ann Langlands of 147, Waverley Street, Lochore, Glencraig, Fife. He was previously S/7439 Private in the Royal Highlanders (Black Watch). He is buried in Bertrancourt Military Cemetery, Plot 1, Row D, Grave 12.

gunners who were happy to fire on previously calculated ranges rather than at targets that needed precision in height, distance and direction to be effective.

Once firing resumed, however, reports from the observers in their cramped front line OPs seemed to suggest progress was being made, at least as far as the wire in front of the 2nd trench and further back was concerned. Lanes had been cut as ordered and were being widened and cleared. The Left Group (165th Brigade) more than doubled the number of shells fired (A = shrapnel, AX = High Explosive):

A/165 – A 571, AX 83
B/165 – A 490, AX 161
C/165 – A 674, AX 142
A/171 – A 689, AX 60

The Brigade War Diary again reported good progress though with a caveat about the work of C/165 Battery which was having trouble observing the results of their firing:

> "A/165 – objective engaged during the day Lane 'Y'. Cut through 2nd, 3rd and 4th lines. This will be widened on subsequent days. 3rd Lane cut through.
> B/165 – objective Lane 'Z'. Cut through 2nd, 3rd and 4th lines. No 3 line needs a bit of clearing up. Good deal wire lying about. This can be done during subsequent days.
> C/165 – Objective 'W' Lane. 2nd line cut. 3rd line: result difficult to see owing to a communication trench false cresting 3rd line parapet, judging from personal observation of CO the bursts of shells and range wire ought to be cut but actual results cannot be seen. It would be well to pay special attention to this during bombardment.
> 4th line reported partially cut and will be attacked during subsequent days. Actual results hard to see.
> A/171 – objective Lane 'X'. Cut through 2nd, 3rd and 4th lines. Will be widened on subsequent days."[6]

One small setback was the loss of one of the 4.5 in. howitzers of D/171 Battery when a premature burst the barrel. Fortunately, there were no casualties. The men were cheered, however, by the arrival of a congratulatory letter complimenting the 31st Division Artillery on its work of the previous day, which was received from the staff at VIII Corps and passed down the system, arriving with the batteries in mid-afternoon. What was unclear, though, was how well the 2 in. trench mortars were getting on with cutting the German front line wire. 'Not well' would soon be the answer.

As the bombardment continued one experienced officer said 'goodbye to all that'. 49 year old Lt. Col. Beauchamp St Clair St Clair-Ford, OC 11th East Yorkshire Regt., Hull Tradesmen, was hurried off to the 93rd Field Ambulance before being sent home. Commissioned into the East Yorkshire Regt. from Sandhurst in 1887, he was a veteran from the South African War, but now he was replaced by another South African 'vet' from the 12th East Yorkshires, Maj. Hugh Robinson Pease. Five years St Clair-Ford's senior, Pease had been commissioned into the East Yorkshire militia in 1881 and was appointed a temporary Captain in the 2nd Hull Battalion of the East Yorkshire Regt. on 8th September 1914 having previously been the Lt. Col. of the 3rd East Yorkshires in the old Militia and then the Territorial Force. He had served in the Orange River and Cape Colonies in 1902, being awarded the Queen's Medal with 3 clasps, and was promoted Major. His advancement to Lt. Col. came in 1907 when he took command of the battalion. He had then retired in March 1913, aged 51. His tenure as OC of the 11th East Yorkshires was to last seven weeks.

IN THE EARLY HOURS OF THE 26TH JUNE the German started the ball rolling at 3 a.m. with a barrage of mortar bombs and rifle grenades. At 5.30 a.m. the German guns shelled Monk and Le Cateau trenches, Observatory Wood and the front line from John to Mark Copse. This was repeated at 10 a.m. as part of a general three hour bombardment that spread from the front lines to the rear areas as the hours passed. Even Bus-en-Artois, more than 6 km behind the front line, received 20 shells from a captured Russian 5 in. gun. The bombardment had probably been in retaliation for a release of gas on the 4th Division's front in the very early hours. It had also been hoped to discharge gas on the 31st Division's front but the gas officer and some of his men were buried by a shell and no gas was released. In the late afternoon and evening the enemy artillery again bombarded the front trenches from John to Matthew Copses and these were beginning to suffer badly from both the heavy shelling and the continuously wet weather.

In response, the Divisional artillery carried on with wire cutting in front of the 2nd, 3rd and 4th German trenches while, on a few occasions, opportunities were taken to bombard known German machine gun emplacements and A/165 and A/171 Batteries both claimed two direct hits on two different MG positions. Reports on the wire cutting were still encouraging and 31st Division received another complimentary message from VIII Corps on the effectiveness of their shooting. It was now thought that the wire in front of the 2nd German trenches was sufficiently cut. All that was required was for the 2 in. trench mortars to clear away the remaining strands and piquets.

The trench mortar batteries were, however, beginning to have troubles of their own and these were materially interfering with their primary task of cutting the front line wire. Such batteries, necessarily positioned close to the front line because of their very limited range of no more than 570 yards with a maximum charge, were prime targets for both German artillery and trench mortar batteries and they were beginning to come under concentrated fire. S/31 Battery had two guns, 14 and 15, in John Copse at the northern end of the Divisional front. The battery was commanded by 2nd Lt. John Mellor who had been attached to the trench mortar batteries from C Battery, 163rd Brigade, Royal Field Artillery. At some time on the 26th June the pit occupied by Gun No. 15 was hit by either a 5.9 in. or heavy trench mortar shell. The gun, 2nd Lt. Mellor[i] and one man were buried and four other men were wounded. It would be several days before their bodies could be recovered as the position was constantly exposed to enemy fire.

---

[i] 2nd Lt. John Lewis Mellor, C Battery, 163rd Brigade, Royal Field Artillery attached S/31 Medium Trench Mortar Battery, was aged 27. He went to France as a sergeant and was commissioned on 29th December 1915. He was the son of John and Selina Mellor, of Manchester. He is buried in Sucrerie Military Cemetery, Colincamps, grave I. C. 9.

This would be but the first of numerous incidents involving the medium trench mortar batteries as the German gunners began to concentrate their fire on their exposed positions. The consequences for the wire cutting programme were, however, immediate. At 11 p.m. the Field Artillery Brigades were notified that they had been given the task of clearing the front line wire with each battery of the Right Group and A/171 Battery of the Left Group being given responsibility for a sector from just north of the Heidenkopf to opposite John Copse.

Today was the day that the heavy guns of the Corps' artillery joined in fully with the bombardment. Up until then, the firing had been mainly restricted to registration and the odd shoot at a German battery position. Now they started to destroy the German defences in earnest – well, parts of them. The heaviest guns firing on the 31st Division's front were No. 3 Gun, Royal Marine Artillery, a 15 in. howitzer, and the two 12 in. howitzers of the 65th Siege Battery. No. 3 Gun fired 37 rounds into Serre, three of which failed to explode, while the two 12 in. howitzers spent the majority of their time obliterating what remained of Serre with the odd bit of counter battery work thrown in. Today, they fired 105 rounds into the village, the surrounding orchards and the trenches that encompassed Serre. The majority of their rounds, 76 in all, were fired either at the heart of the village or the area to the east. The trenches to the west of the village, that is the ones the infantry would approach first, received just nine rounds. Another heavy battery, the four 8 in. howitzers of 36th Siege Battery, also spent most of their time bombarding areas well behind the front line: Puisieux Trench (the German 2nd Position), Serre Trench and the Zwischen Stellung (Munich Trench) south of Serre. Two heavy howitzer batteries, the 55th (Australian) and 54th (Australian) Siege Batteries, did have the front German trench within their sphere of operations. These two batteries, of four 9.2 in. howitzers and four 8 in. howitzers respectively, thus had the opportunity to fire into the crucial forward areas where the front line garrisons sheltered in their dugouts. The only drawback was that their complete bombardment areas took in both the entire 1st German Position back to the Zwischen Stellung, that is, six lines of trenches (for the 55th Siege Battery) and five lines of trenches (for the 54th Siege Battery) as well as the communication trenches linking them. Between them, they fired 380 shells into the large area allocated to them but this total included a proportion used in a special bombardment which took them away from the trench lines they were being asked to demolish.

It is notable, that, although the war diary of the IR 169 records the greatly increased intensity and weight of the British artillery fire from the 26th June onwards, it stresses that the increase was felt mainly in the rear trenches and not on the German front line. These forward trenches did attract the attention of some of the medium mortars but, as they were mainly trying to cut the front line wire, it would hardly have been a concentrated bombardment. Some of the dugouts were damaged but none caved in to trap the occupants. Clearing out entrances and ensuring the connecting tunnels were always clear would become a preoccupation of the German garrison for the rest of the bombardment. The other issue would be communications. Telephone lines, even those laid in special deep trenches, were cut and the communication trenches were often blocked making it difficult to deliver food, ammunition and other supplies to the forward areas. Otherwise, the majority of the men remained safe, if stressed, in their dugouts. Casualties, in spite of the greatly increased British artillery activity, were still relatively slight. Leutnant Schwendemann was killed when an OP on the edge of Serre received a direct hit and another 10 men also died. These losses brought the total for the first three days of the bombardment to 23 dead, one missing and 53 wounded[7].

One German unit which felt the full force of the British long range artillery was the III Battalion of the Reserve Infanterie Regiment Nr. 15 from the 2. Garde Reserve Division. RIR 15 had been asked by 52. Division to take over the position of the Rekrut Kompanie of IR 169 in the 2nd Position south of Puisieux. The fact that Divisions were happy to respond positively to such requests shows the degree of flexibility and co-operation with the German Army. The companies and HQ of III/RIR 15 had been camped in Achiet le Grand (HQ, 9. and 10. Kompanien) and Logeast Wood (11. and 12. Kompanien) and, during the night of the 25th/26th June they set off to march west, through Puisieux, to their allotted dugouts and trenches. The men had spent the previous day digging and improving the rear defences and a night time march was the last thing anyone wanted but off they went. As the sun rose in the early hours, they were spotted by the observer in a lone British BE2c circling above. Lt. Ebeling reported on what followed:

> "Day dawned [on the 26th June]. A British aviator cruised in circles above us. Three companies had already disappeared into Puisieux. Suddenly a signaller dashed out of a dugout and shouted: 'The village is about to be fired on!' Too late! Immediately afterwards a hail of heavy shells came down on the 10.,· 11. and 12. Kompanien. Only the 9. was spared and that was because it was last on the march by a wide margin and had not yet arrived at the village. The pilot had informed his artillery about the battalion. His radio message had been intercepted by our signallers. Unfortunately it took some time to translate. In proportion to the huge weight of fire which came down the casualties were quite bearable."[8]

Apart from the speed of response to the RFC observer's call by the British artillery, what is also interesting about this anecdote is the fact that the radio message was intercepted on the ground by the Germans. As is known, they were adept at intercepting messages sent by telephone and buzzer to units in the front line and this suggest that many of the messages from RFC airplanes were also being routinely intercepted by German radio operators at the front.

After their losses in Puisieux, the III Battalion, RIR 15, occupied the 2nd Position trenches 1.5 km south of the small town. They found them barely fit for purpose[i]:

---

[i] This may be a reflection of the fact that the 52. Division, now concentrated between Serre and Gommecourt, had previously been defending the position all the way to Monchy au Bois in the north towards Adinfer Wood. With their troops stretched so thinly, work on the 2nd Position may have taken second place to strengthening the front lines. On the other side of No Man's Land this same problem had beset the 48th (South Midland) Division when it manned the front from Serre to Monchy au Bois before May. Certain sections of the front line in front of Foncquevillers had been reduced to outposts because of a lack of manpower on such an extended front.

"In many places the unfinished position was full of mud due to the rain. As a result, the 11. Kompanie had to be accommodated in houses, but an immediate start was made at deepening the dugouts which had barely been begun, as well as wiring and clearing the mud out of the position. Excellent assistance was rendered by Bavarian engineers as well as a platoon of Pionier-Kompanie Nr. 104. The latter had spent days carrying heavy mortar rounds to Serre – no easy task!"[9]

Although only two companies of the RIR 15 would be directly involved in the fighting on the 1st July[i], being held in reserve in and around Puisieux, it would suffer several casualties from the long guns and the special bombardments which took place daily. On the 27th, for example, nine men of the 5. Kompanie were killed at roll call and another 12 wounded when a sudden strafe swept the village. Their positioning at Puisieux was, however, crucial as it would enable them to quickly reinforce either the position at Gommecourt or at Serre as required. Throughout the time of the bombardment, however, the men of RIR 15 worked hard to support the regiments of the 52. Division:

"Our soldiers, however, continued to dig, build and carry: 'Many kilometres of [telephone] links must be laid to the command post of IR 66. Rear echelon wagons will transport the material forward. It must then be unloaded, distributed and carried forward'. In other words, right up until the last minute work, which demanded the last ounce of effort, went ahead feverishly, regardless of the fire. At all costs the 5. and 7. Kompanien had to dig a cable trench. But the links were constantly disrupted. For the same purpose, the 9. Kompanie had to make the Signal 'Double Platoon'[ii] available to the 52. Infantry Division and on two occasions the 12. Kompanie had to send a thirty man working party to Division to construct new battery positions. 3,500 hand grenades were brought forward to the Second Position and distributed. Ammunition dumps were established and all types of stores which a major battle demands were carefully stowed away. All the companies suffered casualties…"[10]

The enemy retaliated to this increase in pressure by extending their bombardment of the British front line trenches throughout the afternoon and evening. One of the casualties suffered as a result was the 31st Division's GSO2, Maj. Herbert Stenhouse[iii], who had been up in the front line trenches to inspect

---

[i] The 10. and 11. Kompanien were involved in the counter-attacks against the London Scottish of the 168th Brigade, 56th Division, in their attack on Gommecourt.

[ii] 'Reinforced Signal Platoon' is probably the best approximation.

[iii] Maj. Herbert Wilson Stenhouse, DSO, Queen's Royal West Surrey Regt. att. 31st Division Staff, was aged 36. He was the son of the late Maj. Gen William Stenhouse (Indian Army) and Mrs Mary Jane Stenhouse of 'Tarika', 85 Bristol Road, Weston super Mare, Somerset. Originally commissioned into the 2nd East Yorkshire Regt. in 1898, with which he served in South Africa (severely wounded, MiD, Queen's Medal with 3 clasps, King's Medal with 1 clasp), he was promoted Lt. in the Northumberland Fusiliers in March 1904. He transferred to the Queen's (TF) in 1908. Attending the Staff College on the outbreak of war, he was appointed DAAG in August 1914, GSO3 on 10th February

the effects of the heavy enemy artillery and mortar fire. With the rain also lashing down, considerable damage was done to the fire and support trenches and their muddy condition, exacerbated by the thunderstorm earlier in the week, continued to deteriorate to the extent that men from the 211th Field Company, RE, had to be sent forward to pump out the excess water.

The exchanges of artillery fire carried on until late in the evening and, under cover of the bombardments, various patrols went out to examine the state of the German front line wire. Two of these patrols were mounted by the Sheffield Pals. The patrols, nine men commanded by Lt. Frederick Storry and 12/352 Sgt. Frederick Donoghue, slipped out of the British front line at 11.55 p.m. They found the German wire damaged but with only two clear gaps. They had taken two Bangalore torpedoes with them to help cut the wire but the patrols came under fire. Two men were seriously wounded and there was no opportunity to deploy the torpedoes. Collecting their wounded the patrols returned at 1.10 a.m. only for another man, 12/375 Pte. Thomas Gambles[i], to be wounded helping in one of his wounded mates. Tragically, all three of the casualties would die of their injuries[ii]. Even worse, five of the six other men, as well as Sgt. Donoghue[iii], would die before the war's end, all but one on Saturday, 1st July 1916.

In addition, the 11th East Yorkshires mounted a large scale raid on the enemy trenches. This was one of five raids mounted by the Divisions of VIII Corps that night. The 48th Division was to attempt two and the others one each and all would fail dismally.

The Hull Tradesmen's raid was led by Capt. Stevenson who, with six other officers and 97 men from D Company, left Sap C at 10.30 p.m. The operation was overseen from the front line trench by Maj. Pease. Hung up by uncut wire, the raid was greeted by heavy rifle fire and a flurry of stick grenades and was repulsed without making any entry into the German lines. Casualties were significant: 2nd Lt. Cyril John Oake, 2nd Lt. William Henry Hall and 2nd Lt. Benjamin Hutchinson[iv] were wounded, 2nd Lt. Robert D Caley was slightly

---

1915 and GSO2 on 11th October 1915. He is buried in Bertrancourt Military Cemetery, Plot 1, Row E. Grave 1.

[i] 12/375 Pte Thomas Edward Gambles, B Company, 12th York & Lancaster Regt., died of his wounds on 1st July 1916. Aged 25, he was the son of Edward Wells Gambles and Charlotte Gambles, of 58, Vincent Rd., Sharrow, Sheffield. He is buried in Couin British Cemetery, grave I. B. 17.

[ii] 12/1141 Sgt. Robert Bertram Henderson, 12th York & Lancaster Regt., died of his wounds on 30th June 1916. Aged 39, he was the son of Robert and Elizabeth Henderson, of 41, Curt Road, Wolverhampton; husband of Ida F J Henderson, of 291, Sharrow Vale Road, Sheffield. He is buried on Bertrancourt Military Cemetery, Plot 1, Row D, Grave 19. 12/1378 Pte Harold Storey, D Company, 12th York & Lancaster Regt., died of his wounds on 28th June 1916. Aged 19, he was the son of George and Jessie Storey, of Sheffield. He is buried on Bertrancourt Military Cemetery, Plot 1, Row E, Grave 6.

[iii] 12/352 Sgt. Frederick Donoghue, 12th York & Lancaster Regt., was killed on 1st July 1916. Aged 22, he was the son of Daniel P and Kathleen Donoghue of Maxwell Terrace, New Road, Belper, Derbyshire. He is buried in Railway Hollow Cemetery, grave A. 25.

[iv] 2nd Lt. Benjamin Hutchinson, MC, 11th East Yorkshire Regt., was killed on 3rd May 1917. Aged 23, he was the son of Betsy Hutchinson, of 72, Cannon Hall Rd., Sheffield, and the

wounded but was able to return to duty and 2nd Lt. S Haworth suffered from shell shock. In addition, Sgt. Frank Cox[i] and Ptes. Sawden, Driscoll[ii] and Wells[iii] were killed, and one sergeant, two lance corporals and two privates were wounded.

With all four other raids also failing to achieve an entry into the German trenches, including one to the north on the 48th Division's front which saw one officer and 14 men wounded for no end product, it needed some excellent politician's 'spin' to put a gloss on the evening's events. Hunter-Weston, soon to become a Member of Parliament, was just the man. The 11th East Yorkshire's war diary recorded:

> "Although the Raiders did not succeed in entering the enemy's trenches, the Corps Commander considered that they attained most useful results, as it has been established the enemy's front line trenches are strongly occupied."[11]

It might be thought that such an assessment would result in a re-assessment of the effectiveness and adjustments to the bombardment programme in order to place more and heavier guns on these 'strongly occupied' trenches. It did not.

The German artillery response to this activity had caused significant damage to the already sodden trenches and now, the effects of the shelling led to a shortage of drinking water in the front lines when the water main was again cut. The enemy guns added to the problems by opening up again between 4 a.m. and 5.15 a.m. Meanwhile, the men of all battalions in the Division were alerted to the need to provide working parties to help repair and clear the trenches. In addition to these problems, an anticipated gas release had to be postponed and, with the previous attempt having resulted in nothing more than casualties amongst the men of the Special Brigade, it was concluded that nothing more should be attempted until the new Divisional GSO1, Lt. Col. John Baumgartner[iv], had

---

late Frank Hutchinson. He is remembered on the Arras Memorial, Bay 4 & 5. He was awarded his MC in April 1917.

[i] 11/49 Sgt. Frank Cox, 11th East Yorkshire Regt., was aged 25. He was the son of Alfred and Mary Jane Cox, of Rose Ville, East Acridge, Barton-on-Humber, Lincs. He is buried in Knightsbridge Cemetery, Mesnil-Martinsart, grave H. 65.

[ii] 14/209 Pte. John J Driscoll, 11th East Yorkshire Regt., was never found and his name is inscribed on the Thiepval Memorial, Pier & Face 2 C.

[iii] 11/1393 Pte. Willie Wells, 11th East Yorkshire Regt., was aged 42. He was the son of Mr and Mrs Robert Wells, of Colne, Lancs; husband of Ada Wells (nee Ranch), of 5, Henry's Terrace, Wassand St., Hessle Rd., Hull. His body was never found and his name is inscribed on the Thiepval Memorial, Pier & Face 2 C.

[iv] Lt. Col., later Maj. Gen., Sir John Samuel Jocelyn Baumgartner (Percy), KBE, CB, CMG, DSO, 2nd East Lancashire Regt., was previously the GSO1 of the 48th Division and was swapped with the GSO1 of the 31st Division at Hunter-Weston's suggestion in order to give the 31st Division a GSO1 with a decent level of experience of the Western Front. Born in 1871 and educated at Queen Elizabeth's School, Sevenoaks, he joined the Army from Sandhurst in 1891. He served in Waziristan, Chitral, South Africa and on the NW Frontier. Returning to India he attended the Staff College at Quetta, India, graduating in 1907. He was appointed DAAG, Jullundur Brigade in 1909 and GSO2, Lahore Division. By 1914 he was on the General Staff having been appointed a member of staff and company commander at the Royal Military College, Sandhurst in 1912. BGGS, IX Corps,

interviewed the gas officer responsible for the sector. As a result, a time of 2 p.m. was agreed for the release and VIII Corps was so informed.

Another issue had been raised as a result of the night's escapades out in No Man's Land. Not only had the 11th East Yorkshire's raid been held up by uncut wire it had been discovered by officer patrols sent out by the 93rd and 94th Brigades that the front line wire was uncut in many places. The 94th Brigade's patrols had, in fact, been unable to get close enough to the German wire to inspect it such was the volume of rifle fire they encountered. The 93rd Brigade reported that, though there were some lanes cut in places on the southern edge of their front, the wire to the north was undamaged. One consequence of this discovery was that, in future, wire patrols were ordered to take out Bangalore torpedoes so that they might do a little wire cutting of their own during the night. The other was that, as previously mentioned, Brig. Gen. Lambert, the CRA of the 31st Division, ordered that the job of cutting this wire, previously the responsibility of the 2 in. trench mortars, should now be taken on by the 18 pdrs. With the attack still due to start on the 29th June this gave the Divisional artillery less than two days to cut the front line wire.

The need for all batteries to target this wire was explained at a conference held over lunch at the HQ of the 169th Brigade, RFA. The limitations on their activity were, however, significant. They were still required to participate in the special 'area' bombardments that formed a central part of Rawlinson's overall artillery plan, and they now also needed to take extra care not to fire on their own patrols and raids, the intensity of which was increasing as the need for detailed information about the state of play in the enemy's lines became more pressing. To add to the pressure, two batteries, B and D/171 were not available as they were being moved into new forward positions from which it was intended they should bombard the German furthest trenches as the infantry attack progressed[i]. Furthermore, three batteries of the Left Group, A, B and C/165, still had work to do on cutting their lanes in front of the 2nd, 3rd and 4th line trenches. To add to a sense of impending doom, Brig. Gen. Lambert confided to the OC, 170th Brigade, RFA, on a visit to the OP of C/171 Battery at 5.15 p.m., that the German front line wire could not possibly be cut in one day and that period, broadly speaking, was all the time that was available before the assault on the 29th June.

AS AN INDICATION OF THE PRESSURE now being put on the British field batteries, A/171 Battery, which was engaged on cutting the front line wire

1916. MGGS, Fifth Army, 1917. Chief of Staff, Second Army, 1918. DSO, 1917, CMG, 1918, CB, 1919. Chief of Staff and then commander, British Military Mission, to the Russian White Armies of Denikin and Wrangel. KBE, 1920. Retired to farm in Canada. Inspector General of Albanian Constabulary, 1927-38. Married Inez d'Aguilar, 1902. Their only son, 90025 Flying Officer Alister Charles Jocelyn Percy, 501 Squadron, RAF, was killed on 11th May, 1940, and is buried in Terlincthun British Cemetery, Wimille. Baumgartner changed his name in 1917 to Jocelyn Percy. He died in 1952. [Andy Simpson, *Directing Operations*, page 196, *The Times,* 27th August 1952, and *Hart's Army List 1915*].

[i] B/171 Battery moved to near a hedge at Hittite Trench and D/171 near to La Signy Farm.

throughout 27th June, fired nearly twice as many shells as the other batteries in the group as it endeavoured to make up for lost wirecutting time:

A/165 – A 353, AX 7
B/165 – A 447, AX 55
C/165 – A 442, AX 178
A/171 – A 807, AX 138

One of the reasons for the failure of the trench mortars was that six of their guns were now out of action as a result of enemy shelling. The gun and the bodies of the casualties of S/31 Battery from the previous day were still buried. In spite of this, the remaining three guns managed to fire 210 rounds during the day. At 6.30 a.m. another gun from X/31 Battery received a direct hit. This left only one gun still in action as one had been buried the day before and another destroyed by either an enemy shell of a premature at 10.35 p.m. The remaining gun team managed to fire off 75 of its spherical bombs in an attempt to cut the wire opposite. Y/31 Battery had so far remained unscathed and managed to keep up a regular barrage on the German wire and trenches, firing some 264 rounds but Z/31 was not so fortunate. A 3 p.m. two of the pits were destroyed by direct hits with one man killed and another wounded. A third gun could not fire as the platform had become unusable. Another pit was hurriedly dug nearby in an effort to get the gun back into action on the next day. Lastly, Z/23 Battery, on loan from the 23rd Division, had seen two guns buried the day before and these had still not been recovered. Temp. Capt. Bates, the TMO, was of the view that several of these direct hits had come from heavy trench mortars in the German 1st and 2nd trenches:

> "The enemy's fire throughout the day was particularly accurate and it appears that their heavy TMs in the 1st and 2nd lines have by no means been silenced by our artillery as they merely refrain from shooting whilst being shelled with the light metal we have been sending over."[12]

His comment about the reasons for the artillery's failure to silence these guns is telling as, if 'the light metal we have been sending over' was not damaging exposed trench mortars, then it was hardly likely to cause casualties amongst the garrison in their 20 foot deep dugouts.

Indeed, the damage to the German front lines was appreciable but largely cosmetic. The wire was being systematically worn away and trenches were being blocked, the parapets and parados blown in and dugout entrances regularly collapsed. It was this damage that the men from two Pioneer units attached to IR 169 helped clear while they also repaired the trench network. Pionier Kompanie Nr. 104 was given responsibility for sectors S1 and S2 on the right of the regimental front (almost precisely the area to be attacked by the 94th Brigade) whilst two platoons of the 1. Kompanie of the Kgl. Bayerisches Pionier Regiment Nr. 1 commanded by Hptm. Stahlmann looked after sectors S3 and S4 opposite the 93rd Brigade and the extreme left of the 4th Division. Overall, the IR 169's casualties were still slight. Eight men were killed on the 27th June and 25 wounded, giving a total number of casualties of 110 (32 dead) since the bombardment had started. Given the quantity of ammunition being expended, it is certain that the staff of the 31st Division and VIII Corps would have been dismayed at such small numbers.

The long threatened gas attack eventually took place at 2.45 p.m. after Corps and the neighbouring Divisions were first informed it would be sent over at 1.45 p.m. The cloud was slowly discharged from the canisters in the front lines over a 30 minute period. Apart from bleaching the grass and asphyxiating any remaining wildlife the net effect was a heavy and sustained German artillery barrage on the British front line trenches. The 10th East Yorkshire's war diary tersely recorded after this had ceased:

> "Trenches in an extremely bad condition and front line trenches practically blown level to the ground."[13]

Two of the 92nd Brigade's machine guns were also buried during the barrage. With the 'biggest barrage of the war' being responded to in kind the infantry might have been forgiven if they started to worry just a little about how easy this attack was supposed to be.

HAD THEY SEEN THE REPORT ON THE RESULTS of the seven wire patrols sent out that night, which found its way to VIII Corps at 4.40 a.m. on the morning of the 28th June, their concerns would have sharply increased. On the 93rd Brigade's front the patrols had found just one gap in the wire and that only four yards wide. The rest was impassable. To make matters worse, Lt. Richard Blease[i] and five men of the Leeds Pals were wounded as they returned from their patrol. On the 94th Brigade's front things were better – just. One lane 20 yards wide had been cut and there were one or two other gaps through which small parties of troops might pass. It was probably just as well that yet more heavy rain later in the morning persuaded the British and French High Commands to postpone the attack for 48 hours. Had they not, it seems improbable that the 31st Division would have been in any sort of position to mount a serious attack. The Divisional artillery had only the daylight hours to try to clear sufficient wire for the infantry to stand any chance to getting through to the German trenches. All the while, the front line and assembly trenches from which they were to attack were being flattened and what remained of them was full of water and mud.

Maj. Gen. Wanless-O'Gowan was becoming increasingly alarmed at the state of his sector and the plans for the forthcoming attack. A report about the condition of the German wire and another detailing the failure of an unsuccessful raid had already been forwarded to VIII Corps in the early hours. The raid, 80 men led by Lt. Crabtree of the 12th East Yorkshires attacking Point 10, had suffered the same fate as that of the 11th East Yorkshires the previous night. Stopped by wire, they had been taken under heavy fire and forced to withdraw. The officer in charge, Lt. Stephen Mark Crabtree, came away unscathed. His luck would last just 24 hours. At 11.15 a.m. Wanless-O'Gowan phoned Brig. Gen. Williams, GOC 92nd Brigade, and ordered that a party of 300 men should be detailed to repair the front line trenches between 3 and 9.30 p.m. He then spoke to Hunter-Weston and provided his superior with an assessment of the local situation and of the lamentable state of his front line trenches. Later, at a meeting

[i] Capt. Richard Morris Stanley Blease, 15th West Yorkshire Regt., was killed on 3rd May 1917. Aged 23, he was the son of Ellwood Harrison Blease and Mary Blease, of 30, Canning St., Liverpool. Born at Bowen, Queensland, Australia. B.A. with Honours in Classics, Leeds University. He is buried on Orchard Dump Cemetery, Arleux en Gohelle.

with Capt. William Dobbie[i], RE, a GSO2 at VIII Corps, the worried General explained that he believed the timing of the attack, i.e. 7.30 a.m., was too late a time for the assault to begin. Voicing such concerns so late in the day when there was no chance of the timing being changed is odd behaviour. There was absolutely no chance of the time being brought forward and he must have known that. It does, perhaps, betray his increasing nervousness about his Division's prospects after four days of heavy German artillery fire and after two failed raids.

He also expressed his concerns about German batteries in Biez Wood and behind Rossignol Wood away to the north behind the 2. Garde Reserve Division's front. He wanted these guns to be kept under fire from the time his men entered their assembly trenches on the night of the attack. These batteries were on the front opposite the VII Corps and in position to defend Gommecourt and, according to the too strict divisions of responsibility, were, or should have been, the targets of the VII Corps' heavy guns. If not destroyed or neutralised it would be only too easy for these German guns to change targets and extend their range a few thousand yards in order to enfilade the entire 31st Division. Some of these batteries were ones newly introduced into the Gommecourt sector as a response to the obvious preparations for the attack on that village which Haig had demanded. It may be that at least one senior officer was now beginning to have doubts about the sense of mounting a well-publicised diversion so close to the flank of the main attack.

ALTHOUGH THE DEADLINE FOR WIRECUTTING had been extended with the 48 hour postponement, the Divisional Artillery was still hard at work trying to cut the front line wire and extend and widen the lanes in front of the 2nd, 3rd and 4th German trenches. The batteries attached to the 165th Brigade – A/165, B/165, C/165 and A/171 – fired nearly twice as many rounds on 28th June (4,096) as they had on the 27th (2,427). Three out of the four batteries concentrated on the front line wire, each widening an existing lane. Only A/165 fired on all sets of wire and admitted to 'slow progress' and only 'some damage done' to the front line barrier. The batteries of the 170th Brigade group – A/170, B/170, C/170 and C/171 – also focussed on the front line wire. Their own reports, made by officers in their various OPs, expressed reasonable confidence as to their batteries' performance and little in the judgement of the infantry officers who crept about No Man's Land in an effort to see at first hand the effects of the artillery's shooting. It was, one may recall, on the 93rd Brigade's front that the previous

---

[i] Capt., later Lt. Gen., Sir William George Sheddon Dobbie, GCMG, KCB, DSO, Royal Engineers, was born in Madras in 1879 and was the son of W H Dobbie, CIE. Educated at Charterhouse and the RMA, Woolwich, he joined the Royal Engineers in 1899. Served in South Africa. Staff College, Camberley, 1913. Adjutant, CRE, 4th Division, 1914. GSO3, 1915. GSO1, GHQ, 1918. Staff of Army of the Rhine, Aldershot, War Office, Western Command, 1919-28. GOC, Cairo Brigade, 1928-32. Commandant, School of Military Engineering, 1932-5. GOC, Malaya, 1935-9. Governor of Malta during the siege, 1940-2. Col. Commandannt, RE., 1940-7. DSO, 1916. CMG, 1919. CB, 1930. KCB, 1941. GCMG 1942. Married Sybil Orde-Brown in 1904. One daughter, one son, Maj. Arthur William Granville Dobbie, 237th Field Company, RE., who died on 19th June 1944 and is buried in Orvieto War Cemetery. Lt. Gen. Dobbie died in 1964. A member of the Plymouth Brethren, he wrote to books after 1945: *A Very Present Help* and *Active Service with God.*

night's reports had cast the greatest doubt as to the effectiveness of the artillery's wirecutting. This supporting artillery just happened to be the 170th Brigade group. So, whilst from their own observations made from some hundreds of yards away, they could confidently predict the wire 'entirely cut through in places' and 'wire much damaged', their opinions of the reports from men close to the German wire out in No Man's Land was less charitable:

> "…reports on wire cutting by the infantry patrols and failure of raid which did not reach German front line and brought back non-information. Reports of patrols are valueless. Nothing definite nor particulars of German wire."[14]

That was easy for them to say.

At 3.30 p.m. the Brigade commander, Lt. Col. C B Simonds, made his own reconnaissance of the German wire on the 93rd Brigade's sector. He went with the Battery commanders to each of their own OPs and his findings were comforting. If believed.

> "… the first line had been considerably damaged. The only wire on Brigade front from Serre Road to Point 10 that could be said to form any sort of obstacle to advancing infantry was some 50 yards immediately north of Serre Road (this was defiladed from the fire of all the batteries by a protecting ridge close in front of it in No Man's Land, the TMO Lt. Dann could only reach about 20 yards of it with his 2 in. TMs and so the remaining 30 yards had been left to the 4.5 in. howitzers) and south from Point 10 for about 100 yards whilst in this latter distance one clear gap of 10 yards broad existed 30 yards south of Point 10 and another 50 yards lower down of 3 yards breadth.
> An accurate report from observations made with No. 14 periscope and angular measurement, compass, from Bess Street, Bleneau and Warley Avenue in front line trenches was forwarded to 31st DA and agreed very accurately with reports sent in by patrols later on in the night."[15]

Well, as they say, that was alright then. It must have been pure coincidence that the Commander of the Divisional Royal Engineers, Lt. Col. John Pierre Mackesy, today received an order to make up a 'large number of Bangalore torpedoes for wire cutting'.

While the field gunners carried on trying to cut the wire, the men of the Divisional trench mortar batteries struggled on under consistently heavy enemy fire. Capt. Bates' report for the day is thoroughly detailed and gives an excellent example of the dangers, trials and tribulations faced by the men of the Trench Mortar Batteries:

> "S/31 TMB.
> Guns 16 and 16a in Luke Copse still in action but pits are collapsing from frequent shelling. Near these guns the trenches are hardly discernible as such. No casualties to time of report. The question of ammunition to these two guns is acute as the main trenches are quagmires and blown in every few yards.
> Gun No. 15. Buried. 2nd Lt. Mellor's body still unrecovered as the place is under constant fire and in full view.

Gun No. 14. In action. This battery has done steady, good work and I have nothing but praise for 2nd Lt. Axten[i] and his men.
X/31 TMB.
Gun No. 12. This gun is smashed and is being replaced today by one of the four just received. It should be in action tomorrow.
Gun No. 11. In action though badly shelled.
Gun No. 10. Gun was completely buried but is almost dug out again. Should be in action tomorrow.
Gun No. 9. Gun quite buried. I consider this gun is permanently out of action.
This battery has had a most trying time but officers and men have held on admirably. Lt. Binns[ii], though wounded in the head and badly concussed, has continued to fight his guns. The Copse is almost swept clean by shell and firing is incessant. The wire on this battery's front appears to be cut completely.
Z/31 TMB
Gun No. 13 in action though severely shelled.
Gun No. 8. Direct hits from enemy heavy TM.
Gun No. 7. Direct hits from enemy heavy TM blowing in saps, burying one man and putting both guns out under several feet of earth. I consider these guns permanently out of action and have withdrawn detachments.
Gun No. 6. This gun is in action though severely shelled all the time. This battery whilst in action did good wire cutting. Lt. Alexander and 2nd Lt. Frobisher are both showing signs of the severe strain under which they are working.
Y/31 TMB
Gun No. 4. In action though heavily shelled and pit shaken.
Gun No. 3. This gun in action when I visited it at 10.30 a.m. today but has since been buried by a direct hit.
Gun No. 2. In action though pit is shaken.
Gun No. 1. In action but sap leading out to trench has been blown in.
2nd Lt. Dann and 2nd Lt. Evans have both done very good work on front line wire and have kept up steady fire throughout."[16]

Bates also had quite a day of it. This was not an officer content to linger in his dugout writing reports. He went out to see things for himself. And the things he saw were not good. He found the trenches impassable, forcing him to get from one gun pit to another over the open.

"Whilst going the rounds of the gun positions this morning I was compelled to cross the open frequently and, as can be imagined, orderly communication under such conditions is almost worthless. The German machine guns were quite active and on several occasions the 77s followed me up a trench length. The conditions under which the men are fighting

---

[i] 2nd Lt. Charles Axten, RFA, was awarded the Military Cross in the New Year's Honours List, 1917, *London Gazette*, 29th December 1916.
[ii] 2nd Lt. Percy Charles Binns, 12th King's Own Yorkshire Light Infantry, was awarded the Military Cross, *London Gazette*, 29th December 1916.

are almost incredible. It seems to me as if the TMs are holding the line as the infantry are conspicuous by their absence.
This morning at 1.30 I left Colincamps with S/4 Battery, 2nd Lt. Unwin and 2nd Lt. Curtler and endeavoured to dig a platform in Rob Roy Trench but was shelled out most vigorously. A perfect hurricane of 5.9 shells being sent over also 77 shrapnel. I withdrew the men and sent them back to Colincamps to get two guns to replace the guns damaged in X Battery. The men have been ordered to relieve various detachments of my own.
The officers are relieving 2nd Lt. Axten and 2nd Lt. Frobisher. Total casualties up to noon 28th June:
Killed: 1 officer, 5 OR
Wounded: 3 officers, 15 OR."[17]

Bates' comments about the awful state of the trenches were reinforced by the fact that, for the second day running, the men of the 211th Field Company, RE, were still busily trying to pump the water and mud out of them.

During the night of the 28th/29th June numerous parties of men were wandering around No Man's Land either checking out the state of the wire or attempting an entry into the German trenches. As if in response to the adverse comments by the OC, 170th Brigade, RFA, the wire patrols of the 93rd Brigade made a great effort to be thorough and detailed. All four battalions had patrols out in No Man's Land. The 15th West Yorkshire's patrol was out opposite the end of Ten Tree Alley just to the north of the Serre-Mailly road. They found no clear gap but a lot of low lying, tangled wire along the 20 yards of front they managed to inspect. The 16th West Yorkshires were on their left outside the end of Bleneau trench. They described the wire as very thin and not a serious obstacle though a large number of iron stakes were still standing. Their report covered a distance of 80 yards. On their left by a short distance, the 18th West Yorkshires examined the wire in the shallow re-entrant to the north of the road. Here the wire was damaged but there were no clear gaps. The upper part of the wire had been blown away but the stakes were still standing and trailed a large quantity of loose wire between them. They reported that infantry with wire cutters should be able to get through along the 120 yards frontage they could check. Lastly, the 18th Durham Light Infantry were out opposite Matthew Copse. They found narrow gaps of between three and ten yards every 20 yards they checked. These narrow lanes were, however, cut right through to the German front line. Even where there were no gaps the wire was considerably damaged as was the concertina wire thrown out to block gaps. Along the 150 yards they examined, the wire was between eight to ten yards deep. Only one wire patrol got out on the 94th Brigade front and it was forced to return by 12.30 a.m. so as not to interfere with the raid being mounted. Their cursory inspection suggested the wire was significantly damaged.

The raid was organised by the 12th East Yorkshire Regt. and was again led by Lt. Crabtree. At 1.30 a.m., accompanied by three other officers, he led his men towards the German lines but, as with all of the other raids, they ran into uncut or repaired wire. Where the wire was damaged the German had rather thoughtlessly placed knife rests festooned with wire and no progress could be made. As options were investigated the patrol came under heavy fire and, unlike the previous night, casualties quickly mounted. Two officers, Lt. Stephen Crabtree[i] and 2nd Lt. Charles Drewett[ii], went missing and were later found to have been killed. 2nd Lt. Charles Moncrieff[iii] was wounded and evacuated whilst 2nd Lt. Richard Morgan[iv], who was celebrating his fourth week on the Western Front, was wounded but remained at duty. In addition, two other ranks were killed, two more were missing and 15 wounded. It was another disastrous night for the 31st Division and, what should have worried senior officers most, another night when it was clear that the bombardment was not significantly eroding the morale or performance of the German defenders who were not only able to repel any attacks with apparent ease but had also been out repairing wire previously cut by the British artillery.

The response to the raid by the German artillery also underlined the strength and resilience of the 52. Division. From 2.10 a.m. onwards and for several hours the British front line was pummelled by artillery and trench mortars, rendering all of the work done to repair the trenches during the afternoon and evening a waste of time and effort. It was not until 5.20 a.m. that the 92nd Brigade was able to report that everything was now quiet.

THE 29TH WOULD PROVE TO BE A BUSY DAY for all concerned. The Field Artillery continued to cut the German front line wire but a report from No. 15 Squadron, R.F.C., received late in the afternoon indicated that there was still work to be done on the wire in front of the 2nd, 3rd and 4th trenches. Basically, there were just not enough guns to go round. To assist with the wirecutting it was ordered that all patrols sent out by the 93rd and 94th Brigades had to take Bangalore torpedoes and wirecutters out with them, suggesting that Divisional HQ was not 100% confident in the abilities of the 18 pdrs to cut the remaining wire on their own. VIII Corps had also decided to amend the bombardment programme for the night with everything directed towards the points in the German lines selected for raids. Division was required to co-ordinate its arrangements with the Heavy Artillery and, at 1.15 p.m., the CRA was informed

---

[i] Lt. Stephen Mark Crabtree, C Company, 12th East Yorkshire Regt., was aged 20. He was the son of John and Sarah Crabtree, of Woodside, Ferriby, Hull. He was educated at Hymers College, Hull, where he was in the OTC, and had been living in India before the war. He enlisted in the 1st Hull Battalion and was promoted Sgt. before being commissioned into the 3rd Hull Battalion on 11th September 1914. He is buried in the AIF Burial Ground, Flers, grave VI. J. 27.

[ii] 2nd Lt. Charles Drewett, 12th East Yorkshire Regt., was aged 25. He was the son of Benjamin Bishop and Jane Ann Drewett, of 'Charnley', Coalville, Leicester. His body was never found and his name is inscribed on the Thiepval Memorial, Pier & Face 2 C. His older brother, Capt. Herbert Ben Drewett, 4th East Yorkshire Regt., died on 30th October 1917. He is buried in Poelcapelle British Cemetery.

[iii] 2nd Lt. Charles George Conrad Moncrieff, 9th att. 12th East Yorkshire Regt., died on 24th November 1916 from wounds received in the second attack on Serre. Aged 20, he was the son of Annie Thomson Moncrieff and the late Rev. James Moncrieff, of The Parsonage, Warley, Halifax. He is buried in Abbeville Communal Cemetery Extension.

[iv] 2nd Lt. Richard Godfrey Morgan, 12th East Yorkshire Regt., was killed on 13th November 1916 during the second attack on Serre. Aged 26, he was the son of the Rev. David Richard and Agnes Morgan, of 33, Sunny Gardens, Hendon, London. Native of Chalford, Glos. He is buried in Euston Road Cemetery, Colincamps.

of the areas selected for the raids. The RGA were also asked to be ready to supply counter battery fire on any German guns firing from the areas around Puisieux and in Artillery Lane (Artillerie Mulde) behind the Beaucourt ridge. Given the previous failures of all the raids the Heavy Artillery was also warned that the 94th Brigade might make another raid on the night of the 30th June should the date of Z Day be subject to any further postponement.

The feedback from 92nd Brigade in the front lines was also worrying. They reported the front line, assembly trenches and communication trenches badly damaged and waterlogged and the front line was, in their view, so bad the attacking Brigades should consider abandoning it completely as a jumping off trench. 94th Brigade sent an officer up to inspect their area of front line trench and, reluctant to amend the existing arrangements at the last minute, they concluded that the trench was still fit for purpose. To confirm this, however, late that night it was arranged for a Staff Officer from Division, Capt. Geoffrey Peirson of the 18th Durham Light Infantry, to go up to the trenches first thing on the morning of the 30th to undertake an assessment of their condition.

Others were attempting an equally careful evaluation of the state of the German wire. The 18 pdrs were still firing, though at a far slower rate than the previous days, and much time and effort was spent making careful observations of the front and 2nd line wire. Lt. Col. Simonds of the 170th Brigade was especially assiduous in his efforts to ascertain the effectiveness of his gun teams. He was assisted in this by the absence of any sniping or trench mortar activity on the part of the Germans:

> "…previous day bearings of gaps and cardinal points in condition of enemy's wire were observed with a theodolite. Much progress has been made since the previous day and except for a small space of 300 yards just north of Serre Road the wire was in no way continuous standing. For a distance of 50 yards almost opposite Sap A from which observation was made the wire had been completely driven back against the parapet and was banked there. Nothing more could be done by 18 pdrs or other guns on this. The only thing would be a Bangalore torpedo or it could be bridged with portable bridges and so stamped down. The result of these observations and report furnished agreed very well with reports furnished by patrols the next morning."[18]

Although the front line wire seemed well cut, it was worrying that a bank of wire had been forced up against the German parapet. There were also concerns about the 2nd line wire and the report made clear that a good deal of work was required to clear this obstacle. The war diary also highlighted the impact the heavy firing was having on the guns. Never before had any of the guns or howitzers of the Divisional and Corps artillery been required to fire so heavily over such a prolonged period and the effects of this were being seen in failures, prematures and worn equipment. Two howitzers of D/170 Battery had burst as a result of prematures caused by the 100 fuze. D/171 had seen the same occur earlier. For the 18 pdrs wear and tear was the issue. Some equipment was unavailable with the nearest oscillator pads being at Le Havre. Buffer oil was in short supply and buffer springs were beginning to fail. All contributed to breakdowns and a reduction in accuracy.

The Divisional Trench Mortar Batteries were doing what they could to assist but, as ever, under heavy fire from the German field guns and trench mortars. S/31 had managed to keep three guns in action and they were used during the afternoon to cut the 2nd line wire. X/31 had two guns in action on the same targets and two guns buried but 2nd Lt. Binns was able to report later that a third had been got into action and would be available the next day. Y/31 and Z/31 were in the same position of two guns in action and two buried. Y/31 had a particular problem with its two remaining guns. They were both firing short by more than 100 yards. The wire that was their target was 350 yards distant but even with a charge for 450 yards the bombs still fell short. So severe was the problem that three bombs had actually fallen into the British front line trench killing three men of the infantry. 2nd Lt. Dann had ceased firing as a result. The DTMO, Capt. Bates, suggested that this was because the mortar beds were sinking into the muddy soil and he arranged for two new guns to be sent forward and for the beds to be tested before firing resumed on the 30th.

The soggy ground that was causing the trench mortars such trouble also required the urgent attention of the Royal Engineers. For the third day running the 211th Field Company was trying to pump out the forward trenches. Rain was not the only cause of the flooding, another hole in the water main was contributing its share as well as causing problems with drinking water for the men at the front.

Amongst the parties that needed to get to the front line along the waterlogged and muddy communication trenches was a group of four officers and 38 men from the 18th West Yorkshires. They were dropped off as near as possible to the front line by motor lorries during the late evening. They needed to be in the front line by midnight. The party was led by Lt. Morris Clough. Clough, a clothier's manager, had enlisted as a Private in the Bradford Pals in September 1914 and was commissioned on 26th May 1915. Now he was to lead his men on yet another raid of the, so far, impenetrable German trenches. With him went Lt. Frank Watson, 2nd Lt. John William Worsnop, Lt. George Body McTavish[i], RAMC, three NCOs and 35 men. Their objective was to enter the German lines, take a prisoner and obtain identification of the unit opposite them. This information was crucial as, according to Corps intelligence reports, the German regiment opposing the 31st Division should have been the Infanterie Regiment Nr. 66. Infanterie Regiment Nr. 169 was supposed to be away to the north defending Gommecourt. Instead, this regiment had been moved south and inserted into the line at Serre several weeks earlier after the 2. Garde Reserve Division had taken

[i] Capt. George Boyd McTavish, MC & two Bars, Royal Army Medical Corps, was born in 1883 in Dewart, Ontario. He graduated from Manitoba Medical College in 1915 and joined the Royal Canadian Army Medical Corps. He was appointed the Medical Officer of the 18th West Yorkshire Regt., and was awarded the MC for his conduct on 1st July 1916. The citation in the *London Gazette* of 20th October 1916 reads: "For conspicuous gallantry and devotion to duty. Throughout very severe fighting he was responsible, by his energy, courage and contempt for danger, in saving a large number of severely wounded who had been left in the battered front line trenches or in No Man's Land". He was awarded two Bars to his MC. He returned to Canada where he practised medicine in Winnipeg. He died in 1965.

over the defence of the Gommecourt salient. According to British intelligence this Division was thought to be somewhere in the vicinity but not in the front line. The greatly increased concentration of artillery, machine guns, mortars and infantry was, therefore, unknown to all concerned at GHQ, VIII Corps and 31st Division.

The West Yorkshire's raid was to work as five small parties. Two, each of one officer, one NCO and eight men were to enter the German trenches and move to the left and right. A third party of an NCO and seven men was to block the German communication trench at the point of entry. The fourth party of an officer and six men with stretcher bearers was to wait outside the trench as a covering party and the fifth group, also one officer and six men, was to wait in the British lines at the point of exit as a receiving party. The point of entry was planned to be just north of the Serre-Mailly road opposite the end of Flag Trench. They were timed to enter the German trenches at 12.30 a.m., remain for 20 minutes and then withdraw covered by the artillery.

At 12.28 a.m. the raiders slipped through the British wire and out into No Man's Land. Their advance was substantially slowed by the numerous shell holes and by the Germans constantly sending up flares that turned night into day. Lt. Clough later wrote that they must have been spotted leaving the trenches as, when they got within 30 yards of the German lines, they were met with a shower of bombs. They German response was well co-ordinated. A single green rocket was the sign for the infantry to form a grenade barrage in front of the raiders whilst trench mortars and artillery created another barrage to their rear. Although the wire here seemed well cut and the German parapet much damaged the trenches were deep and full of an aggressive enemy. Lt. Clough made the only sensible decision and gave the order to withdraw. It took his men two hours to re-cross the 200 yards of No Man's Land back to the relative safety of their own lines. In the process, over 75% of the raiders were killed or wounded. Clough was slightly wounded in two places, Lt. Watson[i] and 23 year old 2nd Lt. Worsnop[ii] were never seen again. In all, eleven of the raiders were killed and another nineteen wounded. To add to the sense of shambles, the British artillery, the participation of which had been so carefully planned, had managed to fire well short of the German trenches throughout the time allocated to the raid. Many shells dropped a little over half way across No Man's Land and it seems likely that at least some of the casualties were caused by 'friendly fire'.

THE RAIN THAT FELL IN THE EARLY HOURS OF THE 30TH JUNE greeted a dismal scene on the VIII Corps front. All four Divisions had mounted raids the previous night. One German was known to have been killed on the 29th

---

[i] Lt. Frank Watson, 18th West Yorkshire Regt. att. 93rd Trench Mortar Battery, was never found and his name is inscribed on the Thiepval Memorial, Pier & Face 2A, 2C & 2D. His date of death is recorded on the CWGC as 1st July 1916 but there is no record of him as a casualty in the war diary of the 93rd Trench Mortar Battery to which he was certainly attached. He is recorded as missing in the accounts of this raid.

[ii] 2nd Lt. John William Worsnop, 18th West Yorkshire Regt., was aged 23. He was the son of Mr and Mrs Edwin Worsnop of 16, Redburn Rd., Shipley, Bradford, Yorks. He was commissioned on 6th April 1915. His body was never found and his name is inscribed on the Thiepval Memorial, Pier & Face 2A, 2C & 2D.

Division's front otherwise every other raid failed, held up by heavy enemy fire from the supposedly dead or demoralised German front line garrison. As the information filtered up the chain of command everyone, apart from Hunter-Weston, began to have serious misgivings about the ability of the VIII Corps successfully to achieve their objectives. Haig sent Charteris off to assess their prospects and, according to Charteris, cancel the attack if necessary whilst the CinC confided his doubts to his diary. Rawlinson, too, put on paper his concerns about VIII Corps' preparations. Hunter-Weston, though, was gung-ho! and looked forward confidently to Saturday's attack, feeling, he assured Charteris, 'like Napoleon before Austerlitz'.

The failures of the raids of the 4th and 29th Divisions have been described elsewhere but the 48th (South Midland) Division's performance was just as bad. The troops holding the stretch of front line between the left of the 31st Division and the right of the 56th Division were not to see any fighting on Z Day. It would be a day of smoke screens and artillery and machine gun barrages but, in order to keep up the pretence that an attack would be forthcoming on this front the Division had mounted raids nearly every night since the 26th June. Previous experience had not set a happy precedent. On the night of the 15th June B Company of the 1/7th Worcestershire Regt. had mounted a raid. Its failure was put down to 'bad luck'. As excuses go this one is pretty feeble but it set a marker for the performance of the Division over the next fortnight's activities. Lamentable is a polite way of describing it.

On 26th June, under cover of darkness, three officers, Capt. Walter Archibald Parker Watson, 2nd Lt. R Hambridge and 2nd Lt. Frank Wilfred Marvin accompanied by a group of NCOs and other ranks from the 1/5th Royal Warwickshires, attempted to gain entry to the German lines at the top of Hair Alley to the north of La Louviere Farm. 2nd Lt. Hambridge and 14 other ranks were wounded as they were soundly rebuffed. The following night, Capt. Watson and 2nd Lt. Marvin again led their raiders to the same point and were again harshly treated, 2nd Lt. Marvin and 20 other ranks being injured in the process. On the night of the 28th/29th June the 1/7th Worcesters also tried their luck – and failed. Perhaps it was because they tried to raid the same place as the Warwickshires. If so, their attempted double bluff failed miserably. The raiding party was 75 strong and led by Capts. Harry Willets Adshead and Henry George Westmoreland Wood with Lts. J G Dixon and James Walter Douglas Melhuish along for the ride. The battalion war diary put the failure down to a combination of 'lack of time for reconnaissance and preparations'.

Over complexity might also have had something to do with it. The raiders were split into no less than eight groups:

Two bombing parties of an NCO and eight men each;

Two parties of four men carrying Bangalore torpedoes;

A covering party led by Capt. Wood of 19 men;

Two assaulting parties under Lts. J G Dixon and J D W Melhuish; and

A covering party under Capt. Adshead left at the point of exit.

In addition, Lewis guns were placed on either flank some 200 yards out into No Man's Land. In order to take them to the right place, an officer, two men and a guide from the 1/5th Warwicks helped them on their way. To ensure they found their way across No Man's Land a tape was laid from the British trenches to close up in front of the German wire. The advance of the raiders was to be supported by two field artillery barrages. The first shrapnel barrages was to be laid at 1 a.m. with two batteries firing on the front edge of the German wire for a distance of a couple of hundred yards either side of the planned point of entry. By 1.15 a.m., under cover of this barrage, the raiders were expected to be half way across No Man's Land (which here was over 300 yards wide). At 1.25 a.m. four guns were to lift 250 yards and the two guns on either flank were to lift onto the German front line on either side of the point of entry, the two batteries thus providing a protective pocket around the raiders. In addition, two 4.5 in. howitzers were to bombard two trench junctions and thus block two German communication trenches, Niemeyer Weg and Hair Alley, leading to the planned point of attack. These barrages were to continue until 2.30 a.m. by which time the raiders should have been back in the security of their own trenches.

In spite of the comprehensive and complex planning the raid failed. The explanation given for the failure makes unhappy reading for anyone concerned about the quality of Divisional staff work:

"The enterprise was a complete failure due to various reasons:

a. No one in the party knew the ground;
b. No previous reconnaissance was possible owing to the short notice given;
c. Two of the guides lost their way and did not know their way through their own wire;
d. Owing to c. the party had to cut their way through their own wire;
e. The hour fixed was 1.30 a.m. but party was not in position till 2.10 a.m. due to c. and d.;
f. Daylight came at 3 a.m. so party had to withdraw.

Deductions

a. Enemy were holding their front line in force as this point. Also had cross fire from two machine guns playing on point of entry, also heavy rifle fire from front line trench;
b. Enemy were on the alert as at 2.15 a.m. they kept as many as 4 Very lights in the air over the spot;
c. Enemy wire is good along this piece of ground.

The party were back in our trenches soon after 3.30 a.m. It was then fairly light."[19]

About the only thing that could be said in the favour of this raid was that none of the participants were killed. Other casualty figures were not provided.

The next day it was the turn of the 1/4th Gloucesters. Presumably by way of a triple bluff they too attacked at the same place as the Warwickshires and Worcesters and, predictably, with the same result. The only upside to this event was that only three men were wounded.

The 48th Division's last two raids unsurprisingly achieved nothing. One was again organised by the 1/5th Royal Warwicks. It failed but only at the cost of two men wounded. The other was conducted by the 1/4th Oxfordshire and Buckinghamshire Light Infantry. Incredibly, they too attacked the same point in the German trenches for which nearly every other raid had aimed. The raiding party was 50 strong and was led by 2nd Lts. S Smith and William Lidsey. They were supported by a covering party of two Lewis guns and 25 men with all involved drawn equally from A and D Companies. They came up against uncut wire 20 yards short of the German parapet, were spotted and subject to rifle fire and grenades whilst numerous flares were sent up. They withdrew in good order and, again, no one was killed.

Thus was the 48th Division's catalogue of failure complete. The IR 66 opposite them had comprehensively seen them off and, with little to entertain them on Z Day, the regiment happily interfered with the two British attacks on either side of them thereby making their own small contribution to the catastrophe that was about to unfold in front of Serre and Gommecourt.

As an attempted encouragement, Hunter-Weston sent Maj. Gen. Fanshawe a message which was to be passed on to the men of the Division. It read:

> "Sir Aylmer Hunter-Weston sends his greetings to General Fanshawe and every officer, N.C.O. and man in the 48th Division. He rejoices to be going into battle with so fine a Division as the 48th as his Corps Reserve. He knows that, when the time comes to put them into the fight, he can rely on the men of the South Midland to bear heavy losses from artillery, rifle and machine gun fire and to stick it out and to win though in the end."

The idea that the troops of the Division could be relied on to suffer heavy casualties was not, perhaps, what the men wanted to hear. It was, however, precisely what Hunter-Weston had inflicted on his troops at Gallipoli. So, no change there, then.

WHILE THESE ABJECT FAILURES TOOK PLACE the 93rd and 94th Brigades sent out wire patrols on the night of the 29th/30th, the results of which were forwarded to VIII Corps at 7.34 a.m. on the Friday morning. These reports, at least, contained some encouraging news. Five patrols had been sent out at just after 10.30 p.m. and all agreed that the wire was badly damaged and presented no serious obstacle to the infantry.

Three of the patrols were on the 93rd Brigade's front. No. 1 Patrol under 2nd Lt. Leonard Dick, 18th Durham LI, checked the northern end of the Brigade's front. Ten yards out from the German wire they came across the corpses of two men from the East Yorkshire Regt. who they could not identify. The wire itself had been in cut in several places with gaps eight to ten feet wide but there were the remains of wooden and iron stakes and of knife-rests which might slow down advancing troops. The wire was described as being 'much battered' which is not quite the same was 'well cut' or 'swept away' and the comment that 'it would be possible to go right through in several places' was not completely reassuring. No. 2 Patrol checked the wire in the re-entrant opposite Bleneau Trench. The wire was again described as 'passable' and the officer commanding the patrol saw no need to use the Bangalore torpedoes available. No. 3 Patrol looked at the wire towards the end of Ten Tree Alley and just north of where the Serre-Mailly Road cut the German front line. Here, the 'wire (was) rather thick and strewn with knife-rests'. As a result, they tried to clear an area by exploding a Bangalore torpedo. Later in the afternoon of the 30th June, the 4.5 in. howitzers of D/170

Battery were put onto this area in an effort to clear the remaining wire and knife rests with, it was thought, encouraging results.

For the 94th Brigade Lt. Frank Bailey of the 11th East Lancashires examined the wire opposite Matthew Copse:

> "I went out at 10.35 pm leaving our lines at post No. 6. We walked through our wire and lay in No Man's Land for 5 minutes until our artillery lifted. We then proceeded to crawl out towards the enemy's wire, but were found by the enemy's flares about half-way. We were not fired on by machine guns, but about 3 rifles from slightly to our right kept up fire for about 15 minutes. We then proceeded toward the wire, and examined same for about 40 yards north, but could only find one thickness of concertina wire into which we put the Bangalore torpedo and fired same. We immediately retired as it was now about 11.30 and the artillery were trying to come back. We got back into No. 6 post at 11.45."[20]

On Bailey's left, the wire patrol was taken out by Lt. Cecil Woodhouse of the Sheffield Pals:

> "I went out with a patrol tonight from No. 27 Bay (opp. Luke Copse) at 10.35 p.m. The enemy wire is now considerably damaged opposite this place, but a fair amount of loose wire remains. I do not consider that it would be a serious obstacle to infantry. Another patrol from my party went out opposite Bay 34, and report a similar state of affairs. Two Bangalore torpedoes were placed in position and fired at 11.10, but the one opposite 27 Bay failed to explode. Some flares were sent up from the 2nd German line, but none from the 1st. No other signs of the enemy could be seen or heard."[21]

During the day the field guns kept firing at the wire and co-operated enthusiastically in a special bombardment of the German front trenches between 8.40 and 9.20 a.m. They were joined in the exercise by many of the heavy howitzers and, when the smoke cleared, the 170th Brigade, RFA, war diary recorded the enemy's front line as 'a study in brown'. The appearance was, however, deceiving.

Final arrangements were also being made to ensure adequate supplies of ammunition in the battery shell stores. The batteries of the 165th Brigade group between them took in 4,664 shells from the Divisional Ammunition Column in readiness for Z Day. The 170th Brigade group was also setting in place the liaison officers who would operate at Brigade and Battalion level with the 93rd Brigade during the attack. The rather over-named 2nd Lt. Claud Cleary Harold Maglew Reay was to be at Brigade HQ while three others, 2nd Lt. A Hesketh, 2nd Lt. B Phillips, 2nd Lt. C Reilly, would be attached to the infantry to act as Forward Observation Officers. Final artillery conferences took place in the evening and watches were synchronised at 6 p.m. Everything was ready for the off.

The men of the Trench Mortar batteries were struggling through the final few hours of their ordeal. At Luke Copse, S/31 Battery finally lost the use of 16 and 16a guns during the morning. The exhausted gun crews were withdrawn. An effort was made to direct the fire of their remaining gun, No. 14, onto their targets but this was found to be impossible and the gun fired 40 rounds towards the German 2nd line wire during the day. The two surviving guns of X/31 Battery fired 78 rounds. No. 9 gun, buried the previous day was dug out and got back into action at 2 p.m. In spite of being in the open and continuously fired at by enemy shrapnel it managed to send over 48 rounds on the German 1st and 2nd line wire around Point 46. No. 12 gun, though buried again in the afternoon, fired 30 rounds at the 2nd line wire. Y/31 managed to keep three guns, Nos. 1, 2 and 3 in action throughout the day. From their OP it seemed as though the German wire was 'practically destroyed' with what was left covered by earth thrown up by the bombs. Z/31 used guns Nos. 13 and 6 on the German 2nd line with some success while officers from Z/23 Battery were sent to assist some of the other batteries. 2nd Lt. Charles Coubrough[i] helped Lt. Binns at X/31's guns, having to dig the gun out twice during the day[ii].

Further to the rear and mainly out of harm's way, the gun teams of the heavy howitzers and long guns were getting ready for the big day. The most powerful weapon in the Corps' artillery's armoury was No. 3 howitzer of the Royal Marine Artillery. This 15 in. monster was one of the few guns capable of collapsing the deep German dugouts but spent its entire time firing at the village of Serre rather than the trenches surrounding it. Firing only two rounds a day on the opening two days of the bombardment it swung fully into action on the 26th June, sending over 37 of its 1,500 lb. shells. A further 40 rounds were sent into Serre the following day but then its productivity sharply declined with the gun firing 24 rounds on the 28th June, 20 on the 29th and just 8 on the 30th. To make matters worse, nearly 20% of these shells were 'blinds'. On the day itself, No. 3 howitzer would fire 27 shells, most in the preliminary bombardment, with its targets being Serre, Pendant Copse and Puisieux. The war diary records that 'During the attack no observation was possible'.

The two 12 in. howitzers of the 65th Siege Battery were other weapons which might have caused some serious damage to the German dugouts but, again, they spent most of the five days of the bombardment in which they were active firing at Serre and its immediate surroundings. Its daily targets were:

26th June – Serre 69 rounds, orchard east of Serre 16 rounds, 15 rounds counter battery work. Total 100 rounds.

27th June – Serre 104 rounds, orchard east of Serre 16 rounds, trenches NW of Serre 20 rounds. Total 140 rounds.

28th June – Serre 128 rounds, orchard east of Serre number of rounds not given, trenches north west of Serre 7 rounds. Total 135+ rounds.

---

[i] 2nd Lt. Charles Ellis Merriam Coubrough, MC, was commissioned out of the Duke of Wellington's (West Riding) Regt. before being seconded to the 31st Divisional Trench Mortar Batteries on 27th June 1916 having transferred to the Royal Garrison Artillery in which he achieved the rank of Major in March 1917. He was the son of Ellis Wood and Alice W Coubrough of Ardoch, Northwood. He married Dorsi Gertude Lacy in 1920. Three children. He died in 1967.

[ii] On the 5th July, the officers and men of Z/31 Battery returned to their positions to recover the guns and other equipment. All four guns had been buried and one, No. 8, could not be dug out for several days. Eventually, all guns were recovered and handed over to the 48th Division who took over the sector.

29th June – Serre number of rounds not given, trenches north of Serre 17 rounds.

30th June – Serre and trenches NW and SW of village. Number of rounds not given.

On 1st July, after the preliminary bombardment during which the guns bombarded Serre, the rest of their day was spent firing at targets well beyond any points reached by the British infantry: Pendant Copse, Puisieux and the Bucquoy to Puisieux Road. Late on in the early evening, long after the fighting had died down, the battery, with the assistance of a BE2c and its observer, would claim two German guns destroyed with direct hits. Better late than never, one supposes.

MEANWHILE, DIVISION HAD BEEN SENDING OUT last minutes instructions and was, perhaps belatedly, exhibiting signs of concern over secrecy. At 3 p.m. a message marked 'secret' was sent to the CRE, GOCs of the three infantry Brigades and the CO of the Pioneers:

> "It is of the utmost importance to prevent the enemy from knowing that the Division has assembled in the trenches for attack. The GOC wishes you to take all steps to ensure that all ranks under your command thoroughly understand this. Absolute silence and concealment are necessary and once the positions are taken up there should be no movement in the trenches but men must keep well down and no rifles must be allowed to show over the parapets."[22]

A later secret message to the same list which included code phrases for use by the units when they had reached their assembly positions ended:

> "Remember, Germans can hear what is telephoned or buzzed."[23]

It is interesting to note in light of this comment that a telegram from Rawlinson received at 31st Divisional HQ at 11.48 p.m. was immediately forwarded by wire to the three infantry Brigades and the Royal Artillery. By this time, both the 93rd and 94th Brigades had occupied their new forward battle headquarters close up behind the front line. They were, quite possibly, within listening range of the Germans.

Earlier in the evening the finishing touches were being given to the work of the Royal Engineers under the command of Lt. Col. Mackesy, 31st Division's CRE. His diary recorded the enormous amount of work done by the Field Companies with the help of their infantry working parties:

> "Construction of new support line, three new trenches. 24 bombardment slits off front line trench. New main communication trench. Many trenches cleared, repaired, deepened and where necessary traversed, including front and support lines.
> La Signy Farm connected into strong point.
> Dugouts: 10 medical, 4 for Brigade Battle HQs, 1 for Battalion HQ, 6 for Corps Signals, 1 for RE, 1 for motor lorry all completed. Two excavated but not completed.
> Deep mined dugouts: 36 entrances started to form 18 deep dugouts. Depth reached gives at least 15 feet earth cover. Chambers started at that

depth should have been connected up to form 18 DUs each with two entrances if labour had permitted.
OPs: 3 Divisional OPs, 1 Army Survey Post, numerous Brigade and RA OPs completed.
Miscellaneous: 12 dumps for food, water and SAA completed. 8 RE Dumps completed. Special emplacements for (gas) cylinders constructed in front line.
Roads in forward areas: Forward and Return road marked out and bridged to front line. Cross country tracks marked out and bridged. Extra bridges constructed at Euston. Several spare bridges deposited in forward dumps. Four portable bridges constructed for RA.
Tramways: Decauville track laid in trench between Euston and Colincamps. Wooden tramway overhauled. 16 railway trucks constructed.
Water supply: Wells and pumping plant at Sucrerie protected by steel and concrete double roof. New engine erected at La Signy and installation there put in working order.
Two wells at Bus sunk to depth of 130 feet giving good supply, pumps fixed, tanks erected and stand pipes provided. Couin-Bus supply in working order. New reservoir capacity 12,000 gallons constructed. New 4 in. pipe laid from reservoir to watering place. Watering point much enlarged and separate place being installed for 4th Division.
Hutting: Two huts completed for Divisional School, 1 for officers, Infantry Brigade.
Trees: About 250 cut down for dugouts and gun emplacements. Branches used as revetting posts, entanglement pickets, etc.
Roads: Steady repair to roads. Both watering points metalled. Stone for roads quarried at Warnimont.
Miscellaneous: Russian sap constructed to form flank trench. 8 bomb stores constructed.
Stores: Division kept supplied with RE stores as far as stocks in Parks would permit. Work somewhat hampered owing to motor lorries being withdrawn. Occasional shortage of timber, girders, pickets and shovels."[24]

What must have proved acutely irritating to Mackesy and his men was that, during the night of the 30th June/1st July, the German artillery seemed to specifically target crucial HQ dugouts and many of the stores of key materials and equipment essential to the advance. Their success was commented on by 170th Brigade, RFA:

"Enemy's heavy ordnance very active during the night and mostly directed against material for advance and important dugouts such as the HQ of units. His efforts at putting every obstacle in the way of our advance met with considerable success judging by the havoc made among bridges, ladders, etc., which had been placed in positions of readiness."[25]

Perhaps the warnings about secrecy had come too late.

To repair the damage Nos. 1, 2 and 3 Sections of 210th Field Company, RE, were ordered up to the forward area where they were made available to repair any damaged bridges, the clearly vulnerable water supply and anything else which might need their attention.

Also moving into position were the men and guns of the Brigade Trench Mortar Batteries and Machine Gun Companies. The three sections of the 92nd TMB left Colincamps either side of 6 p.m., their objectives being Sap C and Uriah Trench. It was felt inadvisable for the gun teams to go straight into the front lines as the trenches were too badly damaged to provide sufficient concealment so, while the OC, Capt. Horsley, and Lt. Oake went ahead to reconnoitre suitable conditions, the men remained behind out of sight of the enemy observers. When, eventually, Nos. 1 and 2 Sections[i] reached the front line they found a night's heavy work in front of them. Ammunition which had been stored near the front was now buried as a result of the German bombardment, shell holes had to be adapted as gun positions and all this was done under heavy enemy fire and in damaged and waterlogged trenches increasingly clogged with the infantry awaiting the assault. The area around Sap C was particularly congested as the infantry were using the sap as cover from German shells and it was only with the help of the Royal Engineer officer in charge of the sap that the men were cleared out of the way.

In the front line, the 10th East Yorkshires, who had been holding the Divisional front up to the 30th June, withdrew A, B and C Companies to positions in Palestine Avenue. D Company was left in the front line. With rather odd timing, the battalion's CO, Maj. Daniel Burges[ii], returned to England on this day to become an instructor at the Senior Officers' School at Aldershot. He was replaced by Lt. Col. Walter Bagot Pearson from the 1st Lancashire Fusiliers. The rest of the 92nd Brigade moved into reserve trenches on or just in front of the road from the Sucrerie to Hebuterne, north of La Signy Farm, from which they would have an excellent view of the tragedy about to unfold in the fields to the east.

ON THE 93RD BRIGADE'S FRONT THE ADVANCED BATTLE HQ was opened at 8.30 p.m. and the four artillery officers seconded to the Brigade by the 170th Brigade, RFA, arrived half an hour later to report for duty. The time for the attack was now known and the officer responsible for the writing of the war diary finished the month's account with stirring words:

> "Thus ends the war diary for June 1916 on the eve of the greatest battle of modern times. Every man is confident of victory."[26]

And this in spite of the earlier entry for day bemoaning the fact that 'raids had taken place every night since the commencement of the bombardment with few (actually none) succeeding'. But why let some inconvenient facts get in the way of some martial optimism?

The 93rd Machine Gun Company had taken up their positions at 5 p.m. The OC, Capt. Joseph Pelham Kayll[iii], had sixteen guns at his disposal and 7 officers

[i] No.3 Section stayed in reserve in Uriah Trench.

[ii] Lt. Col. Daniel Burges, VC, DSO, 3rd Gloucestershire Regt., att. 7th South Wales Borderers, won the VC for his conduct in the Balkans on the Doiran Front on 18th September 1918.

[iii] Capt. Joseph Pelham Kayll, 18th Durham Light Infantry att. Machine Gun Corps, was appointed Brigade Machine Gun Officer on 19th June 1915.

and 125 other ranks who made up the company. The guns were distributed as follows:

- Guns Nos. 1-4 under 2nd Lt. Harcourt to provide overhead covering fire when the attack started;
- Attached to the 16th West Yorkshires: Guns Nos. 5 and 6 under 2nd Lt. Baker and Guns Nos. 15 and 16 under 2nd Lt. Dean;
- Attached to the 18th West Yorkshires: Guns Nos. 7 and 12 under 2nd Lt. Barnes, Gun No. 9 under 2nd Lt. Burrows, Guns Nos. 10 and 11 under 2nd Lt. Booth and Gun No. 8 under Sgt. Duke;
- In reserve: Guns Nos. 13 and 14 under 2nd Lt. Charles Luckhoff.

Each of the gun teams consisted of an NCO and seven or eight men. Each of the gun teams advancing with the infantry needed to take forward the tripod, 12 to 14 boxes of ammunition, a First Aid case, spare parts and water for cooling the gun. Given the volume of material and equipment which was to be carried it was obvious that any significant casualties amongst the gun teams would quickly render the gun ineffective, especially if any crucial item was lost as a result. It would quickly become clear that seven men per gun was not enough to keep it operating during an advance, but this lesson was another yet to be learnt.

In the villages to the west the attacking battalions were getting ready to move up to the assembly trenches. The 93rd Brigade was to attack on a one battalion front with the 15th West Yorkshires taking the lead, followed by the 16th Battalion and the 18th Battalion. The 18th Durham Light Infantry had D Company attached to the 16th West Yorkshires while the rest waited to move forward from the reserve trenches. The 15th West Yorkshires were the first to move off but while they paraded in a courtyard in Bus-les-Artois an incident occurred which cast a pall over the men's march to the front. 20 year old 19704 Pte. Robert Henderson was an experienced soldier originally from South Shields and it seems he may have been priming bombs. According to the battalion war diary two grenades exploded killing Henderson[i] and wounding 14 other men of Nos. 14 and 15 Platoons of D Company. It was an inauspicious start to the operation, nonetheless the men set off at 6 p.m., C and D Companies in the lead as they were to form the first line in the attack.

The 16th West Yorkshires moved off from Bus at 6.35 p.m. The war diary tells us the precise strength of the battalion prior to the attack:

HQ 46
A Company 133
B Company 114
C Company 130
D Company 130
Bombers 9
Machine gun 101
Medical staff 19
Total 682

---

[i] 19704 Pte Robert Henderson, 15th West Yorkshire Regt., was aged 20. He was the son of James and Isabella Henderson, of South Shields. He is buried in Bertrancourt Military Cemetery, Plot 1, Row E, grave 9.

In addition, the battalion supplied a carrying party under Lts. Hoffmann and Gibson numbering 68.[27] In support of the battalion was D Company, 18th DLI, and 100 men from the Leeds' Miners Pioneers.

D Company of the 18th Durhams left Courcelles at 8.45 p.m. following on the 16th West Yorkshires and they were followed by the 18th West Yorkshires with the other three companies of the Durhams leaving Courcelles at 10.15 p.m. Their route took them through Colincamps which had come under heavy German artillery fire and, during their march through the village, the 18th West Yorkshires suffered their first casualty – 39 year old Capt. Charles Duckitt[i], OC D Company, being wounded by a shell splinter. Once past the Sucrerie the troops approached their assembly positions down long, wet and muddy communication trenches like Southern Avenue and, as a result, their progress slowed. At Basin Wood a large pit dug by the Leeds' Pioneers waited for the first of the dead with which it would be filled.

The first troops, the men of the Leeds Pals, started to arrive in their allotted positions after midnight on 1st July while the other battalions arrived wet, muddy and tired over the following hours. The 1st Bradford Pals finished arriving in their trenches at 3 a.m. The 2nd Bradford Pals only completed their march at 4.30 a.m. and the Durham Pals were in place in Maitland Trench by 4.50 a.m. Last to reach their appointed place was the company from the Leeds Pioneers who were not settled into Legend Trench until 5.50 a.m. There was less than two hours to go to Zero hour on Z Day.

The assembly trenches to be occupied by the 93rd Brigade's battalions are as shown on Map 27, page 473.

15th West Yorkshire Regt. – C and D Companies the front line (marked **1** to **1** on the map) and A and B Companies in Leeds assembly trench between Bess Street and Southern Avenue (marked **2** to **2**);

16th West Yorkshire Regt. – A and C Companies in North and South Monk between Flag Avenue and Grey Street (**3** to **3**). B (right) and D (left) Companies in Bradford Trench between Flag and Warley Trenches (**4** to **4**);

D Company, 18th Durham Light Infantry in South Monk between Flag and Delaunay (**3** to **3a**);

18th West Yorkshire Regt. – A and D Companies in Dunmow Trench (**5** to **5**), B and C Companies in Landguard Trench (**6** to **6**;

A, B and C Companies, 18th Durham Light Infantry – Maitland Trench (**7** to **7**).

One company, 12th KOYLI (**8** to **8a**), 93rd Machine Gun Company (**8a** to **8b**) and Brigade HQ (**8b** to **8c**) all in Legend Trench.

Immediately after they arrived in the assembly trenches special bombing parties from the 18th Durhams commanded by 2nd Lt. J B Bradford moved up to Sap A and reported to the 15th West Yorkshires.

---

[i] Capt. Charles Stanley Duckitt, 18th West Yorkshire Regt., was killed on 3rd May 1917. Aged 40, he was the son of Charles Atkinson Duckitt and Elizabeth Duckitt, of Bradford; husband of Elaine Duckitt, of 'Yarme', South Walk, Reigate, Surrey. He is remembered on the Arras Memorial, Bay 4.

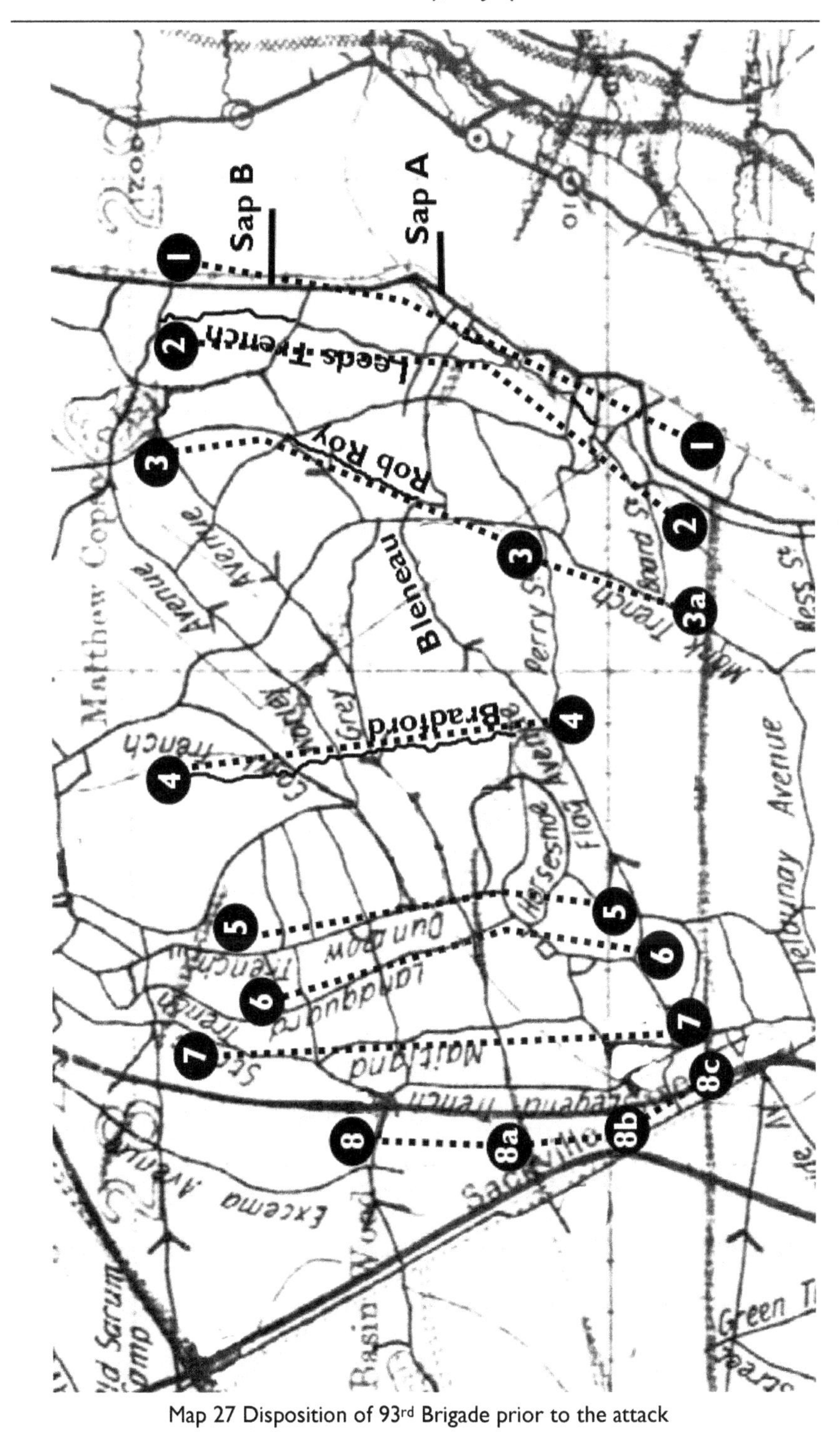

Map 27 Disposition of 93rd Brigade prior to the attack

The men of the battalions settled down as each man tried to find somewhere less wet and muddy than his mate. Last minute letters were exchanged, some slept and others waited for the rum ration to come round. From both sides of No Man's Land the guns still barked and roared and the ground shook under the pounding of shells of all calibres. Above them, shrapnel shells cracked and the bullets whined overhead. And on the far eastern horizon, the sky slowly turned from black to purple and then dark grey as dawn crept over the battlefield. The waiting was nearly over.

THE 94TH BRIGADE WAS TO ATTACK ON A TWO BATTALION FRONT with the Sheffield City Battalion, the 12th York and Lancasters, on the extreme left of the 31st Division's and the Fourth Army front with the Accrington Pals, the 11th East Lancashires, on their right. Broadly speaking, the Sheffield Battalion was to advance from trenches between John and Luke Copse whilst the Accringtons occupied the front line from south of Luke Copse to in front of Matthew Copse. The objective was the village of Serre while the 93rd Brigade swept past the southern edge of the village to take the German 2nd Position. The Division would then turn to face north and north east, presenting a new northern flank for the entire Somme offensive as the main body of the Fourth Army and the French 6th Army progressed north east and east towards Bapaume and Peronne.

The various units of the 94th Brigade were based around Bus-les-Artois and Warnimont Wood and they started the move to the front at about 6 p.m. The Accrington Pals marched via Courcelles leaving for the village at 7 p.m. and arriving at 8.30 p.m. Here they broke the march, were fed and rested before starting to march off at 9.40 p.m. Their route to the front line would be down the very long communication trench Central Avenue. This trench started just north of Colincamps, ran north of La Signy Farm and Observation Wood before reaching the front line at Mark Copse. It was a slow and arduous journey, made under continuous German artillery fire, as the war diary recorded that the trench:

> "… was in a very bad state and over knee deep in mud which had become glutinous."

Key to **Error! Reference source not found.**, page 475.
1 to 1 = Half each of W and X Companies, 11th East Lancashire Regt.
2 to 2 = Half each of W and X Companies, 11th East Lancashire Regt.
3 to 3 = Half each of Y and Z Companies, 11th East Lancashire Regt.
4 to 4 = Half each of Y and Z Companies, 11th East Lancashire Regt.
5 to 5, 6 to 6 and 7 to 7 = A and C Companies, 12th York and Lancaster Regt.
8 to 8 and 9 to 9 = B and D Companies, 12th York & Lancaster Regt.
10 to 10 to 10 and 11 to 11 = A and B Companies, 14th York and Lancaster Regt.
12 to 12 = C Company, 14th York and Lancaster Regt.
13 to 13 = D Company, 14th York and Lancaster Regt.
13 to 14 = 2 Platoons, 13th York and Lancaster Regt.
15 to 15 and 16 to 16 = Rest of 13th York and Lancaster Regt.
17 to 17 = Brigade HQ, company 12th KOYLI and 94th MGC

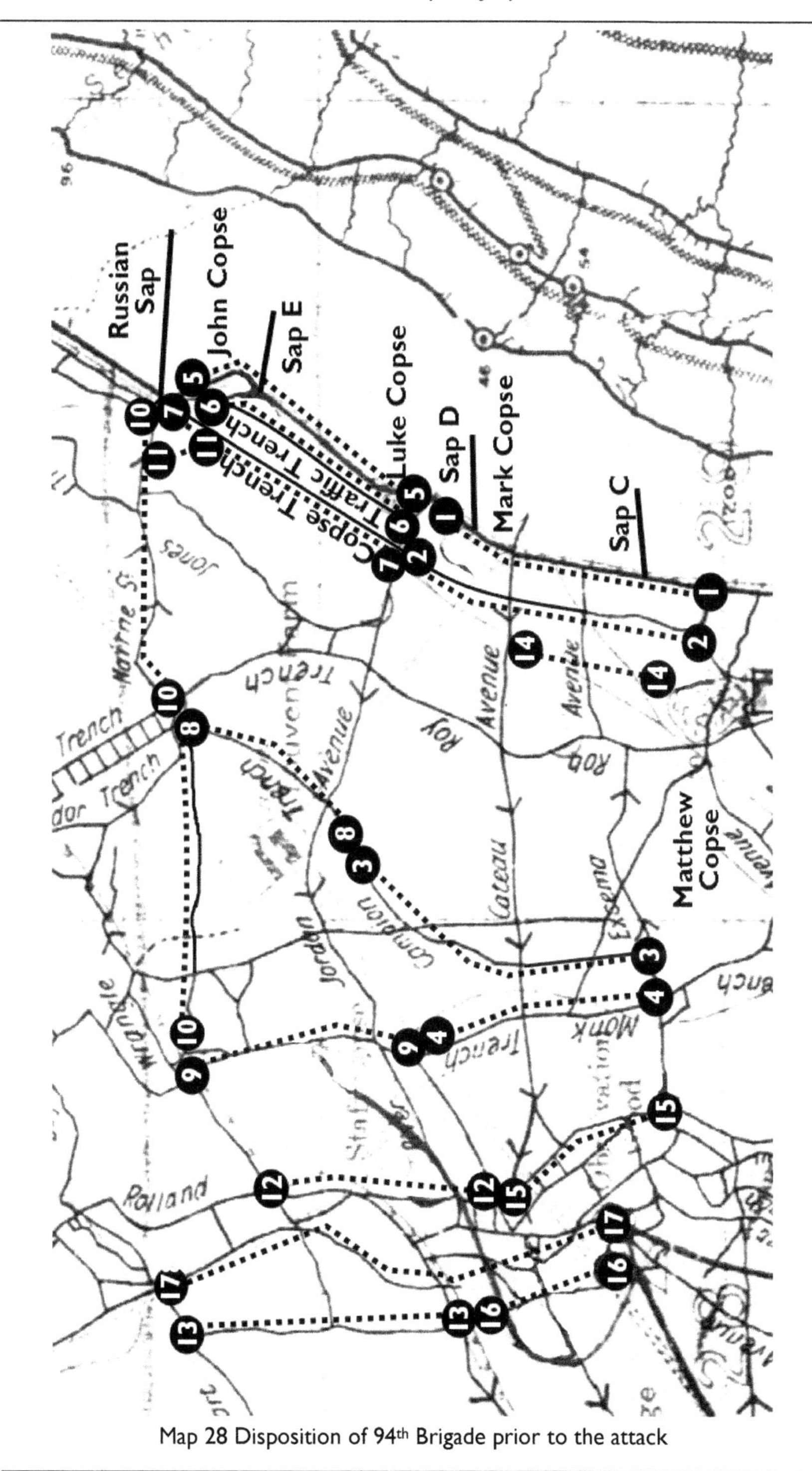

Map 28 Disposition of 94th Brigade prior to the attack

Plate 110 Lt. Col. Arthur Wilmot Rickman, 11th East Lancashire Regt.

By 12.20 a.m. the battalion was still some distance short of a fork in Central Avenue which was itself still some 2,500 yards from the front lines the battalion was to occupy. As a result, Lt. Col. Arthur Rickman moved up the column to the head of the first company due to form the 2nd wave and ordered them to advance over the open. Rickman led the way and he arrived with the head of his column in the front line at 2.40 a.m. Finding places to accommodate his men proved trying as it had been ordered that the tunnels at Sap D and Sap C were not to be occupied by the attacking troops. This Rickman had clearly planned to do as he then spent considerable time changing the dispositions of his 1st wave commanded by Capt. Arnold Tough. Nos. 1 and 2 Platoons of W Company were placed on the right in partially blown in fire bays in the front line and Nos. 5 and 6 Platoons, X Company, were on their left, the battalion's left which stopped at the northern end of Mark Copse. Capt. Harry Livesey's 2nd wave, made up of the remaining platoons of W and X Companies, sought shelter in Copse Trench, with the 3rd wave under 2nd Lt. George Williams[i] in Campion and the 4th wave in Monk Trench under Capt. Henry Riley. These latter two waves were made up of two platoons each of Y and Z Companies. Rickman made his battalion HQ at the end of Sap C. It still took them until 4 a.m. to get organised and all the while they were under fire from the German artillery. [ii]

---

[i] 2nd Lt. George Gabriel Williams transferred to the Royal Engineers where he worked in the Anti-Gas School. He died of pneumonia on 24th February 1919 and is buried in Etaples Military Cemetery.

[ii] Lt. Col. Arthur Wilmot Rickman, DSO, was born on 25th September 1874. He was the son of Maj. Gen William Rickman and Mary Rickman of the Manor House, Barkham, Berkshire. He was educated at Winchester College before being commissioned into 3rd Queen's (Royal West Surrey Regt.) of the Militia before transferring to the 2nd Northumberland Fusiliers in May 1897. He served in the South African War being involved in the defence of Ladysmith. He was awarded the Queen's Medal with 3 clasps and the King's Medal with 2 clasps. He married Florence Cammell in March 1903 and they

Plate 111 2nd Lt. Bartholomew Endean, 11th East Lancashire Regt

It was a shell from one of these guns that nearly brought about the untimely end of 23 year old 2nd Lt. Bartholomew 'Bart' Endean. Endean was a platoon commander in Z Company, part of the 4th wave part, and, during the early hours, he had slipped into a dugout with his sergeant, 15368 Sgt. Benjamin Ingham, to make cups of Oxo on a portable stove. Endean had then left his equipment hanging in the dugout whilst he waited for the off, the better to move around the crowded trenches. Thirty minutes or so before zero hour he and Ingham returned to the dugout where the sergeant started to help the subaltern back into his webbing when a shell landed on and collapsed the roof trapping both men inside. Endean was eventually dug out with a few shell splinter wounds but Sgt. Ingham, who had his back to the dugout entrance, was fatally wounded[i]. For the luckier Endean it was a 'Blighty one' and one that may well have saved his life given the casualties to come[ii].

---

had three children before the marriage was dissolved. He joined the Special Reserve in 1909. He re-joined the Army in Augusts 1914 and was given command of the 11th East Lancashire Regt on 1st March 1915. He married Muriel Joicey Fulton in May 1916. He was awarded the DSO for his conduct on 1st July, 1916. He was invalided home but re-joined the battalion in May 1917. Wounded again on 11th November 1917 he re-joined the battalion on 21st March 1918. He was awarded a second DSO for his conduct on 12th/13th April 1918 during the fighting on the Lys. He was given temporary command of the 92nd Brigade returning to command battalion in January 1919, which position he relinquished in October 1919. He retired from the Army in March 1920 to live in Coombe Bissett, Wiltshire. He died in an accident at his home on 16th October 1925. He is buried in St Michaels and All Angels churchyard, Coombe Bissett.

[i] 15368 Sgt. Benjamin Ingham, 11th East Lancashire Regt., was aged 24. He was the brother of Mary A Ingham, of 15, Spencer Rd., New Southgate, London. A native of Brierfield; he lived at 177 Accrington Road, Burnley. He is buried in Euston Road Cemetery, Colincamps, grave I. D. 9.

[ii] 2nd Lt, later Capt., Bartholomew Endean, 11th East Lancashire Regt., was born on 30th April 1893 in Cramlington, Northumberland. He was commissioned into the 3rd East

The Sheffield City Battalion's journey was no better and, even before they started off from Warnimont Wood, they had already experienced their first setback. It would be one of many. Lt. Col. Joseph Arthur Crosthwaite had been appointed CO of the battalion on 25th September 1915. He came from the 2nd Durham Light Infantry with 26 years' experience with the 3rd Manchester Regt., the DLI and, for a period in the Militia, as Adjutant of the 3rd North Staffordshire Regt. He had commanded the 2nd DLI for five months between January and June 1915 but had been wounded at 2nd Ypres prior to taking command of the Sheffield Battalion during their last months of training. That there was an issue with his health first came to light when he failed to attend an 11 a.m. parade at which the Corps commander was to address the men. Instead, Maj. Alfred Plackett, rushed hurriedly back from his post as commandant of the Divisional School, took his place. The men had then stood to hear a typically gushing and enthusiastic harangue from Hunter-Weston which did not even consider the prospect of anything other than complete success:

> "But your lot is a very heavy one, and a huge responsibility is shared equally by every individual. No individual soldier may say he has no responsibility. The 29th Division performed glorious feats of arms at Gallipoli; the 4th Division, on the right, did wonders in the great retreat from Mons. The feats of these divisions will never be forgotten as long as the world endures. You are Englishmen, even as they, and now you have your opportunity to shine. You will have to stick it. You must stick it. I salute each officer, N.C.O., and man."

The men then returned to their final preparations perhaps wondering what had happened to their gallant CO. He was, in fact, seriously ill, the effects of his wounds still considerable, and was on his way home.

The men, buoyed by the words of the General, were later further encouraged by a Special Order of the Day issued by Brig. Gen. H C Rees[i], DSO, who had

Lancashire Regt. on 8th May 1915. He joined the 11th East Lancashire Regt. in April 1916 and was posted to Z Company which he later commanded. He was wounded at Ploegsteert Wood on 28th September 1918 and resigned his commission in 1919. He trained at Rutherford College and Armstrong College, Newcastle, where he was in the OTC. He married Esther Raine Hall on 11th February 1917. They had three children. He died on 28th December 1986. The Bart Endean Monumental Stonemasonry Company still operates in Morpeth.

[i] Brig. Gen. Hubert Conway Rees, CMG, DSO, was born on 26th March 1882. He joined the 2nd Welch Regt., fighting in South Africa. He had an active and varied war. He was a company commander with the 2nd Welch Regt when it went to France with the 3rd Brigade, 1st Division, in August 1914. He saw action on the Aisne and at 1st Ypres where his battalion was destroyed at Gheluvelt. He had been awarded the DSO for his conduct eight days earlier on the 23rd October 1914. He then joined the 38th (Welsh) Division before being promoted Temp Brig. Gen. in June 1916 when he took over temporary command of the 94th Brigade. He then commanded the 11th Brigade through the autumn fighting on the Somme and was then given command of the 149th Brigade, fighting at Arras. He was taken ill in July 1917 returning to take command of the 150th Brigade, 50th Division, on 27th February 1918. Heavily involved in the defences against the German Michael and Georgette offensives in the Spring, his Brigade was sent to a 'quiet' sector on the Chemin des Dames where they were surrounded on 27th May, the first day of the

taken temporary command of the 94th Brigade. He, too, was overwhelmingly confident of imminent success. Clearly, the results of the raids and the energy and activity of the German infantry and artillery had been completely ignored by senior officers. They seemed convinced that numbers alone, of men and guns, would see the enemy defeated.

"Brigade H.Q.

You are about to attack the enemy with far greater numbers than he can oppose to you, supported by a huge number of guns.
Englishmen have always proved better than the Germans when the odds were heavily against them. It is now our opportunity.
You are about to fight in one of the greatest battles in the world, and in the most just cause.
Remember that the British Empire will anxiously watch your every move, and that the honour of the North Country rests in your hands.
Keep your heads, do your duty, and you will utterly defeat the enemy.

(Signed) F. S. G. Piggott, Captain,
Brigade Major, 94th Infantry Bde."[28]

And so, as the evening drew in, the men from Sheffield marched out of Warnimont Wood towards their assembly trenches at the northern end of the great battlefield. They, along with the other battalions of the Brigade, stopped north of Courcelles for food and tea laced with rum before all the officers synchronised watches and the march resumed. The battalion's point of entry into the front lines was at the far end of Northern Avenue, another enormously long and muddy communication trench. Battalion Headquarters made decent progress and, by 1.40 a.m., Major Alfred Plackett, Major Albert Hoette, second-in-command, Captain and Adjutant Norman Tunbridge, Lt. Henry Oxley, the Signalling Officer, and other Headquarters' details had arrived at John Copse. There they waited for A and C Companies to appear but it took until 3.45 a.m. before all the troops were in position. Nervous, tired and wet, the men settled down to wait for the whistles to blow. The battalion war diary afterwards recorded that their deployment had probably been delayed by 2½ hours by the appalling state of the trenches. The three communication trenches used – Northern Avenue, Pylon and Nairne – were all described as being in 'an exceedingly bad condition'. In places water came over the men's knees. The eastern end of Nairne Street as well as the front line, Traffic Trench and Copse Trench were also 'badly smashed up' and Monk and Campion were in a bad state but mainly because of the rain. To add to their woes, the telephone lines were cut and all information to and from the battalion had to be carried by runners who had to negotiate the water-filled and muddy communication trenches.

Behind them came the two Barnsley Battalions, the 14th York and Lancasters on the left behind the Sheffield Battalion and the 13th Battalion in support of the Accringtons. They started to move away from the stop at Courcelles at about 10.40 p.m. in order to give the preceding battalions time to get into and organised

German Blücher-Yorck offensive. Taken prisoner, he was repatriated in December 1918. He retired from the Army in 1922 and died on 3rd January 1948.

in the front line assembly trenches. But, as the progress of the first wave units slowed in the clinging mud of the congested communication trenches, so the men from Barnsley found their advance grinding to a halt. The 14th York and Lancasters entered the western end of Northern Avenue at midnight. It took them another three hours before they reached the junction with Rolland Trench just short of the assembly trenches. Here they would split into three groups. B Company, commanded by Capt. Frederick Neville Houston, had two platoons under Lt. Harold Bruce Forsdike and 2nd Lt. Harry Strong in Copse Trench close up behind the Sheffield men. A Company under Capt. Gustav Oscar Roos with 2nd Lts. William Hirst, Reginald Dudley Bawdwen Anderson, Walter Kell, and a detachment of the 94th Machine Gun Company with two Vickers Guns was in file in the front end of Nairne Street which ran due west from the northern end of John Copse, passing Toutvent Farm on its northern side. To their rear, also in Nairne Street, were the two remaining platoons of B Company under 2nd Lt. Duncan Fairley and Lt. Rupert Esmond Lowinsky. The other two companies occupied Rolland Trench (C Company, Capt. Henry Edmeades with 2nd Lts. Leslie William Johnson and Albert Edward Holmes) and Babylon Trench (D Company, Capt. Charles Harold Robin, with 2nd Lts. Robert Goodburn and Charles Frederick Moxon). Lt. Col. Walter Backhouse Hulke[i] and Battalion HQ were in Rolland Trench. On their right the 13th York and Lancasters extended down to the south behind the Accringtons except, that is, for two platoons under Capt. Gurney who were close up behind the right of the first two waves of the Accrington Pals just to the north of Matthew Copse.

The tasks of the 2nd Barnsley Pals were dangerous and complicated. A Company under Capt. Roos was to follow the Sheffield men over and occupy and fortify a stretch of German communication trench running from the front line back to Tübinger Stellung and facing north east. This was to be the new front line trench facing the IR 66 in front of Puisieux and would represent the start of the new left flank of Fourth Army which, if all went well during the day, would be extended out as far as the Puisieux to Beaucourt Road. The two platoons of B Company commanded by Forsdike and Strong had the task of clearing the three lines of German trenches running immediately south of the trench occupied by A Company. Behind them, the other two platoons of B Company under Lowinsky and Fairley had the tricky job of opening up Sap F, the Russian sap running facing north east. This would necessitate a lot of standing around in the open in the middle of No Man's Land and would only be achievable if what the Corps

[i] Lt. Col. Walter Backhouse Hulke, DSO, 9th Lincolnshire Regt., att. 14th York and Lancaster Regt. was born in Deal in 1872, the seventh of ten children of Frederick Thomas Hulke, MD, and Charlotte Backhouse. He went to the RMC, Sandhurst, and was commissioned into the Lincolnshire Regt. in November 1892. By 1899 he was a Staff Officer becoming Superintendent of Gymnasia, Eastern District. In 1906 he was appointed Adjutant of the 4th (Hunts) Volunteer Battalion, Bedfordshire Regt., and Adjutant of the 5th Bedfordshire Regt. in 1908 and was put on retired pay in February 1911. He was appointed Adjutant of the 9th Lincolnshire Regt. in November 1914 and was promoted Temp Lt. Col. on 9th July 1915 when he took command of the 14th Y&L. He was awarded the DSO in the New Year's Honours List 1917. He was promoted Temp. Brig. Gen. on 15th April 1918. Married to Elsie Marian Hulke, he died on 9th January, 1923.

commander and the other senior officers had said about the certain destruction of the enemy's machine guns and riflemen turned out to be true.

The rest of the battalion, C and D Companies and Battalion HQ were in reserve in case of unforeseen eventualities. There was one unpredictable element about everything that the Barnsley men had to do. That was the fate of the IR 66 on their left. If the heavy artillery and the weakened firepower of the 48th Division field artillery were unable to suppress the majority of the machine gun and rifle fire coming from this otherwise unoccupied German regiment then the only thing left to protect the 14th York and Lancasters would be a smoke screen. And smoke does not stop bullets.

While the men slogged through the morass in the communication trenches, the men of D Company, 10th East Yorkshires, had been preparing the front line for the attack. Lanes had to be cut through the British wire to allow the attacking troops easy access to No Man's Land. On the Sheffield's front a small party under Capt. William Clark had moved up in advance of the rest of the battalion and they checked the work of the East Yorkshires before crawling out into No Man's Land to lay white tapes parallel to the trenches about 100 yards in advance of the British lines. This was to mark the place where the 1st wave was wait before the attack started. Tapes laid, Clark and his men returned to the British lines at 12.30 a.m. They were not to know that an alert German patrol would find this evidence of an imminent attack and remove it. The Germans scarcely needed any further confirmation that the attack was now due. The laying of the tape would have helped confirm their thinking, but there would be other factors too which resulted in the men of the IR 169 and the IR 66 being placed on high alert.

Out at the ends of the saps work was being done to get the positions ready for the Stokes mortars and at 1.20 a.m. 31st Division was informed that the guns were in position, the 94th TMB at Saps E and D and Eden Trench and the 93rd TMB at Saps A and B and in Leeds Trench. In the front line, the men of the 92nd Trench Mortar Battery were still working hard to uncover and recover the ammunition buried around Sap C as a result of the German bombardment. This work was itself done under fire from the German guns whose flashes could be seen away to the east in a great ring from north of Bucquoy and south to the Ancre valley and beyond.

Such was the weight of the German artillery fire on the British assembly trenches that at 3 a.m. the 16th West Yorkshires reported that half a platoon had been buried by a nearby shell explosion. The general level of activity within the German lines must have given the more perceptive officers and men pause for thought about what awaited them out in No Man's Land. The 92nd Brigade had expected to send out officer patrols for one last minute check on the wire with, perhaps, the judicious use of the odd Bangalore torpedo should it be required. But the constant illumination of the ground between the opposing trenches by flares and the non-stop chatter of machine guns scything across the empty grassland made this impossible and this was reported to Division at 3.43 a.m.

The constant movement of men and equipment in the battered trenches was making nonsense of Wanless-O'Gowan's order that the men should conceal themselves prior to Zero. At 4 a.m. Lt. Col. Baumgartner, GSO1 of 31st Division, telephoned all three Brigade HQs only to be told that none of them had all of their men in position. The 12th York and Lancasters had no reports from B and C Companies and the bombing party from the 18th Durhams had not arrived with the Leeds Pals (they eventually turned up at 5.05 a.m.). Meanwhile, men from various units were wandering all over the trench system trying to find their correct location. And all the while they were under fire. At 4.05 a.m. the Sheffield City Battalion reported shells falling from John Copse along the whole of the already battered front line trench. In spite of this, 31st Division distributed a positive if completely unrealistic situation report to VIII Corps and its Divisional neighbours at 4.15 a.m.:

> "Situation report. Exceptionally quiet night in forward trenches. Front line shelled slightly. Villages of Courcelles and Colincamps shelled between 10 and 11 p.m. Bus Wood and vicinity shelled between 12.30 a.m. and 2.30 a.m. and again at 3.30 a.m. and still continues. Assembly almost complete."[29]

Unfortunately, the activity in the British trenches, the white tapes laid out in No Man's Land and collected in places by German patrols, allied to other intelligence gathered, some from prisoners taken during raids, and yet more intelligence given away through the imprudent use of telephones and buzzers too close to the front line had given the Germans all the noticed they needed of the impending attack. Maj. von Struensee, the CO of IR 169, received a communiqué from 104. Infanterie Brigade at 4.30 a.m. (3.30 a.m. GMT) stating that the long anticipated attack would take place that day. The time given was wrong, 5.30 a.m. (4.30 a.m. GMT) but this may have been more because no-one expected the British to attack in full daylight[30]. Surely they could not make such a huge error? Half an hour later, a particularly enterprising five-man patrol from the 7/IR 169 in sector S4 actually entered the British front line trench. Led by Vizefeldwebel Ackermann, the men investigated a section of the trench and ascertained that there seemed to be plenty going on in the support trench. The sort of activity that suggested something big was to take place in a few hours' time.

IT WAS NOT UNTIL AFTER 5 A.M. that the last Brigade, the 94th, reported that everyone was in position and it was at this time that the British artillery sharply increased the tempo of its firing. In the absence of any wire reports, the 170th Brigade decided to fire at the front line wire anyway. Some repairs had been managed during the night and these were also targeted. By 5.20 a.m., however, Division reported that both assaulting Brigades were:

> "… perfectly satisfied with the way the enemy wire in front of them had been cut."[31]

From then on, a series of comforting reports came in from the units scattered across the Divisional front. Everything seemed 'normal' or 'correct' and, at 6 a.m., the Durham Pals reported that the German guns seemed 'to be inferior to our artillery'. They also noted that the aircraft of the R.F.C. were overhead and seemingly unchallenged.

Behind the attacking battalions, the men of the 92nd Brigade, in reserve, were moving up to their assembly positions. The 12th East Yorkshires occupied assembly trenches in Sackville Street North near to a ruined building known as Red Cottage. Although over 1,200 yards from the British front line, they would still suffer casualties as they waited throughout the day, with 2nd Lt. Sam Daykin Holbrook and two others being wounded by German artillery fire. 300 yards behind them, three companies of the 10th East Yorkshire occupied Palestine Trench off Northern Avenue. The remaining company, D Company, was further forward and was to occupy the old British front line when the other two Brigades moved forward. The 11th East Yorkshires, still smarting from the failed raid of the night of the 27th June, were to occupy another trench the name of which was steeped in Biblical history – Hittite Trench (others similarly named nearby were Babylon, Jeremiah and Uriah Trenches). Although they had nowhere near as far to travel as the leading Brigades, it still took this unit well over nine hours to march from Authie to its assembly trenches and most of the delay was caused by blockages in, and the condition of, the long communication trenches down which they travelled. They would remain in Hittite for the rest of the day, coming under intermittent artillery fire which cost them nine wounded one of whom, 11/1345 Pte. Edward Harrison, died of his wounds the following day at the MDS at Couin manned by men of the 1/3rd South Midland Field Ambulance, 48th Division[i]. The 13th East Yorkshires would also spend most of day huddled in the bottom of a trench, this time Pylon Trench. Their losses from the German guns would total 13 wounded by the end of the day.

Although the weather seemed set fair for later in the day, there was a thick mist at 6 a.m. and this made observation very difficult. Whether this could explain the report of C Company, Sheffield City Battalion, that the British guns were firing into their own front line between John and Luke Copses is not clear. But there was some delay in getting the message through to 94th Brigade HQ as, with the telephone lines cut, the information had been sent by runner, no easy job in the muddy and congested trenches.

Although reports started to come in that the mist had started to rise at 6.10 a.m. the war diary of the 165th Brigade, RFA, flatly contradicts this with its report timed at 6.25 a.m.:

> "Opened fire with HE on German front line trenches… Observation impossible owing to mist."[32]

The 169th Brigade, RFA, reported that A/169 and B/171 Batteries found it impossible to register because of the mist.[33]

In spite of this all of the Division's field guns and medium trench mortars opened fire on the German front line trench and soon the smoke from the guns and the explosions, joined by the entire Corps artillery, smothered the enemy's front line.

As soon as the British guns opened their concerted bombardment the German artillery replied in kind, with the 93rd Brigade reporting heavy shrapnel barrages on the front line and the forward assembly trenches. On the 94th Brigade front they threw in some HE as well and at 6.30 a.m. C Company of the 12th York and Lancasters reported fire bays 31 to 38 heavily shelled and fourteen

---

[i] 11/1345 Pte Edward Harrison, 11th East Yorkshire Regt., died on 2nd July, 1916. Aged 22, he was the son of Hardisty and Emma Harrison, of 86, Goulton St., Eton St., Hessle Rd., Hull. Native of Bradford, Yorks. He is buried at Couin British Cemetery, grave I. C. 17.

men, mainly of No. 12 Platoon, killed or wounded. The British guns were also still firing short. The reply from Brigade was not encouraging:

"Report again at 7.0 a.m. Nothing can be done at present."[34]

They did report again. Their own guns were still firing short.

By 6.53 a.m., 93rd Brigade reported one officer wounded, three other ranks killed and 26 wounded by the German shrapnel barrage. A minute later and the Divisional OP reported that the front line barrage now extended as far back as Sackville Street, a report immediately confirmed by 93rd Brigade. Then, as if they knew they were full of troops, at 7 a.m. the German brought down a heavy HE barrage on the front and assembly trenches.

Concerns were now beginning to grow that the Germans were only too well aware that the attack was about to take place. The writer of the Sheffield City Battalion war diary believed there were several reasons why:

> "The enemy artillery continued shelling heavily from 4.5 a.m., until the attack commenced. In view of the fact that the enemy artillery became active as soon as it was daylight, it would appear likely that the enemy was warned of the attack by observing gaps cut in our own wire and tapes laid out in No Man's Land, thus obtaining at least three and a half hours warning of the attack.
>
> A Company reported no sign of the tape which was laid during the night; it had, apparently, been removed. It served no purpose at all except to give the enemy warning.
>
> The wire in front of our lines had been cut away too much and, as the gaps were not staggered, our intention to attack must have been quite obvious to the enemy."[35]

By 7.04 a.m., 93rd Brigade was describing the German barrage as very heavy. But, at 7.07 a.m., 31st Division reported to VIII Corps that the enemy was putting only a 'light barrage on our front line'.[36] Someone had it wrong. And the front line was not the only area being hit, for some time long range German guns had been firing into the villages in the rear, presumably to interfere with the movement of reserves and reinforcements. The wagon lines of the 170th Brigade, RFA, in Bus Wood had been shelled from 4.30 a.m. onwards causing damage to the wagons and injuries to the horses. At 7.07 a.m. the problem was sufficiently severe for the officer in charge to ask whether he should move the wagons and horses out of range. He was ordered to stay nearby.

At 7.10 a.m. both attacking Brigades reported to Division that they were being shelled, with the right sector of the 93rd Brigade taking a real beating. At the same moment, the 93rd Brigade reported that the British artillery had moved off the enemy front line. The attack was not due for another 20 minutes. Col. Craven, commanding the Reserve Group of the Divisional artillery, reported that two German 15 cm batteries were firing 10 rounds a minute into the area from Matthew Copse south to Bleneau, the left of the 93rd Brigade. In addition, some 10.5 cm and 77 mm shells were battering other parts of the 93rd Brigade's front.

The leading waves of the infantry were now getting ready to move out into No Man's Land where they were to lie out on the tapes, some of which were no longer there. Behind the front line the 2iC of the 2nd Barnsley Pals went forward to supervise the advance of A and B Companies currently sheltering in what remained of Nairne Street and Copse Trench. These units had the task of taking and consolidating the trenches that would become part of the new northern flank of the entire Somme attack. A Company, led by No. 1 Platoon, was to take and hold a German communication trench that ran back across the first four lines of German trenches to the north west of Serre. They were to construct two new strongpoints in a new front line facing north east. Behind them, two platoons of B Company, commanded by Lts. Fairley and Lowinsky, were to enter the Russian sap that ran out from the centre of John Copse, open it up and convert it to a fire trench thus connecting the old British front line with the new one now being held by A Company. Meanwhile, the remaining two platoons of B Company were to clear the first three German trenches running south from this new front line. As they say, it seemed like a good idea at the time.

Their problem was that the German bombardment was not only causing heavy casualties, it was also destroying the trenches in which the men sought shelter. The war diary describes the northern edge of the British lines in these terms:

> "Just before Zero the condition of the front trenches was as follows:
> Nairne Street: From a point about 10yds east of Jones, this trench was completely levelled, and so much exposed that it appeared to form part of No Man's Land.
> Traffic Trench and Fire Bays (Nairne to John Copse). Very much damaged and in places levelled.
> John Copse viewed from front of Nairne resembled a heap of debris.
> Copse Trench. Completely blocked at Nairne end. No communication except over the top."[37]

Most of the damage being done, by both artillery and machine gun fire, was coming from the direction of the IR 66's trenches opposite the 48th Division and batteries around Puisieux and Bucquoy behind them. From here it was possible to enfilade the British fire and assembly trenches in the habitable parts of which were currently squeezed the men of two full Brigades. As Nairne Street was flattened it exposed the Barnsley men within to heavy machine gun fire. Casualties mounted rapidly and it was later estimated that as many as 30% of the assaulting, consolidating and clearing parties of the 2nd Barnsley Pals were killed or wounded before they even reached the British front line. Concentrated machine gun and rifle fire was coming from the II Battalion of IR 66 commanded by Hauptmann Rochlitz[i] who ignored the men of the 1/5th and 1/7th Royal Warwickshire Regt. in the trenches of the 48th Division directly opposite and ordered his men to pour their bullets into the exposed left flank of the 31st Division[ii].

---

[i] The normal OC the II Battalion, Maj. Paulus, had been wounded on the 26th June during the bombardment).

[ii] The 1/7th Royal Warwickshires were on the immediate left of the 31st Division on 1st July. During the day the battalion lost six men killed and 13 wounded (all from a carrying party of 60 men provided by A Company to help move the 4 in. Stokes mortars and ammunition for the smoke screens). During the entire week of the bombardment and the

The only actions designed to assist the advance of the far left of the 94th Brigade was to be a series of smoke screens produced by No. 4 Company of No. 5 Battalion, Special Brigade, Royal Engineers. These were started ten minutes before zero. Six sections of the company armed with 4 in. Stokes trench mortars and a supply of smoke bombs and smoke candles were to attempt to conceal from view the left of the 31st Division and the right of the 56th Division at Gommecourt and, thereby, in some way protect them from the rifle and machine gun fire of the otherwise wholly unengaged IR 66 as well as part of IR 170 further north.

In the main, the men from the Special Brigade did what was asked of them and they thought their job had been done well. The only complete failure was that of Section N37 led by Lt. Mark Henry Vernon. Its four guns were to attempt to extend the smoke screen to the north of Serre and beyond its eastern corner and they had been given 240 mortar rounds with which to achieve this objective. Unfortunately, the 60-strong party came under German artillery fire on the way up to the front line and some of the ammunition being carried was detonated in the trenches. An order was passed round to withdraw and by the time the officers were able to round up the men only thirteen were available and they were exhausted, having carried heavy loads of smoke bombs up and then back down the muddy communication trenches. Another sixteen men were eventually found but the entire operation was subsequently abandoned in mid-morning by which time it would have been too late anyway. For his pains, Lt. Vernon was wounded.

Sections N38 (Lt. Henry George Edwin Wisdom, RFA), N39 (2nd Lt. John Gibson Gibson, RE), Q46 (2nd Lt. John Carroll Johnson, RE), Q47 (Lt. C Smith, RFA) and Q48 (2nd Lt. Adam McCall Robertson, RFA) were all more successful in firing their smoke bombs. They each had between 240 and 256 to fire and every section fired a minimum of 227 (Q47, out of 248) and a maximum of 241 (N38, out of 244). Most of the failures were caused by damp shells and these either misfired or burst in the barrels. The sections also came under heavy artillery fire but the men stuck to their task, being in position from one hour before zero to three hours after. Casualties were mercifully light, however, with the aforementioned Lt. Vernon being joined by 2nd Lt. Edwin Bagshaw (shell shock) and 14 other ranks on a trip to see the medics. All of the OCs believed

---

attack, casualties were Capt. N C Murray and 14 ORs killed, two ORs died of wounds and Lt. Arthur John Field and 2nd Lt. William Arthur Imber and 37 ORs wounded. 2nd Lt. Imber died on 27th August 1917, aged 23. He is remembered on the Tyne Cot Memorial, Panels 23 to 28 and 163A.

Capt. Norman Cairns Murray, 1/7th Royal Warwickshire Regt., was killed on 30th June 1916. Aged 26, he was the youngest son of the late Mr C C Murray of Napier, New Zealand. Educated at Berkhamsted School, where he was in the OTC, he was commissioned on 10th July 1914. He is buried in Hebuterne Military Cemetery, grave I. F. 12.

The 1/5th Royal Warwickshire Regt. were on the left of the 48th Division's front with the battalion's left adjacent to the right wing of the 1/14th London Regt. (London Scottish) of the 168th Brigade, 56th (1st London) Division. On 1st July, the 1/5th Warwicks lost one other rank killed and one other rank missing. Capt. William Charles Coleman Gell (at duty), 2nd Lt. Percival Allan Grove, 2nd Lt. Herbert Henry Pine and 21 other ranks (5 at duty) were wounded.

their job well done. They placed a smoke screen on either flank of the two Divisions they were designed to protect and sustained it for an extended period. The only problem was that it didn't work.

Plate 112 Brig. Gen. Hubert Conway Rees, GOC, 94th Brigade

Brig. Gen. Rees of the 94th Brigade wrote after the war that he had complained to Hunter-Weston about the inadequacies of the preparations on the 48th Division's front on his left:

> "A few days before the attack I pointed out the General Hunter-Weston that the assembly trenches stopped dead on the left of the 94th Brigade and that not a spade had been put in the ground between me and the subsidiary attack at Gommecourt. Worse still, no effort at wirecutting had been made on that stretch either. A child could see where the flank of our attack lay, to within ten yards."[38]

Whilst his comments are not completely accurate there was more than a little evidence to suggest that Rees had serious cause for complaint. It is notable that the last two wire cutting reports forwarded by the 48th Division suggest that the Division's artillery had not been terribly active on their front. 'Partly cut and damaged in places' was the report for Thursday morning while Friday's comment that the wire on their front was in 'about (the) same condition' suggests that 48th Division had not spent much time and effort in trying to persuade IR 66 that their front was about to be attacked. Indeed, according to 2nd Lt. Francis Stanley Gedye[i], the guns of the 240th Brigade, RFA, which had been retained to fire on the wire and trenches in the gap between the 31st and 56th Divisions, ceased firing

[i] 2nd Lt., later Capt., Francis Stanley Gedye, MC, 240th (South Midland) Brigade, RFA, was commissioned out of the Bristol University Contingent, Senior Division, OTC, on 23rd July 1915. He was awarded his MC in the New Year's Honours list of January 1918. His brother, Lt. Edward Leonard Gedye, 240th (South Midland) Brigade, RFA, was killed in action on the 23rd/24th August 1916. He is buried in Aveluy Communal Cemetery Extension.

on this sector after just two days and spent the rest of the bombardment firing at targets on the 31st Division's front[39].

Even the Division's effort at releasing gas earlier in the week had been somewhat half-hearted. The release was due to coincide with similar actions by the 29th and 31st Divisions and, during the mid-morning of 25th June, two Special Brigade officers, Lt. Alexander Fowler and 2nd Lt. G A P Henderson, had supervised the teams ready to turn on the canisters arrayed along the parapet of the 143rd Brigade. At 10.15 a.m. smoke was released along the Corps' front and, two minutes later, the gas canisters were turned on. Or, at least, those of the canisters on which the spanners worked. They proceeded to leak their lethal contents slowly out into No Man's Land where a 4 mph westerly breeze wafted it gently towards the German lines, bleaching the grass as it went. From twenty two of the canisters, however, nothing emerged to trouble the German troops hurriedly donning their gas masks. The valves could not be released whatever the men with their spanners tried. Twenty minutes later the working cylinders were turned off. If the level of German retaliation was an indicator of the threat they felt from the 48th Division's gas discharge then little had been achieved, as the majority of the shells fired by the German guns flew over the heads of the men of the Special Brigade and into the rear areas. Just two fell near the front line trench. There was hardly any rifle or machine gun fire either. In all, the enemy seemed hardly bothered by the entire exercise.

There seems to have been a problem with the conduct of both of the inactive Divisions flanking the attacks on 1st July 1916 as very similar complaints were levelled against the 37th Division which was immediately to the north of the 46th Division when it attacked Gommecourt. They too failed to make any pretence that an attack would take place on their front though, with a No Man's Land nearly 1,000 yards wide, the 37th Division would have had to have been extremely industrious if they were to fool the enemy in any way. Essentially, though, the problem was the same. The Germans on the fronts not being attacked either already knew or very quickly realised that they were not to be attacked and so turned their machine guns, rifles and artillery onto the sectors being assaulted. The fact that the German Divisional commanders had agreed systems for co-operation was also of great assistance to them. Inter-Corps co-operation on the British front would prove to be notable by its absence throughout the day.

So, in spite of the gallant efforts of the Special Brigade smoke bombers, the fact was that the men of IR 66 knew they were not to be attacked and, even better, knew where was being attacked. Smoke screens might conceal but they do not stop bullets and the machine guns of the IR 66 were swiftly re-directed to take the British trenches and No Man's Land in enfilade. They did not need to see the British troops, knowing they were somewhere behind the smoke was good enough. They would have taken ranges and compass readings weeks or months before and could fire using this data in a devastating fashion. This they proceeded to do.

The 14th York and Lancasters out on the extreme left along Nairne Street had the greatest vested interest in the success of the smoke screens. At 7.20 a.m. they watched as the smoke bombs were launched from the mortars whilst, at the same time, smoke candles were lit on the front line parapet and these started to emit their foul smelling green, yellow and black smoke. The wind locally was from the west and moved the smoke at about 2 mph. At 59 yards per minute this was slightly faster than 50 yards a minute at which the infantry was to advance to the attack. The volume of smoke and the direction of the cloud were also good. But, at the first sign of the smoke, the IR 66 opened fire with increasing intensity so that, by zero hour, several machine guns were firing through the cloud and into the flanks of the 31st Division and these weapons were dreadfully effective as they whipped into the flanks of the advancing troops.

The war diary of the 143rd Brigade on the immediate left of the 31st Division states quite frankly how obvious the plan of attack must have appeared to German observers:

> "7.20 a.m. discharge of smoke candles begins from our trenches. This provoked some artillery reply but it soon died down, the enemy apparently realising that no attack was intended from our front. At 7.30 a.m. 31st and 56th Divisions on our right and left respectively assaulted. Thanks to the ample warning the enemy had received (from the demolition of pylons by the road in rear, of all wire on the front to be assaulted which had been removed the previous night as well as from the smoke barrage at 7.20 a.m.) an intense fire from MGs and artillery was at once opened. The 31st Division in particular were mown down by MGs and never reached their objective."[40]

In addition to these problems on the left flank, the weather was still not co-operating. The 165th Brigade, RFA, sent in another report at 7.13 a.m. that, though the mist had cleared a little, it was still impossible to observe the effects of their fire. Field guns and howitzers, medium trench mortars and the heavies of the Corps artillery were effectively firing blind and had been doing so for over an hour.

With the heavy guns lifting off the German front line at 7.20 a.m. it was left to the 18 pdr batteries firing HE and the Brigade Stokes light trench mortar batteries to try to keep the Germans' heads down. The mist, in spite of Division's hopeful comments about an hour later that it was lifting, was still so thick that A/169 and D/171 Batteries could not see their targets and were being forced for fire 'off map'.

The Stokes mortar batteries were due to start their hurricane bombardment from the positions at the head of the saps and from the front line at 7.20 a.m. and, just as they started, the deepest explosion of the day was dimly heard above the hubbub as the Hawthorn Ridge mine erupted. With that, every gun of every calibre set to firing at the fastest possible rate. The noise was indescribable but, on the German front lines bombarded only by the Stokes mortars and light 18 pdr HE, the effect was mainly cosmetic. From the British trenches, however, it appeared as though the gunners were delivering the coup de grace to the battered German defenders. Brig. Gen. Rees, at least, was impressed:

> "…ten minutes before zero our guns opened an intense fire. I stood on top to watch. It was magnificent. The trenches in front of Serre changed shape and dissolved minute by minute under the terrific hail of steel. Watching, I began to believe in the possibility of a great success."

At the same time as the bombardment became intense there was activity in both sets of trenches. The men of the attacking battalions moved out of the front lines to lie down in No Man's Land ready for the assault and the German front line garrison emerged from their dugouts, mounted their machine guns on the parapet and started to pour a withering fire on the horribly exposed men in No Man's Land. At the same time, the German HE and shrapnel barrage on the British front line intensified. Brig. Gen. Rees described the barrage as:

> "…a perfect wall of explosive along the front trenches of my Brigade and the 93rd. It was the most frightful artillery display that I had seen up to that time and in some ways I think it was the heaviest barrage I have seen put down by the defence on any occasion."

It was to be a massacre.

BUT, FOR NOW, ALL EYES WERE ON THE MEN of the Light Trench Mortar Batteries armed with the 3 in Stokes Mortar. Would this weapon be the success everyone hoped? All three Brigades' trench mortar batteries were in action with some placed at the ends of the Russian saps 40 yards from the German front line and others in the British front line. Those in the saps were able to reach the German 2nd and 3rd trenches and, at 7.20 a.m., a rapid fire was opened on these lines while those in the British front line targeted the German first line trench.

92nd Trench Mortar Battery had two guns from No. 1 Section in Sap C with the remaining two guns and the four from No. 2 Section firing from the front line. The targets of these guns were:

Two guns in Sap C the German 2nd and 3rd Trenches; and

Six guns in front line the German front line trench,

In ten minutes each gun fired about 100 rounds before the gun teams in the sap withdrew into the tunnel for protection. The six guns firing from exposed positions in or just behind what remained to the front line trench came under heavy fire but the two officers, Lt. Douglas Oake[i], No. 1 Section, and 2nd Lt. Leonard Hirst, No. 2 Section, each in charge of three guns, kept going from gun to gun encouraging their men, helping to dig out buried ammunition and keeping the men to their task. One mortar was buried by a German shell exploding nearby at 7.30 a.m. but, by that time, the hurricane bombardment of the Stokes mortars was over. The gun was recovered later after the attack had finished. In the meantime, the gun crews withdrew into the comparative safety of Sap C while, all around them, the attack disintegrated.

The 93rd Trench Mortar Battery on the Division's right had two guns in Grey Sap (Sap B) under Lt. Evers, two guns in Bleneau Sap (Sap A) under 2nd Lt. Bobby and eight guns in the trenches, six in Leeds Trench and two in the front line under Capt. Stanley Herbert Titford. Four guns were knocked out before opening fire, including both guns in Sap B which hints at the weight of the German barrage prior to zero hour. The remaining eight guns managed to fire 1,020 rounds in the ten minutes allowed which suggests an incredible rate of fire

---

[i] Capt. Douglas Oake, MC, General List att., 92nd Trench Mortar Battery, was killed on 8th August 1918. He is buried in Le Grand Hasard Military Cemetery, Morbecque. He was awarded the MC in the New Year's Honours List 1917.

of one round every 5 seconds sustained over ten minutes for every gun. Overall, they suffered significant casualties. 2nd Lt. Sidney Bobby[i] was killed at 8.15 a.m. when the mortar position in Sap A was blown in by a German shell and he was replaced by 2nd Lt. Prickett; Capt. Titford was wounded, four men were killed, one died of wounds and 18 were wounded. In total, nine guns were put out of action[ii]. That they stood by their guns speaks volumes about the dedication of the trench mortar teams. Later, between 10.30 and 11 a.m., in an action that clearly showed the Germans still in occupation of their front line trenches, a bombing party entered the head of Sap A and wounded four men with grenades. This local attack was repulsed and the sap barricaded against further attacks.

Details of the actions of the 94th Trench Mortar Battery are sparse. No. 1 Section fired 550 rounds with two guns in Sap D and two in the front line and No. 2 Section, with its guns in Sap E and the front line, fired 600 rounds. By the end of the day they would lose one officer, 2nd Lt. Frank Potter[iii], and three men killed and 19 other ranks wounded. Another officer, Lt. Thomas Rawcliffe of the Accringtons, was awarded an MC for his conduct[iv].

Combined, the three Brigade trench mortar batteries fired some 3,650 rounds containing 8,200 lbs (3,650 Kg) of Amatol into the first three lines of German trenches. This works out as just under 4 lbs of HE per yard of German trench. Of course, we have no idea as to the accuracy of the firing and, given the negligible effect this hurricane bombardment appears to have had on the defenders crowding the front line trenches, one can only assume that many of the rounds either missed their targets completely or failed to explode.

Nevertheless, under cover of this barrage, the 1st waves of the lead battalions crept out into No Man's Land to await the order to attack. On the extreme left the 1st wave of A and C Companies of the 12th York and Lancasters laid down approximately 100 yards from their trench but, with the tapes laid earlier having mysteriously disappeared, this was something of a guess. Behind them, the remaining men of A Company of the 14th York and Lancaster exited the top of Nairne and proceeded to lie down in file behind the left wing of the Sheffield battalion. On the right of the 94th Brigade front the 1st wave of the Accringtons performed the same manoeuvre and waiting for the Stokes guns to cease firing.

---

[i] 2nd Lt. Sidney Fitzgerald Bobby, 18th Durham Light Infantry attached 93rd Trench Mortar Battery, was aged 22. He was the son of William Thomas and Elizabeth Bobby of 7, Wellesley Rd., Leytonstone, London. Educated at Davies Lane School, Leyton, he had joined the Civil Service in 1910 as a temporary Boy Clerk. He was commissioned on 25th April 1915. His body was never found and his name is inscribed on the Thiepval Memorial, Pier & Face 14 A & 15 C.

[ii] All the guns were salvaged and seven made ready for action.

[iii] 2nd Lt. Frank John Potter, 14th York & Lancaster Regt., att. 94th Trench Mortar Battery, enlisted as 2668 Private in the Royal Warwickshire Regt. He was commissioned into the 14th York & Lancaster Regt. on 12th August 1915. His body was never found and his name is inscribed on the Thiepval Memorial, Pier & Face 4C.

[iv] Lt. Thomas William Rawcliffe, 11th East Lancashire Regt., was awarded the MC for his conduct on 1st July 1916. The citation, in the *London Gazette* of 20th October 1916, reads: "For conspicuous gallantry and devotion to duty in bringing four trench mortars into position through a very heavy barrage. By determination and coolness he got his guns into position."

Their commander, Brig. Gen. Rees, watched these green troops go into battle for the first time with the deepest admiration:

> "At the time this barrage really became intense, the last waves of the attack were crossing the trench I was in. I have never seen a finer display of individual and collective bravery than the advance of that brigade. I never saw a man waver from the exact line prescribed for him. Each line disappeared in the thick cloud of dust and smoke which rapidly blotted out the whole area. I saw a few groups of men through gaps in the smoke cloud, but I knew that no troops could hope to get through such a fire."

Plate 113 2nd Lt. Frank John Potter, 14th York & Lancaster Regt. att. 94th Trench Mortar Battery

Plate 114 Lt. Thomas Rawcliffe, MC, 11th East Lancashire Regt. att. 94th Trench Mortar Battery

To the south the 1st wave of the 15th West Yorkshires clambered over the parapet and walked out to a tape which had not been collected by a German patrol. They too lay down, their line spreading out either side of Sap A. Casualties amongst this wave were, as yet, few even though German machine guns had started to fire at about the same time as they entered No Man's Land and other Germans were seen to be manning the front line in large numbers. For the 2nd wave things were not so good. Machine guns swept the parapet as the men emerged and casualties were immediate and heavy and only a few isolated men managed to reach their colleagues lying out by the tape. Within minutes there were crucial losses amongst the officers. The CO, Maj. Redmond Neill[i], was wounded twice and the Adjutant, Capt. Stanley Neil[ii], killed a few minutes later.

---

[i] Maj. Redmond Barry Neill took command of the 15th West Yorkshire Regt. ten days before the attack when the previous CO, Lt. Col. Stuart C Taylor, was wounded. He returned to take command on 16th September 1916.

[ii] Capt. & Adjutant Stanley Thomas Arthur Neil, 15th West Yorkshire Regt., was aged 27. He was the second son of Mr William Warwick Neil of Southampton and Leeds. He was educated at King Edward VI's Grammar School and Hartley University College,

The 31st Division war diary reports that eleven officers of the Leeds Pals were killed and another eleven wounded in the ten minutes they lay out in No Man's Land. They were now not only being fired at by numerous machine guns but, when the remaining British heavy guns moved off the front line and onto the German reserve line at 7.20 a.m., the enemy immediately brought down a heavy shrapnel and HE barrage on the area in front of the trenches, on the front line itself and on the forward assembly trenches.

At 7.30 a.m. Nos. 1, 2, 3 and 4 machine guns of the 93rd Machine Gun Company under 2nd Lt. Harcourt, opened overhead covering fire for the Leeds Pals, the guns firing from emplacements in Fargate Street between Flag Avenue and Delaunay Avenue some 450 yards behind the front line. Then, the 1st wave, at the orders of the few unwounded young subalterns, rose and moved forward. There are some accounts that suggest these leading waves of the 31st Division ignored VIII Corps' instructions and 'rushed'[i] the German trenches. I believe this to be a misunderstanding of the words used to describe the attack where the word 'charge' is also often used. It was nothing of the sort. Had the attack been at the double the result might well have been different. A Musketier Karl Blenk of IR 169 expressed great surprise that the British walked forward, saying they had never seen anyone attack in the manner before. His final comment is telling:

"If only they had run, they would have overwhelmed us."

But the men, overburdened as they were, simply could not run. Fourth Army and VIII Corps' instructions saw to that.

The 1st wave was made up of two platoons, one each from C and D Companies. No. 10 Platoon was commanded by 2nd Lt. Arthur Hutton and No. 13 Platoon by the 19-year-old 2nd Lt. Tom Willey. A product of Harrow School, Willey was the son of Arthur Willey, a leading solicitor and Leeds City Alderman, who had been instrumental in the raising of the battalion. Willey was a popular young man both with his men and his brother officers and with the words, "Come on 13, Give them hell!" he led them forward. According to one eyewitness he was waving his revolver which, if true, was contrary to the instructions given to officers to dress and arm themselves the same as the men so as not to be targeted by the enemy[ii]. It made little difference, however, as he was immediately killed by a shell which, apparently, removed his legs[iii]. His fellow

Southampton. He was employed by Messrs Playfair and Toole, Government contractors of Southampton, and became the resident waterworks engineer to the Leeds Corporation at the New Leighton Reservoir. He enlisted on the formation of the battalion and was commissioned on 5th January 1915. He was promoted Captain in December 1915. His body was never found and his name is inscribed on the Thiepval Memorial, Pier & Face 2A 2C & 2D.

[i] For example, Prior and Wilson in *Command on the Western Front*, page 179.

[ii] In the excellent *'Barnsley Pals'* by Jon Cooksey (Pen & Sword Books, 1986) a number of the veterans interviewed refer to seeing officers carrying revolvers. Either all of these officers explicitly ignored their orders or this is a case of men, a long time after a traumatic event, stating what they or others feel they should remember.

[iii] 2nd Lt. Thomas Arthur Raymond Robert Elliott Willey, 15th West Yorkshire Regt., was aged 19. He was the eldest son of Alderman Arthur Willey of Calverley Chambers, Victoria Square, Leeds. Educated at Roscoe's College, Harrogate, and Harrow School, he

officer, 2nd Lt. Hutton, was luckier. Wounded in the right shoulder, he survived to send a heartfelt letter of condolence to Alderman Willey from his bed in Whitworth Hospital, Manchester[i].

Plate 115 2nd Lt. Thomas Arthur Raymond Robert Elliott Willey, 15th West Yorkshire Regt.

Plate 116 Lt. John Gilbert Vause, 15th West Yorkshire Regt.

Behind Willey and his men the 2nd wave was cut down within yards of leaving their trenches. Amongst them was the OC, No. 15 Platoon, D Company, Lt. John Vause, who had been a childhood friend of 2nd Lt. Willey. Aged 23, he was a graduate of Leeds University and a keen rugby player with Headingley R.F.C. and he had been given an immediate commission on joining the battalion in September 1914. Vause went down as did many of his men. Hit in the elbow on leaving the front line he went forward close to the edge of the German wire. Here he was hit again in the thigh and, with one of his men who was also wounded, he crawled into a nearby shell hole. In the comparative safety of the hole, they talked about the prospects of getting back to Leeds and Vause said he had been recommended for a promotion. Then was hit again in the chin and back. 'This has just about finished me off,' he managed to mutter to the Private lying next to him and he died soon after. Although the man who had shared his

was articled to his father as a solicitor. He joined the 15th West Yorkshire Regt. as a Private in August 1914 and was commissioned into the battalion in December 1914. He went to Egypt in January 1916, returning to France in April. His body was never found and his name is inscribed on the Thiepval Memorial, Pier & Face 2A, 2C & 2D.

[i] 2nd Lt, later Capt., Arthur Norman Hutton, MC, 15th West Yorkshire Regt. was aged 28. He was the son of Charles Hutton of Brentwood, Eccleshall. He was a director of Messrs Smith and Hutton, cloth manufacturers, of which his father was chairman. Educated at Leeds University where he was in the OTC, he was commissioned on 1st April 1915 and was attached to the 15th Battalion, Tank Corps, when he won his MC for his conduct in 1918. It was gazetted on 29th November 1918. He also served in WW2.

last minutes was rescued 36 hours later, Vause's body was not recovered[i]. Initially reported missing it was only when the wounded man was interviewed where he lay with both legs shattered in the Third Western General Hospital in Newport that the death of Lt. Vause was confirmed for his grieving parents.

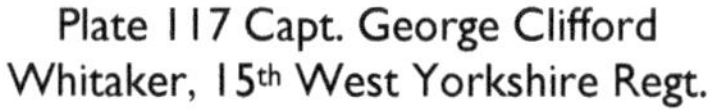

Plate 117 Capt. George Clifford Whitaker, 15th West Yorkshire Regt.

Plate 118 Lt. Evelyn Henry Lintott, 15th West Yorkshire Regt.

Capt. George Whitaker was the OC of C Company. 28 years old he, like Vause, was a Leeds University graduate and member of Headingley R.F.C. He had enlisted on the outbreak of war but was soon commissioned and, on his next leave, he planned to marry his fiancée, Miss Mary Hamilton, the daughter of the manager of the Leeds Tramways. At 7.30 a.m., as the whistles blew along the line he climbed over the parapet at the head of his men. He was wounded almost immediately but, struggling to his feet, he continued forward until seen to be hit once more. He was not seen again. His remains were found by men of his battalion at the end of February 1917 after the German withdrawal. His bones were placed in a sandbag to be buried by his comrades in the quiet village of Sailly-au-Bois[ii].

---

[i] Lt. John Gilbert Vause, D Company, 15th West Yorkshire Regt., was aged 23. He was the youngest son of Frederick William and Sarah Vause of 32, Clarendon Road, Leeds and later 'Meadowfield', Chapel Allerton, Leeds. Educated at Leeds Grammar School and Leeds University, he played rugby for Headingley R.F.C. and worked at Messrs Mortimer & Co.., of Morley. He was commissioned on 25th September 1914. His body was never found and his name is inscribed on the Thiepval Memorial, Pier & Face 2A, 2C & 2D.

[ii] Capt. George Clifford Whitaker, C Company, 15th West Yorkshire Regt., was aged 28. He was the youngest son of Matthew Whitaker, a railway contractor, of The Prospect, Horsforth, Leeds. He was educated at Ilkley Grammar School and Leeds University and was an engineer. He played rugby for Headingley R.F.C. Pre-war he served for two years with the 5th KOYLI but enlisted as a Private in the 15th West Yorkshire Regt. on the outbreak of war and was promoted Lieutenant on 25th September 1914. He is buried in Sailly-Au-Bois Military Cemetery, grave I. A. 1.

2nd Lt. Everitt was part of the 2nd wave. Educated at Malvern College he had initially been commissioned into the 10th King's Own Yorkshire Light Infantry, being posted to the Leeds Pals in June 1915. He commanded No. 14 Platoon of D Company and was killed within yards of the front line[i]. His men thought well of the 19 year old officer as this extract from a letter to his mother shows:

> "I am proud to be able to say that he was always kind, and a gentleman. I admired his principles. He was well liked and admired by his men and the few of them that remain join me in sending our deepest sympathy in your sad bereavement."

Some leading sportsmen were amongst the dead and wounded. Lt. Evelyn Lintott was a former professional footballer and England international having been capped seven times by his country. He was also the first ever head of the Professional Footballers' Association and was the first professional player to hold a commission. He was well known in West Yorkshire having played for both Bradford City and Leeds City but, at age 33, he had returned to being a teacher for which he had trained pre-war. Taking his men 'over the lid' he was hit in the chest but struggled on to be hit again. The third wound took him down. His body was never recovered[ii].

2nd Lt. Major William Booth (Major was his Christian name) was a professional cricketer with Yorkshire County Cricket Club and had gone over the top with D Company. He played twice for England against South Africa and had been the Wisden Cricketer of the Year in 1914 after taking 141 wickets with his off breaks. Four times he had taken eight wickets in an innings, twice he had taken hat-tricks and in 1913 he had done the 'double': scoring over 1,000 runs and taking 158 wickets. At 29, he was at the peak of his cricketing powers, but he died in the fields in front of Serre. He was reported as having been hit in the left shoulder near his heart by a shell fragment and having collapsed a few yards further on. Like Capt. Whitaker, his remains were amongst those recovered in February 1917 and he was laid to rest in Serre Road Cemetery No. 1[iii].

---

[i] 2nd Lt. John Paxman Everitt, 15th West Yorkshire Regt., was aged 19. He was the son of Charles and Elizabeth E Everitt of 12, Inglis Rd., Colchester. He was educated at Malvern College. Commissioned into 10th King's Own Yorkshire Light Infantry in December 1914 he was posted to the 15th West Yorkshire Regt., on 12th June 1915. His body was never found and his name is inscribed on the Thiepval Memorial, Pier & Face 2A, 2C & 2D.

[ii] Lt. Evelyn Henry Lintott, 15th West Yorkshire Regt., was aged 33. He was the second son of Arthur Frederick and Eleanor L Lintott of 'Hazelville', Wolseley Rd., Farncombe, Surrey. He was educated at the Royal Grammar School, Guildford, and studied to be a teacher at St Luke's College, Exeter. He was a former professional football player and England International, playing for Plymouth Argyle, Queens Park Rangers, Bradford City and Leeds City. Throughout he was a school teacher and was teaching at Dudley Hill School, Bradford, before the war. His body was never found and his name is inscribed on the Thiepval Memorial, Pier & Face 2A, 2C & 2D.

[iii] 2nd Lt. Major William Booth, D Company, 15th West Yorkshire Regt., was aged 29. He was the son of James and Louise Booth of Town End House, Pudsey, Yorks. Educated at Fulneck School, he was a professional Cricketer for Yorkshire. He was the Wisden Cricketer of the Year in 1914, a year when he took 141 wickets. Played two Tests against South Africa in 1913-14. He enlisted and was commissioned on 16th July 1915. He is buried in Serre Road Cemetery No.1, grave I. G. 14.

Lt. Stanley Morris Bickersteth[i] was in temporary command of B Company and had managed to get some of his men out into No Man's Land. He ordered them to lie down by the tape laid the previous night as the previous wave had only just moved off. According to two eye witnesses Bickersteth was struck in the back of the head by a shrapnel bullet causing a serious wound and, at the very least, stunning the young officer. A moment later another ball entered the back of his head and exited through his forehead, killing him outright. 'Mr Bickersteth has gone west', a witness, 15/1244 Pte. Edmund Bristow, told the officer's servant Pte. Jenkinson a few moments before he too was hit by shell splinters.

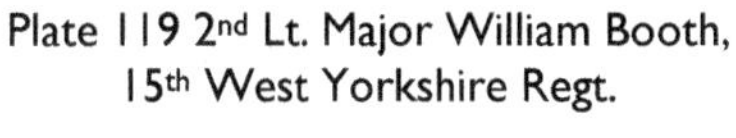

Plate 119 2nd Lt. Major William Booth, 15th West Yorkshire Regt.

Plate 120 Lt. Stanley Morris Bickersteth, 15th West Yorkshire Regt.

Within minutes of the 'off' twenty two officers of the Leeds Pals were either killed or wounded. Such losses were catastrophic and left the men both in the trenches and No Man's Land leaderless before the attack began in earnest. To make matters even worse, the Germans now brought down a triple barrage on the 93rd Brigade front. Described in the Official History as resembling 'a line of Poplar trees' (Brig. Gen. Rees's post-war description) the first barrage fell some 20 yards in front of the British line, the second barrage fell on the British first line and the third barrage plunged into the men crammed into the assembly trenches further back. The posy-battle report would record that no man who attacked from the front line got more than 100 yards beyond the British wire and that not one of those who had assembled further back in Leeds Trench progressed more

[i] Lt. (actg. Capt.) Stanley Morris Bickersteth, B Company, 15th West Yorkshire Regt., was aged 25. He was the fifth son of the Rev. Dr Samuel Bickersteth, D.D., Vicar of Leeds (afterwards Canon of Canterbury), Chaplain to the King, and of Ella Chlora Faithfull, his wife, daughter of Sir Monier Monier-Williams, K.C.I.E., Professor of Sanskrit and Fellow of Balliol College. Born in the Vicarage, Belverdere, Kent, he was educated at St David's School, Reigate, Rugby and Christ Church, Oxford (graduated 1913). Commissioned 25th September 1914, serving first in Egypt and then Salonika. He is buried in Queen's Cemetery, Puisieux, grave E. 19.

than 30 yards from the British parapet. In spite of this, the 93rd Brigade war diary reported at 7.38 a.m. that the Leeds battalion was advancing on their objective, the Green Line. The Green Line was the fourth line of trenches nearly 700 yards deep into the German positions. The nearest living member of the Leeds Pals to this trench line was over 800 yards away to the west, no doubt desperately trying to find shelter in a crater from the murderous fire of the German Maxims.

The report's statements are confirmed by German accounts of the fighting on the 93rd Brigade front. Here, in sectors S3 and S4, the 6. and 7. Kompanien of IR 169 defended the front lines. To their rear, in the third trench, were the 8. and 5. Kompanien. Further back in Tübinger Stellung were three companies of the III Battalion under Hptm. Angel, ready to be used to mount any counter attacks required or to plug holes in the forward defences. The CO of the IR 169, Maj. von Struensee, did not find it necessary to deploy any of these reserve companies on this part of the 31st Division's front. Instead two platoons, led by Lt. der Reserve Gattner and Lt. Friedrich Hoppe, of the 11. Kompanie, were later despatched, although their help was not requested, to assist the RIR 121 in the attempts to throw the 4th Division out of the Heidenkopf[i].

The CO, Major Neill[ii], had been hit in the arm by three shell fragments as he climbed out of the front trench. Nevertheless he carried on until shot through the left thigh some 80 yards into No Man's Land. With the enemy machine guns cutting down anything that moved the Major endeavoured to bring forward two Lewis gun teams from the battalion reserve. Both gun teams were shot down or killed by the shelling. Neill then crawled into a shell crater from where he observed the enemy lines with his binoculars. According to his observations, there were three German machine guns visible on the front line parapet each supported by five or six men with bayonets fixed. One by one they were shot down but still the machine guns fired. A commanding officer might normally be though of as a reliable witness but, as with so many 'observations' on this day there is considerable doubt over precisely what Neill saw as, according to IR 169's own maps, all the machine guns in this sector were set back in the 2nd, 3rd and 4th trenches.

---

[i] It should also be noted that it has only proved possible to identify one man of the 15th West Yorkshires taken prisoner on 1st July 1916, 4526 Pte. Arthur Howard, which fact suggests that very few of the battalion got in to, or even very close to, the German front line trench.

[ii] Maj. Redmond Barry Neill, DSO, 1st Royal Irish Fusiliers att. 15th West Yorkshire Regt., was born in Dunedin, New Zealand, in 1880. He was the son of Percival Clay Neill of Dunedin, a wine and spirits merchant. Commissioned into 3rd Princes of Wales's Volunteers (South Lancashire Regt.), Militia in July 1900. Transferred to the Royal Irish Fusiliers, September 1901. He served on the North West Frontier and in the South African War with the 2nd Royal Irish Fusiliers (Queen's Medal & 5 clasps). Served in India 1903-12. 1913, Captain, General Reserve of Officers. Trained troops in New Zealand, 1914-5. Staff, 4th Reinforcement, NZEF. He took command of the 15th West Yorkshire Regt. on 5th June 1916 after the wounding of Lt. Col. C Dewhurst. After recovering from his wounds he became a Company Commander, Cadet Wing, R.F.C., in late 1916 before commanding a battalion in July 1917. He was awarded the DSO in the New Year's Honours of 1918. He returned to New Zealand where he was a sheep farmer at Barrosa near Canterbury. He died in 1962.

Helping to defend the trenches of sectors S3 and S4 were four guns from Maschinengewehr Kompanie Nr 2. None of these guns were in the front trench, as suggested by Maj. Neill, making it more difficult for any of the attacking troops to get at them with grenades or to attack them physically. One gun was in the centre of sector S3, in the second trench at the apex of a small re-entrant, another was in the third trench at the junction with Ten Tree Alley near the Serre to Mailly Road, a third was further back in Ten Tree Alley at the junction with Roerle Graben, which then ran down into the rear of the Heidenkopf, and the fourth was in Tübinger Stellung just to the south of the Serre to Mailly Road[i].

Of one thing Major Neill was certain – his battalion did not reach the enemy trenches:

> "I did not see a single man of 15th West Yorks enter the German front line and I am practically certain that none of them ever got that far. The German barrage on our front line was very effective and machine gun fire in No Man's Land most intense."

Along with German machine guns in the front line, there was another thing apparently spotted by Maj. Neill and this was an event which was to have long term consequences. He somehow saw two very weak parties of British soldiers, one of eleven men and the other of about 15, entering Serre at about 8 a.m. It would be the 'presence' or otherwise of British troops in Serre which would sustain both Division and Corps in their belief that somehow something positive might be snatched from the jaws of crushing defeat. And, as rumours do, this one grew until even the Commander-in-Chief was being told that two entire battalions were cut off in the village and thus the attack must be renewed.

During the morning Neill struggled back into the British front line. There he found what he believed to be a party from the Leeds Pioneers 'whose morale was nil'. He found no officers or men of his battalion in the trenches. They were all lying out in No Man's Land. He reported his findings to Brigade Battle HQ at 10 a.m. before being hurried off to the Advanced Dressing Station. His place was taken later in the day by Maj. John Cabourn Hartley[ii].

Within ten minutes of the attack starting, the Leeds Pals had ceased to exist as a coherent unit. Initial figures showed 24 officers and 504 other ranks as

---

[i] It is not clear which of the two guns near to the Serre-Mailly Road he refers to but in his book *'Die Schlacht an der Somme'*, Unteroffizier Otto Lais states that the gun commanded by Unteroffizier Koch fired 20,000 rounds during 1st July 1916. One must, however, take some of Lais's somewhat overblown description of the attack with a pinch of salt as he talks about seeing 'Indian Lancers' behind the infantry to exploit the expected victory, an image probably only otherwise seen in Haig's dreams in the nights before the attack.

[ii] Maj., later Col., John Cabourn Hartley, DSO, Royal Fusiliers att. 15th West Yorkshire Regt., was born on 15th November 1874 in Lincoln. He was educated at Tonbridge and Brasenose College, Oxford. He played cricket for Oxford University, Sussex CC, the MCC and England (two Test matches in South Africa 1905-6). In the Varsity Match of 1896 he dismissed the famous Gilbert Jessop and the son of W G Grace, taking eleven wickets in the match. Commissioned into the 1st Cinque Ports Volunteer Rifle Corps (Militia) in 1897. Joined 2nd Royal Fusiliers, 1898. Served in South Africa (Queen's Medal 5 clasps & King's Medal 2 clasps). Resigned commission, 1902 and joined 6th Royal Fusiliers (Militia). Resigned commission, 1914. Appt'd Captain, 25th September 1914. He died in 1963.

casualties. 'Two years in the making, ten minutes in the destroying', as author John Harris has it in his book, *'Covenant with Death'*[41], more than adequately sums up the tragedy of the battalion.

The officers to die were:

Lt. S M Bickersteth
2nd Lt. M W Booth
2nd Lt. J P Everitt
2nd Lt. T Humphries[i]
2nd Lt. C W James[ii]
Lt. E H Lintott
Capt. S T A Neil
2nd Lt. V Oland[iii]
2nd Lt. C Saunders[iv]
2nd Lt. R H Tolson[v]
Lt. J G Vause
Capt. G C Whitaker
2nd Lt. T A R R E Willey

Tragically for the family great uncertainty surrounded 2nd Lt. Tolson's fate. He commanded No. 2 Platoon of A Company and was initially posted as 'missing' but, on 11th July, the *Yorkshire Evening Post* printed the heartening news that the 31 year old officer was wounded and in hospital in France. The following day this information was retracted on the basis of a misunderstanding of a letter received by his wife, Zoe Tolson, from the Rev. Claude Chappell, the Battalion chaplain. The letter stated that her husband had been wounded but no more information was available. His remains were later recovered from the battlefield to be buried amongst the many officers and men of the 31st Division who lie in Serre Road Cemetery No. 1.

---

[i] 2nd Lt. Thomas Humphries, 15th West Yorkshire Regt., was aged 20. He was the second son of Edward Walter and Elizabeth Humphries of 7, Ashburnham Grove, Heaton, Bradford, Yorks. His father was involved in printing with Percy Lund, Humphries & Co. Ltd. He was educated at Bradford Grammar School and St George's, Harpenden. He enlisted as a Private in the 1/6th West Yorkshire Regt., in October 1914 and was commissioned in January 1916. He joined the battalion in June. His body was never found and his name is inscribed on the Thiepval Memorial, Pier & Face 2A, 2C & 2D.

[ii] 2nd Lt. Clement Wilbraham James, 15th West Yorkshire Regt., was aged 26. He was the son of Mrs Ellen Eliza James of 203, Sydenham Rd., Durban, South Africa, and the late Thomas Payne Saint James. He was commissioned i December 1915. His body was never found and his name is inscribed on the Thiepval Memorial, Pier & Face 2A, 2C & 2D.

[iii] 2nd Lt. Valentine Oland, MC, B Company, 15th West Yorkshire Regt., spent most of his life in France. He was commissioned into the 14th (Reserve) Battalion, West Yorkshire Regt., and joined the 15th West Yorkshire Regt., in May 1916. He was awarded the MC for his conduct in driving off a German raid on 22nd May 1916, the award being made by Maj. Gen. Wanless-O'Gowan on 29th June. His body was never found and his name is inscribed on the Thiepval Memorial, Pier & Face 2A, 2C & 2D.

[iv] 2nd Lt. Charles Saunders, 15th West Yorkshire Regt., was never found and his name is inscribed on the Thiepval Memorial, Pier & Face 2A, 2C & 2D.

[v] 2nd Lt. Robert Huntriss Tolson, A Company, 15th West Yorkshire Regt., was aged 31. He was the son of Mr Whiteley Tolson and Mrs Jessy Tolson (née Huntriss) of Oaklands, Dalton, Huddersfield. He was educated at Aysgarth and King William School, Isle of Man and worked at Beckett's Bank, Leeds. He was married to Zoe Tolson and lived at 78, Holly Bank, Leeds. He enlisted in the Public Schools' Battalion and was commissioned into the King's Own Yorkshire Light Infantry. He transferred to the 15th West Yorkshire Regt., in September 1915. Also served in Egypt. He is buried in Serre Road Cemetery No.1, grave I. B. 52. His youngest brother, 2nd Lt. James Martin Tolson, 74th Brigade, RFA, was killed on 20th October 1918.

Plate 121 2nd Lt. Robert Huntriss Tolson, 15th West Yorkshire Regt.

Two more officers later succumbed to their wounds:
2nd Lt. A Liversidge[i], died of wounds, 2nd July 1916
2nd Lt. L Foster[ii], died of wounds, 13th August 1916
The wounded were:
2nd Lt. Briley
2nd Lt. James Gibson
2nd Lt. P H P Gorman
Maj. Redmond Barry Neill, Cdg
2nd Lt. Arthur Norman Hutton
2nd Lt. Major Frederick William Leek
2nd Lt. John Sydney Jones
2nd Lt. Duncan Scott Wells

---

[i] 2nd Lt. Albert Liversidge, 15th West Yorkshire Regt., was aged 23. He was the eldest son of Albert, a bottlemaker, and Elizabeth Ann Liversidge of 39 Newport Street, Jack Lane, Hunslet Road, Leeds. Educated at Wheelwright Grammar School, Dewsbury he won a scholarship to the Leeds Higher Grade School before training to be a teacher at Leeds Training School. He worked as a teacher for the Leeds Education Services at Hunslet Moor School. He enlisted as Private in September 1914 and was commissioned on 26th June 1915. He is buried in Doullens Communal Cemetery Extension No. 1, grave II. A. 6.

[ii] 2nd Lt. Leonard Foster, 15th West Yorkshire Regt., was aged 27. He was the younger son of the late John William Foster, a draper, and Lucy Anne Turvey of The Prospect, Old Pool Bank, Pool in Wharfedale. He was educated at Ilkley Grammar School and was trained as an architect passing the Surveyors' Institute and ARIBA examinations. He worked as an architect and surveyor for Leeds City Corporation. Married Martha Avery Hill on 9th October 1915. He enlisted on the outbreak of war and was commissioned on 26th July 1915. He died in the Empire Hospital for Officers (for Injuries to the Nervous System), Vincent Square, London, and is buried next to his father in the west part of St. Wilfrid's Churchyard, Pool in Wharfedale.

Plate 122 2nd Lt. Albert Liversidge, 15th West Yorkshire Regt.

Plate 123 2nd Lt. Leonard Foster, 15th West Yorkshire Regt.

Perhaps the luckiest officer of all was a 2nd Lt. Stanley. He was admitted to hospital with a sprained ankle suffered on the way up to the front line.

In all, 13 officers were killed, two more died of wounds and eight were wounded (or nine if one counts 2nd Lt. Stanley). Every officer involved was a casualty. Amongst the other ranks the initial report gave the figures as:

56 killed
267 wounded
181 missing
Total 504

This was out of 24 officers and about 650 men who had gone into action, or a casualty rate of 78%. Inevitably these numbers changed as some of the missing lying out in No Man's Land managed to return but the figures for fatalities cannot be challenged. Amongst the other ranks, 222 were killed and another 21 died of wounds before the end of July. A total of 243 deaths or more than one in three of the men who had gone into the attack. What is clear from the nature of the wounds reported by both officers and men is that the Leeds Pals were destroyed as much, if not more, by the German artillery as they were by enemy machine guns.

TO THEIR REAR, THE SUPPORTING BATTALION, the 1st Bradford Pals, were also losing men fast. So heavy were the casualties by day's end that the war diary's description of the events is restricted to the following entry:

> "7.30 a.m. The infantry assault commenced but owing to the large casualties including the loss of all officers no detailed narrative is possible."[42]

The account of the battalion's day is, as a result, taken from the personal accounts of survivors collected after the battle.

Plate 124 Maj. George Sutherland Guyon, 16th West Yorkshire Regt.

Plate 125 Lt. and Adjt. Cecil Talbot Ransome, 16th West Yorkshire Regt.

An advanced party of the Battalion HQ, including the CO, Maj. George Guyon, the Adjutant, Lt. Cecil Ransome, the Intelligence Officer, 2nd Lt. Charles Laxton, and the CO's runner 16/131 Pte. William Carter of No. 1 Platoon, had gone up to the front line five minutes before zero to watch the Leeds Pals go out and to be ready to receive and direct the rest of the battalion as they advanced. They arrived at Sap A to find the area under heavy artillery and machine gun fire. Within two minutes Maj. Guyon was fatally wounded, being struck on the head by a projectile. Guyon had only taken command of the 16th West Yorkshires on the 24th June. He had been given command of the battalion having previously commanded the 2nd Royal Fusiliers in the fighting at Gallipoli where he had been wounded in the head during the landings. Now he was hit in the head again but this time a bullet penetrated his helmet and entered his skull through the temple[i]. Pte. Carter helped prop his unconscious CO up against the side of the trench while Ransome and Laxton bandaged his head but it was clear the wound was fatal and they were forced to leave him while they dealt with even more urgent problems. Pte. Carter started to climb out of the trench when he too was hit on the head by a machine gun bullet. He was luckier than his CO. Although the

[i] Temp. Lt. Col. George Sutherland Guyon, 2nd Royal Fusiliers att. 16th West Yorkshire Regt., was aged 41. He was the son of Lt. Gen. Gardiner Frederic Guyon, Royal Fusiliers, and Mary Elizabeth Guyon (née Sutherland) of Glenvale, St Martin, Jersey. He was educated at Brighton College and married Winifred Mary Ryan in 1908. He joined the 5th Royal Fusiliers (Militia) and transferred into the 2nd Royal Fusiliers on 15th May 1897, promoted Captain 1900 and Major 1912. Served in South Africa being awarded the Queen's Medal with 3 clasps and the King's Medal with 2 clasps. He landed at Gallipoli with the 2nd Royal Fusiliers and was wounded. He took command of the 16th West Yorkshire Regt. on 24th June 1916. His body was never found and his name is inscribed on the Thiepval Memorial, Pier & Face 9A. His second son, Lt. George Edmund Guyon, born October 1916, served with the 1st Battalion, Parachute Regt. at Arnhem where he was OC, Mortar Platoon. He was a PoW.

front of his helmet was smashed, and a piece on the top of his head 'chopped out', he survived – this wound, four others and the war[i].

Back in the assembly trenches, the lead units, A and C Companies, 16th West Yorkshires, and D Company of the 18th Durham Light Infantry, had moved off shortly after zero from Monk and Bradford Trenches and advanced towards Leeds Trench just behind the front line. But, as the 1st Bradford Pals and the Durham Pals clambered up the trench ladders, numerous men were hit as soon as their heads showed above the parapet and these casualties repeatedly fell back into the trench with head or upper body wounds. The survivors then set off towards the front lines, walking down the slight slope towards Railway Hollow, the dip behind the front trench, all the while in full view of the enemy and all the while taking casualties. Meanwhile, the Regimental Aid Post of the Durhams was rapidly overwhelmed with wounded and the newly attached Medical Officer, Lt. J W Macfarlane, and his staff had to work desperately under a stream of German shells to treat the walking wounded and save those more gravely injured.

In the front line the 16th West Yorkshires' Adjutant, Lt. Ransome, and the Intelligence Officer, 2nd Lt. Laxton, were trying to make some sense out of a chaotic situation. The dead and wounded of the Leeds Pals filled the battered trenches and littered the ground either side of the British wire. Behind them advanced the dwindling columns of A and C Companies of their battalion. Laxton noted that one group from A Company was being led by Capt. Robert Pringle as it approached Leeds Trench a few yards behind the front line. Then, according to Laxton:

> "Things seemed to stop. Men were falling and no one advancing over our front line."[43]

Capt. Pringle and his party failed to reach the British front line.

Laxton eventually found 2nd Lt. Ralph Stead with a few men in the front line. Gathering them together he and Stead launched themselves into No Man's Land, scrambling over the parapet in a rush towards a gap in the British wire. The two officers got out but then machine gun fire swept the parapet behind cutting down their small group of men. Laxton lost track of Stead immediately and had advanced no more than 15 yards when a bullet smashed into his left knee and a shell fragment sliced into his right thigh. He crawled back towards a shell hole some five yards to his front and, to his horror, found the crater already occupied by the dead body of his recent companion, 2nd Lt. Stead[ii]. As Laxton composed himself he disposed of all surplus kit and equipment so as not to be encumbered on his dangerous trip back to the British trenches. After 15 minutes he scrambled five yards closer to the front line, falling into another shell hole for cover. But he had been spotted by Lt. Ransome who bravely came out to his assistance. Laxton

---

[i] 16/131 Pte William Henry Townend Carter, 16th West Yorkshire Regt., was sent to hospital in Boulogne. Transferred to the 25th Northumberland Fusiliers and fought at Contalmaison in September. Wounded four times, each time he returned to a different battalion of the Fusiliers. He was discharged as unfit on Christmas Day, 1918.

[ii] 2nd Lt. Ralph Stead, formerly 19th Royal Fusiliers, 16th West Yorkshire Regt., was aged 31. He was the son of Arthur Charles Stead of Necton, Swaffham, Norfolk. Enlisted, Sept., 1914. He is buried in Serre Road Cemetery No. 1, grave I. E. 53.

told him to go back and then to show him the nearest bit of trench into which the wounded officer could crawl. He tried to follow his colleague in but lost sight of him. Writing to the new CO, Maj. Humphrey Hayes Kennedy, Seaforth Highlanders, while on his way to hospital with fellow officers Auty[i], Gray[ii] and Hepworth, Laxton[iii] commented that he had heard that Lt. Ransome was suffering from shell shock along with Lt. Hoffmann[iv] who had been in charge of the carrying parties. Unfortunately, Lt. Cecil Ransome, who had been sent off to reorganise elements of the battalion in Monk Trench, was dead and was later buried in the quickly growing cemetery near the Sucrerie at Euston[v].

Behind them were B and D Companies which constituted the 2nd wave of the battalion. At 7.23 a.m. 16/842 Sgt. Maj. George Cussins, a pre-war Police constable, recalled enemy machine gun, rifle fire and shrapnel sweeping the parapet of the southern half of Bradford Trench where B Company were waiting to advance. Nonetheless, the company struggled up their ladders and formed up in front of Bradford Trench. They too could be clearly seen from all of the gently tiered enemy trenches in front of Serre.

By 7.30 a.m., the time they were due to move off, most of the officers and many NCOs had been knocked out. No. 7 Platoon was led out into the open by 20 year old 2nd Lt. Frank Symonds, a grammar school boy from Norfolk. He nonchalantly smoked a cigarette as he encouraged his men forward. Sgt. Maj. Cussins advanced with Capt. Donald Smith, OC B Company, at the rear of the company but, half way between Bradford Trench and the front line, he found

---

[i] 2nd Lt. Joseph Speight Auty, 16th West Yorkshire Regt., was born in Mayville, Batley in 1884. He was educated at Mill Hill School where he played two seasons in the 1st XI as an all-rounder, being the leading wicket taker in 1901 and scoring 197 against Wellingborough Grammar School in 1902. He played four times for Yorkshire 2nd XI between 1903 and 1913. He was commissioned on 29th April 1915. He relinquished his commission on the grounds of ill-health on 29th November 1916. He died, aged 38, on 27th March 1922.

[ii] 2nd Lt. Francis Martello Gray, 16th West Yorkshire Regt., was aged 31. He was the third son of William Martello Gray, a Bradford accountant and was in business with him before the war. He was educated at Oakham School where he played for the 1st XI for three seasons (1901-3) as an opening bowler, once taking nine wickets for 51 runs against C D Hoffman's XI. He was commissioned into the 16th West Yorkshire Regt. on 18th May 1915. He relinquished his commission on 10th May 1918 because of ill-health contracted on active duty. He died in 1952.

[iii] Lt. Charles Fraser Laxton, 16th West Yorkshire Regt., was aged 22. He was the third son of Mr and Mrs George Wright Laxton of Dewsbury. He enlisted as 15/575 Private in the Leeds Pals in September 1914 with his brother Reginald Earl Laxton and both were commissioned into the 16th West Yorkshire Regt. on 26th June 1915. 2nd Lt. R E Laxton, att. 93rd Trench Mortar Battery, was killed on 10th June 1916. He is buried in Bertrancourt Military Cemetery. Charles Laxton survived to serve in WW2.

[iv] 2nd Lt. James Maximilian Harry Hoffman, 16th West Yorkshire Regt., was the son of the late Frank Hoffman. Born in the USA in 1895 he was educated at Giggleswick School where he played several times for the cricket 1st XI. He was articled with Messrs Beevers and Adjie, accountants of Leeds. He was commissioned on 23rd September 1914.

[v] Lt. & Adjutant Cecil Talbot Ransome, 6th Norfolk Regt. att. 16th West Yorkshire Regt., was aged 26. He was the son of William Fenn Ransome of Norwich. He worked at the Head Office of the Norwich Union Life Insurance Society and was commissioned on 24th December 1914. He is buried in Euston Road Cemetery, Colincamps, grave I. B. 8.

himself leading the entire battalion, with all those in front having been killed or wounded. One of the casualties was Capt. Smith[i], badly wounded in the back, and Cussins had to assume command, leading the remains of his company through the dead and dying of A Company until he reached the shambles of the British front line. Capt. Smith's last message to Battalion HQ, delivered by runner, read 'Company advancing steadily', however, as far as is known, the only men from B Company to reach the front line with Cussins came from No. 8 Platoon. Another casualty at the head of No. 7 Platoon was 2nd Lt. Symonds who was wounded soon after moving off from Bradford Trench. He was last seen sheltering in a shell hole with several other officers and men, amongst them Capt. Pringle of C Company. Symonds' body was never found[ii].

Plate 126 Capt. Donald Charnock Smith, 16th West Yorkshire Regt.

Plate 127 Lt. Robert Sutcliffe, 16th West Yorkshire

66779 Pte. George Gransbury later described how he came across the wounded Captain Pringle and dragged him into a large shell crater. The crater was already well used by casualties. Gransbury noted Capt. Smith from B Company with a bad wound in the back as well as the severely wounded Lt. Robert Sutcliffe

---

[i] Capt. Donald Charnock Smith, B Company, 16th West Yorkshire Regt., was aged 23. He was the son of Mrs Smith of Grange House, Westgate Hill, Bradford, Yorks, and the late Cllr E J Smith, JP. He was educated at Mill Hill where he was in the rugby 1st XV and played rugby for Yorkshire. He was commissioned into the West Yorkshire Regt. in September 1914. His body was never found and his name is inscribed on the Thiepval Memorial, Pier & Face 2A, 2C & 2D. Smith was a tee-totaller and something of a disciplinarian and, just before the attack, had poured some of the rum issued to the men down a sump hole rather than give them more than their usual tot.

[ii] 2nd Lt. Frank James Symonds, B Company, 16th West Yorkshire Regt., was aged 20. He was the son of Ernest and Annie Mary Symonds of 'Brookmead', The Rise, Sheringham, Norfolk. He was educated at Thetford Grammar School and was commissioned on 11th May 1915. His body was never found and his name is inscribed on the Thiepval Memorial, Pier & Face 2A, 2C & 2D.

and a number of injured Privates and the fatally wounded 2nd Lt. Symonds. He had just crawled up to the edge of the crater to sneak a quick look around when a German HE shell exploded close by, blowing the unfortunate Capt. Pringle from one side of the crater to the other where he landed on top of Gransbury who was buried in the process. Fortunately for the Private, another man came and dug him out but Pringle[i] was dead, as was Smith, while Lt. Sutcliffe would die of his wounds on the 5th July on a hospital ship taking him back to Southampton[ii].

Plate 128 Capt. Robert William Hay Pringle, 16th West Yorkshire

Plate 129 2nd Lt. Charles Stuart Hyde, 16th West Yorkshire Regt.

Another officer of the 1st Bradford Pals to die was 25 year old 2nd Lt. Charles Stuart Hyde from Cleckheaton. He had been wounded early in the attack suffering injuries to his arm and leg. The wounds meant he could not walk and he was told to go to the rear with the stretcher bearers. He refused saying he wanted to see the thing through. Instead, he sat on the edge of a shell crater and cheered his men onwards. A German shell abruptly ended the life of this 'conscientious and painstaking officer'[iii].

---

[i] Capt. Robert William Hay Pringle, 16th West Yorkshire Regt., was aged 28. He was the son of David and Agnes Pringle of 171A, Cromwell Road, South Kensington, London. He graduated from Merton College, Oxford, in 1912. Also served in Egypt. His body was found 20 years after the end of the war and he is buried in Euston Road Cemetery, Colincamps, grave I. A. 47.

[ii] Lt. Robert Sutcliffe, 16th West Yorkshire Regt., was aged 36 and was the only son of the late Mr Tom Sutcliffe of Idle. Educated at Bradford Grammar School, he was a partner of Sutcliffe & Trenholme, solicitors, of Bradford. Runner-up Yorkshire Golf Championship 1907. Enlisted on outbreak of war in the 16th Middlesex Regt. Gazetted 2nd Lt. in the West Yorkshire Regt. on 21st October 1914, promoted Lt. Served in Egypt. Died at sea of wounds received in action on July 1st 1916 and was buried in Heptonstall Slack Baptist Chapel Cemetery, grave 330.

[iii] 2nd Lt. Charles Stuart Hyde, 16th West Yorkshire Regt., was aged 25. He was the son of the Rev. Tom Dodsworth Hyde and Mrs Mary Jane Hyde (née Croft) of Whitechapel

By then, the front trench was only occupied by the shocked and disorganised remnants of the 15th West Yorkshires, some men of D Company, Durham Pals, and a few Leeds' Pioneers. There were no officers or NCOs of any regiment to be seen so Sgt. Maj. Cussins attempted to take control. Obviously, something had gone seriously wrong with the Division's attack.

The men of D Company, commanded by Capt. Alan Clough, were somewhat luckier. Their stretch of trench was in dead ground and, although they could not be seen by the enemy infantry, they soon came under heavy shrapnel and HE fire but without sustaining heavy losses. They formed up ready to follow their colleagues in the other companies and, before they left, Capt. Clough penned a hurried note to his CO, Maj. Guyon. He handed the note to a runner, Pte. Drake of No. 13 Platoon, who hurried off to Battalion HQ. Clough's note read:

"To OC, 16th West Yorks
From OC, D Company
D Company advancing. Casualties unknown.
Signed Alan Clough (Capt.)
Place: In front of Bradford Trench
Time 8 a.m."[44]

Drake dashed off to the advanced battalion HQ as quickly as the congested and muddy trenches allowed but found no-one there. Maj. Guyon had already gone forward and was probably dead by this time. Frustrated in his task, Drake attached himself to the 2nd Bradford Pals who were now moving towards the front line in the hope he might catch up with his own unit.

The German artillery observers had obviously marked the locations of the trench bridges over the assembly trenches where the men were forced to bunch and these were receiving particular attention from the enemy guns. By now, the German artillery barrage was described in the 93rd Brigade's diary as 'very heavy'. It not only fell on the British front line but also on the front two lines of assembly trenches and at key junctions of the communication trenches where Monk Trench cut across Flag Avenue and Bleneau, Grey and Warley Trenches.

The really heavy casualties started as Clough and his men approached the British front line and they became exposed to heavy machine gun fire from away to their left. A machine gun from the 93rd Machine Gun Company followed on behind D Company and the company's progress was watched by Pte. Price, a member of the gun team:

"I was last out of the Company, went along Bradford Trench from left to right and there were no wounded in the trench. Got into the preparatory position, saw Capt. Clough in the centre with Company Headquarters. Went forward to the next trench in front of Bradford. No casualties up till

---

Vicarage, Cleckheaton, Yorks. He was educated at Bradford Grammar School and was employed by the Union of London and Smith's Bank, Leeds (taken over by the National Provincial Bank in 1918 and now part of NatWest). He was commissioned on 27th April 1915 and went to France on 19th May, 1916. Originally buried behind the British lines his body was lost and his name is inscribed on the Thiepval Memorial, Pier & Face 2A, 2C & 2D. His younger brother, Lt. Eustace Emil Hyde, 4th att. 1st Royal Irish Fusiliers, was killed on 12th October 1916 aged 23 and is buried in the AIF Burial Ground, Flers.

then. Got the order to move forward and reached Leeds Trench still without casualties. Got the order to move forward, walked up to the front line and contracted a few casualties on our way to the front line. My own section was wiped out as we went into No Man's Land."[45]

The 93rd Machine Gun Company was to perform two main functions: overhead covering from the rear trenches and mobile firepower with which to reinforce and hold the expected haul of captured German trenches. Four of its guns, under 2nd Lt. Harcourt provided the overhead covering barrage fire as the infantry advanced while two more guns were in reserve under 2nd Lt. Charles Luckhoff[i]. All of the others advanced with either the 1st or 2nd Bradford Pals, four with the 1st Battalion and six with the 2nd Battalion. The War Diary provides a detailed commentary for each of the machine gun teams on the day.

2nd Lt. Harcourt's teams had orders to cease fire when the advance reached the German 3rd trench but, as it was obvious that the attack had stalled, they resumed firing on any visible targets. At 8.30 a.m., No. 2 gun under L/Cpl. Redpath was ordered forward to replace gun No. 12 which was supposed to advance to Pendant Copse but which had lost all but one man as they went forward. On arriving at the front line Redpath and his men were ordered by an officer to retire. Having flogged their heavily-laden way down the mud-filled and congested communication trenches they were then forced to make the return journey but, on arriving at Fargate Trench, they were turned round and told to go straight back whence they had come. Redpath's trials were not yet over. He arrived at the front line with just the tripod, the gun being some way behind. An undoubtedly exasperated Redpath then turned back to get the gun. Whilst he was away, a German shell made a direct hit on the tripod, blowing it to fragments. One might imagine the Lance Corporal's oaths when he discovered the bits and pieces on his return though he might also have reflected on how lucky he had just been. His luck had certainly turned as he managed to find a replacement tripod amongst all the discarded equipment in the front line and he now stood to his gun until recalled to Company HQ later in the day.

Back in Fargate Trench, 2nd Lt. Harcourt was ordered by Capt. Kayll, OC 93rd Machine Gun Company, to take his three remaining guns out into the open and to engage any visible targets, which they did successfully and without suffering any casualties.

In the assembly trenches 2nd Lt. Baker was to take forward Nos. 5 and 6 guns with the 1st Bradford Pals but was wounded as soon as he left the cover of the trenches. Sgt. Delaney then took over and brought the men forward to the front line and out into No Man's Land where they were then held up by enemy machine gun fire from the direction of Ten Tree Alley. They were ordered back to the front line trenches in order to provide covering and defensive fire if the feared German counter-attack materialised.

Nos. 15 and 16 guns also went forward with the 1st Bradford Pals. These two guns were under the command of 2nd Lt. Rosser Dean. Dean had already been

[i] Lt. Charles Ferdinand Luckhoff, Enslin's Horse att. 93rd Machine Gun Company. Enslin's Horse was a unit formed in 1915 by Brig. Gen. Barend Enslin to fight the Germans in South West Africa. Luckhoff transferred to the Labour Corps in 1917.

wounded as the men waited in the assembly trenches for the signal to advance. This was given at 8.10 a.m. and Dean[i] was killed immediately on leaving the shelter of the trenches and two men were wounded. 22738 Cpl. Thomas Bruce then took charge of No. 15 gun and, under heavy fire, the two gun teams advanced. As they crossed the parapet of Monk Trench Cpl. Bruce[ii] was killed and command passed to Pte. Ashworth. Ashworth was left with only three men of the team and they took shelter in a shell hole where they found the gun had been damaged by shrapnel or a machine gun bullet. With No. 15 gun unusable they brought it back to Company HQ in Legend Trench along with the tripod, spare parts and all the belt boxes they could carry. No. 16 gun team was hardly any luckier with three men of the team going down before reaching the front line. In the confusion the three men remaining of the gun team lost one another. We will pick up on the story of Ptes Brown, Gardner and Bainbridge later.

Pte. Price of the Machine Gun Company attached to D Company was one of the few men to get beyond the British front line[iii]. As previously reported, five of his six man team had gone down near the British wire and he was now some 60 yards out into No Man's Land. On the way he had passed a man of the Leeds Pals who assured him that no one else had gone past him towards the German lines. Looking around, Price saw the second Vickers attached to D Company off to the left and, somewhat nearer, he saw Capt. Clough, OC, D Company. Somehow, Alan Clough had made it out into No Man's Land unscathed but his luck had run out. Price saw him hit in the left wrist and then hit again as he tried to retire. 16/186 Pte. Ernest Warhurst[iv] confirmed the bullet to the wrist. He saw the Captain regain his feet before being hit in the shoulder and then in the body. He fell again and struggled to his feet three times before collapsing for the final time. His runner, Pte. Chambers, later said Clough had been trying to write a message when he died[v].

---

[i] 2nd Lt. Rosser Fellowes Marriott Dean, 4th Royal Warwickshire Regt. att. 93rd Machine Gun Company, was aged 33. He was the second son of Frederick John and Constance Mary Dean (née Marriott), of 'Enderby', Branksome Hill Rd., Bournemouth. He was educated at Wellington College and Oriel College, Oxford. He was commissioned into the 3rd Devonshire Regt. in May 1900 but resigned in 1903. Acted as Intelligence Officer with the British East Africa Field Force in Kenya Colony in 1914-5. Returned to England, invalided with malaria. Re-joined Special Reserve, Warwickshire Regt., and commissioned into 4th Royal Warwickshire Regt. on 17th June 1915. He is buried on Euston Road Cemetery, Colincamps, grave I. D. 14.

[ii] 22738 Cpl Thomas Gladstone Bruce, West Yorkshire Regt. Att. 93rd Machine Gun Company, was aged 24. He was the son of Richard and Sarah Bruce; husband of Mary Margaret Bruce, of 79, Carrington St., Bradford, Yorks. Born at Manchester. He is buried in Euston Road Cemetery, Colincamps, grave I. A. 50.

[iii] With either No. 5 or No. 6 gun.

[iv] 16/186 Pte Ernest Warhurst, 16th West Yorkshire Regt., was killed on 9th October 1917 whilst serving with the 1/5th West Yorkshire Regt. He is remembered on the Tyne Cot Memorial.

[v] Capt. Alan Clough, 16th West Yorkshire Regt., was aged 21. He was the son of Henry Smith Clough and Elizabeth Clough of Redbolt, Keighley. Educated at Tonbridge School, he was due to attend Trinity College, Cambridge, in September 1914. His body was never found and his name is inscribed on the Thiepval Memorial, Pier & Face 2A, 2C & 2D.

Plate 130 Capt. Alan Clough, 16th West Yorkshire Regt.

With Clough's death, command of the scraps of D Company left standing devolved to 2nd Lt. John Robinson. Robinson's father was the President of the Bradford Chamber of Commerce and he had been at the forefront of the creation of the Bradford Pals battalions. His son, who had initially enlisted as a Private in the Yorkshire Dragoons, was swiftly commissioned into the 1st Battalion. Now, in his first ever battle, he was in the middle of a body-strewn No Man's Land, surrounded by the dead and dying of two West Yorkshire Pals battalions, whilst nominally in command of his Company. His responsibility did not last long. Within a few minutes he too was dead[i].

In the front line, Sgt. Maj. Cussins had received an order to 'ease off to the left' and, as he moved down the trench he found one of the few remaining officers, 2nd Lt. Jowitt, who ordered him to collect as many men as he could find and to prepare for another advance. As he went from traverse to traverse to find men still capable of action the German barrage on the front line sharply increased, killing or wounding many of the men Cussins had found. 2nd Lt. Jowitt was one of those wounded and he ordered Cussins to return to 93rd Brigade HQ with the information that there were no more able bodied men in the front line. He gave the Sgt. Major the encouraging news that he had sent three or four runners back to Brigade but none of them had returned. As Cussins set off, at about 8.30 a.m., he saw a small group of men advancing towards the German trenches where they were met by a flurry of stick grenades and a burst of rifle fire. This was, perhaps, the last gasp of the advance made by Capt. Clough and D

[i] 2nd Lt. John Holdsworth Robinson, 16th West Yorkshire Regt., was the son of Mr J H Robinson, President of the Bradford Chamber of Commerce, of Greenhill Hall, Bingley, Yorkshire., one of the promoters of the movement for the formation of the Battalion. He was educated at Woodhouse Grove School, Bradford. He enlisted as 3072 Private in the Yorkshire Dragoons and was commissioned on 26th October 1914. His body was never found and his name is inscribed on the Thiepval Memorial, Pier & Face 2A, 2C & 2D.

Company. At the end of the day 2nd Lt. Jowitt was reported missing believed killed and this information was published in the Yorkshire Evening Post. He was, however, lying out in the open severely wounded and was not found for 24 hours. He eventually recovered from his wounds and was transferred to the Training Reserve in September 1917. He was posted to the King's Own Royal Lancaster Regt. in July 1918 but would survive the war[i].

Cussins, meanwhile, made his way through the shambles of the trenches now filled with the dead and wounded, piles of discarded equipment as well as mud and water, until he saw a signpost to Brigade HQ. This turned out to be 94th Brigade HQ rather than his own but a staff officer phoned through the information to 93rd Brigade who ordered Cussins to report to the correct HQ. On arriving in Sackville Street he was diverted with some other men to line that trench as rumours were current that the Germans had mounted a counter-attack across No Man's Land. Such was the disarray within VIII Corps along its entire front that rumours (and reports) of such an unprecedented action by the enemy were rampant. Rarely can an offensive mounted with such enormous confidence in success been so quickly reduced to such abject panic and chaos, nor with such crushing casualties.

The 1st Bradford Pals had gone into action with 24 officers, including the MO, and 682 men (including 19 medical staff). Their casualties were reported as:

Officers:

Killed 10	Died of wounds 1	Missing 1	Wounded 10
Total 22			

Other Ranks

Killed 58	Died of wounds 11	Missing 112	Wounded 313
Total 494			

Thus, a battalion, of which probably less than a company entered No Man's Land, had suffered 73% casualties[ii]. 153 officers and men have since been identified as having died on 1st July 1916 and another 13 died of wounds by 12th July, giving a total number of at least 166 deaths within the battalion or nearly one in four of those who went in action. 75% of those described as 'missing' had, in fact, been killed, most of them behind the British front line trenches and many without ever having seen the enemy that killed them.

The officer casualties were:

Killed

Capt. A Clough	2nd Lt. C S Hyde

[i] Lt. Frederick Robert Benson Jowitt, 16th West Yorkshire Regt., was initially reported killed in action by the Yorkshire Evening Post. Aged 24, he was born in Dunedin, the elder son of the late John Herbert Jowitt of Elmhurst, Leeds, and Mrs Rinah M Jowett (née Hales) of Dunedin, New Zealand. He was educated at King's College, Auckland. He returned to Bradford in 1912 to learn the woll trade as part of Messrs R Jowitt & Sons. He was commissioned into the 16th West Yorkshire Regt. on 23rd September 1914. He married Kathleen Margaret Lupton in 1921. Two children.

[ii] The 93rd Brigade's post-battle report states that no-one from the 1st Bradford Pals advanced beyond the British wire.

Lt. A D Maitland[i]	2nd Lt. S B Newlands[ii]
Capt. R W H Pringle	Lt. C T Ransome
2nd Lt. J H Robinson	Capt. D C Smith
2nd Lt. R Stead	2nd Lt. F J Symonds
2nd Lt. E Tweedale[iii]	Lt. M H Webster[iv]

Died of wounds:
Lt. R Sutcliffe, 5th July
Wounded:
2nd Lt. Joseph Speight Auty
2nd Lt. Francis Martello Gray
2nd Lt. Hepworth
2nd Lt. James Maximilian Harry Hoffman (shell shock)
2nd Lt. Frederick Robert Benson Jowitt
2nd Lt. Charles Fraser Laxton
Maj. Sydney Moore
and two others.

THE QUESTION REMAINS AS TO WHAT HAPPENED to D Company, 18th Durham Light Infantry, which had gone forward at the same time as the second wave of the 16th West Yorkshires. D Company of the Durham Pals had assembled in South Monk between Flag and Delaunay Trenches on the extreme right of the 31st Division's position and were intended to leave the British front lines south of Flag Trench and opposite the end of Ten Tree Alley, the long German communication trench which ran away south east. Two thousand yards beyond the German front line lay the small tear-shaped wood known as Pendant Copse. It is this wood with which the Durham Pals (as well as several other units)

---

[i] Lt. Arthur Dudley Maitland, 14th att. 16th West Yorkshire Regt., was aged 21. He was the son of George Arthur and Mabel Kate Maitland of Ferndene, Canonbie Rd., Forest Hill, London. He was educated at Haberdashers' Aske's School, New Cross. He is buried in Serre Road Cemetery No. 3, Puisieux, Sp. Mem. 4.

[ii] 2nd Lt. Sydney Barron Newlands, 16th West Yorkshire Regt., was aged 20. He was the elder son of the Rev. R W Newlands, pastor of the Providence Place Congregational Church, Cleckheaton, and Agnes Newlands of 5, Fairholme Avenue, Romford, Essex. Born at Port Byron, Illinois, U.S.A., he was educated at Glasgow High School and Silcoates School, Wakefield. He worked at the Leeds Education Office. He enlisted in September 1914 and was commissioned in May 1915. He is buried in Serre Road Cemetery No. 2, grave VII. C. 6.

[iii] 2nd Lt. Eric Tweedale, 13th att. 16th West Yorkshire Regt., was aged 20. He was the son of William Henry and Emma Tweedale of 'Serre', Cliff Place, Bispham, Lancs. Born at Monton Green he entered Manchester University to study electrical engineering in 1913. He was a member of the OTC 1914-15. He was commissioned into the 13th West Yorkshire Regt. in May 1915. His body was never found and his name is inscribed on the Thiepval Memorial, Pier & Face 2A, 2C & 2D.

[iv] Lt. Michael Howard Webster, 13th att. 16th West Yorkshire Regt., was aged 22. He was the son of Mr R Webster of the Hollies, Wesley Road, Armley, Leeds. He gained a BA at Leeds University where he was in the OTC. He enlisted in the Highland Light Infantry with which he went to France. He was commissioned into the 16th West Yorkshire Regt. and went back to France on 13th June 1916. His body was never found and his name is inscribed on the Thiepval Memorial, Pier & Face 2A, 2C & 2D.

have become enduringly linked since the morning of 1st July 1916. It has been long held that, somehow and against extraordinary odds, a small group of Durhams fought their way across the six lines of German trenches between the front line and Pendant Copse before entering the wood never to be seen again. It is suggested that, somehow, their path (and that of the men thought to be in Serre) was followed by watching the reflections off the tin triangles on the men's back which, it had been hoped, might give the observers of the R.F.C. some idea as to how far the infantry had advanced. One might have some cause to doubt the plausibility of this claim given the numerous comments about the very poor visibility across the battlefield. One might have even more doubts about the claims given that the sun was in the east and the men's backs were facing west making reflections towards the British lines something of a problem. To add to any reservations one might have about the likelihood of such a small group of men surviving during an advance over 2,000 yards in very hostile territory one should weigh the entry in the 93rd Brigade war diary timed at 8.35 a.m.:

> "So far as is known no one of the 16th West Yorkshire Regt. advanced beyond our own wire and no one of 'D' company, 18th Durham LI advanced more than 20 yards beyond our wire."[46]

The regimental history states that the 'major portion' of D Company had disappeared under the German artillery barrage.

If this is true then where did this gallant band of Durham Pals in Pendant Copse come from? Certainly not from A, B or C Companies which spent most of the day in Maitland and Monk Trenches being shelled intermittently and suffering a steady flow of casualties. None of their men entered No Man's Land.

That leaves the special bombing parties led by 2nd Lt. James Bradford[i]. What of them? They are not mentioned again. Bradford was not a fatal casualty but was wounded on 1st July 1916 with gun shot wounds to the arm and right ankle. He survived later to win the MC but died in 1917. He certainly did not lead his men to Pendant Copse as, with his wounds, he would not have returned. In addition, there are no mentions of such a deep incursion by British troops in any accounts from the German side. Furthermore, there is no mention whatsoever in any of

[i] 2nd Lt. James Barker Bradford, MC, 18th Durham Light Infantry, was aged 26. Born in Witton Park, Durham, he was the son of the late George and Amy Marion Bradford (née Andrews) of Milbanke, Ravenlea Rd., Folkestone. He was married to Annie Bradford (née Wall). He was educated at Darlington Grammar School and Polam Grange School, Darlington. He worked as an engineer at Hawthorn Leslie's Engineering Works in Newcastle and became a director of Dinsdale Wire and Steel Works, Co. Durham. Pre-war he was an Able Seaman in the Royal Naval Reserve and he enlisted in the Northumberland Hussars on the outbreak of war. He was commissioned into the DLI on 25th September 1915. He was one of four brothers who served in WW1. He won the MC (*London Gazette*, 17th April 1917); his oldest brother, Lt. Col. Sir Thomas Andrews Bradford, won the DSO; his older brother, Lt. Cdr. George Nicholson Bradford, Royal Navy, won the VC at Zeebrugge; and his younger brother, Brig. Gen. Roland Boys Bradford, the youngest General in the B.E.F., won the VC and the MC. James, George and Roland were all killed with James dying on 14th May 1917 from wounds received on 10th May in the Battle of Arras. He is buried in Duisans British Cemetery, Etrun.

the war diaries of the day's events, from Corps down to battalion, which might support the notion that men of the Durham Pals reached Pendant Copse.

There can be only one conclusion: no-one from the 18th Durham Light Infantry got anywhere near Pendant Copse. They lay dazed, dead or wounded within the British front line trenches.

Plate 131 2nd Lt. James Barker Bradford, 18th Durham Light Infantry

JUST BEFORE THE FIRST TWO BATTALIONS OF THE 93RD BRIGADE were destroyed on their right, the two lead battalions of the 94th Brigade had been assembling in No Man's Land. At the same time their support battalions started to move forward from the rear assembly trenches. Both the Accrington and Sheffield battalions had their 1st waves lying out in No Man's Land as soon as the 10-minute trench mortar barrage began. At 7.22 a.m. the 2nd wave of the Accringtons left the front line whilst immediately behind them the leading platoons of the 13th York and Lancaster started to move across the open towards the front line trenches.

At 7.25 a.m. 31st Division received a telephone call from the Divisional OP which would be the first of many to make one wonder just what the observers were looking at:

> "7.25 a.m. Divisional OP reports our infantry to have advanced in front of Matthew, Mark and Luke Copses and crossed the German front line."[47]

Other than suggesting that the attack had started five minutes early, what makes this report especially interesting is the one that arrived at the same moment from the 171st Brigade, RFA:

> "7.25 a.m. 171 Brigade RA report: front line heavily shelled in K.35.a. Mist very thick. Observation impossible up to now."[48]

Leaving to one side the fundamental inconsistency of these two reports it is from this point that the 94th Brigade's affairs took a marked turn for the worse. The 2nd waves of the two lead battalions had been seen to clear the front line and lie down 50 yards behind the 1st wave. So far, so good. But then, clearly to the surprise of those watching the attack, dozens of men appeared above the parapet of the German front trench:

> "7.25 a.m. Second wave crossed our front line, and lay down fifty yards in rear of first wave. At this time the German front line was seen to be manned, (about one man per yard), by men who had either been lying behind the parados of fire trench during the bombardment, or who had emerged from shelters. These men, despite our artillery and trench mortar barrage, opened a heavy rifle and machine gun fire, and threw bombs on our first two waves, causing many casualties."[49]

To the observers of the 169th Brigade, RFA, it appeared as if the advanced waves of the 94th Brigade had somehow escaped the worst of the German machine gun fire by keeping up close behind the heavy artillery barrage which had lifted at 7.20 a.m. Their interpretation of what then happened is remarkable:

> "94th Brigade. 1st and 2nd waves appeared to reach Serre without consolidating lines of trenches as they took them but no supports followed and consequently the men who reached Serre were probably cut off and never seen again.
> 93rd Brigade. Held up at 2nd line wire and enfiladed from Quadrilateral which 4th Division had not captured (excepting front line)."[50]

Extraordinarily, none of these 'facts' were true. Any troops that entered Serre, and there are good reasons to believe none did, were numbered, at most, in the tens. We have already heard that the CO of the 15th West Yorkshires was sure none of his men reached even the German front line trench let alone the 2nd line wire. And, for good measure, if there was one part of the 4th Division's attack which had been successful it was at the Heidenkopf (Quadrilateral) which had been overrun. Indeed, so wildly inaccurate was this report that VIII Corps' own comments about the state of affairs at 7.30 a.m. confirmed that the entire 93rd Brigade failed to reach the German front line. It also stated, however, that small parties of the 94th Brigade were seen to cross the first two lines of German trenches whilst, at the same time, admitting that 'Observation of the movements of troops was extremely difficult'.

At 7.29 a.m. the 3rd and 4th waves of the Accringtons and Sheffields were seen to start advancing from Campion and Monk respectively. As they came on, a German artillery barrage started on Monk Trench and slowly rolled forward, following the progress of the men, until it settled on the front line. In addition, these men, who were approaching across the open and bunching as they crossed the various trenches lines on the wooden bridges, came under heavy rifle and machine gun fire. What was left of these waves was seen to cross the front line at about 7.32 a.m. It was estimated that half of them had become casualties before reaching the British front line. In front of them, the remnants of the 1st and 2nd waves got to their feet and advanced stolidly towards the German lines. The British heavy artillery barrage was, by now, already far away battering the 4th line of German trenches. The German barrage of shrapnel and HE, however, was placed firmly on, and just in front of, the British front line.

The 12th York and Lancaster's War Diary provides a breakdown of how the men of the battalion were employed on 1st July. It reveals just how few men were actually in the assault. The total strength of the battalion was 36 officers and 980 Other Ranks. Of these:

18 were sick or had been found to be too young;
33 were in the battalion base detail;
41 were with the 1st Line Transport;
82 were on Brigade or Divisional tasks or were at Schools of Instruction;
25 were attached to the Trench Mortar Battery;
11 were detailed for salvage; and
11 were Battle Police
Total – 207
126 were allocated to the 10% reserve kept behind as a nucleus in the case of very heavy casualties
Total – 333
This leaves 647 men. Of these:
44 were Brigade Bomb carriers;
23 were battalion carriers;
61 were the HQ detail – runners, signallers, observers, stretcher bearers, etc.; and
36 were Company signallers and runners.

This left a total of 483 men plus 24 officers to actually take part in the attack, with the 36 Company signallers and runners going forward with them – a total of 543 officers and men.[51] Many of the other men, the HQ detachment, the Trench Mortar detachment, would have been in the trenches and suffered casualties but these were not men likely to have gone 'over the top', or 'over the lid' as these Northern soldiers would have it. The carriers, many lugging two canvass bags of hand grenades, were to follow the attacking troops over to re-supply the bombers in the enemy lines. How many of them made it into No Man's Land is anyone's guess but, laden as they were, such slow moving targets would have been easy pickings for even an average shot in the German trenches.

The men in the assault were now exposed to heavy enfilade fire from the otherwise unengaged machine guns of the IR 66 on their left. As a result, the left half of C Company of the Sheffield battalion, closest to these guns, was wiped out before reaching the front edge of the German wire. On the right, a few men did reach the German wire and, given the reports about it having been blown away, must have been surprised to find no way through. Instead, they were greeted by a shower of stick grenades thrown from the German front line. Those few men who returned from C Company's front stated that the German wire was almost intact. A few men from A and C Companies entered the German front line on the right of the battalion front but otherwise they were shot down in front of the uncut wire.

Losses amongst officers and NCOs were immediate and catastrophic. In C Company, the officer commanding, 47 year old Capt. William Colley, had been one of the first out of the trench. During the hours of waiting he had imparted to his men the feeling that this would be his last battle but, as the regimental history describes, 'he went to his fate like a brave English gentleman'. Colley, who had first joined the Royal Engineers Volunteers in 1896, was killed by a shell and his body never found[i]. Another loss was an old regular, a veteran of the Matabele Wars, 12/4 CSM Arthur Bilbey. Bilbey had been one of a small group of retired regulars headed by RSM Charles Polden who had returned to the colours to help train the raw recruits of the battalion when first formed[ii].

Plate 132 Capt. William Arthur Colley, 12th York & Lancaster Regt.

Plate 133 Capt. William Spenceley Clark, 12th York & Lancaster Regt.

It did not go any better with A Company. 24 year old Capt. William Clark, OC A Company, fell at the head of his men, killed by machine gun fire and left hanging on some uncut German barbed wire[iii]. Lt. Charles Elam, No. 4 Platoon, was one of a small group of men thought to have entered the German lines on

---

[i] Capt. William Arthur Colley, C Company, 12th York & Lancaster Regt., was aged 47. He was the son of Francis William and Sarah Colley of Sheffield. He was commissioned into the 1st West Riding of Yorkshire (Sheffield) Company, Royal Engineers (Volunteers) in 1896 transferring to the 2nd West Riding Company in 1908 as Captain. He joined the 12th York & Lancaster Regt. in September 1914. He lived with his brother, John Herbert Colley, at 29, Collegiate Crescent, Sheffield. A mason, he was a member of the Ivanhoe No. 1779 Lodge and a Sheffield councillor. His body was never found and his name is inscribed on the Thiepval Memorial, Pier & Face 14A & 14B.

[ii] 12/4 CSM Arthur Thomas Bilbey, 12th York & Lancaster Regt. was aged 42. He was the son of Samuel and Mary (née Keetley) Bilbey who married in Nottingham. Born in Hallam, Sheffield, he lived at 27 Bloor Street, Walkley, Sheffield. Retired from the Army in 1905, he was a postman. His body was never found and his name is inscribed on the Thiepval Memorial, Pier & Face 14A & 14B.

[iii] Capt. William Spenceley Clark, A Company, 12th York and Lancaster Regt., was aged 24. He was the son of William and Margaret Kirkwood Clark of Whiteley Wood Hall, Sheffield, now Annet House, Skelmorie, Ayrshire. His father was the Managing Director of Vickers. He was educated at Glasgow High School and was an engineering pupil for Vickers at Sheffield University. He was commissioned in September 1914 and promoted Captain in December 1915. He is buried in Serre Road Cemetery No. 2, grave XXXIX. J. 7/8.

the right of the battalion front, alongside the Accrington Pals. With him were 12/371 Pte. Albert Fretwell, 12/119 Pte. Harry Glossop and 12/1003 Pte. George Mulford. The three Privates survived but young Charles Elam fell. According to Glossop two bombing parties were trying to work their way up German communication trenches and he was carrying up supplies of bombs to both parties. During one trip he came across Lt. Elam. He had been wounded in the neck. On his next trip the lieutenant had gone. He was never seen again[i].

Plate 134 2nd Lt. Philip Kenneth Perkin, 12th York & Lancaster Regt.

Behind them, 2nd Lt. Philip Perkin was seriously wounded by two grenades near the German wire of which far too much had been left uncut[ii]. An unknown Private described what happened:

> "(2nd Lt. Perkin) was well out in front of his men and was using his revolver and shouting encouragement to them and at the same time trying to work his way through the wire when a hand bomb burst close to him. He reeled and half fell but most pluckily pulled himself together for another effort but another bomb burst which brought him down.

---

[i] Lt. Charles Elam, 12th York and Lancaster Regt., was aged 21. He was the son of Dr and Mrs George Elam of 'Edenthorpe', 41, Wickham Rd., Beckenham, Kent. He worked in the Steel industry and lived at Endcliffe Crescent, Sheffield. He enlisted as 12/1423 Private in the 12th York & Lancaster Regt. on 10th September 1914 but was commissioned on 18th September and promoted Lt. in December. He is buried in A.I.F. Burial Ground, Flers, grave XII. M. 2.

[ii] 2nd Lt. Philip Kenneth Perkin, A Company, 12th York and Lancaster Regt., was aged 22. He was the son of Mr Emil Scales Perkin, ARCA, and Mrs Isabel Lilian Perkin of 97, Lonsdale Rd., Oxford, formerly of The Wilderness, Tiverton, Devon. He was educated at Blundell's School and was employed by William Hutton & Sons. He enlisted as 12/213 Private in the 12th York & Lancaster Regt. and was commissioned on 14th September 1915. He joined the battalion on 23rd April 1916. His body was never found and his name is inscribed on the Thiepval Memorial, Pier & Face 14A & 14B.

Immediately afterwards another bomb exploded which took two pieces out of my leg and peppered me generally and I know nothing beyond this. (He) would have been not more than two or three yards from the German trenches and it is possible that he would have been taken in by them after nightfall."[52]

In a letter to his father, the battalion's chaplain described his end:

"I think that there is little doubt that your brave young son was killed... So much is said of our brave soldiers that some of the force may be lost when applied to individuals. His calmness and coolness were unique... His confidence and courage were infectious and you cannot realise what a blessing this is to others in this difficult time out here. He was last seen sitting on the German line calling his men on. Many of our wounded told me with admiration what he was doing and that he was shot in the head by a machine gun. We are all very sad about it. I cannot tell you officially that he was killed, we do not know, but that is the general opinion, his men saw him fall and spoke of him with pride. I am glad to have known your happy son, I shall always remember his cheery soul in connection with this part of my life and if I am spared to continue my ministry in England, I will remember him in my home church."[53]

Some men, stopped by the uncut wire, exchanged fire with the enemy whilst standing in the open. 12/226 Pte. Robert Seymour fired off round after round until a bullet smashed his jaw. He survived the battle and the war. 12/1123 Sgt. Reginald Gallimore stood and shot at the German bombers and riflemen and somehow escaped unwounded. He then collected some men and retired to a shell hole where they fired at any of the enemy they could see. Gallimore brought his men back under cover of darkness. He too survived 'the war to end all wars'.

Behind the leading waves of the battalion came B and D Companies. Capt. Reginald Moore[i], OC B Company, was hit early in the fighting and put out of action. Two brothers, 2nd Lts. Arnold and Frank Beal, were also in the attack. Arnold was the older of the two, at just 22, and was a student at Sheffield University. He was known as 'Arnie' within his family and he had written a letter to his parents on the 29th June which was only to be sent if he died. The letter arrived a few days later at his home in Sheffield:

"This is a letter to all of you, although I pray that there never be need for you to receive it. You see we are about to attack, part of the Great Advance... Death must come, and can you conceive a finer death...? By God's Grace you still have Frank, and my two sweet little sisters... I pray that England is on the Lord's side, if so I die content and happy... By God's Grace we shall all meet again. Goodbye. Ever your loving son, Arnie"

[i] Writing after the war Maj. Hoette, the 2inC of the Sheffields, stated that Capt. Moore had reached the German wire and, while there, emptied his revolver at the Germans in their trench before being wounded. If true, Moore had ignored the instruction that officers should dress and arm themselves the same as Other Ranks in order not to stand out and make themselves targets for German snipers.

2nd Lt. Arnie Beal's body was recovered in the spring of 1917 and buried in Queen's Cemetery[i]. His younger brother, Temp. Lt. Frank Beal, was attached to the 94th Trench Mortar Battery. He was wounded but survived.

12/562 CSM William Loxley, a veteran of the South African War in which he had served with the King's Royal Rifle Corps, was another to fall as B Company lost its leaders[ii].

D Company was commanded by Capt. Harold Pearson, previously the battalion's Adjutant and one of several Sheffield University students or alumni commissioned into the battalion. He was seriously wounded but stayed to encourage his men on towards the enemy lines. Two of his platoon commanders, Lt. Geoffrey Ingold and Lt. Frederick Storry, were wounded (both survived the war) but 2nd Lt. Eric Carr was not so lucky and he was never seen again[iii].

Plate 135 2nd Lt. Eric Marcus Carr, 12th York & Lancaster Regt.

---

[i] 2nd Lt. Arnold James Beal, B Company, 12th York and Lancaster Regt., was aged 22. He was the son of Arnold James, cutlery manufacturer, and Laura Angwin Beal of 44, Ranmoor Cliff, Sheffield. He was a student at Sheffield University living at Ivy Park Road, Sheffield, and was commissioned on 17th February 1915. He is buried in Queen's Cemetery, Puisieux, grave E. 39. His younger brother, 2nd Lt. Frank Angwyn Beal, survived his wounds but he relinquished his commission on 10th June 1917 as a result of ill-heath. He later married and had a daughter, Catherine Doone Beal.

[ii] 12/562 CSM William Henry Loxley, 12th York & Lancaster Regt., was aged 40. He was the son of Samuel Loxley and Mary Platts. He was the husband of Florence Ada Loxley, of 64, Hammerton Rd., Hillsborough, Sheffield, and had worked as a Postman since 1904. He is buried in Railway Hollow Cemetery, Hebuterne, grave A. 4.

[iii] 2nd Lt. Eric Marcus Carr, 12th York and Lancaster Regt., was educated at King Edward VII School, Sheffield, and played in the Cricket XI in 1913. He was commissioned on 27th June 1915. His body was never found and his name is inscribed on the Thiepval Memorial, Pier & Face 14A & 14B. He is remembered on a memorial in St Oswald's Church, Bannerdale Road, Sheffield.

Although the regimental history suggests that fewer than a dozen men from D Company got through the German barrage at the British wire, it mentions the conduct of one of the bombers, 12/1068 Pte. William Taylor, who leapt into the enemy's trench and drove back its defenders by throwing bomb after bomb. Taylor, always smart and with his hair parted just so, was another lost forever in the fighting[i]. Another bomber, 12/551 Pte. Arthur Wenman, also got into the German front-line trenches where he bombed a dug-out apparently containing eight Germans. Wenman, however, survived and was able to give a detailed description of the construction of the German trench after the battle.

Although Taylor's bravery went officially unrecognised there were several other man whose actions attracted the attention of superior officers and resulted in various decorations – three DCMs and six MMs.

12/1164 L/Cpl. Matthew Burnby, 12/923 Pte. Charles Garbutt and 12/24 Pte. Herbert Arridge were part of a Lewis Gun team supporting the 1st wave of the attack. Although two men from the team were wounded in the advance, these three got their gun into action from a shell hole and took on a German machine gun in the front line. They had collected some grenades on their way across and whoever wasn't firing the gun lobbed these at the MG emplacement. All the while, their hole was peppered with stick grenades and swept by machine gun fire. All three survived to return their gun to the British lines and all three were awarded the MM for their brave efforts[ii].

12/338 Pte. Bertram Corthorn, a 29 year old tailor from Norton Woodseats south of Sheffield, was part of another Lewis Gun team attached to the 3rd wave and they got their gun into action within 20 yards of the German parapet. One by one, the men of the team were shot down by German snipers or machine guns until only Bert Corthorn was left to fight the gun. Taking advantage of the shelter provided by a nearby shell hole he swept the German trenches, concentrating his fire on a German Maxim in the front line. When all of the ammunition panniers were used up he used a rifle. When there was no more ammunition for this weapon he crawled to another shell hole where he found one of his mates from the team, 12/1125 Pte. Reginald Brooks, who had been mortally wounded[iii]. Corthorn, himself wounded, remained with Brooks until he died, collecting water and trying to make him comfortable. As light faded on Saturday, 1st July, Corthorn could have been forgiven for retiring to the British trenches but he stayed with his wounded comrade, unable to move him because of his own wound. Brooks finally died on the afternoon of Sunday, 2nd July, and, as night fell on his second night out in No Man's Land, Corthorn eventually crept back to the British trenches, taking with him the Lewis Gun. Unknown to him, his behaviour had been observed by the badly wounded Capt. Reginald Eric Jennens Moore of B Company and as the Captain was being evacuated on a stretcher he informed

---

[i] 12/1068 Pte William John Taylor, 12th York & Lancaster Regt., from Norton, Sheffield, was never found and his name is inscribed on the Thiepval Memorial, Pier & Face 14A & 14B.

[ii] All three awards were in the *London Gazette*, 14th November 1916.

[iii] 12/1225 Pte Reginald Francis Brooks, 12th York & Lancaster Regt., was never found and his name is inscribed on the Thiepval Memorial, Pier & Face 14A & 14B.

Maj. Plackett, the CO, of what he had seen. 12/338 Pte. Bertram Corthorn was later awarded the DCM[i].

12/1521 Pte. Arthur Greenaway of B Company also went across with the 3rd wave. As the attack broke down in front of the German wire Greenaway started dragging wounded men from the open into the partial shelter of the numerous shell holes that disfigured the ground. There they were at least safe from the predatory snipers who were picking off anyone who moved in No Man's Land. Where he could, Greenaway applied field dressings and gave first aid. His bravery was witnessed by several nearby men but his death was not. Arthur Greenaway died in the fields west of Serre and his body was never found. His bravery did not bring him the recognition of the award he so richly deserved[ii].

Three awards were made to battalion runners, those men who rushed, as far as conditions allowed, from Battalion to Brigade HQs after the telephone wires were cut and who knew not when a German shell or bullet might end their crucial journey.

12/275 Pte. G C Wright took a message from Battalion Headquarters in John Copse to Brigade Headquarters in Dunmow, a distance of nearly half a mile. Three times on his trip he was blown up and partially buried by nearby shell explosions. Undaunted, he delivered his message, although he collapsed on his arrival. He was awarded the DCM in the *London Gazette* of 22nd September 1916[iii].

Two other runners won the MM. 12/443 Pte. Rowland Marsden was partially buried by a shell. He dug himself out and delivered the message. 12/354 Pte. Alexander Downing took two messages from Battalion HQ in John Copse to Brigade Headquarters in Dunmow, all the while under heavy artillery fire.

The Battalion carriers were also recognised if not with awards then with mentions by the CO for their conduct. 12/481 RSM Charles Polden was an ex-Regular who had helped with the training of the original recruits[iv]. At some point during the day he brought up a party of bomb-carriers to Battalion Headquarters from the Battalion dump under heavy artillery fire. Several of the men were killed

---

[i] 12/338 Pte Bertram Corthorn, 12th York & Lancaster Regt., was awarded the DCM in the *London Gazette* of 22nd September 1916. The citation reads: "For conspicuous gallantry and devotion to duty in attack. Being one of a machine gun team held up within 20 yards of the enemy trench, he succeeded, when all the rest of the team had been killed or wounded, in getting the gun to a shell hole, and thence maintaining a heavy fire till his ammunition was exhausted." Corthorn married Winifred Mary Woolhouse in 1916 and they had two children. He was wounded again in 1917 and did not return to the front. He went back to tailoring after the war and died in 1972.

[ii] 12/1521 Pte Arthur Greenaway. 12th York & Lancaster Regt., was aged 36. He was the son of William and Emma Jane Greenaway, of 79, Burnt Ash Rd., Lee, London. He was born in Bermondsey and enlisted in Attercliffe, Sheffield. His body was never found and his name is inscribed on the Thiepval Memorial, Pier & Face 14A & 14B.

[iii] 12/275 Pte G C Wright, 12th York & Lancaster Regt., was awarded the DCM in the *London Gazette* of 22nd September 1916. The citation reads: "For gallantry and devotion to duty when as battalion runner in attack he succeeded in taking a message to brigade headquarters under very heavy fire. He was thrice buried on the way."

[iv] 12/481 RSM Charles Polden, 12th York & Lancaster Regt., was later promoted Lt. and Quartermaster. Whilst still RSM he was awarded the MC for his conduct on 9th March 1917, the award being in the *London Gazette* of 11th May 1917.

on the way. 12/1414 Pte. Willie Dalton was the sole survivor of another carrying party bringing up bombs from the dump to Battalion HQ in John Copse.

If there were gaps in the German wire, and they were few and far between, then they were covered by machine guns from Maschinengewehr-Kompanie Nr. 1 of IR 169. There were four defending Sector S1. One in the front line opposite Luke Copse, a second in the second trench opposite Mark Copse, a third in the third line opposite John Copse and a fourth set back in Tübinger Stellung, the 4th German trench, at the junction with Jahn Graben and able to overlook the entire front of the 94th Brigade. It was from the position occupied by Unteroffizier Kölle's gun team in the second trench that Oblt. Faller, commanding Maschinengewehr-Kompanie Nr 1, oversaw the machine gun support of the I Battalion, IR 169. In Sector S2 two more guns swept the area over which the Accringtons would attack, with one in the front line opposite Matthew Copse and a second in the third line able to cover the area between Matthew and Mark Copse. With the machine guns of IR 66 providing enfilade fire from the north the guns provided excellent interlocking fields of fire through which it was nearly impossible to advance.

Plate 136 2nd Lt. Frank Dinsdale, 12th York & Lancaster Regt.

As with the attack of the Leeds Pals, that of the Sheffield City Battalion was effectively over in a matter of minutes. The view of the survivors was unequivocal:

> "The failure of the attack was undoubtedly due to the wire not being sufficiently cut. Had this been cut the enemy's machine guns could have been dealt with by the men who managed to reach the front line. As it was, they could not be reached and there was no means of stopping their fire. Bombers attempted to silence them with grenades but could not reach them – consequently succeeding waves were wiped out and did not arrive at the German wire in any strength."[54]

The battalion's casualties by the end of the day were truly devastating.

Officers killed:

2nd Lt. A J Beal
2nd Lt. E M Carr
Capt. W S Clark
Capt. W A Colley
2nd Lt. F Dinsdale[i].
Lt C Elam
2nd Lt. P K Perkin
2nd Lt. C Wardill[ii]

Officers wounded:

2nd Lt. Frank Angwin Beal, att. 94th TMB
Lt. Francis Campion Earl
Lt. Geoffrey John Herbert Ingold
Capt. Reginald Eric Jennens Moore
Capt. Harold Ward Pearson
Lt Frederick William Scott Storry
Lt. Cecil Herbert Woodhouse[iii]

In addition, Maj. Alfred Plackett[iv] and Lt. Henry Oxley were evacuated wounded on 2nd July. Including these two, eight officers were dead, nine wounded and only four involved in the action, Capt. & Adjutant Norman Leslie Tunbridge, Lt. Eric L Moxey, 2nd Lt. Cedric Cloud and Lt. Edward Cunnington, RAMC, were unwounded. Three of the officer casualties: Dinsdale, Wardill and Oxley, had been with the battalion for less than a month.

Casualties across the battalion amounted to 83% of those who started the battle. If one includes the estimated 75 men categorised as slightly wounded and who remained at duty then this figure increases to an extraordinary 93%. On the 29th June, the battalion had been 980 strong. After deductions for the 10% reserve, carrying parties, transport, etc., 602 officers and men went into action. Casualties by Company were as follows:

	Overall	In attack	Killed	DoW	Wounded	Missing	PoW	Total	% Casualties
A Coy	264	153	6	1	76	44	1	128	84%
B Coy	247	155	15	2	62	44	0	123	79%
C Coy	234	143	8	2	43	71	0	124	87%
D Coy	235	151	16	7	56	42	1	122	81%
Total	980	602	45	12	237	201	2	497	83%

Table 18 12th York & Lancaster Regt. casualty figures by Company[55]

[i] 2nd Lt. Frank Dinsdale, 12th York and Lancaster Regt., was aged 23. He was the son of James and Sarah Dinsdale of Show Cote, Askrigg. He was a member of the Leeds University OTC and was commissioned in September 1915. He was originally reported as wounded and missing. He is buried in Queen's Cemetery, Puisieux, grave C. 20.

[ii] 2nd Lt. Charles Henry Wardill, 15th att. 12th York and Lancaster Regt., was aged 39. He was the husband of Edith E Wardill of 18, Violet Bank Rd., Nether Edge, Sheffield. He was commissioned on 25th October 1915. His body was never found and his name is inscribed on the Thiepval Memorial, Pier & Face 14A & 14B. His brother, 12/816 Pte Sidney G Wardill, was also killed serving with the Sheffields on 1st July 1916. Like his brother his body was never found and his name is recorded on the Thiepval Memorial.

[iii] Lt. Cecil Herbert Woodhouse, 12th York and Lancaster Regt., died on 6th June 1918. His body was never found and his name is inscribed on the Tyne Cot Memorial

[iv] Maj. Alfred Plackett, 12th York and Lancaster Regt., relinquished his commission on the grounds of ill health on 5th July 1917.

248 men of the the Sheffield Pals, are known to have died on 1st July. Another 15 men died of wounds before the month was out, one of them being one of the two Prisoners of War[i]. Initially, casualties amongst Other Ranks were reported as 468 killed, wounded and missing. By the 3rd July, 21 of the missing had returned unwounded and, on that date, the casualty figures as definitely known revealed a horrible uncertainty about the fate of the overwhelming majority of the men. On this day the war diary gives casualty figures of:

6 killed

67 wounded

373 missing

The enormous number of missing can be explained, in part, by the length of time it took for the wounded to be cleared from the trenches and No Man's Land. By Monday this job was far from complete.

One should not, perhaps, pick out any particular man as being worthy of special note given the scale of these losses. All represent a special personal and family tragedy which should not be diminished. But two men, one a corporal and one a sergeant, in their way represent the extraordinary social makeup of the battalion and embody the heartbreak of promising futures brutally cut short.

12/525 Sgt. John William 'Will' Streets was a 31 year old Derbyshire man who had spent fourteen years working down the local coal mine. An intelligent man with an enquiring mind he turned down a place at Grammar School to help bring in money to a household in which he was the eldest of twelve children. In his spare time he wrote, sketched, played the piano and continued his education with studies of the Classics and French. He also taught at his local Sunday School at Whitwell Wesleyan Chapel. When war came he volunteered and joined the Sheffield Pals. He went to Egypt and then to France. And wherever he went he wrote poetry. At 7.30 a.m. he went forward with his mates to attack the German lines. Wounded, he returned to get his wound dressed and was last seen going to help an injured fellow soldier. His remains were found the following spring when the Serre battlefield was at last cleared of the dead. Unlike many, he was identified and, on 1st May 1917, he was officially declared 'killed in action' and his family could finally mourn their loss[ii]. The same month, a collection of his poems entitled *'The Undying Splendour'* was published. One of its poems is *'A Soldier's Cemetery'*:

Behind that long and lonely trenched line
To which men come and go, where brave men die,
There is a yet unmarked and unknown shrine,
A broken plot, a soldier's cemetery.

---

[i] 12/702 Pte F R Johnston, 12th York and Lancaster Regt., died on 10th July. He was buried in Caudry Old Communal Cemetery, grave A. 11. The other PoW was 12/469 Pte Albert Outram, a signaller.

[ii] 12/525 Sgt. John William Streets, 12th York & Lancaster Regt. was aged 31. He was the eldest son of Mr and Mrs William Streets, of 16, Portland St., Whitwell, Derbyshire. Two books of his poetry were published *'Coal Mining'*, and the War Poems *'The Undying Splendour'*, (May, 1917). He is remembered in Euston Road Cemetery, Colincamps, on Special Memorial A. 6.

There lie the flower of youth, the men who scorn'd
To live (so died) when languished Liberty:
Across their graves flowerless and unadorned
Still scream the shells of each artillery.

When war shall cease this lonely unknown spot
Of many a pilgrimage will be the end,
And flowers will shine in this now barren plot
And fame upon it through the years descend:
But many a heart upon each simple cross
Will hang the grief, the memory of its loss.

Plate 137 12/525 Sgt. John William Streets, 12th York & Lancaster Regt.

Plate 138 12/220 Cpl. Alexander Robertson, 12th York & Lancaster Regt.

Though of lowlier rank, 12/220 Cpl. Alexander Robertson was definitely from 'the other side of the tracks'. A similar age to Streets at 34, he was the son of the late Robert Robertson, M.A., F.R.S.E., and the Headmaster of Edinburgh Ladies' College. Alexander Robertson was educated at one of Edinburgh and Scotland's leading schools, George Watson's College, and he gained a 1st Class Degree in History at Edinburgh University. He returned to Watson's to become a senior history master before going to teach English Literature at the Lycée in Caen. He then went to Oxford University where he graduated with a B. Litt. His thesis was later published as *'The Life of Sir Robert Moray, Soldier, Statesman and Man of Science 1608-1673'*. In February 1914, he became a lecturer in history at Sheffield University and was thus in place to join the Sheffield Pals that September. Like Streets he went to Egypt after basic training before returning with the battalion to France. He was ill for a time with jaundice but returned to the battalion in time for the attack on Serre. He went forward with A Company but no-one who survived saw him die. His name is one of the long list from the battalion inscribed on the Thiepval Memorial to the Missing of the Somme.

Two volumes of Alexander Robertson's poetry were published: *'Comrades'* and *'Last Poems'*. *'Lines Before Going'* is, perhaps, the best known:

Soon is the night of our faring to regions unknown,
There not to flinch at the challenge suddenly thrown
By the great process of Being □ daily to see
The utmost that life has of horror and yet to be
Calm and the masters of fear. Aware that the soul
Lives as a part and alone for the weal of the whole,
So shall the mind be free from the pain of regret,
Vain and enfeebling, firm in each venture, and yet
Brave not as those who despair but keen to maintain,
Though not assured, hope in beneficent pain,
Hope that the truth of the world is not what appears,
Hope in the triumph of man for the price of his tears.

IRONICALLY, IN SPITE OF THEIR APPALLING LOSSES, the Sheffields had achieved more success against the German first trench and their machine guns than they realised and, as a result, it was on their right that they and the Accringtons achieved the only serious incursion into the German line.

A machine gun team under Unteroffizier Ludwig Adelbrecht had been firing furiously into the oncoming ranks of the Sheffield Battalion from a position close to the front line line near the end of a short communication trench which ran forwards from the 3rd German trench. This gun covered the left of sector S1 opposite Luke Copse and had been firing ever since the heavier British guns had moved away from the front line. Somehow, some of the attacking men had managed to get close enough to throw their bombs and engage the enemy with rifle fire. It was now that the Maxim chose to jam. Already, four of Adelbrecht's team were wounded and a nearby bomber, Rfn. Pfähler, had been killed when a stick grenade had gone off prematurely. As Adelbrecht struggled to clear the jam he was shot in the head and killed. An urgent message was sent back to Oblt. Faller 100 yards away down the communication trench advising him that there was now a gap in the carefully deployed machine gun screen. Faller ordered the machine gun team in the third trench away to his right commanded by Unteroffizier Wilhelm to move forward immediately to the front line opposite John Copse where his gun would be able to sweep No Man's Land with enfilade fire while the guns from IR 66 dealt with any men from the 2nd Barnsley Pals still active. The slackening of the German machine gun fire caused by two of the guns in sector S1 being out of action, that is, until Wilhelm's team reached their new position, allowed men of 12th York and Lancasters to creep further forward so that more of them were able to lob their grenades into the front line German trench. It was this scene that greeted the machine gun team as they hurried into position. Worse was to follow. Unteroffizier Wilhelm was immediately hit in the head and the gun was unable to come into action whilst the gun team reorganised. Thankfully, a member of Adelbrecht's gun team, Unteroffizier Reiner, had moved up the front line trench to his right to join the new machine gun and, taking control, he directed the machine gun onto men of both the 12th

and 14th York and Lancasters who were trying to breach the German defences. As the rattle of the Maxim started up again, these groups melted away.

On the far left of the I Battalion, IR 169's front, in sector S2 opposite Matthew Copse, another machine gun of Maschinengewehr-Kompanie Nr. 1 had succumbed to a fault. This gun gun, commanded by Unteroffizier Kaiser, was firing into the Accringtons but, early on, four of his gun team had been wounded. Then the gun failed and the left of sector S2 lost its automatic weapon covering the advancing British. Unteroffizier Schloss had somehow repaired Adelbrecht's gun but it was only briefly in action before failing again. With the British close to the German front trench, Schloss sent the gun to the rear to stop it falling into enemy hands. A large gap had developed in the machine gun defences of the I Battalion, however, with the help of the guns of IR 66 and Reiner's weapon opposite John Copse and the three remaining guns in the third and fourth lines which had views over the front German trenches, No Man's Land and the British lines, the defences held firm except for a brief incursion at the junction of the 3. and 4. Kompanien of IR 169 between Adelbrecht and Kaiser's positions[i].

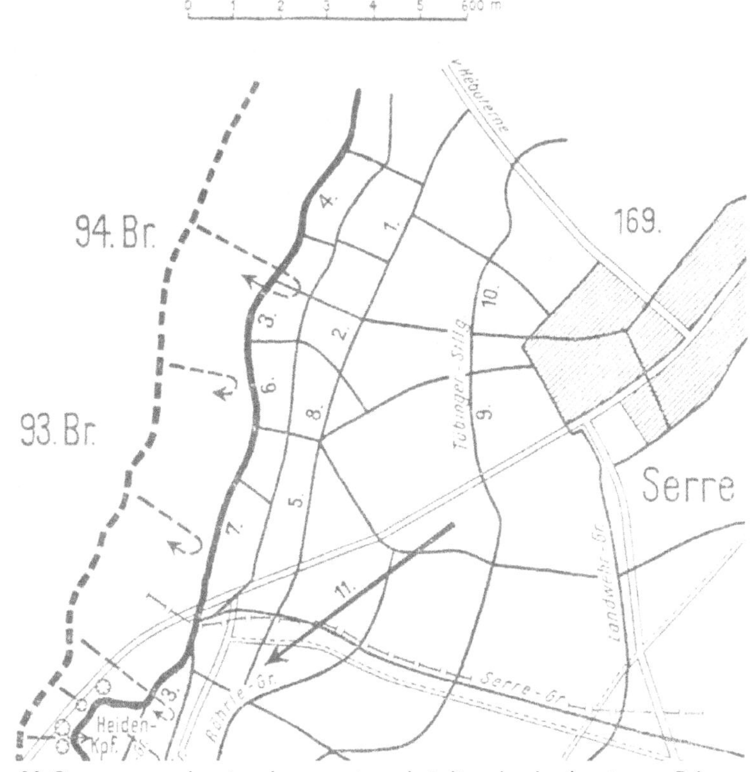

Map 29 German map showing the entry into their lines by the Accrington Pals [Source: *Somme Nord*]

[i] By the end of the day the Maschinengewehr-Kompanie Nr. 1 had lost 5 dead and 14 wounded out of 149.

Being on the 94th Brigade's right the Accringtons suffered somewhat less from the enfilade fire of the IR 66 but the initial volume of fire from the IR 169 in the trenches in front of Serre was undiminished. The waves that had made it out into No Man's Land were faced with a torrent of fire from the regiment's machine guns and a shower of stick grenades if they managed to get close to the German front line. Behind them, the artillery barrage on the British front line was destroying the trenches and killing or maiming the supporting troops trying to advance.

Plate 139 Capt. Arnold Banatyne Tough, 11th East Lancashire Regt.

Plate 140 Capt. Harry Livesey, 11th East Lancashire Regt

The first wave of Nos. 1, 2, 5 and 6 Platoons was commanded by Capt. Arnold Tough, a Manchester University-trained dentist with a practice in Avenue Parade in central Accrington. The son of a local GP, Tough was aged 26 and had been commissioned straight into the battalion on its formation in September 1914. He was now the commander of X Company. He was a popular and efficient officer and held in high regard by his CO, Lt. Col. Rickman, which, perhaps, explains why he was given the task of leading the first wave into action. Tough had led his men out into No Man's Land at 7.20 a.m. where they had waited for zero hour under an increasingly heavy artillery and machine gun fire. He was wounded as they waited for the off but, at 7.30 a.m., he stood and ordered his men forward towards the German trenches 200 yards distant. He was hit again but, ignoring the pain, he led his men until a bullet to the head brought his young life to a brutal end. His remains were recovered and buried the following year in the small battlefield cemetery now known as Queen's Cemetery[i].

---

[i] Capt. Arnold Banatyne Tough, 11th East Lancashire Regt., was aged 26. He was the son of Dr William Robb Tough and Margaret Tough of 34, Delamere Rd., Ainsdale, Southport, previously of Parkside, Blackburn Road, Accrington. He was born at Crook, Co. Durham. He was educated at Accrington Municipal Secondary School and Manchester University from which he graduated as a dentist in 1911. He was in a dental practice with J

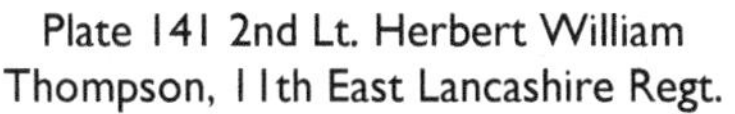
Plate 141 2nd Lt. Herbert William Thompson, 11th East Lancashire Regt.

Plate 142 Lt. Charles Stonehouse, 11th East Lancashire Regt.

The second wave was commanded by Capt. Harry Livesey, OC W Company, and they had been lying up waiting 50 yards behind the 1st wave in No Man's Land. Livesey had, according to reports, led his men with a walking stick in one hand and a revolved in the other. If so, he was flouting in the most outrageous fashion orders for officers to dress and arms themselves like the men but, so far, he had not paid the price for making his rank so obvious. Now he led the few men of Nos. 3, 4, 7 and 8 Platoons who survived the crossing until they came up with the remains of the 1st wave just short of the German lines. With Capt. Tough already dead, it fell to Livesey to take command. He gathered the remnants of the first two waves and led a charge into the German front line supported by 2nd Lt. Herbert Thompson. It was this charge, it seems, which penetrated the German lines at the junction of the 3. and 4. Kompanien of IR 169. Livesey's attack was halted between the 1st and 2nd German trenches and, from here, the wounded Captain sent back a runner asking for reinforcements. The runner and his message failed to arrive at Rickman's HQ and Harry Livesey[i], along with 2nd Lt. Herbert Thompson[ii], was never seen again.

Theakston, Bury & Accrington. He was commissioned 17th September 1914 and promoted Captain on 5th May 1915. He is buried in Queen's Cemetery, Puisieux, grave D. 62. His brother, Capt. John James Tough, 5th Field Ambulance, was killed at Flesquieres on 6th October 1918.

[i] Capt. Harry Livesey, X Company, 11th East Lancashire Regt., was aged 35. He was the son of Robert Crossley Livesey and Corrinna Livesey of Westleigh, Blackburn. He was educated at Rossall School and was a director of the family firm of Henry Livesey Ltd, Greenbank Ironworks, textile machinery manufacturers. He was commissioned into the 11th East Lancashire Regt., in September 1914 and promoted Captain on 20th October 1914. His body was never found and his name is inscribed on the Thiepval Memorial, Pier & Face 6C.

[ii] 2nd Lt. Herbert William Thompson, 10th att. 11th East Lancashire Regt., was aged 21. He was the son of Albert William Thompson of 67, Kenyon St., Fulham Palace Rd., London.

As is so often the case with 'eyewitness' or hearsay accounts of deaths in action, those describing Capt. Livesey's demise have little in common. His servant, 15013 Pte. Clarence Glover, described how, on entering the German front line, they had come face to face with five Germans who the gallant Captain swiftly despatched with his revolver. In return he had suffered a slight wound to the face from a German bomb. They had then clung onto their stretch of trench until their supply of bombs was exhausted and, with no reinforcements coming up, the men made a dash for some shell holes in No Man's Land. Apparently, the last Glover saw of his officer was just before a shell exploded nearby. An alternative version was told by Lt. Jerry Gorst, one of the 10% reserve held out of the battle. He wrote to his sister ten days after the battle suggesting that Livesey was on his way to receiving a posthumous VC[i]. His Company commander had, he wrote, been wounded in the arm going over the parapet, been hit in the chest in the middle of No Man's Land, hit on the head in the German wire from where, notwithstanding any of the foregoing, he got into the German front line, cleared and then held a section of trench before being hit in the face by a rifle grenade and instantly killed. Whatever the truth of it, Capt. Harry Livesey was one of the few men of the Accringtons to enter the German lines and there we must leave him, bravely facing his last battle.

Another officer from W Company to get close to the German trenches was Lt. Charles Stonehouse a 34-year old architect from Blackburn. Stonehouse was seen with his servant, 15216 Pte. Roland Banks, near the German parapet by 20939 Pte. Fred Whitesmith. Whitesmith later reported seeing the lieutenant hit in the wrist and Banks killed while he tried to bandage his wounded officer[ii]. A few moments later Stonehouse was hit in the head and killed[iii].

Men from the 'Other Ranks' also excelled themselves on this terrible day, their first in any major battle. Nothing daunted they followed their orders and then went above and beyond any normal call of duty.

32 year old 15183 CSM Arthur Leeming of Glen View House, Burnley, had been a clothlooker[iv] at Victoria Mill, Trafalgar Street, Burnley before the war[56]. In spite of a bad wound to the shoulder which broke his collar bone in three places, he took control of what was left of his company when all of the officers had fallen and guided his dwindling band through the day. His reward, about which

---

He enlisted as 1464 Rifleman in the 16th London Regt., (Queen's Westminster Rifles) on 23rd September 1912. He was commissioned into the 10th East Lancashire Regt., on 19th June 1915 and attached to the 11th East Lancashire Regt., on 17th June 1916. His body was never found and his name is inscribed on the Thiepval Memorial, Pier & Face 6C.

[i] In the absence of anyone suitably superior to corroborate Glover's or Gorst's stories, Capt. Livesey did not receive any award.

[ii] 15216 Pte Roland Banks, 11th East Lancashire Regt., was aged 22. He was the son of Robert and Eliza Banks, of 6, Aitken St., Accrington, Lancs. His body was never found and his name is inscribed on the Thiepval Memorial, Pier & Face 6 C.

[iii] Lt. Charles Stonehouse, 11th East Lancashire Regt., was aged 34. He was the son of Francis and Mary Ann Stonehouse of Blackburn. An architect, he enlisted as 15360 Private in the 11th East Lancashire Regt. on 17th September 1914. He was commissioned on 18th January 1915. His body was never found and his name is inscribed on the Thiepval Memorial, Pier & Face 6C.

[iv] An inspector of woven materials.

he was told while in hospital in Bristol, was the Distinguished Conduct Medal, listed in the *London Gazette* of 22nd October 1916, the citation reads:

> "For conspicuous gallantry in action. When all his officers became casualties he took command and though severely wounded, handled his company with great coolness and skill."

17922 Pte. William Warburton also won the DCM. Seeing a German bombing party in action against his colleagues he attacked them on his own, killing an officer and sending the rest scuttling away into the refuge of their trenches. His award was listed in the *London Gazette* of 22nd September 1916. The citation reads:

> "For conspicuous courage and gallantry in attacking single handed an enemy bombing party. He killed the officer, wounded others and caused the remainder to retire."

Plate 143 15183 CSM Arthur Leeming, DCM, 11th East Lancashire Regt.

Plate 144 24139 Pte. Holford Speak, MM, 11th East Lancashire Regt.

A third Accrington Pal won the DCM this day. 20 year old 15961 L/Cpl. Esmond Nowell was the son of Dr Thomas and Alice Nowell of Withnell, a small village near Chorley. He was despatched back to the British lines by his company commander with an urgent message. Although wounded, he not only found his way through the intense German barrage to deliver the message, he somehow managed to find his way back to his company out in No Man's Land. Esmond Nowell would survive the war, marry and, in 1923, he and his wife Ellen would have a daughter, Margaret, to join them in the newsagents they now ran. The citation in the *London Gazette* of the 22nd September 1916 reads:

> "For conspicuous gallantry in attack. Being sent by his company commander to deliver a message he performed this duty, although wounded, under very heavy fire, and subsequently returned to his company."

Three men of the Accringtons won the Military Medal. 18048 Pte. Stanley de M Bewsher took the German line under fire with a Lewis gun and survived even though a shell fragment pierced his Brodie helmet. 24139 Pte. Holford Speak was another to receive the MM, gazetted on 1st September 1916. Speak had been wounded in the hand during the advance and sought shelter in a shell hole. When he heard a colleague crying for help he braved the bullets and shell fire to go to his aid but was seriously wounded by several shell fragments. He survived to return to a hospital in Derby via one at Boulogne. He was, no doubt, delighted to be able to return to his father's pub, the Victoria Inn on the Colne Road in Burnley[57]. And finally 15657 Sgt. Austin Lang, too, was awarded the MM though, sadly, posthumously as he was killed on 2nd July 1916[i].

Heroes all.

Two platoons from A Company of the 13th York and Lancasters had followed the 2nd wave of the Accringtons into No Man's Land. Their job was to clear the trenches and dugouts of the enemy as the other troops advanced. The detachment was led by Capt. Stewart Maleham[ii]. He and his men made it a few yards beyond the British wire before the Captain and his men were scythed down by shrapnel and machine gun fire. These men, in spite of the equipment failures of the two nearest German Maxims, were still swept away by the fire from the guns commanded by Unteroffizier Kölle in the second trench, Unteroffizzier Spengler in the third line and Unteroffizier Schumann in Tübinger Stellung. Although the slope up to Serre was slight it still gave every trench a clear and unobstructed field of fire over the entire position laid out in front of them and now these guns took on the task of wiping out the attack of the 94th Brigade.

Plate 145 Lt. George Gabriel Williams, 11th East Lancashire Regt.

[i] 15657 Sgt Austin Lang, MM, 11th East Lancashire Regt., was born in Chorley and was married to Mary Lang. His body was never found and his name is inscribed on the Thiepval Memorial, Pier & Face 6 C.

[ii] Capt. Stewart Maleham, 13th York and Lancaster Regt., was aged 37. He was the son of Henry William and Elizabeth Maleham of 15, Endcliff Avenue, Sheffield. He was commissioned on 7th December 1914. He is remembered on the St Mark's Church, Broomhill, Roll of Honour. He is buried in Queen's Cemetery, Puisieux, grave C. 34.

Behind the unfortunate Capt. Maleham and his men came the third wave of the Accringtons commanded by Lt. George Williams. This wave was made up of two platoons from each of Y and Z Companies and had assembled in Campion Trench nearly 500 yards behind the British front line. In order to reach the front line this wave, and the fourth behind them, had to walk down a gentle slope in full view of the enemy before reaching the slight depression behind the forward positions known as Railway Hollow. They left the relative safety of Campion at 7.29 a.m. and were immediately taken under heavy machine gun and artillery fire, presenting a target that was too good to ignore. At 7.34 a.m. the remains of the wave crossed the front line trench, the survivors clearly having decided to disobey the '50 yards a minute' order in order to reach the trench unscathed. Even so, casualties were already in excess of 50% before a man entered No Man's Land. Few got any further. Lt. Williams was wounded in the calf by a bullet and, after struggling back into the trenches near Mark Copse, he was found several hours later and helped by the then wounded Adjutant, Capt. Anton Peltzer. Together, they apparently walked seven miles before receiving treatment at a dressing station, though quite how they missed the ADS at Euston is something of a mystery. The unfortunate Williams survived his wound only to be carried off by pneumonia in early 1919[i].

The Accrington's fourth and last wave was led by Capt. Henry Riley. He was from an eminent Burnley family who owned a mill in nearby Colne. A county magistrate and a man devoted to 'good works', as his founding of the Burnley Lads' Club[ii] and the membership of the Preston and Mid-Lancashire Discharged Prisoners' Aid Society attests, he was another well respected man who had stepped forward when his country called for volunteers. Along with Capt. Raymond Ross, he had helped raise a body of 250 men from the Burnley area which formed the basis of Z Company in the new battalion. Riley was one of the few officers unconvinced by the confident assertions from the Corps and Divisional commander that 'not a rat would be alive in Serre after the bombardment'. The complexity and inflexibility of the operation concerned him and he also worried about the inactivity of the 48th Division to the north and the exposed flank this created. But, in spite of these reservations, he and his men set forth from Monk Trench at the same time as the third wave up ahead and, whittled away by intense artillery and machine gun fire, the few remaining men crossed into No Man's Land just after 7.35 a.m. Two eyewitnesses, 15650 Pte. Stanley Holgate and 2nd Lt. Arthur Lett, saw Riley caught by machine gun fire beyond the British wire. His body was never found[iii].

---

[i] Lt. George Gabriel Williams, 11th East Lancashire Regt. was born on the 5th June 1886 at Accrington. He was the son of Gabriel and Bessie Matilda Williams of 18, Church St., Accrington. He enlisted on the 14th September 1914 as 15050 Private being commissioned on the 7th December 1914. On recovering from his wounds he became an instructor at the Royal Engineers Anti-Gas School at Etaples on the 30th November 1917. He died of bronchial pneumonia on the 24th February 1919 and is buried in Etaples Military Cemetery, grave XLV. C. 6.

[ii] Now known as the Burnley Boys' and Girls' Club and still going strong.

[iii] Capt. Henry Davison Riley, 11th East LancashireRegt., was aged 34. He was the only son of William John and Annie Eliza Riley of Hawks House, Brierfield, Burnley. Educated at

Plate 146 Capt. Henry Davison Riley, 11th East Lancashire Regt.

Plate 147 Lt. James Foldys Hitchon, 11th East Lancashire Regt.

2nd Lt. Lett was himself wounded soon after. A 22 year old from Oxfordshire, he had enlisted in the Oxfordshire and Buckinghamshire Light Infantry on the outbreak of war. He was commissioned into the 10th (Reserve) Battalion, East Lancashire Regt. on 7th October 1915 and posted to the 11th East Lancashires a few weeks before the attack. Commanding a platoon from Y Company he also advanced from Monk Trench into the face of heavy machine gun and artillery fire. Having witnessed the death of Capt. Riley, Lett was soon after hit by a machine gun bullet. He owed his life to 15560 Pte James Lowe who brought him into the safety of the trenches. It would be nine months before he was able to return to the battalion[i].

Lt. James Hitchon, Y Company, was in one of the last two waves. Just 21, he was training to be an architect but his experience in the OTC at Sedbergh School had seen him rapidly taken from the ranks of the 4th Loyal North Lancashire Regt. and given a commission in the 10th East Lancashires. From there he was one of four young officers, the others were Lts. Gay, Williams and 2nd Lt. Lett, to be attached to the Accringtons on 17th June 1916. Hitchon took his platoon out into No Man's Land where he was hit in the abdomen, a wound with, all too often, a very poor prognosis. Two men saw the young subaltern wounded but,

---

Shrewsbury School, he worked for the family firm of fancy cloth manufacturers, W & A Riley, Houlker Street Mill, Colne and was a director Messers R J Elliott & Co., cigar manufacturers of Huddersfield and Leicester. He founded the Burnley Lad's Club in 1901, was a member of the Preston and Mid-Lancashire Discharged Prisoners' Aid Society and a Lancashire magistrate since 1912. He was appointed Lt. in the 11th East Lancashire Regt. on 17th September 1914 and promoted Captain on 20th March 1915. His body was never found and his name is inscribed on the Thiepval Memorial, Pier & Face 6C.

[i] 2nd Lt. Arthur Robert Cecil Lett, 11th East Lancashire Regt., was gassed during the Battle of Arras but survived. He then transferred to the RFC as an observer. He survived and enlisted in the Pioneer Corps during WW2 and was commissioned in 1941. He served in North Africa and Italy. He died in 1972.

under heavy artillery and machine gun fire, 22104 Pte. James Scot Dalgleish and 15776 Pte. Felix Rawcliff were unable to bring him in. He was another whose remains were discovered in 1917 and buried in Queen's Cemetery[i].

The other casualties amongst officers were heavy. In all, and mainly within the first few minutes of the attack, the battalion lost nine officers killed and another ten wounded.

Officers killed:

2nd Lt. A Beacall	2nd Lt. H N Davies
Lt. J F Hitchon	2nd Lt. W A Kohn
Capt. H Livesey	Capt. H D Riley
Lt. C Stonehouse	2nd Lt. H W Thompson
Capt. A B Tough	

Plate 148 2nd Lt. Arthur Beacall, 11th East Lancashire Regt.

Plate 149 2nd Lt. Wilfred Arthur Kohn, 11th East Lancashire Regt.

Three officers aged between 20 and 22 all died or were mortally wounded in the early minutes of the attack: 20 year old 2nd Lt. Arthur Beacall[ii] from

[i] Lt. James Foldys Hitchon, Y Company, 10th att. 11th East Lancashire Regt., was aged 21. He was the son of George Henry and Margaret Hitchon of The Grove, South Promenade, St. Anne's-on-the-Sea, Lancs. Native of Burnley, he was educated at Sedbergh School where he was in the OTC. Trained as an architect and he lived at Hoghton Bank, Private Road, Brindle. He enlisted as 2333 Private in the 4th Loyal North Lancashire Regt., on 5th September 1914 and was commissioned into the 10th East Lancashire Regt., on 20th January 1915. He was attached to the 11th Battalion on 17th June 1916. He is buried in Queen's Cemetery, Puisieux, grave A. 16.

[ii] 2nd Lt. Arthur Beacall, 10th att. 11th East Lancashire Regt., was aged 20. He was the son of Thomas and Eleanor Rebecca Beacall of 44, Podsmead Rd., Gloucester. He married Edith Maud Brewer in Stroud on 7th June 1916. He was educated at King's School, Gloucester. A bank clerk, he enlisted as 10463 Private in the 6th Somerset Light Infantry on 20th August 1914 and was commissioned into the 10th East Lancashire Regt., on 26th November 1915. He is buried in Euston Road Cemetery, Colincamps, grave I. D. 6.

Gloucester, 2nd Lt. Harry Davies[i], aged 20, from Southend on Sea and the 22 year old Cambridge graduate 2nd Lt. Wilfred Kohn[ii].

Amongst the wounded was Lt. Ernest Ashwell[iii] who spent 16 hours out in No Man's Land about 20 yards from the German parapet. For four hours he was surrounded by explosions and he became so dazed with shell shock that, without thinking, he allowed himself to be seen by the enemy, one of whom shot him in the abdomen. Unlike Lt. Hitchon, his wound was not fatal and, as night fell, he managed to drag himself back to the British lines. Five days later he was admitted to the 3rd London General Hospital in Wandsworth but was discharged within a month. The damage to his abdominal muscles was such, however, that he was found unfit for duty and was transferred nack to the Royal Engineers, in which he had originally enlisted, based at Longmoor Camp in Hampshire.

Plate 150 Lt. Herbert Ashworth, 11th East Lancashire Regt.

Plate 151 Lt. John Victor Kershaw, 11th East Lancashire Regt.

[i] 2nd Lt. Harry Noel Davies, 10th att. 11th East Lancashire Regt., was aged 20. He was the son of John and Louisa Elizabeth Davies (née Baily) of 12, Whitegate Rd., Southend-on-Sea. Student at London University and member of the OTC. He was commissioned into the 10th East Lancashire Regt., on 10th June 1915 and joined the 11th Battalion on 23rd April 1916. His body was never found and his name is inscribed on the Thiepval Memorial, Pier & Face 6C.

[ii] 2nd Lt. Wilfred Arthur Kohn, 11th East Lancashire Regt., was aged 22. He was the only son of Arthur and Rosie Kohn of 79, Queen's Gate, South Kensington, London. He educated at Marlborough and Gonville & Caius College, Cambridge and was a member of the Inner Temple. He enlisted as 1720 Private in the 18th Royal Fusiliers in 1914. He was commissioned into the 11th East Lancashire Regt., on 12th May 1915. He is buried in Euston Road Cemetery, Colincamps, grave I. D. 13.

[iii] Lt. Ernest Ashwell, 11th East Lancashire Regt., was aged 29. Before the war a construction engineer in Walsall he enlisted in as 66882 Sapper, Royal Engineers, in February 1915 before being commissioned into the 11th East Lancashire Regt. on 8th April 1915. He was promoted Lt. on 31st March 1916. On recovering from his wounds he was deemed unfit for active service and he returned to the Royal Engineers in March 1917 serving at home as a Quartermaster and in which he was promoted Captain on 13th March 1918. He married Miriam Gertrude Read in August 1916.

Officers wounded:
Lt. Ernest Ashwell
Lt. Herbert Ashworth
2nd Lt. Bartholomew Endean
2nd Lt. Cecil Douglas Gay
Lt. John Victor Kershaw
2nd Lt. Arthur Robert Cecil Lett
Capt. and Adjt. Anton Peltzer
Capt. John William Nelson Roberts, RAMC
Lt. Leonard Ryden
Lt. George Gabriel Williams

Late in the evening, Lt. Col. Rickman would be added to this list. Only three officers of the Accringtons committed to the battle were not either killed or wounded on 1st July. They were the second in command, Maj. Edward Reiss, the signals officer, Capt. Francis MacAlpine[i] and Lt. John Hardman Heys of Z Company.

Apart from the nine dead officers, 226 NCOs and men are recorded as having died on either the 1st or 2nd July 1916. Another twelve died of wounds during the month. Because of the uncertainty as to the whereabouts of the majority of the battalion – were they holding out in Serre or already dead on the field of battle – 117 of the dead are recorded as having died on 1st July, 24 as dying between the 1st and 2nd July and 85 as having died on the 2nd July. The estimates of the wounded total some 360, giving a total casualty list of approximately 595. It is thought that 720 men from the battalion went into the attack. Their losses represent a strartling 83% of this total.

One key question is: did any of the Accringtons get to Serre alive? Their war diary says not:

> "From information brought back by wounded it appears that only a few reached the enemy front line and were able to enter their trenches owing to the intensity of the Machine Gun and rifle fire. Small parties penetrated as far as the German fourth line, but were not heard of again."[58]

Apart from the unreliable reports of several observers, it is difficult to see how the battalion could know that any of its men even reached the 4th German trench as none of them came back to report having done so. And, to confirm the problems with observation over the battlefield, Brig. Gen. Rees called 31st Division at 8.40 a.m. to report his men across the German front trenches but went on the admit:

[i] Capt. Francis Geoffrey MacAlpine, MC, 11th East Lancashire Regt., was born on 13th May 1894. He was the son of Sir George Macalpine, the Chairman of the Accrington Liberal Association. He was educated at Mill Hill School. He enlisted on 8th September 1914 as Pte. 5254 in the 3rd (Public Schools Battalion), Royal Fusiliers;. Commissioned into the Accrington Batalion., East Lancsashire Regt., 29th September 1914. Promoted Lt. 5th May 1915 and Captain 2nd July 1916. He was awarded the MC for conspicuous gallantry during the Battle of the Lys in April 1918. MiD twice. He lived at Broad Oak, Accrington until 1948. He was the chairman of Accrington magistrates and chairman of directors at Accrington Brick and Tile Co. Ltd. He died on 16th April 1957 at Manchester.

"...but it is very difficult to see what is going on. He (Rees) has no definite information but they are being heavily fired on."[59]

It is the same problem that applies to Serre itself, Pendant Copse and, further south, Beaucourt sur Ancre. None of the troops it was thought reached these positions returned or survived to tell the tale. There may have been burials at Serre, discovered in 1917, but that does not mean the men buried there were alive in Serre. The Germans would have cleared the dead from their own trenches in exactly the same way the British did. The small numbers of British troops found buried on the edge of Serre are just as likely or, to the writer's mind, more likely to be an indication of how few men of the 94th Brigade penetrated the front lines of the German position rather than the graves of men who got into, fought and died in Serre.

IN SPITE OF THIS CARNAGE, AT 7.34 A.M. 31ST DIVISION recorded having received a message from 94th Brigade that the infantry had crossed the German front line one minute after zero. The Divisional OP was not quite so sure. They had seen the waves go forward but had admitted that observation was tricky. Nevertheless, Lt. Col. Baumgartner was on the phone at 7.38 a.m. reporting to VIII Corps that the troops were into the German trenches. 165th Brigade, RFA, then produced two somewhat contradictory reports in the space of two minutes. First, at 7.39 a.m., the war diary recorded seeing two waves of British troops reach the enemy front line. As far as they were concerned there was 'not much fire on No Man's Land'. On the other hand, the thick smoke over the battlefield made 'observation very difficult'. At 7.40 a.m. the 31st Division diary recorded the following:

"7.40 a.m. 165th Brigade RFA report smoke obscures everything. Enemy machine guns being fired hard."[60]

This latter message at least accorded somewhat more closely with the report of the Accringtons at the same which stated that heavy rifle and machine gun fire was still coming from the German 1st line and that there was 'intense fire of all descriptions'.

Advancing steadfastly into this maelstrom at 7.40 a.m. was B Company of the 1st Barnsley Pals under Maj. Thomas Guest[i]. They were following the 4th wave of the Accringtons and their objective was the German 4th trench. Behind them, the two remaining platoons of A Company under Capt. Gurney were to move up to occupy the British front line. As with all the advances of the supporting battalions, B and A Companies moved 'over the top' between the various British trenches and were thus exposed to anything the Germans cared to fling at them. What was flung at them was described in the war diary as a 'perfect tornado of fire' from the German artillery and machine guns. The troops moved forward 'as

[i] Maj. Thomas Heald Guest, 13th York and Lancaster Regt., was aged 41. He was educated at All Saints School, Bloxham. Served in the South African War, twice wounded. A Barnsley grocer, he was commissioned on 19th September 1914, being made Adjutant on 1st February 1915 and promoted Temp. Major on 1st April 1915. He is remembered on the St Peter's (Hale) War Memorial in Altrincham and on a memorial in the Lower Peover (St. Oswald) Churchyard, Cheshire. His body was never found and his name is inscribed on the Thiepval Memorial, Pier & Face 14A & 14B.

if one a drill parade' but with men dropping out step by step. By the time B Company reached the German front line wire it had been reduced to Maj. Guest, Lt. Robert Allatt Heptonstall and three men. Heptonstall went down first, shot in the side followed quickly by the three 'other ranks'. The lieutenant then saw Maj. Guest shot in the right leg close to the German parapet. He lost sight of his superior who was never seen again. Heptonstall managed to roll into a nearby shell hole where he remained until night fell before crawling back to the battered British trenches[i].

Plate 152 Maj. Thomas Heald Guest, 13th York & Lancaster Regt.

Plate 153 Lt. Robert Allatt Heptonstall, 13th York & Lancaster Regt.

ON THE EXTREME LEFT, UNDER THE DUBIOUS COVER of the smoke screen to the north, A and part of B Company of the 2nd Barnsley Pals were endeavouring to achieve their objectives. No. 1 Platoon led the way on the extreme left and quickly lost their platoon commander, 2nd Lt. William Hirst[ii], taken out by a machine gun bullet to the head. But up the shallow slope they went towards Serre, men dropping all the way. The 20 year old 2nd Lt. Reginald Anderson[iii] was

---

[i] Lt. Robert Allatt Heptonstall, 13th York and Lancaster Regt., was commissioned on 28th September 1914. Before the war he was articled to W V Dixon, solicitors of Wakefield. After recovering from his wounds he joined the Tank Corps being promoted Captain. He commanded Tank D10, *'Diana'*, during the 3rd Battle of Ypres. He survived the war becoming a solicitor and a local councillor in the Goole area. He served in the Royal Tank Corps in WW2 and left the Army as an Honorary Lt. Colonel. He died in 1969.

[ii] 2nd Lt. William Hirst, A Company, 14th York and Lancaster Regt., was aged 30. He was the son of John and Jessie Hirst of Wombwell, Yorks; husband of Bertha Hirst of Wath-on-Dearne, Yorks. Educated at the London Institute of Surveying he was the consultant surveyor at Wombwell Main Colliery and a lecturer at Sheffield University. He was commissioned on 7th April 1915. He is buried in Bertrancourt Military Cemetery, Plot 1. Row E. Grave 16.

[iii] 2nd Lt. Reginald Dudley Bawdwen Anderson, 11th att. 14th York and Lancaster Regt., was aged 20. He was the son of Reginald Gustavus Lincoln Anderson and Blanche Gertrude

no more than 50 yards from the British trenches when he too was killed, while the Lewis gun teams, seconded to this party to provide covering fire as they worked on their trenches, went down with the rest. The company commander, Capt. Gustaf Roos, lay fatally wounded somewhere in or close to the German lines. He would die later in the day in German hands.[i]

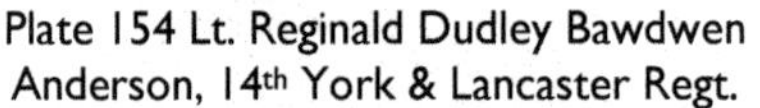

Plate 154 Lt. Reginald Dudley Bawdwen Anderson, 14th York & Lancaster Regt.

Plate 155 Capt. Gustaf Oscar Roos, 14th York & Lancaster Regt.

By 7.40 a.m. the remaining men of A Company had left Nairne Street and got out into No Man's Land but the two platoons of B Company, whose task it was to open out Sap F and convert it into a north facing fire trench, were stuck in an exposed section of Nairne, flattened by the German shelling. It was discovered that the reason for their slow progress was that an order had been sent back that the men were to advance at three pace intervals:

> "If this had been adhered to, the two platoons of B Company would have been held up in the most exposed portion of Nairne under heavy fire, for some time, and would undoubtedly have suffered casualties amounting almost to annihilation. There was also a great risk that in the broken state of the trenches the suggested intervals would have resulted in men losing

---

Anderson of Ashfield House, Wakefield. He played rugby for Wakefield R.F.C. He was commissioned on 18th March 1915. He is buried in Redan Ridge Cemetery No.2, Beaumont-Hamel, grave C. 4.

[i] Capt. Gustaf Oscar Roos, M A., B.C.L, 14th York and Lancaster Regt. was aged 47. He was the younger son of Gustaf and Annie Roos of 7, Queen's Gate Terrace, London. He was a Queen's Scholar at Westminster and was also educated at the United Services College and Balliol College, Oxford, (graduated 1887, 1st Class Jurisprudence). He was a solicitor. He served with Thorneycroft's Mounted Infantry in South Africa and was severely wounded at Spion Kop and Landerspruit. He was awarded the Queen's Medal with two clasps. He became a solicitor in Johannesburg until he was commissioned into the York and Lancaster Regt in October 1915. He was taken prisoner and died of wounds at Fremicourt. He is buried in Douchy-Les-Ayette British Cemetery, grave III. D. 10.

> touch with those in front, and throwing out all those behind them. Orders were therefore given that the men must push on as quickly as possible and without intervals, to the Russian Sap, and Capt. Houston worked his way past the men to see the order carried out. As a result the file commenced to move at a fair pace at 7.52 a.m. and at 7.58 a.m. Nairne was clear of our men."[61]

Having given his orders, Capt. Houston was never seen again.[i]

Whilst the later accounts by the infantry suggest that few if any men had reached the German wire, let alone entered the enemy trenches, optimistic reports from some Artillery observers continued to come in. Others, though, admitted they could see nothing because of the smoke and dust. Within five minutes, between 7.45 and 7.50 a.m., varying artillery reports came in:

> "7.45 a.m. 169th Brigade, RFA: There is very heavy machine gun fire everywhere. Nothing can now be seen." (31st Division)[62]
> "7.45 a.m. C Battery reports our infantry into German front line at 7.42, probably 94th Brigade…" (170th Brigade, RFA)[63]
> "7.50 a.m. FOO reports infantry had reached second line." (165th Brigade, RFA)[64]

This entry into the German trenches referred to by the 165th Brigade FOO, had been affected at a weak point in the German lines between two machine guns which had suffered malfunctions and at the junction between the 3. and 4. Kompanien of I Battalion, IR 169. This was the small scale break-ins made by men of the Accringtons and, perhaps, men of the 12th and 13th York and Lancasters. Certainly, it is the only part of the front line where German sources admit that their front line was breached. Here, not only had their machine gun support been sharply reduced but several of the deep dugouts had been blocked earlier during the intense bombardment and the occupants had struggled to dig themselves out. The I/169 was commanded by Major Berthold whose advanced Battalion HQ was at the north west corner of Serre in Landwehr Stellung (here called Berlin Trench by the British but, south of Serre, Munich Trench). Seeing his front line the scene of serious fighting, Berthold ordered the 1. Kompanie of IR 169, led by Lt. Roth along with Hptm Bohne, Lt. Vogt and Oblt Welsch, which was in the 3rd trench behind the 4. Kompanie, to advance and drive the attackers out. On their left, the 2. Kompanie also helped force out the small number of enemy troops who had managed to occupy a few yards of their front trench. Further back, the 10. Kompanie of III Battalion, IR 169, in Tübinger Stellung to the north west of Serre also moved forward to assist if required. The 12. Kompanie, meanwhile, was withdrawn from the Tübinger Stellung, into the defences around Serre to act as regimental reserve and as a garrison of the village should the minor British incursions develop into a more significant breakthrough.

---

[i] Capt. Frederick Neville Houston, MC, 14th York and Lancaster Regt., was the eldest son of Mr and Mrs W D Houston of Oriental Bay, Wellington, New Zealand; husband of Ellen Marie Houston of Oakwood Lodge, Davigdor Rd., Hove, Sussex. He was educated at St Clair School, Dunedin. He was commissioned into the 3rd South Staffordshire Regt., in 1908 before transferring to the 2nd York & Lancaster Regt., in 1912. His body was never found and his name is inscribed on the Thiepval Memorial, Pier & Face 14A & 14B.

The counter attacks were swiftly mounted and completely successful and, as far as German accounts are concerned, this was the only time British troops entered the positions of IR 169 in front of Serre. There is certainly no mention of any of the 94th Brigade getting into Serre and it must be presumed that the bodies of men of the 31st Division discovered buried in the village in the Spring of 1917 were casualties from the front lines removed when the trenches were cleared and repaired. By 8.20 a.m. (GMT) reports to Maj. Struensee, CO of IR 169, announced that the front line trench was secured and that the defence was going well.

Struensee had, however, warned Oberstleutnant Schwarz, the CO of the RIR 15, of the break-in on his I Battalion's front. Maj. Kiesel and the 5. and 7. Kompanien of the II Battalion, RIR 15, had already moved forward from the 2nd Position at 8.10 a.m. An hour later, Struensee sent another message:

> "Enemy has broken through in S2, H2 and H5. Request that you prepare a counter-attack via Serre Wood (Pendant Copse) in the direction of the Heidenkopf."

Then Schwarz received news of the break-in by the London Scottish in IR 170's sector opposite Hebuterne. Although, part of the 2. Garde Reserve Division, Schwarz had no doubts about splitting his command to help the defenders from two other Divisions – IR 169 and 170 of the 52. Division and RIR 121 of the 26. Reserve Division. The 9. and 12. Kompanien, reinforced by two machine guns, was sent off down Schlüsselgraben, a trench to the north east of Serre, to assist IR 169 and RIR 121 if required, while the 10. and 11. Kompanien went to help the IR 170. With the 7. and 8. Kompanien moving up to be ready to support the RIR 55 in its defence of Gommecourt village, the IR 169 subordinated its Rekrut Kompanie, commanded by Lt. der Reserve Rudolf Neck, to RIR 15[i].

Not needed for the defence of Serre, the 9. and 12. Kompanien were inactive witnesses to the rest of the day in front of Serre as Lt. Ebeling recounts:

> "It was a scene of terrible beauty! It was a wonderful summer's day with a deep blue, cloudless sky, which was only occupied in numbers by British airmen. There was one circling above almost every trench. The company was initially placed in the Landwehrstellung[ii]. In the late afternoon we moved through shot up trenches into the Serre Riegel, which was held until 5th/6th July. During the night we dug and carried forward rations for the 169th."

But that is all they were needed to do. The break-in on the IR 169's front was over, as was the attack of the 31st Division.

---

[i] This company arrived at about midday. Lt. d R Neck and an Offizierstellvertreter were later killed and another officer wounded, presumably by shell fire. Lt. der Reserve Rudolf Neck, commanding the Rekrut Kompanie, 8. Badisches Infanterie-Regiment Nr. 169, is buried in Achiet-le-Petit Cemetery, grave 266.

[ii] The Landwehrstellung was part of the Zwischen Stellung and ran due south from the southern corner of Serre. It was known as Munich Trench to the British.

IN MARK COPSE, THE BATTALION HQ OF THE ACCRINGTONS had been cut off from Brigade HQ when the telephone lines were severed by German shells. The Signals Officer, Lt. Francis MacAlpine, was sent out in an effort to re-establish the link but was forced to abandon the task when it became clear that all lines were cut. Runners became the only form of communication between Lt. Col. Rickman and Brigade for the rest of the day. Rickman had, however, received a report that the left platoon of X Company under Lt. Cecil Gay, part of his 1st wave, had reached and passed the German 1st trench but that Lt. Gay was wounded. Gay had been with the battalion for precisely two weeks and had never before seen action. An undergraduate at Trinity College, Cambridge, he had been commissioned into the 10th East Lancashires on 22nd February 1915 before transferring to the Accringtons on 17th June 1916. Now, this utterly green lieutenant was possibly the most senior British officer within the German lines still standing. But not for long. He was shot through the neck from right to left and his servant, a Pte. Naylor, went down shortly after while trying to dress his wound. Both of them were able to extricate themselves from the German lines in order to avoid becoming Prisoners of War and Cecil Gay somehow managed to struggle back to Mark Copse to report to his colonel before being sent off to the ADS and, eventually, home[i].

It is possible that Gay's men were one of the groups reported by 94th Brigade at 7.55 a.m. to be between the German 1st and 2nd lines and, by 8 a.m. to have entered the 2nd trench. At the same time, Brigade were reporting great difficulties with observation over the German lines as a result of the continuing mist and the drifting smoke screen from the 48th Division's front. Added to the problems of the officers in the various OPs was the increasing intensity of the German barrage on the front line which 165th Brigade, RFA, had reported. In spite of these issues, however, messages continued to come in saying British troops were fighting in the German 1st and 2nd trenches until, towards 8.30 a.m., reports were received that British infantry were now 'advancing through Serre'.

These troops clearly had nothing to do with the 93rd Brigade on the right as, at 8 a.m., 93rd Brigade had two reports confirming the enemy still occupying their front line with Capt. Titford of the 93rd Trench Mortar Battery in the British forward trench stating that the heads and shoulders of German soldiers were clearly visible above the parapet. But, in spite of these reports, 31st Division recorded at 8.02 a.m. that the 1st wave, already wiped out in No Man's Land, was now held up in front of the German 2nd trench. Two minutes later came a report from 94th Brigade that their leading waves were over the first two German trenches on both the left and right of their front. Given that C Company of the

---

[i] 2nd Lt. Gay and 2nd Lt. Lett ended up in the 3rd Southern General Hospital based at Somerville College, Oxford. Gay returned to the 1st East Lancashires, winning the MC at 3rd Ypres. He was wounded again at in August 1918. He returned to Trinity College in 1919 taking the Engineering Science Special Degree, parts 1 and 2 before helping to form a highly successful machine tool company, A C Wickman, in Coventry. He was heavily involved in the supply of machine tools for the aircraft industry in WW2. Cecil Gay's younger brother, 2nd Lt. Frederick Hollington Gay, 16th Squadron, Royal Flying Corps, was killed on 25th March 1917 and is buried in Bruay Communal Cemetery Extension. Cecil Gay died in 1980.

Sheffield City Battalion, on the extreme left of the of the Brigade front, had been pretty much wiped out within the first few minutes, who were these troops on the left? The other battalion out on the flank was the 14th York and Lancasters whose job it was to form the new north facing defences of the Fourth Army. Where were they?

At 8.05 a.m. a rather perplexing entry was recorded in their war diary:

> "At 8-5am. no man of the two Companies, not a casualty, was in sight between Nairne & John Copse, though some may have been hidden by parts of the Traffic Trench & Fire trench still intact."[65]

One can only assume from this double negative infested statement that the men of the 2nd Barnsley Pals were either casualties concealed within what was left of Nairne Street, were taking shelter in the front lines between Nairne and John Copse, were out in No Man's Land or, somehow, had got further forward. At just before 8.10 a.m. observers from the battalion peering out from Nairne watched as a line of troops climbed out of the remains of the front line trench and advanced, in quick time, into No Man's Land. It was later assumed that these men were the 1st wave of the 'second bound'. The 'second bound' was the 3rd and 4th waves of the Sheffield City Battalion who job it was to go through the first two waves and secure the second objective: Serre village. According to previous reports, however, the shattered remnants of the 3rd and 4th waves, which had been decimated within the British lines during their advance from the assembly trenches at Campion and Monk, had disappeared into No Man's Land shortly after zero.

Whoever these troops were the ground made observation difficult for the officers back in Nairne Street and their view of the advance was restricted to the seventh man from the left of the advancing line. These men reached the middle of the British wire when they came under machine gun fire and started to fall. They were all down just two yards beyond the British wire but four of them were trying to crawl back into the British trenches when a shell burst in the middle of them[i].

That still leaves the question about the troops advancing on the left. A and B Companies, 14th York and Lancasters, had eventually gone forward from Nairne during the early minutes of the attack. It was estimated that 30% of them had become casualties before leaving the exposed communication trench in which they were trying to shelter and, later, another estimate was made that, maybe, 20% of these two companies, perhaps 50 men, made it to the German wire, wire that had already been found to be uncut. The remainder of A and B Companies were shot down in No Man's Land. It was thought that some of A Company might have made it to their objective, a German communication trench running back from the front line north of Serre although how this could be ascertained is not clear as the war diary states that:

> "No report or messages of any sort was received back from A or B Companies once they had left Nairne."[66]

---

[i] These may have been men from the 13th York and Lancasters some of whom are recorded in the 94th Brigade war diary as advancing from Copse Trench at 8.10 a.m.

It would seem, therefore, that any information as to the whereabouts of the troops was based on the dubious accuracy of comments of wounded soldiers passing back down the lines towards the Advanced Dressing Station. It should come as no surprise that reports from wounded men could be notoriously unreliable. Understandably, in the heat of battle, men lost all sense of time and location and even very recent events became muddled. And these were men for whom the entire experience of battle was completely new. None had seen the like before and now they were being pestered by officers and men for information they could scarcely recall when all they wanted was to rest, take something for the pain and get away from those blasted German guns. So, whatever the accuracy of the information, it was now assumed that some men of A Company had somehow got through the uncut wire that had stopped C Company of the Sheffields in their tracks and that some men from the clearing party from B Company led by Lt. Forsdike and 2nd Lt. Strong had also entered the first German trench.

Forsdike and Strong had, indeed, got to the German wire with their bombers and found some gaps. Strong and his men tried to bomb the machine gun and riflemen in the front line trenches while Forsdike and some others appeared to enter the German trenches where they disappeared from view[i]. Harry Strong, meanwhile, had been wounded in the head but refused to give in. The *London Gazette* citation for the Military Cross, gazetted on 20th October 1916, describes his actions:

> "For conspicuous gallantry and devotion to duty when in command of a bombing party. Although severely wounded he refused assistance and ordered his men to push on. He then crawled towards the enemy line, endeavouring to join his party, and was again twice wounded."

Strong received additional wounds in the hip and shoulder but was able to return to the British trenches. He survived the war[ii].

Further back, the remaining men of the 14th York and Lancasters in C and D Companies had moved closer to the front line, C Company from Rolland Trench north of Observation Wood to Campion and D Company from Babylon Trench to Monk. On their way they had lost men but nothing to compare with the losses of the two advanced Companies now somewhere in and about the German front line trench.

Throughout this time, reports from observers, or the lack of them, were causing more than a degree of confusion at Division and beyond. At 8.07 a.m., Division was reporting that 169th Brigade, RFA, which had views across the entire Divisional front, could see nothing beyond the German front line. 165th

---

[i] Lt. Harold Brooke Forsdike, 14th York and Lancaster Regt., was aged 24. He was the son of William D and Emily Forsdike of Parkfield House, Sheffield. He was educated at King Edward VII School, Sheffield. He was commissioned on 11th March 1915. His body was never found and his name is inscribed on the Thiepval Memorial, Pier & Face 14A & 14B.

[ii] Lt. Harry Strong, MC, 14th York and Lancaster Regt., was aged 26 and lived at 52, High Street, Wem, Shropshire. He was a bank cashier. He enlisted as 2660 Private in 1/8th Royal Warwickshire Regt. and was commissioned into the 2nd Barnsley Pals on 12th August 1915. After recovering from his wounds he served with the 3rd Reserve Battalion and the 5th Training Reserve Battalion, being demobbed in 1919. Also awarded the Croix de Guerre.

Brigade, RFA, however, was confirming that troops (the 2nd Barnsley Pals?) were over the 4th German trench on the left of the 94th Brigade whilst the 31st Divisional OP stated that, apparently, things were going so well that:

> "… our infantry going forward in columns, when they get into the open lights are dropped apparently from aeroplanes and the guns are then turned on that mark."[67]

This gave all the appearance of a textbook advance just as the planners would have wished. It was utter nonsense.

The contemporaneous comments by Lt. Col. Rickman of the Accringtons were rather more realistic:

> "I … reported I could see odd groups in my front believed to be wounded. Also that I could not see any of my waves. No further report from waves. Heavy artillery barrage on front line."[68]

His remarks about his inability to see 'his waves' would become more plaintive as the day wore on. His report at this time also contained the sorry news about the arrival of the remains of two platoons of A Company, 1st Barnsley Pals, which had started to advance from their assembly trenches at 7.40 a.m. Thirty minutes later Capt. Clement Gurney[i] reported his arrival. He brought with him just nine survivors from the two platoons.

From 8.15 a.m. onwards a flurry of reports came in from the artillery suggesting that, against all the odds, the Division was about to succeed in taking its first two objectives. At 8.14 a.m. the Battery commander of C/170 forwarded two reports from his Forward Observation Officer:

> "8.05 a.m. Our troops are advancing on Green Line and occupying it.
> Our troops are now in Serre (this of course reported to 94th Brigade)."[69]

This first report seemed to reinforce one made a minute earlier that suggested that the 16th West Yorkshires had reached the German parapet in support of the Leeds Pals who, surely by definition, must be ahead of them and moving towards the Green Line. At 8.16 a.m. the FOO of the 165th Brigade reported the glad tidings that infantry appeared to be advancing through Serre. As the same FOO had reported at 7.50 a.m. that the troops had reached the German 2nd line there seemed an inexorable logic about the progress of these reports. And, with the 170th Brigade, RFA, confirming at 8.18 a.m. that the 94th Brigade was 'going well', affairs began to look brighter. Casualties may have been heavy but success was within the Division's grasp.

At the same time, though, 170th Brigade reported 93rd Brigade 'held up'. News had also reached 93rd Brigade about the serious wounding of the CO of the 16th West Yorkshires, Maj. Guyon, and an instruction was sent to Capt. Clough to take command of the battalion and to advance on either side of the apparent blockage in the German front line. It is not clear whether Clough received this order before his death. What is clear is that neither he nor the remnants of his new command were in any fit state to advance anywhere.

---

[i] Capt., later Lt. Col., Clement Henderson Gurney was awarded a DSO in the New Year's Honours of 1916 and Bar when CO of the 11th East Yorkshires on 6th May 1918.

There now occurred one of those events which had so confused the issue on both the 29th and 4th Division's fronts. A BE2c of the R.F.C. reported seeing a flare coming from Serre. The flare was red. To the British this meant that an objective had been taken. To the Germans it was a signal to bring down artillery fire. The Germans had used red rockets for this purpose for weeks on the VIII Corps front. Quite why any British Staff Officer thought it a good idea to use the same colour during the attack is anyone's guess but, as had occurred on the rest of the front, the flare was interpreted in the most positive possible light: Serre had been occupied by men of the 94th Brigade.

By 8.20 a.m. Hunter-Weston had been given the following information by 31st Division:

> "The 94th Brigade have crossed the German 1st and 2nd lines. The last report from the 93rd Brigade reported our first line checked in front of German 2nd line. Impossible to observe well owing to smoke."[70]

The giveaway is, perhaps, the last sentence. With the smoke screen now slowly drifting across the northern end of the battlefield added to the residual mist which had still not completely burnt off and the pall of smoke and dust which now drifted across the fields in front of Serre, proper observation was still almost impossible. Any troops from the 94th Brigade within the enemy lines had to amount to significantly less than 100 men from the various battalions now involved but no-one could put a number on the troops apparently in the German trenches. The impression was, perhaps, that a significant number of men had successfully broken through on the 94th Brigade's front. On the other hand, there was no evidence on the ground that anyone from the 93rd Brigade had breached the enemy line at all, let alone reached the German 2nd line. There was, though, a rumour about a party from the 18th Durham Light Infantry reaching Pendant Copse. It was an unsubstantiated rumour but, all too often, rumours were a good enough basis on which to take firm, if wrong, decisions on 1st July 1916. But, overall, as far as Corps were concerned, British troops had made significant progress. Reinforcements to remove the temporary check on the 93rd Brigade's front was clearly the best way forward and the unit available for this operation was the 18th West Yorkshires, the 2nd Bradford Pals.

At 8.20 a.m. Lt. Col. Maurice Kennard of the 18th West Yorkshire Regt. was ordered by 93rd Brigade to go up to the front line to find out what was holding up the 16th West Yorkshires. Having seen for himself the problems at the front he returned to his battalion and the order to advance was given at 8.40 a.m. and seven minutes later the men were reported as getting over the parapet and forming up, preparatory to the advance. The battalion was assembled in Dunmow and Landguard Trenches, A and D Companies in the lead with B and C Companies to follow. Although these trenches had come under artillery fire, the 2nd Bradford Pals had, until now, been spared the effects of the German machine guns. Dunmow was in dead ground some 500 yards behind the British front line and it was not until about 100 yards from the assembly trenches that the advancing men came into the sights of the German MG gun teams. But, before that, the German artillery started to cause casualties straight away. Capt. Frederick Thomas Williams, the Adjutant, was blown into the air by a shell burst but survived his wounds[i]. The officer commanding A Company, Capt. Cecil Keevil[ii], also went down wounded as he mounted the parapet.

There were some waiting in the trenches convinced their number was up. 31 year old Lt. Harold Foizey was such a man and he shared his fatalistic notion with 18/251 L/Cpl. Norman Goldthorpe[iii]:

> "I remember saying a little prayer and just before we climbed out, our Officer, Lieutenant Foizey, said 'I know that I will not come back'. I told him 'to believe he would as I certainly believed I would'… I scrambled out behind Lieutenant Foizey with his section of Bombers… having not travelled more than 30 yards or so the section was reduced to 4 men. Lieutenant Foizey ordered his small party to take cover behind a small hillock, whilst he went forward to see what was happening, but he was killed covering only a couple of yards."

As was often the case with such recollections, things were not always that straightforward. Foizey was, apparently, badly wounded in the thigh but was found and helped by 15/231 Pte. George Cosby[iv] of the Leeds Pals. He later described Foizey's last moments in a letter to the dead lieutenant's sister:

> "I saw Lieutenant Foizey tumble over the back of a trench, wounded in the thigh, I made him comfortable, and had his wounds dressed, and placed him in a traverse at the back of the trench, soon afterwards a terrible explosion took place, throwing up all the sandbags and earthwork, in the immediate neighbourhood, and burying several men, together with Lieutenant Foizey[v]."

D Company advanced from Dunmow between Bleneau and Flag Trenches. As soon as they became visible the ranks were swept by machine gun fire from the right, around the point where Ten Tree Alley met the Serre to Mailly Road.

---

[i] Capt. Frederick Thomas Williams, 18th West Yorkshire Regt., joined the Training Reserve before returning to the West Yorkshires. He was awarded an MBE in 1919 and, having joined the RAF in April, 1918, was promoted Flight Lieutenant in the 1919.

[ii] Capt. Cecil Horace Case Keevil, 18th West Yorkshire Regt., was aged 36. He was the son of Richard and Georgina Keevil, of Clitter House Farm, Cricklewood, London. He survived his injuries and joined the R.F.C.. He was killed on 13th June 1917 and is buried in Hampstead Cemetery. Keevil was killed whilst flying as observer with Capt. C W E Cole-Hamilton in Bristol F2A A7135 from No. 35 (Training) Squadron, Northolt, whilst attempting to intercept three Gotha bombers engaged in a bombing raid over Ilford.

[iii] 18/251 L/Cpl. Norman Goldthorpe, 18th West Yorkshire Regt., was commissioned into a Transport Worker's Battalion of the East Yorkshire Regt. in 1918 and resigned his commission in 1920.

[iv] 15/231 Pte. George William Cosby, 15th West Yorkshire Regt., later transferred to the Machine Gun Corps and was commissioned into the Tank Corps on 29th September 1917.

[v] Lt. Harold Egbert Foizey, 18th West Yorkshire Regt., was aged 31. He was the son of Benjamin Foizey, a schoolmaster, and Alice Foizey of Tipton, Staffs. He was educated at King Edward VI's High School, Birmingham. He worked for Messrs. Stewarts & Lloyds (Ltd), Iron and Steel Manufacturers, of Neville Street, Leeds, and enlisted as 15/343 Private in the 15th West Yorkshire Regt. (Leeds Pals) in September 1914. He was commissioned into the 18th West Yorkshire Regt. on 24th May 1915. He is buried in Euston Road Cemetery, Colincamps, grave I. D. 42.

They were also caught by long range fire from the north east, i.e. the direction of Serre. At the same time, a curtain of shell fire fell on the front line trenches. All the surviving officers agreed that the field guns were firing shrapnel from behind the village and the heavier high explosive shells came from the numerous batteries dug in around Puisieux. Lt. Col. Kennard led the way, walking ahead carrying a swagger stick and encouraging his men forward until a shell put an end to his life[i].

No. 16 Platoon was the rearmost part of D Company and was to have formed the garrison of strongpoint F in the newly captured German lines. Led by 2nd Lt. F W Whitaker what was left of the platoon managed to get as far as the British front line. This young officer was now one of the few unwounded officers in the front line of the 93rd Brigade and he acted as a magnet for the lost and confused. Amongst these were the three previously mentioned men from No. 16 gun team of the 93rd Machine Gun Company: Ptes. Brown, Gardner and Bainbridge who had become separated when they reached the front trench. Pte. Brown carried the tripod, Pte. Gardner was laden with ammunition boxes and 17 Pte. James Bainbridge, 18th DLI, carried the gun. Bainbridge struggled on with the 25 lb. gun, crossing into No Man's Land with a weapon that was useless without ammunition, tripod and coolant. Somehow, in the total chaos of No Man's Land, Bainbridge then came across Pte. Brown and, with the attack clearly badly hung up, they decided to withdraw to the front line in which the leading survivors of the 2nd Bradford Pals were just arriving. Anxious to know what to do next, Brown then struggled back to Company HQ in Legend Trench before making the 700 yard long return journey to tell Bainbridge they should withdraw to HQ where the company was trying to reorganise.

Pte. Gardner, meanwhile, had lugged his two ammunition boxes into the front line where he met up with the remains of No. 11 gun team which had come forward with the 2nd Bradford Pals. Their officer, 2nd Lt. Percival Booth[ii], who commanded both Nos. 11 and 10 gun teams, had been killed shortly before the gun teams reached the front line trench. By this time, No. 11 gun team had already been reduced to just three men: Pte. Hustwit, Pte. Robinson and Pte. Smith, the others having fallen before reaching Old Monk Trench. On arriving at the front line, the three men reported to 2nd Lt. Whitaker of the 2nd Bradford Pals and, together, they mounted the gun. Fortuitously they now came across Pte.

---

[i] Lt. Col. Maurice Nicholl Kennard, MC, formerly 6th Dragoon Guards (Carabiniers), 18th West Yorkshire Regt., was aged 32. He was the second son of Robert William and Rose N Kennard (née Byass) of North Leigh, Bradford-on-Avon, Wiltshire, and Llwyndu Court, Abergavenny, Monmouthshire. He was educated at Radley College. He joined the 6th Dragoon Guards from the Royal Monmouthshire Royal Engineers (Militia) in 1902, being Adjutant in April 1910. He was an excellent Polo player being the top rated player by the South African Polo Association in 1911. Promoted Captain in 1913, he went to France with the 6th Dragoon Guards and was MiD and wounded Nov. 1914. Appointed 2iC 13th York & Lancaster Regt., November 1915 and took command of the 18th West Yorkshire Regt., on 27th April 1916. His body was never found and his name is inscribed on the Thiepval Memorial, Pier & Face 2A, 2C & 2D.

[ii] 2nd Lt. Percival Edward Booth, 14th Middlesex Regt. att. 93rd Machine Gun Company, was aged 24. He was the son of Walter Scott Booth and Ruth Booth, of 7, Haslemere Rd., Winchmore Hill, London, N. 21. Euston Road Cemetery, Colincamps, grave I. B. 2.

Gardner and his two belt boxes plus another four he had found in a shell hole. With the gun now armed they set to firing at a group of Germans unwisely exposing themselves in an effort to observe No Man's Land. They then shot at any targets of opportunity until ordered by Whitaker to reserve their ammunition in case of a more organised German counter attack.

No. 10 gun team, after the loss of 2nd Lt. Booth, was reduced to four men: Cpl. Dowsett, Pte. Sharp, Pte. Wilson and Pte. Miller. Cpl. Dowsett tried to lead his men to the right of the Brigade front but both he and Pte. Miller were wounded. Pte. Sharp, however, also managed to find 2nd Lt. Whitaker for whom machine guns must have seemed like London buses as, not having seen one all day, out of the blue two had quickly come his way one after the other. Whitaker ordered Sharp and Wilson down to the front line where they mounted their gun. They were, however, lacking a tripod, ammunition and spare parts and they made three trips to recover this equipment dropped by the other members of their team before they started to interfere with some German troops in front of their support line who appeared intent on attacking the men of the 4th Division away to the south. They then dispersed some men thought to be massing for a counter-attack at the end of Ten Tree Alley.

It was about this time that a colleague of Whitaker's in D Company, the recently appointed Intelligence Officer, was likely killed. Aged 20, 2nd Lt. Harold Colley had just started as an assistant master at Skipton Grammar School before gaining his commission and, over the last few nights in his new role, he had spent many hours crawling about in No Man's Land checking on the state of the enemy wire. He had apparently arrived at the front line where he was wounded in the mouth. Discovered lying on the parapet by some of his men he was taken into the front line trench where he was also found to have suffered a probably fatal wound to his back. He was never seen again[i].

Nos. 7, 8, 9 and 12 guns also advanced with the 2nd Bradford Pals. Nos. 7 and 12 guns were commanded by 2nd Lt. Barnes who, like 2nd Lts. Baker and Dean, was hit immediately on leaving his assembly trench, Landguard. By the time No. 7 gun team reached the front line they had been reduced to just L/Cpl. Palmer, Pte. Crouch and Pte. Kemp. Under Palmer's instruction the gun was mounted on the parapet of the front line but, soon afterwards, they were ordered to retire and as they went, Palmer was wounded. Pte. Kemp then somehow returned the gun and spare parts back to Legend Trench while Pte. Crouch attached himself to No. 10 gun to help the now wounded Pte. Sharp with his gun. The other gun of 2nd Lt. Barnes section was No. 12 and two men of the team were killed at the same time as the officer was wounded. When another two men lost touch, the remaining members of the team, L/Cpl. Simpson, Pte. Cherry and Pte. Banks, paused while Banks was sent back to Capt. Kayll in Grey Trench near Fargate Trench for further orders. Whilst he was away, both Simpson and Cherry wounded. With the team now totally hors de combat, Pte. Banks was ordered to return to Company HQ in Legend.

---

[i] 2nd Lt. Harold Colley, 18th West Yorkshire Regt., was aged 20. He was the son of William Henry and Harriet Colley. He was educated at Ermysted's Grammar School, Skipton. He was an assistant master at Skipton Grammar School. His body was never found and his name is inscribed on the Thiepval Memorial, Pier & Face 2A, 2C & 2D.

Plate 156 2nd Lt. Harold Colley, 18th West Yorkshire Regt.

No. 8 gun was commanded by 22764 Sgt. John Duke from the Durham Light Infantry. This gun was earmarked for the advance to Pendant Copse where it would be part of the forward defences of the new front line. The gun team got out into No Man's Land opposite the end of Ten Tree Alley where they occupied the remains of an old trench. From here, L/Cpl. Watson could see into the German trenches to the south and he claimed to have seen 16 German machine guns lining the parapet. This is clearly impossible but it may be that some of the Madsen light machine guns, the German equivalent of the Lewis gun, were in action here. Four members of Sgt. Duke's team had made it this far but amongst the casualties were some of those carrying the belt boxes. They were, therefore, short of Vickers ammunition. Fortunately, they found a Lewis gun and some magazines in the old trench and the four men, Pte. Whitehead, L/Cpl. Watson, Pte. Mitchell and Sgt. Duke took it in turns to fire into the German lines. Duke had just fired on and knocked out an enemy machine gun team when he was killed[i]. With the Lewis gun ammunition spent, and those men of the infantry still able to move retiring past them to the front line, the remaining three men of the team brought their gun and tripod back into the shelter of the trenches having lost four of their seven man team.

The last gun to advance was No. 9, commanded by 2nd Lt. David Burrows. They advanced to the front line at the end of Warley Avenue where Burrows was seriously wounded[ii]. The injury would prove fatal and he died of his wounds on

---

[i] 22764 Sgt. John Duke, Durham Light Infantry att. 93rd Machine Gun Company, was aged 24. He was the son of William and Lucy Duke, of Heatherycleugh, Cornriggs, Wearhead, Co. Durham. His body was never found and his name is inscribed on the Thiepval Memorial, Pier & Face 5 C & 12 C.

[ii] 2nd Lt. David Burrows, Machine Gun Corps att. 93rd Machine Gun Company, died of wounds on 3rd July 1916. Aged 24, he was the son of William Prosser Burrows and Sarah Jane Burrows of Hill Side, Troedyrhiw, near Merthyr. He is buried in Bertrancourt Military Cemetery, Plot 1. Row E. Grave 19.

Monday, 3rd July. Sgt. Richmond took command of the five remaining men and they had just got the gun mounted on the front line parapet when it was knocked into the bottom of the trench. With the area under heavy German artillery fire it seemed prudent to keep the gun and the team as much out of harm's way as possible and Richmond and his men remained in the trench until 6.30 p.m. when they were ordered to return to Landguard Trench.

The 93rd Machine Gun Company lost heavily. In all, two officers were killed, one died of his wounds and two more were wounded along with eight other ranks killed, two missing and 27 wounded out of the seventy men from the ten guns that had taken part in the advance. Overall, they suffered 60% casualties and barely left the British front line.

Coming forward with these four guns, A Company of the 18th West Yorkshires was also cut up by the machine guns to the south east. Lt. Roland Sydney Cross commanded No. 4 Platoon and, as they advanced, he watched the intense battering the front line was receiving:

> "…an intense bombardment was in progress on our front line and support trenches, canister bombers and heavy HE, also shrapnel catching all the men as they reached the support line. This curtain of fire was extended to our assembly trenches."[71]

To this was added intense machine gun and rifle fire and Lt. Cross was certain as to the reasons why so much fire was coming from the German lines:

> "Our artillery seemed to me to have been concentrated mainly on German trenches with good effect in smashing up trenches but evidently did not smash up their dugouts judging by the rifle fire."[72]

A fact, one might have thought, that should have been obvious to senior officers given the aggressive and well co-ordinated response mounted by the German front line garrison to every raid attempted by the 31st Division (and the others of VIII Corps) in the week prior to the attack.

B Company of the 2nd Bradford Pals advanced from Landguard Trench on the left of the battalion and here they were immediately exposed to heavy machine gun fire. Advancing to the north of Grey Trench they were then struck by the artillery barrage as they crossed Monk Trench. Lt. Arthur Howarth was one of more than a few surviving officers who wished that the British artillery had done a better job of counter-battery fire but, as the British intelligence had identified fewer than half of the German battery positions around Puisieux and further north at Bucquoy, it is uncertain that even a greater effort in this direction would have helped his men over much. To Lt. James Akam[i] and some men of B Company goes the credit for having advanced further than anyone else of the 18th West Yorkshires. All are reputed to have reached the German parapet though none survived to tell the tale. Sgt. Bullock, the Signal Sergeant, with one man, apparently became detached and ended up in the 4th Division's sector and he too reached the German lines.

---

[i] Lt. James Rhodes Akam, 18th West Yorkshire Regt., was aged 23. He was a timber merchant. He enlisted in the 16th West Yorkshire Regt., and was commissioned into the 18th West Yorkshire Regt. on 15th March 1915. His body was never found and his name is inscribed on the Thiepval Memorial, Pier & Face 2A, 2C & 2D.

Plate 157 Lt. James Rhodes Akam, 18th West Yorkshire Regt.

C Company on their right was more protected by the lie of the land except, that is, from a heavy shrapnel fire which fell on the left of the position. As they advanced they ran into an area being pummelled by German HE just beyond Dunmow Trench and soon men from the Company were joining those of D Company as casualties littering the ground within the British trenches. At every lateral trench they reached the men were forced to bunch together as there were either not enough bridges on which to cross or the ones there had been destroyed by the German artillery. They thus presented targets too good to miss and, as along the entire Corps front, such choke points could be identified by the piles of dead and wounded surrounding them.

Although the last Company to leave the assembly trenches, C Company managed to get men from all four platoons into the remains of the front line – but no further. Lt. Arthur Stephenson noted with some dismay the numbers of enemy troops in their front line:

> "… there were several seen on the enemy front line parapet. These must have had good cover in their front line during the bombardment either in dugouts or tunnels."[73]

The weight of the German artillery barrage also came as a complete shock:

> "The enemy artillery was a great surprise to our troops who had expected to find most of the enemy guns put out of action."[74]

The junior officers and men had naively believed the confident assurances of Divisional and Corps commanders about the destruction of the German infantry and their defences in spite of all the evidence to the contrary and the men were too inexperienced to know any better. Now, as the Germans stood on their parapet shooting down the advancing British infantry, the consequences of these gross errors of judgement were being made manifest by an ever lengthening butcher's bill.

As with their fellows from the 1st Bradford Pals, the majority of the casualties from the 2nd Battalion occurred between the assembly trenches of Landguard and Dunmow and the British front line. Perhaps a handful of men got beyond this point.

The officers of the 18th West Yorkshires to become casualties were:

Killed:

Lt. J R Akam
2nd Lt. H Colley
Lt H E Foizey
2nd Lt. F J G Walton[ii]
2nd Lt. D Burrows, att. 93rd MGC
2nd Lt. R I Derwent[i]
Lt. Col. M N Kennard
Lt. F Watson, att. 93rd TMB

Died of wounds:

2nd Lt. F P Nowell[iii], 2nd July 1916

Wounded:

Capt. Frederick Thomas Williams
Capt. Cecil Horace Case Keevil
Lt. Walter Peace
And four others

In all, casualties amounted to 16 officers and 400 other ranks out of 23 officers and approximately 570 other ranks who went into action, a casualty rate of about 70% for a battalion not one of which entered the enemy's trenches. Of the casualties, 115, or 28%, were fatal (99 killed and 16 died of wounds).

LET US NOW RETURN TO THE FATE OF THE 94TH BRIGADE. At 8.20 a.m. 31st Division had informed VIII Corps that the 94th Brigade had crossed the first two lines of German trenches while even more encouraging reports from artillery observers suggested they were already into Serre. For the officers and men still in the front line, affairs seemed somewhat less optimistic. Lt. Col. Rickman of the Accringtons had, shortly before, reported that he had completely lost contact with the waves that had gone forward. He had also been rather inadequately reinforced by just one officer and nine men from the 13th York and Lancasters, the only men from two platoons led by Capt. Gurney, who had managed to get through the intense German machine gun and artillery fire. At 8.22 a.m., with no signs of the German barrage slackening, he again confirmed that he had no idea where his men were or what they were doing. 'No information from my waves,' he forlornly repeated.

[i] 2nd Lt. Robert Ivor Derwent, 18th West Yorkshire Regt., was aged 26. He was the son of Henry Casaubon Derwent, J P., and Ann Maria Derwent of Nearcliffe, Bradford, Yorks. He was commissioned on 8th December 1915. He is buried in Euston Road Cemetery, Colincamps, grave I. B. 27.

[ii] 2nd Lt. Francis John George Walton, 18th West Yorkshire Regt., was aged 25. He was the son of Francis James and Annie M Walton; husband of Christina Frances Walton (née Wesson) of 13, First Avenue, Hendon, London. Born at Hampstead, London, he was a Building Contractors Assistant. He was commissioned on 5th November 1915. He is buried in Serre Road Cemetery No. 1, grave IV. B. 11.

[iii] 2nd Lt. Francis Percival Nowell, 18th West Yorkshire Regt., was the son of Mrs E A Nowell of Westfield, Victoria Park, Shipley, Yorks. He is buried in Couin British Cemetery, grave I. C. 20.

But, if the colonel did not know where his men were then there were others who thought they did or, if not the Accringtons, then some men of the Barnsley Pals. At 8.25 a.m. the Divisional OP reported that a small party of British infantry were in Serre. How did they know this? 'Saw sun shining on triangles', was the answer. Again, triangles facing west, reflecting the sun that was in the east. No matter, other information was now forthcoming which appeared to reinforce the idea of some sort of breakthrough on the 94th Brigade front. An observer from the 92nd Brigade reported the enemy to be shelling his own lines in front of Serre. Then, at 8.28 a.m. came the clincher. The 165th Brigade's FOO attached to the 94th Brigade reported clearly that British infantry were advancing through Serre. This was described in the 31st Division's war diary as 'the most definite report'. And it had consequences. Lt. Col. Baumgartner at Divisional HQ immediately called Brig. Gen. Ingles at 93rd Brigade HQ. Baumgartner explained that the 94th Brigade was in Serre and Ingles, though he stated that two battalions were held up and, indeed, currently subject to a German counter attack, also confirmed that he would order more troops forward on either flank of his sector. Thus was the 18th West Yorkshire Regt., ordered forward into the mincing machine of the German barrage between the assembly trenches and the front line.

These were not the only consequences. Two companies of the 13th York and Lancasters were ordered up to support the advance of the Accringtons though, as Rickman repeatedly stated, no-one had any idea where his men were.

And yet, within two minutes of the report from the 165th Brigade's FOO about British troops advancing through Serre, the 31st Division recorded:

> "From 8.30 a.m. onwards it was difficult to arrive at any useful appreciation of the situation. Conflicting reports came in regarding the progress made. The GOC 94th Brigade was unable to get in touch with his leading battalions, the remnants of which were believed to have entered Serre village. The 93rd Brigade was checked and the 18th West Yorkshires had been ordered forward to try and clear up the situation and report. Two companies of the 13th York and Lancs Regt., 94th Brigade, were ordered forward to support the East Lancs Regt. who were reported as having crossed the German second line. These two companies however met a very heavy hostile artillery barrage, lost heavily and got no further than our front line."[75]

Chaos. It is the only word that can best describe the 31st Division's front as the attack entered its second hour. One minute British artillery observers were convinced that the infantry were in Serre and the fact that the Germans were shelling their own lines was seen as confirmation of this breakthrough. The next, all was confusion, reports were conflicting, the prospects uncertain.

How can these initial reports about the Germans bombarding their own lines have emerged? Let us consider the illuminating post-war opinions of Lt. Col. Cecil Simonds, the CO of the 170th Brigade, RFA, whose group was attached to the 93rd Brigade. Simond's OP was to the east of the Sucrerie and just to the south of the Serre-Mailly road where it ran between Roman Road and Taupin Trench. It gave excellent observation over most of the 93rd Brigade's front (except for parts of the German front line on the southern end) and a good view of the ground in front of Serre. He also had an excellent view over the left wing of the 4th Division's front. He could, for example, see all the way to Pendant Copse (when smoke allowed).

In response to a request for comments on the first draft of the Official History, Simonds supplied a highly detailed response covering the effects of the seven day bombardment as well as many aspects of Z Day. One of his concerns, for example, was the precision of the German response. Did they know the details of the Division's attack?

> "The shelling of my wagon lines and the promptitude of the German barrage gave me the impression that the Germans knew more about our scheme of attack than they should have; whether they learnt anything from raid prisoners, or whether their spy system may have been particularly good I know not; but the behaviour of their machine gunners and infantry in getting up and coming out into the open, as they did on the 31st Division front, seems rather to strengthen this impression in my own mind. I still feel that they had an idea of our cut-and-dried scheme and employed efficient means to counter it."[76]

But something else strengthened his view that the Germans were well-prepared for the attack. They appeared to be so well organised in the circumstances for this to be a purely extemporised counter-attack:

> "…this is again strengthened by the fact that at about 9 a.m. the Germans seemed to be concentrating for a counter attack: so much so that General Ingles asked me to bring back my barrage (which had now about reached Pendant Copse) to the German front and support trenches, as the enemy looked like making a counter attack. My instructions were very strict on this point, and definite; I did as he had asked at once, and this dispersed the German formations; at the same time I reported the action to 31st D.A. H.Q. and was told that I had no authority for such action, and that I was at once to return my guns to their allotted place in the barrage time-table. I replied that I would do so as soon as I had the consent of General Ingles, but that in the first instance I must be governed by circumstances as I find them on the spot. It so happened that there was no further threat from the Germans and soon after my guns continued with their allotted time-table."[77]

It is possible that what both Ingles and Simonds had seen was the movement of a platoon of 1. Kompanie, Kgl. Bayerisches Pionier Regiment Nr. 1, commanded by Lt. der Res. Peter von Drathen, who had been despatched from sector S4 on the right of the 31st Division's front of attack to assist the 6. Kompanie, IR 169, in sector S3. If so, it was a relatively minor troop movement in the German lines and it may be that Simonds' batteries had some effect as von Drathen suffered a fatal wound to the head[i], one of just three fatal casualties suffered by the Bavarian pioniers who spent the day in the front line trenches on 1st July.

---

[i] Lt. der Reserve Peter von Drathen, Kgl. Bayerisches Pionier Regiment Nr. 1, was born in Meldorf. He was originally buried in the cemetery at Miraumont but, like most of the men buried there he now has no know grave.

Simonds goes on to explain why he was so determined to respond to Brig. Gen. Ingles's request. He knew, from his own observations, just how badly the attack had failed from the very start. His concern was that the Germans, knowing how the attack was to be made, had not only planned to destroy the assaulting troops but had then put in place the resources to mount a counter-attack of sufficient force to return the front line to its pre-June 1915 line, i.e. once again linking the Heidenkopf (Quadrilateral) with their old trenches to the west of Toutvent Farm, and even, perhaps, straightening the line as far as Gommecourt!

His main problem, though, was in persuading higher authority that the 93rd Brigade's attack had completely failed from the very start. The Divisional Staff was just not interested in such a pessimistic view, however well informed:

> "I found it extremely difficult to get the Divisional Staff to understand that our attack had been held up practically at the start. As a case in point, in spite of my emphatic contradiction, by personal observation, I was told from that quarter that we had occupied Pendant Copse."[78]

So much for the advance of the Durham Pals.

As far as the more encouraging reports coming in from the artillery FOOs on the 94th Brigade front, Simonds is gently sceptical:

> "I am afraid the information sent from some of the Artillery O.Ps on the left of our part of the line must have been misleading by the optimism that was at times implied... (I) was very early convinced that our attack had been a signal failure."[79]

So, what of the news that the Germans were shelling their own lines? Surely this suggested at least some part of the German position occupied by British troops? Sadly not:

> "As regards the remark that it was reported that the Germans were themselves shelling Serre, I think this was an error; the occasion never arose for such a contingency, and the enemy seemed to have their fire well under control. It is possible that the report may have arisen from the observer seeing my batteries shelling the enemy formations in the act of gathering for a counter attack, and, not knowing that I had departed from the regular programme, may have mistaken this fire for that of the enemy: a not unlikely contingency. It will be seen on reference to the 1st Draft sent to me - p.19, 'About this time the Germans were reported to be shelling the village' (meaning Serre) - that the time corresponds fairly well with my co-operation with General Ingles, when he asked me to bring back my barrage to the enemy's front trench system."[80]

Of course, Simonds had reported his departure from the bombardment programme to the HQ of the 31st Divisional Artillery. It appears there was little or no communication of this information to other interested parties as reports of the German's shelling their own trenches continued to come in for nearly half an hour. As a result, as previously mentioned, other infantry units were thrown into the fray with dreadful and unproductive consequences for all concerned. We have heard of the fate of the 2nd Bradford Pals and their abortive advance. What, then, of the two companies of the 13th York and Lancasters sent up to support the Accringtons thought to be beyond the front two German trenches?

At 8.45 a.m. Brig. Gen. Rees ordered these men forward to support Rickman's disappeared troops. He did so, according to his post-war comments, in spite of believing that there were no British troops in Serre except, perhaps,, for a few prisoners. But he had been told that 93rd Brigade was advancing on his Brigade's right and that the 4th Division now occupied the first four German lines and that men from this division were even now bombing northwards to assist the 31st Division. In the face of such information (all completely inaccurate as would be discovered later) Rees had no option but to throw his remaining men into the fight. Fortunately, the German barrage had eased somewhat as the two companies of the 1st Barnsley Pals started to leave the relative safety of their assembly trenches. It would be a short-lived reprieve.

C Company (Capt. Currin) and D Company (Capt. Smith) were told to advance to, and hold, the 1st and 2nd German Lines respectively. They were to support the Accringtons who were then thought to have succeeded in reaching the German 4th Line. C Company was in Campion Trench and D Company behind them in Monk Trench and, after the men had lined up in front of these trenches, they moved forward in two waves at about 9 a.m., immediately taking casualties from the German barrage which increased in strength when these men emerged from their trenches.

The majority of the 94th Brigade was used up, except for the men of the 1st Barnsley Pals now advancing. What, then, of the Divisional reserve, the 92nd Brigade? Could not they provide the necessary weight to break the back of the German defence? At 9 a.m. Wanless-O'Gowan gave his answer. No, he telephoned Rees to say, he did not intend to use his only reserve until the situation was clearer. What then of the men of the Accringtons thought to be at least in the German 2nd line? Rees told his Divisional General that the two companies of 1st Barnsley Pals were, even now, on their way to support them. What of the remainder of the 2nd Barnsley Pals not yet committed? Did the General think it advisable to throw them into the battle? No clear instructions were recorded in the Brigade war diary.

As C and D Companies of the 13th York and Lancasters trudged forward, losing men along the way, two of the Field Artillery Brigades could not even agree on how heavy was the German barrage:

> "9 to 10 a.m. Barrage particularly heavy on No Man's Land and our support lines." (169th Brigade, RFA)[81]
> 9.00 a.m. Hostile barrage not quite so intense." (165th Brigade, RFA)[82]

We shall, perhaps, take Lt. Col. Rickman's word for it. He was under the barrage, after all, and he described it at 9 a.m. as 'heavy'. And, he was also now far better informed as to what had befallen his 'waves':

> "9 a.m. Report from Cpl. Ripley wounded belonging to the 1st wave states that only 7 of his platoon got into 1st lines. They held it for about 20 minutes, bombing Germans back till bombers were exhausted. Capt. Livesey (OC 2nd wave) was with Cpl. Ripley and was wounded.
> Cpl. Ripley saw remnants of 2nd wave in front of our barbed wire.
> Germans still holding out.
> Saw no sign of 3rd or 4th waves."[83]

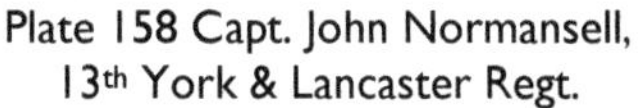

Plate 158 Capt. John Normansell, 13th York & Lancaster Regt.

Plate 159 Capt. George de Ville Smith, 13th York & Lancaster Regt.

It appears as though the information about the failure of the Accringtons was quickly passed to Brig. Gen. Rees as, while the two companies of the 1st Barnsley Pals advanced towards the British front line, an order was sent by runner for them to halt immediately and to re-organise in Monk Trench. The order came not a moment too soon as casualties were growing but, even so, losses were still incurred including Capt. George Smith of D Company.

George de Ville Smith[i] was regarded as something of an oddity by some. Tall and charming, he was also a teetotaller, a disciplinarian and known as 'Devil Smith' to his men. Before the war he had been the curate at St Thomas's Church in Worsborough Dale where he had helped found the local Church Lads' Brigade. The local vicar, the Rev William Banham, described him as 'an acceptable, earnest and faithful preacher' during his address to the congregation after his death. According to his men, though, he had a tendency to swear which seemed a tad incongruous. Earlier that morning, on the way to the assembly trenches, he had given the impression to a fellow officer, 2nd Lt. Philip Brocklesby of No. 13 Platoon, that he would not survive the day. He lived through the now cancelled advance and was in a trench giving out orders along with Capt. John Normansell and a runner when a 5.9 in shell exploded nearby. The runner was badly wounded in the chest, Normansell was left unscathed[ii] and

---

[i] Capt. George De Ville Smith, D Company, 13th York and Lancaster Regt., was aged 33. He was educated at St David's College, Lampeter, and was ordained at St. Anne's Church, Birkenhead, and served there before moving to Barnsley where he became curate of St Thomas's Church, Worsbrough Dale from 1st Sept 1911 to 31st Dec 1914 under the Revd. William Banham. Here he was founding officer of the Church Lads' Brigade. He was commissioned on 28th September 1914. He is buried in Euston Road Cemetery, Colincamps, grave I. A. 15.

[ii] Capt. John Normansell, 13th York and Lancaster Regt., was killed on 10th March 1917 during the advance on Puisieux as the Germans withdrew to the Hindenburg Line. He was

Smith was fatally wounded by a shell splinter. He died 30 minutes later in the bottom of the trench with 2nd Lt. Brocklesby being forced to step over his body as the company changed positions.

Messages were now flying about like confetti at a windswept wedding. From 31st Division's point of view, if one ignored inconvenient information from officers such as Lt. Col. Simonds, the Division was on the cusp of snatching an unlikely victory from the jaws of imminent and ignominious defeat. All that was needed was more men to push through the gap in the German 1st position in front of Serre. Very few were available.

Plate 160 Capt. & Adjt. Hugh Dart, 13th York & Lancaster Regt.

Lt. Col. Wilford[i] of the 13th York and Lancasters had already been shelled out of two positions along with his HQ Staff, in the process losing his Adjutant, Capt. Hugh Dart, to a wound from which he would die the following day[ii]. Dart

commissioned into the Barnsley Pals on 19th September 1914, his forename incorrectly given as James in the *London Gazette.* He was promoted Lieutenant on 1st February 1915 and Captain on 1st August 1915. He is buried in Serre Road Cemetery No. 1.

[i] Lt. Col. Edmund Ernest 'Bullfrog' Wilford, DSO, OBE, 30th Lancers (Gordon's Horse), Indian Army, att. 13th York and Lancaster Regt. Born in London in 1876, he was the oldest son of Col. Edmund Percival Wilford, Gloucestershire Regt., and Constance Mary Hammond. Educated at Clifton College he was commissioned into the East Yorkshire Regt., 1896, transferred to Indian Staff Corps, December 1898. Served as Major and Squadron Commander with 30th Lancers in the Indian Cavalry Corps, 1914. Took command of 13th York and Lancaster Regt. on 11th November 1915. Awarded DSO in New Year's Honours List 1917. Wounded in May 1917, he transferred to Royal Defence Corps, May 1918. Retired from Indian Army 1925.

[ii] Capt. & Adjt. Hugh Dart, 13th York and Lancaster Regt., was aged 34. He was the third son of Richard Dart, JP for the City of Liverpool, and Ellen Dart of 28, Aigburth Drive, Sefton Park, Liverpool. He was educated at Cheam School, Harrow School and Trinity College, Cambridge in 1900 where he was awarded an MA. He worked at Parr's Bank (now a part of NatWest). In the Special Reserve of Officers, he enlisted as a Private in the

was a 34 year old Liverpudlian and highly thought of by his CO, as was shown in a letter to his Adjutant's grieving father:

> "Your son was wounded in the trenches next to me, in the morning of the 1st July, during the attack on Serre. We all felt, and I think he did too, that his wounds were fatal. He died at the Field Hospital later in the day. I can honestly say that he was a most excellent officer, extremely popular with all ranks, and his death is a great blow to us all. I miss him particularly as Adjutant and can get no one successfully to succeed him."[84]

Wilford was something of a character, as his nicknames of 'Bullfrog' and 'The Swashbuckler' suggest. Now the 40 year old Wilford donned the latter persona and, in spite of the already heavy casualties, offered what was left of his battalion to Rees:

> "As far as I can make out, General, I have two companies left. If you would like me to charge at their head I shall be delighted to do so."

Thankfully, Rees had the sense to decline this brave if suicidal offer. A few minutes later, at 9 a.m. Wilford was ordered to collect what men he could of any units and organise Monk Trench as a second defensive line as a German counter-attack was feared! Hardly the order to give when one anticipated a signal success.

Apart from the unfortunate Capt. Maleham and his two platoons who had gone over the top early in the battle, the 13th York and Lancasters had barely reached the British front line let alone seen the enemy. In spite of this they lost five officers killed, one died of wounds and five officers wounded and 40 Other Ranks dead, 163 wounded and 60 missing. 23 officers and 698 Other Ranks went into action and they suffered 38% casualties, almost all of them within the British lines. Six officers and 82 Other Ranks were killed or died of wounds.

The officer casualties were:

Capt. E H Firth[i]
Capt. S Maleham
Capt. G DeV Smith
Maj. T H Guest
Lt. S O Sharp[ii]

Public Schools' Battalion, Middlesex Regt. He was originally going to be commissioned into the 5th Royal Irish Rifles but was instead commissioned into the York & Lancaster Regt on 5th February 1915. Having been promoted Lt. on 1st April he was appointed Adjutant on 15th May 1915. He is buried in Bertrancourt Military Cemetery, Plot 1. Row E. Grave 15.

[i] Capt. Ernest Hartley Firth, 9th Oxfordshire and Buckinghamshire Light Infantry att. 13th York and Lancaster Regt., was aged 42. He was the son of Francis Helme Firth of Mounthill, Beckenham, Kent. He was commissioned into the 9th Oxford & Bucks Light Infantry on 14th August 1915 and transferred to the York & Lancaster Regt. on 30th October 1915. He was promoted temporary Captain on 6th December 1915. He is buried in Euston Road Cemetery, Colincamps, Special Memorial. B. 16.

[ii] Lt. Stephen Oswald Sharp, A Company, 13th York and Lancaster Regt., was aged 26. He was the son of Mr and Mrs H J Sharp of 'Kenilworth', Avenue Rd., Doncaster. B.A. (Cantab.). Educated at Retford Grammar School, where he played for the cricket 1st XI, and Pembroke College, Cambridge (graduated 1909), he was articled to J. H. Cockburn, solicitors, of Rotherham. Joined Sept. 11th 1914, as 1048 Private, 12th York and Lancaster Regt. Gazetted Lt. in same Regt. Nov. 20th, 1914. He is buried in Euston Road Cemetery, Colincamps, V. Q. 3.

Died of wounds:
Capt. & Adj. H Dart, 2nd July 1916
Wounded:
Capt. Edward Arnold Braithwaite
Lt. John Irwin Cooke
Lt. Robert A Heptonstall
2nd Lt. Thomas Henry Hions
2nd Lt. Albert Woodward Knowles

IT WAS NOW OVER 90 MINUTES SINCE ZERO HOUR and Brig. Gen. Rees of the 94th Brigade was in something of a quandary. His right battalion, the 11th East Lancashires, which, until recently, he thought was fighting well inside the German trenches was actually, according to the most recent reports from their CO, back outside the German front line trench. Rees had personally ordered their support battalion back into the assembly trenches once this news had reached him. But what about the Sheffield City Battalion and the 2nd Barnsley Pals? Where were they and what were they doing? At 9.05 a.m. Rees had told Wanless-O'Gowan over the telephone that he had heard nothing from the Sheffield battalion and that he would report back when the situation was clearer. At the same time, 94th Brigade was recording that six platoons of the 2nd Barnsley Pals (A Company and half of B Company) were making good progress with the job of creating a new north facing fire trench. They were under heavy fire but had apparently pushed some men as far forward as the 2nd German trench.

At 9.07 a.m. 93rd Brigade were still continuing to ignore the information from Lt. Col. Simonds, and were insisting they could see two or three of the metal reflectors shining on the outskirts of Serre. This was translated as meaning that British infantry were definitely in the village as well as at Pendant Copse and Munich Trench on the 4th Division's front. Four minutes later, these conclusions were reinforced when British troops were identified as being in shell holes and advancing in front of Serre. At the same time, however, 94th Brigade was hedging its bets by stating that it had no definite information. By 9.18 a.m. this prevarication had changed to a statement, passed to 31st Division by Brig. Gen. Ingles, that Brig. Gen. Rees had told him that his infantry was *not* in Serre. Only a few minutes before, VIII Corps had received reports from Division that the Germans were shelling Serre and their own lines and that this:

"…confirmed the belief that these points were occupied by our men."[85]

Or not, according to Lt. Col. Simonds' earlier account. As the zero + 2 hour mark came and went it seems as though an information overload at the various headquarters was still being filtered through the prism of optimism. It was as if senior officers, still buoyed by their own absolute belief in success, could not quite bring themselves to look beyond what should have been and, instead, examine what actual facts were available and re-assess the state of the attack based on them. The facts were that:

1. the three lead battalions of the 93rd Brigade were shattered and remained in or behind the British front line;
2. the remains of the two lead battalions of the 94th Brigade were either out in No Man's Land or out of contact;

3. the supporting battalion of the Accrington's, the 13th York and Lancasters, had been told to stand fast by personal order of the Brigade commander; and
4. the only reserves available, given that the GOC, 31st Division, was holding back the 92nd Brigade, were three companies of the 18th DLI and two companies of the 14th York and Lancasters.

In the light of these facts, as opposed to observers' reports, it would have seemed prudent to conclude that, at the very best, a proper assessment of the situation was required before further troops were committed to action. But these observer reports continued to come in and continued to have undue influence. Within minutes of 9.30 a.m. a whole series of increasingly contradictory observer reports came in:

> "9:33 a.m. Observation post number 3 reports 'can see clearly as far as Serre. None of our troops west of Serre. They are in Serre.'" (VIII Corps)[86];
>
> 9.33 a.m. 92nd Brigade report that Brigade observer reports Red Line south of Serre in our hands. (31st Division)[87];
>
> 9.33 a.m. Wireless reports: 9.23 a.m. our infantry at K.29.d.57 [the junction of Walter Trench and Stuttgart Lane in the German 3rd trench]. (31st Division)[88];
>
> 9.33 a.m. A/170 Battery reports 'Enemy shelling our front and 2nd line trenches very heavily with HE'. (170th Brigade, RFA)[89];
>
> 9.33.a.m. Enemy seen coming down the communication trenches of their front line system. (93rd Brigade)[90]; and
>
> 9.34 a.m. Our men still held up in front of Pendant Copse, smoke has cleared away and no movement of our troops can be seen in front of Serre (93rd Brigade)[91]."

Just what was a harassed (and inexperienced) Staff Officer to make of all this information? Was the Division on its 2nd objective as the first two reports suggested? Were they held up in front of their 1st objective as the wireless report hinted? Or were the German still actively and aggressively defending the 1st position as the next two messages implied? In short, what on earth was going on out there?

A short time before all of this, 92nd Brigade had asked Division whether it wanted to hear any of the 'definite' information its observers had collected? 31st Division had replied yes to 'definite information'. And so, at 9.45 a.m., the Brigade intelligence officer, sent in a 'definite report'. This report definitely came from an OP in Hittite Trench which was definitely *not* 600 yards behind the British front line as VIII Corps described it. Try 1,200 yards for size (at its closest point. 1,500 yards at its furthest) and, therefore, 2,500 yards from the western edge of Serre. Nonetheless this officer reported that:

> "…he distinctly saw about 100 men of the East Lancashire Regiment on the western edge of Serre at about 9:45 a.m. Red rockets seen later in Serre and Pendant Copse were also believed to have been sent up by our men."[92]

It is, perhaps, surprising that the intelligence officer didn't give the names of a few of the men he had spotted as he had apparently found it so easy to precisely identify this battalion's badges from a mile and a half away. 165th Brigade, RFA, joined in the fun by confirming, at the same time, that, yes, the infantry 'had taken Serre'. Oh, and by the way, six of their guns were out of action with equipment failures.

It was at this moment that Brig. Gen. Ingles decided to pop down to the front line to see things for himself. As he went, he developed a cunning plan. Whilst the 170th Brigade's guns came back to bombard the Red Line south of Serre (yes, the Red Line south of Serre which, at 9.33 a.m., 92nd Brigade had *definitely* stated was occupied by the 93rd Brigade), Ingles thought it might be a wizard wheeze to send the 2nd Bradford Pals (yes, the battalion which had recently suffered 70% casualties getting as far as their own front line) round behind the left wing of the 4th Division so that they could then outflank the Germans and attack Serre from the south! And, whilst all that was going on, the three remaining companies of the 18th DLI might as well come forward to be ready to join in the fun. The order was sent at 9.20 a.m.

Of course, those pesky Germans were having none of it. Just before 10 a.m., Col. Craven of the 169th Brigade, RFA, was on the blower to Division complaining that a very heavy barrage, indeed the heaviest of the day so far, was now (i.e. 9.42 a.m.) falling all over the British front line. Someone was also firing a lot of bullets from near Ten Tree Alley (a location which should have been in British hands were Brig. Gen. Ingles's cunning plan to work). In general, it was all rather inconvenient given that things had been going so swimmingly up until now. On the upside, however, two men were reported as having 'fallen off a haystack in front of Serre'. German observers caught by British machine gun fire it was thought. A few minutes later Col. Craven's report on the German barrage was confirmed by 170th Brigade, RFA, only, by now, it had spread along the communication trenches towards the assembly trenches being vacated by the 18th Durhams. It seems that they had been spotted when A Company started to advance to Monk Trench at 9.47 a.m. followed by B Company at 10 a.m., B Company being delayed as a result of difficulties encountered getting out of the deep Maitland Trench as many of the ladders had been destroyed by German shells. C Company remained in Maitland Trench and awaited orders. A and B Companies would lose heavily during their advance to Monk Trench.

Then some unfortunate news came in from ten wounded men of the Accringtons who had struggled back from No Man's Land and reported to Lt. Col. Rickman on their arrival. He had just again lamented the lack of news from 'his waves' and reported the wounding by shrapnel of his MO, Capt. Jack Roberts[i], RAMC, when the men staggered back. Their news was timely as Capt. Richard Currin and the remains of C Company, 13th York and Lancasters, were just about to wander off across No Man's Land to 'occupy' the German front line trench. 'Wouldn't try it if I were you, squire' was the gist of their report, 'it's still

---

[i] Capt. John (Jack) William Nelson Roberts, M.B., R.A.M.C. was born in 1880. He was educated at Shrewsbury School and Edinburgh University and was commissioned on 19th April 1915 and was promoted Captain on 19th April 1916. After recovering from his wounds he transferred to the 4th South Wales Borderers. He died on 27th October 1960.

full of nasty Germans and their machine guns'. As if to underline the point, the German barrage then crashed down once more on the front line trenches.

The 'definite' 9.45 a.m. report by the intelligence officer of the 92nd Brigade seems increasingly inaccurate in the light of these inconvenient facts. Sensibly, at 10.06 a.m., this Brigade decided they had nothing more to report. But 31st Division were not about to make this intelligence officer appear to be the only idiot in the neighbourhood. At 10.10 a.m. they sent out the following message to 93rd and 94th Brigades:

> "The following information received – 56th Division from Hebuterne have gone right through and are flanking Rossignol Wood [Author: not true]. 165th Brigade RFA report that infantry have taken Serre [wrong]. At 9.45 a.m. our men were seen carrying what looked like machine guns in front of Pendant Copse [incorrect], also 300 to 400 of our men advancing on the line Pendant Copse-Serre [complete nonsense]."[93]

VIII Corps Staff, however, were being somewhat more circumspect in their comments about the current position of the 31st Division, simply stating, in a classic piece of British understatement:

> "The situation in the 31st Division front had not in the meantime become any clearer."[94]

At last, between 10.15 a.m. and 10.27 a.m. the HQs of the two attacking Brigades did their bit to help clear up the 'situation' in front of Serre. 94th Brigade went first with this report:

> "Message from 12th York and Lancs timed at 8.45 a.m. states that no information received from waves. From East Lancs all four waves went on but no reports received from waves. From 13th York and Lancs 3 companies moved forward remainder in Monk amounting to about 70 men at present. 14th York and Lancs have 1½ companies in Campion and Monk, remainder digging Russian sap. 3rd and 4th waves came under very heavy shell fire just behind our front line trench. Fear casualties very heavy."[95]

93rd Brigade's update, timed 10 a.m., was reported by 31st Division at 10.27 a.m.:

> "15th and 16th West Yorkshires lost commanding officer and most of their other officers. 18th West Yorkshires holding front line supported by Durhams on line Monk Trench. Gen. Ingles has gone forward now and proposes to hold front line till more information can bc obtained. 15th and 16th West Yorkshires badly knocked about."[96]

The staff at 31st Division were unable or unwilling to read between the lines of these reports, or indeed, simply read them at all as, a few minutes after receiving 93rd Brigade's report, Division was asking for 'information' about the 15th and 16th West Yorkshires.

Ib spite of this, the concept that British troops were in Serre had taken root and could not be shifted. Thus, at 10.30 a.m., Wanless-O'Gowan ordered Brig. Gen. Rees to:

"… endeavour to get in touch with the 11th East Lancashires and the 13th York and Lancasters."[97]

Sadly, this would have required the services of a medium for a large proportion of the men of these two battalions.

Equally, the conviction that troops from somewhere had taken and were holding Pendant Copse was firmly established at 31st Division HQ. 170th Brigade's guns were, therefore, turned on a point 150 yards beyond the Brown Line, the 3rd objective of the 93rd Brigade and about 2,500 yards in front of where the leading men of the Brigade lay dead in No Man's Land. At 10.20 a.m. no doubt in response to Lt. Col. Simonds deviation from the prescribed programme, the Brigade Major of the 31st Divisional Artillery sent out an instruction that:

"… all guns must catch up their programme (93rd Brigade advancing to Brown Line). No authority to alter other than Division until situation is cleared up."[98]

These misleading ideas of deep penetrations into the German lines, e.g. 93rd Brigade was nowhere near the Brown Line mentioned above, had been reinforced by the unchallenged reports that the German artillery was firing on its own 1st Position and the Zwischen Stellung. Almost certainly, this shelling was coming from the guns of the 170th Brigade, RFA, as explained earlier by Lt. Col. Simonds, however, it was noted that by 10.15 a.m. this firing had ceased as a result of which it was noted that German bombing parties were seen to be working their way up the communication trenches into their front line. This was reported in VIII Corps', 31st Division's and, most importantly, 94th Brigade's war diaries, the interpretation presumably being that the German artillery had done its work (or, in a parallel universe, that the 170th Brigade's guns had temporarily held back/dispersed these bombing parties). The question for the Staff now was: of German bombing parties were seen by the men at the sharp end to be in the German front line what did it say about the prospects of there being many or, indeed, any British troops left behind between the enemy front line or in Serre?

Meanwhile, the German barrage on the front line had steadily increased in intensity and, at about 10.30 a.m., Maj. Albert Hoette was wounded in John Copse trying to find out what had happened to the rest of the Sheffield battalion. 46 year old Hoette was previously an officer in the Imperial Yeomanry and he was something of a yachtsman as, in 1913, he captained the Bristol Channel Pilot Cutter *'Carlotta'* to victory in the 1913 Royal Cornwall Yacht Club Regatta. He had re-joined the Army on the outbreak of war and was now acting as second in command of the battalion[i]. In spite of his wounding another report was furnished to Brigade that there was no contact with any of their companies.

---

[i] Maj. Albert Rudolph Hoette was born in 1870, the son of Emil Hoette, a Liverpool merchant. He was commissioned from Cpl. to 2nd Lt. in the Imperial Yeomanry in April 1901 and joined the 2nd Battalion as Lt. in September 1901. Wounded in the South African War. He relinquished his commission on 28th September 1902. He re-joined the Army as Lt. on 31st August 1914 and was promoted Temp. Major in the 12th York & Lancaster Regt. on 1st February 1915. He joined the Training Reserve on 20th January 1917. He re-joined the York & Lancaster Regt. in December 1917 and relinquished his commission on 21st October 1919. He was married to Johanna Augusta Borberg. He died on 8th July 1935.

Increasingly, German troops dominated No Man's Land, even venturing out to bomb the end of Sap A on 93rd Brigade's front. Others wiled away the time sniping the wounded or, rather pointlessly, shot chunks off the bodies of dead men hung up on the wire. In retribution, the 94th MGC turned some of its guns on the German parapet. Any casualties caused were of small comfort overall.

Further back behind the German lines there was one unit on the receiving end of the some British aggression. The 4., 5. and 6. Batteries of the Kgl. Bayerisches Feldartillerie-Regiment Nr. 19 had been inserted into the defensive system around Puisieux on the 19th June. Some of their emplacements were not as strong or as well camouflaged as others of longer occupation and, at about 10 a.m., one of the batteries, the 4., started to come in for some heavy treatment. The battery was located to the south of Bucquoy, between the town and the small Fork Wood, or Ziegelwäldchen. It was near to the Puisieux road and visible from the trenches around Hebuterne. Someone, either from the air or the ground, had spotted the battery firing and, in response, some gratifyingly accurate counter battery fire fell straight onto the battery position. The left most gun was struck by four heavy calibre shells in quick succession. Then the second from the right received two direct hits. Other damage meant only one gun was still useable and Lt. der Reserve Adam, although wounded, took control and ensured the gun kept firing. He was supported by Utffz. Burkhard and Gefr. Militzer both of whom were later promoted for conspicuous gallantry in the face of the enemy. Lt. der Reserve Adam became the Kgl. Bayerisches Feldartillerie-Regiment Nr. 19's first Battery Officer to receive the Iron Cross, 1st class.

Ammunition wagons had to be brought up one at a time so as not to present too inviting a target for the aircraft and the British artillery. But they got through and the guns kept firing. Evacuating the wounded was also a problem and the injured were, instead, kept at the telephone dugout of the 6. Battery of Badisches Feldartillerie-Regiment Nr. 104 near to the Ziegelwäldchen. When the dugout took a direct hit every available man rushed to help dig out the wounded trapped under the collapsed roof. Thanks to the valiant efforts of the rescuers most of the wounded were released and taken to the rear.

Earlier, the 6. Battery of the FAR Nr. 104, had lost two of its guns and, by the end of the day, the area around the Ziegelwäldchen was a shambles of shell holes and wreckage. In spite of this, casualties amongst the artillerymen were not heavy. The Kgl. Bayerisches Feldartillerie-Regiment Nr. 19, for example, lost two men dead and 15 wounded, half of whom were with the unfortunate 4. Battery.

With the aircraft of the R.F.C. roaming unhindered across the skies over the Somme, some flew increasingly low in order to improve observation and to use their Lewis guns to take on targets of opportunity when the chance arose. This was not without risk from small arms and AA fire from the troops below. One of the BE2cs flying as an infantry contact aircraft in the area north of the Ancre was shot down during the day was unlucky enough, however, to be shot down by one of the few German aircraft willing to contest the skies. BE2c 2578 of No. 15 Squadron was piloted by a 22 year old Australian from Queensland named Lt. Kenneth Selby Henderson. Henderson had initially served in the 5th Australian Light Horse and became a Flying Officer in the RFC in May 1916. Today, his aircraft was shot down by Oblt. Hans-Eberhardt Gandert, the commander of

Jasta 51 and Jagdgruppe 6. This was the fourth of Gandert's eight victories. Both Henderson and his observer, 2nd Lt. N P Tucker, survived.[i]

ON THE EXTREME LEFT OF THE DIVISION'S FRONT the men of the 2nd Barnsley Pals had been beavering away attempting to construct their new flanking trench. Two platoons of B Company had been given the task of opening out the Russian sap, Sap F, constructing a north facing parapet, a firestep and all the other things a new fire trench might wish for. As an idea for a good day out there is, I am sure, nothing quite like wandering around No Man's Land armed with a shovel under heavy machine gun and artillery fire while trying to dig a trench. It is something of a surprise, therefore, that it took as long as two hours before word came back that all had not gone as expected with this task. At 9.30 a.m. Lt. Rupert Esmond Lowinsky staggered back to Battalion HQ to announce that the other platoon commander, Lt. Duncan Fairley[ii], and all of the other officers with those platoons were casualties and that two more platoons needed to be sent up to replace the dead and wounded. He was so severely wounded, however, that no further information could be elicited. Two platoons of C Company commanded by 2nd Lt. Johnson were then ordered to find and assist the remains of the original party or, failing that, they were to consolidate and hold the sap. Johnson proved to be a sensible and brave officer. On reaching the previously flattened section of Nairne Street he told his men to wait while he went forward to reconnoitre. On his return he informed Lt. Col. Hulke that there was no sign of party, sap or trench. Everything, it seemed, had been erased by the German artillery. Hulke decided he must check for himself, then agreed entirely with the subaltern and concluded that, were the men sent out into the open, they would be annihilated. Another officer was sent to find another route forward further south and Johnson and his two platoons retired to slightly safer terrain. A short while after, Brig. Gen. Rees sent orders for C and D Companies to be kept in hand and at his disposal as they constituted his only reserve. This was done.

Not only had most of B Company disappeared but the majority of A Company was gone too. These two parties had been attacked from front and flank. From in front by the men of 4/ IR 169 and in flank by the machine guns and rifles of the II Battalion, IR 66. All that the IR 66 had to contend with was the field artillery of the 48th Division not employed elsewhere and some errant shooting from the VIII Corps heavy guns. Otherwise, it was open season as they picked off the men of the 14th Y&L as they attempted their impossible task of constructing a new north facing trench system.

---

[i] Capt. Kenneth Selby Henderson, No. 1 Squadron, died on 2nd June 1918 when he failed to return from a patrol while flying S.E.5a C1113. Aged 24, he was the son of John Stuart Henderson and Alice Sarah Henderson, of Jedburgh, Yaraka, Queensland, Australia. He is remembered on the Arras Flying Services Memorial.

[ii] 2nd Lt. Duncan Fairley, 14th York and Lancaster Regt., was aged 26. He was the youngest son of Barker Fairley, headmaster of St John's School, and Charlotte Fairley of 84, Ormonde St., Sunderland, and previously Park Grove, Barnsley. A native of Barnsley, he was educated at St John's School, Barnsley, gaining a scholarship to Barnsley Grammar School. He gained a 1st Class Honours degree at Leeds University and became an English master at Scarborough Municipal Secondary School. He was commissioned on 18th May 1915. He is buried in Euston Road Cemetery, Colincamps, grave IV. S. 7.

IR 66 came off relatively lightly. Just two officers fell during the day: Lts. der Reserve Ebers, who died from a stomach wound, and Waldemar Draheim[i] the commander of 5. Kompanie. Draheim was killed early in the day as he observed the beginning of the attack out in the open next to his command dugout in sector M4. A direct hit killed him outright. Another officer, Lt. der Res. Franz Seldte[ii], was severely wounded. He was commanding Maschinengewehr Kompanie Nr. 1 and was firing one of the company's guns when a shell explosion tore of his left forearm. The officer commanding the 8. Kompanie. Lt. der Res. Walter Mende, was wounded in the same incident. Unteroffizier Ackermann took over from the wounded Seldte and continued to direct the flanking machine gun fire which helped destroy the men of the 2nd Barnsley Pals. With the whole of 5. Kompanie occupying the front line in M4, the 8. Kompanie sent two platoons forward to man the support trench from where they too could fire into the flank of the 94th Brigade. Behind them, men of the 2. and 3. Kompanien swarmed into the reserve trench from which they were able to assist in the destruction of the men from Sheffield and Barnsley. According to German sources not one man from either A or B Company of 2nd Barnsley Pals penetrated the front line of either the IR 66 or IR 169. And all this at a cost to the IR 66 of just 36 dead and 92 wounded[iii].

So severe was the concentrated fire of the IR 66's machine guns and rifles into the flank of the 94th Brigade that at 7.50 a.m. the 92nd Machine Gun Company, originally to be kept in reserve, was required to bring forward eight guns to Rolland Trench. From here the machine guns fired intermittently until the end of the day. At one point, another gun was ordered forward to fire on Germans observed to be 'bayoneting and robbing' British wounded at the southern end of the Divisional front[99]. One man from the company was wounded but, at 4 p.m., a stray bullet hit and killed 2nd Lt. Edward White[iv] who was in charge of a section of four guns firing from Rolland Trench.

Information about the actions of the 94th Machine Gun Company is, sadly, limited. Nine gun teams went into action with the Brigade: three gun teams with the 11th East Lancashires, two with the 12th York & Lancasters, two with the 13th York & Lancasters and two with the 14th York and Lancasters, making a total of four officers and 63 men. Of these, only one officer, suffering from shock, and

[i] Lt. Waldemar Draheim, II Battalion, Infanterie Regiment Nr. 66, came from the village of Tokarth, near Briesen in Brandenburg. He is buried in Achiet-le-Petit Cemetery, grave 458.

[ii] Franz Seldte (29th June 1882 – 1st April 1947) was born in Magdeburg. He was co-founder of the German Stahlhelm paramilitary organization made up of World War 1 veterans opposed to the Treaty of Versailles. He became a leading Nazi politician and served as Minister for Labour in the Hitler Government between 1933 and 1945. Seldte was arrested at the end of the war and died in a US military hospital at Fürth before being arraigned on charges. He was awarded the Iron Cross 1st and 2nd Class in the First World War and became a front reporter after the loss of his arm.

[iii] Fourteen of the dead came from the 5. Kompanie which suffered the heaviest casualties.

[iv] 2nd Lt. Edward Beadon White, 11th Yorkshire Regt. att. 92nd Machine Gun Company, enlisted in the North Somerset Yeomanry before being commissioned into the 11th Yorkshire Regt. He joined the Civil Service as a Boy Clerk in 1895 before joining HM Customs in 1899 as a second class clerk at the Outports. He was married to Hellen Mitchell and they had one son, Edward William White. He is buried in Euston Road Cemetery, Colincamps, grave V. G. 7.

22 men returned uninjured. These may have come from amongst the elements Brig. Gen. Rees claimed to have stopped from advancing when he realised that his Brigade had been 'destroyed as a fighting unit'. Of the remainder, two officers were wounded, one was missing and five men were reported killed, 19 wounded and 17 missing. Among the remaining seven gun teams of the 94th MGC there was only one casualty, one man being killed in the trenches while standing by his gun. Amongst the nine gun teams that went forward with the infantry, the casualty rate was 66%. Seven guns were lost.

On their left, on the 48th Division's front, the machine guns of the 143rd Machine Gun Company had been providing long range covering fire. As with most of the actions of the South Midland Division these guns seem not have bothered the Germans unduly as they appear not to have fired very many shells in retaliation for the 143rd MGC's intervention. At least this meant that casualties were for the company were very light with just Lt. John Howatt being wounded.

By the end of the day the 14th Battalion (2nd Barnsley Pals), York and Lancaster Regt. under the onslaught from their left and front, had lost:

Killed:
Lt. H B Forsdike, B Company
2nd Lt. W Hirst, A Company
Missing
2nd Lt. R D B Anderson, A Company
Capt. F N Houston, B Company
2nd Lt. D Fairley, B Company
Capt. G O Roos, A Company
Wounded
2nd Lt. Edward Allen Holmes, C Company
2nd Lt. Walter Kell, A Company
Lt. Rupert Esmond Lowinsky, B Company
2nd Lt. Harry Strong, B Company
Other Ranks:
Killed 24
Missing 149
Wounded 92

Total: 10 officers and 265 Other Ranks, this from a total of 24 officers and just under 700 men or a casualty rate of about 38%. A third of these officers and men were killed on the day, i.e. six officers and 87 other ranks. Another died in the following days, three in German hands: 14/20 Pte. William Clarkson[i] and 14/864 Pte. William Goldthorpe[ii] were both seriously wounded when taken

[i] 14/20 Pte William Henry Clarkson, MM, 14th York & Lancaster Regt., was aged 32. He was born in High Hoyland and worked at the Pywood Colliery, Darton. Married with four children, he lived at 32, School Street, Darton. He died in German hands at Fremicourt on 4th July 1916, and is buried in Achiet le Grand Communal Cemetery, grave IV. Q. 6.

[ii] 14/864 Pte William Greenwood Goldthorpe, 14th York & Lancaster Regt., was aged 24. He was born in Liversedge and was married to Elizabeth Goldthorpe (née Hotchkiss). They had a son, Thomas. He worked at the Darton Colliery. He enlisted on 11th March 1915. He died in German hands at Fremicourt on 4th July 1916, and is buried in Douchy les Ayette British Cemetery, grave III. D. 2.

prisoner. They were taken to a German hospital at Fremicourt just east of Bapaume but both men died on 4th July 1916. 14/452 Pte. Edward Phillips lingered on for another four days, dying on 8th July at the hospital at Caudry where he is buried[i].

Compared to other battalions these casualty figures seem unremarkable, however, the vast majority of the casualties occurred in just two companies, A and B. Only one of the ten officer casualties, the wounded 2nd Lt. Edward Holmes of C Company, did not come from either of these companies. If one apportions the casualties amongst other ranks in the same proportion then it is reasonable to assume that A and B Companies were more or less wiped out. Certainly, a casualty rate in the region of 90% in A Company and the two trench digging platoons of B Company seems fairly certain. The lack of any adequate protection from the 48th Division or the heavy and field artillery from the interference of the IR 66 cost these six platoons very dear.

WHAT OF THE OTHER UNITS THAT HAD BEEN INVOLVED IN THE ATTACK?

The Pioneers, the 12th King's Own Yorkshire Light Infantry, had been split into three sections. A Company, commanded by Capt. John Charlesworth Crawshaw, was attached to the 94th Brigade, D Company, under Capt. Herbert Francis Chadwick, to the 93rd Brigade and B (Capt. William Roberts) and C Companies (Capt. William Cooper) given the rather arduous, if apparently less dangerous, tasks of connecting Saps A, B, C, D and E across the last 40 to 50 yards of No Man's Land to the German communication trenches. Then they were to clear those communication trenches all the way to the new front line on the far side of Serre. The jobs given to A and D Companies were the construction of new strong points and the consolidation of captured trenches. In spite of the fact that every man was to carry the basic equipment of the infantry, i.e. a waterproof sheet and cardigan, two gas masks, full water bottle, iron ration and 24 hours of rations in a haversack, 3 (empty) sandbags, two Mills grenades, 170 rounds of SAA and rifle, they would also carry either a pick or shovel, while every officer and NCO carried four flares, and two men in every platoon a pair of wirecutters. And, of course, their steel helmet. One of the gas masks was to be worn rolled up above the face ready to be lowered should gas be encountered in the trenches. Gas masks had to be lowered if anyone entered a dugout.

Carried in the haversack were a series of items essential to any young man fancying a leisurely day out in the French countryside and a light, al fresco lunch:

1 pair socks
1 towel and soap
1 hairbrush
1 holdall containing knife, fork, spoon, razor, lather brush and tooth brush
1 'house-wife', i.e. a sewing kit
1 ration bag containing 12 ozs biscuits
Mess tin containing 12 ozs meat ration and a tin containing tea, sugar and Oxo cubes.

[i] 14/452 Pte. Edward Phillips, 14th York & Lancaster Regt., is buried in Caudry Old Communal Cemetery, grave B. 1.

Heavily laden, the men of A and D Companies were to follow on close behind the leading waves of the three attacking battalions. Two platoons each of A Company followed the Sheffield City Battalion and the Accringtons while D Company went in after the Leeds Pals. As a result, both companies, but especially A Company, suffered heavy losses. Ninety men of A Company were either killed or wounded and this included the only fatality amongst the battalions' officers, 20 year old 2nd Lt. James Welch, the son of a vicar from Southend on Sea. His Colonel wrote to his father with the less than comforting news that the young officer had first of all been felled by a bullet but, nonetheless, had encouraged his men onwards with the words, "Never mind me; carry on". He had then been killed by a shell immediately afterwards[i].

Plate 161 Lt. James Stanley Lightfoot Welch, 12th King's Own Yorkshire Light Infantry

In total, losses were one officer killed, three officers wounded and 185 Other Ranks killed or wounded. It was not until Tuesday, 4th July, that eight men registered as 'missing' at roll call immediately after the attack managed to find their way back to the battalion at their encampment at Bus-les-Artois. Given that only A and D Companies of the battalion went 'over the top' and the very high casualties recorded by A Company, it is clear that losses were concentrated in these two elements of the battalion. What was left of the two lead companies were joined in the battered front line trenches where A Company was joined by B and D Company by C. They spent the rest of the day under continual shell and machine gun fire rebuilding trenches, bringing up ammunition and supplies and,

[i] Lt. James Stanley Lightfoot Welch, 12th King's Own Yorkshire Light Infantry, was aged 20. He was the son of the Rev Canon Edward A and Edith Marion Welch of Southchurch Rectory, Southend-on-Sea. He was educated at Yardley Court Preparatory School, Somerhill, Tonbridge, Rugby School and Lawrence Saunders School, and was a Scholar of King's College, Cambridge. Born at Toronto, Canada. He enlisted in October 1914 and was commissioned on 24th October 1914. He went to Egypt in December 1915. He was MiD on 13th November 1916. He is buried in Queen's Cemetery, Puisieux, grave D. 66.

later in the evening, helping with the evacuation of the large numbers of wounded scattered all across the 31st Divisional area.

During the fighting several officers and NCOs caught the eye of Lt. Col. Ernest Chambers[i] for their performance. Capt. William Roberts[ii], C Company, Lt. Herbert Gaunt[iii], B Company, 2nd Lt. William Baird, B Company, and 2nd Lt. Leonard Forsdike, C Company, were all commended for their coolness and energy. 9008 CSM Robert Freaks from Chatteris in Cambridgeshire was a ten year veteran of the battalion and he had helped steady some of the men wavering under the heavy German bombardment. In this important task he had been aided by 1165 CQMS Robert Kerr. 242 Sgt. Austin Adams, though wounded early in the day, was reported by his superior as having behaved splendidly[iv].

AS THE HOUR DREW TOWARDS 11 A.M. THE SITUATION along the 31st Division's front was thus:

In the 94th Brigade's sector there were two companies of the 14th York and Lancasters in Monk and Holland Trenches, two platoons of the 13th York and Lancasters in the front line and the remnants of C and D Companies in Monk. The survivors of A Company of the 12th KOYLI less two platoons were in Eden Trench along with the remaining guns of the 94th MGC. This sounds better than the reality on the ground. The 'two platoons' of the 13th York and Lancasters in the front line were the last remaining men of A Company led forward by Capt. Gurney earlier in the day along with a few stragglers from other battalions collected from the vicinity. The 'trench' they occupied had been nearly levelled to the ground by the German artillery.

On the 93rd Brigade, the scattered remains of the 15th, 16th and 18th West Yorkshires were either crammed in and around the front line or widely distributed over various of the assembly trenches to the rear. The Brigade had attempted to estimate its losses. Sadly, the estimate was wildly optimistic:

> "15th West Yorkshires 400 all ranks, 16th West Yorkshires 300 all ranks, 18th West Yorkshires 12, 18th Durham LI 2nd Lt. Harbottle wounded, MG Company 10 wounded."[100]

---

[i] Lt. Col. Ernest Leonard Chambers, MC, Bedfordshire Regt., att. 12th King's Own Yorkshire Light Infantry, was born in 1882, the son of Mr and Mrs Chambers of Nutfield,, Surrey. Educated at Bedford Grammar School and Cambridge, he played rugby for the school 1st XV, gained a rugby (and athletics for the hammer) Blue in 1904 and went on to play for Blackheath, Bedford, Kent, East Midlands and three times for England (1908-10 against France, Ireland and Wales). He was a teacher at Bedford Grammar School (1908-13) where he took charge of the 1st XV. He joined the OTC in 1909. In 1913 he went to work for the Education Department of the Egyptian Civil Service. He returned in 1914 and was commissioned into the 6th Bedfordshire Regt., before being promoted Maj. in the 18th (1st Tyneside), Northumberland Fusiliers. He was made CO of the 12th KOYLI on 13th August 1915. MiD and MC, January 1917. Married Elain Swainston in 1915. He died in 1946.

[ii] Capt. William Howard Roberts was awarded the Italian Silver Medal for Military Valour (*Medaglia d'Argento al Valore Militare)*, the Italian equivalent of the MC, on 25th May 1917.

[iii] Acting Capt. Herbert Douglas Gaunt was awarded the MC in the New Year's Honours List of 1st January 1918.

[iv] 242 Sgt. Austin Adams was awarded the French Medaille Militaire on 1st May 1917.

To make matters worse, at the same time, the Division had informed VIII Corps that both the 15th and 16th West Yorkshires were in the 2nd and 3rd German trenches. Within minutes this assessment would be challenged by some harsh facts of life from closer to the front line.

At 11.05 a.m., 2nd Lt. Trickett of the 93rd Trench Mortar Battery reported that there were only wounded men left in the front line trenches. Then a painfully realistic assessment of the position on the 93rd Brigade's front was forwarded to 31st Division at 11.07 a.m.:

> "15th and 16th West Yorkshires practically non-existent. Adjutant 16th West Yorkshires reports he has only one officer and hardly any NCOs. Cannot get into touch with any officer of 15th West Yorkshires. Remains of both regiments are in front line. Adjutant 18th West Yorkshires was ordered to sort them out. 18th West Yorkshires should be holding front line with 18th Durham LI in reserve. A company of King's Own Regt (4th Division) on our right holding S Monk."[101]

So, whilst VIII Corps was recording the lead battalions of the 93rd Brigade fighting in the German 2nd and 3rd trenches and reports were being sent to Fourth Army that Serre was being consolidated, rather more realistic assessments were beginning to filter through from some of the artillery FOOs:

> "10.50 a.m. Wires from 2nd Lt. Reay and 2nd Lt. Jowell show both 93rd and 94th Brigades probably hung up in German front line trenches. Opposite Mark Copse 94th Brigade barely penetrated German front line. Col. Rickman knows no more." (170th Brigade, RFA)[102]

All were agreed, however, that the German barrage was still heavy and it stretched the entire length of the front line and away to the west with the men sheltering in Monk Trench coming under heavy fire. At 11 a.m., this shelling caught A and B Companies of the 18th DLI as they advanced over the open between Monk and Maitland Trenches

And yet, within minutes of the 93rd Brigade reporting to Division that 'No movement of any troops can be observed in front of Serre either on the left, centre or right', the Divisional OP was reporting that the 14th York and Lancasters were somehow making progress consolidating strong point A in the new north facing front line and that troops were advancing on the Brown Line south of Serre.

Such was the air of unreality amongst all senior officers and their staffs that at 11.15 a.m. 93rd Brigade reported seeing a group of Germans on their front line parapet. It appeared there could be only one reason for their presence:

> "Possibly they may want to surrender."[103]

Evidence to the contrary was now beginning to stack up. At the same time as Germans were apparently giving up, information came to the attention of 93rd Brigade that men from their neighbours, the 4th Division, were crowded into trenches within their sector, unable to get forward and having lost all contact with the rest of their battalions. These were troops from the waves of the 4th Division which should have been pushing onwards, over the Zwischen Stellung towards the German 2nd Position but were now occupying Legend Trench and at a loss to know what to do:

"11.15 a.m. An officer from the Duke of Wellington's Regt. reported at (93rd) Brigade Headquarters that he had failed to advance and was in the southern end of Legend Trench with 150 men and did not know where the rest of his Battalion was. Another Officer of the King's Own Regt. reported that he had failed to advance and was now outside Brigade H.Q. with 12 men which was all that was left of his company."[104]

This information was passed onto Division who were, no doubt, left scratching their heads as the Brigade reported at the same time:

1. British troops advancing on the Brown Line; but
2. The 93rd Brigade held up in front of the German front line; whilst
3. Stretchers were badly needed to clear the front lines of wounded; and
4. There were no more than 1½ battalions available once the Brigade had been sorted out.

Equally confusing was a report from 94th Brigade five minutes later. At 11.25 a.m., whilst Brig. Gen. Rees was stating that '… a field glass reconnaissance shows no movement to his front in the first 4 German trenches', his Brigade observer was reporting that he had seen the sun glinting on the metal reflectors on the backs of British troops in the 4th German trench. On the other hand, work on converting Sap F into a new trench had been abandoned and the Germans had deposited a heavy barrage just in front of the British front line. What was one to think?

What Division decided to do was to 'accentuate the positive'. Rees was ordered to throw more men forward into the German front line and for them to bomb down these trenches towards the 93rd Brigade front. He was made privy to Brig. Gen. Ingles's 'cunning plan' to send the remains of the 93rd Brigade in behind the 4th Division and for them to bomb their way north so that the two Brigades might join hands. It was one of those concepts that looked so lovely on paper and positively marvellous on a map. In practice it was a non-starter. One of the reasons for this was that news was beginning to filter back from No Man's Land about the fate of the leading troops of the 94th Brigade.

We had left Lt. Col. Rickman bewailing the lack of news from 'his waves'. By 11.25 a.m. this had not changed much although Pte. Glover, who had gone forward with the 2nd wave and his officer, Capt. Livesey, and had now returned across the death trap of No Man's Land, reported that the first waves had encountered heavy machine gun, rifle, grenade, artillery and trench mortar fire as they attacked. Of the fate of Livesey and his men Lt. Col. Rickman, as yet, knew nothing. His mind was now occupied with reorganising those troops in the front line and trying to deal with wounded men sheltering in Sap C and Excema Trench. There was a shortage of field dressings such were the numbers.

With most of his men dead, wounded or missing, Rickman was grateful for the work of Capt. Currin of C Company, 13th York and Lancasters, and a few of his men who were occupying the front line from Matthew Copse to Sap C. The 44 year-old Currin was a South African soldier of considerable experience having fought in the South African War[i]. His efforts in the front line now proved

---

[i] Capt. Richard William Currin was later promoted Lt. Col. and commanded a battalion of the Leicester Regt. until February 1918, then the 8th Notts and Derbys from April 1918 to

invaluable and were later rewarded with a DSO for his work (*London Gazette*, 25th August 1916):

> "For conspicuous courage and ability in organising the defence of front line trenches, and by personal example and total disregard of danger securing good work under heavy fire. He was instrumental in bringing in eighty wounded from exposed positions."

At 11.25 a.m. 93rd Brigade corrected their 'Germans want to surrender' report to read:

> "11.25 a.m. Following received from 31st Division: 'Enemy visible on their first line parapet near Point 25. Possibly they want to surrender'. The first portion of the message was unfortunately correct, the latter portion incorrect."[105]

Were this not so tragically absurd one might be tempted to laugh.

Over the next half an hour bizarrely contradictory reports came in from all parts of the Division's front line. The 18th Durham Light Infantry commented on the 'very effective' German artillery fire and reported heavy casualties in all companies, three of which, A, B and C Companies, had not even come close to the British front line. The FOO of B Battery, 165th Brigade, RFA, meanwhile, was blithely reporting that the infantry had taken the 4th German trench just in front of Serre in spite of very heavy casualties to the Sheffield Pals. On the far left flank, a staff officer of the 94th Brigade, a Lt. Grant, had attempted to reach the far end of Nairne Trench but had found it impossible to get beyond Rob Roy Trench, some 400 yards from the front at this point. From there forward, Nairne was swept by machine guns firing from the front of the IR 66 to the north east. As 31st Division digested this 11.45 a.m. report, they were also considering a message from VIII Corps which suggested that, with Serre and Pendant Copse apparently both in British hands, the remains of the 93rd Brigade should shift to the left and push in behind the 94th Brigade. Word went back to Hunter-Weston that Wanless-O'Gowan had already arranged for this to happen. On a map, at least.

This projected manoeuvre would have come as news to Brig. Gen. Ingles at 93rd Brigade HQ. His earlier plan had been to follow behind the right wing of the 4th Division rather than try following the 94th Brigade on his left but even this plan was now academic. He returned to Brigade HQ at 11.45 a.m. having conducted a tour of the forward areas and, having seen conditions on the ground, he had come to a decision. Whilst he was there he had found men abandoning the front line. When asked what they were doing they replied that they had been ordered to leave the front trench. Ingles went to see for himself and found it full of dead and wounded and under heavy shell fire. Getting the able bodied organised simply for defence did not now seem such a bad idea and, with the help of Capt. Jackson, 10th East Yorkshire Regt., and Lt. Clark, 18th Durham L.I., the men retiring were diverted into Bradford and Dunmow Trenches. Ingles then looked out into No Man's Land. There were no troops advancing to left or right

September 1919. Born 14th March 1872 in South Africa, he served in the Langeberg Campaign in the Boer War 1899-1902 and in German West Africa, Egypt and France in the First World War. He died on 12th June 1942.

and the enemy front trench was heavily manned. As he returned to his HQ he came upon some officers and men of the 4th Division who had withdrawn into the 31st Division's sector. They told him that the 4th Division too was badly held up. Generally, the attack was failing.

With such heavy casualties, and in the absence of the majority of his officers and NCOs, Ingles concluded that any further advance was 'fruitless'. His observations of the frontal areas, combined with reports from the various battalions, showed that he had only three officers, Lts. Cross, Peace and Whitaker of the 18th West Yorkshires, and 200 men from various battalions in the front line. The three remaining companies of the 18th DLI were thought to be either in Monk Trench or Maitland Trench. C Company had been left in Maitland Trench while what was left of A and B Companies was supposedly now in Monk Trench. As it turned out, Ingles would discover B Company lying out in the open to the west of Monk and he ordered the company commander, Capt. Douglas Edward Ince, to reorganise his command and get them into Sackville in order to resist any possible German counter attack. Fortunately, not long after, Lt. Col. Hugh Bowes[i], the CO of the Durhams, arrived on the scene and, in the absence of the three other COs of the Brigade who were all now casualties, undertook to organise the mixture of troops currently spread across Monk, Landguard and Dunmow.

A few men from two battalions of the 4th Division, the Duke of Wellington's and the King's Own, had wandered into the right of the 93rd Brigade's front at Legend Trench. Ingles's concern now was to strengthen what remained of the front line trench and to reorganise what was left of his battalions. He therefore issued the following orders:

18th DLI to hold front line where possible with company in support in Monk;
16th West Yorks to organise in Dunmow;
18th West Yorks to organise in Landguard;
15th West Yorks to organise in Maitland;
Company KOYLI, Pioneers, to organise in Legend; and
Duke of Wellington's and King's Own to organise in Legend, south of Flag Avenue.

On their left, the reality of the situation was certainly very much more evident in the front lines than at either 31st Division or VIII Corps HQs. At 11.50 a.m. Lt. Col. Rickman reported two of his few remaining officers, Capt. & Adjt. Anton Peltzer[ii] and Lt. Leonard Ryden, wounded, though Ryden was able to stay

---

[i] Lt. Col. Hugh Bowes, Durham Lifght Infantry, took command of the 18th Battalion in November 1914. He had previously been the OC, 1st Volunteer Battalion, Durham Light Infantry and had served with the 1st Durham Light Infantry in South Africa with the rank of Capt. He left the 18th Battalion on 2nd September 1916 and took command of the 1st Reserve Garrison Battalion, King's Own Yorkshire Light Infantry, on 15th November 1916 until May 1919.

[ii] Capt. Anton Peltzer, DSO, 11th East Lancashire Regt., was born in 1885. He was the son of Charles Armand Peltzer of Spring Hill House, Accrington. Married Ethel Cooper in 1912, a daughter 1915, a son 1918. He was to be commissioned into the 5th East Lancashire Regt. on 3rd October 1914 however this appointment was cancelled after he had been commissioned into the newly formed Accrington Battalion. He was promoted Captain on 15th January 1915. After recovering from his wounds he joined the 9th East

on duty for the time being. He had still had no official news from 'his waves' and was entirely reliant on the dubious accuracy of statements from the returning wounded. He was also concerned about the lack of men holding the front line. Capt. Currin's men were few in number and he again asked for reinforcements to be sent up as soon as possible. For Rickman, his job was now all about defence rather than attack. He ordered men to block Sap C, which had been opened up across No Man's Land, and asked Brigade for a supply of bombs with which he might counter any attacks mounted by the enemy on his front line trenches.

Plate 162 Capt. Anton Peltzer, 11th East Lancashire Regt.

Plate 163 Lt. Leonard Ryden, 11th East Lancashire Regt.

On his left, no news from the Sheffield Pals was bad news as far as the battalion and the attack was concerned. Behind them, the remaining companies of the 14th York and Lancasters waited to move forward and a runner arrived at 11.50 a.m. to tell them that it was thought that the Battalion HQ of the Sheffield Pals had followed the rest of the battalion over the top. This was the signal for the HQ of the 2nd Barnsley Pals to advance from Rolland Trench to John Copse ready for the next phase of the operation, a distance of about 1,000 yards. Such was the German barrage, allied to the threat of the IR 66's machine guns, that it was found impossible to get beyond Rob Roy and the battalion's HQ were forced to return to Rolland. Here they stayed for the rest of the day trying to organise some form of defence should the Germans attempt to take advantage of the chaos and mount an attack on the British lines.

The men of the 94th Trench Mortar Battery were still in the front lines around Sap E and, at 12.10 p.m., they were informed by the Adjutant of the Sheffield Pals that the Germans could be seen bringing up machine guns and ammunition to their front line opposite Nairne. The Stokes mortar in the sap was still useable

Lancashire Regt., and went to Salonika. Took command of the battalion in October 1918. He relinquished his commission on 19th March 1919. His DSO was gazetted on 30th May 1919. He became a director of Howard & Bullough (Securities) Ltd of the Globe Works, Accrington, in 1937. His father had been a director of the company, a major Accrington employer, for 40 years. His wife died in 1939 and he re-married Margaret Winifred Boles in 1943.

and they sent over about 100 bombs in an apparently successful attempt at disrupting the German consolidation of their position.

IN SPITE OF ALL THE EVIDENCE IN THE FRONT LINE TRENCHES that the attack had failed, not the least being the decision to man the front line in case of a German counter-attack, the information coming down from Corps and Division was still laughably optimistic.

At 12.13 p.m. Ingles at 93rd Brigade HQ received a situation report from Division that was incorrect in every particular:

> "We are in Pendant Copse - we are in Serre - 56th Divn. have advanced as far as Rossignol Wood."[106]

Although nothing could have been further from the truth on the 31st Division's front (and no troops from the 56th Division got near Rossignol Wood) the information was relayed on to the Brigade HQs with instructions for action:

> "12.15 p.m. Message as follows went to 93rd Brigade and 94th Brigade: Information from Corps points to fact that we hold Pendant Copse and Serre. Push what reinforcements you have in behind 94th Brigade and in conjunction with GOC 94th Brigade confirm the success at Serre."[107]

The entry in the 31st Divisions' report went on to underline the urgency of this move by the 93rd Brigade:

> "VIII Corps reports that artillery say that there are small bodies of Germans between Serre village and their front line. The Corps Commander hopes that the movement of 93rd Brigade in conjunction with 94th Brigade will be carried out quickly in order that their way may not be barred by these bodies of Germans."[108]

Whatever higher authority expected of 93rd Brigade it was not forthcoming. Ingles stood firm by his decision not to waste any more men by futile advances, especially as the German barrage was still battering his front lines. His only orders were for the remaining organised bodies of men under his command to hold and consolidate their positions. He had seen for himself the state of the ground and his Brigade and any more offensive action was definitely not on his agenda.

This was clearly not apparent to anyone at 31st Division HQ. At 12.35 p.m. they were on the telephone to 94th Brigade in order to ascertain what troops were available for this push through to Serre supported by 93rd Brigade. 94th Brigade's contribution was to be small: 2½ companies of infantry, six machine guns and the Trench Mortar Battery. 93rd Brigade was not in a position to provide anything, though Division seemed not to realise this fact. To occupy the trenches vacated whilst this pathetic force advanced, a battalion of Hull soldiers from the 92nd Brigade was to occupy the old front line.

To confirm the 'need' for this advance another erroneous report came in at 12.40 p.m. from the FOO of B/165 Battery:

> "12th York and Lancs captured 4th line trench and pushing forward. East Lancs very few casualties. Sheffielders of York and Lancs caught it hot."[109]

At the same time as this report arrived another, equally inaccurate but extremely worrying at the time, came in. A Divisional OP had apparently seen small groups of German troops counter-attacking over No Man's Land and into the British lines. The location of these incursions was said to be opposite Point 25, the re-entrant in the German front line opposite the 93rd Brigade front. There was an urgent call to the field guns to barrage this position. These same reports, soon realised to be incorrect, came into 93rd Brigade HQ a few minutes later and were passed to Division. Bizarrely, it was Rees at 94th Brigade who was ordered to sort this situation out by sending a company to bomb the enemy out of the 93rd Brigade's front line. Rees pointed out somewhat testily that the front line trench had long since ceased to exist but the order was confirmed:

> "I therefore ordered seventy men near Brigade headquarters to draw bombs from the dump and take their time about it. A little later I was talking to General O'Gowan and told him that I didn't believe the Germans were in the 93rd's trench at all. He said, to my considerable astonishment, 'Nor do I'. 'In that case', said I, 'I will stop the attack which you have just ordered me to make' and rushed out of the dugout to cancel the order."

It is, however, an indication of the general confusion and uncertainty at the front line that, even if only briefly, it was believed likely that the Germans would abandon the relative security of their trenches in an attempt to take advantage of the chaos in the British lines. Such counter-attacks just did not happen. The Germans had already won the battle by bloodily repelling the British attack. They did not need to suffer unnecessary additional casualties by attacking over the open in an attempt to take trenches they probably could not hold and certainly did not need. But such was the state of affairs that at 12.56 p.m. 93rd Brigade sent Division a report recommending that the Divisional reserve, i.e. 92nd Brigade, be rushed to the front in an effort to repel these non-existent attacks.

With this request came further information from various sources that 93rd Brigade had not only completely failed but had been badly cut up in the process. Lt. Riley, a FOO with C/170 Battery, reported through his Brigade commander to Division that the infantry had not got beyond the German front line. The 93rd Brigade itself admitted to not having left its front line and to losing two battalions in the process. A few minutes later, 169th Brigade, RFA, learnt that, in fact, three battalions of the 93rd Brigade had been destroyed trying to mount the attack.

And yet still Division believed that success was within their grasp. Just after 1 p.m. plans were being put in place for the 94th Brigade to bomb down the German front line trenches whilst the left of the 4th Division bombed northwards. Both Divisions thought this plan eminently reasonable. Even the fact that the 93rd Brigade had stated they would not be able to take part as they were fending off German counter-attacks on their own lines from the area which was to be the subject of these bombing attacks seems not have given any cause for thought. 4th Division was especially gung-ho, stating at 1.15 p.m. that two bombing parties were about to leave on this enterprise.

Of course, if one took the view, as did both Divisional HQs and Corps, that Serre, Pendant Copse and Munich Trench were all taken and that the only German troops in their forward areas were scattered bodies incapable of organised resistance, then these tactics made good sense. Almost all of the evidence from the attacking battalions, however, flatly contradicted this view of events. At 1 p.m. the battered remnants of the Battalion HQ of the Sheffields had left John Copse for Mark Copse. John Copse was too full of wounded to be manageable. When they reported this change of position they also reported to Brigade that that had had no contact with their leading waves. They were out there somewhere but no-one knew where or in what condition.

Meanwhile, the fictional counter-attacks on the 93rd Brigade's trenches were assuming extraordinary proportions. At 1.26 p.m. the CO of the 170th Brigade, RFA, forwarded the following to the Brigade Major of the Divisional Artillery:

> "2nd Lt. Reay reports from Bow Street our front line is now our old 3rd line (Legend Trench). Germans are now in our front line trenches. GOC 93rd Brigade asks me to bombard German front line. I am doing so with all batteries on zones for the front line wire."[110]

It seemed extremely timely that Division had just ordered two companies from the 92nd Brigade to bolster the 93rd Brigade's defences. Or perhaps not as, at 2.30 p.m., by which time it was clear to 93rd Brigade that the Germans were not, and never had been, venturing across No Man's Land, the rather irate Brigade Major of the Divisional Artillery was instructing 2nd Lt. Reay to:

> "… be careful about his reports as 93rd Brigade report that no Germans were seen to enter our trenches."[111]

With the fiction of enemy counter-attacks laid to rest, at least on the 31st Division's front, the Divisional Artillery now started to produce rather more accurate and sober assessments of the situation opposite Serre. By 2.45 p.m. they had caught up with the demise of the 18th West Yorkshires which had occurred several hours earlier. The picture their report painted of the position at the southern end of the Division's front was an unhappy one:

> "Divisional Artillery report 18th West Yorkshire have suffered severely. Col. Kennard killed. Our first line is thinly held and in a bad state. Legend, Bleneau and Flag blocked with wounded. Stretchers badly needed to enable these trenches to be cleared. King's Own and Warwicks (NB: from 4th Division) holding our front. King's Own have only about 200 men left. Trenches above mentioned are accurately barraged by 77mm and 15cm.
> Wire from 93rd Brigade: Will you please ask Heavy Artillery to keep down fire of enemy's batteries on our left, apparently Rossignol or perhaps rather east from there. These are worrying front line considerably."[112]

The awful realisation of the true state of affairs within the two Brigades of the Division appears to have struck home at VIII Corps soon after. Just after 3 p.m. orders were sent to 93rd Brigade to reorganise and to 'adopt a purely defensive attitude'. It was still thought possible that the remains of the 94th Brigade could mount another attack even though barely two hundred men were available for such an assault. And, in spite of 93rd Brigade being ordered onto the defensive, VIII Corps still believed this Brigade could spare men to support the 94th Brigade's attack. Having laid these plans they then consulted the two Brigadiers, Rees and Ingles. They were in no doubt as to the practicalities of any renewed attack and, at last, VIII Corps' report reflected this new reality:

> "After consulting with the Brigadiers of the 93rd and 94th Infantry Brigades, however, the divisional commander came to the conclusion that these two infantry brigades were not in a fit condition to undertake any further offensive operations owing to their heavy losses and disorganised condition."[113]

These Brigades might have been worn out but VIII Corps was still convinced that men of the 94th Brigade, indeed maybe as many as two battalions' worth, were still in Serre and still fighting. They were also certain that troops, whether of the 31st or 4th Division was not entirely clear, had reached and were holding Pendant Copse. This conviction would last the rest of the day and would very nearly lead to yet another disastrous waste of life as Hunter-Weston began to contemplate seriously the idea of a night attack in order to make contact with these supposedly 'cut-off' troops.

Back in the front lines desperate reorganisation was ongoing. Lt. Col. Rickman had withdrawn the two remaining Stokes mortars of the 92nd Trench Mortar Battery in Sap C and put them in emplacements in the front line on either side of the sap. The move was not without its problems and 2nd Lt. Hirst was hit several times by shrapnel as he supervised the movement of the guns and a Pte. Harrison was hit a short time after as he moved ammunition to the new positions. The sap itself was blocked by barricades. Rickman then visited as much of the front line as was still accessible or recognisable. The German artillery had flattened most of the trench and very few bays were defensible and the men had been withdrawn to Excema Trench between Matthew and Mark Copses. Rickman was aware that, on his right, the 93rd Brigade had pulled their men back from the exposed front line trenches and his men, along with the battalion HQ of the Sheffields in Mark Copse, were the only troops still occupying the British front line. Even that occupation was tenuous. Rickman had one officer, the slightly wounded Lt. Ryden, and 25 of his own battalion available along with some details from the Leeds Pioneers and about 30 men from the 13th York and Lancasters commanded by Capts. Currin and Gurney. Rickman had lost all contact with the rest of his battalion at 7.30 a.m. when they went over the top and, he now confirmed, the Sheffields' HQ was in the same position. They had no idea where the rest of the battalion had got to. It was to get worse. Just before 4 p.m. another German barrage crashed down on his positions driving all of his men from the front line and into Excema. Lt. Ryden was hit again, severely wounded in the lung, and his one remaining officer was gone[i] and two men from the 92nd Trench Mortar Battery, L/Cpl. Smith and Pte. Kirby, were wounded.

Rickman sent an urgent message back for more men:

> "I have 55 men in all, some of whom are wounded. 2 Lewis guns only. Two men to work them, one of them wounded. Pans filled by officer's servant."[114]

---

[i] Lt. Leonard Ryden survived the war and lived on until 1977. He was born in 1892 and had enlisted in September as 15056 Private in the Accrington Battalion, East Lancashire Regt. He was commissioned in January 1915. On recovering he was posted to the 3rd East Lancashire Regt. and the Labour Corps being demobbed in February 1919. He served with the Home Guard and the Special Constabulary during WW2.

As the afternoon drew on the battlefield began to fall silent except for the screams and groans coming from the hundreds of wounded scattered the length and width of No Man's Land. The 169th Brigade, RFA, reported that there was 'Hardly a man of either side to be seen anywhere'. The German artillery continued to fire at intervals with 77 mm, 10.5 cm and 15 cm shells coming from both the north east and south east and an observation balloon was slowly winched skywards somewhere near Puisieux in order to improve their observation over the British positions. Machine guns intermittently swept across the British front line. In the assembly trenches elements of the 92nd Brigade had begun to arrive, with a company of the 11th East Yorkshires being attached to the 18th DLI. They joined this battalion's remaining three companies and about 60 men from the 18th West Yorkshires in holding Dunmow, Maitland, Landguard and, subsequently, Legend Trenches some 700 yards behind the old front line.

Strange and unsubstantiated reports continued to come in. At 3.25 p.m. the 31st Division's Northern OP sent in a report from the officer in charge that, during a trip up the front line he had met a man from the Royal Warwickshires (from the 48th Division occupying the trenches to the north). This man insisted there was still fighting going on in the north east corner of Serre and that British troops could be seen 'swinging out to the left flank beyond Serre'. It is not at all clear what this man thought he was seeing. Indeed, it is not at all clear what he could have seen from British trenches some 20 metres below the height of the village. Nonetheless, reports such as this – vague, unreliable, uncorroborated – helped keep the idea alive that British troops were gallantly holding their own deep behind the German 1st position.

On the 93rd Brigade's front the 18th Durham Light Infantry were assuming control over the entire front. C Company was sent forward to man the front line trench but reported it 'blown out of existence' and piled high with casualties. They joined the remains of the various West Yorkshire battalions who had grimly sat out the German bombardment and made the best of the positions they had inherited, sending bombing parties into Saps A and B to defend against enemy incursions. A and B Companies settled down in Maitland Trench where they helped collect stragglers from the 18th and 16th West Yorkshires and here, during the evening, they were joined by Maj. Charles Wynn Tilly[i] and sixty men of the 10% reserve. Brigade instructed them to hold these positions during the night and be prepared for a German counter-attack. When it was confirmed that Lt. Col. Kennard had been killed, they sent forward Maj. Herbert Carter to take command of the 18th West Yorkshires[ii].

---

[i] Maj. later Lt. Col., Charles Wynn Tilly, 18th Durham Light Infantry att. 15th/17th West Yorkshire Regt., died on 14th April 1918. Aged 41, he was the son of Mr. and Mrs. T. H. Tilly, of Seaton Carew, West Hartlepool and the husband of Ruth Tilly, of 19, Lee Terrace, Blackheath, London. He was the Land Agent for the Membland Estate, Devon. His body was never found and he is remembered on the Ploegsteert Memorial. The 15th/17th West Yorkshire Regt. was formed when the 1st and 2nd Leeds Pals were amalgamated in December 1917.

[ii] Lt. Col. Herbert Francis George Carter, MC, King's Own Yorkshire Light Infantry, died of typhus on 28th February 1919 while fighting the Bolsheviks and is buried in the Churkin Russian Naval Cemetery, Vladivostok.

A quick count of the Durham battalion's casualties was made and, apart from D Company which had been attached to the Leeds Pals, this stood at five officers wounded, eleven other ranks killed and 126 other ranks wounded. Not bad for a battalion most of whose men hadn't gone beyond the assembly trenches until nearly eight hours after the attack started. Of D Company there was little news as yet. Four officers and seventeen other ranks were known to be wounded but it would be reported later that only ten men of the company had survived. The fate of the rest was unclear. When the dust settled, the total count was high: 13 officers and 239 other ranks were casualties, a 32% casualty rate of the 789 officers and men who had gone to the front on the evening of 30th June[i]. In D Company, however, this percentage casualty rate must have exceeded 90%.

Some 67 Privates and NCOs are recorded as dying on 1st July 1916 and one officer, 2nd Lt. Sidney Fitzgerald Bobby, attached to the 93rd Trench Mortar Battery, was killed during the morning. 19 year old 2nd Lt. George Kenneth Raine, died of his wounds on Sunday[ii]. Apart from 2nd Lt. J B Bradford, wounded while commanding the special bombing parties, and 2nd Lt. Thomas Milnes Harbottle[iii], no other details of the wounded are available, however, one officer, Lt. Hedworth Williamson Tait[iv], who had been lying out since the first few minutes of the attack, was brought in by 18/483 Sgt. Charles Cross during 3rd July. Cross was later given an inscribed watch by the grateful officer.

---

[i] By the time the battalion was withdrawn from the front line on 5th July it had lost 12 officers and, according to the war diary, some 60% of its Other Ranks.

[ii] 2nd Lt. George Kenneth Raine, 16th att. 18th Durham Light Infantry, was aged 19. He was the son of George and Elizabeth J. Raine, of 61, Percy Park, Tynemouth. He was educated at Tynemouth School and Epworth College, Rhyl. He was a member of the Durham University OTC. Commissioned in November 1914, he had previously been wounded at Hooge in September 1915 while serving with the 2nd Durham Light Infantry. He is buried in Gezaincourt Communal Cemetery Extension, grave I. A. 11.

[iii] Lt. Thomas Milnes Harbottle, CBE, MC, 18th Durham Light Infantry, born in August 1892. He was the son of Thomas Harbottle and Emma Townsley Milnes of Gosforth. He was educated at the Leys School and was a solicitor articled to R. S. Middleton of Sunderland. He enlisted as a Pte. in the 1/14th London Regt. (London Scottish) on 28th August 1914. He was promoted to Lance-Sergeant in December 1914. Commissioned into the 18th Batt. Durham Light Infantry on 14th January, 1915. He was promoted Lt. in July 1916 and transferred to the Royal Engineers in October 1916 serving with the 4th Field Survey Battalion. Awarded the MC. He married Marion Learmount and their daughter, Barbara (b. 1931) worked on the Official History of the Second World War.

[iv] Lt. Hedworth Williamson Tait, 18th Durham Light Infantry, went on to join the RFC and the RAF. He was commissioned on 26th November 1914. He transferred to the Balloon Section, RFC on 17th May 1917. He was awarded the DFC and the Croix de Guerre avec Palme whilst serving with the 11th Balloon Section. On 20th February 1939 he was appointed Squadron Leader and given command of No. 937 (County of Northumberland) Squadron. He was promoted Wing Commander, Balloon Branch, Auxiliary Air Force, in September 1940. He resigned his commission in 1943. He married Dorothy Neville Tait and their son, 1165238 Leading Aircraftman Richard Neville Tait, died on 23rd December 1940 and is buried in Boldon Cemetery in Whitburn where they lived.

WHEN HE ARRIVED, MAJ. CARTER WENT ROUND the forward areas to see who else of the 18th West Yorkshires he could find. The major went round Grey, Bradford, Monk and East Bleneau Trenches as well as Nos. 1, 2 and 3 Posts and A Sap. Except for some wounded there was no-one there. Basically the entire frontal zone of the 93rd Brigade had been abandoned to the dead and wounded. Further back, another two companies of the 92nd Brigade were trying to get forward to support the 93rd. At 4.33 p.m. their Brigade HQ telephoned Division to tell them they were unable to move such was the press of men in the old assembly trenches. They were told to stand fast while attempts were made to reorganise the confused and leaderless men in the trenches and to evacuate the hundreds of wounded who were walking, staggering, limping and being carried to the Advanced Dressing Station at Euston.

Amongst the men adrift in the wreckage of the trenches was Sgt. Maj. Cussins of the 16th West Yorkshires. Since his various trips between the two Brigade HQs he had devoted his time to collecting men from his battalion in Sackville Street. When the rumours of the German attacks across No Man's Land spread during the afternoon he was ordered to take his small group of men to Legend Trench, near to the 93rd Brigade HQ. After 'standing to' for two hours waiting for some Germans to appear he was ordered to take 'the battalion' forward to Dunmow. During the wait he conducted a quick head count and found that 'the battalion' now consisted of some 50 men with no officers and no NCOs above the rank of Lance Corporal. He was pleasantly surprised when some officers and NCOs of the 10% reserve arrived just before the short trip down to Dunmow. Amongst them were Capt. Henry Richard Watling, Lt. Geoffrey Armitage[i] and 2nd Lt. Burnley. By the time Maj. Humfrey Hayes Kennedy[ii], Seaforth Highlanders attached 16th West Yorkshire Regt., arrived to take command, at about 7.30 p.m., Watling and the others had managed to round up another 70 men and the battalion was found to comprise just 20% of the number who had gone into action twelve hours earlier.

BY NOW, THE ONLY FIGHTING ON THE VIII CORPS front was around the Heidenkopf on the 4th Division's front where men of the 2nd Seaforths and half a dozen other battalions were desperately holding out against increasing German counter-attacks. Some of these were led by elements of the 11. Kompanie, IR

---

[i] Capt. Geoffrey Ambler Armitage, 16th West Yorkshire Regt., died on 27th February 1917. Aged 30, he was the son of the late Mr. and Mrs. George Armitage, of Bradford and the husband of Grace L. Armitage, of 14, Chatsworth Avenue, Wembley Hill, Middx. He was commissioned into the battalion on 21st December 1914. He is buried in Owl Trench Cemetery, Hebuterne, Row B.

[ii] Maj. Humfrey Hayes Kennedy, Seaforth Highlanders att. 16th West Yorkshire Regt., was appointed 2iC on 3rd December 1915. He was promoted Temp. Lt. Col. on taking command on 2nd July having commanded the battalion for three months before the arrival of Maj. Guyon. He relinquished his rank and command on 30th January 1917. He took temporary command of a battalion in October 1917 and again in May 1918. Pre-war he was seconded to the Colonial Office and was attached to the Nigeria Regt., West African Frontier Force. He died on 29th July 1918. Lt. Col. Humfrey Hayes Kennedy, 2nd att. 8th Seaforth Highlanders, was aged 36 and was the husband of Mrs H. H. Kennedy, of Inholmes, Dorking, Surrey. He is buried in Raperie British Cemetety, Villemontoire.

169, which had been diverted away from the 31st Division's front to assist their comrades in the RIR 121. Further planned attacks by the 4th Division had failed to materialise as the full scale of the disaster on the 29th Division's front became apparent and it was found that this Division was incapable of any further offensive action. The Seaforths and the remnants of the other battalions which had attacked Redan Ridge were now very much on their own.

At 4.07 p.m. the VIII Corps war diary recorded the reports of an R.F.C. observer whose BE2c had flown the entire length of the Corps front from the Ancre to beyond Serre some 90 minutes earlier. The report plainly showed that the German troops occupied almost their entire front line except for the Heidenkopf and that no British troops were to be seen in the distant positions of Serre, Pendant Copse, Munich Trench and Beaucourt:

> "2:30 p.m. Line River Ancre to Hawthorn Redoubt occupied by German sentry groups.
> 2:33 p.m. German front-line West of Beaumont Hamel very weakly occupied, apparently by Germans. Crater at Hawthorn redoubt occupied on West edge by British troops. Crater a very large one.
> 2:45 p.m. From Frontier Lane end trenches parallel as far as point 94 occupied by small parties thought to be British. Flare seen K.35.c.5.8. (NB: Heidenkopf). Troops in trench from points 77, 92, 55 occupied by small detachments of Germans. Quadrilateral occupied by British.
> 2:50 p.m. Serre apparently unoccupied. Line also unoccupied round here including Munich trench. Pendant Trench at point 72 unoccupied. Trenches between Serre and Mark Copse occupied by small parties of the enemy. No troops visible in Beaumont Hamel. No big movement in communication trenches. Aeroplane was constantly fired at along this line (returned with 40 holes in). Was not fired at over Serre."[115]

Extraordinarily, in spite of this detailed and depressing statement of affairs, VIII Corps still had space to include more unverifiable but optimistic reports in its account, perhaps because they had not, or could not, grasp the scale of the disaster that had befallen its three Divisions:

> "4:27 p.m. 31st Division report East Lancashires are still in Serre. Durhams did not get to Pendant Copse but some of the 4th Division did. Information obtained from a man who has been carrying bombs and has just returned."[116]

Obviously, this unidentified informant could not have 'just returned' from taking bombs to both Serre and Pendant Copse, so how was he supposed to know these details? He could not. Indeed, he had not returned from either place but had, perhaps, picked up some hearsay on the way, at best, to deliver some bombs to men of the 4th Division still holding on in or near to the Heidenkopf. And yet the report is deemed worthy of an entry in the VIII Corps war diary. Wishful thinking was clearly preferable to hard facts amongst Hunter-Weston and his staff.

By 5 p.m. the field guns were reduced to taking pot shots at any Germans foolish enough to show their heads above the parapet. The 165th and 170th Brigades, RFA, both record some success engaging small groups of the enemy on their front and 2nd line parapets. Other members of the Royal Field Artillery were less gainfully employed as, at about 5.08 p.m., the FOO of C/171 Battery reported that there were 'still indications of our forces having joined up beyond Serre'. The trouble was, such reports were still believed at Division and Corps.

At 5.20 p.m. Maj. Gen. Wanless-O'Gowan spoke to Brig. Gen. Rees of 94th Brigade. The Major General wanted to know what arrangements were being made with Brig. Gen. Ingles, GOC 93rd Brigade, to:

> "… bomb the Germans out of the first line German trenches so as to establish communication with our troops in Serre."[117]

Wanless-O'Gowan offered Rees two battalions of the 92nd Brigade to renew the attack. He also promised the support of an entire Brigade of the 48th Division to support the operation. According to Division, Rees voiced the opinion that any advance should be made be entirely fresh troops and his superior told him he would speak to Hunter-Weston and get back to him. Writing later, Rees insisted that, when asked whether renewing the attack with the 92nd Brigade was a good idea, he had answered with a definite 'no'. Whatever the truth of the matter, the idea of another attack aimed directly at Serre was still very definitely on the Corps' agenda.

At 6 p.m. Wanless-O'Gowan spoke to Hunter-Weston on the telephone. The Major General then gave his superior a very fair assessment of the state of affairs on his Division's front and one which seems to support Brig. Gen. Rees' post-battle contention that he opposed any attack by the 92nd Brigade:

> "I have had a long talk with Gen. Rees who has had a consultation with Gen. Ingles and they are both of the opinion that neither of the Brigades are in a fit state to make any further effort. Gen. Rees says that he watched his attack today and that the first three lines went over excellently and then they got it rather stiff. He also says that at present it is his opinion that there are very few, if any, men left on the other side of the enemy's line and that the men who got over are probably killed or captured by now. He thinks that in Serre they are either killed or captured and he is very strong on this point and I have had my signalling people trying to get in communication but cannot get any sign at all. They have got a very good view now – neither of the Brigades are fit to fight and I should like to put it up that the 92nd Brigade should hold the line. We shall have to get the line in order in case of counter attack. If we are to make an attack I think we shall have to do it with 2 new Brigades and a proper preparation tomorrow. We shall have to clear the whole of the area and it would stop any attack at present being launched. Gen. Rees is perfectly certain that any who got over there are either killed or captured by now. If we could hold the line tonight with 92nd Brigade we will see if we can push across raids. I cannot get any information at all about strong point at A. Observation Officer says that the light is good. If we are going to attack it must be regularly done by 2 Brigades. I have only got about 3 companies and they have been shelled this afternoon rather badly and they are in a shaky condition. I have got my 92nd Brigade intact. If we do make an attack there will have to be a proper preparation. We shall probably want a heavier attack than the 92nd Brigade going in. Of course

> now is the best time to see. We have the light behind us. I want to get the remnants of the two Brigades out and we cannot do that until after dark. We shall have to clear the place. A lot of men holding the trenches now are wounded. There are only a few hundred men. 94th Brigade certainly weak."[118]

In spite of this *very* fair and accurate assessment of the conditions on the ground his Corps commander knew better. Hunter-Weston immediately ordered a night time attack by two battalions of the 92nd Brigade:

> "… with a view to clearing up the situation."[119]

Orders to this effect were issued to 31st Division at 6.20 p.m. and passed to a, no doubt, incredulous Rees:

> "The front line is to be held by Lewis guns and the trenches are to be cleared. The 92nd Brigade will attack with 2 battalions; one battalion with its left on John Copse which will advance on Serre and then form a defensive flank facing north. One battalion will advance south of Luke Copse with its right on Serre Road and form a defensive flank facing southwards. One separate company in the centre is to clear up the situation by going along communication trench opposite one of the tunnels."[120]

But, of course. Throwing away another two battalions should just about put the icing on the cake but what, in Hunter-Weston's own words, did he care for casualties? And Hunter-Weston's justification for this extraordinary decision? That he had been told that the Germans were firing shrapnel at Serre. There are no other reports at this time suggesting any such thing.

At 7 p.m. Wanless-O'Gowan was the lucky recipient of a visit from the Brig. Gen., VIII Corps General Staff. He was there to make arrangements for the attack of the 92nd Brigade which, it had been decided, should go ahead in more or less pitch darkness at 2 a.m. on the 2nd July[i].

BACK IN THE REAL WORLD the work of reorganisation, clearance and evacuation went on. The 13th York and Lancasters sent up some of C Company to relieve the survivors of A Company in what passed for the front line. It was estimated that the battalion strength had been reduced to some 280 men of all ranks. In that front line, Capt. Currin had already set to the task of rescuing and evacuating the wounded which would eventually help earn him his DSO.

All along the front line the able bodied and the wounded waited for the light to fade so that the job of evacuation of the wounded could start in earnest. For the time being, the stretcher bearers were mainly occupied clearing the rear trenches and the sections of communication trench away from the front lines. Around the Sucrerie crossroads and near to the Euston ADS crowds of wounded had built up and it was essential they were moved as quickly as possible.

The 92nd Trench Mortar Battery, still in place around Sap C, had found the sap crowded with infantry when they arrived in the early hours before the attack. Now it was crammed with wounded sheltering from the intermittent shelling of

---

[i] Sunrise on the Somme would have been just after 4 a.m. GMT.

the enemy. Injured men sought shelter behind any scrap of cover they could find and the chorus of shrieks and groans coming from this mass of men must have been distressing and unnerving for those still manning the forward areas. With little else to do the men of the 92nd TMB helped the stretcher bearers move the wounded. Such was the congestion that an order for the Battery to place four guns in Uriah Trench in readiness for Hunter-Weston's 2 a.m. attack did not reach them and, rather more usefully, the spare men were used to barricade and guard the entrances to the sap with sandbags in case some enterprising Germans used it as cover to attack the British front lines.

There were still reports coming in of German snipers shooting the wounded in No Man's Land and A/171 Battery was given the task of dispersing one particularly active group of German riflemen. Otherwise, the tasks of the artillery were reduced to firing at long range in an attempt to disrupt the movements of enemy troops which could be seen about Puisieux and Bucquoy. When darkness proper fell they would return to firing on the night lines employed over the previous seven nights.

Reports gradually filtered back as to the status of the battalions in the front line. At 8.21 p.m. the 12th York and Lancasters replied to an enquiry from Brigade about its current strength and supplies. The response must have shocked the Staff officers who received it:

> "Strength of Battalion – 10 men unwounded. These are runners and Signallers. Have no Lewis Guns. 3000 S.A.A., 350 Bombs. Lewis pans – nil."[121]

Twenty minutes later more information came in to Division from the battalions of the 94th Brigade and from the 18th West Yorkshires. The numbers of men available for defence of the front line were pathetic:

11th East Lancashires – 'about 30 all ranks'.
12th York and Lancasters – '3 officers and 6 other ranks'.
13th York and Lancasters – 'about 250 all ranks'.
14th York and Lancasters – 'about 350 all ranks'.

The total of just under 640 men for the entire Brigade was less than the strength of a single battalion just before 7.30 a.m.

The 18th West Yorkshires had managed to rally six officers and 120 other ranks from amongst a battalion that had not got close to the German trenches. The majority of the men – dead, wounded and missing – lay behind the British front lines. One of the six officers, Lt. Walter Peace, had been wounded twice earlier in the day but had collected a small group of men around him and together they had held the front line under the constant German barrage. Now he was looking so ill that Maj. Carter ordered him to return to Bus-les-Artois for treatment[i].

---

[i] Lt. Walter Peace, 18th West Yorkshire Regt., was awarded the MC for his conduct on 1st July 1916. The citation in the *London Gazette* of the 20th October 1916 reads: "For conspicuous gallantry and devotion to duty in attack. Although twice wounded in the early morning, he still held on to a portion of our front line trench with a small party of men for the rest of the day, being completely isolated." He was commissioned into the 18th West

A report at 9.20 a.m. from Lt. Col. Rickman underlined just how thin were the defences directly opposite the Germans:

> "As regards numbers I have at present 58 men including Stokes Mortars and HQ.
> I have also 1 officer and 25 men 18th West Yorks holding 3 posts in 93 area. 1 and 2 posts opposite Warley Avenue. Then there is a gap until you come to Capt. Gurney who holds 4 posts immediately south of Sap C. I have one post between Sap C and Mark Copse.
> There are no Lewis or MGuns in line."[122]

It would be his last report of the day. Twenty minutes later a shell exploded nearby and Lt. Col. Rickman was badly concussed and affected by shell shock. As he was taken to the rear, his 2iC, Maj. Edward Reiss[i] took command of the pathetic remains of the Accrington Pals.

As the evening drew on and the light faded a light mist added to the eeriness of the scene. Behind the nearly empty front lines, men of the 92nd Brigade were trying to work their way up the communication trenches behind John and Luke Copses in order to be ready for the 2 a.m. attack. Their orders had arrived at 9 p.m. and one can only guess at the thoughts of the men as they made their way through the carnage of the trenches towards the front. At 9.30 p.m. four officers of the 92nd Brigade arrived at the 93rd Brigade HQ. They were reporting with regards to finding places in the assembly trenches for the men following on behind. As the attack was due to take place on the 94th Brigade's front this appears somewhat strange. No matter, at 9.35 p.m., as far as 31st Division was concerned, this attack was still on, but this was about to change. Even as the 92nd Brigade advanced, a conference was taking place at VIII Corps HQ between Hunter-Weston, Beauvoir de Lisle and Fanshawe of the 48th Division. Fanshawe was involved because an attack by men of his Division was due to take place on the 29th Division's front the following day. Their discussion was clearly more wide-ranging than just the situation at Beaumont Hamel and, at 9.45 p.m., and much to everyone's relief, the decision was made to cancel the 2 a.m. attack by the 92nd Brigade.

There would still be one advance by some poor souls north of the Ancre in the middle of the night but it would involve the 1/5th Lincolns of the 46th Division, VII Corps, at Gommecourt where there was a similar, if even more far-fetched, belief that British troops were trapped in the German lines. The Lincolns initially lined up facing the wrong way, then got caught up on the German wire and lost two officers killed and one wounded and 11 other ranks killed and 34

Yorkshire Regt., on 24th May 1915. Promoted Major, he relinquished his commission in 1920.

[i] Major Edward Leopold Reiss, 11th East Lancashire Regt., was born in Manchester in 1869. He was the son of James Edward and Jane Francis Reiss of Greenbank, Pendleton. He was commissioned into the 3rd Cheshire Regt. (Militia) in 1888. Trasnsferred to the 6th Dragoon Guards (Carabiniers) on 28th June 1890. Promoted Captain in 1897. Adjutant, 1st Yeomanry Brigade (Berkshire & Middlesex), 1899. Adjutant, Middlesex (Duke of Cambridge's) Imperial Yeomanry, 1901. He retired in 1905. Appointed Adjutant, 4th Western Depot, December 1914. Promoted Major and joined 11th East Lancashire Regt. on 9th November 1915.

wounded in a few chaotic minutes in front of trenches packed with alert and heavily armed Germans. One can but imagine the consequences of sending out two battalions in front of Serre in pitch darkness. It beggars belief that it should even have been considered. But then, much of what happened north of the River Ancre on 1st July 1916 beggars belief.

There was now some debate between Corps and Division about the use of the 92nd Brigade. With the two attacking Brigades reduced to the numbers of two battalions, estimates were that 93rd Brigade could call on 800 men and 94th Brigade 636, Division was concerned at the weakness of the front line. Corps, on the other hand, with plans afoot to use the 48th Division to attack on the 2nd July in the 29th Division's sector, wanted to keep 92nd Brigade available, basically as a Corps reserve. Consequently, Hunter-Weston ordered the Brigade not only to cancel the night attack but to withdraw their men from the 'shelled area' in order to protect them. In practice, this meant withdrawing the 92nd Brigade all the way back to Bus-les-Artois and possibly further. This order was transmitted to Lt. Col. Baumgartner, GSO1 of 31st Division by Capt. Dobbie, GSO2 VIII Corps at 10.35 p.m. Baumgartner explained the weakness of the front line, basically a paper thin crust with no substance to back it up, and Dobbie replied that these facts were 'quite understood' at Corps.

In the intervening period, a report came to the attention of 31st Division at 10 p.m. which, had it been known even thirty minutes earlier, might well have resulted in the 92nd Brigade's attack order being confirmed rather than cancelled. The report came by telephone from the 48th Division who advised 31st Division that a wounded sergeant of an unidentified battalion of the York and Lancasters had been brought into their lines. This man told them that 150 men of the York and Lancasters, presumably the Sheffields, were holding out in the German front line at point K.29.b.4.7., a section of trenches projecting slightly out into No Man's Land opposite Mark Copse. At the same time as this message was received an order had gone out to the Sheffields to withdraw what little was left of the battalion from the front line to Rolland Trench, their place being taken by the remains of the 13th and 14th York and Lancasters. At 10.15 p.m. the Sheffield's HQ made its way to a deep sap off Rolland Trench. Sometime later, the timing is not specific, the information about the 150 men in the German lines was passed to them with the curious instruction that:

> "Every endeavour was to be made to get into touch with them and withdraw them."[123]

Quite what a battalion of less than 50 men now some 900 yards behind the British front line was to do about this is a question only 31st Division's commander and staff can answer.

Of course, Sod's Law, anything that can go wrong will go wrong (which had been operating in over-drive throughout the day on VIII Corps front) meant that by the time this report came through it was too dark and too misty to see anything several hundred yards away. There are, however, no reports of the sounds and sights of fighting coming from this section of German trench, unlike at the Heidenkopf where the Germans were doing their level best to retrieve the last bit of their territory north of the Ancre still in British hands. Here German artillery was still active up to and beyond midnight and nearly all enemy activity reported by 31st Division during the night was to the right of their positions, i.e. on the 4th Division's front. Except for this, the majority of 31st Division's reports described the situation as either 'normal' or 'quiet'.

Division was keen, however, to check the report of British troops in the German lines and, at 1.30 a.m. on Sunday, 2nd July, two officer patrols of one officer and six other ranks from the 14th York and Lancasters under Capt. Lembridge and Lt. Henry Oxley, 12th York and Lancasters (who was slightly wounded during the patrol), were sent into the charnel house of No Man's Land to see what they could find out. They were specifically instructed to get as close to the German lines as possible in the area where the 150 men were supposed to be. The two patrols were out for 90 minutes, creeping around under some very heavy local fire, and came back with a report which stated:

"No indications of occupation other than German."[124]

The patrols also brought in some wounded men who said that any men who had got into the German lines had become casualties until no further resistance was possible. With that, one might have thought that the stories of British troops trapped in the German lines near Serre would have withered and died. Amazingly, they still did not.

Ten hours later, at 11.39 a.m. on the morning of the 2nd July, VIII Corps sent a wire to 31st Division once again reviving the idea that there were still troops in Serre and Pendant Copse. For some reason which this writer cannot explain, they wanted someone in 31st Division to drop off to them some messenger pigeons housed in a loft a Bus-les-Artois. There is no explanation what they planned to use them for. Dinner, perhaps, washed down with a nice drop of Nuits Saint Georges[i].

In the intervening period a message arrived at 31st Division's HQ which must have done a lot to raise dampened spirits. Timed at 8.52 a.m. it read:

> "Well done my comrades of the 31st Division. Your discipline and determination were magnificent and it was bad luck alone that has temporarily robbed you of success."[125]

Perhaps the man responsible for the message truly believed that it was just a spot of 'bad luck' which had robbed the Division of success and so many men of their lives. But then, Lt. Gen. Hunter-Weston always had been an unreconstructed optimist for whom every major setback was just a minor hiccup on the road to ultimate success to be greeted with a hearty slap on the back and some absurd quote plucked from his treasury of mindless platitudes.

Assessments were now coming about the condition of the trenches and the amount of work that was required to clear them of dead, wounded and debris and then rebuild those either badly damaged or completely flattened. 94th Brigade's assessment was that trenches as far back as Monk needed some serious work as did the four main communication trenches – Nairne Trench and Northern, Railway and Central Avenues in the area between Monk and the front

---

[i] There is an instance of a pigeon being used on the 31st Division's front on 1st July. The 14th York and Lancasters sent one off to Divisional HQ which arrived at 4.01 p.m. The message was nothing very useful: 'unable to send any reliable information at present'. No award for the pigeon's bravery appears in the *London Gazette*.

line trench system. One trench, Rob Roy, 200 yards behind the three northern copses, had long since been abandoned. The report went on to say that any digging and consolidation work going on was being hindered by the large numbers of wounded needing evacuation and dead who required burial. Already helping with this latter work were some men of the 10th East Yorkshires of the 92nd Brigade left behind when the rest withdrew.

The report of the 93rd Brigade was rather slower in arriving, indeed it did not arrive at Division until nine hours after the 94th Brigade's report at 2.30 a.m. It described the forwards areas as devastated:

> "Front line with exception of about 50 yards south of Warley is nearly destroyed. Leeds Trench is the same. Monk Trench is badly blown in south of Bleneau. North of Bleneau being used. Bradford nearly destroyed. Dunmow, Landguard, Maitland, Legend and Sackville Street all fairly good are being improved and fire stepped. Communication trenches fair except near first line where all are nearly obliterated. Little work done last night."[126]

Little work was possible because every available man was dealing with the wounded and the dead.

MEDICAL SERVICES WERE SUPPLIED by the 93rd, 94th and 95th Field Ambulances. Col. Alfred William Bewley[i], the ADMS of the 31st Division, had decided upon the following distribution of the resources available to him:

93rd Field Ambulance

A Tent sub-division at the Divisional Rest Station at Sarton;

B and C Tent sub-divisions packed and ready to move at short notice from Sarton;

Bearer sub-division in reserve at Colincamps.

94th Field Ambulance

A Tent sub-division at the Main Dressing Station (MDS) at Bus, B sub-division at the Advanced Dressing Station (ADS) at Colincamps and C sub-division at the ADS at Euston;

Bearer sub-division to remove wounded from 94th Brigade front to ADS, Euston.

95th Field Ambulance

Tent sub-divisions: A and B at MDS, Bus, and C at reserve MDS at the camp in Warnimont Wood;

Bearer sub-division to remove wounded from 93rd Brigade front to ADS, Euston.

71 Sanitary Section in reserve at Bus.

---

[i] Col. Alfred William Bewley, CMG, Royal Army Medical Corps, was born in 1866 at Stillorgan, Rathdown, Dublin, the son of Alfred Bewley. Private education and the Royal College of Surgeons in Dublin. Resident medical officer, National Children's Hospital, Dublin. Capt., 1890. Chitral campaign, 1895 (medal and clasp). Major, 1902. Lt. Col., 1913. Deputy Assistant Director of Medical Services, Northern Command, 1914. Colonel, 1915. MiD three times. CMG, 1917. Retired 1919. He died in 1939.

There was to be a reserve supply of stretchers at the two ADS with fifty kept at Euston and another twenty at Colincamps. In addition, there was motor transport in the form of four Siddeley-Deasy motor ambulances[i] and one Ford.

The plan was for the lightly wounded to be evacuated by reserve motor ambulance, horse-drawn ambulances or GS wagons to Acheux. The more seriously wounded would be processed through the ADS to the MDS and then beyond to the more comprehensive medical services arrayed back towards the Channel ports from where men would be evacuated back to England.

Col. Bewley, perhaps fearing that casualties might be heavier than some estimated, had made an arrangement with the Deputy Acting Adjutant and Quartermaster General (DAA+QMG) of VIII Corps for some emergency stretcher bearers to be made available but, rather at the last minute, i.e. 30th June, the DAA+QMG advised that the men were not available. One assumes that Bewley had hoped for 100 extra bearers as 50 improvised stretchers had been made by 93rd FA for their use. He managed, at least, to get these returned for use by the 31st Division's bearers.

At 6 a.m. on the morning of the 1st July ten motor ambulances from No. 20 Motor Ambulance Convoy (No. 20 MAC) reported for duty. They were barely in time as wounded were already coming in from the assembly trenches as the German artillery started to pound the British positions.

The evacuation process was this:

Severely wounded men were taken by bearers to dugouts at Euston where they were treated, labelled, fed and watered (if appropriate, which it was not for stomach and abdomen wounds) and then sent on by motor ambulance to the MDS at Bus;

Walking wounded received first aid and were then directed to the ADS at Colincamps. Here the same process applied before they were sent on by horsed ambulances and GS wagons to the MDS and from there to the Corps Collecting Station at Acheux.

The most immediate problem for Bewley and the Field Ambulances was a shortage of medical officers. Three had been evacuated sick just prior to the attack and two more ordered to No. 4 Casualty Clearing Station on 28th June. Another, the AQM, had been left seriously ill in Port Said earlier in the year and never replaced. Bewley had sent a telegram to the Director General Medical Services on 29th June asking for three RAMC officers and a QM to be hurried to the 31st Division but they had not yet arrived. To make matters worse, two medical officers were wounded during the day, Lt. Lawrence Ingle, 95th FA, and Capt. J W N Roberts att. 11th East Lancashires, and it was necessary to replace them and wire for substitutes.

On the 94th Brigade's front, Capts. Fraser and King with three bearer sections were available to clear the trenches while Capt. Walker and Lt. Blackmore were in reserve with 14 bearers of B Section. On the 93rd Brigade's front Capt. Cecil McLaren West and Lt. Lawrence Mansfield Ingle were at the ADS at Euston and when Ingle was wounded he was replaced by Lt. Joseph Vincent Duffy, the MO

[i] The Siddeley-Deasy Motorcar Company Ltd. of Coventry merged with Sir W G Armstrong-Whitworth & Co Ltd Motor Car Department in 1919 to form The Armstrong-Siddeley Co Ltd.

of the Royal Engineers of the 29th Division. At the MDS were Capt. G Mitchell and Lt. Arthur Graham Winter of the 95th FA along with Lt. Herbert Wales of the 94th FA. Capt. W Hunt, of the 95th FA, oversaw the overflow MDS in Warnimont Wood. Additional help came in the form of Lt. Thompson of the 71st Sanitary Section, Lt. Craig, MO of the Divisional Ammunition Column and Lt. Johnson, MO of the RE and from 93rd FA when Capt. J R Humphreys and Lt. Charles Evelyn Meryon with 110 rank and file arrived at Bus from Sarton.

Back at Sarton, the 93rd FA had occupied the cinema theatre, the Café de la Place and the Curés presbytery. The cinema was converted into a large dressing station accommodating about 50 cases. The Café de la Place was utilised as an inspection room and in an emergency could accommodate about 20 cases. The Curés presbytery was converted into officers' accommodation which contained medical stores, an operating theatre and two officers' wards.

Very quickly, as the casualties poured in, seven of the nine bearer sections were committed to action with the seventh to be sent down to the trenches from Colincamps ordered to clear Legend, Flag and Bleneau trenches which were crowded with wounded. One of the problems for the stretcher bearers was that, technically, the two 'down' trenches on the 93rd Brigade's front did not reach all the way to the rear around Euston where the first large scale medical facilities were located[i]. To reach them, the bearers had to haul their heavy loads down Grey and Bleneau Trenches as far as Sackville Street where they then had to turn right and struggle towards Red Cottage. Just south of Red Cottage two long communication trenches, Jordan and Cateau, cut across Sackville Street and, along with the western end of Excema, these were the designated 'down' trenches for the 31st Division. All of them lay behind the 94th Brigade front. The walking wounded, of course, failed to adhere to the intended discipline of the 'up' and 'down' trenches. They poured down whichever west-bound communication trench was available where they met these extra bearers as well as carrying parties and others trying to get to the front line. The resulting chaos slowed everyone, whatever their reason for using the communication trenches.

By 4 p.m. there was a danger that the system at Euston might be overwhelmed such were the crowds waiting for treatment and so three motor lorries were sent up to evacuate the slightly wounded direct to the Divisional Rest Station (DRS) at Acheux. VIII Corps helped out too when the DDMS sent down a motor bus to help clear the slight cases.

By 9 p.m. the two front line field ambulances had admitted:

94th FA Officers 47, ORs 634

95th FA ORs 538

A total of 47 officers and 1,172 other ranks of whom 905 had been evacuated. There were, however, hundreds of men still to be evacuated from the front line areas and No Man's Land.

By 6 a.m. on the 2nd July the totals admitted had nearly doubled. 63 officers and 2,103 Other Ranks were admitted in the 24 hours from 6 a.m. on the 1st July and 1,847 had been evacuated. Twenty five of the wounded had gone on the

[i] The only full length communication trench on the 93rd Brigade front was Southern Avenue which was an 'up' trench which ran from Euston, ran just south of La Signy Farm and Basin Wood, ending at front line just south of Matthew Copse.

motor bus direct to No. 29 CCS at Doullens at 6 a.m. and that was the last they saw of this vehicle. It was reported 'missing' at 8 p.m. During the day several additional Casualty Clearing Stations were added to the number dealing with VIII Corps' casualties with No. 19 CCS at Doullens being the first tasked with dealing with the overflow of seriously wounded men. Next Nos. 3 and 44 CCS at Puchevillers were opened and finally two Third Army CCS, Nos. 19 and 41 in Doullens, had to be given over to dealing with the enormous flow of injured.

Most of the rest of the day was spent removing the wounded and getting ready to bury those of the dead who were accessible. The majority of the bodies in No Man's Land would have to wait until the following Spring when the Germans withdrew to their new positions along the Hindenburg Line. The British could, at least, be grateful that, on most days, the prevailing wind would blow the stench of the dead across the German lines rather over theirs.

Almost as if to ensure that there could be no local ceasefires to allow for the removal of the dead and wounded, two special bombardments of the German lines were organised for the 2nd July, one at 3.30 pm. and another at 6.30 p.m. Such bombardments inevitably invited a response and, apart from any of the wounded who may have been finished off during the exchange, C Company, 18th Durham LI, was hit losing two officers wounded, one Other Rank killed[i] and another nine wounded. 2nd Lt. William Bell died of his wounds the following day[ii]. In spite of their losses C Company managed to bring in 40 wounded men, mainly from the 16th West Yorkshires, by the middle of the evening.

The rest of Sunday and Monday was less hectic with another 16 officers and 465 men being admitted in the 24 hours up to 6 a.m. on Monday. 405 of these had also been evacuated. The missing bus was also located. Its driver had independently decided to return it to Corps HQ. Even though the workload was easing, Bewley was relieved when three new medical officers, Lt. Robert Leighton Blenkhorm, Lt. H B Stackpoole and Lt. Alexander Wilson Frew arrived on the 3rd. Blenkhorn and Stackpoole were posted to the 95th FA and Frew to the 94th.

By the 4th July the crisis was over, though wounded would be brought in or would crawl in from No Man's Land for several more days. Most of the exhausted bearer sub-divisions were withdrawn from the front line trenches and the job of re-building the defences could now proceed.

This simple description of the medical services of the 31st Division pays scant regard to the work done at the sharp end by the battalion MOs and orderlies, stretcher bearers and ordinary officers and men of the infantry battalions that had been hit so hard. Every unit had its tales to tell of unrecognised heroes who saved the lives of their comrades as well as those few men who feats were given official recognition with a medal.

---

[i] 18/686 L/Cpl. Thomas Baggott, 18th Durham Light Infantry, was aged 38. He was the husband of Mary E. Baggott, of 69, Southwick Rd., Monkwearmouth, Sunderland. His body was never found and his name is inscribed on the Thiepval Memorial, Pier & Face 14 A & 15 C.

[ii] 2nd Lt. William Bell, 18th Durham Light Infantry, died of wounds on 3rd July 1916. Aged 27, he was the son of John and Margaret Bell of West Farm, Medomsley, Co. Durham. He was commissioned out of the OTC on 21st April 1915. He is buried in Beauval Communal Cemetery, grave A. 11.

With the Sheffields, this roll of honour runs from the Adjutant, Capt. Norman Leslie Tunbridge, to the Medical Officer, Lt. Edward Cunnington to ordinary Privates, all of whom worked tirelessly to help the wounded. Capt. Tunbridge worked indefatigably between 1st and 4th July carrying out both his duties as Adjutant and in assisting the injured. On the night of July 1st-2nd he volunteered to take out a party into No Man's Land in search of wounded and brought in several men. As the senior officer still standing he also had to undertake the work of ensuring the trenches were manned whilst he also kept up the morale and organisation of the few men left to the battalion. Lt. Edward Cunnington, RAMC, spent three days and nights dressing the wounded. Each night he went out into the British wire to bring in wounded lying there, in the process exposing himself to artillery and machine gun fire[i].

Plate 164 Capt. Norman Leslie Tunbridge, 12th York and Lancaster Regt.

12/233 Pte. John Skidmore, an orderly attached to Battalion Headquarters in Mark Copse, collected and assisted wounded men in the front line and in the Sap that became the collecting point for many of the wounded. He worked continuously for 36 hours and helped keep alive twelve severely wounded men until they could receive medical attention.

Going forward with the 1st wave, 12/1376 Pte. Robert Gorrill arrived at the German wire which was uncut and impossible to get through. He took shelter in a shell hole with five other men, one of whom was seriously wounded. Their bolt hole had been spotted, however, by a German bomber who tried to finish them off with his grenades. Gorrill stood in the open and shot the man. After night fell, Gorrill persuaded the unwounded men to go back to the British lines telling

---

[i] Capt. Edward Charles Cunnington, RAMC, 95th Field Ambulance, was killed on 23rd March 1918. Aged 27, he was the only child of Captain Benjamin Howard Cunnington of 33, Long Street, Devizes, and the husband of Maud Edith Cunnington. Educated at Reading and Cambridge. A student at St. Bartholomew's Hospital. He is buried in Cabaret-Rouge British Cemetery, Souchez.

them he would follow on. Instead he stayed with the severely wounded man for three days and nights before being forced to look for help[i].

Another man to stay at the front for three days and nights was 12/727 Pte. Sydney Matthews. He was at the sap in John Copse, or what was left of it, and he dressed and evacuated numerous men. Of his stretcher bearing squad one man was killed and two wounded. He was later awarded the DCM, the citation for which was published in the *London Gazette* of 20th October 1916:

> "12/727 Pte. S Matthews, York & Lanc. R. For conspicuous gallantry as a stretcherbearer. He remained for three days and nights in the front line dressing the wounded under heavy fire."

Lastly, 12/476 Cpl. Frank Peet was recognised for his devotion to duty whilst in charge of the regiment's stretcher-bearers.

The burden placed on these officers and men is starkly brought home by the enormous scale of the casualties incurred.

The initial casualty returns for the 94th Brigade are given in the table below.

	11th E Lancs		12th Y & L		13th Y & L		14th Y & L		94th MGC		94th TMB	
	Off	OR	Off	OR	Off	OR	Off	OR	Off	OR	Off	OR
Killed	7	70	4	44	6	40	5	22	0	5	1	3
Wound	13	450	9	138	6	163	5	136	3	7	0	18
Missing	1	80	3	313	0	60	0	102	1	32	0	0
Total	21	600	16	495	12	263	10	260	4	44	1	21

Table 19 94th Brigade casualty figures[127]

A total of 64 Officers and 1,683 Other Ranks killed, wounded and missing. It should be noted that the relatively low casualty figures amongst the two Barnsley battalions conceal very high rates within the two companies from each battalion actively involved in the attack. Proportionately, their casualties were very similar to the losses amongst the Accringtons and Sheffields.

The casualties suffered by the 93rd Brigade were still greater mainly because of the very heavy casualties suffered by the two follow-up battalions, the 16th and 18th West Yorkshire Regt. With very few of either battalion entering No Man's Land the figures are remarkable as the majority occurred in and behind the British front line[ii].

	15th W Yorks		16th W Yorks		18th W Yorks		18th DLI		93rd MGC		93rd TMB	
	Off	OR	Off	OR	Off	OR	Off	OR	Off	OR	Off	OR
Killed	11	56	14	53	3	50	2	27	2	8	1	0
Wound	12	267	8	303	13	275	11	178	3	31	2	19
Missing	1	181	0	149	0	100	0	34	0	5	0	3
Total	24	504	22	505	16	425	13	239	5	44	3	22

Table 20 93rd Brigade casualty figures[128]

[i] 122903 Pte Robert Gorrill, 12th York & Lancaster Regt. att. 25th Battalion, Machine Gun Corps, was killed on 27th May 1918 and is remembered on the Soissons Memorial.

[ii] Discrepancies between these numbers and those given by particular battalions are explained by the timing of the casualty assessments. 93rd Brigade's figures are an early assessment before the 'missing' were collected or able to return to the British lines.

The total casualties for the Brigade were 83 Officers and 1,739 Other Ranks killed, wounded and missing. The fact that there were over 1,300 casualties (74% of the total) amongst units which barely got into No Man's Land is staggering and shows the effectiveness of the German blocking barrage on the British forward positions.

In addition, the Divisional Pioneers, the 12th KOYLI, lost one officer killed and three wounded and 45 Other Ranks killed, 109 wounded and 5 missing, a total of four officers and 159 Other Ranks.

The combined figures for the two attacking Brigades plus the Pioneers are 151 Officers and 3,581 Other Ranks. In addition, seven men of the 92nd TMB were wounded, one officer was killed and one man wounded with the 92nd MGC, one Other Rank died of wounds and eight were wounded from the 11th East Yorkshires, one officer and two Other Ranks from the 12th East Yorkshires were wounded and 16 Other Ranks of the 13th East Yorkshires. This gives the final casualty figures for the 31st Division as: 153 officers and 3,616 Other Ranks, a total of 3,769.

Interestingly, the Germans only claimed 34 prisoners from the 31st Division on 1st July, a surprisingly low figure if the claims of deep penetrations into Serre and Pendant Copse were to be believed. Had several hundred British troops, let alone the two battalions the numbers were inflated to, actually been trapped in Serre one might imagine rather more Prisoners of War resulting from the action to clear the village. It is far more likely that any PoWs were taken in the vicinity of the shallow and brief incursion in the centre of the IR 169's position or were collected from the areas immediately in front of the German first line trench.

Against these dreadful numbers the casualties suffered by the two regiments involved in the defence of Serre were:

IR 169[i]	141 killed (including five officers)
	219 wounded (including six officers
	2 missing
IR 66	36 killed (including two officers)
	92 wounded (including one officer)

A grand total of:

7 officers killed and 7 wounded: 14 officer casualties

170 Other Ranks killed, 304 wounded, 2 missing: 476 Other Ranks casualties.

Four of the attacking British battalions each suffered higher casualties than the total lost by the German defenders. Overall, the ratio of British to German casualties was 7.5:1.

The officers of the IR 169 to die were: Lts. Beck[ii] (2. Kompanie), Hoff[iii] (2. Kompanie), Jenisch[i] (6. Kompanie), Lt. Der Res. Schwendemann (8. Kompanie),

---

[i] The *'Commemorative Publication for the 1st Regimental Day of the former 8th Baden Inf. Regt. No.169 in Lahr on 30th and 31st August 1924'* gives total casualties for other ranks as 577, rather than 351. This discrepancy may be explained by *Somme Nord* not including the lightly wounded who remained at duty.

[ii] Lt. Heinrich Beck, 8. Badisches Infanterie-Regiment Nr. 169, is buried in Achiet-le-Petit Cemetery, grave 264. He came from Karlsruhe.

[iii] Lt. Karl Hoff, 8. Badisches Infanterie-Regiment Nr. 169, is buried in Achiet-le-Petit Cemetery, grave 263. He came from Trier.

Lt. Kaufmann (7. Kompanie) and Lt. Neck and Lt. der Reserve Imle[ii] (12. Kompanie). Oblt Welsch[iii] (4. Kompanie) died of his wounds on 16th January 1917. The Medical Officer of the I Battalion, Oberarzt Dr Erwin Schmidt, was severely wounded.

Company	Killed	Died of Wounds	Severely Wounded	Slightly Wounded	Total
I Bataillon					
1. Kompanie	19	2	9	20	50
2. Kompanie	29	3	13	48	93
3. Kompanie	61	7	8	102	178
4. Kompanie	25	7	11	43	86
Total	134	19	41	213	407
II Bataillon					
5. Kompanie	11	0	15	25	51
6. Kompanie	23	5	18	72	118
7. Kompanie	21	2	14	56	93
8. Kompanie	9	2	5	20	36
Total	64	9	52	173	298
III Bataillon					
9. Kompanie	8	5	10	23	46
10. Kompanie	11	3	7	30	51
11. Kompanie	17	3	8	33	61
12. Kompanie	10	2	14	27	53
Total	46	13	39	113	211
1. MGK	9	2	1	21	33
2. MGK	3	0	1	8	12
I Batt Staff	0	1	0	1	2
Total	256	44	134	529	963

Table 21 Casualties by Company, IR 169[iv]

Table 21 above shows the total casualties recorded by the regiment defending Serre, IR 169, throughout the bombardment and on into mid July. These numbers necessarily exceed those previously given for just 1st July. What the statistics do show, however, is the concentration of casualties amongst the four

[i] Lt. Ulrich Jenisch, 8. Badisches Infanterie-Regiment Nr. 169, is buried in Achiet-le-Petit Cemetery, grave 262.

[ii] Lt. der Reserve Otto Imle, 8. Badisches Infanterie-Regiment Nr. 169, is buried in Achiet-le-Petit Cemetery, grave 265. He came from Karlsruhe and had been wounded previously at the end of 1914.

[iii] Oberleutnant Hugo Welsch, 8. Badisches Infanterie-Regiment Nr. 169, was born on the 13th June 1891. He is buried in the Kriegsgräberstätte, Constanze, grave 9b. He came from Constanze and had been wounded previously in 1914 and late 1915 when he was the Regimental Adjutant.

[iv] There are no dates for the casualties on IR 169 in the Verlustlisten and it is not possible to identify which of these casualties occurred on, or as a result of, the fighting of 1st July.

companies of the I Bataillon which defended the front lines. 42% of the regiment's losses came from these four companies. Two thirds of the casualties in the I Bataillon came from the two companies, Nos. 2 & 3 Kompanien, defending the area where the only major incursion was made by the men of the Accrington Pals.

Table 22 below shows the casualties suffered by the IR 66. The regiment defending the area to the north of the 31st Division which was not attacked by the 48th Division. Again, these numbers cover a time period greater than just 1st July but, again, the concentration of casualties within the II Bataillon and, within that unit, of the 5. Kompanie shows where the heaviest action took place on the northern flank of the Fourth Army's offensive.

Company	Killed	Died of Wounds	Severely Wounded	Slightly Wounded	Total
I Bataillon					
1. Kompanie	0	0	0	0	1*
2. Kompanie	0	0	0	0	0
3. Kompanie	0	1	0	3	4
4. Kompanie	3	0	2	0	6*
Total	3	1	2	3	11*
II Bataillon					
5. Kompanie	14	6	24	30	74
6. Kompanie	2	0	4	10	16
7. Kompanie	5	4	4	13	26
8. Kompanie	5	2	11	13	31
Total	26	12	43	66	147
III Bataillon					
9. Kompanie	0	0	0	1	1
10. Kompanie	3	0	2	3	8
11. Kompanie	1	0	0	4	5
12. Kompanie	3	0	2	9	14
Total	7	0	4	17	28
1. MGK	0	0	3	3	6
2. MGK	0	0	1	0	1
MGK	1	0	0	1	2
Total	37	13	54	90	194

Table 22 Casualties by Company, IR 66

[1] NA, WO 95/2352/1, *War Diary 210th Field Company, RE.*
[2] NA, WO95/2531/2, *Divisional Trench Mortars.*
[3] NA, WO95/2349/3, *War Diary 165th Brigade, RFA.*
[4] NA, WO95/2350, *War Diary 170th Brigade, RFA.*
[5] *War Diary of IR 169*, Generallandesarchiv Karslruhe 456 EV 42 Vol 108.
[6] NA, WO95/2349/3.

[7] Ibid.
[8] *'Das Königlich-Preussische Reserve-Infanterie-Regiment Nr. 15 1. Band'* Major a.D. Kurt Freiherr von Forstner (Oldenburg 1929) pp 301. Courtesy of Jack Sheldon.
[9] Ibid.
[10] Ibid.
[11] NA, WO95/2357, *War Diary 11th East Yorkshire Regt.*
[12] NA, WO95/2531/2.
[13] NA, WO95/2357, *War Diary 10th East Yorkshire Regt.*
[14] NA, WO95/2350.
[15] Ibid.
[16] NA, WO95/2531/2.
[17] Ibid.
[18] NA, WO95/2350.
[19] NA, WO 95/2759/1, *War Diary 1/7th Worcestershire Regt.*
[20] NA, CAB45/191, *Personal Accounts, Fourth Army.*
[21] NA, CAB45/191.
[22] NA, WO95/2341, *War Diary 31st Division.*
[23] Ibid.
[24] NA, WO95/2348/2, *War Diary, CRE, 31st Division.*
[25] NA, WO95/2350.
[26] NA, WO95/2359, *War Diary 93rd Brigade.*
[27] NA, WO95/2362, *War Diary 16th West Yorkshire Regt.*
[28] NA, WO95/2363, *War Diary 94th Brigade.*
[29] NA, WO95/2341.
[30] NA, CAB45/191.
[31] Ibid.
[32] NA, WO95/2349/3.
[33] NA, WO95/2349/4, *War Diary 169th Brigade, RFA.*
[34] NA, WO95/2365/1, *War Diary 12th York & Lancaster Regt.*
[35] Ibid.
[36] NA, WO95/2341.
[37] NA, WO95/2365/3, *War Diary 14th York & Lancaster Regt.*
[38] NA, CAB45/137, *Comment on the OH by Brig. Gen. H C Rees.*
[39] D J Driscoll, *http://www.thebristolgunners.webspace.virginmedia.com/1st south midland bde anon1.htm.*
[40] NA, WO95/2754, *War Diary 143rd Brigade.*
[41] Harris, J, *'Covenant of Death'*, Hutchinson, 1961. An excellent fictionalised account of the recruiting, training and destruction of the Leeds Pals.
[42] NA, WO95/2362, *War Diary 16th West Yorkshire Regt.*
[43] Ibid.
[44] Ibid.
[45] Ibid.
[46] NA, WO95/2359.
[47] NA, WO95/2341.
[48] Ibid.
[49] NA, WO95/2363.
[50] NA, WO95/2349/4.
[51] NA, WO95/2365/1.
[52] Blundells School website: *http://www.blundells.org/*
[53] Ibid.
[54] NA, WO95/2365/1.
[55] Ibid.

[56] *http://www.burnleygallantry.co.uk/gallantry/leemingdcm.htm.*
[57] *http://www.burnleygallantry.co.uk/gallantry/speakmm.htm.*
[58] NA, WO95/2366/1, *War Diary 11th East Lancashire Regt.*
[59] NA, WO95/2341.
[60] Ibid.
[61] NA, WO95/2365/3, *War Diary 14th York & Lancaster Regt.*
[62] NA, WO95/2341.
[63] NA, WO95/2350.
[64] NA, WO95/2349/3.
[65] NA, WO95/2365/3.
[66] Ibid.
[67] NA, WO95/2341.
[68] NA, WO95/2366/1.
[69] NA, WO95/2350
[70] NA, WO95/2341.
[71] NA, WO95/2362, *War Diary 18th West Yorkshire Regt.*
[72] Ibid.
[73] Ibid.
[74] Ibid.
[75] NA, WO95/2341.
[76] NA, WO95/2350.
[77] Ibid.
[78] Ibid.
[79] Ibid.
[80] Ibid.
[81] NA, WO95/2349/4.
[82] NA, WO95/2349/3.
[83] NA, WO95/2366/1.
[84] *Harrow Memorials of the Great War*, Volume III.
[85] NA, WO95/820.
[86] Ibid.
[87] NA, WO95/2341.
[88] Ibid.
[89] NA, WO95/2350.
[90] NA, WO95/2359.
[91] Ibid.
[92] NA, WO95/820.
[93] NA, WO95/2341.
[94] NA, WO95/820.
[95] NA, WO95/2363.
[96] NA, WO95/2341.
[97] Ibid.
[98] NA, WO95/2345.
[99] NA, WO95/2358/2, *War Diary 92nd Machine Gun Company.*
[100] NA, WO95/2341.
[101] Ibid.
[102] NA, WO95/2350.
[103] NA, WO95/2359.
[104] Ibid.
[105] Ibid.
[106] Ibid.
[107] NA, WO95/2341.

[108] Ibid.
[109] Ibid.
[110] NA, WO95/2350.
[111] Ibid.
[112] NA, WO95/2341.
[113] Ibid.
[114] NA, WO95/2366/1.
[115] NA, WO95/820.
[116] Ibid.
[117] NA, WO95/2341.
[118] Ibid.
[119] NA, WO95/820.
[120] NA, WO95/2341.
[121] NA, WO95/2365/1.
[122] NA, WO95/2366/1.
[123] NA, WO95/2365/1.
[124] NA, WO95/2341.
[125] Ibid.
[126] Ibid.
[127] NA, WO95/2363.
[128] NA, WO95/2359.

10. The Causes of Failure

GIVEN THE SCALE OF THE DISASTER, it is not surprising that those in charge immediately set to scurrying around seeking explanations and scapegoats. Happily for Hunter-Weston and his juniors none of the latter were identified by higher authority within VIII Corps. Instead, his Corps was never again given the responsibility of participating in a major or, indeed, minor British offensive for the duration of the war. Ironically, after the worst day in the history of the British Army, a day on which 57,000 men became casualties within a few hours, the only scapegoat, i.e. the only General publicly humiliated by being sacked and sent home on the first available boat, was to be found leading the Division with the lowest casualties on 1st July. That man was Maj. Gen. Edward James Montagu Stuart Wortley, GOC, 46th (North Midland) Division whose command was severely rebuffed on the northern flank of Gommecourt. The butt of a long standing grudge held by Haig, he was the victim of a move by his Corps commander, Lt. Gen. Sir Thomas D'Oyly Snow, to 'get his retaliation in first' when Snow demanded Stuart Wortley be sacked the day after the attack, a request Haig was only too happy to confirm[i].

Hunter-Weston, meanwhile, was not slow in covering his back. On the Sunday immediately after the attack he wrote to the Chief of the Imperial General Staff, Sir William Robertson, who he had spoken to earlier in the day by telephone. Hunter Weston was clearly getting 'his ducks in a row' when it came to pointing the finger of blame for his Corps' total failure. As the letter shows, he was not beyond telling a few 'porkies' about the reasons for the disaster.

"Private.

> Apropos our conversation this morning I should much like to see you tomorrow if you have a spare moment. May I motor over to you after breakfast, at any hour you may appoint. The bearer will wait for your answer.
>
> We were mistaken in supposing that two battalions had got through to Serre, but had been cut off by the Germans getting up out of dug-outs behind them. Later and more accurate information established the fact that these battalions, and the majority of the other battalions all along this front, were defeated by the enemy's artillery barrage, and by his machine gun fire, which in many cases simply wiped out the battalions before they reached the German trenches.
>
> The gallantry, discipline and devotion of our troops was beyond praise. But we had not knocked the German trenches about nearly enough to block their dug-outs and fill up their trenches in the way the German artillery does to our trenches, and so, as you will see on reading the enclosed interesting notes I have had typed, the German Infantry and

---

[i] A full account of the sacking of Stuart Wortley and background of the dispute between him and Haig can be found in the author's book *'A Lack of Offensive Spirit? The 46th (North Midland) Division at Gommecourt, 1st July 1916'*, Iona Books, 2008.

> Machine Gunners were able to come out of their deep dug-outs, and man their parapets, as soon as our men showed, and were thus able to prevent our men reaching their trenches.
> The reason for the lack of success of the Third Army and left of the Fourth Army is that the Germans here had better trenches, and a much more powerful artillery. It was at Gommecourt, Serre and Beaumont Hamel that they most feared attack.
> A contributory cause was the inadequacy of the artillery and of the ammunition available. The Germans keep up a drum fire with heavy howitzers for many hours. For this we neither have the ammunition nor the howitzers, nor, indeed, could our howitzers stand such continuous fire. We always have to be saving our guns. Of ammunition we had only about 1⅓ heavy howitzer shells per yard run of fire trench, whereas we should have had about 10 per yard run. However, this latter reason is for your ear alone, it is inadvisable to give currency to such unpleasant and dangerous facts."[1]

Hunter Weston's comments about the Germans having 'a much more powerful artillery' is, of course, nonsense. Nor did they have many 'heavy howitzers' in the true sense of the word 'heavy'. Because most of the truly heavy howitzers had been removed to be used at Verdun, the overwhelming majority of howitzers on the German front were the 10.5 cm field howitzer, the equivalent of the British 4.5 in. field howitzer. In terms of sheer numbers and power, the combined heavy and field artillery of VII and VIIII Corps vastly outgunned the enemy opposite. What was the case, however, was that the German gunners had a much smaller target at which to aim and one that was always in the same place, i.e. the British front line and assembly trenches, whereas the VIII Corps artillery had to fire across a huge area and, on the day, provide a moving barrage in front of where the plan said the infantry should be.

The real problem for VIII Corps, however, was the enormous expanse of territory at which they had to fire before the attack and the reason for this was that the Commander in Chief had demanded it. For any sensible officer who valued their rank and position, this was not something which could be explained explicitly in a letter. Far better to whisper it in someone's ear. In this case, Sir William Robertson's lughole. Interestingly, on 5th July, Robertson sent a letter to Kiggell (not Haig, one notes) reciting his firmly held view that attacks should be deliberate and 'exceedingly limited' with a necessary concentration of artillery power[2]. This is, essentially, what Rawlinson had initially proposed and Haig rejected. Furthermore, Robertson's statement that '… we want concentration and not dispersion of artillery fire' echoes the earlier complaint by Noel Birch about Haig's tendency to spread the guns too thin. Robertson seemed only too aware that not all of the responsibility for the failure of the VIII Corps could be put at Hunter-Weston's door. Indeed, his failings were just the icing on a cake recipe already thoroughly spoiled by the intervention of his Commander in Chief.

Whilst Hunter-Weston was distancing himself from the tactics dictated by GHQ and Fourth Army he was also busy sending encouraging messages to his men in his typically extravagant manner:

"From Lt. General Sir Aylmer Hunter-Weston, KCB, DSO
To All Officers, N.C.O.s and Men of the VIII Army Corps
In so big a command as an Army Corps of four Divisions (about 80,000 men) it is impossible for me to come round all front line trenches, and all billets, to sec every man as I wish to do. You must take the will for the deed, and accept this printed message in place of the spoken word.
It is difficult for me to express my admiration for the splendid courage, determination and discipline displayed by every Officer, N.C.O., and man of the Battalions that took part in the great attack on the Beaumont Hamel-Serre position on the 1st July. All observers agree in stating that the various waves of men issued from their trenches and moved forward at the appointed time in perfect order, undismayed by the heavy artillery fire and deadly machine-gun fire. There were no cowards nor waverers, and not a man fell out. It was a magnificent display of disciplined courage worthy of the best traditions of the British Race.
Very few are left of my old comrades, the original 'Contemptibles', but their successors in the 4th Division have shown that they are worthy to bear the honours gained by the 4th Division at their first great fight at Fontaine-au-Pire and Ligny, during the great Retreat and greater Advance across the Marne and Aisne, and in all the hard fighting at Ploegsteert and at Ypres. Though but a few of my old comrades, the heroes of the historic landing at Cape Helles, are still with us, the 29th Division of to-day has shown itself capable of maintaining its high traditions, and has proved itself worthy of its hard-earned title of 'The Incomparable 29th'.
The 31st New Army Division and the 48th Territorial Division, by the heroism and discipline of the units engaged in this their first big battle, have proved themselves worthy to fight by the side of such magnificent regular Divisions as the 4th and 29th. There can be no higher praise.
We had the most difficult part of the line to attack. The Germans had fortified it with skill and immense labour for many months; they had kept their best troops here, and had assembled North, East, and South-East of it a formidable collection of artillery and many machine-guns.
By your splendid attack you held the enemy forces here in the North, and so enabled our friends in the South, both British and French, to achieve the brilliant success that they have. Therefore, though we did not do all we hoped to do, you have more than pulled your weight, and you and our even more glorious comrades who have preceded us across the 'Great Divide', have nobly done your duty.
We have got to stick it out, and go on hammering. Next time we attack, if it please God, we will not only pull our weight, but will pull off a big thing. With such troops as you, who are determined to stick it out and do your duty, we are certain of winning through to a glorious victory. I salute each Officer, N.C.O., and Man of the 4th, 29th, 31st and 48th Divisions as a comrade in arms, and I rejoice to have the privilege of commanding such a band of heroes as the VIII Corps have proved themselves to be.

Aylmer Hunter-Weston, Lt. Gen.
H.Q. VIII Corps, 4th July 1916"[3]

IN THE MEANTIME, OTHER OFFICERS WERE PUTTING PEN TO PAPER in an effort to explain why their attack had failed, and why none of it was their fault.

Ten days after the attack which had reduced his command's infantry strength by not far short of 50%[i], Maj. Gen. de Lisle submitted his report on the operation. It contains a lengthy section entitled *'Causes of Failure'*.[4] It is, in many ways, an extraordinary document. It is a devastating indictment of all senior officers involved in the planning and conduct of the attack including, and perhaps unwittingly, himself. After the war he would point the finger of blame more directly at his Corps and Army commanders and, less directly, at the CinC. He would not be alone in doing so.

But, before setting out his criticisms and complaints, de Lisle made clear that no fault attached to the officers and men of the 29th Division who had actually made the attack. His praise of their dedication, determination and discipline was fulsome, although he did express some concerns about the physical endurance of the recently recruited younger men who made up the mass of the Division:

> "No fault can be found with the behaviour of the troops who did all that was possible. Their bravery and the severity of the engagement are best evidenced by the casualties which I regret to state were very severe, amounting to some 200 officers and 5000 men.
>
> The fact that there were only two stragglers from the Division detained in the Stragglers' Collecting Camp shows also that the discipline of the Division was excellent
>
> It was noticeable that in spite of two attacks having failed on the right the two battalions detailed for the third attack behaved with exemplary bravery. The Newfoundland battalion on the left, for example, attacked 750 strong. Forty odd unwounded returned in the course of the day and the remaining 710 were casualties. This example of discipline and valour was equalled by others but cannot be surpassed.
>
> There is bitter disappointment throughout this Division that in spite of their determination and self-sacrifice they were unable to succeed but the troops were much cheered by the fact that their efforts were having influence on other portions of the line and Gen. Joffre's message to this effect was much appreciated. Though confined at present to the defensive the Division is ready to resume a more active part in the operations as soon as the necessary reinforcements are received.
>
> The spirit of the troops is good but the physical fatigue among the young soldiers who form three fourths of the battalions is marked compared with the stamina of the original troops of earlier days."[5]

---

[i] The total infantry strength of the 29th Division, including the pioneers, the 1/2nd MonmouthshireRegt., prior to the attack was 446 officers and 11,351 other ranks. A total of 8,408 men from the three Brigades went over the top, including the pioneers, of which 226 were officers. Amongst the attacking troops 185 officers (82%) became casualties as well as 4,926 other ranks (60%). Total casualties amongst the infantry, i.e. including the 2nd Hampshires and 4th Worcesters, were 190 officers and 4,999 other ranks giving percentage casualty figures for the infantry of the entire Division of 44%.

In his report De Lisle itemised six reasons why his Division had failed to gain their objectives. There is some overlap between some of the points raised but, broadly, the reasons given are:

1. The strength with which the enemy's defences were held;
2. The strength of the enemy's defensive position;
3. The lack of surprise and speed in the attack;
4. The failure of the heavy artillery to demolish the front line;
5. The early explosion of the Hawthorn Ridge mine; and
6. The performance of the Stokes mortars.

We can dismiss the final point as, if not completely irrelevant, then, at the very best, of tenuous relevance to the outcome. The idea that problems with a ten minute hurricane bombardment by sixteen Stokes mortars can have contributed in any significant way to the failure of the attack is risible. It is, after all, the case that their contribution comprised only a small part of the intense bombardment of the same positions by the entire Divisional field artillery and a third of the Corps heavy artillery. Furthermore, these Stokes mortars only bombarded those sections of the German trench opposite the two tunnels projecting out into No Man's Land, at 1st Avenue and Mary Redan, and the area near Sap 7 on the 1st Lancashire Fusiliers' front. Otherwise, a large number were to be carried forward by the attacking battalions for use in defending their newly won positions.

After the war, Lt. Col. Cuthbert Graham Fuller[i], Royal Engineers, who had been appointed GSO1, 29th Division, in August 1915 and was to remain so until October 1917, repeated this criticism. He believed that demonstrations of the mortars at the Trench Mortar School had raised 'exaggerated expectation' as to their value.[6] With the greatest respect to both de Lisle and Fuller, their comments seem to represent something of a smoke screen. If it is true that senior officers had placed an unwarranted reliance for the success of the attack on such a relatively new weapon, one which had not yet seen significant action in a large scale offensive, then any criticisms as to their 'relative' failure should be placed at their door.

De Lisle, though, also criticised their portability during an attack as witnessed by their minimal benefit at the Hawthorn crater:

> "… the difficulties in conveying ammunition to them, as evidenced at the crater, render them, in my opinion, unsuitable for carrying forward in

[i] Lt. Col., later Maj. Gen., Cuthbert Graham Fuller, CB, CMG, DSO, Royal Engineers, was born in 1874, the son of the late George Fuller. He was educated at St Paul's, Beaumont College and the RMA, Woolwich. Commissioned into Royal Engineers in 1893. Joined 8th Railway Company at Chatham. Served in South Africa in various railway Staff appointments, MiD. OC, 53rd Railway Company, 1904. Deputy Assistant Director of Railways, War Office, 1907. Staff College, Camberley, 1909. GSO3, Military Training Directorate, 1912. GSO2, 1914. Brigade Major then GSO1, 29th Division, 1915. Served at Gallipoli. DSO, 1917. BGGS, III Corps, 1918. CMG, 1919. BGGS, British Army of the Rhine, 1919. GOC 130th Brigade, TF, 1923-5 and Canal Brigade, Egypt, 1925-8. CB, 1926. Maj. Gen. Administration, Eastern Command, 1929-31. GOC, 48th (South Midland) Division, TA, 1931-5. Retired, 1935. Col. Commandant, Royal Engineers, 1937-44. Married Princess Sophia Vladimirovna Shahovskaya, daughter of Prince Vladimir Shahovski, in 1912. Two sons, one daughter, the two sons pre-deceasing him. Died 1960.

> offensive operations until the whole of the enemy's front line in the vicinity has been captured."[7]

Again such criticism is really only of marginal relevance. The Stokes mortar came in three parts, rather like Gaul, and, in addition to the barrel, tripod and base plate, the 11lb (4.48 Kg) shells were not easy to lug across No Man's Land. Lose any one or more members of the team and the guns were useless. But one could make the same point about the Vickers machine gun and, to a lesser extent, about the Lewis Gun. Gun, tripod, water coolant, ammunition belts – all needed transportation during an attack if the Vickers was to function (or gun and ammunition drums in the case of the Lewis gun). It just so happened that, at the crater, the gun teams that suffered critical losses were the Stokes mortar teams whose ammunition carriers went down in unfortunately large numbers. And again, to label a weapon, which was being used in this manner for the first time in large numbers, as a 'cause of failure' seems both rather harsh on the Stokes and the men that manned them and of no great relevance within the bigger picture.

We must, therefore, return to de Lisle's first five points because they constitute the heart of the matter. Let us examine de Lisle's five *'Causes of Failure'* one by one.

THE STRENGTH WITH WHICH THE ENEMY'S DEFENCES WERE HELD

De Lisle's first point actually covers two key areas: the numerical strength of the defenders and the physical strength of the dugouts and caves in which they were accommodated.

> "The enemy were undoubtedly prepared for the attack and had reinforced their line. This was proved during the preliminary bombardment, all our raids and patrols reporting that the German line was strongly held. The enemy had also brought up many additional machine guns which were kept under cover in deep dugouts until required to repel our infantry attack."[8]

This is only partially accurate. The Germans had reinforced their troops north of the Ancre but not on the Beaumont Hamel front. The insertion of the 2. Garde Reserve Division at Gommecourt in May had allowed the 52. Division to sharply reduce its front and, therefore, concentrate their rifle and machine gun power, but this mainly affected the area east of Hebuterne and in front of Serre. The border between the 52. Division and the 26. Reserve Division was not significantly altered by this change though it seems quite certain that the 52. Division was able to assist materially the RIR 121 of the 26. Reserve Division on Redan Ridge in a way that might not have been so effective six weeks earlier. The German artillery north of the Ancre had, however, been reinforced and, as previously mentioned, there were numerous comments about the intensity of both the shrapnel and HE barrage placed on the 29th Division's front, indeed along the entire Corps front, after the attack began. It is the case, however, that batteries from the 52. Division reinforced the artillery of the 26. Reserve Division thereby increasing the strength of the barrage on the 29th and 4th Divisions' front. The German barrage on the 31st Division's front was the most powerful on the Somme front on 1st July 1916.

Certainly, though, his point about the failure of the majority of his Division's raids because of the strength in which the front lines were held is true. Nine raids were mounted by the 29th Division during the period of the bombardment. Seven were complete failures with the raiding parties suffering some significant casualties and the last two were minor successes, one German being shot during each of them. But even these last two raids, mounted just 30 hours before the offensive began, revealed the front line trenches to be actively manned, the entrances to the dugouts unblocked, the trenches still defensible. Given higher commands reassurances that the majority of the German defenders would be either dead or demoralised this surely should have sent alarm bells ringing amongst the Staff officers supervising events.

Apparently not.

De Lisle then goes on to talk about the dugouts and the large mined galleries which helped protect German troops throughout the bombardment. It is clear that they were known to exist before the attack:

> "These dugouts were proof against heavy artillery and from prisoners statements it would appear that they had access to them both from the front and support lines.
> Beaumont Hamel, moreover, is undermined with large caves with some 30 feet of chalk above them and capable of accommodating some two battalions."[9]

Of course, this is not a revelation brought about by British troops discovering these dugouts and galleries as a result of taking the German positions. As Capt., later Major General, Ian Grant, GSO1, 86th Brigade, was to write after the war:

> "We had been in the German front line with a successful raid (1st Lancashire Fusiliers) and knew the dugout and tunnels that existed were more or less bombardment proof."[10]

The raid to which Grant refers is the one conducted on the night of the 3rd/4th June, the report on which stated:

> "Dugouts were about 20 feet deep and connected."[11]

Equally, the British should have known about the mined galleries because at least one was an extension of an underground working which had existed for centuries. These mined galleries are well described in *Somme Nord*:

> "Rhineland and Central German miners had been there in the winter of 1914-15 and had either enlarged or dug anew deep, tunnel-like galleries in which whole companies found shelter. The most famous of these tunnels was the 'Mine' (Bergwerk), one of those famous underground caves and passages of northern France which provided the villagers shelter in previous times of war. Furthermore, teams from the RIR 99 had dug substantial tunnels, the Leiling Schlucht and the Bismarck-Stollen, in what the British called, because of its shape, the Y Ravine."[12]

The Bergwerk or 'Mine', in the RIR 121's sector opposite the Lancashire Fusiliers, was the largest of the existing mined galleries. Surely it is inconceivable that some refugee from Beaumont Hamel had not mentioned the existence of this extensive chalk mine when questioned about the buildings and layout of the village. After all, at Thiepval, the ownership and the detail of every building, out-house and cellar had been noted after interviews with displaced natives. Surely, the same would have been done at Beaumont Hamel. But of course it was, otherwise why would de Lisle know to mention such places in his report?

The Leiling Schlucht and the Bismarck-Stollen might not have been so well known. Dug originally by men of the RIR 99 under the guidance of Hptm. Leiling of the 14. Kompanie, these workings, and others, provided larger scale shelters than the ordinary dugouts themselves. Thus de Lisle's comment about them sheltering, in total, some two battalions.

And so, if the deep inter-connected dugouts and the large mined galleries were both equally well known why were not tactics adapted to meet the challenges they presented?

In short, this first 'cause of failure' concerns issues well known to the British senior command before the attack took place. De Lisle's comments explain why the attack was defeated but not why, having known about these issues well in advance, plans were not laid to deal with them. As they say in sports coaching 'Fail to plan, plan to fail'.

THE STRENGTH OF THE ENEMY'S DEFENSIVE POSITION

De Lisle's second 'cause' again covers more than one issue and, indeed, partially refers back to the previous point:

> "The sector allotted to this Division for attack had been converted by the enemy into a first class fortress and it seems doubtful whether if held by resolute men it can be captured by frontal assault. The second and third lines of the enemy's system also enjoy natural advantages of ground since they are for the most part invisible from our lines."[13]

Leaving to one side the unfortunate point that Beaumont Hamel was taken by frontal assault on 13th November 1916, the issues of the terrain should have been obvious to any trained military eye. The tiered nature of the German defences, which allowed machine guns to cover the whole of the British front from three separate supporting lines of trenches, was there for all to see. The question was: how best to neutralise such weapons so that the infantry might get across No Man's Land and into the German trenches where, by bombing and bayonet, and with covering fire from Vickers and Lewis guns and Stokes mortars, they might work their way methodically through the enemy's trench system?

Maj. Richard Osbaldeston Spencer Smith was the 2ic of the 2nd Hampshire Regt. and he had observed the German position closely. His post-war comments leave one in no doubt as to the great natural strength of their position:

> "The German position was very strong naturally and no labour or skill seems to have been spared to make it much more so artificially.
> I think for defensive purposes the siting of the German trenches, whether by accident of fighting or design, could hardly have been better.
> It possessed the following advantages:
> 1. Front line system almost immune from high velocity shell fire owing to configuration of the ground;
> 2. Irregularity of design, making exact ranging difficult and minor salient and re-entrants giving opportunity for crossfire of MGs from

well concealed positions. And concealment for redoubts and strongpoints;

3. Excellent natural cover for supports and reserves and immunity from shell fire in caves, cellars and dugouts;
4. Covered communications immune from shellfire;
5. The Germans had good observation from high ground in rear of the natural front line system and from ground opposite Thiepval;
6. The trench system was protected by very strong wire entanglements;
7. The British had to advance over a crest line making a splendid target for artillery and MGs."[14]

Maj. Geoffrey Taunton Raikes, the CO of the 2nd South Wales Borderers, provided a detailed description of the German position in the centre of the Division's attack around the Y Ravine:

> "The British front trench, held by the 2nd South Wales Borderers, ran on or just over the crest of the ridge west of the Y Ravine. The German front trench on the western lip of the Y Ravine was sited on the reverse slope of this same ridge. The low ridge between the two branches of the Y Ravine where the German support trench and M. Guns were sited overlooked the front trench while about 1,100 yards behind again the Beaucourt ridge overlooked both the German front and support trenches.
> The result of this was that any advance from the British front trench came at once under fire from the German front, support and Beaucourt trenches and under direct observation from the German artillery OPs.
> As opposed to this, all observation and supporting MG fire from the British side had to come from the front trench. Moreover, the Germans could concentrate their defensive fire on practically one line while the fire in support of the attack had to disperse."[15]

Regarding the dispersal of the artillery's fire, De Lisle makes a similar point at the end of his comments about the physical strength of the Beaumont Hamel position:

> "More success would probably have attended our efforts had we surprised the enemy by an attack at dawn and had we concentrated our artillery fire on the first objective, leaving the second objective to be dealt with in a subsequent operation."[16]

His comments about concentrating the artillery on the first objective, leaving the second objective for a subsequent operation, raise a question about the overall nature of the operation north of the Ancre. Originally, Rawlinson had wanted to take just the German 1st and intermediate positions, effectively stopping at the Beaucourt ridge. It was Haig who insisted on adding the German 2nd Position far to the east to the operation. These three positions were to be taken one after the other during the morning of the 1st July. The requirements of the artillery barrages were, therefore, dictated by the need to be in front of the anticipated infantry attack at all times. Given the rudimentary nature of communications at this date, judging the whereabouts of the infantry in relation to the artillery barrage was not even an art let along a science. Barrages moved to a rigid timetable. It was up to the infantry to keep pace. Should there be *any* hold-up in the progress of the infantry then the artillery barrage, as happened along large swathes of the Somme front on 1st July, would disappear blithely into the distance. Timetables were not be tampered with by battery commanders even if they could see right in front of their noses what was needed in terms of artillery support. Only 'higher authority', i.e. no-one below Division (and then only the field batteries), could change such a timetable and, for reasons yet to be seen, higher authority did not allow this until it was several hours too late.

Then there is the issue of the impact of the bombardment on the front trenches which numerous reports suggest was inadequate. Haig had demanded three German positions be taken during the morning of the attack. That required the Corps artillery to attempt to prepare the infantry's way to and over all three of them. It cannot otherwise be the case that Haig's insistence on taking all three positions diluted the power of the heavy howitzers to demolish the enemy's defences. Where the British and French were most successful on 1st July was in areas where, broadly, the German front line had become untenable. There is more than just the impact of the heavy artillery to explain this link but it is a very good starting point.

THE LACK OF SURPRISE AND SPEED IN THE ATTACK

De Lisle's third point concerns four aspects of the attack across No Man's Land but only mentions two: surprise and speed. The third is discussed under the timing of the Hawthorn Redoubt mine, whilst the fourth is not discussed at all.

> "As hostile lines of this strength can apparently only be captured by surprise, speed in crossing the area between our front trenches and the enemy's is essential. The leading troops should therefore be lightly equipped and should be trained to cross this zone with a rush."[17]

Surprise can be easily dealt with. After seven days' bombardment almost anyone on the German front would have realised that a large scale attack was imminent. The only outstanding questions were precisely when and precisely where. For the men of the RIR 119 this question was certainly resolved when the Hawthorn Redoubt mine exploded ten minutes before zero. Their ability to react to this rather large hint was then materially assisted by the decision to take the heavy guns and, a few minutes later, half of the Divisional artillery off the German front line trench. No one was surprised except, amazingly, the British high command and its soldiers when dozens of German machine guns started to sweep No Man's Land even before zero hour.

Speed. A certain element of 'speed' (by trying to reduce distance) was introduced by moving some of the attacking battalions out into No Man's Land immediately before or after the mine went up, e.g. 2nd South Wales Borderers and the 1st Royal Inniskilling Fusiliers and the leading battalions of the 94th Brigade. As all this achieved was to have the men wandering around in full view of the now firing German machine guns for a few minutes, this initiative was of very doubtful value.

Another element of speed relates to the pace at which the infantry advanced and, indeed, how fast they were capable of advancing. Other historians have pointed out that not every battalion attacked in the slow, methodical manner prescribed by Fourth Army's notes. They did, however, on the 29th Division's front and, indeed on the entire VIII Corps' front[i]. For two reasons.

The first is that they were ordered to. If the infantry was to keep pace with the artillery then a certain speed of advance was required. Too slow and they would lose the barrage, too fast and they would walk into it. For most of the advance the prescribed speed was no more than 50 yards a minute. Try walking at 50 paces a minute. It is a fairly leisurely stroll. Unless you are being fired at by multiple German machine guns in which case it is a death walk.

The second reason is that walking any faster was a real problem. There has been much discussion about the weight of equipment the men were asked to carry. The *Official History* calculates an *average* of 66 lbs per man or nearly 5 stone (or 30 Kg for those of a metric mind set)[ii]. Bear in mind that, though undoubtedly far fitter than when in civilian life and, in some cases, far better fed, the average height and weight of the British soldier in 1916 was significantly less than it is now[iii]. Men who were less than 5 ft. 3 in. tall were recruited into the so-called Bantam battalions for a period and the average height of a British 'Tommy' has since been estimated at between 5 ft. 5 in. and 5 ft. 7 in. tall[18] with a weight of c. 140 lbs. As an example of average male physique, pre-war figures from Southport Borough Council Education Committee Reports show that the average height and weight of 15 year olds who would have been 21 in 1914 was 5 ft. 5 in and 122 lbs.

In other words, this translates into the fact that the average infantryman was being asked to carry half of his own bodyweight across No Man's Land. The *Official History* describes the effects of carrying this load as making it:

> "... difficult to get out of a trench, impossible to move much quicker than a slow walk or to rise and lie down quickly."[19]

A post-war comment by a Captain of the Lancashire Fusiliers who took over as Staff Captain of the 86th Brigade when Capt. Gee was wounded bears this out:

> "I also suggest that it might be matter of historical interest to record the details and weights of equipment which our attacking infantry were expected to carry. I cannot remember the actual details but these could be obtained from orders. I know the weight was so great that the men had great difficulty in getting out of the trenches."[20]

Capt. F A Wilson, 1st Royal Dublin Fusiliers, later commented:

> "Loaded up as the infantry were it was quite impossible for any man to move at any pace faster than a walk, whereas had the troops been able to move quickly across No Man's Land the enemy machine gunners would

---

[i] Words used such as 'rush' and 'charge' to suggest a faster form of attack on, for example, the 31st Division's front are a misreading of the terminology. German observers, e.g. Musketier Blenk, IR 169, on the 31st Division's front commented afterwards on the slowness of the advance which was at walking pace and how they had never seen this before. Also, as mentioned, the VIII Corps order was for an advance at 50 paces a minute.

[ii] Later waves in the attack would have carried more as their function was to consolidate the positions taken.

[iii] Recent research shows the current average height of males in the UK to be 11cm (4.3 in.) taller than in 1870.

> have had much harder shooting. Application was made by one of our officers for the battalion to be allowed to travel as light as possible but permission was refused and the men went over loaded up more like beasts of burden than anything else."[21]

Lastly, there is the comment of 2nd Lt., later Major, Charles James Prior Ball, DSO, MC, then of B Battery, RHA:

> "No mention is made of No Man's Land which was of exceptional width in front of the 29th. To expect infantry to walk across 800 yards with full equipment, carrying parties, with duckboards in the face of a fully alarmed enemy was to invite the massacre that actually occurred."[22]

Which neatly brings us to the point NOT mentioned by de Lisle – distance.

In places, No Man's Land on the 29th Division's front was not excessively wide. It was perhaps 200 to 250 yards across opposite the Sunken Road, the Hawthorn crater, the Mary Redan and the western tip of the Y Ravine. But there were places where it was two or even three times wider. The 16th Middlesex, for example, had a good 400 yards to travel and the right of the 2nd South Wales Borderers upwards of 700 yards. But even crossing just 200 yards of No Man's Land at a pace of 50 yards a minute will take four minutes. In theory a Maxim machine gun can fire nearly 2,000 rounds in that time[i]. For the South Wales Borderers their stroll in the sun would be c. 14 minutes. But they left from the front line. For the next wave of troops you could easily add at least another ten minutes as they moved up from their assembly trenches to reach the British front line.

As to weight, tt is certain that the koad to be carried by the foremost troops of the leading waves could have been reduced. If that had been done then it is arguable that these men could have 'doubled' across No Man's Land and onto the 1st objective.

But, what about the distance? Surely something could have been done about this in certain areas? The answer is: yes it could – but it was decided not to. The reason – so as not to give the game away that the Division intended to attack. By whom and how was this decision made? Why as a result of discussions between Haig, Kiggell, Rawlinson, Hunter-Weston and de Lisle.

Lt. Col. C G Fuller, GSO1 29th Division, tells us this in a letter to the compilers of the Official History after the war:

> "The 29th Division front trenches were situated some 200 yards or more distant from the German front line. Subsequent to the attack this fact was adversely criticised but about a month before the attack the whole question had been discussed by the CinC, CGS, Fourth Army, VIII Corps and 29th Divisional commanders in conference and they had come to the conclusion that it was undesirable to dig trenches closer to the Germans as it would make them realise we intended to attack. After the attack had failed the 29th Division started immediately to advance their trenches closer to the enemy."[23]

---

[i] Theoretically, of course. The gun is fed by a 250 round canvass belt which takes some time to change.

That there was no technical reason why such advanced trenches could not be dug is made clear by the rather guarded post-war comments by the then OC, 1st West Riding Field Company, Royal Engineers. Lt. Col., later Brig. Gen., Atwell Charles Baylay[i] would later write:

> "Criticisms as to the Division being asked to attack across such a No Man's Land would no doubt be out of place but that forward trenches could have been easily made was shown when I and my company went and dug with infantry parties new trenches well in front of the 87th Brigade front commencing the night July 2nd."[24]

Were there any other means by which the infantry could have approached safely the German front line trenches? The short answer is: yes, they could have used the Russian saps dug under No Man's Land on every division's front.

Writing a few days after the attack, Maj. Ralph Shelton Griffin Stokes[ii], Royal Engineers and the Assistant Inspector of Mines, wrote a report on the attack some of which was based on the observations of Capt. Alexander Watt Donald[iii], Highland Light Infantry attached to the 252nd Tunnelling Company. He had witnessed the attack of the 31st Division and 4th Divisions from a position at Bleneau Trench. Stokes' report generally deplored the failure to use imaginatively the numerous Russian saps so painstakingly dug over the previous weeks. Stokes remarked pointedly that:

> "… too much thought seems to have been given to facilities after the occupation of the enemy lines, and too little to the means of getting infantry across 200 yards of good field of fire for machine guns."[25]

---

[i] Brig. Gen. Sir Atwell Charles Baylay, CBE, DSO, Royal Engineers, was born in 1879, the youngest son of the late Col. Frederick George Baylay, RA, and Anna Louisa Murray. Educated at the United Services College, Cheltenham College and the RMA, Woolwich, he was commissioned into the Royal Engineers in 1898. He commanded the 3rd Field Troop, 4th Cavalry Brigade in 1910, taking part in that year's Army Manoeuvres as part of Blue Force. Adjutant, Royal Monmouthshire Royal Reserve Engineers, 1912. He was promoted Major in 1915, Lt. Col. and Brig. Gen. in 1918. He served in Gallipoli and was appointed CRE, 40th Division. He was given command of 59th Brigade of 20th Division in 1918. DSO, 1917, CBE, 1943, Knighted, 1947. He married Maria Edmondson, the daughter of Governor J B Groome of Maryland in 1904. He died in 1957.

[ii] Maj., later Brig. Gen., Ralph Shelton Griffin Stokes, CBE, DSO, MC, Royal Engineers, was born in 1883. Served in South Africa. Assistant assayer, Crown Reef Mine, South Africa, 1902. OC 174th Tunnelling Company, 1915. MiD, 1915. MC, New Year's Honours List, 1916. Assistant Inspector of Mines, 1916. DSO, 1917. Rejoined Royal Engineers, 1939. CBE, 1942. Lived and worked in South Africa before and after both World Wars. The Brigadier Stokes Memorial Award is the highest award given annually by The Southern African Institute of Mining and Metallurgy (He was President in 1936). He died in 1979.

[iii] Capt., later Maj., Alexander Watt Donald, MC & Bar, Highland Light Infantry att. 252nd Tunnelling Company, RE, was married to Jean B Donald of Cambuslang, Lanarkshire. Their son, Flying Officer Alexander Watt Donald, 11 Squadron, RAF, was the observer in Blenheim IV Z7803 and was killed in action near Ceylon on 9th April 1942. On this day nine Blenheims attacked the Japanese Fleeet and five were shot down. Flying Officer Watt is remembered on the Singapore Memorial, Kranji War Cemetery.

This comment by Stokes is telling. It reinforces the view that, all along, VIII Corps had thought of the advance as an 'occupation' of the enemy's trenches rather than a fight to wrest them from the enemy's hand. Hunter-Weston was convinced that the final 65 minute barrage would either kill or neutralise the majority of German troops in the 1st Position and his mis-placed confidence unfortunately infected most other senior officers. Critical evaluation of the intelligence gathered over the previous seven days, in particular the German response to the numerous raids mounted by VIII Corps, seems to have been non-existent. In all, this represents a lamentable failure of command, leadership and staff work which must be laid at the door of Hunter-Weston and his officers.

In the seventeen years or so since the war in South Africa when the British Army had first tried and failed to cross a 'fire swept zone' dominated by the German-manufactured quick firing, long range rifles and quick firing field artillery of the Boers it would seem they had learned little. Learning curve? What learning curve?

THE FAILURE OF THE HEAVY ARTILLERY TO DEMOLISH THE FRONT LINE

De Lisle now came to a crucial issue: the rôle and control of the heavy artillery. The heavy howitzers and long guns were then controlled by the CRA/CHA at Corps level. This meant that, not only was all counter-battery fire the responsibility of Corps, but so was the demolition of trenches and strong points. De Lisle questioned whether the latter, in particular, should not be devolved, at least in part, to the Divisions to control. This was a decision already made by the French.

> "It is essential that the first line system of trenches should be completely demolished and it would appear advisable for certain heavy howitzers to be allotted to the Divisional front for this duty alone and to be placed under Divisional control during the operations. By this means all the local knowledge of the Divisional artillery would be utilised in the important work of the destructions of the enemy's main trench line."[26]

One of the problems about this suggestion is that, had this been the case prior to 1st July, it is difficult to see how the operation could have been organised in such a way that all three objectives could be taken. It is clear from the reports of raids that, even 30 hours from zero, there were significant sections of German front line trenches relatively unscathed and with their dugout entrances unblocked. In these circumstances, it is easy to see local commanders giving priority to the destruction of defences on their immediate front. This would, in fact, have been the sensible thing to do and this is, in practical terms, what the French 6th Army did on their part of the Somme front. There, the German front line trench system was systematically destroyed by a high concentration of trench mortar and howitzer fire such that parts became untenable. This was also achieved on parts of the XIII Corps' front opposite Montauban.

The only other, if over-riding, priority for the French gunners was any active German battery. These were positively battered by all available guns and often swamped with poison gas shells by the 75s. But then the French were only attempting to take the German front line position. They would move onto the switch line the following day, and the 2nd Position the day after that, and this is precisely what they achieved on the Flaucourt plateau south of the Somme[i]. In addition, and because their objectives were limited, control of some of the heavy artillery was devolved to Divisions and, furthermore, the decision makers, the commanders of these batteries, were moved as far forward as practical so that the time delay between receiving information as to the whereabouts of the French infantry and the adjustments of the French barrage was as brief as possible.

VIII Corps, however, had three German positions to take, three sets of priority targets to fire on and a significant dilution of the power of their bombardment as a result. This stemmed from Haig's requirements for a deep advance on the left wing of the attack.

Other than the first-hand evidence provided from the raids late on, others observed the inadequacies of the bombardment of the front line.

Lt. Col. Douglas Evans Forman[ii], CMG, 147th Brigade, RFA, commanded the group of 18 pdr and 4.5 in. howitzer batteries in the Auchonvillers sector (86th Brigade). An experienced artilleryman, his post-war views were forthright:

> "Speaking from a general point of view, however, I consider that one of the chief factors that contributed towards the failure of our infantry in that sector to penetrate the enemy line anywhere was the fact that the enemy front trench had not been sufficiently crumpled up by our heavy artillery beforehand, with the result that the Germans were able to circulate freely in it once our attack was launched.
> I feel sure that if the enemy front trench at Beaumont Hamel had been as effectively treated as the corresponding front trench at Fricourt, which sector I visited a few days later just to see what a line of enemy trenches that our infantry had been able to sweep over looked like, the result of the attack on Beaumont Hamel on 1st July 1916 might have been different."[27]

Whilst it is fair to say that the quality of the German defences at Beaumont Hamel and Fricourt were not directly comparable, the point is still well made. The concentration of heavy shells on the German front line system had been woefully inadequate to achieve the essential results.

Lest one imagine that such concerns have only been expressed by writers after the event, the war diary of the 88th Infantry Brigade records the concerns of Brig. Gen. Cayley about the effectiveness of the British heavy artillery:

---

[i] In the French sector north of the Somme all first day objectives were gained, however, their next advance depended on the ability of the British XIII Corps to drive eastwards through Bernafay and Trones Woods towards Guillemont in order to cover the French left flank. This took some time to achieve and, in the meantime, the German front opposite the French XX Corps was reinforced and somewhat solidified.

[ii] Lt. Col. Douglas Evans Forman, CMG, DSO, Royal Horse Artillery, was born in Edinburgh in 1872. Educated at Edinburgh Academy and St Paul's School, he was commissioned into the Royal Artillery in 1892 from the Royal Military Academy, Woolwich. He served in South Africa in 1902 being awarded the Queen's Medal with four clasps. He was promoted Major in 1909 and Lt. Col. in August 1915. He was MiD in Sir Ian Hamilton's final Gallipoli despatch. His CMG was gazetted on 2nd May 1916. He was awarded the DSO in 1919 and made an Officer of the Order of the Star of Rumania in September 1919. He was placed on retired pay in October 1920. He died in 1949.

"I personally observed this bombardment and took careful note of the apparent damage done to the hostile trenches. It struck me that, though there were shell holes and craters all about them, the actual trenches appeared to have been scarcely touched by the heavy artillery, though there were many signs of direct hits by the Divisional Artillery and the wire seemed to be effectually cut, at any rate in front of the first line."[28]

The writer of the 87th Brigade war diary concurred:

"The actual bombardment by the artillery immediately previous to the assault does not appear to have knocked the enemy trenches about or filled in the deep dugouts."[29]

2nd Lt. Charles Ball, of B Battery, RHA, was in an advanced position, i.e. dug in between Auchonvillers and the White City, and he was in an excellent position to assess the damage done to the German front line trenches:

"The barrage everywhere gave the impression of being far too weak for such a strong position. Looked at every morning it was obvious that there was not enough heavy HE, shrapnel being no good against defences."[30]

Lt. Col. Hamilton-Hall, commander of the 16th Middlesex, the battalion in the 29th Division which suffered the heaviest numerical casualties on 1st July, had concerns about the entire artillery programme. In his view, too much was being asked of too few batteries and thus, by implication, he criticised Haig's demand for the capture of the German 2nd Position:

"The artillery scheme was too ambitious for the amount of artillery employed by us. The Heavy Artillery had too wide a target and got little chance of doing their job thoroughly before the attack. Compared to Ypres, July 1917, the enemy's front wire and lines appeared to be almost untouched. It would have been better if the heavy artillery had been able to concentrate on a more restricted area and the objective of the scheme at any rate for the first day had been more limited in character."[31]

Maj. R O Spencer Smith of the 2nd Hampshires had a comprehensive and highly pertinent list of question concerning the use of the heavy guns prior to and during the attack.

"What were the targets of the heavy howitzers, 15 in., 12 in., 8 in., 9.2 in., positioned near Englebelmer? There is no doubt that our preparatory bombardment did considerable damage to the enemy's trenches and wire but I doubt whether the Germans lost many men from it as they had such excellent dugouts.

During the actual assault I do not think the artillery fire was effective in subduing the enemy's fire. This is not meant as a criticism of the efficiency of the artillery but rather to emphasise the fact that the heavy artillery could not safely find the enemy's front line system owing to the contour of the ground which roughly conformed to the trajectory of the shells.

There were cases during registration when our own gunners failed to clear our crest line in trying to find the German front line trenches and great difficulty was experienced by battery commanders in finding suitable positions. These guns could have been more useful in adding weight to the barrage and where the attack would seem to have more prospect of success.

What assistance did the attack of the Newfoundland and Essex battalions get from our artillery fire at 9.05 a.m., this being the time according to the timetable in orders that the 88th Brigade should have reached Station Road?

The counter battery work does not seem to have been effective as a great many casualties were caused by enemy shell fire to our rear lines of attack before or just after they crossed our front line systems. Also the men bunched owing to only narrow lanes having been cut in our wire. They must have been an ideal target for shrapnel as they came over the skyline.

The Germans undoubtedly changed their battery positions far more frequently than we did, making their guns difficult to locate."[32]

Lt. Col. Ellis, whose 1st Border Regt. suffered huge casualties just getting through the British wire, was equally critical of the British barrage on the 1st July as well as the timing of the lifts:

"You will gather … that I attribute our failure very largely to the fact that our artillery barrage was ineffective.

This is the fact and although it is a platitude to say that we had not at that time learnt the proper way to use an artillery barrage in trench warfare it is none the less true.

Had our barrage gone down at zero just clear of our wire and stayed there long enough for all the attacking troops to form up under it and then moved forward in 50 yard lifts across No Man's Land with a longish halt on each of the German lines we might have brought off a success.

As it was the German machine gunners had it all their own way and the failure was inevitable."[33]

This failure of the timing of the artillery lifts was remarked upon in the post-battle report of the 147th Brigade, Royal Field Artillery:"

We did our allotted task but as our infantry failed except in isolated instances to penetrate the enemy front line our barrage ahead of the infantry represented so much ammunition wasted."[34]

What is interesting is that this report goes on to explain why the artillery barrages could not be brought back safely. The comment is an interesting and illuminating reflection on the numerous inaccurate observers' reports which so muddied the decision making waters at both Divisional and Corps' level:

"… it was impossible, owing to the dust, noise and *difficulty of distinguishing friend or foe* (Author's emphasis), to stop immediately our attack had failed."[35]

The 'difficulty of distinguishing friend or foe' was a crucial problem throughout the day. Is it possible that this was not just because of the smoke that covered the battlefield? It may not be correct but this writer has a 'theory' (don't we all!) as to why this confusion was worse on 1st July than at any other time. The British had been equipped with their Brodie helmets for some months and everyone involved in the attack wore this piece of protective equipment. The Germans, however, had not yet been seen wearing what became the highly recognisable 'coal scuttle' design helmet that became the trade mark of the German Army through this World War and the next. Maj. Philip Neame, VC, the Brigade Major of the 168th Brigade of the 56th Division which fought at Gommecourt, commented that 1st July 1916 was the first time he had ever seen German infantry wearing helmets.[36] Previously it had been either the soft felt cap or the spiked leather helmet, the Pickelhaube. On 1st July, however, the counter-attacking bombing parties came forward from reserve equipped with a large bag carrying stick grenades and wearing a metal helmet. If this were true then it would mean that men wearing helmets, which only the British were known to possess on this front, would have been seen in areas which were the objectives of the attack: Beaucourt, Station Road, Munich Trench, Pendant Copse and Serre; all areas through which counter-attacking German troops would have moved. Allied to the dense smoke clouds which enveloped the battlefield, might this have been the sight which confused observers, many very young and inexperienced, into believing British troops were far ahead of any position actually taken?

In addition, the timing of the early movement of the heavy gun barrage off the German front line was a major cause of bewilderment amongst officers of all arms. Maj. John Houghton Gibbon[i], DSO, commanded D/17 (460th) 4.5 in. Howitzer Battery, wrote later:

> "… we knew (the attack) was foredoomed to failure because of the GOC's orders to lift the heavy guns 10 minutes before zero and the field guns 2 minutes before. We had learned in Gallipoli that the only hope lay in continuing fire until the infantry had actually left their trenches. We carried this out with great success on, I believe, June 28th, 1915, and when the orders for the attack came in I wrote a careful letter pointing out that under such orders the attack could not succeed but, being only a major, there was no result.
>
> There were some bitter words afterwards about the artillery but the CRA (Brig. Gen. Malcolm Peake) had done his best about the lifting and told me that Gen. Hunter Weston was not to be moved from his scheme."[37]

Of all the criticisms of the Corps artillery this one is, perhaps, the most telling. Had the heavy guns only lifted early in the zone immediately surrounding the crater so as to accommodate the charge of the 2nd Royal Fusiliers to the rim, then one could not argue. The fact that this order was, whether by error or design, applied along the entire front of the VIII Corps is nothing short of criminal. It was not only on the 29th Division's front that troops were caught

[i] Maj., later Brig. Gen., John Houghton Gibbon, DSO, Royal Artillery, was born in 1878. He was educated at Eton and Trinity College, Cambridge, where he was awarded an MA. He was commissioned into the Royal Artillery in 1900 and was promoted Captain in 1909 and Major in 1914. He served in the Aro Campaign in West Africa (medal with clasp) and Southern and Northern Nigeria between 1901 and 1908. He served in Gallipoli and was MiD three times and awarded the DSO in 1916. Promoted Lt. Col. in 1925 he was CRA, 42nd (East Lancashire) Division, TA, in 1931-2, CRA, 53rd (Welsh) Division, TA, 1932 and Commandant and Garrison Commander, Royal Artillery Depot, Woolwich between 1932 and 1935. Served as Lt. Col. 4th Field Training Regt., RA, 1940 to 1946. He died in 1960.

forming up in No Man's Land before zero by German machine guns firing unmolested by the heavy guns. The same occurred on the 4th and 31st Divisions' fronts. For sheer incompetence this consumes the entire biscuit tin and yet no-one was brought to book for its tragic consequences.

As Maj. Gibbon relates above, Hunter-Weston was not for turning on the issue of the bombardment. Given the extravagant optimism about the outcome of the attack that permeated VIII Corps HQ at Marieux this is, perhaps, not altogether surprising. Capt. Grant, the Brigade Major of the 86th Brigade, reflected on this after the war:

> "The VIII Corps Staff, reflecting the commander's personality, were saturated with optimism particularly as to the effect of the preliminary bombardment."[38]

As usual, it was the 'Poor Bloody Infantry' who paid the price for such crass stupidity.

THE EARLY EXPLOSION OF THE HAWTHORN RIDGE MINE

It is impossible to find an officer of any rank who believed that the detonation of the mine ten minutes before zero was anything other than a catastrophic mistake. Maj. R O Spencer Smith of the Hampshires described it as 'a blunder' which 'prejudiced our chances of success considerably'.[39] The diary of the 147th Brigade, RFA, described it as 'a fatal error (which) gave away the show all along the line'.[40] Lt. Col. Hamilton Hall of the 16th Middlesex later described the timing of the mine at the Hawthorn Redoubt as 'fatal to the success of the attack as a whole'.[41]

Lt. Albert Whitlock, W Company, 2nd Royal Fusiliers, whose company was devastated trying to follow on the party from Z Company that attacked the crater, believed the early blowing of the mine directly affected any prospects the attack had of achieving success. It was not just the impact further along the Corps' front, it was the immediate impact on the vital tactical position of Hawthorn Ridge:

> "With regards to the firing of the mine, it was indeed very unfortunate that such a long definite notice of the impending attack was notified to the enemy by the firing of the mine under the Hawthorn Redoubt as there is no doubt to my mind that, had this been timed for firing almost simultaneously with the attack, we should, in the general confusion, have been able to overrun the Redoubt with little or no opposition and thus stop the intense direct machine gun fire and permit the following waves to get across No Man's Land subject only to indirect machine gun fire and artillery barrage.
>
> The notice, however, given by the mine was such as to permit the enemy's line being manned and for the crater to be defended with the result that the major portion of the first wave of the three companies of the 2nd RF were placed out of action almost immediately with no one getting into the enemy's trenches.
>
> My own company which followed shortly afterwards as second wave was also put out of action after which no more troops could leave our

trenches mainly owing to the constant machine gun barrage on our parapet from the Redoubt."[42]

De Lisle, as it happens, had been one who went along with Hunter-Weston's original thinking that the mine should have been blown several hours earlier. The idea was that the near rim would be seized and then the Germans lulled into a false sense of security by a return to the relative normality of bombardment life on the Beaumont Hamel front. His report states:

"The explosion of the mine warned the enemy of the time for the assault and better results might have been attained had the mine been fired some time previous to the hour fixed for zero."[43]

It is clear that the mine warned the Germans of an immediate attack. But this was an attack they knew was coming anyway. The idea that, had the mine been blown four or five hours earlier, they might have been persuaded into thinking any attack was a localised affair with limited objectives seems to this writer wishful thinking in the extreme.

Capt. F A Wilson of the Dublin Fusiliers made the case against the earlier blowing of the mine more than eloquently in his comments on the draft of the Official History:

"I agree with you absolutely as to the main cause of our failure namely want of surprise. The Hun must have known for weeks that an attack was pending along this portion of the front: our artillery had been endeavouring to cut his wire; prior to the 1st July gaps had been cut in our own wire; finally the blowing of the mine gave him ample warning of the actual attack."[44]

One assumes, however, that the firing of the mine early would, at least, have meant there was no necessity to lift the heavy guns off the front line trenches ten minutes before the main attack. On the other hand, the Germans everywhere would have been on the alert and then the success or failure of the attack would have been decided by the race to the parapet. As the British were walking and not racing, the German machine gun teams would still have won.

The other option for the mine was to explode it at the same time as all the others further south, i.e. just before zero. The artillery could have been allowed to sit on the German front line until the troops advanced and they might have stood a slightly better chance of success.

The timing of the mine explosion is an issue that has generated much controversy over the years. Lt. Col. C G Fuller's explanation that it was the OC of the 252nd Tunnelling Company who requested the early explosion in case of problems with the fuses only partially explains the 7.20 a.m. timing. Someone, somewhere had to agree to this. Writing after the war, de Lisle described how he had by-passed his Corps commander and gone straight to the top with his concerns about not just the timing of the mine but also the artillery preparation:

"Before the attack Rawlinson came to visit me and I told him I was gravely dissatisfied with the artillery plan which in my opinion was inadequate and too prolonged to be effective. I also highly disapproved of the mine being exploded 10 minutes before the attack as this would give the Germans warning.

> He said he would consider this last point but that I would find that the artillery preparation more than sufficient.
> A few days later Haig came with Rawlinson and I repeated my objections. Haig appeared to agree with me and seemed anxious about the success of the attack north of the Ancre."[45]

Rawlinson was unlikely to accept de Lisle's criticism of the bombardment as it was the Fourth Army commander's recommendation that the bombardment should be of five days' duration (turned into seven by the weather). The inadequacy of the intensity of the bombardment was, however, a different issue and one for which Haig had the primary responsibility when he deepened the required penetration of the VIII Corps and its neighbours to the south.

The timing of the mine was something to which either Haig or Rawlinson could have demanded changes. They knew the timings of the other mines and it is a mystery as to why the OC 252nd Tunnelling Company was not ordered to fall in line with these. Their failure to override this decision allowed de Lisle to develop a post-attack conspiracy theory in which the entire VIII Corps was joined by the VII Corps at Gommecourt in a gigantic sacrificial diversion:

> "Until after the attack we were in ignorance of the fact that the main attack was south of the Ancre and that ours was a subsidiary.
> I then realised that the hour of the mine explosion was intended to draw the enemy's attention to the northern flank and this appears to have been successful as they expected ours to be the main attack.
> The terrible losses in the VIII Corps would not have occurred to the same extent but for the mine which enabled the defenders to leave their dugouts and to man their trenches."[46]

De Lisle was clearly extremely bitter about what he later described as 'the unique failure of the 29th Division'. Scapegoats and excuses were required but the idea that the VIII Corps' attack was a subsidiary attack to ease the passage of the attack south of the Ancre is a classic case of justification 'after the event'. Had the attack to the south been as successful as Haig had hoped then the advance north of the Ancre would have proved a crucial element of the next moves. It was the hinge on which Haig's planned swing north towards the rear of Arras pivoted. It was an essential piece in that grossly over-optimistic jigsaw. Interestingly, though, de Lisle's 'conspiracy' complaint found a home in the Official History where, without any references to support the statement, Edmonds wrote that:

> "It seems to have been in the minds both of Sir Douglas Haig and General Rawlinson that even if the mine – the only one north of the Ancre – did give the alarm it might be to the advantage of the XIII and XV Corps on the right."[47]

Quite what this is supposed to mean is a mystery. Edmonds talks about 'drawing the attention of the enemy to the situation north of the Ancre'. Just what, in ten minutes, was the German Army command going to do while they contemplated the dust cloud over Hawthorn Ridge? Send a warning to all of their troops to expect an attack, one might imagine. But actually do anything in ten minutes that might in any way assist the advance of the XIII and XV Corps? No, but with Haig and Rawlinson both dead by the time of its publication, little flights of fancy like this might appear in the Official History of the Battle of the Somme without attracting too much adverse attention.

As far as the mine was concerned, de Lisle had another complaint. He believed that not only was it fired at the wrong time, it was also fired in the wrong place:

> "On inspecting the ground in November 1917 I noticed the mine was 50 yards short of the Hawthorn Redoubt and only the eastern tip had cut the German front line."[48]

He appended a small sketch of the positioning of the crater in his letter to Edmonds in 1929. A sketch map drawn at the time confirms his view that the majority of the redoubt was left untouched by the blast. Interestingly, the same occurred at the Lochnagar crater at La Boisselle though there the 34th Division managed to keep a permanent grip on the near side of the crater. It has not proved possible to determine whether the positioning of these mines was deliberate of accidental. Suffice to say, pushing them both forward another 50 yards might have resulted in a more dramatic success at each crater. On the other hand, it may be that it was thought inadvisable to tunnel too far under the German trenches for fear the workings might be detected and destroyed by enemy miners.

THESE WERE THE COMPLAINTS RAISED BY THE GOC, 29th Division but there were others just as serious which he failed to address. One of the most pertinent revolves around the question: how much did the Germans know in advance about the detail and timing of the attack?

Even though the Allies had air supremacy on the Somme at this time it is inconceivable that some German airman, in an aircraft or a tethered balloon, did not notice the vast increase in traffic and other activities along the Somme front. The noises of extensive overnight works were, in any event, clearly heard in the German trenches. In addition, the presence in the air of a British tethered balloon for every Division would have indicated an increase in the concentration of troops. Having said that, the German High Command still needed persuading that this was to be the main Allied thrust on the Western Front in the summer of 1916 and this remained the case for several days after the attack started. Locally, however, German commanders were sure they would be the subject of a major attack. The only questions were where and when.

There are two issues worthy of consideration here:

1. How much intelligence was gathered by the Germans from men taken prisoner during the many raids mounted during the bombardment? and
2. How much intelligence was gathered by the various Moritz listening posts located in the German front line?

It has already been recorded how a badly wounded Private from the North Staffordshire Regt., had, unwittingly, given important information about the nature of the attack on Gommecourt after being taken prisoner on the 24th June. On the 29th Division's front, ten men, four from the Newfoundland Regt.[i] and

---

[i] They are believed to be: 945 Pte Peter Barron, 1162 Pte William Frederick Bursey and 747 Pte Thomas Coombs. They were all probably sent to the Minden Mannschaftslager

six from the Royal Dublin Fusiliers, went missing during unsuccessful raids on the German lines. Then there is the case of the desertion of Pte. Josef Lipmann of the Royal Fusiliers on the night of the 27th/28th June, who went with the partial intention of giving information away to the enemy.

As to the missing, Lt. Col. Herbert Nelson, CO of the Dublin Fusiliers, recalls seeing some of his injured men dragged into the German lines on the morning after their raid and, as previously mentioned, he was concerned that, weak through loss of blood and confused by shock, they may have inadvertently given away crucial information about the plan for, and timing of, the attack.

He also makes another interesting and telling comment:

> "It would seem that the raid was expected and there was no element of surprise in it from the moment they went over the top."[49]

Maj. G V Goodliffe of the 2nd Royal Fusiliers echoed Nelson's sentiment that the Germans appeared to know what to expect as well as where and when:

> "Most of the casualties on 1st July were caused by MG fire. These opened fire almost as soon as our men left the trenches. It almost appeared as though the Germans were aware of zero hour but probably the explosion of the mine put them on the qui vive. I remember that at the time we all thought that the mine being blown so long before zero hour was a total mistake."[50]

Maj. Hoette of the Sheffield Pals too felt that the attack was expected though whether he thought it was the obvious preparations or a monitoring of communications which gave the game away is not made clear

> "We certainly had the impression that Germans were expecting the attack and were fully prepared though the original date was postponed 48 hours."[51]

It is now known that the Germans had been listening to British and French front line telephone communications for over a year and that the British (and French) had been aware of this for many months. The listening posts were known as Moritz stations and one, No. 28, was captured at La Boisselle, minus equipment but with copies of several British messages overheard by the German operators. Unfortunately, this would not have been news to the officers and men of the Signal Service of the Royal Engineers in 1916. The problem had first emerged in the summer of 1915:

> "…the enemy did suddenly appear to be extraordinarily well informed of all that was going on behind our lines. This was manifested in many ways. Carefully planned raids and minor attacks were met by hostile fire, exactly directed, and timed to the minute of the attack. Trenches where a relief was taking place were heavily shelled at the very time of the relief, when they were naturally filled with double their complement of men. This occurred too often to be a mere coincidence."[52]

(Prisoner of War Camp). 966 Pte John Joseph Cahill, who was definitely taken prisoner on that night, died of wounds on 5th July 1916.

Intensive experiments had taken place to investigate whether it was possible that the Germans were somehow tapping into British telephone communications and, if so, how were they were doing it. The first experiments took place in June and July 1915 and it was found that spoken phone conversations could be picked up, with the ground conducting the signal, at a distance of 100 yards and buzzer/Morse messages at 300 yards or more. By August, a French Private, an electrician in civilian life, had devised a system for listening in remotely to German telephone conversations. This had shown clearly the prospects for Allied intelligence gathering but, even more importantly, it revealed the danger of loose talk on their own phone systems. Signals Officers were ordered urgently to improve the insulation of signal circuits and put in place other safeguards.

The key problem in the short term, though, was instilling an essential discipline amongst officers and men near the front lines about what could and could not be spoken of during telephone conversations in forward areas. Memoranda were despatched widely insisting that certain subjects were now taboo in positions forward of battalion HQs. They were:

1. Names of units or unit calls.
2. Times of relief.
3. Movements of units.
4. Information regarding results of artillery fire.
5. Location of guns.

Extraordinarily, it took a long time for the need for this discipline to sink in amongst those using telephones near to the front line. Describing the attitude of the officers and men concerned as displaying either 'incredible ignorance or obstinacy', the history of the Signals Service, RE, goes on to say:

> "As late as October, 1916, the main obstacle in the path of the men who were endeavouring to overhear German conversation was the never-ceasing conversation on our own forward lines. Officers could not be made to understand that half their own worries and a considerable proportion of the casualties suffered by their units were due to their own indiscreet use of the forward telephones. Order after order was issued; precaution after precaution was insisted upon; still the leakage continued in slightly less degree only. It was not until disciplinary action was taken and carelessness made the subject of a court-martial charge, that forward telephones were used with any degree of care. Probably more was given away in 1916 than even in 1915; it was certainly to the later year that the classic example of stupidity in this respect belongs."[53]

The example referred to above concerns a set of orders issued by a British Corps for an operation prior to the capture of Ovillers-la-Boisselle. A complete copy of the order was found in a German listening post in the village. It had been transcribed and issued to the local German commanders prior to the proposed attack. It emerged that the order had been read out in its entirety by a Brigade Major to one of his battalions. The Brigade Major had objected to this action but had been over-ruled by his Brigadier. The history of the Signals Section RE, records, 'Hundreds of brave men perished, hundreds more were maimed for life as the result of this one act of incredible foolishness'.

In the light of this ill-discipline one wonders what information might have been leaked to the German Moritz station in the Leiling Stollen in the Y Ravine? Was it such a leak which allowed them to be so obviously ready for the raid of the Royal Dublin Fusiliers and, possibly, all of the other failed raids on the VIII Corps' front?

The fact is that it was known that the Germans were listening in to British transmissions in this area. On 29th May, in a GHQ intelligence report, the final paragraph read as follows:

> "Prisoners Statement: The prisoner of the 121st Res. Inf. Regt. captured north of Beaumont Hamel recently states that the Germans are always aware of impending artillery activity on our part as they obtain this information through the Listening Apparatus. This confirms the statement of other prisoners."[54]

One could speculate about the nature and scope of information given away by indiscreet telephone use in the British trenches opposite Beaumont Hamel in June 1916. What is indisputable is that Moritz Station 28 at La Boisselle sent in a report at 1 a.m. GMT on 1st July 1916 stating that Fourth Army had issued orders for the attack to start at 7 a.m. It was not just the premature blowing of the Hawthorn Redoubt mine that alerted the Germans on the Somme to the imminent attack.

AT THE TIME, AND FOR MANY YEARS AFTERWARDS, the survivors of the attack on Redan Ridge speculated as to the reasons for the spectacular and costly failure of the 4th Division. Certain aspects of a common theme repeat themselves from both contemporary and post-war comments.

There was more than a degree of bitterness in the thoughts of the Rifle Brigade's 2nd Lt. Glover's who had fought so hard in the Heidenkopf. The bitterness was directed mainly at the artillery:

> "The whole day was hopeless, both flanks in the air, continuous bombardment from the Germans and our guns doing nothing. When we saw aeroplanes we burnt flares but it made no difference. The Germans counter-attacking party sent up Very lights at short intervals and their artillery changed to a nicety. Why couldn't ours have held our right flank and put a barrage beyond? We should have held out then. Why didn't they go for the German guns? They were silent all day instead."

Glover is, of course, wrong about the artillery's 'silence' though, given the constant noise and terror around him in the Heidenkopf he was probably completely unaware of the continuous if purposeless firing of the field and heavy guns at targets hundreds and sometimes thousands of yards away to the east. His point about how little use the guns were to the men trapped in the German front line is, however, well made.

Capt. D R Adams, C Company, 1/8th Royal Warwicks, had a similar if less vigorously expressed view. Writing after the war in response to the draft of the Official History his opinion was that:

"The attacking troops could not keep up with the barrage which drew rapidly away from them and as communications had practically ceased to exist the infantry could not get the barrage brought back again."[55]

Lt. Col. Freeth of the 2nd Lancashire Fusiliers reflected on the inadequacy of the final minutes of the bombardment when just the 18 pdrs and Stokes mortars were bombarding the front trenches of the German position:

"Our opening barrage was not successful in keeping the German heads down. We heard their machine guns in action directly the barrage was put down especially on the Beaumont Hamel sector. As the barrage moved off the forward trenches so the machine gun fire increased."[56]

His explanation for the defeat concerned two aspects of the same issue: if the deep dugouts were not destroyed or effectively blocked then not only would the riflemen survive so would the machine gun teams. His explanation, therefore, does not tell us anything that was not already known in advance of the attack by commanding officers and their staffs throughout VIII Corps:

"I attribute the German successful defence to:
a. The strength of their position, especially as regards machine guns;
b. The fact that they had such excellent deep dugouts which even our heavy artillery could not damage. If one entrance was blown in there were always plenty of others available."[57]

An anonymous staff officer of the 4th Division reflected on another aspect of an inflexible Corps-imposed plan:

"The movements of the 10th and 12th Brigades of the 4th Division were, if I am not wrong, to a timetable fixed by the Corps. My recollection of the business was that we in the Division thought it was a mistake as no one could possibly say what would have happened by the time fixed. If, as actually did happen, things did not go well the movement could only make confusion worse confounded. The truth is that the division was not allowed to handle its own reserves or to have a voice as to the frontage they were to move on or the hour at which they were to start. As you say in your text, HQ sent out a message to stop the reserve Brigades. I remember very vividly discussing it with my General and I remember equally that we felt we should probably be blamed heavily. The truth was, of course, that we were right and that we really did it not so much because we were yet convinced we were going to fail but because we realised that to plump two more Brigades into the melee was an unwarranted gamble. In fact we disobeyed orders at the last moment and had to do it because we had been overridden before in the planning stage."[58]

These comments about the Division 'not (being) allowed to handle its own reserves' and of being 'overridden at the planning stage' suggests a Corps' staff riding rough shod over the wishes of more junior members of the organisation. Others, such as Maj. Gibbon of the 29th Division's Field Artillery, voices a similar complaint when commenting on Hunter Weston refusal 'to be moved from his scheme' to lift the barrage off the front lines early in spite of the entreaties of Brig. Gen. Peake, the CRA of 29th Division.

As a result of these hard-line impositions from on high all three Divisions, but most especially the 4th and 31st by nature of the local topography, found every unit involved in the attack simultaneously exposed to German artillery and machine gun fire pretty much from the moment the attack started. Spaced as they were, the 'waves' gave the gunners the chance to deal with each line of men in turn without them advancing sufficiently far to threaten the German defensive line. This was the essential flaw in the 'wave' system and it was exploited ruthlessly by the disciplined artillery and infantry commanders opposite.

Capt. Hugh Frank Dawes[i], Royal Fusiliers and a member of the 12th Brigade staff, expressed a concern already voiced by some officers on the 29th Division front – the suspicion that the Germans knew what to expect:

> "My recollection is that, as soon as the mine went up, that is, without appreciable pause, the rattle of German machine guns was terrific which also tends to show that all this was expected."[59]

Whether this was because they had received advance notice from the listening posts or whether it was simply the obvious preparations being made opposite he does not specify but it is clear that, although a lot of the work was done at night in an attempt to conceal the works from prying eyes, the noise created would have given the game away:

> "These preparations were, so we thought, largely responsible for the stiff resistance put up by the Germans. Heavy gun emplacements were erected in the open behind the trenches and at night the off-loading of the railway irons for these constructions could be heard for miles. It may have been coincidence, but we did not think so at the time, that a long range gun put two shells through the roof of 12th Brigade HQ at Bertrancourt crossroads on the afternoon of 30th June which necessitated our evacuating our HQ. All had been quiet up to that moment.
> The German could not help but know all about the impending attack and were probably waiting for the mine to go up!"[60]

Others, at the time of the attack, expressed concerns about the manner in which the German artillery so accurately targeted essential Royal Engineers' supplies such as trench bridges on the days immediately before the assault.

Dawes shared the well-expressed concerns about the inflexible nature of the artillery programme which so quickly left the infantry behind:

---

[i] Capt., later Brig. Gen., Hugh Frank Dawes, DSO, MC, Royal Fusiliers, was born in 1884. He was educated at Harrow School and attended Staff College, Camberley. He joined The Cardigan Royal Garrison Artillery Militia in 1902. He was commissioned into the 3rd Royal Fusiliers in 1906. He was MiD in the war, awarded the MC in New Year's Honours List of 1917 and awarded the DSO in the New Year's Honours List of 1918. He held staff positions in the 12th Brigade from March 1916, 30th and 39th Divisions, XV Corps and First and Third Armies. He was appointed GSO2 in the Rhine Army in 1930. He commanded the 2nd Royal Fusiliers between 1932 and 1936. He was AQMG, Southern Command, between 1936 and 1939 and served with the BEF 1939-40. He married Adrienne Jean Rathborne in 1920. Their son, Capt. Frank Philip Dawes, 2nd Royal Fusiliers, was killed in action on 10th April 1944 at Monte Cassino and is buried in the Cassino War Cemetery. Brig. Gen. Dawes died in 1965. He left £1,000 in trust for the upkeep of the Royal Fusiliers Regimental Chapel, then at St Sepulchre's, High Holborn.

"'The 29th and 4th Divisions were allowed 3½ hours in which to reach Puisieux Trench and the artillery lifts were arranged accordingly' [Quote from draft of *Official History*]. This was one of the most exasperating things of the day since, owing to the difficulties experienced in penetrating the enemy's front line, the barrage entirely left everyone and could be heard going into the blue... The time table was strictly adhered to throughout and the advance carried out as a drill movement."[61]

Capt. Victor Neville Johnson[i], Gloucestershire Regt., was the GSO3 of 12th Brigade. He watched the attack from the Advanced Brigade HQ which overlooked the Heidenkopf from about 400 yards inside the British lines. He too remarked post-war on the lack of proper artillery support caused, though he does not say so specifically, by the inflexible nature of the artillery programme and the retention of control of all of the guns by Divisional and Corps officers:

"During the progress of the battle we soon lost the use of our barrage as the advance of the infantry was held up so early. We saw good targets for our gunners. One enemy battery came into action in the open east of Pendant Copse but it took a long time for our artillery to fire on it."[62]

This lack of control of the artillery below Divisional level was, in fact, remarked upon soon after the attack by Brig. Gen. Crosbie of 12th Brigade. In his report, dated 15th July, he comments on the delays caused by the need to refer requests for artillery support to Division before they might be acted upon:

"It appears that the artillery followed accurately its clock programme. Artillery support was obtained through the Division.
The affiliation of one battery to infantry brigade would have been helpful in dealing promptly with immediate local needs."[63]

This was a lesson already well learned by the French 6th Army who had taken several measures to ensure that the infantry had access to rapid heavy and field artillery support where and when it was most needed.

In response to these criticisms of the gunners, an officer of the 29th Brigade, RFA, Lt. William Stirling, whilst accepting that the British artillery fire quickly became 'useless', argued that bringing it back in any effective manner was impossible because they simply had no idea where the infantry were:

---

[i] Capt., later Lt. Col., Victor Neville Johnson, DSO, Gloucestershire Regt., was born in 1882. He was the seventh of ten children and the fifth son of Capt. William Johnson, Inniskilling Dragoons, and Rosina Johnson (née Arnoth) of Oddington, Moreton in the Marsh. He was commissioned into the 3rd Wiltshire Regt. (Militia) in 1900 and transferred into the Royal Garrison Regt. in 1902 and then the Gloucestershire Regt. in 1905. Promoted Capt. 1911. Adjutant 1/5th Gloucestershire Regt., 1912. Brigade Major, 1915. Promoted Major 1916. GSO2 1917. GSO1 1918. Staff officer 46th Division and XVII Corps. Served in France and Russia. Five times MiD. Lt. Col. 2nd Gloucestershire Regt. 1919. Commanded 4th Nigeria Regt. 1927. Promoted Colonel and Officer in Charge Infantry Record and Pay Office, Warwick, 1935. Retired 1939. Married Claire Allicia Johnson and lived at Upton on Severn, Worcs. Died 1952. Their son, Capt. Richard Victor Guy Neville Johnson, MC, 1st Gloucestershire Regt., died on 19th April 1942. His body was never found and his name is inscribed on the Rangoon Memorial.

"The barrage on the morning of the 1st July opened according to plan but as is well known soon left the infantry and was therefore useless. There was no question of bringing it back as we could get no information at the time of the position our troops had reached."[64]

This latter comment is somewhat contradicted by the evidence of numerous reports, many inaccurate, from both infantry and artillery observers concerning the advanced positions of the attacking troops. What is does tend to suggest, however, is that these reports, whether optimistic, realistic or pessimistic, were not sufficiently robust for Division or Corps to use them as a basis on which to make changes to the programme until it was already much too late to make any difference. Stirling's statement does, however, confirm how the dearth of accurate communications on the 1916 battlefield so adversely affected the cooperation of the infantry and artillery at the crucial moments. It might be thought that the experiment made by 10th Brigade to advance a radio apparatus into the German third trench made no appreciable difference to the flow of accurate intelligence. Of course, one does not know how long the radio and its operator survived in the German lines. Had they survived and had more radios been shipped across No Man's Land it is conceivable that at least some of the 'fog of war' might have lifted. Success or failure, it was an experiment well worth pursuing.

One of the reasons for the inflexibility of the artillery programme and of the infantry tactics was the hugely detailed set of instructions despatched from VIII Corps to which were added other tactical notes from both Division and Brigade. These documents attempted to provide answers to every possible question that the enemy might ask and to every organisational issue that might arise. The VIII Corps *'Scheme for Offensive'* was 76 pages long to which were added another 15 pages on administrative matters alone by 4th Division's Q Department. Brig. Gen Rees of the 94th Brigade, 31st Division, described the VIII Corps publication as a 'terrible document' and a more lowly officer, Capt. Claude Max Vallentin[i], 27th Battery, 32nd Brigade, RFA, commented that:

"... too much paper was distributed too far down. My Battery Commander gave me all we got in the battery to look after ... at most a

[i] Capt., later Brig. Gen., Claude Max Vallentin, MC, 27th Battery, 32nd Brigade, RFA, was born in 1896. He was the son of Lt. Col. Henry Edward Vallentin, DSO, OBE, RA, and Claudine Vallentin and was educated at Wellington College and the RMA, Woolwich. Commissioned into RFA, September 1914. Joined 27th Battery (then commanded by his father), November 1914. Served in Russia. Awarded MC in New Year's Honours 1919. Staff College, Camberley, 1928. GSO3, War Office, 1932. Major, 1934. Air Staff, 1935. Royal Naval Staff College, Greenwich and GSO2, 1938. CO, 1st Support Group, 1st Armoured Division then Cdr RA, 5th Indian Division, 1940. Lt. Col. 1941. GOC, 5th Indian Division, 1942. Captured in Western Desert but escaped from the Villa Orsini at Sulmona in Northern Italy in 1943 and rejoined the Allied forces. Brig. Gen. Northern Command, 1944. Retired, 1948. Under Sheriff of London, 1951-61. Married first Doris Harvey Blake (died 1956). One daughter, Lisa. He re-married Mrs Winifred Young, the widow of Brig. Gen. Ayerst Young, RA, in 1957. They lived at 30, Kensington Place, Campden Hill, London, W8. He died in 1961. Author of *'A Short History of the 27th Battery, RFA'.*

> quarter of what I lived with ever affected us, the remainder was superfluous."[65]

Unlike the German Army which encouraged personal initiative, every set of instructions produced by Fourth Army downwards seemed intent on stifling such a virtue amongst officers at all levels. Although inexperienced the troops about to attack on the Somme were probably the best educated and most intelligent body of men ever to represent Great Britain on a battlefield. These attributes were to be choked off rather than encouraged in both their training and their application to the grave detriment of all concerned.

WHAT HAD GONE SO BADLY WRONG ON THE 31ST DIVISION'S FRONT to result in such heavy loss for no gain whatsoever?

Brig. Gen. Ingles, GOC 93rd Brigade, initially put it down to three causes:

1. The enemy's artillery barrage;
2. The enemy's machine gun fire;
3. The enemy's rifle fire.

One might regard this as a rather simplistic and, indeed, obvious analysis but, to give the General his due, he did expand on these factors. Clearly, the Germans had a plan and it was one which was effectively employed along the entire front North of the Ancre. It chiefly revolved around the use of their artillery. The plan was very simple: ignore the British artillery, i.e. there was little or no counter battery fire, and concentrate on the British front line trenches and assembly trenches. Anyone who got through the very heavy barrage placed along the front line would be dealt with by the machine guns, riflemen and bombers in the front trenches. What was essential was to prevent any reinforcement or re-supply of any British troops able to get a foothold in the German trench system.

Ingles believed that, on its own, though very severe, the German artillery barrage could have been overcome, although he does not explain how. His description of it was that:

> "It began within 4 minutes of the attack being launched. It was most severe on the front line and 20 yards in front of it, and also on the assembly trenches and the heads of the communication trenches and where those trenches crossed Monk Trench."[66]

He also remarked on the number of casualties caused by men crowding together to cross the trench bridges behind the lines. These locations were then targeted by both the enemy artillery and machine guns.

In other words, with the exception of the waves of the three leading battalions of the 31st Division that had crept out into No Man's Land before zero, the barrage caught all of the troops involved in the attack, killed and wounded many of them behind the British lines and prevented them from supporting the few survivors of the initial advance. The artillery itself was thought mainly to be field guns and howitzers and medium howitzers with the heavier guns firing from the north east around Puisieux and the field guns from behind Serre. Ingles also believed that the Germans had 'unmasked guns they had not previously used'. This is probably true but it is also true that a large proportion of the batteries firing from Serre northwards had simply not been spotted by ground or aerial observers. In the area from Puisieux to Douchy-les-

Ayettes less than half of the German batteries active on 1st July had been previously identified by British Intelligence.

He noted that the German machine guns opened fire before zero, i.e. after the heavy guns and field howitzers had moved off the front lines but during the Stokes mortar 'hurricane bombardment'. Seven machine guns were identified as firing on the 93rd Brigade front, which is a reasonable estimate (we can completely discount the 93rd Machine Gun Company report that there were 16 machine guns on the German front line parapet). The majority of these guns fired from emplacements in the front trenches with others firing from the rear over the heads of the German troops in their front line. Others, it was thought, had been brought into the open.

The enemy riflemen also opened up before zero, another indicator of the weakness of the Stokes mortar and 18 pdr barrage that was all that was used to keep the enemy's heads down in the final minutes before the attack. The view within the 93rd Brigade was that:

> "... the front line was held all through the bombardment and that all, with the exception of one or two sentries, were in deep dug outs immediately in the rear of their front line."[67]

Given the response to every single raid mounted by the 31st Division during the seven day bombardment such a conclusion is hardly rocket science. What is bewildering is that no-one, from Corps downwards, seems to have thought this through and realised that the guns being used to bombard the front line must be inadequate to the task set of killing or neutralising the forward German infantry. At this time, German policy was to keep large garrisons in the front line position. Although this would change as the Somme battle developed and a more elastic, defence in depth was employed, here, now, the German garrison was very much located in deep dugouts in the front trenches. Whilst it was possible to block entrances to dugouts employing the lightweight guns used on these trenches, collapsing the dugouts with such weapons was well-nigh impossible.

Ingles states as much:

> "Our artillery bombardment was apparently not heavy enough to touch the dug-outs or tunnels in the enemy lines. The Stokes bombardment appears to have been equally ineffective...
> ... Although our Artillery bombardment considerably damaged the enemy's trenches it was insufficient to damage his dugouts and I am of the opinion that nothing of less weight than the shell of a 15 in. howitzer would have any effect on these deep dugouts."[68]

Of course, the 15 in. howitzers and others of a similar weight, were mainly used to destroy the villages behind the German front lines whilst the majority of the garrison was either in front of, or to the rear of, these locations. In every case between the Ancre and Serre, two out of the three battalions of the four German regiments involved in the battle were garrisoned in either the front, support or reserve trenches. Perversely, VIII Corps appeared to known this and had stated this as a fact early on. They had then failed to develop this idea by concentrating their heavier guns on these lines but, of course, because of Haig's ambitions for the attack, this would not have been an acceptable deployment of the heavy artillery.

Ingles was impressed, however, by the quality of the New Army men at his disposal:

> "The morale and discipline of the men was most excellent and they advanced through the very heavy enemy artillery barrage and machine gun fire as though on parade.
> The attack never lacked for want of being pushed home and it was only the extremely heavy and accurate machine gun fire and the severe artillery barrage which prevented them attaining their objective…
> The officers proved themselves capable and conscientious in their duties and led their men fearlessly and with confidence."[69]

Brig. Gen. Ingles's final thoughts concerned the lack of any element of surprise. Certainly, a seven day bombardment on any given front was a bit of a giveaway as to Allied intentions, however, as the French showed, if the objective was sensible and the preparation truly comprehensive, then even this was not a barrier to success given the German defensive tactics then employed. But Ingles had concerns in other areas too:

> "I am of opinion that the 10 minutes hurricane bombardment by Trench Mortars gave the enemy warning of impending attack as did also the troops leaving the trenches so early; he was then able to concentrate all his guns to form a barrage prior to hour for assault and all chance of surprise was done away with. Had the leading platoons on leaving our trenches marched direct on their objectives without having to halt I feel convinced that they would have taken the first and probably second and third lines before the enemy's Artillery barrage had been formed and before machine guns could have been produced in any numbers."[70]

This writer does not share the General's optimism given the failure of the preliminary bombardment and the early removal of the heavy guns from the front trenches. These needed to be kept on the front line until the last possible moment but, on the VIII Corps' front, the timing of the explosion of the Hawthorn Ridge mine, and the absurd extension of the local artillery lifts there to the entire Corps' front, rendered this impossible. Only in the circumstances of a far heavier bombardment of the German 1st position and an assault at speed simultaneous with the first artillery lift could one genuinely have held out any hope of a successful attack here or anywhere else north of the Ancre.

Further comments about the failure of the 93rd Brigade were provided in response to the first draft of the Official History by the Brigade Major, Maj. Charles Howard[i], KRRC. Howard is quite clear that the attack was effectively at an end early on:

---

[i] Maj., later Brig. Gen., Sir Charles Alfred Howard, GCVO, DSO, King's Royal Rifle Corps, was born in 1878. He was the grandson of the 17th Earl of Suffolk and 10th Earl of Berkshire. His mother re-married Gen. Sir Redvers Buller, VC. Educated at Eton and Sandhurst, he was commissioned into the King's Shropshire Light Infantry in 1898 serving in India and then South Africa where he served as ADC to Sir Redvers Buller and with the South African Light Horse. Transferred to the KRRC, 1901. Adjutant, 5th KRRC, 1908.

"As far as the 93rd Brigade was concerned the heavy casualties had been sustained and the fighting was over before noon on 1st July. Although it was reported that a few isolated men had reached the German front line trench and even penetrated further ... the attack was held up soon after the troops had left the front line. Very many casualties occurred in the front line trench and many men never even reached this trench."[71]

Howard addressed the issue of D Company, 18th Durham Light Infantry, and their ill-fated and completely unsuccessful mission to occupy Pendant Copse:

"The 4th battalion in this Brigade was the 18th DLI and this battalion, less one company, was the Brigade reserve. The one company had been specially detailed to take Pendant Copse, facetiously known as Pending Corpses beforehand. Of course this company never got there though it was reported that a few men had reached it though I think they were probably men from the 4th Division."[72]

Maj. Howard points the finger of blame for the failure at the inadequacies of the artillery bombardment:

"The failure was undoubtedly due to the ineffectual result of the artillery bombardment, the German trenches were well knocked about but the dugouts must have remained immune. Most of Serre above ground was obliterated but again the dugouts must have been extremely good."[73]

He was also not convinced about the results of the wire cutting, nor with the overwhelming and completely misplaced confidence of Hunter-Weston:

"The Corps commander was extremely optimistic telling everybody that the wire had been blown away (we could see it standing strong and well), no German trenches and all we had to do was walk into Serre."[74]

Like so many of the senior officers of the Division, Howard was extremely impressed by the quality of the men of this New Army Division:

"As far as the 93rd Brigade was concerned the fight was over before noon. The tragedy really was that here was a Brigade, the majority of whom had joined up in 1914, had not left England till the end of 1915 then went to Egypt, returning to France in April 1916 and the first engagement in which they took part was the last for very many.
I've never seen such fine raw material, nearly all well-educated, physically fit young men, nearly all fit to be NCOs and many officers... there was not a single case of shirking or hesitating or turning back and considering it was their first action it was truly fine. Luckily few, if any, understood what was before them."[75]

He occupied Staff positions between 1912 (Brigade Major, Devon & Cornwall Brigade, Southern Command) and 1916, 93rd Brigade, before being given command of the 16th KRRC in August 1916. He was awarded the DSO, 1917, Bar to the DSO while commanding the 1st KRRC in 1918. KCVO, 1955, GCVO in 1957. He commanded the 162nd (East Midland) Brigade, TA, 1929-32 and the 12th Brigade and Dover Garrison 1932-5. Freedom of Dover 1935. Appointed Serjeant at Arms in the House of Commons 1935 in which position he served until 1956. He died in 1958.

Lastly, Howard commented on the weight of equipment each man was forced to take into battle:

> "Another extraordinary and almost incredible thing was the amount each man was forced to carry. In addition to equipment containing spare socks and shirts, etc., unexpired portion of rations, each man was loaded with 200 rounds of ammunition, several bombs and a full size spade or shovel on his back. They could hardly get along the trenches let alone fight."[76]

Brig. Gen. Rees, GOC 94th Brigade, was far more scathing about the planning of the attack both in his own memoirs and in response to the initial draft of the Official History of the war. Rees was only in temporary command. He arrived on the 15th June and left on the 2nd July to replace Bertie Prowse of the 11th Brigade.

Rees was horrified by the quantity of 'bumph' issued at all levels of the VIII Corps:

> "I only arrived at VIII Corps HQ a fortnight before the attack took place. Therefore, as a complete stranger to the scheme, I was faced with this terrible document *'Scheme for the Offensive'* of 76 pages and I found that my Division had issued, I speak from memory, 365 supplementary instructions. It took me three days on reaching my Brigade to reduce this enormous mass of instructions to some 8 pages and 5 maps. The first principles of war were overwhelmed by a mass of detail which dispensed with individual initiative and elasticity."[77]

Having read through the enormous quantity of prescriptive instructions, Rees was even more concerned:

> "The attack was finally fixed to take place on the 29th. One of my criticisms of the general plan of operations was that the time allowed for the capture of each objective was too short. I had a severe argument with Hunter Weston before I induced him to give me an extra ten minutes for the capture of one orchard, 300 yards beyond the village of Serre. I was looked on as something of a heretic for saying that everything had been arranged for except the unexpected, which usually occurs in war."[78]

Rees's final comment is one of the few relating to the lack of a Plan B here and, indeed, almost anywhere on the Fourth Army front on 1st July. The *expectation* amongst senior officers was of complete success everywhere. What need was there of a Plan B? Clearly, Sod's Law was not well known amongst the upper echelons of the B.E.F. whilst it was something of an everyday occurrence lower down the food chain.

The Brigadier was very worried about the speed required to keep up with the artillery timetable although he freely admits he did not foresee the consequences of such a timetable if the infantry fell behind:

> "The short space of time allowed for the capture of each objective made it essential for the whole of my Brigade, with the exception of three companies, to advance at zero hour, otherwise they would not reach the positions assigned to them at the time laid down. In twenty minutes I had to capture the first four lines of trenches in front of Serre. After a check of twenty minutes, I was allowed forty minutes to capture Serre, a village

800 yards deep, and twenty minutes later to capture an orchard on a knoll 300 yards beyond. My criticisms on these points are not altogether a case of being wise after the event. I did not like them at the time, but I do not profess to have foreseen the result of these arrangements should a failure occur."[79]

With their being no chance of surprise, Rees began to worry about the absence of any meaningful activity by the 48th Division on his left. Rees raised this with Hunter-Weston at the time:

"I suggested one day to the Corps Commander that a number of dummy assembly trenches might be dug to attempt to deceive the enemy & cause him to waste shells on that area. Hunter Weston congratulated me on the idea, but whether it was put into execution or not I don't know."[80]

Obviously nothing was done. Writing after the war to the compilers of the Official History, his views are scathing:

"…not a spade had been put into the ground between me and the subsidiary attack at Gommecourt. Worse still no effort at wire cutting was made on that stretch either. A child could see where the flank of our attack lay to within 10 yards."[81]

It is a criminal reflection on the Staffs of both the VIII and VII Corps that on each of their open flanks (of which the VII Corps at Gommecourt had two[i]) nothing realistic was done to persuade the German defenders opposite the inactive 48th and 37th Divisions that they might attack.

Rees later attributed the failure to three main factors:

"The causes of this disaster are lack of secrecy or any effort to mislead, the great success of the German deep dugout system and the failure of our counter battery work.
With regard to the latter the Corps commander assured me that the enemy had only 55 guns north of the Ancre. On 3rd July 66 batteries had been located. The Germans therefore sprang two surprises on us, the deep dugout system and a great quantity of cleverly hidden guns."[82]

As conclusively shown earlier it cannot reasonably be said that the British had no knowledge of the German dugout system. Their existence and the protection afforded to the German garrison really should have come as no surprise to anyone who read the reports of the various raids along the lines which, over several months, had revealed their existence. Even if they had not read these reports, the large numbers of active and aggressive troops who responded to every British raid prior to the attack by VIII Corps should have given senior officers some reason to question the effectiveness of the British bombardment.

The issue about the number of guns available to the German defenders of Serre and Beaumont Hamel is another question. What seems not to have been noticed by British Intelligence was the appearance in the line at Gommecourt of the 2. Garde Reserve Division in early May. As previously mentioned, a map of suspected German units along the front dated 27th June does not have this

[i] Four if one takes into account the decision not to attack Gommecourt Park which lay between the left of the 56th Division and the right of the 46th Division.

Division in the line but has it listed with a question mark as to its position somewhere in reserve. The addition of this Division to the defences north of the Ancre not only strengthened the defences of Gommecourt but strengthened Serre too as the 52. Infanterie Division was able to reduce its front by 50% and concentrate its artillery on a far smaller area.

As a result, north of the Ancre the 26. Reserve Division defending Beaumont Hamel and Redan Ridge could call upon the support of 61 guns from its own resources. The 52. Infanterie Division had the support of a similar number of guns and the 2. Garde Reserve Division slightly fewer, about 50 guns (though they were supported from the north by the otherwise unoccupied artillery of the 111. Infanterie Division at Adinfer Wood). In other words, Serre and Beaumont Hamel were defended by around 120 artillery pieces, more than double Hunter-Weston's estimate, and, if one counts the batteries of the 2. Garde Reserve Division, some of which may have been diverted onto Serre, then the number of German batteries north of the Ancre does, indeed, approach the 66 mentioned by Rees.

The consequences for the 31st Division of this greatly increased concentration of firepower was that, in Rees's own words post-war:

> "This barrage which fell at zero was one of the most consistently severe I have seen. When it fell it gave me the impression of a thick belt of poplar trees from the cones of the explosions. As soon as I saw it I ordered every man within reach to halt and lie down but only managed to stop about 2 companies because all troops had to move at once in order to capture their objectives on time. It was impossible for any but a few men to get through it."[83]

Whatever the precise numbers of guns involved, the intensity of the German barrage came as a severe shock to the officers and men of the 31st Division. Capt. Francis Piggott, Royal Engineers[i], was the Brigade Major of the 94th Brigade, and, after the war, he confirmed that the British were caught by surprise by the number of guns employed against them:

> "The German guns away on our left were, I think, in considerably greater strength than was generally realised and they switched over from the

[i] Capt., later Maj. Gen., Francis Stewart Gilderoy Piggott, CB, DSO, was born in 1883. He was educated at Cheltenham College and the RMA, Woolwich. He was commissioned into the Royal Engineers in 1901. A fluent Japanese speaker he was specially employed in Tokyo during the Russo-Japanese War 1904-5 and was Assistant Military Attaché at the embassy in Tokyo, 1910-13. GSO3, War Office, May 1914. Brigade Major, 94th Brigade. GSO2, 20th Division, 1916. GSO2, Fifth Army, 1917. GSO1 (Intelligence) Fifth Army, 1918, then Second Army. MiD five times, DSO, 1917. Staff College 1919 before returning to the War Office as GSO2, Intelligence. British Empire delegation, Washington Conference on Arms Limitations. GSO1, War Officer, 1927. Deputy Military Secretary, 1931, and Maj. Gen., 1935. Military Attaché, Tokyo, 1936. CB, 1937. Retired 1939. Senior Lecturer in Japanese, School of Oriental Studies, London, 1924-6. Colonel Commandant, Royal Engineers, between 1941 and 1951. He married Jane Smith of Gibraltar in 1909. Their younger son, Lt. John Allen Stewart Piggott, Nigeria Regt., died on 2nd January 1941 and is buried in the Thika War Cemetery, Nairobi. Kenya. Maj. Gen. Piggott died in 1956.

> British lines opposite them in order the enfilade the attack of the 31st Division which was then met by fire both from the front and flank."[84]

Maj. Cyril Mindon Trower Hogg[i], 2/4th Ghurkha Rifles and a graduate of the Staff College at Quetta, was a GSO2 on the 31st Division Staff and he was another to bemoan the lack of accurate intelligence about the strength of the German artillery:

> "Our information regarding enemy artillery was to some extent inaccurate and it was extremely incomplete. Before the action commenced we had drawn up an Artillery Map showing not only the positions of our own guns but also, according to such information as we had received, the positions of enemy batteries which might be expected to oppose the advance. It was this latter information which was so incomplete and therefore misleading and the enemy barrage certainly contained the element of surprise. For the same reason our counter battery work was only partially effective. This combined with the accuracy and unexpected volume of artillery fire directed on our front line at zero hour and subsequently resulted in completely breaking up and disorganising the attack at the very outset."[85]

Hogg was also scathing about the ineffectiveness of the Stokes mortar hurricane bombardment at 7.20 a.m.:

> "The hurricane fire of the Stokes mortars ten minutes before zero was quite ineffective and only helped to 'give the game away'. I saw the Divisional Bombing Officer about midday and he was of the opinion that this bombardment had served no useful purpose. I don't think anyone outside Corps HQ ever expected anything else."[86]

One of the issues not raised by any of the senior and staff officers of the 31st Division apart from Maj. Howard of the 93rd Brigade is the state of the German wire – was it cut or uncut? And, if uncut, how widespread was the problem. There seems to be a significant discrepancy between the wire reports made in the day or so before the attack, the observations made by field artillery officers and the feedback from the attacking infantry.

The wire reports and the artillery observers are seemingly agreed that the German wire, where observable, was well cut and would not present much of an obstacle to attacking infantry. When the infantry arrived in front of the German trenches, however, a regular complaint by those who made it back alive was that there were gaps but that they were too few and too narrow. In some places, for example the extreme left, where the 14th York and Lancasters were to construct

[i] Maj., later Lt. Col., Cyril Mindon Trower Hogg, DSO, 2/4th Gurkha Rifles, was educated at Bedford School. Commissioned into the South Lancashire Regt. Transferred to Indian Staff Corps, 1900. Attended Staff College, Quetta, 1902 & 1914. Promoted Capt. 1907. Promoted Major 1915. GSO2 1916. DSO 1917. GSO1 1920. Lt. Col. cmdg 1/4th Gurkha Regt. Retired 1922. Hon. Flight Lt., 1939, General Duties Branch, RAF Volunteer Reserve, then Temp. Squadron Leader. Resigned commission 1943. Married Winifred Ethel Hogg and lived at The Red House, Church Crookham, Hampshire. Their younger son, Capt. Michael Cyril Trower Hogg, 2/6th South Staffordshire Regt., died on 8th July 1944 and is buried in Cambes-En-Plaine War Cemetery, Calvados, Normandy.

their new flanking trench, there are some suggestions that there were no gaps at all.

The initial draft of the Official History clearly inclined in favour of the infantry's view that the wire cutting was inadequate or the words could be read as such:

> "The bombardment on this sector of the front had not been effective, and the enemy defences were little damaged."[87]

This was, indeed, part of a section critical of the artillery's performance in general. Lt. Col. Simonds, 170th Brigade, RFA, whose comments about independently changing his barrage line in the mid-morning of the attack perhaps explained a lot of the confusion about the German's firing on their own trenches, argued fiercely against an analysis that the field guns had failed the infantry:

> "To say that the bombardment was ineffective and that the enemy defences were little damaged must convey that the wire was not effectively cut. That the wire was effectively cut I have ample evidence to show: I attach copies of reports made at the time on this matter. Apart from these reports, which I still have, there was certainly no complaint from the 93rd Brigade, which my batteries were covering, and I never heard of any from 94th about the enemy wire being any obstacle to their advance."[88]

Though this last point is highly debatable given the testimony of survivors from the Sheffield, Accrington and Barnsley battalions involved in the attack, his other points do have some merit. There are several possible explanations for the existence of uncut wire not properly observed from the British lines. It should be born in mind that the vegetation in No Man's Land had not been cut since the summer of 1914. It seems somewhat inevitable that spring and early summer growth added to the previous year's undergrowth might conceal some of the lower lying wire which, if not through height but through depth, prevented easy access to the enemy's lines. Then there is the question: might the Germans have repaired the wire or somehow filled the gaps cut? Well, they would have had some time to do this unmolested on the final night of the bombardment as the normal machine gun and field gun fire aimed at the gaps cut in the wire was suspended for the period during which the wire patrols were out in No Man's Land. As it is clear that the German front line was heavily manned, making men available for such a task would not have proved an issue. There certainly are examples of places where concertina wire was reported to have been thrown into gaps cut into the more robust staked wire. This could easily have been done in the 90 minutes or so when British fire on the gaps was suspended, assuming, of course, that it had proved possible to bring such supplies forward during the bombardment. As the Germans seem to have planned for most eventualities it would seem unlikely that they would have forgotten to have such material in reserve. As a result, and in spite of Simonds' protestations, it is possible to foresee a scenario where British troops came up against uncut new wire or uncut old wire that could not be seen.

But Simonds' defence of his field gunners is not one designed to cover the artillery in its entirety. About the performance of the Corps Heavy Artillery he is contemptuous:

> "That the artillery were (sic) at fault in not making the bombardment more effective cannot be denied, but the fault lay with the Heavy Artillery of the VIII Corps, and here perhaps I may be able to offer some information which affected the front of the 4th Division. It so happened that I had become acquainted with the Serre front since April, when the Division first went to Maillet Mailly, and never left it until relieved at the end of the first week in July, after the first attack in the Battle of the Somme had been launched. For some time before the opening of the Battle our Infantry had been aware that the Germans had been making use of the sites of two old haystacks near the junction of Serre Trench and Matthew Alley as Machine Gun Nests; the site was marked on the ground by a black patch, the ashes of the burnt haystacks, and it was presumed that the Germans had under this as a camouflage made concrete emplacements. Repeated appeals for heavies to bombard these were met by our being told to employ our own light howitzer fire, which was done with no appreciable effect. It seemed to be the general opinion among the infantry that it would require something bigger than even 6 in. Howitzer fire to reduce these emplacements; but to the last this was neglected, and the penalty for the omission was a heavy one; for not only did these machine guns inflict very heavy losses on our own infantry but brought a most destructive fire to bear on the flank of the otherwise successful advance of the 4th Division. It was from these same emplacements that the destructive fire came from that you mention in the attack of that Division."[89]

FINALLY, ONE MUST ADDRESS THE ISSUE as to who was responsible for the fatal fiasco of the attack of the VIII Corps on 1st July 1916. Most modern historians now view the performance of the generals of all sides in a much kindlier light than during the era of 'Lions led by donkeys' and prior to John Terraine's ground-breaking rehabilitation of Sir Douglas Haig. It is undeniable that these generals were experiencing at first hand and for the first time the complex problems of large scale industrial warfare involving the entire economic and military efforts of the greatest European powers. So, indeed, were those countries' politicians but they, for the time being at least, elicit little sympathy from those who now commend British and, perhaps, some French generals for doing their best and for finally winning the war.

The popular phrase describing the process through which British generals went between late summer 1914 and the early winter of 1918 is 'the learning curve'. The word 'curve' suggests a smooth, and in this case when the word 'learning' is added, a smooth upwards path of increasing knowledge, experience and enhanced tactical acumen. The question is: was this what was on display amongst senior British officers in the period immediately prior to the opening of the Battle of the Somme? Were lessons being drawn from the battles of 1915 and adapted to the new circumstances, new weaponry and new volumes of ammunition now available on the Western Front? What signs were there that the British High Command had taken on board, after a rigorous analysis, the reasons for the failure of every offensive in which they and the French had been involved since the beginning of trench warfare?

Compared to the French, the signs were very few. Foch, Petain and Fayolle had, over the previous nine months, turned on its head nearly every French pre-war tactical concept. No longer was it the role of the infantry to spearhead the defeat of the enemy. Now, whenever possible, the infantry was to be protected from the staggeringly high casualty rates of 1914 and 1915. It was to be the role of the artillery to prepare the way for the infantry to occupy the ground held by the enemy. The time of the grand sweeping advance, the Napoleonic victory, the unstoppable élan of the Poilus sweeping all before it was at an end. Foch and the others looked at circumstances as they were and not as they wished them to be. Breakthroughs were not possible under the current circumstances, was the conclusion. There were not enough guns and not enough ammunition to do the job of rupturing the enemy's lines. Communications systems were too poor to be able to control large battlefields centrally which meant a degree of decentralisation of command and control so that local problems and issues could be dealt with more swiftly at the local level. Communications were so bad that fighting battles outside of the visual range of ground-based observers was no longer practical. This meant that everything had to be done so that officers and men on the ground could see what was happening, with the heavy howitzers firing only at trenches that could be seen from the ground and the infantry being asked only to attack trenches that had been prepared by properly observed artillery fire.

Foch and his colleagues came to several conclusions based on these ideas: limited objectives, overwhelming artillery fire, short distances for the infantry to travel. It meant neutralisation or, even better, destruction of the enemy's artillery capability. It meant clawing back French ground in small and manageable chunks whilst, as far as possible, killing more German soldiers than were lost by the French Armies. Because of the equipment at their disposal, i.e. mainly the obsolete, slow firing heavy guns from the 1880s and 1890s, it meant methodical and, therefore, long artillery preparation. Currently, the French lacked reasonably quick firing heavy howitzers and long guns in any numbers and most of those were being employed at Verdun. In many respects, the British were far better equipped in this department. But then, this country had not lost to the enemy some of the main suppliers of raw materials and industrial manufacturing which had been forfeit with the German occupation of the north of France[i]. British heavy industry was intact and, unlike France, Britain was not attempting to supply its Allies with both equipment and ammunition.

On the Somme, Foch's ideas were translated into a highly circumspect course of action: No Man's Land no more than 200 metres wide; only the first German position as the first day's objective; the width of front determined by the availability of heavy howitzers and their ability to devastate the first three lines of

[i] Lost along with the ten French Departments overrun by the Germans were more than half of French iron and steel production, 40% of its coal production and 21% of its industrial workforce. [Source: Elizabeth Greenhalgh, *Errors and Omissions in Franco–British Co-operation over Munitions 1914-18*, War in History, 2007.]

German trenches; and, finally, the highest priority given to counter battery fire in which all guns within range should participate.

Not one of these ideas was adopted by the Fourth Army prior to the Battle of the Somme although, to give him his due, Rawlinson's initial plan included a depth of attack with which Foch might have agreed. With this exception, an exception blown out of the water by Haig's insistence on a deeper and wider attack than Rawlinson or any of his Corps commanders recommended, the British Army appears to have learnt little. No Man's Land was not narrowed for fear of 'giving the game away' to the Germans. A laughable concern given the British actions over the seven days before 1st July. The width of the front to be attacked was determined by the quantity of infantry available rather than the number of heavy howitzers on hand. The lessons of artillery concentration learned at Neuve Chapelle had still not been re-learned. The artillery was thinly spread rather than concentrated where most needed. Counter battery fire was not a sufficient priority with too few heavy guns and howitzers and too little ammunition utilised throughout the bombardment and the attack. Lastly, and crucially, because of the foregoing, Haig's insistence on a deep penetration of the enemy's lines rendered impossible any chance VIII Corps had of breaking into and then clinging onto the robust German defences north of the Ancre.

It can be argued, and this writer makes that argument, that this directive from the Commander in Chief of the BEF was the single biggest reason why the attacks of the VIII, X and III Corps, were, in the main, so bloodily repulsed. Rawlinson can be accused of attempting to attack on too wide a front with his original plan, however, as even this plan was widened still further at Haig's insistence, it would be unkind to attribute all of this problem to the GOC, Fourth Army. The increased depth, however, was all Haig's idea and this decision was responsible for the deaths of thousands of men.

It can also be argued, and this writer makes that argument, that Haig's decision to so obviously attack Gommecourt was a huge tactical blunder which cost the VIII Corps dear. Allenby's and Bols instincts that the diversion should be sufficiently far away that the German troops defending against it could not directly interfere with the main attack were, undoubtedly, correct. If the German troops and guns defending the Gommecourt salient were not busy fending off VII Corps' assault the question that would then be asked is: what protection could be afforded the left wing of VIII Corps if Gommecourt was not attacked? First, one would answer that VII Corps' diversionary attack made the VIII Corps more vulnerable as a result of the greatly increased power of the defence of Gommecourt and Serre. Then one would answer: the same protection as that offered to the right wing of the French 6th Army about Foucaucourt, i.e. a large concentration of artillery given the task of engaging any batteries firing from the area to the south of the French attack and of firing on any troop movements seen in that area. It should be noted that, employing these tactics, the French achieved their limited objectives on their southern flank on 1st July, objectives which would have been very similar to those of the 31st Division had it been asked to take just the 1st German position south west of Serre, as per Rawlinson's original plan.

It cannot be denied that most senior officers, including Haig and Rawlinson, had concerns about the inexperience and training of the young soldiers that now occupied the ranks of both the New Army divisions and of the Regular and Territorial ones that had seen heavy action with its attendant heavy casualties. Training had been basic, tactics were, therefore, similarly basic – slow moving, long lines of heavily laden troops in successive waves which would wash, like an incoming tide, over the various lines of enemy trenches to be taken. What seems not to have been taken into account is that these new recruits represented the best educated and most intelligent Army that Britain and its Empire had ever put in the field. That they were able to adapt to new tactical ideas was more than adequately shown by their performance on the Somme over the next 4½ months. It was not the fault of the junior officers and other ranks thrown, time after time, into ineptly planned and organised attacks that these attacks failed. It was the fault of the generals and their staffs who planned and organised them.

Had more faith been shown in the battalion officers and men who were to deliver the attack north of the Ancre on 1st July, had more flexible tactics been employed, had objectives been more sensibly chosen and had the artillery been more creatively employed and their use during the attack more adaptable to the needs of the infantry then success might have been achieved. This failure to see the merits rather than just the failings of these new soldiers was a corporate one within the higher echelons of the British Army. No one individual can be blamed. Each and every one of them was blinkered to the potential of the enthusiastic young men of this volunteer, citizen Army.

So, if Haig emerges as the principle culprit for the fiasco on the northern wing of Fourth Army on 1st July who else shares some culpability for the disaster that befell VIII Corps. One need look no further than its commander, Lt. Gen. Hunter Weston.

Hunter Weston is something of an enigma. Pompous, arrogant, a blusterer – certainly. But intelligent too or, at least, sufficiently so that he saw immediately the drawbacks of the Gallipoli strategy and of Haig's deep penetration concept for the initial attack on the Somme. And yet, once given his instructions and in spite of his stated reservations, he was a man who followed orders to the letter irrespective of the likely consequences. He was also, rather like his CinC, an optimist. He was a man who rarely saw the cloud, just the thin thread of silver which sometimes appeared at its edge. He was a true Victorian/Edwardian Army officer who believed, in spite of all the evidence since the Boer War to contradict it, that men of high morale must always overcome whatever firepower was trained on it. He was a man for whom achieving an objective was worth any cost. He was a man who lacked imagination who, seeing the failure of one attack on an enemy position, would happily order ("Casualties? What do I care for casualties?") another in the same manner, over the same ground. From the way in which VIII Corps failed to respond to the relentless failures of its raids, he was a man who, perhaps because of his fondness for the 'silver lining', could not or would not adapt a scheme in the face of adverse news.

In short, he was the last man one would have wanted to command the VIII Corps in its attack on one of the strongest parts of the Western Front. Haig seemed to sense this. His adverse comments in his diary about VIII Corps hint at considerable concerns about both commander and staff. If Charteris's claim about being given the responsibility for cancelling the attack is to be believed then Haig's worries ran far deeper than even his personal diary suggests. But then, Hunter Weston was between a rock and a hard place. He did not agree with the plan he had been ordered to fulfil but his duty as an officer and, probably, a gentleman, demanded he do precisely what his commander ordered. One did not thrive if one argued the toss but then it was not in Hunter Weston's nature or training to do such a thing. He, therefore, enthusiastically embraced his orders, implemented them in a rigid and controlling fashion, persuaded himself and then others that all would be well – and ignored anything to the contrary.

Other than those decisions with which he shares some responsibility with either Haig and/or Rawlinson, e.g. the width of No Man's Land, the failure to concentrate the bombardment, the inflexible infantry attack schemes, what were the particular issues for which Hunter Weston should be called to account?

The timing of the Hawthorn Ridge mine. Although Maj. Trower may have asked for the 10 minute grace period within which to sort out any problems, someone had to agree to it. De Lisle denies all knowledge of this therefore Hunter Weston must take responsibility. Unless, of course, the Trower story is a red-herring in which case Hunter Weston, Rawlinson and Haig, in diminishing order of responsibility, have a case to answer.

Not changing the plans for the attack in spite of the growing body of intelligence which showed the bombardment was not having the required effect on the garrison of the German front line trenches. In spite of this evidence of German strength and resilience, Hunter Weston foolishly pinned all of his hopes, and the lives of his men, on the effectiveness of the 65 minute intense bombardment.

Devising a scheme which involved certain battalions in complex and difficult changes of direction whilst under the fire of the enemy, e.g. the Royal Inniskilling Fusiliers, South Wales Borderers and parts of 94th Brigade.

Refusing the requests of certain battalions to send out at least their initial waves lightly equipped and able to advance at more than a slow walk.

Taking the heavy howitzers of the Corps artillery off the German front line trench at zero -10 and off the support trench at zero -5 which allowed the German machine gun teams to mount their guns while British troops were either forming up in No Man's Land or trying to get through their own wire prior to the advance.

In short, Hunter Weston's performance managed to make a bad situation substantially worse at the expense of the lives of his men.

Where does this leave us in assessing the performance of the three men mainly responsible for shaping the attack of the VII Corps. In this writer's judgement the verdicts would be:

Sir Douglas Haig – guilty
Sir Henry Rawlinson – guilty, but with mitigating circumstances
Aylmer Hunter-Weston – guilty, but possibly insane

FINALLY, NO ONE, BAR ONE MAN, EVER BLAMED OR CRITICISED the young officers and men who had 'gone over the lid' at Serre, Redan Ridge and Beaumont Hamel. Maj. Gen. de Lisle along with Brig. Gens. Rees and Ingles, were tremendously impressed by the steadiness and bravery of the men under their command. Rees also had complimentary word for those who had opposed them:

> "I have never seen a finer display of individual and collective bravery than the advance of that brigade. I never saw a man waver from the exact line prescribed for him. Each line disappeared in the thick cloud of dust & smoke which rapidly blotted out the whole area. I can safely pay a tribute also to the bravery of the enemy, whom I saw standing up in their trenches to fire their rifles in a storm of fire."[90]

In the light of many erroneous reports about the positions achieved by the British infantry one should, perhaps, note Rees's comment that 'Each line disappeared in the thick cloud of dust & smoke which rapidly blotted out the whole area'. And this from the General who occupied an advanced Brigade HQ with 'a splendid view... over the whole of the ground as far as Serre'.

The day after the attack, Brig. Gen. Rees returned command of the 94th Brigade to Brig. Gen. Carter Campbell who had been away sick. For Rees this was a 'bitter blow' in spite of the destruction of much of his temporary command. Rees was not long unemployed as a vacancy had sadly opened with the 11th Brigade of the 4th Division on the death of Bertie Prowse. Rees, therefore, moved from one destroyed Brigade to another and, on 4th July, was given the task of rebuilding this new command. Before he went, he issued a Special Order of the Day to the Brigade:

> "In giving up the Command of the 94th Brigade to Brigadier-General T Carter-Campbell, whose place I have temporarily taken during this great battle, I wish to express to all ranks my admiration of their behaviour. I have been through many battles in this war and nothing more magnificent has come under my notice. The waves went forward as if on a drill parade and I saw no man turn back or falter. I bid good-bye to the remnants of as fine a Brigade as has ever gone into action."[91]

One man might have disagreed with this assessment. A man who spent no time close to the front line on 1st July 1916 but a man more than happy to commit to his diary grossly inaccurate and gratuitously insulting comments about matters of which he had no first-hand knowledge. On a page in his personal diary he wrote in reference to the struggles of the VIII Corps north of the River Ancre:

> "I am inclined to believe from further reports, that few of VIII Corps left the trenches."[92]

The author was the British commander in chief, Sir Douglas Haig, the main architect of the disaster of 1st July 1916.

---

[1] Woodward D, ed. *The Military Correspondence of Field Marshal Sir William Robertson*, Army Records Society, 1989, page 62.

[2] Ibid., page 65.

[3] NA, WO95/2756, *War Diary 1/8th Royal Warwickshire Regt.*

[4] NA, WO95/2280, *War Diary 29th Division.*

[5] Ibid.

[6] NA, CAB45/133, *Comment on the OH by Lt. Col. C G Fuller.*

[7] NA, WO95/2280.

[8] Ibid.
[9] Ibid.
[10] NA, CAB45/134, *Comment on the OH by Capt. I Grant.*
[11] NA, WO95/2280.
[12] *Somme Nord.*
[13] NA, WO95/2280.
[14] NA, CAB45/137, *Comment on the OH by Capt. R O Spencer Smith.*
[15] NA, CAB45/137, *Comment on the OH by Maj. G T Raikes.*
[16] NA, WO95/2280.
[17] Ibid.
[18] Baten, J. (2006), *"Global Height Trends in Industrial and Developing Countries, 1810-1984: An Overview"*. Working Paper, University of Tübingen.
[19] *OH*, page 313
[20] NA, CAB45, *Comment on the OH by anonymous Capt., 1st Lancashire Fusiliers.*
[21] NA, CAB45/138, *Comment on the OH by Capt. F A Wilson.*
[22] NA, CAB45/132, *Comment on the OH by 2nd Lt. C J P Ball.*
[23] Op. cit. *Fuller.*
[24] NA, CAB45/132, *Comment on the OH by Lt. Col. A C Baylay.*
[25] Quoted in Barton, Peter, *The Somme:A Panoramic Perspective*, Constable, 2006, page 88.
[26] NA, WO95/2280.
[27] NA, CAB45/133, *Comments on the OH by Lt. Col. D E Forman.*
[28] NA, WO95/2306, *War Diary 88th Brigade.*
[29] NA, WO95/2303, *War Diary 87th Brigade,*
[30] Op. cit. *Ball.*
[31] NA, CAB45/134, *Comment on the OH by Lt. Col. J Hamilton-Hall.*
[32] Op. cit. *Spencer Smith.*
[33] NA, CAB45/133, *Comment on the OH by Lt. Col. J A Ellis.*
[34] NA, WO 95/2292/2, *War Diary 147th Brigade, RFA.*
[35] Ibid.
[36] NA, WO 95/2951, *War Diary 168th Brigade.*
[37] NA, CAB45/134, *Comment on the OH by J H Maj. Gibbon.*
[38] Op. cit. *Grant.*
[39] Op. cit. *Spencer Smith.*
[40] NA, WO 95/2292/2.
[41] Op. cit. *Hamilton-Hall.*
[42] NA, CAB45/138, *Comment on the OH by Lt. A Whitlock.*
[43] NA, WO95/2280.
[44] Op. cit. *Wilson.*
[45] NA, CAB45/133, *Comment on the OH by Maj. Gen. B de Lisle.*
[46] Ibid.
[47] *OH*, page
[48] Op. cit. *de Lisle.*
[49] NA, CAB45/136, *Comment on the OH by Lt. Col. H Nelson.*
[50] NA, CAB45/134, *Comment on the OH by Maj. G V Goodliffe.*
[51] NA, CAB45/134, *Comment on the OH by Maj. A R Hoette.*
[52] *'The Work of the RE in the European War: Signal Service in France'*, pages 98-99.
[53] Ibid.
[54] NA, WO95/4. *War Diary, GHQ.*
[55] NA, CAB45/132, *Comment on the OH by Capt. D R Adams.*
[56] NA, CAB45/133, *Comment on the OH by Lt. Col. G H B Freeth.*
[57] Ibid.
[58] NA, CAB45/132-8, *Comment on the OH by anonymous Staff officer, 4th Division.*

[59] NA, CAB45/133, *Comment on the OH by Capt. H F Dawes.*
[60] Ibid.
[61] Ibid.
[62] NA, CAB45/135, *Comment on the OH by Capt. V N Johnson.*
[63] NA, WO95/1502. *War Diary 12th Brigade.*
[64] NA, CAB45/137, *Comment on the OH by Lt. W Striling.*
[65] NA, CAB45/138, *Comment on the OH by Capt. C M Vallentin.*
[66] NA, WO95/2359, *War Diary 93rd Brigade.*
[67] Ibid.
[68] Ibid.
[69] Ibid.
[70] Ibid.
[71] NA, CAB45/134, *Comment on the OH by Maj. C Howard.*
[72] Ibid.
[73] Ibid.
[74] Ibid.
[75] Ibid.
[76] Ibid.
[77] NA, CAB45/137, *Comment on the OH by Brig. Gen H C Rees.*
[78] Ibid.
[79] Ibid.
[80] Ibid.
[81] Ibid.
[82] Ibid.
[83] Ibid.
[84] NA, CAB45/136, *Comment on the OH by Capt. F Piggott.*
[85] NA, CAB45/134, *Comment on the OH by Maj. C M T Hogg.*
[86] Ibid.
[87] *OH.*
[88] NA, CAB45/137, *Comment on the OH by Lt. Col. C B Simonds.*
[89] Ibid.
[90] Op. cit. *Rees.*
[91] NA, WO 95/2363, *War Diary 94th Brigade.*
[92] Sheffield & Bourne, op. cit., page 196.

Appendix 1: Prisoners of War

According to the British Official History, 128 men from the VIII Corps were taken prisoner on 1st July 1916. Of these, 32 came from 29th Division (29 of them from 16th Middlesex Regt.), eight from the 31st Division and 88 from the 4th Division.

These figures are indisputably wrong as, for example, they take no account of the four officers of the 2nd Royal Fusiliers taken prisoner after the attack on the Hawthorn Ridge crater[i]. The figures also state that all of the PoWs from the 16th Middlesex Regt. were Other Ranks whilst, in fact, two officers were taken prisoner from this battalion[ii].

Of the 88 PoWs from the 4th Division one was an officer, Lt. Frank Austin Brettell[iii] of the 1/8th Royal Warwickshire Regt. and the rest Other Ranks with 18 coming from the 10th Brigade, 56 from the 11th Brigade (including the two attached Warwickshire battalions) and 14 from the 12th Brigade.

The treatment of Allied Prisoners of War became increasingly scandalous as the war moved towards its climax. Whereas British and French soldiers were treated as well as might be expected in a country suffering an increasingly tight stranglehold on its food supplies as a result of the Allied naval blockade and the needs of the German Army, some of those from the Italian, Russian, Romanian and Serbian Armies were dealt with in a way that presaged the treatment of millions of civilians under Nazi rule during WW2. There was, however, a significant difference in treatment depending on rank. In the main, officers fared far better than lowly Privates and NCOs. Officers did not work, Other Ranks most certainly did and sometimes in dangerous and dirty conditions and, as pressure on the German Army grew in 1918, soldiers were often employed near the front in ways illegal under international conventions to which the German Empire was a signatory.

Irrespective of rank, however, food was poor and supplies meagre. British soldiers quickly became almost totally dependent on parcels from home to stave off starvation and any disruption to this supply caused immediate nutritional problems for the men involved. Soldiers from countries where the organisation of food parcels to PoWs was either poor or pretty much non-existent had to make do with the appalling quality and low quantity provided by their captors. For Italians, Russians and others to starve to death in a camp was not uncommon.

Towards the end of the war, however, the German Army threw away the rule book concerning the treatment and employment of PoWs and started to use them as forced or, rather, slave labour within the battle zone. This infringed all

---

[i] Capt. Cockram, Capt. Hall, 2nd Lt. Starnes and 2nd Lt. Michelmore (who died in the German hands).

[ii] Lt. Russell and Lt. Hedges.

[iii] He is misidentified in the Official History which gives the one officer PoW as coming from the 12th Brigade.

pre-war agreements on the treatment of PoWs[i] and led to an unknown number of Allied soldiers behind the German lines on the Western Front being killed or wounded whilst under Allied artillery fire. The condition of these 'working parties' was pitiful and, again, an unknown number of these prisoners were worked or starved to death.

Several of the PoWs from the VIII Corps were interviewed after their repatriation after the war finished or when they were sent back early because of ill health or they escaped. These officers and men are:

4th Division

18457 Pte. Henry Baker, 1st East Lancashire Regt.

2nd Lt. Frank Austin Brettell, 1/8th Royal Warwickshire Regt.

7390 Pte. Thomas Gill, 2nd Seaforth Highlanders

9795 Pte. John William Kerr, 1st Somerset Light Infantry

29th Division

Capt. Eric Walter W Hall, 16th Middlesex Regt.

1346 Pte. Rupert Robeson, 16th Middlesex Regt.

Lt. Leonard Charles Russell, 2nd Royal Fusiliers

The transcripts of these interviews are printed below in full. They illustrate starkly the dreadful conditions experienced by the ordinary soldiers, the huge discrepancy in the way officers and Other Ranks were treated and the great variations in the attitudes and conduct of the German officers and men who ran the camps.

18457 PTE. HENRY BAKER, 1ST EAST LANCASHIRE REGT. of 6, Stand Street, Liverpool. Taken prisoner at Beaumont Hamel, 1st July 1916.
Nature of wound: Right thigh fractured; nerves of left leg out. I am 21 years of age. Before the war I was employed as porter at an outfitters in Liverpool. I joined the Army in January 1915, and went out to France.

The prisoners in this camp were in huts, There were 152 of us in a hut, cut off in sections; 49 in mine, all English. We slept on planks against the wall one along the other. Each had a blanket only. We ate in the same room. It had only one stove. Our washing was sent to the German laundry. It was very badly done. We only got soap if it came from home, and we used to get water for ourselves as best we could.

The sanitary arrangements were very bad – one long row of seats just outside here, not used in unfavourable weather; the stench was unbearable.

Group Al at this camp worked in coal mines, stone quarries and salt mines. They were badly knocked about by the Germans, and worked 10 or 11 hours a day. One chap was talking to another, when the sentry shot his head off. I was told this sentry was mad. I do not know name of the man who was shot.

---

[i] Articles 6 and 52 of the Hague Regulations on the Laws and Customs of War on Land stated that PoWs should not be used on work connected with military operations and the services demanded of civilians must not involve them in military operations against their own country. These articles had been breached early in the war when both civilians and PoWs had been employed in constructing the German 2nd Position on the Western Front in 1915.

Some of the 'sitting work' was making shell baskets. Prisoners were paid, I think, a very little. I never had anything.

The food consisted of black bread and vegetable soup. I only saw meat once. There was no food at the canteen. They only had cups and saucers. Also wine – this cost 2½ marks a cup.

We got our food from home. It arrived in good condition. We were allowed six parcels a month. The only thing they confiscated was tooth-powder.

I got no clothing at this camp, nor did I ask for it, I do not know whether they supplied it to others.

They never tried to make prisoners here make munitions, as far as I know.

As to exercise and recreation, we were allowed to arrange physical drill for ourselves, and we could play draughts, cards, etc., in the huts. We were not allowed to smoke in the huts, but we could outside. It was not stopped.

There was an outbreak of dysentery just before I got to this camp, but it had finished when I got there.

Religious services were held (Church of England) by a corporal on Wednesdays and Sundays, and there was choir practice every Friday.

I received my letters and parcels regularly during the last few months, and previously also. They were opened by officers, but not in my presence. They were brought to us open. Tooth-powder is the only thing I know was taken out. I do not know that anything in particular was prohibited. We were allowed to write one letter and two postcards a month. The parcels were censored, I think, in the main camp. The tins are not returned to us. We take out the contents from time to time, and they keep them when they are emptied. My parcels were delivered to me in hospital.

I have nothing to say on general treatment beyond what I have said above, nor as to cruelty, but I did hear a German say to one of our chaps, 'The English cannot last'.

As to discipline: we were informed of regulations by one of our own English sergeants. We used to get up at 6 and parade at 6,30. For offences like smoking in barracks or throwing potato peel about the punishment was 14 days in the guardroom. Once because one of our chaps laughed at a German sergeant he made them all bring their beds out into the square and stand at attention for two hours.

I know of no visit from American Ambassador.

There was no change in treatment of prisoners while I was there.

Two working parties, EK1 and EK2, of English prisoners who had been working behind the German lines at Cambrai came to Friedrichsfeld while I was there. There were 200 in one and 150 in the other. I never saw men look like it. They looked like skeletons. The doctor ordered them to go to bed for a week right off. Some (two I know of) died of starvation. I spoke to four or five of them. They were there 10 days. They told me they had been digging trenches and gun pits, filling munitions wagons, and carrying trench mortars.

There was a rumour in camp when they arrived (November 1917) that the Germans had withdrawn all English prisoners from behind their lines.

The men told me they had had nothing but bread and soup, and sometimes had had to eat raw turnip tops from the fields.

I cannot compare the rations issued daring the 18 months I have been a prisoner; and as to the class of men employed as guards, I only know that some were old men, some boys of 16, and some with artificial limbs.

All I can say about the treatment of Russian and Italian prisoners is that I saw two Italians bayoneted by the guards at Friedrichsfeld for coming near the English prisoners to ask for their bread.

I have received my parcels regularly during the last few months, and one was forwarded to me while I was waiting at Aachen.

I left Friedrichsfeld on January 8th, 1918, for Aachen, which I reached the same day. 1 left on 11th January for home via Rotterdam.

Opinion of examiner: I have examined this witness, and he is, in my opinion, intelligent and reliable, but he has spent practically the whole 18 months of his captivity in hospital. I think that his evidence is of chief value on two points, viz.., (1) hospital conditions and (2) as to the condition of the men who had been working behind the German lines, and whom he saw arrive for hospital.

LT. FRANK AUSTIN BRETTELL, 1/8TH ROYAL WARWICKSHIRE REGT.
Captured 1st July 1916

The first Germans I saw were an officer and two soldiers, who entered the dugout where I was lying wounded. I was given biscuits and soda-water by them, and they then left, taking with them three wounded men (British) who were able to walk.

During the night of 1st-2nd July I was carried on a stretcher to a dugout dressing station, where my wound was dressed, and then carried to a headquarter (battalion?) dugout, where I was given food and drink. On the 2nd I was carried out of the trenches and conveyed by horse ambulance to an advance dressing station. During all this time I had been well treated by my captors, who were Saxons, though I am unable to state the number of the regiment.

I lay, with a large number of other British wounded, at the advance dressing station for about six hours before my turn came to be dressed. After another four or five hours I was placed on a farm waggon with a little straw in the bottom, with a wounded British soldier, and conveyed to a large clearing station. During most of the afternoon and evening it rained heavily, and no shelter of any sort was provided for the British wounded, who were naturally the last to be attended to. At the clearing station all the British were put on wet and half-rotten straw. There were two large tents, but these were filled with German wounded. I have since met one or two British officers who were put inside one of these tents. I remained on this straw during a night and most of the following day in the open.

It rained most of the time. I was allowed to keep a wet blanket, with which I was covered when in the waggon, as I had no tunic or shirt, it having been necessary to cut these off when my wound was first dressed.

I was afterwards given instead a British G.S. tunic, which had presumably been taken from a soldier who had died.

During the day following my arrival at the clearing station I was put on a very crowded hospital train and conveyed to Caudry Hospital. I was not on this occasion treated as a stretcher case, although I had to be carried.

I attribute any hardships we had to endure up to this time not to any deliberate desire on the part of the Germans to maltreat us, but owing to wholly inadequate arrangements for coping with so large a number of wounded.

Caudry Hospital, 3rd-11th July 1916.

A large factory converted into a hospital. About 200 British there, I believe, including about 12 officers. Badly under-staffed. About one sister to 25 wounded. Operating theatres were merely curtained off from main wards,

I saw at least 30 men come from these theatres after having had limbs amputated. A large number of minor operations were done without anaesthetic of any sort. Between 25 and 28 British died while I was there.

Journey, 11th-12th July 1916

I left Caudry for Gütersloh on the 11th July 1916. Train journey about 24 hours. During this time we were fed once, with a small bowl of milk soup and a piece of dry black bread.

Gütersloh Stadtkrankenhaus, 12th July- 12th November 1916.

Arrived here on 12th July 1916 and left on 12th November 1916. During all this time I was most excellently treated, and was given good food. I underwent two operations, and I believe that everything possible was done for me.

Camp Lazaret, 12th November 1917-January 1917.

On 12th November I was removed to the Gütersloh Offiziers-Lager. This is probably the best camp in Germany. The grounds are large. During my stay at Gütersloh I was all the time in the lazaret attached to the camp, which was well organised, under the charge of a German Stabsarzt, assisted by British, French, and Russian doctors.

I was able to go into the camp proper, where I found games, amusements, lectures, etc., well organised.

The rooms were a little draughty, and overcrowded.

Bedsteads were what I shall refer to in future as German G.S. bedsteads. They consisted of an iron frame supporting four planks. The mattresses were palliasses stuffed with straw. Electric lighting and rather inadequate steam heating throughout the camp. Half a small cupboard and a chair provided for each officer. Dining hall was a large wooden hut erected in the middle of the camp. Rough trestle tables and forms. Commandant and soldiers usually reasonable, but the senior interpreter, named Langensiepen, was an extremely insolent man, who always worked for the discomfort of the British.

St Elizabeth Hospital, Jan. 1917.

During January 1917 I was sent, with another British officer, to St. Elizabeth Hospital, Gütersloh, as another operation proved necessary. We both underwent operations on the day following, and two days afterwards we were told we were to return to the camp that day. At this hospital we were given comfortable beds and sufficiently good food, but we were left almost entirely in the hands of a German orderly, who did very little for us. We did not have our temperatures taken at all, until, feeling very ill, I asked that this should be done, and it was found that I had a very high temperature indeed. In view of this we were left another three days before being returned to the camp. I mention this as it is typical of cases which are constantly occurring. Officers are sometimes sent to good hospitals, but they are very often not properly cared for, and almost invariably returned to their camps far too soon.

Camp. Jan–March 1917.

The food at Gütersloh Lager was a mere form.

I am quite sure that the ration would not have supported life for three weeks, and it was so filthy arid unpalatable that it was uneatable.

Fortunately all the British and French prisoners had such a good supply of parcels from home that they were not only able to feed fairly well themselves, but, were also able to assist the Russians.

All the British left Gütersloh in the beginning of March for Crefeld. The train journey was about 14 hours.

Crefeld, 22nd May, 1917.

Crefeld Cavalry Barracks. An old-established and well-organised camp. Grounds small for number of prisoners. Rooms overcrowded. Nine officers per room almost 22 feet by 18 feet. One chair and half a small cupboard per officer. German G.S. bedsteads. Mattresses stuffed with seaweed. Not uncomfortable when new. Food wholly inadequate as to quantity, but our lunch on Sundays was always eatable. On other days it was similar to Gütersloh, and never eaten by the prisoners. Commandant very reasonable, and obviously anxious to improve the lot of the prisoners as much as possible. On the 22nd May Crefeld Lager was emptied of all prisoners, and I, with some 390 other British officers, was sent to Schwarmstedt. Train journey about 22 hours.

Schwarmstedt, 23rd May–7th September, 1917.

A collection of rough wooden huts in the middle of the Lüneburger Heath – a vast plain in Hanover composed of a mixture of sandy tracts, pine swamps, and peat bogs. Very small grounds. Rooms very over-crowded. 12 officers in rooms 24 feet by 20 feet, and 16 in rooms very little larger. One stool per officer. No cupboards. German G.S. bedsteads. Mattresses rough sack-cloth palliasses, stuffed with hay, straw, wood-shavings, heather, torn-up newspapers, or any similar rubbish.

Mine contained about half-an-inch thickness of old hay, which had become broken up to chaff. The whole camp infested with every kind of insect: mosquitoes, spiders, beetles, earwigs, bugs, and fleas. Latrine, a large pit covered with a rough wooden structure. Very insanitary and offensive. Food quite uneatable.

Commandant and soldiers extremely unreasonable, insolent, and aggressive, though there was a slight improvement in this respect towards the end.

Everything possible done to annoy the prisoners. Officers put into prison on the most absurdly petty charges. One officer was given three days for patting a dog during roll-call. Two others were given eight days because they came on to roll-call smoking, the German officer being not then on parade. I could cite many similar incidents. I left Schwarmstedt for Holzminden about the 7th September 1917. Train journey about 12 hours.

Holzminden, 7th Sept–2nd October, 1917.

A new barracks. Grounds very small. Rooms very overcrowded, though not so badly us at Schwarmstedt. 10 officers in a room about 18 feet by 26 feet.

One stool per officer and no cupboards provided. German G.S. bedsteads. Seaweed mattresses. Food inadequate as to quantity and uneatable, except for an absolutely starving man. The Commandant was a very old and gentlemanly man, but quite incapable.

The camp was therefore entirely under the control of an ill-bred, insolent bully, Hauptmann Niemeyer. This man escaped from America on America's declaration of war, with the German Legation staff.

We had to suffer the grossest insults at his hands, and from the German N.CO.s and men, and officers were constantly put in prison on the most absurd charges. This camp, in common with all the camps under the X Armeekorps command, may be classed as a thoroughly bad camp, and this is entirely due to the pernicious influence of the G.O.C. – General von Hänisch[i].

Plate 165 Generalleutnant Karl Heinrich Eduard von Hänisch, X Armeekorps

Up to the time I left for Heidelberg on the 2nd October, no heating had been provided. Journey from Holzminden to Heidelberg about 20 hours.

Heidelberg, 3rd Oct–27th November 1917.

Barracks with an extension of hutments. Hutments overcrowded. Nine officers per room about 27 ft. by 14 ft. Grounds fair. Half a cupboard and a stool per officer. German G.S. beds. Mattresses, rough palliasses filled with torn-up newspapers or other rubbish.

Messing arrangements in the hands of a French committee, and the food was always clean and eatable, but the ration was quite inadequate. At this camp I was

---

[i] Generalleutnant Karl Heinrich Eduard von Hänisch was born in Unruhstadt, Posen in 1861. He died in 1921. He entered the army in 1879 as a 2nd Lt. in the 4. Garde-Grenadier-Regiment Königin. He served on the Großer Generalstab in 1890 and on the staffs of the VIII, XV and I Armeekorps between 1891 and 1904. He took command of the Garde-Grenadier-Regiment Nr. 5 in 1908 and the 4. Garde-Infanterie-Brigade in 1910. He was promoted Generalleutnant in 1913 and served as Chief of Staff of the 7. Armee, commander of XIV Armeekorps and as acting commander X Armeekorps in Hannover from November 1916.

treated as an officer for the first time since I left the hospital at Gütersloh. One Feldwebel-Leutnant was inclined to be insolent and overbearing, but he was the junior German officer there, so did not affect us very much.

Sufficient coal was issued to provide heating for about two hours daily. The train journey from Heidelberg to Constance took about twelve hours. At Constance we were provided with quite a good meal.

In concluding this report I would like to make the following comments.

I have made six long railway journeys in Germany. On only two occasions, namely, the first and the last, were we provided with any food whatsoever.

I have always travelled 2nd class. The numbers in the compartments were as follows:

	Officers.	German Soldiers.
Gütersloh to Crefeld	6	2
Crefeld to Schwarmstedt	4	2
Schwarmstedt to Holzminden	6	2
Holzminden to Heidelberg	6	2
Heidelberg to Constance	6	2

In every case a small percentage of the officers have travelled 3rd class, as insufficient 2nd class were provided.

The beds provided at many of the camps are absolutely disgraceful. Very coarse sheets are provided. The pillows were always stuffed with the same rubbish as the mattresses.

The food ration consists for the most part of barley, swedes, turnips, sauerkraut, and horse-beans, with a few potatoes. Almost invariably served as a sort of stew. (The meat ration is negligible.) It is usually so filthy as to be quite uneatable. I am quite convinced that even if eaten it would be insufficient to support life.

7390 PTE. THOMAS GILL, 2ND SEAFORTH HIGHLANDERS of Church View, High Blantyre Road, Burn Bank, Hamilton. Lanarkshire. Aged 26, a miner.
Taken prisoner Mailly, 1st July 1916. Nature of wound: wound in back.

When captured the soldiers in the front line were very kind to me and helped me to the first dressing station where they dressed my wound. I think they were Saxons. They asked me if I could walk a few hundred yards to the next dressing station, as if not I should have to wait till the evening for an ambulance.

I walked about a kilometre, but there was no sign of the dressing station, and by this time I was a bit done up. I struggled on till we came to a village and here the sentry with me tried to see if they could accommodate me there, but they said they were full up, and he could not even get a drink of water for me. By this time I could not stand and they had to help me along. We came to a river, and they got me a drink of water, which quite finished me. They still tried to force me.

A Red Cross ambulance came along and took me to the dressing station, where I got a small piece of bread, but nobody attended me, and I lay for three nights outside; they said they must attend to their own men first. They offered me a little soup, but I was too bad to take it.

After this I was put on a farm cart, with no springs, and jolted along to a place, the name of which I do not know, which took about 10 hours to reach.

Here I lay in a barn for the night, and the next morning was taken by train to St. Quentin. I was too bad to sit up in the carriage and had to lie on the floor.

St Quentin Hospital, 6th-20th July 1916.

I reached St. Quentin about the 5th or 6th of July and was taken to a hospital, where I stayed for a fortnight. I was in a very bad state by this time, and my wound was smelling, A nurse got hold of me, took me to bed, put a bandage on me, but never removed the old bandage. I lay in this state for four days, no one coming near me to do anything.

I got desperate one night and tore the old bandage off and threw it on the floor. The night nurse came along and found it and made a great fuss and brought a doctor. Next morning my wound was dressed properly for the first time; this was 10 days after being wounded.

There was a man in the bed next to mine who had a slight wound in his knee, the sort of wound that, if attended to properly as it would have been at home, would have been all right in a day or two. Nothing was done to him, and at last he lost his leg, and finally died. They did not seem to trouble about the prisoners at all.

Ohrdruf Hospital, 20th July–November 1916.

On about the 20th of July I left St. Quentin and was taken to Ohrdruf Lazaret. I was taken by ambulance train, and was quite comfortable. I was here for about four months, and was more or less decently treated in the lazaret, but this was not due to the Germans, for we had French doctors. My wound was dressed every second day. Ohrdruf Camp was closed.

Langensalza, November 1916-8th January 1917.

In November 1916 I was taken to the camp at Langensalza, and stayed here two days. I was still in bandages, and ought not to have been sent out of hospital. I was sent to a kommando, on a farm; I do not know what it was called. I managed to do a little work, the Germans did not trouble themselves much about us.

Cassel, 8th-15th January 1915.

On 8th January 1917 I was sent to Cassel Camp, where I stayed for a week.

Kommando, 15th January-31st May 1917.

On 15th January 1917, 22 of us were sent to a kommando, working in a forest. My wounds were all right by now and did not require to be bandaged. I do not know the name or number of this kommando, they never would tell us. They gave us no blankets, always telling us that they were being sent on. It was bitterly cold, and after a fortnight we went on strike. After two days the Feldwebel came, and we told him why we were striking, and he promised us that if we would go to work next day he would see that the blankets came. We went to work, and the blankets arrived.

Shortly afterwards they reduced our bread ration, and we went out on strike again. The sentries came in with fixed bayonets and asked each one of us if we would go to work; lots of us said we would not, but when a South African was asked he said he would, so that, of course, finished the strike, as others followed him and we could not hold out.

We were very short of food here, not getting our parcels for April and May. We got a little bit of bread and some coffee before we started to work at about 10 minutes to 7 in the morning, and we got nothing else till we got back at night, and then only a little soup. After six weeks like this some of the men were getting very thin, and many were losing heart.

Cassel, 31st May-2nd June 1917.

Our job finished on 31st May, and we went back to the camp at Cassel, but I only stayed here until 2nd June 1917, when I got a fine job. Six of us were sent to work in Mr Henschel's private garden.

Rothenditmold, 2nd June 1917-17th May 1918.

He is a big locomotive manufacturer, and also makes guns and other things, and has a great many factories in Cassel, and has about 500 prisoners working in them, the majority being Russians. There is a barrack attached to one of the factories, and we lived there, going every day to Mr Henschel's private house, the address of which, I think, is No. 25, Weinburg Strasse. The barrack was very uncomfortable, the place was very verminous, and there were only four men to look after it. I was here for 11 months and my mattress, which was dirty to start with, was never changed. We complained to Mr Henschel about the condition of things here, but he could do nothing; he told us it was a Government concern and we were under charge of the military.

After the beginning of the offensive of this year a number of English guns were brought up to one of his factories, in good condition. I did not see them myself, but heard of them from some of the other men who were working there.

We left the barrack about 7 in the morning, and returned at 8 at night, and we fed the same as the other men who worked in the factories. At noon our dinner was brought down to another factory and one of our party fetched it for us.

We were getting our parcels all right again now, so did not do so badly for food, the more so as we took plenty of fruit, potatoes and other vegetables from the garden. The sentry complained about this, but we did it all the same.

It was a very large garden, flowers, fruit, and vegetables grown just for Mr Henschel's own house. He was very good to us, as far as was in his power: he lent us English books to read, and would come and talk to us. I gathered that his first wife had been an English lady.

I did not have much opportunity of talking to Germans; you are not allowed to really. There were only two German boys working in the garden, and the sentry, who was really a gardener, and did more work than the six of us together ever did. We heard very little news. For instance, we never knew the exchange of prisoners was going on until we got into Holland. We had heard a talk of it coming off at some time, but did not know it had actually begun.

Escape, 17th May 1918.

I escaped from Cassel with another prisoner who was working with me on 17th May 1918, and reached Holland on 22nd May.

Opinion of Examiner. This man seems very intelligent, and gave his information in a straightforward manner.

9795 Pte. John William Kerr, 1st Somerset Light Infantry of 24, Queen's Buildings, Montague Street, Borough, S.E.

Taken prisoner Mailly, 1st July 1916. Nature of wound: Wounded just below left eye and in right thigh; bullet wound in cye and shrapnel in thigh.

I enlisted on the 1st August 1914 as a regular, previously I had been a carman. I was 20 years old at the time I enlisted.

Just before we attacked I picked up some bullets being fired from the German machine guns, which were converted into dum-dums; they had dropped in our trench. We had received the order to attack. I was with the bombing section of my battalion. We had got between the second and third line of the enemy trenches when I received bullet in the eye; it rendered me unconscious, and before I came to, the enemy had counter-attacked and driven our men back to the German first line, and I found myself with about eight other men of different regiments, a prisoner in the German hands. We were taken to a dug-out. This was between 2 and 3 o'clock in the afternoon. We were quite well treated. It was the 221st Württemberg Regiment (sic: 121st), We were all wounded. The Germans dressed our wounds and gave us some food and rum; they, however, stole our money and valuables, I lost my watch and about 20 francs in money. We spent that night in the dug-out, and next morning, 2nd July, they marched us about 15 km. to a hospital in a park. This was a kind of clearing station; there were about 200 British and 3,000 or 4,000 Germans. They were lying about on the ground and anywhere. We British remained out in the open. We were well treated and our wounds dressed by German women nurses. The food consisted of four slices of black bread and coffee, and a kind of soup for dinner. We stayed here several days and were eventually sent by train to Le Cateau, where we arrived on 10th July, The journey lasted from 8 a.m. to 3 p.m. We were in third-class carriages, not very comfortable; no food, no attendants. The guards left us alone. We had about six British officers with us; I do not know their names or regiments, one belonged to the R.F.C. They were all badly wounded, one had his nose shot off. These were in third-class carriages with us. I saw no German Red Cross during the journey.

Le Cateau Hospital, 10th-25th July, 1916.

We were placed in a hospital which had been a cotton mill. It was a large place and held about 1,000 or more. We were well treated here. The medical treatment was good. The doctor was a German who could speak English; he was clever and humane. I do not know his name. The nursing was done by German women, who were good. There were about 80 men in my ward, all British, including the officers. We used to get five meals a day: 6 a.m., bread and butter, bacon and coffee with milk ; 10 a.m., same again; 12.30, a two-course dinner, a little meat and soup ; 3 p.m., two slices of bread and butter or jam, and coffee; 6 p.m., same again. The sanitary arrangements were quite good. I had no operation. We got ordinary blue hospital clothing. The bedding was clean and changed about once a week. We were allowed to write one postcard but not allowed to say where we were, only that we were alive; my card arrived home all right. I should describe the general treatment as very good, all nationalities were treated alike. We were allowed to smoke.

Journey, 25th-26th July, 1916.

On 25th July they collected all those who were able to walk, about 100, and took us to the station and embarked us on board a Red Cross train for Minden. The accommodation was good; the journey lasted from 3 a.m. to 6 p.m. on the 26th. We received no food on the way.

Minden Hospital, 26th July-2nd August, 1916.

On arrival at Minden we were fallen in, some half dead from the fatigue of the journey, and had to wait about an hour and a half in the street, No one attended to us at all. One poor fellow had an open vein bleeding; he fell down and was lying bleeding for the best part of an hour, when at last two policemen arrived with a stretcher and took him off to hospital; his name was Private Spencer, I think, of the Manchester. I never saw him again. At about 7 p.m. we were marched off about 5 miles to Minden Lager; it was a terrible march, the lads were so weak they kept falling down; the guards shoved us along but did not ill-treat us. One lad was forced to march without boots; they had not been returned to him when he left Le Cateau Hospital.

Minden, 2nd-20th August, 1916.

On arrival at Minden Lager, when they saw that we were all wounded, we were taken to the lazaret. It was a wooden hut. The accommodation was a little better than the camp but very poor. We were placed on wooden beds with straw mattresses, We lay on these till the next morning without any food. There were about 20 in each ward. Next morning we were given a pound of black bread and some coffee. About 9 a.m. the doctor came and looked at us; did not dress our wounds; he did not know much and could not speak English. I do not know his name. He only visited us occasionally and did not seem to care if we got well or not. We were here altogether about seven days. Our wounds were dressed by Russian orderlies, who were pretty good. We had two blankets, no sheets or pillow slips. No clothing was supplied. The food was very bad, plenty but uneatable. The sanitary and washing facilities were good.

About the 2nd of August almost 20 of us were shifted into the big lager. It was a large place – accommodation for about 5,000 prisoners, arranged in blocks; the usual kind of huts, built of wood and arranged in such a way that we could not see the country round, the windows all opening inside into the squares. There were two Generals at the head, one in command and the other acting as second in command. I do not know their names. The former would listen to complaints, but the latter would not.

In my hut there were 250, all British. We lay on wooden beds, straw mattresses, two blankets. The straw was never changed and got lousy. The heating was insufficient. We could get a bath once a week and also be fumigated. The latrines were too near the hut and very offensive and insanitary. I was employed in helping to drain the camp, no payment. The food was very bad; in the morning, coffee. 1 lb. of bread for the day; mid-day, sandstorm soup, un-drinkable; evening, coffee. It was simply starvation, never any meat. At this time we were getting no parcels, There was a canteen, only cigarettes and apple wine on sale. I had no money. We got no clothing, although asked for. For exercise we could walk about the camp and there was a field where we could play football. Indoors we could play cards. We could smoke anywhere outside but not inside the huts. It was never stopped. There was no epidemic but I saw plenty of Russians dying from starvation. A Canadian chaplain, prisoner of war, used to conduct services in a room set apart for the purpose. We could write two letters and four postcards a month; they arrived all right. I received letters and parcels regularly. As regards general treatment at this camp, the chief complaint was against the under-officers, who used to beat the men with their rifles. I saw no ill-effects. The French were treated best, ourselves and Russians worst. The rules of the camp were printed in all languages and posted up; they were the ordinary military rules, except that we were supposed to tell the Germans if we thought anyone was going to escape. Punishments consisted of darkened cells and dry bread and water, up to 28 days. Standing to attention facing a wall six hours a day called stiller-stand – and being sent to 'Strafe' camps.

Once a man who passed himself off as the American Ambassador came to visit us. I spoke to him and complained of various things, and from his speech I was convinced he was a German; he tried to speak with an American accent but failed. He was accompanied by German officials.

I never saw or heard anything of the Irish Brigade. One man, Private King (I think of the Gordons), went mad and was sent to a mad-house near Berlin. I saw several men besides who were 'queer' from long confinement.

Vornhagen, 20th-26th August, 1916.

On the 20th August 1916, I and two other British were sent by train to Vornhagen Commando, attached Minden. It was about an hour's journey. On arrival we were taken to a small lager consisting of what had been a Post Office, a brick building, one large room in which were 8 Frenchmen, 12 Russians, 6 Belgians, and we 3 British. A German lance-corporal was in command. I do not know his name.

The accommodation was the same as at Minden. The sanitary, heating and washing arrangements were good.

We worked on different farms. We three British were on the same farm. We were doing ordinary harvesting work, hours 7 a.m. till 7 p.m., pay 3d a day. We had our food with the farmer during the day, and this consisted of, at 7 a.m., bread and butter and coffee and, twice a week, eggs; 10 a.m., coffee again; mid-day, potatoes, vegetables and bacon; 4 p.m., coffee and two slices of bread; 7 p.m., soup with vegetables and meat. We could live on the food all right. We were well treated. We worked with some German people, two old men and the rest women. They seemed well nourished and confident that Germany would win but they wished it was over. I have no complaints to make about this place.

1st Escape, 26th August, 1916.

On the 24th August I planned to escape with one Belgian, one Russian, and one Frenchman. We arranged for 1 p.m. on 26th. We were to meet the Belgian and Frenchman at our farm. We had civilian clothing. We just walked off. There were no sentries on the farm; the farmer was responsible for us. We followed the road up in a N.W. direction intending to make for the Dutch frontier. We had a compass and map which the Russian had got. When we had got about 20 km. the farmer telephoned our escape, and we were arrested by a policeman in a village we had got to. We were not ill-treated, and marched back to Vornhagen to be identified; there the lance-corporal in charge gave me a smack over the head, and we were sent back at once by train to Minden, the parent camp.

Minden, 26th August-26th September, 1916.

At Minden I was punished first and sentenced afterwards to 21 days cells. At the expiration of my sentence I was sent with four other Britishers by train to Crefeld Commando. The journey lasted about four hours.

Crefeld, 26th September-6th October 1916.

Crefeld Commando is under the Minden Command. We were placed in a dancing room attached to a public house. There were eight British, the remainder were French and Russians. We had cots, straw mattresses, fairly clean, and two blankets. The heating was insufficient, sanitary arrangements very good, washing facilities very good; we could get a warm bath when we liked. A German Feldwebel was in charge; he was not bad and I had no special complaints to make about him. I do not know his name.

There was no hospital, and if anyone was very ill or met with an accident at the works a doctor was sent for from Crefeld, and the man would then be taken to the hospital at Crefeld about 3 km. off. No doctor came regularly to visit the place.

We were set to work at boiler making; there was also attached a plant for making munitions, but we did not work at that. The hours of work were from 6 a.m. to 6 p.m., pay 3d a day. We worked under civilian foremen; they were not allowed to talk to us; they were all old men of over 45. There were about 10 women working in the place. I got very little information out of them; they seemed underfed. The food consisted of coffee, bread and soup, very much the same as we had at Minden. I was now getting my parcels, they were censored at Crefeld, there was no delay. They were opened in my presence. They arrived in good condition and came regularly, letters also. The treatment here was quite good and I have no complaints to make. After a bit we discovered that the boilers we were making were intended for ships of war, so on 6th October 1916 we refused to work, and were sent back to Minden, all four of us British.

Minden, 6th October-12th December, 1916.

On arrival at Minden we were given 'stille-stand' six hours a day for 10 days, We were made to stand strictly to attention the whole six hours and no easy at all.

Ten of our men came in from working behind the German lines in France. I cannot give their names or regiments. They were in a terrible state; they said that they had been wounded on the Somme and forced to work digging trenches under fire; they were starved, ill-treated and given no clothes. Several died of starvation and ill-treatment. They had not been allowed to write any letters. The poor fellows were in a most pitiable condition and were taken to hospital.

Crefeld, 12th-15th December 1916.

On the 12th December 1916. we four British were sent back to Crefeld on another commando. We were housed in a sort of barn containing three Frenchmen besides ourselves, under a German corporal whose name I do not know. He was not bad and treated us all right. We slept on beds, straw mattresses and two blankets. The washing, heating and sanitary arrangements were good. We could get a warm bath when we liked. We were here only three days. The work was tinning food for the front. Our work consisted of unloading trainloads of mangel-wurzels, potatoes and carrots, which were taken to the factory to be tinned. I never saw anything else; no meat.

2nd Escape, 15th December, 1916.

On the 15th December, I and another Britisher, Private Humphrey, K.O.R.L., got through the barbed wire and started for the frontier. We had a compass and a map. We started due north and got during that night close to the frontier, and while passing through a wood got to a canal, which we had to swim. On the opposite bank we ran into a German post and were caught. We were not ill-treated but were escorted back to Crefeld to be identified, and from there we were sent back to Minden.

Minden, 15th December, 1916-6th March 1917.

On arrival back at Minden we were sentenced to 21 days' cells. When a man gets cells he never gets his parcels. I think he should be given his Swiss bread whenever he is given 10 days' cells or more, as one gets so terribly weak on bread and water and only one bowl of soup every fourth day. I received letters and parcels regularly. Parcels were opened in my presence and the contents given to us; later on they kept our tins and only gave them out as we wanted them, and then tipped the contents into a basin and kept the tins. The parcels arrived in good condition. The bread from Switzerland was good; the biscuits that were sent afterwards in the place of bread in the summer were quite satisfactory. I never heard any complaints about the new system of parcels or the contents thereof; all seemed pleased with them.

Westerholt, 6th March 1917-11th January 1918.

On the 6th March 1917, I was sent with a party of 180 British to Westerholt, a journey of about six hours. On arrival we were taken to the camp, which is under the Friedrichsfeld command and about 50 km. off. The camp is built in the ordinary way, wooden huts, and holds about 1,300 prisoners of war, commanded by a Lieut.-Feldwebel, under him a corporal and about four Gefreiters and 30 Postern. I do not know the names of any of them.

Our hut held about 180 men, all British. The nationalities were kept separate – there were about 200 French, 355 Russians, roughly 100 Serbians, about 200 British and about 200 Italians who came in in January 1918. We lay in hammocks, two blankets, heated by hot-water pipes which were seldom warm. Washing facilities very poor, one long trough and only cold water. No bath in the camp, but we could get one at the pits. Clothes were sent out to be washed. Latrines almost adjoining our hut; trenches flushed with water and cleaned out by the men who were sick and excused duty; very insanitary.

We were employed in a coal mine below the ground, pushing waggons. We were in eight-hour shifts, and twice a week we did 12 hours. The pay ranged from 30 pfg, to two marks a week according to the work done.

The food was the same as at Minden, but not quite so good.

We got our parcels pretty regularly, they were censored in the camp.

There was a canteen, but the prices were very dear.

We were given work clothes. We had a band and a gymnastic bar. We could smoke. There was no epidemic. There was a sick-room. A doctor visited us twice a week. The treatment was very bad; the first night we arrived the 180 British refused to work, and after standing out for a couple of hours the German Feldwebel ordered the guard to charge us with their rifles, lumps of iron, sticks, and rubber tubing. I was hit in the back. One man was knocked senseless – Private Brooks, of the 1st Gordons. We were driven to the barrack room, and next day we had to go down the pits. All the time we were here we were ill-treated by the foremen. About 10th November 1917, at 8 a.m., 15 of us went for a sleep, dodging work; a German foreman caught us, took our numbers and lifted his hand at one of our fellows. Private Shand, Gordons, caught hold of the foreman and shoved him down the steps, a drop of about 10 feet. We left him there and went along the main road, and we were all chased about the pit till about 12.30. A foreman, not the one who was sent down the steps, came up to Private Gordon Denny, of the Gordons, and hit him over the bead with a testing hammer; he was knocked senseless and afterwards taken back to the lager and had his bead dressed. At 12.30 I was caught and four Germans started beating me with sticks and rubber piping. I was black and blue from head to foot; several of the others were knocked about the same sort of way. When we got to the top we were made to 'stille stand' for 24 hours. If any prisoners escape from here and are brought back the Feldwebel starts beating them; he is a regular brute and is still there. Once he beat a Russian to such an extent that he was in hospital for three months after it. The ill-treatment is common to all the prisoners on the part of the Feldwebel and the civilian foremen in the works. I did not see much of the Italians nor how they were treated; they seemed well clothed in their uniform. They were not working in the same pit as us. I was never asked to make munitions.

The Dutch Ambassador came to visit us once in September 1917. The place was cleaned up before his arrival. We were able to speak quite freely with him. He could speak English and seemed a nice man. We told him all about our bad treatment, and there was a marked improvement in our treatment after he left. I have not heard of any camp in Germany where prisoners are not allowed to write or receive letters. Latterly, I noticed that the treatment of prisoners is worse than it was when I was first in Germany I attribute this to their being obliged to be stricter in making their prisoners work as they are so short of workmen themselves. The food is more scarce and worse in quality.

The guards at first were ordinary Landsturm men, but now they are either boys or old men or cripples from the front.

I heard of a riot at Essen in which the military had to charge and kill several people before it was stopped; this was the latter end of 1917. I was also told that the civil population are starving and sick of the war.

On three occasions on the railway between Friedrichsfeld and Westerholt the civilians raided the parcels for the prisoners and stole several. The tins were taken from the parcels and handed to us as wanted; that is to say, the contents were handed to us, the tins were kept. Our parcels were withheld from us whenever we were doing punishment and given out afterwards. Collective punishments were often inflicted: 15 men escaped one week, and all parcels were stopped for a month. Parcels were coming regularly up to the time I left. I never heard of any British prisoner who either assumed German nationality or showed any German sympathies. I never saw any American prisoners. Patients in hospitals get their tinned stuff sent to them, and their bread is distributed amongst the British prisoners of war in the camp.

3rd Escape, 11th January 1918.

I escaped on 11th January 1918, with Private Shand, 1st Gordons, Private Shane, Cameron Highlanders, and Private Mullins, Sherwood Foresters.

Opinion of examiner: This man is not intelligent, very dull, and with no powers of observation. His statements, however, in my opinion are reliable. He was not inclined to be bitter about his treatment.

CAPT. ERIC W HALL, 16TH MIDDLESEX REGT.
Mürren, 23rd February 1917

I was taken prisoner about 5 p.m. on the evening of July 1st, 1916. I had been lying out all day since 7.45 in the morning and was unable to move as I was wounded in the knee. About 5 the Germans put up a white flag with a red cross on it and sent three Red Cross men out to collect the wounded. These men. were armed with revolvers. All this took place about 80 yards in front of the German first-line trench at Beaumont Hamel. After being carried in by four of our men, I was taken on a stretcher by two German Red Cross men to a dressing station in the village, where after an hour or two I was attended to by a doctor, who dressed my wound and gave me a glass of wine. I was there till the evening of the 2nd, when I was conveyed in a horse ambulance to a dressing station at Miraumont.

Miraumont, 2nd-3rd July 1916.

This place was crowded with German and our own wounded, and as there was no accommodation indoors, I was left outside in a yard with many others all night. The next day, as there seemed to be no chance of being attended to – the doctors were working continuously all the time – I pressed hard to be allowed to go on somewhere else. This was allowed me about 4 in the afternoon, and that evening I found myself at Vélu, in the grounds of a big chateau.

Vélu, July 1916.

Again there were hundreds of our own and German wounded, and no place could be found for me in the two tents they had there, so I had to spend another night in the open – but this time on the stretcher and only straw to lie on. Unfortunately, it rained hard that night, and I presume the exposure must have affected me, for I have been told since that when I was carried off to the doctor next morning people thought I was in a dying condition. The doctor put my leg in a splint, and that evening I was sent by a Red Cross train to Caudry.

Journey, 4th-5th July 1916.

The train was crammed, and many who should have got beds were unable to do so. The next morning we arrived at an improvised hospital at Caudry which was almost full.

Caudry, 5th-10th July.

Here, again, many men who ought to have been bed cases had to spend their time on the floor. There were only two doctors, and I can guarantee they were working from 7.30 in the morning till 9.30 at night, and yet my wound was never dressed. There were worse cases that needed immediate attention. The nurses there were excellent though much overworked. The food was bad, i.e., for wounded, but there was plenty of it. We were visited nearly every day by Red Cross officials, and on one occasion by the Princess of Pless, who seemed to take great interest in many of the English patients. On July 10th, about 8 p.m., as many of us as were able to stand the journey were moved in a Red Cross tram to Germany.

Journey, 10th-12th July 1916.

The journey was long and tedious; we only had two platesful of soup and some bread all the time till we reached Gütersloh about 1 a.m. on July 12th. We were met at the station by stretcher bearers, and four other officers and myself were taken to the town hospital in Gütersloh.

Gütersloh Town Hospital, 12th July-11th September 1916.

The doctor was up to attend to us, and we were given hot tea and clean clothes, and for the first time had a comfortable bed. The next day the doctor dressed our wounds and X-rayed those who needed it, including myself. It was decided after the X-ray that an operation was not necessary on my leg, but there was 7 inches difference between the two legs. I accordingly had weights attached to my left leg to draw it out. I was in this hospital till September 11th, and throughout was treated with consummate care. Nurses and doctor alike did all in their power to get us well, and though at times conversation had to be carried on in the Latin and even Greek tongue, there were no signs of that irritation which often arises from an incomplete understanding, and the doctor never left the room till he was positive that we had explained to him what we wanted.

Camp Hospital, 11th September-15th November 1916.

On being moved from the town hospital I was taken to the Lager of Gütersloh and then put in hospital – a building which was within the camp itself. Gütersloh, from all accounts, including that of the first Secretary at the American Embassy in Berlin, is the best camp in Germany for officers. Letters and parcels came regularly, and I don't think I have missed any, and I think I received a good deal more than the average. Heating and sanitary arrangements were good both here and in the town hospital. The money exchange was 750 marks for 10*l.*

As there was so much sport of every kind at Gütersloh, I do not consider the mentality of British prisoners had been affected much. As I was there such a short time, I did not notice any improvement in prison life. Indeed, except for the food, which was, of course, execrable, very little improvement could have been rightly asked for: though it must be remembered that most of the improvements in the camp had been brought about by the prisoners themselves and not by our captors. There was a restaurant where you could have your own food cooked, but where nothing was supplied to you.

Most kinds of drink could be procured except spirits. The drink was not good; indeed, it was thoroughly bad, and any excesses in that line were dearly paid for.

On November 15th I was sent with eight others to Constance, there to go before the final Swiss Commission. We were not seen for a fortnight, and then after that were kept another fortnight. Eventually 11 of us were sent to a French lager at Vöhrenbach, in the Black Forest, where we stayed a week. On December 20th we came through to Mürren.

Constance, 15th Nov-13th December 1916.

There is no doubt that the last month at Constance was my worst experience. Letters and parcels were not sent to us, and we had to live on German rations. Fifty officers were packed together in a ward, and only a small room to have meals in. We were only allowed out in the square twice during the day for a period of two hours.

From my point of view this is the one complaint I wish to make during my captivity: that thousands of men were brought as far as the border at Constance and then were rejected and had to return back to camp. I can well imagine the disappointment killing certain men. With regard to everything else, I can only say that if I had to be taken prisoner in a war I would always choose the German nation to be my captor.

1346 PTE. RUPERT ROBESON, 16TH MIDDLESEX REGT., from Chile. An auditor. Taken prisoner Beaumont Hamel, 1st July 1916. Nature of wound: Shrapnel wound in right leg. Capture and journey, 1st-2nd July, 1916.

I was hit about 8 o'clock in the morning of the 1st July 1916, and lay there until about 7 o'clock in the evening, when I was taken prisoner by the Germans.

I was taken back over their lines and put in a dug-out. They gave me some coffee, and treated me decently. I saw the German doctor at the field dressing station. He just looked at my leg (which bad been bound up, but was bleeding) and said I was able to walk, I walked 8 kilometres to a church in a village (name unknown) and there had my wound dressed by a British Red Cross man. I had to walk back about 12 kilometres next day to another village (name unknown), where we entrained for Cambrai.

Cambrai, 3rd-13th July.

At Cambrai I was kept for 13 days in barracks. Some of the British Red Cross men dressed my wound and took out the shrapnel, which was on the surface. In about a fortnight my wound was healed.

We had to sleep on straw without any blankets. We had the usual food – soup made from vegetables, blank coffee and a thin slice of black bread. I have nothing to complain about with regard to treatment. We asked whether we could write a postcard from Cambrai, but were told we should be able to write from Dülmen, where we went on the 15th July 1916.

Dülmen, 15th July-August, 1916.

The newly-captured prisoners were separated from the others so as to prevent the latter from giving the former tips, such as lance-corporal putting on second stripe to make himself a full corporal and hiding his pay-book.

Heuberg, August, 1916-February 1918.

I left Dülmen for Heuberg towards the end of August 1916. This is a camp with 9,000 prisoners of all nationalities, 250 British. I do not know the names of the commandant or second in command. The commandant did not like the English and would not grant them any favours. We asked if we could have a boxing match in the theatre, but this was refused. At first he would not allow concerts for the English but when the French asked for permission, he gave it them. We were in huts, and had beds and two blankets for us, fairly clean. In the winter we had an allowance of coal which lasted only about two hours; consequently, the huts were nearly always cold. There was a pump with cold water for washing, but no trough or basins. The sanitary arrangements were pretty good.

Everybody at this camp had to work, and if they refused they were put in cells on bread and water until they did work. They were employed on the land at the various surrounding farms, and on road making. The pay was 30 pfennigs a day. The first two weeks I was at the camp I was sent out road making; we started at 7 in the morning and worked until 4 in the afternoon, with a break of one hour, when soup was given us. After about two months a man was wanted for work in the office to make out the pay sheets. I was selected, and had to work from 8 a.m. to 11 a.m. and from 2 to 6 p.m. I had no privileges at all, but was treated all right. I worked the same hours on Saturdays, but not on Sundays. I did this work for about 14 or 15 months, when I heard a man was wanted at a farm at Schildach, near the frontier. I volunteered, thinking I might be able to escape. There was no attempt to force prisoners to make munitions at Heuberg.

The food in the camp was the same as over all Germany – coffee substitute and bread in the morning, soup middle day, and coffee at night; occasionally very thin soup again at night. There was a canteen where we could buy apples in the summer, cigars and lemonade, but the prices were very high. Parcels arrived in good condition, except that the bread in the summer-time was bad. My parcels commenced to arrive three months after I was captured, and then came regularly, as also did the letters. All letters and parcels were censored at Immingen, which was the main station for different railways. The parcels were opened in the presence of four Englishmen, but letters were censored before we received them. Curry powder, pepper and marmite (a kind of Oxo) were taken from the parcels. We were not informed as to what articles were prohibited. We were given the tins from our parcels, which we smashed up,

I had no clothing from the Germans, and never asked for them, as I received supplies from England. We could play football on Sundays, and indoors we were allowed to play cards. Smoking was never stopped. There was an epidemic of diphtheria in the summer of 1917. There were seven English cases, also some Russian and French. We had one or two religious services, conducted by travelling clergymen, in eighteen months. I have not heard of any complaint of ill-treatment or cruelty to prisoners. Discipline was very strict; we had to salute all non-commissioned officers as well as officers. The regulations were read out in English, and practically everything was considered an offence. The usual punishment was cells, bread and water.

I saw a representative of the American Embassy once, at the beginning of 1917. I was one of the deputation who spoke to him. We complained that corporals who had refused to work were put in cells. The representative insisted on their being released. The Germans contended that they were only lance-corporals, but the representative said it was for the Germans to prove it. Corporal Broadbent (regiment unknown) complained that the commandant had torn his stripes off. The American representative told the commandant he could not degrade an English soldier, and the stripes were again put on. The German officers were present when we were speaking to the American representative. Special preparations were made for the American's visit; the camp was cleaned and everything put in order. For a few days after his visit the food was a little better, but soon deteriorated. I was never asked to join the Irish Brigade or assume German nationality, and never witnessed any cases of insanity.

The treatment of prisoners improved during my stay in the camp. At first the Germans called us pigs, and swore at us; now they call us by our numbers and have more respect for us. I think this is because they now recognise that the English are stronger than they imagined them to be.

Schildach, February 1918.

Having volunteered to work, I was sent to a camp at Schildach, where I stayed only two days before I escaped.

1st Escape, February 1918.

The farm of Schildach was about 40 kilometres from the frontier, and I escaped only two days after my arrival there. I got within 7 kilometres of the frontier, when I ran into a German patrol, and was retaken.

Heuberg, February-2nd March 1918.

I was taken back to Heuberg Camp, and put in cells on bread and water as a punishment. A month or so before I escaped 30 men arrived at Heuberg who had been working behind the German lines. They did not complain of their treatment, and said they had been given the same rations as the German soldiers. They had been employed in making roads.

Just after Christmas 250 Italian prisoners arrived at the camp. They said they had only received half the ration which was served out by the Germans to the British, French and Russians. They looked in very bad condition, and complained of their treatment generally. Three Italian prisoners died within three weeks of their arrival in the camp, and one of the English prisoners told me it was nothing but starvation.

Kirchdorf, 2nd-19th March, 1918.

After 14 days they sent me to another farm at Kirchdorf. I had to sleep in the neighbouring village in a barrack with two English and 19 Russians, I was there for two weeks, and had to work from 5 a.m. until 8 p.m. We had no break at all. They wanted me to plough, clean out the stables, and, in fact, do everything I had not been used to farm work, and the farmer complained of the way I did my work. I had my parcels from the barracks, and did not touch any of the farmer's food, though it was better than at the camp. The pay was the same. I was put in civilian cells in the village for three days for not working hard enough for the farmer. At the end of three days I was told to go back to the farm, and that if I did not work harder I should be given another three days in cells. The rations were worse at this time than they were when I was captured. The bread ration was smaller; formerly we had two potatoes latterly only one. I went back to the farm.

Final escape, 19th March 1918.

The same night I escaped (March 19th, 1918), and got over the Swiss border on March 22nd near Schaffhausen.

When I was captured the men guarding the camps were men getting on for 50, but now they are very old and have lost an eye or leg.

German papers were smuggled into the camp, and we read therein of food riots in Germany. The farmer I was working for at Kirchdorf complained bitterly and said that if the war did not finish in three months there would be a revolution in Germany.

Opinion of examiner: The witness is very intelligent and reliable.

LT. LEONARD CHARLES RUSSELL, 2ND ROYAL FUSILIERS, of 44, Hillcourt Road, East Dulwich, London SE. Aged 25, accountant.

Capture, 1st July 1916. Captured at Beaumont Hamel, 1st July 1916. Wounded in the head and in both shoulders.

On the night of June 30th my battalion went up to the front-line trenches. I was in command of Z Company, to which were attached four Stokes mortars, four machine guns, two Lewis guns and a section of bombers. On the following morning – the first day of the battle of the Somme – at 7.20 a.m., a mine exploded just in front of our trench and I went over with half the company. About half of us went to the right of the crater and the remainder to the left; I was on the right. When we got to the German trenches there were only about 15 men with me, and no guns. Our bombers put three enemy machine guns out of action, but we were forced to retire owing to the British barrage, and I remained in the German frontline trenches with three men, doing my best to hold it. Here I was wounded three times, in the head and in both shoulders. The Germans came up to where I was lying, and I pretended to be dead, hoping that I might be able to get back to our lines. After about two hours had passed I was discovered and taken to a dressing station in the trenches, where my wounds were dressed. The men who captured me belonged to the 119th Regiment of Württemburgers, and they treated me very well. After my wounds had been dressed I was taken to the officers' dug-out. The officers there were considerate and polite, and I was given a good meal of meat and wine and beer.

When I was lying on the ground I saw soldiers firing bullets into the bodies of the dead, but not hitting the wounded, and I noticed no infraction by the enemy of the laws and usages of war.

There were about a dozen officers in the dug-out amongst whom was an Artillery officer who spoke English, and who interrogated me, but I gave him no information. I remained in this dug-out until the morning of July 2nd, when a wagon came, in which I was taken to a dressing station in Beaumont Hamel. Here I remained until the evening, when they took me to another dressing station about four miles to the rear, where I spent the night in company with some other wounded British officers. The arrangements in this dressing station were bad, only dirty straw to lie on in an uncomfortable marquee. The next morning we went on to another dressing station, where we were joined by some more wounded officers and men. We left this last dressing station in the morning of July 4th and went by train to Caudry, There was no cause for complaint in the way in which we were treated at the dressing station or during our journey by wagon and rail.

Caudry Hospital, 5th-9th July, 1916.

We reached the hospital at Caudry at 4 a.m. on July 5th and on my arrival I was put to bed and my wounds were dressed. This hospital was a converted lace factory. The arrangements were good, but it was very much understaffed, for there were not more than two doctors and about six nurses to attend to the 400 wounded, and there were many men who received no medical attention. The food also was very poor – only substitute coffee, bread and soup. I was allowed to write home from here.

Journey, 9th-10th July 1916.

On the 9th July I was sent off with nine other wounded officers and about 100 wounded men. Our train started at 5 p.m. We (the officers) were to go to Gütersloh, but I do not know where the men were sent to. The journey occupied over 30 hours, and we were given some soup and a piece of bread twice on the way. Second-class carriages were provided for the officers, and the men travelled 3rd and 4th class. Our guards, who were young men, treated us quite well.

Gütersloh Hospital, 10th-17th July 1916.

We reached Gütersloh about 3 a m on July 10th and on our arrival were taken to the hospital and put to bed. On the following morning we were taken before an officer, who asked us questions about our regiments, brigades, divisions, etc., but we refused to answer. After a week in the hospital I was discharged. The hospital arrangements were quite good, and I was looked after principally by a British officer who was, by profession, a doctor and who helped in the hospital.

Camp, 17th July 1916-22nd March 1917.

At Gütersloh there were about 600 Russian officers, 400 French and 200 British. The accommodation was very good indeed. There were five other officers in my room, and we were most comfortable. There was nothing to complain about as regards lodging, heating, washing facilities and the sanitary arrangements.

There were excellent arrangements for study, and ample opportunity given to attend lectures and to learn languages. We could play any games, smoking was allowed anywhere, and there was a theatre. We were allowed to go out for walks on parole, and there was a good canteen where most things could be bought at reasonable prices, and which we were allowed to run ourselves, the profits being divided among the officers of all nationalities.

The food was very bad indeed. For breakfast substitute coffee and two slices of nasty bread; dinner, two slices of bread and vegetable soup; and at supper, soup and bread. A little fish and some cheese were given occasionally, and this was all. We lived entirely on our parcels.

Parcels came very regularly, and also letters. The treatment we received was very good. The commandant, Major von der Gröben, was quite popular with the prisoners. He was rather excitable, but I never heard any serious complaint about him. I do not know the name of the second in command. We saw very little of these officers. The interpreter, an unteroffizier named Langensieben, seemed to have a great deal of influence and almost to run the camp. This man, who spoke English well and was reported to have an English wife, was very unpleasant and most offensive in his conduct towards the British prisoners. Whilst I was at Gütersloh there were no punishments.

There was no epidemic during my stay. Religious services were held every Sunday. There was no visit from the American Ambassador, nor did I hear any mention of the Irish Brigade. I saw no case of insanity, and I was never asked nor did I hear of anybody being asked to assume German nationality.

There was a Russian doctor a prisoner at Gütersloh who seemed to be in great favour with the authorities, and whose wife lived in the town, I cannot remember this man's name, but he was allowed to go in and out of the camp, and we looked upon him as a spy.

On March 20th, 1917, the British prisoners were told that they would be moved to Crefeld, as it had been arranged that nationalities should be kept separate, and on the 22nd we left Gütersloh. We were given facilities for packing and removing our belongings, and every consideration was shown us. I was very sorry indeed that we had to change our prison.

Crefeld, 22nd March-22nd May 1917.

We reached Crefeld on March 22nd, 1917. The British adjutant allocated us rooms, and I was put in a room with seven other officers. There were about 900 British prisoners at Crefeld.

The commandant, Courth, was a very nice man, most kind and extremely popular. The accommodation was excellent; also heating, washing facilities and sanitary arrangements were good.

We formed classes for study, and lectures were given which kept us fully employed; and although there were no Russians nor French to teach their languages, some officers who knew them held classes and taught their fellow prisoners.

The food was much better than at Gütersloh, and almost sufficient, but we ate very little of it, preferring to live on our parcels. For breakfast we had coffee substitute and bread, which was quite good, two slices; at dinner we were given either soup or meat and potatoes; for supper we had coffee, soup and bread. The canteen was well run, and one could buy practically anything except boots and shoes and rubber articles.

The opportunities for recreation were not so good as at Gütersloh, but there were tennis and football, and we had a good theatre. Smoking was allowed everywhere, and we could go out for walks on parole.

Isolation Hospital, five days.

There was no epidemic at Crefeld whilst I was there and I never heard of any case of insanity. I was never at the hospital, but I spent five days in the isolation hospital for skin trouble, from which I also suffered when I was at Gütersloh. The treatment given me was quite successful, and I thought the arrangements in the isolation hospital quite good.

Parcels came regularly, and only those which were sent through the American Express Company were ever tampered with. These generally arrived with only about half of their contents, and I lost many things that were sent to me through this agency. The ordinary parcels nearly always arrived intact. There was a good deal of uncertainty about the letters, and several of mine miscarried.

Punishments were not frequent, and I was never punished at Crefeld.

There was no visit from representatives of either the American Embassy or the Dutch Legation whilst I was here, but I remember that all Irish officers were warned that they would be taken to a separate camp; nothing, however, came of this.

About May 20th when the guards were increased and the machine guns brought, we were told that the camp was to be broken up, and on the 22nd, at 7 a.m. we left. Some went to Ströhen, others to Schwarmstedt. and the senior officers were distributed amongst various other camps. I noticed when the prisoners were divided that the members of different messes and rooms were separated, and this seemed to me to have been done purposely by the authorities, possibly in view of future attempts to escape.

Ströhen, 22nd May-19th November 1917.

I was sent to Ströhen, and we arrived there about 8.30 on the night of May 22nd. The commandant when he received the officers treated them rudely and did not acknowledge their salutes when he called out their names, and as soon as this was noticed the British officers went up to him without saluting.

I can corroborate all that Lieutenant Wingfield, Captain Fitzgerald and Captain Somerville have said with regard to the filthy and verminous condition of the huts and their state of repair, as well as their description of the general state of the camp.

I was put in a hut with six other prisoners, and the accommodation was very bad indeed: mattresses stuffed with paper and cardboard; the only place for washing was at the pump, and the sanitary arrangements were disgusting.

As regards employment, the only place where classes could be held was the dining room, and it was not easy to work there, nor convenient. There was scarcely any space for recreation. Smoking was allowed, but British cigarettes were stopped, and the only tobacco obtainable was what could be bought at the canteen. Not much could be obtained there: some very bad wine, soda, braces and a few things of that sort, but no food and no boots.

The food was atrocious and quite insufficient. For the first two weeks or rather longer there were no parcels and we suffered much from hunger for, except for the small quantity of food that we were able to bring away from Crefeld in our handbags, there was nothing for us to eat except the rations. These consisted at that time of half a loaf of very bad bread per week; for breakfast, some substitute coffee or very bad cocoa; swede soup for dinner, and the same soup again for supper. On Sunday we were given a small piece of meat and some potatoes. After our parcels began to arrive we got on better, but for the first fortnight we were literally starving. The things which we had to leave at Crefeld to follow us did not get to Ströhen for quite two weeks after our arrival.

I can confirm all that has been said by Lieutenant Wingfield and the other officers about the conduct of the two first commandants towards the prisoners and the frequency of the punishments. The commandant who was at Ströhen when we arrived, and who was most severe and unreasonable, left in July 1917. I cannot remember his name. His successor as commandant was a man just as bad, if not worse. His name I also forget, but it was this officer who gave the order to the sentry to bayonet Downes and Woodhouse. He was only at Ströhen for two months. The third commandant, to whom I spoke on more than one occasion, seemed to be very different in manner to his predecessors, and I expect is much better. The second in command did all that was possible to irritate and exasperate the prisoners. He was a great bully, and his manner was most offensive. I do not know his real name, but he was always called 'I guess you know', being evidently an American German. I am sure he was responsible for much of the friction and unpleasantness. He left Ströhen at the beginning of September, and he is now commandant at Holzminden. After 'I guess you know' left, a very nice man became second in command; he was most considerate, but he only remained two months, and we were all sorry when he left. Under the third commandant and this new second in command, punishments – except those for attempted escape – became quite rare. There was a slight improvement also in the washing arrangements, although the number of baths allowed was curtailed, but the sanitary arrangements were just us bad and the drinking water just as nasty.

The Dutch representative came twice whilst I was at Ströhen.

Towards the end of August the epidemic of diarrhoea which had been prevalent all the time, more or less, became worse, and just before the second visit of the Dutch representatives we were warned not to drink the water unboiled. A charge of 5 pfennigs per litre was made for water supposed to be boiled, but as there were no proper facilities for boiling the water it was never really boiled.

The rations became even worse than they were when we first arrived, and eventually an arrangement was made by the camp adjutant that officers should be charged only for the midday ration, and that we should live entirely on our parcels.

Parcels came irregularly towards the end, and occasionally food was missing out of them. Letters came pretty regularly. On November 17th a new order was given out that in future no letters would be delivered in their envelopes. A list was posted of the officers from whom there were letters, and they were desired to call for them after evening Appel. My letters frequently arrived undated, and when I called for them I asked that the date of the postmark might be noted on the letter when it was taken out of the envelope, but I was told that this would give too much trouble and could not be done.

Although punishments were so frequent. I was only once punished. This perhaps was because I was the junior officer in my room and punishments were usually given to the seniors. The ground on which I was punished was very unreasonable; it was for smoking on parade. We had been kept standing at Appel for over two hours, and as leave was given to the unteroffiziers to smoke, I supposed that the officers were also allowed to do so.

I remember the case of Captain Coulson. He certainly was in prison on November 19th, the day on which I escaped, and, so far as I knew, he had not been sentenced for the supposed offence of having assaulted on unteroffizier.

The case of Captain Sloper (Northumberland Fusiliers) was a very hard one. One evening in August we were kept standing on Appel for quite an hour and a half, and we were not allowed to move. Captain Sloper moved and proceeded to walk across the parade. One of the guards followed him and let the butt of his rifle down on Sloper's foot. Sloper was at once marched off to prison, and he also was in prison on November 19th.

Captain Onslow, who attempted to escape on the day following the escape of Insall, Templer and Harrison (August 21st), was imprisoned for two weeks at Ströhen, and then sent to Holzminden, and in a letter which he wrote from there in October, and which I saw, he stated that he was still in prison and had not had a bath for six weeks.

I remember the incident of Lieutenant Knight being bayoneted, and I saw him after he was wounded. I saw the bayoneting of Lieutenant Downes and Captain Woodhouse, and the account given by Captain Somerville is quite correct. I was present on the occasion when the sentry charged Lieutenant Wilson and ran his bayonet through Wilson's coat.

There were two most objectionable unteroffiziers. Feldwebel Pohlmann was one who did all in his power to annoy the prisoners. On the same day that Knight was wounded this man ordered the sentry to charge another officer and myself because we happened to be walking near the ponds whilst they were being pumped dry for the recovery of the helmets which had been thrown in by the prisoners. Another very offensive Feldwebel was named Müller. This man habitually kept the officers standing at Appel for an unnecessarily long time, and lie was overbearing and rude.

Very frequent searches of the prisoners' rooms were made at Ströhen almost once a week, and about November 15th, a day or two before my escape, a staff of detectives in plain clothes with officers in uniform made a two days' search of the whole camp.

The guards at Ströhen were elderly men, badly clothed and badly fed, but nearly all of them were friendly and inclined to be civil and obliging.

The censoring of parcels as at present carried on at Ströhen causes great inconvenience and waste. Bread, bacon and cheese are much damaged by being cut, and the opening of all unsoldered tins and the delivery of the contents to the consignees seems to be unnecessary and unreasonable. All parcels are opened in the presence of a Feldwebel, and if they happen to contain any unsoldered tins these are emptied into whatever receptacle the prisoner may happen to bring, the tins being kept by the Feldwebel. Soldered tins, however, are put in each prisoner's locker and opened only when he asks for them. I heard many complaints of damage to food, etc., through this regulation, and I strongly advise that all tins sent in parcels should be soldered. The arrangements for getting out parcels from the office were most inconvenient, for we often had to stand in a queue for a couple of hours before our turn came. If the parcel office could be kept open for a longer period the prisoners would be spared this annoyance.

I escaped from Ströhen on November 19th, 1917.

Diary kept by Lieutenant Russell.

November 1916 to March 1917 – Winter passed at Gütersloh; no particular events. January and February very cold. Skating for six weeks; played ice hockey. Gave carnival to Allies – very enjoyable.

March 22nd – Moved to Crefeld; very sorry to leave Gütersloh and all my French friends. Journey very interesting after seeing so little of the outside world.

First impressions of Crefeld: bad. No hockey except on very dangerous ground. Preferred to take exercise in form of running, gymnasium, polo, etc. Beginning to like Crefeld; heaps to do; lectures, concerts, theatres ('You never can tell').

April – In a very comfortable room furnished quite nicely, very cosy, month passed quietly. Arras battle.

May 10th – Commenced to make tennis courts.

May 20th – Told to pack up and leave for camp No. III Tried to transfer to camp No. II., as nearly all my friends sent there.

May 21st – Packing. Evening 'Appel' lasted from 8.30 to 11.30 owing to several attempted escapes, bonfires and general excitement, guards turned out, etc. 12 p.m., bed.

May 22nd 2 a.m. – First party called, viz.. No. II., got up, had breakfast. 3 a.m., said good-bye to all my friends; very fed up. 5,30 a.m. No. III. numbers and baggage checked. 7 a.m.,, walked to station; handbag very heavy; very pleased when train reached. Left Crefeld Station at 7.30; journey uninteresting; reached Ströhen 8 p.m. (passed Gütersloh); appeared very desolate. Walk to camp with heavy handbag very trying. Camp of huts. Germans rather offensive and inclined to shout. Took several hours to allot rooms. I got to bed 1 a.m.

May 23rd – Appel 8 a.m. By day camp appears even more desolate; no baths. Bathed under pumps; water very bad. There are two pumps, with troughs running into filthy pools. Camp surrounded with marshes, altogether very unpleasant and should think unhealthy; no sports; beds staffed with dirty paper and cardboard, etc. Food very bad; cup of so-called coffee for breakfast, filthy soup for lunch and same for dinner. Half loaf of terrible bread for one week. We all have numbers, and have been put in rooms in numerical and alphabetical order. Many applications made for changes.

May 24th – Two men put in jug for bathing. Great excitement and mutinous spirits; everyone ripe for anything. Germans agree to make as many changes as possible, and we agree to meet them halfway. Got baggage from baggage office. Germans agree to let us change rooms.

May 24th – Changed rooms. Got a small room for two. A. L. Russell stable companion, now a bit more comfy. Lists started for classes. No excitement or rumours; life very dull and hopeless.

May 26th – Started physical jerks and feel little better; pantomime game of cricket with stick and soft ball; evening, played a little cricket with proper things. Life is getting interesting again. Lice reported, and confirmed free in my room no far.

May 27th – Physical jerks and little cricket. Jones, of 9th Battalion, arrived; invited him to dinner; half-way through went to get his bread ration and finished his dinner in dining hall – extraordinary beggar. Newcomers think war will end this year – hope so.

Following subjects discussed with Inspector-General:

Sanitation – It is not possible to change present latrine arrangements. Great care would be taken to disinfect. Water was proved good by analysis. Fresh samples were being analysed to reassure us. Filters were refused.

Accommodation. – Mattresses stuffed with sea grass will be substituted for those stuffed with paper, (b) Ventilation. The order re: closing of lower windows at night be rescinded or amended. The question is being re-submitted, and it is expected that an improvement in ventilation will result, (c) Baths. The IG. offered to install 12 cold showers within the lager, expense to be borne by us. (d) Parcel room is to be enlarged and German parcel staff doubled. Vessels for contents of tins will be stocked in canteen. The present regime re: tobacco and cigarettes are enforced as precautionary measure. Another appeal to Hanover is being submitted against them. The I.G. asked for a written report re: confiscation of potatoes. (e) Canteen. Management by us requested. Improved stock promised. (f) Cooking and rations. Management by us refused; better cooking facilities promised. Extra stove at our expense. It is expected that permission will be given for the erection of more stoves. (g) Stools will be gradually replaced by chairs. Benches will he placed about the lager, Washstands will be erected in corridors.

Arrest – The I.G. agreed that to deprive officers in arrest on remand of parcels was unjust, but written representations must be submitted to Hanover on the subject.

Recreation – Games on parole without lager refused. Separate room for chapel, theatre, music and cards cannot be granted. Parole card will have photograph, which will take the place of word of honour; not transferable.

June 1st, 1917, 5 a.m. – awakened by G.O. presumably D.; counted us and went out again; continued stamping for some time. 10 a.m., drink stopped, smoke stopped. Search for tins (how they love us!). 2.30, French lesson; search still continues. Given option of having windows opened at night and parcels stopped or windows closed at night and parcels continued. Germans decided to take out top windows. Storm, violent rain.

June 2nd 1917 – Physical jerks 9.45-10.20. Hindustani 1st lesson 10.30-11.45. Reported big offensive to take place soon all fronts. It will be the last? Rumour all yearers to go to Neutral countries, remainder of prisoners of war to be concentrated in one big camp. One top window taken out. Change in weather; cloudy and windy.

June 3rd – Very windy and cold. Rumour we shall leave here within three weeks. Evening service 8.30. Sewed on numbers (washing). Weather improved.

June 4th,1917 – Monday. Perfect day. Gymnasium. Bath. Strong rumour we shall go to Königsberg. New German officer; seems quite tame. Report 18 months with three children shortly to go to Switzerland. . .

June 5th – Very stormy and a missing Appel. Several speeches by G.; shouting by G. returned by Coulson. Perfect weather. Gymnasium, very strenuous. Visit G. general. Many rumours ; mainly camp is unfit for B.O.'s ; many alterations to be made. I would rather leave the camp, and hope it is closed down. No letters since 29th May; anxiously awaiting one from Maude.

June 6th – Speeches on both 'Appels', more shouting (expect transfer before long); all seniors of rooms going to 'jug' for three days for open windows. Most of our requests submitted Inspector-General refused. News from all fronts good. Gymnasium in morning. Hindustani lesson. Luggage arrived from Crefeld.

June 7th – Gymnasium. French lesson. Letter from home. Very fed up this evening. Hope the great offensive will soon come off. Wrote to Maude. 52,000 prisoners since 19th April, 1,000 officers.

June 8th – Physical jerks; very strenuous this morning. Received two old letters from Maude, 5th and 21st April. Great offensive reported commenced France; the sea to the south bank of Scarpe. Fear the Russians will not do much – withdrawn by French on account of their bad discipline. Italians appear to have had a knock. China about to declare war on Germany. Germans demand all tin hats.

June 9th – Tins and parcels stopped until German belt returned. Extra 'Appel' at 10 a.m.. a perfect scream; lessons in 'how to salute'. First news of great offensive; very good; 5,000 prisoners. Messines, Wytschaete and several villages taken on a front of nine miles. Commenced at 5 a.m. on 7th June.

June 10th – Sunday. Very long 'Appel'. All rooms searched; dismissed at 10.15 a.m.; very small breakfast.

November 18th, 1917 – Sunday. (Diary from 10th June to 18th November 1917 at Ströhen.) 'Appel' early – 4.30. Ready to escape by 5.15. Vogg cut wire at 5.30 and got through; remainder of us too late, as extra sentry came out at same moment. Stopped in old Bold Mates hut all night; no opportunity until 7.30 a.m.

Then Lonsdale, myself, followed by Johnson, crowded through; clear away and in cover by 8 a.m. on 19th.

November 19th – Spent day in wood; no alarm; moved off 5.30 p.m.; skirted round Wogenfeld, entering on road N.W. of village; immediately spotted by three men. Johnson and I bolted; don't know what happened to Lonsdale, Got into cover, and lay up for two hours. Very fed up and longing for Ströhen comforts; escaping is an overrated pastime. Moved on about 9.30 p.m., met several people, but took cover each time. Very hazy about road and impossible to examine map or compass, so lay up in ditch in wood near railway, presumably Diepholz.

November 20th – Quiet day. Pushed off at 9.30 and struck Diepholz road at once; lots of people about, so lay up until 11.30 just outside Diepholz; passed over railway at 12 p.m., alarmed signalmen, but got away without suspicion. Priceless walk to Vechta; passed a few people for first 2 kilometres, but afterwards clear road. Passed through Vechta 3.45-4.15, very large place and cobbled; had a little trouble in finding right turning and wind up through noise; several people about: got our right road and lay up in topping cover to left of road; about 6.15 a-m. raining.

November 21st – Cover so good, were able to make cocoa and Oxo; pushed off 8,30; passed a few people and aroused their suspicion, so lay up again for an hour; pushed on about 11.30, found misleading signpost, wandered along wrong road for some time and had to get into thick wood to read map; got on right road again, passed Essen about 6 a.m., put up in small wood about 3 kilometres along road in ditch covered with heather; warm but uncomfortable.

November 22nd – Thursday. Pushed off at 9 p.m., reached Lonnger (?) about 11.30; some trouble in finding right turning, got on N.E. road and had to strike across country to get proper track; walked to Lindern, passed through about 6 and put up in very bad cover; difficult to find a good place; lots of rain, very cold and wet; escaping no joke.

November 23rd – Pushed off after uncomfortable day at 8 p.m. Splendid march to cover near Lathen and second day, without meeting a soul.

November 24th – Last day; very tired; had enough. Alarmed at 4 p.m. by man with gun and dog passing near our cover, so cleared off to new spot; fortunately very cold, so pushed off earlier than intended and crawled lot of way to canal just west of Mestrop and struck river just north, not more than 50 yards broad; pleasant surprise – water not so awfully cold; got over, dressed, and started on final stage of journey at 1 a.m. Left Johnson on far side of Emms; terrible march across moor; rain, gale and terrible swamps, thunder and lightning. Reached Terapel at 6 a.m. wet through and tired, but very elated and relieved. Didn't see a sentry all way, but have an idea passed near one with torch near border,

November 25th, 1917 – Free. Partially dried clothes before fire 10 a.m.; sent off to Colvorden ; just started, when Johnson rolled up; delighted to see each other, 12 o'clock arrived Colvorden; went to bank and cashed cheque, afterwards to Van Wely Hotel. Ripping lunch; best wine have had for months. After lunch Van Wely escorted us to shops; bought underclothes, cigarettes, etc., two good liqueurs before dinner and steak for dinner. One dream realised. After dinner sat round fire with family, mother, father and two dear girls aged 15 and 17, very bright and clever. Charmed with Dutch people. Finished drying clothes round fire; to bed at 9 p.m. Best day of my life.

November 26th, 1917 – Monday, Up at 5 a.m. Loth to leave my lovely soft warm bed. Train for Enschede at 6 a.m., arrived at 9 a.m. Curious eyes of people quite disconcerting. Taken to internment camp – had glorious bath, all clothes taken away and disinfected, good lunch, interviewed Director, charming man, spoke to Rotterdam (Consul); arranged for us to leave tomorrow; should be interned for 16 days. Wrote postcards and diary. To bed 10 p.m. not too warm.

November 27th – Tuesday. Up at 8 a.m.; rather cold, so got back to bed. Visit by Mr Tattersall 9 a.m.—dear old man!—gave us some most excellent cigarettes. Photographed, leaving for Rotterdam at 4 p.m.

Appendix 2: British Order of Battle

British Expeditionary Force
Commander in Chief, British Armies in France – **General Sir Douglas Haig**
Artillery Adviser – **Maj. Gen. (later General) Sir James Frederick Noel Birch**
Chief of Intelligence – **Brig. Gen. John Charteris**

Royal Flying Corps
Commander, RFC – **Maj. Gen. Hugh Montague Trenchard, Royal Scots Fusiliers**
Ninth (HQ) Wing – **Lt. Col. Hugh Caswall Tremenheere Dowding, Royal Garrison Artillery** Fienvillers

No 21 Squadron	Maj. John Robert Campbell-Heathcote, Cameron Highlanders	14 R.E.7., 4 B.E.2c., 1 B.E.2e.	Fienvillers
No 27 Squadron	Maj. Amyas Eden Borton, DSO, Royal Highlanders	17 Martinsyde Scout	Fienvillers
No 60 Squadron	Maj. Francis Fitzgerald Waldron, 19th (Queen Alexandra's Own Royal) Hussars (KiA 3rd July 1916)	4 Morane Biplane, 9 Morane Scout	Vert Galand
No 70 Squadron (2 Flights)	Maj. George Aubrey Kennedy Lawrence DSO, Royal Artillery	4 Sopwith two-seater	Fienvillers

Fourth Army
Commander, Fourth Army – **Lt. Gen. Sir Henry Seymour Rawlinson**
Chief of Staff, Fourth Army – **Maj. Gen. (later Field-Marshal) Sir Archibald Armar Montgomery (later Montgomery-Massingberd)**
Commander, Royal Artillery, Fourth Army – **Maj. Gen. Charles Edward Dutton Budworth**

Royal Flying Corps
IV Brigade, RFC – Brig. Gen. Edward Bailey Ashmore, CMG, DSO, Royal Artillery

Third (Corps) Wing	**Lt. Col. Edgar Rainey Ludlow-Hewitt, MC, Royal Irish Rifles**		Bertangles
No 3 Squadron	Maj. Hubert Dunsterville Harvey-Kelly, DSO, Royal Irish Regt. (KiA 29th April 1917)	12 Morane Parasol, 4 Morane Biplane	Lahoussoye
No 4 Squadron	Maj. Thomas Walter Colby Carthew, DSO, 4th Bedfordshire Regt.	17 B.E.2c., 1 B.E.2d.	Baizieux
No 9 Squadron	Maj. Arthur Burdett Burdett, York & Lancaster Regt.	18 B.E.2c.	Allonville
No 15 Squadron	Maj. Henry le Marchant Brock DSO, Royal Warwickshire Regt.	B.E.2c.	
No 1 Kite Balloon Squadron Attached	Maj. Carlos Bovill, Royal Garrison Artillery	Nos 1, 3, 11, 12 & 14 Kite Balloon Sections	Contay
	Maj. H R Hunt	Nos 4, 6 & 13 Kite Balloon Sections	
Fourteenth (Army) Wing	**Lt. Col. Cuthbert Gurney Hoare, 39th Horse, Indian Army**		Bertangles

No 22 Squadron	Maj. Rutter Barry Martyn, Wiltshire Regt.	18 F.E.2b.	Bertangles
No 24 Squadron	Maj. Lanoe George Hawker, VC, DSO, Royal Engineers (KiA 23rd November 1916)	19 D.H.2, 3 Bristol Scout, 2 Morane Scout	Bertangles
Fourth Army Aircraft Park		Maj. A Fletcher (Beauval)	

Attached Troops
Special Section, Special Brigade, RE — Capt. William Howard Livens

Casualty Clearing Stations
Nos 3, 4, 5, 21, 29, 34, 35, 36, 38, 39, 44, 45, South Midland & B Section, Lucknow CCS
Ambulance Flotillas
Nos 3 & 4

2nd Indian Cavalry Division – Maj. Gen. Henry John Milnes MacAndrew
Attached Troops
9th Armoured Motor Car Battery (6 Rolls Royce Armoured Cars)

3rd (Ambala) Cavalry Brigade
- 8th (King's Royal Irish) Hussars
- 10th Duke of Cambridge's Own Lancers (Hodson's Horse)
- 18th King George's Own Lancers
- X Battery, RHA
- 14th Machine Gun Squadron

9th (Secunderabad) Cavalry Brigade – **Brig. Gen. C L Gregory**
- 7th (Princess Royal's) Dragoon Guards
- 20th Deccan Horse
- 34th Prince Albert Victor's Own Poona Horse
- N Battery, RHA
- 13th Machine Gun Squadron

Canadian Cavalry Brigade – **Lt. Col. John Edward Bernard Seely**
- Royal Canadian Dragoons — Lt. Col. C M Nelles
- Lord Strathcona's Horse — Lt. Col. J A Hesketh
- Fort Garry Horse — Lt. Col. R W Paterson
- Royal Canadian Horse Artillery Brigade
- Canadian Cavalry Brigade Machine Gun Squadron

VIII Corps
GOC, VIII Corps – **Lt. Gen. Sir Aylmer Hunter-Weston of Hunterston**
Commander, Royal Artillery, VIII Corps – **Brig. Gen. (later Maj. Gen.) Thomas Angus Tancred, CMG**
Commander, Heavy Artillery, VIII Corps – **Brig. Gen. David Finlay Hosken Logan**
VIII Corps Heavy Artillery

1st Heavy Artillery Group Maj. Robert Norman Lockhart	No 1 Howitzer, RMA	15 in howitzer	
	65th Siege Battery	2 x 12 in howitzers	Maj. George Francis Stratford Tuke
	46th Siege Battery	4 x 9.2 in howitzers	Maj. T S N Hardinge
	55th (Australian) Siege Battery	4 x 9.2 in howitzers	Maj. John Hurst
	54th (Australian) Siege Battery	4 x 8 in howitzers	

	71st (Transvaal) Siege Battery	4 x 6 in howitzers 26 cwt	Maj. Percy Nugent George Fitzpatrick
	29th Siege Battery, Left Section	2 x 6 in Mk VII guns	
	1/1st Highland Heavy Battery	4 x 4.7 in guns	
	1/1st Welsh Heavy Battery	4 x 4.7 in guns	Capt. George Brymer
4th Heavy Artillery Group Lt. Col. Charles Fosbett Phipps	No 3 Howitzer. RMA	15 inch howitzer	Capt. W Lidyard
	112th Siege Battery	4 x 6 in howitzers 26 cwt	Maj. John Connor Hanna
	23rd Siege Battery	4 x 6 in howitzers 26 cwt	
	16th Heavy Battery	4 x 60 pdr guns	Capt. I Cumming
	112th Heavy Battery	4 x 60 pdr guns	
16th Heavy Artillery Group Lt. Col. Hugh Robert Palmer	No 5 Howitzer, RMA	15 in howitzer	Capt. Hugh W Boffey
	36th Siege Battery	4 x 8 in howitzers	Maj. Arthur Cecil Hamilton Dean
	14th Siege Battery	4 x 6 in howitzers 30 cwt	
	81st Siege Battery	4 x 6 in howitzers 30 cwt	
	60th Siege Battery, Left Section	2 x 6 in Mk VII guns	
	19th Heavy Battery	4 x 60 pdr guns	Maj. E L Caldecott
	25th Heavy Battery	4 x 60 pdr guns	
	139th Heavy Battery	4 x 60 pdr guns	
17th Heavy Artillery Group Lt. Col. Thomas Richard Phillips	79th Siege Battery	4 x 9.2 in howitzers	
	77th Siege Battery	4 x 8 in howitzers	Maj. Wilfred Noel Leggett
	56th Siege Battery	4 x 8 in howitzers	Maj. Hugh Wallace Lockhart
	16th Siege Battery	4 x 6 in howitzers 30 cwt	
	29th Siege Battery, Right Section	2 x 6 in Mk VII guns	
	48th Heavy Battery	4 x 60 pdr guns	Maj. Maurice Alexander Beattie
	111th Heavy Battery	4 x 60 pdr guns	
	113th Heavy Battery	4 x 60 pdr guns	
	D/242 Battery RFA (attached)	4 x 4.5 in howitzers	

2e Groupe, 37e Regiment d'Artillerie de Campagne (4e, 5e & 6e Batteries)	3 batteries each 4 x 75 mm guns	Chef d'Escadron Charron
9th AA Battery (9th & 41st Sections	4 x 13 pdr 9 cwt guns	
15th AA Battery (15th & 43rd Sections)	4 x 13 pdr 9 cwt guns	

Chief Engineer, VIII Corps – **Brig. Gen. George Strachan Cartwright**

252nd Tunnelling Company, RE	Maj. Reginald Graham Trower
No 4 Company, No 5 Battalion, Special Brigade RE	

Attached Troops
Royal Flying Corps

No 15 Squadron, RFC	No 13 Kite Balloon Section

No. 20 Motor Ambulance Convoy

4th Division – Maj. Gen. Hon. Sir William Lambton
Commander, Royal Artillery, 4th Division – **Brig. Gen. Cyril Prescott-Decie**

Divisional Troops

14th Bde RFA (68th & 88th [18 pdr] and 86th [How] Batteries RFA)*	Lt. Col. H G Lloyd
29th Bde RFA (125th, 126th & 127th [18 pdr] and 128th [How] Batteries RFA)*	Col. Norman Eccles Tilney
32nd Bde RFA (27th, 134th & 135th [18 pdr] and D/32 [How] Batteries RFA)*	
4th Divisional Trench Mortars: Heavy V4 & W4, Medium S4, T4, X4, Y4 & Z4	
9th Field Company RE	Capt. E E F Homer
406th (1/1st Renfrew) Field Company RE	Capt. H McC Hodgart
526th (1/1st Durham) Field Company RE	Maj. Arthur Michael Terry
10th Field Ambulance	Lt. Col. Basil Fenton Wingate
11th Field Ambulance	Lt. Col. D Ahearn
12th Field Ambulance	Lt. Col. F G Fitzgerald
Pioneers 21st West Yorkshire Regt. (Wool Textile Pioneers)	Lt. Col. Sir Edward Henry St Lawrence Clarke

* The 18 pdr batteries of the 4th Division contained six guns per battery rather than the normal four guns. The Howitzer batteries had four guns as normal.

10th Brigade – **Brig. Gen. Charles Arthur Wilding**

1st Royal Warwickshire Regt.	Lt. Col. George Norman Bowes Forster
2nd Seaforth Highlanders	Lt. Col. John Oliver Hopkinson DSO, MC
1st Royal Irish Fusiliers	Lt. Col. William Alexander Victor Findlater
2nd Royal Dublin Fusiliers	Lt. Col. Harold Martin Cliff, Royal Irish Rifles
10th Machine Gun Coy	
10th Trench Mortar Battery	

11th Brigade – **Brig. Gen. Charles Bertie Prowse**

1st Somerset Light Infantry	Lt. Col. John Audley Thicknesse
1st East Lancashire Regt.	Lt. Col. James Edward Green DSO
1st Hampshire Regt.	Lt. Col. Hon Lawrence Charles Walter Palk, DSO
1st Rifle Brigade	Lt. Col. Donald Wood
11th Machine Gun Coy	Capt. Francis George Ross Mockler, MC, 2nd Royal Irish Regt.
11th Trench Mortar Battery	

12th Brigade – **Brig. Gen. James Dayrolles Crosbie**

1st King's Own Royal Lancaster Regt.	Maj. John Nisket Bromilow
2nd Lancashire Fusiliers	Lt. Col. George Henry Basil Freeth CMG, DSO
2nd Duke of Wellington's Regt.	Lt. Col. Robert Napier Bray
2nd Essex Regt.	Lt. Col. Sir George Murray Home Stirling

12th Machine Gun Coy	Capt. G Basil Sleigh King's Own Royal Lancaster Regiment
12th Trench Mortar Battery	Lt. F D Roberts

29th Division – Maj. Gen. (later Lt. Gen.) Sir Henry de Beauvoir De Lisle
Commander, Royal Artillery, 29th Division – **Brig. Gen. Malcolm Peake**

Divisional Troops

15th Bde RHA	Lt. Col. Theodore Montgomery Archdale DSO
B [18 pdr] Battery RHA	Maj. Cecil Dudley Woodgate Uniacke
L [18 pdr] Battery RHA	Capt. George Edward Mervyn Thorneycroft
Y [18 pdr] Battery RHA	Capt. Herbert Geoffrey Lush-Wilson
17th Bde RFA	Lt. Col. William Percival Monkhouse CMG, MVO
13th [18 pdr] Battery RFA	Capt. Robin Secly Leach
26th [18 pdr] Battery RFA	Capt. Denis Daly
92nd [18 pdr] Battery RFA	Maj. Robert Carlisle Williams DSO
D/17 (460th) [How.] Battery RFA	Maj. John H Gibbon DSO
132nd Bde RFA	Lt. Col. Harry Reginald Walter Marriott-Smith DSO
369th [18 pdr] Battery RFA	Capt. C G Lawson
370th [18 pdr] Battery RFA	Maj. Miles Rafe Ferguson Courage
371st [18 pdr] Battery RFA	Capt. C G Hetherington
D/132 [How.] Battery RFA	
147th Bde RFA	Lt. Col. Douglas Evans Forman CMG
10th [18 pdr] Battery RFA	Capt. J de H Chisholm Batten
97th [18 pdr] Battery RFA	Capt. Kenneth Moore Ball
368th [18 pdr] Battery RFA	Maj. Harry Denison
D/147 [How.] Battery RFA	Lt. H L Holmes
29th Division Trench Mortar Batteries: X29, Y29 and Z29	
Attached: Y23	2nd Lt. D F P Coles, 3rd East Yorkshire Regt
455th (1/1st West Riding) Field Company RE	Maj. Atwell Charles Baylay
497th (1/3rd Kent) Field Company RE	Maj. Alfred Francis Gerald Ruston
510th (1/2nd London Field) Company RE	Maj. William Macrae
87th (1st West Lancashire) Field Ambulance	Lt. Col. Creighton Hutchison Lindsay
88th (1st East Anglian) Field Ambulance	Lt. Col. Alfred Edward Weld
89th (1st Highland) Field Ambulance	Lt. Col. John G Bell
Pioneers	1/2nd Monmouthshire Regt.

86th Brigade – **Brig. Gen. (later Maj. Gen.) Weir De Lancey Williams**

2nd Royal Fusiliers	Lt. Col. Allen Victor Johnson
1st Lancashire Fusiliers	Lt. Col. Meredith Magniac
16th Middlesex Regt (Public Schools')	Lt. Col. John Hamilton Hall
1st Royal Dublin Fusiliers	Lt. Col. Herbert Nelson, DSO, Border Regt.
86th Machine Gun Coy	
86th Trench Mortar Battery	

87th Brigade – **Brig. Gen. (later Maj. Gen.) Cuthbert Henry Tindall Lucas**

2nd South Wales Borderers	Maj. Geoffrey Taunton Raikes Egyptian Army
1st King's Own Scottish Borderers	Lt. Col. Alfred John Welch
1st Royal Inniskilling Fusiliers	Lt. Col. Robert Campbell Pierce
1st Border Regt.	Lt. Col. Archibald Jenner Ellis

87th Machine Gun Coy	Capt. Harold Ruthfen Burrill, Dragoon Guards
87th Trench Mortar Battery	

88th Brigade – **Brig. Gen. Hon. (later Maj. Gen.) Douglas Edward Cayley**

4th Worcestershire Regt.	Lt. Col. Edward Thomas John Kerans
2nd Hampshire Regt.	Lt. Col. William Henry Middleton
1st Essex Regt.	Lt. Col. Arthur Crosby Halahan
1st Newfoundland Regt.	Lt. Col. Arthur Lovell Hadow Norfolk Regt.
88th Machine Gun Coy	Capt. Alfred Morris, Royal Fusiliers
88th Trench Mortar Battery	Capt. L W Vicars Miles, 2nd Hampshire Regt.

31st Division – Maj. Gen. Robert Wanless-O'Gowan
Commander, Royal Artillery, 31st Division – **Brig. Gen. Edward Parry Lambert**
Commander, Royal Engineers, 31st Division – **Lt. Col. John Pierre Mackesy**

Divisional Troops

165th (County Palatine) Bde RFA (A, B, C [18 pdr] and D [How] Batteries RFA)	Lt. Col. G J Henderson
169th Bde RFA (A, B, C [18 pdr] and D [How] Batteries RFA)	Lt. Col. Waldemar Sigismund Dacre Craven
170th Bde RFA (A, B, C [18 pdr] and D [How] Batteries RFA)	Lt. Col. Cecil Barrow Simonds
171st Bde RFA (A, B, C [18 pdr] and D [How] Batteries RFA)	Col. Hon. Harold William Addington
31st Divisional Trench Mortar Batteries	Capt. Henry Brian Bates
S31 Medium Battery	2nd Lt. Charles Axten RFA
Y31 Medium Battery	2nd Lt. Walter Dann, RFA
X31 Medium Battery	Lt. Percy Charles Binns, 12th KOYLI
Z31 Medium Battery	Lt. Reginald Murray Alexander, RGA
V31 Heavy Trench Mortar Battery	Capt. Frederick Joseph Haney, RFA
Z23 Battery (23rd Division attached)	Lt. George
210th (Leeds) Field Company RE	
211th (Leeds) Field Company RE	Capt. Anderson
223rd (Leeds) Field Company RE	Capt. F S Collin
93rd Field Ambulance	
94th Field Ambulance	
95th Field Ambulance	Lt. Col. E B Knox
Pioneers 12th King's Own Yorkshire Light Infantry (Leeds Miners)	Lt. Col. Ernest Leonard Chambers

92nd Brigade – **Brig. Gen. Oliver de Lancey Williams**

10th East Yorkshire Regt. (Hull Commercials)	Lt. Col. Walter Bagot Pearson, Lancashire Fusiliers
11th East Yorkshire Regt. (Hull Tradesmen)	Maj. Hugh Robinson Pease
12th East Yorkshire Regt. (Hull Sportsmen)	Lt. Col. Harold Robinson Pease
13th East Yorkshire Regt. (T'Others)	Lt. Col. Robert Henry Dewing Indian Army
92nd Machine Gun Coy	
92nd Trench Mortar Battery	Capt. Wilfred Palmer Horsley

93rd Brigade – **Brig. Gen. John Darnley Ingles**

Unit	Commander
15th West Yorkshire Regt. (Leeds Pals)	Maj. Redmond Barry Neill
16th West Yorkshire Regt. (1st Bradford Pals)	Maj. George Sutherland Guyon, Royal Fusiliers
18th West Yorkshire Regt. (2nd Bradford Pals)	Lt. Col. Maurice Nicholl Kennard, 6th Dragoon Guards (Carabiniers)
18th Durham Light Infantry (Durham Pals)	Lt. Col. Hugh Bowes
93rd Machine Gun Coy	Capt. Joseph Pelham Kayll, 18th Durham Light Infantry
93rd Trench Mortar Battery	Capt. Stanley Herbert Titford, 18th West Yorkshire Regt.

94th Brigade – **Brig. Gen. Hubert Conway Rees**
(in the absence of Brig. Gen. G T C Carter-Campbell)

Unit	Commander
11th East Lancashire Regt. (Accrington Pals)	Lt. Col. Arthur Wilmot Rickman, 3rd Special Res Bn, Northumberland Fus.
12th York and Lancaster Regt. (Sheffield City Battalion)	Maj. Alfred Plackett
13th York and Lancaster Regt. (1st Barnsley Pals)	Lt. Col. Edmund Ernest Wilford, Indian Army
14th York and Lancaster Regt. (2nd Barnsley Pals)	Lt. Col. Walter Backhouse Hulke, 9th Lincolnshire Regt.
94th Machine Gun Coy	Capt. W Dunne
94th Trench Mortar Battery	Capt. Hutson

48th (South Midland) Division (T.F.) – Maj. Gen. Sir Robert Fanshawe
Commander, Royal Artillery – **Brig. Gen. Henry Dudley Ossulston Ward**

Divisional Troops

Unit	Commander
240th South Midland Bde RFA (A, B and C [18 pdr] and D [How] Gloucester Batteries RFA)	Lt. Col. Lord Philip George Wynford
241st South Midland Bde RFA (A, B and C [18 pdr] and D [How] Worcester Batteries RFA)	
242nd South Midland Bde RFA (A, B and C [18 pdr] and D [How] Warwick Batteries RFA)	Lt. Col. Arthur Raleigh Blandy Cossart
243rd South Midland Bde RFA (A, B and C [18 pdr] Batteries	Lt. Col. F C B West
48th Divisional Trench Mortar Batteries: V48, X48, Y48 and Z48	Capt. R H Willan, King's Royal Rifle Corps
474th South Midland Field Company RE	Maj. Harry Clissold
475th South Midland Field Company RE	
477th South Midland Field Company RE	
1/1st South Midland Field Ambulance	Lt. Col. Cyril H Howkins
1/2nd South Midland Field Ambulance	Lt. Col. Seymour Gilbert Barling
1/3rd South Midland Field Ambulance	Maj. J A Green
Pioneers 1/5th Royal Sussex Regt.	Lt. Col. F G Langham

143rd Brigade – **Brig. Gen. Bertie Coore Dent**

Unit	Commander
1/5th Royal Warwickshire Regt.	Lt. Col. Gerald Carew Sladen, Rifle Brigade
1/6th Royal Warwickshire Regt.	Lt. Col. William Hodgson Franklin, Newfoundland Regt.
1/7th Royal Warwickshire Regt.	Lt. Col. James Meldrum Knox
1/8th Royal Warwickshire Regt.	Lt. Col. Edgar Arthur Innes
143rd Machine Gun Coy	
143rd Trench Mortar Battery	

144th Brigade – **Brig. Gen. George Harvey Nicholson**

Unit	Commander
1/4th Gloucestershire Regt.	Lt. Col. Herbert Thomas Dobbin, DCLI
1/6th Gloucestershire Regt.	Lt. Col. K Micklem, Rifle Brigade
1/7th Worcestershire Regt.	Lt. Col. Alexander Ramsay Harman, Rifle Brigade
1/8th Worcestershire Regt.	Lt. Col. Walter King Peake, R. Berkshire Regt.
144th Machine Gun Company	Capt. Borlase
144th Trench Mortar Battery	

145th Brigade – **Brig. Gen. Herbert Richard Done**

Unit	Commander
1/5th Gloucestershire Regt.	Lt. Col. John Henry Collett, CMG
1/4th Oxfordshire and Buckinghamshire Light Infantry	Lt. Col. Alfred James Napier Bartlett, DSO & Bar
1st Buckinghamshire Regt. (Ox and Bucks Light Infantry)	Lt. Col. Lewis Leslie Clayton Reynolds
1/4th Royal Berkshire Regt.	Lt. Col. Robert Joyce Clarke, CMD, DSO, TD
145th Machine Gun Company	Capt. N Long
145th Trench Mortar Battery	

36th (Ulster) Division (T.F) – Maj. Gen. Oliver Stewart Wood Nugent (Part)

108th Brigade – **Brig. Gen. Charles Richard Jebb Griffith, CMG, DSO**

Unit	Commander
12th Royal Irish Rifles	Lt. Col. George Bull
9th Royal Irish Fusiliers	Lt. Col. Stewart Ward William Blacker, RA

APPENDIX 3: BIOGRAPHICAL DETAILS OF SENIOR BRITISH OFFICERS

COMMANDER IN CHIEF, BRITISH ARMIES IN FRANCE – GENERAL SIR DOUGLAS HAIG

1st Earl Haig.

CB 1900; KCVO 1909; KCIE 1911; KCB 1913; GCB 1915; GCVO 1916; KT 1917; OM 1919

Viscount Dawick 1919; Baron Haig and 29th Laird of Bemersyde

Born 19th June 1861 at 24, Charlotte Square, Edinburgh, died of heart failure at 21, Prince's Gate, London on 29th January 1928. Fifth son and eleventh child of John Haig, JP, of Cameronbridge, Fife (1802–1878), whiskey distiller, and Rachael Mackerras (d. 1879), 4th daughter and co-heiress of Hugh Veitch of Stewartfield, Midlothian. Married the Hon. Dorothy Maud Vivian (d. 1939), daughter of Hussey Crespigny Vivian, 3rd Baron Vivian; maid of honour to Queen Victoria and then to Queen Alexandra; one son, three daughters.

EDUCATION Preparatory school, Orwell House, near Edinburgh, and Warwickshire; Clifton College; Brasenose College, Oxford (Hon. Fellow, 1915); Royal Military College, Sandhurst, awarded Anson Memorial Sword

CAREER

1885 – Joined 7th Hussars. Went to India, appointed adjutant, promoted captain, and undertook staff work with the headquarters of the Bombay army at Poona.

1893 – Applied to Staff College, Camberley but rejected because of colour blindness and poor performance in the mathematical examination.

1896 – Entered Staff College by nomination of Sir Evelyn Wood.

1898 – Sudan, including Atbara and Khartoum (MiD, Bt-Major, British Medal, Khedive's Medal with two clasps). Then Brigade Major at Aldershot under Maj. Gen. John French.

1899 – South Africa with French's cavalry division; DAAG for Cavalry, Natal; CSO to General French during the Colesberg operations; AAG Cavalry Division, 1900; commanded group of columns, 1901–02 (MiD, ADC to King, Brevet Col, CB, Queen's Medal with seven clasps, King's Medal)

1901–03 – Lt. Col. Comdg 17th Lancers

1903–06 – Inspector-General of Cavalry, India. Appt'd Major-General 1904

1906–07 – Director of Military Training, India. Published *'Cavalry Studies'*, 1907

1907–09 – Director of Staff Duties at Army Headquarters, India. Created KCVO, 1909

1909–12 – Chief of Staff, India. Lt-General, 1910.

1912–14 – General Officer Commanding, Aldershot

1914–15 – Commanding 1st Army; General, 1914, for distinguished service

1915–19 – Commander-in-Chief of the Expeditionary Forces in France and Flanders

1914–18 – MiD five times, Field-Marshal, GCB, GCVO, KT, Grand Cordon Légion d'Honneur; Médaille Militaire; Grand Cross Order of Leopold; Grand Cross St Maurice and St Lazarus; Obolitch Gold Medal (Montenegro) and 1st Class Order of Danilo, 1917; 4th Class of St George (Russia)

1919–20 – Field-Marshal Commander-in-Chief the Forces in Great Britain

1916–19 – Lord Rector, St Andrew's University

1921 – Chairman of Council of the United Services Fund

1922 – Chancellor of St Andrew's University, President, Royal British Legion

Colonel of RHG, 17th Lancers, KOSB and London Scottish

CHIEF OF THE GENERAL STAFF – LT. GEN. SIR LAUNCELOT EDWARD KIGGELL

CB 1908; KCB 1916; KCMG 1918; LLD (Hon.) St Andrew's University
Born Wilton House, Ballingarry, Co. Limerick, 2nd October 1862, died 23rd February 1954. Son of Launcelot John Kiggell, JP, and Meliora Emily, daughter of Edward Brown. Married Eleanor Rose (d 1948), daughter of Col Spencer Field in 1888. Three sons.
EDUCATION Ireland; Royal Military College, Sandhurst
CAREER
1882 – Joined Royal Warwickshire Regt.
1886–90 – Adjutant of 2nd Battalion
1893–94 – Staff College
1895–97 – Instructor RMC
1897–99 – DAAG South Eastern District
1899–1902 – South Africa (MiD, brevet Lt. Col., Queen's medal 6 clasps, King's medal 2 clasps)
1904–07 – DAAG, Staff College
1907–09 – GSO, Army HQ
1909 – Brig. Gen. i/c Administration, Scottish Command
1909–13 – Director of Staff Duties, War Office
1913–14 – Commandant Staff College, Camberley
1914–15 – Director of Home Defence, War Office
1915–18 – Chief of General Staff to British Armies in France (prom. Lt-Gen., 1917)
1914–18 – Légion d'Honneur (Grand Officer); Belgian Order of the Crown (Grand Cordon); Italian Order of St Michael and St Lazarus (Grand Officer); Obilitch gold medal and Order of Danilo, 1st Class, Montenegro, 1917; Japanese Order of the Sacred Treasure (Grand Cordon)
1918–20 – GOC and Lt-Gov., Guernsey
1920 – Retired
Publication
Revised Sir E Hamley's *'Operations of War'* for 6th edition

ARTILLERY ADVISER – MAJ. GEN. (LATER GEN) SIR JAMES FREDERICK NOEL BIRCH

CB 1916; KCMG, 1918; KCB, 1922; GBE, 1927
Born 29th December 1865, died 3rd February 1939. Son of the late Richard Frederick Birch, Maes Elwy, St Asaph, and Euphemia Mercer, eldest daughter of James Somerville, of Edinburgh. Married Florence Hyacinthe (d 1938), daughter of Sir George Chetwode, 6th Bt, of Oakley, Staffs, and Chetwode, Bucks and sister of the future Field Marshal Lord Chetwode in 1903. Two sons.
EDUCATION Giggleswick; Marlborough; Royal Military Academy, Woolwich
CAREER
1885 – Entered Royal Artillery
1890 – Royal Horse Artillery
1895–96 – Ashanti Expedition (star)
1899–1902 – South Africa (MiD, Queen's medal with 6 clasps)
1905–07 – Commanded Riding Establishment, Royal Artillery
1912 – Lt. Col.
1914 – Commander, VII Brigade, RHA
1915 – Brig. Gen., General Staff Cavalry Corps then GOC RA 7th Div., then GOC RA I Corps and IV Corps
1916 – GOC RA 4th Army then Artillery Adviser to the CinC, France to 1919
1914–18 – KCMG, MiD 11 times, ADC to the King, Bt Col, CB, prom. Maj. Gen.; prom. Lt. Gen.; Croix de Commandeur Légion d'Honneur, Croix de Guerre with 2 palms; Croix de Commandeur Order of Leopold, Croix de Guerre (Belgian); American Distinguished Service Medal

1920–21 – Director of Remounts
1921–23 – Director-General of the Territorial Army
1923–27 – Master-General of the Ordnance and Member of the Army Council
1920 – Col Commandant, Royal Artillery
1927 – Retired
1928 – Col Commandant, Royal Horse Artillery
Publications:
Modern Riding; Modern Riding and Horse Education

CHIEF OF INTELLIGENCE – BRIG. GEN. JOHN CHARTERIS

DSO 1915; CMG 1919
Born 8th January 1877, died 4th February 1946. Son of the late Prof. Matthew Charteris, Senior professor of materia medica at Glasgow University, and his wife, Elizabeth (née Greer). Married Noel Emily Beatrice, daughter of C D Hodgson, in 1913. Three sons (Lt Euan Charteris was killed in action in Tunisia on 3rd December 1942)
EDUCATION Kelvinside Academy; Göttingen; Royal Military Academy, Woolwich
CAREER
1896 – Joined Royal Engineers
1909–10 – Staff Capt. HQ, India
1910–12 – General Staff Officer, 2nd Grade
1912–14 – AMS to General Officer commanding Aldershot (i.e. Douglas Haig)
1914 – ADC, Douglas Haig then Chief of Intelligence I Corps, 1st Army and GHQ to
1918 – Deputy Director of Transportation
1914–18 – MiD, CMG, DSO, Bt Col, Légion d'Honneur, Commander of Order of the Couronne of Belgium, Rising Sun of Japan, Croix de Guerre, American Distinguished Service Cross
1920 – DQMG, India
1921–22 – DA and QMG, Eastern Command, India
1922 – Retired
1924–29 – Conservative MP for Dumfriesshire
Publications:
Field-Marshal Earl Haig, 1929; *At GHQ* 1931; *Haig*, 1933

FOURTH ARMY – LT. GEN. SIR HENRY SEYMOUR RAWLINSON

1st Baron Rawlinson of Trent, Dorset.
CB 1900; KCB 1915; GCVO 1917; KCMG 1918; GCB 1919 GCSI 1924
Born 20th February 1864, died 28th March 1925. Elder son of Maj. Gen. Sir Henry Creswick Rawlinson (1810–1895), 1st Bt, and Louisa Caroline Harcourt (d. 1889), daughter of Henry Seymour of Knoyle, Wilts; married Meredith Sophia Frances (d. 1951), oldest daughter of Coleridge John Kennard in 1890.
EDUCATION Eton; Royal Military College, Sandhurst; Staff College, Camberley
CAREER
1884 – Entered 60th KRRC
1887–90 – ADC to Sir Frederick Roberts, Commander-in-Chief in India. Served with Mounted Infantry, Burma campaign (medal and clasp)
1892 – Staff College. Exchanged into Coldstream Guards
1895 – Brigade Major, Aldershot
1898 – Sudan campaign as DAAG to Maj. Gen. Horatio Herbert Kitchener present at battles Atbara and Khartoum (medal and two clasps, MiD twice)
1899 – South Africa (two medals and eight clasps); AAG (Ladysmith siege) Natal
1900 – AAG Headquarters, South Africa
1901–02 – Commanded Mobile Column (MiD three times)
1903–06 – Commandant Staff College

1907–09 – Commanded 2nd Brigade, Aldershot
1910 – Commanded 3rd Division, Salisbury Plain
1914 – Director of Recruiting, War Office
1914 – GOC 4th Division then IV Corps
1916 – GOC 4th Army
1917 – Promoted full General
1914–18 – MiD eight times, KCB, GCB, KCVO, GCVO, KCMG;
1919 – Commanded Forces in N Russia
1920 – GOC Aldershot
1920 – CinC Indian Army
Publication:
The Officers' Note-book

CHIEF OF STAFF – MAJ. GEN. (LATER FIELD-MARSHAL) SIR ARCHIBALD ARMAR MONTGOMERY (LATER MONTGOMERY-MASSINGBERD)

KCMG, 1919; KCB, 1925; GCB, 1934; LLD (Queen's University, Belfast), 1934
Born 6th December 1871, died 13th October 1947. 2nd son of the late Rt Hon. Hugh de F Montgomery, PC; assumed name of Montgomery-Massingberd 1926. Married Diana, youngest daughter of the late Edmund Langton in 1896. No children
EDUCATION Charterhouse; Royal Military Academy, Woolwich
CAREER
1891 – Joined Royal Field Artillery
1899–1902 – South Africa (MiD, Queen's medal four clasps, King's medal two clasps, wounded)
1905 – Staff College
1914 – Instructor, Staff College then Staff Officer, 4th Division and Chief of Staff, IV Corps
1916 – Chief of Staff, 4th Army
1914–18 – MiD nine times, Bt Lt. Col., Bt Col, Maj. Gen., CB, KCMG; Commander Légion d'Honneur, Croix de Guerre, American DSM
1920–22 – Deputy Chief of General Staff, India
1922–23 – GOC 53rd Welsh Division, TF
1923–26 – GOC 1st Division
1927–41 – Col-Commandant RA
1928–31 – General Officer Commanding-in-Chief, Southern Command
1931–33 – Adjutant-General to the Forces
1931–35 – ADC General to the King
1933–36 – Chief of Imperial General Staff
1935 – Field-Marshal and Col Comdt 20th Burma Rifles
1934–39 – Col Comdt Royal Tank Corps
1937–41 – Col Comdt Royal Malta Artillery
1940–46 – Vice-Lt of Lincolnshire
Publication:
The Story of the Fourth Army in the Battles of the Hundred Days (1919)

COMMANDER, ROYAL ARTILLERY – MAJ. GEN. CHARLES EDWARD DUTTON BUDWORTH

MVO 1903; CB 1916; CMG 1917
Born 3rd October 1869, died 15th July 1921. 3rd son of the late P J Budworth, JP, DL, of Greensted Hall, Ongar, Essex. Married Winifred (d 1914), daughter of late Sir Patteson Nickalls then Helen, only daughter of Maj. Gen. W E Blewitt in 1918. Two sons.
EDUCATION Royal Military Academy, Woolwich

CAREER
1889 – Joined the Royal Horse Artillery
1899 – Captain & Adjutant, Honourable Artillery Company
1899–1902 – South Africa, City of London Imperial Volunteers, Field Battery (MiD, Queen's Medal and 3 clasps, Bt Major)
1904 – Instructor in Gunnery, Royal Horse and Field School of Gunnery
1907 – Chief Instructor, Royal Horse and Field School of Gunnery
1909 – Major
1914 – Commander, H Battery, RHA
1914–18 – MiD ten times, CB, CMG, Bt Col, Maj. Gen.

2ND INDIAN CAVALRY DIVISION – MAJ. GEN. HENRY JOHN MILNES MACANDREW

KCB 1918; DSO 1900
Born 7th August 1866, Aisthorpe, Inverness. Died 16th July 1919, Aleppo, Syria. Son of Sir Henry and Lady MacAndrew. Married Esther, youngest daughter of Henry Rictchie Cooper, 1892. One son, one daughter.
EDUCATION Inverness College
CAREER
1884 – Joined 2nd Cameron Highlanders
1886 – Lincolnshire Regt
1888 – 5th Bengal Cavalry, Indian Army
1897– 1898 – Tirah Campaign (MiD, Indian Frontier Medal with 2 clasps)
1900–1902 – South Africa; Kitchener's Horse, General Clement's Column. DAAG Intelligence Gen Hon. Neville Lyttleton and Gen Sir Bruce Hamilton May; DAAG Intelligence, Army Headquarters; South African Medal and 4 clasps, King's Medal and 2 clasps, DSO, MiD twice)
1903–1905 – Brigade Major, Inspector General of Cavalary in India
1909 – 2iC, 5th Cavalry Regt., Indian Army
1916 – Commander, 2nd Indian Cavalry Division
1917 – Maj. Gen., commander 5th (Indian) Cavalry Division
1914–18 – MiD four times, CB

VIII CORPS – LT. GEN. SIR AYLMER GOULD HUNTER-WESTON OF HUNTERSTON

DSO 1900; CB 1911, KCB, 1915
Born 23rd September 1864; died 18th March 1940. Elder son of Lt. Col. Gould Hunter-Weston, 26th Laird of Hunterston and his second wife, Jane. Married Grace, oldest daughter of William Strang Steel of Philiphaugh, Selkirkshire in 1905.
EDUCATION Wellington College; Royal Military Academy, Woolwich; Staff College
CAREER
1884 – Entered Royal Engineers
1891 – Miranzai Expedition
1894–95 – Waziristan Field Force (wounded, MiD, Bt of Maj., medal with clasp)
1896 – Dongola Expeditionary Force (MiD, 4th class Medjidieh, Khedive's medal with clasp, Queen's medal)
1898 – Staff College, Camberley
1899–1901 – South Africa (MiD, medal with 7 clasps, DSO, Brevet Lt. Col.)
1904–08 – General Staff Officer Eastern Command
1908–11 – Chief General Staff Officer Scottish Command
1911–14 – Assistant Director of Military Training, War Office
1914 – Brig. Gen.. commanding 11th Infantry Brigade; Maj. Gen.. for Distinguished Service in the Field, 1914
1915 – Maj. Gen. commanding 29th Division; VIII Corps

1914–18 – MiD ten times, KCB, promoted Lt. Gen. for distinguished service in the field; French and Belgian Croix de Guerre, Commander Légion d'Honneur; Officer Order of Medjidieh; Grand Officer of the Order of the Belgian Crown
1916–35 – MP (Unionist) North Ayrshire, and then for Buteshire and North Ayrshire

COMMANDER, ROYAL ARTILLERY, VIII CORPS – BRIG. GEN. (LATER MAJ. GEN.) THOMAS ANGUS TANCRED

CMG 1915; CB 1917; DSO 1918
Born 16th September 1867; died 8th July 1944. Third son of George Tancred and Mary Anne née Lumsden of Weens, Hawick, Roxburghshire
EDUCATION Harrow; Royal Military Academy, Woolwich
CAREER
1886 – Entered Royal Artillery
1893–96 – Bechuanaland Border Police; served Matabeleland, 1893–94
1896 – Captain
1899 – Adjutant, Royal Garrison Artillery, India
1900 – China (medal)
1904 – Major
1914 – Retired
1914 – Major, cdg 38 Company, RGA, Plymouth; Lt. Col. Commander, 3rd Heavy Battery, RGA
1915 – Brig. Gen.
1914–18 – MiD six times, CMG, CB, DSO, Bt Col, 1914 Star, Comm. Légion d'Honneur
1921 – Maj. Gen.

COMMANDER, HEAVY ARTILLERY, VIII CORPS – BRIG. GEN. DAVID FINLAY HOSKEN LOGAN

CMG 1916; CB 1917
Born 28th December 1862; died 17th June 1923. Son of the late David Logan, Chief Engineer, South Indian Railway, and Jean Hosken. Married Ethel Mayzod Evans. One son, one daughter.
EDUCATION Private school, Reading; Royal Military Academy, Woolwich
CAREER
1883 – Joined Royal Artillery
1890 – Captain & Adjutant, 1st Glamorgan Volunteer Artillery
1899 – Adjutant, Cape Garrison Artillery
1899–1902 – South Africa (King's and Queen's medals)
1901 – Major
1911 – Lt. Col.
1914 – Cdg Portsmouth Garrison Company, RGA
1916 – Brig. Gen.
1914–17 – MiD, CB, CMG

CHIEF ENGINEER, VIII CORPS – BRIG. GEN. GEORGE STRACHAN CARTWRIGHT

CB 1916; CMG 1918
Born 29th August 1866; died 15th January 1959. Son of late Rev Conway Cartwright, Vancouver, Canada. Married Kate Mary (died 1943), older daughter of late Robert A Stevenson, MD, Toronto, Canada, in 1898. One son killed in action, November 1942; one daughter deceased.
EDUCATION Private school; RMC, Canada
CAREER
1885 – Received Commission Royal Engineers, RMC, Canada
1888 – Aden
1891 – India

1892 – Isazai Expedition, Indian Frontier
1895 – Chatham, Exeter and Plymouth
1903 – Halifax, Nova Scotia
1906 – Commanded 17th Field Company, RE, Aldershot
1907 – India
1912 – UK
1914–18 – CRE, 15th (Scottish) Division (MiD, CB, CMG, Officer Légion d'Honneur)
1918 – Chief Engineer, Aldershot
1920 – Retired
1927–1937 – Director of Military Studies, University of Toronto

4TH DIVISION – MAJ. GEN. HON. SIR WILLIAM LAMBTON

DSO 1900; CMG 1904; MVO 1907; CVO 1914; CB 1915; KCB, 1918
Born 4th December 1863; died 11th October 1936. Son of 2nd Earl of Durham. Married Lady Katherine de Vere Somerset, daughter of 10th Duke of St Albans in 1921
EDUCATION Eton; Royal Military College, Sandhurst
CAREER
1884 – Joined Coldstream Guards
1896 – Staff, Brigade of Guards
1898 – Seconded to Egyptian Army
1899 – To Gibraltar with 1st Coldstream Guards
1899–1902 – Egyptian campaign; Atbara & Omdurman; South Africa with 3rd Coldstream Guards (wounded, MiD twice, Queen's medal, four clasps, King's medal, two clasps, DSO)
1900–04 – Military Secretary to Lord Milner
1909 – Commanded 1st Batt. Coldstream Guards
1910 – Groom-in-Waiting to the King, Col. cdg Coldstream Guards and 3rd London Infantry Brigade
1912–14 – AA and QMG, London District
1914 – Military Secretary to Commander-in-Chief in France
1915–17 – GOC 4th Division
1920 – Retired

10TH BRIGADE – BRIG. GEN. CHARLES ARTHUR WILDING

CMG 1915
Born 13th June 1868; died 9th July 1953. Married Mabel Charlotte, daughter of Mr F Simpson of Perton, Staffs, in 1901
EDUCATION Wellington; Royal Military College, Sandhurst
CAREER
1887 – Commissioned into Royal Inniskilling Fusiliers
1889–92 – Burma (medal)
1893–94 – Nigeria (medal)
1897 – Captain & Adjutant, 4th Royal Inniskilling Fusiliers
1898 – Sudan
1905 – Major
1914 – Lt. Col. commanding 2nd Royal Inniskilling Fusiliers
1916 – Brig. Gen.. cdg 10th Brigade
1914–18 – CMG, MiD three times
1918 – Retired

11TH BRIGADE – BRIG. GEN. CHARLES BERTIE PROWSE

DSO 1916
Born 1869; died 1st July 1916. Son of Captain George James William Prowse, J.P., and Emmeline Lucy Prowse, of Bromham, Wilts. Born at West Monkton, Taunton, Somerset.

Husband of Violet Stanley Prowse of Bromham, Fleet, Hants. One son. His brother, Captain Cyril Prowse RN, was killed when his ship, the battlecruiser *HMS Queen Mary*, blew up and sank at the Battle of Jutland, 31st May 1916.
EDUCATION Marlborough College
CAREER
1889 – Commissioned into 3rd Somerset Light Infantry (Militia)
1892 – Joined 2nd Somerset Light Infantry
1900 – Adjutant, 2nd Somerset Light Infantry, Railway Staff Officer
1899–1902 – South Africa, MiD, Queen's Medal & 5 clasps, King's Medal & 2 clasps
1904-09 – Adjutant of the 1st Volunteer Bn. Somerset Light Infantry then 4th Somerset Light Infantry, TF.
1914 – Lt. Col. 1st Somerset Light Infantry
1915 – OC 1st Leinster Regiment then GOC 11th Brigade

12TH BRIGADE – BRIG. GEN. JAMES DAYROLLES CROSBIE

DSO 1917; CMG 1919
Born 19th August 1865; died 18th December 1947. Son of the late Col J Crosbie of Ballyheigue Castle, Co. Kerry, and daughter of Sir John Lister-Kaye, Bart Married May, daughter of Major Leith, VC. One daughter
EDUCATION Harrow; Royal Military College, Sandhurst
CAREER
1885 – Joined 2nd Royal Welch Fusiliers
1891-3 – Adjutant
1893 – Resigned to live on his estate in Co. Kerry
1915 – Rejoined, commanding 11th Lancashire Fusiliers
1916 – Brig. Gen. 12th Infantry Brigade
1917 – Commanded 16th The Queen's Regt in UK
1914–18 – MID five times, CMG, DSO
1918 – Base Commandant to Archangel
1938–45 – Chairman Fife County Council

29TH DIVISION – MAJ. GEN. (LATER LT. GEN.) SIR HENRY DE BEAUVOIR DE LISLE

DSO 1885; CB 1900; KCB 1917; KCMG 1919
Born 27th July 1864, died 16th July 1955. Fourth son of Richard Francis Valpy De Lisle, MRCS, honorary deputy inspector-general, and his wife, Clara Ella de Lisle. His father served as assistant surgeon of the 96th Foot (1841–51), and 1st (Royal) Dragoons (1851–2), and as surgeon of the 4th (King's Own) Foot (1852–9) including the Crimean War. Married Leila Annette (d. 1938), eldest daughter and heir of Wilberforce Bryant of Stoke Park, Stoke Poges, Buckinghamshire in 1902. One son, Christian de Beauvoir.
EDUCATION Privately on Jersey, Royal Military College, Sandhurst
CAREER
1883 – Gazetted into 2nd Durham Light Infantry in 1883
1885–6 – Sudan (DSO after recommendation for the VC)
1887 – India
1898–99 – Staff College, Camberley
1900–02 – South Africa commanding 6th Mounted Infantry (MiD four times, Queen's Medal & 5 clasps, King's Medal & 2 clasps
1902 – Transferred to 5th Dragoon Guards
1903 – Transferred to 1st Royal Dragoons. To India.
1906 – Lt. Col.
1910 – GSO1, 2nd Division Aldershot
1911 – Brig. Gen. 2nd Cavalry Brigade
1914 – Maj. Gen. 1st Cavalry Division in October 1914

1915 – GOC 29th Division and temporary command of the IX Corps
1918 – Acting Lt. Gen. XIII Corps then XV Corps
1914–18 – Promoted Maj. Gen. and Lt. Gen. in the field; KCB and KCMG; Commandeur, Legion of Honour; Grand Officier, Order of Leopold; Grand Cross, Serbian Order of White Eagle
1919–23 – General Officer Commanding-in-Chief, Western Command
1926 – Retired
1928–34 – Colonel, Durham Light Infantry

COMMANDER, ROYAL ARTILLERY – BRIG. GEN. MALCOLM PEAKE CMG

CMG 1900
Born 27th March 1865; died 27th Aug 1917. 3rd son of Frederick and Charlotte Peake of Burrough, Melton Mowbray, Leicestershire. Married Louisa, eldest daughter of Patrick H Osborne, NSW in 1900.
EDUCATION Charterhouse, Royal Military Academy, Woolwich
CAREER
1884 – Commissioned into Royal Artillery
1896 – Dongola Expedition (4th class Medjidie, British medal, Khedive's medal with two clasps)
1897 – Commanded a battery of Egyptian Artillery (MiD, clasp)
1898 – Atbara and Khartoum, (MiD, brevet major, two clasps)
1899 – Operations against Khalifa, (4th class Osmanieh, clasp)
1900 – Opened the Upper Nile, (3rd class Medjidie, CMG)
1911 – Lt. Col.
1914 – Commanding X Battery, RHA; Assistant Adjutant-General, War Office
1915 – Bt-Col; Officer Légion d'Honneur
1916 – CRA, 29th Division then BGRA I Corps
1917 – Killed by German shell on Hill 70 near Loos

86TH BRIGADE – BRIG. GEN. (LATER MAJ. GEN.) WEIR DE LANCEY WILLIAMS

DSO 1899; CMG 1917; CB 1921
Born 2nd March 1872; died 28th November 1961. Son of Sir W J Williams, KCB, of Pembroke, Wales. Married Nina Henrietta, daughter of Col Field, late 6th Foot, in 1899. One daughter
EDUCATION United Services College, Westward Ho!, Royal Military College, Sandhurst
CAREER
1891 – Joined Hampshire Regt.
1898 – Captain
1897 – Tirah Expedition (severely wounded)
1898 – Benin Hinterland & Siama Expedition, West Africa (severely wounded)
1900 – South Africa (severely wounded, MiD, Queen's Medal & 3 clasps, King's Medal & clasp)
1903 – Station Staff Officer, Indian Army
1904 – Brigade Major, Indian Army
1908 – Brigade Staff , Indian Army
1909 – Major
1913 – GSO2, Welsh Division, Western Command
1914 – Temp. Lt. Col., GSO1, 1/1st Welsh Division, Central Force, Home Defence
1915 – GSO1, Headquarters, Mediterranean Expeditionary Force, Temp. Brig. Gen. 86th Brigade
1914–18 – MiD, Bt Col, CMG
1923 – Retired

87TH BRIGADE – BRIG. GEN. (LATER MAJ. GEN.) CUTHBERT HENRY TINDALL LUCAS

DSO 1917; CMG 1918; CB 1921
Born 1st March 1879; died 7th April 1958. Son of the late William Tindall Lucas of Foxholes, Hitchin. Married Joan, daughter of late Arthur F Holdsworth, Widdecombe, Kingsbridge in 1917. Two sons, one daughter
EDUCATION Marlborough; Royal Military College, Sandhurst
CAREER
1898 – Joined 2nd Royal Berkshire Regt
1900–02 – South Africa (Queen's Medal & 3 clasps, King's Medal & 2 clasps)
1905–09 – Egyptian Army and Sudan Civil Service
1909 – Captain
1913 – Staff College
1914 – OC 1st Royal Berkshire Regt
1915 – Brigade Major, Temp. Lt. Col. 87th Brigade
1916 – Temp. Brig. Gen.
1918 – Commander Machine Gun Training Centre, GOC 4th Division
1920 – GOC, 11th Infantry Brigade in Ireland where he was taken prisoner by the IRA before escaping
1923 – AAG, Aldershot
1927-32 – HQ Staff, British Army of the Rhine
1929 – Maj. Gen.
1932 – Retired

88TH BRIGADE – BRIG. GEN. HON. (LATER MAJ. GEN.) DOUGLAS EDWARD CAYLEY

CMG 1915; CB 1919
Born 15th July 1870; died 19th December 1951. Son of late Deputy Surgeon-General H Cayley, CMG, Indian Medical Service, and late Letitia Mary, daughter of Rev. Nicholas Walters. Married Jessie, daughter of late Sir W D Gibbon in 1906. One son lost on active service Royal Navy in 1943 (DSO & 2 Bars).
EDUCATION Clifton College, Royal Military College, Sandhurst
CAREER
1890 – Gazetted into 2nd Worcestershire Regt., Limerick
1st Worcestershire Regt., India
1899 – Captain
1900–02 – South Africa (Queen's medal 3 clasps, King's medal 2 clasps)
1904 – Major
1905 – Ceylon, 2nd Worcestershire Regt.
1914 – Lt. Col. commanding 4th Worcestershire Reg., Burma
1915 – GOC 88th Brigade, Temp. Brig. Gen.
1918 – GOC 29th Division, Temp. Maj. Gen.
1914–18 – Wounded three times, MiD ten times, CMG, CB, Bt Col
1920 – Retired

31ST DIVISION – MAJ. GEN. ROBERT WANLESS-O'GOWAN

CB 1915; CMG 1919
Born Robert Wanless-Smith, 5th September 1864; died 15th December 1947. He was the eldest son of Edward John Smith and Dorcas Maria Smith (née Kelley) of Clonard, Co Dublin. Married 1887, Alice Phillis (d 1940), daughter of F C Bland of Derryquin Castle, Co. Kerry. One son, one daughter. He changed his name by deed poll in 1895 from Smith to Wanless-O'Gowan.
CAREER
1886 – Entered Army from Militia joining 2nd Cameronians (Scottish Rifles) from 8th KRRC

1899–1901 – South Africa (severely wounded, MiD twice, Bt Major; Queen's medal & 5 clasps)
1901–03 – District Inspector of Musketry, Southern District
1903–05 – DAAG, NE District
1906 – Transferred to East Lancashire Regt.
1909 – CO, 1st East Lancashire Regt.
1914 – AQMG, No. 12 Regimental District, Ireland; AAG Lines of Communication, BEF; AA and QMG 6th Division
1915 – Temp. Brig. Gen. commanding 13th Brigade, 5th Division then Temp. Maj. Gen.
1915–18 – GOC 31st Division
1914–18 – MiD six times, CB, CMG, 4th Class Order of Vladimir with swords, French Croix de Guerre avec Palme, Commander Belgian Ordre de la Couronne
1920 – Cannock Chase Reserve Centre then Retired

COMMANDER, ROYAL ARTILLERY, 31ST DIVISION – BRIG. GEN. EDWARD PARRY LAMBERT

CB 1915; CMG 1918
Born 9th Oct. 1865; died 26th May 1932. Oldest son of late Col Parry Lambert, RE, and grandson of late General Burnett, of Gadgirth, Tarbolton, Ayrshire. Married Thomasine Caroline, daughter of late Maj-Gen George Shaw, CB, RA, and widow of Major C A Ryan, RA in 1901
EDUCATION Wellington College; Royal Military Academy, Woolwich
CAREER
1884 – Entered Royal Artillery
1894 – Captain
1898 – Seconded to Hyderabad contingent, India
1900 – Major
1911 – Lt. Col.
1914 – 35th Brigade, RFA, Lahore
1915 – Brig. Gen.
1914–18 – MiD, CB, CMG
1921 – General Staff, Eastern Command, Indian Army; Retired

COMMANDER, ROYAL ENGINEERS, 31ST DIVISION – LT. COL. JOHN PIERRE MACKESY

DSO
Born 1873, Died 28th September 1950
EDUCATION Mottingham House, Eltham; Royal Military Academy, Woolwich
CAREER
1891 – At RMA, Woolwich won prizes for Fortifications (Engineer Division) & Landscape Drawing
1896 – Served in West Africa, cdg Section, West India Fortress Company, Royal Engineers in Sierra Leone
1898-9 – Protectorate Expedition, Sierra Leone (Medal & clasp)
1900-1902 – South Africa (MiD, Queen's Medal & 3 clasps, King's Medal & 2 clasps)
1902 – Captain
1906 – Staff College, Camberley
1911 – Major, Pretoria
1918 – Commander, Royal Anglesey Company, Royal Engineers, and GSO2
1920 – Colonel
1923 – Retired

92ND BRIGADE – BRIG. GEN. OLIVER DE LANCEY WILLIAMS

DSO 1915; CMG 1917

Born 5th November 1875; died 27th November 1959. Son of late Lt. Gen. Sir W G Williams, KCB. Married Mildred Lota Ramsay-Hill, Oberland, Guernsey, daughter of A H Baines, Bournemouth and Rosario, in 1924.

EDUCATION Oxford Military College; Royal Military College, Sandhurst

CAREER

1894 – Joined 2nd Royal Welsh Fusiliers
1899–1900 – South Africa (Queen's medal 5 clasps)
1901 – Seconded to the Chinese Regiment of Infantry
1903 – Captain
1912 – Issued Aviator's Certificate No. 356 on 16th November 1912 by the Royal Aero Club
1913 – Major
1914 – CO, 2nd Royal Welsh Fusiliers
1915 – Lt. Col.
1914–17 – Wounded, MiD, DSO, CMG, brevets Lt. Col. and Col.
1921 – Retired

93RD BRIGADE – BRIG. GEN. JOHN DARNLEY INGLES

DSO 1917; CMG 1918

Born Torcross, S. Devon, 18th December 1872 died 9th March 1957. 2nd son of late John Chamberlayne Ingles, DIG, RN

EDUCATION Cheltenham College; United Services College, Westward Ho!

CAREER

1894 – Commissioned into Devonshire Regt
1899–1902 – South Africa (MiD, Queen's Medal & 4 clasps, King's Medal & 2 clasps)
1900 – Captain
1912 – Adjutant, 2nd Devonshire Regt.
1916 – Temporary Brig. Gen.
1914–18 – MiD five times; Bt Lt. Col. June 1915, DSO, CMG
1922 – Lt. Col.
1926 – Retired

94TH BRIGADE – BRIG. GEN. HUBERT CONWAY REES

DSO 1914; CMG 1918

Born 26th March 1882; died 3rd January 1948. Only son of late Canon Henry Rees, The White Cottage, Shanklin. Married Katharine Adelaide, daughter of late John Loring, The Cottage, Doddington, Nantwich in 1914. Three daughters.

EDUCATION Charterhouse

CAREER

Joined 3rd East Surrey Regt. (Militia)
1903 – Joined 2nd The Welch Regiment
1901–02 – South Africa (Queen's medal four clasps)
1912 – Captain
1914 – Company commander 2nd Welch Regt.
1915 – GSO2, Staff 43rd Division, promoted Major
1916 – Temp. Brig. Gen. 94th Brigade and then 11th Brigade
1917 – GOC 13th Reserve Brigade then 149th Brigade
1918 – GOC 150th Brigade
1914–18 – MiD five times, DSO, CMG, Col
1922 – Retired

48TH (SOUTH MIDLAND) DIVISION (T.F.) – MAJ. GEN. SIR ROBERT FANSHAWE

DSO 1900; CB 1915; KCB 1917
Born 5th November 1863; died 24th August 1946. Son of Rev. H L Fanshawe. Married Evelyne Katherine Isabel Knox (d 1943) in 1903.
EDUCATION Marlborough
CAREER
1883 – Joined 2nd Oxfordshire Light Infantry to India
1897–98 – NW Frontier (Indian Frontier medal and two clasps)
1899 – Staff College
1901–02 – South Africa, 6th Regt., Mounted Infantry (MiD twice, Queen's medal 5 clasps, King's medal 2 clasps, DSO),
1903 – Bt Lt. Col., DAAG 4th Division
1907–11 – Commanded 2nd Oxfordshire Light Infantry
1911–14 – GSO1, 1st Division
1914–15 – GOC 6th Infantry Brigade
1915–18 – GOC 48th South Midland Div.
1914–18 – MiD eight times, KCB
1918–19 – GOC 69th Div.
1919 – Retired

COMMANDER, ROYAL ARTILLERY – BRIG. GEN. HENRY DUDLEY OSSULSTON WARD

CMG 1916, CB 1918
Born 23rd May 1872; died 7th Dec 1947. Married Mary, daughter of late Right Hon C G Milnes Gaskell in 1919. One son.
CAREER
1899–1900 – South Africa, (MiD, Queen's medal five clasps)
1914–18 – MiD seven times, CMG, Bt Col, CB, Chevalier Légion d'Honneur. Order of St John
1926–30 – Commanded Presidency and Assam District
1930 – Retired

143RD BRIGADE – BRIG. GEN. BERTIE COORE DENT

DSO 1918; CMG 1919; CB 1921
Born 22nd March 1872 died 20th May 1960. Eldest son of late Lt. Col. H F Dent. Married Violet, eldest daughter of G A Duff, Folkestone in 1909. One son
EDUCATION Charterhouse; Royal Military College, Sandhurst
CAREER
1892 – 2nd Lt., Leicestershire Regt
1896 – Matabeleland Campaign (medal and clasp)
1898–99 – Garrison Adjutant, Natal
1899–1902 – South Africa (Queen's and King's medals and clasps, MiD twice)
1904 – Somaliland (medal and clasp)
1916 and 1918–19 – Brigade Comdr, France
1914–18 – CMG, DSO, Légion d'Honneur, 5th Class, MiD six times
1920 – Iraq (medal and clasp, CB, MiD)
1920–22 – Mesopotamia E Force
1923 – Eastern Command
1927 – Retired

144TH BRIGADE – BRIG. GEN. GEORGE HARVEY NICHOLSON

CB 1916; CMG 1919
Born 5th Dec 1862; died 13th June 1942. Son of W S Nicholson, JP, Eastmore, Isle of Wight. Married Blanche, daughter of Capt. F. C. Annesley, 28th Regt., in 1892. One son. JP Hants

EDUCATION Charterhouse
CAREER
1882–1913 – Hampshire Regt
1887–89 – Burmese War, (medal with clasp)
1909–13 – Commanded 2nd Hampshire Regt
1914 – Commanded Hampshire Brigade TF
1914–18 – CB, CMG, Mid three times

145TH BRIGADE – BRIG. GEN. HERBERT RICHARD DONE

DSO 1915; CMG 1919
Born 23rd Sept 1876; died 17th Jan 1950. Youngest son of Richard Done. Married Elsie, daughter of late Samuel Kingan, DL, of Glenganagh, Co. Down, in 1916. Two daughters. Late of the Norfolk Regiment
EDUCATION Harrow
CAREER
1896 – Entered Army
1900–02 – South African War (Queen's medal 3 clasps, King's medal 2 clasps)
1914–18 – MiD nine times, DSO and bar, Bt. Lt. Col. and Col., CMG)
1919 – Retired

108TH BRIGADE – BRIG. GEN. CHARLES RICHARD JEBB GRIFFITH, CMG, DSO
DSO 1901; CMG 1915; CB 1918
Born 4th October 1867; died 4th August 1948. Son of Col. R Griffith.
EDUCATION Clifton College; Oundle; Royal Military College, Sandhurst
CAREER
1887 – Bedfordshire Regt.
1895 – Adjutant, 2nd Bedfordshire Regt.
1899-1902 – South African War (MiD, Queen's medal 2 clasps, King's medal 2 clasps)
1901 – DSO
1906 – Major
1913 – Lt. Col.
1914 – CO, 1st Bedfordshire Regt.
1915 – GOC, 108th Brigade
1918 – 20th Training Reserve Brigade, No 1 Machine Gun Corps
1914-1918 – MiD 8 times, CMG, CB, Officer, Légion d'Honneur
1919 – Member, War Office Standing Committee of Enquiry, re Prisoners of War
Member, Historical Section, Committee for Imperial Defence

Appendix 4: German Order of Battle

German Second Army – Gen. Fritz Theodor Carl von Below

Chief of Staff – GenMaj. Paul Grünert (Replaced by Oberst von Lossberg, 3rd July)
General of Foot (Heavy) Artillery – GenLt. Leo Limbourg
General of Pioneers – GenMaj. Friemel

XIV Reserve Corps – GenLt. Hermann Christlieb Matthäus von Stein

Chief of Staff – Major Kirch
General of Foot (Heavy) Artillery – GenMaj. Stüve

Corps Troops

II Abteilung (Feld-Haubitze[i]), Württembergisches Reserve-Feldartillerie-Regiment Nr. 116
Fußartillerie-Bataillon Nr. 51 Hptm Ritscher (att 26. Reserve Division)
Fußartillerie-Bataillon Nr. 229:
- 749 Batt att 26. Reserve Division
- 750 Batt att 28. Reserve Division
- 751 Batt att 28. Reserve Division

Artillerie Messtrupps[ii] Nr. 1, 2, 3, 4 and 6
Schall Messtrupps[iii] Nr. 1 and 49
M Flak Zug[iv] Nr. 4
K Flak[v] Geschütz Nr. 36
K Flak Batteries Nr. 5 and 7
Reserve Fernsprech Abteilung[vi] Nr. 14
Artillerie Scheinwerferzug[vii] Nr. 1
Feldluftschiffer Abteilung[viii] Nr. 2
Artillerie Feldflieger Abteilung[ix] Nr. 221
Feldflieger Abteilung[x] Nr. 32
Kgl. Bayerisches Feldflieger Abteilung Nr. 1
Staffelstäbe[xi] Nr. 152, 153, 266, 267 and 268

2. Garde Reserve Infanterie Division — **Gen. der Inf. Richard Freiherr von Süsskind-Schwendi (HQ – Gomiecourt)**

General Staff Officer — Hptm. von Stünzner

Divisional Artillery

Reserve-Feldartillerie-Regiment Nr. 20 — Oberstleutnant Hohnhorst (Recruited from Hannover/Oldenburg)

ATTACHED:
1 & 3/Kgl. Bayerisches Feldartillerie-Regiment Nr. 19 (10. KB Division)
2/Fußartillerie-Bataillon Nr. 52 (52. Division)
ATTACHED ARMY TROOPS:
II Abt & ½ 5/2. Garde-Fußartillerie-Regiment — Hptm. Matschke

---

[i] Light Field Howitzer
[ii] Artillery Survey Sections
[iii] Sound Ranging Sections
[iv] Flug-Abwehr-Maschinenkanonenzug = 3.7 cm anti-aircraft gun section
[v] Flugabwehrkanone auf Kraftwagen = Motorised anti-aircraft gun
[vi] Telephone section
[vii] Searchlight section
[viii] Balloon detachment
[ix] Artillery Flight
[x] Reconnaissance Flight
[xi] Divisional train echelons

3/II Kgl. Bayerisches Landsturm Fußartillerie-Bataillon Nr. 1
Fußartillerie-Batt. Apel. | Fußartillerie-Batt. Nr. 517
Fußartillerie-Batt. Nr. 692 | Fußartillerie-Batt. Nr. 706
Fußartillerie-Batt. Nr. 212 (½) | Three 5.7 cm Belgian guns
K Flak Zug Nr. 38

DIVISIONAL TROOPS

4/Hannoverisches Pionier-Bataillon Nr. 10
2. Garde-Reserve-Minenwerfer-Kompanie
3. Eskadron/Reserve-Ulanen-Regiment Nr. 2 (Demmin)
Flak Zug Nr. 58
Scheinwerferzug Nr. 260
Garde Reserve Sanitäts Kompanie[i] Nr. 2
Feldrekrutendepot[ii]

ATTACHED ARMY TROOPS:
3/Armeriungs-Bataillon[iii] Nr. 31 | 4/Armeriungs-Bataillon Nr. 69
Reserve Eisenbahn Bau Kompanie[iv] Nr. 22

26. RESERVE INFANTRY BRIGADE | **GENMAJ. WILHELM ERNST HERMANN VON DRESLER UND SCHARFENSTEIN**

Reserve-Infanterie-Regiment Nr. 15 | Oberstleutnant Schwarz (Recruited from Bielefeld/Detmold/Minden)
I Battalion
II Battalion | Maj. Kiesel
III Battalion | Maj. Ritter
Maschinengewehr-Kompanie[v] | Maschinengewehr-Ergänzungs-Zug[vi] Nr. 662
Maschinengewehr-Scharfschützen-Abteilung[vii] Nr. 73

Reserve-Infanterie-Regiment Nr. 55 | Oberstleutnant von Laue (Recruited from Detmold/Paderborn/Soest)
I Battalion | Maj. von Bothmer
II Battalion | Hptm. d L. Minck
III Battalion | Maj. Tauscher
Maschinengewehr-Kompanie | Maschinengewehr-Ergänzungs-Zug Nr. 663

38. RESERVE-INFANTERIE-BRIGADE | **GENLT. OTTO VON ETZEL**

2. Hannoverisches Reserve-Infanterie-Regiment Nr. 77 | Oberst Rücker (Recruited from Hameln/Hildesheim)

Maschinengewehr-Kompanie | Maschinengewehr-Ergänzungs-Zug Nr. 331
Maschinengewehr-Scharfschützen-Abteilung Nr. 106

Hannoverisches Reserve-Infanterie-Regiment Nr. 91 | Oberstleutnant von Heynitz (Recruited from Hameln/Göttingen)

---

[i] Medical or Bearer Company
[ii] Recruit Depot.
[iii] Companies of Labour battalions
[iv] Railway construction company
[v] Regimental Machine Gun Company
[vi] Machine Gun Section
[vii] Machine Gun Marksman Detachment

I Battalion	Hptm. von Eckartsberg
II Battalion	Hptm. von Beerfelde
III Battalion	Maj. Lorenz
Maschinengewehr-Kompanie	Maschinengewehr-Ergänzungs-Zug Nr. 352

52. INFANTERIE DIVISION — **GENLT. KARL JULIUS WILHELM VON BORRIES (HQ – BIHUCOURT)**

General Staff Officer — Hptm. Prager

DIVISIONAL ARTILLERY

52. FELDARTILLERIE-BRIGADE — **GENMAJ. KÖRNER**

Badisches Feldartillerie-Regiment Nr. 103	Maj. Knorr
Badisches Feldartillerie-Regiment Nr. 104	Maj. Von Laer
Fußartillerie-Bataillon Nr. 52 (less 2nd Abt)	Hptm. Haccius
Flak Zug Nr. 108	

ATTACHED:
II/Kgl. Bayerisches Feldartillerie-Regiment Nr. 19 (10. KB Division)
2/Kgl. Bayerisches Fußartillerie-Regiment Nr. 10 (10. KB Division)

ATTACHED ARMY TROOPS:

1, 2 and 3 Batterie, Fußartillerie-Regiment Nr. 7	Hptm. Dorn
7/Garde Fußartillerie-Batt Nr. 2 ($\frac{1}{2}$)	Fußartillerie-Batt. Nr. 471 ($\frac{2}{3}$)
Fußartillerie-Batterie Nr. 472 ($\frac{1}{2}$)	Fußartillerie-Batt. Nr. 10

1 & 2/ II Kgl. Bayerisches Landsturm Fußartillerie-Bataillon Nr. 2

2/Ersatz Fußartillerie-Regiment Nr. 18	Three 5.7 cm Belgian guns

DIVISIONAL TROOPS

Pionier-Kompanie Nr. 103	Pionier-Kompanie Nr. 104
Minenwerfer-Kompanie Nr. 52	Radfahrer Kompanie[i] Nr. 52

4. Eskadron/Ulanen-Regiment Hennigs von Treffenfeld (Altmärkisches) Nr. 16

Scheinwerferzug Nr. 103	Sanitäts Kompanie Nr. 52
Feldrekrutendepot	

ATTACHED ARMY TROOPS:
Kgl. Bayerisches Pionier Regiment Nr. 1

2/Armeriungs-Bataillon Nr. 31	3/Armeriungs-Bataillon Nr. 78

104. INFANTERIE BRIGADE — **GENMAJ. ARNOLD LEQUIS**

3. Magdeburgisches Infanterie-Regiment Nr. 66	Maj. von Stoeklern zu Grünholzek (Recruited from Magdeburg)
I Battalion	Maj. Kiesel
II Battalion	Hptm. Rochlitz (Maj. Paulis w. 26.6.16)
III Battalion	Hptm. Trenck
Two Maschinengewehr-Kompanien	

8. Badisches Infanterie-Regiment Nr. 169	Maj. von Struensee (Recruited from Lahr, II Vilingen)
I Battalion	Maj. Berthold
II Battalion	
III Battalion	

[i] Cyclist company

Two Maschinengewehr-Kompanien
9. Badisches Infanterie-Regiment Nr. 170 — Maj. von Ihlenfeld (Offenburg, III Donaueschingen)
I Battalion — Hptm. Wulff
II Battalion — Maj. Fischer
III Battalion
Maschinengewehr-Ergänzungs-Zug Nr. 13 + one MGC
Maschinengewehr-Scharfschützen-Abteilung Nr. 74

26. RESERVE INFANTERIE DIVISION (1. WÜRTTEMBERGISCHE) — **GEN. DER INF. FRANZ FREIHERR VON SODEN (HQ – BIEFVILLERS)**
General Staff Officer — Hptm. Fischer

DIVISIONAL ARTILLERY

26. RESERVE FELDARTILLERIE-BRIGADE — **GENMAJ. HEINRICH VON MAUR**

Württembergisches Reserve-Feldartillerie-Regiment Nr. 26 — Oberstleutnant Erlenbusch
I Abteilung — Maj. Bornemann
II Abteilung — Hptm. Graf von Preysing
Württembergisches Reserve-Feldartillerie-Regiment Nr. 27 — Maj. Reiniger
I Abteilung — Hptm. Wiedtmann
II Abteilung — Hptm. Jäckh
Flak Zug Nr. 137

ATTACHED:
Kgl. Bayerisches Feldartillerie-Regiment Nr. 20 (10. KB Division)
2/Kgl. Bayerisches Feldartillerie-Regiment Nr. 19 (10. KB Division)
Kgl. Bayerisches Minenwerfer Company Nr. 10 (10. KB Division)
I/Feldartillerie-Regiment Nr. 104 (less ½ 2nd Batterie) (52. Division)
I/Reserve Feldartillerie-Regiment Nr. 12 (12. Reserve Division)

ATTACHED CORPS TROOPS:
1, 2 & 3 Batt, Fußartillerie-Bataillon Nr. 51
749 Batt, Fußartillerie-Bataillon Nr. 229

ATTACHED ARMY TROOPS:
Fußartillerie-Batt. Nr. 471
7 Batt, Garde Fußartillerie-Regiment Nr. 2 (½)
Fußartillerie-Batt. Nr. 683
Fußartillerie-Batt. Nr. 235 & 236
Four Belgian 5.7 cm Guns
Fußartillerie-Batt. Nr. 551
Fußartillerie-Batt. Nr. 550 (½)
Fußartillerie-Batt. Nr. 709
1 Batt, Fußartillerie-Regiment Nr. 20

DIVISIONAL TROOPS

4 & 6 Kompanie/Württembergisches Pionier-Bataillon Nr. 13
Württembergisches Minenwerfer-Kompanie Nr. 226
Württembergisches Reserve Dragoner Regt (3 Squadrons)
Württembergisches Radfahrer Kompanie Nr. 2
Württemberg Scheinwerferzug Nr. 256
Württembergisches Reserve Sanitäts Kompanie Nr. 26
Württembergisches Sanitäts Kraftwagen Kolonne[i] Nr. 5
Württembergisches Feldrekrutendepot

[i] Sanitäts Kraftwagen Kolonne = Motor Ambulance Column

ATTACHED:

Kgl. Bayerisches Reserve-Infanterie-Regiment Nr. 8	Oberstleutnant Bram (10. KB Division)
I Battalion	Maj. Prager
II Battalion	Maj. Roesch
III Battalion	Maj. Beyerköhler
One Maschinengewehr-Kompanie	
Maschinengewehr-Scharfschützen-Abteilung Nr. 45	
Maschinengewehr-Scharfschützen-Abteilung Nr. 88	

ATTACHED ARMY TROOPS:

1/Musketen Bn[i] Nr. 1	5th Kgl. Bayerisches Pionier-Mineur-Kompanie[ii]
5/Armeriungs-Bataillon 31	

51. WÜRTTEMBERG RESERVE INFANTERIE BRIGADE	**GENLT. THEODOR VON WUNDT**
Württembergisches Reserve-Infanterie-Regiment Nr. 119	Oberst Freiherr von Ziegesar (Recruited from Stuttgart)
I Battalion	Hptm. von Breuning
II Battalion	
III Battalion	Maj. Schäfer
Two Maschinengewehr-Kompanien	
Württembergisches Reserve-Infanterie-Regiment Nr. 121	Oberst Josenhantz (Recruited from Ludwigsburg)
I Battalion	Hptm. Winter (Hptm. Freiherr von Ziegesar dow 26.6.16)
II Battalion	
III Battalion	
One Maschinengewehr-Kompanie	Maschinengewehr-Kompanie Fassbender
Maschinengewehr-Scharfschützen-Abteilung Nr. 198	

52. WÜRTTEMBERG RESERVE INFANTERIE BRIGADE	**GENLT. FRIEDRICH VON AUWÄRTER**
(Defending Thiepval & Ovillers La Boisselle)	
Reserve-Infanterie-Regiment Nr. 99	Maj. von Fabeck (Recruited from Mönchengladbach)
I Battalion	Maj. Sauer
II Battalion	Maj. Frhr. von Meerscheidt-Hüllessem
III Battalion	Hptm. Mandel
Two Maschinengewehr-Kompanien	
10. Württembergisches Infanterie Regiment Nr. 180	Oberstleutnant Alfred Vischer (Recruited from Tübingen)
I Battalion	Hptm. Heyberger
II Battalion	Maj. Keerl
III Battalion	Maj. Scupin
Two Maschinengewehr-Kompanien	

[i] Armed with the Danish Madsen Light Machine Gun.

[ii] Mining (Tunnelling) Company

APPENDIX 5: BIOGRAPHICAL DETAILS OF SENIOR GERMAN OFFICERS

SECOND ARMY – GENERAL DER INFANTERIE FRITZ THEODOR CARL VON BELOW

Born 23rd September 1853, Danzig, West Prussia. Died 23rd November 1918, Weimar. Son of Gen Ferdinand von Below (killed at Pont a Musson, 1870, in the Franco-Prussian War) and Therese née Mauve. His brothers Ernst and Nikolaus were also Generals in the war. Pour le Merite: 16th February 1915, Oakleaves, 11th August 1916

CAREER

1873 – Lt, 1. Garde-Regiment zu Fuß
1881 – Prussian War Academy (Preußische Kriegsakademie – Berlin)
1885 – Großer Generalstab – Berlin
1887 – Hauptmann
1888 – Generalstab, Gardekorps
1892 – Major; General Staff, 5. Infanterie Division
1896 – Battalion commander, Königin Augusta Garde-Grenadier-Regiment Nr. 4
1898 – General Staff, III Armeekorps
1901 – Oberst, commander Königin Elisabeth Garde-Grenadier-Regiment Nr. 3
1904 – Commander, 4. Garde-Infanterie-Brigade
1905 – Generalmajor
1906 – Deputy Chief of the General Staff
1908 – Generalleutnant, Commander, 1. Garde-Infanterie-Division
1912 – General de Infanterie, commander XXI Armeekorps, Saarbrücken
1914 – Commander, XXI Armeekorps
1915 – Commander, 2. Armee
1916 – Commander, 1. Armee
1918 – Commander, 9. Armee

CHIEF OF THE GENERAL STAFF – GENMAJ. PAUL FERDINAND ALEXANDER GRÜNERT

Born 12th January 1861, Magdeburg. Died 11th December 1936, Munich.
Pour le Merite: 3rd May 1918

CAREER

1881 – Lt, Dragoner-Regiment König Karl I von Rumänien (1. Hannoverisches) Nr. 9
1895 – Großer Generalstab, Berlin
1901 – Staff, 15. Infanterie Division
1904 – Staff, VII Armeekorps, Köln
1906 – Instructor, Preußische Kriegsakademie, Berlin
1908 – Chief of Staff, VIII Armeekorps, Koblenz
1912 – Commander, Magdeburgisches Dragoner-Regiment Nr. 6
1913 – Commander, 13. Kavallerie-Brigade
1914 – Quartermaster, 8. Armee; Chief of Staff, 9. Armee
1915 – Chief of Staff Heeresgruppe 'Prinz Leopold'
1916 – Commander, 25. Reserve Division; Chief of Staff, 2. Armee; commander 3. Infanterie Division; commander 119. Infanterie Division
1917 – Instructor – Generalstabs-Schule
1918 – Generalleutnant; commander 21. Infanterie Division; commander XXXIX Armeekorps; commander XXXX Armeekorps

XIV RESERVE ARMEEKORPS – GENLT. HERMANN CHRISTLIEB MATTHÄUS VON STEIN

Born 12th September 1854, Weddersted, Sachsen. Died 26th May 1927 in Lehnin. Son of Hermann Robert Stein and Julie Friederike née Meyer. Pour le Merite: September 1916
CAREER
1873 – Feldartillerie-Regiment General Feldzeugmeister (1. Brandenburgisches) Nr. 3
1875 – Lt.
1883 – Preußische Kriegsakademie – Berlin
1886 – Oberleutnant, Feldartillerie-Regiment General Feldzeugmeister (1. Brandenburgisches) Nr. 3
1888 – Großer Generalstab – Berlin
1890 – Hauptmann
1894 – General Staff, 34. Infanterie Division
1896 – Major; General Staff
1901 – Commander, 1. Lothringisches Feldartillerie-Regiment Nr. 33
1905 – Oberst
1908 – Senior Quartermaster, General Staff
1910 – Generalmajor
1912 – Generalleutnant; Commander, 41. Infanterie Division
1914 – Deputy Chief of the General Staff of the Field Army; Commander, XIV Armeekorps
1916 – Minister of War, Berlin

2. GARDE RESERVE INFANTRY DIVISION – GEN. DER INF. RICHARD KARL GOTTLIEB WILHELM FRIEDRICH PHILIPP FREIHERR VON SÜSSKIND-SCHWENDI

Born 3rd July 1854, Schwendi. Died 20th December 1946, Bächingen. Son of Max Theodor Freiherr von Süßkind and Karolina Freiin von Woellwarth-Lauterburg. Married Ilse von Winterfeld, 1901. Three sons, one daughter
CAREER
Military attaché, Paris
General der Infanterie
Commander, 2. Garde Reserve Infanterie Division

38. RESERVE-INFANTERIE-BRIGADE – GENLT. OTTO FRANZ HERMANN KARL VON ETZEL

Born 17th May 1860, Naumburg, Saxony-Anhalt. Died 1934. Son of Hermann von Etzel and Gattin Augusta née Koch. Married Margarete von Klingspor, 1912. Two sons. His brother, Günther, was a General der Kavalerie.
CAREER
1880 – Entered Army
1902–1908 Military attaché, Washington DC
Commander, 75. Infanterie Brigade
1914 – Commander, 38. Infanterie Brigade
1916 – Commander, 206. Infanterie Division

26. RESERVE INFANTRY BRIGADE – GENMAJ. WILHELM ERNST HERMANN VON DRESLER UND SCHARFENSTEIN

Born 9th July 1857, Liegnitz. Died 13th April 1942, Göttingen. Son of Otto von Dresler und Scharfenstein and Emilie née von Schachtmeyer. Married Elfriede Elisabeth Müller, 1889. Five children.
Pour le Merite (1917)
CAREER
1876 – 2nd Lt, Füsilier-Regiment von Gersdorff (Kurhessisches) Nr. 80

1886 – 1st Lt, Infanterie-Regiment Großherzog Friedrich Franz II von Mecklenburg-Schwerin (4. Brandenburgisches) Nr. 24
1891 – Hauptmann, 6. Pommersche Infanterie-Regiment Nr. 49
1902 – Major
1904 – Commander, III Bataillon, 6. Rheinischen Infanterie-Regiments Nr. 68
1909 – Oberstleutnant
1912 – Oberst; commander 3. Magdeburgischen Infanterie-Regiments Nr. 66
1914 – Commander, 13. Reserve Infanterie Brigade
1915 – Commander, 26. Reserve Infanterie Brigade
1916 – Commander, 25. Infanterie Division
1918 – Generalleutnant

52. INFANTRY DIVISION – GENLT. KARL JULIUS WILHELM LEO VON BORRIES

Born 26th November 1854, Bilstein (Lennestadt). Died 3rd March 1938, Lüneburg. Son of Adolf Friedrich Ludwig Karl Anton Wilhelm August von Borries and August Johanne Marie née Crome. Married Elise Hulda Werner, 1877. 1 son, 2 daughters.
Pour le Merite (1918), Commander of the Baden Military Order of Karl Friedrich (1918)
CAREER
1870 – One year volunteer, 1. Proviant-Kolonne , XIII Armeekorps
1872 – Cadet, Füsilier-Regiment Prinz Heinrich von Preußen (Brandenburgisches) Nr. 35
1876 – Preußische Kriegsakademie – Berlin
1879 – Rheinische Jäger-Bataillon Nr. 8
1882 – General Staff then Pommersche Jäger-Bataillon Fürst Bismarck Nr. 2
1886 – Garde-Jäger-Bataillon then Company commander, Kurhessischen Jäger-Bataillon Nr. 11
1887 – Company commander, Garde-Schützen-Bataillon
1896 – Major, 1. Badische Leib-Grenadier-Regiment Nr. 109, commander II Bataillon
1897 – Commander, Kurhessische Jäger-Bataillon Nr. 11
1904 – Commander, 3. Posenschen Infanterie-Regiments Nr. 58
1909 – General Major cdg 84. Infanterie Brigade
1911 – Generalleutnant, cdg Altona, Hamburg and Wandsbek
1914 – Commander, 33. Reserve Infanterie Brigade
1915 – Commander, 52. Infanterie Division
1918 – Commander II Armeekorps

104. INFANTRY BRIGADE – GENMAJ. ARNOLD LEQUIS

Born 2nd February 1861, Dillenburg, Hesse. Died 16th February 1942, Wiesbaden.
Pour le Merite (1917, October, Oakleaves (1917 December)
CAREER
1880 – 1. Rheinisches Pionier-Bataillon Nr. 8
1891 – Oberleutnant
1896 – Hauptmann
1898 – Großer Generalstab – Berlin
1900 – Major; German Expeditionary Force to China
1902 – Preußische Kriegsakademie – Berlin
1904 – General Staff, Colonial Forces, South West Africa
1912 – Oberst
1913 – Commander of Pioniere, 1. Armeekorps
1914 – Oberqartiermeister, 2. Armee
1914 – Generalmajor
1916 – Commander, 104· Infanterie Brigade; commander 12. Infanterie Division
1918 – Generalleutnant
1919 – Commander XV Armeelorps

26. RESERVE INFANTRY DIVISION (WÜRTTEMBERG) – GEN. DER INF. FRANZ LUDWIG FREIHERR VON SODEN-FRAUNHOFEN

Born 9th March 1856, Stuttgart. Died 29th November 1945, Überlingen. Son of Alfred Karl August von Soden-Frauenhofen and Emilie née von Rom. Married Amelie Charlotte Frenn Hugo von Spitzemberg, 1890. Two daughters.
Pour le Merite (1917), Military Merit Cross, 1st class (Austria-Hungary 1918)
CAREER
1873 – One year volunteer, Grenadier-Regiment Königin Olga (1. Württembergische) Nr. 119
1880 – Preußische Kriegsakademie – Berlin
1883 – Premierleutnant, Grenadier-Regiment König Karl (5. Württembergisches) Nr. 123
1884-86 – Großer Generalstab – Berlin
1889 – Staff, X Armeekorps
1890 – Staff, 19. Infanterie Division
1891 – Company commander, Grenadier-Regiment Königin Olga (1. Württembergische) Nr. 119
1893 – Staff, 26. Infanterie Division
1895 – Staff, XIII. Armeekorps (Königlich Württembergisches)
1898 – Battalion commander, Infanterie-Regiment von Wittich (3. Kurhessisches) Nr. 83
1900 – Chief of Staff, X Armeekorps
1903 – Commander, Infanterie-Regiment Kaiser Friedrich König von Preußen (7. Württembergisches) Nr. 125
1906 – Commander, 51. Infanterie-Brigade (1. Königlich Württembergische)
1910 – Commander, 26. Infanterie-Division (1. Königlich Württembergische)
1911 – General de Infanterie
1914 – Commander, 26. Reserve-Division (1. Königlich Württembergische)
1916 – Commander, VII Reservekorps
1917 – Commander, XI Armeekorps; commander V Reservekorps

51. WÜRTTEMBERG RESERVE INFANTRY BRIGADE – GENLT. THEODOR KARL WILHELM VON WUNDT

Born 21st April 1858, Ludwigsburg. Died 16th August 1929, Stuttgart. Son of the Württemberg War Minister Theodor von Wundt and Christiane Auguste Franziska née Huber.
CAREER
Pre-war – Commander 59. Infantry Brigade, Saarburg
1914 – Commander 51. Reserve Infanterie Brigade
1916 – Commander, 18. Reserve Infanterie Division

52. WÜRTTEMBERG RESERVE INFANTRY BRIGADE – GENLT. FRIEDRICH VON AUWÄRTER

1901 – German Expeditionary Force to China, Boxer Rebellion
1908 – Commander, Infanterie-Regiment Kaiser Wilhelm, König von Preußen
(2. Württembergisches) Nr. 120
1912 – Commander, 54. Infanterie Brigade
1914 – Commander, 52. Reserve Infanterie Brigade
1916 – Commander, 6. Reserve Infanterie Division
1917 – Commander, 5. Reserve Infanterie Division

APPENDIX 6: FIGHTING STRENGTH, VIII CORPS, 30TH JUNE 1916

4th Division		
10th Brigade	Officers	Other Ranks
1st Royal Warwickshire Regt.	33	938
2nd Seaforth Highlanders	42	1022
1st Royal Irish Fusiliers	41	1024
2nd Royal Dublin Fusiliers	44	1085
	160	4069
11th Brigade		
1st Somerset Light Infantry	40	1065
1st East Lancashire Regt.	42	1004
1st Hampshire Regt.	38	1050
1st Rifle Brigade	42	1070
	162	4189
12th Brigade		
1st King's Own Royal Lancaster Regt.	41	983
2nd Lancashire Fusiliers	42	1031
2nd Essex Regt.	41	1033
2nd Duke of Wellington's (West Riding) Regt.	42	1051
	166	4098
Pioneers		
21st West Yorkshire Regt.	29	993
Divisional Total	**517**	**13249**

29th Division		
86th Brigade		
2nd Royal Fusiliers	46	1064
1st Lancashire Fusiliers	43	1065
1st Royal Dublin Fusiliers	40	1027
16th Middlesex Regt.	42	912
	171	4068
87th Brigade		
2nd South Wales Borderers	44	794
1st King's Own Scottish Borderers	44	1065
1st Royal Inniskilling Fusiliers	46	1019
1st Border Regt.	39	1096
	173	3974
88th Brigade		
4th Worcestershire Regt.	41	966
2nd Hampshire Regt.	43	1105
1st Essex Regt.	44	1028
1st Newfoundland Regt.	54	990
	182	4089
Pioneers		
1/2nd Monmouthshire Regt.	44	990
Divisional Total	**570**	**12899**

31st Division		
92nd Brigade		
10th East Yorkshire Regt.	29	858
11th East Yorkshire Regt.	36	919
12th East Yorkshire Regt.	37	998
13th East Yorkshire Regt.	36	915
	138	3690
93rd Brigade		
15th West Yorkshire Regt	34	953
16th West Yorkshire Regt.	33	1015
18th West Yorkshire Regt.	37	1019
18th Durham Light Infantry	40	1118
	144	4105
94th Brigade		
11th East Lancashire Regt	40	1034
12th York & Lancaster Regt.	33	977
13th York & Lancaster Regt.	38	1004
14th York & Lancaster Regt.	37	1020
	148	4035
Pioneers		
12th King's Own Yorkshire Light Infantry	31	1082
Divisional Total	**461**	**12912**
48th (South Midland) Division		
143rd Brigade		
1/5th Royal Warwickshire Regt.	25	831
1/6th Royal Warwickshire Regt.	32	787
1/7th Royal Warwickshire Regt.	23	803
1/8th Royal Warwickshire Regt.	34	1027
	114	3448
144th Brigade		
1/4th Gloucestershire Regt.	33	996
1/6th Gloucestershire Regt.	33	1001
1/7th Worcestershire Regt.	33	875
1/8th Worcestershire Regt.	36	855
	135	3727
145th Brigade		
1/5th Gloucestershire Regt.	34	906
1/4th Oxfordshire & Buckinghamshire Light Infantry	36	1072
1st Buckinghamshire Battalion, Oxfordshire & Buckinghamshire Light Infantry	29	1010
1/4th Royal Berkshire Regt.	29	878
	128	3866
Pioneers		
1/5th Royal Sussex Regt.	42	1040
Divisional Total	**419**	**12081**
Corps Total	**1967**	**51141**

BIBLIOGRAPHY

British Regimental and Unit Histories

Atkinson C T, *The Royal Hampshire Regt.*, Vol. 2, Robert Macklehose, 1952

Atkinson, *The History of the South Wales Borderers 1914-18*, Medici Society, 1931

Berkeley R, *History of the Rifle Brigade in the War of 1914-19,* Vol. 1, The Rifle Brigade Club Ltd., 1927.

Bilton D, *Hull Pals*, Pen & Sword, 1999

Cooksey J, *Barnsley Pals*, Pen & Sword, 1986

Farndale, Gen. Sir M, *History of the Royal Regiment of Artillery, Western Front 1914-18*, Royal Artillery Institution, 1986

Gibson R & Oldfield P, *Sheffield City Battalion*, Pen & Sword, 1988

Gillon, Capt. S, *The Story of the 29th Division*, Naval & Military Press, 1925

Hudson, R N, *The Bradford Pals*, Bradford Libraries Archives and Information Service, 2000

Latter, Maj. Gen. J C, *The History of the Lancashire Fusiliers, 1914-18*, Gale & Polden, 1949

Lowe, Lt. Col. W D, *The War History of the 18th (S) Durham Light Infantry*, OUP, 1920

Milner L, *Leeds Pals*, Pen & Sword, 1991

Nicholson, Maj. Gen. Sir L, & McMullen, Maj. H T, *History of the East Lancashire Regiment in the Great War*, Littlebury Brothers, 1936

O'Neill H C, *The Royal Fusiliers in the Great War*, William Heinemann, 1922

Turner W, *Accrington Pals*, Pen & Sword, 1987

Wyrrall E, *The History of the Somerset Light Infantry (Prince Albert's), 1914-19*, Methuen & Co., 1927

Wyrall, *The Die Hards in the Great War. A History of the Duke of Cambridge's Own (Middlesex Regt.,) 1914-19*, Harrison & Sons, 1926

German Histories

Anonymous, *Die 26. Reserve-Division im Weltkrieg*, Stuttgart, 1920

Anonymous, *Die 26. Reserve-Division im Weltkrieg*, Stuttgart, 1936

Forstner, Frhr. K v., *Das Königlich – Preussische Reserve-Infanterie-Regiment Nr. 15*, Sporn Zeulenroda 1931

Gerster M, *Die Schwaben an der Ancre*, Heilbronn, 1918

Gerster, *Das Württembergische Reserve-Infanterie-Regiment Nr. 119 im Weltkrieg.* Stuttgart, 1920

Holtz, Freiherr, G v., *Das Württembergische Reserve-Infanterie-Regiment Nr. 121 im Weltkrieg.* Stuttgart, 1921

Lais, Otto, *Die Schlacht an der Somme,* Karlsruhe

Klaus, Max, *Das Württembergische Reserve-Feldartillerie-Regiment Nr. 26 im Weltkrieg*, Stuttgart, 1929

Soden, Freiherr v. *Die 26. (Württembergische) Reserve-Division im Weltkrieg*, 1. Teil, 1914-16, Stuttgart, 1939

Stosch, A v., *Somme Nord,* 1 Teil, Reichsarchiv, Oldenburg 1927

Official Accounts

Edmonds, Brig. Gen. Sir James E, *Official History of the War: Military Operations, France and Belgium, 1915*, Vols 1 & 2 and *1916*, Vol. 1 and Maps and Appendices

Jones, H A, *The war in the air : being the story of the part played in the Great War by the Royal Air Force*. Volume 3, Naval & Military Press, 1928

Various, *Der Weltkrieg 1914 bis 1918: Die Operationen des Jahres 1916*, Berlin, 1936

Various, *Les Armées Françaises dans la Grande Guerre,* Tome IV, Vols 1 & 2 and Appendices, Paris, 1936

General Accounts

Barton, P, *The Somme*, Constable, 2006

Brown M, *The Imperial War Museum Book of the Somme*, Sidgwick & Jackson, 1996

Cave, N, *Beaumont Hamel*, Pen & Sword, 1994

Churchill, Winston, *The World Crisis*,

Duffy C, Through *German Eyes: The British and the Somme, 1916*, Weidenfeld & Nicholson, 2006

Farrar-Hockley, Gen. Sir A H, *The Somme*, B T Batsford 1966

Hart, Peter, *The Somme*, Weidenfeld and Nicholson, 2005

Horsfall J & Cave N, *Serre*, Pen & Sword, 1996

Keegan, John, *The Face of Battle*, Penguin, 1976.

Macdonald, Lyn, *Somme*, Michael Joseph 1983 and Papermac 1984

Mace M & Grehan J, *Slaughter on the Somme*, Pen & Sword, 2013

Middlebrook, Martin, *The First Day on the Somme*, Penguin 1971

Philpott. W, *Bloody Victory*, Little Brown, 2009

Prior R & Wilson T, *The Somme*, Yale University Press, 2005

Renshaw, M, *Redan Ridge*, Pen & Sword, 2004

Sheffield, G, *The Somme*, Cassell, 2003

Sheldon, J, *The German Army on the Somme 1914-16*, Pen and Sword 2005

Sheldon, *The Germans at Beaumont Hamel*, Pen & Sword, 2006

Whitehead R J, *The Other Side of the Wire*, Vols 1 & 2, Helion Press, 2010/13

Wynne, Capt. G G, *If Germany Attacks*, Greenwood Press, 1976

Biographies and Diaries

Blake, R, *The Private Papers of Douglas Haig*, Eyre & Spottiswoode, 1952

Boraston J.H., O.B.E., ed. *Sir Douglas Haig's Despatches, Dec. 1915 - Apr 1919*. J. M. Dent, 1919

Charteris, Brig. Gen. J, *Field Marshal Earl Haig*, Cassell, 1929

Charteris, *At GHQ*, Cassell, 1931

Dewar G A B, *Sir Douglas Haig's Command 1915-18*, Constable, 1922.

Duff Cooper, *Haig*, Faber & Faber, 1935

De Groot G J, *Douglas Haig, 1861-1928*, Unwin Hyman, 1988

Falkenhayn, Gen. E von, *General Headquarters 1914-16*, The Battery Press, 1919

Harris J P, *Douglas Haig and the First World War*, Cambridge University Press, 2008

Lloyd George D, David, *War Memoirs*, 1931

Maurice, Maj. Gen. Sir F, *The Life of General Lord Rawlinson of Trent*, Cassell, 1928

Prior R & Wilson T, *Command on the Western Front: The Military Career of Sir Henry Rawlinson 1914-18*, Blackwell Publishers 1992

Sheffield G & Bourne J, *Douglas Haig, War Diaries and Letters*, Weidenfeld and Nicholson, 2005
Terraine, John, *Haig: The Educated Soldier*, Leo Cooper, 1990
Warner, Philp, *Field Marshal Earl Haig*, Bodley Head, 1991
Woodward, *The Military Correspondence of Field Marshal Sir William Robertson*, Army Records Society, 1989

Weapons and Equipment

François, Gen. G, *Les Canons de la Victoire 1914-18, Tome 2: L'Artillerie Lourde a Grande Puissnace,* Histoire & Collections, 2008
François, *Les Canons de la Victoire 1914-18, Tome 3: L'Artillerie de Côte et L'Artillerie de Tranchée,* Histoire & Collections, 2010
Hogg I V & Thurston L F, *British Artillery Weapons and Ammunition 1914-18,* Ian Allan, 1972
Jager, H, *German Artillery of World War One*, The Crowood Press, 2001
Marble, S, *'The Infantry Cannot Do with a Gun Less' The Place of the Artillery in the B.E.F., 1914-1918*, Gutenberg-e, Columbia University Press, 2005
Tauzin P & Vauvillier F, *Les Canons de la Victoire 1914-18, Tome 1: L'Artillerie de Campagne*, Histoire & Collections, 2006

Miscellaneous

Gray, Lt. Col. H M W, *The Early Treatment of War Wounds*, Oxford Medical Publications 1919
Pelling, H, *Social Geography of British Elections 1885-1910*, MacMillan, 1967
German Military Terms, Imperial War Museum
The Times Digital Archive
Who was Who, Oxford University Press (http://www.ukwhoswho.com)
The London Gazette (http://www.london-gazette.co.uk/)
Hart's Army List 1914 and *1915*
De Ruvigny's Roll of Honour (5 volumes), N & MP

Sources

National Archives

WO95 Series

GHQ General Staff	4-5	2nd Essex Regt.	1505/1
4th Army Gen Staff	431	2nd Duke of Wellington's Regt.	1508/1
VIII Corps Staff	820	21st West Yorkshire Regt.	1472/3
VIII Corps Cdr RA	824	29th Division Staff	2280
VIII Corps Cdr Heavy Artillery	825	29h Division Adjt Qmaster	2286
4th Division Staff	1444-5	29th Division Cdr RA	2287
4th Division Adjt Qmaster	1450	15th Brigade, RHA	2291/2
4th Division Cdr RA	1458	17th Brigade, RFA	2291/3
14th Brigade, RFA	1466/4	132nd Brigade, RFA	2292/1
29th Brigade, RFA	1466/5	147th Brigade, RFA	2292/2
32nd Brigade, RFA	1467/1	455th Field Coy, RE	2293/1
4th Division/TM Bty	1468/2	497th Field Coy, RE	2293/2
9th Field Coy, RE	1469/2	510th Field Coy, RE	2293/3
406th Field Coy, RE	1470/1	29th Division ADMS	2289
526th Field Coy, RE	1470/2	87th Field Ambulance	2296/1
4th Division ADMS	1461-2	88th Field Ambulance	2296/2
10th Field Ambulance	1473/3	89th Field Ambulance	2297/1
11th Field Ambulance	1475/1	86th Brigade	2298
12th Field Ambulance	1474/3	86th MGC	2302/6
3A Sanitary Section	1475/2	2nd R Fusiliers	2301/3
10th Brigade	1478-9	1st R. Dublin Fusiliers	2301/1
10th MGC	1485/1	1st Lancs Fusiliers	2300
10th TMB	1485/2	16th Middlesex Regt.	2302/2
1st R. Warwickshire Regt.	1484	87th Brigade	2303
1st R. Irish Fusiliers	1482/1	87th MGC	2305/6
2nd Seaforth Highlanders	1483	2nd South Wales Borderers	2304/2
2nd R. Dublin Fusiliers	1481/4	1st King's Own Scottish Borderers	2304/1
11th Brigade	1490	1st R. Inniskilling Fusiliers	2305/2
11th MGC	1500/1	1st Border Regt.	2305/1
11th TMB	1500/2	88th Brigade	2306
1st Somerset Light Infantry	1499	88th MGC	2309/7
1st East Lancashire Regt.	1498/1	1st Newfoundland Regt.	2308/1
1st Hampshire Regt.	1495	2nd Hampshire Regt.	2308/3
1st Rifle Brigade	1496	4th Worcestershire Regt.	2309/2
12th Brigade	1502	1st Essex Regt.	2309/1
12th MGC	1509/1	1 /2nd Monmouthshire Regt.	2295
12th TMB	1509/2	31st Division Staff	2341
1st King's Own Royal Lancaster Regt.	1506/1	31st Division Adjt Qtr	2344

2nd Lancashire Fusiliers	1507
165th Brigade, RFA	2349/3
169th Brigade, RFA	2349/4
171st Brigade. RFA	2349/5
170th Brigade, RFA	2350
31st Division/TM Bty	2351/2
210th Field Coy, RE	2352/1
211th Field Coy, RE	2352/2
223rd Field Coy, RE	2352/3
31st Division ADMS	2348/1
93rd Field Ambulance	2354/1
94th Field Ambulance	2354/2
95th Field Ambulance	2354/3
92nd Brigade	2356/1
92nd MGC	2358/2
92nd TMB	2358/3
10th East Yorkshire Regt.	2357/1
11th East Yorkshire Regt.	2357/2
12th East Yorkshire Regt.	2357/3
13th East Yorkshire Regt.	2357/4
93rd Brigade	2359
93rd MGC	2362/3
93rd TMB	2362/4
15th West Yorkshire Regt	2361/3
16th West Yorkshire Regt.	2362/1
18th West Yorkshire Regt.	2362/2
18th Durham Light Infantry	2361/1
94th Brigade	2363
94th MGC	2366/5
94th TMB	2366/6
11th East Lancashire Regt	2366/1
12th York & Lancaster Regt.	2365/1
13th York & Lancaster Regt.	2365/2
14th York & Lancaster Regt.	2365/3
12th King's Own Yorkshire Light Infantry	2353/1
48th Division Staff	2745/3-4
48th Division Adjt Qtmastr	2747
48th Division Cdr RA	2747
31st Division Cdr RA	2345/1
240th Brigade, RFA	2749/3
241st Brigade, RFA	2749/4
242nd Brigade, RFA	2750/1
243rd Brigade, RFA	2750/2
48th Division/TM Bty	2750/3
48th Division ADMS	2748/1
1/1st South Midland Field Ambulance	2752/1
1/2nd South Midland Field Ambulance	2752/2
1/3rd South Midland Field Ambulance	2752/3
143rd Brigade	2754
1/5th R. Warwickshire Regt.	2755/1
1/6th R. Warwickshire Regt.	2755/2
1/7th R. Warwickshire Regt..	2756/1
1/8th R. Warwickshire Regt.	2756/2
144th Brigade	2757
145th Brigade	2760

CAB45 Series

Military: Western Front: Battles: Comments, Letters, Personal Accounts: The Somme

Authors A-C	132
D-F	133
G-H	134
I-L	135
M-P	136
R-S	137
T-Y & Unidentified	138

Original letters, comments, personal accounts, and extracts from War Diaries: Fourth Army:

Authors A-F	188
G-L	189
M-R	190
S-Y	191

INDEX

Alan MacDonald was born in London in 1951 and was educated at Dulwich College. His various careers as rock and roll musician, political organiser and director of a market research company were an imperfect preparation for writing books about the First World War, or any other book for that matter. Encouraged by his late brother, the music writer Ian MacDonald, to turn some rambling and half-hearted research into a book, he published the first edition of *'Pro Patria Mori – The 56th (1st London) Division at Gommecourt, 1st July 1916'* in June 2006. Somewhat carried away by the results he decided to research and write a companion volume about the involvement of the 46th (North Midland) Division at Gommecourt. The result, *'A Lack of Offensive Spirit?'*, happily took less time to write, although 170 pages longer. It was published in March 2007. In the meantime, various factors necessitated the withdrawal of *'Pro Patria Mori'* and this opportunity was used to considerably update and expand the book into a revised edition which was published in 2008.

Since 2008 he has been researching and writing what will be a series of books covering the planning and conduct of the opening attack of the Battle of the Somme by the British Fourth and French Sixth Armies. *The Attack of the VIII Corps* is the first of a planned four books.

Alan MacDonald lives in South East London with his wife, Helen, daughter, Kate, and a cat called Twiglet. A sports fan, he supports Wolverhampton Wanderers, Harlequins RFC and all teams Scottish. Like writing these books, supporting such teams is a genuine labour of love.

Lightning Source UK Ltd.
Milton Keynes UK
UKOW04f0923010716

277405UK00001B/132/P